GAZETTEER
OF THE
PERSIAN GULF, 'OMĀN,
AND
CENTRAL ARABIA

II A

GEOGRAPHICAL
AND
STATISTICAL

GAZETTEER

OF THE

PERSIAN GULF,

'OMĀN,

AND

CENTRAL ARABIA

BY

J. G. LORIMER, C.I.E.
INDIAN CIVIL SERVICE

VOL. II
GEOGRAPHICAL AND STATISTICAL

CALCUTTA
SUPERINTENDENT GOVERNMENT PRINTING, INDIA
1908

All rights reserved. No part of this publication may be reproduced, stored in a retrieval system, or transmitted in any form or by any means, electronic, mechanical, photocopying, recording, or otherwise, without the prior permission of Gregg International Publishers Limited and Irish University Press.

Reprinted from an original
in the India Office Library

The map which in the original was bound in with this volume is to be found in Volume I part 3, containing the genealogical tables and maps

ISBN
Complete set 0 576 03451 7 and 0 7165 0993 8
This volume 0 576 03456 8 and 0 7165 1325 0

Republished in 1970 by Gregg International Publishers Limited
Westmead, Farnborough, Hants., England
and
Irish University Press, Shannon, Ireland

Printed in Holland

INTRODUCTION

THIS second volume of the Gazetteer of the Persian Gulf, 'Omān and Central Arabia is a geographical dictionary, presenting, in a series of alphabetically arranged articles, a detailed account of the physical and political conditions of the Persian Gulf and its surrounding countries. For a description of the Gulf region as a whole, however, the reader is referred to the Introduction to the first volume of this Gazetteer, some of the Appendices in which also deal with subjects of a general or statistical nature. The information contained in the Gazetteer has been specially collected or compiled, and much of it is entirely new.

Of the articles composing the present volume those that are enumerated below, relating to the chief political divisions of the Gulf region and covering among them the whole of its extent, are the most important; they stand, in fact, on a different footing from the remainder, which are subordinate and explanatory; and they contain in themselves all that it is most essential to know in regard to the Persian Gulf.

The principal articles in question are these:—

'Omān Sultanate	Pages 1382—1425.
'Omān (Trucial)	Pages 1425—1451.
Qatar	Pages 1505—1535.
Bahrain Principality	Pages 233—253.
Hasa Sanjāq	Pages 657—679.
Kuwait Principality	Pages 1058—1077.
Najd	Pages 1313—1351, supplemented by articles on Najd (Southern), pages 1351—1359; Qasīm, pages 1485—1503; and Shammar (Jabal), pages 1732—1748.
'Irāq (Turkish)	Pages 759—882.
'Arabistān	Pages 115—151, supplemented by articles on 'Arabistān (Northern), pages 151—157; and 'Arabistān (Southern), pages 157—165.

INTRODUCTION.

Persian Coast . . . Pages 1455—1468, supplemented by the articles on the component districts, mentioned in the article itself and too numerous to be specified here.

Makrān (Coast of Persian) . Pages 1130—1155.

All these articles follow similar though not identical lines; and the topics discussed in each, though the order of arrangement is not invariable, are generally as follow :—

Boundaries and sub-divisions of the tract.

Physical character and main features, *viz.*, mountains, rivers, etc.

Climate and seasons.

Natural products, vegetable, animal and mineral.

Agriculture and crops.

Livestock, including transport animals.

Inhabitants, with reference to racial and tribal distinctions, religious differences, mode of life, character, language, customs, dress and arms; also estimates of population.

Trade, internal and external, with a notice of currency, weights and measures; also shipping, manufactures and industries, and miscellaneous occupations.

Communications by land and water, with descriptions of routes and estimates of transport.

Administration and government, especially police, justice, military resources, taxation and finance, and political constitution.

International position and foreign interests, especially British, and their representation in the country.

Some of the principal articles contain in addition a paragraph on topography, dealing with that subject in so far as it has not been exhausted in subordinate articles; and a list of useful authorities and maps is given in a footnote at the beginning of each principal article. The fullest and most general information in regard to meteorology and health, date culture, transport animals and livestock, religions and sects, trade, sailing vessels, fisheries, pearl fisheries and postal and telegraphic communications will be found, however, not in the articles above cited, but in Appendices, which the reader will have no difficulty in finding, in the first volume of the Gazetteer.

The subordinate articles deal in greater detail with the districts, places, tribes, etc., of which mention is made in the principal articles; and, to facilitate reference, names which form the subjects of separate articles have been printed in bold type throughout this volume. In subordinate articles on districts and tracts the arrangement and method of treatment are somewhat the same as in principal articles; but, so far as possible, repetition of the information already given in principal articles is avoided. Topographical information has generally been thrown into tabular form in order to avoid an excessive multiplication of separate articles, and most wells, villages of minor importance, etc., will be found described in the article on the district to which they belong, or on the river, valley, etc., where they are situated. It has not been possible to prepare an index of these smaller places, and they should accordingly be looked for first in the article on the appropriate district or, in a few cases, the main division, and then in the other articles containing topographical tables to which the article first consulted may afford a clue. The map issued with this Gazetteer will be found useful in tracing the articles in which minor features and places are described.

The reader should understand that estimates of distance, where they depend on native information only, are not very reliable; and that a good deal of the geography—especially of the remoter Arabian districts—is more or less conjectural, though no pains have been spared in testing, where possible, the account of one native informant by that of another. Estimates of population are necessarily very rough and have generally been derived, subject to other checks, from numbers of houses and from reputed tribal fighting strengths; it appears to be the general opinion that on the average there are about five souls to a " house " in settled populations, and that among nomads the proportion capable of bearing arms is about two-sevenths of the whole tribe. The figures for livestock and other agricultural resources have generally been obtained through untrained native reporters and cannot be regarded as altogether trustworthy, but they explain the general character of tracts and help to determine the relative importance of villages in the same neighbourhood. The common statement that water is " good " must be received with caution, for in many cases it probably means no more than that its taste is not disagreeable and that it may be drunk with impunity by natives of the country.

It remains to define the sense in which some of the terms used in this Gazetteer are employed. When distances are computed by the " hour," a pedestrian's hour of about three miles in ordinary ground is meant; but, when " days " are mentioned without a qualifying adjective, the reference is to the daily journey of a caravan, which may be anything from

25 to 30 miles. A "day" by riding camel may be taken as the double or more, in mileage, of a caravan day. "Miles" are common land miles, except where it is stated that they are geographical or nautical. By the "right" and "left" banks of rivers and valleys are meant those banks which a traveller would have on his right and left hand, respectively, in descending with the stream or slope. The term "foot" is used to indicate the end furthest from the sea of a bay or inlet; and "depth", in the same connection, sometimes refers not to the soundings but to the depth of the indentation formed in the coast line, the sense in this case depending on the context.

The system of transliteration followed in this volume is that explained in the Introduction to the first volume.

J. G. LORIMER.

STRATHMARTINE,
    DUNDEE:
24th December 1908.

GEOGRAPHICAL AND STATISTICAL GAZETTEER

OF THE

PERSIAN GULF,

'OMĀN,

AND CENTRAL ARABIA.

'ABĀDILAH عبادله
Singular 'Abdūli عبدولي : a tribe of Trucial 'Omān who have 200 houses at Shārjah Town, 20 at Ghāllah in Shamailīyah, and 15 at Khalaibīyah adjoining Wādi Hām; some of them are found also as settlers on Shaikh Shu'aib island. In all they may number about 1,200 souls. In politics they are Ghāfiris, and in religion Hanbali Sunnis. They are not connected with the Sharqiyīn, and they claim, it is said, to be Shurafa from Makkah. Another account assimilates them to the 'Obaidli tribe of the Shībkuh district in Persia, deriving them from the 'Abdah branch of the Shammar of Najd; it is possible that this theory has no foundation except in the partial resemblance of the names.

ABBĀDĀN عبادان
Also called Jazīrat-al-Khidhar * جزيرة الخضر from a shrine near its centre, is a large and valuable island enclosed by the Kārūn river on the north, by the Shatt-al-'Arab on the west, by the Persian Gulf on the south, and by the Bahmanshīr on the east. Its length is about 40 miles, and its width varies from about 1½ miles at the middle to 12 miles near its southern end. The centre is mostly desert, but the margins adjoining the rivers, as far as creeks extend inland, are cultivated and planted with dates: much land is now being reclaimed in the Ma'āmareh neighbourhood near the south end. A submarine prolongation of the island into the Persian Gulf forms the great reef called Maraqqat 'Abbādān مرقة عبادان.

The inhabitants of 'Abbādān are almost all Ka'ab Arabs, of the Drīs division of the tribe, and those in the southern part of the island nearly all belong to the Nassār subdivision.

A considerable tract in the north-eastern corner of the island is known by the name of Maharzi مهرزي; its limits are at Shākhat-al-Hayāk on the northern, and at Hūz 'Umar on the eastern shore of the island.

---

* Both names are in common use.

B

The shrine of Khidhar* stands a little nearer to the north than to the south end of the island, about 2 miles from the Shatt-al-'Arab and 1 mile from the Bahmanshīr: it is largely visited by the Shī'ahs of the surrounding districts.

We proceed to give a list of the villages with which the shores of 'Abbādān are studded :—

Villages on the north shore of 'Abbādān island from the bifurcation of the Kārūn and Bahmanshīr rivers to the confluence of the Kārūn and Shatt-al-'Arab.

Name.	Inhabitants.	Remarks.	Position.
Būzat Maharzi بوزة محرزي or Shākhat-al-Būzah شاخة البوزة or Pūzeh Shaikh 'Abdullah پوزه ش ح بدالله	Ka'ab.	40 mud houses and huts.	(In the fork between the Kārūn and Bahmanshīr rivers.)
Shākhat Abarteh شاخة عبرته	Mutūr uhaisin).	30 huts.	Adjoins the last.
Shākhat-as-Sādeh شاخة السادة	Bait Kana'ān (Muhaisin).	10 huts.	Do.
Shākhat Hāji 'Arrāk شاخة جاجي عرّاك	Mutūr (Muhaisin).	20 mud houses.	Do.
Shākhat Hāji Dighaifij شاخة جاجي دغيفج	Do.	20 huts.	Do.
Hūz Ridh-yo حوز رضيو	Do.	10 huts.	Do.

* Muhammadan theologians are not agreed whether this mysterious personage is a prophet or not. Some of them even deny his existence; but there are, on the other hand, Sūfi mystics who affirm that they have seen him. He is believed to have existed in the time of Abraham, to have been a companion of Moses, and to be still alive in consequence of having drunk of the water of life. Some Muhammadan commentators identify him with the prophet Elias, others with Saint George of England: one even makes him a general in the army of Alexander the Great.

'ABBADĀN

Villages on the north shore of 'Abbādān island from the bifurcation of the Kārūn and Bahmanshīr rivers to the confluence of the Kārūn and Shatt-al-'Arab—contd.

Name.	Inhabitants.	Remarks.	Position.
Shākhat-al-Hayāk شاخة العياك or Hayākeh حياكه	Bait Ghānim (**Muhaisin**) and Saiyids.	40 mud houses. Opposite **Muhammareh** Town.	Adjoins the last.
Fārsīyeh فارسيه	Dawālim (**Muhaisin**).	15 huts. Opposite **Muhammareh** Town.	Do.
Kūt-ash-Shaikh كوت الشيخ	Bahraini settlers, Persians, and a few mixed Arabs.	150 mud houses; opposite **Muhammareh** Town. There are about 15 shops; Ballams and sailing craft are built, and water-pots, jars and 'Abas are manufactured. Kūt-ash-Shaikh was formerly called Kūt Fāris and belonged to the **Ka'ab** Shaikhs in the time of their supremacy.	Do.
Umm-al-Jaraidīyeh (1) ام الجريديه	Descendants of Bahrain refugees.	10 huts.	½ a mile below Kūt-ash-Shaikh.
(2) Do.	Nassār (**Ka'ab**).	10 mud houses and huts.	Adjoins the last.
(3) Do.	**Balūchis** and mixed Arabs.	30 mud houses and huts.	½ a mile below the last.
Ruwais رويس	Ahl-al-'Aryadh (**Muhaisin**).	100 mud houses. The residence of Hāji Faisal, Shaikh of the Ahl-al-'Aryadh.	½ a mile inland, south of Umm-al-Jaraidīyeh.
Būzat-as-Sanqar بوزة الصنقر	……	Not a village, but the angle between the **Kārūn** river (left bank) and the Shatt-al-'Arab (left bank), in which the Persian quarantine station and doctor's house are situated.	¾ of a mile below Ruwais

'ABBĀDĀN

Villages on the east shore of 'Abbādān island from the bifurcation of the Kārūn and Bahmanshīr rivers to the mouth of the latter on the Persian Gulf.

Name.	Inhabitants.	Remarks.	Position.
Shākhat Bait Sālim شاخة بيت سالم	Mutūr (Muhaisin).	12 huts.	Contiguous to Būzat Maharzi.
Shākhat Abul Khadhair شاخة ابو الخضير	Do.	13 huts.	Adjoins the last.
Hūz 'Umar حوز عمر	Do.	10 huts.	Do.
Shākhat Bait Hanūn شاخة بيت حنون	Drīs (Ka'ab).	30 mud houses and huts.	Do.
Mahyūb محيوب	Do.	15 huts.	...
Bait Hāji 'Abdullah بيت حاجي عبدالله	Do.	40 mud houses and huts.	Adjoins the last.
Shanneh شنه	Bait Kana'ān (Muhaisin).	10 mud huts.	...
Shinaineh شنينه	Do.	6 huts.	Adjoins the last.
Faiyādhi فياضي	Mutūr (Muhaisin).	6 mud huts.	...
Bait Bin 'Ataiwi بيت بن عتيوي	Bait Kana'ān (Muhaisin).	20 mud huts.	...
Faiyeh فيه	Drīs (Ka'ab).	30 mud huts.	...
Suwainikh-as-Sādeh صوينخ السادة	Baghlānīyeh (Muhaisin) and Drīs (Ka'ab).	35 mud huts.	...
Suwainikh صوينخ	Do.	22 mud huts.	4 miles below Faiyādhi.
Āl Bū Hamaid آل بو حميد	Do.	50 mud huts.	1 mile below Suwainikh.

'ABBĀDĀN

Villages on the east shore of 'Abbādān island from the bifurcation of the Kārūn and Bahmanshīr rivers to the mouth of the latter on the Persian Gulf—contd.

Name.	Inhabitants.	Remarks.	Position.
Sha'aibīyeh شعيبيه	Drīs (**Ka'ab**).	20 mud huts.	3 miles below **Āl Bū Hamaid**.
'Abdullah-bīn-Da'būleh عبدالله بن دعبوله	Nassār (**Ka'ab**).	21 mud huts.	1 mile below Sha'aibīyeh.
Qabāneh قبانه	Thawāmir (**Ka'ab**).	6 mud huts.	2 miles below 'Abdullah-bin-Da'-būleh.
Shākhat Hāji Is-hāq شاخة حاجي اسحاق	Drīs (**Ka'ab**).	40 mud houses.	3 miles below Qabāneh.
Nahr-al-Khidhar نهر الخضر	Drīs (**Ka'ab**) only.	30 mud houses.	1 mile below Shākhat Hāj Is-hāq.
Bakhākh-at-Tura بخاخ الطرا	Bakhākh (**Muhaisin**).	...	...
Bakhākh بخاخ	Do.	50 mud houses.	About 7 miles below Bakhākh-at-Tura.
Kuwaibdeh كويبده	Mutūr (**Muhaisin**).	30 houses.	About 4 miles below Bakhākh and 15 miles from the mouth of the **Bahmanshīr**.

Villages on the west shore of 'Abbādān island from the confluence of the Kārūn river and Shatt-al-'Arab to the sea.

Name.	Inhabitants.	Remarks.	Position or distance, in miles, below last village.
Arādhīyeh عراضيه	Ahl-al-'Aryadh and tribesmen from the Turkish side of the river (**Muhaisin**).	25 mud huts.	1 below the mouth of the **Kārūn** river.
l Bū Nāji آل بو ناجي	Baghlānīyeh (**Muhaisin**).	10 mud huts.	¼

Villages on the west shore of 'Abbādān island from the confluence of the Kārūn river and Shatt-al-'Arab to the sea—contd.

Name.	Inhabitants.	Remarks.	Position or distance, in miles, below last village.
Tuwaiqāt طويقات	Drīs (Ka'ab).	8 mud huts.	¼
Bait Zāir Hamaid بيت زائر حميد	Āl Bū Farhān (Muhaisin).	20 mud houses.	¼
Bait Zāir Muhammad بيت زائر محمّد	Drīs (Ka'ab).	20 mud huts.	¼
Hārtheh هارثه	Do.	20 mud huts. Hāji Salbūq island begins just below this village.	1
Shākhat Mahyūb شاخة محيوب	Do.	35 mud huts.	1½
Juruf جرف	Do.	30 mud huts.	1½
Juruf Bait Hāji Jarrāh جرف بيت حاجي جراح	Do.	30 mud huts.	½
Āl Bū Burqa' آل بو برقع	Bait Kana'ān (Muhaisin).	8 mud huts.	½
Baraim بريم	Thawāmir (Ka'ab).	50 mud houses. Hāji Salbuq island ends at this village.	2
'Arūsīyeh عروسيه	Baghlānīyeh (Muhaisin).	12 mud and date-stick huts.	2
Bawairdeh بويردة	Āl Bū Ma'arrif (Muhaisin).	20 mud huts.	½
Shatait شطيط	Mutūr (Muhaisin).	30 mud huts.	3
Shākhat Zāir Husain شاخة زائر حسين	Āl Bū Ma'arrif (Muhaisin).	45 mud huts.	10
Nāsirīyeh ناصريه	Thawāmir (Ka'ab)	50 mud huts.	...

'ABBĀDĀN

Villages on the west shore of 'Abbādān island from the confluence of the Kārūn river and Shatt-al-'Arab to the sea—concld.

Name.	Inhabitants.	Remarks.	Position or distance, in miles, below last village.
Manyūhi مَنوحي or Manjūhi مَنجوحي	Bakhākh and Āl Bu Ma'arrif (**Muhaisin**) and Nassār and Thawāmir (**Ka'ab**).	A stretch of date-plantations, extending 15 miles along the Shatt-al-'**Arab** and containing about 300 mud huts scattered here and there in small groups. The yield of these plantations is over 50,000 baskets annually.	...
Qasbeh قصبة or Çasbat-an-Nassār قصبة النصّار	Nassār Ka'ab, Bahrainis, Persians and negroes; also '**Idān** who have recently immigrated from Turkish territory.	Date-plantations reaching 20 miles along the Shatt-al-'**Arab** with a depth of 2 to 3 miles. They contain 600 mud huts scattered about in small groups, and produce about 100,000 baskets of dates annually. Till 20 years ago there were few inhabitants owing to constant wars with **Muhammareh**.	...
Ma'āmareh معامره	Chiefly Nassār Ka'ab.	A stretch of date-groves, 6 miles in length on the Shatt-al-'**Arab**, containing about 150 scattered huts.	Adjoins the last.

Villages on the south coast of 'Abbādān island.

The sea coast appears to be fairly firm and well marked, but there are no fixed villages, only temporary huts used by shepherds.

The total population of the island appears to be about 24,000 souls.

The two southern administrative divisions of 'Abbādān, which is itself included in the **Muhammareh** District of Southern '**Arabistān**, are Manyūhi and Qasbat-an-Nassār; in each of the villages bearing these names there is a representative of the Shaikh of **Muhammareh**. The part of the island north of Manyūhi was formerly under the chief Shaikh of the Drīs **Ka'āb**, but it is now in charge of the Shaikh of the Ahl-al-'Aryadh **Muhaisin**.

'ABBĀS (BANDAR)*
بندر عباس

An important town on the **Persian Coast** at the entrance of the Persian Gulf; it constitutes in itself an administrative district and is surrounded, except on the south side which is to the sea, by the district of **Shāmil**. Bandar 'Abbās is situated about 280 miles north-north-west of **Masqat** and 96 miles east-north-east of **Lingeh** Town.

Site and buildings.—Bandar 'Abbās stands at the foot of a bay upon a low, sandy, shelving beach; the buildings approach within 100 yards of the water's edge and at high spring tides the sea washes their walls. The town looks out, between the islands of **Hormūz** and **Lārak**, upon the junction off the **Ruūs-al-Jibāl** promontory of the Gulfs of Persia and **'Oman**: its background, as viewed from the sea, is formed by the massive pile of Kūh-i-Ginau, which at a distance of only 18 miles north by west of the town attains an altitude of 7,783 feet. The immediate surroundings of Bandar 'Abbās are utterly bare; even garden cultivation and the usual drapery of a few palms are here wanting. The anchorage for ships drawing up to 18 feet of water lies south of the town at a minimum distance of 2½ miles; it has good holding-ground and is well sheltered from every direction except the south-east, but the landing is bad on account of shallows which extend a long way off the beach. Large vessels lie as much as 4 miles out. Opposite the town the distance between high water and low water mark is about ¼ of a mile, and rowing boats ground at as much as 100 yards from the shore. At the middle of the town a pier 100 yards in length and 20 in readth extends seawards; but it is left high and dry at low tide, and at high water boats drawing 6 feet or more can only reach the seaward end of it.

The bulk of the town consists of houses of sun-dried brick plastered with mud or Gach, but there are a few old Portuguese and Dutch houses

---

* Bandar 'Abbās, so named by Shāh 'Abbās in the 17th century, was known at the time of the Portuguese occupation of **Hormūz**, when it was the place of embarkation for that island, as Gombrūn, a name which continued to be current among Europeans till the end of the 18th century. "Gombrūn" is believed to be a corruption of Gumruk-customs. See LeStrange's *Lands of the Eastern Caliphate.*

of better material and a large number of huts ; the frontage on the sea is about half a mile. A number of the houses possess Bādgīrs, which here take the form of low square towers like those of English country churches, but more squat and with vertical slits in all four sides towards the top; each of these Bādgīrs is divided into 4 internal compartments or shafts by vertical walls which start from the corners and meet in the middle of the tower. Bandar 'Abbās was formerly enclosed by walls upon the landward side ; but these, where they still exist, are concealed by the quarters which have sprung up outside them. At the head of the pier stands the old Dutch factory, now called the Kulāh-i-Farangi * کلاه فرنگی and used as a residence by the Deputy-Governor, who shares it with the Imperial Customs Department; the courtyard contains an extraordinary number of solidly built warehouses.

The condition of the town and foreshore is highly insanitary : there are no scavengers and no system of conservancy.

Climate.—The climate of Bandar 'Abbās is notorious for its heat and unhealthiness ;† but there is no meteorological station and precise data are not available. The summer heat is almost intolerable ; this is due, doubtless, to the combination of the moist air from the stagnant bay in front of the town and the heat reflected or radiated by the mountain wall behind. Even in the depths of winter the mercury seldom falls below freezing point, and, when on the morning of the 29th of January 1905‡ pools were found covered with a slight coating of ice, the oldest inhabitants professed themselves unable to recall any similar occurrence. The months of January and February are cool and salubrious with occasional showers of rain, which are sometimes heavy ; in March, April and May the temperature rises, the surrounding country becomes dried up, and malaria prevails ; in June, July, August and September the heat is intense and most of the inhabitants desert the town to escape it, but at the same time fever diminishes ; during October, November and December the heat is again upon the wane and malarial fevers are once more rife. Mosquitoes are troublesome in the spring and autumn months.

Water and supplies.—The town contains wells, but the water is invariably bad and brackish and seems to conduce to guinea-worm and

---

* Or " European Hat."

† A selection of remarks by travellers on the Bandar 'Abbās climate will be found in Lord Curzon's Persia (II, 421). See also the Historical Volume of this Gazetteer (Chapter First).

‡ The winter of 1904-05 was exceptionally severe in the Persian Gulf as well as in Upper India.

kidney disease; the former complaint seems to be most prevalent in May, June and July. The better-off among the inhabitants obtain their supply for drinking from wells at Nāiband village, 3 miles to eastwards of the town, and their demand has given rise to a regular traffic. Water from reservoirs at the town is used for drinking by the poorer classes, but by others only for washing.

Fish are generally abundant, being caught with seine nets, wicker baskets, cages, and lines; but they become scarce in summer and in stormy weather. Grain is not obtainable in very large quantities; vegetables are scarce; firewood is scanty and expensive; and fodder is almost unobtainable. About 250 cattle and 150 sheep and goats are owned in the town.

Population.—Bandar 'Abbās is described as at present consisting of over 2,000 houses and huts, the more substantial structures outnumbering the slighter in the proportion of 3 to 2. The cold-weather population is about 10,000 souls; the summer population, as already explained, is very much less. The bulk of the inhabitants belong to a hybrid race of mixed Persian, **Balūchi,** Arab and negro descent and are known as 'Abbāsis; the lower orders of them speak a patois—also called 'Abbāsi—which is a compound of Persian, Balūchi, Arabic and Swahīli ingredients. The 'Abbāsis are a poor-spirited race and hardly, it is said, regard truth, honesty or charity as virtues. The poorer classes lead a squalid life in date-leaf huts. A cheap diet of fish and dates is all that they require, and, when this has been provided, laziness and independence alike forbid them to work; this apathetic spirit among the labouring classes greatly impedes business and affords some justification for a local saying to the effect that nothing begun at Bandar 'Abbās is ever finished. Apart from the merchants and shopkeepers, who are mostly strangers from abroad, the people are boatmen, fishermen or labourers, and in the date-season they all become harvesters.

The immigrants, upon whom the life of the place chiefly depends, are Persians from Lār (500 souls), from 'Avaz (300 souls) and from Bastak (150 souls); also Hindus (66 souls), **Khōjahs** (67 souls) and Arabs (50 souls). The Hindus here are not accompanied by their families, but of the **Khōjahs** half the number mentioned are females. Sunnis at Bandar 'Abbās are about half as numerous again as Shī'ahs and mostly belong to the Shāfi'i school, but some are Hanafis. About 300 or 400 persons, chiefly Lāris and 'Avazis, possess arms.

Trade and commerce.—Local trade with the surrounding district of **Shamīl** is inconsiderable; and the Bandar 'Abbās bazaar, which contains about 200 shops, is only moderately well supplied with goods. There are no local manufactures, and practically no skilled labour is available.

The export and import business of Bandar 'Abbās, though its pre-eminence as the port of Southern Persia has disappeared since the rise of **Būshehr** and the development of the Shīrāz route to the interior, is still valuable. Kirmān and even Yazd still fall within the commercial radius of Bandar 'Abbās; and so also, to some extent, do Sīstān and Khurāsān.

About 1903-04 the average annual value of the export trade of Bandar 'Abbās was approximately £130,000, more than half of which was with India, the United Kingdom being the customer of next greatest importance. The chief exports during the 7 years preceding 1906 were (in lakhs of rupees per annum) the following: fruits and vegetables (6), opium (3), wool (1½), drugs and medicines (1⅓), gums (1⅓) and carpets (1¼). Except opium sent to China, nearly all of these went to India.

Imports at the same time (1903-04) were worth about £390,000 a year, among which goods to the value of £160,000 were from India, and to that of £125,000 from the United Kingdom. The principal imports during the period 1899—1906 were (in lakhs of rupees per annum) cotton piece-goods (14½), tea (13¾), yarn and twist (9½), sugar (6½), grain and pulse (2), dyeing and colouring materials (1¾) and spices (1). Except the cotton piece-goods, which were from Britain, and the sugar, which was from France, nearly all these imports were derived from India. A considerable import trade in rifles which was formerly carried on here has been either extinguished or forced into other channels by the vigilance of the Imperial Persian Customs Department.

Drafts on Bombay and Karachi are obtainable at Bandar 'Abbās.

Currency, weights and measures.—The currency of Bandar 'Abbās, which is typical of this part of Persia, consists principally of silver and nickel. The silver coins are pieces of 1, 2, and 5 Qrāns, the double Qrān being the commonest. The nickel coins, minted in Belgium, are of 100 and 50 Dīnārs each and are used as small change; they are styled respectively Dūshāhi (or Chahārpūl) and Yakshāhi (or Dūpūl). The money table runs as follows:—

    50 Dīnārs دينار = 1 Shāhi
    20 Shāhis شاهي = 1 Qrān
    10 Qrāns قران = 1 Tūmān تومان

Indian rupees are also current: in 1905-06 the rate of exchange varied between 415 and 350 Qrāns to the hundred rupees.

The official standard of weight at Bandar 'Abbās, as elsewhere in Persia, is now the Tabrīz Man of 640 Misqāls, equal to 6·547 lbs. English avoirdupois. The unit generally employed in trade, however, is the so-called 'Abbāsi Man of about 9 lb. English, which is subdivided as follows:—

1 Man 'Abbāsi	من عباسي	=	4 Chahāraks
1 Chahārak	چهارك	=	6 Qiyās
1 Qiyās	قياس	=	37½ Misqāls مثقال

The silver one and two-Qrān pieces are supposed to weigh 1 and 2 Misqāls respectively, but those of the most recent mintage are slightly under weight.

Measures of length are as below:—

4 Girehs	گره	=	1 Chahārak
4 Chahāraks	چهارك	=	1 Zara'-i-Shāh ذرع شاه
			or 41·143 English inches.

There is also a Zara'-i-Dast ذرع دست or cubit of 18 inches, a Zara'-i-Bandari ذرع بندري of 9 Girehs or about 22 inches, and a Zara'-i-Lār ذرع لار of 12 Girehs. The English yard is used by cloth-merchants under the name of Vār وار and is taken as equivalent to 14 Girehs. There are no liquid measures, fluids being sold by weight, and no measures of capacity. Square measurements are expressed in terms of length and breadth, and there is no separate table of square measure.

Shipping and sea communications.—The native craft of Bandar 'Abbās are:—

Class.	Number.	Total tonnage.	Total hands employed.
Baghlahs	3	1,250	114
Ghunchahs	3	375	48
Zārūqehs	25	250	100
Māshuwahs	15	80	90
Jolly-boats	10	50	50
Horis	50	20	100
TOTAL	106	2,025	502

Apart from this small mercantile marine, and from native boats of other ports which call here, Bandar 'Abbās is dependent for over-sea communication upon the visits of European vessels.

In 1905-06 steam vessels to the number of 158 with a tonnage of 241,000 entered the port. All but 8 were under the British flag.

Transport and communications.—Transport owned in Bandar 'Abbās is small, amounting to only 10 horses and 350 donkeys; there are no camels or mules. The town is dependent for pack-carriage on the surrounding district of **Shamīl**, of which the resources are estimated in the article under that name. Between November and April there is a large influx of Afghans with camels, and at that season the number of camels in the neighbourhood sometimes rises to 2,000 or more.

The inland routes which have their starting point at Bandar 'Abbās are dealt with in the article on the **Shamīl** District.

Bandar 'Abbās is now connected with **Hanjām** island by telegraph. The shore end of the cable is landed about ¾ of a mile east of the pier at the centre of the town.

Administration.—Bandar 'Abbās is one of the **Gulf Ports** and as such is subject to the Governor who has his head-quarters at **Būshehr** Town. The local representative of that authority is a resident Deputy-Governor who is his nominee; this individual appears to be entitled in theory to exercise official influence over the Kalāntar of the **Shamīl** District, whose seat is at **Ziyārat**; but in practice the Kalāntar generally succeeds in maintaining a position of equality and the Deputy-Governor is ruler of the town only. The Deputy-Governor is an unsalaried official, who pays a premium for his post and recoups himself as best he can by the collection of dues and taxes; the predecessor of the present incumbent paid 5,000 Tūmāns for his appointment for one year, and the highest annual sum ever contracted for is said to have been 14,000 Tūmāns. From the Deputy-Governor's sources of income the revenue of the sea customs, collected by the staff of the Imperial Persian Customs, are of course excepted. His chief items of revenue are a shop tax called Asnāfīyeh اضنافیه at the rate of 7½ Tūmāns per annum on each shop, and a passport tax called Tazkireh تذکره at 14½ Qrāns for each person. Attempts are made from time to time to increase the revenue by the imposition of various irregular imposts under the names of Dallāli دلالي or brokerage, collected at the rate of 2½ per cent. from both seller and buyer; of Sar-i-Rīgi سرریگي, a tax levied on goods placed in position for loading on transport animals; of Maidāni میداني, a kind of octroi duty, at ½ a Qrān to 2 Qrāns per package according to size; and of Askalīyeh اسکلیه

or pierage, nominally for the upkeep of the pier or Askaleh, at 2½ to 5 Qrāns per package according to size. Rāhdāri (رهداری) or road tolls, nominally for the maintenance of roads and the provision of road guards, are not at present levied in the neighbourhood of Bandar 'Abbās. The Deputy-Governor in fact has *carte blanche* to make what he can out of the place during his lease, subject only to the restraints imposed by the presence of the Director of Customs and of the consular representatives of foreign Powers. The town produces no land or agricultural revenue.

Incidentally the Deputy-Governor conducts the general administration of the town and decides criminal and civil cases. He maintains no regular police, and his settlement of cases appears to be determined chiefly by corrupt or partisan considerations. As a criminal authority he has power to inflict fine, torture or imprisonment, but death sentences cannot be carried out without the sanction of the Governor of the **Gulf Ports.**

The religious authorities, who in some districts of the **Persian Coast** are respected and administer at least the semblance of civil justice, appear at Bandar 'Abbās to be utterly venal and are not spontaneously resorted to by litigants even as an alternative to the court of the Deputy-Governor. Fanaticism is absent and the ecclesiastical element at Bandar 'Abbās is a negligible quantity. There are no leading families: the most influential of the local notables at the present time is the Amīn-ul-Tujjār, Hāji Husain, who belongs to a family from Galehdār.

The Persian Government is represented at Bandar 'Abbās by the officials of the Imperial Customs Department, at the head of whom is a Belgian Director, and by a Nāib Kārguzār (نائب کارگذار) or deputy agent of the Persian Foreign Office. The office of the Customs Director has become a general court of appeal from the decisions of the Persian Deputy-Governor, and relations between the Director and the general body of Persian officials in the place are strained. The duties of the Nāib Kārguzār are nominal. The subjects and representatives of foreign Powers are supposed to have their dealings with him; but in fact he merely plays the part of a spy in the interests of the Persian Government upon the proceedings of the Customs officials and of the consular representatives of foreign Powers. His salary is 50 Tūmāns a month.

The place is undefended. The only armed men are 8 artillery-men, charged with the duty of firing the sunset gun, and about 40 Tufangchīs or armed levies who are under the orders of the Deputy-Governor or the Director of Customs.

Foreign interests.—Except Great Britain no European power possesses any tangible interests at Bandar 'Abbās. The Indian Government maintain at Bandar 'Abbās a Consul, who is a member of their Political Department; and there are also an Indian post office and savings bank, of which the operations are exempt from Persian interference unless in the matter of parcels, which are treated as imports and pass through the hands of the Persian Imperial Customs. The British Consulate is situated at Nāiband, on the coast 3 miles east of the town, and is surrounded by a garden and some trees which constitute almost the only trace of verdure in the locality. To the British Consul are confided the interests of 21 Hindu and 9 Muhammadan traders, British subjects, some of whom own trading vessels and pearl boats: the Hindu community have in addition a Sarāi (or residential quarter) and temple of their own. One European British firm has a branch at Bandar 'Abbās, and there are 3 native houses which act as agents for various British firms and shipping companies. The only other foreign power locally represented is Russia, who maintains a Consulate with a staff of a Consul, a Persian Agent, an Armenian clerk, a Persian Mīrzā and 10 Cossacks. Russian trade however at Bandar 'Abbās is very small, and there is not a single resident Russian subject.

'ABDULLAH (KHOR) *

خور عبدالله

An important inlet running north-westwards, between the mouth of the Shatt-al-'**Arab** and **Būbiyān** island, from the head of the Persian Gulf to **Warbah** island. It is 12 miles wide at the entrance, and in the channel the soundings are from 4 to 5 fathoms, except at the east end of **Warbah** island where, for a short distance, they decrease to between 3 and 4 fathoms. A deep channel passing to the north of **Warbah** connects Khor 'Abdullah with Khor-ath-Tha'lab خور الثعلب on which stands Umm **Qasr**, while another, styled apparently Khor Būbiyān, leads from Khor

---

* A report by Commander T. W. Kemp, R.N., on Khor 'Abdullah will be found in the Government of India's Political Proceedings for February 1905. See also a report by Commander W. G. Beauchamp, R.I.M., forwarded to the Government of India by Major P. Z. Cox, Resident in the Persian Gulf, with a demi-official letter dated 20th November 1906.

'Abdullah, south of **Warbah**, into the Khor-as-**Sabīyah**.* The northern shore of Khor 'Abdullah from the mouth of the Shatt-al-'**Arab** to **Warbah** consists of very low alluvial land, in some places bare mud, in some places covered with grass and reeds; at high tide the sea runs inland upon this side, in places for several miles, forming a broad sheet of shallow water. The southern shore is formed by **Būbiyān** island, off which, at the entrance of the Khor, lies a detached bank of hard sand, 8 miles long and nearly parallel to the island: this bank is called 'Aik عيك. The entire Khor could be traversed by the largest ships at high water; and there are good anchorages for large vessels, in any state of the tide, both below **Warbah** island and in the northern continuation of the Khor above it. When the shores are overflowed by the tide, the navigation of Khor 'Abdullah, especially at the east end of **Warbah** island, is somewhat difficult owing to the absence of beacons and buoys.

'ABRIYĪN
عبريين

Singular 'Abri عبري. A tribe of Nizāri descent in the **'Omān** Sultanate, belonging to the Ghāfiri political faction; in religion they are mostly Ibādhis, but a small minority are Sunnis. They are found in **Dhāhirah** at **'Arāqi**; in Western **Hajar** at **'Awābi**, at 'Aqair in Wādi **Shāfān**, at Zāmmah and Hāt in Wādi Bani **'Auf**, at Bait-al-Qarn in Wādi **Fara'**, at Tabāqah in Wādi Bani **Ghāfir**, and at 'Amq, Fashah, Maqamma and Mabu in Wādi **Sahtan**; in **'Omān** Proper at **Bahlah**, Farq, Ghamr and Hamrah: their number is estimated at 6,500 souls. They cultivate dates and corn and are generally a well-behaved and peaceable tribe. They are the real masters of **'Awābi**, but **Bahlah** is their capital, and Hamrah their largest separate village. Their Tamīmahs are Muhanna-bin-Hamad and Rāshid-bin-Hamaid.

'ADAI (WĀDI)
وادي عدي

A valley in the **Masqat** District of the **'Omān** Sultanate; it rises in the northern slopes of the Eastern **Hajar** and runs north-east till near **Ruwi**, when it turns to the north-west and enters the sea 2 miles south-west of Rās-al-Hamar: it contains a running stream. The valley in the

---

* This southern channel also is apparently navigable for vessels of some size. *Vide* footnote to article on Khor-as-**Sabīyah**.

'ADAI (WĀDI)

first 12 miles of its course is uninhabited; the places upon its lower course are the following:—

Place.	Position.	On which bank.	Houses and inhabitants.	Remarks.
Bīrain بيرين	12 miles south-south-east of **Matrah**.	Right.	A village of 3 or 4 houses only with some 30 acres of cultivation and constant irrigation from a sweet-water Falaj. Grain, lucerne and water-melons are grown; there are also dates.	The whole is an estate of Muhammad-bin-Sa'īd, son of a late Wazīr of the Sultān: a **Khōjah** is partner with him in the property. Bīrain belonged originally to the Bani **Wahaib**.
Mahaj محج	1 mile below Bīrain.	Do.	There was a village here but it has ceased to exist.	There is cultivation but no live-stock.
Mutahaddamāt or Mit-haddamāt متهدمات	3 miles below Mahaj.	Do.	20 houses of Jabūr.	There is a considerable date-grove on the north side of the village.
Bajarīyah بجريه	1 mile below Mutahaddamāt, a short distance up a side valley.	Left.	4 houses.	Resources are 10 donkeys, 20 sheep and goats, and some dates, belonging to a resident of **Nakhl**.
Ruwi روي	5 miles below Bajarīyah, 1 mile up a side valley.	Right.	......	See article **Ruwi**.
Wataiyah وطيه	2 miles below **Ruwi**.	Do.	Half a dozen houses of Bani **Wahaib**.	Here are date-plantations, arable land and a large house, belonging to the present Sultān of **'Omān**, and assigned by him to his eldest son Taimūr. The annual value of these is $2,000. Irrigation is by a Falaj from the Wādi.

Name.	Position.	On which bank.	Houses and inhabitants.	Remarks.
Quram قُرم	1 mile below Wataiyah and 1½ from the coast.	Right.	15 houses of Hādiyīn and Bani Hasan.	A few cattle and goats are kept.

The portion of Wadi 'Adai from Birain to Mutahaddamāt is considered to be in **Saih Hatāt**. The population of the whole valley is about 500 souls.

ADAM
ادم

The southernmost town in the **'Omān** Sultanate, situated in **'Omān** Proper, 20 to 25 miles south-south-west of **Manah**. To the northward is open country, without human inhabitants, sloping gradually down towards Adam; on the southward the **Ruba'-al-Khāli** begins immediately outside the town. The road from **Manah**, as it approaches Adam, passes between two arid hills of considerable elevation, namely Jabal Salakh سلخ on the west, and Jabal Madhmār مضمار on the east. The town stands some 850 feet above sea level and has extensive date plantations irrigated from warm springs. The principal defence is a large fort built by the Imām Ahmad, the founder of the present Āl Bū Sa'īdi dynasty, who, according to one tradition, was born here: it was repaired in 1869 by Saiyid 'Azzān. The population is about 3,000 souls, comprising about 300 houses of Mahārīq, 150 of Āl Bū **Sa'īd**, 30 of Hawāshim and 20 of Bani Rāshid. The only trade is in dates, which are exported to **Mahōt**. The inhabitants of Adam are too remote to take much part in the faction wars of **'Omān** and maintain feuds among themselves instead.

'ADĀN
عدان

A district in the principality of **Kuwait**, enclosed between the district of **Qrā'ah** on the north, that of **Shaqq** on the west, that of **Salū'** on the south, and the sea on the east. By some authorities 'Adān is considered to include the district of **Qrā'ah**; if, however, we adopt the view that the two are distinct, 'Adān commences 16 miles south of **Kuwait** Town, immediately beyond Malah which is in **Qrā'ah**, and extends 22 miles southwards to the **Qrain** hill which marks its boundary with the district of **Salū'**. Mi'aidniyāt and Subaihīyah, mentioned below, are situated in the north-western and south-western corners respectively of 'Adān, from which it appears that the breadth of the district from the sea inland varies from 10 to 20 miles. On the coast, 'Adān reaches rather further north than Malah and includes Fanaitis, mentioned further on.

'Adān is a plain of softish sand, but elevated so as to form a sort of ridge: there is very little fuel, and almost the only serviceable product is Thamām grass of bad quality.

The nature of such agriculture as exists is described in the articles on **Fahaihīl**, **Fantās**, Abu **Halaifah** and **Shi'aibah**, the only villages in the district. These are virtually dependencies of **Kuwait** Town, to which merchants and others resort in the Aiyām-ar-Rabī' or period preceding the pearling season; the inhabitants are generally unrelated to one another and have been attracted to the service of some prosperous man who has dug a well.

The character of the district may be learned from the following alphabetical table of villages, wells and physical features :*—

Name.	Position.	Nature.	Remarks.
'Aqailah عقيله	Near the coast several miles south of Shi'aibah.	Wells.	Also called Umm-al-'Ausaj عوسج, from the plant, which is abundant here.
'Araifjān عريفجان	1 mile north of Subaihīyah.	Do.	12 feet deep; water brackish. There is also another group of wells similarly named about 3 miles west of Qalai'at-al-'Abīd on the coast.
Burqān برقان	28 miles south of Kuwait Town and 13 miles from the coast.	Hill.	350 feet high; easy of ascent.
Dasht دشت	Reaches southwards along the coast for several miles from Qalai'at-al-'Abīd and extends about 3 miles inland.	A barren plain of sand and swamp, with here and there tufts of Tarfah (a small bushy tamarisk with a handsome feathery pink flower) and of 'Ardiq (a plant with a white flower and a red berry, closely resembling 'Ausaj).	About 5 miles from Qalai'at-al-'Abīd and ¼ of a mile from the coast is a white sand hill known as Banīyat-ad-Dasht بنية الدشت.

* For coastal features see article on Kuwait Principality.

Name.	Position.	Nature.	Remarks.
Dasmah دسمه	9 miles west of Shi'aibah.	Wells.	Brackish water.
Fahaihīl فحيحيل	On the coast, 21 miles south-south-east of Kuwait Town.	Village.	See article Fahaihīl.
Fanaitis فنيطس	On the coast, 8 miles south of Rās-al-Ardh in Qrā'ah.	6 or 7 wells.	12 feet deep; water sufficient for 15 households and slightly brackish, but compares favourably with the water of Kuwait Town.
Fantās فنطاس	On the coast, 16 miles south-south-east of Kuwait Town.	Village.	See article Fantās.
Ghalāb (Niqa'ah) نقعه غلاب	Near the coast, south of the 'Aqailah wells, between them and Qalai'at-al-'Abīd.	Swampy ground covered with Haram bushes.	To the eye this tract appears to be below sea level.
Halaifah (Abu) ابو حليفه	On the coast, 18 miles south-south-east of Kuwait Town.	Village.	See article Abu Halaifah.
Hanaidhil حنيضل	On the coast, 2 miles north of Fantās.	Wells.	Many, but only 2 contain water; depth 18 feet. There is melon cultivation surrounded by walls.
Hilu حلو	2 miles south of Dasmah.	Do.	Two have good water at 18 feet.
Hīmān (Umm-al-) الحيمان	1 mile west of Laqīt.	About 80 wells.	Water good; depth 18 feet. There is also a small group of brackish wells bearing the same name near the coast about 3 miles south of Shi'aibah.
Laqīt لقيط or Lıqait لقيت	25 miles south by east of Kuwait Town and 8 miles west-south-west of Shi'aibah on the coast.	About 50 wells.	Water good, only slightly brackish; depth 20 feet; would suffice for 60 or 70 households. Melon cultivation covers about 1 square mile. A route runs from this point across the desert to Zilfi in Najd.

'ADĀN

Name.	Position.	Nature.	Remarks.
Majū'ah مجوعه	1 mile south of Malah.	5 wells.	Depth 18 feet; water good.
Manīfah منيفه	On the coast between **Fantās** and Hanaidhil.	9 wells.	21 feet deep; good water.
Marair مرير	Less than 1 mile south of Dasmah.	Wells.	Brackish water.
Mazāra' مزارع	3 miles north-west of Laqīt.	Cultivated tract several miles in extent.	Contains numerous wells, 8 of which have good water at 17 feet. Melons are grown in the hot weather.
Mi'aidnīyāt معيدنيات	4 miles west of Malah in **Qrā'ah**; at the north-west corner of 'Adān.	Group of 2 or 3 inconsiderable hills.	...
Mishāsh Habainān مشاش حبينان	Immediately on the west of Mazāra'.	5 wells.	Passable water at 18 feet.
Qābji قابجي	1 mile north of Dasmah.	Wells.	Brackish water.
Qairīyah قيريه	1 mile north of Burqān.	A hollow about 1 mile square.	The depression contains numerous wells, also springs of bitumen or Qīr, whence the name.
Qutqatai قطقطي	2 miles south-east of Dasmah.	Do.	Sweet water.
Safāwi صفاري	Adjoins Laqīt on the north-west.	About 100 wells.	Depth 18 feet; water good; there is some cultivation of melons.
Shi'aibah شعيبه	On the coast, 24 miles south-south-east of **Kuwait Town**.	Village.	See article **Shi'aibah**.

Name.	Position	Nature.	Remarks.
Subailiyah صبيحيه	32 miles south of **Kuwait** Town and 20 miles from the coast.	About 100 wells.	Scattered irregularly over a plain about 1 mile square; in some the water is good, in others brackish; water is struck at 18 feet, but "owing to its strong flow" rises to within 6 feet of the surface; 5 of the wells are lined with stone. The soil here is a white clay covered with white sand. There is no camel-grazing or wood within 1½ miles of the wells.
Tawīl or Tawāil طويل	6 miles west of Wārah.	About 12 wells.	Depth 30 to 40 feet. Water sweet.
Umm Safaq ام صفق	2 miles north-west of Laqīt.	Wells.	Good water at 18 feet; melons are cultivated.
Uqsubah (Umm) ام اقصبه	Near the coast about 5 miles south of **Shi'ai-bah**.	A small group of brackish wells.	...
Wārah واره	9 miles north of Burqān.	About 100 wells.	Good water at 18 feet. There was formerly cultivation here, watered by hand from the wells; it was begun by 'Uthmān of the **'Awāzim** tribe who died 10 years ago. One mile to the west is Nafūd Wārah نفود واره, a hill of black stone 200 feet high and in shape resembling a tower. The top, about 60 feet square, is accessible by a path practicable for mules. The hill commands an extensive view.
Warwar ورور	Immediately on the east of Wārah.	About 40 wells.	18 feet deep; water good.

Rās-al-Qalai'ah and the northern part of Dōhat-az-Zarq, both described in the article on the **Kuwait** Principality, are features upon the coast of this district.

The inhabitants of 'Adān, except in the fixed villages of **Fahaihīl, Fantās,** Abu **Halaifah** and **Shi'aibah,** are wandering Arabs who encamp now at one well, now at another.

The 'Adān district contains the only relics of antiquarian interest which have as yet been discovered in **Kuwait** Principality; these consist of some sarcophagi at a spot 6 miles from the Wārah hill, from which that hill lies at 258° and the westernmost part of the Burqān hill at 214°. The tombs lie east and west and are therefore not Muhammadan: they occupy a plot of high ground about 100 feet square. The sarcophagi are of gypsum cement, about 5 feet long, 1 foot 8 inches broad and 2 feet deep; the thickness of the sides is about 4 inches; they are buried 3 to 4 feet below ground and a large number of stones of irregular shape, each about 2 cubic feet in volume are piled over them. There are no inscriptions. A copper coin found here seemed to be Persian, of **Baghād** mintage, belonging to the 17th or 18th century A.D.*

As used in **Bahrain** and **Hasa** the term 'Adān designates the whole desert tract which extends along the coast between the **Qatīf** Oasis and **Kuwait.** See Barr-al-'**Adān.**

'ADĀN (BARR-AL-)
بر العدان

A term sometimes applied by mariners to the entire coastal region between the towns of **Kuwait** and **Qatīf** in Eastern Arabia. Bedouins, however, seem to be unaware of any such general application of the name; and among them, as among the settled population of the **Kuwait** Principality also, the term 'Adān is only understood as referring to the small tract near **Kuwait** Town which is described in this Gazetteer under the title '**Adān.**

The shore between **Kuwait** and **Qatīf** is a low sandy and stony desert with occasional date-groves owned by Bedouins and a few isolated hills at intervals; it is fronted throughout almost its entire length by extensive reefs, which in places have a passage between them and the mainland; the bottom of the sea in many parts consists of white clay, and the water in consequence is not generally so clear as it is further to the south.

---

* This spot was first visited and described by Captain S. G. Knox, Political Agent at Kuwait, in March 1906.

The pearl banks decrease in number off this coast, and, though there are some small pearl fisheries further to the northwards, they may be said to end near Abu 'Ali island. The districts composing Barr-al-'Adān are enumerated in the articles upon the **Kuwait** Principality and the **Hasa** Sanjāq, and most of them form the subject of separate articles under their own names.

'ADI (BANI) بني عدي

Singular 'Adwāni عدواني. A Hināwi tribe of the **'Omān** Sultanate, found chiefly in the Western **Hajar** district where they occupy the villages of Sawālih, Murbah, Qasra, Ghashab and Wabil in Wādi **Fara'**. They are found also on the coast at **Quryāt** and at Ghuwaisah in the sub-Wilāyat of **Saham**. Those at Ghashab belong to a section called Bani Bakr بني بكر. Their total number is about 5,000 souls. At present they have no Tamīmah or other recognised chiefs.

AFLĀJ افلاج

Or Aflāg, sometimes called with greater precision Aflāj (or Aflāg) ad-Dawāsir افلاج الدواسر. A district of Southern **Najd** descending from Jabal **Tuwaiq** on the west to the **Dahánah** desert on the east; north of it lie the districts of **Hautah** and **Kharj**, and on the south a great depression called Maqran مقرن divides it from the **Ruba'-al-Khāli**. There is no means of determining the real size or exact position of Aflāj, but it is stated to be several caravan days in length from east to west; and the centre of Farshah, which is one of its subdivisions, is said to be 2 or 3 days south of the centre of **Kharj**.

Divisions and physical features.—The Aflāj district consists of several tracts differing in their characteristics and distinguished by names. Near the western end is Hadhāfah حضافه, a region enclosed by Jabal **Tuwaiq** on the west and by Jabal Birk برك —probably, but not certainly, a spur of Jabal **Tuwaiq**—on the north; Hadhafah is described as uninhabited and covered with thorny jungle and is perhaps the part of Aflāj which lies between the hill villages mentioned in the topographical table below and the other villages further to the east. If this assumption is correct, Hadhāfah is seamed by a series of parallel valleys which run eastwards from the hill villages of

Aflāj to those of the plain, conveying the drainage of the hills. Of these, the northernmost is one which descends to Wusailah from Harādhah and is joined between Wusailah and Ghail by another coming from Stārah and Ghail; the third passes Hamar and Wāsit on its way to **Kharfah** and **Saih**; a fourth has its rise near Haddār and ends near **Badī'**; the southernmost begins at Shutbah, and arrives by way of 'Ijlīyah at Hinu, which is also in the neighbourhood of **Badī'**.

On the east of Hadhāfah is Aflāj proper, the most important subdivision of the Aflāj district; it resembles Hadhāfah in being bounded on the north by Jabal Birk, a pass in which—called Salāmīyah سلامية— connects it with the district of **Hautah**. The plain villages of Aflāj are all situated in this part of the district; their names and positions will be found in the topographical table at the end of this article. Besides the numerous wells irrigating date plantations and gardens, Aflāj proper is said to contain as many as 14 springs. One of these, called Yahmūm يحموم, rises a short distance to the east of Rajaijīyah village and forms a stream, which, after flowing about 3 miles, leaves a tall black hill on its left bank and continues on its way through stony ground until it is absorbed by sandy soil at a distance of about 20 miles from its source.

Next below and to the east of Aflāj proper is the Farshah فرشه tract, on the northern side of which the Jabal Birk spur at length dies away and ceases to form a barrier between Aflāj and **Kharj**. Farshah has numerous wells and some wheat is grown, but there are no trees or villages; cultivation, where it exists, is defended by small forts.

Farshah is followed on the east by Biyādhah بياضه, a tract which is adjoined on the north by **Sahábah**. Biyādhah contains no springs or wells, but there are Sidr and other wild trees and some grazing. Apparently at the south-eastern corner of Biyādhah is a prominent, dark-coloured hill named Da'ajah دعجه, having wells to which Bedouins resort.

East of Biyādhah again is Haraisān هريسان; Da'ajah, just mentioned, marks the point of transition from the somewhat sandy surface of Biyādhah to the more pebbly ground of Haraisān. The flood water of Haraisān is carried eastwards into the **Dahánah** by a depression, called Mahammil مهمل, which is barren but contains some grazing.

Shutbah شتبه, a tract situated in a recess in the eastern flank of Jabal **Tuwaiq** and containing a village of the same name, is generally reckoned to Aflāj; but it lies in the direction of Widyān **Dawāsir** and is included by some authorities in that district; its drainage appears to escape north-eastwards into the neighbourhood of **Badī'** in Aflāj proper.

We may note that the Aflāj district is apparently skirted on the south throughout a considerable proportion of its length, by a depression called Jadwal جدول which is to the north of Maqran and parallel to that valley, but of much smaller size. The beginning and end of Jadwal have not been successfully located; but it appears to be shorter than Maqran, which is said to extend the whole way from Jabal **Tuwaiq** to the **Dahánah**, and it is positively asserted that Jadwal and Maqran do not communicate with one another. According to some authorities the Jadwal depression receives a torrent called Harim حرم from the direction of **Badī'** and swallows up the Yahmūm stream which, as we have seen, rises near Rajaijīyah. Maqran is said to contain large Sidr and other trees, and wells at which animals can be watered.

Population.—As will be apparent from the topographical table which concludes this article, the settled inhabitants of Aflāj are mostly **Dawāsir** landowners and their cultivators of the Bani **Khadhīr** tribe; but there are also a few representatives of the **Fadhūl, Sahūl** and **Sabai'**, and possibly of the **'Anizah** and of other smaller but still distinct tribes, besides negro and half caste slaves.* The total number of the fixed population of Aflāj may be roughly estimated at 22,000 souls. The people are Wahhābis.

Agriculture and general resources.—The topographical table at the end of this article and the related articles to which it affords a clue contain some information as to the crops and livestock of Aflāj. It appears that the agricultural staples are dates, wheat, barley and lucerne, and in a lesser degree fruits, maize and millet. The fruit trees of the hill villages are superior to those of the plains; but, in regard to livestock, the lower lying villages are the better provided with horses. The domestic animals are those of Southern **Najd** generally, *viz.*, camels, donkeys, horned cattle, sheep and goats.

Administration.—In comparison with the more northern districts of the Wahhābi dominions Aflāj is backward and uncivilised; and, in common with the neighbouring but still more remote district of Widyān **Dawāsir**, it seems to play but a small part in the political life of the country. Aflāj appears to have been but little affected by the internecine struggle, since 1880, between the rulers of **Hāil** and **Riyādh**; but it is

---

* According to Palgrave the half caste population at **Kharfah** in 1862 almost equalled the Arab in numbers and, like full negroes, frequently wore nothing but a waist cloth. Hospitality was meagre, and a want of sociability and a coarseness of manners were observable. It should be added that Palgrave's account of his journey to **Kharfah** does not inspire confidence, chiefly on account of the position which he assigns to it and to Aflāj with reference to adjoining districts.

stated that the Wahhābi Amīr now extracts an annual revenue of about $20,000 from the district, of which ⅓ is paid by the Bedouins and ⅔ by the villagers. The control of the settled villages of the plain appears to be vested in the headmen (here called Amīrs) of the principal villages of **Badī'**, **Kharfah, Lailah, Raudhah** and **Saih,** each of them being answerable for the component hamlets of his own group: in the hills, however, each village is independent of the others and subject to its own Shaikh, the only exception being Wāsit which is under Hamar.

Topography.—The following is a table, alphabetically arranged, of the inhabited places in Aflāj :—

Name.	Position.	Houses and inhabitants.	Remarks.
'Amār عمار	In the middle of the triangle formed by Lailah, Saih and Kharfah and about 3 miles from each of those places.	60 houses of Mughairah, a shaikhly section of the Fadhūl, and 40 of Bani Khadhīr who cultivate for them. The people are said to have come from Raudhah 30 years ago, on account of a quarrel, and settled here.	This village is independent of Saih and its name has no connection with the 'Ammār section of the Dawāsir. There are 2,000 date palms, all young, and the usual fruit trees and cereals. Lucerne and melons grow freely. Water is at 6 fathoms. The ordinary animals of Aflāj are kept, but there are no horses. The Amīr of 'Amār is 'Abdur Rahmān-bin-Shabīb of the Mughairah.
Badī' بديع	The southernmost village in Aflāj.	...	See article **Badī'**.
Ghail غيل	In the hills of Aflāj 15 miles to the north-west of Lailah, upon a depression which runs down eastwards to Wusailah.	160 houses, of which about 20 belong to slaves.	The place is described as extremely unhealthy for Arabs, and the date plantations, which are very large, are said to be tended by hired cultivators from the plain villages. Water is from springs. The usual fruits, cereals and lucerne are grown. Bedouins pillage the date-groves of the absent owners.

AFLĀJ

Name.	Position.	Houses and inhabitants.	Remarks.
Haddār هدار	In the hills of Aflāj at a distance of 30 miles (or possibly more) due west of **Badī'** and perhaps 15 miles south-west of Hamar. The drainage of Haddār apparently runs to **Badī'**.	20 houses of Intaifāt, 50 of Musārīr and 100 of Widā'īn, all sections of the **Dawāsir** tribe; also 20 houses of Bani **Khadhīr**. Besides these houses there are many detached Qasrs possessed by the same tribes.	This is the highest in elevation of the hill villages of Aflāj and also, apparently, the most remote. The march from **Badī'** is said to occupy 15 hours and to be broken generally at Dhaba'īyah ضبعيه, where there are wells and an abandoned Qasr and where the plain ends and the hills begin. Water is at 4 to 5 fathoms below the surface. There are said to be 7,000 date palms and a few fruit trees, besides the usual crops and domestic animals of Aflāj.
Hamar حمر	In the hills, about 20 miles west of **Saih** to which its drainage descends.	300 houses of **Dawāsir** of the Ishkarah section, 100 of the Hanābijah section, and 80 of Bani **Khadhīr**. Besides these there are a number of isolated enclosures.	The name is said to be due to the fact that the hills from which floods reach the village are of a blood-red colour and that the flood water itself is red. There are extensive date-groves, besides the usual fruit trees, cereals, lucerne and melons; also the ordinary domestic animals and 25 horses. Water stands 6 to 7 fathoms below the surface.
Harādhah حراضه	In the hills about 9 miles north-west of Stārah, at the head of a valley which runs down to Wusailah joining that from Stārah and Ghail before it reaches Wusailah.	100 houses of **Sahūl** of the 'Anājīd section and 25 of Bani **Khadhīr**.	There are two routes between Ghail and Harādhah, one direct and one by Stārah. The date trees here are estimated at 8,000 and the fruit trees are specially good. Water is at 3 to 4 fathoms. Lucerne and the usual cereals grow and there are 10 horses besides the ordinary livestock of Aflāj.

AFLĀJ

Name.	Position.	Houses and inhabitants.	Remarks.
Kharfah خرفه	In the middle of the district, 3 miles north of Raudhah and 5 or 6 miles south-south-west of Lailah.	...	See article Kharfah.
Lailah ليله	Towards the north end of Aflāj, about 4 miles north-west of Saih and 5 miles south of Wusailah.	...	See article Lailah.
Marwān مروان	About 6 miles north-east of Badī'.	30 houses of Dawāsir of the Māna' sub-section of the 'Ammār, and 40 of Bani Khadhīr cultivators living in the date gardens. Large numbers of Bedouins resort but do not reside here.	There are 6,000 date palms, but no fruit trees; the usual cereals, lucerne, melons and water-melons are grown, and the ordinary livestock of Aflāj, besides some horses, are kept. The resident Dawāsir own half the date-groves and the Bedouins the other half. Water is abundant at 4 fathoms. Southwest of Marwān, in the direction of Badī', is a spot Qā'iyah قاعيه where there are no fixed habitations, but cultivators from Marwān raise crops of wheat and barley.
Rajaijīyah رجيجيه	2 miles north of Marwān.	10 houses of Idghamah Dawāsir and 30 of Bani Khadhīr; the latter are cultivators but reside within the village enclosure.	Date palms are about 4,000, but there are no other fruit trees; of the date groves about $\frac{3}{4}$ are owned by Bedouins who resort here in large numbers in the season. Lucerne, melons and cereals are cultivated and there are the usual livestock, also 12 horses. The water in the wells is at 4 fathoms from the surface. The Yahmūm stream, described above, rises to the east or north-east of Rajaijīyah; but the cultivation of its banks is prevented by the Bedouins.

Name.	Position.	Houses and inhabitants.	Remarks.
Raudhah روضه	About 3 miles south of **Kharfah** and 10 miles north by west of **Badī'**.	...	See article **Raudhah**.
Saih سيح	About 4 miles south-east of **Lailah** and 7 miles north-east of **Raudhah**.	...	See article **Saih**.
Shinādhir (Umm) ام شناضر	1½ miles north of **Wusailah**.	20 houses of **Fadh-ūl**, forming a Qasr, and 10 of inferior tribes.	There are about 500 date palms. Water in the wells is at about 9 fathoms.
Shutbah شتبه	At the head of a valley which drains down north-eastwards to Hinu, a place connected with **Badī'**.	40 houses of **Bani Khadhīr**, cultivators. The owners are Khadhrān Dawāsir who reside elsewhere and only visit the place to collect their share of the produce in the harvest.	There are 2,000 date palms here, but no fruit trees of other kinds. There is also ordinary cultivation of cereals and lucerne. The village is described as capable of much improvement, but greatly neglected by its present owners.
Stārah ساتاره	In the hills of Aflāj, in the same valley as Ghail, but perhaps 12 miles further up it and westwards.	20 houses of **Sahūl** of the Qubābinah section and 60 houses of inferior tribes.	Cultivated date palms are estimated at 3,000 and wild ones at 1,500. The cultivation and livestock are the same as in the other hill villages of Aflāj. The water level is 2 to 3 fathoms below the surface of the ground.
Wāsit واسط	In the same valley as Hamar, but perhaps 5 miles further east and further down.	30 houses of **Dawāsir** of the Huqbān section and 20 of Bani **Khadhīr**.	Date palms number about 7,000 and are partly owned by inhabitants of Hamar. Other fruits and crops are average; so also are livestock, except that there are no horses. Water occurs at 4 fathoms.

Name.	Position.	Houses and inhabitants.	Remarks.
Wusailah رسيله	About 5 miles north of Lailah.	30 houses of **Dawāsir**, *viz.*, 20 of the 'Arfaj and 10 of the Ishkarah section; also 8 of Bani **Hājir** and 20 of inferior tribes.	There are no ordinary fruit trees and only about 500 date palms; but there is good cultivation of barley and wheat, and melons, watermelons, onions and lucerne are raised. Irrigation is from wells and the water is raised by camel, bullock or donkey power from a depth of 6 fathoms. There are no horses; but sheep and goats are numerous. Wusailah is under **Lailah**. In the middle of the Wusailah lands is some high ground called Rifā'ah رفاعه with ruins of houses; it is now uncultivated as well as uninhabited.

'ĀHIN (WĀDI)
وادي عاهن

A valley in the Sultanate of **'Omān** which has its head at Najd Wuqbah in the Western **Hajar** and reaches the sea about half an hour west of **Saham** Town in **Bātinah**. The inhabited part of the valley is in **Hajar**, where it is small and narrow: the houses are of mud and stone. Dates are grown on terraces on the hills; other crops are wheat, bajri and lucerne. The people, who are mostly Bani' **Īsa**, also own some sheep and cattle. The market-towns of Wādi 'Āhin are **Sohār, Saham** and **Khābūrah** in **Bātinah**. The following are the villages of this Wādi in order from the coast upwards:—

Name.	Distance in hours from the coast.	On which bank (proper).	Houses and inhabitants.	Resources.
Falaj-ash-Shakhāriyīn فلج الشخاريين	5	Right.	50 houses of Shakhāriyīn.	100 camels, 150 donkeys and 800 sheep and goats.

'ĀHIN (WĀDI)

Names.	Distance in hours from the coast.	On which bank (proper).	Houses and inhabitants.	Resources.
Gharaifah غريفه	8	Left.	200 houses of Bani 'Īsa.	100 camels, 80 donkeys and 1,000 sheep and goats.
Ghadhaifah غضيفه	8	Right.	Do.	70 camels, 50 donkeys and 600 sheep and goats.
Wuqbah ربقه	12	Do.	100 houses of Bani 'Ali.	200 camels, 150 donkeys and 2,000 sheep and goats.

The population of Wādi 'Āhin is thus about 3,000 souls. Najd Wuqbah is 2 hours above the village of the same name and about 4 north of Yanqul in **Dhāhirah**. The valley contains a flowing stream.

AHRAM
اهرم

The chief place in the **Persian Coast** district of **Tangistān**; it is situated 27 miles east-south-east of **Būshehr** Town and 17 miles north-north-west of **Khurmūj**, the capital of the adjoining district of **Dashti**. Ahram stands at a short distance from the right bank of the Ahram or Bāhūshi stream, a little below its exit from the hills, and is overlooked by the Kūh Gūgardi mountain a few miles to the north-east; its elevation above the sea is 360 feet.

The town, which is not now walled, covers an area of nearly ½ a square mile; it is enclosed by date-groves on the north and south, and palms partially mask its western face also. On the south-west side is a stone fort; the residence of the Khān of **Tangistān**, which has walls 40 feet high and round towers at the four corners. The town within is crowded with mud and stone houses and contains many mat huts, but a large proportion of the houses are ruinous and uninhabited.

The inhabitants number about 1,500 souls and belong to the various tribes which, under the common denomination of Tangistānis, compose the population of the surrounding district. They depend on the cultivation of wheat, barley, dates and water-melons and have no industrial or commercial resources; communication with **Būshehr** however is maintained by constant caravans. Animals are 20 horse,

5 mules, 40 camels, 200 donkeys, 70 cattle and 1,500 sheep and goats, and the date palms are estimated at 20,000. Grazing in the neighbourhood of Ahram is excellent, but water though abundant is very brackish.

AHWĀZ* اهواز DISTRICT

The largest but not the most important district in Southern 'Arabistān.

Position and boundaries.—Ahwāz district reaches on the west almost to the **Karkheh** river, meeting there the district of **Hawīzeh**; on the south it is bounded by the districts of **Muhammareh** and **Fallāhīyeh**, on the south-east by the district of **Jarrāhi**, on the east by the district of **Rāmuz**, on the north-east by the **Bakhtiyāri** country, and on the north by the districts of **Shūshtar** and **Dizfūl**.

Natural features and general topography.—The great plain between the **Kārūn** river and the **Rāmuz** District, which has no general name though parts of it are distinguished and designated, lies entirely in the Ahwāz District, of which it forms about half; this plain is generally grassy, and in favourable years it is sprinkled with patches of wheat cultivation. After rain it becomes swampy, and in some seasons the mosquitoes are very troublesome. The **Gūpāl** stream enters the plain at its eastern end and forms a marsh at Shākheh towards its centre; and the principal hills are those of Ahwāz and Bunneh, elsewhere described. A considerable strip of country, parallel to the **Kārūn** river on its east side, is drained by the **Mālih** hollow which begins near **Ahwāz** and ends near Gharaibeh in the **Fallāhīyeh** District; a ridge of higher country divides the marshes formed by the Mālih in its lower course from the overflow southwards towards the **Jarrāhi** of the surplus waters of the **Gūpāl** stream. The main feature, however, of the Ahwāz District is the **Kārūn** river bisecting it, which is the subject of a separate article. The part of the district to the west of the **Kārūn** is still, except for information from native sources, virtually a *terra incognita*.

---

* It has been suggested that اهواز (Ahwāz) is a corruption of احواز, the plural of the word حوز (Hūz) common in Southern 'Arabistān in the sense of a cultivated area or estate. The conjecture is plausible, and furnishes an explanation at the same time of the origin of the name Hawīzeh, and possibly even of that of "Khūzistān"——the old name of 'Arabistān——which may have been in the beginning "Hūzistān." Another derivation of Ahwāz is given in Curzon's *Persia*, II, 351 (footnote): see also Le Strange, p. 232.

D

The following is a table of the principal natural features and localities having names which occur in the district* :—

Name.	Position.	Nature.	Remarks.
'Adhām (Tubaij Umm-al-) تبيج أم العظام	Adjoining the range of hills near Ahwāz Village.	A small rocky hill.	The outliers of the Ahwāz hills, of which this is one, lie more or less parallel to the main range.
Ahwāz (Kūh-i- or Jabal-al-) كوه اهواز or جبل الاهواز	Cross the Kārūn river at Ahwāz Village and extend in the direction of Banneh.	Hills.	See article on Southern 'Arabistān.
'Araibīyeh عريبيه	11 miles north of Thiniyeh, close to Tawīleh, etc.	A locality.	Bāwīyeh of the 'Amūr section frequent this place.
Asad (Shaikh) شيخ اسد	8 miles east of Ismā'īli on the Kārūn.	A camping ground.	So named from the Shaikh—still alive—of a Bāwīyeh section who are accustomed to pitch here.
Banneh بنه	Several, perhaps 9 or 10, miles south or south-south-east of the point where the Nāsiri-Rāmuz route crosses the Gūpāl Stream.	A group of hills with the lands adjoining.	The hills appear to be a continuation of the ridge which crosses the Kārūn river at Ahwāz Village. Bāwīyeh of the Bait Sunhair section camp and cultivate at this place; also numerous Ka'ab of the Muqaddam division. The presence of two lions here was reported in 1904.
Bu'airish بعيرش	On the Nāsiri-Rāmuz road, beginning about 3 miles east of the Gūpāl Stream and ending 3 miles further east at the border of the Rāmuz District.	A level plain with vestiges of a deserted village.	Bāwīyeh of the 'Amūr section and others are to be found here in winter. The name of the place is also given as Libairish لبيرش.
Buaa' بدع	16 miles south by east of Nāsiri, on the left bank of the Malih.	A locality.	This spot is upon the direct route from Nāsiri to Gharaibeh in the Fallāhīyeh District.

* Except those on the Kārūn river, the article on which may be consulted.

AHWĀZ DISTRICT

Name.	Position.	Nature.	Remarks.
Būmeh (Tal) تل بومه	About 4 miles north-east of **Wais**.	A locality.	The inhabitants are **Hōtah** or shepherds not belonging to any particular tribe.
Buwairdeh بويرده	4 to 5 miles east of **Wais**.	Ditto.	This is a habitat of **Salāmāt** Arabs of the **Māsakh** section.
Chinaibeh چنيبه	On the right bank of the **Kārūn** 4 miles above Karaishān.	Ditto.	Frequented by **Bāwīyeh** of the Bait Khaz'al section.
Fāris (Tubaij) تبيج فارس	Adjoins the Ahwāz hills, apparently to the westward of Thinīyeh.	A rocky hill.	See remarks under Tubaij Umm-al-'Adhām.
Faqaisāt (Chāi) چاي فقيسات	2 miles north of Shākheh.	A locality.	The Farātiseh tribe are found here.
Gharaibeh (Umm-al-) ام الغريبه	7 miles east by north of **Wais**.	A place with shallow wells, where there are generally 15 to 20 households of **Hamaid** Arabs, apparently poor. The population varies with the season.	The routes from **Ahwāz** Village and **Wais** to 'Alwānīyeh unite here. After rain there is a large body of standing water at this place which to travellers is better known as Kunār, on account of a large tree which forms a landmark.
Gūpāl Stream گوپال	Enters the district on its eastern side towards the north and ends in the marsh at Shākheh.	...	See article **Gūpāl**.
Hauzi (Shaikh) شيخ حوزي	12 miles south-south-east of **Nāsiri**.	A camping ground.	**Bāwīyeh** Bedouins pitch here, and the place takes its name from one of their former Shaikhs.
Hilweh خلوه	About 8 miles north of Shākheh.	A locality.	There is fresh water here on which the Jāma' tribe in the neighbourhood depend for their supply.
Hisān (Dōb-al-) دوب الحصان	Between **Nāsiri** and **Fallāhiyeh** Town, about 20 miles from the latter.	Ditto.	One of the seats of the Āl Bū 'Atuwi and Āl Bū Balid sections of the **Bāwīyeh**.

D 2

AHWĀZ DISTRICT

Name.	Position.	Nature.	Remarks.
Imbāraki الا مباركي	11 miles east of Ismā'īli on the Kārūn and close to Khudhairiyāt.	A locality.	Bāwīyeh of the Bait Rahāmeh section occupy this neighbourhood.
Ishtīreh (Khar) خر اشتيره	On the right bank of the Kārūn nearly opposite Ahwāz Village.	A depression forming a line of drainage.	The 'Anāfijeh tribe formerly extended as far south as this point.
Jarbeh جربه	11 miles south-east of Nāsiri.	A locality.	Bāwīyeh are found here of the Hilaichīyeh sub-section of the Nawāsir section of the tribe. The name of this place is pronounced Yarbeh.
Jarrāh (Nasir-bin-) ناصر بن جرّاخ	12 miles south-east of Muzaffari on the Kārūn.	A camping ground.	The name is pronounced Yarrāh. Nomad Bāwīyeh frequent this spot which is named after one of their Shaikhs, now deceased.
Jāsim (Saiyid) سيد جاسم	In the Bu'airish plain towards its north-west side.	Ditto.	Occupied in winter by Saiyid families.
Kādhim كاظم	...	Ditto.	A resort of Bāwīyeh nomads, taking its name from one of their former Shaikhs.
Karaid كريد	2 miles north of Thinīyeh.	A locality.	Frequented by the Āl Barūmi subsection of the Nawāsir section of the Bāwīyeh, but often unoccupied even in winter. There is a well of fresh water and, after rain, a standing pool here.
Kārūn River كارون	Traverses the district with a south-westerly course.	...	See article Kārūn.
Khudhairiyāt الخضيريات	11 miles east of Ismā'īli on the Kārūn and close to Imbāraki.	A locality.	Frequented by Bāwīyeh of the Bait Rahāmeh section.

AHWĀZ DISTRICT

Name.	Position.	Nature.	Remarks.
Luqbair لقبير	On the right bank of the **Kārūn** adjoining and including the village of Kūt Saiyid Ismā'īl.	A tract.	The Marawuneh tribe have their head-quarters here. The correct form of the name is Al-Qubair القبير
Mālih مالح	Begins in the Thinīyeh or gap in the Ahwāz hills and ends at, or just short of, Gharaibeh on the **Jarrāhi** River.	A hollow running from north to south and carrying the drainage, after rain, of a large extent of country; at such times it becomes a flowing stream of slightly brackish water.	From the neighbourhood of **Nāsiri** to a point 6 miles north of Gharaibeh the Mālih has a canal-like bed, beyond this it has no banks and after wet weather spreads over the country westwards and south-westwards as far as the eye can see.
Mandīl (Tubaij) تبيج منديل	Adjoins the Ahwāz hills.	A stony hill or hillock.	As at Tubaij 'Umm-al-'Adhām.
Mārid (Shaikh) شيخ مارد	2 miles south of Shaikh Asad.	A camping ground.	Nomad Bāwīyeh occupy this place, which takes its name from one of their present Shaikhs. About 1 mile to the east of Shaikh Mārid is a ruined Imāmzādeh called Maghrūr.
Miz'al (Bait) بيت مزعل	13 miles east by south of Ismā'īli on the **Kārūn**, upon the right bank of an old canal which ran from **Nāsiri** in the direction of **Fallāhīyeh** Town.	Ditto.	A resort of Bāwīyeh nomads, called after a Shaikh now deceased.
Musarbeh (Jabal) (spelling uncertain).	...	...	See Kūh-i-Ahwāz above. The name is also pronounced Umsarbeh.
Qāmīsh قاميش	4 miles south of Thinīyeh.	A locality.	Bāwīyeh of the Awāudeh subsection of the Nawāsir section are found here.

Name.	Position.	Nature.	Remarks.
Rashid (Shaikh) شيخ راشد	On the right bank of the Gūpāl Stream at the point where the Nāsiri-Rāmuz route crosses it.	A camping ground.	200 houses of the Bāwīyeh tribe may be found here in the cold weather.
Sawaiseh سويسه	8 miles east of Braikeh on the Kārūn.	A locality.	There is another spot bearing the same name a little way south of Thinīyeh.
Shākheh شاخه	On the west side of Banneh.	The tract irrigated by the Gūpāl Stream below the point where the stream breaks up: its limits are not precisely defined but it appears to be several miles in extent. A village also generally known as Shākheh, is situated in this tract near the route from Nāsiri to Rāmuz and about 6 miles west of the Gūpāl Stream.	The village stands on the bank of a very brackish canal from the Gūpāl stream, is adjoined by several square miles of indifferent wheat cultivation, and consists of about 40 houses of Ka'ab of the Muqaddam division. Besides the village the tract contains large semi-permanent settlements of Ka'ab. The Shākheh tract is also inhabited by Bāwīyeh of the Āl Bū 'Atuwi and Bait Sunhair sections.
Shārtāgh شارتاغ	7 miles east of Kūt Nahr Hāshim on the Karkheh.	A locality.	The inhabitants are Hardān of the 'Abūdeh, Hardān and Bani Tamīm sections.
Shawweh شوه	East of Shākheh on the borders of the Rāmuz District.	Ditto.	Frequented by the Shawākir tribe.
Sīdīyeh (I) سيديه	On the right bank of the Kārūn river below Li'aimi.	Ditto.	A principal residence of the Shijairāt section of the Hardān tribe.
Sīdīyeh (II) سيديه	11 miles south-south-east of Nāsiri.	Ditto.	Bāwīyeh encamp here.

AHWĀZ DISTRICT

Name.	Position.	Nature.	Remarks.
Sūdān (Chāi) چاي سودان	About 11 miles north of Thinī-yeh.	A locality.	Bāwīyeh of the 'Amūr section are found here.
Tarfeh (Umm-at-) ام الطرفه	About 11 miles north of Thinīyeh. Adjoins the last.	Ditto.	A resort of Bāwīyeh of the Āl Bū 'Atuwi and Al Bū Bālid sections.
Tawīleh طويله	Ditto.	Ditto.	Bāwīyeh of the 'Amūr section occur here.
Thidīyain ثدييں	4 miles east of Qrāneh on the Kārūn river.	2 mounds close together on the track of an old canal.	Zarqān of the Āl Bū Lahaiyab and Āl Bū Subti sections have huts of mud and mats at this place.
Thinīyeh ثنيه	About 7 miles east-south-east of Nāsiri.	A gap in the Ahwāz hills, q.v. above.	The Mālih begins here. Immediately to the north-east of Thinī-yeh is ground which is swampy in the cold weather and forms the head of the Mālih.
Yarrāt (I) يرات	Near Buwairdeh, 5 or 6 miles east of Wais.	A locality.	Zarqān of the Bait Muhārib and other sections are found here. Also called Jarrāt.
Yarrāt (II) يرات	Between Thidīyain and Ahwāz Village.	Ditto.	Visited by Zarqān of the Āl Bū Fādhil section.
Zuwair زوير	4 miles east of Naddāfīyeh on the Kārūn river.	Ditto.	A habitat of Hamaid of the 'Awāmir section.
Zūwīyeh زويه	On the left bank of the Kārūn river, about the village of Kūt Saiyid 'Abbās which it includes.	Ditto.	...

To the foregoing may be added the features and localities that follow below; but these, it should be noted, though closely connected with the district, are really outside its limits, being situated either in the

AHWÁZ DISTRICT

Bakhtiyāri country or in a tract adjoining the Gargar of which the position, administratively, appears to be doubtful.

Name.	Position.	Nature.	Remarks.
Alwānīyeh علوانیّة	On the Bakhtiyāri Road between the Raghaiweh tract on the west and the Gypsum Hills, which here bound the Ahwāz plain on the east; its nearer edge is thus about 23½ miles east by north of Wais and the further one about 25 miles. It is divided from Raghaiweh by the Shūr watercourse.	A tract of land of which the limits are imperfectly defined; it appears to include other smaller tracts known as Darrehbīd, Umm-al-Gharab, Sālmīyeh, and Umm-at-Tarfeh; and it contains a white oil spring at its eastern end near the foot of the hills. Sālmīyeh is sometimes used as halting place by travellers on the Bakhtiyāri Road.	Wheat and barley are cultivated about 'Alwānīyeh by nomads, chiefly Hamaid Arabs, in the winter months; and in spring there is good pasture in the neighbourhood. The place is also visited by so-called Turkish tribes under the protection of the Bakhtiyāris. 'Alwānīyeh is in the jurisdiction of the Bakhtiyāri Khāns.
Darrehbīd درّه بید	Included in the 'Alwānīyeh tract.	A locality.	...
Gharab (Umm-al) امّ الغرب	Ditto.	Ditto.	...
Haddām هدّام	On the east side of the Gargar, striking that river about 8 miles by water above Band-i-Qīr.	A hollow which after rain contains water and becomes a left bank tributary of the Gargar.	The neighbourhood of Haddām is frequented by various tribes. Salāmāt are found to the north of it and Hamaid on both sides; south of it are the Āl Bū Harmeh, who are perhaps a branch of the Muhaisin.
Hasanīyeh حسنیّة	11 miles east of Saiyid Hasan on the Gargar.	A locality.	The inhabitants are Hamaid of the 'Attāb section.
Hubaishiyāt حبیشیات	5 miles from Raghaiweh in the direction of Nāsiri.	Ditto.	Salāmāt of the 'Abdu Wais section and others are to be found here. This place formerly belonged to the Hamaid.

AHWAZ DISTRICT

Name	Position.	Nature.	Remarks.
Kharrān خرّان	On the east side of **Gargar** from Būlaiti down to Saiyid Hasan.	A tract seamed by numerous drainage hollows, whence its name.	Frequented by the Bait Sha'aibath subsection of the Dilfīyeh section of the 'Anāfijeh and by the Bani Na'āmeh division of the **Hardān**. There is a Qadamgāh here called Shiraif.
Linhairi لنهيري	...	...	See Nihairīyeh below.
Nihairīyeh نهيريه	11 miles east by north of **Wais**, on the north side of the Bakhtiyāri Road.	Wells and a small permanent Arab camp similar to those at **Umm-al-Gharaibeh**.	Also called Linhairi. The occupants are **Hamaid** of the Kharāmizeh section and pay revenue to the Samsām-as-Saltaneh, Īlkhāni of the **Bakhtiyāris**.
Qaswān قصوان	About one mile from Nihairīyeh, apparently eastwards.	A locality.	**Hamaid** of the 'Abdu Wais and other sections and with them 'Anāfijeh of the 'Abādāt section resort to this place.
Raghaiweh رغيوه	On the Bakhtiyāri Road, between the Shūr watercourse and a point $3\frac{1}{2}$ miles to the west of it; 'Alwānīyeh is immediately to the east of it, divided from it by the Shūr.	A tract of open country with a well of fresh water towards its western end.	Raghaiweh was formerly included in the territories of the Shaikh of **Muhammareh**, but jurisdiction over it was gradually acquired by the Khāns of the **Bakhtiyāris** and for some years a dispute existed which was a cause of heart-burning. During this period Raghaiweh became a place of refuge for discontented subjects of the Shaikh emigrating from his jurisdiction. Eventually in 1905 an arrangement was reached between the Shaikh and the Īlbaigi of the **Bakhtiyāris** by which the former was permitted to remove his subjects and also

Name.	Position.	Nature.	Remarks.
			obtained a lease of the tract. This arrangement is not agreeable to the Īlkhāni of the **Bakhtiyāris** who is the owner of the land. At the end of 1906 the only inhabitants were **Hamaid** occupying a tribal camp which the Shaikh of **Muhammareh** had established at the west end of the tract for the protection of the Bakhtiyāri Road. So-called Turkish tribes under **Bakhtiyāri** protection also visit Raghaiweh.
Sālmīyeh سالمیة	In the 'Alwānīyeh tract at its west end, adjoining the Shūr watercourse.	A camping ground with wells.	This is the ordinary halting place in 'Alwānīyeh for travellers by the Bakhtiyāri Road. At times a few tents or shelters of **Hamaid** Arabs are to be found here and water is obtainable; at others the place is deserted and waterless.
Shūr شور	Between the 'Alwānīyeh and Rāghaiweh tracts, the former being on its left and the latter on its right bank.	A watercourse crossed by the **Wais Rāmuz** road at $23\frac{1}{2}$ miles from **Wais**.	The bed is saline and generally dry.

Villages and population.—The fixed villages of the district are almost without exception situated upon the **Kārūn**, the largest being **Nāsiri**, Muzaffari, **Ahwāz**, Braikeh and **Wais**; and the settled population of the district, including besides the **Kārūn** villages the large semi-permanent settlements of Banneh and Shākheh, may be estimated at 13,000 souls. The sedentary population consists chiefly of **Bāwīyeh**, Āl Bū **Kurd**, Dizfūlis, Shūshtaris and Ma'āwīyeh; but among them there are **Hamaid**, **Zarqān**, Hawāshim and **Muhaisin**, and a very few 'Ikrish and Sabians. The Ka'ab of Banneh and Shākheh are here reckoned among the fixed inhabitants of the district, and there is proportion of miscellan-

AHWĀZ DISTRICT

cous Arabs and Persians. The mud brick used in domestic architecture is of the same pattern as in the **Jarrāhi** District.

The nomad population is very much larger, amounting to about 37,930 souls, and includes the bulk of the **Bāwīyeh** tribe and of the **'Anāfijeh**; besides these there are Farātiseh, **Hamaid, Hardān,** Hawāshim, Jāma', **Ka'ab,** Marawuneh, **Muhaisin,** Āl Bū Rawāyeh, Bait **Sa'ad, Salāmāt,** Shawākir, Bani **Tamīm** and **Zarqān**; of these the **Hamaid, Hardān** and **Salāmāt** are chiefly found on the outskirts of the district, in the quarter to which the second of the topographical tables given above refers.

The following is a tabular account of the principal among the minor tribes which have their headquarters in, or are peculiar to, this district:—

Name.	Location.	Fighting strength.	Remarks.
Farātiseh فراطسة	Chāi Faqaisāt.	60, of whom 20 are mounted and 20 are armed with rifles.	The Farātiseh are politically allied to the **Bāwīyeh**, but they are said to be of Bani **Lām** stock and to have immigrated from the neighbourhood of **'Amārah** on the **Tigris**.
Hawāshim هواشم	Muwailheh and Amīnīyeh on the **Kārūn**, and scattered.	150, of whom 130 have rifles; but none are mounted.	The Hawāshim have 100 mules and donkeys and pay in their revenue at **Wais**. The tribe are said to be related to the Kinānah section of the Bani **Lām**.
Jāma' جامع	On the **Gūpāl** stream.	150, of whom 60 are mounted and 60 have rifles.	They are politically connected with the **Bāwīyeh**; but pay revenue at Kūt-ash-Shaikh to the Samsām-ud-Dauleh, Īlkhāni of the **Bakhtiyāris**. They draw their fresh water at Hilweh. Their livestock are 100 camels, 200 cattle and 2,000 sheep and goats.
Ma'āwiyeh معاوية	Braikeh on the **Kārūn**.	200, of whom 60 have rifles and 30 are mounted.	At one time subordinate to the **Bāwīyeh**, but now recognised as a separate tribe.

Name.	Position.	Fighting strength.	Remarks.
Marawuneh مرونه	Right bank of the Kārūn between Amīnīyeh and Li'aimi and to 20 miles inland; their focus is at Luqbair.	200, all with rifles, of whom 60 are mounted.	This tribe pay half their revenue through the 'Anāfijeh and the other half direct to the Shaikh of Muhammareh's Deputy-Governor at Nāsiri. They own 100 camels, 400 cattle and 5,000 sheep and goats.
Rawāyeh (Āl Bū) آل بو روایه	Li'aimi on the Kārūn and Khairābād on the Karkheh, the latter in the Dizfūl District.	200, of whom 50 are mounted and all are armed with rifles.	The position of the Āl Bū Rawāyeh in revenue matters is the same as that of the Marawuneh. Their livestock are 100 camels, 200 cattle and 2,000 sheep and goats. They bear an evil reputation as thieves and robbers.
Shawākir شواکر	Shawweh.	50, of whom 10 are mounted and 20 have rifles.	They are subjects of the Shurafa of the Hawīzeh District, but their revenue is paid through the Shaikh of the Bāwīyeh, with whom they are politically allied. They have 20 camels, 60 cattle and 800 sheep and goats.

Apart from the Hawāshim and Ma'āwiyeh, all of whom are settled, and from 20 families of Āl Bū Rawāyeh in the Dizfūl District, these minor tribes appear to be entirely nomadic and to represent a Bedouin population of about 2,250 souls. They all cultivate wheat and barley, and some of the Hawāshim are weavers.

Agriculture, trade and communications.—These subjects are dealt with in the general article on 'Arabistān; but here it may be noted that there is an old disused canal leaving the Kārūn at Ahwāz Village, which runs southwards for 30 miles and is lost in the marshes on the right bank of the Jarrāhi west of Gharaibeh. On the western side of the Kārūn a canal, it is said, formerly took off at Maqtū' and ran to Hawīzeh.

Administration.—The district is subject to the Shaikh of **Muhammareh** who manages it through a Deputy-Governor with head-quarters at **Nāsiri**—at present a nephew named Hāji Shaikh Rahmah; the Deputy Governor only acts on orders from the Shaikh and has little real power outside the village in which he resides. The Shaikh of **Muhammareh** is also represented in the district by various political agents: the principal of these at the present time are Mulla Thāni at Kūt-an-Naddāfīyeh Kabīr, through whom the revenue of the **Hamaid** and Farātiseh and that of a few of the '**Anāfijeh** is collected; Mulla Abus Saiyid at Muzaffari, who is responsible for the Āl Bū **Kurd** community in that neighbourhood; and Shaikh 'Anāyeh at Umm-at-Tamair, who is in charge of the right bank of the **Kārūn** generally and through whom part of the **Hardān** tribe pay their revenue. These agents usually deal with their master direct and not through his representative at **Nāsiri**, but there is no fixed rule in the matter. The Shaikh of **Muhammareh** maintains police posts on the **Kārūn** in this district at Kūt-an-Naddāfīyeh Saghīr (10 rifles), at Milaihān (20 rifles, of whom 10 are mounted) and at Qājārīyeh (60 rifles, of whom 50 are mounted). For administrative purposes the Ahwāz district is roughly divided into two tracts, that of Bāwīyeh on the east, and that of Kārūn upon the river. So much of the district as lies west of the **Kārūn** is claimed by the Nizām-as-Saltaneh as his property, and it is understood that the Shaikh of **Muhammareh** pays him 3,000 Tūmāns a year on account of the tract but does not admit the validity of his title.

AHWĀZ
اهواز
VILLAGE

A considerable village on the left bank of the **Kārūn** river, situated at the head of the rapids to which it gives its name and at the western end of a range of sandstone hills which subside before reaching it but re-appear at some distance on the opposite side of the river. The elevation of Ahwāz is 220 feet above the sea, and it stands upon a somewhat high bank; the country behind it is desert. At the north end of the village, on an elevated salient of the river bank, there was until recently a large, dilapidated, rectangular Persian fort, but it has now been pulled down for the sake of the materials: an Imāmzādeh shrine is still a feature of the place. In the stream, opposite to the lower end of the village, are some mills which are removed in time of flood; and a little below these again is a bluff or rock, forming part of the bank and traversed by galleries which probably carried mill races in former times. Immediately below this rock is a garden on the bank belonging to the Mu'ín-ut-Tujjār. Houses number about 160, and, except a few which are of stone, are built of sun-dried bricks. The population is about 800 souls; most of them are Arabs of mixed tribes, but there are some Persians; the majority are engaged in agriculture, but about 60 mules are kept. To Ahwāz belong 17 sailing boats of 10 to 15 tons burden, besides the river steamer "Shushan" of 30 tons capacity and her barge of 50 tons; there is also an iron barge belonging to the Mu'ín-ut-Tujjār. Without the help of sails the native boats, which can be and are towed up the rapids when necessary, drop down the river from Shalaili on the **Gargar** to Ahwāz in 3 days, or with a good stream sometimes in 24 hours, and from Ahwāz to **Muhammareh** in from 4 to 6 days; some pilgrims to **Karbala** adopt this means of conveyance, especially those from **Shūshtar** and the **Bakhtiyāri** country and a few from Isfahān. There is a ferry at Ahwāz with two small boats. The rapids are fully described in the article on the **Kārūn** river. Ahwāz is situated in the Southern **'Arabistān** district of **Ahwāz** and its revenues are equally divided between the local headman and the Shaikh of **Muhammareh**.

Ahwāz, under the name of Hurmuz-Ardashīr, was in early times the capital of **'Arabistān**; but it suffered greatly during the rebellion of the Zanj in the 9th century A.D., and was for a time the residence of their leader. It was partially restored by the Buyids in the 10th century; and the main town, situated on the east bank of the **Kārūn**, was then connected by a masonry bridge with a quarter which stood on an island in the river.*

The principal tribe, Bedouins being excluded, of the **Kharj** district in Southern **Najd**; they are found in the villages of 'Adhār, **Dilam**, Sulaimīyah and Yamāmah. They are possibly identical with the section called 'Iyādah عیاد of the great **'Anizah** tribe; but some authorities would identify them with the 'Āidh section of the **Qahtān**. A very few 'Āid are found also in the **'Āridh** District, and there are some 'Aid or 'Āidh in **Zilfi** in **Sadair**.

---

* *Vide* Le Strange.

'AIN (WĀDI-AL-)   'AIN (WĀDI-AL-) وادي العين

A valley in the **Dhāhirah** district of the **'Omān** Sultanate, which, rising in Jabal-al-Kor at the eastern end of **Dhāhirah**, runs westwards to the neighbourhood of **'Ibri** where it joins Wādi **Sanaisal**. Its villages in order from its head downwards are as follow :—

Name.	Position.	Bank.	Houses and inhabitants.	Remarks.
Hail Bani Hina حيل بني هنا	3 hours to westward of Najd-al-Barak.	Right.	100 houses of Bani Hina.	Stands under a jagged square perpendicular cliff called Jabal Misht جبل مشط : resources are 25 camels, 50 donkeys and 600 sheep and goats.
Dham ضم	5 hours below Hail Bani Hina.	Do.	80 houses of Bani Hina.	Livestock are 30 camels, 20 donkeys and 700 sheep and goats.
'Ain Bani Sārikh عين بني صارخ	3 hours below Dham.	Do.	70 houses of Bani Sārikh.	Animals are 20 camels, 20 donkeys and 400 sheep and goats.
Kubārah كبارة	3 hours below 'Ain Bani Sārikh.	Do.	40 houses of Bani Jissās.	This hamlet with its date groves suffered severely from drought in 1902. There are 20 camels, 20 donkeys and 600 goats and sheep.
Salaif سليف	20 miles below Kubārah.	Both.	150 houses of Manādharah and 200 of Suwāwifah.	Salaif is practically a suburb of 'Ibri, from which it is distant 2 miles to the east-south-east. There is a small fort on the east bank of the Wādi overlooking an aqueduct. Dates and lucerne are grown. There are 40 camels, 100 donkeys and 600 sheep and goats.

The population of Wādi-al-'Ain is approximately 3,000 souls.

'AINAIN
آل بو عينين

A branch of the Āl Subaih section of the **Bani Khālid** tribe, found in **Qatar** and **Bahrain**: in the former they have 400 houses at **Wakrah**, and in the latter 75 houses at 'Askar and 20 at **Muharraq** Town. In religion they are Māliki Sunnis. The Āl Bū 'Ainain gain their livelihood as pearl-divers, pearl-merchants and boatmen. None of them are pastoral; but a proportion, though smaller than in the case of the other settled tribes of **Qatar**, live in tents in the interior during part of the cold season.

The Dōhah quarter of **Dōhah** is said to have been founded early in the 19th century by Āl Bū 'Ainain, who did not remain there long but were removed in 1828 to **Ruwais** and **Fuwairat** and subsequently settled at **Wakrah**.

AJA
or
IJA
(JABAL)
جبل اجا

A range of mountains in the Jabal **Shammar** principality and one of the chief physical features of northern **Najd**; it bounds the Batn plain in which **Hāil** stands on the north-west, being interposed between Batn and the **Nafūd** and divided from the latter by a strip of hard gravelly ground in places 2 hours wide. The length of Aja is about 75 miles,* its breadth is about 15, and its general direction is from north-east to south-west. Its elevation is fairly constant and about 1,000 feet above the surrounding plains, but one peak (Jabal Fara' فرع) immediately to the west of **Hāil** is 5,550 feet high† and so rises fully 2,000 feet above the town. There are no subordinate ranges or spurs of importance. The material of Jabal Aja is a coarse-grained granite of grey, pink or reddish-brown colour; the strata are inclined to the horizon at an angle of 55°; and the sides of the hills, in places vertical, are generally so steep that the number of points from which they can be ascended is limited. Wells and springs abound; the hills bear brushwood and, in valleys where there is water, fine palms; there is also a tree, resembling a tamarisk in appearance, which yields gum mastic and is perhaps the Talh. A species of wild goat is found. Snow is seen, but not often, upon Jabal Aja.

The principal features of the range are two: first a remarkable enclosed valley in the east flank of the range near **Hāil**, called 'Aqdah,

---

* According to Huber (*Journal de Voyage*, page 638) only so much of the range as is red is called Aja (viz., the portion north-west of Jafaifah) and the remainder is called Hazām حزام

† As calculated by Lieutenant F. Fraser Hunter from an observation by Huber (see footnote to article Jabal **Shammar**).

described elsewhere under its own name; and second, a defile known as Rī'-as-Salf ربع السلف which pierces the range about 4 miles south-west of 'Aqdah and carries the ordinary route from Hāil to Taimah and the west. The entrance of the Rī' on the east is close to Qafār and the exit on the west is near Mūqaq; the distance between these points may be 20 miles in a straight line. The crest of the intermediate pass is about 1,000 feet above the level of Hāil; the descent from it on the west is steep and rugged, and at some distance below the top on the western side is a place where cold springwater falls from a cliff.

Minor valleys which descend from Jabal Aja on its east side are in order from south to north: Umm Sinām أمّ سنام, Taraf طرف, Jau جو, Khashmat 'Awād خشمة عواد, Ghamr غمر, Ratāwīyah رطاويه, Ratāwi رطاوي, Mishlah مشلح, Sūq سوق, 'Ariki عركي, Shahrīz شهريز, Baidhā بيضاء, Taraiq طريق, Dabbi دبي, Hijiri هجري, Fahaidi فهيدي, Jārdi جاردي, Ahaimir احيمر, Jasha'ami جشعمي, 'Atūn عتون, Ghalghal غلغل and Tawārin توارن. Those on the west face are Ruwaihli ربيحلي, Wubāri ربّاري, Dhalmah ظلمه, Hōmah حومه, Nuwaiyah نويه, Baidhatain بيضتين, Daqalah دقله and Wākah واكه. All these glens, except the first four near the south-eastern corner, are said to contain trickling springs at which the wild goats drink. In most of them are date palms, owned by **Shammar** Bedouins,[*] which flourish on the water of the subsoil; the owners, who live elsewhere at other times, camp in the groves to enjoy the fruit from May to September and obtain their drinking water from wells which are numerous and often very shallow. The large valley of 'Aqdah is the only one permanently inhabited. Tuwārin contains Himyaritic inscriptions and ancient drawings on the rocks.

'AJAIRĀ-WĪYAH
العجيراريه

Also known as Quarantine Island, a long narrow island in the Shatt-al-'**Arab** beginning about two miles below the British Consulate at **Basrah** and ending at 10½ miles below the same place; its length is thus 8¼ miles, while its breadth, which is fairly uniform, is on the average about ¼ of a mile only. 'Ajairāwīyah is divided from the left bank of the Shatt-al-'**Arab** by a channel called Sālhiyah صالحيه, which is navigable by launches, lighters and boats at high tide, and by the main stream from

---

[*] For a list of the palm groves and their owners see Huber's *Journal de Voyage*, pages 664—667.

the right bank of the river; the island subtends all the villages on the left bank from Kūt-al-Jū' to Nahr Jāsim, and those from Khorah to Abul Hamad on the right bank.

The following is a table of the places on 'Ajairāwīyah in order from the upper to the lower end of the island :—

Name.	Position.	Inhabitants and houses.	Remarks.
Sālbīyah صالحيه or Lisān لسان	The tip of the island nearest to Basrah.	Now occupied by the Basrah Lazaret.	The lazaret and quarantine station of Basrah, from which the whole island derives its alternative name, are situated here on land belonging to Hāji Ibrāhīm-az-Zahair. There are about 4,000 date palms.
Shamālīyah شماليه	About one mile below Lisān, opposite to the mouth of the Sarāji creek on the right bank of the Shatt-al-'Arab.	100 souls of 'Īdān, inhabiting huts.	A tract containing about 4,000 date trees. The inhabitants own a few livestock.
Sa'aiwān سعيوان	About one mile below Shamālīyah, opposite to the Mina creek on the left bank of the Shatt-al-'Arab.	80 souls of 'Īdān. The dwellings are huts, except one large stone house on the north shore which belongs to the principal Shaikh of the island.	Do.
Sidrah سدره	About $\frac{3}{4}$ of a mile below Sa'aiwān, opposite the Za'īr creek on the left bank of the Shatt-al-'Arab.	50 souls of 'Īdān, occupying a few huts.	The inhabitants own about 2,500 date palms and a few cattle, sheep and goats. The place is owned by Hāji Dāwud-al-Fadāgh.
Fadāghīyah فداغيه	$\frac{1}{3}$ of a mile below Sidrah, opposite to Yūsifān on the right bank of the Shatt-al-'Arab.	130 souls of 'Atub, inhabiting huts.	Resources are described as 5,000 date palms, 30 cattle, 30 sheep and goats, and 5 horses.
"Amukdas" (spelling uncertain).	On the north shore, $\frac{1}{3}$ of a mile below Fadāghīyah and facing the Gawām creek on the left bank of the Shatt-al-'Arab.	150 souls of 'Atub, dwellers in huts.	Do.

'AJAIRĀWĪYAH

Name.	Position.	Inhabitants and houses.	Remarks.
Yāmīn يامين	On the south shore, level with "Amukdas" and opposite the mouth of the Hamdān creek on the right bank of the Shatt-al-'Arab.	350 souls of 'Atub and other tribes. The habitations are huts except for several stone houses.	Oats, wheat, rice and fruit are grown and there are 1,000 date palms. Livestock are 100 cattle, 70 sheep and goats and 3 horses. There are here an ice factory and flour mills erected by Yāmīn Hārūn, a Jew, in 1905-06.
Hiramtān (Kūt) كوت حيرمطان	½ a mile below Yāmīn.	130 souls of 'Īdān, living in huts.	There are about 1,000 date palms, and other fruits are grown and wheat is cultivated. Livestock are one or two horses and about 25 cattle and 30 sheep and goats.
Wa'aibāl وعيبال	On the north shore of the island, ½ a mile below Hiramtān and nearly opposite the Kūt-ash-Shaikh creek on the left bank of the Shatt-al-'Arab.	80 souls of 'Atub, occupying huts.	Do.
Sangar صنگر	On the south shore of the island, opposite to Sangar on the right bank of the Shatt-al-'Arab.	Do.	Do., except that the date palms are only half as numerous.
Dirrah درّه	On the south shore of the island, one mile from its lower extremity and opposite to Sabīliyāt on the right bank of the Shatt-al-'Arab.	130 souls of 'Atub, dwellers in huts.	As at Sangar above.
Mufraz-ad-Da'aiji مفرز الدعيجي	The tip of the island furthest from Basrah: it is called Mufraz on account of the reunion here of the Sālhīyah channel with the main stream of the river.	180 souls of 'Atub. The habitations are huts.	Date palms number about 2,000 and wheat, barley and other fruits are grown. Livestock are 50 cattle, 50 sheep and goats, and 8 horses.

E 2

Some date plantations on the island are owned by nephews of the present Shaikh of **Kuwait**.

It will be seen that the total population of 'Ajairāwīyah is about 1,500 souls, and that they belong chiefly to the **'Īdān** and **'Atub** tribes. The present total number of date trees seems to be about 30,500.

'AJĀJ (QAL'AT-AL-)
قلعة العجاج

Sometimes pronounced 'Ayāy. This is the only name by which the Portuguese Fort on **Bahrain** Island is known among the surrounding villages; but the townspeople of **Manāmah**, especially the Persians among them, generally call it Qal'at-al-Farangi قلعة الفرنجي. The fort, a regular bastioned Portuguese construction of the 16th century, is now an untenanted ruin. It is situated on the north coast of **Bahrain** Island, 3½ miles west of the **Manāmah** fort, stands about 150 yards from the beach, and covers nearly 2 acres of ground. The top of the highest portion still standing is 80 feet above sea level; and there is a deep well in the centre, lined with excellent masonry, but now dry.

AJĪRUB
عجيرب

Or 'Ajairub; by Persians called Āb-i-Gīrub آب گيرب. A considerable permanent stream in the **Dizfūl** District of **'Arabistān**, having its source in a spring near the village of Qal'eh Qāzi, and joining the **Diz** river on its left bank some 3 or 4 miles below Kūt 'Abdush Shāh. The villages of Qāzi, Shama'ūn and Biyāwtiyūn are irrigated by the 'Ajīrub, which also forms the border between the portion of the **Kāthīr** tribe under Shaikh Farhān Asad on the east and those under Shaikh Haidar on the west.

'AJMĀN
عجمان
TOWN and PRINCIPALITY*

Sometimes pronounced 'Aimān. A town on the coast of Trucial **'Omān** forming, with its immediate environs, a small independent principality of which the political position is defined in the article on Trucial **'Omān**. It is situated 6 miles south-west of **Hamrīyah** and

* For authorities, maps, charts, etc., see first footnote to article Trucial **'Omān**.

5 miles north-east of **Shārjah** Town, on the south side of the entrance to a creek which, having a bar of sand and not of rock with 5 feet of water on it at low tide, is one of the most accessible on this part of the coast; the sea anchorage off 'Ajmān, however, is bad. Fresh water for drinking is obtained from wells 9 feet deep, of which the locality is constantly changing.

The population of 'Ajmān is about 750 souls, composed of 25 houses of **Na'īm** of the Qarātisah, Hamīrat, and Āl Bū Dhanain sections, 80 houses of Āl Bū **Mahair,** 12 houses of **Sūdān,** 14 of Āl Bū Kalbi, 5 of Masāibah and 12 of Shāqōsh. All the inhabitants are pearl divers and fishermen: they own about 40 pearl boats and 25 fishing boats, besides some 60 camels, 20 horses, 100 donkeys, 100 cattle and 400 goats. The plantations of the town contain about 1,900 date trees: there is no other cultivation. One or two boats are built here each year, but most of those in use have been obtained from **Shārjah** or **Dibai.**

The authority of the Shaikh only extends 2 miles inland, and, upon the sea, 1½ miles south-westwards and 2½ miles north-eastwards, embracing on the last-mentioned side part of the tract called **Zora**: his dominions are thus an enclave in **Shārjah** territory. There is no dependent village, and no Bedouin tribe owes allegiance to the Shaikh, who is of the Qarātisah section of the **Na'īm**: a political alliance and friendly relations, however, generally subsist between the inhabitants of 'Ajmān and the people of **Baraimi;** and the present Shaikh of 'Ajmān is a maternal uncle of the present Shaikh of Umm-al-**Qaiwain.** The Shaikh of 'Ajmān derives a revenue of about Rs. 4,600 a year from the pearl fishers of his port, and he owns some date gardens at **Dhaid** of which the yield is inconsiderable.

'AJMĀN
عجمان
TRIBE

An important nomad Arab tribe in Eastern Arabia. The singular is 'Ajmi عجمي ; and in the mouth of Bedouins the name generally becomes 'Aimi (singular) and 'Aimān (plural).

Distribution.—The head-quarters of the tribe are in the Sanjāq of **Hasa,** where the tract of **Taff,** the southern half of **Habl,** all **Jauf,** and **Biyādh** as far south as **'Oqair** Port are recognised as being 'Ajmān territory. The 'Ajmān also occupy the northern confines of **Jāfūrah** and are generally found in **Kharmah,** especially about Zarnūqah; their winter quarters are partly in **Summān**; in the cold weather a few of them occasionally visit **Qatar**; and some of the Āl 'Arjah and Āl Shāmir sections habitually camp in the **Kharj** district of Southern **Najd**. These are the ordinary limits of the tribe, but, when as at present they are on good terms with the Bani **Khālid**, they wander over the whole country as far northwards as **Kuwait** Town. Some settled 'Ajmān detached from the tribe are found in **Kuwait** Town and there are a few in the fixed villages of Wādi-al-**Miyāh**.

Religion, character and mode of life.—In religion the 'Ajmān are Hanbali Sunnis. As a tribe they are reputed hospitable, steadfast, and trustworthy according to Bedouin standards; and their women enjoy a considerable degree of social freedom, even in the presence of strangers.

By occupation the 'Ajmān are pastoral; and they own many horses, camels, sheep and goats, but have not a large number of cattle; their camels are bought by merchants from the north, and even from Syria, who visit their country for the purpose every year. The dealings of the 'Ajmān are principally with the **Hasa** Oasis, where they dispose of their marketable wares, including horses, and supply themselves with the products of civilisation; part of their dates, however, they obtain from the **Qatīf** Oasis. Some of the tribe own date plantations in the oasis of **Hasa**, but none of them have any in **Qatīf**. The tents of the 'Ajmān are next in size to those of the Bani **Khālid** and are generally black with a white lining.

Divisions, numbers and arms.—The following table shows the principal divisions of the tribe, together with some particulars concerning them:—

Section.	Sub-section.	Alleged fighting strength.	Present sub-sectional Shaikh (etc.).
'Arjah (Āl) آل عرجه	'Arjah (Āl) آل عرجه	400	...
Do.	Mirja' (Āl) آل مرجع	100	...
Do.	Rizq (Al) آل رزق	150	...

'AJMĀN TRIBE

Section.	Sub-section.	Alleged fighting strength.	Present sub-sectional Shaikh (etc.).
Dhā'in (Āl) آل ضاعن	'Ajāmah or 'Ajaimah (Āl) آل عجامة - عجيمة	100	...
Do.	Dhā'in (Āl) آل ضاعن	200	...
Do.	Kharmān (Āl) آل خرمان	100	...
Hādi (Āl) آل هادي	'Āsi (Āl) آل عاصي	250	...
Do.	Sāil (Āl) آل سائل	250	...
Hairaf (Āl) آل حيرف	...	100	...
Haiyān or Hajjān (Āl) آل حيان - حجان	...	100	...
Hamad-bin-Rāshid (Āl) آل حمد بن راشد	...	300	Closely connected with the Āl Sifrān section and with the Āl Nāja' sub-section of Āl Ma'idh section (see below).
Hitlān (Āl) آل هتلان	Dahāmish (Al) آل دهامش	300	Mirdās-bin-Habāb.
Do.	Jāhil (Āl) آل جاهل	50	Fahad-al-Jāhil.
Do.	Kharsān (Al) آل خرسان	200	Sālih-bin-Arhab.
Do.	Ma'ataq (Āl) آل معتق	100	Suwaiyid-al-Faqad.
Do.	Sa'adah (Āl) آل سعدة	200	'Abdullah-bin-Sa'adah.
Do.	Sharyah (Āl) آل شرية	100	Sa'īd-bin-Sharyah.

Section.	Sub-section.	Alleged fighting strength.	Present sub-sectional Shaikh (etc.).
Khuwaitir (Āl) آل خويطر	...	50	...
Maḥfūdh (Āl) آل محفوظ	Dabasah (Āl) آل دبسه	200	Biqyad-bin-Maqtūf.
Do.	Maḥfūdh (Āl) آل محفوظ	700	Hamad-bin-Muqrād.
Do.	Shāfah (Āl) آل شافه	300	Hashar-bin-Jahdah.
Ma'idh (Āl) آل معيض	Habaish (Āl) آل حبيش	400	Muhammad-bin-Tawīl.
Do.	Nāja' (Āl) آل ناجع	700	Muhammad-bin-Hazām-bin-Hithlain, chief of the whole 'Ajmān tribe.
Do.	Sālih (Āl) آل صالح	800	Tāhūs-bin-Thuwaini
Do.	Silbah (Āl) آل سلبه	200	Muhammad-bin-Suhdah.
Do.	Zaiz (Āl) آل زيز	600	...
Miflih (Āl) آل مفلح	...	100	...
Misra' (Āl) آل مصرع	...	200	'Abdullah-bin-Suwaid.
Rushaid (Āl) آل رشيد	...	200	...
Salaifi (Āl) آل سليفي	...	100	...
Salūm (Āl) آل سلوم	...	100	...
Shāmir (Āl) آل شامر	Husain (Āl) آل حسين	250	...

'AJMĀN TRIBE

Section.	Sub-section.	Alleged fighting strength.	Present sub-sectional Shaikh (etc.).
Shāmir (Āl) آل شامر	Khadhair (Āl) آل خضير	200	...
Do.	Shāiqah (Āl) آل شائقه	150	...
Shawāwlah شواوله	...	80	...
Sifrān (Āl) آل سفران	'Amir-bin-Sifrān (Āl) آل عامر بن سفران	150	Khumaiyis-bin-Munaikhir. (See also next entry.)
Do.	Hādi-bin-Sifrān (Āl) آل هادي بن سفران	150	This sub-section together with the last—in other words the Āl Sifrān section as a whole—are considered the most redoubtable of the whole tribe and are closely related to the Āl Nāja' sub-section of the Āl Ma'īdh.
Sulaimān (Āl) آل سليمان	Baghawwar بغوّر	60	...
Do.	Dharwān (Āl) آل ضروان	200	Mubārak-bin-Haqrab.
Do.	Hamrah (Āl) آل حمرة	300	Hajaiyir-bin-Hishshah.
Do.	Hasnah (Āl) آل حسنه	250	Hattāb-bin-Shuwaiyir.
Do.	Jibāl (Āl) آل جبال	60	...
Do.	Jibār (Āl) آل جبار	100	...
Do.	Sulaimān (Āl) آل سليمان	300	...
Saraih (Āl Umm-as-) آل ام الصريح	...	100	..

To these may be added the Āl Jiblān section of the **Mutair**, who have separated from their own tribe and at present form part of the 'Ajmān; and it may be noted that the Marāzīq of the **Shībkūh** District of the **Persian Coast** lay claim to 'Ajmān descent. In Arabia the various sections of the tribe are intermingled throughout their whole territory and have not separate locations.

The estimate of fighting strength, amounting to 10,000 men, appears high; it indicates a total tribal strength of about 35,000 souls, but regard being had to the wideness of the area over which the tribe extend the number is perhaps not excessive. The 'Ajmān are said to muster 2,000 mounted men, all of whom are armed with Martini rifles, for spears and swords are now hardly to be found in the tribe.

Political position.—The 'Ajmān, whom some authorities would connect with the **Qahtān**, state that they are descended from Shurafa of Najrān; but their pretensions are generally disallowed, or at least ignored, for no special consideration is shown them in virtue of the origin to which they lay claim. On the other hand, their tribal strength makes their alliance valuable and their enmity a serious danger; but in politics they are a shifting and inconstant factor, being, as they themselves have been known openly to profess, "the friends of those who treat them best."

At the present time the 'Ajmān are on good terms with the Bani **Khālid**, the two tribes being mutually free of each other's country; and they have somewhat similar relations with the Bani **Hājir**, who, after providing themselves with Rafīqs from the 'Ajmān, range as they please in the 'Ajmi districts. With the Āl **Morrah**, whose camps intermingle with theirs on the south side of the **Hasa** Oasis, the 'Ajmān are presently at feud; and they were also at enmity with the late Ahmad-bin-Thāni, Shaikh of the **Ma'ādhīd** of **Qatar**, but with Jāsim, the senior Shaikh of that tribe, their dealings are amicable. As a body, they are particularly well disposed to Ibn Sa'ūd, whose cause they supported throughout the recent wars in **Najd**; and they are friendly as a rule, though not at the present time (1907), with the Shaikh of **Kuwait**.

In the desert the 'Ajmān do not acknowledge the authority of the Turkish Government; but in the vicinity of **Hofūf**, where a large number of them are encamped for 6 months in the year, they are more submissive; and those who actually enter the bounds of the **Hasa** Oasis pay as Government revenue in each season 1 Riyāl on account of every 5 camels and the same on account of every 10 sheep and goats. The Shaikhs, however, are subsidised by the Porte, the more important among them receiving in this manner $50 a month in cash and monthly rations of the value of $15 or further cash in lieu of the rations; and it is calculated that the Turks in this manner pay more to the tribe than they receive from it.

The principal Shaikhship of the tribe is vested in a family of the Āl Nāja' division of the Āl Ma'īdh. The present holder of the position is Muhammad-bin-Hazām-bin-Hithlain, who attained to it in 1905 by the murder of his relation Shabīb-bin-Hithlain.

AKHDHAR (JABAL) جبل اخضر

Position and extent.—A mass of mountains in the Western **Hajar** of the **'Omān** Sultanate, forming the highest portion of the **Hajar** range and dividing the district of **'Omān** Proper on the south from that of **Bātinah** on the north. Its axis lies west-north-west and east-south-east, its eastern extremity being at Najd-al-Mughbārīyah, the head of Wādi **Samāil**, and its western at or near the head of Wādi Bani **Ghāfir**. The length of the range proper is thus about 50 miles and its breadth on the average about 20; but it throws off from its eastern end a great unnamed spur which runs for nearly 30 miles to the north-east and forms a barrier dividing Wādi **Samāil** from the Wādi-al-Hammām branch of Wādi **Ma'āwal**.

Configuration.—The top of Jabal Akhdhar is described as a table-land which is highest, throughout its length, upon the side next the sea. From the crest the fall on the northern side is abrupt and precipitous; but inland the plateau first declines gradually to southwards and then drops, by cliffs less remarkable than those of the seaward face, to the plains of **'Omān** Proper. The chief peak of Jabal Akhdhar is Shām شام or Wishām وشام, nearer to the west than to the east end of the range; it is 9,940 feet high and is visible from the sea at a distance of over 100 miles. Another peak is Khadhar خضر, 7,500 feet high, at the south-east corner between Wādi **Mi'aidin** and Wādi **Halfain**, above Muti in the latter. One of the highest points on the limb of Jabal Akhdhar which reaches to the north-east is Jabal Nakhl, 7,000 feet. The northern

* A distant view of Jabal Akhdhar from the sea will be found in Chart No. 2373 – 2837A.

flank of Jabal Akhdhar gives birth to the Wādis Bani **Kharūs, Fara', Sahtan** and Bani **Ghāfir** which descend to **Bātinah**; while Wādi **Mi'aidin** and Wādi Tanūf, both draining to **'Omān** Proper, are the principal hollows that furrow its southern slopes.

Routes.—Routes across Jabal Akhdhar are neither numerous nor easy. The best known is one which leaves Wādi Bani **Kharūs** near the village of 'Aliya (2,400 feet), and rises by an extremely steep and partly artificial road to the top of the 'Aqabat-al-Hajar عقبة الحجر (8,000 feet), the ascent occupying, if local donkeys are used, about 5 hours; from this pass it traverses an undulating plain to the head of a ravine containing **Saiq** village, to which it descends about 400 feet by a stairway cut in the rock; the way beyond **Saiq** lies through the adjacent village of **Sharaijah**, whence it drops into Wādi **Mi'aidin**.

The other principal route across the main mass of Jabal Akhdhar is one called Tarīq-ash-Shass طريق الشص which leads from **'Awābi** to **Saiq** and **Sharaijah** and thence to Tanūf; it is narrow and inconvenient but, like that already described, it is passable by animals.

Sharaijah is connected with Tanūf, 21 miles distant to the westward, by a route practicable for mules and donkeys, which could be rendered passable for camels; to the east a difficult track, fit only for men and local donkeys, leads from **Sharaijah** over the southern slopes of Jabal Khadhar and thence for about 3,000 feet down a steep stone staircase to Muti in Wādi **Halfain**.

To these routes may be added a footpath called 'Aqabat-al-Qatt عقبه القت by which a strong walker can cross the hills between **Nakhl** and Wādi **Samāil** in about 6 hours, and 'Aqbat-al-Fīq عقبة الفيق, an inferior route by which Jabal Akhdhar can be ascended from the north.

Geology and natural products.—Jabal Akhdhar consists, so far as is known, entirely of limestones of the 'Omān series: regarding these the Appendix on Geology* may be consulted. In some places the rock lies exposed in large tabular masses; in others it has hollows containing a shallow earthy deposit; in others again it is covered with good soil. The high plateau is stony, intersected by ravines and covered with grass in tussocks which must afford good grazing after rain; it bears evergreen bushes and even some trees of considerable size. Animals are the wolf, hyæna, wild cat and Wa'al or Jayakar's wild goat; birds are few, principally kites and vultures.

---

* See the other volume of this Gazetteer.

Wādi Bani Habīb in Jabal Akhdhar.
(Maj. P. Z. Cox.)

Population, villages and agriculture.—The inhabitants of Jabal Akhdhar nearly all belong to the Bani **Riyām** and **Habūs** tribes. The principal villages are Bani **Habīb, Saiq,** and **Sharaijah** in the hills and Musairah, Mi'aidin and Misfāh in Wādi **Mi'aidin** ; of these **Sharaijah** is the largest and most important. The cultivated lands of these villages are generally terraced and irrigated ; the crops include wheat and leguminous plants, but most attention is given to fruit culture. The hillsides in some places are covered with vineyards, producing white and black grapes which are made into wine or raisins; and pomegranates are grown in great profusion and exported. Peaches, apricots, figs, mulberries and melons are among the other fruits. There are also walnut-trees, and a kind of coriander called Būt بوت which grows wild. Outside the villages possessing irrigation the people are pastoral, depending for subsistence on their flocks and herds, but they are not nomadic. The total population of Jabal Akhdhar, the upper villages of Wādi **Mi'aidin** being included, is about 3,500 souls.

'ĀLI عالي

A considerable village on **Bahrain** Island, 6 miles south-west of **Manāmah** fort and near to the south-west end of the date groves which cover the north end of the island. 'Āli consists of 200 houses of **Bahārinah**, who are lime-burners, potters and cultivators of dates. The largest of the prehistoric tumuli of **Bahrain** adjoin this village on the south side. Date palms are estimated at 8,250 trees and livestock include 35 donkeys and 10 cattle.

'ALI (ABU) ابو علي

An uninhabited island, about 12 miles long from east to west, lying off the coast of the **Hasa** Sanjāq about 16 miles south-east of Rās-al-Bidya'. The nearest point on the mainland is the extremity of the so-called Jazīrat-al-Bātinah in **Biyādh** (I), distant 2 miles to southward ; the passage between the two, known as Maqta'-ar-Raiyāfah مقطع الريافة is not navigable. The eastern point of Abu 'Ali, named Rās Abu 'Ali, is low and rocky; it has an anchorage on its south side, protected from the Shamāl, in a bay which is known as Dōhat Abu 'Ali. A cape on the south side of the island near its western end is known as Rās-ar-Raiyāfah, and another on the same side but near the opposite end as Rās Barābakh برابخ. Abu 'Ali island is closely surrounded by pearl banks: on its north side, at about ⅓ of the distance from its west to its east end, is a bank known as Dhahr-al-Baidhah; a short distance off its north coast, rather nearer to the eastern than to the western end, is another called Dhahr Abu 'Ali; adjoining Rās Abu 'Ali is a bank named after that cape; and in the strait between the island and the mainland are the bank of Batīn at the eastern entrance and that of Barābakh farther in.

'ALI (ĀL or AHL) آل—اهل علي

Singular 'Alīyi علیي. An Arab tribe of Trucial **Omān** and the Shībkūh district in Persia: they belong to the Ghāfiri faction and are described as Hanbali Sunnis in religion, but are virtually Wahhābis. The bulk of the tribe are now settled in towns,—1,000 families residing at Umm-al-**Qaiwain**, 200 at **Shārjah** and 150 at Rās-al-**Khaimah**. The Bedouin portion of the tribe in Trucial **Omān** number about 140 families and frequent the country from Umm-al-**Qaiwain** to Jazīrat-al-**Hamrah** and as far inland as Falaj Āl 'Ali. The Āl 'Ali of the Persian side are separately described in the article on **Shībkūh**: by them the Āl 'Ali of Trucial **Omān** are regarded as forming a division called Bin Mu'alla بن معلّی. The Āl 'Ali generally claim connection with the **Mutair** of **Najd**, and by some authorities the Bani Bū **'Alī** of the **'Omān** Sultanate are considered to be of one stock with the Āl 'Ali.

'ALI (ĀL BIN-) آل بن علي

One of the largest Arab tribes in **Bahrain** and fairly numerous also in Qatar. In Bahrain they are found at **Muharraq** Town (400 houses) and at **Hadd** (100 houses); in **Qatar**, exclusive of some of the **Ma'ādhīd** section, they number 350 households at **Dōhah**.

Below follow the principal sections and sub-sections, according to the best information obtainable, of the Āl Bin-'Ali; but it is not certain that all the divisions specified originally belonged to the tribe, and there is even reason to think that some of them are separate tribes which have

'ALĪ (ĀL BIN-)

undergone affiliation. The peculiar case of the **Ma'ādhīd** * is discussed in a separate article.

Section.	Sub-section.	Families.	Remarks on families.
Salim (Āl) آل سالم	Lahdān (Āl Bin-) آل بن لحدان	Ghānim (Āl) آل غانم	Represented in both **Bahrain** and **Qatar**.
Do.	Do.	Hitmi (Āl Bin) آل بن همتي	Do.
Do.	Do.	Tarīf (Āl Bin) آل بن طريف	Do.
Do.	Ma'ādhīd معاضيد	*'Ali (Āl)* آل علي	Found only in **Qatar**.
Do.	Do.	'Asīriyīn عسيريين	Do.
Do.	Do.	Fādhal (Āl) آل فاضل	Do.
Do.	Do.	*Muqbil (Āl Bin)* آل بن مقبل	Represented in both **Bahrain** and **Qatar**: in the former they are few.
Do.	Do.	Salāmah (Āl) آل سلامة	Became extinct in 1905.
Do.	Do.	*Talah (Āl)* آل طلح	Occur only in **Qatar**.
Do.	Do.	*Thāni (Āl)* آل ثاني	Do.
Do.	Shabūq (Āl Bū) آل بو شبوق	None of distinction.	The most numerous sub-section of the Āl Sālim. They are found in both **Bahrain** and **Qatar**.
Shadhaib (Āl Bū) آل بو شظيب	The sub-sections and families, except the Āl Bin Durbās, are unimportant.	Durbās (Āl Bin) آل بن درباس	Represented in **Qatar** only.

The predominant sub-sections in **Bahrain** are the Āl Bin-Lahdān and the Āl Bū Shabūq.

The list of **Ma'ādhīd** families given above is not exhaustive. Some of the Āl Bū Shadhaib are said to live with the **Manāsīr** in Trucial

* The leading families of the **Ma'ādhīd** whose names are printed in italics in the table are those who, either in whole or part, repudiate or do not claim membership of the Āl Bin-'Ali tribe.

'Omān; and one of the Āl Bin-Durbās family of the Āl Bū Shadhaib is reported to have succeeded, on the ground of affinity by marriage, to a tribal Shaikhship left vacant by the extinction of the Āl Salāmah family of the **Ma'ādhīd**. All the sections and sub-sections of the Āl Bin-'Ali are so much intermarried and such stress is at the same time laid on female descent that a majority of the tribe now describe themselves indifferently as belonging to one division or another, and that there is considerable doubt even among tribesmen as to which divisions include, and which are included in, others. The number of the Āl Bin-'Ali, apart from the **Ma'ādhīd** families who disclaim connection with the tribe, is probably about 4,500 souls. These **Ma'ādhīd** families alone excepted, the Āl Bin-'Ali fly on their boats a distinctive flag of 5 red and 5 white stripes alternating; it is called the Salaimi flag, and the bulk of the tribe for this reason are known also by the alternative name of Āl Salaim آل سليم.

By profession the Āl Bin-'Ali are pearl divers, pearl merchants, cultivators of dates, and sailors voyaging to all parts of the Persian Gulf and even to places beyond; none of the tribe are pastoral. In religion they are Māliki Sunnis.

The Āl Bin-'Ali are variously derived by different authorities from the **'Anizah, Qahtān** and Bani **Tamīm**, all Arab tribes of **Najd**; the truth, perhaps, is that they are of mixed origin. The greater number of the Āl Bin-'Ali of **Bahrain** arrived in 1783 with the **'Utūb** and have ever since been closely connected with that tribe, but in a subordinate capacity. A considerable number of them again emigrated to **Qatar** in 1894 to escape the tyranny of the Shaikh of **Bahrain**. There is at the present time a serious feud, arising out of bloodshed, between the Āl Bin-'Ali and the **'Amāmarah**.

'ALI
(BALAD
BANI BŪ)
بلد بني
بر علي

The principal Ghāfiri settlement in the **Ja'alān** district of the **'Omān** Sultanate: it is situated about 40 miles south-south-west of **Sūr** and 7 miles to the south-south-east of the rival Hināwi township of Balad Bani Bū **Hasan**. The houses number about 600, and the population which consists entirely of the Bani Bū **'Ali** tribe may number about 3,000 souls. The settlement boasts about 2,000 camels, 800 donkeys and 4,000 sheep and goats, but only a few horses; the date palms are estimated at 30,000.

'ALI (BANI BŪ) بني بو علي

Singular is 'Alawi علوي. The principal Ghāfri tribe of the Ja'alān and **Sharqīyah** districts in the Sultanate of 'Omān. They are partly nomadic and partly sedentary: the Bedouin portion of the tribe inhabit **Ja'alān** only and possess considerable herds of camels and goats, while the settled portion cultivate dates and grain in the Balad Bani Bū 'Ali oasis and are found also at **Sūr** and at Rās-ar-Ruwais, Suwaih, Khor Bani Bū 'Ali, Jumailah and Lashkharah on the South-Eastern Coast of 'Omān where they are mostly mariners and fishermen. A few occur also at Khabbah in Wādi **Khabbah**.

Some authorities connect the Bani Bū 'Ali with the Āl 'Ali of Trucial 'Omān and the **Shībkūh** district of Persia.

The following are the chief sections and sub-sections of the tribe :—

Section.	Sub-section.	Fighting strength.	Habitat.	Remarks.
Fahūd فهود	Fahūd فهود	50	Balad Bani Bū 'Ali.	Cultivators of grain.
Ditto	Muwāridah مواردة	60	Lashkharah.	Ditto.
Ditto	Ruwātilah رواتله	50	Rās-ar-Ruwais and Sūr.	Fishermen.
Ja'āfarah جعافرة	Ghanābīs غنابيس	200	The Ja'āfarah have their headquarters at Lashkharah and are found at Suwaih, their country extending for a considerable distance along the coast, and at Sūr. They catch sharks, seer-fish, etc., and salt them for export to Sūr and Makalla. They have only 1 or 2 trading vessels but own a number of large fishing-boats. They are comparatively poor in animals.	
Ditto	Ibrāhīm (Bani) بني ابراهيم	120		
Ditto	Muqbil (Āl Abu) آل ابو مقبل	200		
Ditto	Sakhīlah (Aulād) اولاد سخيله	40		
Ditto	Salābikhah سلابخه	50		
Razīq (Bani) بني رزيق	Hamūdah (Āl) آل حمودة	200	Balad Bani Bū 'Ali and Sūr.	The principal Shaikh of the tribe belongs to this section.
Ditto	Hasan (Aulād) اولاد حسن	100	Ditto	Cultivators.
Ditto	Jalīl (Aulād 'Abdul) اولاد عبد الجليل	40	Ditto	Cultivators and fishermen.
Ditto	Khanjar (Aulād) اولاد خنجر	40	Balad Bani Bū 'Ali.	Cultivators.

Section.	Sub-section.	Fighting strength.	Habitat.	Remarks.
Sinadah سندة	Majāghamah مجاغمة	60	In Ja'alān and at Sūr.	...
Ditto	Mazāmilah مزاملة	100	Ditto	About 1,000 Bedouin souls in addition belong to these two subsections: they own some 100 camels, 40 cattle, 50 donkeys and 300 sheep and goats.
Ditto	Saif (Aulād) اولاد سيف	50	Ditto	

The total number of the tribe appears to be about 7,000 souls. The Bani Bū 'Ali became Wahhābis at the time of the Najdi invasions of **'Omān** nearly a century ago; and as late as 1845 they were strict, if not fanatical, in the observance of Wahhābi principles. They have since relaxed something of their rigour and have resumed the smoking of tobacco; but they continue to be exact in their observance of the forms and times of prayer and are accounted the most religious tribe in the **'Omān** Sultanate. They belong to a Wahhābi sect known as Azraqah ازرقة.

The Bani Bū 'Ali are on the average men of middle size, with short features and quick deep-set eyes. A gloomy and determined expression which characterises some of them does not belie their natural character. They are a warlike, independent race and bear a high reputation for courage and dash. Their favourite weapon was originally a thin, straight, two-edged sword, sharp as a razor and attached by a leather thong to a shield 14 inches in diameter, in addition to which they carried matchlocks; their armament is now of a more modern character, but they still have few breech-loaders.

The Bani Bū 'Ali are the only tribe of the **'Omān** Sultanate that have met a British force on land. On the 9th of November 1820, as related in the historical portion of this Gazetteer, they defeated a force of British Indian sepoys at their village of Balad Bani Bū 'Ali, and on the 2nd March 1821 suffered severe retribution near the same place. On the latter occasion the tribe lost heavily in killed and wounded, the town and fort were destroyed and a large number of prisoners were taken including the principal Shaikh, Muhammad-bin 'Ali; but the date groves belonging to the place were spared,—an act of clemency that was much appreciated and is still remembered. The prisoners after being kept for two years at Bombay were repatriated and received grants of money from the Indian Government to enable them to rebuild their houses and restore irrigation. Since this episode the tribe have uniformly shown themselves well-disposed to the British nation and have treated hospitably more than one British traveller visiting their country; but they have never fully regained their position in tribal politics. The Bani Bū 'Ali have a chronic feud with their neighbours the Bani Bū Hasan; their present Tamīmah is 'Abdullah-bin-Sālim of the Hamūdah sub-section, who resides near Lashkharah but sometimes visits Sūr, where he has a house.

ALI-AL-GHARBI علي الغربي

A small town in Turkish 'Irāq, on the right bank of the Tigris about half-way by river between 'Amārah and Kūt. There are about 300 brick houses and a population of perhaps 2,000 souls. The inhabitants are of mixed origin, but almost entirely Shī'ahs by religion; they live by agriculture and petty trade. Wheat and barley grown in the surrounding country are exported; also ghi, wool, skins and other Kurdish products, for 'Alī-al-Gharbi is a depôt of the Kurdistān trade, besides being a market town of the Bani Lām tribe. A small business in Manchester goods is carried on, chiefly by Jewish merchants who barter them for grain. 'Alī-al-Gharbi is the headquarters of a Nāhiyah of the same name in the Qadha of 'Amārah and is consequently the seat of a Mudir: it has also a telegraph office, a customs house and two Khāns. The town takes its name from a mosque dedicated, it is said, to 'Ali, a son of the Imām Mūsa whose tomb is at Kādhimain.

The name of 'Ali-ash-Sharqi علي الشرقي, a place on the left or eastern bank of the Tigris about three-sevenths of the way from 'Ali-al-Gharbi to 'Amārah, has a similar derivation; it also is the headquarters of a Mudīrate in the 'Amārah Qadha and exports some grain, but it is much smaller than 'Ali-al-Gharbi, in fact there is only a shrine and a few tents. There is a Government reserved forest at 'Ali-ash-Sharqi.

'AMĀMARAH عمارة

Singular 'Ammāri عمّاري. A comparatively poor, seafaring tribe of **Bahrain** and **Qatar,** by some supposed to belong to the **'Ammār** division of the **Dawāsir** of **Najd.** In **Bahrain** the 'Amāmarah have 40 houses at **Muharraq** Town and 100 at **Budaiya'**; in **Qatar** they have 20 at **Dōhah** and 20 at **Wakrah.** Their total number may be about 900 souls. They are Māliki Sunnis by religion and live by pearl diving and by navigation in all parts of the Persian Gulf. They are closely connected with the **Āl Bū Kuwārah** and **Ma'ādhīd** and originally came to **Bahrain** from **Qatar** along with the **'Utūb.** At present they have feuds with the Al Bin-'Ali and with the Āl Bahaih section of the Āl **Morrah.**

'AMĀRAH عمارة
QADHA

A division of the Sanjāq of 'Amārah in the Wilāyat of Basrah in Turkish **'Irāq.**

Position and boundaries.—The Qadha is situated on both banks of the **Tigris** chiefly above, but also for a short distance below, the town of 'Amārah: it is bounded on the north-west by the Qadhas of **Kūt-al-Amārah** and Badrah, on the north-east by the Persian frontier, on the south-east by the Qadha of **Shatrat-al-'Amārah,** and on the south-west by that of **Hai.**

Topography and inhabitants.—The town of 'Amārah and the villages of **'Ali-al-Gharbi, Kumait** and **Majar** are the only considerable centres of population in the Qadha. Above, that is to the north-west of the town of **Amārah,** the people are mostly of the Bani **Lām** tribe, but those about **Kumait** are Āl Bū Darāj; below **'Amārah** Town the principal tribe are the Āl Bū **Muhammad.**

The chief physical features of the district are the river **Tigris,** which flows through it, and the **Jahálah** canal derived from the same.

Population.—The total fixed population of the 'Amārah Qadha is estimated, inclusive of **'Amārah** Town, at 41,000 souls. It is calculated that of these about 34,000 are Shi'ah Muhammadans, 4,500 Sunni Muhammadans, 1,000 Jews, 1,000 **Sabians** and 500 Christians: the classes other than Shi'ah Muhammadans are practically confined to the town of **Amārah.**

Resources.—Above **Amārah** Town the principal crops are wheat, barley and millet; below it rice and maize predominate. Sesame and **Māsh** are also grown; and cotton, linseed and opium have been cultivated with success. The district is important for its livestock, especially horses and sheep, and for its pastoral products such as ghi, wool, skins and hides.

Among the more productive estates in the district are those of Akhdhar اخضر, Bahāthah بحاثه, Jahálah جهله (on the canal of the same name), Misharrah مشرّح and Shatt شطّ, all of which belong to the Dāirat-as-Sanīyah.

Administration.—'Amārah is the headquarters Qadha of the Sanjāq of the same name. It consists—the Markaz Nāhiyah of 'Amārah, which is administered by the Mutasarrif of the Sanjāq personally, being excluded—of four rural Nāhiyahs, namely 'Ali-al-Gharbi علي الغربي, 'Ali-ash-Sharqi علي الشرقي, Majar-al-Kabīr مجر الكبير and Majar-as-Saghīr مجر الصغير. Each of these is governed by a Mudīr who has his seat at the place from which his charge takes its name.

'AMĀRAH عماره TOWN

This important and rising town of Turkish 'Irāq, not to be confounded with **Kūt-al-Amārah** كوت الامارة, is situated upon the left bank of the **Tigris** about 130 miles by water above **Basrah** and is distant some 30 miles from the Turco-Persian land frontier: it is the *chef-lieu* of the Sanjāq and Qadha similarly named in the Wilāyat of Basrah.

Site and buildings.—'Amārah stands on a strip of land enclosed on the west by the **Tigris** and on the north and east by the **Jahálah** canal; while to the south of it, but at some distance, are the marshes of the **Āl Bū Muhammad** tribe. To the east of the **Jahálah** are extensive swamps and waterways, by means of which some boat communication is maintained with the **Hawīzeh** District and with Persian **'Arabistān** as a whole. On the right bank of the **Tigris** opposite 'Amārah are flourishing plantations of dates, other fruit trees and poplars, amidst which is the village or suburb of **Daffās** دفّاس,—so called from a shrine which it contains,—united to the town of 'Amārah by a boat bridge formerly of about 40 pontoons, but now (it is reported) reduced to about half that number by the employment of larger boats. 'Amārah has a river frontage of more than half a mile upon the **Tigris**; and a good embankment or wharf faced with brick, alongside of which steamers can lie, runs the whole length of the town. The northern quarter is the older and extends the whole way from the **Tigris** to the **Jahálah**, which is spanned behind the town by a boat bridge of several pontoons. In the northern quarter is situated a fine building belonging to the Dāirat-as-Sanīyah; here also are the military barracks and, upon the quay, the principal government offices. The main street of the town traverses the northern quarter from the **Tigris** to the **Jahálah** running at right angles to both streams: it contains the chief bazaar, of which the end next the **Tigris** was destroyed by fire in 1903 and has now been rebuilt in a more modern and commodious style. The southern quarter consists of a row of 27 new houses of uniform pattern and handsome appearance which face the river and form 6 large blocks: 15 of them were built as a speculation by the Dāirat-as-Sanīyah and the remainder by local Shaikhs in emulation of the Department's example. There are at 'Amārah two public baths.

Inhabitants.—The population of 'Amārah is estimated at 10,000 souls, of whom 4,500 may be Sunnis, 3,000 Shī'ahs, 1,000 Jews, 1,000 **Sabians**, and 500 Christians; most of the Muhammadans with the exception of the Turkish officials are town Arabs, but there are also a good many **Kurds** and a few Persians. The country Arabs to the north of 'Amārah are Banī **Lām**, and to the south Āl Bū **Muhammad**. The townspeople—apart from the officials, some well-to-do Persian merchants and the representatives of **Baghdād** and **Basrah** firms—are mostly petty traders and artisans.

Products, manufactures and trade.—The gardens of the town produce citrons, pomegranates, quinces, figs and grapes.

Arab cloaks, Kurdish rugs and silverware are among the manufactures of the place; the silverware is the work of the **Sabians** and one variety of it, inlaid with antimony, is unusual and not inelegant.

Ghi, wool, hides and skins, various kinds of nuts, also walnut and other woods are imported from the Kurdish hills, while wheat, barley, maize, rice and sesame are brought in from the surrounding country. The imports of 'Amārah from foreign countries are the same as those of Turkish **'Irāq** generally. Live cattle are exported by land in great numbers from 'Amārah to Syria. 'Amārah supplies **Baghdād** and **Basrah** with ghi, rice and barley; a considerable quantity of the barley is shipped to Europe and the greater part of the ghi to Bombay and the

Levant ports. 'Amārah wool, which is of excellent quality, is for the most part baled in a press belonging to Messrs. Lynch Brothers, and goes chiefly to London and Marseilles. In matters of trade 'Amārah is dependent to a great extent upon **Baghdād** through which it receives nearly all its imports from abroad. Skins and hides are usually sent to **Baghdād** to be pressed for exportation : there are, however, two native hand-presses for hides. The currency of 'Amārah consists chiefly of Persian silver Qrāns. Shops are said to number 150.

Administrative and official matters.—'Amārah is a place of administrative importance, being the headquarters of the Sanjāq of 'Amārah and the residence of the Mutasarrif : it has ordinarily a military garrison amounting to one infantry battalion, one squadron of cavalry and three or four field guns, and it is the headquarters of the 3rd battalion of the 85th Radīf regiment. The Dāirat-as-Sanīyah has a head office here; and the Customs, Public Debt and Sanitary Departments and the Tobacco Régie are each represented by a Mamūr, while a harbour master superintends shipping and river conservancy. There is a telegraph office linked with **'Ali-al-Gharbi** on one side and Qal'at **Sālīh** on the other. The Persian Government are represented at 'Amārah by a Nāib-Kārpardāz or Consular Agent. The town is constituted as a municipality.

General.—'Amārah did not exist at the time of Colonel Chesney's survey in 1836 : it is said to have grown up since 1860 in consequence of the pacification and material development of the country around. It is believed to mark the site of a battle field on which a Turkish commander broke the power of the local Arabs and afterwards encamped, and for this reason it is still sometimes called Ordu or The Camp. The present thriving condition of the town is largely due to the operations of the Dāirat-as-Sanīyah, whose local manager at the present time (1905) is a man of progressive ideas. A Committee of Management, subordinate to the Central Committee at **Baghdād,** and the principal offices of the Dāirat-as-Sanīyah in Turkish **'Irāq** are now located here. There is a Government reserved forest near 'Amārah.

'ANĀFIJEH
عنافجة

Singular 'Anaifiji عنيفجي. An Arab tribe, said to be related to the Āl **Kathīr,** once powerful and of first-rate importance in Southern **'Arabistān,** but now diminished in numbers to about 5,000 souls of whom about 1,000 are settled and 4,000 are nomadic. The former boundary of the 'Anāfijeh ran along the right bank of the **Shatait** from its confluence with the **Diz** to a little above Chahārdingeh; thence it crossed to Kūt Bandar on the **Diz** and, passing by Khairābād to the left bank of the **Karkheh** followed the **Karkheh** to a point some 10 miles above Kūt Nahr Hāshim: from this point it ran to Khar Ishtīreh خرا شتیره opposite **Ahwāz** village on the **Kārūn** river and then kept along the right bank of the **Kārūn** to the mouth of the **Diz** river. The 'Anāfijeh now chiefly occur on the lower course of the **Shatait**, on the banks of the **Diz** within 20 miles of its mouth, and on the right bank of the **Kārūn**: a few are found however on both banks of the **Gargar**. The 'Anāfijeh are mostly tent-dwellers and they own livestock in considerable numbers, but they depend chiefly for their livelihood on the cultivation of wheat, millet and barley. The tribe can still muster some 1,140 fighting men, of whom about 150 are mounted, and the majority are armed with rifles. Except the 'Abādāt section the 'Anāfijeh pay revenue direct to the Shaikh of **Muhammareh** through their own Shaikh, at present Alwān. In bad years the Shaikh of **Muhammareh** remits his demands and even finances the tribe. The sections are :—

Name.	Location.	Fighting strength.	Remarks.
'Abādāt عبادات	With the Āl Hamaid, east of the **Kārūn** river.	100, of whom 15 are mounted.	They inhabit tents and possess 10 camels, 100 cattle and 2,000 sheep and goats. They migrated to their present quarters 13 years ago.
Anāfijeh عنافجه	Usually on the right bank of the lower **Diz** about Abu Tayūr.	40, of whom 30 are mounted.	The chief Shaikh belongs to this section. They live in tents and have 200 cattle and 4,000 sheep and goats.
Dailam دیلم	At 'Arab Hasan and Abu 'Amūd on the **Shatait**, and in **Miyānāb** 2 miles from 'Arab Hasan.	400, of whom 30 are mounted.	The Dailam are now in a transition stage between tent and hut life. Their livestock are 300 cattle and 15,000 sheep and goats. The Dailam include some Maiyāh میاح who are said to be of Bani **Lām** descent.

Name.	Location.	Fighting strength.	Remarks.
Dilfīyeh دلفیه	At Bait Simaich and Bait Saiyid Ahmad, localities in Miyānāb, and at Bait Sha'aibath and Kharrān east of the Gargar.	200, of whom 20 are mounted.	They live in tents and possess 50 cattle and 1,000 sheep and goats.
Hamaid Bait Tarfeh حمید بیت طرفه	South of the Diz, about Abu Jazīreh and Abu Tayūr.	40, of whom 15 are mounted.	Tent dwellers. They own 20 camels, 100 cattle and 10,000 sheep and goats. Their sheep are said to be all white and of a specially good stock.
Ightufān اغتفان	In the same part as the 'Anāfijeh section above.	40, of whom 10 are mounted.	They live in tents. Their livestock are 40 cattle and 4,000 sheep and goats.
Mahdīyeh مهدیه	At Sōzi and Adhāfeh on the Gargar.	60, of whom 10 are mounted.	This section have huts. They own 80 cattle and 4,000 sheep and goats.
Nais نیس	About Abu Qrānīyeh on the right bank of the Shatait and on the lower Diz.	200; none are mounted.	The Nais inhabit tents: they have 300 buffaloes, 600 cattle and 1,000 sheep and goats. They really belong to the tribe of the same name in the Hawīzeh District.
Wahabīyeh وهبیه	At Sōzi on the Gargar.	60, of whom 10 are mounted.	They live in huts and possess 60 cattle and 3,000 sheep and goats.

The Āl Bū Hāji section of the **Hardān** tribe pay their revenue to the Shaikh of **Muhammareh** through the 'Anāfijeh, among whom they reside.

'ANAIZAH
عنیزه

The principal town of **Qasīm** and in fact of all **Najd**; it is situated about 150 miles south-east by east of **Hāil**, 200 miles northwest of **Riyādh** and 12 miles south of **Buraidah**. It is thus about half way between **Basrah** and Makkah, being distant about 400 miles from either, and lies nearly in the straight line, and not far from midway, between the capitals of Northern and Southern **Najd**. With good reason it is regarded by its inhabitants as being the centre of the whole Arabian peninsula and is styled by them Umm **Najd** اُمّ نجد or "Mother of Central Arabia."

Site and buildings.—The site of 'Anaizah is a loamy hollow 2 or 3 miles from the right bank of Wādi-ar-**Rummah**, underlain by sandstone rock and surrounded by sandy desert. To the south-east, at no great distance, are some very barren hills covered with loose stones. The height of 'Anaizah above the sea is probably about 2,500 feet. The town is walled and stands in the middle of an oasis which is also walled, or formerly was so; the space between the outer and the inner enceinte is filled with date groves, gardens and cultivated fields. On the north of the town this cultivated belt has a depth of 1 to 2 miles, and the aspect which the place presents to a traveller approaching from this side is imposing in its extent as well as in its richness. Both walls are strengthened by towers set at intervals, and the agricultural resources and abundant supply of well-water which the oasis contains would render its reduction by blockade a difficult if not impossible task. Internally the town is divided into three principal wards, each of which has its own separate banner in time of war; they are Kharaizah خريزه on the north and west, Hofūf حفوف on the south, and Umm Himār اُمّ حمار on the east. The houses, even the best, are clay-built, but pleasant and clean: a large proportion of them have upper storeys.

Population.—The inhabitants of 'Anaizah are mostly of the Bani **Tamīm** tribe; but the town is said to have been founded by **Sabai'** from **'Āridh**, to whom Bani **Khālid** refugees were added at a later date. There are also some **'Anizah**. The total population is probably between 10,000 and 15,000 souls. The people have a free bearing and are well clad; they are industrious and not unintelligent, but their disposition has been somewhat soured by the Wahhābi form of religion, which is still in the ascendant, though not universal, among them. The poorer townsmen resemble Bedouins in garb, and wear the Kafiyah and 'Aqāl of the desert; while the richer classes use the fez, over which a gay-coloured kerchief is loosely thrown. The well-to-do dress in light worsted 'Abas from Turkish **'Irāq**, with sometimes an embroidered collar; and persons of good birth, when walking in the street, carry in their hands long rods that are brought from Makkah.

'ANAIZAH

The women are not visible in the day time, but go out to visit at one another's houses between twilight and the last prayer. Friday is the market day, and the Friday prayers in the congregational mosque are attended by all and sundry residing in the oasis. More aged men are to be seen here than in north-western Arabia generally. The principal diseases are fever, enlarged spleen, catarrh, and cataract. In 1880 the mosques of 'Anaizah numbered 15, including the Jāmi' in the public square; and there were four schools, of which one was for girls. The residents of the town have an agreeable custom of camping *en famille* in the surrounding desert for change of air.

Agriculture.—'Anaizah, though it possesses a considerable trade, is largely dependent on its agriculture. On the town lands wheat is grown year after year in the same fields, and the crops are dense but light; fresh loam and the dung of the camels which work the water-lifts are the only manures in use. The fields are levelled, embanked, and irrigated from wells; the date trees stand in channels which are flushed with water twice daily. The ordinary cereals, fruits and vegetables of **Qasīm** are cultivated. Most of the small owners are burdened with debt and cannot afford sufficiently to irrigate their ground. Animals are horses, camels, donkeys, cattle, sheep and goats, the horses are estimated at 60, the camels at 1,000, the donkeys at 300 and the horned cattle at 1,500.

Internal trade and supplies.—Supplies of many kinds are abundant. In the main bazaar are sold piece-goods, clothing, drugs (including occasionally English medicines such as cod-liver oil), camel medicines, loaf sugar, spices, Syrian soap imported through Madīnah, and Yaman coffee brought by caravans from Makkah. This principal bazaar is called Maskaf مسكف ; it contains about 120 shops, but only a small part of it is roofed over. Most of the imported commodities are received through **Kuwait**; the remainder come through **Hasa** or, as already mentioned, from Makkah or Madīnah. In the outlying quarters of the town are small shops which deal in sundries, such as iron, nails, matches, salt, onions, eggs, girdle-bread and milk; and on Fridays veiled women sell chickens in the market place and dispose of skins for holding milk or water which they have tanned and prepared with their own hands. Common food, Arabian coffee and clothing from the Persian Gulf side are cheap; and dates, sold by weight sometimes at 30 lbs. for a dollar, are excellent; but grain is dear. There is only one well of perfectly fresh water, and it is observed that the wells near the desert yield as a rule sweeter water than those lower down in the Qā' قاع or basin in which the town stands.

Occupations and industries.—Numerous handicrafts and industries are exercised in 'Anaizah: there are goldsmiths, silversmiths, armourers and tinkers; turners of wooden bowls and makers of wooden locks, of camel-saddles and of wheels for wells; stone-cutters, who seldom live more than three or four years at their trade on account of its unhealthiness; sinkers and liners of wells, workers in marble and manufacturers of coffee-mortars; house builders and plasterers; seamsters and seamstresses; embroiderers and sandal makers. The goldsmiths and silversmiths of 'Anaizah are renowned for their filigree and thread work, and some who have settled at Makkah are said to surpass all their competitors there.

External trade.—Trade on the large scale is represented by about 15 merchants of substance, some of whom have representatives at **Basrah** and Jiddah; the capital of the wealthiest among them may be worth £24,000. Among the leading merchants are a family named Bassām who are said to be of **Washam** origin. There is no horse-breeding at 'Anaizah itself, but horses are purchased from the Bedouins in winter and brought into condition for export to India. Ghi also is collected from the Bedouins in spring by 'Anaizah merchants and stored in marble troughs till summer or autumn, when it is sent by caravan to Makkah; one such caravan may carry as much as 30 tons of ghi worth £2,000.

Political position and administration.—The history of 'Anaizah is that of **Qasīm**, in which it has ever occupied the leading position. Before the capture of the place by the Amīr of Jabal **Shammar** in 1891, 'Anaizah was ruled by its own Amīrs; they possessed arbitrary powers, but wielded them in a constitutional manner, deferring to some extent to their Majlis or council. Capital punishment was then but rarely inflicted. Common offences and theft were visited with a beating; cutting off of the hand for theft, according to Muhammadan law, was not in vogue. Hardened felons were expelled from the township. In case of a military expedition the lists for service were made up by the Amīr, only the better-off classes being required to serve; those who were called out were obliged to send a camel and back-rider each, the front place on the animal being filled either by the sender or, if he preferred it, by an efficient substitute. The poorer classes remained at home for the defence of the town, and on such occasions it was customary to discontinue the morning market, to prohibit the killing of butchers'-meat, and to close by order all places of business except small general shops. A typical expedition sent out by the town in 1878 against Bedouins consisted of 400 men with 20 mares and 200 camels.

It is probable that, after the liberation of **Qasīm** from the yoke of Jabal **Shammar** in 1902, the old order of things was in most respects re-established under the present Amīr, 'Abdul 'Azīz-bin-'Abdullah-bin-Yahya; nor does it appear that it has been seriously modified since the nominal Turkish occupation of **Qasīm** in 1905. The sole sign of Turkish influence in 1906 was a Nuqtah or military post garrisoned by a detachment of less than 100 Turkish soldiers under a Yūzbāshi; this detachment occupied a house belonging to the Amīr of 'Anaizah in the Umm Himār quarter, it seemed to have no police or other duties in the town, and according to the accounts received its presence was virtually ignored by the Arabs. The Amīr held the honorary rank of Mudīr, but he drew no salary and maintained no relations with the Turks. He was understood to profess allegiance to Ibn Sa'ūd alone and to pay him occasional tribute.

'ANDĀM (WĀDI) وادي عندام

A valley of considerable importance in the Sultanate of **'Omān**: it begins in the Eastern **Hajar**, in a part of the hills called Jabal 'Ulya علیا, and runs southwards across the western end of the **Sharqīyah** district to Wādi **Halfain**, which it joins.

The following are the villages, in descending order, of this valley:—

Name.	Position.	On which bank situated.	Houses and inhabitants.	Remarks.
'Ulya علیا	At the head of the Wādi.	Right.	100 houses of Bani Ruwāhah.	Possesses the ordinary livestock of 'Omān (viz., camels, donkeys, cattle, sheep and goats) and 3,000 palms.
Washāl رشال	1 hour below 'Ulya.	Left.	50 do.	Do. and 1,000 palms.
Mahalyah محليه	2 miles below Washāl.	Do.	100 do.	Do. do.

'ANDĀM (WĀDI)

Name.	Position.	On which bank situated.	Houses and inhabitants.	Remarks.
Hibāt حباط	4 miles below Mahalyah.	Right.	70 houses of Bani **Ruwāhah** of the Wilād Sulaimān-bin-'Umr and other sections.	Possesses the ordinary livestock of **'Omān** (*viz.*, camels, donkeys, cattle, sheep and goats) and 2,000 palms.
Ghiryain غريين	1 mile below Hibāt.	Do.	120 do.	Do. and 2,500 palms. (At this point Wādi **Mahram** comes in from the right or western bank.)
Khadhra Bin-Daffā' خضرا بن دفاع	2½ hours below Ghiryain and 10 or 12 miles south-west of **Samad** Town.	Do.	See article **'Omān** Proper.	Do. and 4,000 palms. (Here this valley is joined by Wādi **Samad** from the left or eastern bank.)
Majāzah مجازه	2 miles below Khadhra.	Do.	180 houses of Bani **Jābir** of the Bani Harb section.	Do. and 2,000 palms. (Here Wādi Qant, described below, joins Wādi 'Andām from the west.)
Washihi واشحي	2 hours below Majāzah.	Do.	50 houses of Bani **Ruwāhah**.	Do. and 600 palms.
Mukhtari' مختزع	1½ hours below Washihi.	Do.	100 houses of Shurūj.	Do. and 2,000 palms.
Ukhaidhir اخيضر	2 hours below Mukhtari'.	Left.	60 houses of Bani **Ruwāhah**.	Do. and 1,000 palms.
Wāfi وافي	1 hour below Ukhaidhir.	Do.	70 houses of **Habūs**	Do. and 1,500 palms.
Mutaili' مطيلع	2 hours below Wāfi.	Do.	80 do.	Do. do.

Wādi 'Andām issues from the hills about midway between 'Ulya and Washāl, and its junction with Wādi **Halfain** is said to take place 2 miles below Mutaili'.

The Bani Ruwāhah of this valley belong to the Aulād 'Aqīd, 'Awāmir, Wilād Harmal, Wilād Hasan, Wilād Husain, Bani Na'amān and Wilād

Sulaimān-bin-'Umr sections of the tribe. The total number of inhabitants is about 6,000 souls. Among them are some of the Hādiyīn tribe.

Livestock are estimated in all at about 200 camels, 350 donkeys, 350 cattle and 2,500 sheep and goats: these are divided approximately in proportion to the size of the villages.

Wādi 'Andām forms, from Khadra Bin-Daffa' downwards, the boundary between the districts of **'Omān** Proper on the west and **Sharqīyah** on the east.

The affluent called Wādi Qant قنت , which comes in at Majāzah, has its head at Saddi in **'Omān** Proper and forms the boundary, from that place to Khadhra Bin-Daffa', between **'Omān** Proper and **Sharqīyah**. It apparently contains three or four of the villages described in the article on **'Omān** Proper.

ANGĀLI
انگالي

A small district on the mainland of Persia immediately to the north-east of **Būshehr** Town; it is enclosed between the **Rūd-hilleh** River on the north, the **Rūd-hilleh** District on the west, the **Būshehr** harbour on the south and the **Dashtistān** District on the east, and is in the jurisdiction of the Governor of the **Gulf Ports**. Angāli is said to have been at one time a part of the **Dashtistān** District and to have been detached from it for administrative reasons.

Extent and physical characteristics.—The length of Angāli is about 15 miles from north to south, but its breadth is only 5 to 10 miles.

The whole is a plain; and the portion about Shīf, Hasan Nadu and the two Nūkāls (mentioned below) is a barren waste. The climate in winter is cold, and in summer from June to August a very hot wind blows in the middle of the day.

Population.—The people numbering only some 2,700 souls are a mixed race, the blood of Behbehāni **Lurs** probably predominating; there is a small Arab infusion. The men of Angāli are described as brave and hard-working. They wear the ordinary Persian knife and are well-armed with Martini rifles, nearly 400 of which are owned in the district. All the people follow agricultural pursuits and their dwellings are mostly built of sun-dried bricks and mud, but some are huts of wood and matting. They are Shī'ahs by religion.

80   ANGĀLI

Agriculture, transport and trade.—Wheat and barley are, with the exception of a few dates and melons, the only crops.

It is calculated that the district possesses about 100 horses, 500 donkeys and 2,000 sheep and goats. Communication with **Būshehr Town** is by boat from Shīf.

The Hāshim Man of Angāli, consisting of 16 ordinary local Mans of 8 lbs. 4 oz. each, is equal to 132 lbs. English. Trade is small and of a commonplace character. Building materials, chiefly Zanzibar timber and **Muhammareh** matting, are imported through **Būshehr Town.**

Administration.—The villages of Angāli are ruled by a hereditary Khān, at present Ahmad Khān, who is subject to the Governor of the **Gulf Ports**: his family are said to have been originally Nūi **Lurs** who immigrated from **Behbehān** 60 or 70 years ago, but they have absorbed some Arab blood. The administration is of the same type as in the neighbouring districts ruled by Khāns. The only tax is one of 65 Qrāns per Gāu of cultivation, the Gāu being here a plot measuring 250 by 250 yards and requiring 6 Hāshim maunds of seed to sow it. The annual sum at present payable to the Persian Government as revenue is 1,500 Tūmāns exclusive of the farm of the tolls at Shīf.

Topography.—The villages of the district are:—

Name.	Position.	Houses and inhabitants.	Remarks.
Bahi (Tul-i-) طل بهي	Near the south-east corner of the district.	30 houses of Persians.	Wheat and barley are grown; there are 40 donkeys.
Barkhurdār (Khashm-i-) خشم برخوردار	5 miles south-east of **Mahmad-shāhi.**	20 houses of **Lurs** of Behbehāni extraction.	Wheat, barley and a few dates are grown: there are 7 horses, 40 donkeys, 20 cattle and 100 sheep and goats.
Barkhurdār (Khashm-i-Shaikh) خشم شيخ برخوردار	Adjoining Haft-jūsh on the south.	12 houses of Persians, tribe not ascertainable.	Ordinary cultivation.
Gazi (Nūkāl-i-) نوكال گزي	8 miles south-south-east of **Mahmad-shāhi** and 10 miles north-east of Shīf	40 do.	Wheat and barley are grown: there are 50 donkeys, 200 sheep and a few horses.

ANGALI

Name.	Position.	Houses and inhabitants.	Remarks.
Haftjūsh هفت جوش	On the left bank of the Rūd-hil-leh River, 2 miles above **Mahmad-shāhi**.	150 houses of the descendants of immigrants from **Burāzjān, Dāliki, Kāzarūn**, etc.	Wheat and barley are grown. There are 100 donkeys and a considerable number of horses.
Haidari حيدري	On the left bank of the Rūd-hil-leh River, 1 mile above **Mahmad-shāhi**.	35 houses of the descendants of Ka'ab immigrants from the **Hindiyān** district.	Wheat and barley are grown, and there are about 600 date palms. There are a few donkeys. The people are Sunnis.
Hasan (Khashm-i-Kal) خشم كل حسن	4 miles east-south-east of **Mahmad-shāhi**.	25 houses of Lurs and others.	There is ordinary cultivation. Animals are 10 horses, 5 mules, 40 donkeys, 25 cattle, 100 sheep and goats.
Hasan Nadu حسن ندر or Hasan Nadūm حسن ندوم	7 miles north-east of Shīf.	20 houses of Lurs.	The people grow wheat and barley and have about 20 donkeys.
Mahmadshāhi محمد شاهي	...	...	See article **Mahmad-shāhi**.
Muhammad Quli (Khashm-i-) خشم محمّد قلي	1 or 2 miles south of Haftjūsh.	20 houses of Arabs calling themselves Bani **Tamīm**.	The crops are wheat, barley and dates: there are about 30 donkeys.
Mukhi (Nūkāl-i-) نوكال مخي	1½ miles north-west of Nūkāl-i-Gazi.	45 houses of Lur and supposed Bani **Tamīm** Arabs.	The people have 50 donkeys and 200 sheep, and grow wheat and barley.

Name.	Position.	Houses and inhabitants.	Remarks.
Shīf شيف	On the coast 5 miles north-east of Būshehr Town.	There are no inhabitants.	Also called Tul-i-Shīf طل شيف on account of a rocky knoll by which it is distinguished. This is a low rocky point and landing-place on the mainland at the north-east end of Būshehr harbour. Goods passing between Būshehr and the interior are transferred from boat to caravan or *vice versâ* at this spot when the road by Ahmadi is closed. Shīf is visible from the high part of the Būshehr Peninsula. There is no water at Shīf and mules required there must be ordered previously through the muleteers' agents in Būshehr Town. The Persian Imperial Customs established a post here in 1904.
Suhaili سهيلي	1 or 2 miles south of Khashm-i-Barkhurdār.	20 houses of Persian tribes.	Cultivation is ordinary.
Zandān زندان	6 miles south-south-east of Mahmadshāhi.	15 houses of Nūi Lurs from Behbehān.	The village grows wheat and barley and has 35 donkeys.
Zardaki Buzurg زردكي بزرگ	On the left bank of the Rūd-hil-leh River, 1 mile below Mahmadshāhi.	30 houses of Bani Tamīm Arabs and Lurs intermingled.	This village has dates as well as wheat and barley, and there are a few horses and 40 donkeys.
Zardaki Kūchik زردكي كوچك	To the north-east of Zardaki Buzurg which it adjoins.	20 houses of the same.	Possesses wheat, barley and a few dates, also 35 donkeys.

'ANIZAH عنزة

Singular 'Anizi عنزي: there is also a plural 'Anūz عنوز: a great Arab tribe of Northern and Central Arabia.

Distribution.—Their original seat is believed to have been a little to the north of Madīnah on the water-shed between the Red Sea and the basin of Wādi-ar-**Rummah**, but the Dīrah of their Bedouins now extends from **Qasīm** and Madīnah on the south to the Haurān in Syria on the north, while on the east it reaches to the main route between **Hāil** and **Najaf** and, further north, to the **Euphrates** valley. Some of the Bedouin 'Anizah occupy the neighbourhood of **Musaiyib** in Turkish **'Irāq** for about two months in the year, and make their annual purchases of food and clothing there and at **Tawairīj**. The greater part of the Syrian desert belongs to the 'Anizah, and they come in contact with the Persian Gulf basin chiefly to the west of the **Euphrates** between **Karbala** and **Najaf** and further south on the borders of Jabal **Shammar**, where they camp in Hajarah and dispute the possession of Batn with the **Shammar** tribe. They frequent **Wadyān** and the **Nafūd**; in the latter Jubbah is one of their chief centres. The Bedouins around **Taimah** are 'Anizah, and numbers of the tribe collect during the date harvest at Khaibar, which formerly belonged to them and where they still own plantations. Besides these Bedouins a very considerable proportion of the sedentary population in the districts of Southern **Najd** and in **Qasīm** appear to be of 'Anizah blood.

Divisions and numbers of the Bedouin 'Anizah.—The internal organisation of the 'Anizah tribe is a subject of great difficulty, and comparison of the various authorities who have written on the subject yields no clear or consistent result.

According to information collected recently at **Kuwait**, the more southern 'Anizah fall into two main divisions, the 'Amarāt عمرات and the Bishr بشر.*

The 'Amarāt are sub-divided into Dahāmishah دهامشه and Hilbān حلبان, and these again into the sections and sub-sections below:—

Dahāmishah sub-division of the 'Amarāt.

| 'Ayāsh عياش | { Dhuwaidah ضوائده
Sumair سمير
Suwālim سوالم | Tawātihah طواطحه | 'Adalāt عدلات
Khamīs خميس
Mahuwwis مهوس
Marwān مروان
Mirābidah مرابده
Qahūs قحوس
Shtaiwi شتيوي |

---

* Doughty however (I. 331) treats the 'Amarāt as a sub-division of the Bishr and does not mention the Dahāmishah and Hilbān whom our **Kuwait** authority treats as important.

Dahāmishah sub-division of the 'Amarāt—contd.

Suwailmāt سلويمات	{	Bakr	بكر		Zibnah زبنه	{	Balālīz	بلاليز
		Diyādibah	ديادبه				Ghirrah	غره
		Muhaisin	محيسن				Mahaināt	محينات
		Munāhirah	مناهره				Qumaishāt	قميشات
		Mutair	مطير				Rikā'ān	ركعان
		Rubdhāt	ربضات				Sabābīh	سبابيح
							Salātīn	سلاطين
							Shilkhān	شلخان

Hilbān sub-division of the 'Amarāt.

Bisaisāt	بسيسات	Salqah	سلقه	{	'Awāsi	عواصي
Ghashūm	غشوم				Kāsib	كاسب
Hayāzah	حيازه	Saqūr	صقور		Dhalā'īn	ضلاعين
Matārifah	مطارفه				Marzūq	مرزوق
Midhyān	مضيان				Mutair	مطير

The sub-divisions of the Bishr are the Fida'ān فدعان, Sabā'ah سباعه or Saba'ah سبعه, and Wald Sulaimān ولد سليمان, and the following table shows their sections:—

Fida'ān sub-division of the Bishr.

Hadaib	هديب	Mizahlif	مزحلف
Jidā'īn	جداعين	and	
Mahaid	مهيد	Shtaiwi	شتيري

Sabā'ah sub-division of the Bishr.

Faqaqāt	فققات	Misāribah	مصاربه
Haraimīs	حريميس	and	
Mirshid	مرشد	Qa'aishish	قعيششي

Wald Sulaimān sub-division of the Bishr.

'Awājīyah	عواجيه	Khumishah	خمشه
Fuqarah	فقره	Yidyān	يديان

Of the large Bishr division generally it may be stated that, except their Sabā'ah sub-division, they adjoin the **Shammar** tribe on its south-west frontier and that their ordinary range is from **Qasīm** to the western end of the **Nafūd**. The pasture of their Dīrah is excellent, but their good watering-places are few and their wells are deep. In person the Bishr are robust and resemble the Bedouins of the north; for dress they wear clothes imported from Turkish **'Irāq** and sometimes don as head-gear a worsted band wound fold upon fold like a turban.

The Sabā'ah sub-division of the Bishr are said to be found chiefly in the direction of **Najaf** and **Karbala**; on the average they are short of stature but carry long spears. Batn is on the border between them and the **Shammar**.

The Wald Sulaimān* sub-division of the Bishr is said by some to include, as well as the sections given above, the Bajāidah بجائده, a portion of the 'Anizah tribe of whom a good deal is heard. It seems certain that the Fuqarah section of the Wald Sulaimān together with a number of rather strong sections collectively known as the Wald 'Ali† ولد علي compose a group known as the Bani Wahab ‡ بني وهب; but whether this group includes other sections of the Wald Sulaimān besides the Fuqarah cannot, on present data, be determined. The 'Awājīyah section of the Wald Sulaimān are described as inhospitable and violent in their dealings; they are found between the **Nafūd** and **Qasīm**. The Fuqarah § section of the Wald Sulaimān, in number about 800 souls, inhabit the country between **Taimah** and Khaibar and extend to the west of the pilgrim-route from Syria to Madīnah. They live generally in the Bedouin manner, but their Shaikhs have houses at Khaibar, where the tribesmen sell querns of their own manufacture at the autumn fair. In religion the Fuqarah are somewhat fanatical; yet they eat the hedgehog and the fox, and their women go unveiled. In 1878 they were subject to Ibn Rashīd, to whom they paid tribute of $400 a year at the rate of one dollar per 5 camels or 30 head of cattle. They were then on bad terms with the Muwāhīb مواهيب another section of the 'Anizah who are variously described as belonging to the Hilbān and to the Sabā'ah.

---

* It may be noted here that there is little or no agreement between Guarmani's division of the Wald Sulaimān and that furnished by our authority.

† Regarding the Wald 'Ali there is considerable agreement between Doughty and Huber. The largest section of the Wald 'Ali appears to be the Tuwālah and the most aristocratic the Alāidah.

‡ By some accounts the Bani Wahab include also all the Bishr, Ruwalah and Qalās: see Doughty, I. 229.

§ Doughty divides the Fuqarah into 8 sub-sections, Huber into 9: only 3 names in the two lists appear to correspond—an apt illustration of the difficulty of tribal questions in Arabia. It is not clear that our Kuwait authority, in classing the Fuqarah as Bishr, has Doughty's support.

86 'ANIZAH

The 'Amarāt and the Bishr, except the Sabā'ah, mainly belong to the south: the best known 'Anizah of the north are the Ruwalah روله, the Qalās قلاس or Jalās and the Sha'alān شعلان. A close connection exists between these three, but it has not been satisfactorily explained. The Ruwalah are certainly a large body; their range is from the **Nafūd** northwards to the Syrian Haurān and from Wādi **Sirhān** on the west to the Hāil-Najaf route on the east. The Ruwalah, it is said, can ordinarily be distinguished from their southern neighbours the **Shammar** by their smaller horses and shorter spears.

Portions of the 'Anizah tribe who cannot, on the information available, be correlated with any of the foregoing are the—

'Ajail	عجيل	Makāsirah	مكاسره
Alāidah *	الائده	Masā'ib	مصاعب
Daghaiyim (Āl)	آل دغيّم	Matūtah	مطوطه
Dahmān	دحمان	Muwaijah	مويجه
Dhayān (Bani)	بني ضيان	Nūri	نوري
Dilimah	دلمه	Rūs	روس
Hasani	حسني	Shiblān † or Shimlān	شملان شبلان
Idhn	اذن	Shumailah	شميله
Jalā'id	جلاعيد	Taiyār	طيار

Probably a number of these are fractions of the larger and smaller units already enumerated.

The total strength of the Bedouin 'Anizah may, on various considerations,‡ be roughly estimated at 36,000 souls.

Character and life of the Bedouin 'Anizah.—The 'Anizah are respected by their neighbours and enemies the **Shammar** as being, next to themselves, the noblest of the Bedouins in descent and character; nevertheless the more southern 'Anizah are perhaps the most evilly disposed tribe, except the **Qahtān**, of Central Arabia. The features of

---

* Possibly a section of the Wald 'Ali group. See second footnote, page 85.

† The Shiblān are said to include the Nāif نائف who appear to be identical with a clan mentioned by Wallin as belonging to the north. On the other hand, Guarmani appears to include the Shimlān with the Wald Sulaimān of the south-west.

‡ This estimate is partially based on Kuwait reports of the fighting strength of the southern 'Anizah, which, though containing useful indications, were not sufficiently reliable to be included in the article. Doughty placed the total of the tribe at 25,000 souls only; the present Shaikh of Kuwait on the other hand would raise the 'Anizah to a frankly impossible figure.

the northern 'Anizah are often of a Syrian or even Jewish caste. Some 'Anizah families, for the sake of a more comfortable life, live among the **Hataim**; but they do not intermarry with them. The tents of the 'Anizah are high compared with others, and the apartment of the wife is upon the left in entering.

Political sympathies.—In the recent struggle in Central Arabia the Bedouins, at least, of the 'Anizah took part with Ibn Sa'ūd and the Shaikh of **Kuwait** against Ibn Rashīd.

Settled 'Anizah.—The foregoing remarks relate to the Bedouin 'Anizah; but, as already observed, a large part of the settled population of **Najd** claim to be, and many of them probably are, of the 'Anizah. In Jabal **Shammar** they are not mentioned except at **Jauf-al-'Āmir** and Ghazālah; but in **Qasīm** settled Arabs who call themselves 'Anizah are apparently found at **'Anaizah, Buraidah,** Dhalfa'ah, Dharās, 'Ain-ibn-Fahaid, Ghāf I, **Khabrah,** Khadhar, **Qusaibah,** Muraid Saiyid, **Rass,** Raudhat-ar-Rubai'i, Saib, Shaihīyah, Shiqqah, Ta'amīyah, Watāt and Wathāl, and possibly at Khabb, Mudhnib and Qisaiya'ah. In **Sadair** they are said to occur at Dākhilah, Dhalmah, Harmah, Ijwai, Janūbī-yah, Khīs, **Majma'**, Ruwaidhah, Tuwaim and **Zilfi**; in **'Āridh** at Barrah, Haraimlah and Malham in Mahmal, at Bātin-ash-Shuyūkh, Manfūhah and **Riyādh** on Wādi **Hanīfah,** and at Dhrumah town, Mizāhmīyah and Rōdhah in the **Dhrumah** tract. In **Harīq** their presence is reported at Harīq town and Mufaijir, and in **Hautah** at Hautah town and Hilwah. In **Aflāj** they are found at **Raudhah** and in Wādi **Sabai'** at Khurmah and Raudhah. They also occur in **Kharj**.

The sections to which the settled 'Anizah belong have not been investigated in many cases, but the following are mentioned:—

'Askar عسكر: in **Kharj,** and at Dhalmah and **Majma'** in **Sadair.**

Dāūd دأود: at Hautah town in **Hautah.**

Harqān حرقان: at Malham in **'Āridh.**

Hawaidi هويدي at **Majma'** in **Sadair.**

Hawaishān هويشان in **Zīlfi.**

Hazāzinah هزازنه: at Harīq town and Mufaijir in **Harīq.**

Ifqahah افقهه: at the town of **Dhrumah.**

Ijdaimāt اجديمات: at Raudhah in **Aflāj.**

Rabā' (Āl Bū) آل بو رباع: at Dākhilah in **Sadair.**

Of these the Hazāzinah are said to be a branch of the Ruwalah, already mentioned in the paragraph on Bedouin divisions. Among the settled 'Anizah mention must also be made of the Misālīkh مصاليخ. According to some authorities these are a branch of the Wald 'Ali; and the Āl Maqran آل مقرن, the family of the rulers of Southern Najd, together with the family of the Shaikhs of Buraidah in Qasīm, are said to be sprung from them.*

'AQAL†
العقل

A small littoral district at the base of the Qatar peninsula upon the east side; it is bounded by Khor-al-'Odaid on the north-west and by Dōhat-an-Nakhalah دوحة النخلة on the south-east, the distance between which in a direct line is nearly 35 miles. Inland the depth of the district is on the average about 20 miles. On the landward side 'Aqal is enclosed by Mijan on the east, by the Jāfūrah desert on the south and south-west, and by Qatar on the north-west.

The coast of 'Aqal is embayed by a great opening, Khor-adh-Dhuwaihin خور الضريهن, which is 20 miles deep and, being about 16 miles wide at its entrance, occupies nearly a half of the whole sea frontage of 'Aqal; this inlet is rather nearer to the Khor-al-'Odaid end of the district than to the other. The depth of the bay varies over the greater part of its extent from 4 to 10 fathoms, but in different parts of it there are shoals.

The soil of 'Aqal in the proximity of the sea is fairly firm, and the land rises in steps to a height of several feet; behind the ridges thus formed, which are of a reddish colour, lies a tract of heavy dark sand with hillocks of light-coloured sand occurring at intervals.

The principal camping grounds in the district are the following:—

Name.	Position.	Remarks.
Dhuwaihin الضريهن	About 10 miles inland, south-westwards, from the foot of Dōhat-adh-Dhuwaihin.	The principal camping place in the district. There is 1 well about 2 fathoms deep, surrounded by 10 smaller ones each a fathom deep: the water of all is good.

* Others however give a different account of the origin of the Wahhābi ruler. See Doughty, I. 229.

† The information contained in the article was supplied by Captain F. B. Prideaux, Political Agent in Bahrain. His map may be consulted (*Map of Jāfūrah, etc.*); see first footnote in article Trucial 'Omān.

Name.	Position.	Remarks.
Nakhalah ('Aqalat-an-) عقلة النخله	5 to 10 miles inland, south-south-westwards, from the foot of Dōhat-an-Nakhalah. The spot lies among sand hills.	Good water occurs near the surface over a considerable area. The place is frequented by the **Mānāsīr** and **Āl Morrah**.
Nathīl (Saudah) سوده نثيل	20 to 25 miles inland, westwards, from the foot of Khor-al-'Odaid.	Wells yield good water at 1 fathom.
'Odaid العديد	On the south shore of Khor-al-'Odaid, at a little way from the entrance.	See article Khor-al-'Odaid.
Rims ('Aqalat-ar-) عقلة الرمس	5 to 10 miles inland, westwards, from the foot of Khor-al-'Odaid.	Water is good, in wells 1 fathom deep.

The Bedouins do not regard 'Aqal as geographically included in **'Omān,** which in their view is terminated on the west by the Sabákhat **Matti**; but the district has been recognised by the British Government as forming part of the territories of the Shaikh of Abu **Dhabi** and it must therefore be considered to belong, in the political sense, to Trucial **'Omān.**

'AQDAH
عقده

A remarkable amphitheatre or bay in the eastern slopes of Jabal **Aja** in Northern **Najd**; it is formed by the junction of several small valleys within the mountains. The elevation of its floor is 4,020 feet above the sea or about 500 feet above **Hāil**, but the climate is exceedingly hot in summer. The hills which surround 'Aqdah are inaccessible from the outside, and the only entrance to the place is by a narrow gorge, called Rī'-al-'Aqdah ريع العقدة, 6 miles west-south-west of **Hāil**, which is 100 yards wide at the mouth but contracts, further in, to 50 or less. At the narrowest part it is barred by a dry-stone wall, about 10 feet high and 3 feet thick, in which at the southern end is a gateway with a heavy iron gate, broad enough for 4 camels to pass through abreast. The approach is capable of defence by a small number of riflemen posted behind the wall and upon the hill on its flanks. The various interior valleys of 'Aqdah are overhung by naked granite crags, and their floors are of granite covered with 12 to 15 feet of a gravel which contains much moisture and supports plantations of date trees aggregating about 75,000 palms. The various groves are walled, and each contains a hamlet named after the clan of the **Shammar** tribe which inhabits it; they are :— 'Abaid عبيد, 'Abdullah عبدالله, Aqni اقني, 'Ali علي, 'Atā عطآ, Fādhil فاضل, Dhiyāb ذياب, Hāmil هامل, Jabar جبر, Jinidah جنده, Mufadhdhal مفضل, Rakhīs رخيص, Salīṭ سليط, Shīrah شيره, Shumailah شميله and Zuwaimil زويمل. The total number of houses, which are of sun-dried brick, is about 460; and the largest villages are 'Abdullah and Mufadhdhal with 40 houses each, 'Abaid with 35, and Shumailah with 30.* The fixed population is estimated at 1,500 souls and this is increased by 500 during the date season when Bedouins who own some of the date groves are encamped in them. About ½ the palms belong to the permanent inhabitants, ¼ to Bedouins of the **Shammar** tribe and ¼ to the Amīr of Jabal **Shammar**; the plantations belonging to the Amīr and his relations are situated in the middle of the valley where the subsoil contains most water. Besides dates, limited quantities of maize, millet and fruit are grown. 'Aqdah is regarded by the Āl Rashīd as their ancestral stronghold, and various members of the family own forts in it large enough to accommodate their households in time of danger. In spite of the abundance of its dates 'Aqdah, it is believed, could not on account of the paucity of its other resources stand a siege of more than 3 months.†

The correct spelling of this name is uncertain; it is frequently pronounced as if written اغيلي, or اخيلي. 'Aqīli is a rich district, mostly plain, situated on the left bank of the **Kārūn** river between its exit from the hills at Tang-i-Qal'eh-i-Dukhtarān and the town of **Shūshtar**; a part of it is enclosed on the west by the loop which the **Kārūn** forms near the villages of Gotwand and Jallakān in the **Shūshtar** District. The riverain lands of 'Aqīli are probably the most valuable upon the **Kārūn**; they bear luxuriant crops of wheat, barley, tobacco and cotton, and the whole surface is cultivated. Cattle and sheep are fairly numerous, and there are some buffaloes and a few horses and donkeys. The supply of firewood for **Shūshtar** Town is drawn partly from 'Aqīli.

In the absence of a survey it is impossible to determine the precise limits of the tract or to explain its topography in detail, but the table

---

* Huber gives several names, which are probably true village names; but it is impossible to identify them with the tribal names in the text, or to know how to transliterate one of them.

† Large and small scale plans of 'Aqdah will be found at the end of Huber's *Journal de Voyage* and two good sketches of the entrance in Euting's *Tagbuch* (I. 216-7).

below embodies all that is known of the prosperous villages* which it comprises :—

Village.	Position.	Population and arms.	REMARKS.
Badīl بديل	Near Muhammad-ibn-Zaid.	100 huts of mixed Lurs.	This is a Bunneh or permanent encampment. There are 100 date palms.
Batwand بتوند	About 30 miles from Shūshtar Town, beyond the last wells in 'Aqīli.	80 houses. The people have 20 rifles.	Owned by the Sarum-ul-Mulk, one of the Bakhtiyāri Khāns.
Dasht-i-Buzurg دشت بزرگ	9 miles from Shūshtar Town and 2 miles from the left bank of the Kārūn.	250 houses. There are 50 rifles.	Water is from the river and from springs. The proprietor is the Shahāb-us-Saltaneh, at present Īlba:gī of the Bakhtiyāris.
Īstagi ايستگي	Between Simāleh and Qāidān.	120 huts with 50 rifles.	This is a permanent camp only, but it has a strong tower. It shares two water mills with Simāleh.
Kamari (Bunneh-i-Muhammad 'Arab-i) بنه محمد عرب كمري	Close to the left bank of the Kārūn above Jallakān.	40 houses with 5 rifles.	The inhabitants have an evil reputation as thieves and robbers. The village belongs to the Shahāb-us-Saltaneh.
Kangarpaz كنگرپز	On the river.	The people are $\frac{1}{3}$ Kangarpaz and $\frac{2}{3}$ descendants of immigrants from Shīrāz, still known as Shīrāzis.	There are 3 Bunnehs or permanent encampments of this name, all connected with Bunneh-i-Muhammad 'Arab-i-Kamari.
Kūh Zard كوه زرد	7 miles from Shūshtar Town, at the foot of Kūh-i-Fidalak, and 4 miles from the Kārūn.	120 houses. The inhabitants have 30 rifles.	Water is from springs. The proprietor is the Shahāb-us-Saltaneh.
Makandawān مكندوان	Between Simāleh and Turk Khāliqi.	100 huts of mixed Lurs.	This is a Bunneh or permanent encampment.

* A later report (1907) mentions only the villages of Badīl, Dasht-i-Buzurg, Īstagi, Mūndani, Qāidān, Rūdani, Simāleh and Turk Khāliqi, given in the text, but adds others viz., Gūizar, Haidarābād, Murtazaābād, Saiyidān and Zulmābād. It greatly decreases the number of houses, giving no village more than 150.

Village.	Position.	Population and arms.	Remarks.
Māmīzard ماميزرد or Muhammad-ibn-Zaid محمد ابن زيد	At the foot of the Gypsum Hills.	250 houses with 20 rifles.	Māmīzard belongs to the Shahāb-us-Saltaneh. There is a good spring. Adjacent is Kūh-i-Nārdungaki ناردنگكي, on the summit of which a place called Haft Shāhidān هفت شاهدان is said to exist, with gardens, mills and much excellent cultivation watered by springs.
Mūndani موندني	Close to the river.	120 houses and 10 rifles.	The owner is the Shahāb-us-Saltaneh.
Qāidān قائدان	Adjoins Rūdani.	60 houses and 10 rifles.	Do.
Rāhdārān راه داران	About 20 miles from Shūshtar Town.	200 houses, among which are 15 rifles.	Water is from a spring. This place belongs to the Sarum-ul-Mulk, one of the Bakhtiyāri chiefs.
Rūdani رودني	About 12 miles from Shūshtar Town and nearly opposite to Jallakān on the other side of the Kārūn.	120 houses; the people have 12 rifles.	The village stands partly on a hillock and has a newly built fort. The famous salt of Shūshtar is obtained as a deposit along the banks of a stream which passes this place. Rūdani is owned by the Shahāb-us-Saltaneh.
Saiyideh صيده	...	120 houses. The people are mostly Saiyids and have 15 rifles.	Water is from the Kārūn river. The owner is the Shahāb-us-Saltaneh.
Shāhin (Bunneh Hāji Saiyid بنه حاجي سيد شاهين	...	300 houses. Half of the inhabitants are Saiyids and there are 35 rifles.	Do.
Simāleh سماله	About 15 miles from Shūshtar Town.	400 houses. The people own 300 rifles.	This place is the property of the Shahāb-us-Saltaneh and enjoys his favour in a special degree. There are a dozen shops and a fine garden called Bāgh-i-Nargisi: date palms number 1,000. Water is from the Kārūn river; and two water mills are shared with Īstagi.

Village.	Position.	Population and arms.	Remarks.
Turk Khāliqi ترک خالقي	On the east side of the Kārūn 1½ miles below Gotwand on the other side.	500 houses and 300 rifles.	Owned by the Shahāb-us-Saltaneh.
Waisi (Bunneh) بنّه ريسي	Between Simāleh and Turk Khāliqi.	100 huts of mixed Lurs.	This is a Bunneh or permanent encampment.

The inhabitants of these villages are, where not otherwise stated, **Lurs** of the **Bakhtiyāri** stock; they pay one-third of the produce as rent to their landlords.

'Aqīli, as will be apparent from the table that precedes, is virtually a private estate of the **Bakhtiyāri** Khāns, but it is attached to the **Shūshtar** District; the revenue payable by the Bakhtiyāri Khāns to the Persian Government is 12,150 Tūmāns in cash, 300 Kharvārs of grain and 280 Kharvārs of straw. At the beginning of 1907 a contest was in progress between the Khāns and the Persian Governor of Northern **'Arabistān** for the direct administration of the district.

The population of 'Aqīli is apparently about 15,000 souls.*

'AQQ (WĀDI-Al-) وادي العق

This name appears to denote not one valley in the Eastern **Hajar** district of the **'Omān** Sultanate but two, of which the eastern enters Wādi **Samāil** 1 mile and the other 2 miles above Sarūr, both on the right bank; the second is the true Wādi-al-'Aqq. In the last 4 or 5 miles of their course the two valleys run parallel and close together.

The eastern valley contains the villages of Lizugh لزغ and Mizra' Bū Ba'arah مرزع بو بعره; Lizugh is 1½ miles up the valley on the right bank and consists of 100 houses of **Nidābiyīn**, while Mizra' Bū Ba'arah, also on the right bank, is 8 miles above Lizugh and comprises 80 houses of **Nidābiyīn**. At each of these villages the usual livestock are found and about 1,000 date palms.

The villages of the western valley are three: Fankh فنخ, on the right bank, 4 miles from Wādi **Samāil**, 50 houses of **Nidābiyīn**; Da'asar دعسر or 'Aqq, on the left bank 5 miles from Wādi **Samāil**, 50 houses of **Nidābiyīn**; and Sinsilah سنسله, 5 miles further up, 40 houses of **Nidābiyīn**. These villages also have the usual complement of livestock and from 500 to 700 date palms each.

* According to the recent report already cited in a footnote (page 91), the population is much smaller than this, perhaps only half or even less.

The total population of Wādi-al-'Aqq is about 1,500 souls.

Wādi **Saijāni** joins Wādi-al-'Aqq at Fankh, apparently from the western side.

A pass at the head of Wādi-al-'Aqq, 3 miles south of Sinsilah, leads into **Sharqīyah** and is one of the best routes thither: the topography of this part is not well understood, but the route after crossing the watershed falls into Wādi **Samad**.

The command of Wādi-al-'Aqq is of high importance to the Sultān of **'Omān** as it is one of the principal routes by which **Sharqīyah** insurgents have been accustomed to enter Wādi **Samāil** and advance against his capital. The Sultān has no post in the valley and controls it, so far as he is able, by keeping the **Nidābiyīn** tribe upon his side.

'ARAB (SHATT-AL-)
شط العرب

The largest, or, if small native sailing vessels be excluded from consideration, the only navigable river that enters the Persian Gulf; it carries the whole drainage of Turkish **'Irāq** and a large part of that of Persian **'Arabistān** as well.

Course and general characteristics.—The Shatt-al-'Arab is formed by the confluence at **Qūrnah** Village of the **Tigris** and the **Euphrates**; in winter the swift brown **Tigris** and the feeble transparent **Euphrates**, the latter strained of its sediment in a journey of many days through marshes, present a remarkable contrast at their junction. At about 40 miles below **Qūrnah** village the Shatt-al-'Arab leaves the celebrated city of **Basrah** upon its right bank; 22 miles further on it passes the smaller and less ancient but important town of **Muhammareh**, situated at a short distance from its left bank within the embouchure of the **Kārūn**; immediately below **Fāo**, at a distance of about 50 miles from **Muhammareh** and 112 miles from **Qūrnah**, it ends in the waters of the Persian Gulf. The average direction of the river is to the south-east, but in the reach between **Basrah** and **Muhammareh** it has a more easterly and a less southerly inclination.

The width of the Shatt-al-'Arab at **Basrah** as measured in 1905 is 600 yards, and from **Basrah** to **Muhammareh** its mean breadth is probably about the same; but after receiving the **Karūn** at **Muhammareh** it expands at once to half a mile, and its dimensions thereafter gradually increase to a maximum of about one mile in the neighbourhood of its mouth.

The sea tides affect the level of the Shatt-al-'Arab throughout its entire length, raising and lowering it by 6 to 9 feet in the neighbourhood of **Basrah** and by about 4 feet at **Qūrnah** Village; and they are stronger than the current of the river. Sea water, however, does not reach further than about 20 miles above **Fāo**. The temperature of the Shatt-'al-'Arab stream is sometimes as much as 16° Fahrenheit higher than that of the **Kārūn** which enters it near **Muhammareh**.

Tributaries.—Tributaries of the Shatt-al-'Arab deserving of mention are two only,—the Suwaib سويب or Shwaiyib شويّب and the **Kārūn**: of these the latter is by far the more important.

The Suwaib, which enters the Shatt-al-'Arab from its left bank about 4 miles below **Qūrnah** Village, comes from the direction of **Hawīzeh** and consists of the mingled waters, so far as not expended in irrigation, of the **Karkheh** river from **'Arabistān** and of the **Jahálah** canal which taps the **Tigris** at **'Amārah**.

The **Kārūn**, the only really navigable river in all Persia, joins the Shatt-al-'Arab, also from the left bank, at a point about 22 miles by the course of the stream below **Basrah**. The **Kārūn** is described in a separate article.

Here may be mentioned—though it is not exactly a tributary—the creek or backwater, known as Gurmat 'Ali گرمة علي, which cuts the right bank of the Shatt-al-'Arab at a point about 8 miles above **Basrah** Town and is said to communicate through marshes with the right bank of the **Euphrates** near Hammār. It is also stated that water which leaves the **Euphrates** near Khamīsīyah below **Sūq-ash-Shuyūkh** reaches the Shatt-al-'Arab by a creek immediately above Kūt-al-**Farangi**.

Islands.—Above **Basrah** the river now contains no islands worthy of note; between **Basrah** and **Muhammareh** on the contrary the islands of **'Ajairāwīyah, Tawailah, Shamshamīyah** and Umm-al-**Khasāsīf**, which are separately described under their own names, form a continuous chain reaching nearly the whole way; and below **Muhammareh** also there are several islands, namely **Bahrīyah, Gat'ah,** Hāji **Salbūq** or Muhilleh, **Ziyādīyah** and **Dawāsir**; these form the subject of separate articles. Comparison of the most recent charts with those of Colonel Chesney's expedition shows that the islands of the Shatt-al-'Arab are somewhat unstable, or, in other words, that the main channel of the river is not constant.

In 1836 **'Ajairāwīyah** included part of the present **Tawailah**; the rest of **Tawailah** had not then been formed; **Shamshamīyah** did not exist; Umm-al-**Khasāsīf** was smaller than at present and belonged to the left instead of to the right bank; Hāji **Salbūq** on the contrary belonged to the Turkish and not to the Persian side; and **Zīyādīyah** was still a part of the mainland.

Navigation.—The Shatt-al-'Arab is in most respects a fine example of a navigable river. It forms as it were a spacious vestibule to Turkish **'Irāq** while the **Tigris** and **Euphrates** resemble long but narrow corridors in the interior. An impressive though common spectacle on the Shatt-al-'Arab is that of a tall ocean steamer ascending or descending the river with swiftness and confidence.

The great blemish of the river as a waterway is the undredged and unlighted bar, 12 miles in breadth, which obstructs the entrance. The passage over the bar is marked by a line of 5 buoys belonging to the British India Steam Navigation Company of which the positions are occasionally changed; at the present time the buoys* extend from about 6 to about 15 miles from **Fāo**, the innermost or Bar Buoy alone being situated within territorial waters at a distance approximately of 1·7 (nautical) miles from the Persian and 2·8 (nautical) miles from the Turkish shore. Steamers can cross the bar daily with a draft of 18, and at spring tides (or once a fortnight) with draft of 21 feet; but in both cases the combination of daylight and high tide must be awaited, a necessity which is liable to cause a delay of as much as 14 hours. Moreover, the soundings on the bar do not depend on the tide alone but are liable to be considerably reduced by a wind from the north, and the position and depth of the channel are variable. The bar itself consists of soft mud, stiffer on the Persian than on the Arab side: a powerful steamer may sometimes plough through even when the water is less than her draught, but she will list to one side when inequalities of bottom are encountered and will not steer: in this way a turbine steamer of the British India Company has been known to force her way out on an actual draft of 16 feet when there were only 13 feet of water on the bar. Any vessel which can pass the bar can also ascend to **Basrah** without difficulty, the intermediate soundings being commonly 24 feet or more and the worst places not difficult: it is believed that such vessels might even reach **Qūrnah** Village without let or hindrance. In 1047 A.D., the

---

* Detailed information in regard to these buoys will be found in the Political Proceedings of the Government of India for December 1905.

A Creek near Basrah from the Shatt-al-'Arab.
(Maj. P. Z. Cox.)

entrance of the Shatt-al-'Arab was marked by a teak-wood beacon on the east bank, 120 feet high, on a stone platform at the top of which a fire was kindled at night.

In the autumn of 1841, when the water was at its lowest, a small steamer ascended the Suwaib tributary of the Shatt-al-'Arab to a distance of 10 miles.

Irrigation and cultivation.—The value of the Shatt-al-'Arab as a natural irrigation canal and as the fertiliser of a date-growing region, probably the most prolific and extensive in the world, is not inferior to that which it possesses as a highway of travel and commerce. Below **Muhammareh** the river is rich in silt, contributed chiefly by the **Kārūn**; and the fertility of even the higher reaches is considered by an expert authority (Sir W. Willcocks) to depend largely on mud from the **Kārūn** carried upstream by the action of the tides.

Everywhere the banks of the Shatt-al-'Arab are extremely low, and in places the water must—as in Holland—be kept out at high tide by means of dykes. The watering of the plantations is a simple operation; it depends solely on the existence of creeks and distributaries up which twice a day the tide forces the fresh river water, generally making it rise to within 2 feet or less of the general ground level.

Between **Basrah** and **Muhammareh** the date groves are practically continuous on both sides of the river and have a depth inland of half a mile to 2 miles; the number of trees upon this reach in Turkish territory alone is estimated at over 1,900,000, including those on the islands. On both banks above **Basrah** and on the right bank below **Muhammareh** there is generally a fine palm belt, but it is not so dense or unbroken as between **Basrah** and **Muhammareh**. The number of trees on the right bank and its islands below **Muhammareh** appears to be about 250,000.

Political importance.—The Shatt-al-'Arab in the lower half of its course is an important political boundary, dividing Turkish **Arabia** from the Persian province of **'Arabistān**. Since 1847, in consequence of the Erzeroum Treaty of that year, the left bank from the **Shamshamīyah** island downwards together with the islands of Hāji **Salbūq** and **Dawāsir** has been recognised as belonging to Persia. The rights of Turkey and Persia upon the river below **Shamshamīyah** island are in theory equal; nevertheless Turkish influence is more conspicuous upon the stream than Persian.

Topography of the banks from Qūrnah Village to Basrah.—The table below shows the principal places passed on either bank in descending the section of the river, 40 miles in length, from **Qūrnah** Village to **Basrah** :—

Right bank.		Left bank.	
Sharish شرش	A village with date groves; it is 10 to 15 miles below **Qūrnah** Village. It is the headquarters of a Nāhiyah in the Qadha of **Qūrnah**, and the seat of a Mudīr.	Suwaib سويب or Shwaiyib شويب	About 6 miles below **Qūrnah** Village; a creek forming the mouth of the stream, similarly named, which has been described in the paragraph on tributaries above.
Mazar'ah مزرعه	Also called Mazar'iyah مزرعة, a stretch of date gardens upon the river.	Maiyāh (Nahr) نهر مياح	A stretch of date plantations upon the river.
Dair الدير	About 17 miles by river below **Qūrnah**; a village with date groves. A creek called Nahr-al-Ghumaiyij نهر الغميج leaves the river at this point and runs inland to the marshes.	Nashwah نشوة	About 5 miles below Maiyāh; a village of many houses inhabited by Ahl-al-Jazāir and other tribes. It is the headquarters of a Nāhiyah in the Qadha of **Qūrnah**.
Shāfi (Nahr) نهر شافي	A large creek on which there is military post.	Hamrah الحمرة	An uninhabited locality.
'Umr (Nahr) نهر عمر	Another large creek with a village which is the property of the Naqīb of **Basrah**. Dates and rice are cultivated. The place is about 22 miles by river below **Qūrnah**.	Kataibān كتيبان	About 15 miles above **Basrah** Town; a creek and large village inhabited by **Muhaisin, 'Atub, Qatārnah and 'Idān**. Mr. Stephen Lynch owns property here.
Hārthah الهارثه	A stretch of date groves and rice fields upon the river.	Kilāb (Nahr Abul) نهر البو كلاب	A creek, about 10 miles by water above **Basrah** Town.

	Right bank.		Left bank.
Māgidīyah (Nabr-al-) نهر المايديه	A large creek near which are several brick kilns.	Jazīrat-as-Saghīr جزيرة السكر	An insulated tract inhabited by the same tribes as Kataibān above.
Gurmat 'Ali كرمة علي	This creek or backwater, about 8 miles above Basrah Town, is mentioned in the paragraph on tributaries above.	Fīrūzīyah فيروزيه	Date gardens and a village.
Fulīwān فليوان	Brick kilns. Opposite Shi'aibīyah.	Shi'aibīyah الشعيبيه	A creek and village.
Sabūr (Abus) ابو الصبور	A large creek extending from the river to the desert.	...	...
Farangi (Kūt-al-) كوت الفرنكي	See article Kūt-al-Farangi.	Kibāsi-as-Saghīr كباسي الصغير	A large creek running behind Jazīrat-al-'Ain جزيرة العين, an islet immediately opposite Kūt-al-Farangi. Upon it is a village with date plantations. The inhabitants are of the same tribes as at Kataibān. The chief Shaikh of the 'Idān lives here or upon Jazīrat-al-'Ain.
Silq سلق	Pronounced Silij. Date groves belonging to 'Ali Pāsha, Zahair.	Kharāb الخراب	An island.
Jubailah الجبيله	A large creek with gardens and a village; it is about a mile below Kūt-al-Farangi.	...	...
Sūfīyah الصوفيه	A village and gardens. Here also is a creek called Nahr-al-Jinn نهر الجن.	Ma'āf معاف	Date gardens owned by Hashel Khiyem.
Basrah Town البصرة	See article Basrah Town.	Dependencies of Basrah Town.	See article Basrah Town.

The following table* of the same reach brings out additional facts connected with irrigation and navigation and the geography of the banks and presents those already given in a different light :—

Direction of the river.	Names of river-side tracts (right bank).	Names or number of tributaries or irrigation creeks (right bank).	Names of river-side tracts (left bank).	Names or number of tributaries or irrigation creeks (left bank).	Remarks.
South-East and South-South-West	Sharish شرش	...	Al Bū Ghirbah آل بو غربه	Suwaib سويب	...
South	Do.	...	Umm-ash-Shilb ام الشلب	...	There is an island here called Umm-ash-Shilb.
South-South-East	Dair الدير	...	Do.	...	...
Do.	Shāfi الشافي	Shāfi الشافي	Nashwah نشوة	Nashwah نشوة	...
South-South East and South-East	Sāhib-az-Zamān صاحب الزمان	2	'Azairij عزيرج	...	...
East-South-East	Nahr 'Umr نهر عمر	...	Do.	...	...
East	Khaimah الخيمه	...	Buqchah بقچه	...	...
South-East	Do.	1	Hamrah الحمره	...	...
South	Hārithah هارثه	Mīyādīyah ميّاديه	Kataibān كتيبان	Kataibān كتيبان	...
Do.	Do.	...	Shalāhi شلاهي	...	There is an island here called Saghīr صغير.

* Supplied by Major J. Ramsay, Political Resident at Baghdād. It is based on the observations of Lieutenants A. Hamilton and Gardner, R.I.M., of the "Comet," who surveyed this part of the river in 1906-07.

Direction of the river.	Names of river-side tracts (right bank).	Names or number of tributaries or irrigation creeks (right bank).	Names of river-side tracts (left bank).	Names or number of tributaries or irrigation creeks (left bank).	Remarks.
South-South-East	Gurmat 'Ali كرمة علي	Gurmat 'Ali كرمة علي	Jazīrat-al-Kibāsi جزيرة الكباسي	Saghīr صغير	...
South-East	Jubailah جبيله	Sūfīyah and Jubailah صوفيه جبيله	Dependencies of Basrah Town.	Shi'aibīyah, Kibāsi and Kharāb شعيبيه كباسي الخراب	...

Topography of the right bank from Basrah to Muhammareh.*—The following is a list of the villages and settlements which succeed one another upon the right bank of the river on the way from **Basrah** to a point opposite the mouth of the **Kārūn**, a distance of 22 miles by water:—

Name.	Nature and position.†	Inhabitants and houses.	Remarks.
Khorah خوره	A village about 2 miles up a creek of which the mouth is 2½ miles below the British Consulate at **Basrah**.	4,000 souls of various tribes. There are about 30 brick houses here: the other dwellings are huts.	Estimated resources are 200,000 date palms, 1,000 cattle, 2,000 sheep and goats, 20 horses and 8 camels. The Khorah creek is said to reach to the dry desert behind. **'Ajairāwīyah** island begins a short distance above the mouth of this creek.
Barādh'īyah برانعيه	A village, about 1 mile up a creek of which the mouth is ¼ of a mile below the mouth of the Khorah creek.	600 souls of the 'Idān and other tribes inhabiting huts.	The date plantations of this village are very dense. Estimated resources are 100,000 palms, 200 cattle, 500 sheep and goats and 10 horses.

* The topographical tables which compose the remainder of this article have been compiled from a valuable report submitted by Captain Bowden of the R. I. M. S. "Lawrence" in 1906 after a close local inquiry: the report is illustrated by a map which is cited in a footnote to the article Turkish **'Irāq**.

† The terms right and left bank are used of creeks as if the latter were streams flowing into the river.

Name.	Nature and position.*	Inhabitants and houses.	Remarks.
Sarāji سراجي	A village, about 2 miles up a large creek of which the entrance is ¼ of a mile below the Barādh'īyah creek.	2,000 souls of the 'Idān and other tribes inhabiting huts. As the creek is entered from the river there is a large house on the right belonging to 'Abdul Wahhāb-al-Qirtās, and another on the left which is the property of Agha Ja'far, Agent of the Bombay and Persia Steam Navigation Company.	At low water the creek is almost dry at 1 mile from the river. Estimated resources are 60,000 date trees, 300 cattle, 400 sheep and goats and 10 horses.
Mahaulat-az-Zahair محولة الزحير	A village on the bank of the river, 4 miles below the British Consulate at Basrah.	200 souls of Muhaisin of the Bait Kana'ān section and of other tribes. There are 2 or 3 well built stone houses here; the rest of the habitations are huts.	Resources are estimated as 5,000 date trees, 20 cattle, 35 sheep and goats, and 6 horses.
Muhaijarān مهيجران	A village, 2 miles up a creek similarly named which leaves the river 1 mile below Mahaulat-az-Zahair.	1,500 souls of the 'Idān and other tribes, occupying huts. There are several brick houses.	The dates grown here have a high reputation, and the area under cultivation is steadily increasing. The estimate of resources is 180,000 palms, 500 cattle, 1,000 sheep and goats and 20 horses.
Bait Na'amah بيت نعمه	A settlement on the river bank, ½ a mile below the mouth of the Muhaijarān creek.	250 souls, chiefly of the 'Idān tribe. The principal building is a palatial mansion with a frontage of about 400 feet erected by the late Hājj Ahmad-an-Na'amah: it is now occupied by his 4 sons, who were till lately among the wealthiest Muhammadan notables of Basrah, but have now lost most of their money.	The date palms, which number about 15,000 belong to the family of Na'amah. Livestock are estimated at 20 cattle, 50 sheep and goats, 20 horses and 5 camels, those of the next place (Yusifān) being included.

* The terms right and left bank are used of creeks as if the latter were streams flowing into the river.

Name.	Nature and position.*	Inhabitants and houses.	Remarks.
Yusifān يوسفان	A settlement on the river bank, about 600 yards below the mansion of Bait Na'amah.	120 souls, chiefly 'Idān. There are 3 well-built houses, one of which belongs to a member of the Na'amah family: the rest are huts.	The resources of this place are included in the foregoing entry.
Hamdān حمدان	A town, about 2½ miles up a creek of the same name of which the entrance is 6¼ miles by river below the British Consulate at Basrah, and opposite to Yāmīn, which is about the middle of 'Ajairāwīyah island.	...	See article Hamdān.
Fajat-al-'Arab فجت العرب	A village, on the left bank of the Hamdān creek at ⅓ a mile within the entrance.	450 souls of various tribes. Many huts are in ruins and the remainder are scattered and straggling.	Resources are estimated at 1,000 date trees, 60 cattle, 100 sheep and goats and 2 horses.
Hamdān-as-Saghīr حمدان الصغير	A village, on the bank of the river 1 mile below the mouth of the Hamdān creek.	100 souls of Muhaisin of the Bait Kana'ān section. The hamlet consists of 2 well built stone houses round which cluster a number of huts.	The Shaikh of Hamdān resides here occasionally. There are about 800 date palms, and livestock are 20 sheep and goats and 3 horses.
Yahūdi يهودي	A village, 1½ miles up a very tortuous creek, of which the mouth is nearly 2 miles below the entrance of the Hamdān creek.	1,600 souls of 'Idān, inhabiting huts.	The Yahūdi creek is easily distinguished by a nameless tomb which stands in the angle between its right bank and the right bank of the river. Date palms are estimated at 90,000, and there are about 100 cattle, 200 sheep and goats and 3 horses.

* The terms right and left bank are used of creeks as if the latter were streams flowing into the river.

Name.	Nature and position.*	Inhabitants and houses.	Remarks.
Sangar صنگر	A village which extends for ½ a mile down the bank of the river from the tomb immediately below the Yahūdi creek.	1,300 souls of 'Atub. There are several well built brick and mud houses: the other dwellings are huts.	Some of the villagers are fishermen and they own about 20 boats. The date plantations here, though dense upon the river bank, are not deep and they contain only about 9,000 trees: there are 10 cattle and 100 sheep and goats. Pottery is manufactured and boats are built of timber imported from India.
Sabīliyāt سبيليات	A village on the river bank, upon a creek similarly named which is 9½ miles by river below the British Consulate at Basrah.	4,000 souls, mostly 'Atub, inhabiting huts. The Naqīb of Basrah generally resides here in a well built and fairly large house.	Resources are placed at 55,000 date palms, 200 cattle, 500 sheep and goats, 20 horses, 5 camels and 42 donkeys.
Abu Mughairah ابو مغيره	A village, 2½ miles up a creek which enters the river just below Sabīliyāt.	About 5,500 souls of Bani Mālik of the Bani Nahd section. The dwellings are all huts.	The creek is the largest between Basrah and Fāo and is said to reach inland to the desert, a distance of 2 hours by Ballam; it communicates with the creek of Abul Khasīb mentioned below. The inhabitants refused to reply to questions about their resources; but date trees may be estimated at 100,000, and animals at 250 cattle, 400 sheep and goats and 10 horses.
Abul Hamad ابرالحمد	A hamlet, on the river about 1 mile below Sabīliyāt and opposite to the lower end of 'Ajairāwi- yah island.	The inhabitants, about 70 in number, are Muhaisin of the Bait Kana'ān section. There is a well built mansion, the property of Abul Hamad, from whom the place takes its name: the other habitations are huts.	Resources are 2,000 date palms, 10 cattle, 20 sheep and goats, 4 horses, and 2 camels. Abul Hamad is a rich landowner.

* The terms right and left bank are used of creeks as if the latter were streams flowing into the river.

'ARAB (SHATT-AL-)

Name.	Nature and position.*	Inhabitants and houses.	Remarks.
Nahr Khōs نهر خوص	A village, 2 miles up a creek of the same name which enters the river 100 yards below Abul Hamad.	1,300 souls of 'Idān and Bani Mālik of the Bani Nahd section, living in huts.	There are about 120,000 date palms, 80 cattle, 250 sheep and goats and 4 horses. In this estimate are included the palms of the next village.
Labāni لباني	A small village on the river bank, about 11¼ miles by water below the British Consulate at Basrah: the island of Tawailah begins a short way above it.	350 souls of 'Idān. There are 3 well-built mud and brick houses; the rest of the village consists of huts.	The palms, which are on the right bank of the Nahr Khōs creek, are included in the estimate for that village. Livestock are 40 sheep and goats, 8 horses and 2 camels.
Abul Khasīb ابو الخصيب	A considerable town, situated 2 miles up a creek of which the mouth upon the river is 1 mile below Labāni and which communicates inland with the creek of Abu Mughairah.	...	See article Abul Khasīb.
Abu Ibgai' ابو ابگيع	A tract reaching from the Abul Khasīb creek to a point 1½ miles further down stream.	The inhabitants are about 2,000 souls and belong to various tribes. There are 8 or 9 hamlets consisting of huts.	There are about 50,000 date palms; animals are 200 cattle, 200 sheep and goats and 30 horses. The Shaikh is agent to the Naqīb of Basrah who owns most of the land in this neighbourhood.
Abul Fulūs ابو الفلوس	A tract beginning immediately below Abu Ibgai' and extending about 1½ miles down stream.	1,800 souls of mixed tribes, occupying about a dozen small hut villages.	Agricultural resources are 25,000 date palms, 300 cattle, 300 sheep and goats and 110 horses. The date palms in this tract are comparatively sparse, but every year more land is being brought under cultivation. Bricks are made, but the industry is a decaying one. There is a small military post at this place.

* The terms right and left bank are used of creeks as if the latter were streams flowing into the river.

Name.	Nature and position.*	Inhabitants and houses.	Remarks.
Baljānīyah بلجانيه	A tract similar to Abu Ibgai' and Abul Fulūs but larger; it begins at 15½ miles below the British Consulate at **Basrah** and extends down stream for 3½ miles. The island of **Shamshamīyah** is opposite the middle of it and the island of **Tawailah** ends off its upper, while that of Umm-al-**Khasāsif** begins off its lower part.	900 souls of tribes described as Mashid and Shaikh Hasan, inhabiting 8 small villages of huts. There is one well-built brick house upon the river owned by Hāji Mahmūd Pāsha and two others have been built lately by Hāji Ibrāhīm 'Abdul Wāhid and Ahmad Chalabi 'Abdul Wāhid.	Resources are estimated at 15,000 palms, 200 cattle, 100 sheep and goats and 4 horses.
Faiyādhi الفياضي	A tract extending along the river for a mile from the lower limit of Baljānīyah: it is subtended throughout its length by the island of Umm-al-Yabābi.	500 souls of various tribes, inhabiting 5 distinct villages of huts.	The date palms here only number about 5,000 and they appear to be below the average in productiveness. About half the population are engaged in fishing. Animals are 20 cattle, 50 sheep and goats and 20 donkeys.
Zain الزين	A tract, beginning immediately below Faiyādhi and extending for one mile down stream to the Mutāwa' creek which enters the river almost opposite to (but a little higher up than) the **Kārūn** river on the other bank.	The population is about 1,300 souls distributed among 7 small villages of huts. The largest, Zain, which gives its name to the district, consists of nearly 100 huts and is opposite Umm-ar-Rasās on Umm-al-**Khasāsif** island.	Resources are estimated at 35,000 palms, 30 cattle, 50 sheep and goats and 4 horses. Practically the whole of the tract belongs to nephews of the Shaikh of **Kuwait**. A step-mother of the present Shaikh of **Muhammareh** lives here in a house near the bank of the river and owns some property.

The population of this section of the right bank appears to be about 53,000 souls, and the number of date palms about 1,618,000.

* The terms right and left bank are used of creeks as if the latter were streams flowing into the river.

'ARAB (SHATT-AL-) 107

Topography of the left bank from Basrah to the Persian frontier.—A tabular account is given below of the villages and cultivated estates on the left bank of the river in the order in which they occur from **Basrah** down to the end of Turkish territory on this side, a distance about 16½ miles.

Name.	Nature and position.	Inhabitants and houses.	Remarks.
Kūt-al-Jū' كوت الجوع	A village, 300 yards up a small creek which enters the river 3¼ miles below the Tanūmah Hospital at **Basrah** and about 1½ miles below the upper end of 'Ajairā-wīyah island.	1,700 souls of the 'Īdān, inhabiting huts. The village is a crowded one.	The date palms number about 20,000, and there is fair pasturage for livestock which amount to some 140 cattle, 140 sheep and goats, 4 horses and 50 donkeys. It is proposed to locate the new quarantine station for **Basrah** at this place.
Kūt-as-Saiyid (I) كوت السيد	A village, 500 yards up a creek which opens into the river ¾ of a mile below the Kūt-al-Jū' creek.	250 souls of 'Īdān, whose dwellings are huts.	Resources are estimated at 10,000 date palms, 20 cattle, 40 sheep and goats and 2 horses.
Kūt Bin—Mina (spelling uncertain)	A village, 500 yards up a creek of which the mouth is 600 yards below that of the Kūt-as-Saiyid creek.	250 souls of 'Īdān, whose dwellings are huts.	This village is surrounded by a well-built mud wall 10 feet high and 2 feet thick. There are about 20 cattle, 30 sheep and goats and 8,000 palms.
Majma' مجمع	A village, 200 yards up a small creek which is ⅓ a mile below that of Kūt Bin-Mina.	160 souls of 'Īdān, inhabiting huts.	Resources are estimated at 6,000 date palms, 10 cattle and 20 sheep and goats. The village belongs to M. Asfar, who has bought the whole of it.
Kūt-az-Za'īr كوت الزعير	A village, 200 yards up a creek of which the entrance is ⅓ a mile below that of the Majma' creek.	130 souls of 'Īdān, dwellers in huts.	The inhabitants own about 5,000 date palms, 8 cattle and 10 sheep and goats.

Name.	Nature and position.	Inhabitants and houses.	Remarks.
Gawām (Kūt-al-) كوت الگوام	A village, ½ a mile up a creek of the same name which takes out of the river at a point 6 miles below the Tanūmah Hospital at Basrah.	250 souls of 'Īdān, occupying huts.	The village is walled. There are about 10,000 palms, 20 cattle and 30 sheep and goats.
Mōhīyah موحيه	A village about ⅓ a mile east of Kūt-al-Gawām, on an eastern branch of the Kūt-al-Gawām creek.	50 souls of **Muhaisin** of the Bait Kana'ān section. The habitations are huts.	The village is surrounded by a ruined wall and there are many deserted huts; it is owned by Shaikh 'Abdullah, Bāsh A'yān. Resources are estimated at 1,000 date palms, 5 cattle and 10 sheep and goats.
Ghadhbān (Kūt) كوت غضبان	A village, ¼ of a mile up a creek which joins the river ½ a mile below the Kūt-al-Gawām creek.	150 souls of **Muhaisin** of the Bait Kana'ān section, dwellers in huts.	Date palms number about 5,000, and livestock are 20 cattle, 20 sheep and goats, 2 horses and 10 donkeys.
Shaikh (Kūt-ash-) كوت الشيخ	A village, ½ a mile up a creek which enters the river ¾ of a mile below the Ghadhbān creek.	Do.	This village and the date groves in its neighbourhood are partly the property of the Naqīb of Basrah, Saiyid Rajab; other part-owners are Messrs. Lynch Bros. and the families of Hāji Mansūr and Matos Iskandar. Resources are 7,000 date palms, 6 cattle, 20 sheep and goats and 6 donkeys.

'ARAB (SHATT-AL-)

Name.	Nature and position.	Inhabitants and houses.	Remarks.
Suwādi (Kūt) كوت سوادي	A village, ⅓ a mile up a creek which joins the river ¼ of a mile below the Kūt-ash-Shaikh creek.	600 souls of **Muhaisin** of the Bait Kana'ān section. The habitations are huts.	A good view of the surrounding country is obtained from this place, the date groves being here less dense than the average, though the trees are productive. The palms are estimated at 6,000; and the livestock are 100 cattle, 50 sheep and goats, 6 horses and 10 camels.
Dahaimat-al-Kabīr دحيمة الكبير	A village, ⅓ a mile up a creek of which the entrance is ⅓ a mile below that of the Suwādi creek.	200 souls of **Muhaisin** of the Bait Kana'ān section, dwellers in huts.	Date palms, which are sparse, number about 4,000; and there are 15 cattle and 20 sheep and goats. About 20 acres of land are cultivated with wheat and barley. The village is enclosed by a ruined wall.
Dahaimat-as-Saghīr دحيمة الصغير	A village, ⅓ a mile up a creek which enters the river ¼ of a mile below the Dahaimat-al-Kabīr creek.	600 souls of **Muhaisin** of the Bait Kana'ān section, occupying huts.	The resources in palms and animals are about half those of the last village. Here also some wheat and barley are grown.
Sinni (Kūt-as-) كوت السذي	A village, at the same distance inland as the last, upon a small eastern tributary of the same creek.	60 souls of **Muhaisin** of the Bait Kana'ān section, inhabiting huts.	There are about 1,000 date palms, and livestock are 10 cattle, 10 sheep and goats and 2 donkeys.
Saiyid (Kūt-as-) (II) كوت السيد	A village, about ½ a mile up a small creek which joins the river ½ a mile below the last creek.	100 souls of **Muhaisin** of the Bait Kana'ān section, occupying huts.	At this place are 10 to 15 acres of arable land cultivated with wheat and barley. The inhabitants own about 2,500 palms, 10 cattle and 15 sheep and goats.

Name.	Nature and position.	Inhabitants and houses.	Remarks.
Daghaimāt دغيمات	A village, about ¼ of a mile up a creek of which the mouth is ½ a mile below the mouth of the Kūt-as-Saiyid creek.	120 souls of **Muhaisin** of the Bait Kana'ān section, dwellers in huts.	There are about 4,000 palms: animals are 6 cattle and 10 sheep and goats. The village belongs to the family of Hāji Mansūr.
Jāsim (Nahr) نهر جاسم	A village, ½ a mile up a creek which enters the river ½ a mile below the Daghaimāt creek. **'Ajairāwīyah** island ends off this creek.	500 souls of **Muhaisin** of the Bait Kana'ān section. The dwellings are huts.	Date trees are estimated at 10,000, and livestock at 30 cattle, 40 sheep and goats and 2 horses.
Da'aiji دعيجي	A large village, situated about 2½ miles up a great creek, of which the mouth is nearly 11 miles by water below the Tanūmah Hospital at **Basrah** and about opposite to **Labāni** on the right bank of the river: **Tawailah** island begins a little above this point.	Including several small hamlets on the creek, of which the largest (18 huts) is ¾ of a mile within the entrance, the population amounts to about 3,000 souls. The people are **Muhaisin** of the Bait Kana'ān section and live in huts.	There is a Turkish Custom House at this place. Palms number about 50,000, and livestock are 250 cattle, 600 sheep and goats, 10 horses and 20 camels. Two-thirds of the village belong to the Dāirat-as-Sanīyah: the remainder is the property of Saiyid Hāshim and others.
Sulaimānīyah سليمانيه	A district, with a frontage of 1¼ miles upon the river, commencing immediately below the Da'aiji creek.	450 souls of the **'Atub** tribe distributed among 6 small villages of huts, no one of which is more than ¾ of a mile from the river bank. The houses are all huts.	Resources are estimated at 10,000 date palms, 10 cattle, 20 sheep and goats and 5 horses. The late Shaikh of the **'Atub** had his abode in the largest of the hamlets. The estate is Waqf property.

Name.	Nature and position.	Inhabitants and houses.	Remarks.
Kharnūbīyah خرنوبيه	A village, about 1 mile up a creek of the same name which enters the river a little over a mile below the Da'aiji creek.	200 souls of **Muhaisin** of the Bait Kana'ān section, inhabiting huts.	The people possess about 3,000 date palms besides 10 cattle, 20 sheep and goats and 5 horses. This village also is Waqf.
Buwārīn البوارين	A district, with a frontage of 3½ miles upon the river, extending from the Kharnūbīyah creek to that of Khaiyain الخيين, the latter marking the boundary between Turkey and Persia. (It is a question here of the upper or principal mouth of the Khaiyain creek, which is opposite **Shamshamīyah** island, not of the branch which joins the river 2 miles further down in the direction of **Failīyeh**.)	This district contains 8 villages and 6 hamlets and the total population is about 3,500 souls. The largest village, consisting of 150 huts and several more substantial houses is situated on the Kharnūbīyah creek at ¼ of a mile within the entrance. The people of Buwārīn belong to the so-called Shaikh Hasan tribe. With the exception noted the houses are all huts.	There are about 50,000 date palms, and livestock are estimated at 1,000 cattle, 1,500 sheep and goats and 120 horses.

The remainder of the villages upon the left bank of the Shatt-al-'Arab in this section are described in the article on **Muhammareh** District: the population of those in Turkish territory, given above, is apparently about 12,000 souls, while the date palms belonging to them amount to nearly 215,000.

Topography of the right bank from Muhammareh to Fāo.—Here we may resume our account of the villages and tracts upon the right bank of the river, taking them in the order in which they occur from a point nearly opposite the embouchure of the **Kārūn** down to the sea, the distance by river being approximately 50 miles:—

Name.	Nature and position.	Inhabitants and houses.	Remarks.
Mutāwa' مطاوع or Mutawa'īyah مطوعية	A tract; it begins immediately below Zain from which a creek (leaving the river 1 mile west-south-west of the mouth of the **Kārūn** and exactly opposite Umm-ar-Rasās on Umm-al-**Khasā-sīf** island) divides it; and from this creek, which is known as the Mutāwa' creek, it extends down the bank for nearly 1½ miles.	About 500 souls of mixed tribes distributed among 5 small villages of huts.	There are about 10,000 date palms and live-stock are about 60 sheep and goats. At the lower extremity of the tract is a Turkish police post on the river bank. It may be noted that the Mutāwa' creek, after passing inland of this tract and the succeeding tracts of Umm-al-Gharab and Ruwais, rejoins the river at a point 3¾ miles by stream from the point where it left it. This creek is full of fish traps.
Gharab (Umm-al-) أم الغرب	A tract, extending downstream from the Turkish police post on the border of Mutāwa' for nearly a mile to a group of 7 conspicuous palm trees, well known as As-Saba' السبع or The Seven. The inland boundary is formed by the Mutāwa' creek which runs behind this tract at a distance of 1½ miles from the river.	1,600 souls of various tribes living in scattered and isolated huts; on the Mutāwa' creek, however, there are 3 small villages or groups of huts known as Kilāl, Rasbān and Badr, this being their order from north to south.	Resources are estimated at 30,000 date palms, 200 cattle, 50 sheep and goats and 10 horses.
Ruwais رويس	A tract, extending for ¾ of a mile from the border of Umm-al-Gharab to the southern extremity of the Mutāwa' creek, and bounded on the inland side by the Mutāwa' creek.	850 souls of a tribe described as Mashid, occupying 3 small villages of huts in different places.	Date palms are estimated at 20,000 and the inhabitants own some 200 cattle, 80 sheep and goats and 20 horses.

'ARAB (SHATT-AL) 113

Name.	Nature and position.	Inhabitants and houses.	Remarks.
Gat'ah الگطعه	A tract, reaching from the southern entrance of the Mutāwa' creek for 4¾ miles to the entrance of another creek, known as the Gat'ah creek, which enters the river opposite the centre of Hāji Salbūq island. The islands of Bahrīyah and Gat'ah lie off this tract.	1,300 souls of various tribes, occupying huts which compose 7 separate hamlets.	The date trees, which here grow only on the bank of the river, number about 25,000. Livestock are some 300 cattle, 150 sheep and goats and 30 horses. There is a Turkish customs house on the north side of the entrance of the Gat'ah creek; and a Turkish guard house on the river bank about 1½ miles above that creek.
Sanīyah السنیه	A tract, extending from the Gat'ah creek for 2½ miles down to the Saihān creek.	350 souls of mixed tribes; they live in scattered huts, except in one place where about a dozen huts are collected to form a hamlet.	This district was originally part of the next (Saihān), but it is now the property of the Sultān of Turkey and takes its separate name from the Dāirat-as-Sanīyah, by which it is administered. The date groves, which are extremely valuable, contain about 10,000 trees. The livestock of the cultivators amounts to some 30 cattle, 100 sheep and goats and 4 horses.
Saihān سیحان	A tract, of which the upper boundary is the creek called Saihān, while the lower is the entrance of the Ziyādīyah creek dividing Ziyādīyah island from the bank: its extent is thus about 2 miles and it subtends the southern end of Hāji Salbūq island.	350 souls of mixed tribes, inhabiting huts. There is only one village worthy of the name; it consists of about 40 huts, is situated on the river about midway between the two ends of the tract, and is known as Khast خسمت.	The country hereabouts is open and barren. Date palms are about 5,000 in number, and animals are estimated at 60 cattle, 100 sheep and goats and 8 horses.
Dawāsir District دواسر	A district, extending downstream for about 18 miles	...	See article **Dawāsir District**.

I

Name.	Nature and position.	Inhabitants and houses.	Remarks.
	from a point opposite the upper or northern end of Ziyādīyah island.		
Dorah, or Dorat Bin-Ibrāhīm دورة - دورة بن ابراهيم	A tract, beginning immediately below the Dawāsir District and extending from a point 15 miles by river to another 10½ miles by river above the Fāo civil station.	1,500 souls of the 'Īdān and 'Atub tribes, occupying huts which form about 12 distinct hamlets.	This is a prosperous tract containing about 12,000 prolific palms: grapes, oranges and figs are cultivated as well as dates. Livestock are estimated at 120 cattle, 200 sheep and goats and 160 horses. Bricks were ormerly made here and a large kiln is still a conspicuous object a little below the middle of the tract, but the industry has now ceased in consequence of the cost of transport to Basrah. This was the starting point of a boat expedition sent by Yūsuf-bin-Ibrāhīm against Kuwait in 1902.
Ma'āmir المعامر	A tract, with a frontage of 7½ miles on the river, beginning 10½ miles by stream, and ending 3½ miles by stream, above the Fāo civil station. A creek which divides it from Dorah is known as the Ma'āmir creek.	1,500 souls of mixed tribes, partly Muntafik, distributed among about 25 small hut villages, each of which as a rule stands on a separate little creek of its own. The district has a small population for its size. It is thus somewhat similar to Fāo.	Date palms are estimated at 6,000, and livestock at 450 cattle, 300 sheep and goats, 50 horses and 30 donkeys. The tract is not fully developed having come into existence as a settlement only during the last 30 years. At the lower end of Ma'āmir, on the border of Fāo, are date plantations owned by nephews of the present Shaikh of Kuwait and known as Sūfīyah صوفيه.
Fāo فاو	A tract occupying the last 8 miles of the right bank, between Ma'āmir and the mouth of the river.	...	See article Fāo.

The population of the right bank villages of this reach would seem to be about 12,500 souls and the number of their date palms is probably 150,000 at least.

'ARĀBAH (BANI)
بني عرابه

The singular form of the word, which is 'Arābi عرابي , is avoided as it is ambiguous, meaning also a hill-donkey. The Bani 'Arābah are a Ghāfiri tribe of the **'Omān** Sultanate, found chiefly in Wādi **Tāyīn**, where their principal places are Sibal, Qurr, Hammām and Shāt. Twenty years ago they are said to have been a large tribe; but they are now much less numerous in consequence, chiefly, of the ravages of cholera, and probably do not exceed 1,000 persons. They have been on bad terms with the **Siyābiyīn** for more than 30 years, but the feud is now less acute than formerly.

'ARABI
عربي

An island, only 3 feet above sea level, situated about 60 miles east-north-east of **Musallamīyah** bay and 15 miles south of **Fārsi** island. It consists of a sandbank with a rocky foundation and is visited by fishermen to catch turtle. It swarms with cormorants, being covered in the season with their nests and young ones; and there is a deposit of guano, a few inches thick, all over it. The question of the ownership of 'Arabi has never arisen, and there is apparently no reason for regarding it as the property of one territorial power rather than of another.

'ARAB-ISTĀN *
عربستان

An important province of South-Western Persia; it consists chiefly of the alluvial plains which are either drained or watered by the **Kārūn** River and its affluents the **Diz** and the **Jarrāhi**. 'Arabistān falls

---

* Notwithstanding the existence of a large number of previous works on this province, the portions of the Gazetteer relating to 'Arabistān have involved more laborious investigations than almost any other. A beginning was made in November 1904 by the issue, in the form of 27 printed foolscap pages, of an abstract of the information at that time available: this collection of materials was supplied to the

naturally, in its tribal and narrower administrative aspect, into two parts or sub-provinces which may be styled Northern 'Arabistān and Southern 'Arabistān respectively ; and each of these, in so far as it differs from the other, is described in the article bearing its name in this Gazetteer.

Questions of boundaries, physical geography, climate, and internal government,—and to some extent that of inhabitants,—having been disposed of elsewhere, the subjects of the present article will be flora and fauna ; agriculture and livestock ; external and internal trade ; currency, weights and measures ; communications of all kinds ; administration in the wider sense ; foreign relations and interests : these are all subjects which are common to the province as a whole.

But first of all we may consider, in a more general and comprehensive way than was possible in the articles on the two sub-provinces, the matter of population and tribes.

local officers and was used by them, and by the writer while on tour at Muhammareh, as a basis for fresh inquiries. During the earlier part of 1905, a large quantity of new information was supplied by Mr. W. McDouall, Consul at Muhammareh, in regard to the **Muhammareh** and **Fallāhīyeh** Districts, and by Captain D. L. R. Lorimer, Vice-Consul in 'Arabistān, in regard to the remainder of the province ; a number of reports were furnished also by Mr. J. C. Gaskin, Political Assistant. The material obtained appeared in September 1905 as 156 printed octavo pages, and, having been sent in this shape to Major P. Z. Cox, Political Resident in the Persian Gulf, to Mr. McDouall and to Captain Lorimer, was very greatly amplified and improved by the further efforts of those officers and of Major Morton, R.E., then on special duty for irrigation matters in 'Arabistān. A number of journeys were made by Captain Lorimer in connection with this work, and in the autumn of 1905 the districts of **Hindiyān** and **Fallāhīyeh** and the **Bahmanshīr** were explored by Major Cox and Lieutenant C. H. Gabriel, I.A., a number of doubtful points being thus settled. The observations of Major Cox on land were supplemented by those of Commander C. G. Sinclair, R.I.M., along the coast, which were made at the same time. The result of the further investigations, which continued during 1906, was that most of the articles on the province had to be re-written, and when they were reprinted at the beginning of 1907 they had expanded to nearly 300 octavo pages. Most of the new articles underwent further revision during 1907, and in some instances were extensively added to and corrected. A second journey to Khor **Mūsa** and **Qubbān**, visited by him in 1905, was made by Major Cox, accompanied by Captain Birdwood, Assistant Resident, in 1907 ; and the **Kārūn** in the **Muhammareh** District and the **Bahmanshīr** were examined by Mr. J. H. Bill, Assistant Resident, with a view to solving certain difficulties. Information on particular points was supplied also by Ahmad Khan, Nāib Tahsīldār, Captain Lorimer's assistant at Nāsiri. The articles in their present shape represent a very large amount of work, especially on the part of Captain Lorimer.

The following are the principal sources of information in regard to 'Arabistān apart from those which came into existence with the Gazetteer operations : Kinneir's *Geographical Memoir of the Persian Empire* (with map), 1813 ; Mignan's *Account*

Population and tribes.—The following is an estimate, by districts, of the settled population of the province of 'Arabistān :—

NORTHERN 'ARABISTĀN.		SOUTHERN 'ARABISTĀN.	
District.	Souls.	District.	Souls.
Dizfūl	61,500	Ahwāz	13,000
Shūshtar	35,000	Fallāhīyeh	45,000
		Hawīzeh	5,000
ATTACHED TO NORTHERN 'ARABISTĀN.		Hindiyān	14,000
		Jarrāhi	4,000
District.	Souls.	Ma'shūr	1,500
'Aqīli	15,000	Muhammareh	23,000
Rāmuz	12,000	Total for Southern 'Arabistān.	105,500
Total for Northern 'Arabistān.	123,500		

of the *Ruins of Ahwaz*, 1830; Stocqueler's *Fifteen Months' Pilgrimage* (with map), 1832; Whitelock's *Remarks on the Endian (Tab) River*, 1838; Ainsworth's *Researches*, 1838; Rawlinson's *Notes on a March from Zohab to Khuzistan*, 1839; Selby's *Account of the Ascent of the Karun and Dizful Rivers*, 1844; De Bode's *Travels in Luristan and Arabistan* (with map), 1845; Layard's *Description of the Province of Khuzistan* (with map), 1846; Chesney's *Expedition for the Survey of the Rivers Euphrates and Tigris* (with map), 1850; Loftus' *Travels and Researches* (with map), 1857; Monteith's *Notes on the Routes from Bushire to Shiraz* (notwithstanding the title), 1857 (but refers to 1810); Colonel L. Pelly's *Remarks on the Tribes, etc.*, 1865; Colonel Pelly and Dr. Colvill's *Recent Tour* (with map), 1865; General Chesney's *Narrative of the Euphrates Expedition*, 1868; Mr. Robertson's *Memorandum on the Topography, etc., of Khuzistan*, 1879; General Houtum Schindler's *Historical and Archæological Notes*, 1880; Lady Anne Blunt's *Pilgrimage to Nejd*, 1881; Captain Well's *Surveying Tours in Southern Persia*, 1883; Sir H. Layard's *Early Adventures*, 1887; Mme. Dieulafoy's *La Perse*, 1887; Lieutenant Maunsell's *Communications in South-Western Persia*, 1888; Colonel Bell's *Visit to the Karun River*, 1889; Mr. Ainsworth's *River Karun*, 1890; Lord Curzon's *Karun River* (with map), 1890; Lord Curzon's *Persia*, 1892; the *Gazetter of Persia*, 1892; M. De Morgan's *Mission Scientifique en Perse* (Vol. II) (with photographs and sketches), 1895; the *Persian Gulf Pilot*, 1898; *Routes in Persia* (with Index map), 1898, and *Appendix* to the same, 1899; *Military Report on Southern Persia*, 1900; and various other military works; Lady Durand's *Autumn Tour*, 1902; also an article which appeared in Petermann's *Mitteilungen*, Nos. 3 and 4 of Vol. 53, 1907.

There are also a number of recent official reports, especially by Commanders T. W. Kemp and H. B. T. Somerville, R.N., by Major E. B. Burton, Consul at

From this table it would appear that the fixed inhabitants of 'Arabistān number about 229,000 souls altogether.

In the statement below will be found all the principal tribes of the province, whether settled or nomadic :—

Name of tribe.	Number of settled members.	Where chiefly settled.	Number of nomadic members.	Where chiefly wandering.
Ābād آباد	1,100	**Hindiyān** District.	...	...
Afshār افشار	...	Dizfūl Town. (See article Northern 'Arabistān.)	...	...

Muhammareh, and by Captain Lorimer, which were prepared otherwise than in connection with the Gazetteer; some of these are quoted in footnotes to the appropriate articles. A valuable memorandum on the *Rivers of Arabistan* and a general description of the **Jarrāhi-Fallāhīyeh** country by Major Burton will be found in the Government of India's Political Proceedings for February 1905 and in the same for June 1904; also remarks on the comparative political importance of **Ahwāz, Dizfūl** and **Shūshtar** by Captain Lorimer in the Proceedings for May 1905.

The writings of Ainsworth, Rawlinson, Layard, Loftus, Houtum Schindler and De Morgan, above, have special reference in part to antiquities and ancient geography; and these subjects are expressly treated of in Vincent's *Voyage of Nearchus*, 1797; in Loftus' *Determination of the River Eulaeus*, 1857, and in Mr. Le Strange's *Lands of the Eastern Caliphate*, 1905.

Full information in regard to trade is afforded by the annual Consular Reports on the trade of 'Arabistan; and the special reports of Messrs. Maclean and Newcomen, cited in a footnote to the article **Persian Coast**, may be consulted.

The best general map of the province on a small scale is that issued with the present Gazetteer, which takes the place of *Parts of Arabia and Persia*, 1883. The country is shown on a large scale in sheets Nos. 71 S. W. and 72 N. W. and S. W. of the *South-Western Asia* series of the Survey of India, but the present edition of these is now out of date. Useful surveys or maps relating to portions of the province are: Map of the *Turco-Persian Frontier, made by Russian and English Officers* (Sheet VIII), 1849—55; Captain Well's *Sketch of the Karun River at Ahwaz*, 1881 (Map No. 1378 in the Foreign Department Library, Simla); Lord Curzon's map of the *Karun River and Branches* in the Proceedings of the R. G. S. for 1890; Captain L. E. Hopkins' *Route from Ahwaz by Behbehan to Shiraz*, 1903, in the Intelligence Branch, Simla; Major Burton's *Sketch of the Route from Ram Hormuz to Fellahieh*, 1904, in the Government of India's Political Proceedings for July 1904; a *Rough Diagram showing Positions of Villages on the Bahmishir River*, by Major Cox and Lieutenant Gabriel, 1905 Library No. 1379); *Rough Diagrams explanatory of River Systems in Southern Arabistan*, by the same, 1905 (Library No. 1380); *Map of Parts of the Behbehān, Hindiyān, Jarrāhi and Fallāhīyeh Districts*, by Surveyor Jamna Parshad, Survey of India, 1905; Major Morton's *River Jarrāhi from Mansoura to Fellahia*, 1906 (Library No. 1381); and a preliminary map by Major Morton of *Part of*

ARABISTĀN

Name of tribe.	Number of settled members.	Where chiefly settled.	Number of nomadic members.	Where chiefly wandering.
'Anāfijeh	1,000	On the Gargar and Shatait rivers.	4,000	Ahwāz District.
'Atub	100	Muhammareh District.	...	...
'Aushār عوشار	400	Hindiyān District.	...	...
Bahrakūn بهركون	750	Do. do.	...	...
Bāji (Āl) آل باجي	...	...	Uncertain.	Hawīzeh and Dizfūl Districts.
Bakhtiyāri بختياري	12,000	Dizfūl, Shūshtar, Rāmuz and Hindiyān Districts.	Fluctuating.	Dizfūl and Shūshtar Districts.
Balūchi بلوچ	A few	Failīyeh.	...	...
Bandari بندري	1,000	Ma'shūr and Jarrāhi Districts.	...	...
Bāwīyeh باوية	1,500	Ahwāz District.	18,500	Ahwāz District.
Dailami ديلمي	125	Hindiyān District.	...	...
Dizfūli دزفولي	39,000	Dizfūl District, chiefly in Dizfūl Town.	...	...

'Arabistan adjoining the Karun River, 1906. A map has also been published by M. De Morgan.

The two naval Charts into which parts of 'Arabistān enter are No. 2374-2837B., *Persian Gulf*, and No. 2380-1235, *Mouth of the Euphrates, Shatt-el-Arab and Bahmishir:* the latter contains as an inset a sketch survey of the Kārūn River to Ahwāz dated 1899. Marine surveys made in connection with the present Gazetteer are a *Rough Sketch Survey of Part of the Khor Musa and the Entrance to Hindian River*, 1905, by Commander Sinclair, R.I.M. (Library No. 1383); a *Sketch Survey of the Creek between Muhalla and Abadan Islands*, 1905, by Commander Sinclair, R.I.M. (Library No. 1382); a *Sketch Survey of Kannaka Creek, Khor-Musa*, 1907, by Commander C. W. Shearme, R.I.M. (Library No. 1384); and a *Topographical Sketch showing Dry Bed of Blind Karun River*, 1908, by the same, correcting and extending the last (Library No. 1397)

Name of tribe.	Number of settled members.	Where chiefly settled.	Number of nomadic members.	Where chiefly wandering.
Farātiseh فراطسه	...	...	200	Ahwāz District.
Ghālibi غالبي	125	Hindiyān District.	...	...
Gūndazlu گوندزلو	1,000	Shūshtar District. (See article Northern 'Arabistān.)	...	...
Gurgi گرگي	200	Hindiyān District.	...	...
Haidari حيدري	500	Do. do.	...	...
Haiyādir حيادر	300	Jarrāhi District.	...	...
Halāf حلاف	...	...	(8,500, but these are included in the Bani Sāleh and Bani Turuf below.)	Hawīzeh District.
Hamaid حميد	...	...	6,000	Between the Ahwāz District proper and the Bakhtiyāri country.
Hardān حردان	100	On the Gargar River.	2,400 (exclusive of the Bani Na'āmeh in the Hawīzeh District below.)	Ahwāz District.
Hawāshim هواشم	500	Ahwāz District.	...	...
Hiyādir حيادر	...	...	2,000	Hawīzeh District.
Iblāl (Bait) بيت ابلال	150	Fallāhīyeh District.	...	...
'Ikrish عكرش		Ahwāz District.	5,000	Hawīzeh and Ahwāz Districts.

'ARABISTĀN 121

Name of tribe.	Number of settled members.	Where chiefly settled.	Number of nomadic members.	Where chiefly wandering.
Ja'fari جعفري	850	Hindiyān District.	...	...
Jāma جامع	...	...	500	Ahwāz District.
Juruf (Ahl-al-) اهل الجرف	500	Hawīzeh Town.	900	Hawīzeh District.
Ka'ab كعب	55,000	Fallāhīyeh, Muhammareh, Jarrāhi, Ahwāz and Hindiyān Districts.	...	...
Kangarpaz كنگرپز	...	'Aqīli.	...	...
Kathīr كثير	1,000	Dizfūl District.	7,000	Dizfūl and Shūshtar Districts.
Khamīs (Āl) آل خميس	2,500	Rāmuz District.	...	...
Khawānīn خوانين	1,000	Dizfūl and Shūshtar Towns.	...	...
Kurd كرد	750	Dizfūl District.	...	...
Kurd (Āl Bū) آل بوكرد	1,700	Ahwāz District.	...	...
Kūt (Ahl-al-) اهل الكوت	1,200	Hawīzeh Town.	...	...
Laki لكي	1,000	Hindiyān District.	...	...
Lām (Bani) بني لام	500	Rāmuz District.	...	...
Lur (Eastern) لر	3,500	Rāmuz and Hindiyān Districts.	...	...
Lur (Western) لر	5,000	Dizfūl District.	Fluctuating.	Dizfūl District.
Ma'adān عدان	...	...	Ditto	Muhammareh and Fallāhīyeh Districts.

'ARABISTĀN

Name of tribe.	Number of settled members.	Where chiefly settled.	Number of nomadic members.	Where chiefly wandering.
Ma'āwiyeh	770	Ahwāz and Fallāhīyeh Districts.	...	...
Maqātīf مقاطيف	400	Jarrāhi District.	...	...
Marawuneh مرونه	...	...	700	Ahwāz District.
Mashāikh مشائخ	1,700	Dizfūl and Shūshtar Towns.	...	...
Mazra'eh مزرعه	...	...	(1,400, but these are included in the Bani Turuf below.)	Hawīzeh District.
Miyānāb Arabs ميانآب	600	Miyānāb.	...	...
Muhaisin محيسن	12,000	Muhammareh and Ahwāz Districts.	...	...
Na'āmeh (Bani) بني نعامه	...	...	900 (not included in the Hardān).	Hawīzeh District.
Nais نيس	300	Hawīzeh Town and Dizfūl District.	1,200	Hawīzeh District.
Nidhārāt نظارات	1,000	Hindiyān District.	...	...
Qanawāti قنواتي	5,250	Hindiyān and Ma'shūr Districts.	...	...
Qāti' (Āl) آل قاطع	...	...	350	Hawīzeh District.
Rāmuz (Ahl-i-) اهل رامز	4,800	Rāmuz District.	...	...
Rawāyeh (Al Bū) آل بو رايه	...	...	700	Ahwāz District.

'ARABISTĀN

Name of tribe.	Number of settled members.	Where chiefly settled.	Number of nomadic members.	Where chiefly wandering.
Sa'ad (Bait) بيت سعد	100	On the Gargar River and in Miyānāb.	14,000	Dizfūl and Shūshtar Districts.
Sabians صبّا	350	The towns of Muhammareh, Hawīzeh and Buziyeh, Amīnīyeh village on the Kārūn, and Shāhwali in the Shūshtar District.	...	...
Saiyids سادات	10,000	Dizfūl and Shūshtar Towns, also villages of the Rāmuz, 'Aqīli and Dizfūl Districts.	...	...
Sākīyeh ساكيّة	...	...	1,000	Hawīzeh District.
Salāmāt سلامات	350	On the Gargar River.	1,250	Ahwāz District.
Sāleh (Bani) بني ساله	...	...	15,000	Hawīzeh District.
Sharīfāt شريفات	500	Hindiyān and Jarrāhi Districts.	500	Hindiyān District.
Shawākir شواكر	...	...	180	Ahwāz District.
Shurafa شرفا	...	...	1,800	Hawīzeh District.
Shūshtari شوشتري	19,500	Shūshtar Town and District.	...	...
Suwā'id سواعد	...	...	1,400	Hawīzeh District.
Sawāri سواري	...	...	3,200	Do.
Tamīm (Bani) (I) بني تميم	...	...	10,000	Do.
Tujjār نجّار	2,500	Dizfūl Town.	...	...

Name of tribe.	Number of settled members.	Where chiefly settled.	Number of nomadic members.	Where chiefly wandering.
Turuf (Bani) بني طرف	...	...	20,000 (including the Halāf and Mazra'eh above.)	Hawīzeh District.
Zarqān زرقان	500	Ahwāz District.	1,000	Ahwāz District.

This table shows the total number of the nomadic inhabitants of 'Arabistān to be about 119,680 souls, and, as the settled population have already been estimated at 229,000, it would seem that the total number of persons resident in the province must be about 348,680. The manner in which these numbers are distributed between Northern and Southern **'Arabistān** and among the districts of the same is explained in the articles on the two sub-provinces. The great bulk of the nomads inhabit the Southern **'Arabistān** districts of **Ahwāz** and **Hawīzeh**.

In the above figures no account is taken of **Bakhtiyāris** and **Lurs**, who only enter the districts as winter visitors: the most important of these numerically are probably the Sagwand **Lurs**, who encamp annually in the **Dizfūl** District, sometimes to the number of 15,000 souls. Wandering Turkish tribes who, under **Bakhtiyāri** protection, enter the north-western corner of the province have likewise been neglected. Similarly a large number of the **'Īdān** tribe who have recently immigrated from the right bank of the Shatt-al-'**Arab** into the **Muhammareh** District have been omitted from the calculations, their sojourn being possibly temporary. *Per contra* it is probable that a proportion of the nomads of the **Hawīzeh** District, who have been treated as permanently domiciled there, belong as much to Turkish **'Irāq** as to Persian **'Arabistān**. It is needless to remark that the estimates of numbers are in a high degree conjectural.

To speak generally, the tribal system of 'Arabistān does not,—like that of the North-Western Frontier of India for instance,—rest upon a rigid basis of race; nor is the tribal or sectional position of the individual determined immutably by his descent upon the male side. On the contrary tribesmen can, in 'Arabistān, be made as well as born; and the strength of the tribe or section is liable to be increased by addition to its numbers from without or diminished by desertion from within. Whole tribes are sometimes merged and disappear, or are distributed as sections among two or more other tribes; while at the same time the process of disintegration is actively bringing fresh tribes, or at least sections, into existence. * New sections generally take the names of the Shaikhs under whose auspices they are formed, and the result shows itself in perpetual variation and much confusion of tribal nomenclature. Another consequence of the looseness of the tribal system is a constant transfer of fighting power from one tribe or section to another,—a fact which goes far to explain the discrepancies between the numerical estimates that have been formed of the same body at different periods. In the present Gazetteer an endeavour has been made to present as accurately as possible the grouping of the tribesmen at the present day; but it is probable that the account will soon be out of date. An explanation of the want of permanency in tribal matters in 'Arabistān may be found perhaps in the migratory habits of some of the tribes, who constantly change their place and are obliged, as a guarantee for their safety amid new surroundings, to affiliate themselves to strong tribes already established there.

The important tribes of 'Arabistān, with the notable exception of the **Bakhtiyāris** and **Lurs,** are all Arab, but they have a strain of Persian blood, which has increased perceptibly since the famine of 1872, when many Arabs bought Persian girls as wives. The vast majority, indeed practically all, are Shī'ahs; and until recent years Sunnis, being considered infidels, had difficulty in obtaining justice.

Some of the tribes of 'Arabistān are settled, others are nomadic; and some are difficult to class, being at present in a transitional stage between the two modes of life. The settled or semi-settled tribes are mainly agricultural, and the nomadic mainly pastoral; but even the latter cultivate a certain amount of grain in winter. Dwellings are houses, huts and tent. A mud house having a roof of timber and mud is called in Arabic Bait-at-Tain بيت الطين and in Persian Dār دار; and every other habitation, except a tent, appears to be included in the term Kipar (Arabic, Kibar كبر, plural Kubārah كبارة), though strictly speaking a

* Obvious illustrations of these statements could be collected from the articles on particular tribes of 'Arabistān: here it may suffice to recall that besides the Nais tribe there are sections styled Nais belonging to the 'Anāfijeh, Bait Sa'ad and Bani **Turuf**; that Dailam are found among the 'Anāfijeh, Kathīr and Bait Sa'ad; that Āl Bū 'Adhār are common to the Bani **Sāleh** and Bani **Turuf**; that Halaf occu among the Bani **Sāleh**, Bani **Tamīm** and Bani **Turuf**; that Hamdān and Sitātleh belong alike to the Bait **Sa'ad** and to the Bani **Turuf**; and that the **Hamaid,** Bani **Lām,** Bani **Turuf** and **Ka'ab** have sections called Maiyāh. It is not contended that in all these cases community of name indicates community of blood, but in some of them it certainly does.

Kipar is a hut of Bardi or Qassāb reeds only. A mat hut is properly styled Kūkh كوخ (plural, Kuwākheh كواخه), but may also be spoken of as Kipar Buwāri. On the nomenclature and classification of huts composed in various ways of mud, matting, grass, reeds and tent cloth a manual might be written; but it is sufficient to note that Kipar is the most comprehensive term.

In character and customs the Arab tribes of 'Arabistān are all more or less alike. Shaikhs or headmen are generally chosen, by the greybeards of the tribe or section, from a family in which the office is hereditary; but the greybeards are not fettered in their selection by the wishes, or even by a nomination, of the late Shaikh: in deciding between claims they pay much attention to fitness and experience. When the greybeards are not unanimous the tribe or section frequently break up and follow different Shaikhs. A dispute between men not belonging to the same tribe or section is arranged, if possible, by their respective chiefs in consultation. If the minor chiefs cannot agree a reference is made to a common superior having authority over both tribes or sections; and in Southern **'Arabistān** the Shaikh of **Muhammareh** thus generally becomes arbiter when the disagreement is between two of the larger tribes. In case of a murder, the blood money payable by the murderer is fixed in the above manner; and, if the culprit has not the wherewithal to meet the demand, the adult males of his tribe or section must contribute rateably, according to the tribal books, to make up the deficiency. A case once settled by tribal custom cannot be re-opened by an appeal to the Shara' or ecclesiastical law.

Religious shrines are numerous in the country and are of two kinds, Imāmzādehs امامزاده and Qadamgāhs قدمگاه; the difference appears to be that the Imāmzādeh is (or is supposed to be) the actual tomb of a Shī'ah saint, while the Qadamgāh is merely a cenotaph erected, as tradition usually relates, on a request from the spectre of the sacred personage whom it commemorates.

Flora and fauna.—We now return to the subjects which have not been dealt with at all in the subprovincial articles.

The most widely distributed trees are the **Kunār** or ber and the **tamarisk**, the dwarf species of the latter being included; they seem to occur almost everywhere that any natural wood exists. Smaller brushwood is confined chiefly to the banks of streams and consists, besides **dwarf tamarisk**, of **Gharab** or **Euphrates poplar**, **Sarīm** (a medium-sized thorny bush), **liquorice**, **willow**, **a kind of blackberry**, and similar shrubs.

Other plants are the 'Ausaj, the Qāqilah, the Rimth—a plant which in habit somewhat resembles ling heather and is found growing near salt-water creeks,—and a kind of Salsola which is burned for potash. The swamps produce Qassāb, a reed of which matting is made, and Bardi or Labbūn, a coarse marsh grass used for hut building.

Of animals, and especially of birds, there is a large variety. There are said to be a few lions still in the jungles on the **Karkheh** and **Diz** Rivers and in the marshes near **Fallāhiyeh**; and the presence of a pair at Banneh in the **Ahwāz** District was reported in 1904. The lynx certainly exists, one having been seen near **Shūsh** in 1905, and the Arabs of the **Ahwāz** neighbourhood state that there are wolves. Marks of hyæna have been seen near **Nāsiri**; and the jackal, fox, hare and porcupine are found there, and probably everywhere throughout the province. Wild pigs are numerous wherever there is cover; of the fallow deer only a few remain in the jungles on the **Diz**, but gazelle—said to be of two kinds—are not uncommon, especially about Shākheh in the **Ahwāz** District, whence they sometimes approach **Nāsiri** in the hot weather. Natives say that there are otters, and a badger was killed at **Rāmuz** in 1905. Water rats are seen, of more than one sort. The mongoose lives in date plantations, and in the open plains near Ahwāz there is a small kind of jerboa. Bats exist.

There are scorpions, including a variety called Jarrār; also centipedes. Snakes of several kinds are found everywhere and lizards of more varieties than one in **Nāsiri** alone. Locusts occasionally make their appearance, and appeared as jumpers in May 1905, subsequently developing wings. Mosquitoes are numerous in the damper parts of the province: in the drier districts their place is taken by sand-flies. There is also a fly like the ordinary house fly, but it stings sharply.

Sharks frequent the **Kārūn**, and even the **Gargar**, and a fish called 'Anz, which is said to run to 185 lbs. in weight, abounds in the **Karkheh** and is present, though in smaller numbers, in the **Kārūn**. A small kind of turtle, about a foot long, lives in the **Gargar** and the **Diz**.

Among land birds the sandgrouse is one of the most common; it is found everywhere in the open country, especially in the plains of the **Hindiyān** and **Jarrāhi** Districts. The large kind (*pterocles arenarius*) and the small or pin-tailed kind (*pterocles alchata*) are both represented, the former being the more numerous; the local names for these are Kōkar كوكر and Kharkharah خرخره respectively. The black partridge (*francolinus vulgaris*), by natives of the country called Durāj دراج,

occurs wherever water and brushwood are found together, as at many places on the **Kārūn, Jarrāhi, Hindiyān** and **Diz** rivers: there appears to be also a distinct kind of brown partridge, which might easily be mistaken for the female of the black. The Sisi (*ammoperdix Bonhami*), locally styled Tīhu تيهو, frequents suitable stony grounds, as upon the **Gargar** and in the valley of the **Hindiyān** River; and the chikore (*caccabis chukor*), in Persian Kabk كبك, is found in the hills. The Houbarah bustard may be shot on the **Hindiyān** and **Jarrāhi** plains, and it is said that the great bustard also has been seen. Quail visit the country in their season, and blue rock pigeons inhabit the banks of the **Gargar.** Swifts and sparrows are common; but the crow is rare at **Nāsiri** and the rook, kite and mynah are said not to be seen there.

Water birds include several kinds of duck; the snipe (*gallinago scolopax*), here called Tapūk تپوك; the common curlew, especially near the sea; the great and small grebe; the purple and ordinary coot; the bittern, and a bird called Baiyūdhi بيوضي which is probably an egret. The woodcock is said not to be unknown.

Agriculture and livestock.—'Arabistān is a fertile and productive country and the variety of crops is considerable; wheat and barley are the most general in their distribution, but rice, cotton, sesame and beans also are grown in a number of the districts. Linseed, maize or millet, and different kinds of pulse are produced in some localities. Special crops are indigo in the **Dizfūl** District, opium and pepper in the **Shūshtar** District, and tobacco in **'Aqīli** and **Rāmuz.** Vegetables include lettuce, tomatoes, cucumbers, Lūbiya (a kind of French bean), garlic and onions: in the **Shūshtar** District all of these are obtainable. The most widely distributed fruits are dates, pomegranates, figs and grapes; but limes (both sweet and bitter), oranges, citrons, quinces, apples, pears, apricots, plums, peaches, mulberries, water melons, musk melons and almonds are grown in various places. **Dizfūl** and **Rāmuz** appear to be two of the best fruit-producing districts; yet it is reported that in **Rāmuz** all the fruit trees, except dates, are of recent introduction.*

Cultivation in 'Arabistān is either by rainfall, when it is called Daimi ديمي, or by irrigation, in which case it is described as Pāryāb پارياب. The most heavily irrigated districts are those of **Fallāhīyeh, Hawīzeh** and **Muhammareh,** in which is grown the bulk of the dates and of the

---

* In the 10th century A.D. sugarcane was the most important crop of **'Arabistān** and the province supplied the whole of Persia, Mesopotamia and Arabia with sugar (*vide* **Le Strange**). The disappearance of this staple is not a little remarkable.

rice; while among the driest districts are **Ahwāz** and **Jarrāhi,** important wheat and barley-growing tracts. Local terms relating to irrigation are Shākheh شاخه, a main canal; Naqreh نقره, a branch of the same; Nahr نهر, a canal smaller than a Shākheh; Jūb جوب, an ordinary open water channel; and Qanāt قنات, a subterranean aqueduct like the "Karez" of the Indo-Afghan frontier. The courses of these Qanāts are sometimes difficult to trace, and it often happens that the ultimate source of the water supply of a village is not discoverable at a glance. Cham چم, a word which enters into the composition of many names, means a piece of alluvial land by a river and generally one so situated at a bend as to be enclosed by the stream on three sides. Dōb دوب is apparently a long shallow depression in which water tends to collect.

Domestic animals are horses, mules, camels, donkeys, buffaloes, cattle, and sheep and goats. The distribution of these, like the distribution of the crops, follows to some extent the character of the country; buffaloes, for instance, occur only in the wetter tracts such as the **Fallāhīyeh** and **Hawīzeh** Districts and parts of the Districts of **Dizfūl** and **Hindiyān,** while camels and mules are kept chiefly in the drier districts. Camels are not ridden in 'Arabistān, and "mounted men" in this province are generally mounted on mares: almost all colts are intentionally destroyed. Of sheep and goats the former are the more numerous, and in some parts there is only a sprinkling of goats. The cattle of the Sagwand **Lurs** are small and are used chiefly as beasts of burden. Not only oxen but horses, mules, buffaloes and even donkeys are used for drawing the plough, which in 'Arabistān is generally woodenshared.

External trade.—The foreign trade of 'Arabistān is carried on almost exclusively through the single port of **Muhammareh,** which is situated upon the **Kārūn** River at a short distance from its junction with the Shatt-al-'**Arab.** Small ports exist at **Buziyeh** and **Ma'shūr,** but they are without steam communication; at both the amount of shipping and of business transacted is inconsiderable, and **Ma'shūr** is partially dependent for its trade upon **Muhammareh.** **Buziyeh** serves the **Fallāhīyeh** and part of the **Jarrāhi** District, the remainder of the **Jarrāhi** District being commercially attached to **Ma'shūr;** but **Muhammareh** is the port of all '**Arabistān** and even, to a slight extent, of parts of Persia beyond it. In 1905-1906 the steamers which called at **Muhammareh** numbered 143, of which 140 were British, and their tonnage aggregated 137,070. No exact estimate is possible of the native sailing craft that visit **Muhammareh** annually, but it is stated that about 100 such

K

vessels ranging from 30 to 150 tons burden call there in the date season and a similar number during the remainder of the year.

The average annual value of the merchandise (other than specie) exported from **Muhammareh** in recent years has been about £100,000. The chief articles of export are dates, wool, gum, oil-seeds and opium, and in some years wheat. The dates exported are mostly of the miscellaneous inferior sorts called Sāir: the best kind of local date, known as Qantār, is not sent out of the country, and the proportion of the superior Khadhrāwi and Halāwi varieties is small in proportion to the quantity of Sāirs. Dates go chiefly to India, the United Kingdom and America, but some are carried by native sailing boats to **Masqat**, the Red Sea and other places. The date trade is influenced by a prohibition in consequence of which no private owner may bring his dates on the market until those of the Shaikh of **Muhammareh** have been cleared off: one result of this rule is that the smaller merchants are sometimes obliged to part with their stocks to the Shaikh's broker at a very low price. The grain trade is uncertain and fluctuating: in the past it has been greatly hampered by embargoes on exportation suddenly and arbitrarily imposed in the interest of local officials and notables. A large quantity of the good wheat sold at **Basrah** is from 'Arabistān, and in favourable years such as 1903 the native merchants of **Basrah** send agents to **Nāsiri** to buy. The destination of the wheat exported is generally the United Kingdom; that of the wool, India and the United Kingdom. Gum includes gum tragacanth from the direction of Isfahān and ordinary gums collected at **Nāsiri**: both are sent chiefly to the United Kingdom. Of the oil-seeds, linseed goes mostly to India, the United Kingdom and Germany; and sesame to India and France. Opium from the side of Isfahān is nearly all consigned to Hong Kong: local opium from **Shūshtar** is said not to go beyond **Masqat**. Other exports are raw cotton to India and Turkey, bugloss and almonds to India, barley to ports of the Persian Gulf, tobacco chiefly to Egypt, and madder root to the United Kingdom and to France; there are also carpets of Isfahān origin. Altogether about half the exports from **Muhammareh** are to India and nearly a quarter to the United Kingdom: the shares in the remainder of countries not under the British flag are separately inconsiderable, especially when a further deduction has been made for the large quantities of opium that are shipped to Hong Kong.

The import trade of **Muhammareh** is worth, at the present time, about £225,000 annually. The most valuable items, in their usual order of importance, appear to be: cotton goods, sugar, metal and metal goods, thread and twist, tea, silk, and wood for making date boxes. The cotton goods are chiefly from Bombay or Manchester, and the Indian article—which is chiefly grey or indigo-dyed—exceeds the English in quantity but not in value. The sugar is from various European countries, chiefly France, Belgium, Germany and Austria; but some is received from Egypt, and a small quantity from Mauritius. Metals are chiefly iron and steel from India and the United Kingdom, whence also come most of the thread and twist. The tea is mostly Indian : the silk goods are Indian, British, French and Japanese. Other imports are rice, drugs, spices and indigo from India, and kerosine from Russia and America. The imports at **Muhammareh** in recent years from countries forming part of the British Empire has amounted on the average to more than four-fifths of the whole.

Internal trade.—The only considerable centre of internal trade is **Muhammareh** Town, whence distribution of imported goods is carried on and where local merchandise is collected for exportation. After **Muhammareh** the most important commercial entrepôt in the province is **Nāsiri**, which, since the opening of the **Kārūn** to navigation, has superseded **Ma'shūr** as the port of the landlocked **Rāmuz** District.

The mercantile position of the towns of **Dizfūl** and **Shūshtar** deserves notice with reference to the surrounding hill and other tribes and to the general trade of the province. The Arab tribes of Northern **'Arabistān** have their dealings with both **Dizfūl** and **Shūshtar**, and **Dizfūl** is also the market town of the Western **Lurs**. The commodities with which the tribes supply themselves at these centres include sugar, tea, dates, date syrup, rice, beans, onions, garlic, tobacco, matches, candles, locally-made soap, henna, ready-made clothes of European material, block-printed cloth of Persian manufacture, leather shoes, cotton shoes, felt, hair rope, horse and mule saddles, copper vessels, spades, horse shoes and other articles of iron; also lead, gunpowder and rifles. Besides these the Arabs take kerchiefs and the **Bakhtiyāris** felt hats; while the Arabs purchase some wheat and barley, as do also the **Bakhtiyāris** and the **Lurs,** and that in greater quantities than the Arabs. At **Dizfūl** and **Shūshtar** the Arab tribes bring in ghi, curds, wool and live sheep for sale; they also supply wheat, barley, millet, mules and horses to the **Dizfūl** market, and skins and hides to that of **Shūshtar.** At both places the **Bakhtiyāris** bring in ghi, wool, live sheep, gum, charcoal and bitter almonds : **Dizfūl** they also supply with curds, goats, lime and a few rugs, and **Shūshtar** with goats' hair. The **Bakhtiyāris** of Māl Amīr,

K 2

Murgheh and Anteh Kūh are among those who have dealings with **Shūshtar**; and the more neighbouring **Bakhtiyāris** of **'Aqīli** provide the town with donkeys, hides, linseed, rice, firewood, honey, pomegranates, water melons and salt; also ashes—said to be of dung—which are used for mixing with a lime made from boulders found in the bed of the **Kārūn**. The commodities brought by the Western **Lurs** to the **Dizfūl** market are chiefly live goats, ghi, firewood and charcoal. Both towns deal with **Muhammareh** Town by way of the **Kārūn**, goods for **Dizfūl** passing in this case through **Shūshtar** *en route*. Piece-goods are the most valuable of the imports by river; but sugar, tea, matches, candles, iron, copper, lead and German silver are also imported in considerable quantities by this line; and letter paper, liquors, boots and shoes, glassware and henna are also received, though on a smaller scale. Both **Dizfūl** and **Shūshtar** have trade relations with Isfahān and obtain thence native fabrics with block-printed patterns called Qalamkār قلمكار and cotton shoes known as Gīwehs گیوه: besides these, dark cloth for women's veils, linen cloth, waist-cloths, and a sweetmeat styled Halwa Gaz حلوا گز, compounded from a sticky exudation of the tamarisk tree, are brought from Isfahān to **Dizfūl**; and **Shūshtar** receives from the same source various native textile fabrics, dried fruits, walnuts, pipe tobacco and tea samovars. **Dizfūl** has dealings with a number of other places besides Isfahān and is provided with lacquered boxes, spoons and tobacco from Khōnsār; with tanned leather from Hamadān; and, when the route—which has been closed to trade for some years—is open, with wheat, barley, gram, dried fruits, pistachios, saddle-fittings, samovars and trays from Khurramābād and Burūjird. There is also some direct trade between the Towns of **Dizfūl** and **Shūshtar**, the latter supplying the former not only with foreign merchandise brought from **Muhammareh**, but also with pottery, sieves, local soap, local petroleum and dates; while **Dizfūl** in return provides **Shūshtar** with raw cotton, indigo, rice, beans, Māsh, fruit, felt cloth, pencases, and in some seasons with wheat. The production of raw silk, an industry which seems to have flourished in **'Arabistān** in the 10th century A. D.,[*] appears to have ceased.

Salt is sent to **Dizfūl** from the village of Gotwand near **Shūshtar**. Wool, linseed, hides, gums and sometimes wheat form part of the contribution of both the **Dizfūl** and the **Shūshtar** Districts to the export trade of 'Arabistān; and in addition to these the former produces indigo, raw cotton and pen-reeds for the foreign market, while the **Shūshtar** District is a source of opium.

---

[*] *Vide* Le Strange.

The commercial characteristics of the remaining districts of 'Arabistān may be described in a few words.

The **Ahwāz** District produces grain : its river port is **Nāsiri** and its sea port **Muhammareh**. **Nāsiri** is a centre for the collection of ordinary (or so-called insoluble) gums.

The exports of the **Fallāhīyeh** District are dates, rice, wheat, barley, wool, ghi, hides and the skins and feathers of the Baiyūdhi and other birds found in the marshes. The dates are mostly disposed of to sailing boats from the Persian Gulf at the local port of **Buziyeh**; the wheat and barley are purchased by visitors from **Kuwait, Būshehr, Bahrain** and **Masqat; Kuwait** is the destination of most of the rice; the remaining articles are sent to **Muhammareh** Town. Imports into **Fallāhīyeh** are chiefly piece-goods from **Muhammareh** Town, and metals, coffee, tea, sugar and spices from **Kuwait**. **Buziyeh**, besides being the port, is the only trade centre in the district; at **Fallāhīyeh** Town, though it is the political capital, business is inconsiderable.

The trade of the **Hawīzeh** District is mostly with **'Amārah** on the **Tigris** River by way of the marshes and the **Jahálah** canal : rice and fish constitute the sole exports.

Of the **Hindiyān** District the only valuable exports are grain and wool, which are sent abroad in considerable quantities from the similarly named capital and port upon the **Hindiyān** River. Imports consist of necessities of life and simple luxuries which the district does not itself produce.

Jarrāhi is a pastoral district with a small population : wheat, barley and a little sesame are the only agricultural exports. It imports dates from the neighbouring district of **Fallāhīyeh** and rice from that of **Rāmuz**, while its small demand for piece-goods, tea, sugar and spices is met by the sea ports of **Buziyeh** and **Ma'shūr**.

Ma'shūr is merely a port, though it ranks as a district, and it is unnecessary to repeat here the facts about its trade which are fully stated in the article under its name. **Ma'shūr**, as already mentioned, has lost to **Nāsiri** the foreign trade of the **Rāmuz** District; and little now remains to it beyond a share in the trade of **Jarrāhi**.

Dates and date-syrup are the most important products of the **Muhammareh** District, of which the port is naturally **Muhammareh** Town : for the latter reason it is difficult to discriminate the trade of the district from that of 'Arabistān as a whole.

Rāmuz Town is a market and dépôt of exportation for the produce of the district of which it is capital and also for that of the adjacent

Bakhtiyārī and Eastern Lur hills. The exportable products of the plain are wheat, barley, sesame, rice, beans, linseed, ghi, wool and hides: those of the mountains are wool, gums, various nuts, a kind of logwood and some carpets. Piece-goods, metals, sugar, tea, coffee, spices, crockery and candles are among the chief imports of the district. The trade of **Rāmuz** with places abroad is now conducted chiefly through **Nāsiri**, but a part of it is still carried on direct with **Muhammareh** Town by way of the **Jarrāhi** River.

Manufactures.—There are no manufactures of any importance in 'Arabistān. Such handicrafts as exist are exercised chiefly at the towns of **Dizfūl** and **Shūshtar**, in the articles on which they are described.

Currency and accounts.—The currency of 'Arabistān is much the same as that of the **Persian Coast**, but it has a somewhat different nomenclature. The Qrān, worth ordinarily about $4\frac{1}{4}d.$ English, is not the commonest coin in actual circulation, but it is the most convenient to take as a basis for the money table of 'Arabistān. The coins actually current in the province are the following:—

Name.	Nominal value in Qrāns.	Material.	Remarks.
Siyāh Pūl سياه پول	Variable. At one and the same time the Siyāh Pūl has been known to stand at 1·54 of a Qrān at Shūshtar, at ·56 at Dizfūl and at 1·61 at Nāsiri.	Copper.	Or "Black Cash." By Arabs called Ghāzi غازي and Shāhīyeh شاهيه: the latter name is not to be confounded with Shāhi below.
Shāhi شاهي	1·20	Nickel.	Of Belgian mintage. By Arabs called Nus Qamari and Nus Baljīki.
Qamari قمري	1·10	Do.	Also of Belgian manufacture, and for that reason called Baljīki بلجيكي by the Arabs.
Qrān قران	1	Silver.	This coin is not abundant; it is die-struck, but the edges are not milled. Some Qrāns of old and clumsy mintage, known in English as "Dump" Qrāns, are current in upper Persia; but in 'Arabistān merchants only receive them at a discount.

Name.	Nominal value in Qrāns.	Material.	REMARKS.
Dū Hazār دو هزار	2	Silver.	This is the commonest coin in circulation, corresponding to the rupee in India. It is very badly minted; and though die-struck, is not mill-edged.
Dū Hazār در هزار	2	Gold.	Cannot be described as current; when it changes hands, it does so at a valuation of $3\frac{1}{2}$ to 4 Qrāns.
Panj Hazār پنج هزار	5	Silver.	Uncommon in 'Arabistān: it is die-struck, mill-edged and altogether well minted.
Panj Hazār پنج هزار	5	Gold.	Not really in circulation and passes when available at a valuation of $10\frac{1}{2}$ to 11 Qrāns.
Ashrafi اشرفي	10	Do.	The material counterpart of that Persian unit of account which is known as the Tūmān. The Ashrafi is not really a current coin and its market value is $20\frac{1}{2}$ to 22 Qrāns.

Besides these actual coins there is an imaginary unit called a Dīnār دينار equal to the one-thousandth part of a Qrān; for this reason the Qrān itself is often spoken of simply as "Hazār" or a thousand (sc. Qrāns). At **Dizfūl** and **Shūshtar** the single Qrān is sometimes also called "Riyāl"—a very misleading abuse of terms.

Persians ordinarily work out Qrān sums in Tūmāns and Dīnārs, but they express fractions of a Qrān in Qamaris and Shāhis and not in Dīnārs. Europeans and Arabs reckon in Qrāns, the Arabs making use of the Qamari and half Qamari to express fractions, and Europeans of "cents." Some native merchants are said to keep their accounts in Qamaris.

For Turkish gold Līrahs and for Indian rupees there is always a demand; and Maria Theresa dollars and Turkish Majīdis also can generally be disposed of. The value of these foreign coins is liable to fluctuations. The Līrah is nominally worth 20 Qrāns only, but it ordinarily changes hands for 50 to 60 Qrāns, and many merchants and others in the bazaar make their calculations in Līrahs or, as they are here sometimes called, Lairahs. The Indian rupee has acquired a conventional value of 3·85 Qrāns, and the word "Rūbīyah" is sometimes (it is said) used by Arabs to express this amount even in transactions into which the rupee as a coin does not itself enter. The rupee is to all intents and purposes current at **Muhammareh** Town : in the bazaars of **Nāsiri, Shūshtar** or **Dizfūl,** the case is otherwise; but even at those places merchants willing to purchase Indian rupees can ordinarily be found.

At **Nāsiri** a coin with the slightest crack or defect is invariably refused, but such coins are current at **Dizfūl** and to a lesser extent at **Shūshtar** and **Rāmuz.**

Weights and measures.—The only weight common to the whole of 'Arabistān is the Misqāl مثقال, which is used like the English grain as a standard for comparing different weights that are neither multiples nor aliquot parts of one another: 97·744 Misqāls are equal to 1 lb. avoirdupois English. The only larger weights in general use are the Man-i-Tabrīz من تبريز of 640 Misqāls or 6·5478 lbs. English, which under the name of " Batman "* has been adopted by the Persian Imperial Customs as their unit of weight in all parts of Persia, and the Man-i-Shīrāz من شيراز of 720 Misqāls or 7·3662 lbs. which is not altogether unknown in general trade. Besides these there is a Man-i-Shāhi من شاهي of 1,280 Misqāls or 13·095 lbs. English, which appears to be used only in arranging transport on the Bakhtiyāri Road, and the British steamship company on the **Kārūn** do their business everywhere in an " Oke " or Huqqah of 2·87 lbs.

The weights used at **Ma'shūr** are described in the article on that place. The other local standards which still hold the field in native trade are those given in table below :—

District where used.	Name.	Equivalent in English lbs. av.	Remarks.
Ahwāz	Huqqah-al-Ahwāz حقه الاهواز	2·87	...
Do	Waqīyah-al-Ahwāz وقيه الاهواز	4·30	Is equal to 1½ Huqqah-al-Ahwāz.
Do.	Man-i-Shūshtar من شوشتر	15·478	Its subdivisions are described after this table. It is the standard weight for ordinary purposes in the district.

* The writer has not been able to discover the origin of this term or to what language it belongs.

'ARABISTAN

District where used.	Name.	Equivalent in English lbs. av.	REMARKS.
Ahwāz	Man-i-Ismā'īli (or Simāīni) من اسماعيلي	392	Used for transactions in grain. It apparently fluctuates and is at present over 400 lbs.
Do.	Taghār-al-Ahwāz تغار الاهواز	7,840	Considered to be equal to 20 Man-i-Ismā'īli.
Do.	Kārah كاره	39,200	Described as the equivalent of 100 Man-i-Ismā'īli.
Dizfūl	Man-i-Dizfūl من دزفول	16·969	...
Fallāhīyeh	Man-i-Fallāhīyeh من فلاحيّه or Man-i-Dōraq من دورق	248	Divisible into 12 local Waqīyahs.
Hawīzeh	Man-i-Hawīzeh من حويزه	108·35	If it is equal, as is stated, to 7 Man-i-Shūshtar; but possibly it is a good deal less, *viz.*, 26 Ahwāz Huqqahs.
Hindiyān	Man-i-Hindiyān من هنديان	240	...
Do.	Man-i-Dih Mulla من ده ملّا	247½	...
Jarrāhi	Man-i-Khalfābād من خلف آباد	124	...
Muhammareh	Man-i-Bāzār من بازار	147·3	Consists of 24 Waqīyahs of 600 Misqāls each. In practice this weight is variable.

District where used.	Name.	Equivalent in English lbs. av.	Remarks.
Muhammareh	Man-i-Sīf من سيف	159·6	Consists of 26 Waqīyahs of 600 Misqāls each. In practice this weight is variable.
Do.	Man-i-Basrah من بصره	168	Used in the export trade.
Do.	Taghār-i-Basri تغار بصري	3,360	Employed also at Nāsiri by European merchants.
Rāmuz	Man-i-Rāmuz من رامز	106	...
Shūshtar	Man-i-Shūshtar من شوشتر	15·478	The subdivisions of this Man are described below: by Arabs it is sometimes called the Man-al-Khān.

Grain is in some places estimated (but not bought or sold) by the Kharwār خروار or Khalwār خلوار, which is considered to be equal to 100 Man-i-Tabrīz or 654·78 lbs. English; and in the **Muhammareh** District date crops are computed by means of the Kārah of 1½ tons English, which is mentioned above as used in the **Ahwāz** District.

At **Nāsiri**, **Dizfūl** and **Shūshtar**, and possibly in some of the other districts, the local Man من is subdivided as below :—

    4 Sanār سنار = 1 Chārak.
    2 Chārak چارك = 1 Pashti.
    2 Pashti پشتي = 1 Dahsi.
    4 Dahsi دهسي = 1 Man.

Liquids are sold by weight or, if in small quantities, by the reputed quart bottle.

Units of linear measurement are the Gaz-i-Shāh گزشاه of 40 to 41 inches and the double cubit; the latter, called by Persians Zar' ذرع and by the Arabs Dharā' ذراع, varies in 'Arabistān between 32 inches in **Shūshtar** and **Fallāhīyeh** and 37 inches or even more in other districts. Persians subdivide this measure into Nīm نيم or halves and Rub' ربع or quarters; by Arabs these are styled Nuss نّص (for نصف) and Ruba' ربع. The Rub' or Ruba' is also called a Chārak چارك and the Chārak is said to consist of 4 Gireh گره. Piece-goods are sometimes sold by the English yard: otherwise they are measured by the actual cubit (*viz.*, the combined length of a man's forearm and hand), or, usually, by the actual double cubit (*viz.*, the distance from a man's nose to the tip of his fingers when the arm is extended). In some parts of the country, and especially in Northern **'Arabistān,** distances are estimated by the Farsakh فرسخ (Persian) or Sā'at ساعة (Arabic), which is equal to something between 3½ and 4 English statute miles.

Areas are generally described in terms of their dimensions; but a rudimentary unit of square measurement for land exists on the Shatt-al-**'Arab** in the Jarīb جريب; the Jarīb is supposed to accommodate 200 date palms and on the average it appears to have a superficies of about 2½ acres, but in practice its size is somewhat variable. There is also the Faddān فدّان (Arabic) or Khīsh* خيش (Persian), a somewhat indefinite measure of land, but one more generally understood than the Jarīb: it is described as being that area of land which can be ploughed over with one pair of bullocks during the season of ploughing, or which requires 100 Shūshtar Mans (13 cwts. English) of seed to sow it. It is evidently the same as the Gāo of the Persian Coast and in the **Hindiyān** District it is even called by that name.

Commercial usages and obstacles to trade.—Importation of goods from abroad generally takes place at the order of the larger merchants, and from these the petty dealers and shopkeepers obtain their stocks. Traders, whether on the large or on the small scale, frequently keep their merchandise—especially the more valuable articles—at their private residences instead of at their places of business. In the date-growing districts credit is ordinarily allowed for goods purchased until the following date season, and in other parts until the ensuing harvest of cereals.

The principal difficulty with which foreign traders in 'Arabistān have to contend is the uncertainty (and frequent impossibility) of recovering sums due. This difficulty arises from the absence of proper tribunals and is common to the whole of Persia. It is probable that if adequate arrangements were made in 'Arabistān for enforcing the just

---

* For the Rāmuz Khīsh, however, see article **Rāmuz District.**

claims of foreign merchants a portion at least of the European trade with Western Persia which at present passes through **Baghdād** would enter the country through **Muhammareh** instead.

Water communications.— Access from the sea to **Muhammareh** Town is afforded by the Shatt-al-**'Arab,** and to the minor ports of **Buziyeh** and **Ma'shūr** by Khor **Mūsa**: the river and the inlet are described in articles under their own names.

The principal waterways in the interior of the province are the **Kārūn** and **Jarrāhi** and, to a lesser extent, the **Hindiyān** River: a steamer is run on the lower **Kārūn** by the (British) Euphrates and Tigris Steam Navigation Company, and another on the upper **Kārūn** by the same Company on behalf of the Persian Government. The **Karkheh** and **Diz** do not appear to be utilised for purposes of travel or of carriage, except that at certain seasons wood is made into rafts and floated down the **Diz** by Arabs, chiefly to **Ahwāz** on the **Kārūn**. The Fallāhīyeh-Mārid canal or Shākheh, which connects the **Kārūn** and **Jarrāhi** rivers and so provides water communication—though at present of an unsatisfactory character—between the towns of **Muhammareh** and **Fallāhīyeh,** is noticed in the article on the **Fallāhīyeh** District.

The navigational features of the streams of 'Arabistān are described in the separate articles which are devoted to them, and for statistics of river (as well as of seagoing) craft the articles on the appropriate towns and villages may be consulted. Here however we may mention that the native cargo boats on the lower **Kārūn** amount to 19 Mahailahs and a dozen Nassāri Ballams, owned at **Muhammareh** Town; and that there are 17 native cargo boats at **Ahwāz** which ply upon the upper river. The carrying power of the Mahailahs is from 200 to 600 gunny bags. Besides these about 80 passenger Ballams are obtainable at **Muhammareh** Town, and about 40 small ferry boats are stationed at different villages on the **Kārūn** and **Gargar** between **Muhammareh** and **Shūshtar**. There are also a number of small Ballams in the **Fallāhīyeh** District. On the **Kārūn** native sailing boats maintain a not unsuccessful competition with the steamers, especially in the carriage of grain; this may be explained by the facts that the owners accept grain in bulk and do not insist on bagging, that for petty collections from point to point small craft have a natural advantage over large, and that the boat of the country is able to some extent to evade the embargo when imposed.

Land communications.—With one or two notable exceptions, especially the Bakhtiyārī Road and the route between **Shūshtar** and **Dizfūl** Towns, land communications are subsidiary to the **Kārūn** and **Jarrāhi** rivers and are of comparatively slight importance. The main obstacles to movement by land are rivers and marshes, and, in places, the lawless state of the inhabitants. In wet weather long détours must often be made in order to avoid impassable ground; whereas in dry weather, on the contrary, the possibility of obtaining water sometimes becomes the governing factor in a choice of routes.

The principal routes in 'Arabistān may be arranged in 6 groups according as they start from (1) **Muhammareh** Town, (2) **Nāsiri**, (3) **Shūshtar** Town, (4) **Dizfūl** Town or (5) **Ma'shūr** or lie in the (6) **Hindiyān** District. It will be sufficient to indicate the courses of these routes, leaving the distances in most cases to be roughly determined by map and the probable nature and amount of supplies available to be gauged by means of the articles on the districts, etc., traversed; the majority of the routes being described from native information only it seems inexpedient to enter into greater detail.

1. (*a*) *Route from Muhammareh Town to Dizfūl Town.*—This caravan route follows more or less the right bank of the **Kārūn** passing by Rahwāli (about 20 miles), Sab'eh (about 30 miles) and Umm-at-Tamair (about 35 miles). Leaving the river at the last-named place the route strikes northwards and crosses the Khārūr and Sharish branches of the **Shāūr** River, which travellers must bridge for themselves with local timber; beyond this point the route runs between the left bank of the **Shāūr** and the right bank of the **Diz** and finally crosses to the left bank of the **Diz** at or near **Dizfūl**. Until 1892 about one caravan from **Dizfūl** used to arrived at **Muhammareh** by this route every 6 weeks: it was then preferred to the river route as enabling merchants to escape the extortions of Persian officials.

Troops moving up the **Kārūn** by land from **Muhammareh** would follow the right bank, at least until the marshes on the left bank, in the **Muhammareh** District, were left behind.

1. (*b*) *Route from Muhammareh Town to Fallāhīyeh Town.*—The ordinary route is by water *viâ* the **Kārūn** River and the Mārid-Fallāhīyeh Canal; but there are also winding paths, practicable for transport animals, which conduct from the left bank of the **Kārūn** to **Fallāhīyeh** Town.

2. (*a*) *Route from Nāsiri to Dizfūl Town.*—Travellers between **Nāsiri** and **Dizfūl** ordinarily go by **Shūshtar** Town, but—the state of tribal politics permitting—it is possible to march by the right bank of **Diz**. The total distance is said to be about 90 miles, and it seems probable that this route falls into route No. 1 (*a*) at a short distance from **Nāsiri.**

2. (*b*) *Route from Nāsiri to Shūshtar Town.*—The route runs up the left bank of the **Kārūn** to **Wais** (16 miles), and continues along the same to a point opposite **Band-i-Qīr** (10 miles), where it crosses the **Gargar** into **Miyānāb**. From **Band-i-Qīr** the way lies by 'Arab Hasan on the **Shatait** (14 miles) and thence to **Shūshtar** Town (16 miles). The nature of the latter part of this route will be better understood on reference to the article on **Miyānāb**, where also some unimportant variants are mentioned. Supplies are scarce, but water of course is plentiful, between **Nāsiri** and **Shūshtar**.

In connection with this route may be mentioned a horse tramway, owned by a Persian merchant, which runs from **Nāsiri** to **Ahwāz** Village; it is 2,500 yards in length and the gauge is 3 feet. It passes through **Nāsiri** and then behind (that is inland of) the village of **Ahwāz**. There are 2 new and 2 old trucks, each of which can carry 2 tons and is drawn in good weather by a single horse. At present there are 6 trained horses. The permanent-way is unballasted and the wooden sleepers are crooked; but for practical purposes the line is efficient. The sole function of this tramway is to transfer goods from vessels on the lower to those on the upper **Kārūn** and *vice versâ*.

2. (*c*) *Route from Nāsiri to Isfahān.*—This line of communication consists of a road constructed by the firm of Messrs. Lynch Brothers through the **Bakhtiyāri** hills on behalf of the **Bakhtiyāri** Khāns: it was opened for traffic in December 1899. Among natives it is generally known as the Rāh-i-Bakhtiyāri or the Bakhtiyāri Road, but its name at Isfahān is Rāh-i-'Arabistān. The first 40 miles only of this route lie in 'Arabistān: they present no difficulties to wheeled transport except in wet weather. From **Nāsiri** the road follows the left bank of the **Kārūn** by Qrāneh and Kūt Saiyid 'Anāyeh to **Wais** (16 miles) which is the first stage; from **Wais** it runs by Umm-al-Gharaibeh, Linhairi and Raghaiweh to 'Alwānīyeh (24 miles): these places are described in the article on the **Ahwāz** District. One and a half miles beyond Alwāniyeh the road enters the hills.*

---

* This route has been minutely described by Captain D. L. R. Lorimer, Vice-Consul in 'Arabistān, and his report is in possession of the Intelligence Branch, Simla. As the route does not properly belong to 'Arabistān it is only mentioned here.

2. (*d*) *Route from Nāsiri to Rāmuz Town.*—The length of this route, which runs across the plains of the **Ahwāz** and **Rāmuz** Districts, is about 60 miles in actual travelling. It breaks off, as does also the Persian telegraph line to **Rāmuz** and **Burāzjān,** from route No. 2 (*c*) at 2 miles from **Nāsiri**: it lies at first along the north side of the Kūh-i-Ahwāz across plains which are sometimes cultivated with wheat, but in places are grassy and trackless, and in others swampy. At 26 miles the village of Shākheh in the tract of the same name is passed, and at 32 miles the **Gūpāl** stream is crossed near the place where the camp of Shaikh Rāshid generally stands on its right bank; the nature of the crossing, which is sometimes difficult and after rain impassable, is described in the article on the **Gūpāl** stream. Beyond the **Gūpāl** the route after traversing a belt of sandhills, crosses the level plain of Bu'airish and at 39 miles reaches the administrative border between the **Ahwāz** and **Rāmuz** districts. At 8 miles from this border, or 47 miles from **Nāsiri,** the route crosses the Muwailheh affluent of the **Gūpāl,** and at 49 miles the village of **Mīrbacheh** is passed; at 4 miles beyond **Mīrbacheh** the Zarnīni stream is encountered; and finally, at 7 miles from the Zarnīni and 60 from **Nāsiri,** the track enters **Rāmuz** Town, having lain after **Mīrbacheh** across cultivated grassy and swampy plains. The Muwailheh and Zarnīni are described in the article on **Rāmuz** District.

Cart caravans of the D'Arcy Oil Concession Syndicate now leave the **Kārūn** River at Shikāreh and proceed by **Nāsiri, Wais** and 'Alwānīyeh* in the **Ahwāz** District, and along the foot of the Kuh-i-Gach which bounds the **Rāmuz** District on its north-eastern side, until the valley of the Rāmuz River is reached 5 miles east of **Rāmuz** Town. The route then runs up the valley, crossing the river 3 times, to Shārdīn شاردين, Māmātain, etc., where there are oil borings. For 10 miles beyond **Wais** the track is very soft in wet weather, and for the next 5 miles there are sandy hills; but beyond this, along the foot of the Kūh-ī-Gach, the going is good, except for the crossing of the Kindak tributary of the **Gūpāl** which is difficult after rain. The Rāmuz River is not uncrossable for ridden animals for more than a few days at a time; but vehicles may be greatly delayed there.

2. (*e*) *Route from Nāsiri to Fuziyeh and Ma'shūr.*—This route runs to Ruda' in the **Ahwāz** District (16 miles) and thence to Gharaibeh on the **Jarrāhi** River (22 miles). The Mālih stream accompanies the route on its western side for the first two-thirds of the second march and then expands into a large Hor or swamp; from this point for about 2½

---

* See Route 3 (*b*) below.

miles there is a Hor on the eastern side also, and the track follows an elevated strip of land between the two. This narrow strip is cut across by one or two channels connecting the two bodies of water, and it appears that at times it is itself submerged : in fact the practicability of this route depends in part on weather and season. Between the marshes and Gharaibeh there is only one easy canal to be crossed.

From Gharaibeh communication with **Fallāhīyeh** Town and **Buziyeh** is maintained chiefly by boat. Cotton goods manufactured at **Shūshtar** are regularly sent by this route, and the forwarding charge is 15 to 20 Tūmāns per 100 Shūshtar Mans for the whole journey by road and river.

If the **Jarrāhi** be crossed at Gharaibeh and the left bank be then followed upstream for some distance it brings the traveller into one of the routes to **Ma'shūr**. (See Route No. 5 (*a*) below.)

3. (*a*) *Route from Shūshtar Town to Dizfūl Town.*—The most direct route between these two important centres is *viâ* **Kāunak**, 22 miles from **Shūshtar** and 16 from **Dizfūl**, which affords a convenient halting place and has flowing but rather brackish water. Some caravans travel by Āb Bīd, skirting the right bank of the **Kārūn** for the first half of the first march : water is obtainable at Āb Bīd, which divides the journey into two equal stages of 21 miles each. Travellers from **Dizfūl** to **Shūshtar** by Āb Bīd may strike the **Kārūn** at Gotwand and complete their journey by water.

3. (*b*) *Route from Shūshtar to Rāmuz.*—This route runs along the outer foot of the Gypsum Hills which extend in a continuous line from the one place to the other. The total distance is said to be about 70 miles, and it is divided into 3 stages of which the first is perhaps rather shorter than the two others; the intermediate halting places are ordinarily at Darreh Naft درّه نفط and at 'Alwānīyeh in the **Ahwāz** District (or on the banks of the Kindak affluent of the **Gūpāl** a few miles beyond 'Alwānīyeh). In wet weather a different route appears to be followed from a point 8 miles from **Shūshtar** Town to the neighbourhood of 'Alwānīyeh : travellers by this variant usually make the first halt at a place called Mazzabanūr مزّبنور instead of at Darreh Naft.

3. (*c*) *Route from Shūshtar Town to Hawīzeh Town.*—The intermediate stages on this route are given as **Band-i-Qīr**—see route No. 2 (*a*) above—and Kūt Nahr Hāshim ; and the total distance is stated at about 80 miles.

4. (a) *Route from Dizfūl Town to 'Amārah.*—The following are given as the stages upon this route:—a camp known by the name of Shaikh Mushattat of the Bani **Lām** tribe, 18 miles; Qiraizīyah, where there is a small spring, 16 miles; the **Dawairīj** stream, where there is water (but bitter), 24 miles; Sifsāfāt صفصافات on the left bank of the **Tigris**, 28 miles. From Sifsāfāt the route is said to follow the **Tigris** bank to **'Amārah** for 16 miles, the total distance being thus 102 miles.

4. (b) *Routes from Dizfūl Town to Khurramābād.*—There are apparently 4 routes from **Dizfūl** Town to Khurramābād of which the 3 easternmost partially coincide with one another: in length they vary from 8 to 12 stages. The easternmost of all, which is also the most direct, is known as the Kiyālan كيالن route and is about 150 miles in length; it was once provided with caravansarais, but insecurity has completely closed it to traffic since six or seven years. These routes lie outside of 'Arabistān and it is enough to mention them here.*

4. (c) *Routes from Dizfūl Town to Isfahān.*—Dizfūl is said to be connected with Isfahān by two routes through the hills, one of which (by Khōnsār خونسار) consists of 18, and the other (by Gulpāigān كلپايكان) of 20 stages.

4. (d) *Route from Dizfūl Town to Hawīzeh Town.*—The first few stages on this route are the same as the last ones upon route No. 1 (a) above: the present route then diverges to the right and follows the **Karkheh** River to **Hawīzeh**.

5. (a) *Routes from Ma'shūr to Fallāhīyeh Town.*—One route runs north-westwards from **Ma'shūr** until it strikes the left bank of the **Jarrāhi** River at two miles above Saraimeh: Saraimeh, at 15 miles from **Ma'shūr**, is a convenient halting place. The second stage is from Saraimeh along the left bank of the **Jarrāhi** to the take-off of the **Janjīreh** canals (15 miles). From **Janjīreh** to **Fallāhīyeh** Town the distance by the river and its continuation the Fallāhīyeh-Mārid canal is 13 miles; and from the fact that boat is usually taken at **Janjīreh** it may be inferred that progress by land on the river bank is difficult below that point, on account of the numerous canals which are thrown off.

---

* The most recent reports on these routes are by Captain D. L. R. Lorimer, Vice-Consul in 'Arabistān, and will be found in the Government of India's Political Proceedings for October 1904.

From **Ma'shūr** to **Janjīreh** the route is passable to all arms in ordinary weather; supplies are obtainable and water is abundant.*

The other route from **Ma'shur** to **Buziyeh** and so to **Fallāhīyeh** Town lies by Imāmzādeh 'Abdul Hasan in the **Fallāhīyeh** District (20 miles) and its total length is perhaps 30 miles: a variant of it passes by Ran leh which is four miles south-east of the Imāmzādeh. This second route to **Buziyeh,** sometimes called the 'Aquleh route after a locality through which it passes at eight miles from **Ma'shūr,** is interrupted in winter by flooded country between Imāmzādeh 'Abdul Hasan and **Buziyeh;** and the traveller may then, if irrigation in the **Shatūt** tract permits, make from Imāmzādeh 'Abdul Hasan for Nahr-ash-Shaikh on the **Jarrāhi** River (12 miles) and then follow the left bank of the river down to a place opposite Gharaibeh, where boats can be obtained. The 'Aquleh route has fresh water and its course is very nearly straight.†

5. (*b*) *Route from Ma'shūr to Rāmuz Town.*—The stages are Rahāneh on the **Jarrāhi** River (16 miles), Cham-as-**Sābi** (19 miles), and **Rāmuz** Town (about 25 miles); the total distance is about 60 miles. The route crosses from the right to the left bank of the **Jarrāhi** at Rahāneh; it then runs to Cham-as-**Sābi,** keeping within 3 miles of the river all the way; 4 or 5 miles beyond Cham-as-**Sābi** a gorge in low mud hills is entered, and for 10 miles or so thereafter the ground traversed is more or less broken and hilly; at 7 miles before **Rāmuz** Town the track diverges from the river bank; and at 1 mile before the end of the stage the village of Kīmeh is passed. The principal obstacle on this route is the **Jarrāhi** River; at the crossing place at Rahāneh it is about 50 yards wide and has perpendicular banks 15 feet high; the current here is not generally rapid, but in winter a maximum depth of 13 feet of water may be attained. At 10 miles beyond Rahāneh there is a deep ravine which requires ramping for wheels, and at 4 or 5 miles beyond Cham-as-**Sābi** some cutting and widening would be necessary. With the exceptions noted the route is good throughout and passable to all arms; some supplies also are obtainable, and there is plenty of fresh water from the **Jarrāhi** by the way.

* An exact description of this route by Major E. B. Burton (with a map) will be found in Government of India's Proceedings in the Foreign Department for July 1904.

† This route has been more fully described by Captain D. L. R. Lorimer, Vice-Consul in 'Arabistān, in a letter No. 412, dated 22nd March 1906, to the Political Resident in the Persian Gulf.

This route is used by caravans in summer and autumn after the wheat and rice harvests; at other times there is but little traffic on it.*

6. (*a*) *Route from Hindiyān Village to Ma'shūr.*—A track runs from **Hindiyān** village along the right bank of the **Hindiyān** River to ' Abbād Ilāhi village a few miles further down; it then strikes away north-westwards to **Ma'shūr**. The distance by this route cannot be less than 40 miles, but some miles might possibly be saved by travelling in a more direct line between the two termini. The ground crossed appears to be a plain, fairly level, of which parts are grassy.†

6. (*b*) *Routes from Hindiyān Village to Behbehān Town.*—The principal line of communication within the **Hindiyān** District is a track that everywhere skirts the right bank of the **Hindiyān** River. Travellers from **Hindiyān** to Behbehān either follow this track to Cham **Zaidān** and thence strike direct for Behbehān, or proceed by Gargari on the **Hindiyān** to Cham Siyāh on the **Mārūn** and thence up the valley of the **Mārūn** to Behbehān. The distance by the former of these routes appears to be 75 or 80 and by the latter 60 or 65 miles.

6. (*c*) *Routes from Hindiyān Village to Dīlam.*—The way lies by **Shāh Abul Shāh** (at about 25 miles) and the total distance is between 30 and 35 miles over plains. An alternative route is up the right bank of the **Hindiyān** River to Chihl Mani (6 miles); thence, crossing the river, to **Shāh Abul Shāh** (24 miles); and so to **Dīlam** (about 8 miles). Beyond Chihl Mani the track first crosses good grazing land with numerous flocks of goats and sheep; at about 14 miles it traverses a plain with sparse herbage, which is muddy in wet weather; and as **Shāh Abul Shāh** is approached it follows a line of sandhills which are hemmed in between mud-flats on the landward side and the sea upon the other.‡ This route appears to be free of obstacles except in wet weather.

Telegraphic communications.—The telegraphic system of 'Arabistān is entirely under Persian management and extremely inefficient; the wires are frequently interrupted — sometimes for weeks together, the

---

* This route has been minutely described by Major E. B. Burton—*vide* Government of India's Proceedings in the Foreign Department for July 1904, where also a map will be found.

† See Pelly and Colvill's *Recent Tour.*

‡ From a report by Colonel Bailward, R.F.A.

L 2

signalling is defective, and messages are only sent in the Persian language;* consequently the lines are of little service to Europeans except for the simplest purposes. The central telegraph office in 'Arabistān is at **Nāsiri**, from which place one branch line runs to **Muhammareh** Town and another *viâ* **Shūshtar** Town to **Dizfūl** Town: **Nāsiri** itself is connected with **Būrāzjān** on the Indo-European Telegraph Department's Būshehr-Shīrāz line by a wire on which the intermediate stations are **Rāmuz** Town, Behbehān Town, **Dīlam** and **Rīg**. The only telegraph offices in 'Arabistān are those at **Nāsiri** and the towns of **Muhammareh, Shūshtar, Dizfūl** and **Rāmuz**. The Telegraph Masters at these places all hold the military rank of Sarhang سرهنگ.

Political constitution.—The systems of internal administration in Northern and Southern **'Arabistān** are explained in the articles on those sub-provinces; and the exceptional position of the **Rāmuz** District, which is attached to Northern **'Arabistān**, is mentioned in the article under the name of the district. It remains to describe the political constitution of the 'Arabistān province as a whole.

The leading political authorities are three in number, namely, the Persian Governor of 'Arabistān in Northern **'Arabistān**, the **Bakhtiyāri** Khāns in the **Rāmuz** District, and the Shaikh of **Muhammareh** in Southern **'Arabistān**. The Persian Governor is nominally ruler of the whole province, but outside of the Northern **'Arabistān** districts of **Dizfūl** and **Shūshtar** his authority is slight or non-existent, and in the **'Aqīli** tract in **Shūshtar** it is disputed by the **Bakhtiyāri** Khāns. The Shaikh of **Muhammareh** holds his position as Governor of Southern **'Arabistān** directly from the Shāh, and the Persian Governor cannot summon the Shaikh to his presence. The position of the **Bakhtiyāri** Khāns with reference to the Persian Governor is similar; at least in practice the latter would not venture to send for them.

The only establishments which are general to the province are those of the Persian Foreign Office, the Persian Army, the Persian Telegraphs, the Imperial Persian Customs, the Persian Posts, the Treasury and the Land Revenue Accounts.

The Foreign Office is represented by a Kārguzār کارگذار or Agent who has his residence at **Muhammareh** Town. This official is supposed to possess copies of all the treaties into which Persia has entered with

---

* In autumn 1906, however, a signaller able to transmit English messages was posted to **Nāsiri**.

foreign powers, and he is in theory the only medium of communication with Foreign Consular representatives; it is his duty to try cases which may occur between Persian and foreign subjects and to protect the interests of foreigners whose countries may be without consular representation in the province. In practice the functions of the Kārguzār are much more restricted, for Foreign Consuls deal directly in many cases with the local administrative authority, especially with the Shaikh of **Muhammareh** and the **Bakhtiyāri** Khāns, and disputes between natives and foreigners are but seldom referred to the Kārguzār for settlement.

The Persian army is represented only by a skeleton garrison at **Shūshtar** Town, at the present time probably not more than 20 men,* and by a Qurkhānehchi قرخانه‌چي (or captain of ordnance) and a few artillery men under the command of a Nāib at **Muhammareh** Town: this **Muhammareh** detachment is under the orders of an artillery officer at **Shūshtar**. The Persian military arrangements in the province cannot be regarded seriously.

The Telegraph Department in 'Arabistān has been described in the paragraph above on telegraphic communications.

The head of the Imperial Persian Customs in 'Arabistān is a Director General, at present a Belgian, who has his headquarters at **Muhammareh** Town. The establishment under his control is detailed in the Appendix on the Persian Imperial Customs. Posts and treasuries in the province are also subject to this official. Treasuries exist only at the towns of **Dizfūl, Shūshtar** and **Muhammareh** and their character is as yet somewhat informal: land revenue payments, not collected by the Customs, as well as customs receipts, are understood to be now deposited in these treasuries; and all official disbursements such as salaries are regularly made from the same.

The accounts of land revenue for the whole province are believed to be kept and adjusted by the Persian Governor of 'Arabistān.†

For the remaining branches of administration,—such as police, justice, and revenue collection as distinguished from revenue accounts, —the local administrative authorities are responsible; and for information in regard to these the articles on Northern and Southern **'Arabistān** and the **Rāmuz** District may be consulted.

---

* While the Sālār-i-Mukarram was here (1906) there were several hundred — perhaps 1,000 — Persian soldiers at **Shūshtar**.

† According to a statement furnished by the Mustaufi in 1907, the total annual revenue of Northern and Southern 'Arabistan, including everything paid by the **Bakhtiyāri** tribe, is 135,725 Tūmāns; but the items, given by him separately, aggregate 139,217 Tūmāns.

Foreign interests.—Foreign interests in 'Arabistān are almost entirely British and are principally represented by the Euphrates and Tigris Steam Navigation Company, by the firm of Messrs. Lynch Brothers, and by the Persian Transport Company, all of which are closely connected with one another. The Navigation Company maintain a steamer service on the **Kārūn** between **Muhammareh** and **Nāsiri** and also run, on behalf of the Persian Government, a steamer on the upper **Kārūn** from **Ahwāz** Village to the neighbourhood of **Shūshtar**. The Nāsiri-Isfahān Road was constructed and is kept in repair by Messrs. Lynch as agents of the **Bakhtiyāri** Khāns, who hold a 60 years' concession for its management dating from 1897. Messrs. Lynch are also the chief trading firm in 'Arabistān and the only one which maintains a European establishment. The Transport Company are holders of a 60 years' concession, beginning in 1890, for the construction and working of a road from **Nāsiri** *viâ* **Dizfūl**, Khurramābād and Burūjird to Qum, with a branch from Burūjird to Isfahān. The D'Arcy Oil Exploitation Company, also British, have recently commenced operations in 'Arabistān under a concession obtained by them in 1901. Various British trading and steamship companies and one or two Jewish firms of which the headquarters are in England have agents at **Muhammareh**.

British subjects at the present time resident in 'Arabistān number nearly 50, exclusive of Indian military consular guards; of these about 20 are Europeans and only 1 is a Hindu. The number is at present above normal in consequence of the operations of the Oil Syndicate.

The only monopoly enjoyed in 'Arabistān by Europeans other than the British is one for antiquarian research, conferred on the French Government, in virtue of which the ruins of **Shūsh** have been excavated since 1897 by a French scientific mission under M. De Morgan. The principal non-British commercial concerns in 'Arabistān are the Russian Steam Navigation and Trading Company, who have offices at **Muhammareh**, and that of a Dutch merchant who is settled at **Nāsiri**.

Representation of foreign interests.—The British Government is represented in 'Arabistān by a Consul, whose functions are almost entirely commercial, and also by a Vice-Consul whose duties are exclusively political. The Consul is a member of the British Consular Service, his headquarters are at **Muhammareh**, and his jurisdiction extends to the whole province; the Vice-Consul belongs to the Indian Political Department, is stationed at **Nāsiri**, and is charged with all political matters

'ARABISTĀN (NORTHERN)

relating to 'Arabistān or to the country of the **Bakhtiyāris** and Western **Lurs**. The Consul is under the authority of His Majesty's Minister at Tehrān only, while the Vice-Consul receives orders from the Minister at Tehrān or from the Political Resident of the Indian Government at **Būshehr** according to the nature of the case.

The only other European power represented in 'Arabistān is Russia, who has a consular agent at **Nāsiri** in the person of the Dutch merchant already mentioned: this official is subordinate to the Russian Consul-General at **Būshehr**.

Northern 'Arabistān is a division of the Persian province elsewhere described as a whole under the title of **'Arabistān**; it is composed of the districts of **Dizfūl** and **Shūshtar** and includes also, in one sense, those of **'Aqīli** and **Rāmuz**. The boundaries of Northern 'Arabistān may be ascertained by referring to the articles on the districts mentioned, in which also the topography of the country is detailed; and for particulars of flora and fauna, agriculture, trade, communications, political constitution, and foreign interests and representation the reader is referred to the general article on **'Arabistān**. But the differences in physical geography, climate, population and internal administrative organisation between Northern and Southern 'Arabistān are so considerable as to demand separate treatment of the two divisions in these respects, and we accordingly proceed to deal with Northern 'Arabistān under heads corresponding to these subjects.

'ARABISTĀN
عربستان
(NORTHERN)

Physical geography.—For a few miles within the northern border the country slopes gently downwards from the foot hills of Western Luristān and the **Bakhtiyāri** country, and the soil contains shingle; elsewhere it is a level, rich, and stoneless alluvium.

The principal exception to this general rule is a system of ranges, collectively known as Khadhar خضر, which extend for about 60 miles in a north-westerly direction from the right bank of the **Karkheh** a little above Kūt Nahr Hashim to the left bank of the **Dawairīj**. A very low ridge of earth-covered hills called Kūh-i-Khāk كوه خاك is also deserving of mention: it begins 3 or 4 miles east of **Dizfūl** Town and, following a direction parallel to the hills of Western Luristān, reaches Jallakān on the **Kārūn**, becomes rocky, skirts the right bank of the **Kārūn** at a distance of 2 or 3 miles from it, and finally dies away in the plain a few miles to the west of **Shūshtar** Town. An important prolongation of this ridge begins on the left bank of the **Kārūn** River some two or three miles above **Shūshtar** Town, where it attains a height of nearly 1,000 feet and bears the name of Kūh-i-Fidalak فدلک. To these accidents of surface may be added the rocky ridge styled Umm-al-'Ayāi which crosses the **Diz** River obliquely at Kūt Bandar; as seen from that point it appears to run north-west and south-east and to be nowhere more than 100 feet high.

The principal rivers of Northern 'Arabistān are the upper **Karkheh,** the **Shāūr,** the **Diz,** and a portion of the **Kārūn** including the **Shatait** and **Gargar** branches of that river. The course of the **Diz** below Kūt 'Abdush Shāh is marked by an almost continuous belt of scrub with a sprinkling of trees, and there is some insignificant brushwood at places on the **Gargar** and **Shatait** and in the neighbourhood of Shāhābād on the **Dizfūl-Shūshtar** Road; elsewhere the country is bare of natural wood.

The preceding remarks apply only to the districts of **Dizfūl** and **Shūshtar**; the **Rāmuz** District lies detached from the others, with which it has physically little in common, and is fully described in a separate article under its own name. The **'Aqīli** district also forms the subject of a distinct article.

Climate and seasons.—The hot weather in Northern 'Arabistān is absolutely rainless, the cold weather as a rule moist and long; but even in winter protracted droughts may be experienced. The rains ordinarily begin at the end of October, the weather at the same time becoming cooler, and continue at intervals until the end of March; in 1905-06, however, hardly any rain fell before the spring. The rainfall decreases from north to south, **Dizfūl** Town receiving more rain than **Shūshtar**, and **Shūshtar** again more than places to the south of it. In ordinary years, though very high temperatures are registered by day, the nights, at least in the open country, are generally cool. The climate, except where it is marred by bad sanitation as in the towns of **Dizfūl** and **Shūshtar,** is not an unhealthy one.

Population.—Northern 'Arabistān, if we exclude the **Rāmuz** and **'Aqīli** Districts of which the population is described elsewhere, is inhabited chiefly by three races: first, an indigenous breed known as Dizfūlis and Shūshtaris; then certain Arab tribes; thirdly, various representatives of the great **Lur** family of clans.

The Dizfūlis and Shūshtaris, who are more particularly noticed in the articles upon the towns from which their names are drawn, appear to be of mixed origin, Persian blood however predominating in their veins; the dialects spoken by both are debased forms of Persian, yet differ to a certain extent; in appearance as well as in language these two classes somewhat resemble one another and are distinguishable from the natives of other parts of Persia.

Politically the most important of the Arab tribes are the **Kathīr,** who are settled upon the **Diz** and who are at present broken into two rival groups. Numerically the strongest of the Arabs are the Bait **Sa'ad,** who also have their headquarters upon the **Diz** and are intermingled, both geographically and politically, with the **Kathīr.** The only other considerable Arab tribe are the Āl **Khamīs** of the **Rāmuz** District.

The **Lurs** of Northern 'Arabistān are partly **Bakhtiyāris** and partly Western **Lurs**; regarding the distribution of both of these the articles under their names may be consulted.

Of the above tribes the Dizfūlis and Shūshtaris alone are never nomadic; they are not, however, confined to the larger towns, but are found besides in many of the country villages. The Arabs, except some of the **Kathīr** and the mixed Arabs in general of **Miyānāb,** are still Bedouin in their habits; but the **Kathīr,** besides owning livestock, cultivate wheat and barley. The **Lurs** are mostly nomadic, except a certain proportion of the **Bakhtiyāris** and Sagwands who occupy fixed villages. The nomadic **Bakhtiyāris** mostly encamp in winter between Āb Bīd and the **Diz** River, while the wandering Sagwands in the same season occupy the country to the west of **Dizfūl** Town as far south as **Shūsh,** but never cross to the east of the **Diz.**

Minor tribes of Northern 'Arabistān are the **Kurds,** who form the subject of a separate article, the Afshārs and the Gūndazlus. The Afshārs افشار appear to be found only in **Dizfūl** Town, where they are practically merged in the general body of Dizfūlis; and, though they now claim descent from Nādir Shāh, they are possibly identical with the Afshār Turks, from whom the **Ka'ab** are said to have conquered **Fallāhīyeh,** and even with the 'Aushārs عوشار of the **Hindiyan** District. The Gūndazlus کوندزلو, who occur at Būlaiti on the **Gargar** and 'Arab Hasan on the **Shatait,** are stated to be a branch of the Turkish tribe of Afshār, but there is no evidence that they ever spoke Turki and their present dialect appears to be Lurish.

The following is an estimate of the population and a statement of the tribes of Northern 'Arabistān, condensed from the corresponding paragraph in the general article on **'Arabistān** :—

District.	Number of settled inhabitants.	Characteristic or dominant settled tribes.	Number of nomadic inhabitants.	Characteristic or dominant nomadic tribes.	Total number of inhabitants.
'Aqīli	15,000	**Bakhtiyāris,** Western **Lurs,** Saiyids and Kangarpaz.	...	...	15,000
Dizfūl	61,500	Dizfūlis, Western **Lurs, Bakhtiyāris** and **Kathīr.**	15,000	Bait Sa'ad and Kathīr.	76,500
Rāmuz	12,000	Ahl-i-Rāmuz, Āl **Khamīs,** Eastern **Lurs** and **Bakhtiyāris.**	...	...	12,000
Shūshtar	35,000	Shūshtaris, **Bakhtiyāris** and Gūndazlus.	6,000	Bait Sa'ad and Kathīr.	41,000

From this abstract it would appear that the settled inhabitants of Northern 'Arabistān number about 123,500, and the nomadic about 21,000 souls: the total population is thus approximately 144,500 souls. In this account the very large numbers of **Lur** and **Bakhtiyāri** nomads who visit the district in the cold weather only are omitted, as they are temporary visitors and their numbers fluctuate.

The nomads of Northern 'Arabistān are avowedly predatory, and the same tendency, partly mitigated by civilisation, manifests itself among the settled population in the shape of grasping avarice. The people treat foreigners tolerably well, but only in expectation of rewards which shall be adequate according to their own exorbitant standards. The town populations are quarrelsome and turbulent, especially at **Shūshtar**; but it is probable that under an efficient Government they would, after the removal of their self-constituted leaders, subside into a litigious orderliness. Shi'ism is almost the only form of Islām here current, and in the towns it is of an extreme type in consequence of the numbers and influence of the local religious leaders. Customs vary from tribe to tribe, and the only observances common to all are those founded on religion, such as the Muharram and Rōzehkhwāni.

The weapons chiefly in use are rifles—almost entirely trade Martinis of English make—and long, rather heavy sticks carried by Arabs and

Lurs who cannot afford to buy rifles. Rifles are still scarce among the **Bakhtiyāris**, and there are not many in **Miyānāb**; but the townsmen of **Shūshtar** possess several hundreds. Cartridges are all of the solid-drawn brass pattern and are repeatedly recapped and reloaded by the owners or by tradesmen in the towns. Swords and daggers are rare. In the **Dizfūl** District the villages are usually fortified against sudden attack, but the towers are inferior to the solidly built Burjs of the North-Western Frontier of India.

General internal administration.—The province of Northern 'Arabistān is ruled by a Governor who is appointed by the central government at Tehrān; he is generally (from the situation of his headquarters) described as Governor of **Shūshtar**, but his proper official style is Hukmrān-i-'Arabistān حکمران عربستان. The position of this individual in regard to Southern **'Arabistān** is defined in the article on that division of the province. The **Rāmuz** District, though its revenue is paid into the **Shūshtar** treasury, is ruled in all respects by the **Bakhtiyāri** chiefs who hold it in farm; its administration is described in the article under its name, and the remarks which follow here do not apply to it. The position of the **'Aqīli** tract, attached to the **Shūshtar** District, is likewise somewhat ambiguous.

Until recently the telegraph masters at **Dizfūl** and **Shūshtar** were Deputy-Governors, each with the title of Nāib-al-Hukūmat, of the districts of which those towns are capitals; but these appointments have been abolished since the advent of the present Governor, the Sālār-i-Mukarram, in 1905. The Governor is now represented by a special agent at **Dizfūl**, and when he leaves **Shūshtar** upon tour a temporary agent is appointed at that place also. In the former régime the chief object of the Governor was to secure the goodwill of a few influential personages whose assistance might enable him to make a living, and normally the power which a Governor possessed did not extend to any distance from the towns of **Dizfūl** and **Shūshtar**, while even within the walls of those places it was subject to the competition of the Mujtahids, whose wishes carry immense weight with the populace. Outside the two principal towns matters were entirely controlled by the chiefs of the **Kathīr** Arabs and the **Bakhtiyāri** and Sagwand **Lurs**. To the state of matters thus outlined there will always be a tendency to revert; but for the present there is a partial improvement due to the personality of the new and vigorous Governor.*

Police and justice.—There are still no regular police in Northern 'Arabistān and arrests are made by the orderlies or Farrāshs of the Governor. Similarly there are no criminal or civil courts, but justice—or a travesty of it—is administered in the towns by the religious leaders, and in the country is dispensed by the local chiefs in their own jurisdictions.†

Revenue.—The collection of revenue, in so far as revenue is realisable, takes place through Mustaufis, of whom there are two, one for the **Shūshtar** and one for the **Dizfūl** District; these officials are strictly accountants and removable annually, but in practice they are more or less permanent collectors and farmers of the revenue with authority to sublet the demand in portions. Revenue defaulters are reported to the Governor, who takes such action against them as he finds convenient.

In the country the revenue consists of taxes on produce, not on land; in the towns it takes the shape of taxes on industries and taxes on shops; in each tract or area it is imposed as a lump sum, which appears to have been arbitrarily fixed at some time in the past, and it is subdivided and apportioned by local arrangement. The revenue proper is collected in cash, but in the **Dizfūl** District there is a surtax which is exigible in grain. In the **Dizfūl** District the annual demand amounts to 26,000 Tūmāns,‡ and in the **Shūshtar** District it is 20,000 Tūmāns; but in the latter district, at least until lately, not so much as half the nominal amount was actually recovered; the figures given include the urban as well as the rural assessments, also miscellaneous taxes on mills, indigo works, rafts, etc. In the **Dizfūl** District there is, in addition to the foregoing, an impost in kind of 600 Kharvārs of wheat and 600 Kharvārs of barley. Of the total annual revenue for the two districts, of 46,000 Tūmāns, no less than 4,725 Tūmāns is payable by the **Kathīr** tribe, who are partly under **Dizfūl** and partly under **Shūshtar**. More detailed in-

---

* The Sālār-i-Mukarram, while he has not broken with the Mujtahids, does not allow them to dictate to him, and he has completely subjugated the towns of Dizfūl and Shūshtar. Naturally he has not been able to effect so much in regard to the Arab and Lur tribes in the open country, but with them also he has made some progress. He maintains a sort of Border Police composed of **Bakhtiyāris** and Sagwand **Lurs**.

† The Sālār-i-Mukarram, who has the defects of his qualities, has now taken the administration of justice in the towns into his own hands and is energetically exploiting it as a source of private income (1906).

‡ A recent report (1907) gives the assessment of Dizfūl (town and villages) as 19,577 Tūmāns in cash, 1,150 Kharvārs of grain, and 700 Kharvārs of straw.

formation regarding urban revenue will be found in the article on **Shūshtar** Town. The annual revenue of the **Rāmuz** District is 15,000 Tūmāns or less, and of **'Aqīli** 12,150 Tūmāns.

Miscellaneous departments.—The Imperial Persian Customs have posts, each under the superintendence of a native Mudīr who is locally called Raīs Gumrukāt, in the towns of **Dizfūl** and **Shūshtar**; these are under the orders of the Director-General of 'Arabistān Customs, whose seat is at **Muhammareh**. At each of the towns mentioned there are also a post office and a treasury, both of which are now—as elsewhere throughout Persia – in charge of the Imperial Persian Customs; from the latter are disbursed all the salaries and pensions which are payable locally.

Southern 'Arabistān forms part of the Persian province of **'Arabistān**, to which a separate article in this Gazetteer is devoted, and greatly exceeds in extent the remainder to which the name of Northern **'Arabistān** has been given. The botany, zoology, agriculture, trade and communications of the country as a whole are discussed in the general article on **'Arabistān**, as are also the general political position and foreign relations and interests; here it is only necessary to refer to the boundaries by which Southern 'Arabistān is defined, and to give some account of its physical features, climate, inhabitants and government—the respects in which, chiefly, it differs from Northern **'Arabistān**.

Boundaries and divisions.—On the north, Southern 'Arabistān includes the village of **Band-i-Qīr**, which is situated in **Miyānāb** in the angle between the **Gargar** and the **Shatait** streams at their confluence; and from that neighbourhood its border runs westwards in such a manner as to take in the territories of the **'Anāfijeh** tribe upon the lower **Diz**, and the town of **Hawīzeh** together with the marshy district surrounding it. On the west, the limit of Southern 'Arabistān is the undemarcated frontier between Persia and Turkey which becomes definite only at the place where it reaches the left bank of the Shatt-al-'Arab at the larger Khaiyain creek opposite to the Turkish island of **Shamshamīyah**; from this point to the Persian Gulf the frontier, as fixed by the Treaty of Erzeroum in 1847, is the Shatt-al-'**Arab**. The whole southern boundary of the sub-province, from the mouth of the Shatt-al-'**Arab** eastwards as far as a point between **Shāh Abul Shāh** and **Dīlam**, is supplied by the waters of the Persian Gulf. The eastern limit is unfixed, but corresponds approximately with an imaginary curved line drawn from the extremity, upon the coast, of Southern 'Arabistān to the intersection of the 50th meridian of east longitude with the 31st parallel of north latitude: another imaginary line drawn from this intersection to the point immediately north of **Band-i-Qīr**, from which we started, completes the perimeter. The actual point where the boundary crosses the **Gargar** seems to be immediately below the village of Naghaishi, which is 8 miles upstream from **Band-i-Qīr**. In a few cases the course of the boundary is explained with greater precision in the articles on the component districts.

The regular districts included in Southern ' Arabistān are **Ahwāz, Fallāhīyeh, Hawīzeh, Hindiyān, Jarrāhi** and **Muhammareh**, all of which are separately described under their own names; and the village of **Ma'shūr** with its few square miles of dependent territory may, as not forming part of any of the others, be reckoned a separate district.

Physical geography.—The natural divisions of Southern 'Arabistān are nearly identical with the administrative districts specified in the last paragraph, each of which has a physical character peculiar to itself. The main features are the **Kārūn, Jarrāhi, Hindiyān** and **Karkheh** rivers; and the articles under these names, and under the names of the administrative districts, contain the bulk of the information available regarding the nature of the country.

Southern 'Arabistān consists, as a whole, of open alluvial plains which in some places are barren or thinly sprinkled with desert scrub, but in others are grassy and in spring diversified with patches of wheat and barley. In the **Fallāhīyeh** and **Ma'shūr** tracts there are, however, considerable swamps and saline tracts; and of such the south-eastern part of **Ahwāz** District also is not altogether free, while the neighbourhood of **Hawīzeh** is entirely a marsh. Belts of tamarisk, willow and other bushes fringe the banks of the rivers, but as a rule there are no large trees; in the valley of the **Hindiyān** River, however, are scattered Kunār trees of considerable size; and dense plantations of dates clothe the lower course of the **Jarrāhi** River and its canals, the upper part of the **Bahmanshīr**, the banks of the **Kārūn** from Qisbeh downwards, and the Persian shore of the Shatt-al-'**Arab**.

The generally level surface of the sub-province is broken chiefly in the **Hindiyān** District, in the east and north of which there is a considerable hilly tract, and in the **Ahwāz** District by the Kūh-i-Ahwāz. This last is a range running in a west-north-westerly and east-south-easterly direction which is pierced by the Kārūn River at Ahwāz Village : the hills are of red tertiary sandstone, oblique in stratification and jagged in outline, and they rise to a height of 200 feet above the plain. It is believed that the entire length of the Ahwāz range is about 30 miles and that the **Kārūn** divides it into two almost equal parts : the portion to the east of the **Kārūn** is interrupted, however, at 5 miles from the river by a gap or Thinīyeh and the part east of this gap is distinguished by the name of Jabal Musarbeh.* Another group of hills in the **Ahwāz** District, known as Banneh, is perhaps an isolated continuation of the Kūh-i-Ahwāz—or rather of Jabal Musarbeh—but is separated from the latter by an interval of at least 10 miles ; and it is possible that the low hills through which the **Jarrāhi** River breaks between the **Rāmuz** and **Jarrāhi** Districts are a sort of link between the hills of the **Ahwāz** and those of the **Hindiyān** District.

Climate and seasons.—The temperature at **Muhammareh** Town ranges, in the course of the year, from 32° to 115° F. on shore, and from 27° to 120° F.—the last under double awnings—on board ship. The usual daily range of temperature on shore in July is from 85° to 110° F., and in January from 40° to 57°. In January 1906 the temperature in the open near **Muhammareh** is said to have dropped on one occasion to 24° F.

Rain may fall at any time between the middle of October and the middle of May, but the principal rains generally occur at the end of December or in January, and heavy local showers are usual about the time of the vernal equinox. The total annual rainfall is, however, insignificant.

About the middle of May a dry north-west wind generally blows for 10 days and is followed by a calm of similar duration before the setting in of the Bārih or great north-wester, which lasts for about 40 days. After the Bārih come, as a rule, 10 days of light southerly breezes ; and thereafter hot winds from the north-west and damp winds from the south-east blow alternately till the end of August.

The summer heat in the plains of Southern 'Arabistān is intense, but (except in the marshes) dry and not unhealthy; and from the middle of October to the end of April the climate is pleasant. Such is the ordinary, but not invariable, course of the seasons.

---

* Properly speaking the part of the range to the west of the river is not " Kūh-i-Ahwāz." It seems to be sometimes called Manyūr (but see article **Hawīzeh** District).

Inhabitants.—The following is an estimate of the population and a statement of the tribes of Southern 'Arabistān, condensed from the corresponding paragraph in the general article on **'Arabistān** :—

District.	Number of settled inhabitants.	Characteristic or dominant settled tribes.	Number of nomadic inhabitants.	Characteristic or dominant nomadic tribes.	Total number of inhabitants.
Ahwāz	13,000	Bāwiyeh, Ka'ab and Āl Bū Kurd.	37,930	Bāwiyeh, 'Anāfijeh and Hamaid.	50,930
Fallāhīyeh	45,000	Ka'ab.	Some.	...	45,000
Hawīzeh	5,000	Ahl-al-Kūt, Ahl-al-Juruf and Nais.	60,250	Bani Turuf, Bani Sāleh, Bani Tamīm (II) and 'Ikrish.	65,250
Hindiyān	14,000	Qanawāti.	500	Sharīfāt.	14,500
Jarrāhi	4,000	Ka'ab.	Some.	...	4,000
Ma'shūr	1,500	Bandari and Qanawāti.	Do.	...	1,500
Muhammareh	23,000	Muhaisin and Ka'ah.	Do.	...	23,000

From this abstract it would appear that the settled inhabitants of Southern 'Arabistān number about 105,500 and the nomadic about 98,680 souls: the total population is thus approximately 204,180 persons.

The great dominant tribes of Southern 'Arabistān are the **Muhaisin** and the **Ka'ab**—the former politically, the latter numerically: of these the **Muhaisin** with their centre at **Muhammareh** Town should certainly, and the **Ka'ab** whose focus is **Fallāhīyeh** Town should probably, be regarded as settled. The only other sedentary tribe of importance is the **Qanawāti** in the **Hindiyān** District and at **Mā'shūr**. The principal nomad tribes are the Bani **Turuf**, Bani **Sāleh** and Bani **Tamīm** (II) all of the **Hawīzeh** District, and the **Bāwīyeh** who are almost confined to the district of **Ahwāz** : of less importance, but yet substantial nomad tribes, are the **Hamaid** between the **Ahwāz** District and the **Bakhtiyārī** hills, the **'Ikrish** on the border of the **Ahwāz** and **Hawīzeh** Districts, the **'Anāfijeh** at the frontier between **Ahwāz** and **Dizfūl**, the **Āl Khamīs** (semi-settled) in the **Rāmuz** District, and the **Hardān** in the district of **Ahwāz**. The institutions and characters of these tribes are dealt with from a general point of view in the article on **'Arabistān** and detailed information will be found in the separate articles upon particular tribes. In religion all are Shi'ahs.

The fighting strength of Southern 'Arabistān was calculated in 1902 at 54,500 men ; this estimate was founded partly on the tribal books, but it is in remarkable accord with the figure given above for total population, which was obtained by entirely different methods. The principal arm of the fighting man is here the Martini carbine ; of these there are at least 20,000, and probably more, within the limits of the sub-province, and cartridges for the same are refilled locally with native powder. Percussion guns, generally fowling-pieces, are also used. In the neighbourhood of **Muhammareh** Town arms are not generally carried by private persons except on journeys.

General internal administration.—The whole of Southern 'Arabistan is governed by the hereditary **Muhaisin** Shaikh of **Muhammareh***— now Khaz'al Khān, Sardār Arfa', Mu'izz-as-Saltaneh ارفع معزّ السلطنه خزعل خان سردار—who bears the title of Governor of the Shatt-al-**'Arab** and **Kārūn**, and also of Sarhadd-dār سرحدّدار or Warden of the Marches. The rule of the present Shaikh is personal and extremely stringent, but, while his severity inspires awe, his justice commands respect, and tribal opinion is fully consulted by him through tribal councils. He has two principal advisers or ministers : the first is Hāji Muhammad 'Ali, a Persian merchant of Behbehāni family, but settled at **Muhammareh**, whom he utilises in his affairs generally and in negotiations with the Persian Government or with communities and persons not Arab ; the other is Mīrza Hamzah, an Arab of **Hillah**, who generally resides at **Basrah** but is entrusted by the Shaikh with much of his Arab

---

* The political position and extent of jurisdiction of the Shaikh are explained by Major Burton and Captain Lorimer in the proceedings of the Government of India (Political) for June 1904, January 1905, and August 1905. His resources are described in the Proceedings for June 1900. For the principles of succession to the Shaikhship, see the Government of India's Foreign Proceedings for November 1898.

business. The relations of the Shaikh and his two advisers among themselves are not well understood, and it is doubtful to which of the three the ability and determination that have distinguished the present Shaikh's policy since his accession should in the main be ascribed.

The following table explains the connection of the Shaikh with the various districts for the government of which he is responsible:—

District.	Annual amount payable by the Shaikh as farm.	From whom farmed and nature of farm.	Representatives of the Shaikh in the district.
Ahwāz	See next column.	Chiefly from the Persian Government, to whom apparently nothing is paid; but the Nizām-as-Saltaneh receives 3,000 Tūmāns a year from the Shaikh on account of the part to the west of the Kārūn, the whole of which he claims as his property. The Shaikh is said to obtain about 6,000 Tūmāns a year as revenue from the tribes of the district.	A Deputy-Governor at Nāsiri, also agents with local connections at Kūt-an-Naddāfīyeh Kabīr, Muzaffari and Umm-at-Tamair, all on the Kārūn River.
Fallāhīyeh	Do.	From the Persian Government, who have apparently granted this district to the Shaikh free of payment, in compensation for the transfer to the Imperial Customs of the customs at Muhammareh. The realisations are said to amount to 14,500 Tūmāns per annum.	An agent, who is a local man, at Fallāhīyeh Town.
Hawīzeh	30,000 Tūmāns.	From the Persian Governor of Northern 'Arabistān.	A Deputy-Governor at Hawīzeh Town, who is a member of the old ruling family of Hawīzeh.
Hindiyān	23,000 Tūmāns.	...	Agents at Hindiyān Village and Dih Mulla, who are perhaps subordinate to the Shaikh's agent at Ma'shūr.

'ARABISTĀN (SOUTHERN)

District.	Annual amount payable by the Shaikh as farm.	From whom farmed and nature of farm.	Representatives of the Shaikh in the district.
Jarrāhi	14,000 Tūmāns.	From the Nizām-us-Sltaneh and the Mushīr-nd-Daulah who are jointly owners.	The Shaikh's agent at Ma'shūr visits Khafābād when necessary.
Ma'shūr,	...	Do. do.	An agent at Ma'shūr who is also responsible for the Jarrāhi District and apparently supervises the agents in the Hindiyān District.
Muhammareh	20,000 Tūmāns.	From the Persian Government.	Agents at Ruvais, Manyūhi and Qasbat Nassār on 'Abbādān Island.

The incompleteness of the table is due to the difficulty of obtaining reliable information locally in matters of the kind.* It should be added that the Shaikh has a joint interest with the **Bakhtiyāri** Khāns in part of the **Behbehān** sub-province, which is outside the limits of 'Arabistān, and that he maintains an agent at Cham Zaidān to watch his interests in that quarter. The Shaikh, it may be mentioned, is a trader on a large scale in dates and grain and keeps his own accounts. He also owns large properties on the Turkish side of the Shatt-al-'Arab and has a large private income which he uses to strengthen his administrative position and push his political interests.

In describing the relations of the Shaikh with the districts under his charge no mention has yet been made of the local chiefs through whom, and not through the special agents, the work of executive Government is carried on.

These headmen, generally called Qilīds قليد or Qilaits قليت, are the real medium of communication with the people: the most important of the class are two Shaikhs of the **Ka'ab** through whom the **Fallāhīyeh** District is managed. The Qilīds are as a rule appointed by the Shaikh of **Muhammareh** from the family in each tribe in which the post is hereditary, and by him also they may be removed; such appointments and removals, however, are not usually made without consultation of other headmen. The Shaikh of **Muhammareh** seldom or never goes on tour in

* According to a recent report, based on information supplied by the Mustaufi, the Shaikh of Muhammareh pays 71,670 Tūmāns a year for the **Ahwāz, Fallāhīyeh, Hawīzeh, Hindiyān Jarrahi, Ma'shūr** and **Muhammareh** districts (1907).

the districts, but in winter he frequently camps at Muzaffari or some other place on the **Kārūn** in order to attend to the affairs of the **Bāwīyeh** and Bani **Turuf** tribes.

Military forces.—Besides the whole force of tribal levies which is at his disposal, the Shaikh of **Muhammareh** maintains a corps of Makrāni and Arab mercenaries, called Balūch-i-Shāh بلوچ شاه, which is about 400 strong and furnishes guards for **Muhammareh** Town, the customs houses, and the Shaikh's own residences at **Failīyeh** and elsewhere. The expenditure on this corps is chargeable to the Persian Government and is adjusted by means of deductions from the annual revenue which is payable by the Shaikh into the Persian Treasury. In addition to the tribal levies and the Balūch-i-Shāh, there is a sort of militia in character intermediate between the two others, of uncertain strength, and known as the Ghulāms غلام: it consists partly of the Shaikh's Mamlūks—who are either negro slaves or half-caste or "white" (*i.e.* Arab) serfs from the neighbourhood of **Basrah**—and partly of villagers on whose services the Shaikh has some special claim: the peasant Ghulāms are paid by assignments of dates from the Shaikh's share of the crop and receive them regularly whether they are employed or not. The only military details under the direct control of the Persian Government in Southern 'Arabistān are a Nāib or lieutenant and a few men of the Persian Artillery and a Qurkhānehchi or captain in the Ordnance Department; these are stationed at **Muhammareh** Town and receive their orders from the officer commanding the artillery in the **'Arabistān** province.

Police and justice.—There is no separate police force, and crime is dealt with by the Shaikh through the civil and military agencies already described above. The official at **Muhammareh** Town known as the Nāib-al-Hukūmeh is, however, virtually a head of police. The criminal procedure is generally severe. Persons accused of theft, especially if they belong to the town population, are often beaten to make them confess; and in serious cases, such as piracy, the Shaikh seldom requires witnesses but proceeds upon information obtained by means best known to himself.

In civil cases affecting tribesmen only tribal custom is followed, and that to the exclusion of ecclesiastical law; such suits are decided by oaths which no tribesman can take falsely, as to do so would be treason to the tribe. Commercial cases are settled by the Shaikh's Persian adviser, Hāji Muhammad 'Ali already mentioned, whom the Persian Government have recognised as Rais-ut-Tujjār or official head of the mercantile community.

'ARAQI 165

Revenue.—The rates and character of agricultural and other taxation vary from one part of the sub-province to another. They are described in the separate articles upon the component districts. Small Mahailahs ascending the **Kārūn** pay a toll of 2 Qrāns in the **Haffār** reach and an additional 2 Qrāns on arrival at **Nāsiri**; in the case of large Mahailahs these rates are doubled. Every Mahailah plying on the river is required to bring down gratis, twice in the year, a load of firewood for the Shaikh of **Muhammareh**.

Miscellaneous departments.—Apart from Telegraphs, which are noticed in the general article on **'Arabistān,** the principal departments are Customs, Posts and Treasuries: of these the management is at present combined in the hands of a Belgian Director-General of Customs in **'Arabistān**. This official is nominally subordinate—except in departmental matters—to the Shaikh of **Muhammareh** and enjoys his support, which has been purchased by concessions on the part of the Persian Government: without the co-operation of the Shaikh the Customs officials would be helpless. Custom houses exist at **Muhammareh** Town, **Nāsiri, Buziyeh, Ma'shūr** and **Hindiyān** Village, and post offices at these places and at **Fallāhīyeh** Town. The only treasury in the sub-province is at **Muhammareh** Town. The position of the Kārguzār or representative of the Persian Foreign Office at **Muhammareh** Town is explained in the general article on **'Arabistān**.

'ARAD
عراد

An old disused name for the whole of **Muharraq** Island in **Bahrain**; it is now applied only to one of the villages which are described in the table in the article on **Mūharraq** Island.

'ARĀQI
عراقي

A village in the **Dhāhirah** District of the **'Omān** Sultanate, situated in a plain on the right bank of Wādi **Sanaisal** about 2 miles above **'Ibri** and between Ghabbi and Bait-al-'Ainain, both of which it adjoins. The place consists of about 100 houses of **'Abriyīn**, 90 of Bani Rāshid, and 35 of **Balūchis**: it derives its importance from the existence of a fort which came into the possession of the Sultān of **'Omān** in 1904 and constitutes his only foot-hold in the district of **Dhāhirah**. A Wāli resides at 'Arāqi on the part of the Sultān and about $100 is collected annually as Zakāt and locally expended. There are about 150 camels, 20 horses, 200 donkeys, 300 cattle, 500 sheep and goats and 3,000 date palms.

ĀRIDH عارض DISTRICT

The central and from every point of view the most important district of the Wahhābi dominions, of which the capital, **Riyādh**, is situated within its borders.

Boundaries and extent.—'Āridh reaches westwards from the **Dahánah** desert to the principal range of Jabal **Tuwaiq** and even to some distance beyond it; on the north it is separated from the district of **Sadair** by a hollow called 'Ajsh عجش, and on the south from the districts of **Hautah** and **Harīq** by the mountainous mass of Jabal 'Alaiyah. The only data for determining the dimensions of the 'Āridh district are those deducible from the information about routes which is contained in the articles on **Najd** and **Dhrumah** and from the facts that are known about Wādi Hanīfah. From these it would appear that the district, to neglect a portion on the north-east which lies outside the **Tuwaiq** system and should not perhaps be reckoned to 'Āridh, measures about 80 miles from north to south and the same from east to west.

Physical features and geographical divisions.—The physical conformation of the district is by no means simple. The chief range of Jabal **Tuwaiq** traverses it, as we have seen, from north to south towards its western end and may be used as a base from which to describe the district. A subsidiary range belonging to the **Tuwaiq** system leaves the principal range in the **Sadair** district and, gradually inclining away from it in a south-easterly direction, ends somewhere between **Riyādh** and the **Dahánah** desert. Part of 'Āridh, that which was left out of account in estimating the extent of the district, lies to the north-east of this subsidiary range on the side towards the **Dahánah**; and another portion, containing numerous villages, is included between the lesser and the greater range. Towards the south end of the district Wādi **Hanīfah** takes its rise in the eastern slopes of the main **Tuwaiq** range and, travelling eastwards with a southerly inclination, leaves 'Āridh by the south-eastern corner. Still further south, but on the western side of Jabal

Tuwaiq, is the plain of **Dhrumah** from which a valley descends eastwards, piercing Jabal **Tuwaiq** on its way, to join Wādi **Hanīfah** in its lower course. Between Wādi **Hanīfah** and **Dhrumah**, Jabal **Tuwaiq** appears to extend considerably further eastwards than it does in the north.

The recognised geographical divisions of the 'Āridh District are not, unfortunately, altogether determined by the physical features—in themselves sufficiently perplexing—which have just been described. It has been possible to describe the southern parts of the district under the titles Wādi **Hanīfah** and **Dhrumah** without in any way violating native usage; but it is more difficult to know how to deal with the remainder to the north of Wādi **Hanīfah** which consists of two hill ranges, inclined towards one another at their northern ends, and of three plains, one of which is between the ranges while the others lie outside them on the extreme east and extreme west.

The plain on the extreme east is named ' Urmah عرمه. It is bounded on the south-west by the subsidiary range already mentioned, and on the north-east by the **Dahánah** desert; its breadth between the two is 1½ days' journey with laden camels or about 45 miles. On the north 'Urmah is said to reach to a locality called Batainiyāt بطينيات and it extends far enough south and east to include the wells of Abu Jifān on the route between **Hofūf** and **Riyādh**. A dry water-course, commencing in the subsidiary range and named Thamāmah ثمامه, intersects the plain from south-west to north-east and is eventually lost in the **Dahánah** desert; to the south of it, in a parallel dry torrent bed, are two groups of wells called Rumāh رماح and Rumhīyah رميحه, of which the latter is about 8 miles nearer to the source of the torrent than the former. In the neighbourhood of these wells is a customary halting place on the route from **Kuwait** to **Riyādh**; **Riyādh** lies about 70 miles or two long camel marches to the south-south-west of Rumāh, and on the way thither the village of Banbān is either passed through or left some distance to the right. Also to the south of Thamāmah another torrent bed called Misājidi مساجدي, which has its rise in the same hills, crosses the plain in a similar direction and is also lost in the **Dahánah**. The plain of 'Urmah is itself stony and barren and broken up into low hillocks, some of which are flat and some conical, with intervening hollows.

The remainder of the district, consisting of the principal chain of Jabal **Tuwaiq** north of Wādi **Hanīfah** together with the plains on the east and west of it, is sometimes included in the term Mahmal محمل, to which however certain authorities would assign a much more restricted meaning. The village topography of Mahmal will be found in a table at the end of this article; at present we are only concerned with its more outstanding physical features. The true centre of Mahmal is a large depression named Khafs خفص, in which rain water is said to collect and stagnate for as much as a year together; it lies between the main range of **Tuwaiq** and the subsidiary range, and it is fed by the drainage, after rain, of valleys coming down from both. The southernmost and most important of the valleys on the western side of Khafs is Wādi Wutar وتر which comes down from Sidūs; at Salbūkh, perhaps 20 miles below that place, it receives on its left bank a tributary coming down from Qasr Harqān and Ghiyānah; and before reaching Khafs it is joined, again on the left, by the Abu Kithādah ابو كثادة torrent bed of which the head is near Haraimlah, while Malham is situated on its middle course. Wādi Wutar is a deepish, well-defined valley, and between Sidūs and Salbūkh it cuts through a mass of hills: in its lower course it contains, at least at times, a certain quantity of running water. North of Wādi Wutar another hollow carrying the drainage of Uqalah, Diqail and Mahrīqah finds its way to Khafs. The outlying part of **Tuwaiq** on the east side of Khafs appears to overlook the Khafs basin from a short distance and to send down to it no less than 6 hollows of which the names, in order from north to south, are Khanāsar خناصر, Hifnat-at-Tairi حفنة الطيري, Tauqi طوقي, Hamāmah حمامة, Hamaiyim حميّم and Thamāmah ثمامة; of these the last named has its origin in the same part of the range as the torrent similarly named which goes down to the 'Urmah plain upon the opposite side. This eastern range of **Tuwaiq** rises less than 1,000 feet above 'Urmah, and it is pierced by a remarkable gap, through which runs the route between **Kuwait** and Sidūs.

Somewhat further north than Khafs and the drainage hollows connected with it is a depression, on which are situated the three villages of Safurrah and further down the hamlet of Hasi; its course is at first north and then north-east and it ends a short distance to the east of Hasi at a hill named Khātilah خاتلة, which is described as standing solitary in the desert like a ship at sea. This hill is said to be about the same height as Jabal **Sanām** near **Safwān**, and on the east side of it are wells, 4 fathoms deep, known as Qulbān-al-Khātilah قلبان الخاتلة. Beyond this hollow of Safurrah and Hasi, but rather perhaps to the **west** than to the north of it, are two others which convey the drainage of Bīr and Thādiq away in a direction which has not been exactly ascertained but is probably northerly.

Another interesting feature of Mahmal that calls for notice is a depression furrowing the plateau (apparently styled Sad-hah سدحة) between Sidūs and 'Ayainah on Wādi **Hanīfah**; this hollow is named Ghāllah غالة, it begins a mile or two from Sidūs, and it eventually enters Wādi **Hanīfah** just above the village of Jabailah. At about 10 miles from Sidūs Ghāllah is blocked by a masonry dam forming a reservoir called Haqar حقر which is close to the road from Sidūs to 'Ayainah upon its north-east side; when this reservoir is filled by rain it is expected that a spring at 'Ayainah, called 'Ayainat Bin-Mu'-ammar عيينة بن معمر, will begin to flow. Part of the rest of the country between Wādi Wutar and Wādi **Hanīfah** drains to Banbān and not to Khafs.

It remains to mention that, on the western side of Jabal **Tuwaiq**, a hollow descending from the neighbourhood of Haraimlah passes Barrah and ends in the swamp of Mufidh in the **Washam** district; while another, also from the direction of Haraimlah, runs down to **Washam** by way of Rghabah. The western Haisīyah, which is to the south of the valleys just mentioned, is described in the article on Jabal **Tuwaiq**.

Inhabitants.—The 'Urmah subdivision of the 'Āridh district contains no settled inhabitants: from a consideration of the appropriate articles it will appear that the fixed population of Mahmal is about 12,500, of Wādi **Hanīfah** (inclusive of **Riyādh**) about 15,000, and of **Dhrumah** and its dependencies about 2,500 souls, making up a non-Bedouin total for 'Āridh of some 30,000 persons. In the whole district, **Riyādh** town being left out of consideration, the predominant tribe of respectable lineage appear to be the **Dawāsir**, with about 3,600 souls, who are particularly strong in Mahmal; they are followed by the **Sabai'** and the Bani **Tamīm** with about 2,600 persons each, and by the **'Anizah** and **'Ataibah**, whose numbers are about 2,000 and 1,000, respectively; after these come the **Fadhūl** and **Qahtān**, and after these again the Bani **Hājir, Sahūl, Mutair, 'Āid, Harb** and Bani **Khālid** whose numbers are extremely small. More numerous than any single Arab tribe, however, are the low caste cultivators, generally grouped together under the common designation of Bani **Khadhīr**, who appear in this district to number nearly 6,000 persons. The people of 'Āridh are restless and not unwarlike and their district is the headquarters of Wahhābism.

The ordinary Bedouins of 'Āridh are **Sabai'**, **Sahūl** and, in a minor degree, **Dawāsir**; but nomads of the **Harb**, **'Ataibah** and **Qahtān** and a few **Mutair** also visit the district.

Agriculture and resources.—The character of agriculture in 'Āridh will be understood on reference to the village lists of its various divisions, from which it will be seen that the people depend chiefly on the cultivation of dates, wheat, barley, millet, melons and lucerne, all of which are grown for the most part by irrigation from wells. There are also, in most places, fruit trees of the various sorts met with in **Najd**, especially citrons, limes, pomegranates, figs and vines; vegetables also are raised in considerable variety. A large part of the district consists of pastoral uplands or downs, and the ordinary livestock of **Najd** are owned, in the usual proportions, by most villages. The flocks and herds graze on the lower levels in winter and the hill grass is reserved for consumption in summer and autumn.

Communications.—The routes which traverse the **'Āridh** District are described in the article on **Najd**.

Administration.—The political importance of the district is proved by the fact that, despite political convulsions and foreign wars, one of its towns has always remained the capital of the Wahhābi dominions. The revenue of 'Āridh, then mostly collected in kind, was valued in 1865 at $50,000; at the present time the revenue from dates is estimated at $12,000 and that from cereals at $4,000 only. The decrease is said to be due to the damage done by both sides during the recent wars in **Najd**.

Topography.—The villages of Wādi **Hanīfah** and of the **Dhrumah** neighbourhood are tabulated in the separate articles on those subdivisions of the district: those of the remaining Mahmal tract are as follow:—

Name.	Position.	Houses and inhabitants.	REMARKS.
'Awainidh عوينذ	About 3 miles east of Barrah on the way to Riyādh.	A Qasr containing 15 houses of **Sabai'** of the Āl Khanaizān section.	Close to 'Awainidh is a hill called Jabal Abuz Zidd جبل ابو الزّد. There are a few dates and some cultivation of wheat. Wells are 2 to 3 fathoms deep: the water is rather bitter.

Name.	Position.	Houses and inhabitants.	Remarks.
Banbān بنبان	One and a half days by caravan (say 45 miles) north by east of Riyādh and about midway between the chief range of Tuwaiq and its eastern offshoot.	20 houses, viz., 5 of 'Ataibah and 15 of inferior tribes. To these are added about 5 houses of inferior tribes from Dara'īyah when there is scarcity of water at that place.	There are no date palms, but wheat, barley, millet, musk melons and water melons are grown. The wells vary in depth from 4 to 12 fathoms. Good grass grows in the neighbourhood and the place is a favourite camping ground of Bedouins, especially of Sabai'.
Barrah برة	On the western side of the chief range of Tuwaiq about midway between Dara'īyah and Shaqrah and about 35 miles north-west of Dhrumah.	150 mud houses, of Sabai', Sahūl, 'Ataibah and 'Anizah.	There are some date palms; and citrons, pomegranates, musk melons, water melons, barley, wheat, millet and lucerne are grown. The date crop is not sufficient for the support of the inhabitants who in the hot weather disperse to the larger villages of 'Āridh. The wells of Barrah are 6 to 7 fathoms deep. There are about 40 camels and 100 cattle besides sheep and goats.
Bīr بير	Probably about 10 miles north-west of Haraimlah.	About 200 houses, viz., 160 of Dawāsir of the Badrāni section, 4 of Fadhūl and 40 of other tribes.	On the west side of the village the wells are 8 fathoms deep, and on the east 6 fathoms. There are many dates; and wheat, barley, lucerne and millet are grown: fruit trees are not numerous and there are no vines.
Diqail دقيل	Adjoins Dqalah, apparently on the south-east.	In summer there are about half-a-dozen cultivators from Dqalah who sleep armed; in winter no one spends the night at Diqail for fear of robbers.	Date palms number about 300; there are no other fruit trees. The other crops are the same as at Dqalah, except that lucerne is not grown. The wells are 3 fathoms deep.

Name.	Position.	Houses and inhabitants.	Remarks.
Dqalah دقله	Immediately under the chief range of Jabal **Tuwaiq** on its eastern side, in the extreme north of the district.	40 houses of **Dawāsir**.	There are about 2,000 date palms, besides citron and fig trees. Crops are barley, wheat, millet, lucerne, musk melons and water melons, irrigated from wells 5 fathoms deep.
Ghiyānah غيانه	Perhaps 3 miles west of albūkh on a drainage hollow which joins Wādi Wutar just above Salbūkh.	20 houses of **Sabai'**.	The date groves contain about 200 trees. Wheat, barley, millet and lucerne are cultivated. Water stands at 3 fathoms ordinarily, but in time of drought the wells dry up.
Haraimlah حريمله	About 20 miles south of Thādiq and 12 miles north-north-west of Sidūs, at the head of the Abu Kitlalah depression which drains by Malham to Wādi Wutar. Haraimlah is apparently situated almost on the main watershed of Jabal **Tuwaiq**, for torrents descend from its vicinity both westwards and eastwards.	About 465 houses, viz., 20 of **'Āid**, 150 of **'Anizah**, 25 of **Bani Hājir**, 35 of **Sabai'**, 70 of **Bani Tamīm**, and 150 of inferior tribes.	Haraimlah blocks the southern end of a hollow which extends half a day's journey in Jabal **Tuwaiq** in the direction of Thādiq. A large fort built by the Egyptians during their occupation stands on rising ground inside the town and there is a small bazaar. Haraimlah is surrounded by date plantations, and the other fruit trees and usual crops of the 'Āridh district are grown and flourish. Irrigation is from numerous wells of good water, 15 fathoms deep or probably less. The present Amīr is Nāsir-al-'Amrāni appointed by Ibn Sa'ūd; he is not a native of the place. Haraimlah is two days by caravan from **Riyādh** and 9 from **'Anaizah** in Qasīm. It is said to have been the birth place of Muhammad-bin-'Abdul Wahhāb, the founder of the Wahhābi sect.

'ĀRIDH DISTRICT

Name.	Position.	Houses and inhabitants.	Remarks.
Ḥarqān (Qaṣr) قصر حرقان	Perhaps 3 miles west of Ghiyānah, at the head of a drainage hollow which goes down by Ghiyānah to Wādi Wutar at Salbūkh.	Visited, in the seasons of agriculture only, by as many as 20 families of cultivators from Malham, Jarīnah and Haraimlah.	There are no dates and very little water: cultivation is by rainfall. Some wheat and barley and (in good years) millet are grown.
Ḥasi حسي	Apparently a few miles to the north of Dqalah, on a line of drainage coming down from Safurrah.	A Qasr containing 4 families of Dawāsir of the Widā'īn division.	Inhabited all the year round.
Ḥizwah حزوة	Adjoins Sidūs or forms part of it.	About 25 houses, viz, 6 of Sabai', 10 of Bani Tamīm and 8 of inferior tribes.	The agriculture is the same as that of Sidūs.
Jarīnah جرينه or Qarīnah قرينه	Apparently between Haraimlah and Malham, considerably nearer to the former.	240 houses, viz., 160 of Dawāsir, 40 of Fadhūl and 40 of inferior tribes.	There are many dates and all the other fruit trees and usual crops of the district. Water stands in the wells ordinarily at 8 fathoms, but falls in time of drought to 18.
Maḥrīqah محرقة	A few miles below Dqalah, on the drainage hollow which runs thence to Khafs; it is just below the main range of Tuwaiq on the east side.	35 houses, viz., 20 of Bani Tamīm and 15 of Fadhūl.	Date palms number 3,000 and there are also citrons, grapes and figs. Crops are barley, wheat water melons and musk melons, but lucerne is not cultivated. Irrigation is from wells, 5 fathoms deep, which become considerably deeper in time of drought.

Name.	Position.	Houses and inhabitants.	Remarks.
Malham ملهم	At the foot of the chief range of Jabal Tuwaiq on its east side probably about 15 miles north-east of Haraimlah.	About 300 mud houses, viz., 6 of **Dawāsir**, 20 of **Fadhūl**, 30 of '**Anizah** of the Harqān section, 8 of **Sabai'** of the Āl Bin Rāshid section, 4 of Bani **Khālid** of the Qamuāz section, 3 of **Sahūl** of the Āl Sulaimān section; also 150 houses of mixed tribes, and the following (included under the common denomination of Bani **Khadhīr**, or inferior tribes) Hamadāt 20, Muhārib 30, Had-hūd 5, Marsbūd 10.	The date groves are considerable and grapes, figs and pomegranates grow, but not in profusion. The supply of water for irrigation and other purposes is from wells which vary in depth, according to rainfall, between 8 and 18 fathoms. Water lifts are worked by camels, buffaloes and donkeys. The cultivated area is described as about 8 times that of **Jahrah** in **Kuwait** territory. The Imārat or headship of the village belongs to the **Fadhūl** and was held till 1905 by Hasan-bin-'Abdullah, a very aged man, who then on account of the troubled state of the country resigned in favour of his nephew 'Abdullah-bin-'Abdul 'Azīz, aged 60.
Rghabah رغبة	On the western side of the chief range of Tuwaiq, about 18 miles east by north of Tharmidah in **Washam**.	About 315 houses, viz., 100 of '**Ataibah**, 100 of **Sabai'**. 15 of **Harb** and 100 of inferior tribes.	Date trees are numerous and the ordinary crops of 'Āridh are all grown. Water in the wells stands ordinarily at 8 fathoms.

Name.	Position.	Houses and inhabitants.	Remarks.
Salbūkh ملبوخ	Apparently near the north-western bank of Wādi Wutar a little below the point where the drainage of Ghiyānah joins it, and perhaps 15 to 20 miles north-east of Sidūs. The main range of Jabal Tuwaiq rises immediately to the west of this village.	35 houses, *viz.*, 20 of Sabai' and 15 of inferior tribes.	Date trees are numerous and there is abundance of water, which does not fail even in the driest years. Citrons, musk melons water melons, wheat, barley and millet are all grown.
Sidūs سدوس	About 12 miles south-south-east of Haraimlah and 15 west-north-west of 'Ayainah in Wādi Hanīfah, at the head of Wādi Wutar. To the east of the village is a plateau, 300 feet higher, which the route to Riyādh ascends by a narrow but not difficult path. The main range of Jabal Tuwaiq passes a little to the west of this place.	160 houses, *viz.*, 80 of Bani Tamīm of the Bin Mu'ammar section, 20 of Sabai' and 60 of inferior tribes. There are two quarters, an upper and a lower, of which the latter is the older but is now half abandoned on account of floods. The people in 1865 were civil and quiet, but they seemed poor and had a dingy, unwholesome appearance not commonly characteristic of an agricultural community.	The hamlets forming the village are neat and pleasant in appearance, with large date groves and enclosed patches of cultivation. There are good wells for irrigation and a fine flow of fresh water; but cattle in 1865 were few and poor. The usual fruits and cereals are grown and the ordinary domestic animals are kept. In 1865 a small fort stood in the middle of the village, from the vicinity of which a good view could be obtained westwards across the Mahmal plain in the direction of Jabal Tuwaiq. Near the fort was a mound, formed by the débris of considerable buildings, on which stood an elegant stone column 3 feet in diameter and, though broken, still 20 feet high with two crosses engraved on the shaft.*

* For a sketch of this column and further details of the village, see Pelly's *Report on a Journey to the Wahabee Capital*. According to a recent report the pillar fell (or was dismantled by order of the Wahhābi Amīr) soon after Colonel Pelly's visit, but has since been re-erected.

Name.	Position.	Houses and inhabitants.	Remarks.
Sufurrah صفرّة	In the northern part of the district, probably several miles to the south-east of Thādiq. It consists of 3 villages disposed in order from south to north upon the same drainage hollow, viz., 'Aliya علیا Wastah وسطه and Siflah سفله Some of the drainage of the village lands which does not escape by this hollow north-eastwards to Khātilah is said to go westwards to some sand hills called Iswār اصوار.	About 135 houses, viz., 30 of Dawāsir in 'Aliya, 60 of Dawāsir and 6 of Bani Tamīm in Wastah, and 40 of Dawāsir in Siflah.	There are date palms in all three villages, and some citrons, figs, limes and a few vines are seen; but on the whole fruit trees are fewer than in the other villages of 'Āridh. Crops are wheat, barley, millet, lucerne, musk melons and water melons. The depth of the wells is 8 fathoms at 'Aliya, 7 at Wastah and 6 at Siflah.
Thādiq ثادق or Thādik ثادك	Between Tuwaim and Haraimlah, probably 25 miles from the former and 20 from the latter.	About 300 houses. The details are: Dawāsir of the Suwailim section 40, and of the Al 'Īsa section 40; Bani Tamīm of the Mājid section 60; Bani Hājir 20; inferior tribes 23, viz., Jidā'ah 4, Mizai'al 4, Rabaiya' 10 and Jamai'ah 5: the balance belong to miscellaneous tribes.	The date plantations are extensive: other fruit trees are the fig, pomegranate, peach, lime, citron and vine. Wheat, barley, millet, lucerne and melons are cultivated. The wells, which are 8 fathoms deep, yield excellent water. The name is generally pronounced Tḥādij or Thādich.

'ĀRIDH عارض **VILLAGE**

A village in the **Dhāhirah** District of the **'Omān** Sultanate: it is situated on the right bank of Wādi-al-**Kabīr** between Hayāl and Darīz. 'Āridh consists of about 320 mud houses: it is inhabited by Bani **Kalbān** of the Jarāwinah section (300 families) and by Bani **Shakail** (20 families). It possesses dates and other cultivation. The people are carriers as well as cultivators and own some 40 camels and 100 donkeys: there are about 50 cattle and 1,000 sheep and goats.

ARZANAH
ارزنه

An island off the coast of the Abu **Dhabi** Principality in Trucial **'Omān**, 72 miles east by north of the entrance of Khor-al-**'Odaid** and belonging to the Shaikh of Abu **Dhabi**. It is 1⅜ miles long by 1 mile broad: the northern part is hilly, one point having an elevation of 200 feet above the sea; the southern part is a plain. There is an anchorage, in 4 or 5 fathoms, to the east of the southern tip of the island: no fresh water is obtainable. Some pearl banks exist in the vicinity of Arzanah, of which we may here mention Sutūh Arzanah, a large group extending eastwards towards Zirko Island; Batin Arzanah, 16 miles to the east-south-east; and Maiyānah, 4 miles to the south.

'ASALU
عسلو

One of the **Shībkūh** ports of the **Persian Coast**; it is situated 22 miles south-east of **Tāhiri** and 4 miles north of **Nāband** at the north entrance point of **Nāband** bay. The village, which consists of about 200 stone houses and a certain number of huts, occupies more than ½ a mile of the coast and has a large date-grove behind it. The ship anchorage at 'Asalu is exposed to the Shamāl, but small boats find shelter by running over a reef which fronts the place and anchoring inside. The inhabitants are Sunnis and belong to the Harami or Āl Haram tribe. They own 4 pearling Sambūks and a score of fishing Baqārahs in which they go pearl-diving on the banks near **Nāband**; they also fish, especially on a ground in **Nāband** bay off Baidheh Khān village, and cultivate grain and dates. 'Asalu was, till his death by violence in 1906, the residence of Shaikh Ahmad-bin-Saif, the Āl Haram Shaikh, who till recently ruled over the villages of Nakhl Taqi, 'Asalu, Baidheh Khān, Hālat Nāband, **Nāband**, Barku, Tabin and 'Amārīyeh in subordination to the Khān of **Dashti** by whom they were held in farm; in 1906, however, the group were brought directly under the authority of the

Governor of the **Gulf Ports,** and the connection of the **Dashti** Khān دشتی with them was terminated. The Persian Imperial Customs have now a post here.

ASHRĀF
اشراف

Singular Sharīf شریف : there is also a plural Shurafa شرفا . A sacred or semi-sacred tribe, tracing their origin to the Hijāz province and claiming kinship with the prophet Muhammad through descent from the Imām Hasan; they are found in small numbers at various points in Arabia and in the Persian Gulf region, as for instance at Na'ām in the district of **Harīq**, and possibly at Sabhah in Widyān **Dawāsir.** Some who live at **Lailah** in **Aflāj** belong to a section called Saqar سقر, while others at **Saih** in the same district are Hāmid حامد .

ASIS (BADD-AL-)
بدّ الاسیس

A tract in the Sanjāq of **Hasa,** immediately to the north-west of the Hasa Oasis; it is about 30 miles in length, stretching from Jabal-ad-Dām on the north to the border of the **Ghuwār** tract on the south, and its average breadth between Jau-as-**Sa'adān** on the west and **Jauf** on the east is about 18 miles. Its boundaries are further defined by the Gharaimīl hill on its east side, by the Qārat-ar-Rukbān hill at its south-east corner where it meets the oasis of **Hasa,** by the Ghār-ash-Shuyūkh hill at its south-western extremity, and by the Barāim hill on its western border towards the north end. Badd-al-Asīs is described as a plain of sand interspersed with undulating rocky ground; the sand is reddish and the rocks are dark-brown in colour. Grazing consists of Thamām grass and of 'Arfaj and Rimth bushes, of which the last is particularly favoured by camels. The only well in Badd-al-Asīs is Shatqam ستقم, about 5 miles north-west of Qārat-ar-Rukbān, which is 2 fathoms deep and contains good water. It should be noted that according to some authorities the district described is mostly a part of Ghuwār, and that Badd-al-Asīs is merely the name of a track leading across **Ghuwār** in the direction of **Taff** and **Wādi-al-Miyāh.**

'ATAIBAH

ĀSŪH (DARVEH
درهٔ آسوه

A valley in the **Shībkūh** District of Persia, in the article on which its position and course are fully described.

Darveh Āsūh contains the following villages:—

Name.	Position.	Population, resources, etc.
Bihdih بهده	In the western branch of the valley, about 4 miles above the point of junction of the two branches.	200 houses; 80 camels, 200 donkeys, 230 cattle, 3,000 sheep and goats, and 8,000 date palms.
Hashnīz هشنيز	In the eastern branch of the valley, about 6 miles above the point of junction of the two branches.	100 houses; 70 camels, 200 donkeys, 150 cattle, 2,000 sheep and goats and 3,000 date trees.
Kunārdūn کناردن	In the western branch of the valley, about 4 miles above Bihdih.	40 houses; 20 camels, 50 donkeys, 30 cattle, 3,000 sheep and goats and 200 palms.

From this table the population of the valley would seem to be about 1,500 souls.

Darveh Āsūh has a close political connection with the upper part of the **Gābandi** Valley and forms part of the territories for which the Nasūri Shaikh pays revenue to the Governor of **Bastak**.

'ATAIBAH
عتيبه

The singular is 'Ataibi عتيبي and the collective plural 'Ataibah; but to designate a number of individuals there is a plural 'Utbān عتبان.

Range and territory.—An important Bedouin tribe of **Najd**, occupying the vast wilderness, 300 miles in extent, between **Qasīm** and the Makkah country; the Bedouin tribes which adjoin them are the **Mutair** on the east, the **Shammar** on the north, the **Harb** on the north-west and the **Buqūm, Qahtān,** and **Sabai'** on the south. A great part of the routes from **'Anaizah** and **Buraidah** to Makkah lies in their territory and Qasīmi caravans travelling by those lines are accustomed to enlist Rafīqs of the 'Ataibah. Their camps are seen especially at Dhariyah, Dukhnah, Miskah and Shibīrmah. On the north their limit is at Wādi-ar-

Rummah, and they are found as far east as the Qatan hill in that valley, and as Wādi-as-Sirr and Washam; they are also among the Bedouins who frequent the district of Kharj, they are sometimes seen in 'Āridh, and a few poor 'Ataibah occasionally visit Kuwait in search of a livelihood. Ihe opposite direction they are known to encamp at Huwaiyah in Wādi Sabai'. The Dīrah proper of the 'Ataibah consists of sandy or gravelly plains, sprinkled with isolated bergs of granite and basalt, but containing excellent desert pasture.

Life and subsistence.—The majority of the tribe are nomads wandering dispersed through their vast domains; but the 'Ataibah have also some fixed villages, with palm groves, in the hills 100 miles to the north of Makkah, and colonies of settled 'Ataibah exist at different places in Najd, especially in Middle Najd or Qasīm. The 'Ataibah live chiefly by the camels, sheep and goats of which they own large numbers; the wool of their flocks is short and coarse and suitable only for making ropes and Bedouin tents. Forty years ago the 'Ataibah owned some of the best horses in Arabia, and good horses are even now said to be sold *within the tribe* for $200 each. The prices of camels, sheep and goats are lower among the 'Ataibah than among the Mutair; the best riding camels fetch only $60 to $70, the best baggage camels $40, and sheep and goats $3 a head. The 'Ataibah eke out their subsistence by raiding, especially to the north of Wādi-ar-Rummah, and by protecting pilgrims on their way to Makkah.

Character.—As a tribe the 'Ataibah are honourable, hospitable, and not inclined to treachery; more stable in mind than most Bedouins; better fighters than even the redoubted Qahtān; in religion moderate and free from fanaticism.

Number and divisions.—Their total number within the limits of Central Arabia may be roughly estimated at 6,000 souls.

The 'Ataibah consist of two large divisions, the Ruwaqah or Rōqah رُوقة and the Barqah برقة.*

The war cry of the Rōqah is انا بن رزق and the Wasm of their chief Shaikh is a snake branded below the left eye of the camel.

---

* The composition of the tribe as given ¡ below from Kuwait information differs considerably from that attributed to it by Doughty (II. 427) on a western authority.

'ATAIBAH

The Rōqah are divided into the following sections:—

'Adhyān	عضيان	Hanātishah	حناتشه
'Afārīn	عفارين	Hizmān	حزمان
'Ali (Dhī)	ذي علي	Jidha'ān	جذعان
'Awāzim	عوازم	Jisāsimah	جساسمه
Barārīq	براريق	Kharārīs	خراريص
D ll	ذيبه	Khlāwīyah	خلاوية
Dilābihah	دلابحه	Mihādilah	مهادله
Ghanānīm	غنانيم	Mirāshidah	مراشده
Gharbīyah	غربية	Murja	مرجا
Habardīyah	هبردية	Sa'adah	سعده
Hafa	حفا	Simrah	سمرة
Hamāmid	حمامد	Zirqān	زرقان

The main sections of the Barqah are the 'Asumah عصمه, the Da'ājīl دعاجيل or Da'ajīn دعجين, the Daghālibah دغالبه, the Dahasah دهسه, the Miqatah مقطه or Imqatah امقطه, the Milābisah ملابسه, the Nafa'a نفعا, the Nakhasah نخسه, the Rūsān روسان, the Shiyābinah شيابنه, the Thibitah ثبته and the Tufahah طفحه. Of these the Shiyābinah have recently lost two successive Shaikhs at the hands of the **Qahtān** and **Mutair**. Some sections of the Barqah are divided again into subsections as below:—

'Asumah.

'Alwāt	علوات	Nāshir	ناشر
'Amrīyah	عمرية	Rakaibāt	ركيبات
Ghazāl	غزال	Rūsān	روسان
Jalāmidah	جلامده	Sumhān	سمحان
Jilādīn	جلادين	and	
Maghārīyah	مغارية	Tahmān	طحمان

Da'ājīl.

'Adhādīn	عضادين	Hidf	هدف
'Aqāilah	عقائله	Ma'aliyah	معليه

'ATAIBAH

Daghālibah.

Hinādīyah	هناديه	Qaba'ah	قبعه
Mawāsilh	مواسله	Qamū	قمول

Miqatah.

'Alābīyah	علابيّة	Khanāfirah	خذافره
Aqafah	عقفه	Khuniyān	خنيان
Ghazāila	غزائله	Qimizah	قمزه
Hamidah	حمده	Rūsān Miqatah	روسان مقطه
Hawābīyah	هوابيّه	and	
Hawārinah	هوارنه	Silifah	سلفه

Milābisah.

Bisāisah	بصائصه	Rahmah (Dhī)	ذي رحمه
Hawāmilah	هوامله	and	
Hayādhila	حياذله	Rubiqah	ربقه

Nafa'a.

Dharā'in	ذراءين	Majāwilah	مجاوله
Falatah	فلته	Misā'id	مساعيد
or		Mufarrij	مفرج
Aflatah	افلته	Qumaishāt	قميشات
Faqahah	فقعه	Ziyād (Dhī)	ذي زياد

Rūsān.

'Amrah (Dhī)	ذي عمره	Majarri (Dhī)	ذي مجرّي
Habūr	هبور	and	
Jawāma'ah	جوامعه	Miqāhisah	مقاهصه

Shiyābinah.

'Abdullah (Dhī)	ذي عبدالله	Khalīfah (Dhī)	ذي خليفه
'Amr (Dhī)	ذي عمر	Sakhalah	صخله
Fahaid (Dhī)	ذي فهيد	Shaibah (Dhī)	ذي شيبه
Hafārah	حفاره	Zabālijah.	زبالجه

The Barqah appear to have no general war cry, but some of the sections have distinctive war cries and also Wasms of their own. Such are the following:—

Section.	War cry.	Wasm.
'Asumah	خيّال رحمان ابن عاصم	§ Half-way up the near side of the animal's neck.
Da'ājīl	سقم الحريب ابن مفلح	⊓ Half-way up the off side of the animal's neck.
Daghālibah	خيّال الشرفة عالي	‖— Half-way up the near side of the animal's neck.
Miqatah	خيّال رحمان كريزي	I— On the off foreleg of the animal.
Nafa'a	خيّال الحرشه زيود	O— On the off hind-leg of the animal.
Rūsān	خيّال البلهه امرح	O On the off cheek of the animal.
Shiyābinah	خيّال رحمان ابن مشيب	☾ On the off cheek of the animal.

Political position.—The 'Ataibah have from early times paid allegiance to the Wahhābi power and in 1865 their annual contribution to the treasury of **Riyādh** was estimated at $12,000. In the civil war in Southern **Najd** about 1871 they sided with 'Abdullah against Sa'ūd and, assisted by the treachery of the **Qahtān**, defeated Sa'ūd when he attempted to subdue them. Subsequently, when the fortunes of **Hāil** were in the ascendant, they came under the authority of the **Shammar** Amīr, who severely enhanced their taxation; but in 1902, on the recovery of the Wahhābi power, they again became subjects of Ibn Sa'ūd whose cause they always favoured and to whom they now render tribute at the rate of $1 on every 5 camels and $2 on every 10 sheep. The 'Ataibah are fairly well armed with trade rifles.

Settled 'Ataibah.—Up to this point we have been concerned with the 'Ataibah as a tribe of nomads, but it is necessary to observe that residents of a number of fixed villages in **Najd** are described as 'Ataibah by descent. In **Qasīm** the following villages are said to be wholly or partially possessed by 'Ataibah:—Qasr-bin-'Aqaiyil, Athlah, Badāyah,

Basr, Bitāh, Bukairīyah, Ab-ad-Dūd, 'Ain Ibn-Fahaid, Ghāf I, Ghammāsh, Haid, Jau'i, Quwai'ah, Nafi, Rass, Saib, Shaihīyah and Wuzākh, to which should perhaps be added Mudhnib. In Jabal **Shammar** territory **Baqa'a** is said to be occupied by 'Ataibah of the Sa'adah section; and in **Sadair** the people of **Zilfi**, and in **'Āridh** those of Banbān, Barrah and Rghabah, are mentioned as being to a greater or less extent 'Ataibah. Those of **Zilfi** belong to sections known as Farāhīd فراهيد and Masā'idah مساعدة.

'ATUB
عطب

An Arab tribe of Turkish **'Irāq**, who have their headquarters upon the Shatt-al-**'Arab** between **Basrah** Town and **Muhammareh** Town; in religion they are Shi'ahs, and like all their neighbours they are addicted to robbery. Nearly all the villages upon **Ajairāwīyah** island towards its lower end are inhabited by 'Atub, as are also the large villages of Sangar and Sabīliyāt upon the right bank of the Shatt-al-**'Arab** opposite; and the 'Atub are (with the **'Īdān** and the Qatārnah) the principal element of the population in the mixed villages generally of the right bank. They are also found at Sulaimānīyah on the left bank of the river below the Da'aiji creek. Outlying colonies of 'Atub are found at Kataibān and one or two other villages on the left bank of the river above **Basrah** Town; also at Dorah which is a short distance above **Fāo**. Some 'Atub also occur on the Haffār reach of the **Kārūn** who probably belong to this tribe. The principal Shaikh of the 'Atub was till lately Alag-al-Humaiyid, who lived in one of the Sulaimānīyah hamlets; but he is dead, and his son Sultān is now in prison in connection with offences committed on the river.

AUDHĀN (ZOR AL-)
زور الاردان

A tract in the **Hasa** Sanjāq, forming its extreme north-eastern corner upon the sea. On the coast it extends from Jabal Manīfah on the north, where it meets the **Kuwait** district of **Sūdah**, to **Musallamīyah** bay which forms its southern limit. Inland it is bounded by the marshy depression known as Sabákhat-al-**Mutāya** سبخة المطايا. It is in fact the irregularly shaped strip cut off by a line joining Jabal Manīfah to the foot of **Musallamīyah** bay, and its extent measured in any direction hardly exceeds 20 miles and is generally much less.

The principal features of the Zor-al-Audhān coast are the capes of Rās-al-Ghār راس الغار, Rās-al-Musainah راس المسينة and Rās al-Bidya' راس البديع; of these the first is about 14 miles south-east of Jabal Manīfah, the last is 8 or 9 miles further to the south and forms the northern entrance point of **Musallamīyah** bay, and the second is about midway between the other two but rather nearer to Rās-al-Bidya'. Off Rās-al-Ghār is a pearl bank similarly named.

The wells of the Zor-al-Audhān tract are Ruwāqīyah رواقية on the coast half way between Rās-al-Ghār and Rās-al-Musainah; Bahajah بجة in the centre of the tract; and Sūdah سودة about 3 miles inland from the north-western side of **Musallamīyah** bay. The water of all three is indifferent in quality.

'AUF (WĀDI BANI) وادي بني عوف

A valley in the 'Omān Sultanate, connected with Wādi **Fara'**, which it is said to leave in the neighbourhood of **Rustāq**, and subsequently reaching the sea at Sha'ibah near **Masna'ah** by an independent course to the east of Wādi **Fara'**. The villages in this valley are, apparently in descending order, the following:—

Name.	Proposition.	House and inhabitant.	REMARKS.
Qasmītain قصميتن	1 hour from Wādi Fara.'	10 houses of Bani 'Auf.	Wheat and lucerne are cultivated. There are 15 camels, 30 cattle, 150 sheep and goats.
Taikha تيخا	1 hour from Qasmītain.	40 houses of Bani 'Auf.	Crops are wheat and lucerne, and there are 60 camels, 10 cattle and 50 sheep and goats.
Zammah زامّة	3 hours from Taikha.	100 houses of 'Abriyīn.	The only crop is wheat. There are 100 camels, 70 cattle and 200 sheep and goats.
Hāt هاط	1 hour from Zammah.	50 houses of 'Abriyīn.	No cultivation; the people are shepherds and carriers owning 10 camels, 50 donkeys, 80 cattle and 1,000 sheep and goats.

AWĀBI
عوابي

A town or large village in the Western **Hajar** of the **'Omān** Sultanate on the left bank of Wādi Bani **Kharūs** within the hills; it lies about 15 miles west of **Nakhl** and somewhat less (13 miles) to the east of **Rustāq**. The elevation is 1,850 feet above the sea and the settlement covers a fairly large area. There are about 300 houses in the town proper, mostly of mud and stone, but some of them mere huts; and another 150 stand outside upon lower ground. The place is defended by a fort called Bait-al-'Awābi بيت العوابي which occupies a position of natural strength commanding the approach from **Nakhl**. The population is about 2,500 souls, belonging chiefly to the **'Abriyīn** (120 houses), Bani **Kharūs** (70 houses), Bani **Harrās** and Dhahūl; but there are also some **Siyābiyīn**, Bani Bahri and Bani 'Auf. The bazaar contains over 50 shops kept by Arabs of the place. Every available spot in the vicinity is reclaimed for tillage, and the neat regular fields attest good husbandry. Dates, lucerne, maize, millet, wheat and barley are the principal crops; the palms are estimated at 4,000. Livestock are 100 camels, 150 donkeys, 100 cattle and 4,000 sheep and goats; the cattle are of a small hump-backed sort; they are not sent to graze on the coarse grass of the hills, but are stall-fed on barley, dates and lucerne. 'Awābi is a position of great natural importance dominating as it does Wādi Bani **Kharūs**, up which lies the best route to Jabal **Akhdhar** from the north: it has been perpetually in dispute between the Bani **Riyām** and the **'Abriyīn**, but the political influence of the 'Abriyīn, who number 120 households, has generally been predominant. In 1900 the **'Abriyīn** transferred possession of the fort from themselves to the Sultān of **'Omān** who still retains it by means of a garrison of 30 men. The route called Tarīq-ash-Shass leads direct from 'Awābi over Jabal **Akhdhar** to Wādi Tanūf in **'Omān** Proper.

AWĀL
اوال

The old name of **Bahrain** Island, disused, but still remembered. According to tradition Awāl was the name of the first occupier, the brother of a certain Na'asān whose name also is supposed to survive in that of Jazīrat Umm **Na'asān**. The name Awāl occurs in the annals of the earliest Muhammadan conquest.[*]

'AWĀMIR
عوامر

Singular **'Āmiri** عامري. A large Arab tribe of **'Omān**, by race Nizārīyah, but now in politics Hināwīyah. About one-third of them are

---

[*] *Vide* Le Strange's *Lands of the Eastern Caliphate.*

Bedouins ranging the borders of the **Ruba'-al-Khāli** from Trucial **'Omān** in the north, which they occasionally visit in small numbers, to the district of **Dhufār** on the southern coast of Arabia.

The other two-thirds are now settled, chiefly in **'Omān** Proper where they possess the villages of 'Aqīl, Qal'at-al-'Awāmir, Falaj, Hamaidhah, Qurīyatain, Qārūt, Khurmah, Shāfa', Saiyāhi and Sūq-al-Qadīm and are found at **Nizwa**: they occur also at **Masqat** Town, **Bait-al-Falaj** and **Ruwi** in the **Masqat** District; at Ghallah and Sād in Wādi **Bōshar**; at Hail Āl 'Umair, **Sīb** and Ma'bīlah in **Bātinah**; at Khōdh in Wādi **Samāil** and at Khubār and Luwīz in **Daghmar**. In **'Omān** Proper the settled 'Awāmir number about 2,500 souls and are divided into the following sections: Ahmad (Aulād) اولاد احمد, 'Ali-bin-Hamad (Aulād) اولاد علي بن حمد, 'Ali-bin-Khalf (Aulād) اولاد علي بن خلف, Amīr (Aulād) اولاد امير, Harāmilah حراملة, Ja'āfarah جعافرة, Jā'id (Aulād-al-) اولاد الجاعد, Khanājirah خناجرة, Muhammad محمد, Mūsa (Aulād) اولاد موسى, Rakhbah رخبة, Rāshid (Aulād) اولاد راشد, Saba (Aulād) اولاد سبا, Saif (Aulād) اولاد سيف, Salīm (Aulād) اولاد سليم, Sand (Aulād) اولاد سند, Sarāhīn سراحين, Sarāhīn-al-Muwailah سراحين المويلة and Shīrāz (Aulād) اولاد شيراز; those at **Nizwa** are of the Aulād Saif section, and at **Sīb** a section called Aulād Mahaiyi محيي are found. The settled 'Awāmir outside **'Omān** Proper are about 4,000 persons.

Their migratory habits and the slightness of their contact with civilisation renders a close estimate of the strength of the Bedouin portion impossible; but, regard being had to the wideness of their distribution, they may safely be assumed to be numerous and perhaps amount to 3,500 souls. The total strength of the tribe is thus probably about 10,000 souls.

A term 'Afār عفار, frequently used in connection with the 'Awāmir, appears to denote a portion of the tribe inhabiting a particular territory, called 'Afār or Dhafrah ضفرة, between **Mahōt** and **Dhufār**; it includes representatives of many sections.

The 'Awāmir are reputed brave and warlike, but crafty, treacherous and predatory; they are said to plunder indiscriminately all whom they meet, not excepting members of their own tribe with whom they happen to be unacquainted. The 'Afār are popularly supposed to feed upon carrion: they deny this, but admit that they are not infrequently reduced to devouring the animals' skins with which some of them are clothed. The 'Awāmir speak a peculiar dialect of Arabic and the language of the westernmost sections is hardly intelligible to their settled brethren in **'Omān** Proper. The tribe is Ibādhi in religion: they are at feud with the **Jannabah** and the **Darū'**. The tribal capital is **'Aqīl**, and the present Tamīmahs are Suhail-bin-Aswad and Bībān-bin-Bībān.

AWĀZIM
عوازم

Distribution.—Singular 'Āzimi عازمي. A preponderantly Bedouin tribe now hardly found in Eastern Arabia outside the limits of the **Kuwait** Principality, within which they range from **Kuwait** Town and **Jahrah** on the north to the borders of the **Hasa** Sanjāq on the south, and from the sea on the east to the beginning of **Summān** on the west; some, however, exist in the neighbourhood of **Qatīf**, where they breed horses and camels and take menial service under various Shaikhs; and a few are settled in the fixed villages of Wādi-al-**Miyāh**. About 250 non-nomadic families of the tribe are established in **Kuwait** Town, where one of the quarters is called after them; and 25 others possess the village of **Dimnah**.

'Awāzim or Hawāzim are apparently found in various parts of Central Arabia, especially at **Jauf-al-'Āmir**, Sakākah, **Taimah** and Baidha Nathīl in Jabal **Shammar**, and at Ghāt in the **Sadair** district of Southern **Najd**; but these 'Awāzim or Hawāzim are possibly not identical with the **Kuwait** 'Awāzim and may belong to the **Hataim** tribe (*vide* article) or to the **Harb**.*

Origin and traditions.—The Shaikh of **Kuwait** says that the name 'Awāzim means the "segregated," and that they are sprung from the bastard children of a victorious Turkish army in Central Arabia, who were collected and formed into a tribe. This story appears improbable, especially as it is not supported by anything peculiar in the physical characteristics of the 'Awāzim and involves the difficult supposition that the word 'Awāzim was originally 'Awāzil عوازل: it serves, however, to

---

* This is a difficult question which it has not been possible to clear up at the present time, though the names 'Awāzim عوازم and Hawāzim حوازم could hardly, one might suppose, be confounded by Arabs. The "Hawâzim" of Wallin, the "'Azzāmees" of Palgrave, and the Howeysin of Lady Anne Blunt must apparently all be the same people; and the first and the last, at any rate, resembled the 'Awāzim of the **Kuwait** in being of undistinguished origin. Wallin found the Hawāzim living intermingled with the **Sharārāt**, despised and poor, and robbed of almost all their animals by raiding parties of the Southern **Shammar**. The latest reports however state that the 'Awāzim, the Hawāzim section of the **Harb** and the Hawāzim section of the **Hataim** are entirely distinct from and independent of one another.

illustrate the slight esteem in which the 'Awāzim are held socially. The tribe themselves claim to be an offshoot of the **Harb**, and say that their name means "quick in starting" and refers to a sudden tribal dispersion, of which their accounts are various and conflicting; it is generally ascribed to a difficulty with the Sharīf of Makka. Some of the 'Awāzim admit the descent of their tribe from a Harb foundling adopted by the **Mutair**. The 'Awāzim appear to have immigrated into **Kuwait** territory about three generations ago and the island of Umm-an-Namal was granted to the Adhyaibāt subdivision by the grandfather of the present Shaikh of **Kuwait**.

Numbers and divisions.—The 'Awāzim Bedouins of **Kuwait** are divided into two main sections, the Kū'ah كوعه, 'Aiyāl Kuwai' عيال كويع or Aulād Kuwai' اولاد كويع, and the 'Aiyāl Ghiyādh عيال غياض. The Kū'ah, who on account of their supposed descent from an elder brother take precedence of the 'Aiyāl Ghiyādh, are subdivided into the Hadhālīn هذالين, Braikāt بريكات, and Shqufah شقفه, each of which sections has a Shaikh of its own: the Braikāt are not considered to be true descendants of Kuwai'. The 'Aiyāl Ghiyādh are subdivided into the Malā'ibah ملاعبه, Musāhimah مساهمه, Misā'idah مساعده, Adhyaibāt اذيبيات, Jawāsirah جواسره, Muhālibah محالبه, Muwaijīyah or Mwāiji مواجي, Aghrubah اغربه, Karāshah كراشه, and Sawābir صوابر. One authority mentions a subdivision called Tuwalīn توالين, without indicating to which of the divisions it belongs. The Aghrubah and Muhālibah are so much scattered that they hardly possess a corporate existence. The 'Adhyaibāt and Muwaijīyah admittedly have no Shaikhs of their own and are variously represented as being included with the Malā'ibah or the Sawābir; and the Shaikh of the Sawābir appears to be also Shaikh of the Misā'idah. The strongest subdivision are the Misā'idah, and the Hadhālīn are among the weakest. The number of the Bedouin 'Awāzim in **Kuwait** territory may amount to 4,000 souls.

Occupations and resources.—The 'Awāzim of **Kuwait** are pastoral nomads, fishermen and pearl divers, and some of them cultivate melons at Wārah in the **'Adān** district. Their camels are estimated at 7,000 and their sheep and goats at 140,000, but these numbers are probably exaggerated: they have some donkeys, but no cattle and only 15 horses.

Religion, social position and customs.—Vague stories are current that the 'Awāzim in other parts of Arabia have a strange religion of their own; but those in **Kuwait** territory are now without exception Sunnis of the Māliki persuasion. By the Arabs the 'Awāzim are regarded as an inferior tribe, and they intermarry only among themselves and with the **Rashāidah**. The Mihr or price paid for wives among them was formerly only 40 Riyāls, of which half was given in kind; it has now risen to 100 and even 200 Riyāls. The 'Awāzim can recognise one another by their pronunciation or Nutaq.

Political position.—The tribe are at present loyal subjects of the Shaikh of **Kuwait** and, from the military point of view, the backbone of his state; the Shaikh regards them, despite their dubious origin, as good fighting men —and with justice, for about 50 of them were killed in his invasion of Jabal **Shammar** in 1901, including three sons of the Shaikh of the Sawābir and several men of mark among the Jawāsirah. The real head of the tribe is now the Shaikh of **Kuwait**, but a representative of the old tribal authority exists in Is'ūd-bin-Habīb-bin-Jām'ah اسعود بن حبيب بن جامعة of the Hadhālīn subdivision. The 'Awāzim are politically allied to the **'Ajmān**.

AYŪN
عيون

An important village or small town in **Qasīm**, the most populous place between **Hāil** and **Buraidah**; it is situated about 25 miles west-north-west of **Buraidah**. The emplacement of 'Ayūn is a large depression, some miles in extent, in a bay on the southern side of Jabal Sārah. The plantations cover a space 3 miles in length and nearly 1 mile broad, and the palms are among the best in **Qasīm**. The groves are said to be 40 in number: some of the palms are planted in excavations in sandstone rock. On the west side of the town is a large and growing sand dune, retained by a mud wall of which the height has frequently to be increased. Water is very abundant and though not good is drinkable; the depth of the wells is from 5 to 6 fathoms. The people, about 2,500 souls, are said to be of **Shammar** descent. They are small, thin and ugly, with hollow eyes and projecting cheek-bones; they wear a red Kafīyah without an 'Aqāl and are Wahhābis by religion, but they are reputed to be of a humorous disposition. 'Ayūn has about 20 shops and is the market town of Ghāf, Raudh and Wathāl. Politically it is dependent on **Buraidah**. The rocks at the entrance of the 'Ayūn depression at its north-western end bear some Himyaritic inscriptions.

'AZĪZĪYAH QADHA

'AZAIR
عزير

The reputed tomb of the prophet Ezra, domed and having a row of Jewish houses attached to the precincts: it stands on the right bank of the **Tigris** midway between **Qurnah** and Qal'at **Sālih** about 30 miles by river from each. 'Azair is within the limits of the **Tigris** marshes and is included in the Qadha of **Shatrat-al-'Amārah**: the surrounding Arabs are of the Āl Bū **Muhammad** tribe. There are some trees and gardens, but no village.

'AZĪZĪYAH
عزيزيه
QADHA

A division of the Sanjāq of Baghdād, which is a part of the Wilāyat of the same name in Turkish 'Irāq; it was constituted in 1884, at the time of separation of the Basrah Wilāyat from that of Baghdād, out of territory formerly included in the Qadha of **Kūt-al-Amārah**.

Position and boundaries.—The 'Azīzīyah Qadha is situated on the left bank of the **Tigris** some distance below **Baghdād** City, and is enclosed by the Qadhas of **Baghdād** and Khurāsān on the north-west, by that of Badrah on the north-east, by that of **Kūt-al-Amārah** on the south-east, and by that of **Jazīrah** on the south-west. 'Azīzīyah apparently reaches up the **Tigris** to the junction with that river of the **Diyālah**.

Topography and tribes.—The Qadha contains only two villages of any importance: of these one is **'Azīzīyah**, described elsewhere under its own name; the other is Salmān Pāk, which is mentioned in the article on the **Tigris**.

The following is an alphabetical table of the principal Muqāta'ahs or tracts in 'Azīzīyah and of the tribes occupying them:—

Tract.	Tribe.	Tract.	Tribe.
1. Bādi بادي	Dilaim.	10. Qutnīyat-ash-Sharqīyah قطنية الشرقيه	Shammar Tōqah of the Hadail section.
2. Dabūni دبوني (The private property of an Armenian family.)	Shammar Tōqah of the 'Atbah, Khawālid and Qarāghōl sections.	11. Safi صافي	Shammar Tōqah of the Manāhīr section.

Tract.	Tribe.	Tract.	Tribe.
3. Dair دير	Shammar Tōqah of the Banwah section.	12. Samrah سمره (On the large bend of the Tigris at Ctesiphon.)	Zubaid of the Bani 'Ajīl and Battah sections.
4. Dāwar-al-Gharbī داور الغربي	Shammar Tōqah of the Qufaifān section.	13. Shadhif سظف	Shammar Tōqah of the Dāwud and Majli section.
5. Dāwar-ash-Sharqi داورالشرقى	Shammar Tōqah of the Mardān and Zakaitat sections.	14. Shādi شادي	Shammar Tōqah of the Sud'ān section and Da'ajah.
6. Diyālah دياله	Dafāfi'ah, who are perhaps a section of the Shammar Tōqah.	15. Tuwaithah توينه	Jabūr.
7. Hamīnīyah همينيه	Shammar Tōqah of the Dāwar section.	16. Zaljah زلجه	Shammar Tōqah of the Majābilah section.
8. Khanāsah خناسه	Shammar Tōqah of the Manāhīr section.	17. Zara' (Zāwiyat-as)- زاوية الزرع	Shammar Tōqah of the Dāwar section.
9. Qutnīyat-al-Gharbīyah قطنية الغربيه	Shammar Tōqah of the Shuwaiqi section.		

Population.—The total fixed population is estimated at 20,000 souls: nearly all the people are Shī'ah Muhammadans, but there are a few Jews.

Resources.—The district is entirely agricultural and pastoral. The principal crops are wheat and barley; livestock include horses, donkeys, camels, cattle and buffaloes in considerable, and sheep in large, numbers; and there are a few mules.

In the Shādi tract there are extensive deposits of good white salt, said to be formed by the evaporation in the sun of water from certain brackish streams. Some 15 or 20 miles to the east of 'Azīzīyah Village these deposits reach down towards the Tigris bank, and the salt is removed in boats by a contractor to whom they are leased. Wild liquorice is another asset of some value.

Administration.—The Qadha of 'Azīzīyah belongs to the 2nd class. 'Azīzīyah Village was until recently the seat of the Qāim-Maqām, while the only Mudīr in the Qadha was located at Salmān Pāk and was of the 1st class ; now however it is reported that since 1905 Salmān Pāk has become the headquarters of the Qadha, and **'Azīzīyah** Village (on account of its inconvenient situation and the encroachments of the river) that of a Nāhiyah only. The Dāirat-as-Sanīyah owns the Shādi tract together with the Mamlahah المملحة or salt-field which it contains.

'AZĪZĪYAH VILLAGE

عزيزية

A village in Turkish **'Irāq**, on the left bank of the **Tigris** about midway between **Baghdād** and **Kūt-al-Amārah**; it is about 50 miles from either in a direct line, but by river it is 117½ miles from **Baghdād** and 110 miles from **Kūt**. Prior to 1860 there was at most only a police station upon the site now occupied by 'Azīzīyah ; but some years later the place began to develop in consequence of the acquisition of land in the vicinity by the Dāirat-as-Sanīyah ; and in 1884 from being the headquarters of a Nāhiyah it became those of a Qadha. About this time the population of 'Azīzīyah amounted to 1,000 souls, of whom three-fourths were Sunni Muhammadans and the remainder Shī'ahs with a few Jews. After 1884 'Azīzīyah again retrograded, partly in consequence of the inroads of the river upon the bank ; and in 1905 it exchanged places administratively with Salmān Pāk, the latter becoming the *chef-lieu* of the Qadha while 'Azīzīyah again descended to the status of a Nāhiyah. The population of 'Azīzīyah is now under 200 persons : there are about 30 small mud houses only, and half a dozen shops. The means of artificial irrigation being wanting, there is consequently no cultivation ; and the few inhabitants who remain draw their supplies chiefly from the adjoining **Shammar Tōqah** tribe. The chief and almost sole kind of trade at 'Azīzīyah is an export of liquorice ; it is carried on by a Jew who holds a monopoly of it from the Government.

The only civil executive official at 'Azīzīyah is now a Mudīr—an old man of the Jamīl family—with a single clerk and two Dhābitīyahs under his orders. There is a telegraph office at 'Azīzīyah, which is connected by a double wire with **Baghdād** on the one side and by a single one with **Kūt-al-'Amārah** on the other : 3 mounted Dhābitīyahs are posted to the office as line guards. The Hamīdīyah (Turkish) river steamers stop in passing 'Azīzīyah to receive and deliver mails. A Government reserved forest exists on the **Tigris** bank near this place.

BADI'
بديع

The southernmost village in the **Aflāj** district of **Najd**; it is situated about 10 miles south, and perhaps a little east, of **Raudhah** in the same district. Badī' consists of two quarters, a northern called Batīnah and a southern called Taraf, which are separated by a mile or two miles of date plantations and cultivated land. The population of Badī' is about 3,000 souls and consists of 300 houses of the Sukhābirah and 200 of the Ishkarah (Āl Bū 'Ali) sections of the **Dawāsir** and of 100 houses of the Bani **Khadhīr**. Date palms are said to number 25,000 and the common fruits of **Najd** are grown. The other crops are wheat, barley, maize, millet, lucerne, musk melons and water melons. The wells are 5 to 6 fathoms deep. Horses are few among the settled population, but other livestock are in the usual proportions. The following is a table of the component parts and dependencies of Badī':—

Name.	Position.	Houses and inhabitants.	Remarks.
Batīnah بطينه	See above.	The people are Sukhābirah **Dawāsir**.	The northern quarter of Badī'.
Hinu حنو	At the lower end of a hollow which comes down from Shutbah at the south-west corner of **Aflāj**.	No permanent habitations, but some cultivation by inhabitants of Badī'.	There is a date grove, practically wild. Crops are cultivated only in promising seasons when they are likely to be worth protecting against Bedouins.
'Ijlīyah عجليه	In the hollow which comes down from Shutbah, above Hinu.	Do.	There is a date grove and melons are grown; cereals also are cultivated but are apt to suffer by the depredations of Bedouins.
Mishrif مشرف	In the middle of Badī'.	A fort containing only a few households of slaves.	The fort belonged originally to the Hijji of Lailah, but about 35 years ago the other **Dawāsir** of the neighbourhood attacked and ejected them.
Qarainah قرينه	On the west of Taraf and closely adjoining it.	15 houses of **Dawāsir** of the Ishkarah (Harāthmah) section.	A small hamlet forming a suburb of Badī'.
Taraf طرف	See above.	The people are Ishkarah (Āl Bū 'Ali) Dawāsir.	The southern quarter of Badī'.

BADĪYAH

BADĪYAH
بدية

An important and populous division of the **Sharqīyah** district of the **'Omān** Sultanate. It consists of a plain several miles in extent, having its centre about 25 miles south-east of **Ibra** and 35 miles north-west of Balad Banī Bū Hasan in **Ja'alān**; it is bounded on the north and east by the hills of Eastern **Hajar**, on the south and west by ranges of sand-hills beyond which all is desert. In the plain stand several villages, each with a separate fort and with date plantations watered by a separate spring; the intermediate spaces are sandy and barren. About half of the houses are built of mud and stone; the remainder are huts of date branches. Badīyah produces the most valuable dates in **'Omān**, mostly of the Mibsali variety, which are exported to Bombay by way of **Sūr**. The people, except a few Banī Bū **Hasan**, are all **Hajriyīn**. The following is a list, in alphabetical order, of the places in this oasis:—

Name.	Houses.	Camels.	Donkeys.	Cattle.	Sheep and goats.	Date palms.	REMARKS.
Dabīk دبيك	80	20	30	160	1,000	4,000	Nil.
Ghabbi غبي	200	20	20	200	2,000	20,000	Do.
Haili حيلي	20	15	10	10	20	1,000	Do.
Hātūh هاتوه	40	20	30	60	1,200	10,000	Do.
Hawiya حويا	100	20	20	100	1,000	8,000	Bedouins of the Hajriyīn and Al Wahībah tribes are always encamped at this place.
Jafar جفر	...	...	...	...	...	...	A watering place without fixed inhabitants.
Mintirib منترب	400	100	300	250	5,000	60,000	Nil.
Qā' قاع	50	12	20	20	200	4,000	Do.
Rākah راكه	30	40	30	...	6,000	6,000	Do.
Shāhik شاحك	30	70	60	100	1,000	6,000	Do.
Carried over	950	317	520	900	17,420	119,000	

Name.	Houses.	Camels.	Donkeys.	Cattle.	Sheep and goats.	Date palms.	REMARKS.
Brought forward	950	317	520	900	17,420	119,000	
Shāraq شارق	40	20	25	80	1,000	10,000	There are permanent encampments here of Suwāwifah and other Bedouins.
Wāsil واصل or Sūq Badīyah سوق بدية	300	80	150	200	3,000	20,000	Nil.
Yāhis ياحس	40	8	30	20	2,000	9,000	Nil.
TOTALS	1,330	425	725	1,200	23,420	158,000	

The population of Badīyah is probably about 6,500 souls. Trade is centred at Wāsil, the only one of the villages which possesses a bazaar.

BAGHDĀD بغداد **CITY***

The city of Baghdād, the capital of the Wilāyat of the same name and the largest and most important place in Turkish 'Irāq, is also styled Dār-as-Salām دار السلام or the Abode of Safety and Madīnat-al-Khulafa مدينة الخلفا or the City of the Khalīfahs; sometimes it is even mentioned by the ancient and possibly pre-Islamic name of Zaurā† زورا. The name Baghdād appears to be ancient Persian, meaning "the God-given place." Ruins of a solid brick embankment discovered on the right bank of the **Tigris** in 1848 prove that Baghdād, no doubt under a different name, already existed as a place of some importance in the days of Nebuchadnezzar; and (with an interval of 56 years from 836 to 892 A.D., during which its place was taken by Sāmarrah) Baghdād was for about 3 centuries under the 'Abbāsid Khalīfahs the political capital of the whole Muhammadan world. The Muhammadan city of Baghdād, which supplanted Hāshimīyah near the present **Hillah**, was founded by Mansūr, the second of the 'Abbāsid Khalīfahs, in 762 A.D., and was originally on the right bank of the **Tigris** only.

Although its administrative pre-eminence was somewhat impaired by the erection of the Mūsal and Basrah regions into independent

---
* The best map is *Plan of Baghdād revised to 1906*, numbered 1388 in the Foreign Department Library, Simla.

† The semi-official local newspaper is called "Zaura."

Wilāyats in 1878 and 1884, and although the rapidly growing port of **Basrah** is thought by some to threaten its commercial ascendency, Baghdād is still the true capital of all Turkish **'Irāq**. The civil governorship of Baghdād even now enjoys a higher prestige than that of **Basrah**; and to the Wāli of Baghdād are still accredited the consular representatives of highest rank maintained by foreign powers in Turkish **'Irāq**. Baghdād moreover remains the headquarters of the 6th Army Corps of the Turkish Army; and to Baghdād also are posted the officials who superintend the working throughout Turkish **'Irāq** of the departments, such as Customs, which are directly controlled from Constantinople. Again, if from the trade of **Basrah** be subtracted so much as depends directly or indirectly upon Baghdād, the commercial subordination of **Basrah** to Baghdād will at once become apparent; and in matters of education and religion, likewise, **Basrah** occupies a merely secondary place.

Position, site and climate.—Baghdād is situated in latitude 33° 19' 7" north and longitude 44° 25' 33" east; it is further north than Jhelam and not so far north as Rawalpindi in the Punjab province of British India. From Damascus it is distant 480 miles very slightly to the south of east, and from **Basrah** 282 miles in a north-westerly direction; but its distance by the rivers Shatt-al-**'Arab** and **Tigris** from **Basrah** is 500, and from the Persian Gulf about 570 miles. Its elevation above the sea is about 220 feet.

The city stands on both sides of the **Tigris**, which flows through it from north-west to south-east, with a breadth varying from less than 250 to more than 350 yards: opposite the present British Residency the width is 390 yards. The banks of the river at Baghdād and to a considerable distance both above and below the town are of good clay soil and stand both firm and high; in places beyond the walls they are bordered by rich cultivation irrigated from water-lifts, and in others they are fringed with date plantations in which fodder crops are grown between the palms; sometimes they even carry a sprinkling of natural wood, chiefly dwarf poplar. These fertile waterside belts however are narrow, and upon the sides away from the river Baghdād is closely hemmed in by parched clay deserts of dreary aspect; the north-eastern desert reaches away towards the **Diyālah** river and the hills of the Persian frontier and is high lying and waterless, but the other, between the **Tigris** and the **Euphrates**, is liable to be inundated by the spill of the latter river and is not altogether uncultivated. From each of these deserts the part of Baghdād which it approaches is cut off by a depressed tract surrounding the town, imperfectly protected by embankments and liable to be flooded by the Tigris at certain seasons; when this occurs the city itself becomes, as it were, a low island crowded with houses and divided into two parts by the broad and rapidly flowing river.

The climate of Baghdād, owing to the proximity of arid and treeless deserts, is extreme, and upon the whole dry. The summer maximum at 8 A.M. ranges from about 114° to 121° Fahrenheit, and the winter minimum from about 26° to 31°; but the thermometer has been known to rise to 123° and to fall to 20°. The rainy days, mostly in winter, vary from 5 to 20 per annum; the normal rainfall for the year is 9·04 inches; and the mean humidity for the whole year is about 56 per cent. of saturation.

Perimeter and area.—Until the time of Mid-hat Pāsha, who was Wāli now nearly 40 years ago, Baghdād possessed a complete enceinte of earthworks and brick fortifications; but they were dismantled by the reforming governor, and the débris now forms an almost continuous embankment along which runs a path or road. Except for this raised (but unfortunately shadeless) boulevard surrounding it, Baghdād is now a perfectly open town. *

On the left bank of the Tigris these remains, together with the river, enclose a rough parallelogram about two miles in length and somewhat over 1 mile in average breadth. About ⅓ of this area on the side next the desert is empty or occupied only by graveyards and ruins, and towards the southern end a good deal of space is still occupied by date groves, which are however rapidly making way for houses; the rest is covered by the main town of Baghdād. To the old fortifications belonged 4 gateways which still exist and preserve their ancient names; these are the Bāb-ash-Sharqi باب الشرقي at the present south-eastern, and the Bāb-al-Mu'adhdham باب المعظّم at the present north-western corner of this part of the town, and the Bāb-at-Tilism باب الطلسم or Talismanic Gate and the Bāb-al-Wastāni باب الوسطاني or Middle Gate in the long face towards the desert of the former fortifications, the first towards its south-eastern and the other near its north-western end. The Bāb-at-Tilism, which was bricked up after the exit through it in 1639 of the conquering Sultān, Murād IV, has recently been converted into a military

---

* The defensibility of Baghdād is discussed by Captain H. Smyth in his *Reconnaissance Report*, 1904.

magazine: both it and the Bāb-al-Wastāni now stand isolated in the open at a long distance from the houses of the town. The names of a number of Tābiyahs (bastions and redoubts) which have disappeared remain attached to the mounds that mark their sites.

The quarter on the right bank of the **Tigris** begins somewhat further upstream than the main town on the other side; but its length is not so great and its depth is a good deal less. On this side the outline of the former fortifications was more irregular and the area enclosed much less considerable; but the vacant spaces within are not now so large, proportionally, as they are in the main town. On the south side there seem to have been four gateways, the Bāb-al-Karaimāt باب الكريمات at the east end, the Bāb-al-Hillah باب الحلّه near the south-eastern corner, the Bāb-al-Kādhimain باب الكاظمين at the north-western extremity, and the Bāb Shaikh Ma'rūf باب شيخ معروف midway between the two last; but some of these are possibly modern.

Apart from the uncompleted demolition of the fortifications, from the building over in the south-eastern quarters of the main town of lands formerly arable, and from the construction outside the Bāb-al-Mu'adhdham of some military and other government buildings, Baghdād has changed but little since it was surveyed by Jones and Collingwood in 1853-54.

General aspect.—The general appearance of Baghdād, seen from the top of a high building such as the Roman Catholic Church, is flat and monotonous. The narrow and crooked streets are invisible from such a point of view; the height of the houses, which in the better residential quarters is considerable, cannot be appreciated; and there are few inequalities of ground or striking edifices and but little verdure to break the clay-coloured superficies of terraced roofs and insignificant upper storeys. Some rising ground occurs in the trans-Tigris suburb, and one of the quarters in the west centre of the main town appears to stand on higher ground than the rest. Conspicuous single objects are the isolated minaret of the Sūq-al-Ghazal سوق الغزل or Thread Market, rising to the height of about 100 feet in the very centre of the main town; the Latin Church, with a cupola of brick, 150 yards to the west of it; the domed shrine of Shaikh 'Abdul Qādir شيخ عبدالقادر near the south-eastern extremity of the town; and, lastly, the fine blue cupola of the Jāmi'-al-Maidān جامع الميدان towards the west end, with the summit of the Jāmi'-as-Sarāi جامع السراي mosque somewhat nearer the middle of the town, close to the government offices, and the Azbak ازبك mosque nearer the circumference, just within the Bāb-al-Mu'adhdham or westernmost gate of the town.

In all, Baghdād is said to possess 145 mosques. The trans-Tigris suburb is devoid of architectural features.

Views of Baghdād from the river or from the ground level are less disappointing; the better houses, built of soft yellow brick, are sometimes three storeys high and are frequently ornamented with projecting balconies or windows of carved wood called Shanāshīl شناشيل . The long, vaulted brick bazaars are dark, but their very obscurity only increases the picturesqueness of the effect. The poorer quarters of the town contain low and commonplace houses of unburnt brick.

Shrines, monuments and inscriptions.—The most famous shrine at Baghdād is the tomb and mosque of Shaikh 'Abdul Qādir, Gīlāni, near the east end of the town; it was once a centre of political intrigue and was regarded as a place of sanctuary from the law and from the civil arm; but the Turks have now brought it under proper control. A well-known tomb is that of Shaikh 'Umr, with a fretted tapering top, which stands in the vacant space between the town and the old northern wall; the individual commemorated whose full name was Shaikh 'Umr-as-Suhrawardi, Shahāb-ad-Dīn شيخ عمر السهروردي شهاب الدين , was an eminent Muhammadan teacher and preacher who was born at Suhraward in 539 A. H., taught at Baghdād and **Basrah**, and died at Baghdād in 632 A. H.

We may mention also, though it possesses no sacred character, the tomb of the Lady Zubaidah زبيدة, consort of the Khalīfah Hārūn-ar-Rashīd; it is situated on the edge of the desert beyond the southern suburb and consists of an octagon surmounted by a shaft which suggests the inverted cone of a pine-tree.

The minaret of the Sūq-al-Ghazal bears an inscription in the **Kufic** character, but it is reported undecipherable. Another, on the wall of what is now the Customs House, is in excellent preservation and fixes the date of that building as 630 A. H.

Thoroughfares and communications.—The streets of Baghdād are generally ill-kept and too narrow for the passage of a wheeled vehicle. There is no main street unless a road, somewhat wider than the others, which leads from the main bazaar past the military barracks and government offices to the Bāb-al-Mu'adhdham may be so termed; this road shortly before it reaches the city gate traverses the Maidān الميدان or principal piazza of the town.

The two sides of the river are connected about the middle of the town by a Jisr جسر or bridge of boats 240 yards in length, composed

Bridge of Boats, Baghdād.
[MAJ. G. ARBUTHNOT]

of 24 strongly-built wooden pontoons ; these are lashed together and are moored not only to the banks, but also to buoys in midstream. The roadway laid across the bridge is fit for any kind of vehicle and is provided with a parapet or handrail. A section of 3 boats near the right bank can be disconnected and swung down stream to allow the passage of steamers or masted vessels, and the bridge can be opened at the other end also. The whole bridge is removed in case of high floods, especially if the wind is blowing up the river ; for such a wind, if strong, sometimes raises quite a sea. Numerous Quffahs ply as ferry boats between the two parts of the town.

A horse tramway to **Kādhimain** starts from a station in the south-western part of the town not far from the head of the bridge of boats. *

Water supply.—About 300 houses in the Maidān and 3 other quarters of the town are supplied by means of pipes with water from the **Tigris** ; the water for these is pumped from the river by an oil engine of 20 horse power, but no attempt is made to filter it, and the silt even is not allowed to settle. In other parts of the town water is furnished by carriers who bring it in single skins balanced on the backs of donkeys, not in pairs of skins loaded so as to counterpoise one another as in India : the present cost of water so fetched is from Rs. 2-8-0 to Rs. 4-11-0 per 100 skins according to the distance of the house from the river. The shrine of Shaikh 'Abdul Qādir, Gīlāni, and part of the quarter in which it stands are provided with water by means of pipes that are fed by lifts worked by horses. Many houses in the town have private wells, but the water in these is not sweet and is only fit for such purposes as watering the roads ; the level of the water in the wells varies with the level of the **Tigris.** Estimates are now being prepared by the local authorities for a scheme to supply the whole town with water automatically.

Inhabitants, religions, mode of life, and health.—From the ethnical standpoint Baghdād is a remarkable place : situated in an Arab country it is governed by Turks and inhabited chiefly by Jews, and so polyglot and cosmopolitan is its character that as many as 13 languages may occasionally be heard in the same assembly. The population of the town is believed to amount, at the present time, to about 140,000 souls ; if so, it is apparently more than double what it was fifty years ago, when the ravages of the great plague of 1831 and other losses had not been fully repaired. Jews are about 55,000 and out-number every other racial group ;

---

* Fully described by Captain H. Smyth in his *Reconnaissance Report,* 1904.

Arabs are next with a strength of about 38,500, of whom some 7,500 are Bedouin sojourners; then come real or reputed Turks, 30,000; **Kurds,** 5,500; and Persians, 5,000. There are also about 8,000 native Christians who belong to various races. Some Pathans are found and a few Muhammadan Indians, but no Hindus.

The Turks inhabit chiefly the western part of the main town, while the Jews and Christians still partially adhere to their ancient quarters, adjoining the Sūq-al-Ghazal on the north and west respectively. The original Christian quarter, however, is being rapidly overrun by Jews, while the Christians are spreading simultaneously into the more eastern quarters. The Arab, Persian and Kurdish elements live commingled throughout the remainder of the town, except that the quarters on the right bank of the river are predominantly Persian and almost altogether Shī'ah.

Of the Muhammadan population about five-ninths are Sunnis and four-ninths Shī'ahs. Among the leading Muhammadan inhabitants are the Naqīb of Baghdād, who has a house on the left bank of the river immediately above the new British Residency, and Kāzim كاظم Pāsha, a brother-in-law of the Sultan of Turkey who resides here as a political détenu in a mansion on the right bank of the Tigris nearly opposite to the French Consulate.

The native Christians are divided into the following sects: Gregorian Armenians and Chaldæan Catholics, each about 2,000; Syrian Catholics, 1,400; Roman Catholics or Latins, 1,200; Catholic Armenians, 1,000; Protestants, 200; Greek Orthodox, 60. The Christians are mostly Christians by descent; few are recent converts or the children of such. The first five of the Christian communities specified have each a church of their own. The enclosure belonging to the church of the Gregorian Armenians was used for the burial of British Christians until the right to a separate British cemetery was conceded by the Turkish Government. It contains the grave of a British Residency Surgeon, Dr. Ross, who died in 1849. The present Armenian, Roman Catholic and British cemeteries succeed each other upon the right of the road from the Bāb-ash-Sharqī to the north-east corner of the old fortifications. A school and orphanage, managed by the Carmelite order, are attached to the Roman Catholic Church, and a social club and library to that of the Gregorian Armenians. The Roman Catholic, Syrian Catholic and Catholic Armenian churches are closely associated with one another and are subject in common to the Bishop of Babylon, whose seat is at Baghdād. Advocates and lawyers are nearly all Christians.

Fuller information about some of the classes of Baghdād society will be found in the general article on Turkish 'Irāq which should be consulted.

Some characteristic features of life at Baghdād depend on the extreme climate of the place. Such is the habit of living in Sardābs سرداب or subterranean cellars during the heat of the day in summer, and of existing entirely on the roof between sunset and sunrise during the same season. Among institutions of public utility at Baghdād are, according to the Turkish official almanac, 12 libraries, 1 reading room, 28 baths, 7 gymnasia and 2 hotels. Schools are noticed in the general article on Turkish 'Irāq.

The "Baghdād boil" or "date-mark" is a disease peculiar to Baghdād city, and a large proportion of the inhabitants bear its traces in the shape of permanent oval scars. It is a slow, sloughing, rodent ulcer, which generally attacks the face, hand, wrist or ankle, and is not generally amenable to treatment, but disappears of itself after running a tedious course of months; in these respects it resembles the "Aleppo button" and the "frontier-sore" of India; its cause is believed to be the entrance of dust from the streets through an abrasion in the skin.

Trade.—The trade, manufactures and commercial position of Baghdād are dealt with at length in the article on Turkish 'Irāq. The principal bazaar runs parallel to the left bank of the river, at a short distance from it, from the bridge of boats to a point a little above the old British Residency. There is a smaller bazaar, also parallel to the river, in the southern suburb; it extends both above and below the bridge of boats and contains a number of grain stores or 'Alwahs. The only bank is a branch of the Imperial Ottoman.

In the whole town there are reported to be 4,000 shops, 208 Khāns or caravansarais, 235 coffee houses, 182 'Alwahs, 116 flour mills worked by horses, 179 weavers' hand looms, 22 silk weaving machines, 68 dyeing establishments, 4 wool presses, and a soap factory. To these we may add 13 potteries, a number of sweetmeat and treacle factories, 3 oil mills, and an ice machine. There are also 3 printing presses.

Civil, military, and municipal administration.—Baghdād is the *chef-lieu* at once of the Wilāyat, of the Sanjāq and of the Qadha—all similarly named—in which it is situated. Its position in regard to the general administration of Turkish 'Irāq in all its departments is discussed in the article under that name.

The law courts, including the mercantile court, and the civil and military offices of government form a block of buildings known as the

Sarāi السراي on the left bank of the **Tigris**; the Sarāi begins about 350 yards above the bridge of boats and has a considerable frontage on the river; it contains also the public reception rooms of the Wāli. Immediately above the Sarāi is the local office of the Dāirat-as-Sanīyah. One court-house at a distance from the others is the Shara' court, which stands on the left bank of the **Tigris** about ¼ of a mile below the bridge of boats. The Customs House is on the left bank of the river a short distance below the bridge of boats; near to it is the mooring place of all the river steamers. Baghdād is the centre of the telegraph system of the Basrah, Baghdād and Mūsal Wilāyats, which is described in the article on Turkish **'Irāq** and the head office, which is accommodated under the same roof with the principal post office, is situated in a back street a little way from the Maidān on its north side. There is a harbour master at Baghdād who superintends shipping and river conservancy. **Baghdād** is the seat of the Central Committee of the Dāirat-as-Sanīyah administration in **'Irāq**.

The military importance of Baghdād as the headquarters of the 6th Turkish Army Corps will be apparent from the article on Turkish **'Irāq**, in which also the strength and composition of the local garrison are noticed. It is the headquarters of the 1st, 2nd and 3rd battalions of the 81st regiment of the Radīf and also of the 41st brigade of the same. The town, as already explained, is now practically unfortified. The infantry of the garrison, with the exception of certain guards such as that over the magazine at the Bāb-at-Tilism, are quartered in barracks having a large parade ground with a clock tower in the centre; these are called the Qīshlah قیشله —a corruption from Qīshlāq قیشلاق —and extend up the left bank of the **Tigris** almost all the way from the bridge of boats to the Sarāi. The eastern end of the Qīshlah contains a secondary military school, but the local Government now propose to sell the building and transfer this school to another site. The cavalry lines are outside the Bāb-al-Mu'adhdham at no great distance from the river or the town: they adjoin the road to **Mu'adhdham** and are surrounded by an ordinary wall. There are also quarters for marines. The town contains 19 small military posts or guard houses.

The Qal'ah القلعه or ancient citadel still exists, retaining its military designation, in the corner of the main town between the Bāb-al-Mu'-adhdham and the river; it comprises the artillery lines known as Tōp-khānah توپخانه, a military prison, a prison for ordinary life-convicts, a large open space, and possibly an ordnance store. The Turkish official almanac shows that there are two arsenals and two arms depôts. A military hospital, known as the Majīdīyah المجيديّة, is situated outside the town on the river bank just above the Qal'ah, and a military bakery exists.

Baghdād is a municipality, and as such its affairs are supposed to be regulated by a Municipal Council working under the supervision of the civil authorities. In point of fact the committee can do little beyond offering suggestions to the Wāli; they cannot of themselves expend any sum larger than 200 gold piastres and in the circumstances it is not extraordinary that few signs of their activity should be observable. They maintain a hospital just outside the Bāb-al-Mu'adhdham which is known as the Ghuraba Khastahkhānahsi غربه خسته خانه سي and is resorted to by the very poor. There were formerly 3 separate municipalities in the town, but now they have been combined into one by order of the local Government.

Foreign consular buildings, etc.—The question of foreign interests and their representation at Baghdād is sufficiently dealt with in the article on Turkish 'Irāq; here it only remains to mention the tangible evidences of the same which exist in the shape of buildings.

The former British Political Residency and Consulate-General, a hired building given up in 1905, stands on the left bank of the river about ½ a mile below the bridge of boats; it is a rambling old building in the native style of architecture with some remarkable interior decorations and a garden on the side towards the river, and it has now been converted into a hotel. The new British Residency, which is the property of the Indian Government, is on the same bank but at twice the distance below the bridge of boats; along with its dependencies (which include a separate house for the Residency Surgeon, a dispensary, a post office and lines for the native infantry guard) it is situated not far from the south-eastern end of the town and was originally one of the last buildings in this direction, but already a number of houses have sprung up between it and the open country. The new British Residency and edifices connected with it are certainly the largest, finest and most commodious buildings in Baghdād. The English Club is about 100 yards to the east of the former British Residency.

Most of the foreign consular buildings are situated on or near the left bank of the river below the bridge of boats. The Russian Consulate-General, a good house, is about ⅜ of a mile below the bridge of boats; next below it is the French and Austrian Consulate, a very old building, part of which subsided during the floods of 1907 ; then comes the German Consulate, about 250 yards below the Russian Consulate-General and the same distance above the new British Residency, of which the river wall has recently been advanced so as to give a considerable space between the house and the river : the American Vice-Consulate is about 200 yards inland from the German Consulate. These residences are all rented from private owners, except the German which is the private property of the German Consul.

The Persian Consulate-General is on the right bank of the river about 150 yards above the bridge of boats : it also is a hired building.

The consular representatives of Belgium and Norway, being private merchants charged with consular functions, have no official residences.

BAGHDĀD
بغداد
QADHA

A division of the Sanjāq, similarly named, in the Baghdād Wilāyat of Turkish 'Irāq.

Position and boundaries.—The Qadha of Baghdād is situated on both banks of the **Tigris**, partly above and partly below **Baghdād** City. It is bounded on the east by the river **Diyālah** in its lower course, and on the south and west—except that it includes the trans-Tigris suburb of the City—by the **Tigris**: on the north and north-west it is in contact with the Qadha of **Kādhimain** and on the north and north-east with that of Khurāsān.

Topography.—The only points of any importance which the Qadha contains, besides the city of **Baghdād** itself, are **Mu'adhdham** and **Qarārah**, each of which is described in a separate article under its own name.

Population.—The fixed population of the Qadha may be estimated at 150,000 souls. Of these about 55,000 are Jews by religion, while 50,000 are Sunni Muhammadans, 37,000 are Shi'ah Muhammadans, and 8,000 are Christians. The articles on **Baghdād** City and **Mu'adhdham** give the composition by races of almost the whole population of the Qadha.

Resources.—Most of the wealth in the Qadha belongs to the city of **Baghdād**, the article on which may be consulted. It remains to add that a considerable cultivation of fruit and vegetables is carried on upon the banks of the river immediately above and below the town, and even within the municipal limits. The gardens are irrigated from the **Tigris** by means of water lifts or pumps, and in many of them are situated country or pleasure houses belonging to wealthy residents of the town. The fruits grown are dates, grapes, peaches, nectarines, pomegranates, figs, plums, mulberries, quinces, limes, citrons, oranges, apples and apricots, but only the oranges are of the first quality ; the vegetables include ladies' fingers, brinjols, cucumbers, musk melons, water melons, pumpkins, beetroot, carrots, cabbages, cauliflowers, turnips, cress, lettuce, beans, tomatoes, onions, garlic and radishes. Some of the vegetables are of recent introduction ; on the whole they are good, but, as successive sowings are not regularly made, they are obtainable only during a short season. According to Turkish official statistics there are 769 water lifts in the immediate environs of **Baghdād** City, while date palms within the same limits number 177,800 and other fruit trees 130,000. The area of cultivation in the Qadha has been estimated at 1,850 Faddāns.

Administration.— In this Qadha there is no Qāim-Maqām; the administration is carried on by the Wāli of the Wilāyat, whose residence is within its limits, in **Baghdād** City. There is only one Nāhiyah, that of **Mu'adhdham**, belonging to the 2nd class ; another which formerly existed at **Qarārah** has been suppressed.

BAHĀRINAH

بحارنه

Singular Bahrāni بحراني . The name of the race or class to which nearly all the Shī'ahs of the **Bahrain** Islands, of the **Hasa** and **Qatīf** Oases and of the **Qatar** promontory belong. The mistake of supposing that Bahārinah means "natives of **Bahrain**" must be carefully guarded against ; on the contrary the Sunni inhabitant of **Bahrain** repudiates the name of "Bahrāni" and describes the class to which he himself belongs as "Ahl-al-Bahrain." As employed along the western coast of the Persian Gulf the term Bahrāni is practically a synonym for a Shī'ah Muhammadan whose mother tongue is Arabic.

Numbers and distribution.—In **Bahrain** the number of the Bahārinah appears to be about 38,000 souls ; in the **Hasa** Oasis, if we include the Shī'ah population of the towns of **Hofūf** and **Mubarraz**, they are about 30,000 persons ; in the **Qatīf** Oasis, inclusive of **Qatīf** Town, they are perhaps 28,000 souls. In **Qatar** they have about 60 houses at **Dōhah** and 40 at **Wakrah**, representing in all about 500 heads. Some of the tribe have emigrated at various times to other parts of the Gulf, especially to some of the districts of the **Persian Coast,** such as **Dashti** and perhaps **Dashtistān**; about 250 Bahārinah are settled at **Sohār** Town in the Sultanate of **'Omān** and about 600 at the towns of Abu **Dhabi** and **Dibai** in Trucial **'Omān**; and the total number of the Bahārinah cannot now be assessed at much less than 100,000 persons.

Religion and character.—All Bahārinah are Shī'ahs. They are unwarlike in character and tend to peaceful pursuits, the richer among them living by trade and the poorer by husbandry, pearl diving and various handicrafts.

Leading families.—The Bahārinah have no tribal cohesion or organisation, but some of their leading families are distinguished by names. The prominent Bahrāni families of the **Hasa** and **Qatīf** Oases,—if we except the 'Alaiwāt عليوات, who are found at 'Anik in the **Qatīf** Oasis, and the Āl Bin-Ghānim آل بن غانم, whose Shaikhs ruled **Qatīf** Town until they were subverted by the Wahhābis,—have not been ascertained; but among the wealthier and more important in the **Bahrain** Principality are the following:—

'Anābirah	عنابره	Mājid (Āl)	آل ماجد
'Asāfirah	عصافره	Muslim (Āl)	آل مسلم
(or Āl 'Asfūr	(آل عصفور)	Rafyah (Āl)	آل رفيه
'Asākirah	عساكره	Rahmah (Āl)	آل رحمه
Ghabārah	غباره	and	
Hadādīd	حداديد	Suwār (Āl Bin-)	آل بن سوار;

besides numerous families of Saiyids who are now recognised as Bahārinah. The above are mostly large families of which branches are found in different parts of **Bahrain**. The **Baqāqalah** of **Bahrain**—but not those of **Qatar** who are Sunnis — are considered to be Bahārinah; so are the **Hamidah**.

Origin.—The Bahārinah are generally stated to have come into existence by the conversion of certain Arab tribes, including one called the Bani Rabī', to Shī'ism about 300 years ago; this is the local Muhammadan tradition. Some European writers on the other hand have manifested an inclination to regard the bulk of the Bahārinah as an aboriginal tribe conquered by the Arabs. In the absence of sufficient ethnological data it is impossible to pronounce in favour of or against either theory.

BAHLAH
بهله

A town of the 'Omān Sultanate in 'Omān Proper towards the west end of that district and about 20 miles west of Nizwa; it is situated 1,600 feet above sea level. The site with the surrounding cultivation forms an irregular parallelogram about 2 square miles in extent, which is enclosed by a wall and stands on the left bank of Wādi Bahlah, a tributary probably of Wādi Halfain. The town, composed of a number of distinct villages or walled quarters, is in appearance one of the most striking in 'Omān. On an eminence in the centre of it rises a huge white fort with two towers, one of which is very lofty and commands a splendid view of the whole valley; while around, on various sides, the plain is broken by low hills less than two miles distant. The inhabitants of Bahlah are Mahāriq (35 houses), 'Abriyīn (200 houses), Bayāsirah (100 houses), Jannabah (30 houses), Miyāyihah of the Maqārishah section (30 houses), Bani Jissās (30 houses), Bani Kalbān (30 houses), Bani Rāshid (50 houses), Bani Shakail (40 houses) and mixed tribes, amounting to about 3,000 souls in all. The crops grown on the town lands include wheat, barley, jowari, sugar, beans, gram and cotton; there are also plantains and mangoes and the number of date palms is estimated at 3,000. There are 40 horses, 300 camels, 400 donkeys, 600 cattle and 1,000 sheep and goats. Cloaks called Manāsīl مناسيل are manufactured of fine goats' hair, some earthenware is made, and lungis are woven as in most of the larger places in 'Omān. Bahlah is believed to be a very ancient place and was for a time under the Nabhāni dynasty, who ruled at the beginning of the 17th century, the capital of all 'Omān. The principal Shaikh is Nāsir-bin-Hamaiyid, a man of forcible character who attained his position about 1885 by the murder of two elder brothers, Barghāsh and Rāshid. In March 1885 a destructive flood occurred in the Wādi by which many date trees and houses were swept away.

BAHMAN-SHĪR
بهمشير

Or Bahmishīr بهمشير, but the forms Bahmanshīr and Bahmānshīr بهمانشير are locally more prevalent. By European geographers this name is applied to the stream which leaves the left bank of the Kārūn 2 miles above Muhammareh Town and forms the eastern boundary of 'Abbādān island all the way from that point to the sea. We must however warn the reader that in the neighbourhood of Muhammareh Town the term Bahmanshīr is applied to the last reach of the Kārūn, by Europeans wrongly called "Haffār"; and that the river now in question, having among natives no general name, is described by various local terms

P

in its different reaches —such as Shatt Silaikh سليخ or Silaich, and Shatt Tura طرا, taken from villages on its banks.*

The total length of the Bahmanshīr, as we in accordance with European usage shall call it, is 54 miles by its winding course and 40 in a straight line; its mouth in the Persian Gulf is about 10 miles east of the mouth of the Shatt-al-'**Arab**. There are two remarkable bends rather below the middle of its course. The breadth of the river varies from 300 yards in the upper reaches to 600 yards and even ½ a mile as it approaches the sea.

Towards the middle of the nineteenth century it carried about two-fifths of the water of the **Kārūn** and its depth at low water was nowhere less than 9 feet; but by 1890 the uppermost 15 miles of its course had become obstructed by banks which in places dried almost across the channel at low water, and the R.I.M.S. "Comet," drawing only three feet, grounded twice in making the passage: the 30 miles of the river nearest to the sea however then continued navigable for vessels of not more than 7 feet draft. Native sea-going boats cannot now pass the shoals of the upper Bahmanshīr without assistance from the tide. The rise and fall of the tide, which is felt throughout the whole length of the Bahmanshīr, is about 9 feet. The channel between the mouth of the river and the open sea is called Khor Bahmanshīr; at its north end it had, in 1890, 15 feet at low water diminishing to 12, 10 and finally to 8 feet on the bar, which is of soft mud and 10 miles distant from the river mouth; the river was then accessible, at low water, to craft drawing not more than 7 feet. When there was no steamer service at **Kuwait** and **Muhammareh** was the steam-port of that place, the native sailing boats by which communication was maintained frequently made use of the Bahmanshīr channel in order to escape Turkish interference upon the Shatt-al-'**Arab**.

From the **Kārūn** downwards the banks are lined with villages and date-plantations to within about 10 miles of the sea; low grassy plains follow, the banks for some distance remaining firm and steep; finally, the stream enters a region of shelving mud-flats, covered above the water line with coarse grass and reeds. Islands are easily formed in the Bahmanshīr by staking the stream and so causing a deposit of silt, and this is frequently done; the new island is at first used for pasturage and ultimately brought under cultivation.

---

* Of these two names, that of Silaich is perhaps sometimes used by natives to describe the whole stream to which the present article relates. But the term is open to objection as leading to confusion with Khor Silaich—see article Khor **Mūsa**—which enters the sea between the Bahmanshīr and Khor **Mūsa**.

The villages upon the right bank of the Bahmanshīr are enumerated and described in the article on 'Abbādān island: those on the left bank are:—

Name.	Position.	Houses and inhabitants.	Remarks.
Munīkh منیخ	From the head of the Bahmanshīr down to a point opposite Mahyūb on 'Abbādān island.	20 houses of Mutūr Muhaisin, partly scattered and partly forming a hamlet.	Near by is a place called Ma'aibar معبر where there is sometimes a ferry kept by a family of Nassār Ka'ab. The Imperial Persian Customs have a post at the lower end of Munīkh, at a place where there is a bar across the river.
Silaik (Upper) سلیك	Opposite Shanneh and Shinaineh on 'Abbādān island.	A few houses of Hilālāt Muhaisin.	Pronounced Silaich. There is an island here called Ma'amareh.
Kharkhareh خرخره	Opposite 'Abdullah-bin-Da'būleh on the 'Abbādān side.	10 houses of Bakhākh Muhaisin.	Above this place, opposite Suwainīkh on 'Abbādān island, but close to the left bank of the Bahmanshīr, is an island called Saiyid 'Abūd.
Silaik (Lower) سلیك	Follows Kharkhareh.	30 houses of Ka'ab of the Thawāmir section.	Pronounced Silaich. The place appears to have the alternative name of Hasawīyeh.
Āl Bū 'Abbādi آل بو عبادي	Opposite Qabāneh on the 'Abbādān side.	30 houses of Ka'ab of the Āl Bū 'Abbādi section.	...
Malākeh ملاكه	About a mile above Shākhat Hāji Is-hāq on the opposite side.	20 houses of Ka'ab of the Drīs division.	...
Bū Shānak بو شانك	Opposite Shākhat Hāji Is-hāq on 'Abbādān island.	Do.	...
Dalgeh دلگه	Opposite Bakhākh-at-Tura on the 'Abbādān side.	10 houses of Mutūr Muhaisin.	...
Tingeh تنگه	Opposite to open desert on 'Abbādān island.	20 houses of Nassār Ka'ab and Mutūr Muhaisin.	A few miles below Tingeh and opposite to Kuwaibdeh on the 'Abbādān side is a Customs post.

BAHRAIN

البحرين

ISLAND *

This island, formerly called **Awāl,** is the largest in the **Bahrain** archipelago and lies almost in the middle of the unnamed V-shaped gulf which divides the Turkish territories of **Hasa** and **Qatīf** from the promontory of **Qatar.**

Shape, size and physical characteristics.—The shape of the island corresponds with that of the gulf, the coasts that front the mainland being approximately parallel to it throughout. From the northernmost point near **Manāmah** town to the southern extremity at Rās-al-Barr, Bahrain Island measures 30 miles: its maximum breadth from Rās-al-Jufair to **Budaiya'** is 10 miles. The total area of the island is 208 square miles, and about 18 square miles are covered by date plantations.

The principal date belt is at the north end of the island; it is almost continuous from **Manāmah** to Būri, with a length north-east and south-west of 7 and a maximum breadth at the middle of 3 miles; and it thus occupies most of the space north of the great marine indentation, known as Khor-al-**Kabb,** which penetrates from the east coast almost to the centre of the island.

The greater part of Bahrain Island is flat and low, but the surface rises gradually from all sides towards the centre to form a plateau 100 to 200 feet high; in the middle of the plateau is an oval-shaped depression, about 13 miles long from north to south by 4 broad, containing in its centre the solitary hill of Jabal-ad-**Dukhān,** 440 feet high, the most elevated point on the island. The descent inwards from the plateau to the depression is in most places too steep to be practicable for animals; it consists at the northern end of a nearly vertical drop of 20 feet followed by a steep slope of 30 feet. The plateau itself is extraordinarily stony and presents a line of low cliffs, perhaps 15 feet high, to the north, below which is a sandy plain extending in all directions to the coast and draining from west to east. Jabal-ad-**Dukhān** is of a dark hue, but elsewhere the rocks are light yellow or light pink, indeed almost white, in colour.

Features of the coasts.—We need not dwell here on the geology of Bahrain Island, which is dealt with at length in the article on the **Bahrain** Principality; but it will be convenient to give at this point, in alphabetical order, a list of the chief features and points of interest

---

* The more important authorities, maps, charts, etc., are specified in a footnote to the general article on **Bahrain** Principality.

—other than inhabited or cultivated spots—which occur upon the coast:—

Name.	Position.*	Nature.	Remarks.
'Aqāriyah العقاريه	On the west coast 8 miles below **Budaiya'**. Mālikīyah village lies a little way inland.	Landing place.	The usual point of embarkation and disembarkation for passengers between **Bahrain** and the mainland of **Hasa**. There are one or two huts here for the accommodation of travellers.
Barr (Rās-al-) راس البرّ	The southern extremity of the island.	Cape.	Also known as Rās Hadd-al-Bahrain راس حدّ البحرين. About a mile long and very narrow.
Bartúfi (Fasht) فشت برطفي	Adjoining the north-west corner of Bahrain Island.	A coral reef.	Has a spring of fresh water.
Buqshi (Rās-al-) راس البقشي	On the east coast 6 miles from the southern extremity of island.	Cape.	...
Dūbās (Rās) راس دوباس	On the west coast 7 miles south-south-west of Jabal-ad-**Dukhān**.	Do.	A short distance off it, at sea, is a deep-water hole famous for its fish.
Hasam (Rās Umm-al-) راس امّ الحصم	2 miles south-east of **Manāmah** fort.	Do.	The north-east entrance point of the Khor-al-**Kabb** behind **Manāmah** town.
Haiyān (Rās) راس حيّان	On the east coast 5 miles east of Jabal-ad-**Dukhān**.	Do.	Carries an old and prominent building, said to have been erected as a memorial or as a tomb; this promontory is called also Rās Sa'sa'ah. صعصعه
Jarjūr (Rās Abu) راس ابو جرجور	On the east coast 5 miles east-north-east of Jabal-ad-**Dukhān**.	Do.	...
Jasrah (Rās-al-) راس الجسره	On the west coast 3 miles below **Budaiya'**.	Do.	Rās-al-Jasrah is also a alternative name of Rās-al-Jufair below.

*In this column "above" means to the north, and "below" to the south, of the point specified.

BAHRAIN ISLAND.

Name.	Position.*	Nature.	Remarks.
Jazāir (Rās-al-) راس الجزائر	On the west coast 6 miles south-west of Jabal-ad-**Dukhān**.	Cape.	Has a well, frequented by fishermen, and gives its name to a hamlet near by.
Jidi (Jazīrat) جزيرة جدي	3 miles west-south-west of **Budai-ya'**.	Islet.	Nearly a mile long from east to west, rocky, and reaching a height of 52 feet.
Jufair (Rās-al-) راس الجفير	On the east coast 2 miles east-south-east of **Manā-mah** fort.	Cape.	Called also Rās Qazqaz راس قزقز and Rās-al-Jasrah راس الجسره
Kabb (Khor-al-) خور الكبّ	...	...	See article Khor-al-**Kabb**.
Libainat-al-'Alīyah لبينة العليه	8 miles west-north-west of **Budai-ya'**.	Islet.	Sandy and covered with low scrub; the surface is 2 feet above sea-level at high water.
Libainat-as-Sāfi-līyah لبينة السافليه	8 miles west-south-west of **Budai-ya'**.	Do.	Do.
Mattalah (Rās-al-) راس المطله	On the west side of Bahrain Island, 8 miles south by west of Jabal-ad-**Dukhān**.	Cape.	Inland 1½ miles from the cape is a well called 'Ain-al-Mat-talah. A salt plain called Mimlahat-al-Mattalah مملحة المطلا about 4 miles in length, extends from Rās-al-Mattalah to Rās Dūbās: here the people of Bahrain extract salt for domestic consumption.
Mōj (Rās Abul) راس ابو الموج	On the west coast 4½ miles west-south-west of Ja-bal-ad-**Dukhān**.	Do.	...
Na'aijā النعيجات	2 miles west-north-west of **Budai-ya'**.	Rocks.	They rise 2 feet above high water mark.

* In this column " above " means to the north, and " below " to the south, of the point specified.

Name.	Position.*	Nature.	Remarks.
Nōmah (Rās) راس نومه	On the west coast, 6 miles south-west by west of Jabal-ad-Dukhān.	Cape.	A short distance inland is the village of 'Adāim.
Qadhaibīyah (Dōhat-al-) دوحة القضيبيه	On the north-east coast of Bahrain between Jufair and Hālat Bin-Anas villages.	A large bay with a clean sandy beach.	In summer an encampment, extending a mile along the shore and having 2 or 3 wide streets which run throughout its length, is formed here. The occupants are people of Muharraq Town, Hadd and Hālat Abu Māhur; they inhabit 'Arīshes of date fronds having compounds walled in with the same materials, and their water is fetched from the Umm-ash-Sha'ūm wells.
Qarain (Rās-al-) راس القرين	On the east coast, 7 miles south-east of Jabal-ad-Dukhān.	Cape.	...
Qazqaz (Rās)	...	...	See Jufair above.
Raqah (Jazīrat-ar-) جزيرة الرقه	1¼ miles south-west of Budaiya'.	Islet.	Rocky and about 5 feet above high water; covered with low scrub. Also known as Umm-as-Subbān ام الصبان
Rummān (Rās-ar-) راس الرمان	The northernmost point of Bahrain Island, near its north-eastern corner.	Cape.	Entirely built over and now forms the eastern quarter of Manāmah Town.
Sa'sa'ah (Rās)	...	...	See Rās Haiyān above.
Sahailah (Jazīrat) جزيرة سهيله	1½ miles north-west of Budaiya'.	Islet.	Sandy; said to be increasing in elevation, but is still covered at high tide.
Subh (Rās Abu) راس ابو صبح	On the north-west coast about midway between Budaiya' and Sharaibah.	Cape.	...

* In this column "above" means to the north, and "below" to the south, of the point specified.

Name.	Position.*	Nature.	REMARKS.
Sulaisil. سليسل	Begins 4 miles north-west by north of **Manāmah** Town and runs landwards.	The passage used by large native vessels between the outer and the inner anchorages at **Manāmah**.	Arabs call the inner buoy "Bōyat Sulaisil."
Tūbli (Rās) راس توبلي	On the south side of the Khor-al-**Kabb**, 1½ miles from the foot of it.	Cape.	...
Yaman (Rās-al-) راس اليمن	On the east coast, 5 miles from the southern extremity of island.	Do.	Prominent.
Ya'sūf (Jazīrat) جزيرة يعصرف	2½ miles west of 'Aqārīyah.	Islet.	Small and barren.
Zallāq (Rās-az-) راس الزلاق	4 miles west by north of Jabal-ad-**Dukhān**.	Cape.	The village of the same name stands on this point.
Zuwaiyid (Rās) راس زويد	On the east coast 6 miles north-east of Jabal-ad-**Dukhān**.	Do.	Nil.

*In this column "above" means to the north, and "below" to the south, of the point specified.

Hills.—To these features of the coast we may add the following hills, which are the principal, and indeed the only conspicuous, natural objects in the interior of Bahrain Island:—

Name.	Position.*	Nature.	REMARKS.
Dukhān (Jabal-ad-) جبل الدخان	...	...	See article Jabal-ad-**Dukhān**.
Hisai (Jabal-al-) جبل الحسي	2 miles east of **Rifā'-ash-Sharqi**.	Hill.	About 2½ miles in length and slopes downwards in a south-easterly direction almost to the seashore.
Lughaibrāt (Jabal) لغيبرات	1¼ miles north of Jabal-ad-**Dukhān**.	Group of hillocks.	In the central depression of Bahrain Island.
Rumāmain (Jabal) رمامين	Near the foot of Jabal-ad-**Dukhān** on the north-east side.	Couple of hillocks.	...

*In this column "above" means to the north, and "below" to the south, of the point specified.

Towns, villages, etc.—The following alphabetically arranged list exhibits in a convenient form the towns, villages and other inhabited or cultivated places on Bahrain Island :—

Name.	Position.	Houses and population.	Remarks.
'Adāim عدائم	5½ miles south-west of Jabal-ad-**Dukhān**.	15 stone and mud huts.	The place is between Rās Nōmah and some sand mounds. Empty in summer, it is occupied in winter by fishermen from Zallāq.
'Ain-ad-Dār عين الدار	Adjoins Jidd Hafs on the south-west.	50 houses of **Bahārinah**, cultivators, masons and barbers.	Practically a suburb of Jidd Hafs. Animals are 7 donkeys and 2 cattle.
'Ajāj (Qal'at-al-) قلعة العجاج	...	...	See article Qal'at-al-'Ajāj.
'Āli عالي	...	...	See article 'Āli.
Anas (Hālat Bin-) حالة بن انس	On a point at a very short distance due east of **Manāmah** Town.	85 huts of Sunnis, some Mālikis, some Shāfi'is; they are pearl divers and fishermen. Most of the people are non-tribal Arabs, but there are about 10 houses of **Hūwalah** and 20 of free negroes. Donkeys number 7.	There are 9 pearl boats at this place, of which 6 are Māshuwahs.
'Aqur العقر	On the east coast, opposite the centre of **Sitrah** Island.	30 reed huts of **Bahārinah**, cultivators, fruit and grass-sellers, fishermen and pearl divers.	Situated on very low-lying ground. There are 8 donkeys and 5 cattle here; also 6 pearl boats of which 3 are Shū'ais or Sambūks.
'Askar العسكر	On the east coast, 4½ miles east-north-east of Jabal-ad-**Dukhān**.	75 stone houses and reed huts of Āl Bū **'Ainain** pearl divers.	1 Batīl, 1 Baqārah and 17 Māshuwahs or jolly boats are owned here, of which 16 are pearl boats; and there are 6 donkeys and 16 cattle. Date palms are estimated at 1,500.

Name.	Position.	Houses and population.	Remarks.
Bada'ah بدعه	On the north coast between Sanābis and Karbābād.	...	A favourite hot weather resort of townspeople who erect date-stick huts for themselves here.
Bahām (Abu) ابو بهام	2½ miles west-south-west of Manāmah fort.	30 huts of Bahārinah, date growers and cultivators.	The village is surrounded by plantations irrigated by a fine stream of water from the 'Adāri spring; the stream flows through the village. There are 7 donkeys and 2 cattle.
Baijawīyah البيجويه	2 miles west-south-west of Manāmah fort.	20 huts of Bahārinah, date growers.	There are here 9 donkeys and 1 head of cattle. Date trees number about 750.
Baqaishi (Qal'at-al-) قلعة البقيشي	On the west coast, 4 miles west-north-west of Jabal-ad-Dukhān.	...	A ruined fort.
Bārbār باربار	½ a mile south-east of Sharaibah.	60 mean reed huts occupied by Bahārinah, weavers, cultivators and fishermen.	A village with date groves adjoining. Several Shū'ais or Sambūks, employed in pearling, are owned here. Donkeys number 19 and cattle 8. There are about 2,400 date palms, besides some peaches and pomegranates and a few tamarinds and mulberries.
Barbūrah بربوره	2 miles north-east of Rifā'-ash-Sharqi.	20 small stone huts of Bahārinah, agriculturists.	A fine spring to the north of the village irrigates the cultivation. Donkeys number 15 and there are 2 cattle. Date palms are estimated at 1,760.
Bilād-al-Qadīm بلاد القديم	...	...	See article Bilād-al-Qadīm.
Budaiya' البديع	..	...	See article Budaiya'.
Buquwwah بوه	4 miles west-south-west of Manāmah fort.	20 huts of Bahārinah who live by selling firewood.	Donkeys are 55 and cattle 5 and dates about 5,500.

Name.	Position.	Houses and population.	Remarks.
Būri بوري	7 miles south-west of **Manāmah** fort.	A few stone houses and 150 huts of **Bahārinah**, all growers of dates.	The village is surrounded by date plantations and is at the south-western extremity of the great date belt. Donkeys number 17 and cattle 13 · dates are estimated at 10,500.
Dirāz الدراز	1 mile east-north-east of **Budaiya'** and ¾ of a mile from sea.	Several well built houses and about 150 huts of **Bahārinah**, cultivators, weavers and pearl divers.	The dwellings are scattered amongst various adjacent date clumps. The weaving industry is considerable and the cloth manufactured is chiefly that used for making 'Abas. Several Shū'ais or Sambūks, employed in pearling, are owned here. Livestock include 30 donkeys and 12 cattle, and dates are about 1,500.
Dumistān دمستان	4¼ miles west of **Rifā'-al-Gharbi** and ¾ of a mile from the west coast.	20 huts of **Bahārinah**, cultivators and pearl divers.	There are 17 donkeys and 5 cattle, and date palms are estimated at between 2,500 and 3,000.
Falāh الفلاح	On the north coast, 1½ miles east of **Qal'at-al-'Ajāj**.	About 30 huts inhabited by **Bahārinah** who are pearl divers and date growers.	Practically an eastern suburb of Sanābis. It stands between the shore and the date gardens. Animals are 9 donkeys and 2 cattle.
Fārsiyah فارسيه	On the east coast, 3 miles east-south-east of **Rifā'-ash-Sharqi**.	30 huts of **Bahārinah**, all cultivators.	There are 5 donkeys here and 5 cattle. Palms are about 1,900.
Ghuraifah الغريفه	On the east coast midway between Rās al-Jufair and Rās Umm-al-Hasam.	30 mean reed huts of **Bahārinah**, cultivators and fishermen.	Stands at the east end of the date groves which line the north shore of Khor-al-**Kabb**. Animals include 6 donkeys and 1 head of cattle.

Name.	Position.	House and population.	Remarks.
Habshi (Jabalat) جبلة حبشي	3 miles west by south of **Manāmah** fort.	20 huts of **Bahārinah**, agriculturists.	There are 17 donkeys and 3 cattle here. Palms are about 1,800.
Hajar الهجر	1½ miles south of **Qal'at-al-'Ajāj**.	40 huts of **Bahārinah**, cultivators.	The village lands are irrigated from numerous good wells. There are 18 donkeys and 4 cattle. Dates are estimated at 12,000.
Halaitān حليطان	...	...	See **Jazāir** below.
Hamalah الهمله	¼ of a mile from the west coast 5 miles below **Budaiya'**.	40 huts of **Bahārinah**, cultivators and fishermen.	There are 8 donkeys and 1 head of cattle.
Harbadīyah الهربديّة	On the north coast ½ a mile west of **Qal'at-al-'Ajāj**.	20 huts inhabited by **Bahārinah** who are cultivators and fishermen.	...
Hujair الهجير	4½ miles north of **Rifā'-ash-Sharqi** and ½ a mile south of the **Kabb** creek.	15 huts of **Bahārinah**, date growers.	Situated on the western fringe of the date groves between Kawarah and Tūbli. Donkeys number 18 and cattle 2. Date palms are estimated at 4,000.
Hūrah الحورة	Between **Manāmah** town and **Hālat Bin-Anas**, close to the Christian cemetery.	50 reed huts of **Bahārinah** who are stone-cutters, lime-burners, blacksmiths and pearl divers.	There are 8 donkeys here and 2 cattle, but only about 300 palms.
Iswār (Hālat Bin-). حالة بن اسوار	On the coast between **Rās-ar-Rummān** and **Hāl-at Bin-Anas**.	40 huts of **Bahārinah**, who are pearl divers, fishermen, rope-makers, carpenters and donkey-men.	Livestock are 3 donkeys and 4 cattle and there are 16 pearl boats, of which 3 are **Māshuwahs** or jolly-boats.
Jabailāt الجبيلات	4½ miles north of **Rifā'-ash-Sharqi** and ½ a mile south of the **Kabb** creek.	15 huts of **Bahārinah**, date growers.	There are large date plantations, and most of the fruits acclimatised in **Bahrain** are grown here.
Jabalah الجبله	On the north coast 1 mile west of **Manāmah** fort.	20 reed huts of **Bahārinah**, date growers, pearl divers and boat-builders.	Date plantations adjoin. Animals are 4 donkeys and 1 head of cattle.

BAHRAIN ISLAND

Name.	Position.	Houses and population.	Remarks.
Jamrah (Bani) بني جمرة	¾ of a mile east of Budaiya'.	50 huts of **Bahārinah**, who are date growers and weave cloth of which 'Abas are made.	Near by is the well from which is procured some of the drinking water used in Budaiya'. Several Shū'ais or Sambūks, employed in pearling, are owned here. Donkeys number 25 and palms are about 1,300.
Janābīyah الجنابية	Near the west coast 1½ miles below Budaiya'.	20 huts of **Bahārinah**, cultivators and fishermen.	Stands in a date-clump. There are 8 donkeys, 2 cattle and not quite 1,000 date trees.
Jannūsān جنوسان	Near the north coast, 1½ miles west of Qal'at-al-'Ajāj.	30 huts of **Bahārinah**, pearl divers and fishermen.	There are 15 donkeys and 5 cattle. Date palms are estimated at 5,500, and there are some peaches and pomegranates, besides, it is said, a few vines and apricots.
Jasairah الجسيرة	On the east coast, 7½ miles from the south end of the island.	35 reed huts of Sunnis, viz., 30 of **Ka'abān** and 5 of **Kibīsah**, pearl divers and fishermen.	There are 11 pearl boats here.
Jau جو	On the east coast, 5 miles east-south-east of Jabal-ad-Dukhān.	A few well built houses of stone, mud and gypsum mortar and about 400 huts. The people are all Sunnis and are mostly engaged in the pearl fisheries. There are 80 households of Āl Bū **Rumaih**.	There are no dates, but about 30 boats are owned here, viz., 4 Baqārahs and 28 Māshuwahs and jolly-boats, of which 23 are pearl boats. Donkeys number 8, and cattle 25. There are 2 routes to Jau from **Manāmah** town, one along the coast, the other by **Rifā'-ash-Sharqi**. Jau was the abode of the Āl Bū **Samait** while in Bahrain.
Jasrah الجسرة	On the west coast, 3 miles below Budaiya'.	50 reed huts of Bani **Khālid** of the Dawāwdah section, engaged in the pearl fisheries.	There is a small date clump here, adjoining the sea. Donkeys number 9 and cattle 2.

Name.	Position.	Houses and population.	Remarks.
Jazāir الجزائر	On the west coast, 6 miles south-west of Jabal-ad-Dukhān, near Rās-al-Jazāir.	Resembles 'Adāim above.	It is also called Halaitān حليطان.
Jidd 'Ali جدّ علي	Near the east coast, 4 miles north of Rifā'-ash-Sharqi.	30 squalid reed huts inhabited by **Bahārinah** who cultivate dates.	Here there are 13 donkeys and 3 cattle, and date trees are placed at 3,430.
Jidd Hafs جدّ حفص	1½ miles south-east of Qal'-at-al-'Ajāj.	300 houses of **Bahārinah** who are date growers, carpenters, lime-burners and pearl-merchants.	The village is prosperous, with large vegetable and lucerne gardens irrigated from a number of good springs. 'Ain-ad-Dār is practically a suburb of Jidd Hafs. There are 50 donkeys and 13 cattle. Date palms are estimated at 16,500, and fruits of all sorts are grown.
Jidd-al-Hajj جدّ الحاج	On the coast, 1 mile west of Qal'at-al-'Ajāj.	15 huts of **Bahārinah**, date growers and fishermen.	There are 17 donkeys and 3 cattle and about 1,400 palms.
Jubailāt الجبيلات	Between Qal'at-al-'Ajāj and Rūzakkān, adjoining the latter.	10 houses of **Bahārinah**, cultivators.	Animals include 3 donkeys and 3 cattle. There are some boats (see Ruqa'ah below).
Jufair الجفير	On the north side of the cape similarly named.	80 reed huts of **Bahārinah**, cultivators and fishermen.	¼ of a mile east of the village, near the point of the cape, is a large stone house, the property of 'Abdur Rahmān-bin-'Abdul Wahhāb, the Wazīr of **Bahrain**. On the south-west side of the village are a large date clump and some lucerne fields. Livestock are 2 horses, 7 donkeys and 4 cattle. There are about 900 date trees. There are 15 pearl boats here, of which 13 are Māshuwahs and jolly-boats.

Name.	Position.	Houses and population.	Remarks.
Jurdāb جرداب	On the east coast, opposite Nabi Sālih Island.	30 reed huts inhabited by **Bahārinah** who are date growers.	Date palms are estimated at 2,230.
Karbābād كرب آباد	On the west coast, ½ a mile east of Qal'at-al-'Ajāj.	50 mean reed huts of **Bahārinah** who fish, dive for pearls, and cultivate dates.	There are 23 donkeys and 3 cattle. Dates are estimated at 8,500, besides which are oranges, pomegranates, peaches, almonds, tamarinds, bananas, etc.
Karānah كرانه	¾ of a mile west-south-west of Qal'at-al-'Ajāj.	60 huts of **Bahārinah**, cultivators.	There are 15 donkeys and 12 cattle.
Karzakkān كرزكّان	¾ of a mile from the west coast, 7 miles below **Budaiya'**.	150 huts of **Bahārinah** who are cultivators and sailmakers.	The houses stand amidst date groves and gardens which are watered, along with those of Mālikīyah, by Falajs. Animals include 24 donkeys and 8 cattle; dates are about 16,500.
Kawarah كوره	4¼ miles north of **Rifā'-ash-Sharqi** and ¾ of a mile from the east coast.	50 reed huts of **Bahārinah** who are cultivators.	Situated on the fringe of the date groves furthest from the sea. There are here 14 donkeys, 3 cattle and about 2,150 palms.
Khafīr (Abu) ابو خفير	1½ miles south-west of **Manāmah** fort.	30 mat huts inhabited by **Bahārinah**, cultivators.	Donkeys here number 4 and cattle 2.
Khuraiyān خريّان	1½ miles south-west of **Manāmah** fort.	30 huts of **Bahārinah**, cultivators and makers of a black cement.	Close to the highroad between Manāmah town and Rifā'. Animals are 11 donkeys and 1 head of cattle.
Kulaib (Dār) دار كليب	3 miles north-west of Jabal-ad-**Dukhān** and 1½ miles from west coast.	50 reed huts of **Bahārinah**, cultivators and sailmakers.	There are 25 donkeys and 12 cattle and about 4,000 dates.

Name.	Position.	Houses and population.	Remarks.
Ma'āmīr المعامير	On the east coast, opposite to **Sitrah** island a little below its centre.	130 houses, including a number of masonry buildings. The people are **Bahārinah**, all engaged in the pearl fisheries and owning a considerable number of large boats.	2 Baqārahs and 22 Shū'ais and Sambūks are owned here, 17 of these being used for pearling; livestock include 9 donkeys and 3 cattle.
Māhūz الماحوز	1 mile south-west of **Manāmah** fort.	30 reed huts of **Bahārinah**, cultivators.	There are several good wells and a spring. The village stands surrounded by lucerne fields on the north shore of Khor-al-Kabb. Livestock include 19 donkeys and 2 cattle, and dates are estimated at 9,000.
Makhrūq المخروق	1 mile south-east of **Rifā'-ash-Sharqi**.	A small group of huts, now deserted, belonging to **Bahārinah**, agriculturists.	There are fields of lucerne watered from a spring. The cultivation here is going to ruin.
Mālikīyah المالكية	Near the west coast 8 miles below **Budaiya'** and just inland of 'Aqārīyah.	100 huts of **Bahārinah**, engaged in cultivation.	The dwellings stand amidst dates and there is a prominent stone-built Shī'ah shrine close by. Among the livestock are 18 donkeys and 10 cattle. Dates are about 6,000.
Manāmah town المنامة	...	...	See article **Manāmah**.
Mani مني	On the north coast 1½ miles west of **Manāmah** fort.	20 reed huts of **Bahārinah**, date growers and fishermen.	There are 19 donkeys and 4 cattle here. Dates are estimated at over 19,000.
Maqāba مقابا	2 miles east of **Budaiya'**.	20 huts of **Bahārina**, cultivators.	This village possesses one of the finest springs on the island. Donkeys number 20 and cattle 8. Date trees are about 4,000.
Markh المرخ	1⅓ miles east of **Budaiya'**.	25 huts of **Bahārinah**, weavers, and of Saiyids who are religious beggars.	Situated in the middle of a date clump. There are 15 donkeys and 3 cattle; also about 1,350 date trees.

Name.	Position.	Houses and population.	Remarks.
Marwazān مروزان	1½ miles east-south-east of Qal'at-al-'Ajāj.	25 huts of Bahārinah.	Surrounded by date gardens. Animals are 10 donkeys and 3 cattle.
Muqshā' المقشاع	1 mile south of Qal'at-al-'Ajāj.	20 huts of Bahārinah, date growers.	There are 9 donkeys and 8 cattle here, also about 1,500 date-palms.
Musalla المصلا	2¼ miles west-south-west of Manāmah fort.	40 huts of Bahārinah, cultivators.	There are 5 donkeys and 4 cattle here.
Muwailghah المويلغه	Almost adjoins the south-west corner of Bilād-al-Qadīm.	40 stone and mat huts of Bahārinah, date cultivators and gardeners.	There are 5 donkeys and 1 head of cattle.
Na'īm-al-Kabīrah نعيم الكبيرة	...	...	See article Manāmah.
Nūr Juruft نور جرفت	1 mile west of Qal'at-al-'Ajāj.	20 huts of Bahārinah, date growers.	Livestock include 15 donkeys and 2 cattle. There are some 2,500 date-palms and many other kinds of fruits.
Nuwaidrāt النويدرات	2 miles north-east of Qal'at-al-'Ajāj.	60 reed huts of Bahārinah, mat-makers, cultivators and pearl divers.	There are 11 donkeys and 2 cattle here, and about 1,730 date-palms.
Portuguese Fort	...	...	See article Qal'at-al-'Ajāj.
Qadam القدم	1¼ miles south of Qal'at-al-'Ajāj.	30 huts of Bahārinah, cultivators.	There are date plantations on the east side of the village, and a large number of prehistoric tumuli to the west. Donkeys are 12 and cattle 2.
Qal'ah القلعه	Adjoins Qal'at-al-'Ajāj.	30 huts of Bahārinah date growers.	There are 9 donkeys and 3 cattle. Trees are 1,400 dates, some pomegranates and a few oranges, tamarinds, almonds, peaches and mulberries.
Quraiyah قريه	½ a mile from the west coast, 1 mile below Budaiya'.	50 reed huts of Bahārinah, mostly weavers of sailcloth for the Manāmah market.	Animals include 9 donkeys and 5 cattle. There are less than 1,000 palms.

Name.	Position.	Houses and population.	Remarks.
Rifāʾ-al-Gharbi رفاع الغربي	...	...	See article Rifāʾ-al-Gharbi.
Rifāʾ-ash-Sharqi رفاع الشرقي	...	...	See article Rifāʾ-ash-Sharqi.
Rummān (Rās-ar-) راس الرمان	...	...	See article Manāmah.
Ruqaʿah الرقعه	¾ of a mile west of Qalʾat-al-ʾAjāj.	10 houses of Bahārinah, divers and cultivators.	Surrounded by date groves. With Jubailāt this place boasts 23 Shūʾais and Sambūks, used as pearl boats. There are 18 donkeys and 3 cattle. Date-palms are put at 8,000 and there are many citron and other fruit trees.
Rūzakkān روزكان	¼ of a mile west of Qalʾat-al-ʾAjāj.	20 huts of Bahārinah, cultivators and fishermen.	There are 13 donkeys and 1 head of cattle. Date-palms are placed at 5,000 and there are numerous citrons besides other fruit trees.
Sadad صدد	Near the west coast, 9 miles below Budaiyaʾ.	40 reed huts of Bahārinah, cultivators.	Stands in the midst of date plantations which are watered by a Falaj from a spring called Sakhārah, and contain about 10,500 palms. There are 16 donkeys and 5 cattle.
Saibiʾ (Abu) ابو صيبع	1½ miles south-west of Qalʾat-al-ʾAjāj.	45 huts of weavers, cloth-dealers and cultivators.	There are 8 donkeys and 3 cattle here, also about 1,400 date trees.
Sahlat-al-Fūqiyah سهلة الفوقيه or Sahlat-al-ʾAudah سهلة العدة	3 miles west-south-west of Manāmah fort.	50 reed huts of Bahārinah who keep sheep and cultivate.	The village stands on comparatively high ground and is surrounded at a short distance by date groves situated upon a lower level. Here there are 2 horses, 23 donkeys, and 5 cattle. Along with that following, this village possesses about 15,000 date-palms.

Name.	Position.	Houses and population.	Remarks.
Sahlat-al-Hadrīyah سهلة الحدريه or Sahlat-as-Saghīrah سهلة الصغيرة	3 miles south-west by west of **Manāmah** fort.	30 reed huts of **Bahārinah**, cultivators.	The village is in the midst of a date grove on the longer road from **Manāmah** to **Rifā'**. A good stream of water runs through the village, and there is considerable cultivation round it. There are 7 donkeys and 3 cattle.
Sakhīr الصخير	1½ miles north-west of **Jabal-ad-Dukhān**.	...	A camping ground near which are 3 large masonry houses, the property of two sons of the Sheikh of **Bahrain**.
Salbah سلبه	On the east coast, 3½ miles east of **Rifā'-ash-Sharqi**.	30 huts of the Āl Bani **Yatail**, fishermen.	...
Sālih (Hillat 'Abdus) حلة عبد الصالح	½ a mile south of **Qal'at-al-'Ajāj**.	20 huts of **Bahārinah**, date growers.	There are several good streams of water emanating from springs. Donkeys here number 5 and cattle 4.
Salmābād سلمآباد	3½ miles south of **Qal'at-al-'Ajāj**.	30 huts of **Bahārinah**, date growers.	This village is about 1 mile west of the ordinary route from **Manāmah** to **Rifā'** and is far from any other village. It is on the southern fringe of the great date-belt and to the south-east of it a stony plain stretches to **Rifā'**. A good stream of water, utilised for irrigation, passes close to the village. Livestock include 15 donkeys and 5 cattle. There are about 5,500 dates.
Sanābis سنابس	On the north coast, midway between **Manāmah** and **Qal'at-al-'Ajāj**.	The inhabitants are about 1,500 **Bahārinah** engaged in boat-building, fishing and the pearl trade.	The village has a long straggling front to the sea occupying, with intervals, about ½ a mile. There is a prettily situated mosque in the centre

Q 2

Name.	Position.	Houses and population.	Remarks.
			of the place. Livestock include 16 donkeys and 10 cattle. Date-palms are about 900. The people own 30 pearl boats, of which 2 are Baqārahs and 23 are Shū'ais and Sambūks.
Sanad سند	2⅓ miles north-north-east of Rifā'-ash-Sharqi.	20 huts of Bahārinah, cultivators.	Livestock include 25 donkeys and 7 cattle, and there are about 5,250 palms.
Sār سار	3 miles east-south-east of Budaiya'.	30 huts of Bahārinah, cultivators.	The people have 17 donkeys, 7 cattle and about 10,000 palms.
Shahrakkān شهركان	1 mile from the west coast, 10 miles below Budaiya'.	50 reed huts of Bahārinah, date growers and sail-makers.	There are 15 donkeys and 7 cattle. Date-palms are 2,500 to 3,000.
Shākhūrah الشاخورة	1¾ miles south-south-east of Qal'at-al-'Ajāj.	The inhabitants are now only 10 or 12 houses of Bahārinah, cultivators.	Once a flourishing village with numerous well built stone houses; now for the most part ruins, but still covering a large area. Donkeys number 31 and cattle 6. Palms are estimated at 6,000.
Sharaibah الشريبه	On the north coast 3 miles west of Qal'at-al-'Ajāj.	40 reed huts with one good masonry house on the seashore. The people are Māliki Sunnis, chiefly 'Utūb, and all engaged in the pearl fisheries.	There are 23 donkeys and 6 cattle here; boats are 10 Shū'ais and Sambūks and 3 others, all used for pearling.
Sūq-al-Khamīs شوق الخميس	...	...	See article Bilād-al-Qadīm.
Suqaiyah السقيه	200 yards south-east of Manāmah fort.	40 huts of Bahārinah, date growers.	The houses are scattered amidst cultivation bordered by date groves. Lucerne is extensively grown and palms number about 700. On the east side of the village is a well, enclosed by a wall, belonging to the Hindus of Manāmah.

Name.	Position.	Houses and population.	Remarks.
Tashshān طشّان	2 miles south-west by west of Manāmah fort.	50 huts of Bahārinah, cultivators.	Close to the west side of Bilād-al-Qadīm, and has a fine spring of water. Animals are 6 donkeys and 3 cattle.
Tūbli توبلي	4½ miles north by west of Rifā'-ash-Sharqi and ½ a mile from the Kabb creek.	30 reed huts of poor Bahārinah, cultivators.	Stands on the inland edge of the great date belt. Livestock include 22 donkeys and 4 cattle. Trees are 50 pomegranates and 8,150 date-palms.
Tūbli(Murāqīb-at-) مراقيب التوبلي	Begins a short distance south of Tūbli and extends south-eastwards for a couple of miles.	...	A camping ground frequented in summer by Na'īm Bedouins, who draw their water, while there, from Jalīb-al-Qumri.
Zallāq الزلّاق	On the west coast, 11 miles below Budaiya'.	3 masonry houses and about 200 mud houses, inhabited by Dawāsir who are all engaged in the pearl fisheries.	This is the second most important place of the Dawāsir in the Bahrain Principality. There is a ruined fort. Vessels are 5 Baqārahs, 19 Shū'ais and Sambūks and 9 Māshuwahs and jollyboats, 16 of which are used for pearling; there are 15 donkeys and 15 cattle.
Zinj الزنج	1 mile south-west of Manāmah fort.	30 huts of Bahārinah who cultivate and manufacture a black cement.	There is extensive cultivation in and near the date groves, which are irrigated from several good wells. Livestock are 15 donkeys and 3 cattle. There are about 12,000 date-palms and a good many figs.

It should be noted that in the above table negroes have been shown as belonging to the tribe among whom they live or whose slaves they are.

Springs.—The springs characteristic of Bahrain Island and the other islands of the archipelago are described generally in the article on the **Bahrain** Principality. Those which are situated on Bahrain Island itself, or on the reefs connected with it, are enumerated below in alphabetical order: along with them are mentioned the principal wells, which in many cases are doubtless low-level springs, in character not differing from those that reach the surface :—

Name.	Position.	Remarks.
Adāri or 'Adhāri عداري - عذاري	A little to the east of Sahlat-al-Hadrīyah village, close to the shore of the **Kabb** inlet.	A magnificent spring of which the water is extensively utilised for cultivation.
'Aqala عقلا	$\frac{3}{4}$ of a mile from west coast and 7 miles from Rās-al-Barr.	A well of fresh water.
'Amar العمر	3 miles south-south-west of Jabal-ad-**Dukhān**.	Do.
Bartúfi (Fasht) فشت برطفي	See table of coast features above.	There is a spring on this reef.
Dār دار	Close to south-east corner of Jidd Hafs, in its suburb called 'Ain-ad-Dār.	A fine spring.
Dār-al-Manādīl دار المناديل	$\frac{1}{2}$ a mile south of Jau on the east coast.	A well of fresh water.
Faraihah فريحه	In Māhūz village.	A fine spring of fresh water extensively used for irrigation.
Fasht (Kaukab Fasht Khor) كوكب فشت خور فشت	...	See article Fasht Khor **Fasht**.
Ghuwaifah (Umm) ام غويفه	On the west side of **Rifā'-al-Gharbi** village.	A deep well on the high plateau from which the people of **Rifā'-al-Gharbi** draw their own drinking water and from which much water is sent to **Manāmah**. Its water is considered by natives to be the best in **Bahrain**.
Hafīrah حفيره	$3\frac{1}{2}$ miles south-east of Jabal-ad-**Dukhān**.	A well of fresh water.
Hanaini حنيني	Immediately below **Rifā'-ash-Sharqi** on the west side, in the central depression of Bahrain Island.	Two wells close together, each situated in a small enclosure closely packed with green palm trees. The wells are 17 fathoms deep in winter and more in summer. One is used for irrigation only; from the other most of the well-to-do people of **Manāmah** Town obtain their drinking water.

The Hanaini well, Bahrain Island.
(Mr. J. C. Gaskin.)

COPYRIGHT.

Name.	Position.	Remarks.
Harta هرتا	½ a mile south-east of Māhūz village.	A fine spring of fresh water, which is carried inland and applied to irrigation.
Ijra-i (Umm) ام اجرئي	3⅓ miles west of **Rifā'-al-Gharbi**.	A spring of which the waters are conveyed by Falaj to the date groves of Karzakkān.
Khālid خالد	On the high plateau, inside the village of **Rifā'-ash-Sharqi**.	A deep well from which the people of the village obtain their drinking water.
Mālikīyah مالكيه	2 miles north-east of the village of the same name.	This spring waters the lands of the village by means of a Falaj.
Maqāba مقابا	Close to the village of the same name.	One of the finest springs on the island.
Mattalah مطله	1¼ miles inland from Rās-al-Mattala.	A well.
Muwailghah مويلغه	Near the village of the same name.	The water is brackish, but valuable for irrigation.
Qār قار	3 miles south-south-west of Jabal-ad-**Dukhān**.	A good well of drinking water adjoined by bitumen deposits, whence its name.
Qarain-adh-Dhabbān قرين الذبان	½ a mile inland from Rās-al-Qarain.	A well of fresh water.
Qassāri قصاري	Within the limits of **Bilād-al-Qadīm**, the one to the north, the other to the south of the village.	2 large springs of good water. The name is also pronounced Gassāri and Jassāri.
Qumri (Jalīb-al-) جليب القمري	2 miles south of Tūbli, amidst prehistoric tumuli.	A small spring which supplies with water the Bedouin encampments at Murāqīb-at-Tūbli.
Rumaidhah رميظه	7½ miles south by east of Jabal-ad-**Dukhān**.	A well of fresh water.
Sabīyah سبيه	2½ miles east of **Rifā'-ash-Sharqi**.	A spring and underground water-channel by means of which many date groves are irrigated.
Sāfa سافا	3 miles north-north-east of **Rifā'-ash-Sharqi**, on the east coast.	Do.
Sāfirah صافره	2 miles south-west of **Rifā'-ash-Sharqi**.	A well in a meadow-like Raudhah, with ruins of some houses beside it.

Name.	Position.	Remarks.
Saiyid (I) سيد	In Tūbli village.	A fine spring of fresh water forming a valuable source of irrigation.
Saiyid (II) سيد	On the north side of Sār village.	Do.
Sha'ūm (Umm-ash-) ام الشعوم	Close to Māhūz village.	Do.
Shabāfah شبافه	3 miles east of Rifā'-ash-Sharqi.	A spring. There are date gardens here belonging to the people of Nuwaidrāt, who encamp beside them in the hot weather. The nearest permanent village is Salbah.
Sharaibah الشريبه	In the sea opposite the village of this name.	A spring.
Summān صمان	6 miles north of Rās-al-Barr and 2 miles inland from the east coast.	A well of fresh water.
Tashshān طشان	At the village of the same name.	A fine spring.
Yādar (Umm) ام يادر	7 miles north of Rās-al-Barr and 2 miles inland from the east coast.	A well of fresh water.
Yūsuf يوسف	2 miles east of Jabal-ad-Dukhān.	Do.
Zaidān (Abu) ابو زيدان	Close to Bilād-al-Qadīm village.	A fine spring of fresh water which issues from beneath a mosque.

The wells described are all situated in small Rōdhahs surrounded by desert. A few Bedouin tents or some flocks and herds belonging to the Shaikh of Bahrain are generally to be found in the vicinity of each of them.

Miscellaneous.—The article on the **Bahrain** Principality may be consulted in regard to all matters not dealt with above which concern Bahrain Island. Here however we may mention that in Bahrain Island a space of more than 12 square miles is covered by fields of prehistoric tumuli, by the Arabs called Murāqīb مراقيب : they lie for the most part on the glacis of the plateau to the north of the central depression, and those of the largest size and seemingly greatest importance are close to the village of 'Āli.

Ancient Tumuli, Bahrain Island.
(Mr. J. C. Gaskin.)

BAHRAIN PRINCIPALITY

BAHRAIN
البحرين
PRINCI-
PALITY*

The term Bahrain once embraced the promontory of **Qatar** and the Oases of **Qatīf** and **Hasa** as well as the islands of the archipelago: some authorities indeed would attribute to it in the past an even more extended application, affirming that it once denoted the whole western side of the Persian Gulf from **Ruūs-al-Jibāl** to the mouth of the Shatt-al-'**Arab**. The derivation of the name is uncertain. Its apparent

* This leading article on the Bahrain principality and the minor articles on places in the same are founded chiefly upon systematic and careful investigations made on the spot during the years 1904-1905. The information available from sources existing before 1904 was arranged by the writer and was issued in November of that year in the form of 9 printed foolscap pages intended to serve as a basis for further inquiry. The inquiry proper was begun by the writer on tour in Bahrain early in 1905; but it was carried out chiefly by Lieutenant C. H. Gabriel, I.A., who personally travelled over the greater part of the islands, and by Captain F. B. Prideaux, Political Agent in Bahrain, who supplied very full information regarding all places in his jurisdiction. A set of draft articles founded on the notes and reports of 1905 was then prepared by the writer; it was finished in January 1906 and extended to over 60 octavo pages of print. These drafts were sent to Captain Prideaux, by whom they were very carefully revised with the assistance of Mr. In'ām-al-Haqq, the Agency Interpreter, a graduate of the Aligarh College. Early in 1907 the drafts were reissued, with modifications and additions, and some points which remained doubtful or obscure were disposed of by Captain Prideaux and his assistant during the year. Geological information was kindly furnished by Mr. G. Pilgrim of the Geological Survey of India. The articles in their final form now occupy over 70 octavo pages.

Bahrain has from an early time attracted the attention of travellers in the Persian Gulf, and the following are some of the older authorities on the islands: Niebuhr's *Description de l'Arabie*, 1774; Buckingham's *Travels in Assyria, Media and Persia*, 1829; Whitelock's *Description of the Arabian Coast*, 1838; Mignan's *Winter Journey*, 1839; *Bombay Records, XXIV*, 1856; Whish's *Memoir on Bahreyn* (with map), 1862; and Palgrave's *Central and Eastern Arabia*, 1865. More recent are: Captain E. L. Durand's *Description of the Bahrein Islands*, 1879, and his *Extracts from a Report on the Islands and Antiquities of Bahrain*, 1880; Mr. T. Bent's *Bahrein Islands in the Persian Gulf*, 1890; Captain J. A. Douglas's *Journey from the Mediterranean to India*, 1897; the *Persian Gulf Pilot*, 1898; the Reverend S. M. Zwemer's *Arabia*, 1900; Mrs. T. Bent's *Southern Arabia*, 1900; and Captain A. W. Stiffe's *Ancient Trading Centres of the Persian Gulf—Bahrain*, 1901. Captain Durand's second paper and the contributions of Mr. and Mrs. Bent deal partly with the subject of antiquities; the *Persian Gulf Pilot* is concerned chiefly with maritime features; and the remainder of the authorities are general in their scope.

In matters relating to trade, the annual commercial reports of the Political Agent in Bahrain are the chief source of information.

A large scale map of the Bahrain Islands (except Jazīrat Umm Na'asān) exists in the Survey of India's sheet *Bahrain* 1904-1905, the result of a survey undertaken in connection with the Gazetteer inquiries; and Admiralty Plan No. 2377-20, *Bahrain Harbour*, shows some detail of the northern half of the islands and their coasts as well as all marine features on the northern side of the meaning is "the Two Seas," but the reference is not clear and is interpreted in different ways.

Extent and importance.—The present Shaikhdom of Bahrain consists of the archipelago formed by the **Bahrain, Muharraq,** Umm **Na'asān, Sitrah** and Nabi **Sālih** islands and by a number of lesser islets and rocks which are enumerated in the articles upon the islands: taken all together these form a compact group almost in the middle of the gulf which divides the promontory of **Qatar** from the coast of **Qatīf** and which, as it has no recognised name, may appropriately be styled the Gulf of Bahrain. Connected with the sovereignty of Bahrain, or possibly appertaining to the Shaikh as hereditary personal property, are certain ill-defined rights upon the mainland of **Qatar,** at present (1905) under discussion. Whatever the nature or extent of these rights our attention will be confined, in the present article, to the undisputed insular possessions of the Shaikh.

On the western side of the Persian Gulf, Bahrain is, agriculturally and commercially, the most valuable district. Its position moreover as regards the Persian Gulf is central, for the distance of its port and capital from the entrance of the Gulf is only a little greater than its distance from the mouth of the Shatt-al-'**Arab.** On the Arabian side of the Gulf, Bahrain has no rival in political importance except the principality of **Kuwait;** and the Turkish province of **Hasa,** although it affords the best and shortest approach from the Gulf to **Najd,** is itself commercially dependent upon Bahrain.

Marine surroundings.—The most striking feature of the Bahrain group of islands is the lowness and levelness of the land and the shallowness of the environing sea. The whole Gulf of Bahrain from Rās Rakan to Rās **Tanūrah,** a distance of 73 miles, is, except for one clear and fairly wide channel which runs north and south off the east coast of **Muharraq** Island, a mass of reefs and shoals. The most extensive obstacles to navigation in the archipelago are the Fasht-ad-Dibal فشت الديبل, between **Muharraq** Island and Rās Rakan, four miles

---

group. The general chart for Bahrain is No. 2374—2837-B., *Persian Gulf;* both this and the Plan mentioned contain distant views of the Bahrain Islands from the sea. There are two recent marine surveys of the waters to the west and east of the Bahrain islands, respectively, namely, *Bahrain to Ojar* and *Bahrein to Ras Rakkin,* Preliminary Charts Nos. O. 1 and O. 2, Poona, 1902. Two charts relating to Khor-al-Qalai'ah accompany a report by Lieutenant H. C. Somerville, R.N., which was printed for the Government of India in the Foreign Department, Simla, in July 1905.

long from north to south by three miles broad, and the Fasht-al-Jārim فشت الجارم, 15 miles long north and south by 9 miles broad towards its northern end, which shelters the harbour of **Manāmah** from north and west winds. Many of the reefs of the Bahrain islands are partially dry at low water. On the side towards the open sea the shallow waters of Bahrain may be considered to end at the Rennie Shoal, 54 miles north of **Muharraq**. There is a passage, called the Khor-al-Bāb خور الباب, from **Manāmah** to **Qatīf** south of the Fasht-al-Jārim, which is practicable for vessels drawing not more than 15 feet. Many pearl banks are situated in these waters: their names and positions are given in the Appendix on the Pearl Fisheries.

Geology.—The main island of Bahrain forms a striking geological contrast to the other islands of the Persian Gulf. The rocks are chiefly white or pale-coloured limestones of the eocene age, sometimes sandy or argillaceous, and so disposed as to form a low anticlinal dome of which Jabal-ad-**Dukhān** is the summit. In the hollow between the girdling plateau (described in the article on **Bahrain** Island) and this central peak the rock has been denuded by marine agency and forms a plain. In places the eocene limestone rocks are highly fossiliferous and contain foraminifera, echinids and mollusca: as a whole they are characterised by an abundance of siliceous material, occurring as flint, as cherty concretions or as quartz geodes, and by the dissemination of gypsum and salt throughout the series in a marked degree. The presence of the salt and the gypsum is most conspicuous in certain places where they have been leached out of the rock and have formed vast accumulations of saliferous or gypseous soil. The most distinctly marked areas of this character are one towards the south end of **Bahrain** Island and another on the island of Umm **Na'asān**, and the gypsum fields of the latter supply practically all the mortar that is used in Bahrain. The coastal portions of **Bahrain** Island, as also of the other islands of the group, are overlaid with sub-recent coral rocks or shelly concrete; and sandstone of the same age is found in the central depression of **Bahrain** Island. This depression, as well as the littoral flats, has in fact emerged from the sea in comparatively recent times, and the remains of the old sea-beaches are well marked. A small deposit of asphalt is found penetrating the eocene rocks 3 miles south-south-east of Jabal-ad-**Dukhān**.

The Bahrain islands are famous for a remarkable set of springs, beautifully clear and but slightly brackish, some of which are submarine; the majority of them are enumerated in the articles on the principal islands, and here it will be sufficient to mention that in the northern part of **Bahrain** Island, north of Khor-al-**Kabb**, they are warm, copious and nearly fresh, the best known in that district being those of 'Adāri, Qassāri and Abu Zaidān. The most noteworthy springs in the sea are that of Abu **Māhur** close to **Muharraq** Island and the Kaukab on Fasht Khor **Fasht**. The best water in the islands is obtained from the Hanaini wells, at the north end of the central depression of **Bahrain** Island, and from the Khālid and Umm Ghuwaifah wells on the plateau adjoining. There can be little doubt that the springs of Bahrain, like those of the **Hofūf** and **Qatīf** Oases, are fed by the drainage of part of **Najd** which, temporarily lost in **Dahánah** and **Sahábah**, travels thence eastwards by subterranean passages.

Climate and seasons.—The climate of Bahrain is by no means the worst in the Persian Gulf, and some travellers have emphasized its less pleasant features in terms which the facts do not warrant. Daily observations have been taken only since October 1901, and since that time the highest temperature registered has been 107·5° F. and the lowest 40°. The weather from October to April inclusive is pleasant, the temperature indoors ranging between 60° and 85° F.; January and February however, in which north winds blow and it is cold enough to light housefires, are sometimes rainy and unhealthy. From the beginning of May till the middle of June the weather is hot; but the heat is still tempered by the sea-breeze or Bārih, and the nights are fairly cool. From the middle of June until the end of September the heat is oppressive; land breezes from the west, south-west and south, it is true, continue irregularly all summer; but in the intervals the thermometer remains persistently above 100° F. The average rainfall between 1902 and 1906 was 3·25 inches a year; but the atmosphere of Bahrain, in consequence of irrigation and the nearness of the sea, is damp and heavy, as is evidenced by the mean humidity which ranges from 79 to 80 per cent. of saturation. The rainy season is considered to begin at the middle of October and to end at the middle of May; the rainy days however are ordinarily 3 to 6 only. In Bahrain only the Shaikhs, who own flocks and herds, welcome rain; to the poorer classes in their frail huts of date fronds it causes serious discomfort. The prevailing wind is the Shamāl or north-wester, which in winter is violent and dangerous to shipping; after it the north wind is the most frequent; the only strong wind besides the Shamāl is the Qaus from the south-east which blows irregularly between December and April. On the whole

BAHRAIN PRINCIPALITY

the climate of Bahrain is probably superior to that of **Masqat** or Bandar **'Abbās** and it certainly excels that of the neighbouring shores of **Qatīf**, but rheumatic affections are very common, and so also are diseases of the heart and lungs. A grey-headed negro is hardly ever seen, and the pearl divers of Bahrain are notoriously a short-lived race, though this possibly is due rather to their occupation than to the climate.

Natural products and wild animals.—The only minerals of value in Bahrain have been mentioned already in the paragraph on geology. There is almost no natural vegetation; mangroves in the creeks and a few ber trees in other places appear to be the only exceptions; there is not even grass except what is artificially cultivated. A kind of small gazelle (believed to be Arabica) is not uncommon in the less inhabited parts of the main island; and hares and mongoose are fairly numerous. The Houbara bustard is a winter visitor, and the Shaikhs keep hawks (imported from Persia) for hunting it. Sandgrouse also are sometimes seen, but are not apparently sought after by native sportsmen.

Population and tribes.—No census has ever been taken of the population of Bahrain, but we subjoin here a rough estimate based on the reported number of houses. The totals of souls have been calculated on an assumed average of 5 persons to a house; and if, as is not improbable, the figure assumed is too low in the towns, the totals for urban population must be proportionally increased.

Island.	Towns.	Sunni towns-people.	Shi'ah towns-people.	Sunni villages.	Sunni villagers.	Shi'ah villages.	Shi'ah villagers.
Bahrain	Manāmah	9,800	15,000	10	6,275	73	19,450
	Budaiya'	8,000	Nil.				
Muharraq	Muharraq	19,000	1,000	8	7,775	3	2,750
	Hadd	8,000	Nil.				
Na'asān (Umm)	Nil	Nil.	Nil.	Nil.	Nil.	Nil.	Nil.
Nabi Sālih	Do.	Do.	Do.	Do.	Do.	2	375
Sitrah	Do.	Do.	Do.	1	150	7	1,500
TOTAL		44,800	16,000	19	14,200	85	24,075

The principality then contains, on such an estimate as it is possible to form, 4 towns with a population of 60,800 souls and 104 villages with a population of 38,275; in all 99,075. To these must be added about 200 non-Muhammadans at **Manāmah,** making a grand total of 99,275 settled inhabitants. The only nomads are **Na'īm** Bedouins, who frequent the island in varying numbers, and a few **Ka'abān** who have no settled residence.

Of the whole population of about 100,000 souls some 60,000, chiefly townsmen, are Sunnis and about 40,000, mostly villagers, are Shī'ahs.

The largest community—for it cannot be called a tribe—in the principality is undoubtedly that of the Bahrānis or **Bahārinah,** who compose nearly the whole of the Shī'ah community and more than three-fifths of the rural population. The remainder of the people, except a few foreigners such as Persians and **Basrah** Arabs, Hindus, Jews, etc., belong to various Sunni tribes or classes, of which the most important, numerically or for other reasons, appear in the following synopsis :—

Name.	Number of houses.	Where located.	Remarks.
'Ainain (Āl Bū)	95	'Askar and **Muharraq** Town.	Belong to the Māliki sect of Sunnis.
'Ali (Āl Bin-)	500	**Muharraq** and **Hadd** Towns.	Do.
'Amāmarah	140	Budaiya' and Muharraq Town.	Do.
Dawāsir	1,000	Budaiya' and Zallāq.	Do.
Dhā'in (Āl)	10	Muharraq Town.	Do.
Hūwalah	3,080	Manāmah, Muharraq Town, Budaiya', Hadd and Hālat-bin Anas.	Like the Shī'ah Bahārinah the Hūwalah are a class, not a tribe. All are Sunnis, but some are of the Māliki and some of the Shāfi'i persuasion.
Janā'āt	3	Manāmah.	Belong to the Māliki sect of Sunnis.
Ka'abān	60	$\frac{1}{2}$ at Jasairah and $\frac{1}{2}$ wandering near Jabal-ad-**Dukhān.**	Do.

BAHRAIN PRINCIPALITY 239

Name.	Number of houses.	Where located.	Remarks.
Khālid (Bani) of the Dawāwdah section	50	Jasrah.	Belong to the Māliki sect of Sunnis.
Kibīsah	8	Jasairah and Rifā'-al-Gharbi.	Do.
Kuwārah (Āl Bū)	20	Muharraq Town and Hadd.	Do.
Madhāhakah	150	Busaitīn.	Do.
Maqla (Al Bin-)	100	Hālat Abu Māhur.	Do.
Manāna'ah	120	Qalāli, Muharraq Town and Hadd.	Do.
Mu'āwadah	20	Muharraq Town.	Do.
Muraikhāt	15	Hālat Umm-al-Baidh.	Do.
Musallam (Āl)	25	Muharraq Town, Hadd and Hālat Abu Māhur.	Do.
Na'īm	Fluctuating	Mostly nomad, but 154 settled families are found at Hālat-an-Na'īm, Umm-ash-Shajar, Umm-ash-Shajairah, Hālat-as-Sulutah and Rifā'-al-Gharbi.	Do.
Negroes (free)	860	Manāmah, Muharraq Town, Budaiya', Hālat Abu Māhur and Rifā'-ash-Sharqi.	There are free negroes in other places also, but in the lists of villages they have been treated as of the tribe or class among whom they dwell. Only about 50 of the free negroes in Bahrain formerly belonged to Shī'ah masters and are now themselves Shī'ahs.
Negroes (slaves, but living separately from their masters)	1,160	Budaiya', Muharraq Town, Hālat Abu Māhur, Manāmah and Rifā'-ash-Sharqi.	Negro slaves at places other than those mentioned have not been distinguished in the tables of villages from the tribe to which their masters belong. Only about 20 of

Name.	Number of houses.	Where located.	Remarks.
			the negro slaves in Bahrain are owned by Shī'ahs and are Shī'ahs themselves.
Qumárah	10	**Muharraq** Town.	Belong to the Māliki sect of Sunnis.
Rumaih (Āl Bū)	115	Jau, **Busaitīn** and **Muharraq** Town.	Do.
Sādah	150	**Hadd**.	Belong to the Hanafi and Shāfi'i sects of Sunnis.
Sūdān	10	Do.	Belong to the Hanbali sect of Sunnis.
Sulutah	10	**Hālat-as-Sulutah**.	Belong to the Māliki sect of Sunnis.
'Utūb	930	**Muharraq** Town, **Manāmah**, both **Rifā's**, Sharaibah, **Busaitīn**, Hālat Abu **Mahūr** and Hālat Umm-al-Baidh.	Do.
Yās (Bani) of the Āl Bū Falāsah section	120	Mostly at **Hadd**; a few at **Hālat-as-Sulutah**, **Busaitīn**, Umm-ash-Shajar, Umm-ash-Shajairah and **Muharraq** Town.	Do.
Yatail (Al Bani)	10	Salbah.	Do.
Ziyāinah	150	**Muharraq** Town.	Do.

Besides the above there are 69 Hindus in Bahrain, unaccompanied by their families; their number rises in the pearling season to about 175 souls.

Although the **Bahārinah** are numerically the strongest class they are far from being politically the most important; indeed their position is little better than one of serfdom. Most of the date cultivation and agriculture of the islands is in their hands; but they also depend, though to a less extent than their Sunni brethren, upon pearl diving and other seafaring occupations.

The **Hūwalah** are the most numerous community of Sunnis; but they are all townsmen living by trade and without solidarity among themselves;

consequently they are unimportant, except commercially. The **'Utūb**, the **Sādah** and the **Dawāsir** are the most influential tribes in Bahrain; the first on account of their connection with the ruling family, the **Sādah** by virtue of their sacred origin, and the **Dawāsir** because they are comparatively wealthy, united, and obedient to their chiefs, and partly, perhaps, that as the most recent immigrants from **Najd** they enjoy a certain prestige. The remainder of the Sunni population are mostly settled on or near the coast, and depend chiefly on the sea, and in a lesser degree on cultivation, for their subsistence.

The races inhabiting Bahrain are generally insignificant in appearance and there is nothing remarkable in their character. The pearl diving sections of the community seem to be distinguished by weak eyes and raucous voices. The huts in which the bulk of the rural population live are constructed of date or reed mats and have gable roofs.

In concluding this paragraph we may notice that, though negroes are numerous in Bahrain, a mixture of Arab and negro blood is here less frequent than in the ports of **'Omān** and Trucial **'Omān**. The analysis of population given above shows that there are nearly 5,000 free negroes and 6,000 negro slaves in the principality, and these figures are probably much below the mark as it has been impossible, except in the larger places, to distinguish negro families from the communities among whom they live or by whom they are owned. The reason given for the non-mixture of blood is that in Bahrain a full-blood negro slave is more valuable than a half-caste son. The services of slaves are hired out by their masters for the pearl fishery, and in winter the slave and his family are left to support themselves. In some cases the slave is married to a free woman with whom his master has no concern; but in others the master provides the slave with a slave wife and takes possession of the offspring.

Agriculture and domestic animals.—The agricultural products of Bahrain are chiefly fruits, lucerne and a few vegetables; the last, including brinjals, cucumbers, carrots, leeks and onions, are almost the only non-arboreal crops. The supply of vegetables is sufficient for local consumption and none are imported. Plant growth generally is rank, but the produce is poor. The citrons of Bahrain are, it is true, the best in the Persian Gulf, and there is a kind of small and luscious banana; but the date palms are here of a dull green and have a poor and stunted appearance, while the other fruits, whether almonds, apricots, figs, grapes, limes, melons, peaches or pomegranates, fall below mediocrity. There are some tamarinds, and the mango and mulberry are seen, but are rare.

The soil is perhaps not sterile, although, without cultivation, it does not ordinarily produce even grass; deficiency of rainfall is probably the chief reason, for in exceptionally wet years grass is said to grow knee-deep all over the central depression of the main island to the edge of the Mimlahat-al-Mattalah. All cultivated land is irrigated from springs or wells. The springs are many and copious, but the low level at which many of them lie makes it necessary to conduct the water to the plantations in very deep cuttings, which in places are lined with stone and in others are carried through outcrops of rock. Irrigation is of 3 kinds, and date plantations are distinguished as Nakhl-as-Saih نخل السيح, Dūlāb دولاب and Nakhl-al-Gharrāfah نخل الغرّافه ; of these the first kind is watered by gravitation from flowing channels, the second by a lift of 1 or 2 skins raised by bullocks or donkeys walking down a slope, and the third by a Gharrāfah or lever and skin with a counterpoise.* Fish-manure is used to fertilise the date groves. Agricultural produce is brought to market daily in the **Manāmah** bazaar, and weekly at the Sūq-al-Khamīs fair (on Thursdays) and at a place near Qal'at-al-'**Ajāj** (on Mondays).

The most valuable of the domestic animals are donkeys of a particular breed, from 12 to 13·1 hands in height; they are generally white but a few incline to greyness, probably on account of impure breeding. The stock was originally imported from **Hasa** and is perhaps the finest kind of donkey in the world. The females, being less noisy than the males, are sold at higher prices, and a good one sometimes fetches as much as R500; the stallions are all sold to professional donkey boys, who hire them out in the towns for riding or carrying loads. Only about 200 of these donkeys, it is said, now exist upon the islands; but the number of donkeys of all sorts, according to the statistics obtainable, is nearly 2,000. The ordinary donkeys, about 1,800 in number, are of all colours— white, grey, black and brown—and vary in height from 12 to 10 hands and less; they are useful and capable of hard work. The provender of donkeys is chiefly lucerne, dates and grass. Horses are only kept by the family of the ruling Shaikh: they are generally of pure Najdi blood, but have somewhat deteriorated through being bred in an unsuitable climate. No horses are bred for exportation: those owned are about 50 in number. About 100 camels are owned by the Shaikh and his family and perhaps 50 others belong to private individuals at the two **Rifā's**, who employ them in carrying water to **Manāmah** for sale. There is a small but fine local breed of cattle, famous even on the Persian coast for their milking

---

* The Gharrāfah is handled by one man. The counterpoise is generally a basket of earth.

qualities: the beef of Bahrain however, which sells locally at about 6 annas per lb., is by no means first-rate. Cattle of all sorts in the islands are reported to amount to about 850 head; they are stall-fed upon dates, lucerne, bhoosa, dried fish and old bones and are sometimes unable to walk on account of their over-grown hoofs. Sheep and goats are few and are hardly owned outside the principal island, there being no grazing elsewhere except upon Umm **Na'asān;** it is estimated that there are in all about 500 sheep and 700 goats, of which 600 belong to the leading members of the Āl Khalīfah or ruling family, 400 to the larger Arab tribes, and 200 (stall-fed) to individual townsmen of **Manāmah** and **Muharraq.** Mutton and goats' flesh, mostly imported, sells locally at 7 to 8 annas per lb. according to quality.

Pearl and sea fisheries.—The pearl fisheries of Bahrain are the most important in the Persian Gulf except those of Trucial **'Omān**; they employ 917 boats and afford occupation to over 17,500 men, the Bahrain pearl boat being thus manned on the average by about 19 men.

The local sea fisheries are productive and afford a livelihood to a considerable proportion of the coast population. The fish are taken both with nets and in tidal weirs or enclosures called Hadhras حظرة, made of reeds, some of which surround large areas.

Communications and navigation.—The Bahrain islands are traversable in most directions with riding and pack animals: in irrigated tracts the water channels, which would otherwise seriously impede movement, are generally sufficiently well bridged. The most important route in the islands is that from **Manāmah** to the two **Rifā's**: wayfarers travelling by it either ford the Maqta'-at-Tūbli creek or go round the head of it, 1 mile further west, according to the state of the tide.

A table * of the various kinds of craft owned in the ports of Bahrain is given below.

Island.	Port.	Baghlahs.	Batils.	Būms.	Baqārahs.	Shū'ais and Sambuks.	Māshuwahs or Jolly boats.	Totals.
Bahrain Island	Anas (Hālat Bin)	...	...	...	...	...	6	9
,, ,,	'Aqur	...	...	...	...	3	...	6
,, ,,	'Askar	...	1	...	1	...	17	19
Carried over		...	1	...	1	3	23	34

* This table may be compared with the estimate given by Pelly in his *Report on the Tribes, etc.*, 1863.

Island.	Port.	Baghlahs.	Batils.	Būms.	Baqārahs.	Shū'als and Sambuks.	Māshuwahs or Jolly boats.	Totals.
Brought forward		...	1	...	1	3	23	34
Bahrain Island	Bārbār, Dirāz and Bani Jamrah	...	...	...	...	15	...	17
,, ,,	Budaiya'	...	11	...	10	56	37	114
,, ,,	Iswār (Hālat Bin-)	...	...	...	...	...	3	16
,, ,,	Jau	...	...	...	4	...	28	32
,, ,,	Jufair	...	...	...	...	...	13	15
,,	Ma'āmir	...	...	...	2	22	...	24
,, ,,	Manāmah	2	...	6	...	1	100	109
,, ,,	Rummān (Rās-ar-)	1	...	2	1	...	15	19
,, ,,	Ruqa'ah and Jubailāt	...	...	...	...	23	...	23
,, ,,	Sanābis	...	...	...	2	23	...	30
,, ,,	Sharaibah	...	...	...	...	10	...	13
,, ,,	Zallāq	...	...	...	5	19	9	33
Muharraq Island	Busaitīn	...	...	...	8	12	26	46
,, ,,	Dair	...	...	...	1	25	...	26
,, ,,	Hadd	...	3	...	42	183	21	249
,, ,,	Muharraq Town	...	40	14	68	189	396	707
,, ,,	Na'īm (Hālat-an-) and Sulutah (Hālat-as-)	...	5	...	12	50	4	71
,, ,,	Qalāli	...	...	...	...	55	4	59
,, ,,	Samāhij	...	...	...	...	6	6	12
,, ,,	Shajairah (Umm-ash-)	...	...	...	1	14	...	15
,, ,,	Shajar (Umm-ash-)	...	...	...	2	15	...	17
Nabi Sālih Island	Kāflān and Quryah	...	...	...	1	...	8	10
Sitrah Island	Muhazzah	...	...	...	...	30	1	31
,, ,,	Quriyah	...	...	...	...	19	...	19
,, ,,	Sufālah	...	...	...	...	19	...	19
	Total number of vessels	3	60	22	160	789	694	1,760
	Total tonnage	365	1,847	563	3,182	9,615	4,473	20,720
	Total hands employed	99	2,010	167	3,090	9,748	2,942	18,390

The column of totals in the table above includes some vessels of which the class has not been ascertained.

A word is necessary as to the uses for which these various types of vessels are suitable; a certain number are convertible and are not restricted to one form of employment. Trading vessels are Baghlahs, Būms, Shū'ais and Māshuwahs; pearl boats are chiefly Baqārahs, Māshuwahs, Sambūks and Batīls; cargo lighters are Būms of a wide flat-bottomed species called Tashāshīl تشاشيل ; ferry boats are Māshuwahs and Shū'ais, and so are fishing boats. It has been ascertained that there are in Bahrain about 100 vessels used for trade which run to **Qatīf, 'Oqair, Qatar,** Trucial **'Omān** and the **Persian Coast**, some of them even to India, Southern Arabia and Zanzibar; 917 which proceed to the pearl banks; 30 cargo lighters in **Manāmah** harbour, of which half are Būms; 300 ferry-boats plying chiefly between **Manāmah** and **Muharraq** Town; and 600 fishing boats. The total of these figures is 1,947, clearly illustrating our statement as to partial convertibility.

Manufactures and industries.—The leading handicrafts of Bahrain are sailmaking and the manufacture for local sale of woollen 'Abas, lungis both white and coloured, and checked sheeting. Matting is woven from fine **Hasa** reeds and is the best obtainable in the Persian Gulf. A new textile industry has recently sprung up in the manufacture of a striped cotton cloth from which Qabas and Zabūns are made, and the output of this material now amounts to about 100 pieces weekly.

Bahrain is famous throughout the Persian Gulf for its boat building, and this industry gives employment to about 200 carpenters. In 1903-04 nearly 130 boats, ranging in price from R300 to R3,000, were sold to purchasers in **Qatar** and Trucial **'Omān**. The timber and nails used in construction are chiefly from India.

Foreign trade.—Bahrain is the principal pearl market of the Persian Gulf. It is also an emporium of general trade with the mainland of Arabia; but its former function is the more important, and it is probable that, if the pearl beds were to fail, the Shaikhdom would shortly be reduced to comparative insignificance. Imports are oyster shells and pearls from the neighbouring seas and coasts; rice, cotton piece-goods, silk piece-goods, embroidery, spices, coffee, sugar, tea, coir-rope, timber, metals, hardware and haberdashery from India; barley, wheat, ghi, carpets, rosebuds, rosewater, firewood, almonds, currants, gram, walnuts, live cattle, sheep and goats and some henna from Persia; fruit and sweetmeats from the Sultanate of **'Omān**; 'Abas, dates, ghi and hides from **Hasa**; dates, fruits and some sheep and ghi from **Qatīf**: ghi, sheep, a few 'Abas and a little wool from **Kuwait**; dates, ghi, Māsh, wheat, barley, tobacco and coarse reed-mats for roofing from Turkish 'Irāq; rafters and cocoanuts from East Africa. Of these the most important with their values (in lakhs of rupees) in 1905 were pearls (118), rice (26½), cotton piece-goods (9⅓), dates (9¼), coffee (4¾), wheat (4½), ghi (2¾), sugar and tobacco (2½ each), 'Abas (1¾), silk piece-goods (1½), slaughter animals (1⅓) and timber and wood (1). The slaughter animals are chiefly sheep and goats imported periodically by about 15 Persian butchers from the **Persian Coast**; in 1905 no less than 14,000 sheep and goats were thus brought over from Persia and 2,050 from **Qatīf**. An import of arms, worth 4 lakhs of rupees annually only a few years ago, has now entirely disappeared. The total value of the imports for 1905 was 243 lakhs, of which 103 lakhs were from India and 102 lakhs from Turkish possessions. In the same year 65 steamers in cargo, all British and with an aggregate tonnage of 95,097, entered **Manāmah**, the only steam port of Bahrain.

The principal exports with their values (in lakhs of rupees) in 1905 were pearls (161), rice (6), cotton piece-goods (3¾), dates (3¾) and coffee (1½). The pearls go chiefly to Bombay; the dates (of which some are dried and some, called Salūq سلوق, are boiled) to Karāchi and the ports of Kathiawar. Oyster shells are sent to the United Kingdom, to Germany, and a few to France. Some sail cloth is exported, mostly to **Basrah**; fine reed matting is sent to Persia and Turkish 'Irāq; and a portion of the striped fabrics, already mentioned as locally manufactured, is disposed of in **Hasa** and **Qatīf**. In 1905 the total value of exports from Bahrain was 204 lakhs of rupees, of which 129 lakhs' worth went to India and 62 lakhs' worth to Turkish territory. In the same year 35 steamers * cleared from **Manāmah** with cargo; all were British and they had a total tonnage of 54,666.

It is calculated that about ⅓ of the total goods imported eventually leave the island again for various destinations; and this at least is clear that the trade of Bahrain is largely a transit trade. In particular **Manāmah** is the steam port for the **Qatar** promontory, for the Oases of **Hasa** and **Qatīf** and, through **Hasa**, for part of **Najd** as well; the goods despatched to the mainland are chiefly piece-goods, rice, barley, metals, coffee, sugar and spices.

About 50 horses per annum pass through Bahrain *en route* from **Najd** and **Hasa** to the Indian market. Until a few years ago donkeys

---

* This does not mean that only half the steamers which called at Bahrain found cargo there. The explanation is that not all the steamers which call take out clearance certificates.

BAHRAIN PRINCIPALITY

also were largely exported from Bahrain to Persia; but the diminution of their numbers, together with the rise of their price in the Bahrain islands, has brought about a cessation for the present of this trade. The trade with **Qatar** is divided between the towns of **Manāmah** and **Muharraq**: that with **Hasa** and **Qatīf** is concentrated at **Manāmah**.

Currency, weights and measures.—The currency of the Bahrain principality is mixed. Indian coins of all denominations are the most popular and circulate freely; but Maria Theresa dollars or Riyāls ريال are largely current during the pearl season, as the divers, who are mostly Arabs from the mainland, prefer them; and quantities are imported from Bombay to meet the demand. The Riyāl is at present (1905) worth normally Re. 1 As. 5, but it is liable to fluctuations in value of as much as 1 or 2 annas either way. The Turkish Līrah passes at a valuation of Rs. 14. The ordinary unit of small values is however an imaginary coin called the Bahrain Qrān قران which is worth ⅖ths of a rupee. The Tawīlah طويله of the **Hasa** Oasis is seen and is valued at ½ an anna, but it is not readily accepted. A large quantity of specie from abroad enters Bahrain. In 1903 the value of the coin imported was 43 lakhs of rupees, and coin worth 4½ lakhs is known to have left the islands in the same year.

The ordinary weights of Bahrain are:—

Ruba' Mithqāl	ربع مثقال	·04	lb. English.
Nisf Mithqāl	نصف مثقال	·08	do.
Mithqāl	مثقال	·16	do.
Nisf Ruba'-ath-Thamīn	نصف ربع الثمين	·32	do.
Ruba'-ath-Thamīn	ربع الثمين	·64	do.
Thulth Thamīn	ثلث ثمين	·86	do.
Nisf Thamīn	نصف ثمين	1·29	do.
Qiyās	قياس	1·54	do.
Thamīn	ثمين	2·57	do.
Alf	الف	3·09	do.
Ruba'	ربع	4·11	do.
Mann	من	57·60	do.
Rafa'ah	رفعه	576·00	do.

The table of lineal measure runs:—
6 Sha'arāt Bardhūn
  شعرات برذون
  or "mule-hairs" = 1 Habbat Sha'īr or "barley-corn."
  حبّة شعير
6 Habbāt Sha'īr = 1 Asba' اصبع or "finger-breadth."
4 Asābi' = 1 Qabdhah قبضه or "fist."

6	Qabdhāt	= 1 Dhirā' ذراع	or "cubit."
4	Dhirā'	= 1 Bā' باع	or "fathom."
1,000	Bā'	= 1 Mīl Hāshimi ميل هاشمي	or "mile."
3	Amyāl	= 1 Farsakh فرسخ	or "hour's-walk."
4	Farsakh	= 1 Barīd بريد	or "postal runner's stage."
3⅓	Barīd	= 1 Darjah درجة	or "degree."
360	Darjah	= 1 Dāirat-al-Ardh دائرة الارض	or "circuit of the earth."

Of these only the Qabdhah, Dhirā', Bā' and Farsakh are known to ordinary illiterate people. The Dhirā' is equivalent to 18¾ English inches.

General administration.—The Government of Bahrain is of a loose and ill-organised character. It is ruled by a Shaikh—at present 'Īsa bin-'Ali—who, with the assistance of a Wazīr or principal adviser, disposes of matters of political or general importance and personally governs, unless when absent on sporting expeditions to the mainland, the island of **Muharraq** and the part of **Bahrain** Island which is adjacent to **Manāmah**. During four months in the hot weather the Shaikh has his seat at **Manāmah**: his headquarters during the rest of the year are at **Muharraq** Town, but he indulges in frequent journeys. A brother, sons, nephews and other near relations hold fiefs in various places, of which they have almost independent possession for life; upon these estates they collect taxes for their own behoof and exercise magisterial and seignorial jurisdiction. The most important semi-independent holding of this sort at the present time is in the hands of the Shaikh's brother Khālid; it includes the islands of **Sitrah** and Nabi **Sālih**, as well as all the villages on the east side of **Bahrain** Island to the south of Khor-al-**Kabb** and the inland villages of **Rifā'-ash-Sharqi** and **Rifā'-al-Gharbi**. These fiefs are resumable at the death of the holder: in theory, at least, there is no obligation to continue them in favour of heirs.

Class disabilities and privileges.—Under the régime of the Shaikh and his relations the condition of the **Bahārinah**, who form the bulk of the cultivating class in the principality, is unhappy. They are subject to a constant Sukhrah سخرى or corvée which affects their persons, their boats and their animals; their position in regard to the land is that of serfs rather than of tenants at will; and if they fail to deliver a certain amount of produce, which is often arbitrarily enhanced by the Shaikh's servants and relations, they are summarily evicted from their homes and in some cases are beaten and imprisoned as well. Some of the **Bahārinah** are in theory landowners, having been allowed in the past to purchase gardens and obtain Sanads for the same; but their estates are often resumed for no valid reason: even the sons of the present ruler have been guilty of this injustice. The crops of the **Bahārinah** are frequently stolen by the Bedouins who range the island, or are damaged by their animals. It does not appear that the **Bahārinah** are ever put to death without a regular trial by a Qādhi; but there is reason to suspect that deaths due to ill-treatment sometimes occur among them, and their women are apt to be molested by the Shaikh's servants. If oppressed beyond endurance the **Bahārinah** might emigrate to the **Qatīf** Oasis, and a consciousness of this possibility is the principal check upon the inhumanity of their masters.

The position of the **Dawāsir** of **Budaiya'** and Zallāq is somewhat peculiar. With their neighbours the **Bahārinah** they have little to do; and their relations with the Shaikh of **Bahrain** are distant though not unfriendly. They insist on being dealt with through their own chiefs, and they have given the Shaikh of Bahrain clearly to understand that, if he should take any action affecting them of which they disapprove, they will quit Bahrain in a body. It is considered, however, that the extensive purchases of date plantations which four or five of their headmen have made of late years in the vicinity of their settlements now render this threat difficult, if not impossible, of fulfilment.

The Bedouins, chiefly **Na'īm**, of whose presence the islands are never free and whose number reaches its maximum in the hot weather, are a cause of much trouble and annoyance to the settled inhabitants; but they are patronised and encouraged by the Shaikh from an idea, probably erroneous, that they would rally to his side in an emergency.

Religious and legal institutions.[*]—The Shaikh of Bahrain and his family and tribe are Sunnis, and the Sunni form of Islam consequently enjoys, as it were, official recognition and preference.

Serious cases of a criminal ture and important cases of civil law not relating to mercantile transactions or to the pearl fisheries are referred by the Shaikh to an official chief Qādhi—at present Jāsim-bin-Mahza' of **Manāmah**—who is a Sunni; and, provided that the whole of the parties are Bahrain subjects, the fact that some of them may be Shī'ahs does not affect the established procedure in this respect.

Minor cases, especially those of a civil character, are sent for settlement, if both parties are Sunnis, to Shaikh Sharaf bin-Ahmad of **Muharraq**, Sunni; and, if both parties are Shī'ahs, to Shaikh

---

[*] The Foreign Proceedings of the Government of India for April 1901 contain some information under this head.

Ahmad-bin-Hurz of **Manāmah**, Shī'ah: to this extent the right of Shī'ahs to have their cases disposed of by co-religionists is recognised. The secular arm is brought into play by the Shaikh to enforce the findings, on the criminal side, of these various judges; the latter, unfortunately, are reported to discharge their functions "with the maximum of injustice."* Besides the legal experts whose names have just been mentioned, there are at the present time in Bahrain 7 other Sunni Qādhis and 2 Qādhis of the Shī'ah persuasion who are permitted by the Shaikh to adjudicate on cases which the contesting parties may agree to refer to them. It is believed that, in criminal matters, the headmen of Sunni tribes other than those residing in the towns of **Manāmah** and **Muharraq** wield considerable magisterial powers; and it is probable that landowners of the Shaikh's family and their agents exercise a similar authority in regard to the agricultural **Bahārinah**. It is understood that the **Bahārinah**, who, as we have seen, are not generally landowners, are accustomed to submit their matrimonial cases and petty disputes about moveable property for settlement to their village Mullas.

Mercantile cases, especially those in which foreigners are concerned, are decided by a tribunal † called variously the Majlis-al-'Urfī مجلس العرفي or Majlis-at-Tijārah مجلس التجارة, that is the Customary or the Commercial Court. This body, of which the permanent members are nominated by the Shaikh in consultation with the British Political Agent, possibly had its origin in arrangements made long since for settling by arbitration claims which arose between British subjects and persons amenable to the jurisdiction of the Shaikh of Bahrain ‡; but it has now existed for at least 50 years, and has come to be regarded as the only authority in the islands competent to settle mercantile suits. In practice such suits, if both parties are Bahrain subjects and the dispute is one of fact only, are often irregularly settled by the relations or servants of the Shaikh; but all questions of principle, by which the interests of foreigners might afterwards be affected, are referred to the Majlis for decision, and the Shaikh admits a moral obligation to make use of the Majlis on all suitable occasions. When one or more of the parties to a case is a British subject, or when none of the parties are Bahrain subjects, the Majlis is ordinarily convoked by the British

---

* Since the political crisis of February 1905 the administration of justice in Bahrain has somewhat improved. Public opinion on the subject is growing more powerful, largely in consequence of a steady influx of protected foreigners.

† Regarding the Majlis, etc., see letters from Major P. Z. Cox, Resident in the Persian Gulf, No. 76 of 25th February and No. 516 of 4th March 1906; the Government of India's Foreign Proceedings for April 1901 may also be consulted.

‡ Some authorities, however, suppose it to be a purely indigenous institution.

Political Agent and sits at the British Political Agency, but a representative of the Shaikh is allowed to be present, and his presence is occasionally requested by one of the parties; the finding in such circumstances becomes operative only after it has been approved by the British Political Agent.

Cases arising out of pearl diving operations or the pearl trade are determined by a board of arbitration, known as the Sālifat-al-Ghaus, of which the constitution and powers are described in another place. *

Judicial fees (called Khidmah خدمة) are levied, sometimes by the Qādhis, sometimes by the Amīrs or Bazaar Masters of the **Manāmah** and **Muharraq** towns, and sometimes (particularly in large cases) by the Shaikh himself. In small cases the plaintiff generally pays Khidmah on the amount of his decree; but sometimes he is made to pay 10 per cent. on the amount of his claim, even if he does not obtain a decree in full. If the plaintiff loses his case Khidmah is not taken, unless it had been recovered in advance. In large cases the Shaikh is careful always to take Khidmah in advance.

Finance.†—The budget of the Bahrain principality is at the present time, in rough outline, as follows ‡ :—

Receipts.	Rs.	Expenditure.	Rs.
Sea customs.	1,50,000	Personal expenses of the Shaikh (including salaries of bodyguard).	1,00,000
Agricultural dues (*viz.*, the produce of state gardens and a tax called Nōb نوب on the gardens of private individuals from whom it can be collected).	1,00,000	Special expenses (in connection with marriages, journeys, etc.).	30,000
Tax on pearl boats.	12,000	Allowances to members of the Shaikh's family.	1,00,000
Judicial fees, succession duty (at 10 per cent.) on all estates transferred by inheritance, etc.	20,000	Expenses of the administration	14,000
Rent of town lands, shops and Khāns.	14,000	Subsidies and presents to Bedouins.	56,000
Miscellaneous (including secret extortions).	4,000		
TOTAL	3,00,000	TOTAL	3,00,000

* See the Appendix on the Pearl Fisheries.
† The Foreign Proceedings of the Government of India for October 1905 may be consulted.
‡ The table below may be compared with that at page 66 of the **Persian Gulf Administration Report for 1873-74.**

In addition to monetary taxes the Shaikh takes for himself one-twentieth of the slaughter animals imported from abroad; this particular trade is considered not to be included in the lease of the sea customs.

It will be observed that the above is the budget of the Shaikh of Bahrain alone, and that the column of receipts does not include the amounts which are wrung by fief-holders of the Shaikh's family from the villages situated in their estates. A poll tax called Tarāz طراز is among the additional imposts to which the agricultural **Bahārinah** are at times subjected. In the Sunni villages as a rule, and especially in those where one tribe largely predominates, there is either no taxation at all or the proceeds go to the tribal chief instead of to the Shaikh of Bahrain or members of his family.

Military and naval resources.—Altogether the Shaikh of Bahrain and his principal relations and servants maintain about 540 armed men, distributed somewhat as follows:—

Shaikh 'Īsa-bin-'Ali, Shaikh of Bahrain	200
Shaikh Khālid, brother of 'Īsa	100
Shaikh Hamad, son of 'Īsa	80
Shaikh Muhammad, son of 'Īsa	30
Shaikh 'Abdullah, son of 'Īsa	30
The Bazaar Master of **Manāmah**	50
The Bazaar Master of **Muharraq**	50
Total	540

Of this force about 200 men are armed with rifles, but the remainder, if they possess firearms at all, have only matchlocks: all, however, carry swords. For the defence of his dominions from foreign aggression, however, and for the maintenance of order within, the Shaikh depends not so much on these retainers as on the **Na'īm** tribe, of whom he professes to have large numbers at call. In point of fact the **Na'īm** of Bahrain and **Qatar** only amount to about 400 fighting men all told, and of these more than half are generally absent in **Qatar**, while not more than 100 out of the whole number are mounted. The Shaikh, as already mentioned, has a small but excellent stud of Arab mares, and he and his family own about 100 riding camels.

Till lately he possessed several fast-sailing but unarmed Batīls, of which 2 or 3 were ordinarily placed at the disposal of the customs contractors for the prevention of smuggling; these, however, have now disappeared, and when the Shaikh requires a boat he takes one by Sukhrah.

Political position and foreign interests.—The treaty relations of the Shaikh of Bahrain are exclusively with the Indian Government, who maintain at **Manāmah,** as their local representative, a European officer of their Political Department having the local rank of Agent : this Agent is subordinate to the British Political Resident in the Persian Gulf. The maintenance of a charitable medical dispensary, built by local contributions and known as the Victoria Memorial Hospital, was undertaken by the Government of India from 1905, and the institution itself has been attached to the Political Agency. There is also a British post office connected with the Agency.

British subjects ordinarily resident in Bahrain at the present time, inclusive of officials but exclusive of an Indian military guard for the Agency, are : European British subjects, 2 ; Eurasians, 4 ; Native Christians, 2, Hindus, 69 ; Muhammadans, 122 ; Jews, 5. In the hot weather the number of Hindus under British protection rises to about 175, and that of Muhammadans to 150. One British mercantile firm and 2 British steamship companies are represented in the islands ; and there are 22 resident Hindu and 11 resident Muhammadan traders who are under British protection.

After the political and commercial interests of Britain in Bahrain, the interests of the United States, arising from a mission of the Reformed (Dutch) Church of America, are the most important; this mission, which is at **Manāmah,** was founded in 1893.

Of more recent origin, and less extensive, are the German interests represented by a commercial firm.

BAHRĪYAH

بحرية

A small island in the Shatt-al-'**Arab** close to its right bank at a little more than 6 miles below the mouth of the **Kārūn** ; immediately below it is **Gat'ah** Island, from which a small channel only divides it; and opposite to it, on the other side of the main stream, is the upper end of Hāji **Salbūq** Island. Bahrīyah lies off the centre of the tract called Gat'ah on the right bank of the Shatt-al-'**Arab** ; its length, up and down stream, is a little over half a mile ; its breadth is considerably less. The inhabitants, who belong to various tribes and live in huts, number about 80 souls. They possess about half a dozen cattle, a score of sheep and goats and 30 date trees besides fruit trees of other kinds. Bahrīyah is in Turkish territory: it is owned by the present Shaikh of **Muhammareh** and by the family of 'Abdul Wahhāb.

BAI'AH or BĪ'AH بيعه

A village on the coast of the **Ruūs-al-Jibāl** District in the **'Omān** Sultanate; the mountains rise behind it at a distance of about 1½ miles. It consists of about 450 houses of **Shihūh**, nearly all of the Bani Shatair, but a few of the Bani Hadīyah section, and is situated in **Dibah** bay about 1 mile north of Hisn-ad-Dibah حصن الدبه or **Dibah** proper, but it is sometimes regarded as a part of **Dibah**. From the sea the two places appear to form one town with a background of date palms, but in reality they are separated by a watercourse up which the sea runs for about 200 yards. The inhabitants live by date-cultivation and fishing and own about 14 sea-going Sambūks which carry dates and fish to **Masqat** Town and places in the Persian Gulf. A little wheat, barley and sweet potato is grown both in the date gardens and behind the town, and dates are exported. There is one provision shop kept by a Persian. Bai'ah is the southernmost village in **Ruūs-al-Jibāl** on the eastern side of the **'Omān** Promontory, but it is controlled by a Shaikh appointed from **Kumzār**.

BAIDHAH خور البيضه **(KHOR-AL-)**

A creek on the coast of Trucial **'Omān** which, leaving the sea halfway between Jazīrat-al-**Hamra** and Umm-al-**Qaiwain**, runs parallel to the coast for 4 miles at a distance of 1 mile inland and terminates in the bay of Umm-al-**Qaiwain**, entering the same at its north-eastern corner. The island thus formed is known as Sinīyah سنيه and belongs to the Umm-al-**Qaiwain** Principality: it has no date trees but contains the ruins of two deserted villages, namely Mallāh ملّح at the north-east end, where there is an unoccupied fort belonging to the Shaikh of Umm-al-**Qaiwain**, and Sinīyah at the south-eastern extremity, where an old mosque may be seen. It is said that scarcity of water obliged the inhabitants to migrate to Umm-al-**Qaiwain** Town. The Shaikh of Umm-al-**Qaiwain** sometimes goes hawking on the island.

BAIT-AL FALAJ (WĀDI) وادي بيت الفلج

A very short valley in the **Masqat** District of the **'Omān** Sultanate: it begins 3 or 4 miles south and a little west of **Masqat** Town, runs 3½ miles to the north-west and then turns due north reaching the sea at Dārsait 2½ miles from the bend. The only places in this Wādi are Dārsait at its mouth and Bait-al-Falaj, from which it takes its name, 1½ miles from the sea. **Ruwi** is close to the left bank of Wādi Bait-al-Falaj at a point 3 miles from the sea; but its lands mostly drain to Wādi **'Adai**, in which we have included it.

Bait-al-Falaj village is 1½ miles from **Matrah** Town; its main feature (and raison d'être) is a large fortified residence of the Sultān of **'Omān**, who comes to live here in the hot weather. There are young date plantations watered by **Falajs** from the Wādi, Saih-al-Harmal, and **Ruwi**. A village has sprung up on the north-east side of the fort; it contains some stone houses and a considerable number of less substantial dwellings, about 30 in all. The inhabitants are **'Awāmir** and are mostly connected with the garrison: they possess 60 camels, 30 donkeys, 70 cattle and 200 sheep and goats. The situation of Bait-al-Falaj is open and airy for this district and there is convenient access to the sea both at Dārsait and at **Matrah**; with the latter Bait-al-Falaj is connected by a road running through a natural opening in the hills which is called Kharāshīf خراشيف.

BAKHTIYĀRI TRIBE بختياري

An important division of the **Lur** race; they have their headquarters in the mountains between **Shūshtar** and Isfahān, but are found also in the districts of **Dizfūl, Shūshtar** and **Rāmuz** in Northern **'Arabistān** and in the plain of **'Aqīli**. In all these localities some Bakhtiyāris are permanently settled, while others make their appearance as cold weather visitors and camp mostly to the south of Āb Bīd between that place and the **Diz** river. The plural of the name is Bakhtiyārīhā بختياريها.

Divisions and distribution in 'Arabistān.—The sections of the Bakhtiyāri tribe form two groups known as the Haftlang هفت لنگ and the Chahārlang چهارلنگ; the ruling chiefs of the whole tribe at the present time belong to a section which is included in the Haftlang group. The sections most frequently met with in Northern **'Arabistān** are perhaps the Shīr 'Ali شیر علي and Talāwari طلاوري, who belong to the Chahārlang group, as do also a section or incorporated tribe called Zanganeh زنگنه. These three sections are all represented in the **Rāmuz** District, of which the population is largely Bakhtiyāri; but in the **Shūshtar** District the settled Bakhtiyāris, almost without exception, are members of the Shīr 'Ali section. Bakhtiyāris are found in the **Dizfūl** District permanently established in the villages of Āb Bīd, Asad Khān (I), Biyāwtiyūn, Chūgheh Sabz, Chūgheh Surkh, Dūbandar, **Kāunak**, Khusrauābād, Kūtiyān, Najafābād, Sālārābād, Sar Bīsheh, Shāhābād, Shalgahi Buzurg and Kūchik, Shāmi, Shamsābād and Siyāh Mansūr, of some of which they have exclusive possession. In the **Shūshtar** District they occur at the villages of Gotwand, Jallakān and Pahwindeh; at Shalaili Buzurg and Kūchik, Qurūmizi, Hasmāwa, Chahārgāweh, 'Abdullah Jarrāh, Sūfān, 'Abbās, Hilāleh, Sōzi and Saiyid Hasan on the **Gargar**; at Kunārpīr, Lungur, Mahdiābād, Qal'eh Nau, Kūt Saiyid and Tabatti in **Miyānāb**; and at Burāki and Yissāreh on the **Shatait**: a few live also in **Shūshtar** Town. There are a few Shīr 'Ali Bakhtiyāris in the **Hindiyān** District at Gargari Bālāi.

Political organisation and position in 'Arabistān.—The political headship of the Bakhtiyāris is vested in two chiefs, the Īlkhāni ایلخانی or paramount chief and the Īlbaigi ایلبیگی or second chief, both of whom are recognised by the Persian Government; the present Īlkhāni is Najaf Quli Khān, Samsām-us-Saltaneh, while the Īlbaigi is his cousin, Ghulām Husain Khān, Shahāb-us-Saltaneh. The Īlkhāni and Īlbaigi are however only two, out of a large number of Khāns, relations, all of whom are deemed to be chiefs of the tribe.

To the Khāns belong, besides almost the whole of the **Rāmuz** District, the villages of Āb Bīd, Kūtiyān and Sar Bīsheh, part of the village of **Kāunak** and a water mill at 'Abdush Shāh, all in the **Dizfūl** District; the plain of 'Aqīli, Gotwand and Jallakān in the **Shūshtar** District; and 'Arab Hasan, Shaikh Jarrāh and the site (at present deserted) of Chahārdingeh on the **Shatait**. Each Khān is accustomed to administer the tracts which he owns, and in spring the principal Khāns generally encamp in the neighbourhood of Āb Bīd and take charge of the whole surrounding country; during the anarchy which prevailed in 1904 they even undertook the protection of the route between **Shūshtar** and **Dizfūl** and maintained an armed guard at **Shūshtar**. The Bakhtiyāri Khāns are responsible to the Persian Government for the revenue and administration of the **Rāmuz** District, where they own much property and enjoy a good reputation as considerate and progressive landlords; and 'Alwānīyeh and Raghaiweh on the borders of the **Ahwāz** District of Southern **'Arabistān** are also within their jurisdiction. In **Rāmuz** the Āl **Khamīs,** and at 'Alwānīyeh and Raghaiweh the **Hamaid** tribe are subject to them and pay them taxes. Apart from land revenue in agricultural districts, the Bakhtiyaris are said to pay an annual assessment of 16,700 Tūmāns to the Persian Government.

General.—A favourable opinion was formerly entertained by British officers of the Bakhtiyāris, who were described as a manly and spirited tribe; but closer political relations with them in recent years have caused them to appear rather in the light of truculent, avaricious and quarrelsome savages. They are submissive to the authority of their Khāns, but the only bonds are those of money and fear, recalcitrant subjects being coerced by spoliation and force of arms; little, if any, loyalty towards the chiefs is apparent which is not due to the dictates of immediate self-interest. The Khāns appear to greater advantage as landlords in the **Rāmuz** District. They are not always at accord among themselves. The total fighting strength of the Bakhtiyāris is about 20,000 men: of these a very few are armed with rifles of recent patterns, perhaps 7,000 have Martinis, and the rest carry smooth-bore muzzle-loading guns of native manufacture. About 2,000 men are serviceably mounted and some others possess inferior ponies. A good many mules and horses are bred by the tribe and some of these find their way to India through **Muhammareh.** The speech of the Bakhtiyāris is a dialect of Persian.

For more exact information in regard to the distribution of the Bakhtiyāris in **'Arabistān** and the property owned there by the chiefs the reader is referred to the articles in this Gazetteer on the districts mentioned. The "Bākhtiyāri Road" from **Nāsiri** to Isfahān, which lies through the Bakhtiyāri country, is noticed in the paragraph on communications in the article on **'Arabistān.** A more general account of the Bakhtiyāri tribe will be found in the Gazetteer of Persia.

BALĀRŪD or BILĀRŪI
بلارود

A stream of Northern **'Arabistān**; it rises near Qilāb قيلاب, a place situated in the hills of the Western **Lurs** about 30 miles north and slightly west of **Dizfūl** Town; the name Qilāb is derived from a bitumen spring. The Balārūd, after irrigating the tract known as Mazra'eh Sālihābād in the **Dizfūl** District, passes 5 miles west of **Dizfūl** Town and then 1 mile east of Bunwār Nāzir; it finally joins the **Diz** river from the west at a point 11 miles below **Dizfūl** Town. The village of 'Amleh Karīm Khān is partly irrigated from the Balārūd. The bed of the Balārūd is coarse shingle; in summer the Balārūd is dry except in pools; in autumn it becomes a flowing stream supplying many camps of Sagwand **Lurs;** after heavy rain it is apt to become impassable for one or two days.

BALŪCHI TRIBES.

Throughout this Gazetteer the name Balūchi, sanctioned by English usage, is used to designate the race or tribes which form the subject of this article: but the correct form of the word in Balūchistān is Balōch بلوچ, both for the singular and for the plural, and there the term Balōchi refers only to the language spoken by the Balōch. In Arabic the name is Balūsh بلوش in the plural and Balūshi بلوشي in the singular.

In Balūchistān the name Balōch is strictly employed to designate certain respectable middle-class tribes of the country only; but in the Gulfs of Persia and **'Omān,** and consequently throughout this Gazetteer (except in places in the articles relating to Persian **Makrān**), it is used in a wider sense to include immigrants from Balūchistān generally and persons whose mother tongue is the Balūchi language. The principal tribes of Balūchis proper represented in the area covered by this Gazetteer are the Buzdārs, Hōts, Kalmatis, Lattis, Mullāis, Raīs, **Rinds,** Sangurs and Shaizadahs, who are scarcely if ever mentioned by their tribal names outside the limits of Persian **Makrān,** also the **Jadgāls** who in Balūchistān are reckoned Balūchis, but elsewhere, and especially in the **'Omān** Sultanate, are generally distinguished under their proper name from other Balūchis.

In the political divisions of the Gulfs of Persia and **'Omān** Balūchis are found chiefly in the Sultanate of **'Omān,** where their number is roughly estimated at 20,000, or, including **Jadgāls,** at 30,000 souls. In Trucial **'Omān** they appear to number about 1,400, and in Turkish **'Irāq** about 3,000 persons; in the intermediate regions of **Qatar, Bahrain, Hasa** and **Kuwait** they are a negligeable element; and in **Najd** they are apparently not found. A few occur in Southern **'Arabistān,** chiefly as mercenaries and dependents of the Shaikh of **Muhammareh.** On the **Persian Coast** they are few until the district of **Shamīl** is reached, in which and in the **Mīnāb** District they form an appreciable part of the population. The district of **Biyābān** is, like the whole of Persian **Makrān,** almost altogether a country of Balūchis in the wider sense of the term as explained above.

The Balūchis even abroad are seldom Shī'ahs, and they settle more readily among Arab than among Persian communities. Some remarks on

BAND-I-QĪR
بند قير

BANDAKĪI
بند كيل

or BANAU-DEH
بنوده

A village of about 40 mud houses, situated at the southern apex of the **Miyānāb**, between the **Gargar** and **Shataīt** branches of the **Kārūn** river just above their junction. The banks here, which stand about 18 feet above the **Gargar** at low water, are submerged in floods. There is a ferry with 3 small boats, and a land route leads through the **Miyānāb** to **Shūshtar** Town. The inhabitants of Band-i-Qīr are 'Anāfijeh Arabs who cultivate wheat and barley and own about 20 mules and some donkeys. The land revenue of the village was farmed for 1,500 Qrāns in 1904. Band-i-Qīr sends most of its produce to **Nāsiri** and receives most of its imports from **Shūshtar**. Traces of the ancient city of Lashkar or 'Askar Mukram exist on both banks of the **Gargar** from a mile above Band-i-Qīr upwards.

BAQA'A†
بقعا

A village in the Jabal **Shammar** principality about 45 miles north-east of **Hāil** on the route to **Najaf**: it is also known by the name of Taiyibat-al-Ism طيبة الاسم. Baqa'a is picturesquely situated in a large basin of whitish sandstone, which receives the drainage of a plain between it and Jabal Jildīyah and also, it is believed, forms the conclusion of Wādi Da'aijān on which stands **Hāil**. The village consists of two main parts, Uwaimi اويمي at the north and Sahabi at the south side of the basin, and the plain between them is covered with a thick layer of very bitter salt. These quarters consist each of a stone-walled enclosure containing a number of miserable hovels, the inhabitants being of the Sa'adah section of the **'Ataibah** tribe. A little to the east is a small intermediate hamlet called Sharqi شرقي or Maraiqib مريقب; it is inhabited by **Shammar** of the Ja'afar section and is believed to be very ancient. The total population of Baqa'a is about 400 souls. The date-groves are 5 miles in circuit and their produce excellent; corn and

---

* A view of Band-i-Qīr is given in Chesney's *Expedition*.

† A sketch-map which includes the Baqa'a basin will be found at the end of Huber's *Journal de Voyage*, but it does not entirely agree with his earlier description of the place.

barley also are sown every year. Water, bad and brackish, is at 40 feet below the surface. Only one well, in Uwaimi, yields passable water; and even that is bluish and milky in appearance.

BAQĀ-QALAH
بقاقله

Singular Baqqāli بقالي. A community represented by about 12 households at **Manāmah** in **Bahrain** and by 10 at **Dōhah** in **Qatar**. They perform menial service in the houses of the **Bahrain** and **Qatar** chiefs, cultivate gardens, and are petty shopkeepers. Those of **Bahrain** are Shi'ahs and are reckoned to the **Bahārinah**; those of **Qatar** are Māliki Sunnis.

BARAIMI
بريمي
OASIS*

In English formerly spelt "Brymee," a remarkable oasis in the district of **Jau**, in a tract situated between the **'Omān** Sultanate and Trucial **'Omān** which may be described as Independent **'Omān**; it was formerly known also as Tuwāmīyah تواميّة, but this name has fallen into disuse.

Position and extent.—The exact situation by latitude and longitude of Jīmi, one of the most central villages in the oasis, is given in the table of villages below; it shows the oasis to lie a little south of a straight line drawn between the towns of **Sohār** and Abu **Dhabi**, about 65 miles west by south of the former, and 85 miles east by south of the latter. The plain of Baraimi is bordered on the north by the wilderness of Ramlat Kahal; on the east by well-wooded plains and small ridges of hills belonging to the district of **Jau**; on the south by Jabal Hafīt; and on the west by the first dunes of an ocean of sand that stretches without interruption to the coast of Abu **Dhabi**. The oasis is nearly circular and its diameter is about six miles.

Inhabitants and villages.—The population of Baraimi amounts to about 5,500 souls, of whom the greater number are **Dhawāhir**, some are **Na'īm** and a few are Bani **Yās**. The general condition of the people is poor, probably in consequence of tribal warfare and chronic insecurity

---

* The map for the Baraimi Oasis is *Route taken by Major P. Z. Cox, etc., 1905*; see first footnote in article Trucial 'Omān.

rather than of the natural conditions of their existence, and the prosperity which seems to distinguish the place is said to be more apparent than real. The food of the inhabitants is mainly dates and coarse bread or rice, but they vary their diet with salt fish and goats' or camels' flesh. Milk is abundant, and a hard cream cheese is made, the juice of the euphorbia being sometimes used instead of rennet. The women wear an unbecoming black veil and high-heeled shoes: their work is to spin, to weave, to make felt, and to tend the goats and kine.

The following is a table, alphabetically arranged, of the villages of the Baraimi Oasis:—

Name.	Position.	Nature.	Remarks.
'Ain Dhawāhir عين ظواهر	About 3 miles south of Baraimi Village.	A village of 280 houses of Dhawāhir of the Jawābir section.	Sometimes merely called 'Ain. The lands are watered by 2 Falajs, one of which comes from the east and the other (called Dāwudi داودي) from Jabal Hafīt. Date palms are estimated at 20,000, and livestock are said to be 40 horses, 150 camels, 100 donkeys, 100 cattle and 1,000 sheep and goats.
Baraimi Village بريمي	1½ miles east-south-east of Jīmi, of which the position has been astronomically determined.	...	See article Baraimi Village.
Hīli هيلي	2 miles north-north-east of Baraimi Village.	A village of 80 houses of Dhawāhir of the Darāmikah section.	Irrigation is by a Falaj coming from the hills to the north-east. Resources are 2,000 date palms, 40 camels, 20 donkeys, 20 cattle and 60 sheep and goats: there are no horses.
Jāhali جاهلي	4 miles south-west of Baraimi Village.	A date plantation with a few huts of care-takers.	The place belonged originally to the Dhawāhir, but it is now owned by the Shaikh of Abu Dhabi who reclaimed it about ten years ago.

Name.	Position.	Nature.	Remarks.
Jīmi جيمي	Situated, according to careful observations by circum-meridional altitudes of the sun, in latitude 24° 16' 10" north and longitude 55° 42' 30" east, Madras observatory being 80° 14' 51" east of Greenwich. It is nearly in the centre of the oasis.	A village of 200 houses of Dhawāhir of the Bani Sa'ad section.	The water supply is from the east. Date trees are estimated at 6,000 and livestock at 6 horses, 60 camels, 40 donkeys, 40 cattle and 100 sheep and goats.
Ma'ataradh معترض	3 miles south-west of Baraimi Village.	A village of 200 houses of Dhawāhir of the Darāmikah section.	Water is from Jabal Hafīt by Falaj. There are said to be here 4,000 date palms, 40 camels, 20 donkeys, 20 cattle and 70 sheep and goats, but no horses.
Mas'ūdi مسعودي	2⅓ miles north-north-west of Baraimi Village.	An encampment of Bani Yās, lately started by Khālifah, the eldest son of the Shaikh of Abu Dhabi.	The lands are watered by a Falaj which first passes Muraijib. As yet there are no resources except a few recently planted date trees.
Muraijib مريجب	2½ miles west-north-west of Baraimi Village.	An old abandoned fort, adjoining the Falaj which goes to Mas'ūdi.	The fort was built and used by the grandfather of the present Shaikh of Abu Dhabi.
Qatārah قطارة	1½ miles north-west by north of Baraimi Village.	A village of 120 houses of Dhawāhir of the Darāmikah section.	The lands are irrigated by a Falaj coming from the hills on the north-east. Resources are estimated at 5,000 date palms, 60 camels, 30 donkeys, 40 cattle and 100 sheep and goats: there are no horses.
Su'arah صعره	1 mile east by south of Baraimi Village.	A village of 100 houses of Na'īm of the Qarātisah section.	The Falaj by which the date groves are irrigated comes from the north-east. There are said to be 10,000 date trees here; also 100 camels, 50 donkeys, 50 cattle and 500 sheep and goats.

Village of Qatārah Baraimi Oasis.
(Maj. P. Z. Cox.)

The villages are unwalled and consist of houses, built of mud and date branches, which are scattered and concealed among the plantations. Besides those occupied there are many empty and dilapidated habitations.

Agriculture.—The general aspect of the oasis is verdant and fruitful. The soil though thin is fertile, and streams of running water abound on every side; these are brought by Falaj from the hills, sometimes several miles distant, and supply the deficiency of the slight rainfall. Each village has its separate belt of date groves; within the village the sub-division of arable land among owners is minute, and individual holdings are on the average extremely small.

Attention has been devoted with success to the culture of dates and other fruits; of cereals and vegetables the quantity and quality are at best moderate. Some of the best varieties of date are grown, including the Fard, Khalas and Mibsali sorts; but they are not held in equal estimation with the produce of Wādi **Samāil** and **Badīyah** in the **'Omān** Sultanate. The palms of the oasis number about 60,000. Fruits other than dates are lemons, sour and sweet limes, pomegranates, water melons, musk melons, bananas, mangoes, grapes, figs and olives : the papai also exists. Cereals are wheat and barley in spring, and jowari and millet in autumn ; vegetables include sweet potatoes, radishes, brinjals, beans, onions and garlic. Pulse, cotton—both of the white and the red flowered varieties—and lucerne yielding 8 to 9 crops a year are among the other products. Leguminous plants are not here sown among cereals, but follow them in rotation on the same ground ; stubble, too, is ploughed in and never burnt. It is said that coffee was once cultivated on the slopes of Jabal Hafīt, but the plantations, if any ever existed, have now disappeared.

Livestock.—Horses are only seen in the possession of Shaikhs, and cattle too are somewhat scarce ; but camels are cheap and abundant, and donkeys are largely in use both as riding animals and as beasts of burden. The villages of the oasis are reckoned to possess in the aggregate about 50 horses, 550 camels, 300 donkeys, 300 cattle and 2,500 sheep and goats. Besides these a number of horses, said to be as many as 100, are ordinarily kept by the Shaikh of Abu **Dhabi** in the Oasis.

Trade.—There are few or no professional traders, but a primitive local market is held each afternoon in one of the quarters of **Baraimi** Village ; here commodities mostly change hands by barter. The foreign trade of Baraimi passes chiefly through the port of **Shārjah**, which is distant nearly 80 miles north-north-westwards, but also to some extent through the other coast towns of **Dhabi, Dibai** and **Sohār.**

Political position.—Baraimi is independent, but the influence of the Shaikh of Abu **Dhabi** in the district is |strong and increasing. The ruins of the fort at Muraijib bear witness to the hereditary connection of his family with Baraimi, and he has recently acquired (and is now engaged in developing) an estate at Jāhali, while Mas'ūdi is being formed into a village by his eldest son. Moreover a regular tribute, of which the form and amount are mentioned in the article on the Abu **Dhabi** Principality, is paid him by the **Dhawāhir** who are numerically a majority in the oasis. At the present time the Shaikh could probably seize Baraimi if he wished to do so, but his policy appears to be one of pacific penetration. The **Na'īm** are the original owners of the oasis, and possession of the fort in **Baraimi** Village still gives them prestige and a local superiority over the **Dhawāhir**. A few **Manāsīr** of the Abu Khail subsection frequent the Baraimi Oasis or its neighbourhood in summer.

BARAIMI
بريمي
VILLAGE*

The original and most central village of the **Baraimi** Oasis. It consists of 9 quarters stretching northwards from a fort which may be regarded as one of them. The quarters are given below in alphabetical order; they are mostly inhabited by **Na'īm** of the Qarātisah and other sections, and the population may be estimated at 500 souls altogether.

Name of quarter.	Houses and inhabitants.	Remarks.
'Azzāzinah (Hārat-al-) حارة العزازنه	7 houses.	...
Darāmikah (Hārat-ad-) حارة الدرامكه	11 houses.	This is the quarter furthest from the fort.
Fudhah (Hārat-al-) حارة الفضه	17 houses.	...
Hillah حله or Sūq سوق	7 houses of Khidāmah of the **Na'īm**.	This quarter contains the market place, where there are a few booths of the ubiquitous Persian shopkeeper, but most of the wares are displayed on the ground; they include grain, handkerchiefs, lungis, matches, locks, bottles, etc. Several hundred people collect here in the afternoon and the sight is an interesting one.

* *Authorities.*—Reports by Major P. Z. Cox, Political Resident in the Persian Gulf, from personal observation: also Col. Miles in his *Route between Sohar and el Bereymi in 'Oman.*

Name of quarter.	House and inhabitants.	Remarks.
Kunūd (Hārat-al-) حارة الكنود	9 houses of **Kunūd**.	...
Muhammad-bin-'Ali (Hārat) حارة محمد بن علي	17 houses.	...
Qasr القصر	Contains a few houses occupied by a tribal garrison of **Na'īm**.	A fort. Described below: its possession is the source of the strength of the **Na'īm** in **Baraimi**.
Shindaghah شندغه	16 houses.	...

There is also a quarter called Hamāsah حماسه on the west of the Qasr.

Except the fort none of these quarters are walled: some of the houses are of mud and some are huts of date branches. There is no bazaar except that mentioned as situated in the Hillah quarter.

The resources of the village are estimated at 100 camels, 50 donkeys, 50 cattle, 500 sheep and goats and 10,000 date palms.

The Baraimi fort consists of a square with sides about 150 feet in length: the whole construction is of sun-dried brick. At each corner stands a tower about 40 feet high; but the curtains connecting the towers are less than 20 feet in height. A ditch 25 feet broad surrounds the place: both the scarp and counter-scarp are steep and faced with brick. Two wells in the interior yield water, apparently of good quality and sufficient for a large garrison. The situation of the fort, standing in a plain, is generally good; but on the north and west it is too nearly adjoined by houses and cultivation, and on the opposite side the ruins of another fort were (in 1875) capable of affording shelter to an attacking force. A wooden gate in the south face was (in 1875) the weakest feature of the work. The Baraimi fort is not equal to the best of those in the Sultanate of 'Omān, but it is the key of the 'Omān Sultanate on the west, and must necessarily, as has been observed, be reduced or masked by an invader of the Sultanate approaching from that direction.

BARKAH بركه

A considerable town on the coast of the **Bātinah** district of the 'Omān Sultanate: it lies about 43 miles west by north of **Masqat** Town and is on the east side of Wādi **Ma'āwal** at its mouth. The place extends along the shore for about 3 miles and consists mostly of huts scattered among the date-plantations. There is no harbour, only an open roadstead. In the centre of the place rises a lofty fortress with flanking-towers at the angles. The houses surrounding the fort on east, south and west number about 1,200, but some of them are empty and the population of the town may be estimated at about 5,000 souls. The inhabitants of the eastern quarters are chiefly Dawakah, Muwālik and Mashāfirah with some Āl Hamad and **Siyābiyīn**; in the neighbourhood of the fort the population is mixed; the western quarters are tenanted by **Hirth**, Ghawārib, **Ma'āwal**, Muwālik, Āl Badar, **Hikmān** and Bani Bū **Hasan**. There are also some **Darū'**. These Arab tribes (except the Muwālik, most of whom are found here) number on the average only 20 households each and their number is exceeded by that of the **Balūchis** and **Jadgāls** who form the remainder of the population. A few **Khōjahs** also are found, and there are 11 Hindus, the latter representing 6 commercial concerns and enjoying British protection. Many of the Arabs are Bedouins,—still owning cattle, sheep and camels,—who have settled down and acquired date-plantations; and some should be classed as a rural rather than as an urban population, occupying as they do a great part of the country between the town and the promontory opposite the **Suwādi** islands. Temporary Bedouin visitors are also numerous. In the date-season the population of Barkah is swelled by immigrants from **Masqat** Town and elsewhere who come to work as harvesters. Barkah is celebrated chiefly for its dates. The groves extend continuously from Wādi Manūmah وادي منومه, 6 miles east of the town, to Wādi-al-Qāsim some 10 miles to westward of it, and the trees number 40,000 or more. There is also some ordinary cultivation; and in the month of August large quantities of a shell-fish called Dōk دك, resembling a cockle, are collected and dried in the sun for export to the interior. Live-stock are 6 horses, 700 camels, 200 donkeys, 500 cattle and 3,000 sheep and goats. The bazaar contains over 100 shops dealing in ordinary wares. Barkah possesses 20 large Badans and is the port of the villages in Wādis **Lājāl** and **Ma'āwal** and partially of those in Wādis **Tau** and Bani **Kharūs**, as also of the town of **Nakhl**. The place is governed by a Wāli with a salary of $1,800 a year on behalf of the Sultān of **'Omān**, who also maintains in the fort a garrison of 20 men commanded by an 'Aqīd. The customs of the port produce about $3,000 a year and $1,800 is realised as Zakāt; the former amount is locally expended, and of the latter only $1,200 reaches the Sultān's treasury. The customs here have been under direct management, instead of being farmed, since 1901-02.

BASIDU 267

BA'RŪR (UMM-AL-)
ام البعرور

A village, formerly *chef-lieu* of the Qadha of **Shāmīyah** in Turkish 'Irāq; it is situated 17 or 18 miles east by south of the town of **Najaf** in the marshes which compose the **Shāmīyah** district. The population of Umm-al-Ba'rūr is now very small, and the majority of the inhabitants, though the place was till lately the administrative headquarters of a Qadha, merely inhabit reed huts. Umm-al-Ba'rūr is regarded as unhealthy and was abandoned by the administration for this reason. Its place has been taken by Hamīdīyah حميديه, a town which has sprung up on the left bank of the Abu Kufūf canal about 2 miles above Umm-al-Ba'rūr. Hamīdīyah is said to contain 800 houses, 150 shops, 3 mosques, 3 Khāns and 10 granaries, also a Government Sarāi and barracks.

BĀSĪDU*
باسيدر

Anglice "Bassadore," a British station situated on the westernmost point, similarly named, of **Qishm** Island and about 25 miles east by north of **Lingeh** Town. It includes a native village called Bandar Singau بندر سنگو about 1 mile to eastward of the remains of the principal settlement described below. The village of Nakhlistān, mentioned in the article on **Qishm** Island, lies just outside the station and to the east of it.

Bāsīdu Point is of low cliff rising 20 feet above high-water mark, is level on the top, and carries a few date-trees; it is an airy position open to all the winds that blow. The station has been practically unoccupied since the abolition of the Indian naval squadron; but three reservoirs, a jetty extending to low-water mark, and a rifle-range laid out to 600 yards still exist. There are also a small building on which the Union Jack is hoisted daily, ¼ of a mile south of the point, and a graveyard which is maintained in good order. The former officers' quarters, hospital, sepoy lines, bazaar and store houses have been allowed to fall into decay, being no longer required. There were never any permanent defences, and the only establishment now existing for the public service is a small coal depôt in charge of a Native Agent who is also responsible for the flag and receives a salary from the Indian Government. The

---

* Plans of Bāsīdu and its immediate surroundings are included in the Government of India's Foreign Proceedings for July 1902. See also Admiralty Chart, No. 2376-35, *Bāsidu*. A discussion of the boundaries of the British station will be found in the former place (as also in the Proceedings for January 1902), and a view of the approach from seaward in the latter. Some remarks on Bāsīdu by Sir L. Dane and Admiral Atkinson-Willes are contained in the Foreign Proceedings of the Government of India for June 1904 and a general report by Lieutenant V. Hunt in those for August 1901.

population of this part of the station is now only about 30 souls: it consists of natives who inhabit some scattered mat huts.

Bandar Singau, above mentioned, falls within the bounds of British jurisdiction. The people are fugitive slaves and gain a living as fishermen and weavers of Lūngis: they possess 6 boats. The village has no trade and affords few supplies except water, for the collection of which there are 8 reservoirs. There were formerly about 200 huts here, but now nearly all are in ruins, and the population has fallen to about 20 souls. The reason for the decline of Bandar Singau is that residence there is now discouraged by the British authorities lest the place should become a base for the operations of smugglers in Persia.

The anchorage at Bāsīdu extends parallel to the shore on the north side of the point and consists of a belt $\frac{1}{4}$ of a mile broad at $\frac{1}{4}$ of a mile from the shore: the depth is 5 to 7 fathoms and the bottom, of clay, is good holding-ground. The landing is inconvenient in a swell on account of the rockiness of the coast, and at low water on account of a mud-flat which is then uncovered. Outside the anchorage lies a channel 12 to 16 fathoms deep called the "Gut," in which vessels avoid anchoring. Protection against the Shamāl, which here blows from south-west by west, is given by the northern point of Beacon Shoal, a narrow bank which curves round the west end of **Qishm** Island from Bāsīdu point for two-thirds of the way to Rās Dastakān; of this bank the northern half, about $2\frac{1}{2}$ miles long, is dry at low water and has its extremity marked by a beacon. There is a deep but narrow and unnavigable channel between Beacon Shoal and the coast of the island. Other important features of the approaches to Bāsīdu are the North Bank and the Flat. The North Bank is a westward prolongation of the middle shoal of **Clarence Strait** which has its final ending in the sea 7 miles west-south-west of Bāsīdu point. The Flat is a great bank carrying 2 to 3 fathoms at low water and lying round the whole south-western corner of **Qishm** Island. It extends for more than 20 miles along the coast, about $\frac{1}{3}$ of its length covering the western and the remainder the southern side of the island, and its northern end overlaps the south end of Beacon Shoal and is outside it. The main entrance to the Bāsīdu roadstead begins between the Flat and the North Bank where it is 2 miles wide and has $3\frac{3}{4}$ fathoms of water; it then runs between Beacon Shoal and the North Bank, deepening as it goes to 7, and eventually to 9 fathoms. There is a passage between the south coast of the island and the Flat joining the ordinary entrance at Beacon Shoal; it contains a channel of 4 to $4\frac{1}{2}$ fathoms, but this channel is not easy to find nor is it suitable for vessels so large as a second-class cruiser, though it might be used by such in clear weather.*

BASRAH بصرة QADHA

The headquarters division of the Basrah Sanjāq of the Basrah Wilāyat in Turkish 'Irāq.

Position and boundaries.—The Qadha of Basrah is situated on both sides of the Shatt-al-'Arab and extends from a few miles above **Basrah** Town down to Zain on the right and down to the Persian frontier upon the left bank. It is bounded by the Qadha of **Qūrnah** on the north, by Persian territory upon the east, by the Qadha of **Fāo** upon the south, and by deserts upon the west.

Topography and inhabitants.—The most populous and important place in the Qadha is the town of **Basrah**, to which a separate article is devoted; but **Hamdān**, Abul **Khasīb** and **Zubair** also are towns of considerable size and consequence, and there are numerous large villages such as Khorah, Muhaijarān, Sabīliyāt and Abu Mughairah upon the right bank of the Shatt-al-'Arab and Da'aiji upon the left bank. The region is probably the most densely inhabited in Turkish 'Irāq and even in the whole Persian Gulf. The main feature of the district and that to which it owes its entire character is the Shatt-al-'Arab, in the article upon which and its islands will be found detailed topographical information about the whole Qadha. The rural tribes in the settlements irrigated by the river are chiefly 'Atub, 'Īdān and **Muhaisin**.

Population.—The fixed population of the Qadha appears to be as follows, according to the Nāhiyahs of which the positions are explained in the paragraph on administration below:—

Nāhiyah of 'Arab (Shatt-al-)	. . . .	17,000
„ Basrah (*i.e.*, **Basrah** Town)	. . . .	58,000
„ Hārtbah	. . . .	12,500
„ Khasīb (Abul)	. . . .	56,500
„ Zubair (*i.e.*, **Zubair** Town)	. . . .	6,000
	Total	150,000 souls.

About half the population of **Basrah** Town together with the

---

* *Vide* Admiral Atkinson-Willes' memorandum of the 8th December 1903.

entire population of **Zubair** Town are Sunni Muhammadans, and nearly the whole remainder of the people are Shī'ahs; but there are about 2,500 Christians of various sects and about 2,000 Jews, both of which communities are located chiefly in **Basrah** Town.

Resources.—The Zubair Nāhiyah is situated in the desert, but the other Nāhiyahs together constitute one of the richest date-producing tracts in the world. Some cereals are grown in the more open lands, and lucerne and vegetables are cultivated among the date trees. Livestock also are abundant and include buffaloes.

Administration.—This large as well as populous Qadha has no separate Qāim-Maqām; being the Markaz Qadha of the Basrah Sanjāq—which is the Markaz Sanjāq, in its turn, of the Wilāyat—it is, according to the usual Turkish arrangement, in direct charge of the Wāli of Basrah. The Qadha is subdivided, as we have already seen, into 5 Nāhiyahs. Two of these are simply the towns of **Basrah** and **Zubair**: the others are Hārthah, which extends along the right bank of the Shatt-al-'**Arab** from the borders of the Qadha of **Qūrnah** to **Basrah** Town; Abul Khasīb, which reaches along the same bank from **Basrah** Town to Zain, the latter being included,—that is to the commencement of the **Fāo** Qadha; and Shatt-al-'Arab, which occupies the left bank of the river from the limits of the **Qūrnah** Qadha down to the Persian frontier.

BASRAH
بصرة
TOWN.*

The name is believed to mean "the Black Pebbles." Basrah is the second town of Turkish '**Irāq** in political and commercial importance and perhaps in population; in all these respects it is inferior to **Baghdād,** and in the last it is possibly equalled by **Karbala**. Basrah is the *chef-lieu* of the Turkish Wilāyat similarly named, and such influence as the Ottoman Government possess in Eastern Arabia and even in **Najd** is exerted chiefly from Basrah. Old Basrah, which occupied a different site from the modern, was famous for its schools of theological and philosophical learning; but the present Basrah can lay no claim to any kind of erudition.

Position and site.—Basrah,—the position of which, as the town is rather scattered, we may take to be that of the British Consulate,—is

---

* The best map is *Plan of Basrah and its Environs from a Turkish Survey,* 1905 numbered 1389 in the Foreign Department Library, Simla.

situated about 282 miles, as the crow flies, south-east of **Baghdād**; about 22 miles west by north of the neighbouring Persian provincial capital of **Muhammareh**, and about 80 miles north by west of the Arab town of **Kuwait**. By river it is 72 miles distant from the head of the Persian Gulf, and by way of the Shatt-al-'**Arab** and **Tigris** it is 500 miles from **Baghdād**.

The town stands, enveloped in and interspersed with date groves, partly near and partly upon the right bank of the Shatt-al-'**Arab**, which here flows from north-west to south-east and has a breadth of 600 yards; the surrounding country is flat and is intersected in every direction by tidal creeks and irrigation channels.

After the Shatt-al-'**Arab** the dominant features of Basrah are two creeks, the Nahr-al-'Ashār نهر العشار and the Nahr-al-Khandaq نهر الخندق which leave the right bank of the river about 300 and 1,200 yards respectively above the British Consulate; both run inland, with slightly winding courses, for 3 miles or more in a general south-westerly direction; and their breadth, which is about 50 yards at the entrance, diminishes as they go.

Climate and water-supply.— In December and January the weather at Basrah is cold, sometimes with frost at night; the months of July, August and September on the other hand are intensely hot. The greatest heat experienced in summer is ordinarily about 112° Fahrenheit and in winter the thermometer falls to 35° or lower. The hottest weather is generally in July, and the coldest in January; in 1901 the thermometer rose to 113·2° on the 8th of July, and in 1902 in winter it fell as low as 32·5°. The annual average rainfall appears to be about 6 inches. Basrah was once reputed very unhealthy, but it is now less so than formerly; nevertheless the climate is extremely trying during the summer months, and it is malarious all the year round.

The drinking water of all who can afford it is fetched from the open stream of the Shatt-al-'**Arab**. Only the poorest classes of Basrah town proper drink the water of the 'Ashār, but of these it has been remarked with truth that they "use the canal from which they draw their drinking water as a wash-tub, a bath, a dust-bin and a cesspool combined."

We now proceed to describe the divisions and suburbs which in their *ensemble* compose Basrah.

The town of Basrah proper.—The main town, which alone is properly called Basrah, extends along the south-eastern bank of the 'Ashār creek, beginning at about two miles from the Shatt-al-'Arab and ending 1 mile further on at a bridge called Jisr-al-Ghurbān, جسر الغربان beyond which the 'Ashār is narrow and unfrequented. Some of the best native residential houses at Basrah, occupied by officials and rich merchants, are on the 'Ashār just below this bridge. The main bazaar runs from near the 'Ashār creek southwards through the busiest part of the town to a suburb called Mishrāq مشراق; it is about ¾ of a mile long and is built of brick and roofed all the way: at the end towards the 'Ashār are a few shops which deal in European commodities. The town is said to contain 7 mosques besides several shrines and Imāmzādahs.

Dōb and Maqām.—The spit between the 'Ashār and Khandaq creeks is called Dōb دوب; it is about half a mile broad and is overgrown with dates except so much of it as is within a mile of the Shatt-al-'**Arab**. In this lower and open extremity there stands, upon the 'Ashār creek at ¼ to ½ a mile from its entrance, an important quarter of the town which is generally known as Maqām 'Ali مقام علي or Maqām, but by the Turks (together with the whole clear end of Dōb) is styled 'Ashār. Maqām contains houses, shops, cafés and a considerable population, and it has a post office and telegraph office, the latter only for messages in oriental characters; here too were a flour mill and an ice factory belonging to a Jew, but they have lately been transferred to '**Ajairāwīyah** island. Behind Maqām, more in the direction of the Khandaq creek, are the unfinished barracks of the Turkish military garrison.

The 'Ashār creek.—The 'Ashār creek has been partially described above. It remains to mention that superior houses are now springing up along its south-eastern bank; some of these are occupied by Europeans and one is the private residence of the present Wāli of Basrah. Opposite the middle of Maqām the 'Ashār creek is spanned by a wooden bridge on piles which can be crossed by horses and vehicles and of which part can be removed to allow boats with masts, etc., to pass.

The Khandaq creek.—The Khandaq creek, of which the general character has already been outlined, is the seat of the grain trade; its banks are lined with yards and depôts, and many Mahailahs and other boats constantly lie moored within its entrance. The Khandaq is bridged in two places, which are on a level with the upper and lower ends respectively of Maqām. The lower of the two bridges, near to the grain

The 'Ashshār creek in Basrah Town.
(Mr. A. C. Wratislaw.)

BASRAH TOWN

market, is inferior to the 'Ashār bridge; the other is of brick, but it is broken in the middle and only planked across.

The banks of the Shatt-al-'Arab at Basrah.—A number of localities which may fairly be considered as included in Basrah Town are situated on the banks of the Shatt-al-'Arab, partly above and partly below the British Consulate. These we enumerate, in the order in which they are passed by the river, beginning with the furthest up-stream:—

Right bank.		Left bank.	
Rubāt (Nahr-ar-) نهر الرباط	A creek, the next above the Nahr-al-Khandaq, from which it is about 500 yards distant. On the north side of it are a new house belonging to Mīrza Hamzah, the Arab Secretary of the Shaikh of **Muhammareh**, and a house belonging to Raphael Sayegh; below it is a house belonging to Asfar and Co.	Gardilān گردلان	A creek and large village about 1 mile up-stream from the British Consulate. Below Gardilān are 3 large houses owned by Ibn-al-Faraib, Sālim-al-Badr and Muhammad-ash-Sha'aibi; the last of these 3 proprietors is now in exile and his house remains unfinished. Some date plantations at Gardilān are owned by nephews of the present Shaikh of **Kuwait**.
Khandaq (Nahr-al-) نهر الخندق	This creek, 1,200 yards above the British Consulate, has already been fully described. On the north side of the entrance are the premises of the Basrah Trading Co., known as "Bait Muir" but owned by Asfar and Co.	...	...
'Ashār (Nahr-al-) نهر العشار	This creek opens into the river 300 yards above the British Consulate and has been described at length above.	Khastahkhānah 'Askari خسته خانه عسكري	A Turkish Government hospital exactly opposite the entrance of the 'Ashār creek; it was originally a naval hospital, but is now used also by the military authorities and resorted to by the general public. In maps it is generally shown as Gardilān, but it should rather be called Tanūmah.

T

Right bank.		Left bank.	
British Consulate (by Arabs called Bait-al-Bālyōz بيت الباليوز or Qunsulkhānah (قنصل خانه)	A large handsome building with a high flagstaff upon the bank of the river: it contains, besides the residence and offices of the Consul, a British Indian Post Office. Immediately above the Consulate are the offices of Messrs. Gray, Mackenzie and Co., and just below it and a little further inland are those of Messrs. Lynch Bros.	Tanūmah تنومه	A small village with some cultivation about opposite to the British Consulate. During the crisis between Turkey and Kuwait in 1901-02 about 8,000 troops were encamped here on ground generally used as golf links by the British community of Basrah.
Gazàrah (Nahr-al-) نهر الگزاره	A large village; next below it is a house belonging to Saiyid Hāshim, a nephew of the present Naqīb of Basrah, about 500 yards below the British Consulate: this house is now leased to Messrs. R. Wönckhaus and Co., the agents of the Hamburg-American Line of steamers.	...	...
Sarāi (Nahr-as-) نهر السراي	A creek about 750 yards below the British Consulate: on the south side of the entrance is the house of the Turkish Commodore with the naval barracks behind it.	...	...
Quarantine Office or Karantīnah كرنتينه	This office is only a short way below the Commodore's house and stands on land belonging to Asfar and Co. It is immediately followed by a house belonging to M. Asfar, at present leased to Manashi Kārah, a Jew; and below this again is Mr. Hamilton's house, where there is a liquorice press.	...	...

The British Consulate, Basrah, from the Shatt-al-'Arab. (Consulate building on the right of picture)

(Mr. P. Z. Cox.)

COPYRIGHT.

Right bank		Left bank.	
Manāwi-al-Pāsha (Nahr) نهر مناوي الپاشا	A creek, about a mile below the British Consulate, in which Turkish Government vessels sometimes lie. A short distance up it is situated a considerable village suburb of Basrah, consisting of about 400 houses.	...	...

It will be seen that if any quarter of Basrah can claim to be a European quarter it is that on the right bank of the Shatt-al-'Arab below the 'Ashār creek. The houses in this part are generally large and stand in their own grounds.

Communications by water and land.—The Shatt-al-'Arab connects Basrah by water with the Persian Gulf, and on the other side, continued by the **Tigris**, with **Baghdād**. Basrah is at present the head of navigation for ocean steamers which usually anchor in the stream, in a depth of 5 to 6 fathoms, from the British Consulate downwards: but river steamers lie by preference near the mouth of the 'Ashār. The rise and fall of the river and creeks under the influence of the sea tides is from 6 to 9 feet, but the water is always fresh.

For the service of the town itself the Shatt-al-'**Arab**, the 'Ashār and the Khandaq are all highways, and the Ballam is to Basrah what the gondola is to Venice. The 'Ashār and Khandaq become shallow when the tide is out, but they are crowded with boats and full of life and activity at other times. These two are connected at intervals by transverse irrigation cuts; but the last are not passable even for small Ballams except at high water, and they are consequently little used unless for removing dates in the date season. A driving road follows the south-eastern bank of the 'Ashār creek from the Shatt-al-'Arab up to the town of Basrah proper, and a few flies and omnibuses ply upon it; but most passengers between the two prefer to go by water. The wooden bridge at Maqām gives access from this road to Dōb.

General character of the town and buildings.—From the foregoing account of quarters and suburbs it will be evident that the modern Basrah is a straggling town: it might even be called a disjointed collection of places. The walls and gates of the town proper which until recently existed in a dilapidated state have now practically disappeared, leaving the place undefended except by its dense forest of date palms and its labyrinth of muddy tidal canals.

The better houses in the residential quarters are mostly built of a soft yellow burnt brick; but timber, at least in the town proper, enters largely into the construction of the upper storeys. Rooms on the ground floor are not generally inhabited except in the hot weather.

Inhabitants.—The population of Basrah, in the sense in which the name is used in this article, is now roughly estimated at 58,000 souls, but it may be less. Of the people about one-eighth are Persians and most of the remainder Arabs; the rival Muhammadan sects of Sunni and Shī'ah are said to be here about equally balanced in numbers. There are also many Jews—probably more than 1,000—among whom are some of the wealthiest merchants. Resident Indian Muhammadans, mostly Sunnis, number about 50; and there are about half a dozen Hindu traders. Negroes of servile origin are fairly numerous.

Among institutions of general convenience are 4 public baths in the town proper and 2 in Maqām. Schools are noticed in the general article on Turkish 'Irāq.

Trade.—The trade and commercial position of Basrah are fully described in the general article on Turkish 'Irāq, where also will be found some remarks on the native shipping of the port. Khāns or caravansarais are estimated at 25 in the town proper and 10 in Maqām, and there are said to be 33 coffee houses in the former and 27 in the latter. Soda water and ice are manufactured locally and there are various wool presses and one liquorice press. The only bank is a branch of the Imperial Ottoman.

There are no wharves or pontoons at Basrah for the discharge of cargo from sea-going vessels; ships are laden and unladen in the stream by means of lighters, and during the date season the harbour is much congested. Steamers have commonly to complete their lading outside the bar of the Shatt-al-'**Arab** or even (in bad weather) at **Kuwait**.

General, military, marine and municipal administration.—Basrah is the headquarters of the Wilāyat of Basrah and its position in the civil administration of Turkish 'Irāq will be understood on reference to the article under that name. The Sarāi or principal group of government buildings stands upon the 'Ashār creek in the town of Basrah proper towards its lower end; and the principal telegraph office is also in the main town.

The branch telegraph office in Maqām (by the Turks called the 'Ashār office), accepts messages in Turkish or Arabic only. The principal customs house is in Maqām at the junction of the 'Ashār creek with the Shatt-al-'**Arab**, the port office being near it; there is also a customs house upon the Khandaq creek. The Dāirat-as-Sanīyah have a workshop on the south bank of the 'Ashār near its entrance where there are a few machine tools and where small castings can be made and ordinary engineering repairs executed. A mud dock at the same place is useless as it cannot be emptied; but the Dāirat-as-Sanīyah have also a dry dock on the north bank of the Khandaq at ¾ of a mile from the Shatt-al-'**Arab**, and here 2 new river steamers were put together in 1904. The site of the quarantine office has been mentioned above and that of the lazaret is described in the article on '**Ajairāwīyah** island. There are at Basrah about 100 Astarsuwārs or gendarmes mounted on mules. Shipping and river conservancy are in the charge of a harbour master; the Dāirat-as-Sanīyah is represented by a Mamūr and subordinate staff; and the principal offices, etc., of the navigation branch of that department are located here and are under a director who is subordinate to the Central Committee at **Baghdād**. There is also a local Sanīyah Committee.

The military position of Basrah is explained generally in the article on Turkish '**Irāq**. There is now no defensive military work of any sort at Basrah; but a field battery of 6 guns is permanently located in the angle between the south bank of the 'Ashār creek and the right bank of the Shatt al-'**Arab** and partially commands the river both above and below that point. Two battalions of regular infantry form the bulk of the normal garrison, and a detachment of engineers also is said to be stationed at Basrah. No cavalry are ordinarily present, but there are about 40 horses belonging to the artillery. The principal barracks, two in number, are in Dōb behind Maqām: in the town proper there are 9 military stations or posts. Basrah is the head-quarters of the 1st battalion of the 85th regiment of the Radīf and also of the 43rd brigade of the same.

The marine establishments are described in the article on Turkish '**Irāq**, and the position of the naval and military hospital on the left bank, and that of the Commodore's quarters and of the naval barracks upon the right bank of the Shatt-al-'**Arab** have already been specified above.

The municipal affairs of Basrah are regulated by a Municipal Council which in powerlessness and inefficiency resembles that of **Baghdād**. The streets are unpaved and the main town is notoriously insanitary.[*]

---

[*] For a full account of the sanitary condition of Basrah and its surroundings, also of the nature of the water supply, see Dr. Borel's *Report on the Sanitary Defence of the Persian Gulf and the Shatt-al-Arab*, 1901.

Foreign consular and other buildings.—In regard to foreign interests at Basrah the general article on Turkish **'Irāq** may be consulted. Of the foreign communities the British is the most numerous and important and possesses a club; reference has been made already to the British Consulate and to its situation upon the right bank of the Shatt-al-**'Arab** a little below the mouth of the 'Ashār. An American Consular Agency and an American Presbyterian Mission exist; the latter stands upon the south bank of the 'Ashār above Maqām, where also are the Russian Consulate and the office of the Russian Steam Navigation and Trading Company. A small hospital and free dispensary managed by the American missionaries are near the English club, and there is also a school attached to the Mission, but it is not recognised by the Turkish authorities who are taking steps to have it closed if possible. A Roman Catholic church and school are under the direction of the Carmelite Fathers.

The Persian Consulate, which has much business in consequence of the passage of Persian pilgrims to the Shī'ah shrines through Basrah, is situated in the town proper.

Shrines and antiquities.—In the Mishrāq quarter at the south end of the town proper is the mosque of Shaikh 'Abdullah Bāsh A'yān شيخ عبد الله باش اعيان which was built about 1729 A.D.; its minaret commands the only good general view that is obtainable of Basrah and its environing sea of palms.

The ruins of the ancient Basrah, founded in 638 A.D., begin about 6 miles south-west by west of the modern town and extend for about 3 miles farther in the same direction up to the walls of **Zubair,** in the article upon which they are described. The site of the present town is divided from that of the old by a depression liable to inundation by the **Euphrates.** The names of the streets and quarters of Old Basrah are said by local literati to be preserved in those of the modern town. Under the 'Omaiyids Basrah was one of the 'Irāqān or twin capitals of 'Irāq, the other being **Kūfah.** The greater part of Old Basrah was burned in an insurrection in 871 A.D., and in 923 it suffered a 17 days' sack at the hands of the Carmathians; by 985 A.D. a considerable portion of it had gone to ruin, but by 1052 it appears to have been once more in a fairly flourishing condition. In 1123 A.D. the town wall was rebuilt with a smaller perimeter than before. The port of Old Basrah on the Shatt-al-**'Arab** was Ubullah ابلّه, which had existed from Sassanian or even earlier times and had become, by the 10th century, a place of considerable size. Ubullah was probably the Greek "Apologos" and it seems to have occupied the site of the present Maqām quarter of Basrah.

BASTAK

BASTAK
بستك

A division of the sub-province of Lār لار in the province of Fārs in Persia; the greater portion of the district lies inland at a distance from the Persian Gulf. Bastak has nevertheless a partial connection with the Persian Gulf and is held, in a sense, to extend to the shore of the Gulf on both sides of the **Lingeh** District. To the west of the **Lingeh** District the revenue of the territories subject to the chiefs of **Gābandi, Mugām, Chīru, Chārak,** and **Mughu** has now for some time been payable to the Deputy-Governor of Bastak. To the east of the **Lingeh** District again, the town of **Khamīr** together with the coast from the border of the **Lingeh** District at Purghār to the frontier of the **Shamīl** District at the mouth of the Rūd-i-Kul is recognised as belonging geographically to Bastak. This recognition however is of no practical significance, for **Khamīr**, the only place of importance, is actually subject for administrative purposes to the Governor of the **Gulf Ports**, while its revenues are farmed by the Mu'īn-ut-Tujjār of Tehrān: the powers of the Governor of Bastak in relation to this part of his territories are consequently nominal.

The coast of the district from Purghār to the mouth of the Rūd-i-Kul is about 34 miles in extent; its average direction is from west-south-west to east-north-east, and it forms the north shore of the **Clarence Strait** between **Qishm** Island and the main; it is a low coast and the greater part of it has not as yet been satisfactorily examined. The town of **Khamīr**, situated 14 or 15 miles west of the Rūd-i-Kul, divides the coast into two portions, of which the western is the mouth of a great valley from the interior, namely, the long trough which lies behind the maritime range of the **Shībkūh** and **Lingeh** Districts and contains Galehdār, Tarākameh and Ishkani. Off this part of the coast line lie miles of swamp, from which most of the firewood used in the lower part of the Persian Gulf is obtained; the marshes, thickly grown with mangroves, are intersected by numerous creeks and difficult of passage except for small boats.

The maritime range which forms the northern boundary of the **Lingeh** District and has already been described in the articles on that district and on **Shībkūh** encloses this part of Bastak on the south; and the district appears to be intersected by a higher range, similar in direction, which leaves the coast at **Khamīr**. This last range has two principal summits near **Khamīr**; one, which is 9 miles north-east of the village and nearer to the coast, is 3,700 feet high; while another, 12 miles north-west of **Khamīr**, is even loftier but is less bold in outline. From the higher peak a spur runs off south-eastwards in the direction of **Khamīr**; its foot-hills contain deposits of sulphur.

The following are the principal places on or near the Bastak coast:—

Name.	Position.	Houses and inhabitants.	Remarks.
Khamīr خمیر	On the coast 12 miles west-north-west of Lāft on Qishm Island.	...	See article **Khamīr**.
Lashtaghān لشتغان	2 miles west of **Khamīr**.	40 houses. The people are mostly Sunnis.	The inhabitants own 6 fishing-boats and engage in petty trade. The village is under the Kalāntar of **Khamīr**.
Mahtābi (Bandar) بندر مهتابي	On the coast about 20 miles north-east of **Lingeh Town**.	20 houses.	This is a port of the Ishkani district and also a mart for firewood, charcoal and sail-cloth made at Dishkūn, the trade being mostly with Trucial **'Omān**. There are some fishing boats and a good harbour to keep them in. The Imperial Persian Customs have a post at this place.
Puhal-i-Kōsh پهل کوش	On the coast 11 miles east by north of **Khamīr** and 2 miles west of the mouth of the Rūd-i-Kul.	30 houses, mostly of Sunnis.	There are 4 camels, 20 cattle and 150 sheep and goats. Cultivation is insignificant. There are 5 water reservoirs and 1 or 2 fishing-boats.
Puhal-i-Qibleh پهل قباه	1 mile west of Puhal-i-Kōsh.	20 houses of Sunnis.	There are a few dates, a little cultivation and a few cattle and sheep, also 4 water reservoirs, a ruined caravansarai and a few fishing-boats. In the neighbourhood is a salt mine which is worked.

BĀTIH
باطح

A considerable tract of land in **Kuwait** territory between **Kuwait** Bay and the Turkish outpost of **Safwān**: Bātih begins 23 miles north of **Jahrah**, its extent from south to north is 22 miles; and its end 11 miles south of **Safwān**. On the east it is separated from **Khor-as-Sabīyah** by a low-lying tract called Rōdhatain, and on the west it reaches to the locality known as Umm-al-**Khīlān**. Bātih consists of undulating perfectly waterless desert and lies somewhat high, its elevation above the sea varying from 130 to 210 feet. Numerous slight ridges cross it from west to east, the more northern appearing to be included under the common name of Hamār*حمار , and the slope of the country downwards from west to east is uniform but gradual. Bātih is traversed from west to east near its northern extremity by a broad, shallow depression called Bil Jirfān بي الجرفان, and towards its southern end by a series of sandy runs, through which the rainfall drains from the higher ground in the west down to Rōdhatain: between these two, on the southern side of a well-marked ridge, is a locality which appears to be generally known under the name of Bātih-al-'Aud باطح العود or Great Bātih. A few gazelle are to be seen in Bātih.

BĀTIN
باطن
or
BATAIN
بطين

The final and lowest section of the great Wādi-ar-**Rummah**, of which the middle and upper course lies in **Najd**. The Bātin may be considered to reach the **Kuwait** frontier first at **Hafar**; from **Hafar** it runs for about 61 miles north-eastwards to **Riqa'i** and from **Riqa'i** it continues in the same direction for about 95 miles further to the neighbourhood of Jabal **Sanām**, to the westward of which it passes at a distance of 15 miles, thereafter vanishing altogether.†

The Bātin is generally a well marked depression, varying in breadth from 8 miles (as at **Hafar**) to 2 miles (as at **Riqa'i**). The actual bottom or bed of the valley measures about 3 miles across at **Hafar**, but it is ordinarily much less, and for some distance above **Riqa'i** its width does not exceed ½ a mile: it shows no signs of water action, but it is covered with a level deposit of dark-coloured clay which may have been gradually washed down from the higher ground on either side. The level bed bears large patches of low scrub which give cover to gazelle and bustard.

Between **Hafar** and Jabal **Sanām** the Bātin is approximately the north-western boundary of the Shaikhdom of **Kuwait**, but the Shaikh asserts that his influence extends some distance beyond it.

* The Hamār ridges have a slightly reddish tinge (whence their name) and are said to curve southwards between Bātih and the sea ending somewhere near Mdairah. The drainage, nevertheless, of the country towards Khor-as-**Sabīyah** is apparently not intercepted by these ridges. It is from the highest part of Hamār crossed by the road that **Safwān** is first descried by the traveller from **Kuwait**.

† A later report, from Bedouin information, states that the Bātin below Jabal **Sanām** passes south of a place called Barjisīyah, and then a little north of Zubair Town, and finally ends in a marsh in Turkish 'Irāq.

The routes from **Basrah** and **Kuwait** to **Qasīm** run along the Bātin, the former joining it near Jabal **Sanām** and the latter at **Riqa'i**.

In the following table the principal features of the Bātin are enumerated and are described in descending order :—*

Name.	Position.	Nature.	Remarks.
Hafar حفر	In the middle of the Bātin, about 160 miles west-south-west of Kuwait Town.	...	See article **Hafar**.
Ballāl (Qasr) قصر بلال	In the middle of the Bātin, about 25 miles below **Hafar**.	The remains of an old mud fort, about 50 yards square, with some outlying débris There is nothing impressive about these ruins though the Arabs attribute them to the prehistoric Bani Hilāl.	The bed of the valley is here of greater breadth and bears more vegetation than near **Riqa'i**, but there is no water, and the existence of the ruins is somewhat difficult to account for.
Dharābīn ضرابين	On both sides of the Bātin, about 17 miles below Qasr Ballāl.	Two groups of mounds opposite to each other.	The mounds are low.
'Ādhariyāt عاذريات	On the right bank of the Bātin from Dharābīn to Riqa'i, a distance of 19 miles.	A series of half a dozen dry water courses which enter the Bātin from the higher ground on the south-east.	In some of these there is water underground.
Riqa'i رقعي	Between the deepest part of the Bātin and its right bank, about 19 miles below Dharābīn.	...	See article **Riqa'i**.
Kharjah خرجه	Near the left bank of the Bātin opposite **Riqa'i**.	A number of knolls.	The knolls form groups.
(No name)	On the right bank of the Bātin 10 miles below Riqa'i.	A conspicuous hill forming a good landmark.	...
Mahzūl مهزول	Near the right bank of the Bātin at an uncertain distance to the north-west of Jahrah.	A hill.	**Mahzūl** marks the western extremity of the **Kuwait** district of **Shiqqaq**.

* A portion of the Bātin below Jabal **Sanām** was examined by Major Knox in January 1908. The results were unfortunately received too late for incorporation in this Gazetteer and were transferred to the Foreign Department.

BĀTINAH

BĀTINAH*
باطنة

Limits.—An important maritime district in the Sultanate of 'Omān; its coast forms a great hollow curve between **Masqat** Town and the promontory that divides the Gulf of 'Omān from the Persian Gulf. Its extreme points are Khatmat Milāhah خطمة ملاحة, a spur coming down close to the sea nearly 3 miles north-north-west of Murair, and Hail Āl 'Umair on the south-east, which are 150 miles apart in a direct line; its boundary inland is the foot of the Western **Hajar** hills which run roughly parallel to the coast at a distance varying from 10 to 20 miles. The exact boundary with the Qāsimi district of **Shamailīyah** beyond Murair is marked at the present time by a stone wall which runs seawards for a quarter of a mile from the extremity of the hills and through a gap in which the road from Murair to **Ghāllah** passes.‡

Physical geography.—The whole of Bātinah is a low-lying plain, sandy towards the sea, clayey in the interior, and stony as the hills are approached. There are no springs, but water is everywhere obtainable from wells which are generally 15 to 20 feet deep. The great valleys of the seaward slope of Western **Hajar** all traverse Bātinah on their way to the coast; but their courses within the limits of Bātinah are often ill-defined, and in some cases their channels are so broken up and dispersed as to render uncertain the point at which they reach the sea. A list of the principal of these valleys, in order from east to west, will be found in the article on Western **Hajar**: some of them bear in Bātinah names different from those by which they are distinguished in the hills. The coast of Bātinah is destitute of prominent capes, and the only islands that lie off it are those of the **Daimānīyāt** and **Suwādi** groups.

Climate.—The Bātinah coast is much cooler in summer, especially at night, than the rocky coastal tract to the east of it in which **Masqat** Town is situated. The months of May, June and July are healthy, but fever begins with the date harvest.

---

* The principal villages of Bātinah are shown in Black's *Sketch of the Bātinah Coast*. For authorities on the district see article 'Omān Sultanate (foot note).

The etymology of the names of Bātinah and Dhāhirah is not free from difficulty. Bātin باطن ordinarily means that which is hidden or inward, Dhāhir ظاهر that which is evident or external; but unless we suppose the districts in question to be viewed from the west instead of the east—a supposition which appears unnatural—the names in these senses are clearly inappropriate. It is possible that Dhāhirah is so called because it is high and prominent, while Bātinah has received its name because it is low-lying and not visible from a distance. Or the names may be referred to other senses of the Arabic roots, and we may connect Bātinah with the "belly" بطن which is in front, and Dhāhirah with the "back" ظهر which is behind.

‡ See plan No. 1363 in the Foreign Department Library, Simla.

Inhabitants.—The largest and most important tribes of Bātinah are the Yāl **Sa'ad** and the **Hawāsinah**; the remainder may be ascertained from the paragraph on population in the article on the **'Omān** Sultanate. Bātinah is an exceedingly populous district in the neighbourhood of the coast; and a number of the tribes represented in the towns and villages are understood to have Bedouin sections which wander in the interior of the district with their flocks and herds. Practically the whole of the people belong to the Hināwi faction.

The following is an estimate of the settled population of Bātinah:—

Eastern Bātinah, *viz.*
Places on the coast (see end of this article)	51,200
Wādi Bani **Ghāfir** (Lower)	2,800
Western Bātinah, *viz.*, the sub-Wilāyats of	
Liwa	12,500
Saham	12,800
Shinās	6,200
Sohār	20,000
Total	105,500 souls.

The nomads of Bātinah, whose number is quite uncertain, belong chiefly to the important **Hawāsinah**, Bani **Kharūs** and Yāl **Sa'ad** tribes and to the less important tribes of the Bidūwāt, Āl Hamad, Yāl Jarād, Muwālik, Nuwāfil, Āl Bū Qarain, Āl Bū Rashaid and Shabūl.

Agriculture, animals and fisheries.—Bātinah is celebrated principally for its dates, and the Arabs have a saying that a man can walk along the coast from one end of the district to the other without leaving the shade of the palms: the statement is not literally true, but it conveys without much exaggeration an idea of the magnificent date belt which fringes the sea-shore almost continuously and has sometimes a depth of 7 miles inland. There is also much ordinary cultivation along the coast; the chief crops are wheat, barley, cotton, sugar, and lucerne, and some tobacco is grown in the north-westernmost villages. Fruits include—besides dates—mangoes, bananas, pomegranates, figs, limes, melons, quinces, olives and Lōz almonds. All crops are irrigated from wells which are copious and, as already mentioned, not deep. The interior of Bātinah, with the exception of a few spots, appears to be uncultivated and barren.

The domestic animals are camels, horses, cattle, goats and dogs, but horses are few; wild animals include the gazelle and the hare. The country, though suitable enough for wheeled traffic, has no vehicles.

The fisheries of the coast are productive. The commonest kind of fishing-boat is the Shāshah شاشة, composed of a bundle of date stalks held together with string, which floats by the buoyancy of its materials and not by excluding water; in these slight but unsubmersible craft the people of Bātinah put to sea in all weathers and perform journeys of 50 miles and more.

Trade.—The only article of exportation is the date. Imports are principally rice, cotton goods, sugar and coffee, received for the most part from India through **Masqat** Town; and the trade, in consequence of the denseness of the local population and of the fact that the valleys of Western **Hajar** are supplied through the Bātinah ports, is not inconsiderable. The coast of Bātinah possesses no harbours, nor even any creeks that are accessible to boats except of the smallest size; it lies quite open to the Shamāl and is a dead lee-shore in a Na'shi. Nevertheless some sea-going and coasting craft belong to Bātinah, and the following table of its ports, in order from east to west, contains particulars regarding them:—

Port.	Inland area served by the port.	Vessels owned at the port.	Places to which the larger vessels run.
Sīb	Wādi Samāil and Wādi Tau.	30 Shāshahs and 40 small boats.	Masqat Town only.
Barkah	Wādis Tau, Lājāl, Ma'āwal and Bani Kharūs.	20 large Badans and 20 small boats.	Ditto.
Masna'ah	Wādis Bani Kharūs and Fara'.	4 Baqārahs, 12 Badans and 20 Shāshahs.	The coast of Trucial 'Omān and Masqat Town.
Wudām	Wādi Bani Ghāfir.	40 Baqārahs, Batīls and Ghunchahs.	Persian Gulf, India and Yaman.
Suwaiq	Ditto	10 Baqārahs, 5 Badans and 20 small craft.	Masqat Town and Persian Gulf.
Sūr Haiyān	The adjacent villages.	40 Baqārahs, Batīls and Ghunchahs.	Persian Gulf, India and Yaman.
Khābūrah	Wādis Hawāsinah, Bani 'Umr and 'Āhin.	5 Badans, 30 Shāshahs and 15 small boats.	Masqat Town and Persian Gulf.
Saham	Wādis 'Āhin, Sarrāmi and Shāfān.	30 Badans and 70 small boats.	Masqat Town, Shinās Town and the Persian Gulf.

Port.	Inland area served by the port.	Vessels owned at the port.	Places to which the larger vessels run.
Sohār	Wādis 'Āhin, Hiltī, Jizi and Bani 'Umr-al-Gharbi.	8 Badans and 30 smaller boats.	Masqat Town and Makrān.
Harmūl	Liwa Town.	None of its own.	Boats from Khābūrah bring cargoes for Liwa, which is the trade centre of this part.
Shināa Town	Wādis Hatta and Faidh.	4 Baqārahs.	Masqat Town.
Murair (Saghīrah and Kabīrah)	Wādi-al-Qor.	33 Baqārahs and Batīls.	Masqat Town and Persian Gulf.

Administration.—The Sultān of 'Omān is represented in Bātinah by Wālis at Sīb, Barkah, Masna'ah, Suwaiq, Khābūrah and Sohār Town. The Sohār Wilāyat is divided into the sub-Wilāyats of Saham, Sohār Proper, Liwa and Shinās, each of which is described under its own name. The other Wilāyats are smaller and less organised. At present the Sultān derives almost no revenue in excess of local expenditure from his possessions in Bātinah.

Topography.—The topography of the western part of Bātinah is set forth in the articles on the Wilāyat of Sohār and its subdivisions; the following are the principal places in eastern Bātinah in order from the east westwards :—

Place.	Position.	Houses and inhabitants.	REMARKS.
Hail Āl 'Umair حيل آل عمير	On the sea 5 miles south-east of Sīb.	50 to 60 houses of 'Awāmir and Āl 'Umair.	The inhabitants live by dates, other cultivation and fishing.
Sīb سيب	......	......	See article Sīb.
Laghshībah لغشيبه	4 miles west of Sīb and 1 mile inland.	60 houses of Aulād Hadīd, Āl Wahībah and Bani Haya.	The people fish and own 20 Shāshahs; they have also 80 cattle, 250 sheep and goats and 2,000 date palms.

BĀTINAH

Place.	Position.	Houses and Inhabitants.	Remarks.
Ma'abīlah معبيله	A little west of Laghshībah, near the sea, on the left bank of Wādi Qaṭīb قطيب which comes down from a place about 13 miles inland.	40 houses of 'Awāmir.	The inhabitants are cultivators and own 10 camels, 12 donkeys, 30 cattle, 200 sheep and goats and 3,000 palms: they have no boats.
Shakhākhit سخاخيط	On the coast, 4 miles west of Ma'abīlah.	40 houses of Muwālik and mixed tribes.	Here are 25 Shāshahs, 30 camels, 20 donkeys, 300 sheep and goats and 3,000 palms.
Rumais رميس	On the sea 10 miles west of Sīb.	30 ditto, including Mashāfirah.	Wādi Lājāl reaches the sea half a mile west of this place and Wādi Tau still further to the west. There are 30 Shāshahs, 15 camels, 20 cattle, 150 sheep and 2,000 palms.
Wādi Manūmah وادي منومه	At the coast 6 miles east of Barkah.	150 houses of Hikmān and Jannabah.	Nil.
Harādi حرادي	On the coast 4 miles east of Barkah.	100 dwellings of Matārīsh: one is a fortified house; the rest are huts.	There are dates and wells. The people are fishermen and sailors and dive for pearls at the Daimānīyāt islands.
Barkah بركه	......	......	See article Barkah.
Falaij فليج	About 6 miles inland from Barkah.	One stone-built plastered house belonging to the Sultān of 'Omān and about 20 huts of nomads of various tribes.	20 camels, 30 cattle, 200 sheep and goats and 600 palms.
Mahār (Bū) بو محار	About 4 miles west of Barkah and 3 miles inland.	85 huts of the Muwālik tribe.	30 camels, 50 cattle, 400 sheep and goats, and 3,000 palms.
Billah بله	About 3 miles inland and 4 miles west of Barkah, to the west of Wādi Ma'āwal.	A fort and over 300 huts of the Āl Badar.	Besides dates there is cultivation of sugar, wheat and melons. Palms are about 2,000.
Na'amān نعمان	About 7 miles south-west of Barkah and the same distance inland.	......	......

Place.	Position.	Houses and inhabitants.	Remarks.
Hadhīb (I) حضيب	A short distance inland, about 1 mile west of Billah.	40 houses of Bani Bū Hasan.	90 camels, 30 cattle, 200 sheep and goats and 5,000 palms.
'Abāli (Bū) بو عبالي	On the coast 3 miles east of Masna'ah.	A large scattered village of Ghafailāt, Ghawārib, Yāl Jarād and Nuwāfil, inhabiting date-branch huts.	Sugar and lucerne are cultivated as well as dates. There are 500 palms. Wādi Bani Kharūs reaches the sea a mile or two east of this place.
Marāghah مراغه	A mile or more inland between Bū 'Abāli and Masna'ah.	60 huts of Yāl Jarād.	Dates are grown: there are about 1,000 palms.
Sha'ībah سعيبه	2 miles east of Masna'ah.	40 houses of Yāl Khamīs and Nuwāfil.	Grain is cultivated and there are 3,000 date palms. Wādi Bani 'Auf reaches the sea here.
Masna'ah مصنعه	......	.....	See article Masna'ah. Here Wādi Fara' falls into the sea.
Tau-ash-Shawi طو الشوي	On the right bank of Wādi Fara,' 3 miles inland from Masna'ah.	20 houses of Yāl Sa'ad.	Wheat and lucerne are grown; there are 50 cattle and 100 sheep and goats, also about 400 date trees.
Tarīf طريف	On the left bank of Wādi Fara' opposite Tan-ash-Shawi, but rather higher up and clear of the Masna'ah date groves.	60 houses of Yāl Sa'ad.	The inhabitants subsist by their dates and other cultivation; there are about 12,000 palms. There are a few sheep and cattle.
Muladdah ملده	7 miles inland, south-westwards of Masna'ah.	Town consisting of a few mud houses and some 400 huts. The people are all Yāl Sa'ad except a few Balūchis.	There is a bazaar of 50 shops, and a large fort belonging to the Yāl Sa'ad. The place depends on its extensive date plantations which are divided only by a narrow Wādi from those of Masna'ah and contain about 5,000 palms.

Place.	Position.	Houses and inhabitants.	Remarks.
Shirs شرص	On the coast, divided from **Masna'ah** only by the mouth of Wādi **Fara'**.	A large double village consisting of two quarters; the eastern contains 300 houses of the Hadādabah; the western, separated from it by a distinct interval, is composed of 200 houses of the Yāl Braik.	The people live by date cultivation and fishing. There are wells, but no cultivation except of dates. Palms are about 3,000.
'Awaid عويد	On the sea between Shirs and Wudām.	80 houses of various tribes.	The inhabitants are fishermen and possess about 80 Shāshahs.
Wudām ردام	On the sea 8 miles from **Masna'ah** and 6 from **Suwaiq**.	A town of 400 huts, chiefly of the **Balūchi**, Maqānnah, and Bani Hammād tribes. One of the quarters is called Sūr-al-Maqānnah.	Besides fishing-boats some 40 sea-going craft running to Bandar **'Abbās**, **Lingeh**, the Makrān ports and Karāchi are owned here. Wudām is the port of Muladdah, Gharaifah, Qarat and Tharmad and of Wādi Bani **Ghāfir**. There are no shops; business is done in private houses.
Raqqās رقاص	About 6 miles inland from Wudām.	100 huts of the Yāl Sa'ad.	There are date plantations containing about 2,000 trees.
Gharaifah غريفه	Inland, a few hundred yards east of Sūr-al-Qarat.	500 huts of Yāl Sa'ad.	There are 6,000 date palms.
Qarat (Sūr-al-) سور القرط	5 miles inland of Wudām southwestwards, between Gharaifah and Tharmad.	200 dwellings of the Yāl Sa'ad, most huts, but some mud houses.	There are about 3,000 date palms; no other cultivation. About 40 camels are kept, but few cattle or sheep.
Tharmad ترمد	Inland, a few hundred yards west of Sūr-al-Qarat.	250 houses of Yāl Sa'ad.	There is abundance of dates, palms numbering about 5,000, but little other cultivation. The people are many of them camelmen.
Khabbah خبه	On the sea about half way from Wudām to Suwaiq.	300 to 400 houses of **Ma'āwal**, Yāl Sa'ad and Yāl Khamīs.	The people live by the cultivation of dates, wheat and lucerne: there are 4,000 palms.

Place.	Position.	Houses and inhabitants.	REMARKS.
Suwaiq سويق	......	......	See article **Suwaiq**.
Bat-hah Yāl Sa'ad بطحه يآل سعد or Bat-hah Suwaiq بطحه سويق	On the coast about 2 miles west of **Suwaiq**.	600 houses of Yāl Sa'ad, very much scattered.	There are wells, and the date-groves belonging to the place extend about 6 miles along the sea-front and reach about 3 miles inland. The trees possibly number 10,000. Wādi Bani Ghāfir reaches the sea here.
Khadhr خضرا	On the sea, about 7 miles west of Suwaiq.	400 houses of Yāl Sa'ad and Āl Bū Rashaid. There are 2 quarters, that inland being detached from the other.	The people fish and grow large quantities of dates: the palms number about 5,000.
Haiyān (Sūr) سور هيان	On the coast 4 miles west of Khadhra.	250 houses of Marāzīq, Bani Khammārah, Yāl Sa'ad, Balūchis, etc.	The date plantations are very fine, containing about 4,000 palms, but the people have no other agriculture or live-stock. They own about 40 large boats which carry dates to Karāchi and Makrān.
Dhiyān ضيان	On the sea, 9 miles east-south-east of **Khābūrah**.	200 houses of Āl Bū Qarain, Āl Bū Sa'īd, Huyūd and mixed tribes.	There are about 3,000 palms.
Hajairah حجيرة	On the sea to the west of Dhiyān.	40 permanently inhabited huts of date branches, besides a large fluctuating Bedouin population in tents. The Bedouins are Āl Bū Qarain and the place belongs to them: the fixed inhabitants are fishermen of various tribes including Bani Khālid.	The place is really a camping-ground of the nomad Āl Bū Qarain with wells and dates: they have many camels and sheep here.
Hadhīb (II) حضيب	On the sea, 5 miles east of **Khābūrah**.	50 houses of Manāwarah and Yāl Sa'ad	The people live by the cultivation of dates and cereals: they have 1,000 palms.

Place.	Position.	Houses and inhabitants.	Remarks.
'Abbāsah عباسه	On the sea 1½ miles east of Khāburah.	150 huts of Bani Khālid and Āl Bū Rashaid.	There are 500 date palms; the people also fish and have many small boats. Wādi-al-Hawāsinah falls into the sea between this place and Khāburah.
Khāburah خابوره	...	...	See article Khāburah.
Qasaf قسف	One hour inland from Khāburah on the right bank of Wādi-al-Hawāsinah.	40 houses of Hawāsinah.	Livestock are 14 horses, 20 camels, 40 donkeys, 20 cattle and 1,000 sheep and goats; and there are 8,000 date palms.

The number of date palms has perhaps been generally underestimated in the above table.

The following places in Bātinah have not been exactly located:—

Place.	Position.	Houses and inhabitants.	Remarks.
Ghalīl غليل	Uncertain.	Masā'id and Hinādīs.	Firewood is exported to Masqat Town.
Sabaikhi سبيخي	Do.	50 houses.	The people are fishermen and cultivators owning 1,000 date palms.

Singular Battāshi بطاشي. A tribe of the 'Omān Sultanate; they are of Yamani descent, belong to the Hināwi faction, and are Ibādhis in religion. Their principal seat is in Wādi Tāyīn, where they occupy a large number of villages including Hail-al-Ghāf, but they are found also in Wādi Maih, Wādi-al-Hilu and Wādi Bani Bttaāsh, at Daghmar and Quryāt, and at one or two other places on the

BATTĀSH (BANI)
بني بطاش

coast of the **Masqat** District; full details are given in the table below. The Bani Battāsh are divided into the following 10 sections :—

Section.	Fighting strength.	Location.	Remarks.
Dhakar (Bani) بني دكر	150	Wādi Bani Battāsh.	Nil.
Fāris (Wilād) ولاد فارس	200	Do.	Do.
Ghasain (Bani) بني غسين	80	Madairah in Wādi Tāyīn.	Shepherds.
Hazam (Wilād) ولاد هزم	60	Do.	Do.
Juma'ah (Wilād) ولاد جمعه	50	Mazāra' in Wādi Tāyīn.	Carriers and cultivators of dates.
Ma'āshirah معاشرة	550	Yiti, Bandar Khairān and Khaisat-ash-Shaikh on the coast of the **Masqat** District; Mizra'-al-'Alowi, Mizra'-al-Hadri and Rija' in Wādi **Maih**; and Hiwar and Falaj-al-Hilam in Wādi-al-Hilu.	Singular is Ma'ashari معشري
Malik (Wilād) ولاد مالك	120	'Aqair, etc., in Wādi Bani Battāsh.	Carriers and cultivators of dates.
Salt (Wilād) ولاد سلط	120	Do.	Do.
Umr (Bani) بني عمر	650	Hida, 'Uqdah, 'Ajma, Malahlah, Ghaiyān, Sīdafi and Rikākīyah in Wādi Tāyīn.	Singular is Ma'amri معمري
Ward (Wilād) ولاد ورد	30	Lashkhar in Wādi Tāyīn.	Cultivators of dates.

The total number of the tribe is now about 7,000 souls ; formerly they were more numerous. The Bani Battāsh bear a good character and are peaceably disposed; they concern themselves chiefly with trade and the cultivation of dates. In ancient times, it is said, they used to breed horses for the Indian market on grazing grounds near **Quryāt**; but this occupation has long been discontinued.

The Bani Battāsh are sometimes at feud with the **Siyābiyīn**. Their Tamīmah or chief Shaikh belongs to a family called Wilād Shimās ولاد شماس and has his residence at **Mazāra'**.

BATTĀSH (WĀDI BANI) وادي بني بطّاش

A valley in the **Masqat** District of the Sultanate of **'Omān**; its course is from south-west to north-east, its length is about 20 miles, and it reaches the sea at the south end of **Quryāt**. The inhabitants are all of the Bani Battāsh tribe, and the following are their villages in order from the head of the valley down to **Quryāt** upon the sea :— Mazāra' مزارع (left bank, 150 houses); Mihya محيا (right bank, 100 houses); Misfāh مسفاه (right bank, 100 houses); 'Aqair عقير (left bank, 50 houses); Khadhra خضرا (right bank, 80 houses); Hail حيل (left bank, 70 houses); Sakhbari سخبري (left bank, 10 houses); Khilaiyif خليّف (left bank, 20 houses). The population of the valley is thus about 3,000 souls. Resources are estimated at 200 camels, 280 donkeys, 360 cattle and 4,500 sheep and goats, which are distributed among the villages roughly in proportion to the size of the latter. Date palms amount altogether to some 21,000, of which about 7,000 are at Mazāra' and 7,000 at Misfāh.

BĀWĪYEH باويّه

Singular Bāwi باوي. A large and powerful Arab tribe of Southern **'Arabistān**; they claim descent from Muhalhal, an Arab hero, and consider their ancestry superior to that of the **Ka'ab**. The Bāwīyeh number perhaps 20,000 souls and occupy, along with certain small tribes dependent on them, the whole of the region between the **Jarrāhi** on the east and the **Kārūn** on the west, from the confluence of the Haddām with the **Gargar** in the north to 'Ali-ibn-al-Husain or even Mārid on the **Kārūn** in the south. A few are found also on the right bank of the **Kārūn**. The tribe are mostly nomads living in tents and owning large flocks and herds; but on the **Kārūn** they possess the permanent villages of Kūt 'Abdullah, Kūt Saiyid Sālih, Kūt-al-'Amaireh, Umm-at-Tamair and Ghazzāwīyeh, also the more than temporary settlements of Kūt Saiyid Sālih, Kūt Saiyid 'Anāyeh and Morān. The residence of the chief Shaikh, at present Husain-bin-'Ali whose father died at an advanced age in 1907, is at Kūt-al-'Amaireh where he has a fort and house. The number of settled Bāwīyeh is probably about 1,500 souls, as against 18,500 who are nomads. The Farātiseh, **Hamaid**, Jāma', Al Bū **Kurd**, **Salāmāt**, Shawākir and **Zarqān** tribes which are politically connected with the Bāwīyeh are described elsewhere, and the detailed analysis which follows below relates only to the divisions of the Bāwīyeh proper. From this table it would appear that the Bāwīyeh have 2,710 fighting men, of whom 920 are mounted on horses (or rather mares) and 800 are armed with rifles, but in practice they seem unable to put as many as 2,000 warriors in the field; on the other hand the estimated fighting strength appears small in proportion to the alleged total number of the tribe.

Section.	Habitat.	Fighting strength.	Remarks.
'Amūr عمور	'Araibīyeh, Bu'airish, Chāi Sūdān and Tawīleh. They also visit the Jarrāhi District.	400, of whom 150 have rifles and 100 are mounted.	They own 200 camels, 100 cattle and 6,000 sheep and goats. A smaller division called Chūl are included in the 'Amūr section.
'Atuwi (Āl Bū) آل بو عطوي	Shākheh, Dōb-al-Hisān, and Umm-at-Tarfeh. They are still under the Bairaq or flag of the **Muhaisin**, to which tribe they properly belong, but it is now about 20 years since they settled at Shākheh.	500, of whom all have rifles and 50 are mounted.	This section have no camels, but they own 200 donkeys and 300 cattle and have in their possession about 10,000 sheep and goats, many of which belong to other tribes such as the **Muhaisin**, the Āl Bū 'Atuwi being hired to pasture them. The Āl Bū 'Atuwi pay 200 Tūmāns a year to the Shaikh of **Muhammareh** and 150 Tūmāns to the chief Shaikh of the Bāwīyeh on account of the land they occupy.
Balid (Al Bū) آل بو بالد	Dōb-al-Hisān and Umm-at-Tarfeh.	100, of whom 50 have rifles and 20 are mounted.	This section own 100 camels and 200 cattle and have charge of

BÂWIYEH

Section.	Habitat.	Fighting strength.	REMARKS.
			about 10,000 sheep and goats, but of these many belong to the **Muhaisin** and other tribes. They are said to pay 100 Tūmāns a year as revenue to the Shaikh of **Muhammareh**.
Khālid (Bani) بني خالد	Cham-as-Sābi.	150, all mounted and armed with rifles.	The Bani Khālid own 300 camels, 400 cattle and 10,000 sheep and goats. They are probably of a different origin from the Bāwiyeh proper, and it is reported that they have recently begun to pay their revenue direct to the Shaikh of **Muhammareh**.
Khaz'al (Bait) بيت خزعل	Chinaibeh.	60, all mounted, of whom 20 have rifles.	This section is named, in compliment, after the Shaikh of **Muhammareh** whose maternal uncle's son is head of it. They have 40 camels, a few cattle and 1,000 sheep and goats, besides 60 mares.
Lijbārāt لجبارات or Libārāt ليبارات	Kūt-al-'Amaireh and Ghazzāwīyeh.	50, of whom 20 are mounted and armed with rifles.	The Lijbārāt only possess 500 sheep and goats. They are said to be descended from the kitchen-servants of a chief Shaikh of the Bāwiyeh.
Nawāsir نواصر	The places mentioned in the column of remarks.	1,000, of whom 100 are mounted and 170 possess rifles.	The Nawāsir are said to pay 800 Tūmāns as annual revenue to the Shaikh of **Muhammareh** and to be divided into 6 subsections, viz.:— (1) Nawāsir proper (30 rifles) at Ghazzāwīyeh. (2) 'Awāudeh عوائده (30 rifles) at Qāmīsh: annual revenue 100 Tūmāns.

Section.	Habitat.	Fighting strength.	Remarks.
			(3) Barūmi (Al) آل بروي (20 rifles) at Karaid: annual revenue 20 ر Tūmāns.
			(4) Hilaichīyeh هليچيه at Jarbeh.
			(5) Husain (Āl Bū) آل بو حسين (30 rifles) at Ghazzāwīyeh.
			(6) Musabbi (Al Bū) (20 rifles) at Morān.
Rahāmeh (Bait) بيت رحامه	Khudhairiyāt and Imbāraki.	200, of whom 100 are mounted and 50 are armed with rifles.	This section have 400 camels and 5,000 sheep and goats.
Sunhair (Bait) بيت صنهير	Shākheh and Banneh.	200, of whom 100 have rifles and are mounted.	Also called Āl Bū Rashdi آل بو رشدي. Livestock are 100 camels, 200 cattle and 4,000 sheep and goats. The present Shaikh is Rāshid.
Zahrāo (Al) آل زهراو	Kūt-al-'Amaireh.	150, all mounted, but only 60 with rifles.	The Shaikh of the whole Bāwīyeh tribe belongs to this section. They own 400 camels, a few cattle, 15,000 sheep and goats and 200 mares.

There is also a section styled Simairāt سميرات who are scattered among the other sections and number about 60 fighting men. Most of them are at present attached to the Bait Rahāmeh section above and are dependents of Shaikh 'Anāyeh, nephew of the principal chief of the Bāwīyeh.

It is affirmed that the Bāwīyeh as a whole pay annual revenue to the Shaikh of **Muhammareh** through their own Shaikh, but that certain sections are exempt and even receive allowances.

BAYĀSIRAH بياسره Or Bayāsir بياسر: singular Baisar بيسر. A community or tribe of inferior social status, found everywhere in **'Omān**, but especially at **Nakhl**,

BGHAILAH

Bahlah and **Nizwa** and in the coast towns of **Masqat, Matrah, Saham** and **Sohār**; they occur also at various places in Wādi **Samāil**, and at Misinnah and Mali in Wādi Bani **Ghāfir**. Their origin is doubtful; some authorities state that they are a tribe of Hadhramauti origin, but it appears to be the case that most of them are merely the children of 'Omāni Arabs by slave mothers. Some are Ghāfiris and some Hināwis and there is no agreement among them in religious matters. They are peaceable and industrious and some have accumulated wealth, but the Arabs do not entrust them with authority or command; and they are accustomed to remove their sandals, after the manner of servants and inferiors, before kissing the hands of Shaikhs. Those who regard the Bayāsirah as a regularly constituted tribe divide them into the following 4 sections: Aulād Barakain اولاد بركين and Aulād 'Abdu اولاد عبد with headquarters at **Nakhl**, Aulād Subāh اولاد صباح with headquarters at **Nizwa**, and Āl Khasaib آل خسيب with headquarters at **Masqat** Town: there are also at **Nakhl** sections or subsections called Aulād Hamad حمد and Aulād 'Ubaidān عبيدان The Bayāsirah number perhaps 10,000 souls and are connected, among others, with the following tribes:—with the Bani Hasan, 400 houses; with the Bani **Ruwāhah**, 70 houses; with the Bani **Battāsh**, 30 houses; and with the **Habūs**, 20 houses. A few Bayāsirah have emigrated to **Dhufār** Proper and are to be found there cultivating at Hamrān.

BEHBE-HĀN بهبهان

This sub-province of **Fārs**, with the town of Behbehān as its capital, lies for the most part beyond the limits of the Gazetteer: the only portions included are the coast district of **Lirāvi**, which is described in a separate article under its own name, and the Zaidān plain which, with its villages, is noticed in the article on the **Hindiyān** River. The town of Arrajān, famous in the 10th century, seems to have been situated within a few miles of the site of the present town of Behbehān, by which it was superseded before the end of the 14th century A. D.*

BGHAI-LAH بغيله

A small town in the **Jazīrah** Qadha of Turkish 'Irāq, on the right bank of the **Tigris** about 50 miles above **Kūt-al-Amārah** and 60 below

---

* Arrajān declined after its capture by the Ismailians in the 13th century A. D. and by the end of the 14th century had fallen completely to decay. See Le Strange's *Lands of the Eastern Caliphate*. The name of Behbehān is first mentioned in connection with a march made by Tīmūr in 1393 A. D.

'Azīzīyah by river: it stands on Dāirat-as-Sanīyah land and belongs entirely to that Department. The population is about 2,000, of whom more than one-third are **Kurds** and a majority are Shī'ahs. The town is situated on the boundary between the country of the Bani **Rabī'ah** on the east and that of the **Zubaid** on the west, and it is much frequented by the surrounding Arabs. It is the centre of a cultivated tract which produces wheat, barley, oats, rice, sesame, maize, millet, beans and Māsh in profusion and the lands are watered by a large canal, called Bad'ah بدعة, which takes off below the town and runs into the desert behind it. There are as yet no dates; but gardens of fruit trees, including peaches, have been laid out. Supplies not locally produced are brought from **Hillah, Daghārah** and the 'Afaj district in the **Euphrates** valley. Sheep are numerous, but larger animals scarce. There is a bazaar of about 50 shops. A manager of the Dāirat-as-Sanīyah, who is said to be invested with executive powers, resides here, and there is a small police post of 7 mounted and 3 unmounted Dhābitīyahs. Trade and cultivation are both on the increase. The local Arabs are nearly all employed as cultivators by the Dāirat-as-Sanīyah and pay ¼ of the gross produce as rent. The income of the Department from this estate is said to be 4,000 Līrahs annually and the annual expenditure 500 Līrahs.

BIDYAH
بديه

A coast village of the **Shamailīyah** tract in Trucial **'Omān**, subject to **Shārjah** and situated 5 or 6 miles north of Khor **Fakkān**. A small island, also called Bidyah, lies off the coast a little to the southward: it is 200 feet high. Bidyah consists of about 300 houses of **Sharqiyīn** who are fishermen and cultivators of dates, wheat and maize. There are 3 shops, but no Indian traders. Some 10 sea-going boats running to **Sīb** and **Masqat** are owned here and 8 fishing boats. Livestock are estimated at 15 camels, 30 donkeys, 200 cattle and 100 sheep and goats, and date palms number about 3,500. There is a suburb or dependent hamlet called Haqīl حقيل.

BILĀD-AL-QADĪM
بلاد القديم

A large scattered village on **Bahrain** Island, about 1½ miles south-west of **Manāmah** fort. It consists of about 350 mud and reed huts, along with the ruins of many well built houses. There is a south-western suburb called Bilād-ar-Rafī' بلاد الرفيع, and the ground on the north-west side of the village, called Sūq-al-Khamīs سوق الخميس, is the scene of a largely attended market which is held every Thursday throughout the year. About ½ a mile west of the existing habitations are the ruins of the Madrasah Abu Zaidān مدرسه ابو زيدان mosque, with two slender and not inelegant minarets, 70 feet high, still standing: in combination with Jabal-ad-**Dukhān** these minarets form the leading mark for vessels entering **Manāmah** harbour. In the midst of the ruined part of the village is the Abu Zaidān spring, over which is built a modern Shī'ah mosque; its beautifully clear waters fill a tank to which all the notabilities of **Bahrain** resort for bathing in the hot weather. The people of Bilād-al-Qadīm are **Bahārinah** who gain a livelihood as pearl merchants, cultivators and tailors. Livestock include 21 donkeys and 7 cattle. Date palms are estimated at 11,500 trees, and there are also some figs, almonds and pomegranates. The rose and jessamine grow.

BIYĀBĀN
بيابان

A district of the **Persian Coast,** included in the administrative province known as the **Gulf Ports**; it is intermediate between the district of **Mīnāb** on the north and the district of **Jāshk** on the south, and it flanks upon the eastern side the passage which connects the Gulf of 'Omān with the Gulf of Persia. Geographically Biyābān is considered to belong to Persian **Makrān**.

Boundaries.—The Biyābān District is bounded on the west by the sea, and on the east by the crest of a range of hills which runs parallel to the coast at a distance of 10 to 15 miles inland, dividing Biyābān from the districts of Rūdbār and Bashākard. On the north the boundary with **Mīnāb** District is a line which passes between the **Mīnāb** villages of Ziyārat, Dūdar, Qal'eh-i-Gāt and Taling and the Biyābān villages of Bundrām, Guwāsmand and Garūk; on the south the boundary with the **Jāshk** District passes between the Biyābān villages of Būnji and Bāshīb and the **Jāshk** village of Kūh Mubārak. The district is thus about 50 miles in length from north to south and from 10 to 20 miles in breadth.

Physical features.—The chief range of hills is that forming the eastern boundary of the district; it is known as the Kūh-i-Biyābān كوه بيابان.

In the north near Guwāsmand it reaches an altitude of 1,962 feet, and in the south it has a peak 3,946 feet in height. Between Kūh-i-Biyābān and the sea are several minor ranges which begin near the coast and trend gradually away from it in a south-easterly direction towards the main range; these ridges have no general names and are called after the villages near which they pass. They are entirely of sandstone, assuming in places curious and grotesque shapes and lending themselves to varied uses as forts, store houses for grain, etc. In one peak these subsidiary ranges attain a height of 899 feet.*

The principal streams of Biyābān, in order from north to south, are the Gaz گز, Hiwāi هواي, Karāi كراي, Birīz بريز and Zangali, all of which, except the Karāi and the Birīz, flow down from the main range to the sea. The Gaz, which passes about a mile north of the village of Gaz, derives its name from the tamarisks which grow in profusion along its banks. The Hiwāi reaches the sea approximately in north latitude 26° 15′; the Karāi is about 7 miles south of the Hiwāi, and the Birīz about 8 miles south of the Karāi; and the Zangali, which is the southernmost of all, has its course immediately to the south of the villages of Tūjak and Gawān. All these streams have steep banks which are about 20 feet high and from 50 to 70 yards apart. In winter the Gaz, Hiwāi, Karāi, Birīz and Zangali are sometimes impassable, but in summer they either fall to a low level or dry up altogether. In spring the Gaz river has been known to run 6 feet deep with a current of 6 miles an hour, and travellers are sometimes delayed by it for as much as a week at a time. Besides these large streams there are a number of hill torrents, varying in width from 10 to 30 yards, which after rain would undoubtedly become difficult, if not impassable, for transport animals.

The coast line is low and sandy except for a short distance southwards from Birīz, where it is said to be rocky and bold. There are few inlets or creeks, and none of consequence except that which forms an anchorage for Sirīk.

The soil of Biyābān is clayey in parts and sandy elsewhere. A feature of the district are Mīns مين or dangerous quicksands, formed by the sun drying the surface of the ground while below the soil remains in a semi-fluid condition; they occur chiefly upon the coast between the firm, damp strip near the water's edge and the soft, dry ground further inland. The commonest wild trees are the camel thorn and the tamarisk.

---

* A delineation of some of the hills in this district as seen from the sea is given in Chart No. 2373—2837-A., *Persian Gulf.*

People.—The inhabitants of Biyābān are all **Balūchis**, chiefly of the Raīs and Hōt tribes; in religion they are Sunnis, and they are not in any degree Persianised. They are extremely poor, ignorant and uncivilised. Almost all of them inhabit date leaf huts; there is hardly a dwelling of any other kind in the whole district. The people are date growers, stock owners and cultivators; a few upon the coast, however, eke out their livelihood by working as fishermen and sailors. The total population of Biyābān is about 8,000 souls.

Agriculture, livestock and trade.—Dates, wheat and barley are grown for local consumption and the surplus for export is inconsiderable; a little produce, however, from the smaller villages finds a market in the larger, especially in those at the coast and most of all at Sirīk. Cattle, sheep, goats and fowls exist only in numbers sufficient to meet local requirements.

The only commercial centre is Sirīk, from which agricultural products are exported in small quantities to the islands of **Qishm, Hormūz,** etc., and to the ports of Trucial **'Omān** and **'Omān**. Sarkand and the landing places for Sirīk and for the village of Gunāri near the mouth of the Hiwāi stream are also points of call for vessels of light draft. Native vessels which are too large to enter the creeks or to be hauled up on the beach generally avoid the exposed shores of Biyābān.

Communications and transport —Two main routes between **Mīnāb** Town and **Jāshk** traverse the Biyābān District lengthwise; they divide at Kalāwi in the **Mīnāb** District and unite again at Gangān in the **Jāshk** District. One of them, known as the Rāh-i-Daryā راه دريا follows the coast; the other, called Rāh-i-Kūh راه كوه runs further inland through the lower hills. The Rāh-i-Daryā,* starting from Kalāwi passes by Kūhistak (6 miles) and Ziyārat (12 miles) in the **Mīnāb** District, and then by Tāhrūi (9 miles), Sirīk (4 miles), Kardar (6 miles), Gaz (3 miles), Gāo or Namurdi (4 miles), Zarāwat (5 miles), Sīkūi (4 miles), Karāi (3 miles), Birīz (8 miles), Gawān (5 miles), Mukhjangān (3 miles), and Gatān (6 miles) in Biyābān to Kūh Mubārak (10 miles), in the **Jāshk** District, and so to Gangān (12 miles). The points through which the Rāh-i-Kūh runs after leaving Kalāwi are Shāhmurdi شاه مردي, Kunārzu كنارزو, Dūdar, Bangūrman بنگورمن, and Hunzām هنزام, most if not all of which are in the **Mīnāb** District, and

---

* This route is fully described by Preece in his *Notes of a Journey between Shiraz and Jashk.*

the villages of Maihmāni, Sarzeh, Qalamūi, Gōshki, Agushki, Zahraki, Shīrāhan, Sarkūh and Bāshīb in Biyābān; Gangān in the **Jāshk** District is reached after the last named. The Rāh-i-Darya is frequently impassable in winter in consequence of floods, otherwise it presents no difficulties of a physical nature; it is a mere track, however, sometimes not even visible, across the sandy deserts which divide the villages and date groves situated upon it. The Rāh-i-Kūh is described as hilly and difficult, and water, at least in summer, is scanty and bad. It follows that the Rāh-i-Darya is used in summer and the Rāh-i-Kūh in winter. It should be noted that the inhabitants of Biyābān consider all water "good" which can be drunk without immediate evil results: this fact should be borne in mind in consulting the table of villages given below.

The district possesses about 300 camels and 500 donkeys, but these are only sufficient for the requirements of the owners, and no considerable demand for transport could be enforced without hardship to the people.

Administration.—The district is governed by a Kalāntar of local influence appointed by the Governor of the **Gulf Ports**. At present the Kalāntarship is in dispute between Mīr Hāji and Mīr Barkat who both belong to the family of the Mīrs of **Jāshk**. The revenue for which the Kalāntar is responsible appears to be about 2,500 Tūmāns a year. The seat of Government has ordinarily been Sirīk; but Mīr Barkat, when in power, has made Namurdi his headquarters. The state of the district is lawless and about 1,200 rifles of various kinds are said to be in the hands of the inhabitants. The Kalāntar has authority to order any punishment, except death, without reference to the Governor of the **Gulf Ports**; and in practice he may be said to inflict even the extreme penalty at will, for persons obnoxious to him are liable to be shot out of hand on pretext of their having attempted to escape from custody. Civil cases are nominally decided by the Shara' courts, but in reality they are generally settled by force. The Imperial Persian Customs are now represented in Biyābān by Mudīrs at Sirīk, Birīz, Sarkand and Būnji; these officials are at present directly subordinate to the Director-General of Customs at **Būshehr** and their duties as yet are far from onerous.

Topography.—The following is an alphabetically arranged table of the principal villages in Biyābān :—

Name.	Position.	Houses.	Remarks.
Agushki اكشكي	5 miles east-north-east of Mukhjangān.	25	Wheat and barley are grown and there are 150 date palms. Livestock are 10 camels, 12 donkeys, 20 cattle and 150 sheep and goats. There are wells of good water, 6 fathoms deep.
Bailāi بيلاي	2 miles south of Tāhrūi, near the coast.	50	Resources are 700 date trees, 10 camels, 20 donkeys, 70 cattle and 100 sheep and goats. There are 3 wells of good water, 2 fathoms deep.
Bāshīb باشيب	6 miles south-east of Gatān.	20	There are 200 date palms and a little wheat and barley is grown. Animals are 10 donkeys, 10 cattle and 100 sheep and goats. Water is good, from 3 wells, 6 fathoms deep.
Bauni برني	3 miles south of Tāhrūi, near the coast.	2	1 date palm, 1 donkey, 2 cows and a well, 1 fathom deep, of good water.
Bāzgar بازگر	3 miles west of Namurdi.	20	Livestock are 20 camels, 15 donkeys, 10 cattle and 20 sheep and goats; date trees number 150. There are 5 wells, 4 fathoms deep; the water is fairly good.
Birīz بريز	11 miles north-north-west of Gatān and 4 miles from the coast.	100	Wheat and barley are grown and there are 200 date palms. Some of the people are fishermen and possess 4 small boats. Animals are 20 camels, 20 cattle and 100 sheep and goats. There are 7 wells, 3 fathoms deep; the water is poor.

Name.	Position.	Houses.	Remarks.
Bundrām بندرام	2 miles north of Girau, on the coast.	15	A little wheat and barley are cultivated and date trees number 300. Livestock are 10 camels, 7 donkeys, 50 cattle and 300 sheep and goats. Water is good, from 4 wells, 1 to 2 fathoms deep.
Būnji بونجي	5 miles south by east of Gatān and 3 miles from the coast.	10	There are 100 date palms, 2 or 3 donkeys, 10 cattle and 25 sheep and goats. There are 2 wells of good water, 1 fathom deep.
Dardān دردان	In the low hills, near the right bank of the Gaz river about 6 miles above Gaz.	7	A little wheat and barley only are grown. Animals are 2 camels, 3 donkeys, 4 cattle and 20 sheep and goats. There are 2 wells, 6 to 7 fathoms deep: the water is fairly good.
Faig فیگ	In the low hills, 4 miles east of Gaz.	Nil.	There are no houses and no date palms, but a little wheat and barley is cultivated by the inhabitants of Gaz.
Gābnān کابنان	1½ miles south-west of Mukhjangān.	15	Resources are 300 date trees, 4 camels, 8 donkeys, 15 cattle and 100 sheep and goats. There are 5 wells, 3 fathoms deep, of good water.
Gāo گار	3½ miles south-south-east of Gaz.	8	There are 100 date trees and 2 wells, 3 fathoms deep, of good water. Animals are 3 camels, 6 donkeys, 10 cattle and 50 sheep and goats.
Gārindahu گارندهر	5 miles west-south-west of Gaz and 2 miles from the coast.	3	A little wheat and barley are grown and there are 50 date trees. Livestock are 2 camels, 1 donkey, 5 cattle, 15 sheep and goats. Three wells, 3 fathoms deep, yield water of poor quality.

BIYĀBĀN

Name.	Position.	Houses.	Remarks.
Garūk گروک	In the low hills 14 miles east-north-of Kūhistak in the **Mīnāb** District and near the right bank of the Mazāvi stream.	10 houses of Bashā-kardi Persians.	Wheat and barley are grown to a small extent. Water is from the Mazāvi stream.
Gatān گتان	9 miles north of Kūh Mubārak in the **Jāshk** District and 4 miles from the coast.	100	There are a few donkeys, 150 cattle, 250 sheep and goats and 2,000 date palms; wheat, barley and Indian corn are grown. The annual Mālyāt is 30 Tūmāns.
Gawān گوان	4 miles south-east of Birīz.	80	A little wheat and barley are grown and there are 300 date palms, also 6 wells of good water, 3 fathoms deep. Animals are 4 cattle, 20 donkeys, 30 cattle and 80 sheep and goats. A mile or two to the north of this village the **Mīnāb-Jāshk** road passes through fantastic sandstone hills.
Gaz گز	Near the left bank of the Gaz river, at 8 miles from the coast.	50	Wheat and barley are grown in winter by irrigation from the Gaz river and there are 500 date trees. Livestock are 10 camels, 15 donkeys, 60 cattle and 100 sheep and goats. There is good water in 3 wells from 2 to 5 fathoms deep. The annual Mālyāt is 32 Tūmāns.
Gazpīr گزپیر	1½ miles west of Namurdi.	20	Animals are 5 donkeys, 15 cattle and 100 sheep and goats, and there are 6 wells, 5 fathoms deep, of good water. Date palms number 300.

Name.	Position.	Houses.	Remarks.
Gidu کدر	6 miles east of Zarāwat.	20	Resources are a little cultivation of wheat and barley, 200 date trees, 3 camels, 5 donkeys, 20 cattle and 100 sheep and goats. There are 4 wells of indifferent water, 4 fathoms deep.
Girau کرو	On the south bank of a small creek at about ½ a mile from the coast and 16 miles south of Kūhistak in the **Mīnāb** District.	100	Date palms number 1,000 and there are 20 camels, 30 donkeys, 100 cattle and 200 sheep and goats. Wheat and barley are grown. Good water is obtainable from 6 wells, 1 fathom deep. The village lies among sand hills 30 or 40 feet high and has a white fort which is visible from the sea. The inhabitants own a few boats which are kept hauled up in the creek. The annual Mālyāt of the village is 100 Tūmāns.
Gōshki گرشکي	4 miles east-north-east of Zarāwat.	100	Wheat and barley are grown, and there are 300 date trees. Livestock are 20 camels, 25 donkeys, 25 cattle and 200 sheep and goats. Good water is obtainable from 5 wells, 4 fathoms deep.
Gunāri گناري	4 miles south-west of Namurdi and 4 miles from the coast.	9	A little wheat and barley is grown and there are 180 date trees. Animals are 2 camels, 5 cattle and 10 sheep and goats. There are 3 wells 3 fathoms deep; the water is of poor quality. Some of the inhabitants are fishermen and the landing place is a point of call for small coasting vessels.
Guwāsmānd گواسمند	About 12 miles north-east of Girau.	...	...

Name.	Position.	Houses.	Remarks.
Kahūrchilān كاهور چلان	3½ miles west of Namurdi and 4 miles from the coast.	8	Resources are 100 date palms, 4 camels, 3 cattle, 15 sheep and goats, and 3 wells of 3 fathoms depth containing good water.
Karāi كراي	2½ miles south of Sīkūi and 5 miles from the coast.	50	Wheat and barley are grown and there are 400 date palms. Livestock are 7 camels, 12 donkeys, 20 cattle and 100 sheep and goats. Water is good from 10 wells, 5 fathoms deep.
Karatān كرتان	On the left bank of the Hiwāi stream, 4 miles west-north-west of Sīkūi and the same from the coast.	20	A little wheat and barley is grown and date trees number 300. Animals are 5 camels, 2 donkeys, 8 cattle and 60 sheep and goats. Water of poor quality is found in 4 wells, 2 fathoms deep.
Kardar كودر	1 mile from the right bank of the Gaz river at 7 miles from the coast.	10	Resources are cultivation of cereals (watered by the Gaz river in winter), 400 date palms, 6 camels, 10 donkeys, 40 cattle, 200 sheep and goats and 2 wells of good water, 2 fathoms deep.
Kargūshki كرگوشكي	4 miles south by east of Karāi.	50	Wheat and barley are grown and date trees number 1,000. Livestock are 10 camels, 20 donkeys, 15 cattle and 100 sheep and goats. There are 6 wells, 1½ fathoms deep, of good water.
Kilingi كلنگي	3 miles south-east of Sirīk.	3	Animals are 2 camels, 3 donkeys, 10 cattle, and 100 sheep and goats, and a little wheat and barley is cultivated. There are 3 wells, 3 fathoms deep, of good water.

x 2

Name.	Position.	Houses.	Remarks.
Maihmāni میهمانی	In the low hills near the right bank of the Gaz river about 8 miles above Gaz.	25	There are 500 date trees and cultivation of wheat and barley. Livestock are 4 camels, 10 donkeys, 20 cattle and 200 sheep and goats. One well, 20 fathoms deep, contains good water.
Mishi مشی	½ a mile south of Sirīk, of which it is a dependency.	20	Resources are 400 date trees, 10 camels, 8 donkeys, 50 cattle, 200 sheep and goats and 4 wells, of good water, 2½ fathoms deep.
Mukhjangān مخ جنگان	5 miles north of Gatān and 6 miles south-east of Birīz.	15	There are 150 date palms and a little wheat and barley is cultivated. Animals are 10 camels, 7 donkeys, 12 cattle and 100 sheep and goats. Water is good, from 3 wells, 3 fathoms in depth.
Namurdi نمردی	3½ miles south of Gaz.	15	The inhabitants own 200 date palms, 3 camels, 15 donkeys, 20 cattle and 50 sheep and goats. There are 2 wells, 3 fathoms deep, of good water. The annual Mālyāt is 40 Tūmāns.
Farāiband فرای بند	3 miles south-east of Zarāwat.	18	Resources are 200 date palms, 4 donkeys, 15 cattle and 40 sheep and goats. Water is indifferent from 3 wells, 3 fathoms deep.
Qalamūi قلموی	6 miles north-east of Zarāwat.	20	A little wheat and barley is grown and there are 100 date trees. Livestock are 5 camels, 4 donkeys, 10 cattle and 100 sheep and goats. The water, from 3 wells 4 fathoms deep, is fairly good.

Name.	Position.	Houses.	Remarks.
Salāwi سلاوي	2 miles north of Mukhjangān.	5	There are 1,000 date trees and a little cultivation of wheat and barley. No livestock except one camel. Water is good, from 6 wells, 5 fathoms deep.
Sarkand سرکند	On the coast 4 miles north of Kūh Mubārak in the **Jāshk** District.	...	A small port, or rather landing place, where the Persian Customs now maintain a post.
Sarkūh سرکی	6 miles east by south of Gatān.	12	Date trees number 100, and animals are 4 camels, 4 donkeys, 10 cattle and 50 sheep and goats. There is one well, 7 fathoms deep, of which the water is brackish.
Sarzeh سرزه	Near the left bank of the Gaz river, 5 miles above Gaz, in the low hills.	40	There are 1,500 date palms and livestock are 12 camels, 20 donkeys, 25 cattle and 200 sheep and goats. There are 20 wells, 15 fathoms deep, from which the water is raised by bullocks: it is of fair quality.
Shambīrān سمبیران	2 miles west of Mukhjangān.	4	A little wheat and barley is grown and there are 100 date palms. Livestock are 3 camels, 4 donkeys, 6 cattle and 40 sheep and goats. The wells are 4 fathoms deep and contain good water.
Shīrāhan شیراهن	5 miles east by south of Gatān.	20	There is a little cultivation of wheat and barley and date palms number 350. Animals are 5 camels, 10 donkeys, 25 cattle and 100 sheep and goats. There are 4 or 5 wells, of good water, 6 to 7 fathoms deep.

Name.	Position.	Houses.	Remarks.
Sīkūi سيكري	10 miles south by east of Gaz and 7 miles from the coast.	150	This village has 2,000 date trees besides some cultivation of wheat and barley. The wells, 7 in number, are 5 to 6 fathoms in depth and contain good water. Animals are 20 camels, 25 donkeys, 20 cattle and 20 sheep and goats.
Sirīk سريك (N.B.—The name Sirīk is sometimes used in a general sense to designate all the villages lying within a radius of 5 miles of Sirīk proper.)	$3\frac{1}{2}$ miles south-south-east of Tāhrūi and about the same distance from the coast.	150	The only approach to a port in Biyābān; the landing place, known as Bandar Sirīk, lies upon a creek due west of the village where small Būms and other light vessels can anchor; goods are carried by land between the Bandar and the village. Wheat and barley are cultivated and there are 2,000 date trees. Animals are 10 camels, 70 donkeys, 100 cattle and 100 sheep and goats. Good water is obtainable from 10 wells, 2 fathoms in depth. Some of the inhabitants are fishermen and 7 small boats are owned here.
Tāhrūi تاهرري	3 miles south of Girau and 1 mile from the coast.	100	There are 7 or 8 wells of good water, 2,000 date trees and a little cultivation of wheat and barley. Livestock are 10 camels, 20 donkeys, 150 cattle and 400 sheep and goats.
Tūjak ترجك	$3\frac{1}{2}$ miles south of Birīz and 4 miles inland from the coast.	10	A little wheat and barley is grown and there are 200 date trees. Livestock are 4 camels, 6 donkeys, 10 cattle and 50 sheep and goats. There are 3 wells, $2\frac{1}{2}$ fathoms deep, of good water.

Name.	Position.	Houses.	Remarks.
Tūmrāhi تومراحي	3 miles south-east of Sirīk.	20	The only crops are a little wheat and barley; animals are 3 camels, 10 donkeys, 50 cattle and 100 sheep and goats. There are 2 wells, 1½ fathoms deep, containing good water.
Zahraki زهركي	4 miles east by north of Gatān.	10	Wheat and barley are cultivated and there are 400 date trees. Water is from 4 wells, 6 fathoms deep, and is good. Animals are 10 donkeys, 30 cattle and 30 sheep and goats.
Zarāwat زارت	4 miles north-north-east of Sīkūi.	10	There are 200 date palms and a little cultivation of wheat and barley. Animals are 3 donkeys, 7 cattle and 20 sheep and goats. Good water is obtainable from 2 wells 4 to 5 fathoms in depth.

BIYĀDH
بياض

The largest tract in the Sanjāq of **Hasa** that is included under one name: on account of its desolate character, however, its importance is not in proportion to its size nor comparable with that of the oases of **Hasa** and **Qatīf**.

Boundaries.—On the coast Biyādh reaches from the cape off which lies Abu 'Ali island in the north to Rās-as-Safairah, a promontory opposite the south end of **Zakhnūnīyah** island on the south—a distance of 130 miles. Biyādh is bounded on the north by the tract called **Huzūm**; on the west of it lie in succession from north to south the tracts of Jau **Shamīn**, **Habl**, **Jauf**, Badd-al-**Asīs** and the **Hasa** Oasis; on the south it meets **Jāfūrah** inland and Barr-al-**Qārah** near the coast.

The maximum breadth of Biyādh is between the sea and **Habl** where it amounts to about 50 miles.

The **Qatīf** Oasis, which lies upon the coast about midway between the two ends of Biyādh, is regarded as a separate tract, surrounded on the landward side by Biyādh but not forming a part of it. Certain other areas also, which fall within the limits above described, but are distinguished by names and characteristics of their own, are scarcely to be taken as included in the term Biyādh; these are dealt with in separate articles and their names will be found in the following paragraph.

Physical characteristics and divisions.—Biyādh, considered generally, is a tract of light-coloured sandy soil and abounds in low white sandhills called Naqiyān نقيان . Qasba, Subat and Thamām are among the grasses, and 'Andal, Rashād and Tarfah are among the shrubs which grow, and they are found in great profusion. Almost everywhere water is obtainable by digging a very few feet beneath the surface, and the Bedouins say that the wells of Biyādh are numbered "by thousands."

There are several areas which call for notice as differing in character from the rest of the tract. The northernmost of these is the Sabákhat-as-Summ سبخة الصم , a large saline plain or nitrous depression covered with sandhills, which almost reaches the sea in the neighbourhood of Jabal Dhalaifain and extends inland for many miles with a very considerable breadth. To the south of it, and divided from it only by a narrow strip of the ordinary Biyādh, is a second Sabákhah of similar character known as Sabákhat Salāliyāt سبخة سلاليات ; on the east this marsh nearly touches the confines of the **Qatīf** Oasis. The two areas containing the best groups of wells in Biyādh are known as **Dabaisi** and **Hushūm** and have their centres respectively 10 miles south-west and 30 miles west by south of **Qatīf** Town. Next to these in excellence are two coastal strips, the Barr-adh-**Dhahrān** which extends from the **Qatīf** Oasis to the large bay of Dōhat **Ruhum**, and the Barr-al-'**Oqair** which reaches southwards from Dōhat **Ruhum** to the end of the Biyādh tract. The least inviting part of Biyādh after the Sabákhahs is said to be Habail حبيل , a region some miles in extent which is traversed at 30 or 40 miles from **Hofūf** on the route to **Qatīf** Town; water is obtainable, however, and Bedouins sometimes encamp here. Jau-al-Ajal جو الاجل is a small similar tract between Jubail-al-Barri and Qasr Āl **Subaih**.

BIYĀDH 313

Features and wells.—For the purpose of more minute description it is necessary to divide Biyādh into the following parts :—

  I. The part north of Sabákhat-as-Summ.
  II. The part between Sabákhat-as-Summ and **Hushūm, Dabaisi** and the **Qatīf** Oasis.
  III. The part between **Hushūm, Dabaisi** and **Jauf**.
  IV. The part between **Dabaisi** on the west and the **Qatīf** Oasis and Barr-adh-**Dhahrān** on the east.
  V. The part inland of Dōhat **Ruhum**.
  VI. The part westwards and south-westwards of Barr-al-'**Oqair**.

Each of these artificial divisions we now proceed to describe: but **Hushūm, Dabaisi,** Barr-adh-**Dhahrān** and Barr-al-'**Oqair**—whether they ought to be regarded as belonging to Biyādh or only as enclosed by it—are dealt with separately under their own names; and so, of course, is the **Hasa** Oasis.

I. The following is a table, alphabetically arranged, of the principal features in the division of Biyādh north of Sabákhat-as-Summ :—

Name.	Position.	Nature.	Remarks.
Bahri (Jubail-al-) جبيل البحري	On the coast 23 miles south-east of Abu 'Ali island and 37 miles north-west of Rās Tanūrah.	A hill forming a landmark of some importance.	A small creek known as Khuwair-al-Jubail runs inland immediately on the north side of the hill.
Barri (Jubail-al-) جبيل البري	5 miles inland south-westwards from Jubail-al-Bahri.	Do.	...
Bātinah (Jazīrat-al-) جزيرة الباطنة	South of Abu 'Ali island from which it is divided by the unnavigable channel Maqta'-ar-Raiyāfah, 2 miles broad.	The seaward end of the promontory which juts out from the mainland towards Abu 'Ali island; at high tide it is cut off from the remainder by a small arm of the sea, called Maqta'-al-Bātinah, and becomes an island; it is described as being about the same size as the island of Umm Na'asān in Bahrain.	The so-called island is rocky and rises in two or three peaks. It has no named capes.

Name.	Position.	Nature.	Remarks.
Dafi (Dōhat-ad-) درحة الدفي	6 miles south of the west end of Abu 'Ali island and about 20 miles south-east of **Musallamīyah** bay.	A small bay.	From the foot of Dōhat-ad-Dafi the boundary between **Huzūm** and **Biyādh** runs inland due westwards.
Dafi (Rās-ad-) راس الدفي	On the coast apparently in the corner between the eastern end of Maqta'-al-Bātinah and the coast of the mainland running south from it.	A small cape.	...
Dhalaifain (Jabal) جبل ضليفين	On the coast, 12 miles south-east of Jubail-al-Bahri.	A hill.	...
Ja'ailīyah (Rās-al-) راس الجعيلية	On the coast, 16 miles north-west of Rās **Tanūrah**.	A small cape.	Sometimes pronounced Lij'ailīyah. A pearl bank, similarly named, adjoins this cape.
Tanūrah (Rās) راس تنوره	About 10 miles north-east of **Qatīf** Town.	...	See article Rās **Tanūrah**.

The pearl banks along this coast are given in the Appendix on the pearl fisheries of the Gulf.

The principal Bedouin camping places in this division where water is obtainable are given below, the relative positions being stated from native information:—

Name.	Vernacular equivalent.	Position.
'Ainain	عينين	At the north end of Jubail-al-Barri.
Ajal (Jau-al-)	جو الاجل	Midway between Jubail-al-Barri and Qasr Al **Subaih**.
'Arūq (Umm-al-)	ام العروق	15 miles south-west of Qasr Āl **Subaih**.
'Awāzim ('Aqalat-al-)	عقلة العوازم	6 miles south-south-west of the Murair hill.
Dafi	دفي	3 miles east by south of the foot of Dōhat-ad-Dafi.
Dhalaifain	ضليفين	At the hill of the same name upon the coast.

BIYĀDH

Name.	Vernacular equivalent.	Position.
Faṣal	فصل	6 miles west-south-west of the foot of Dōhat-ad-Dafi.
Jarār (Umm-al-)	أم الجرار	In the centre of the division, 11 miles south-south-west of the foot of Dōhat-al-Dafi and 23 miles west by south of Jubail-al-Bahri.
Madhārib	مضارب	6 miles south-south-west of the foot of Dōhat-ad-Dafi.
Marāghah	مراغه	7 miles south-west of the Murair hill.
Nabhānīyah	نبهانيه	18 miles west by south of Umm-al-Jarār.
Nafail	نفيل	10 miles west by north of Umm-al-Jarār.
Qarain (Umm)	أم قرين	14 miles south-west of Umm-al-Jarār.
Ruqq	رقّ	Midway between 'Ainain and Umm-al-Jarār.
Sa'ādah	سعاده	14 miles south-south-west of Umm-al-Jarār.
Sabāb	صباب	At the coast between Jubail-al-Bahri and Jabal Dhalaifain, slightly nearer to the former.
Sabhah Sabīhah	صبحه صبيحه	15 miles west by south of Umm-al-Jarār.
Sadīyah	سديه	4 miles north-east of Umm-al-Jarār.
Sharūf (Abu)	أبو شروف	2 miles south of Jubail-al-Barri.
Subaih (Qaṣr Āl)	قصر آل صبيح	See article Qaṣr Al Subaih.
Summ	صمّ	4 miles inland from a point on the coast which is rather nearer to Jabal Dhalaifain than to Jubail-al-Bahri.
Tuwaiyah	طويه	3 miles west and slightly north of Jubail-al-Bahri.
Wāsat	واسط	7 miles south by east of the Murair hill.

II. The only features of interest in the division of Biyādh immediately south of the Sabákhat-as-Summ are two hills named Mubārakīyah مباركيه and Qarain قرين respectively; of these Qarain is about 28 miles west of Lājām in the Qaṭīf Oasis, while the Mubārakīyah is about 9 miles to the north of Qarain and appears to be situated between the Sabákhat-as-Summ and the Sabákhat Salālīyāt at or near their inland extremities.

The camping grounds with water in this division are the following :—

Name.	Vernacular equivalent.	Position.
'Ardhūmīyah	عرضومية	8 miles north-west of Safwa in the Qatīf Oasis.
'Arīsh (Umm)	ام عريش	14 miles west by north of Safwa in the Qatīf Oasis.
'Arqūbah	عرقوبه	19 miles west by north of Safwa in the Qatīf Oasis.
Birdi (Umm-al-)	ام البردي	On the south side of the Sabákhat-as-Summ, 8 miles east of the Qarain hill.
Daraidi	دريدي	6 miles west of Safwa in the Qatīf Oasis.
Dasmah	دسمه	2 miles east-south-east of the Mubārakīyah hill.
Dhūmain ('Aqalat)	عقلة ضومين	5 miles west of the Qarain hill.
Ghumailah	غميله	14 miles west of Lājām in the Qatīf Oasis.
Hail (Abul)	ابو الحيل	3 miles west of Lājām in the Qatīf Oasis
Ja'aimah	جعيمه	8 miles north-east of Safwa in the Qatīf Oasis, and about 1 mile from the sea and the same from the north shore of Qatīf bay.
Jō'ān	جوعان	6 miles north-north-west of Safwa in the Qatīf Oasis.
Ma'an (Abu)	ابو معن	10 miles west by north of Safwa in the Qatīf Oasis.
Rahīmah	رحيمه	On the coast between Rās Tanūrah and Rās-al-Ja'ailīyah, 11 miles from the former and 5 miles from the latter.
Sa'alūl	سعلول	5 miles north-north-west of Lājām in the Qatīf Oasis.
Salālīyāt	سلاليت	9 miles east of the Qarain hill.
Shāb	شاب	8 miles north by west of Safwa in the Qatīf Oasis and 3 miles from the sea.
Shaham (Kawākib)	كواكب شحم	10 miles west-north-west of Safwa in the Qatīf Oasis.
Shaqm	شقم	3 miles north-north-west of Safwa in the Qatīf Oasis.
Shumailah (Bū)	بو شميله	6 miles north-west of Safwa in the Qatīf Oasis.
Subaghāwīyah	صبغاويه	10 miles west of Lājām in the Qatīf Oasis.

BIYĀDH

At Ja'aimah is a clump of date trees belonging to Bani **Hājir**.

Here may be mentioned 3 other watering places which, though not situated in this division, are adjacent to it, lying to the west of **Hushūm**. They are :—

Name.	Vernacular equivalent.	Position.
Jafain	جفين	10 miles west-south-west of the Qarain hill.
Jarthāmah	جرثامه	8 miles south-south-west of the Qarain hill.
Nuwaisah	نويسه	12 miles south-south-west of the Qarain hill.

III. The central division of Biyādh has no outstanding natural features, but the following camping grounds with water are situated in it :—

Name.	Vernacular equivalent.	Position.
Abāl (Abul)	ابو الابال	13 miles west by north of Munīfah.
Baqaiq	بقيق	7 miles south-west of Munīfah.
Baqqah	بقه	14 miles south-south-west of Munīfah.
Dhabbīyah	ضبيه	15 miles west of **Qatīf** Town.
Ghubaiyah	غبيه	9 miles west-north-west of **Qatīf** Town.
Ghuwailāt	غويلات	3 miles north-east of Munīfah.
Halaiwīn (Bani)	بني حليوين	16 miles south-west of Munīfah.
Jidō-ai	جدوئي	3 miles east of Munīfah.
Mulaihah	مليحه	5 miles west of Bani Halaiwīn.
Munīfah	منيفه	21 miles south-west of **Qatīf** Town and the same west of Jabal Mudrah in Barr-adh-**Dhahrān**.
Naba'ah	نبعه	16 miles west by south of Munīfah.
Safāwīyah	صفاويه	5 miles south of Naba'ah.
Sha'aibah (Abu)	ابو شعيبه	7 miles west by north of Munīfah.
Tiyānah (Abu)	ابو تيانه	4 miles west-south-west of Baqqah.
Tuwailah	طويله	6 miles south-south-east of Munīfah.

IV. The strip of Biyādh on the east side of Dabaisi resembles the central division in its lack of prominent features; it has only 5 camping grounds which are well known, with water :—

Name.	Vernacular equivalent.	Position.
Badrāni	البدراني	3 miles west-south-west of Qatīf Town.
Baqailah	بقيله	6 miles south-west of Qatīf Town.
Nabyah	نبيه	8 miles south of Qatīf Town and 4 miles west of Dammān.
Suwāba'	صوابع	2 miles south of Nabyah.
Tāba	طابا	2 miles south of Suwāba' and the same west-north-west of Jabal Mudrah in Barr-adh-Dhahrān.

V. Except for the objects described in the article on the bay itself, the part of Biyādh inland of Dōhat Ruhum is featureless. The following points in it, where water is procurable, are Bedouin resorts :—

Name.	Vernacular equivalent.	Position.
Baqarrah	بقرة	14 miles west of Niqa-al-Mahāraf on Dōhat Ruhum.
Dhabbān (Umm)	أم ضبان	18 miles north-west of Niqa-al-Mahāraf on Dōhat Ruhum.
Dirā'	دراع	6 miles north-west of Niqa-al-Mahāraf on Dōhat Ruhum.
Ghūnān	غونان	6 miles north-north-east of Umm Dhabbān.
Haiyāt (Abul)	ابو الحيات	12 miles west by north of Niqa-al-Mahāraf on Dōhat Ruhum.
Hujairi	حجيري	7 miles north-north-west of Niqa-al-Mahāraf on Dōhat Ruhum.
Ruhum	رحم	2 miles north-north-west of Niqa-al-Mahāraf on Dōhat Ruhum and 1 mile from the shore of the bay.
Sarair	صرير	2 miles west of Zughail.
Sarrah	صرة	5 miles west of Sarair.
Zughail	زغيل	17 miles west-north-west of Niqa-al-Mahāraf on Dōhat Ruhum.

VI. The only considerable feature of the division of Biyādh that lies inland of Barr-al-'Oqair is a nitrous marshy depression, known as Sabákhat Shātar سبخة شاطر, which is close to the eastern border of the Hasa Oasis and has its centre about 30 miles south-west of 'Oqair Port. The length of this depression from north to south is probably 20 miles, and its breadth where it is crossed by the route between 'Oqair and Hofūf is 4 miles; it is fairly clear of sand and the surface is covered with saltpetre.

The principal Bedouin camping grounds with wells in this division are:—

Name.	Vernacular equivalent.	Position.	Remarks.
'Alāh	علام	About 16 miles inland south-westwards from a point on the coast opposite Zakhnūniyah island.	These wells are situated in a tract of the same name which is several miles in extent and adjoins the southern boundary of Biyādh.
Athlah (Umm)	ام اثله	18 miles west by north of 'Oqair Port.	...
Baraimān	بريمان	14 miles south-west by south of 'Oqair Port.	The first halting place on the ordinary route from 'Oqair Port to Hofūf when the journey is performed in 4 stages. There are 3 wells, but the water is brackish. Grass and camel grazing are available, but no fuel. Remains exist of a Qasr, similar to that at Khuwainij below, but older.
Bisaitīn	بسيتين	3 miles north-east by north of Baraimān.	There is some grazing here, and by digging sweet water is obtainable.
Dannān	دنان	22 miles north-west of 'Oqair Port and 7 miles inland from Dōhat Dhalūm.	...

Name.	Vernacular equivalent.	Position.	Remarks.
Dharr (Umm-adh-)	ام الذّر	1 mile north-north-east of Bisaitīn.	Near by is a group of mounds where in 1902 Al Morrah tribesmen lay in wait for a Turkish military detachment, afterwards surprising and cutting it up at Qōfdīyah. In 1906 the whole incident was repeated.
Hīshah (Umm)	ام حيشة	11 miles west by south of Khuwainij.	...
Kharāiq	خرائق	10 miles inland westwards from Rās-al-Qaraiyah in Barr-al-'Oqair Port.	...
Khuwainij	خوينج	22 miles south-west of 'Oqair Port.	The halting place on one route between 'Oqair and Hofūf when the journey is performed in 2 stages. There are remains here of a Qasr built by the Turks; it was about 20 yards square, with a bastion at each corner, and had rooms against all four walls inside. On the east side, only a few yards distant, is a well of good water, $2\frac{1}{2}$ fathoms deep.
Māris (Abul)	ابو المارس	10 miles south-west of Baraimān.	...
Mijām'ah	مجامعة	9 miles west-north-west of 'Oqair Port.	...
Muwaih	مريح	$1\frac{1}{2}$ miles north-north-east of Baraimān.	...
Qōfdīyah	قوفدية	4 miles south-west of Umm-adh-Dharr.	The scene of 2 mishaps to Turkish troops. See Umm-adh-Dharr above. The place is also called Quff-al-Yasrah قفّ اليسرة
Rizqān	رزقان	18 miles west by south of 'Oqair Port.	...

Name.	Vernacular equivalent.	Position.	Remarks.
Rughwān	رغوان	15 miles north-west of 'Oqair Port and 7 miles inland from the coast.	...
Shātar	شاطر	3 miles south of Abul Māris on the eastern border of the Sabákhat Shātar.	The middle stage on the ordinary route between Hofūf and 'Oqair Port; by road it is 21 miles from the former and 28 from the latter place. The wells, 3 in number, are small and the water is brackish. There is no grazing or fuel.
Sūwād	صواد	8 miles south-west of 'Oqair Port.	Good water for 'Oqair Port is fetched from this well.
Taba'āt	طبعات	18 miles inland westwards of Dōhat Dhalūm.	...
Zaghaimah	زغيمه	3 miles west by south of Baraimān.	...

Population.—Except for the one recently formed settlement of Qasr Āl **Subaih,** Biyādh is without fixed inhabitants, but it is much frequented by nomads. The northern half of the tract is understood to belong to the Bani **Khālid** and the remainder to the **'Ajmān;** but when, as at present, the two tribes are on terms of amity the Bedouins of both make use indifferently of the entire tract. The Bani **Hājir** also visit Biyādh under the auspices of the **'Ajmān.**

BŌSHAR*
(WĀDI)
وادي بوشر

A tract of country in the **Masqat** District of the **'Omān** Sultanate, forming a plain on the north-west side of a spur which the Eastern **Hajar** sends down to the sea between **Masqat** Town and Wādi **Samail.** Although the tract is spoken of as Wādi Bōshar there is no valley properly so called, but the drainage of the plain finds its way to the coast by

---

* See map *Maskat District* (Survey of India, 1904-05) and **Stiffe's** *Visit to the Hot Springs of Bosher.*

various outlets between Hail Āl 'Umair in **Bātinah** and Khuwair in the **Masqat** District. The Bōshar villages extend in a string about 14 miles long from north-east to south-west: in the table which follows they are given in order, beginning at the end nearest **Masqat** Town:—

Name.	Position.	Houses and inhabitants.	Remarks.
Fath Al Bū Sa'īd فتح آل بو سعيد	9 miles west-south-west of **Ruwi**.	30 houses of Āl Bū Sa'īd.	There are a few date trees.
Jāl جال	Adjoins Fath.	40 houses of Bani Hasan.	The people are shepherds.
Sād صاد	Do.	30 houses of 'Awāmir.	Do.
Bōshar Bin-'Amrān. بوشر بن عمران	Adjoins Sād.	100 houses of Bani Hasan.	A few cattle, sheep and goats are procurable.
Filij فلج	Adjoins Bōshar Bin-'Amrān.	200 houses of Bani Hasan.	The owners, as distinguished from the occupiers of this village, are Āl Bū Sa'īd. There are 350 donkeys, 300 cattle and 250 sheep and goats.
Ghallah غلة	1 mile south-west of Filij.	200 houses, *viz.*, Bani Hasan (60), Bani Jābir chiefly of the Salūt section (70), Bani Raqād (20), **Siyābiyīn** (15), 'Awāmir (25) and Āl **Wahībah** (10).	Most of the village is owned by **Khōjahs**. There are 5 hot springs here: the hottest is 115°F., and the largest discharges about as much as a 5-inch pipe. Dates, mangoes, plantains, pomegranates, limes, corn and vegetables are grown and there are about 3 camels, 90 donkeys, 30 cattle and 100 sheep and goats.
Lansab لنصب	3 miles west of Ghallah.	60 houses of Bani Jābir, Bani Raqād and others.	A convenient halting-place for the night for travellers who have made a late start from **Matrah** for Wādi **Samāil**. There are 25 camels and 250 sheep and goats.
Jifār جفار	Less than a mile west of Lansab.	35 houses of Shabūl.	50 camels, 15 donkeys and 200 sheep and goats.

Name.	Position.	Houses and inhabitants.	REMARKS.
Falaij-ash-Shām فليج الشام	3 miles south-west of Ghallah.	30 houses of Bani **Ruwāhah** and mixed tribes.	Part of this village belongs to 'Ali-bin-Juma', one of the Sultan's secretaries. There are 20 donkeys, 10 cattle and 100 sheep and goats.
Sunub صنب	2 miles south of Falaij-ash-Shām.	80 houses of **Nabāhinah**.	10 camels are owned here, also 25 donkeys, 30 cattle and 60 sheep and goats.
Hammām-al-'Āli حمام العالي	2 miles south of Falaij-ash-Shām and west of Sunub.	30 houses of **Nabāhinah** and others.	The people are cultivators and carriers; they possess 16 camels, 40 donkeys, 35 cattle and 100 sheep and goats.
'Awābi عرابي	4 miles south-west of Falaij-ash-Shām.	10 houses of Tamātimah.	7 donkeys and 20 sheep and goats.
Misfāh-al-'Āli مسفاة العالي Misfāh-as-Sāfil مسفاة السافل	Adjoin one another 2 miles west of 'Awābi.	80 houses of Bani **Raqād** and Tamātimah, also **Rahbiyīn** and **Siyābiyīn**.	45 donkeys, 40 cattle and 60 sheep and goats.
Sa'āl سعال	2½ miles west of Misfāh.	20 houses of **Siyābiyīn**.	This village is famed for a vegetable antidote to snake-poison which the inhabitants are said to possess.

These hamlets, with the exception of Bōshar Bin-'Amrān, in which the houses are mostly of stone, consist of date-branch huts with one or two buildings each of a better class, constructed for purposes of defence. The total population of the whole tract is apparently about 4,800 souls. The villages have separate date-groves.

Wādi Bōshar is celebrated for its hot springs, of which the best and most frequented for medical baths are those at the village of Ghallah: there is a spring also at one of the Misfāhs but it is too hot for use. In 1888 Barghāsh, Sultān of Zanzibar, who was then suffering from a fatal disease, visited **'Omān** chiefly with the object of bathing in the Bōshar springs.

The distance of the nearest part of Bōshar by road from **Matrah** is seven or eight miles.

BŪBIYĀN
بوبيان

A large, low island, about 26 miles in length by 12 in breadth, at the north-western corner of the Persian Gulf; Khor **'Abdullah** divides it from the mouth of the Shatt-al-**'Arab** and from Turkish territory, Khor Būbiyān from the island of **Warbah**, and Khor-as-**Sabīyah** from the possessions of the Shaikh of **Kuwait** north of **Kuwait** Bay. The easternmost point (or nearly so) of Būbiyān is called Rās-al-Qaid راس القيد; the southern point, 7 miles north-north-west from **Failakah** island, is known as Rās-al-Barshah راس البرشه. The island has no date trees or villages, and is destitute of fresh water. The northern end of it is very low and is sometimes broken in upon by the sea; the south end also is partially overflowed at high water. In summer some of the **'Awāzim** of **Kuwait** visit Būbiyān and catch fish upon its north-eastern coast by means of tidal weirs or Hadhrahs; and, chiefly on this ground, the Shaikh of **Kuwait** claims the island as his property. A storehouse, guarded by a small military detachment under an officer, was established by the Turks near Rās-al-Qaid in 1902 and still remains.

BUDAIYA'
البديع

A town on the coast of **Bahrain** Island near its north-western corner: it stretches for about a mile along the sea and is about 300 yards deep. It consists of 3 quarters named Farīq-al-'Amāmarah, Farīq-ad-Dām دام and Farīq-al-Budaiya': of these the last is the oldest and southernmost. Farīq-al-Budaiya' is adjoined on the north by Farīq-ad-Dām, which stands on Rās Budaiya' or Budaiya' point; and Farīq-ad-Dām is adjoined in its turn by Farīq-al-'Amāmarah on the east. Waste spaces which divided these quarters have now entirely disappeared. There are a considerable number of stone houses, including 5 or 6 buildings of solid masonry with upper storeys, besides a large number of reed huts; and Farīq-al-Budaiya' contains a tower. The inhabitants of Budaiya' are all Sunnis, comprising **Dawāsir** (800 houses), **'Amāmarah** (100 houses), **Hūwalah** (50 houses), free negroes (200 houses) and a large number of negro slaves (perhaps 450 houses). The total population is estimated at 8,000 souls. The Budaiya' and Dām quarters are mostly **Dawāsir**; their water supply is from wells in the date plantations of Dirāz and Bani Jamrah villages; that of the quarter of the **'Amāmarah** is from a well a little to the east of their houses. Most of the people are engaged in the pearl fisheries. Over 100 boats, some of considerable size, are owned here; they are 11 Batīls, 10 Baqārahs, 56 Shū'ais and Sambūks and 37 Māshuwahs and jollyboats; of these 57 are used for pearling. Livestock include 2 horses, 55 donkeys and 25 cattle. There are 3 day schools kept by Mullas. The internal administration of the place is conducted by the Shaikh of the **Dawāsir** without any interference from the Shaikh of **Bahrain**.

BUQŪM بقوم

An Arab tribe, partly settled and partly nomad, found in the extreme south-western corner of **Najd** and beyond. Wādi Bīshah is one of their seats, and Rumadān and Turabah in Wādi **Sabai'** are among their villages. Bedouin Buqūm encamp in large numbers near Turabah in the summer. The singular of the name is Buqūmi بقومي.

BURAIDAH بريده

An important town of **Najd**, situated in **Qasīm** and second in that district to **'Anaizah** only. Buraidah stands on the opposite side of Wādi-ar-**Rummah** from **'Anaizah**, at some distance from the left bank, and is distant 12 miles from **'Anaizah** northwards.

Site.—Buraidah is almost surrounded by desert, and palm groves and cultivation are found only on that side of it which is next the Wādi. On the west side of the place the sand of the desert appears to be constantly accumulating to a greater and greater height. The sub-soil is a sedimentary deposit of bluish-white clay; but in some places three strata of sandstone, each from 3 to 6 feet thick, are encountered within 30 feet of the surface. The elevation of Buraidah above the sea is slightly less than that of **'Anaizah.**

Arrangement and buildings.—The town is surrounded by a strong mud wall with square towers at intervals, and contains, at its north end, a large but not lofty fort called Qasr Mahanna قصر مهنا which also possesses towers. The houses of Buraidah are of clay, but many have upper storeys; they cover on the average a larger area than those of **'Anaizah**, and their size, together with the greater width of the Buraidah streets, makes the town appear more extensive than **'Anaizah.**

The central feature of the town is the main bazaar, called Majlis مجلس, which runs north and south and is divided by sections among the various trades. At the northernmost end are blacksmiths and tinsmiths; next them are cobblers and shoemakers; then tailors and vendors of ready-made clothes and of piece-goods; then green-grocers; then butchers; finally a miscellaneous collection of shops belonging to dealers in piece-goods, confectioners, arms and ammunition merchants, and gold and silver smiths. A street running eastwards leaves the main bazaar near its southern end and is given up to female traders who traffic in collyrium, henna, toilet requisites, dresses, gold thread, rings, etc. In two places, one in the tailors' quarter and the other in that of the butchers and miscellaneous dealers, the bazaar widens out and forms an open space; both these spaces are used as camel and cattle markets, and in the latter auctions are also held.

The various wards of the town surround the Majlis and are as follows: on the north-east, Jaradah جردة; on the south-east, Jadīdah جديدة; on the south-west, Būtah بوطة; on the west, Duwash دوش; and on the north-west Shamāl شمال. Of these Jaradah is by far the largest, amounting perhaps to a third of the whole town.

The Jāmi' or principal mosque, which is situated to the east of the Majlis near the northern of the two cattle markets, has a high square tower; it is a large building but like other Wahhābi mosques can lay no claim to elegance. There are five other considerable mosques, one of which has a tall minaret; this minaret and the tower of the Jāmi', though attached to places of worship, are used as ordinary look-out stations by the town watchmen.

Inhabitants.—The population of Buraidah amounts to about 7,500 souls; they are mostly **'Anizah** but partly Bani **Tamīm**. Galla slaves, dependents of the Amīr of Buraidah, were formerly numerous. A number of the fighting men are mounted on the Amīr's horses. There are seven schools in which Muhammadan jurisprudence and Quranic lore are taught, also a number of elementary schools; five schools for girls exist at which instruction in reading, writing, needlework and the Qurān is imparted by female teachers.

Agriculture and supplies.—The date groves of Buraidah are very extensive and ordinary fruit trees are numerous. Cereals also are grown in the vicinity of the town, and desultory cultivation is carried on by Buraidah agriculturists at outlying places such as Duwairah and Naqīb. The date belt to the south of the town is called Subākh; it is full of wells of good water, on which the irrigation depends, and lucerne is raised in large quantities among the palms. Livestock are estimated at 1,000 camels, 200 donkeys and 600 or more horned cattle. The Amīr owns about 50 good horses and mares and his relations have 10 or 15 more, but there are few or none among the ordinary townsmen. Camels for transport are supplied by the adjacent Bedouins, those of the town itself being mostly employed on the wells.

Buraidah is a stage on the route between **Kuwait** and **Makkah**. All kinds of supplies are plentiful. The water of Buraidah, however, is generally dull and brackish; its level varies from 20 to 40 feet below ground and rises after floods in Wādi-ar-**Rummah**. The wells in the town are lined with dry-stone masonry.

Commerce and industries.—The shops in the main bazaar number about 300. Buraidah is a great commercial centre, but its trade and activity are at their height only during the four months following the date harvest, when nomads resort to the town to buy dates, rice and cloth; sometimes as many as 1,000 of their tents may be seen at one time pitched outside the walls. At other seasons of the year a considerable proportion of the shops are closed. Buraidah is celebrated for its horse market; the animals mostly come from the **Mutair** and are more numerous than in the **'Anaizah** market but not so good. Buraidah is partly dependent on **Kuwait** for food-stuffs and entirely so for cotton goods. There are richer merchants at Buraidah than at **Hāil**, among them being some prosperous camel masters who have made their money by transporting grain in Turkish 'Irāq, by importing rice and clothing into **Najd**, and by exporting ghi to Makkah or, in some years, dates and corn to Madīnah.

The chief indigenous handicrafts are those of the blacksmith, goldsmith and silversmith. Swords of good temper and workmanship are still turned out, and in former days Buraidah was celebrated for the manufacture of fire-arms.

Political position and government.—The history of Buraidah is inseparable from that of **Qasīm**; it is a record of rivalry with **'Anaizah** varied by occasional coalitions between the two places to meet a common danger. The constitution of Buraidah under its own Amir has hitherto resembled that of **'Anaizah**, political relations with the surrounding Bedouins being however less close; and it appears to be as little in abeyance, notwithstanding the nominal Turkish occupation of **Qasīm** established in 1905, as that of the larger town. The Turkish Nuqtan or military post at Buraidah consisted in 1906 of 60 rifles and was accommodated in a large house without an upper storey in the Jaradah quarter, which belonged to the Amīr of Buraidah. The Amir, at present Sālih-bin-Hasan-bin-Mahanna, received in 1905 the rank of Qāim-Maqām in the Turkish service ; but his appointment, in so far as his employers are concerned, is an unpaid sinecure, and he is understood to own allegiance to Ibn Sa'ūd.*

BURĀZ-JĀN
برازجان

Ordinarily pronounced Burāzjūn. The principal place in the district of **Dashtistān** and the seat of the Khān who under the Governor-General of **Fārs** rules tne greater part of that district: Burāzjān is situated about 28 miles north-east of **Būshehr** Town. The ordinary route from **Būshehr** Town to Shīrāz passes by Burāzjān, which by land is distant 43 miles from **Būshehr** and 16 from **Dāliki,** the next stage beyond it ; but the land-journey from **Būshehr** can be reduced to 28 miles by taking boat from **Būshehr** to Shīf.

Burāzjān stands on the plain of **Dashtistān,** at an elevation of only 250 feet above the sea and dominated by the lofty crests of the Gīsakān mountain less than 10 miles to the eastward ; it is surrounded by date-groves which are most extensive upon the west side. The ordinary houses are poor but there is a fine stone-built Sarāi with loopholed walls, commanding the town and capable of being utilised as a fort ; it was in fact occupied in 1906 by a Persian military detachment of 150 infantry with one mountain gun. High Persian officials passing through Burāzjān treat the Sarāi as a residence. Water is from deep wells and is good and abundant.

The town contains about 500 houses and the population may be estimated at 2,500 souls ; the people are mostly cultivators, traders, or muleteers. The only prominent tribes are the Pāpāris پاپري, who have dominated the place since they expelled the original Bag owners less than a century ago ; the Qāidān قائدان, also comparatively recent immigrants ; and some Saiyids : the remainder of the townspeople are a medley of immigrants from other places, such as Būshehris, Dashtis, Khishtis and Kāzarūnis. The standard of civilisation is higher at Burāzjān than is usual in the coast districts about **Būshehr,** but the inhabitants avoid needless display of well-being and even allow their houses to remain unrepaired lest the Persian Government should be tempted to quarter a high official permanently among them ; at the same time their attitude towards the Government is somewhat defiant.

* In 1906 the son of Ibn Sa'ūd seized and deported him, undeterred by his Turkish official status.

The opium-habit is very prevalent. There are several religious shrines of slight importance.

There are no local manufactures, but the bazaar contains about 170 shops. Burāzjān depends upon dates and agriculture and upon the transit through it of the Shīrāz and up-country trade. About 300 mules belonging to Burāzjān are employed on the Shīrāz route; formerly there were over 500, but many were sold in consequence of scarcity in 1903-04. Burāzjān is the only trade centre in **Dashtistān** and its trade is consequently an epitome of the trade of the district. The exports all go to **Būshehr** Town and comprise wheat, barley, beans, melons, tobacco, gum, wool, firewood, charcoal and lime: the imports in the contrary direction, for the consumption of town and district, are chiefly prints, rice, coffee, sugar, tea, opium and spices. The currency is Persian, chiefly silver Qrāns; and the Man of Burāzjān is equal to 18 lbs. 11 oz. English, giving a Hāshim Man (13 ordinary Mans) of 139 lbs. English.

Burāzjān, though at present farmed along with its dependencies by the Governor of the **Gulf Ports,** belongs to the Government of **Fārs** and is the seat of the Khān who administers the greater part of the **Dashtistān** District. He is not himself a Pāpari but belongs to a tribe called Maiman میمن. A Deputy-Governor also resides here on behalf of the Governor-General of **Fārs.**

The Indo-European Telegraph Department's line from **Būshehr** Town to Shīrāz passes through Burāzjān and is connected at this place with the Persian Government telegraph which goes by **Rīg, Dīlam, Behbehān** and **Ahwāz** to **Muhammareh, Shūshtar** and **Dizfūl.**

BUSAITĪN
البسيتين

A village on the west coast of **Muharraq** Island in **Bahrain,** 1 mile north of **Muharraq** Town. East of the village is a date grove about 300 yards in length by 200 in breadth, in which are situated two wells that supply the village with slightly brackish drinking water. Beneath the date palms carrots and lucerne are extensively cultivated. Busaitīn contains about 400 dwellings; some are of masonry, but the majority are date-mat huts. The inhabitants are Sunnis, chiefly **Madhāhakah** (150 houses); but a few are Āl Bū **Rumaih** (20 houses), **'Utūb** and Bani Yās of the Āl Bū Falāsah section. The inhabitants own 8 Baqārahs, 12 Shū'ais and Sambūks, and 26 Māshuwabs and jollyboats; of these 32 are used as pearl boats. Date palms number less than 1,000 : there are a few pomegranate and lemon trees. Donkeys number 8, and cattle 4 only.

BŪSHEHR بوشهر PENINSULA

A torpedo-shaped promontory lying parallel to the coast of the Persian district of **Tangistān** at a distance of 4 or 5 miles; the intervening space is occupied by a grass and reed-grown swamp or Mashīleh مشيله across which, at about midway between the extremities of the peninsula, runs a caravan route to the mainland.

Extent.—The peninsula measures exactly 12 miles from its north-western tip on which stands **Būshehr** Town to Rās Halīleh at the opposite end : between these points the outline on each side is a convex curve and the maximum breadth, at midway, is about 3½ miles. A small tail running eastwards from Rās Halīleh almost cuts off the Mashīleh from the sea. The peninsula is surrounded by the sea on north, west and south; on the east it is bounded by the Mashīleh which at its northern end merges in Khor Sultāni, a creek entering Būshehr harbour.

Physical features, water and vegetation.—The site of **Būshehr** Town is rocky and slightly elevated above the sea, but immediately south of it a strip of very low land runs across the peninsula from coast to coast; beyond this low strip the ground gradually rises again, and the remainder of the peninsula is a sort of turtle-back attaining its maximum elevation of 150 feet in the centre at Imāmzādeh village. There is a stretch of low cliff along the coast at the south-west corner of **Būshehr** Town and again in the neighbourhood of Rīshehr: south of Rīshehr the high ground falls away abruptly, at some distance inland, both on the west towards the sea and on the east towards the Mashīleh and there are several considerable ravines. One hollow called Andar-i-Buneh Dareh اندر بنه دره or Āndar Bāndar آندر باندر runs down from the middle of the peninsula to its east side, a little south of the telegraph line to the mainland; and parallel to this, on its south side, is a Qanāt which taps a subterranean water-supply. The low parts of the peninsula are sandy, the higher are generally of a firm, arable soil; but there are protrusions at numerous places of a soft, porous sandstone rock in horizontal strata, and elsewhere there are considerable stony tracts.

Wells are numerous, but there is no really good drinking water in the peninsula; the best is obtained from a shallow well near the beach at Bandar Halīleh and some of respectable quality at a spot called Naidi نيدي between 1 and 2 miles south of **Būshehr** Town.

Here and there a little grass is found. An occasional ber and tamarisk are the only naturally growing trees; but the Bābul and cypress are found, also a tree with yellow flowers called Gul-i-Abrīsham and another with red of which the name is Panjeh-i-'Arūs. Roses grow, but not well: the jasmine, Bougainvillea and oleander flourish.

Climate.—The climate resembles that described in the article on **Būshehr** Town, but on the higher parts of the peninsula the heat is less oppressive in summer. The cold weather is frequently ushered in by dust-storms. In winter white clouds, formed by exhalations from the Gulf meeting the cold air of the mountains, cling to the summits and seaward slopes of the great maritime range to the east of the town* and are sometimes carried by a change of wind down to the coast itself. Storms are frequent in December and are sometimes accompanied by thunder and hail.

Population.—The inhabitants of the Būshehr peninsula, apart from **Būshehr** Town which forms the subject of a separate article, number about 8,500 souls and belong to mixed tribes. A number of the wealthier natives of **Būshehr** Town have gardens and country houses in the northern part of the peninsula and live there, driving or riding every day to their business in the town. The inhabitants of the villages of the peninsula own about 300 rifles exclusive of those in the possession of the Kadkhuda of Rīshehr's levies.

Agriculture and trade.—A large proportion of the peninsula consists of arable land, which in part is cultivated regularly by means of wells, and in part after a more desultory fashion by rainfall. The ordinary crops are wheat and barley, sown about December after the beginning of the winter rains and reaped after 4 months. The seed is scattered on the surface of the unprepared ground and is then turned in with a light plough drawn by a single bullock or even donkey. In places there are date-groves, but not of a thriving appearance. A peculiar feature of the peninsula is its viticulture, conducted after a somewhat curious method. The vines are planted in deep pits or wells, led to the surface of the

---

* A sketch of these hills as seen from the sea will be found in Chart No. 2378-27, *Abu Shahr.*

ground, and then trained over rockeries of loose stones; each vine-pit and mound is surrounded by a low dry-stone wall and forms a circular enclosure with an average diameter of about 20 yards, some being less and some considerably more. The vines of Rīshehr are particularly prolific and it is said that one at that place used to yield nearly 2,000 lbs. weight of fruit every year. The grapes find a market in **Būshehr** Town. The number of date palms in the peninsula is from 15,000 to 20,000. Other fruits are water melons, marsh melons, oranges, lemons, pomegranates, citrons and figs, and there are a few Purtuqāl برتقال or Baghdād oranges. Vegetables of all sorts are grown, including cucumbers, pumpkins, brinjals, tomatoes and bindis in summer, and carrots, beetroot, cabbage, cauliflower, turnips, beans, mint, lettuce and chillies in winter; the lettuce of Būshehr has a high reputation in Persia. Potatoes are very little grown and are imported from Shīrāz and Karāchi.

There is no trade apart from that of **Būshehr** Town, and no other port exists except a few small boat-harbours which are little used except by the fishing craft of adjoining villages.

Communications.—The only road in the peninsula fit for vehicles—and those of strongly built types—is one 6 miles in length from **Būshehr** Town to Sabzābād; it is maintained at the expense of private subscribers, under the supervision of the British Residency, and has a branch to Rīshehr. The land routes* from **Būshehr** Town to Bandar **'Abbās, Muhammareh** and Shīrāz all leave the peninsula by one common crossing about 5 miles south-east of **Būshehr** Town. Here it may be noted that the Shīf route was closed in 1906 by the Governor of the **Gulf Ports** in favour of the route by Ahmadi, and that caravans from up-country were then obliged to come to **Būshehr** Town and encamp outside the walls. This change was due chiefly to the extortions practised at Shīf by the Khān of **Angāli,** who paid 4,800 Tūmāns a year for the right to collect tolls at Shīf; but in 1906 it was intended to continue the new arrangement and to build a large caravansarai just outside the town. The Shīf route was always unpopular because there was no warehouse for goods at Shīf, and transport animals could not be kept nearer to that place than at Khushāb whence it was necessary to fetch them when required.

Three cables of the Indo-European Telegraph Department, 2 from **Jāshk** and 1 from **Fāo,** are landed a few hundred yards to the west of Rīshehr fort and conducted overland for about one mile north-eastwards to the telegraph station which consists of 6 or 7 large buildings. The

---

* See *Routes in Persia* I, Nos. 20, 21 and 23.

European signalling staff, formerly 25 strong, has been reduced to 14 since the introduction of automatic long-distance instruments which render manual repetition unnecessary. From the Rīshehr telegraph office three land lines run across the peninsula and the Mashīleh to the coast and thence to Shīrāz. A short line runs direct from the office to the British Resident's house at Sabzābād, and another line accompanies the Shīrāz line to the coast of the peninsula and then strikes northwards to **Būshehr** Town where instruments in the British Residency and the Persian telegraph office are connected with it. The British town Residency is thus placed in communication with Sabzābād, and the Persian telegraph office with Shīrāz, through the Rīshehr office; and the Persian office in the town is almost continuously in possession of one of the 3 wires to Shīrāz.

Administration.—The present Kadkhuda of Rīshehr, a refugee of the family of the Khān of **Angāli**, farms the land revenue of the peninsula for 500 to 600 Tūmāns a year. He maintains a body of 35 to 40 men armed with rifles, who act as a sort of police in the villages and supply personal escorts to the Governor of the **Gulf Ports**. The Būshehr peninsula is naturally under the jurisdiction of the Governor of the **Gulf Ports** who has his head-quarters at **Būshehr** Town.

Topography.—The following are the principal places and points of interest on the Būshehr peninsula:—

Name.	Position.	Houses and inhabitants.	Remarks.
Asalu عسلو	About 2½ miles south of Būshehr Town.	15 huts.	There are a few donkeys and cattle and about 1,000 date palms forming several plantations.
Bin Māna' بن مانع	About 2 miles south of Būshehr Town.	100 huts, chiefly of Arabs.	This is a summer camping ground chiefly, and the place is reduced to about 20 huts in winter. There are 15 cattle and 30 donkeys.
Būshehr Town بوشهر	On the northern tip of the peninsula.	...	See article **Būshehr** Town.
Dallāka (Khashm) خشم دلاکه	Nearly 2 miles south of Būshehr Town.	12 huts.	Two bungalows are being built here by Jews.

Name.	Position.	Houses and inhabitants.	REMARKS.
Davās دراس	One mile north of the Būshehr fort.	45 clay houses.	There are 30 donkeys, 20 cattle and 100 sheep here.
Halīleh حليله	10 miles south and slightly east of Būshehr Town, and less than a mile from the point of the same name which is considered to be the southern extremity of the Būshehr peninsula.	40 houses.	Some of the houses are of masonry, the rest of clay. The village stands on a low, stony coast a few feet above sea level and has date-groves on its north side which extend to the first ridge of higher ground about a mile to the northward. There is some cultivation, most of which is irrigated from wells.
Halīleh (Bandar) بندر حليله	About 1½ miles east-south-east of Halīleh village, on the opposite or eastern side of Halīleh point.	4 or 5 huts.	There is a good anchorage here for small boats, sheltered from the Shamāl but not much used; also a well of water, better than any procurable at Būshehr Town, which is only 3 feet deep and is at 80 yards from the beach. The Imperial Persian Customs have a post at this spot, and the guards cultivate. Behind the place are date plantations which reach to the Mashīleh at the back of the peninsula.
Husainku حسينکو	On the sea beach on the south-west side of the Russian Consulate-General.	12 houses.	There are 5 fishing boats here.
Imāmzādeh امام زاده	5½ miles south by east of Būshehr Town and ½ a mile north of Sabzābād, on the highest part of the peninsula about 150 feet above sea level.	The shrine of Shāhzādeh 'Abdul Muhaiman عبد المهيمن with 25 houses of Saiyids.	It is supposed that diseases are cured by sleeping one night in the precincts of the shrine. The place is frequented by visitors from Būshehr Town and from Tangistān. Nothing is known of the history of the saint. The present hereditary keeper of the shrine is one Saiyid 'Ali.

Name.	Position.	Houses and inhabitants.	Remarks.
Jabri* جبري	On the west bank of Khor Sultāni less than ½ a mile above the Chahār-burj.	200 houses (30 of which are upper-storeyed) and 100 huts.	A village or detached suburb of Būshehr Town close to its south-east corner: boats are built here. There are 15 shops and (with Sitamābād and Zulmābād) 150 fishing boats. Animals are 20 donkeys and 10 cattle. The size of this place is increasing, and it is now almost joined to the town. The new settlers are chiefly from Tangistān.
Juffareh جفره or Hafrah حفره	About 3 miles south of Būshehr Town near the sea.	12 huts, etc.	There is one fairly large bungalow and a small house of stone and mud. The French Consulate has a house on the north-east side of this place.
Khājah (Khashm) خشم خواجه	¼ of a mile north of the Rīshehr fort and the same distance from the sea.	1 large house and 15 huts.	The village possesses cultivated lands which lie in a hollow between it and the sea and are irrigated from a well. There are 10 donkeys, 7 cattle and about 50 sheep and goats.
Khashm Bāla خشم بالا	A short distance to the north of Khashm Khājah.	20 houses.	There are a few donkeys and cattle and 50 sheep and goats.
Khashm Nau خشم نو	Closely adjoining Khashm Bāla and to the north of it.	15 huts.	There are 15 donkeys and a few cattle.
Līl ليل	¾ of a mile north-west of Bāgh Muqām.	35 houses.	The village consists of two parts, Līl 'Ajamah عجمه and Līl Bahraini بحريني; the latter is somewhat the larger and is inhabited by the descendants of immigrants from Bahrain. There are 30 donkeys, 30 cattle and 50 sheep and goats.

* The names Jabri, Sitamābād and Zulmābād, all signifying "tyranny," refer to some incident in the Anglo-Persian war, but its precise nature cannot now be ascertained.

Name.	Position.	Houses and inhabitants.	Remarks.
Mahmūdābād محمود آباد	Immediately next the graveyard on the south side of the Turkish Vice-Consulate.	5 stone houses and 15 huts.	This is practically a part of Būshehr Town.
Mufqa'eh مفقعه	On the west coast of the peninsula, 2 miles south-south-west of Būshehr Town.	40 houses.	The people are fishermen and own about 12 boats. Immediately to the north of Mufqa'eh is the base of an unfinished beacon or lighthouse 40 feet high. To the village belong about 500 date palms.
Muqām (Bāgh) باغ مقام	Near the east coast of the peninsula, slightly north of the point where the Shīrāz telegraph line enters the Mashīleh, and 3 miles north-east of Rīshehr fort.	Half a dozen houses. The present chief Mulla of Būshehr, Shaikh Muhammad, Imām-i-Juma', resides here in summer.	A disconnected block on the north side is called Bāgh Jims جمس after Mr. James Edwards, Extra Assistant Resident, who built a house and resided here after taking his pension. Muqām is so named from being the site of a shrine. The people are gardeners and have charge of about 10,000 date palms (including young trees).
Pūdar پودر	1½ miles south-east of the south-east corner of Būshehr Town, on the south bank of the Khor Sultānī near its head.	40 houses, to which 80 huts belonging to inhabitants of Būshehr Town are added in summer.	Some rising ground and high trees adjoin the village and to the south of it are about 100 acres of cultivated land. The village contains a number of masonry houses. There are a few horses and cattle and a dozen donkeys.
Ravanī رونی	Between Sabzābād and Rīshehr village.	25 huts	There are a few cattle and donkeys and about 50 sheep and goats.
Rīshehr ریشهر (in English generally "Reshire")	Near the west coast of the peninsula, 6 miles south of Būshehr Town and ¾ of a mile south of the Rīshehr telegraph buildings.	15 houses of Bahrainis, forming a block called Bahrainiyān, and 10 of Saiyids and others. Shaikh Husain, a Bahraini who was chief Mulla of Būshehr 40 or	On the coast ¼ of a mile west of the village are the ruins of the old Rīshehr fort, by natives called Qal'eh Bahman Shāh بهمن شاه. It is in the form of a square

Parade of British and Persian troops at Rîshehr, 1905.

Name.	Position.	Houses and inhabitants.	Remarks.
		50 years ago used to live here in summer, as did also his two immediate successors Shaikh Khalaf and Shaikh 'Abdul 'Ali.	with sides over 300 yards long, and the ramparts still rise about 80 feet above the sea-level. The site belongs to the Persian Government and is surrounded by a ditch 70 to 100 feet wide which is cultivated by forced labour under the orders of the Governor of the **Gulf Ports**. The fort was taken by storm by a British Indian force in the Persian war.
Sabzābād سبزآباد	6 miles south of **Būshehr** Town, 1 mile east of Rīshehr fort and ¼ of a mile south of Imāmzādeh.	...	This is the country house of the British Political Resident in the Persian Gulf. It stands on the highest part of the peninsula and is surrounded by a good garden.
Sangi سنگی	In the middle of the peninsula, 1¼ miles south of **Būshehr** Town.	300 houses, mostly of stone.	Most of the inhabitants work in **Būshehr** Town. They have about 400 donkeys on which they bring water for sale, also mud and stone (whence the name Sangi) for building purposes. When there is a scarcity of mules they also act as carriers to Shīrāz. They have besides about 50 cattle.
Sar-i-Tul سرطل	¼ of a mile southwest of Sabzābād.	10 houses.	The people are cultivators, vine-growers and quarrymen. It is said that they formerly inhabited the Rīshehr fort. They have 100 sheep and goats and a few other animals.
Shaghāb شغاب	On the west coast of the peninsula, ⅜ of a mile northwest of Rīshehr fort.	A small Persian hamlet of about 6 houses.	There are two small date groves and 10 donkeys, besides a few other animals.

Name.	Position.	Houses and inhabitants.	Remarks.
Shakari (Bāgh) باغ شكري	In the middle of the peninsula, slightly to the east of Sangi.	20 houses of stone and mud, to which are added in summer about 30 huts.	The village consists of two or three small blocks. Stone is quarried here. There are a few horses and cattle, and 3 or 4 date plantations containing in all about 4,000 palms.
Shambu شمبو	Near Sangi, on the west of the road which passes that place.	20 stone houses.	The houses belong to inhabitants of Būshehr Town: they are not fully occupied except in summer.
Sitamābād ستم آباد	On the west bank of Khor Sultāni, $1\frac{1}{4}$ miles above the Chahārburj.	300 houses.	This place is growing and will shortly coalesce with Zulmābād. There are 20 donkeys, 10 cattle and (with Jabri and Zulmābād) about 150 fishing boats.
Tangak تنگك	On the east coast of the peninsula, $1\frac{1}{2}$ miles east of Imāmzādeh.	Altogether 100 houses.	Six villages lying close together. The northernmost is $\frac{3}{4}$ of a mile south of the point where the telegraph line enters the Mashīleh and the southernmost is $1\frac{1}{2}$ miles from it. The inhabitants possess about 120 donkeys, 90 cattle and 300 sheep and goats, and there are about 1,500 date palms.
Zāir Ghulām Husain (Khashm) خشم زائر غلام حسين	On the east side of Khashm Dallāka.	Half a dozen houses.	There are very few donkeys and cattle. Immediately to the southeast is a clump of dates situated near ground which has been bought by the British Residency.
Zulmābād ظلم آباد	On the west bank of Khor Sultāni, immediately to the east of Sitamābād from which it is divided by a road only.	150 houses.	A number of the inhabitants are sailors and fishermen. They own about 20 large and (with Jabri and Sitamābād) 150 small boats. There are 20 donkeys and 10 cattle. The place is increasing by immigration from Tangistān.

The Russian Consulate-General and the German Consulate at **Būshehr** are situated on the west coast of the peninsula, the former ¾ of a mile, and the latter (just south of the village of Mufqa'eh) at 2¼ miles, from the south-west corner of **Būshehr** Town.

Būshehr, in English generally called "Bushire," is the chief seaport of Persia; it is also the principal town on the eastern side of the Persian Gulf and the headquarters of the Persian administrative division known as the **Gulf Ports**. Its position on the **Persian Coast** is about 190 miles north by east of **Manāmah** in **Bahrain**, 170 miles east by south of **Kuwait** and 150 miles east-south-east of the mouth of the **Shatt-al-'Arab**. The earliest mention of Būshehr, at least under that name, occurs apparently in the works of Yāqūt, who wrote in the 13th century A. D.†

BŪSHEHR
بوشهر
TOWN*

Situation and harbour.‡—The town occupies the extreme northern tip of a promontory, elsewhere described under the name of **Būshehr** Peninsula. The peninsula projects from the southward into a large bay of which the muddy, ill-defined edges are on the north in the district of **Rūdhilleh**, on the north-east in **Angāli**, and for a short distance on the east in **Dashtistān**. The width of the bay is 5 miles north by west from Būshehr town, which may be regarded as its southern entrance point, to the nearest part of the **Rūdhilleh** coast; its depth, from the entrance inland in an east-north-easterly direction, is 6 or 7 miles. The greater part of the bay is very shallow, and east of a line drawn across it north-north-eastwards from Būshehr town nearly the whole area is occupied by mud-flats and islands. The innermost anchorage attainable by vessels of moderate draft is at the head of a channel called Khūr Daireh دیره and is situated in the middle of what we have called the entrance of the bay. It lies nearly 3 miles north-north-west of Būshehr town and is sheltered on the north-west by a great submerged sandbank called Raq'at-al-'Ālī رقعة العالي which runs out southwards from the **Rūdhilleh**

---

* A plan of the Būshehr harbour is given as an inset in Chart No. 2374-2837-B, *Persian Gulf*; but the principal plan is No. 2378-27, *Abu Shahr*, which will shortly be improved in accordance with the results of a fresh survey by the Royal Indian Marine in 1904.

† See Le Strange's *Lands of the Eastern Caliphate*.

‡ Recent information regarding the harbour will be found in the Government of India's Foreign Proceedings for February and July 1905.

coast, while on the south-east it is adjoined by a long narrow wall of sand called Lakfeh لقفة, only 1 to 3 feet below water. The holding ground in Khūr Daireh is good and the soundings 3 to 4 fathoms, but the approach in many parts has only 15 to 17 feet of water and the anchorage is a rough one in a Shamāl. The bottom being very soft steamers drawing 15 feet can reach Khūr Daireh in any state of the tide unless a Shamāl be blowing, when it becomes necessary to wait for high tide. Steamers drawing from 19 to 20 feet can generally be brought in upon the highest high water of the 24 hours. The outer anchorage, that ordinarily used by steam vessels calling at Būshehr but exposed both to the Shamāl and to the Sharqi, is in 5 fathoms at about 5 miles west by south of the town. Here steamers drop anchor and wait to be relieved of their mails and cargo and to receive fresh shipments by a fleet of native sailing boats which, if it suits the convenience of the boatmen and the Hammālbāshi, immediately put off from the town under a full press of canvas.

A deep creek about 200 yards broad, called Khūr Sultāni سلطاني, runs past the east side of Būshehr town in a south-easterly direction towards the Mashileh; it is unfortunately divided from the inner anchorage by a bank 1½ mile broad on which the soundings are only 5 and 6 feet; the bottom here is hard sand and a good channel could probably be dredged. At Pūdar 1½ miles above the town this creek, which has many soundings of over 20 and some of more than 30 feet, forks; one branch continues south-eastwards to the Mashileh, while the other, styled Khūr Shakari شكري, bearing at first to the north-east, sweeps round in a great semi-circle and eventually rejoins the bay at its northern end. On this creek, near the place where it opens again into the bay and is called Khūr Bandargāh بندر, is Shīf in the **Angāli District**, a landing-place for travellers to the interior. Between the curving creek just described and the open bay is enclosed a mass of mud-flats, sand-flats and low islands. The principal island, divided into two parts—*viz.*, Shaikh Sa'ad سعد to the north and 'Abbāsak عباسك to the south—which are separated by a shallow channel named Khūr-i-'Abbāsak, easily fordable at low water, is long and narrow with an extent from north to south of over 4 miles; it forms a low plain covered in places with coarse grass and is largely overflowed by the sea at the highest spring-tides. At the northern extremity of Shaikh Sa'ad, not far to the west of Shīf, is a village called Jazīrah جزيرة of 50 houses of boatmen and fishermen, Arabs of the Bani **Tamīm** or Dumūkh **Dawāsir** tribe, or originally from **Kuwait**, who are all Sunnis and speak both Persian

Part of the town of Būshehr.

and Arabic. On the eastern shore of 'Abbāsak towards the end nearest Būshehr town, are a hospital and the Būshehr quarantine station. Between 'Abbāsak and Pūdar is a small island called Muharraq محرق or Shāh Zangi شاه زنكي , which is covered at the highest springs and whence mud is brought for house building in the eastern part of the town ; and west of this, facing Būshehr town across Khūr Sultāni, are mud and sand flats which are dry at low water springs. These flats end westward in a seaweed-covered spit called Alafdān الفدان which forms the northern side of the Khūr Sultāni entrance, the southern side being constituted by a sand bank, called Raq'at-as-Sāfli, رقعة السافلي , that dries in patches and is a subaqueous prolongation of the **Būshehr Peninsula**. These marine surroundings of Būshehr are at once so indefinite in their outline, so flat and so extensive, that the eye is of little aid in arriving at a comprehension of them, and even on the spot recourse must frequently be had to a map or chart.

Site, buildings and topography.--Būshehr is a compact town, and the closeness of the houses together, their height and the elevation of the rocky ground on which they stand—the last being in parts 40 feet above sea-level—impart to it an appearance somewhat more distinguished than is usual in towns of the Persian Gulf littoral. The lofty Bādgīrs which were once a distinctive feature of the place have, however, ceased to be conspicuous ; there are now only 3, of which 2 are old, and it is considered unlucky to build new ones. The houses are of stone and nearly all have an upper storey : none have 2 storeys and few have only a ground floor. Altogether there are only about 1,400 houses, but the population is dense and out of proportion to the number of dwellings. The ordinary building material is a friable conglomerate of sand and shells from adjacent quarries in the peninsula ; it is rapidly eroded by the action of the weather and the aspect of the older houses is consequently one of decay. The town contains no open spaces deserving of mention, and such courtyards as the larger mansions may possess are enclosed and hidden from view. The winding lanes, which are the only streets, though narrow, are not inconvenient in ordinary weather ; but in rain the trench which runs down the centre of each becomes a mere sewer of mud. The town was formerly walled on the landward, that is on the south side; but the rampart, where not actually demolished, is now almost altogether concealed amid the recent extensions of the town in this direction, and only traces of it are here and there visible.

The town is divided into four principal wards or Mahalleks محلة styled Behbehāni بهبهاني , Dehlashti دهـ دشتي , Khashshābi خشّابي and Kūti كوتي ;

Behbehāni is the most northern, Dehdashti is on the east, Kūti is at the south-west corner and contains the British Residency from which it is named, and Khashshābi appears to be more or less central. Besides these there are two small quarters inhabited by Jews, the more important being at the north-west corner of the town and the other at the south-east corner near the Chahārburj. At the northern end of the town is a solitary open space, called Bāsīdūn باسیدون, between which and the water's edge is situated a block of buildings containing the Persian Imperial Customs establishment and the Persian post office. The premises of the Imperial Bank of Persia are in the town, but they front upon this welcome piece of unencumbered ground; from the latter diverge the two principal thoroughfares of Būshehr, one skirting the sea face on the west side of the town and the other following more or less closely the bank of the Khūr Sultāni upon the opposite side.

The esplanade upon the seaward side runs at some height above the beach; it is narrow and crumbling but can boast some of the handsomest edifices in Būshehr. Among them are—to proceed from the north southwards—the Amīrīyeh امیریه a large mansion built by the Darya Baigi when he was Governor of the **Gulf Ports** and at present inhabited by the principal Customs officials, two blocks of buildings occupied by the Russian Steam Navigation and Trading Company, and finally the British Political Residency. The last is a large walled tenement consisting of two courtyards, one behind the other and each completely surrounded by buildings; the buildings face inwards and on two sides of each courtyard they rise to an upper storey. A little beyond the British Residency, on the sea face, is an Āb Ambar آب امبار or water reservoir constructed for the public benefit, by the Qawām-ul-Mulk, who was Governor of Būshehr, about 60 years ago; and beyond this again is the Turkish Vice-Consulate, where the town ceases and there is a native cemetery on ground supported by a sea cliff about 15 feet in height.

The way round the opposite side of the town is more confined and obstructed, and the pedestrian may either pass from the Customs yard along the busy quays of Khor Sultāni or plunge into the main bazaar to emerge finally at the Chahārburj or Persian Government offices, there rejoining the Khor Sultāni at the extreme south-eastern corner of the town. The Chahārburj is a large building with a flagstaff; and outside it, on the Maidān which extends towards Jabri, stand the time-guns which regulate the meals of the populace in the month of the Ramazān fast, are fired daily at dawn and sunset, and are used also for saluting purposes.

The Sea Front, Būshehr Town.

Climate and sanitation.—The hottest month at Būshehr is August and the coldest months are January and February; in summer the thermometer has been known to rise to 115·5° F. in the shade, the moistness of the atmosphere rendering this temperature much more trying than in other places, and in winter to fall to 32° F. The period most dreaded is between the 20th of July and the 15th of September, when the temperature seldom rises much above 100° F. but the difference between the wet and dry bulb readings is sometimes only 2°. The normal rainfall is about 12 inches per annum, but as little as 4 inches may be received. The most frequent winds are northerly, those from the north-west apparently predominating, and after them those from the north-east and north. December, January and February are stormy and cold months; March and April are pleasant; May is hot and dry; during June and part of July the increasing heat is mitigated by the Shamāl; then follows the period of extreme discomfort, already described; after the middle of September the weather gradually becomes cooler. The sanitary condition of Būshehr is bad, for the subsoil is riddled with cesspools which are seldom cleaned out, and in the vicinity there are cemeteries where the dead are buried in shallow graves; yet the place is not unhealthy. Malarial fever is the most prevalent disease among the native population. Ophthalmia and other eye diseases are rife, caused by flies, glare, dust and the insanitary habits of the people.

Population.—The present population of Būshehr Town is estimated at 15,000 souls. As will appear from the table below, which is not exhaustive, it is composed of extremely heterogenous elements; but it is predominantly Persian, and Persian is almost the only language heard, for though about ⅓ of the people know Arabic few of them speak it habitually. The following are the most important, numerically or otherwise, of the classes represented at Būshehr :—

Persians.		Other Orientals.	
Būshehrīs بوشهري	5,000	Jews يهودي	600
Shambadīs شمبدي	2,500	Armenians	35
Behbehānīs بهبهاني	1,000	Goanese كواني	20
Kāzarūnīs كازروني	1,000	Baghdād Muhammadans	20
Khanasīrīs خنسيري	300	Do. Christians	18

Persians.		Other Orientals.	
Shirāzis شيرازي	200	Memons	4
Tangasīris تنكسيري	200	Bohrahs	3
Duvvānis دّواني	200	Other British Indians	10
Dehdashtis دهدشتي (supposed to be immigrants from a place, now deserted, between the Rāmuz Behbehān Districts)	150	*Europeans.*	
Dashtis دشتي	100	British	24
Samghūnis صمغوني	40	Eurasians	10
Khāragis خارگي	30	French	5
Isfahānis اصفهاني	10	Russians	5
Tehrānis طهراني	10	Belgians	5
Gabrs گبر	5	Germans	2
Lingavis لنگوي	5	Greek	1
Arabs.			
Local	200		
Bahrainis بحريني	20		
Kuwaitis كويتي	10		
Hasāwis حساري	10		

The above are all permanent residents; and among a large floating population of travellers, traders, temporary labourers and other visitors there may be on the average about 200 Kāzarūnis and 100 Behbehānis.

The labouring class are mostly immigrants from **Dashti**, and are known of Khanasīris, but many are Tangistānis and Duvvānis.

The most characteristic article of Persian garb is the head-dress which is of several kinds; one is the familiar felt hat or Kulāh-i-Namadi كلاه نمدي,

which may be black, grey or white; another is the Kulāh-i-Māhūti ماهوتي of black broad-cloth mounted on cardboard; a third is the light cloth cap known by the name of 'Araqchīn عرق چين or " perspiration catcher," and worn with a coloured **Masqat** turban. There are also a Kulāh-i-Tarmah ترمه or soft hat, which goes with a white turban styled 'Amāmeh عمامه or Shāl شال, and a Kulāh-i-Safīd سفيد made of white shirting; the latter is used by Mullas and merchants and is covered by a white turban of local pattern. The ordinary costume of well-to-do men at Būshehr now consists of a long coat, waistcoat, pantaloons, woollen socks and imported shoes; but elderly and religious persons still affect the robe confined at the waist by a Kashmīr or Calcutta shawl, the loose drawers, the white Shīrāz socks, and the broad-cloth cloak which were universal 20 years ago. The females of Būshehr wear a black mantilla and sometimes a black netted veil; those of the lower classes have stockings of yellow leather called Chakmeh چکمه; and those of the upper classes use, outside their houses, a kind of silken trouser which fits like a stocking over the foot and lower leg and is baggy above the knee.

If it be permissible to include in one general description so mixed a body as the population of Būshehr, it may be said that they are physically well-developed and mentally quick and intelligent; but that their naturally well-bred and agreeable manners conceal an unreliable and ungrateful disposition, and that they are inclined to be uncivil to foreigners, though less so than formerly.

Trade and manufactures.—Būshehr, despite the natural disadvantages under which its harbour labours, is still the chief gateway of foreign trade in Southern Persia; and the volume of business depending on this circumstance is increased by the consumption of its own not inconsiderable population. The market of Shīrāz is chiefly, and that of Isfahān to a great extent, supplied with imported goods through Būshehr.

The imports of Būshehr were valued, between 1901 and 1903, at £701,000 per annum. The principal commodities imported from 1899 to 1906 were the following, of which the average annual values in lacs of rupees are given in brackets: cotton piece-goods (63$\frac{1}{3}$), sugar (18), tea (11$\frac{3}{4}$), grain and pulse (6), metals (5), dyeing and colouring materials (3$\frac{1}{3}$), provisions (3), woollen goods (2$\frac{1}{4}$), silk piece-goods (2), hardware and cutlery (2), yarn and twist (1$\frac{3}{4}$), spices (1$\frac{3}{4}$), drugs and medicines (1$\frac{1}{2}$), glass and glassware (1), haberdashery (1), and silverware and jewellery (1). Of these principal imports, cotton piece-goods were chiefly from the United Kingdom, while the remainder—except sugar and silk piece-goods from France and glass and glassware from Germany—were mostly of Indian origin.

The annual value of Būshehr exports during the period 1901-03 was estimated at £350,000, or half that of the imports. During the 7 years 1899—1906 the chief articles of export were, according to the same notation as has been used for imports above: opium (35½), gums of all sorts (8), carpets (6½), wheat (5½), almonds and kernels (3¾), hides and skins (2¾), tobacco (2), raw cotton (1⅓), cotton piece-goods (re-exported) (1¼) and rosewater (1). In most of these commodities the principal customer was the United Kingdom; but the destination of the opium was for the most part China, of the tobacco Turkey and Egypt, of the cotton piece-goods Turkey and Bahrain, and of the remainder India.

The only manufacture at Būshehr is of copper coffee-pots which find a market at various places in the Persian Gulf.

Local trade at Būshehr is conducted in the bazaars which are situated on the east side of the town adjoining the Khor Sultāni; the principal of these is clean, lofty, roofed over, and some 200 yards in length; it is somewhat winding and at its south-eastern end breaks up into several smaller bazaars chiefly occupied by dealers in food. In all, the bazaars contain about 600 shops, and the goods exposed for sale, consisting mainly of provisions, clothing materials, hardware and miscellaneous articles, are varied and of passable quality: Manchester prints, Shīrāz tobacco, Java tea described as Chinese, Shīrāz and Bandar 'Abbās carpets and Russian teapots, together with grains, spices, vegetables and fruit, are the commodities most in evidence.

Standards of weight are a Būshehr Man of 7¾ lbs. English and a Hāshim Man consisting of 16 Būshehr Mans and equal to 124 lbs. English.

Shipping.—The shipping of Būshehr comprises 50 to 60 Māshuwahs of 10 to 15 tons and manned by 6 or 7 men each, which run only between the town and the harbour; about 50 Sambūks, Būms and large Māshuwahs of 30 to 40 tons, which make voyages to all the principal Gulf ports; 4 Baghlahs of 50 to 60 tons; and about 20 still larger vessels which visit Karāchi, Bombay and Zanzibar. Besides these there are about 350 fishing boats.

The port of Būshehr was visited in 1905-06 by 158 steamers with a tonnage of 198,278: of these all but 5 were British.

Supplies.—The water of Būshehr town is bad. Every house almost has a well, but the fluid which it yields is bitter; about 10 per cent. of the houses are provided with reservoirs. The better classes obtain their drinking water from Bahmani بهمنى, Andar Bandar اندر بندر Dahmiru دهميرر and Bōjīkdān بوجيكدان or Gunjashkdān كنجشكدان, places in the peninsula at considerable distances from the town; but even this water is slightly brackish and cannot be drunk with impunity except by persons habituated to it: in fact the water from whatever source in the Būshehr peninsula has been pronounced unfit for human consumption by the Chemical Analyist to the Government of India. Drinking water for the British Residency is brought from **Basrah** by the R.I.M. vessel attached to the Residency. Other supplies available in the town depend chiefly on the state of the export or import trade at the moment; the adjoining districts of **Rūdhilleh, Angāli** and **Dashtistān**, besides the remainder of the **Būshehr** Peninsula, can also be drawn on at short notice for articles which they produce.

The British Government keep steam coal for their own use at Būshehr, and a little is stocked for sale by some private firms. Repairs to ships cannot be executed here.

Communications.—The adjoining mainland can be reached by boat, disembarkation taking place at Shīf on the northern coast of the bay * which is reached in about 3 hours; or, with land carriage, by following the eastern edge of the **Būshehr** Peninsula for about 4 miles and then crossing the Mashīleh at the same place as the telegraph line.† The Shīf route, as stated in the article on **Būshehr** Peninsula, is at present out of use. The number of harbour boats has already been mentioned above under the head of shipping; some of them, it should be observed, belong to Jazīrah village and not to Būshehr town. The amount of transport ordinarily present at or near Būshehr town may be estimated at 250 to 300 mules when the Shīf route is closed, but when it is open there is none. The adjacent districts, however, of **Būshehr** Peninsula, **Dashtistān, Angāli** and **Rūdhilleh** possess transport resources which are described in the articles under their names; and recourse can be had, if time and circumstances permit, to more distant but still not remote districts such as **Dashti**.

The telegraph system which has its focus at Rīshehr is described in the article on **Būshehr** Peninsula. There are two telegraph offices in Būshehr town, a British one in the Residency and a Persian one in the centre of the town, both situated on a short branch from Rīshehr.

---

* See *Routes in Persia*, I, No. 21 (footnote).
† See *Routes in Persia*, I, No. 23.

Administration.—Būshehr is the seat of the high official known as the Governor of the **Gulf Ports**, whose jurisdiction is defined in the article on the **Persian Coast** of the Persian Gulf. Here it is only necessary to refer to his headquarters establishment and that of the Persian Imperial Customs which is independent of his control.

The force at the disposal of the Governor in Būshehr consists nominally of one battalion of regular Persian infantry and 50 artillerymen, but in fact, in addition to a few mounted irregulars whom he maintains as a personal escort, he has only 200 infantry and 20 gunners under his orders. Six breech-loading mule guns belong properly to Būshehr, but one of them is now (1906) at **Burāzjān** and another at **Shūshtar**;* there are also about 25 muzzle-loading guns, but these are practically useless. The regular garrison seldom receive pay and for the most part gain a livelihood by working as labourers, barbers, etc., in the town, an arrangement which is facilitated by their having no professional duties to perform: though dressed in ragged uniforms of blue cloth with red facings, their appearance is unmilitary and spiritless, promising little advantage to their employers in any kind of warfare. The Governor's power at sea is represented by the "Persepolis" gunboat of 600 tons and 450 horse-power; she was launched at Bremerhaven in 1885, her extreme speed is now 6 knots, and she carries 6 guns (4-inch B. L. Krupps) and 24 Snider rifles.

The offices of the **Gulf Ports** administration are situated in the Chahārburj building, already mentioned, which is also the private residence of the Governor unless he is accompanied by his family; in the latter case he hires a house in the town or near it. The Governor is supposed to attend to business at the Chahārburj every day except Friday from early morning until the middle of the afternoon; and here the bastinado or Falak فلك is still administered under his orders according to Persian custom. There are no regular tribunals. Civil disputes are ordinarily settled by the ecclesiastical authorities, nominally in accordance with the law of the Qurān. Such criminal and other cases as come before the Governor are disposed of by executive order, according to his caprice, and without reference to any code of law.

The Imperial Persian Customs, at present under Belgian management, have their principal office in the Persian Gulf at **Būshehr**. The customs wharf is at the northern extremity of the town, as already mentioned; and the European officials are accommodated in the Amīrīyeh mansion, once before alluded to. Employés of the Customs wearing a black uniform

---

* These detached guns have now been returned to Būshehr (1907).

The British Political Residency, Būshehr.

and a white metal badge on the front of a black Persian cap are now met with at every corner in Būshehr: in appearance at least they are the least discreditable part of the administration.

The Persian telegraph, like the Customs, is exempt from the control of the Governor; it is subject to the Minister of Telegraphs at Tehrān.

The British Residency Surgeon is Port Health Officer, and the penalties for infraction of quarantine regulations are enforced by the Customs authorities; the latter now hold charge of the local treasury also and pay all official salaries. The quarantine station is on the 'Abbāsak island in Būshehr bay.

Foreign representation and interests.—Great Britain is represented by a Consul-General, a member of the Indian Political Service, who is also British Political Resident in the Persian Gulf. To his staff belongs the Residency Surgeon, just mentioned in his capacity of Port Health Officer, a member of the Indian Medical Service; this officer usually enjoys a considerable private practice in the town and many natives have recourse to the charitable hospital in the Residency, of which he is in charge, for medical and surgical treatment. The Resident has also 2 Assistants of the Indian Political Service. A British Vice-Consul of the Levant Consular Service was posted to Būshehr for the first time in 1904 and arrived in November of that year; he is subordinate to the Consul-General, and his special functions are to attend to commercial matters and to protect the interests of British trade, especially during the frequent inevitable absences of the Consul-General from headquarters on political duty elsewhere. A British post office is maintained in the Residency, the mails being shipped and landed direct without passing through any Persian office; and there was until recently a treasury of the Government of India in charge of the Resident, but in 1905 it was abolished and the financial business of the Residency was transferred to the Imperial Bank of Persia.

There are at Būshehr (including officials) 34 European British subjects, 48 Muhammadan British subjects, and 25 British subjects of other races (Armenians, Goanese, etc.). Apart from the military guard and a few domestic servants there are no Hindus. European British firms represented at Būshehr are 8 in number, and there are 4 Muhammadan houses of business and 2 others which enjoy British protection.

Russia is the only other Power represented by a Consul-General. The principal Russian interest, not purely political, in Būshehr is the Russian Steam Navigation and Trading Company which occupies a double block of buildings on the sea front. France, Germany, the

Netherlands and Turkey are each represented by a Vice-Consul. There is a small French school for the teaching of the French language.

BUZIYEH
بزيه
or
BIZĪYEH
بزيه
or
BŪZI
بوزي

The largest town in the **Fallāhīyeh** District of Southern **'Arabistān**, more populous than the capital town of **Fallāhīyeh**, from which it is distant 3 miles eastwards. Buziyeh is situated on both banks of Khor Dōraq within a mile of its head, 2 miles south of the end of the **Jārrahi** River at Khazīneh, and at a distance of about 35 miles *via* Khor Dōraq from Khor **Mūsa**, but it is accessible to native sea-going craft of as much as 150 tons; at Buziyeh the creek is wide enough for two good-sized native vessels to pass one another at high tide, and is spanned by a narrow timber bridge, 60 feet in length, which connects the two parts of the town. At Buziyeh the water of Khor Dōraq is drinkable, but only when the sea ebbs; its level varies with the state of the tide, of which the range is about 6 feet. The Khulfi and Buziyeh canals from the **Jarrāhi** River separate from each other about 1½ miles northwards of Buziyeh and a little above the head of Khor Dōraq; after dividing they pass the town at a few hundred yards distance on the east and west sides respectively and eventually both fall into Khor Dōraq, the former from its left and the latter from its right bank, at some distance below the town. The nucleus of Buziyeh consists of a bazar of about 25 shops situated on the western bank of the Khor; the remainder of the settlement is scattered amidst interminable date groves and intricate water-courses, making its size difficult to estimate; but the total population is placed at about 8,000 souls. The inhabitants, except some **Kuwait** Arabs and some Persians who have settled here for trade, and a few **Sabians** who are chiefly goldsmiths, all belong to the **Ka'ab** Arab tribe; the sections to which they belong, chiefly of the Āl Bū Ghubaish subdivision, are shown in the article on the **Ka'ab**. The chief occupation is date culture, but Buziyeh is also the only port and the chief centre of trade in the **Fallāhīyeh** District; to some extent it serves the **Jarrāhi** District also. The principal exports are dates, rice, wheat, barley, matting, palm leaves, trunks for firewood, etc., melons and a little wool.

With the rest of the district the town is subject to the Shaikh of **Muhammareh** who administers it through an agent, at present Shaikh Rizaij of the Āl Bu Ghubaish section of the **Ka'ab** tribe. The Imperial Persian Customs have a post here, with premises at both ends of the bridge over Khor Dōraq, but it is believed that the smuggling of arms and other goods, for which the place was once notorious, has not yet entirely

Bridge at Buziyeh
(Maj. P. Z. Cox.)

ceased; the local Mudīr of Customs is under the orders of the Director-General at **Muhammareh** Town. There is also a Persian post office. The thick date groves and steep-sided canal which surround Buziyeh are its only defences: by manipulation of the canals it could be rendered even more difficult of approach than it is in ordinary circumstances.

Buziyeh may perhaps be identical with the Bāsiyān باسیان of the mediæval Arab geographers.*

A considerable village in the **Dashtistān** district of the **Persian Coast** and the head-quarters of an Arab Shaikh who rules it, along with several adjoining villages, in subordination to the Governor of the **Gulf Ports**. Chāh Kūtāh is situated about 15 miles south by west of **Burāzjān** and 18 miles east by north of **Būshehr** Town. It consists of about 150 houses of Dumūkh Arabs, who are connected with the **Dawāsir** of **Bahrain** and were until recently all Sunnis but are now many of them Shī'ahs; there are also a few Persians of the tribe called Zanganeh. Wheat, barley, melons and dates are grown, and the people own 300 donkeys and some camels. There are two small mud and stone forts and about 70 of the fighting men of the place are said to be mounted. There are no shops, but a little trade is carried on in private houses. The other villages in the jurisdiction of the **Chāh Kūtāh** Shaikh are Davīrah, Husainaki, Kunārābādi, Muhammad Ahmadi, Tul Ashki and Abu Tavīl.

CHĀH KŪTĀH
چاه کوتاه

The best, and indeed the only, harbour on the coast of Persian **Makrān**: the part of it which can be used by large vessels is however entirely open to southwards. The bay is of horse-shoe form, slightly wider within than at the entrance, of which the eastern and western points, called Rās Chahbār and Rās Puzim, پزم respectively, are 8 miles apart; Chahbār point is low and rocky with sandhills and a rocky spit, while Puzim is cliff, about 200 feet high, and has no reef off it; on Chahbār point there is a small square tomb. The maximum depth of the bay from the entrance northwards is about 11 miles, and the shore on both

CHAHBĀR
چهبار
BAY †

---

* *Vide* Le Strange

† A plan of this bay is given as an inset in Chart No. 2383—38, *Maskat to Karachi*; and a minute description and naval appreciation of the bay by Commanders T. W. Kemp and H. B. T. Somerville, R.N., will be found in the Government of India's Political Proceedings for June 1904.

sides is generally rocky, with cliffs in places, for about 4 miles within the entrance. Between Chahbār point and **Chahbār** Town, however, there is a sandy beach which increases in breadth from 10 yards at the point to 200 yards at the town; the town is 1½ miles within the point, on the eastern side of the bay. On the same side the land rises to a plateau which behind **Chahbār** Town attains a height of about 400 feet; but the rest of the perimeter of the bay is low and swampy. The soundings diminish from 8 fathoms at the entrance to 6 fathoms at the place where the shores cease to be rocky and become low; the whole inner part of the bay is very shallow. The bottom is sand of various degrees of fineness; nowhere does deep water approach the beach. The monsoon blows here as a fresh south-south-easterly breeze which dies away at night, and during its continuance a strong swell runs into the bay and breaks heavily all round its circuit except at the town of **Chahbār**. A Shamāl causes inconvenience at Chahbār, but good shelter can then be found on the Puzim side of the bay: Shamāls are fairly frequent in winter. Tidal streams are hardly felt in the bay; the rise and fall of the tide is about 9 feet. On the east side of the bay are the town of **Chahbār** and the village of Tīz; at the head of it, a few miles inland, the village of Pārag; and on the west side the village of Kunarak. North-north-east of the head of the bay, at 13 miles inland, is a peak of the maritime range 2,259 feet in height.

CHAHBĀR
چاہ بار
TOWN

The name is said to be a corruption of the Persian Chāh Bāgh چاہ باغ, but the derivation is doubtful: by Persians it is sometimes spelt Chahārbār چہار بار. Chahbār, the most central and at present the principal port of Persian **Makrān**, is situated in a small cove in **Chahbār** Bay 1½ miles within the eastern point, and is distant 180 miles east by south from New **Jāshk** and 55 miles west by north of **Gwatar**, the two other ports of the country: the important town of **Gwādar** is 106 miles east by south of Chahbār. Chahbār belongs to the Gaih district.

Site and surroundings. — The town stands on low ground less than quarter of a mile from the beach, at half a mile from which native vessels find an anchorage in 2 fathoms of water: the anchorage for larger vessels is at double the distance off shore in 4 fathoms of water with a sandy bottom. Along half a mile of the shore opposite the town boats of 5 feet draught can approach to within 20 yards of the shore at low tide. To the north of the town, at a distance of less than 2 miles, rises the escarpment, nearly vertical n places, of a table land over 700 feet high; while close to the southward are orchards and date plantations, reaching part of the way to Chahbar point.

Climate.—Chahbār is regarded as a healthy place: the climate is more equable and considerably cooler than that of New Jāshk, but in June and July it is somewhat trying. In 1903, the maximum cold weather temperature in the shade was 87° and in 1904 it was 90°: the hot weather maxima in 1903 and 1904 were 99° and 94°. The minima were not registered. The normal rainfall is 5 to 6 inches a year, but the amount fluctuates. The rainy season is from December to February.

Inhabitants.—The population of Chahbar is about 2,300 souls, chiefly Maids and Buzdārs. Hindus number 60 and Khōjahs 140 souls, including women and children. The language spoken is a Makrāni dialect of Balūchi, but Hindustani is generally understood. Persian is rarely heard and is unintelligible to the majority of the people. The houses are chiefly mat huts, except the residences and shops of the British Indian traders which are of stone and mud. A mud fort, which was once a distinctive feature and stood in the centre of the town, is now a hopeless ruin.

Resources and supplies.—The drinking water of the place is sweet and abundant; it is obtained from numerous wells among the gardens. About 500 sheep and goats are kept by the inhabitants, but there are no cattle. It is believed that with a month's warning about 2,500 camels could be collected here for transport. Large quantities of fish are netted in the bay, but they are generally coarse and of poor quality. Grass is unobtainable, but camel grazing is abundant throughout the year, and fodder is procurable from the interior in large quantities. Fuel is scarce. Good stone for building and roadmaking can be quarried at a place half a mile west of the Telegraph Office.

Trade and shipping.—Chahbār is the principal port of Persian **Makrān** and the character of its business will be apparent from the paragraph on trade in the article on Persian **Makrān**. The value of the exports is about Rs. 150,000 and that of the imports about Rs. 100,000 annually; the exports are barley, wheat, jowari, raw cotton, dal, ghi, fish, sharkfins, isinglass and hides and to a small extent dates; the imports are cotton, silk and woollen goods, sugar, rice, flour, kerosine and cocoanut oil, and (in small quantities) spices, indigo, iron, copper, tobacco, alum, beads and teak planks. To the place belong 12 vessels of 20 to 100 tons burden carrying crews of 8 to 20 men; these ply to Karāchi, Bombay, **Masqat** and **Bahrain**; they draw 7 to 9 feet of water:

used as lighters they are capable on the average of carrying about 100 men each. Besides these there are 7 smaller boats. Trade is chiefly with India, and 5 Hindu and 1 Muhammadan Indian merchants under British protection are engaged in general business here.

Administrative and political matters.—The local executive authority is a Wāli, and the Persian Imperial Customs are represented by a Mudīr and his subordinates; the Wāli was formerly nominated by the Chief of Gaih, but the present incumbent of the post received his appointment from the Persian Imperial Customs. The Indo-European Telegraph Department have an office here on their land line between **Gwādar** and New **Jāshk**, with both of which places telephone communication is mentioned; the telegraph building is a substantial one and is situated about half a mile south of the town. There are also stone barracks built by the Government of India in 1902 for the accommodation of a native officer, 50 men and a Hospital Assistant of the Indian Army. The head of the telegraph establishment is the local representative of the British Government, in subordination to the Director of the Persian Gulf Telegraphs who has his head-quarters at Karāchi.

CHĀRAK
چارک

One of the **Shībkūh** ports on the **Persian Coast**; its position is 34 miles east of **Chīru** and 16 miles west-north-west of **Mughu**. About a mile to the east of the town the **Gulshan** valley reaches the sea forming a considerable creek, beyond which again is swampy land; the creek is 300 yards wide, and impassable at high tide and after heavy rain. The village has several towers and there are date-groves behind it, over which rises a fort, on a hillock inland of the town, nearly 100 feet high: this fort is reckoned the strongest in all the **Shībkūh** ports and enables the Chāraki̇s to hold their own against the Marzūqi and Hamadi Shaikhs, their neighbours. The general appearance of the place is clean and attractive. Water is partly from tanks and partly from wells 15 feet deep. The anchorage is good in easterly winds but some swell is experienced in a Shamāl.* The population consists of 170 houses of Āl 'Ali, who are Sunnis. The people have some cultivation of dates and other crops, but the majority are Nākhudas, sailors and pearl-divers, and a few are merchants. They own about 8 trading vessels (Baghlahs, Ghunchahs and Sambūks) which run as far as **Basrah** on the one side and **Masqat** on the other, occasionally even visiting India; and

---

* A plan of the anchorage and coast adjoining **Chārak** forms an inset in Admiralty Chart, No. 2373—2837-A., *Persian Gulf.*

they have also about a dozen regular pearl-boats which cross the Gulf, and rather more than a dozen smaller craft which are used for fishing and for pearl-diving off the neighbouring island of **Qais**. The revenue of Chārak, together with Tāvuneh and the island of **Qais**, amounts to 1,600 Tūmāns per annum and is payable to the Governor of **Bastak**. The Shaikh of Chārak and its dependencies, *viz.*, Tāvuneh, the villages of **Gulshan**, Bavirdūn, and part of the village of **Duvvān** in the district of **Lingeh**, is Sālih-bin-Muhammad Sālih, a childless man who has associated a nephew with him in his government: he is noted for his greed, and his control over his subjects is insecure. The Imperial Persian Customs have a post at Chārak.

CHĪRU
اچیرر

One of the **Shībkūh** ports on the **Persian Coast**; it is situated about 43 miles south-east of **Shīvuh** and 34 miles west of **Chārak**. Chīru has a fort and a large date-grove, and lies facing the east in a small bay formed by a low sandy projection running southwards from the main line of the Persian coast; the village is a mile north of the point of the promontory. The bay is easy of access and forms a capital anchorage in a Shamāl, but it is exposed to easterly and south-easterly winds *; the shore is flat and sandy, the water is deep close to the beach, and little or no tidal stream is felt in the anchorage. A very small pearl bank is said to lie east of the village at about ½ a mile off shore. There are steep hills inland of the village, which is amply supplied with water from 5 reservoirs filled by their drainage. Chīru village consists of about 200 houses of the 'Obaidli Arab tribe, who are Sunnis. They possess some 5 trading vessels, which run all over the Gulf, to **'Omān**, and occasionally to **Basrah**; also 5 pearl boats which visit the western coast of the Gulf, and a dozen fishing Baqārahs and Shū'ais which are used for sea-fishing and in summer for pearling operations off the adjoining island of **Hindarābi**. The local authority is 'Abdullah-bin-Muhammad 'Abdur Rasūl, 'Obaidli, but he ordinarily resides at Baikheh Armaki بیخه ارمکی, a place 30 miles distant, leaving a brother in charge of Chīru. The revenue of the Chīru Shaikhdom, amounting to 1,600 Tūmāns a year, is payable to the Governor of **Bastak**. There is a post of the Imperial Persian Customs at Chīru.

---

* A plan of the anchorage is given as an inset to Admiralty Chart No. 2373—2837-A., *Persian Gulf*. For naval considerations connected with Chīru, Commanders T. W. Kemp and H. B. T. Somerville's report of 20th June 1903 may be consulted. (See the Proceedings of the Government of India for June 1904.)

CLARENCE STRAIT * This is the English and only general name of the passage between **Qishm** Island and the coast of the mainland; it is navigable for vessels, but a pilot is indispensable as it is very intricate besides being incompletely surveyed.

The Strait may be divided into 3 reaches. The first is from the eastern entrance between **Qishm** Town and Bandar **'Abbās** to **Lāft** point which is exactly midway between **Qishm** Town and **Bāsīdu**; it is 36 miles in length and it contracts from a width of 15 miles at the entrance to only 1 mile in the neighbourhood of **Lāft**. The navigable channel, at its western end called Khūr Masakeh مسكه, hugs the **Qishm** coast and is for the greater part of the way very much narrower than the Strait.

The second reach begins at Lāft point and continues to a little beyond the village of Gūrān, a distance in a direct line of 17 miles; its direction is more southerly than that of the other two reaches. In this part the strait consists of two branches which separate at Lāft point and reunite slightly below Gūrān; the western is Khūr Masakeh مسكه, the eastern Khūr Gūrān کوران or Saiyid Ahmad سيد احمد. Khūr Masakeh has a minimum depth in the fair-way of 5 fathoms and does not narrow to much less than half a mile, but the banks, which are steep, are submerged and have nothing to mark their position and this branch is consequently seldom used by pilots. Khūr Gūrān is in places only ¼ of a mile wide and its course is winding, but the banks are well-defined for most of the way by mangroves and the minimum depth, like that of Khūr Masakeh, is not less than 5 fathoms. The two Khūrs are separated by a mangrove swamp intersected by creeks. Khūr Masakeh gives access to the town of **Khamīr** near its right bank and Khūr Gūrān to **Lāft** village on **Qishm** Island. The length of both Khūrs is over 20 miles, that of Khūr Gūrān being the greater by a few miles.

The third and last reach of the strait, called Khūr Ja'afari جعفري, reaches from the junction of Khūrs Masakeh and Gūrān to **Bāsīdu** and is 19 miles in length. As **Bāsīdu** is approached there is a mud flat extending along the shore of **Qishm** Island, and also a shoal in mid-channel by the northern side of which ships pass.

There is an anchorage off Lāft point which is thoroughly well protected from all winds and would form a good harbour for the largest ships; the bottom is fine sand and shell and appears to be good holding

---

* Clarence Strait is best shown in Chart No. 2375—753, *Entrance of the Persian Gulf.*

ground* The tidal stream here runs about 2 knots an hour at springs. The land at Lāft point slopes upwards to a height of 60 feet; on the mainland opposite the ground is low and quite flat for a distance inland of about 3 miles.

An area surrounded on all sides by the larger tract known as **Biyādh**: **DABAISI** it is uncertain whether it should be regarded as forming part of the latter دبيسي or not. The centre of Dabaisi is approximately at the Qarāin wells mentioned below. Northwards the tract extends to the latitude of **Qatīf Town** and southwards to a mile or two beyond that of Jabal Mudrah in Barr-adh-**Dhahrān**; its eastern border runs nearly parallel to the sea shore at a distance of about 7 miles from it, and its western border is on the average 7 miles further to the west. The best known wells in Dabaisi and the positions assigned to them by the Bedouins are as follow:—

Name.	Vernacular equivalent.	Position.
'Arīsh (Ummahāt)	امّهات عريش	Possibly outside of the Dabaisi tract, to the westwards.
Bahair (Bu)	ابو بحير	4 miles south of Qarāin.
Bataikhi	البطيخي	5 miles east-south-east of Qarāin.
Hathrūsh (Kaukab Bin)	كوكب بن حذروش	11 miles west of Qatīf Town.
Hasni (Niqa)	نقى حصني	9 miles south-east by south of Qarāin.
Jabānīn	الجبانين	2 miles north-north-east of Qarāin.
Jaib 'Owaiyid	جيب عويد	3 miles south-west of Qarāin.
Jamrah	الجمرة	7 miles south-south-west of Qarāin.
Mustadill	مستدلّ	8 miles west-south-west of Qatīf Town.
Qarāin	القرائن	11 miles south-west of Qatīf Town, almost in the centre of the Dabaisi tract.
Rifāqah	الرفاقه	10 miles west by south of Qatīf Town.
Salām	سلام	7 miles south of Qarāin.
Shaddād (Abu)	ابو شداد	3 miles east of Qarāin.

The wells of Dabaisi are superior to those of the tracts enclosed by or forming part of **Biyādh**, excepting **Hushūm** only which is equal to Dabaisi in respect of water supply.

---

* The naval advantages of the anchorage off Lāft point are discussed in Commander Kemp and Somerville's report of 20th June 1903 in the Proceedings (Foreign) of the Government of India for June 1904.

DAGHĀ-RAH
دغاره

An important canal in Turkish 'Irāq taking off from the left bank of the **Euphrates** about 35 miles below **Hillah**. At its mouth it is about 70 yards wide and of considerable depth, and it runs at first in an easterly or south-easterly direction for about 12 miles to a town or group of villages called Daghārah which stands on its left bank. The tribes inhabiting this settlement are the Āl Sa'īd, the Āl Shibānah, the Āl 'Umr, the Āl Bū Nail, the Hamad, the Āl Zaiyād, the Hilālat and the Mujāwir, all of whom are included under the common designation of Aqra', also the Farāhinah, Āl Bū Rīshah and Sindān. At the Daghārah villages the canal divides and subdivides into a number of branches and so creates a moist area producing wheat, barley and rice, inhabited by settled cultivators whose reed-hut villages are scattered here and there over the waterlogged soil. A few miles further on its waters recombine into a large reed-bearing marsh with an open space in the centre. From the lower end of this swamp issue small runlets, which, rapidly uniting one with another, bring back the remaining water of the Daghārah into one channel called Mikhrīyah مخريه near a collection of villages known as 'Afaj عفج, distant about 16 miles in a straight line from the village of Daghārah and like it situated on the left bank of the stream. The inhabitants of 'Afaj belong to the Bahāhithah, Makhādahah, Shaibah, Hamzah, Āl Bū Nāshi, 'Ajārij and Āl Bū Rashīd tribes, and they are spoken of collectively as the 'Afaj, as if that also were the name of a tribe. Below 'Afaj the Daghārah curves round to the southward, and possibly rejoins the **Euphrates** a little above the westernmost mouth of the Shatt-al-**Gharāf** under the name of Shatt-al-Kār شط الكار. The celebrated ancient site of Nifar نفر is 4 or 5 miles to the north of the principal of the 'Afaj villages. The Daghārah tract is a Nāhiyah in the **Dīwānīyah** Qadha, as is also Shatt-al-Kār in that of **Shatrat-al-Muntafik**. Besides the tribes domiciled at Daghārah and 'Afaj, Āl Budair also are found upon the course of the Daghārah canal and give their name to a Nāhiyah of the **Dīwānīyah** Qadha.

DAGHMAR
دغمر

A group of small villages upon the coast of the **'Omān** Sultanate in the Eastern **Hajar** district: it is situated about four miles southeast of **Quryāt** on a maritime plain that is bounded inland by steep and rugged hills of limestone and is divided down the centre by a chain of low, stony knolls, on one of which is a small ruined tower.

DAHÁNAH

The drainage of Wādi **Tāyīn** reaches the sea here by several channels passing between and round the villages.

The hamlets of the group, which extends four miles, are in order from north-west to south-east:—

Name.	Houses and inhabitants.	Remarks.
Khūbār خربار	10 huts of **'Awāmir**.	The hills are two or three miles distant from this village.
Luwīz لويز	15 huts of **'Awāmir**.	Nil.
Sallān صلان	20 huts of mixed Arabs.	Do.
Bilād بلاد	30 huts of mixed tribes.	Do.
Janāh جناه	30 huts of Bani **Battāsh**, Bani **Wahaib**, etc.	Do.
Hājir حاجر	50 huts of Bani **Jābir** of the Ghazāl section.	The hills closely adjoin this village.

All these villages consist of huts only: among the mixed population Bani **Battāsh** predominate. Dates, fruits, lucerne and cotton are cultivated, and fowls, vegetables and water are obtainable: livestock are 50 donkeys, 30 cattle and 600 sheep and goats. Water, which is good and plentiful, is drawn from wells 15 to 20 feet deep. Twenty to 25 fishing-boats, but no coasting vessels, are owned here.

DAHÁNAH
دهنة

A belt of sandy desert which runs north-west and south-east between Central Arabia and the Arabian districts of the Persian Gulf and forms a clear and continuous line of demarcation between the two. The Dahánah is also known, particularly towards its southern end, by the less specific name of Nafūd.* Its average breadth is about 50 miles, and it extends from about the 29th degree of north latitude to the tropic in the neighbourhood of **Jabrīn**, or somewhat further. It is flanked on the east throughout the greater part of its length by the non-sandy but almost equally inhospitable tract of Summān: south of Summān it has first Wādi **Farūq** and then probably the **Jabrīn** oasis upon its eastern

---

*We may note that conversely a small portion of the great Northern **Nafūd** is distinguished by the name of Dahánah: see **Najd**, Route No. III, *ad fin.*

border. Where it is crossed by the route between **Kuwait** and **Riyādh** it has a breadth of two ordinary marches and consists of seven great sand ridges (with smaller intermediate ones), separated from one another by plains; the ridges vary from a quarter of a mile to several miles in width and the plains from 1½ to 7 miles. The sand of this part has a light-red or reddish-orange tint; the subsoil, where exposed, consists of light clay, pebbles and sandstone débris; there is some vegetation, and the fauna include gazelle, hare, bustard, snakes, lizards and beetles. The southern Dahánah is also crossed in two average marches by the route between **Riyādh** and **Hofūf**; it has a more confused configuration than the northern, cones and domes of many shapes taking the place of parallel ridges, and the sand is of an orange or deep-red colour. In crossing it here from the west, steep ascents are first encountered, alternating with nearly perpendicular descents down which camels slide bodily; these are followed by an interval of firmer sand with scattered brushwood; near the centre of the tract patches of soil with dark-coloured stones begin to appear through the sand; beyond the centre the sandhills pass from the form of eminences and hollows to that of long rollers and then to that of steps; finally progress ceases to be heavy and the country is sprinkled with vegetation. In this part the Dahánah is separated from **Summān** by a well-defined valley. The nomads of Dahánah, as of **Summān**, are almost entirely **Mutair**.

DAIMĀNI-YĀT
ديمانيات

Also called Saba' Jazāir سبع جزائر. A chain of islets and rocks, 12 miles in length, at a distance of nine miles from the **Bātinah** coast of the 'Omān Sultanate between **Sīb** and **Barkah** and nearly parallel to it. The chain may be divided into three sections. The easternmost section consists of one islet ¼ of a mile long and 25 feet high called Kharābah خرابة, and of several detached rocks which belong to it. A channel three miles wide divides the eastern from the central section which is four miles long, and comprises seven islets of different sizes in a row, 30 to 40 feet high, with low cliffs of a light brown colour: of these seven islets the largest and westernmost is ¾ of a mile long by ¼ broad. The western section is divided by a channel 3½ miles wide from the central; it consists of one islet, Jazīrat Jūn جون, and 3 rocks above water and extends 1½ miles east and west in a straight line. The main islet of this section is ¾ of a mile long, very narrow and 107 feet high near its west end: it has a tolerable anchorage in eight fathoms on its south side. All the islets are barren and destitute of fresh water, but they are frequented by fishermen who come over from the mainland in Badans and Shāshahs, and pearl-diving is carried on round them on a small scale.

DAIR
الدير

A village on the north-west coast of **Muharraq** Island in **Bahrain**, 2 miles north by east of **Muharraq** Town: it stands on comparatively high ground and is surrounded by date groves and lucerne fields. Irrigation is from several large wells in which the water stands at about 15 feet from the surface. There are some 300 houses of mud and mats, also three mosques. The people are **Bahārinah**, all engaged in the pearl fisheries; they own 1 Baqārah and 25 Shū'ais and Sambūks and employ 21 of these in pearling. There are 30 donkeys, 13 cattle and about 1,700 date palms. The full name of the place is said to be Dair-ar-Rāhib دير الراهب, or the Monk's Cloister, and ruins still exist of what the Arabs suppose to have been a Christian settlement.

DAIYĪNAH
ديينه

An island off the coast of the Abu **Dhabi** Principality in Trucial 'Omān near its western end, and about 29 miles north by east of **Dalmah** island. Daiyīnah is low, flat and sandy, bearing scanty grass; the highest part is a black detached rock at the north end, rising about 9 feet above high water. The length of the island is 1½ miles from north-north-west to south-south-east and the breadth about 600 yards. A fair anchorage in a Shamāl exists close to the south end of Daiyīnah. There are several pearl banks in the vicinity, of which the more important are:—Tubābāt Daiyīnah, 11 miles to the north; Hawād-bin-Mansūr, 10 miles to the north-east; Dhahr Daiyīnah, 3 miles to the north-east; Batn Daiyīnah, 2 miles to the south-east; and Hawād-ar-Raddād, 4 miles to the south-west. Daiyīnah belongs to the Shaikh of Abu **Dhabi**.

DAIYIR
دير

A considerable place on the coast of the **Dashti** district in Persia, 104 miles south-east of **Būshehr** Town and 9 miles west of **Kangūn**; it stands at the edge of the sea with a low range of sandstone hills behind it, and on the east side is a large date-grove. One mile off-shore is an excellent anchorage in a Shamāl, but a reef makes landing difficult; the inhabitants use as their boat harbour the Bardistān creek which comes down to the sea at 2 miles to the eastward. Daiyir consists partly of stone houses and partly of huts and is protected by a fort with towers. The population is about 5,500 souls, including some Āl Nasūr, some Bahrainis who discharge the functions of Mullas and 'Ālims, and some Jews; but the bulk of the people say they are from the neighbouring village of Bardistān in **Dashti** and claim to have come originally from **Kūfah**. The inhabitants of Daiyir mostly live by agriculture; but they own, besides a few fishing-boats, half a dozen sailing-vessels (Sambūks, etc.) which make voyages to **Bahrain** and other places. As a port Daiyir is the natural outlet of a considerable grain-growing tract, and horses from the Shīrāz district were formerly (but are not now) embarked here to escape export duty. At times, when its neighbour and rival **Kangūn** has been temporarily destroyed, Daiyir has managed to secure a large amount of trade; but it has itself suffered vicissitudes of fortune and has twice been burned by the Nasūri Khān of **Gābandi**. In 1865 Daiyir was ruled by a lady who appeared in public and was able to write: she was the mother of the present Khān of Dashti. It is now governed by a son of the Khān as his father's deputy and there is a post of the Imperial Persian Customs.

DĀLIKI*
دالکي

A village in the **Dashtistān** district of the **Persian Coast**, and a stage on the **Būshehr**-Shīrāz route; it is situated at an elevation of 400 feet about 13 miles north-north-east of **Burāzjān**, being adjoined by hills on the north-east and surrounded on the other sides by date-plantations. The heat in summer is excessive. Dāliki consists of about 35 houses of bilingual Arabs, who are Shi'ahs and are said to be the descendants of immigrants from **Bahrain**; they cultivate dates, wheat and barley and own about 40 mules and 40 donkeys. A short distance to the south of the village is a green sulphurous stream. A bitumen pit exists in the plain about 4 miles from Dāliki and 1 mile from Qarāwal Khāneh, and a deep boring has been made for petroleum by European concessionaires, but without success.

---

* Goldsmid's *Telegraph and Travel* deals with Dāliki and its neighbourhood at pages 183—184.

DAM

DALMAH
دلمه

An island off the coast of Abu Dhabi territory in Trucial 'Omān, a little to the south of an imaginary line connecting Abu Dhabi Town with the entrance of Khor-al-'Odaid and rather more than twice the distance from the former that it is from the latter. Dalmah is elliptical in shape, with its longer axis running north and south, and it has a narrow projection at its southern end. Its length is 5 and its breadth 2½ miles, and the surface, except for a very low, narrow plain at the south end, is hilly, the highest point being 244 feet above sea level. Plenty of brackish water is obtainable from wells, and there are deposits of red oxide of iron which are not at present considered worth removal. A small settlement of about 15 families of the Qubaisāt section of the Bani Yās tribe exists on the west side of the southern plain; the inhabitants wade for pearls in winter, besides diving for them in summer, and are keepers of goats. Dalmah is a place of some importance at the end of the pearl season, when a temporary bazaar of some 10 shops springs up, and a number of persons engaged in the pearl trade meet there to settle their accounts. Among these are the majority of the Indian traders on the coast of Trucial 'Omān, who come here to recover debts and make purchases of pearls. Several pearl banks exist in the vicinity, among which are:—Umm-as-Sulsul and Manyōkh, 8 and 5 miles respectively to the north; Hawād Bin-Musammih, 9 miles to the south-east; Abu Dastūr 4 miles to the south-west; and, besides several others which are nearer, Hālat Dalmah 27 miles to the north-west. Dalmah belongs to the Shaikh of Abu Dhabi.

DĀM
دام
or
ILDĀM
الدام

The administrative capital and principal town of the district of Widyān Dawāsir in Southern Najd; it appears to be situated about midway between the eastern and western ends of that part of the district which is known as Wādi Dawāsir.

Site and buildings.—The town is surrounded by a wall in which there are four gateways: internally it is divided into two wards, 'Ayaidhāt عييضات and Shawāiq شوائق, to each of which a bazaar or Sūq of the same name is attached. 'Ayaidhāt is apparently on the west side of the town and Shawāiq on the east, while Sūq Shawāiq is almost in the centre. The two bazaars, which are open squares, are connected by a street that widens out between them to form the meat market, known as Maqsab مقصب. On the east side of the town near one of the gateways is the combined fort and residence of the Amīr, called Qasr-al-Hasaiyin قصر الحصين

which has several high towers. There are four large mosques, two in the 'Ayaidhāt quarter and one at each end of the Sūq-al-Shawāiq; but, as is usual in this part of Arabia, they are without decoration or architectural features. The ordinary houses of the town are frequently of brick and mortar and rise to an upper storey; sometimes they are whitewashed, and sometimes the lower part of the walls is painted green or red. The façades of the upper storeys are often ornamented with a balcony projecting considerably over the entrance door.

Inhabitants.—The people are **Dawāsir** of the Rijbān division and number perhaps 5,000 souls. They are described as independent in politics, bold in war, and enterprising in trade; they are reported to be well armed with rifles, and Dām merchants are said to make journeys to both India and Africa in the ordinary course of business. In religion the inhabitants of Dām are Wahhābis or Hanbali Sunnis; the mosques of the town are not many, apparently on account of a local preference for large over numerous congregations. There are about five much frequented schools, of which the Madrasat-bin-Dharmān is the best known, and about 15 smaller ones. Female education is unknown here except in the family of the Amīr and the houses of religious teachers.

Agricultural and other resources.—The date groves are very extensive and contain an enormous number of palms. Other fruits are grown in abundance, and there is some cultivation also of wheat, barley, maize and lucerne, but almost entirely as secondary crops among the palms in the date gardens. Wells are numerous both within the town and outside it; the ordinary depth is about five fathoms, and the water as a rule is only fairly good; inside the walls however there are some excellent wells, notably those of Atainah, Hamaili, Jalīb and Mathlah. A large number of camels are owned here and a considerable number of horses; but cattle are scarce and donkeys very few.

Trade and industries.—Imported goods, except arms and ammunition which are brought from **Qatar** through **Aflāj**, are received by way of Yaman and Hijāz. Merchants from Yaman and Najrān are said to visit Dām but maintain no permanent business agencies there. Among the crafts exercised in the town are those of goldsmith, blacksmith, tinsmith, carpenter, potter, tailor and oil-presser. The number of shops in the bazaar is said to be very large, but the statistics obtained are not reliable. Swords and daggers of fine temper are made, but the daggers are not equal to those of Hadhramaut. Dām appears to be a rifle-repairing and cartridge loading centre for a large tract of country, including Wādi **Sabai'** as well as the whole of Widyān **Dawāsir**. It is reported that an attempt was lately made by some mechanics, who had gained experience abroad, to start a rifle factory; but it proved impossible to turn out weapons which could compete either in quality or in price with those imported from Europe.

Administration.—Dām is the seat of an Amīr whose power is absolute in the town and extends in a modified degree to all the villages of Wādi Dawāsir and Salaiyil. His political position is described in the article on Widyān **Dawāsir**. The quarters of 'Ayaidhāt and Shawāiq have each a Shaikh of their own; both of these Shaikhs are of course in strict subordination to the **Amīr**.

DARA'ĪYAH

درعيه

A considerable village in the 'Āridh district of Southern **Najd**; it is situated chiefly on the left bank of Wādi **Hanīfah** about 9 miles above **Riyādh**. The country immediately to the north of Dara'īyah consists of open downs. A quarter of Dara'īyah on the right bank of the Wādi is called Taraif طريف, those on the left are Saraihah سريحه and Ghasībah غصيبه, and the bed of the valley between the two is known as Bātin باطن. Each of the quarters is walled and defended by towers. The place is surrounded by extensive date groves containing perhaps 20,000 palms, and by gardens which produce apricots, figs, grapes, pomegranates and citrons. There are also lucerne, vegetables and the usual cereals. The present population may be about 1,300 souls, *viz.*, 110 houses of Bani **Tamīm**, 50 of **Dawāsir** and 100 of inferior tribes. There is some ordinary trade by resident merchants in coffee, piece-goods, etc., imported from **Hasa, Kuwait** and **Hijāz**.

Dara'īyah, which was at the time the capital of **Najd**, was completely destroyed by the Egyptians in 1818, and remained practically uninhabited until 1865 or later. Since then it has regained part of its population and some of its former prosperity. The ruins of the old town are chiefly on the right bank of the Wādi. According to local tradition, when Dara'īyah was at the height of its prosperity a shop there used to let for $30 a month. By the older Arab geographers the name of the place is spelt Dharīyah ضريه.

DARŪ'
درع

Singular Dara'i درعي. A tribe of the **'Omān** Sultanate belonging to the Ghāfiri faction: originally they were all nomads of the **Ruba'-al-Khāli**, but some are now settled at Tana'am and other places in **Dhāhirah**. Estimates of their numbers differ very widely: those in **Dhāhirah** may amount to 3,000 souls of whom about one-third are settled. There are also a few at **Barkah** in **Bātinah**. The Bedouin portion now frequent the neighbourhood of Jabal Hamrah. They are a wild and predatory race and hardly a rising of the eastern tribes occur in which the Darū' are not involved. The Bedouin portion are said to belong to the Ibādhi, the settled portion to the Sunni sect. The Bedouin Darū' rear large numbers of camels which they graze on the confines of the Great Desert. The following are the sections of the Darū': Badiwai بدري, Batūn بطون, Farādīs فراديس, Hādi (Hāl Bū) حال بو هادي, Janīn جنين, Khamīs (Hāl) حال خميس, Khamīs (Yāl) يال خميس, Mahābinah محابنة, Mahāridah محاردة, Majāli مجالي, Makhādir مخادر, Marāziqah مرازقة, Muhammad (Hāl) حال محمد, Mutāwihah مطاوهة, Nafāfi ('Ayāl) عيال نفافي, Salīm ('Ayāl) عيال سليم, Shamātah شماطة, Sultān ('Ayāl) عيال سلطان, Thuwail ثويل and Zuwaiyah زوية. Their Tamīmah is Saif-bin-Hamad of the Hāl Muhammad section.

DĀS
داس

The northernmost of the islands in the great bay between Abu Dhabi and Qatar; it lies about 100 miles west-north-west of Abu Dhabi Town, 67 miles north of the nearest part of the Abu Dhabi coast and rather further from Qatar. Dās is only 1¼ miles long by ¾ of a mile broad, with hills of regular outline that reach an elevation of 145 feet in the northern half; the south of the island is low. There is no water on Dās and it possesses no anchorage of any value. It is considered to belong to the Shaikh of Abu Dhabi and therefore to be included in Trucial 'Omān. The following pearl banks are situated in the vicinity of Dās:—Riqqat Dās, 2 miles to the south-east; Riqqat Mani, 9 miles to the south-east; Umm-al-Bunduq, 6 miles to the south-west and Abul Qamaqīm, Kharaiyis and Abul Hanainūn at 7 and 5 miles and a very short distance, respectively, to the north-west.

DASHTI
دشتي

A large and important district of the **Persian Coast** of the Persian Gulf, inland it begins at 'Arabi, 27 miles east-south-east of **Būsheh**

Town, and on the coast at a point 40 miles south-south-east of the same place; its termination is at the mouth of the Bardistān valley, 105 miles south-east of **Būshehr** Town.

Limits.—Dashti is bounded on the west by the sea, and on the east, approximately, by the seaward face of the main maritime range; some places connected with it lie in valleys within that range, but none of them are important and they fall beyond the scope of a Persian Gulf Gazetteer. On the north Dashti meets the district of **Tangistān**, its extreme inland village on this side being 'Arabi, as already mentioned, and the extreme coast village Qalāt. On the south Dashti meets the district of **Shībkūh**, in which the place nearest to Dashti is **Kangūn**.

Physical characteristics.—The physical features of Dashti are few and simple. The principal one is, of course, the great maritime range which runs south-eastwards and forms an almost continuous background to the district. Six miles to the north-east of **Khurmūj** it rises in a grand peak 6,430 feet high which is generally known as Kūh-i-Khurmūj, but possesses also the more distinctive name of Kūh-i-Bairami بيرمي, probably a corruption of Bahrāmi بهرامي. South of **Khurmūj** town for 15 or 20 miles the main range is fronted, towards Dashti, by an outwork of low sandstone hills called the Kūh-i-Kāki كاكي, terminated at its south-eastern end by a gap, 4 or 5 miles wide, through which the **Mūnd** river issues from the highlands of **Fārs**. South of this gap the main range, at first under the name of Kūh-i-Namak نمك, resumes its course; and finally it impinges on the coast at **Kangūn**, a few miles beyond the end of the district. Kūh-i-Bairami is a huge mass of limestone having a quaqua-versal dip and is sometimes crowned with snow for 2 or 3 days in winter. Kūh-i-Namak, 4,000 feet high, is of sandstone below, and towards the summit consists largely of salt which is visible from afar as glistening streaks of white or grey.

A minor but important feature is a sandstone coast range, reaching a height of over 2,500 feet, which bears the name of Kūh-i-Mūnd or Kūh-i-Kār كار and is described in the article on the **Tangistān** district, to which it partly belongs. The trough contained between this subordinate range and the main range is the Khurmūj plain or valley, extending from near **Ahram** to the **Mūnd** river, with a length of 30 and a breadth of several miles; a string of palm-leaf villages extends along its western side and there are a few upon the east also; it drains by a longitudinal channel called Shūr شور, which is 10 yards broad and contains above 2 feet of brackish water in places, to the **Mūnd** river at Chaghāpūr.

Kūh-i-Namak is adjoined on its southern side by a range of which the highest point (3,270 feet) is Kūh-i-Darang درنگ, not far from Kūh-i-Namak. This range runs first southwards for 16 miles and then eastwards for an equal distance: the result is the enclosing between it and the main range of a triangular valley called Bū Saif بو سيف which has no open exit except at its south-eastern corner on the coast between **Daiyir** and **Kangūn**. Kūh-i-Darang is of sandstone and is connected with Kūh-i-Namak by mounds of sandstone and gypsum intersected by ravines containing brackish water.

Dashti thus consists of two plains or valleys that both drain south-eastwards and are separated from one another by the plain or serpentine valley of the **Mūnd** river, of which the average direction is at right angles to theirs.

Coast.—The coast of Dashti has not been thoroughly explored and part of it is unapproachable by vessels owing to extensive shoals. Six miles off the mainland at about 27 miles south-south-east of Khor Ziyārat and approximately the same distance west of **Daiyir** is a low islet, ½ a mile in diameter, called Nakhīlu نخيلو: it appears to be a meeting-place of several hydrographical features and it marks the point where the direction of the coast changes from south-south-east to full east. From Nakhīlu a great shoal, called Rās-al-Mutāf راس المطاف, runs for nearly 20 miles to the east-south-east with a deep channel inside which is open to the east but blind at the other end except for a boat passage round the north side of Nakhīlu; and between this shoal and the mainland again is a second shoal with yet another deep channel inside. The inner channel appears to be called Khor Umm-al-Karam ام الكرم, from the name of a small island at the head of it: the outer is called Khān خان: both Umm-al-Karam and Khān are excellent havens for native boats and are used as such by the people of the nearest mainland villages. On the north side of the Nakhīlu boat passage, already mentioned, begins a narrow strip of sand called Jabrīn جرين which runs north-north-west for 6 miles and then joins, or almost joins, the mainland. From Nakhīlu northwards to Khor Ziyārat the coast is a mass of swamps and small creeks of which little is known.

Climate.—The climate of Dashti is accounted good; both on the coast and inland it is cooler in summer than that of the **Būshehr** Peninsula.

Population.—The population of the district, between the mountains and the sea, is probably not less than 20,000 souls.

The following are the better known tribes of the Dashti district:—

Name.	Approximate number of souls.	Remarks.
'Amrānis عمراني	600	This tribe is said to have immigrated from the neighbourhood of **Sūq-ash-Shuyūkh** in Turkish 'Irāq.
Bahrainis	A few.	Mostly at **Daiyir**.
Faqīha فقيها	1,000	A well behaved tribe. They are believed to be indigenous.
Hājiyān حاجيان	2,500	Reputed the bravest of the Dashti tribes. Like the Faqīha they are considered to be indigenous.
Jatūt جتوت	1,000	Camelmen of unknown origin. They are found also in **Tangistān** District.
Khājaha جواجها	550	They are said to have immigrated from **Behbehān** about a century ago.
Lurs لر	Very few.	See article **Lurs**. These also are said to have come from **Behbehān**.
Mīrzāha ميرزاها	Not numerous.	They are said to be descended from a family of brothers whose mother was a Saiyid, hence the name.
Mullāha ملاها	550	Better educated than their neighbours, but depend on charity for their support.
Ruūseh روسه	1,500	Have always been faithful to the present Khān and his father: the Khān consequently appoints all his deputies from this tribe.
Sādāt سادات	600	Saiyids.
Sālih Ahmadis صالح احمدي	150	The Khāns of the dynasty preceding the present one belonged to this tribe.

Most of these tribes are said to be of Arab descent, but nearly all are now Shī'ahs in religion and speak Persian only. Besides the above there are a number of small and obscure tribes, including the Dabāshīhā دباشيها, Dehdārhā دهدارها, Kabgānis كبگاني, Khanasir خنسير, Muhallis محلي, Qāidān قائدان, Shaikhānis شيخاني, Shaikhhā شيخها, Tangasīr تنگسير, and 'Umrūhā عمروها; and at some villages, especially on the coast, are found colonies of Arab immigrants from **Shībkūh** and elsewhere, who are mostly bilingual and belong to the Sunni denomination. The largest place in the district is **Daiyir**, and after it are **Khūrmūj** and **Kāki**. The Dashtis differ from their northern neighbours, the Tangistānis, in being peacefully inclined, partially civilised, and comparatively amenable to management. In the larger places their houses are often of stone and mud, but the ordinary villages consist of date-frond huts only; most villages however are defended by one or more Burj Tufangchi برج تفنگچي or rifle towers of stone and mud. The great bulk of the people are agriculturists or, on the coast, sailors and fishermen; a few live by trade. They have a number of Martini rifles, but on the whole the Dashtis are not so heavily armed as the residents of the other districts of the **Persian Coast**; the proportion is about 3 rifles to 5 houses on the coast, and 2 rifles to 3 houses inland. The Dashtis are a healthy, sturdy race, and many of the labourers and boatmen at **Būshehr T**own are of their number.

Agriculture and trade.—The chief crops are wheat, barley and dates; the date plantations are everywhere watered from wells. There is not the same quantity or variety of fruit as in **Tangistān**. The waterlift used is called Charkh-i-Chahāb چرخ چهاب and is worked by a bullock which is made to walk down an inclined cutting in the ground. Cattle are fairly numerous, and sheep and goats are kept in great numbers.

Trade on a small scale is general; but there is nowhere any large bazaar or mercantile centre, unless the towns of **Khurmūj** and **Daiyir** may be accounted such. The exports of the district are cattle, ghi, wheat, barley, dates, tobacco, onions, firewood, charcoal and earthenware, also some 'Abas of local manufacture. Imports are cotton piece-goods, rice, coffee, sugar and tea. External trade in both directions is with **Būshehr Town, Bahrain, Lingeh** and Bandar **'Abbas**. The ordinary currency consists of Persian Qrāns, but the Indian rupee circulates in some of the coast villages. The standards of weight are a local Man of 5 lbs. 13 oz. English and a Hāshim Man of 16 local Mans or 93 lbs. English. The chief port is **Daiyir**.

Communications and transport.—The only known routes in the district are a section of the **Būshehr**-Bandar **'Abbās** route *, which passes through **Khurmūj** town and leaves Dashti by the gorge of the **Mūnd** river, and a route † which runs from **Khurmūj** town by **Kāki** to **Daiyir** on the coast: neither apparently presents any difficulties.

---

* See *Routes in Persia*, I, No. 20.

† *Vide* Colvill's report forwarded to the Government of India by the Political Resident in the Gulf with his letter No. 46, dated 4th May 1866.

The total transport of the district is estimated at about 250 horses, 250 mules, 1,250 camels and 3,500 donkeys.

Administration.—The Dashti district belongs to **Fārs**, but it is sometimes farmed from the Governor-General of **Fārs** by the Governor of the **Gulf Ports**. It is administered by a hereditary Khān of reputed Arab descent, at present Jamāl Khān, who has his residence at **Khurmūj** and became master of the district after numerous smaller Khāns or Shaikhs had reduced themselves to impotence by their internecine feuds. The Khān pays 16,000 Tūmāns a year for the district of Dashti to the Governor of **Fārs** or the Governor of the **Gulf Ports**, as the case may be. There is no organised police force; but the Khān's personal retainers maintain order on the roads, and village affairs are regulated through the headmen. In the larger places there are some highly respected Mullas, whose decisions in civil disputes are accepted by the people. Land revenue is assessed at the rate of 50 Qrāns per Gāu (250 by 250 yards) of cultivation, and a tax of ½ a Qrān to 2 Qrāns is levied per date-palm according to value. There is also a poll tax of 5 to 20 Qrāns; this tax is recovered (at the rate of 8 Qrāns per annum) from Dashtis at **Būshehr** Town by agents whom the Khān sends for the purpose. The poll tax is unpopular and, in conjunction with general misgovernment resulting from the incompetence and age of the present Khān, has been responsible for much emigration from the district in recent years. The Khān formerly held in farm and administered several of the **Shībkūh** ports to the southward which are outside the Dashti district, and for these he paid 8,000 Tūmāns a year.

Topography.—The following are, in alphabetical order, the villages of Dashti:—

Name.	Position.	Houses and inhabitants.	REMARKS.*
Abādān آبادان	23 miles north-west of Bardistān, near the head of the Bardistān valley.	100 houses of Hājiyān and 'Amrānis.	12 horses, 80 camels, 120 donkeys, 6 mules, 60 cattle, 1,500 sheep and goats and 4,000 date-palms.
'Ali (Chāh) چاه علي	9 miles west-north-west of Khurmūj.	70 houses of Hājiyān and Faqīha.	Some of the houses are of stone. There are 6 horses, 30 camels, 40 donkeys, 2 mules, 20 cattle, 700 sheep and goats and 2,000 date trees.

* NOTE.—The resources in this column appear to be in many cases exaggerated and are to be regarded with caution.

Name.	Position.	Houses and inhabitants.	Remarks.
'Arabi عرابي	13 miles north-west of **Khurmūj**.	25 houses of Mullāha and Sādāt.	There are 2 or 3 stone and mud towers. This village is on the road from **Ahram** to **Khurmūj**. Resources are 25 camels, 40 donkeys, 30 cattle and 1,200 sheep and goats, also 2,500 date-palms.
Bahrām Asad بهرام اسد	On the southern extremity of **Kūh-i-Mūnd**, where it is turned by the **Mūnd** river.	40 houses of Ruūseh and Hājiyān.	There are 500 date trees: livestock are 40 donkeys, 20 cattle and 500 sheep and goats.
Bālingistān بالنگستان	On the coast 6 miles north of **Lāvar**.	20 houses.	The people are poor; they cultivate corn.
Bardistān بردستان	1½ miles north-north-east of **Daiyir** and the same distance from the mouth of a valley which comes down from **Kūh-i-Darang** to the sea 2 miles east of **Daiyir**.	100 houses of Faqīha, Jatūt and 'Amrānis.	There is a tall Bādgīr. Resources are 7 horses, 30 camels, 50 donkeys, 5 mules, 25 cattle, 1,000 sheep and goats and 1,250 date trees.
Barīku باريكو	On the coast, ⅓ a mile south of **Zīrahak**.	25 houses of Kabgānis and Khanasīr.	There are 15 Varjis. Agricultural resources are 2,500 date-palms, 20 donkeys, 10 cattle and 100 sheep and goats.
Batūneh بطونه	On the coast, 9 miles west of **Daiyir**.	50 houses of immigrants from **Kung** near **Lingeh** and **Bustānu** in **Shībkūh**, all Arabs and Sunnis; they speak Arabic as well as Persian.	The people grow dates and corn. There is a small domed tomb on the hill behind. There are 15 fishing boats and 2,000 date-palms. Animals are 50 camels, 50 donkeys, 40 cattle and 1,500 sheep and goats.
Bun (Chāh) چاه بن	4 miles east-north-east of Burdakhān Nau on the **Mūnd** river plain.	15 houses of Muhallis and Hājiyan.	Livestock are 30 donkeys, 20 cattle, and 500 sheep and goats. There are 300 date-palms.

DASHTI

Name.	Position.	Houses and inhabitants.	Remarks.
Burdakhān Kuhneh برد خان کهنه	On the **Mūnd** river plain, 7 miles north-east of Burdakhān Nau.	30 houses of Mullāha, Sādāt, Jatūt and Bahrainis.	There are said to be 10,000 lemon trees and 20,000 date-palms here. Animals are 100 camels, 400 donkeys, 20 horses, 15 mules, 150 cattle and 3,000 sheep and goats. The Chief of Dashti once resided here.
Burdakhān Nau برد خان نو	On the **Mūnd** river plain, 14 miles south-east of Khor Ziyārat.	60 houses of Mullāha, Sādāt and Bahrainis.	Here are 1,000 lemon trees a$_n$d 1,500 date-palms. Livestock are 6 horses, 300 donkeys, 7 mules, 70 cattle and 2,500 sheep and goats.
Chaghāpūr چغاپور	10 miles north-west of **Kāki**, on the right bank of the **Mūnd** river just below the point where the drainage of the Khurmūj plain enters it.	50 houses of Hājiyān and Muhallis.	Stock are 5 horses, 6 mules, 25 camels, 70 donkeys, 30 cattle and 1,500 sheep and goats. Date-palms number 4,000.
Chāhpūl جاه پول	9 miles from the coast, between Burdakhān and **Daiyir**.	A village of Ruūseh.	There are 20 camels, 40 donkeys, 30 cattle and 500 sheep and goats, also 1,500 date-palms.
Chārak چارک	10 miles west-south-west of **Khurmūj**, on the western side of the **Khurmūj** valley.	40 houses of Ruūseh.	Date-palms number 1,000, and there are 15 camels, 35 donkeys, 20 cattle and 500 sheep and goats.
Chāwashki چارشکی	8 miles west by north of **Khurmūj**, on the west side of the Khurmūj valley.	50 houses of Ruūseh.	Animals are 40 donkeys, 20 cattle and 600 sheep and goats, and there are 2,500 date-palms.
Chughāwār چغاوار	8 miles north-north-west of **Kāki**, near the right bank of the **Mūnd** river.	A village of Hājiyān and Ruūseh.	Animals are 10 horses, 25 camels, 80 donkeys, 8 mules, 50 cattle and 2,500 sheep and goats. Date-palms are 4,000.
Daiyir دیر	...	...	See article **Daiyir**.

Name.	Position.	Houses and inhabitants.	Remarks.
Danaki دانكي	On the coast between Daiyir and Batuneh.	15 houses of Arabs from Bustāneh, near Lingeh, Sunnis, and speaking both Arabic and Persian.	The people are fishermen and cultivate dates and corn. They have 2 large Māshuwahs and 6 fishing boats. Livestock are 30 donkeys, 20 cattle and 200 sheep and goats.
Dam-i-Gazi دم گزي	On the coast 19 miles west of Daiyir.	10 houses of the same.	10 fishing boats and 6 Varjis are owned here. Livestock are 20 donkeys, 15 cattle and 2,500 sheep and goats.
Darak درك	6 miles north of Bardistān, on the east side of the Bardistān valley.	20 houses of the same.	There are 30 donkeys, 20 cattle and 270 sheep and goats.
Darāzi درازي	9 miles west by south of Khurmūj, on the west side of the Khurmūj plain.	100 houses of Ruūseh.	Resources are 15 horses, 60 camels, 120 donkeys, 10 mules, 150 cattle, 4,000 sheep and goats and 1,200 date-palms.
Dashu دشو	In a plain immediately north of Khurmūj town.	20 houses of Hājiyān and Ruūseh.	There are 10 camels, 30 donkeys, 20 cattle, 1,000 sheep and goats and 700 date trees.
Dam Nālu دم نالو	10 miles south-south-west of Khurmūj town, on the west side of the Khurmūj valley.	50 houses of Sādāt, Khājahā and Jatūt.	There are 7 horses, 10 mules, 30 camels, 80 donkeys, 40 cattle and 1,500 sheep and goats. Date-palms are 6,000.
Faqīh Hasanān فقیه حسنان	13 miles south-south-west of Khurmūj, on the west side of the Khurmūj plain.	70 houses of Ruūseh, Faqīha and Jatūt.	There are 1,800 date-palms. Animals are 20 camels, 60 donkeys, 8 horses, 10 mules, 40 cattle and 3,000 sheep and goats.
Gankhak Shamāli گنخك شمالي	3 miles south-east of Kāki, on the Mūnd river plain.	50 houses of Ruūseh, Faqīha and Jatūt.	There are 8,000 date-palms; animals are 80 camels, 6 horses, 15 mules, 80 donkeys, 60 cattle and 1,500 sheep and goats.
Gankhak Hīrāni گنخك هیراني	1½ miles south-south-east of Gankhak Shamāli.	10 houses of the same.	Resources are 20 camels, 20 donkeys, 10 cattle, 200 sheep and goats and 1,000 date-palms.

Name.	Position.	Houses and inhabitants.	Remarks.
Gināwi گناوي	9 miles north of Bardistān, on the east side of the Bardistān valley.	15 houses of Hājiyān and Mullāha.	There are 500 date-palms. Animals are 10 camels, 20 donkeys, 10 cattle and 150 sheep and goats.
Gizak گزک	8 miles west-north-west of Kāki, on the right bank of the Mūnd river.	50 houses of Hājiyān.	There are 4,000 date-palms. Animals are 7 horses, 12 mules, 25 camels, 55 donkeys, 30 cattle and 1,500 sheep and goats.
Gulaki گلکي	11 miles north-west of Khurmūj town, on the west side of the Khurmūj valley.	30 houses of Ruūseh and Tangasīri.	Resources are 4 horses, 6 mules, 50 donkeys, 30 cattle and 700 sheep and goats; there are 3,000 date-palms.
Gulbīta گل بیتا	6 miles east of Ziyārat.	40 houses of Hājiyān, Faqīha, Mullāha and Jatūt.	Animals are 60 camels, 40 donkeys, 20 cattle and 250 sheep and goats. There are no dates.
Hadaku هدکو	On the coast immediately south of Qalāt.	30 houses of Kabgānis.	The people are fishermen and growers of dates and corn: they own 3 Māshuwahs and 10 Varjis. There are 400 date-palms, also 40 donkeys, 30 cattle and 100 sheep and goats.
Haidari حیدري	11 miles south-west of Khurmūj town, on the west side of the Khurmūj valley.	50 houses of Ruūseh, Faqīha and Jatūt.	Date-palms number 6,000 and there are 5 horses, 6 mules, 25 camels, 75 donkeys, 40 cattle and 2,000 sheep and goats.
Hasan Kā Muhammad (Ihshām) احشام حسن کا محمد	10 miles south-west of Khurmūj town, on the west side of the Khurmūj valley.	30 houses of Qāidān and Mullāha.	There are 2,000 date-palms, also 30 donkeys, 15 cattle and 700 sheep and goats.
Husain Jamāl (Chāh-i-) جاه حسین جمال	7 miles south-west of Kāki.	20 houses of Hājiyān, Shaikhānis, 'Amrānis and Faqīha.	There are 4 horses, 5 mules, 12 camels, 25 donkeys, 15 cattle, and 3,000 sheep and goats, also 4,000 date-palms.

Name.	Position.	Houses and inhabitants.	Remarks.
Jamarak جمرک	3 miles north-west of Bardistān, near the south end of the Bardistān valley.	20 houses of Hājiyān and Sālih Ahmadis.	There are 6,000 date, 1,000 pomegranate, 600 lemon and 200 orange trees. Animals are 25 horses, 30 mules, 35 camels, 200 donkeys, 100 cattle and 4,000 sheep and goats.
Kabgān کبگان	On the coast 1 mile north of Lāvar.	A village of Khanasīr.	There are 3,000 date-palms and much cultivation, and the people own 3 good sized boats. Animals are 40 donkeys, 20 cattle and 500 sheep and goats.
Kāki کاکي	26 miles south-south-east of Khurmūj town, in the Mūnd river plain.	...	See article Kāki.
Khār Kuhneh خار کهنه	10 miles north by west of Bardistān, on the north side of the Bardistān valley.	Half-a-dozen houses of Tangasīr.	There are 400 dates, 15 donkeys and 100 sheep and goats.
Khurmūj خرموج	40 miles south-east of Būshehr Town and 20 miles from the coast.	...	See article Khurmūj.
Kulul کلل	1 mile north of Chāh 'Ali, on the west side of the Khurmūj plain.	40 houses of Ruūseh, Sālih Ahmadis and Faqīha.	Wheat, barley and dates are grown: there are 6,000 date-palms, 17 horses, 4 mules, 12 camels, 80 donkeys, 30 cattle and 300 sheep and goats.
Kunāvi کناري	8 miles south by east of Kāki, in the Mūnd river plain.	30 houses of Hājiyān, Sālih Ahmadis, Sādāt and Jatūt.	Resources are 5 horses, 4 mules, 15 camels, 70 donkeys, 60 cattle and 1,500 sheep and goats, also 4,000 dates.
Kurdavān کرادرن	On the right bank of the Mūnd river at 2 miles from the coast.	100 houses of Hājiyān, Ruūseh, Shaikhha and Mullāha.	There are 12,000 date-palms, 4 horses, 4 mules, 25 camels, 60 donkeys, 30 cattle, 400 sheep and goats.

DASHTI

Name.	Position.	Houses and inhabitants.	Remarks.
Lāvar (I) لاور	12 miles south of **Khurmūj** town.	A village of Mīrzāha and Ruūseh.	(See *Routes in Persia*, I. 86.) There are 5,000 date-palms. Animals are 7 horses, 5 mules, 12 camels, 40 donkeys, 30 cattle and 1,500 sheep and goats.
Lāvar (II) لاور	On the coast, 12 miles north of Khor Ziyārat.	20 houses of Khanasīr and Kabgānis.	There are 5 large boats. Livestock are 30 donkeys, 15 cattle and 200 sheep and goats. Date trees number 3,000 and fig trees 2,000. The Imperial Persian Customs have a post here.
Malangu ملنگو	9 miles east by north of Burdakhān Nau, on the slopes of Kūh-i-Darang.	15 houses of Hājiyān, Ruūseh and Jatūt.	There are 5 horses, 4 mules, 40 donkeys, 20 cattle and 700 sheep and goats. Date trees number 2,000.
Mankal منکل	5 miles south of **Khurmūj** town, on the east side of the Khurmūj valley.	40 houses of Sādāt, Mullāha and Shaikhānis.	Resources are 5 horses, 4 mules, 40 donkeys, 20 cattle, 500 sheep and goats and 2,500 date-palms.
Mashīleh Akbari مشیله اکبری	4 miles north-west of **Khurmūj**.	30 houses of Hājiyān.	Resources are 6 horses, 5 mules, 25 camels, 30 donkeys, 25 cattle, 400 sheep and goats and 2,000 date-palms.
Mashīleh Haidar Muhammad 'Ali مشیله حیدر محمد علی	1 mile south of Mashīleh Akbari.	25 houses of Hājiyān.	There are 1,500 dates. Animals are 4 horses, 3 mules, 20 camels, 25 donkeys, 20 cattle and 30 sheep and goats.
Miyānkhareh میانخره	8 miles south-west of **Khurmūj** town, towards the west side of the Khurmūj valley.	40 houses of Sādāt and Shaikhānis.	There are 2,000 date-palms. Animals are 6 horses, 3 mules, 40 donkeys, 20 cattle and 700 sheep and goats.
Muhammadābād محمد آباد	3 miles south by west of **Khurmūj** town, on the east side of the Khurmūj valley.	20 houses of Mīrzāha and Ruūseh.	Animals are 4 horses, 4 mules, 40 donkeys, 20 cattle and 800 sheep and goats. Date-palms number 6,000.

DASHTI

Name.	Position.	Houses and inhabitants.	Remarks.
Mukhdān مخدان	On the left bank of the **Mūnd** river at 16 miles from the coast.	Some houses of Hājiyān, Shaikhānis, Sādāt and Jatūt.	There are 8,000 date-palms. Livestock include 5 horses, 7 mules, 100 camels, 120 donkeys, 40 cattle and 2,000 sheep and goats.
Naukān نوكان	2 miles north by west of Bardistān, in the middle of the Bardistān valley.	15 houses of 'Amrānis and Faqīha.	Animals are 3 horses, 20 donkeys, 10 cattle, 300 sheep and goats. Date trees number 1,000.
Qaidān قائدان	1 mile south-east of Faqīh Hasanān.	10 houses of **Lurs** and Faqīha.	30 donkeys, 15 cattle, 500 sheep and goats, also 2,000 date-palms.
Qalāt قلات	On the coast, 12 miles north-north-west of Lāvar and immediately south of the Bāraki group of villages in the **Tangistān** District.	25 houses of Khanasir and Kabgānis.	The people are fishermen and grow corn and dates. They have 2 large boats.
Raīs (Bāgh) باغ رئيس	8 miles west of Khurmūj town at the west side of the Khurmūj valley.	A village of 200 houses.	Some of the houses are of stone. Resources are 5 horses, 4 mules, 12 camels, 60 donkeys, 40 cattle, 800 sheep and goats and 6,000 date-palms. Also called Gaz Darāz گز دراز and Maqtal مقتل.
Sahal سهل	15 miles north-north-west of Bardistān, at the north side of the Bardistān valley.	30 houses of Faqīha and 'Amrānis, immigrants from Bustānu, in **Shībkūh**, who are Sunnis and speak both Persian and Arabic.	Animals are 20 donkeys, 10 cattle and 400 sheep and goats, and there are 700 date-palms.
Sarvistān سروستان	20 miles north-west of Bardistān, towards the head of the Bardistān plain.	60 houses of Hājiyān, Faqīha, Shaikhānis and Jatūt.	There are 4,000 date-palms. Animals include 12 horses, 10 mules, 50 camels, 70 donkeys, 50 cattle and 1,200 sheep and goats.
Shahri شهري	3 miles west of Kāki, in the **Mūnd** river plain.	30 houses of Hājiyān and Jatūt.	There are 100 date-palms, 10 horses, 5 mules, 25 camels, 70 donkeys, 30 cattle, and 700 sheep and goats.

Name.	Position.	Houses and inhabitants.	Remarks.
Shībarm شیبرم	About 12 miles north of **Daiyir**.	20 houses of Hājiyān.	There are 1,000 date-palms, also 10 camels, 30 donkeys, 20 cattle, and 400 sheep and goats.
Trāvi تراوي	6 miles north-west of **Khurmūj** town, in the middle of the Khurmūj plain.	20 houses of Hājiyān.	Date-palms number 2,000 and animals are 15 camels, 20 donkeys, 15 cattle and 200 sheep and goats.
Vāli والي	On the coast, 3 miles west of **Daiyir**, on a small rocky point of low cliff.	25 houses of Hājiyān and Faqīha.	There is a high round tower, also a boat-harbour inside some rocks. Animals are 15 donkeys, 10 cattle and 1,200 sheep and goats, and there are 300 date-palms.
Varāvi وراوي	9 miles south-west of **Khurmūj** town, on the west side of the Khurmūj plain.	30 houses of Sunni immigrants from **Shībkūh**.	Resources are 20 donkeys, 15 cattle, 300 sheep and goats and 3,000 date-palms.
Zaizār زیزار	9 miles south-south-west of **Khurmūj** town, on the west side of the Khurmūj plain.	20 houses of Hājiyān and Sādāt.	There are 3,000 date trees. Animals are 40 donkeys, 20 cattle and 800 sheep and goats.
Zīrahak زیرهك	On the coast, 6 miles north of **Lāvar**.	Half a dozen houses of Kabgānis and Khanasīr.	There are 2 large boats and 4 Varjis. Agricultural resources are 10 donkeys, 5 cattle, 700 sheep and goats and 1,200 date trees.
Ziyārat زیارت	Near the coast, 6 miles north of Khor Ziyārat, the mouth of the **Mūnd** river.	40 houses of Hājiyān Mīrzāha, Shaikhānis and Jatūt.	There are 4,000 date-palms. Animals are 60 camels, 70 donkeys, 30 cattle, and 2,000 sheep and goats.

A district of the **Persian Coast** in the vicinity of the **Būshehr** Peninsula; the principal place in Dashtistān is **Burāzjān**, situated exactly in the middle of the district and about 28 miles north-east of **Būshehr** Town. The districts of **Mazāra'i, Zīra, Angāli** and **Shabānkāreh** are

DASHT-ISTĀN
دشتستن

considered to belong geographically to Dashtistān, and it is said that they once formed parts of it in the administrative sense also.

Limits.—The length of Dashtistān from Bībara in the north to **Chāh Kūtāh** in the south is about 30 miles; and its breadth, which is greatest towards the southern end, averages 10 to 15 miles. On the south Dashtistān reaches to the coast opposite **Būshehr** Town; on the west it is enclosed by the districts of **Angāli** and **Zīra**, and on the north-west by the district of **Mazāra'i**; on the north-east and east it is bounded by hills of which the Gīsakān mountain is a part.

Physical characteristics.—The whole of Dashtistān is a plain, forming a slight declivity between the mountains on the north-east and the sea coast on the south-west,— a circumstance determining the direction of the various streams and hollows by which the district is crossed. The principal stream is that which passes **Dāliki** and, by uniting with the Rūd Shīrīn, forms the **Rūd-hilleh** River. Of secondary importance are the Ahmadi water-course, which rises in a part of the hills called Bairami بيرمي, passes the village of Ahmadi, and reaches the sea a couple of miles to the east of Shīf; and the **Chāh Kūtāh** salt stream which pursues a parallel and similar course a few miles further to the south-eastward. The part of the district adjoining the hills enjoys less of the sea breeze and suffers from scorching winds in summer between the end of May and the beginning of October; otherwise the climate resembles that of **Būshehr**. Traces of sulphur, bitumen and petroleum occur at the north end of the district. Water nearly everywhere is from wells varying between 30 and 50 feet in depth; these ordinarily contain 4 to 10 feet of water and they never dry up.

Inhabitants.—The population of the district is exceedingly composite and amounts to about 15,000 souls; at most places they are described as Persians, and in many cases they are believed to be descendants of immigrants from neighbouring Persian districts, especially from **Dashti** and the direction of Shīrāz. Deserving of special mention are the Persian tribe of Bag بگ, who inhabit the villages of Jīmeh, Khushāb and Khushakān in the centre of the district; they were originally the masters of **Burāzjān**, but were expelled by the Pāparis about two generations ago and have now sunk to the level of ordinary cultivators. The Pāpari and Qāidān tribes are noticed in the article on **Burāzjān**. A few Zanganeh زنگنه or Zangūis زنگوي are found, especially at **Chāh Kūtāh**; this is a Persian tribe of uncertain origin, but reputed courageous. There are also a number of Arab settlements in the district, the most important being a group in the south-east corner of which **Chāh Kūtāh** is the largest; this group is inhabited by Dumūkh who are a section of the **Dawāsir** tribe of **Bahrain** and until recently were all Sunnis; now about ¾ of them are Shī'ahs. Other Arabs, said to be of **Bahrain** origin but not belonging to any known tribe, are found north of **Burāzjān**; and Arabs calling themselves Bani Hājir هاجر , who are believed to have come from the **Hindiyān** district, occur at three or four scattered points. With the exception of the Dumūkh and a few of the other Arabs the whole population is Persian-speaking and Shī'ah. Further details of the population are given in the table of villages at the end of this article. Except in **Burāzjān** the dwellings of the people are nearly all huts or mud houses of an unpretentious kind. **Burāzjān** is the district capital.

Agriculture.—The chief products of Dashtistān are wheat and barley, which are grown in winter by rainfall; in summer water melons, musk melons, cucumbers, maize, a little cotton, castor oil, beans, onions, garlic and sesame are cultivated by irrigation from wells. The soil is rich and suitable for the growing of opium; dates also flourish. Livestock is represented by an ordinary proportion of cattle, sheep and goats. The unit of land-measurement is the Gāu or that area of land which requires 6 Hāshim Mans of seed-grain and can be ploughed by one yoke of animals (whether cattle, horses, mules or donkeys) in about 25 days; it is represented by a square of which the side measures about 250 yards. In a good year the return to cultivation in Dashtistān is from 8 to 16-fold. Dashtistān agriculturally resembles **Dashti,** but it is considered the superior district. The cultivators of Dashtistān are many of them embarrassed with debts originating in loans taken at exorbitant rates of interest for the purpose of buying seed-grain.

Trade.—**Burāzjān** is the commercial centre of Dashtistān, and the article on it may be consulted for an account of the trade of the district. The standard of weight is a local Man equal to 8 lbs. 11 oz. English, and the Hāshim Man of the district (=16 local Mans) is equivalent to 139 lbs. English.

Communications and transport.—The district contains no natural obstacles to movement; within it lie the first three stages on the ordinary route from **Būshehr** to Shīrāz.* The transport resources of the district are estimated at 200 horses, some camels, 350 mules and 2,500 donkeys. Some

---

* See *Routes in Persia,* I, No. 23.

quantity of wheat and barley is purchasable locally, but not as a rule until the prospects of the coming harvest are assured; until this occurs the stocks in hand are hoarded.

Administration.—The political organisation of Dashtistān is a patchwork of extraordinary complexity. The bulk of the district is under the Governor-General of **Fārs**; but some of the southern villages, including a group for which the Shaikh of **Chāh Kūtāh** is responsible, are subordinate to the Governor of the **Gulf Ports**. The system of farming the revenues is responsible for further confusion, especially as an indefinite degree of executive power is conferred on the farmer along with the right to collect the taxes, and the more so in the present case that the farmer of the greater part of Dashtistān is the Governor of the **Gulf Ports** and that he holds it on lease from the Governor-General of **Fārs**. Half or more of the villages to the north of **Burāzjān** are held on a Tiyūl or royal grant by the Sālār-i-Mu'azzam, who is accountable for them to the Shāh only. **Burāzjān** and its dependent villages, forming the greater part of the district, are ruled by the Khān of **Burāzjān** (at present Mīrza Husain) who also collects the revenues, a drivilege for which he pays the sum of 5,000 Tūmāns annually; he is properly answerable to the Governor of **Fārs**, to whose jurisdiction **Burāzjān** has always nominally belonged, but, in consequence of the farm in favour of the Governor of the **Gulf Ports**, the relations of the Shaikh are at present, it would seem, exclusively with the **Būshehr** Government. The Shaikh of **Chāh Kūtāh**, who is in executive charge of that place and of several adjoining villages, is subject, both in theory and in practice, to the Governor of the **Gulf Ports**. The Governor-General of **Fārs** is represented by a Deputy-Governor at **Burāzjān**, where also there is a Persian telegraph staff.

The lot of the subjects of the Khān of **Burāzjān** is not a happy one; they are rack-rented and are obliged to yield their master military service whenever he may require it, supplying their own arms and ammunition. The subjects of the Sālār-i-Mu'azzam and of the Shaikh of **Chāh Kūtāh** are probably little better off, and of late years there has been a good deal of emigration from the district. The nominal land revenue averages 50 to 60 Qrāns per Gāu; but the Khān of **Burāzjān**, at least, endeavours to extort more.

There is no sort of criminal justice, and civil justice is synonymous with the good offices of Mullas in arranging private disputes. Quarrels between villages are either adjusted by Saiyids or else fought out to the bitter end.

DASHTISTĀN

Topography.—The following are the villages of the Dashtistān district: the present political position of those not subject to the Khān of **Burāzjān** is indicated in the column of remarks:—

Name.	Position.	Houses and inhabitants.	Remarks.
Ahmadi احمدي	9 miles east of Shīf.	120 houses of Dumūkh Dawāsir Arabs.	Under **Būshehr**. Wheat and barley are grown; there are no dates. Animals are 20 horses, 10 mules, 200 donkeys, 100 cattle and 800 sheep and goats. There is a caravansarai with 50 rooms for travellers and capable of accommodating about 2,000 animals; also a tower for defence.
Ashki ('Tul) طل اشكي	½ a mile east of **Chāh Kūtāh**.	20 houses of Dumūkh Dawāsir Arabs.	Under **Būshehr** in the jurisdiction of the Shaikh of **Chāh Kūtāh**. Wheat, barley, water melons and dates are grown, and there are some donkeys.
Bandārūz بندا روز	3 miles south of **Burāzjān**.	50 houses of Burāzjānis.	Wheat and barley are grown and there are 150 donkeys.
Bargāhi برگاهي	4 miles north of **Burāzjān**.	30 houses. ¾ of the inhabitants are Pāparis of **Burāzjān** and the rest are Bahraini immigrants who speak Arabic as well as Persian.	Wheat and barley and a few dates are grown. Bargāhi is an ancient place.
Bībara بيبرا	4 miles north-west of **Dāliki**.	200 houses of Burāzjānis, Dashtis and Kāzarūnis.	Farmed by the Sālār-i-Mu'azzam to the Khān of **Shabānkāreh**. Wheat and barley are grown; there are about 300 donkeys, a few horses and 400 sheep. The hot winds are very trying here in summer.
Bunār بنار	3 miles south of **Burāzjān**.	80 houses of Burāzjānis.	There are 20 horses, 15 mules, 25 camels, 200 donkeys, 100 cattle and 400 sheep and goats, and wheat, barley and dates are cultivated.

Name.	Position.	Houses and inhabitants.	Remarks.
Burāzjān برازجان	28 miles north-east of Būshehr Town.	...	See article Burāzjān.
Chāh 'Arabi چاه عربي	1 mile north-west of 'Īsavand.	30 houses of Arabs called Bani Hājīr and said to have come from the Hindiyān District. They are Sunnis and speak both Persian and Arabic.	There is cultivation of wheat and barley and a little dates; about 100 donkeys are kept.
Chāh Khāni چاه خانی	2 miles south of Chāh 'Arabi.	30 houses of Burāzjānis.	Wheat and barley are grown, but there are only about 200 date-palms; there are 100 donkeys.
Chāh Kūtāh چاه کوتاه	15 miles south by west of Burāzjān and 18 miles east by north of Būshehr Town.	...	See article Chāh Kūtāh.
Chītu (Dar-i-) در چیتو	4 miles north of Chāh Kūtāh.	40 houses, half of Zanganeh and half of mixed tribes.	There is a tower. Wheat and barley are grown; and animals are 15 horses, 100 donkeys, 50 cattle and 400 sheep and goats.
Dāliki دالکي	13 miles north-north-east of Burāzjān.	...	See article Dāliki.
Davīreh دویره	2 miles north of Chāh Kūtāh.	20 houses of Dumūkh Dawāsir Arabs: they are Sunnis and speak Arabic as well as Persian.	Under Būshehr and administered by the Shaikh of Chāh Kūtāh. Wheat, barley and dates are cultivated. Livestock are 15 horses, 100 donkeys, 50 cattle and 400 sheep and goats.
Dih Nau ده نو	7 miles west of Burāzjān.	20 houses of Burāzjānis.	Wheat and barley are grown and there are 35 donkeys.
Gazbīd گزبید	1 mile east of Khushāb.	50 houses of Burāzjānis.	Wheat, barley and dates are grown; there are 20 mules and 100 donkeys.

DASHTISTĀN

Name.	Position.	Houses and inhabitants.	Remarks.
Gīsakān گیسکان	High up on the mountain of the same name, a few miles to the east of Burāzjān.	In all 80 houses of Kāshkulis and Lurs.	This place has springs of sweet water. It consists of 4 separate hamlets of about equal size, each protected by a tower. Jointly the hamlets possess about 40 horses, 200 donkeys, 100 cattle and 800 sheep and goats. Insoluble gum, charcoal and wild almonds are exported.
Hamad (Buneh) بنه حمد	$4\frac{1}{2}$ miles west of Dāliki.	A village of 20 houses	Closely connected with Bibara. There is a tower. Date-palms number 5,000. Animals are 40 donkeys, 25 cattle, 100 sheep and goats and a few horses.
Hisār (Bāgh-i-) باغ حصار	$4\frac{1}{2}$ miles west of Burāzjān.	20 houses of Burāzjānis and Tangistānis.	Wheat, barley and dates are grown and there are 40 donkeys, 25 cattle, 80 sheep and goats and a few horses.
Husainaki حسینکي	6 miles west-north-west of Chāh Kūtāh.	20 houses of descendants of Bani Hājir Arab immigrants from the Hindiyān District and of Dumūkh Dawāsir Arabs from Bahrain: some are still Sunnis and all speak Arabic as well as Persian. The Dumūkh outnumber the Bani Hājir.	Under Būshehr and administered by the Shaikh of Chāh Kūtāh. Wheat, barley and melons are grown and there are a few dates.
'Īsavand عیسوند	10 miles south-west of Burāzjān.	30 houses, $\frac{1}{4}$ of Bani Hājir from Hindiyān and $\frac{3}{4}$ of Burāzjānis, mostly of the Pāpari tribe.	Wheat, barley, tobacco and a few dates are grown. There are 100 donkeys.
Ismā'īl (Buneh) بنه اسماعیل	6 miles south-west of Dāliki, on the right bank of the Dāliki stream.	20 houses of Dashtis, Burāzjānis, etc.	Wheat, barley and dates grow and there are some donkeys.

2 c

Name.	Position.	Houses and inhabitants.	Remarks.
Jarrañ جراڧي	10 miles west by south of **Burāzjān**.	25 houses of immigrants from the **Angāli** and **Tangistān** Districts.	Wheat and barley are grown and there are 40 donkeys.
Jīmeh جيمه	3 miles west of **Khushāb**.	30 houses of settlers from Khushāb *q. v.*	The village has a tower. Livestock are 10 horses, 100 donkeys, 50 cattle and 200 sheep and goats.
Khushāb خوش آب	4 miles west-south-west of **Burāzjān**, situated on rising ground on the west side of the road to Shīf.	50 houses mostly of Bags who were expelled from **Burāzjān** 2 or 3 generations ago.	Wheat and barley are grown and a few dates. Khushāb was the scene of a Persian defeat in the Anglo-Persian war of 1857.
Khūshakān خوشكان	5 miles west-south-west of **Burāzjān**, upon a hill, on the west side of the road to Shīf.	60 houses of Bags, the former rulers of **Burāzjān**.	Wheat, barley and a few dates are cultivated: there are some donkeys.
Kulal كلل	7 miles west-north-west of **Burāzjān** and 1 mile from the **Rūdhilleh** River.	60 houses of aboriginal Persians.	Wheat and barley are grown and there are 60 donkeys.
Kunārābād كنار آباد	On a plain to the south of **Chāh Kūtāh**.	25 houses of Dumūkh **Dawāsir** Arabs.	Closely connected with **Chāh Kūtāh**. Livestock are 40 donkeys, 20 cattle and 300 sheep and goats. This village has a tower.
Lardeh لرده	In the hills, 8 miles east-north-east of **Burāzjān**.	20 houses of Bahrainis, **Lurs** and other Persians.	There is a tower here.
Mīrza (Buneh) بنه ميرزا	Near the left bank of the **Dāliki** stream, mid-way between **Dāliki** and **Burāzjān**.	20 houses: ⅓ of the people are **Lurs** and ⅔ are Bahraini Arabs.	This village is closely connected with **Sarkuvardān** and like that place is farmed by the **Salār-i-Mu'azzam**. Wheat, barley and dates grow, and there are some donkeys.

Name.	Position.	Houses and inhabitants.	Remarks.
Muhammad Ahmadi محمد احمدی	⅓ a mile south of Chāh Kūtah.	20 houses of Dumūkh (Dawāsir) Arabs; they are Sunnis and speak both Arabic and Persian.	Under Būshehr and administered by the Shaikh of Chāh Kūtah. This village has dates, wheat and barley and a few donkeys.
Nanīzak ننیزک	8 miles south of Burāzjān.	40 houses of no particular tribe.	The inhabitants grow wheat, barley and dates, collect gum, and own some donkeys and camels.
Nazar Āghāi نظر آغای	2 miles south-west of Dāliki.	150 houses of Burāzjānis, Dashtis and Kāzarūnis.	Wheat and barley are cultivated and some donkeys owned.
Qāid (Dih) ده قائد	3 miles north-north-west of Burāzjān.	200 houses of Burāzjānis and Khishtis.	Wheat, barley, tobacco and dates grow; there are 40 donkeys, also 30 mules and some camels. The elder son (Mīrza Muhammad Khān) of the Khān of Burāzjān resides here as his father's deputy. There is a large but old and dilapidated fort with 4 towers.
Qarāval Khāneh قراول خانه	5 miles south of Dāliki, on the east of the road to Burāzjān.	20 houses of Burāzjānis.	The people have 50 donkeys and a little cultivation of wheat and barley, but they are inclined to depend rather on robbery for their livelihood.
Rāhdār راه دار	5 miles north-north-west of Burāzjān, on the east side of the road from Dāliki to Burāzjān.	20 houses of Burāzjānis, Lurs, Khishtis and Kāzarūnis.	The people cultivate wheat and barley and own 50 donkeys and some mules, but they are mostly robbers.
Sādeh ساده	2 miles west-north-west of Dāliki.	20 houses, ½ of Bahraini Arabs and ½ of aboriginal Persians.	Under Dāliki. The crops are wheat and barley; there are some donkeys. This village is closely connected with Sarkuvardān, ½ a mile distant, and like it is farmed by the Sālār-i-Mu'azzam.

Name.	Position.	Houses and inhabitants.	Remarks.
Samal سمل	6 miles east of Chāh Kūtāh.	100 houses of mixed Tangistānis.	There are 2 towers here. Livestock are 15 horses, 150 donkeys, 75 cattle and 600 sheep and goats. Formerly this village belonged to **Tangistān**, but the Khān of **Burāzjān** has succeeded in attaching it to his jurisdiction.
Sarkureh سرکره	5 miles south of Burāzjān.	50 houses of Burāzjānis, Khishtis and Dashtis.	Wheat, barley and tobacco are grown; there are 100 donkeys.
Sarkuvardān سرکوردان	2 miles south-west of Dāliki.	100 houses of mixed tribes from other districts.	Wheat, barley and dates grow and donkeys are kept.
Sarmal سرمل	6 miles north-east of Chāh Kūtāh.	40 houses of Bani-Hājir immigrants from the **Hindiyān** District. They are Sunnis.	This village has 1 tower. Livestock are 60 donkeys, 30 cattle and 400 sheep and goats.
Sufiābād صفي آباد	1½ miles south-east of Haftjūsh.	70 houses of mixed Persian-speaking tribes.	Wheat and barley are grown, and livestock are 15 horses, 60 donkeys, 40 cattle and 300 sheep and goats.
Tavīl (Abu) ابو طویل	5 miles north-north-west of Chāh Kūtāh.	30 houses of Dumūkh (Dawāsir) Arabs, who are Sunnis and speak Arabic as well as Persian.	Under **Būshehr**, in the jurisdiction of the Shaikh of Chāh Kūtāh. Dates, tobacco, water-melons, wheat, and barley are grown. There are 30 horses, 200 donkeys, 150 cattle and 600 sheep and goats.
Ziyārat زیارت	8 miles west by north of Burāzjān.	200 houses. The people are descendants of Dashti immigrants of no particular tribe.	Wheat, barley and dates are the crops, and there are 200 donkeys and some mules. There is a small shrine called Shaikh Mansūr.

DAWAIRIJ   A division of the 'Amārah Sanjāq of the Basrah Wilāyat in Turkish
دورريج   'Irāq.

Position and boundaries.—The Dawairīj Qadha comprises a good part of the plains to the north-east of '**Amārah** Town between that place and the Persian hills. Dawairīj is understood to be bounded by the 'Amārah Qadha on the west and by the Persian frontier on the north and east: on the south it is adjoined by the Qadha of **Zubair**.

Topography and inhabitants.—There are no fixed villages in Dawairīj: Tafrah طفرة, the administrative headquarters, is merely a mud fort; it is reported to be situated about 30 miles to the east and somewhat to the north of '**Amārah** Town. The district is traversed by a brackish stream of the same name (Dawairīj) which comes down from the Persian hills and contributes to form the marshes between 'Amārah and **Hawīzeh**. Dawairīj is the headquarters of the Bani **Lām** tribe and their principal Shaikh has his residence in the district.

Population.—The entire fixed population is estimated at 50,000 souls who, with the exception of a few Sunni officials, are all Shī'ah Arabs.

Resources.—The Dāirat-as-Sanīyah has acquired some of the best land in the district, and there are now flourishing date plantations at Tafrah which owe their existence to that department: the arable land under its management is generally leased to tribesmen of the neighbourhood for cultivation. Rice, maize and wheat are grown; camels, cattle and sheep are abundant; and there are some buffaloes. The excellent grazing in the neighbourhood has in the past been a cause of dispute not only between different sections of the Bani **Lām**, but also between the Turkish and Persian Governments.

Administration.—The class of the Dawairīj Qadha has not been ascertained and there are no Nāhiyahs. The Qāim-Maqām and his staff generally manage to live at 'Amārah Town instead of at Tafrah, leaving the Bani **Lām** to their own devices.

DAWĀSIR DISTRICT and ISLANDS

دواسر

A district extending for a considerable distance along the right bank of the Shatt-al-'**Arab** between Saihān and Dorah; its upper extremity is about 16 miles by river below the mouth of the **Kārūn**, while its lower is 15 miles by river above the **Fāo** telegraph station: its own length between the two is nearly 19 miles. In the whole district there are about 50 hamlets of 5 to 15 huts each, inhabited by various tribes;

the people are somewhat nomadic in their habits and many old deserted huts are to be seen. One place, known as Kūt-al-Khalīfah كوت الخليفه, is inhabited by **Muntafik**. Palms are comparatively scarce and the crop poor, but native sailing boats call to collect inferior dates for exportation.

The island of **Ziyādīyah** lies between the Shatt-al-'**Arab** and Dawāsir in the uppermost 6 miles of its extent; and, where it terminates, a chain of low and narrow islands called Dawāsir begins on the opposite or Persian side of the river and continues for about 6 miles.

Exclusive of the part, apparently uninhabited, opposite **Ziyādīyah** island, Dawāsir consists of the following tracts in order as the river is descended:—

Name.	Extent upon the river.	Inhabitants.	Remarks.
Dawaib دويب	3 miles.	About 1,250 souls of mixed tribes.	Resources are estimated at 10,000 palms, 100 cattle, 250 sheep and goats and 6 camels.
Sanīyah السنيه	4 to 5 miles.	About 450 souls of various tribes.	There are about 3,000 date palms. Animals are 50 sheep and goats and 12 horses. This tract owes its name to the circumstance that it is the property of the Sultan of Turkey and is managed by the Dāirat-as-Sanīyah.
Faddāghīyah فداغيه	Ditto.	1,000 souls of Muhaisin of the Bait Kana'ān section.	The date palms of this tract are estimated at 5,000, and the live-stock at 100 cattle, 150 sheep and goats and 100 horses. A creek which forms the upper boundary of this tract, dividing it from Sanīyah, is known as the Faddāghīyah creek and has at times been notorious as a resort of river pirates.

From this table it would appear that the total fixed population of Dawāsir is about 2,700, and that date palms number some 18,000.

DAWĀSIR TRIBE

دواسر

Singular Dōsiri دوسري. An important Arab tribe of Southern **Najd**, having settlements also on the coasts of the Persian Gulf.

Distribution.—The districts *par excellence* of the Dawāsir are those of Widyān **Dawāsir** and **Aflāj** in Central Arabia : the Bedouins as well as the settled inhabitants of those regions are chiefly of this tribe. The numerous villages of the Salaiyil and Wādi Dawāsir divisions of the Widyān **Dawāsir** district belong entirely to the settled Dawāsir, whose fellow tribesmen in **Aflāj** are owners of **Badi'**, Haddār, Hamar, **Kharfah**, **Lailah**, Marwān, Rajaijīyah, **Raudhah**, Shutbah, Wāsit and Wusailah. The populations of Hautah town and Hilwah in the **Hautah** district and of Harīq town in the **Harīq** district are partly Dawāsir, and the tribe is represented in **Kharj** both by settled villagers at **Dilam**, Sulaimīyah and Yamāmah and by Bedouins who encamp in the district. In **'Āridh**, where nomadic Dawāsir also are seen, fixed Dawāsir occur at Bīr, Dqalah, Hasi, Jarīnah, Malham, Safurrah and Thādiq in Mahmal ; at 'Ammārīyah, **Dara'īyah**, and Manfūhah on Wādi **Hanīfah** ; and at Dhrumah town and Mizāhmīyah in the **Dhrumah** tract : in **Sadair** they are found at 'Audah, Ghāt, Hasūn, Jalājil, Ma'āshibah, Raudhah, Ruwaidhah, and **Zilfi**, and in **Washam** at Marāt. The settlements of the Dawāsir scarcely extend further north than **Sadair**, and in **Qasīm** their presence is reported at Hatān, Huwailān, Quwai'ah and Shamāsīyah only. On the south-west their limit appears to be in the Wādi **Sabai'** district, where some exist at Hazam, Khurmah, Raudhah, Rumadān and Suwaiyid.

In **Bahrain** the Dawāsir are the most numerous Sunni tribe after the **'Utūb**, and are the second of all the **Bahrain** tribes in political importance, being inferior in this respect to the **'Utūb** only. The Dawāsir of **Bahrain** are said to have immigrated from **Najd**, whence they gradually moved eastwards and, after spending several years by the way on **Zakhnūnīyah** island, finally arrived in **Bahrain** about 1845 under the leadership of the grandfather of their present Shaikh. They have now about 800 houses at **Budaiya'** and 200 at Zallāq, both places on the west side of **Bahrain** Island. About 30 households of the tribe are settled at **Dōhah** in **Qatar** and perhaps the same number in the town of **Kuwait**. Offshoots from the **Bahrain** community of Dawāsir exist in the Persian coast district of **Dashtistān** at **Chāh Kūtāh** and its dependent villages and at the village of Jazīreh in **Būshehr** harbour.

Divisions.*—The principal divisions of the Dawāsir tribe are said to be :—

1. Braik (Āl)	آل بريك	5. Riyāyithāt	ريايثات
2. Hasan (Āl)	آل حسن	6. Suhabah	صهبه
3. Makhārīb	مخاريب	and	
4. Rijbān	رجبان	7. Widā'īn	وداعين

Some of these call for further remark or for minuter classification.

1. The Āl Braik are possibly not a main division of the Dawāsir; according to one account they are included in a larger unit known as the Misā'irah مساعره, to which sections called Āl Abul Hasan آل ابو الحسن, Āl Bū Sabbā' آل بو سباع and a group of sections known as Musārīr مسارير also belong. Āl Braik are found at Nuwaimah, Āl Abul Hasan at Quwaiz, and Āl Bū Sabbā' at Nazwah, all places in Widyān **Dawāsir**. Mu'addi-bin-Iqwaid, at present the chief Shaikh of the Bedouin Dawāsir of Central Arabia, himself belongs to the Misā'irah. The Hanābijah حنابجه of Bilād-al-Hanābijah in Wādi Dawāsir are Misā'irah; so also are the Intaifāt انتيفات at Haddār in **Aflāj**, the Āl Rishdān آل رشدان at Ruwaisah in Wādi Dawāsir, the Sharāfah شرافه at Sabhah and Thamāmīyah in Wādi Dawāsir, the 'Uwaidhāt at Thamāmīyah in Wādi Dawāsir and the 'Uwaimir عويمر at Huwaizah in Wādi Dawāsir. Some of the Dawāsir in **Zilfi** also are Misā'irah.

2. The Al Hasan division consists of two subdivisions, the 'Ammār عمار and the Farjān فرجان, which in turn are composed of the sections given in the table below. Numerically small sections are distinguished

---

* A list by Col. E. C. Ross of Dawāsir sections will be found in the Persian Gulf Administration Report for 1879-80.

DAWĀSIR TRIBE

by an asterisk, and in a few cases localities in which the sections are known to be represented are specified.

'Ammār subdivision of the Āl Hasan.

Ajab عجب	Idghamah ادغمه at Rajai-jīyah in **Aflāj**.	Nifal نفل
'Ajlān عجلان or 'Ajālīn عجالين at **Lailah** in **Aflāj**.	Imdhaikhar امذيخر	Nimshān نمشان
		Nishair نشير
'Ali (I) علي	Ishkarah اشكره at **Badī'**, Hamar and Wusailah in **Aflāj** and Dārsah in **Wādi Dawāsir**. They include two subsections named Āl Bū 'Ali آل بو علي and Harāthmah هراثمه.	Qainān قينان
Batair بتير		Sa'ab صعب
Burās براس or Āl Abu hās آل ابو راس at **Lailah** in **Aflāj**.	Jabail جبيل	Sa'ad * سعد at Asail in Widyān **Dawāsir**.
Dawai'ij دويعج	Ja'afar جعفر	
Dramah درمه	Jawā'id * جواعد	Sawādirah سوادره
Fahad فهد	Khirfān خرفان	Sawāhilah سواحله
Fahaid فهيد	Māna' مانع at Asail in Widyān **Dawāsir** and at **Lailah** in **Aflāj**.	Shāfān شافان
Faraj فرج		Sharaim شريم
Ghānim غانم	Mubārak مبارك at **Raudhah** in **Aflāj**.	
Hamāmah حمامه or Mabkhūt مبخوت	Muhammad محمد	Shawāhīn شواهين
Hijris هجرس	Muwājidah مواجده	Sukhābirah صخابره at **Badī'** in **Aflāj**.
Huqbān حقبان at **Raudhah** and Wāsit in **Aflāj** and at Kamidah in Widyān **Dawāsir**.	Nibqān نبقان	Wāsit واسط

Among the 'Ammār the Qainān are one of the largest sections.

Farjān subdivision of the Āl Hasan.

'Ali (II) علي	Fuwārīn فوارين	Mas'ūd مسعود
'Arfaj عرفج at Wusailah in Aflāj.	Hāif هائف	Miznah مزنه
'Awād عواد	Hājis حاجس	Mufarrij مفرج
Badrah بدره	Hamdān حمدان at Lailah in Aflāj.	Nādir نادر
Badrāni بدراني at Bīr in 'Āridh	Hawāmilah هواملـه	Nahadh نحض
Bidārīn بدارين : at Jalājil and Zilfi in Sadair possibly identical with the Badrāni.	Huwāshilah هواشله	Nāif نائف
	Jadhālīn جذالين at Lailah in Aflāj	Sa'adūn سعدون
	Khafīr خفير	Salaiyim سليم
Basmān بصمان	Mahl محل	Sālim سالم and
Dahash دهش	Mannā' منّاع	
Dawaihis دويحس	Maqtūf مقطوف	Sa'ūd سعود

The 'Arfaj are a large section among the Farjān. The Dawāsir in **Dashtistān** and some of those in **Bahrain** belong to a section known as Dumūkh دموخ, who are stated to belong to the Āl Hasan division of the tribe.

It should be added that a Ghaiyithāt غيثات section, who are found at **Kharfah** in **Aflāj** and at Hautah and Hilwah in **Hautah,** are of the Āl Hasan; but the subdivision to which they belong is uncertain.

3. One village in which the Makhārīb (also called the Makhārīm مخاريم) division are represented is Ma'talah in Wādi Dawāsir. The Ju'aid جعيد, who are Bedouins found only in **Kharj,** are said to belong to this division.

4. The Rijbān are found at **Dām,** which is the capital of the settled Dawāsir of Central Arabia, and at other places. One of the sections of the Rijbān are the Khatātibah خطاطبه who inhabit Muqābil in Wādi Dawāsir.

5. The Widā'īn division comprises, among other sections, the 'Araimah عريمه at Bilād Āl Hāmid in Wādi Dawāsir, the Dawwās دراس at Mathnah in Salaiyil, the Āl Dhuwaiyān آل ضويان at Bilād Āl Dhuwaiyān and Khataijān in Salaiyil, the Farrāj فراج at Khairān in

Salaiyil, the Āl Hāmid آل حامد at Bilād Āl Hāmid in Wādi Dawāsir, the Āl Hanaish آل حنيش at Dahlah in Salaiyil, the Hijji حجّي at Tamnah in Salaiyil and at **Lailah** in **Aflāj**, the Āl 'Īsa آل عيسى at Thādiq in **'Āridh**, the Jibārīn جبارين or Āl Jābir آل جابر at **Lailah** in **Aflāj**, and in **Bahrain**, the Khadhrān خضران who own Shutbah in **Aflāj** but do not reside there, the Khamāsīn خماسين at Mishrif in Wādi Dawāsir, the Midbal مدبل or Midābilah مدابله in **Dhrumah**, the Āl Muhammad آل محمّد at Bilād Āl Muhammad in Salaiyil, the Āl Nāhish آل ناهش at Fara'ah in Wādi Dawāsir, the Al Suwailim سويلم at Thādiq in **'Āridh** and Muqābil in Salaiyil, the 'Umūr عمور at Kabkābīyah and Tamrah in Salaiyil, and the Walāmīn at Nafjān in Wādi Dawāsir. The Walāmīn have two subsections known as Māna' and Sa'ad.

Character and life.—Little is known, in consequence of the remoteness of their country and its inaccessibility to European travellers, of the main body of the Dawāsir; but they appear to be of consequence as a settled rather than as a nomad tribe. A party of Dawāsir from the far interior, who supplied at **Kuwait** in 1905 most of the information about tribal divisions given above, wore a somewhat distinctive dress in which different shades of red and brown were blended, and they carried silver-mounted swords. Their kerchiefs and shawls were red, of European manufacture; their mantles were brown, some light, some dark in colour; their swords, they said, were from India, **Baghdād** and **Makkah**. In their **Bahrain** settlements none of the tribe are pastoral; there they are chiefly engaged in pearl diving, in pearl dealing and in the culture of dates.

The Dawāsir of Central Arabia profess to be followers of Ibn Hanbāl, but in reality they are Wahhābis in the modern acceptation of the term; in **Bahrain** they are Māliki Sunnis; and in **Dashtistān** about one-fourth are still Sunnis, while the remainder have recently been converted to Shī'ism.

Political position.—The district of Widyān **Dawāsir** forms a principality which is almost purely Dōsiri in population, is ruled by a Dōsiri chief with his capital at **Dām**, and is but slightly attached to the Wahhābi state; **Aflāj**, on the other hand, though all but exclusively a Dōsiri district, appears to be an integral part of the dominions of Ibn Sa'ūd. The political organisation of Widyān **Dawāsir** is noticed more fully in the article on that district. In the other districts of **Najd** where Dawāsir occur they are not of political importance in a tribal sense. The Dawāsir of **Bahrain** are a practically independent community; they pay no revenue to the Shaikh of **Bahrain** on account either of their pearl boats or their date gardens, and under the weak régime of the present ruler they would certainly resist any attempt by him at interference in their affairs.

DAWĀSIR (WIDYĀN)
ودیان دراسر

The most inaccessible and the least known, except Wādi Sabai', of the districts of **Najd.***

General.—Widyān Dawāsir is described as a hollow district or system of depressions, sandy and monotonous, filling a great part of the space enclosed between Jabal **Tuwaiq** on the north-east, the **Ruba'-al-Khāli** on the south-east, and Wādi **Sabai'** on the west. Its general slope is downwards from west to east, and Salaiyil, the lowest lying and most easterly of its subdivisions, affords a common outlet towards the **Dahánah** desert for the drainage of its component valleys except Hamām.

Salaiyil subdistrict.—The Salaiyil سليل subdistrict is situated among confused outliers of Jabal **Tuwaiq**, thrown off at the point where that range ceases to run southwards; it lies about 5 days' journey, perhaps 80 or 100 miles, south and somewhat to the west of the populous part of the **Aflāj** district.† The south side of Salaiyil is formed by a detached mass of hills which a chain of eminences, not too continuous to prevent the escape of the Widyān Dawāsir drainage eastwards, connects with the corner of Jabal **Tuwaiq**, some 15 or 20 miles to the north. The part of the hills of Salaiyil immediately west of the village of Tamrah is called Jabal Tamrah, and one of its spurs, over which a track runs westwards into the subdistrict of Wādi Dawāsir, is styled Fird-al-Jūbah فرد الجوبه .

Salaiyil is not a large tract and it contains only about a dozen villages situated, with their palm groves, at intervals of a few miles apart upon hollows coming down from the southern hills. The villages and other chief points of interest are said to be as follows:—

---

* It does not appear that Widyān Dawāsir has as yet been visited by any European traveller and the whole of our information concerning it is derived from native sources.

† It is possible that, as apparently stated by another authority who has been followed in the map issued with this Gazetteer, the distance between the villages of **Aflāj** and **Salaiyil** is very much less than 80 or 100 miles.

DAWĀSIR (WIDYĀN)

Name.	Position.	Houses and inhabitants.	Remarks.
Dahlah دحله	Near Bilād Āl Muhammad.	100 houses of Al Hanaish Dawāsir.	The village is surrounded by hills which make its position one of some strength. Water is at 6 fathoms, and there are some date groves in the middle of which other cultivation is carried on.
Dhuwaiyān (Bilād Āl) بلاد آل ضويان	Several miles south-west of Bilād Āl Muhammad.	100 houses of Āl Dhuwaiyān Dawāsir.	An ordinary village. The wells contain good water at 4 fathoms.
Fara'ah فرعه	...	...	Possibly identical with Bilād Āl Dhuwaiyān above, or with Khataijān below.
Jāhilīyah (Qaryat-al-) قرية الجاهلية	On the west side of Jabal Tamrah, at the western border of Salaiyil.	A place where Bedouin Dawāsir encamp in summer.	There are 8 wells with good water at 12 fathoms. Ruins said to be those of a pre-Islamic town exist here, and report mentions a number of inscribed and sculptured stones. According to local tradition a route once ran from this place to the realms, somewhere in the Ruba'-al-Khāli, of a certain King 'Ād.
Kabkābīyah كبكابية	Several miles north of Tamrah.	100 houses of 'Umūr Dawāsir.	Some of the dwellings are huts and are scattered among the date groves. Water is at 3 fathoms.
Khairān خيران	A mile or two east of Tamrah.	20 houses of Āl Farrāj Dawāsir.	...
Khataijān خطيجان	A few miles north-east of Tamrah.	50 houses of Al Dhuwaiyān Dawāsir.	The dwellings are dispersed among the date plantations. Water is at 4 fathoms.
Mathnab مثنه	To the west of Bilād Āl Muhammad.	75 houses of Dawwās Dawāsir.	...

Name.	Position.	Houses and inhabitants.	Remarks.
Muhammad (Bilād Āl) بلاد آل محمد	The easternmost village (with the possible exception of Dahlah) in Salaiyil.	200 houses of Āl Muhammad Dawāsir.	There are 4 regular shops dealing in 'Abas, piece-goods, coffee, arms and ammunition; some trade is done also in private houses. A number of houses have an upper storey. There are considerable date groves, containing perhaps 5,000 trees; and cultivation of wheat, barley, maize and lucerne is carried on both among the palms and in the open fields. There is a big Jāmi' mosque, near which are 3 large wells with good water at 5 fathoms.
Muqābil مقابل	Between Bilād Āl Muhammad and Tamrah.	100 houses of Āl Suwailim Dawāsir.	...
Murqāb مرقاب	Some miles east of Tamrah.	25 houses of Āl Nāsir Dawāsir.	...
Qila'āt (Umm-al-) أم القلعات	At the foot of Jabal Tamrah on its east side.	A camping ground of Dawāsir Bedouins.	There are several hollows here in which rain water collects.
Tamnah طمنة	Between Bilād Āl Muhammad and Tamrah.	50 houses of Āl Hijji Dawāsir.	...
Tamrah تمرة	The westernmost of the fixed villages in Salaiyil, about 30 miles west of Bilād Āl Muhammad.	150 houses of 'Umūr Dawāsir.	Ordinary cultivation and livestock, except horses of which there are none. The water, in wells, is good; it is at 4½ fathoms.

From this table the whole fixed population of Salaiyil would appear to be less than 5,000 souls.

In Salaiyil the soil is sandy and the water-supply is exclusively from wells. Wheat, barley and dates, however, are grown and are irrigated by means of lifts worked by camels and bullocks. The houses are nearly all of mud and stone.

Hamām subdistrict.—Between Salaiyil and **Aflāj**, but nearer to Salaiyil and perhaps only 20 or 25 miles distant from it, is Hamām حمام, a small not unfertile tract yielding wheat and dates by irrigation and possessing a camping ground, several wells, and two Qasrs ; each of the enclosures is occupied by a family of Widā'īn **Dawāsir** from Salaiyil. Although Hamām is counted a part of Widyān Dawāsir, its drainage has an independent outfall to the eastern desert ; it neither combines with that of Salaiyil and the rest of the district to the south-west nor runs north-eastwards to the Maqran depression, which is regarded as the boundary between **Aflāj** and Widyān Dawāsir upon that side.

Wādi Dawāsir subdistrict.—The principal subdistrict of Widyān Dawāsir is Wādi Dawāsir which drains down into Salaiyil from the west ; the position of its head is uncertain, but the valley is said to be about 100 miles in length. According to one account it is entered at some point in its course by the drainage of Wādi **Sabai'**, the westernmost district of Southern **Najd**. The following is a list of the principal inhabited and frequented places which it is reported to contain :—

Name.	Position.	Houses and inhabitants.	Remarks.
Asail اسيل	West of Dām at perhaps 9 miles.	500 houses of Walāmīn **Dawāsir** of the Māna' and Sa'ad sections.	The town is divided into two quarters, Farīq-al-Māna' and Farīq-as-Sa-'ad, each presided over by a Shaikh of the section to which it belongs. Many of the houses have upper storeys and are built of sun-dried brick and mud, and some are whitewashed or painted. There are 2 large mosques and 2 schools of importance. The place has no bazaar, and goods are brought from **Dām** or purchased at the Thursday fair at Mishrif. The date plantations are very extensive ; and figs, peaches, pomegranates, grapes and almonds are produced as well as dates ; cultivation of wheat, barley and maize also is carried on among the date-palms. Water is good and stands at 5 fathoms. There are a number of horses besides other livestock.

Name.	Position.	Houses and inhabitants.	Remarks.
Dām دام or Ildām الدام	About the middle of Wādi Dawāsir.	...	See article Dām.
Dārsah دارسه	East of Dām at a distance of 15 to 20 miles.	100 houses of Ishkarah Dawāsir.	An ordinary village. There are 2 large gateways.
Dhāin ضائن	At the western extremity of Wādi Dawāsir, perhaps 35 miles west of Dām.	A camping ground frequented by Dawāsir Bedouins.	There are a dozen wells of good water 5 fathoms deep.
Fara'ah فرعه	About 20 miles west and somewhat south of Dām; it is the westernmost permanent village in Wādi Dawāsir.	150 houses of Āl Nāhish Dawāsir.	The village has only one entrance. There are the ordinary dates, cereals and livestock. The wells are 5 fathoms deep and slightly brackish.
Hāmid (Bilād Āl) بلاد آل حامد	About 12 miles west of Dām.	150 houses of Dawāsir of the Āl Hāmid and 'Araimah sections.	Like Asail this village is divided into two quarters, each belonging to one of the sections and controlled by a Shaikh of that section, and each has its own mosque. Date-palms are very numerous and among them wheat is grown. Wells are $5\frac{1}{3}$ fathoms deep and the water is good. There are some horses besides other animals.
Hanābijah (Bilād) بلاد حنابجه	About 20 miles east by north of Dām.	200 houses of Hanābijah Dawāsir.	An ordinary village without a bazaar of its own; goods are bought at Dām. There are large date groves amidst which wheat and lucerne also are grown. Water, which is at 5 fathoms, is fairly good. There are some horses as well as ordinary livestock.

DAWĀSIR (WIDYĀN)

Name.	Position.	Houses and inhabitants.	Remarks.
Huwaizah حويزه	About 12 miles from Dām in the direction of Fara'ah.	150 houses of Āl 'Uwaimir Dawāsir.	This village has 3 gateways, otherwise nothing distinctive.
Kamidah كمده	About 25 miles east of Dām, the easternmost of the fixed villages in Wādi Dawāsir.	50 houses of Huqbān Dawāsir.	Date-palms are very few, but cultivation of wheat and lucerne in open fields is considerable. Water is at 3 fathoms and brackish.
Ma'talah معتله	About 8 miles south-east of Dām.	300 houses of Makhārib Dawāsir.	The water in the wells is at 3 fathoms and fairly good. The date plantations are large.
Mishrif مشرف	2 or 3 miles north-west of Dām.	350 houses of Khamāsīn Dawāsir.	There is a bazaar here containing about 80 shops; it is in the form of a parallelogram running north-east and south-west, and in the centre is a market to which Bedouins bring ghi and wool. A Qādhi has his seat at Mishrif. In other respects this is an ordinary village.
Muqābil مقابل	5 or 6 miles east and somewhat to the south of Dām.	150 houses of Khatātibah Dawāsr.	An average village.
Mustajidd مستجد	Far to the west and somewhat to the south of Dām, possibly beyond the limits of Wādi Dawāsir.	A summer camping ground of Dawāsir Bedouins.	There are about 25 wells within an area of 4 or 5 miles; they are 3 to 4 fathoms deep and the water is good.
Nafjān نفجان	West of Mishrif at no great distance.	400 houses of Walāmīn Dawāsir.	Possibly identical with Asail above.
Nazwah نزوه	About 15 miles east and slightly north of Dām.	200 houses of Āl Bū Sabbā' Dawāsir.	The date groves are described as enormous: figs, grapes and melons are also produced, and wheat is grown both among the dates and in the open. Wells are 5 fathoms deep and the water is fairly good. There are said to be about 60 horses here.

Name.	Position.	Houses and inhabitants.	Remarks.
Nuwaimah نويمه or Nuwai'amah نويعمه	About 12 miles east and a little south of Dām.	150 houses of Āl Braik Dawāsir.	There are huge date plantations and some wheat and barley are grown, chiefly among the dates. The wells are 4 to 5 fathoms deep and contain fairly good water. There are about 30 horses besides other animals.
Quwaiz قويز	A mile or two west of Nuwaimah.	300 houses of Āl Abul Hasan Dawāsir.	The date groves are extensive and there is some cultivation of cereals. In addition to other livestock there are horses numbering about 60. The wells in the fields and gardens are 5 fathoms deep and their water is slightly brackish; a very large well called Dabbūs in the village is slightly deeper and yields better water.
Rākah راكه	Between Kamidah and Ruwaisah.	A shady spot with a cluster of Rāk trees.	There is no water here.
Ruwaisah رويسه	About 15 miles east and rather north of Dām.	70 houses of Āl Rishdān Dawāsir.	An ordinary village, except that dates are few; there were formerly more, but the plantations are said to have been ravaged by 'Abdullah-bin-Faisal, the Wahhābi Amīr, in a retirement from Wādi Dawāsir.
Sabhah صبهه	Further west than Kamidah and further east than Ruwaisah.	150 houses of Sharāfah Dawāsir.	Possibly identical with one of the divisions of Thamāmīyah below.
Subaihah (Spelling uncertain)	Some miles east of Dhain.	A summer camping ground of Dawāsir Bedouins.	There are half a dozen wells of good water about 4 fathoms deep.

Name.	Position.	Houses and inhabitants.	Remarks.
Thamāmīyah ثمامية	About 20 miles east of Dām.	350 houses of Dawāsir.	This place is composed of two separately walled villages a short distance apart: one (containing 150 houses) is called Qasr-al-'Uwaidhāt and the other (of 200 houses) Qasr-ash-Sharāfah, from the sections of the Dawāsir by whom they are respectively inhabited. Each village has its own Shaikh. Water is good at 5 fathoms; agriculture and livestock are average.
Wu'aifrah وعيفرة	15 to 20 miles south-east of Dām.	Now a camping ground only of Bedouin Dawāsir.	There are the remains of an old village and a dozen wells, 4 fathoms deep, which contain good water.

According to this table the settled population of Wādi Dawāsir would appear to be about 22,000 souls.

Wādi Dawāsir has no water except in wells, but it is full of palm groves; dates, wheat and barley are the chief products.

Other subdistricts.—A tract called Lughaf لغف said to contain 3 hamlets, also belongs to Widyān Dawāsir. It lies to the west of Jabal **Tuwaiq**, but like most of the districts it drains to Salaiyil, sending down along with its own drainage that of Fara'ah فرعة, a place still further to the west. Fara'ah is described as a settlement with extensive cultivation of dates, wheat and barley; the waterlifts there are worked by camels.

Daham دهم is the name of a tribe and their district; the latter is sometimes reckoned to Widyān Dawāsir and lies, it would seem, to the south of Salaiyil, presumably in the desert.

Population.—The Arab inhabitants, both nomadic and non-nomadic, of Widyān Dawāsir belong almost entirely to the **Dawāsir** tribe, from whom the district has received its name; but it is said that about one-fourth of the population is composed of negro slaves (included in the above statistics in the tribe of their masters). The total fixed population of the whole district probably does not exceed 27,000 souls and must be considerably less if, as is probable, the numbers of houses in the villages have been greatly exaggerated. The people are described as hospitable, but they are all Wahhābis. Adjoining villages are frequently at feud and nearly all villages are walled.

Agriculture and trade.—There is apparently nothing distinctive in the agriculture or trade of the Widyān Dawāsir district. The staples of cultivation, as will be apparent from the tables of villages above, are dates, wheat, barley, maize and lucerne ; and the fruits include figs, peaches, pomegranates, grapes and almonds. Camels are very numerous, and everywhere there are cattle and some donkeys ; a few horses are found in nearly all the villages, and in some the number is considerable. Such information as has been obtained about the trade of Widyān Dawāsir will be found in the article upon the town of **Dām**.

Political organisation.—The Amīr of **Dām** is paramount chief of Widyān Dawāsir, as well as absolute ruler of his own town. He represents the district in its dealings with external powers and receives tribute from all the villages. He does not interfere in the domestic affairs of the villages, but he settles cases which are referred to him and mediates in disputes ; cases which involve points of law are referred by him to the Qādhi of **Dām**, an official who is altogether under his influence. The Amīr has a treasury and maintains a staff of several secretaries or clerks. It is reported that the Amīr and his subjects regard themselves as independent of outside control and that a Turkish army advancing on **Dām** from the direction of Yaman was once repulsed by the **Dawāsir** with great slaughter ; two guns taken on that occasion can still, it is added, be seen at **Dām**. It is not denied that Zakāt was formerly paid to the house of Ibn Sa'ūd and, though discontinued during the supremacy of Ibn Rashīd in **Najd**, its renewal shortly in favour of the restored Wahhābi ruler is regarded as probable ; but the Wahhābis have never, it is alleged, meddled in the internal affairs of Widyān Dawasir, nor would they ever be permitted to do so. The present Amīr is one Masri-bin-Wuthailah ; he is described as tall, broad-shouldered and muscular, with a long beard, and is said to be extremely popular among his subjects.

DHA'ĀIN
الضائن

A village on the eastern coast of **Qatar** about 20 miles north of **Dōhah**. It is closely connected with the village of **Sumaismah**, which is distant from it only about 1 mile westwards. Dha'ain consists of about 150 houses, mostly of Āl Bū **Kuwārah** with some of **Hamaidāt** and a few of **Madhāhakah**. About 70 pearl boats belong to the place, besides 10 trading vessels and 10 fishing boats. Transport animals are 10 horses and 60 camels. Drinking water is from 'Awainat Bin-Husain, 6 miles inland.

An Arab principality, the most extensive and one of the two most important in Trucial '**Omān**.

Boundaries and divisions.—Upon the coast Abu Dhabi reaches from Khor-al-Ghanādhah, which divides it from the Shaikhdom of **Dibai**, on the east to Khor-al-'**Odaid** on the west—a distance of over 200 miles. The Shaikh of Abu Dhabi in 1895 claimed that his frontier extended to the bay of Umm-al-Hūl near **Wakrah** in **Qatar**, but his claim was not approved by the Government of India: Bishairīyah has also been named as the limit of his state in this direction, but no good reason has been adduced for supposing that his jurisdiction ever extended beyond Khor-al-'Odaid, though the northern shore of that inlet should perhaps be reckoned as included with the inlet itself in his territories. Inland the frontiers of Abu Dhabi are not defined: it is asserted that on the east they reach to the **Baraimi** Oasis, but without taking it in; and on the south they may presumably be placed at the margin of the **Ruba'-al-Khāli**.

The principal divisions of Abu Dhabi upon the mainland in order from west to east are '**Aqal, Mijan**, Sabákhat **Matti, Dhafrah** (including Bainūnah, Līwah and other minor tracts), possibly **Khatam**, and finally what may be called the home district in which the capital, Abu **Dhabi** Town, is situated: these tracts, except the last, all form the subjects of separate articles. The insular possessions of the Shaikh of Abu Dhabi are the islands of **Arzanah, Daiyīnah, Dalmah, Dās, Qarnain, Salāli, Yas** and **Zirko**, and, these also being described elsewhere under their own names, it only remains to deal here with the geography of the home division.

Physical characteristics and topography of the home division.—This part of the principality apparently consists altogether of undulating sandy desert with scanty grazing and a poor water-supply.

DHABI (ABU)*

ابو ظبي

PRIN-CIPALIT

---

* For authorities, maps, charts, etc., see first footnote to the article Trucial '**Omān**.

The following are the inhabited places and other points in it of which the names are most frequently heard :—

Name.	Position.	Nature.	Remarks.
Batīn بطين	On the northern shore of Khor-al-Batīn, about 1½ miles within the entrance.	A village of 130 date branch huts, of which 100 belong to the Āl Bū Mahair and the remainder to the Sūdān tribe.	There are some date plantations in which are situated the wells that yield the drinking water of the place. The inhabitants own 50 pearl boats, but no seagoing vessels.
Batīn (Khor-al-) * خور البطين	The north side of the entrance is about 1½ miles south-west of the nearest part of Abu Dhabi Town.	A creek of which the extent is probably great, but has not been ascertained; at high tide it is a large lagoon, at low tide it is full of uncovered sand banks; the 3 fathom line does not appear to reach its interior. Khor-al-Batīn communicates by way of Khor-al-Maqta' with the sea 2 or 3 miles north of Abu Dhabi Town.	Batīn village is on the north side of this Khor at 1½ miles inside the entrance; immediately in front of the village is a narrow channel which is 3 feet deep at low water. One of the islands in the lagoon carries a mound called Jabal Fataisah فطيسه which is 4½ miles south-south-west of Batīn village : on the north-western end of the same island, 1 mile from the mound is a hut. Another island lying 3 or 4 miles to the west of the last is known as Jazīrat-al-Bahrāni بحراني
Dhabi (Abu) ابو ظبي Town	...	...	See article Abu Dhabi Town.
Ghanādhah (Khor-al-) خور الغناضه	42 miles south-west of Dibai Town and 36 miles north-east of Abu Dhabi Town.	An inlet of the sea.	It marks the boundary between the Shaikhdoms of Dibai and Abu Dhabi, the north bank belonging to the former and the south bank to the latter.
Huwail (Bul) بو الحويل	35 to 40 miles west by north of the Baraimi Oasis.	Well.	One route between Abu Dhabi Town and the Baraimi Oasis passes this way.

* For a representation of part of this inlet see Commander G. Sinclair's *Part of Khor-al-Batin*, 1906.

DHABI (ABU) PRINCIPALITY 407

Name.	Position.	Nature.	Remarks.
Iblīs (Sūq) سوق ابليس	About 25 miles by road from Abu Dhabi Town on the way to the Baraimi Oasis.	An outcrop of light coloured sandstone, fantastically shaped, rising from the sand.	There is no water here, but the projection serves as a landmark for caravans. The name means " The Devil's Market."
Juhar الجحر	12 miles west of the Baraimi Oasis.	Wells containing good water.	There is some acacia jungle near. The country belongs to the Dhawāhir. The name is generally pronounced Yahar.
Maqta' المقطع	10 miles inland of Abu Dhabi Town, on the route to the Baraimi Oasis.	A ford on a creek which connects the interior of Khor-al-Batīn with the sea at a point 2 or 3 miles beyond Abu Dhabi Town.	Men on foot can cross only at low tide. A fort built on a sand bank in the middle of the creek commands the passage to the mainland. South of this ford the creek is called Khor-al-Maqta', and north of it Khor-as-Sa'aidiyāt سعيديات.
Mashairif مشيرف	About 16 miles south-east by east of Maqta'.	Wells.	Surrounded by desert.
Raknah ركنه	20 miles north-west of the Baraimi Oasis.	A camping ground with Ghāf trees.	Frequented by Bani Yās nomads, especially those of the Qumzān section.
Samaih سميح	6 or 7 miles east and somewhat south of Khor-al-Ghanādhah. The place is in Abu Dhabi territory.	A locality characterised by stony hills interspersed with sand: there are some 7 wells about 15 feet deep, but the water is drinkable only after rain.	Samaih is a convenient rendezvous for Bedoins and is used as such by the Shaikhs of both Abu Dhabi and Dibai when preparing for war. Bani Yās of the Rumaithāt section camp about here.
Silmīyah سلميه	Between Khatam and the sea, about 20 miles south-south-east of Abu Dhabi Town.	Wells.	...

Inhabitants.—The settled population of the principality are merely the residents of Abu **Dhabi** Town and Batīn village in the home division, the occupants of fixed settlements in the Līwah tract of the **Dhafrah** division, and the inhabitants of **Dalmah** island. The composition of the non-nomadic population is therefore as follows:—

Tribe.	Place.	Number of souls.
Bani Yās	Abu Dhabi Town	2,800
Do.	Līwah tract	5,100
Do.	Dalmah island	75
Al Bū Mahair	Abu Dhabi Town	500
Do.	Batīn	500
Sūdān	Abu Dhabi Town	375
Do.	Batīn	150
Persians	Abu Dhabi Town	500
Marar	Do.	200
Bahārinah	Do.	120
Miscellaneous	Do.	635

The total is thus about 11,000 souls.

The Bedouins of the principality are the remainder of the Bani **Yās** and nearly the whole of the **Manāsīr** tribe, or together about 3,300 persons. It is probable that the nomads of the **Dhawāhir**, Bani **Qitab** and **Na'īm** sometimes cross the indefinite eastern border into the Abu Dhabi Shaikhdom, but they can hardly be reckoned to belong to it.

Resources and trade.—There is no cultivation except a little of dates. Camels abound; but cattle, sheep and goats are few; and pearl diving is the principal occupation even of the Bedouins. In the whole of the Shaikhdom there are about 410 pearl boats, of which the majority are owned at Abu **Dhabi** Town and 50 at Batīn, the remainder being kept in creeks along the coast, or on islands; they are as a rule of small size and work on banks adjoining the coast or islands. There are about 10 seagoing vessels at Abu **Dhabi** Town, of which 2 are Sambūks and the rest large jollyboats merely: these run to **Bahrain, Basrah, Lingeh** and **Masqat,** but not to India.

DHABI (ABU) PRINCIPALITY

There is no trade worthy of mention outside the town of Abu Dhabi, in the article on which the subject is treated of. The villages of Muzaira'ah and Taraq in Līwah are small local centres for the distribution of goods.

Communications.—The routes in the principality are described in the article on Trucial 'Omān.

Administration.—The present Shaikh of Abu Dhabi, Zāid-bin-Khalīfah, rules his principality absolutely within the limits to which his powers of coercion extend; and, though his control over the Bedouin portion of his subjects is incomplete, as is the case more or less in all Arab Shaikhdoms, his authority over them is unusually great. His is by far the most powerful personality in Trucial 'Omān at the present time, and his influence is not only dominant throughout that region but extends to the independent Baraimi Oasis and even to 'Ibri in the Sultanate of 'Omān.

An estimate of his annual revenues, in so far as they are ascertainable, follows below: the principal item, it will be observed, is that derived from the pearl fisheries:—

Item.	Amount. $
Dues on pearl boats and operatives and other income dependent on the pearl industry	57,000
Commission levied by his son on transactions in pearls at Dalmah island	5,000
Agricultural taxes paid in kind by the Bani Yās of Līwah in Dhafrah	2,500
Five thousand Jirābs of dates worth $1 per Jirāb, rendered as tribute by the Dhawāhir of the Baraimi Oasis	5,000
Lucerne supplied by the same Dhawāhir for 100 tribal horses maintained by the Shaikh in the Baraimi Oasis	3,000
A cash subsidy paid him by the Sultān of 'Omān for restraining the Bedouins of the Baraimi Oasis and Dhāhirah and preventing raids by them on the villages of Bātinah, perhaps	3,000
TOTAL	75,500

The last item, though it has been in existence for at least 10 years, has only recently come to notice: the payment is of a private and personal nature and its amount is necessarily uncertain, but the fact that it is regularly made throws much light on the present political position in 'Omān.

Foreign relations and interests.—The ruler of Abu Dhabi is one of the Trucial Shaikhs, whose position is described in the article on Trucial

'Oman. The only foreign interests in the principality are British, and these are described in the article on Abu Dhabi Town.

DHABI (ABU) ابو ظبي TOWN

The capital of the Abu Dhabi Principality in Trucial 'Omān and the only settlement of importance which that principality contains.

Abu Dhabi Town is situated on the coast of Trucial 'Omān about 88 miles south-west of Shārjah Town: it extends for about 1½ miles along the low sandy coast and consists chiefly of mat huts with a few stone buildings. At sea, 15 miles to the northward, is Hadd, the nearest of the Persian Gulf pearl banks. The largest edifice is the fort of the Shaikh at a little distance inland behind the town; not far from it, on the outskirts of the town proper, is the separate bazaar of the Indian traders. The anchorage* for large vessels is totally unsheltered and lies more than two miles off the shore. At the back of the town are some stunted date trees and water is obtained from wells: 35 years ago most of the drinking water of the place used to be fetched from Dibai, but recently potable water has become obtainable in the vicinity of the town, especially at a place 3 or 4 miles from it; pits are dug in which the water collects at 4 to 5 feet below the ground level. Immediately to the south of the town is the large shallow lagoon of Khor-al-Batīn, and to the east a creek connected with it, both of which are described in the article on the Abu Dhabi Principality.

The population of the town may be about 6,000 souls, about ½ Bani Yās and the rest other tribes. The Bani Yās sections are Āl Bū Falāh, 40 persons; Qubaisāt, 380; Mahāribah, 300; Āl Bū Falāsah, 200; Qumzān, 250; Āl Bū Hamīr, 300; Rumaithāt, 500; Mazārī', 300; and Hawāmil, 500. The other tribes are Āl Bū Mahair, 500; Sūdān, 375; Marar, 200; Thamairāt ثميرات, 120; Āl Bin Nāsir آل بن ناصر, 120; Āl Bū 'Amīm آل بو عميم, 120; Khamārah, خمارة (said to be originally from Khamīr in Persia), 375; Halālamah, حلالمه, 75; Dahailāt دحيلات, 200; and Bahārinah, 120. To these must be added a Persian community of about 500 persons and 65 Hindus.

The inhabitants of Abu Dhabi live almost entirely by pearl diving and fishing or in a few cases by petty trade: they have no ordinary

---

* A plan of this anchorage is given in Chart No. 2373—2837-A.

The Fort of the Shaikh at Abu Dhabi.
(Herr H. Burchardt.)

COPYRIGHT.

cultivation and very few dates. Particulars of shipping are given in the article on Abu **Dhabi** Principality. About 750 camels belong to the place, and there are 85 horses; but of the horses all except 5 belong to the Shaikh and his family. Trade with the interior is insignificant, being only with the **Baraimi** Oasis and with the Bani **Yās** and **Manāsīr** tribes. There are over 70 shops of all sorts in the Abu Dhabi bazaar; 40 are kept by Persians, 19 by Hindus and 10 by Arabs. Pearls are the sole export. The Hindus import cloth, rice, coffee and sugar besides dealing in pearls.

British interests are represented here by the Hindu trading community, all from Tatta in Sind; the majority have their families with them, and most of them take leave to India at intervals of about a year. In the pearl season the number of Hindus is about doubled. No Muhammadan Indians do business at this place.

DHAFĪR*

ظفير
ضفير

An important Bedouin tribe whose territory extends from the right bank of the **Euphrates** about **Samāwah** and **Sūq-ash-Shuyūkh** westwards to the **Birāk** or **Darb Zubaidah**, a section of the pilgrim route between **Najaf** and Makkah, and south-eastwards to **Kuwait**. They are sometimes found in the **Nafūd** as far west as the route between **Jauf-al-'Āmir** and **Hāil** and they maintain occasional relations with the latter place. Their neighbours on the north-west are the **'Anizah**; on the west the **Shammar** of Jabal **Shammar**, with whom they are at feud; on the south the **Mutair** and **'Ajmān**; and on the east the **Muntafik**. They are said to visit places on the **Euphrates** occasionally for the purpose of obtaining supplies, but to a great extent their dealings with Turkish **'Irāq** are carried on indirectly through other tribes.

The principal sections of the Dhafīr who live in the direction of **Kuwait** are the Batūn بطون, Samīd صميد, and Ma'ālīb معاليب: with them are found a small section, called Kathīr, of the once celebrated Bani **Khālid** tribe. The Dhafīr are all nomads and do not engage in trade, but they own large flocks and herds besides camels. In religion they are Sunnis of the Māliki sect. They are at present (1905) on good terms with the Shaikh of **Kuwait**, where their smiths'

---

* A genealogical table of the Shaikhs of the Dhafīr by Captain Knox, Political Agent at Kuwait, forms an appendix to his diary No. 19 for the week ending 8th May 1907.

work is executed ; and, perhaps for this reason, the subsidies formerly paid to them by the Turkish Government in the Basrah Wilāyat, generally at **Nāsirīyah**, have been suspended for the last four years. They have no property in Turkish territory. The tribe is now well armed with modern rifles.

DHAFRAH*
الضفرة

The westernmost and least known part of **'Omān**, a subdivision of Trucial **'Omān**.

Boundaries.—Dhafrah lies between the Persian Gulf on the north and the **Ruba'-al-Khāli** or Great Desert of Southern Arabia on the south ; on the west it is bounded by Sabákhat **Matti** and **Jāfūrah**, and on the east by **Khatam**.

Divisions.—The huge area thus defined comprises at least 5 separate tracts which are distinguished by names, but the absence of striking natural features makes it difficult to determine their relative positions and extent. Indeed there is reason to think that the internal boundaries of Dhafrah are somewhat vague, and that the names of the tracts are not employed by all Bedouins in strictly the same sense. The 5 tracts in question are Taff طف, Dhafrah proper, Bainūnah بينونه, Qufa قفا and Līwah ليوه, of which last name the correct form is said to be Al-Juwa الجوا; of these Līwah and Bainūnah are the most important.

All authorities agree that Līwah is the southernmost and furthest inland of the divisions of Dhafrah; that its length, which is eastwards and westwards, approaches, if it does not exceed, 175 miles ; that its breadth is insignificant in comparison with its length ; and that the village of Shāh is situated in it almost exactly midway between its two extremities. To determine the position of Līwah it is therefore only necessary to determine the position of Shāh, but here we are confronted by serious discrepancies of evidence ; the most probable view, however, appears to

---

* *Authorities*—Major P. Z. Cox, Political Resident in the Persian Gulf, Captain F. B. Prideaux, Political Agent in **Bahrain**, and 'Abdul Latīf, Residency Agent at **Shārjah**, all from native information ; also Col. Miles in his *Route between Sohar and el-Bereymi* in 'Omān. The most reliable map of the interior is *Map of Dhafrah, Līwah, etc.*, 1906, compiled by Major P. Z. Cox from native information. Charts of the coast are specified in the footnote to article Trucial **Omān**, especially cancelled **Chart No. 19-B**.

be that Shāh is situated 50 to 55 miles inland from the coast upon a line drawn due south from Rās Miqaishit, the western point of the Salāli group of islands, and that it is about 90 miles south-west by south of Abu **Dhabi** Town. If this opinion errs, it is probably by bringing Shāh somewhat too near to the coast and too far to westwards.

The position of Bainūnah depends upon that of a well Da'afas, which undoubtedly belongs to this tract, though its position in the same is not, perhaps, so central as that of Shāh in Līwah. According to the report which for several reasons appears most reliable, Da'afas is about 30 miles south-east of Jabal Dhannah (on the coast opposite **Yās** island) and about 20 miles inland from the nearest point on the sea. The alternative position attributed to Da'afas is very much more southerly and more easterly than that just described. It is not disputed that Bainūnah is between Līwah and the sea, nor that it reaches to the westernmost extremity of Dhafrah, in other words to the border of Sabákhat **Matti**.

Of the remaining tracts Qufa is undoubtedly interposed between Līwah and Bainūnah and is long from east to west and narrow from north to south.

Taff is, by general consent, a maritime strip extending the whole length of Dhafrah with an average depth inland of about 15 miles. Its westernmost section, that reaching for about 25 miles on either side of Jabal Dhannah, is possibly particularised as Taff Bainūnah.

The last tract requiring to be located is Dhafrah proper, and the name may be taken to signify so much of Dhafrah in the wider sense as is not included in any of the foregoing divisions. The position of Dhafrah proper with reference to Bainūnah is doubtful; but it is probably on the east while Bainūnah is on the west and the distances of the two from the sea are similar. The wells of Kafaifah, it may be added, seem to be near the point at which the tracts of Bainūnah and Dhafrah proper meet one another and the tract of Taff.

Following then the opinion which seems most worthy of acceptance we may provisionally arrange the divisions of Dhafrah as follows:—

1. Along the coast a strip 15 miles wide, which for nearly 100 miles on the east is called Taff, and for 50 miles on the west Taff Bainūnah.
2. Behind the coastal strip a belt 40 miles wide composed of Dhafrah proper, Bainūnah and Qufa: of these Dhafrah proper (30 miles broad) adjoins Taff throughout its length, and Bainūnah (20 miles broad) adjoins Taff Bainūnah, also

throughout its length, while Qufa fills the space remaining on the south of these two.

3. Inland of Qufa, and like Qufa roughly parallel to the sea, another belt measuring about 175 miles in length and perhaps 20 miles in breadth: this belt is Līwah.

Physical characteristics.—The maritime tracts of Taff and Taff Bainūnah contain no features of interest except a few small hills, which are possibly volcanic. The shore is stony, and at a little distance inland swamps are said to exist, interspersed with stony mounds. Vegetation is chiefly Abal and Hams.

Dhafrah proper and Bainūnah are said to resemble one another in character: they form, apparently, a fairly level expanse of heavy red sand or reddish soil with occasional sand dunes of lighter colour and gravelly patches. Dhafrah proper, at least, is somewhat higher in level than Taff. Neither tract possesses any trees; but in Dhafrah proper there is some vegetation of Arta and Hādh, and in Bainūnah the Arta, Markh and Abal are found: both districts afford a considerable amount of grazing for camels. The wells of Dhafrah proper seem to vary in depth between 1 and 2 fathoms and those of Bainūnah between 1½ and 7 fathoms, the average in the case of the latter tract being 3 fathoms.

Qufa is an inhospitable region of sandy ridges with no vegetation except a few shrubs of Arta and very little water; but the few wells that occur are shallow, not exceeding 2 fathoms.

Līwah is the most remarkable of all the tracts. It consists mainly of white undulating sand dunes, altogether without vegetation; but it contains over a score of small depressions, disposed in series or chains from east to west. These depressions are divided from one another by sandy wastes; but at the bottom of each depression there is fertile soil, supporting the cultivation of a village which generally stands upon a sandy eminence near by. These low-lying oases contain plantations of date palms, which in a few cases are of considerable extent. The water level in Līwah, doubtless in the depressions, appears to be on the average at 2 fathoms beneath the surface; and except at Tharwānīyah a depth of 4 fathoms is not, it would seem, ever exceeded.

Throughout Dhafrah, to speak generally, the water of the wells is of fairly good quality, and not very scarce. The wells themselves are either unlined or lined only with date sticks and leaves; the only exceptions to the rule appear to be the Bābah well in Bainūnah, which is reported to be half lined with masonry, and a well called Saqar صقر, also in Bainūnah but not precisely located, which is said to be entirely so lined. This

DHAFRAH

peculiarity is no doubt due largely to the shallowness of the wells, but it also seems to indicate firmness in the soil.

Inhabitants.—In the whole of Dhafrah only two tribes are found, the Bani Yās and the **Manāsīr**; the former are settled rather than nomadic, while the latter are altogether Bedouins. Of Līwah they are jointly occupants, but the permanent villages, called Mahdhar مـحـضـر, all belong to the Bani Yās, the settlements of the **Manāsīr** being untenanted except in summer while the date harvest is in progress. Among the **Manāsīr** date plantations are joint tribal property, but with the Bani Yās they belong to individual owners. The Bani Yās of Dhafrah are semi-civilised; some of them trade with Abu **Dhabi** and even **Dibai** and correspond with those places. The dwellings of both tribes are huts of date sticks and leaves: the **Manāsīr**, when their sojourn in Līwah is over for the year, close theirs up and stop the adjacent wells, it is said, with sand. Dhafrah proper is the principal grazing ground of the **Manāsīr** while Bainūnah contains the favourite pastures of the Bani Yās; but in winter the **Manāsīr** range as far west as **Qatar** and in summer their camels are left with those of the Bani Yās in Bainūnah. The Bani Yās of Dhafrah take a share in the pearl fishery and own a number of boats which are kept at Bandar Radaim, Khor Mughairah and Bandar Mirfah upon the coast. The number of the Bani Yās ordinarily in Dhafrah may be reckoned at 5,100 souls, while that of the **Manāsīr** is the entire strength of the tribe or 1,400 persons; and besides these there are about 70 Bedouin families of the **Marar** tribe who are accustomed to wander in Līwah. The whole population of Dhafrah may therefore be estimated at 6,500 souls, but it is fluctuating.

Topography.—The following is a detailed list of the villages, settlements, wells and other principal points in Dhafrah according to the best information available:—

Name.	Position.	Nature.	Remarks.
Abyadh (Abul) ابو الابيض	...	The middle portion of the island of which the east end is called Salāli.	See article Salāli.
'Ajūz (Bada'-al-) بدع العجوز	About 12 miles south-south-east of Da'afas. In Bainūnah.	A well.	This well is 7 fathoms deep and at present out of repair.

Name.	Position.	Nature.	Remarks.
'Aqailah العقيله	Inland, about 10 miles south of Jabal Barākah on the coast. Probably in Bainūnah.	A well.	The depth is 5 fathoms. Also called 'Aghailah عغيله .
'Asi العصي	About 10 miles north-west of Hamaim. In Qufa.	Do.	The depth is $1\frac{1}{4}$ fathoms.
'Attāb عطاب	About 10 miles north of Muzaira'ah. In Līwah.	A permanent hamlet of 20 huts of Banī Yās of the Qubaisāt section.	The present headman is Buti-bin-Khādim, who is also over Muzaira'ah and Qarmidah but generally resides at Abu Dhabi Town. There are a fair number of date palms and 20 wells of 2 fathoms depth.
Ayih عايه	About 30 miles east-south-east of Da'afas and the same north-north-west of Shāh. In Dhafrah proper.	A well and camping place of 25 families of Banī Yās of the Mazārī'section.	The depth is 2 fathoms.
Bābah البابه	About 12 miles east of Da'afas. In Bainūnah.	A well.	The water is good. The well is about 3 fathoms deep and to half its depth it is lined with masonry.
Barākah (Jabal) جبل براكه	On the coast about 16 miles south-west of Jabal Dhannah.	A hill.	...
Bārid (Bū) بو بارد	A mile or two north of Muhibbi. In Bainūnah.	A well.	Water is at 2 fathoms.
Bazam (Khor-al-) خور البزم	Off the coast of Taff and Taff Bainūnah, its entrance being off Rās Ijlā', which is described below, and its head between Salāli Island and the mainland. The east end is 50 miles from Abu Dhabi Town	An extensive blind channel, parallel to the shore and situated between it and a great reef called Bazam; it is accessible to small vessels and contains the anchorages of Bandar Mirfah, Khor Mughairah and Bandar Radaim which are separately	Or Bazummi بزمي This inlet is 50 miles long, and the width at the entrance is 5 miles diminishing to 1 mile at the head: it is open to the west and closed to the east. The soundings diminish irregularly from 10 fathoms to 1; in 1907, in an attempt

DHAFRAH

Name.	Position.	Nature.	Remarks.
	and the west end is the same distance from the border of Sabákhat Matti.	described in this table.	to explore it, a cast of 5 fathoms was immediately followed by another of 1½.
Da'afas دعفس	The position of this place is discussed in the text above. It is admitted by all authorities to be in Bainūnah and is a convenient point from which to fix others.	A well.	The water, at 1½ fathoms, is good.
Dāhin داهن	About 10 miles north-west of Qa'aisah. In Līwah.	A summer hamlet of 6 houses of Manāsīr of the Al Bū Mindhir section.	The headman is Rāshid-bin-Māni'. There are about 250 date palms. Wells are 4 in number and only 1 fathom deep.
Dhabaibah ضبيبه	15 to 20 miles east-north-east of Tharwānīyah. In Qufa.	A well, at present out of repair.	The depth is 2 fathoms.
Dhafīr ظفير	About 10 miles south-west of Muzaira'ah. In Līwah.	A permanent village of 30 huts of Bani Yās of the Maharibah section.	The chief man is Hamad-bin-Aghtail who is also over Taraq. There are large date plantations and about 30 wells 4 fathoms deep, but the water is brackish.
Dhannah (Jabal) جبل ظنه	On the Taff Bainūnah coast, on the promontory which runs out towards Yās island.	A hill.	The height is 350 feet. Two or three miles to the east of this hill is a small inlet known as Barqah Hāiz برقه حائز; 3 miles to the east of Barqah Hāiz is a small promontory called Ruwais رويس; and 4 miles east of Ruwais is another slight headland styled Rās Dhubai'ah ضبيعه. The sea from Jabal Dhannah to Rās Dhubai'ah forms a bay of which the name is Dōhat Dhannah.

2 E

Name.	Position.	Nature.	Remarks.
Dhawaihir ظريهر	About 25 miles west by south of Shāh. In Līwah.	A village of 30 huts of Bani Yās of the Āl Falāh and Qubaisāt sections.	...
Hādhi الحاضي	Some 10 or 12 miles east of Subakhah. In Līwah.	A permanent hamlet of 15 huts of Bani Yās of the Hawāmil section.	Rāshid-bin-Humaid is the chief man, as he is also of Shāh, Subakhah and Wazīl. Here are 25 wells 1 fathom deep and considerable date plantations. It is remarked that the inhabitants irrigate their fields by manual labour instead of employing animals and that they are purely Hadhar.
Hafīf الحفيف	About 12 miles east-north-east of Khannūr. In Līwah.	A permanent village of 50 huts of Bani Yās, of the Mazāri' section.	The date groves are extensive and there are about 30 wells 3 fathoms deep. The place is under Fāris-bin-'Ali of Khannūr and Mārīyah.
Halīb الحليب	25 or 30 miles north-east of Qa'aisah. On the border of Khatam.	A well.	The depth is about 2½ fathoms.
Hamaim حميم	Between 85 and 90 miles east of Shāh. The easternmost village in Līwah.	A summer village of 30 huts of Manāsīr of the Āl Taraif subsection.	There are 5 wells, about 1½ fathoms deep, and a good many date trees. The present headman is Suwīd-bin-Ghadaiyar, under whom also is Qa'aisah.
Hamrah (Bada'-al-) بدع الحمرة	15 to 20 miles north of 'Attāb. Probably in Dhafrah proper.	A well.	One fathom deep.
Hawāya الحوايا	About 15 miles north-east of Bada'-al-Hamrah.	Do.	The water is at less than 1 fathom.
Huwailah الحويلة	In the extreme west of Līwah.	A permanent village of 40 huts of Bani Yās of the Mazāri' section.	The depth of the wells is 2½ fathoms.

DHAFRAH

Name.	Position.	Nature.	Remarks.
'Idd العد	About 12 miles west of Khannūr. In Līwah.	A summer village of 50 huts of **Manā-sīr** of the Āl Bū Mindhir section.	There are some 60 wells with an average depth of 2 fathoms. The date plantations are fairly extensive. The place is under Rāshid-bin-Māni' who generally lives at Sarait and is over that place and Tharwānīyah also.
Ijlā' (Rās) راس اجلاع	On the coast 20 miles east of Jabal Dhannah: it marks the entrance of Khor-al-Bazam.	A headland shaped like a fort with towers.	To the west of this cape at 4 or 5 miles is a small inlet called Khor Manāif مناىف; and to the east, at about 2½ and 5 miles respectively, are a small inlet known as Khor Thumairīyah خور ثميريه and a rock which goes by the name of Qassār Bū Khinn قصار بو خن.
Jarairah جريره	About 2 miles south of Jarrah. In Līwah.	A summer hamlet of 6 huts of **Manāsīr** of the Āl Bū Sha'ar section.	There are some date palms and 4 wells of 1 fathom deep. The headman of this place and of Jarrah and Mōsal is Muhammed-bin-Jaraiw.
Jarash (Bada') بدع جرش	About 25 miles south-west of Bandar Mirfah. In Taff Bainūnah.	A well.	1½ fathoms deep.
Jarrah جرّ	About 20 miles south-west of Hamaim. In Līwah.	A summer hamlet of 10 huts of **Manāsīr** of the Āl Bū Sha'ar section.	Or Yarrah يرّ. Wells number 8 and are 1 fathom deep: there are a good many date palms. Three horses are owned here. Muhammad-bin-Jaraiw is chief man of this place and of Jarairah and Mōsal.

2 E 2

Name.	Position.	Nature.	Remarks.
Kafaifah الكفيفه	About 16 miles south-west of Khor Mughairah on the coast. It appears to be in Taff, but it is sometimes said to be in Bainūnah or Dhafrah proper; from this it may be inferred that it is near the meeting place of the 3 tracts.	A well.	Often pronounced Chifaifah. The water, at 1½ fathoms, is good.
Kaiwrah كيوره	15 to 20 miles east of Hamaim. In Līwah.	A spot, marked by 10 Ghāf trees, which is a rendezvous for parties of marauding Manāsir when about to enter 'Omān.	There are 8 wells less than a fathom deep: the water is brackish.
Kaiyih كيه	About 8 miles north of Khannūr. In Līwah.	A settlement of 20 huts of Bani Yās of the Āl Bū Falāh, Āl Falāh and Āl Sultān sections.	Do.
Khannūr خنور	About 55 miles west by south of Shāh. In Līwah.	A permanent village of 100 huts of Bani Yās of the Mazāri' section.	There are about 80 wells here, 2 fathoms in depth; and the date groves are extensive for Līwah, including according to one account as many as 14,000 palms. Fāris-bin-'Ali, who lives here, is head-man of Hafīf and Mārīyah as well as of this place. A fort which once existed at Khannūr was destroyed by Shaikh Jāsim-bin-Thāni of Qatar in one of his invasions of Līwah.
Lashtān (Umm) ام لشطان	About 30 miles west of Da'afas. In Bainūnah, at its western extremity.	A well.	The water is brackish and the depth 2 fathoms or more. This halting place is much frequented by Bedouins passing between Dhafrah and Qatar, Hasa or Jabrīn.

Name.	Position.	Nature.	Remarks.
Latīr (I) لطير	30 or 35 miles west-south-west of Shāh. In Līwah.	A permanent village of 15 huts of Bani Yās of the Qanaisāt section.	The depth of the wells is 3 fathoms.
Latīr (II) لطير	About 35 miles south-east of Bandar Radaim on the coast. In the centre of Dhafrah proper.	A well and camping place of 30 families of Bani Yās of the Mazārī' section.	The depth is 1 to 2 fathoms.
Lidāmah لدامه	...	A camping ground of 20 families of Bani Yās of the Mazārī' section.	...
Ma'asār معصار	15 to 20 miles north and somewhat west of Qa'aisah. In Dhafrah proper.	A well.	The depth is 1 to 2 fathoms.
Mārīyah ماريه	About 7 miles north-west of Khannūr. In Līwah.	A permanent village of 70 huts of Bani Yās of the Mazāri and Qubaisāt sections.	There are about 30 wells, 2 fathoms deep, and dates are cultivated on a considerable scale. With Hafīf this place is under Fāris-bin-'Ali of Khannūr.
Miqaishit مقيشط	...	The western part of the island of Salāli.	See article Salāli. The western tip of Miqaishit is called Rās Miqaishit.
Mirfah (Bandar) بندر مرفه	On the coast of Taff, in Khor-al-Bazam, about 7 miles east-south-east of Rās Ruwaisīyah.	An anchorage where some of the pearl divers of Dhafrah keep their boats.	Bani Yās of the Bani Shikr section make this place a base of pearling operations.
Mōsal موصل	About 20 miles west of Jarrah. In Līwah.	A summer hamlet of 10 huts of Manāsīr of the Āl Bū Sha'ar section.	There are 5 wells of 1 fathom deep and some dates. The inhabitants own 3 horses. With Jarrah and Jarairah this place is under Muhammad-bin-Jaraiw.
Mughairah (Khor) مغيره	On the coast of Taff, in Khor-al-Bazam, midway between Bandars Mirfah and Radaim, and about 8 miles from either.	An inlet and anchorage where some of the boats of the pearl fishers of Dhafrah are kept.	Bani Yās of the Mahāribah, Qanaisāt, Qubaisāt and Āl Sultān sections make this a base for their pearling operations.

Name.	Position.	Nature.	Remarks.
Muhibbi مهيبي	About 8 miles south-east of Rakaiyah. In Bainūnah.	A well.	The depth is 2 fathoms.
Mulaisah مليسه	About 12 miles inland, south-eastwards, from the coast at Jabal Barākah. In Taff Bainūnah.	Do.	Do.
Mūqab موقب	About 12 miles east by north of Khannūr. In Līwah.	A permanent village of 80 huts of Bani Yās of the Bani Shikr section.	The people are pearl fishers in the season, working chiefly from Bandar Mirfah. The wells at Mūqab are 3 fathoms deep.
Mutawwa' (Bada'-al-) بدع المطوع	About 15 miles west of Da'afas. In Bainūnah.	Do.	The well is 5 fathoms deep, but the water is good.
Muzaira'ah مزيرعه	About 12 miles south-south-west of Shāh. In Līwah.	A permanent village of 80 huts of Bani Yās of the Mahāribah and Qubaisāt sections.	There are over 100 wells of an average depth of 4 fathoms; the water is said to be very pure and transparent. The date groves are the most extensive in Līwa. There are some storerooms or Makhāzin at which the villagers and Bedouins of the neighbourhood buy what they require. The headman is Buti-bin-Khādim, who generally resides at Abu Dhabi town and under whom are also the villages of 'Attāb and Qarmidah.
Nimairīyan النميريه	About 33 miles south from the easternmost foot of Khor-al-Batīn which is near Abu Dhabi Town. In Dhafrah proper.	A well.	The depth is between 1 and 2 fathoms.
Nishāsh نشاش	About 8 miles north-west of Jarrah. In Līwah.	A locality with water.	Frequented by Bani Yās. The wells are 2 fathoms deep.

Name.	Position.	Nature.	Remarks.
Qa'aisah قعيسه	About 12 miles west-south-west of Hamaim. In Līwah.	A summer hamlet of 15 huts of Manāsīr of the Āl Bū Rahamah section.	There are 6 wells: about 2 fathoms deep and a few date trees. The inhabitants have 5 horses. The chief man is Suwīd-bin-Ghadaiyar, to whom Hamaim also is subject.
Qarmidah قرمده	About 9 miles east by north of Muzaira'ah. In Līwah.	A permanent village of 40 huts of Bani Yās of the Mahāribah, Qubaisāt and Āl Sultān sections.	There are about 10 wells of a fathom depth, also a few date palms. This village, with Muzaira'ah and 'Attāb is under Butibin-Khādim who usually lives at Abu Dhabi Town.
Qumzān (Bada'-al-) بدع القمزان	About 20 miles south-west by west of Da'afas. In Bainūnah.	A well, at present out of repair.	Water is at 3 fathoms.
Qutūf قطوف	About 25 miles east and somewhat south of Khannūr. The southernmost village in Līwah.	A village of 25 huts of Bani Yās of the Qubaisāt section.	...
Radaim (Bandar) بندر رديم	On the coast of Taff, in Khor-al-Bazam near its head and about 14 miles east of Bandar Mirfah.	An anchorage where some of the boats of the pearl diving inhabitants of Dhafrah are kept.	This is a base of pearling operations to the Hawāmil, Mazāri', Qasal and Āl Sultān sections of the Bani Yās. Some of the Āl Falāh and Āl Bū Falāh who have no boats of their own also go pearling from this place.
Rakaiyah الركيّه	About 12 miles south of 'Aqailah. In Bainūnah.	A well.	The depth is 2 fathoms.
Rakaiz (Ghait-ar-) غيت الركيز	Between Mughīlat-ar-Rakaiz and Subakhah. Perhaps in Līwah.	Do.	One fathom deep.
Rakaiz (Mughīlat-ar-) مغيلة الركيز	About 12 miles north-north-east of Subakhah. In Qufa.	Do.	Between 1 and 2 fathoms in depth.

Name.	Position.	Nature.	Remarks.
Ramrāmah رمرامه	Inland, about 25 miles south of Bandar Radaim on the coast. In Dhafrah proper.	A well.	The depth is 2 fathoms.
Riksah الركسه	15 to 20 miles west of 'Idd. In Līwah, at its extreme western end.	Do.	Water is at 1 fathom. There is a small date plantation here belonging to the villagers of 'Idd.
Ruwaisīyah (Rās) راس اويسيه	On the coast about half way up Khor-al-Bazam and 13 miles west of Rās Miqaishit.	A small cape.	...
Salāli سلالي Island	...	...	See article Salāli.
Sālimi سالمي	Nearly 10 miles north-north-east of Muzaira-'ah. In Līwah.	A village of 30 huts of Bani Yās of the Mahāribah section.	...
Sarait صريط	About 15 miles east-south-east of Shāh. In Līwah.	A summer village of 20 huts of Manāsīr of the Āl Bū Mindhir section.	There are 5 wells 2 fathoms deep, and a few date palms. The headman is Rāshid-bin-Māni' who generally lives here but is also over the villages of 'Idd and Tharwānīyah. He has 10 horses and in winter goes as far as Qatar.
Sawāmi' (Rās) راس صوامع	On the coast midway between the nearest parts of the islands of Salāli and Yās, about 30 miles from either.	A bluff headland.	About 4 miles west of Rās Sawāmi' is a small cape known as Rās Qurain-al-'Aish قرين العيش; to the east at 4 and 8 miles are Khor Khasaifah خصيفه and Khor Haramiyah هرميه between which at a short distance inland is a small hill called Jabal Khasaifah.

Name.	Position.	Nature.	Remarks.
Shāh شاه	The position of this place, which is universally admitted to be central in Līwah, is discussed in the text above.	A permanent village of 60 huts of Bani Yās of the Āl Bū-Falāh, Hawāmil and Qasal sections.	Wells number about 30 and are 1 to 2 fathoms deep; there are extensive plantations of dates. The headman is Rāshid-bin-Humaid who is also over Hādhi, Subakhah and Wazīl.
Shawaibir (Badu'-ash-) بدع الشويبر	About 40 miles south-east of Abu Dhabi Town. In the north-eastern corner of Dhafrah proper.	A well.	Depth is 1½ fathoms.
Shidaq-al-Kalb شدق الكلب	About 10 miles west of Muzaira'ah. In Līwah.	A village of 40 huts of Bani Yās of the Āl Falāh, Qubaisāt and Āl Sultān sections.	The name means "Corner of the Dog's Mouth."
Shwaihāt شويهات	On the coast of Taff Bainūnah, about midway between Jabal Barākah and Jabal Dhannah.	A locality where water is not obtainable except after rain.	This place has been used by the Shaikh of Abu Dhabi as an advanced base for military operations against Qatar.
Subakhah صبخه	About 15 miles east of Shāh. In Līwah.	A permanent village of 30 huts of Bani Yās of the Hawāmil section.	There are 30 wells of about 2 fathoms depth and the date plantations are extensive. The headman is Rāshid-bin-Humaid, to whom also Hādhi, Shāh and Wazīl are subject.
Suhail سهيل	About 25 miles north of Hādhi. In Dhafrah proper.	A camping ground of 15 families of Bani Yās of the Mazāri' section	...
Taraif الطريف	About 6 miles inland from Bandar Radaim, southward. In Taff.	A well, at present disused.	Water, when obtainable, is at 1 fathom.
Taraq الطرق	About 7 miles north-east of Muzaira'ah. In Līwah.	A permanent village of about 40 huts of Bani Yās of the Mahāribah section.	There are 40 wells about 2 fathoms deep, and extensive plantations. Two storekeepers sell rice and coffee. The headman is Hamad-bin-Aghtail who is also over Dhafīr.

Name.	Position.	Nature.	Remarks.
Thāmir (Kharaijat) خريجة ثامر	About 10 miles south-east of 'Aqailah. In Bainūnah.	A well.	The depth is 2 fathoms.
Tharwānīyah الثروانيه	About midway between Shāh and Hamaim in a straight line between the two. In Līwah.	A summer village of 30 huts of **Manāsīr** of the Āl Bū Mindhir section. There are also permanent Bani **Yās** of the Hawāmil section, about 25 households.	The wells, about 30 in number, are 6 fathoms deep and the date groves are extensive. There are 4 horses. Rāshid-bin-Māni' is over this settlement as well as over Sarait (where he generally lives) and 'Idd.
Thāih ثائك	About 15 miles inland, southwards from the sea; and 50 miles west by south from Shawaibir. In Dhafrah proper.	A well.	Water is at 2 fathoms.
Wahaidah الوهيده	6 or 7 miles south-east of Sarait. In Līwah.	A village of 25 huts of Bani **Yās** of the Hawāmil section.	Depth of wells is 3 fathoms.
Waralah الوره	About 20 miles east of Ghait-ar-Rakaiz.	Do.	Water is at 1 fathom. The place is much frequented by **Manāsīr**.
Wazīl وزيل	3 or 4 miles south of Shāh. In Līwah.	A permanent village of 20 huts of Bani **Yās** of the Hawāmil section.	Wells number 10 and are 1 fathom deep. There are a few date palms. Rāshid-bin-Humaid of Shāh, etc., is Shaikh also of this place.
Wutaid (Jabal) جبل وتيد	On the coast, at the extreme west end of Taff Bainūnah.	A hill.	It marks the boundary between Dhafrah and Sabákhat **Matti**. ...
Yaif اليف	About 35 miles west of Shāh. In Līwah.	A village of 25 huts of Bani **Yās** of the Qubaisāt section.	
Yās ياس Island	...	...	See article **Yās** Island.

Communications.—Desert routes from Bandar Mīrfah, Khor Mughairah and Bandar Radaim connect the villages of Līwah with the coast. The usual stages are given as follows:—

(1) Bandar Mīrfah, Bada' Jarash, Bābah, Majmūlah مجموله, Bada' Muhammad محمد and Kaiyih in Līwah.

(2) Khor Mughairah, Kafaifah, Bābah, Badī'ah بديعه ' Mashairib مشيرب, and Muzaira'ah in Līwah.

(3) Bandar Radaim, Bazummi برمي, Dhuwannain ذونين, Qaryān قريان, Bada' Saif بدع سيف, Mughailah مغيله, Istāl استال and Shāh in Līwah.

Political position.—Dhafrah, as already remarked, is a part of Trucial 'Omān, and the whole of it falls within the political sphere of the Shaikh of Abu Dhabi to whose principality it may accordingly be considered to belong. The Bani Yās of Līwah count themselves subjects of the Shaikh, but the extent to which the Manāsīr are amenable to his influence is doubtful. Dhafrah has been at times the scene of prolonged contests between the Shaikh of Abu Dhabi and the principal Shaikh of Qatar, the latter making raids into the Līwah tract, and the former retaliating by means of expeditions against Qatar, in the course of which he has been known to utilise Shwaihāt upon the coast as an advanced base for his operations.

DHĀHI-RAH* ظاهره

Limits and extent.—A large district of the 'Omān Sultanate lying between the Western Hajar on the north-east and the Ruba'-al-Khāli or Great Desert on the south-west: it is divided from 'Omān Proper by Jabal-al-Kor at its south-eastern end and meets the district of Jau at its north-western extremity. Dhāhirah thus forms an elongated parallelogram about 100 miles in length from north-west to south-east and about 50 in breadth from north-east to south-west.

Physical characteristics.—Dhāhirah consists of a plain of uneven surface sloping down from the hills of Hajar to the Ruba'-al-Khāli, in which the whole of its drainage is lost. It has two principal valleys, Wādi Dhank, which comes down from Hajar to the town of Dhank and

---

* For the signification of the name see footnote under Bāṭinah. For authorities and maps see article 'Omān Sultanate (first footnote).

thence runs to the **Ruba'-al-Khāli** preserving throughout its course a general direction from east to west, and Wādi-al-**Kabīr** which, descending from **Hajar** west-south-westwards towards '**Ibri**, becomes in the neighbourhood of that town Wādi **Sanaisal** and receives from the east Wādi **Sharsah** and Wādi-al-'**Ain**, the former joining it a little above, and the latter a little below '**Ibri**. The hills which diversify the surface of Dhāhirah are outliers of **Hajar**; chief among them are detached or semi-detached eminences around '**Ibri** which attain an elevation of 300 or 400 feet above the plain, an isolated group of low hills called Jabal Falaij which lies some 25 miles to the north-west of '**Ibri**, and some scattered hillocks between '**Ibri** and Jabal Falaij on the side towards the Great Desert. The north-western slopes of Jabal-al-Kor may be regarded as pertaining to Dhāhirah along with a ridge called Jabal Haddah جده which runs west-north-west from the southern extremity of Jabal-al-Kor and forms an acute angle with it.

The elevation of the district varies from 1,200 feet above sea-level at '**Ibri** to 2,750 feet at **Miskin**. To the west of **Dhank** Town the plain is generally stony or shingly with a sparse growth of mimosa and acacia that affords winter grazing for thousands of Bedouin goats. South of **Dhank** Town a more sandy and less stony region begins. The south-east corner of the district between Jabal-al-Kor and Jabal Haddah is a plain sprinkled with mimosa and débris from the hills. Scrub jungles cover the open plains through which Dhāhirah merges along its entire length into the **Ruba'-al-Khāli**. Everywhere water is derived from springs.

Population.—Full particulars of the settled inhabitants of Dhāhirah will be found in the articles on the Wādis mentioned in the preceding paragraph, in those on the towns which they contain, and in the table of villages given at the end of this article. In this place it is sufficient to recall that '**Ibri** is mainly a town of the Ya'āqīb and **Dhank** of the **Na'īm**, while considerable settlements of Bani 'Ali, Bani Zīd and Bidāh occur in Wādi **Dhank**; Bani **Kalbān** are found in Wādi **Dhank** and Wādi-al-**Kabīr**; '**Abriyīn** in Wādi **Sanaisal**; Bani **Hina**, Manādharah and Sawāwifah in Wādi-al-'**Ain**; and **Maqabīl** in Wādi **Sharsah**. Towards the north-western end of the district there are communities of Bani **Qitab**, and **Balūchis** and other tribes are represented in various places in numbers not entitling them to special mention here. Regarding the nomadic inhabitants of Dhāhirah less is known; but they seem to be chiefly **Na'īm** and '**Awāmir** in the north-west and **Darū'** in the

DHAHIRĀH

south: there are also **Bani Zafait**. The Bedouin element is in Dhāhīrah highly important, but its numerical strength is not ascertainable.

The following is an estimate of the settled population of Dhāhīrah:—

Wādi-al-'Ain	3,000
Wādi **Dhank**	7,300
Wādi-al-**Kabīr** with its tributary Wādi Bilād Shahūm	8,000
Wādi **Sanaisal**	6,400
Wādi **Sharsah**	1,400
Remainder of the district (see the table at the end of this article)	5,000
Total	31,100 souls

Agriculture, industries and trade.—The products of Dhāhirah include all the typical products, of the **'Omān** Sultanate, and the wheat is reputed better than that of the other districts. The soil, where cultivable, is described as a rather heavy clay mixed with stones. **'Ibri** is the centre of the richest cultivation; in its vicinity are produced wheat, millet, indigo, sugar and lucerne, besides dates, mangoes, limes and other fruits. The chief industry is indigo-dyeing. Wheat and fruits are exported to the **Sharqīyah** and **Sohār** districts.

Administration.—The hold of the Sultān of **'Omān** on the Dhāhirah district is slight; but he maintains a Wāli, supported by a garrison of 20 men, at **'Arāqi** in Wadi **Sanaisal**.

Topography.—The following is an alphabetical list of the principal places in Dhāhirah exclusive of those, among which are the most important, that are described elsewhere in the articles on Wādis **Kabīr, Sanaisal, Sharsah, 'Ain** and **Dhank**:—

Name.	Position.	Houses and inhabitants.	REMARKS.
Aflāj Bani Qitab أفلاج بني قتب	Twenty-five miles north-west of 'Ibri and 15 miles south of Dhank Town.	A cluster of 7 hamlets of the Bani Qitab, situated on the plain immediately south of Jabal Falaij and comprising some 600 houses altogether. Two hamlets, that of Māzim, which is walled and fortified, and that of Subaikhi are inhabited by a Balūchi colony. Each hamlet is	The names of the hamlets are Falaj-al-Faranji فرنجي, Falaj-al-Māzim مازم Falaj as-Subaikhi صبيخي Falaj-al-Ma'mūr معمور, Falaj-al-Hamaidhi حميضي, Falaj-al-Qafaiqif قفيقف and Falaj Abu Khābi أبو خابي The road from Dhank to

Name.	Position.	Houses and inhabitants.	Remarks.
		within shouting distance of the next.	'Ibri, descending from Jabal Falaij, passes through the village of Māzim. The external trade of the place is mainly with Trucial 'Omān. Livestock are 15 horses, 400 camels, 150 donkeys, 250 cattle, and 4,000 sheep and goats.
Bizaili بزيلي	Ten miles west of Dhank.	40 houses of Āl Bū Shāmis Na'īm.	There are some wells at which Bedouins encamp and the village itself is not permanent. Livestock are 25 camels, 20 donkeys, 20 cattle and 500 sheep and goats.
Mūfiyah مرفيه	Twenty-six miles west-north-west of Dhank.	Watering place with a large well.	A village of 30 blanket and mat wigwams of Āl Bū Shāmis Na'īm is generally pitched here in winter. They have 150 camels, 20 donkeys, 20 cattle and 400 sheep and goats.
Sanainah سذينه	Four miles south of Bizaili.	200 houses of Āl Bū Shāmis Na'īm.	Stands on a plain which has much mimosa vegetation but merges, at no great distance, into the Ruba'-al-Khāli. Livestock are 10 horses, 200 camels, 30 donkeys, 50 cattle and 1,200 sheep and goats.
Tana'am تنعم	About 3 miles south of Dabai-shi on Wad Sanaisal.	Tract or group of villages, the headquarters of the Darū' tribe, with a population of perhaps 1,000 souls. The settlement is said to extend 7 miles.	Seen from a distance the Tana'am oasis resembles that of 'Ibri. The houses are scattered through the plantations in the same manner. The principal hamlets are said to be Daraiz دريز, 'Arāqi عراقي, Ghabbah غبه, Salmi سلمي, 'Ibri عبري, Naqīs نقيص, Hijār حجار, Akhdhar اخضر and Salaif سليف but their relative sizes and positions have not been ascertained.

DHAHRAN (BARR-ADH-)

DHAHRĀN (BARR-ADH-)
بَرّ الظَّهران

A littoral tract in the **Hasa** Sanjāq; though included within the boundaries of the larger tract known as **Biyādh** it is distinguished therefrom by its natural characteristics and by the possession of a separate name. **Bahrain** Island lies off the coast of Barr-adh-Dhahrān at 15 to 25 miles distance.

Boundaries.—Upon the coast Barr-al-Dhahran extends from Dammām on the north—that is from the southernmost outpost of the **Qatīf** Oasis—to the entrance of Dōhat **Ruhum** on the south; its length is thus rather less than 30 miles. Its depth inland is indeterminate, but does not exceed a few miles.

Physical features.—The only striking accident of surface in Barr-adh-Dhahrān is Jabal-adh-Dhahrān, from which, it is said, the name of the entire tract is derived. This is a range running parallel to the shore between Dammām and Qal'āt-al-Husain, which are 12 miles apart, at a distance of only 2 or 3 miles from the sea. The principal summit, flat-topped and 500 feet high, is situated 5 miles inland from the coast and 17 miles approximately south-south-east of **Qatīf** Town. About 3 miles nearer to **Qatīf** Town and 6 miles south of Dammām is a conical peak, belonging to the same range, which is 446 feet in height and bears the name of Jabal Mudrah مدرة. On the south side of Jabal-adh-Dhahrān is an area called Madārah مدارة containing many wells. The land on the eastern side of Jabal Dhahrān, which slopes down to the sea, is actually higher upon the average than that on the western side. Barr-adh-Dhahrān contains numerous small clumps of date trees scattered about in all directions.

Wells and other named places.—The following are the objects having names which are of most importance in Barr-adh-Dhahrān:—

Name.	Position.	Nature.	Remarks.
qdān (Bin) بن عقدان	5 miles inland west-north-west wards from the foot of Dōhat-as-Saih.	A well.	Shaikh Salmān-bin-Di'aij, a near relation of the Shaikh of Bahrain, was murdered here with a large party in 1900 by a gang of Al Morrah Bedouins of the Al Bahaih section.

Name.	Position.	Nature.	Remarks.
Buraiqat (Rās) راس بريقط	The entrance point on the north side of Dōhat Ruhum.	A cape.	To this headland, in the present Charts, the name of "Kureya" has been erroneously given. See article Dōhat Ruhum.
Dhahrān (Maqta'-adh-) مقطع الظهران	One mile inland from the northern shore of Dōhat Ruhum.	A well.	...
Husain (Qal'āt-al-) قلعات الحسين	Near the coast 12 miles south-east of Dammām and the same distance north of Dōhat 'Ain-as-Saih.	Some wells of good water and a number of date plantations.	This place is separated from the sea only by a narrow line of sandhills. There is a small ruined fort. The dates belong to the Bani Hājir.
Khashaibīyah الخشيبيه	Two miles inland north-westwards from the foot of Dōhat 'Ain-as-Saih.	A well.	...
Lalyah لليه	On the coast 3 miles north-north-east of the entrance of Dōhat 'Ain-as-Saih.	A well and date plantation.	...
Mudhbā المذباع	Several miles west or north-west of Bin-'Aqdān; possibly in Dabaisi.	A well.	...
Rākah الراكه	On the coast 1 mile north-west of Qal'-āt-al-Husain.	Do.	...
Saih (Dōhat 'Ain-as-) دوحة عين السيح	About 28 miles south-south-east of Qatīf Town and 36 miles north of 'Oqair Port.	A shallow bay of no great extent.	...

Inhabitants.—The date groves of Barr-adh-Dhahrān are owned an tended by Bani **Hājir** Bedouins, but Āl **Morrah** also wander in the trac

DHAHURIYIN
ظهوريين

A tribe of the **Ruūs-al-Jibāl** district in the **'Omān** Sultanate, numbering about 1,750 souls, to whom belong the villages of Film (60 houses), Habalain (25 houses), Mansal (6 houses) and Maqāqah (100 houses) in **Ghubbat Ghazīrah**; Midah (1 house), Qānah (40 houses), Sham (25 houses) and Sībi (7 houses) in Khor-ash-**Sham**; Balad (20 houses) in Ghubbat Shābūs; and Muntaf (15 houses) and Shīsah (15 houses) in Ghubbat Shīsah: **Lārak** island also is inhabited by about 200 souls of Dhahūriyīn who are closely connected with the people of **Kumzār**.

In the cold weather the **Dhahūriyīn** of **Ruūs-al-Jibāl** live by fishing; in spring they migrate bodily, leaving only caretakers behind. to Khor **Fakkān, Dibah** and **Khasab**, where they attach themselves to some of the permanent residents and bivouac in the date plantations.

The Dhahūriyīn are practically a part of the **Shihūh** tribe, by whom they are surrounded and with whom they are closely identified, but they claim connection with the **Dhawāhir** of **Baraimi**; the **Dhawāhir**, however, it must be observed, are Mawālik and Hināwīyah, while the Dhahūriyīn are mostly Hanābilah and Ghāfirīyah, a circumstance which renders somewhat doubtful the validity of the claim. The Dhahūriyīn do not admit that they are in any way subordinate to the **Shihūh**: they appear, except those of Maqāqah, Qānah, Sham and Sībi, who have perhaps closer relations with the Bani Hadīyah, to be connected with the Bani Shatair section of that tribe. The Dhahūriyīn of Film and Mansal are Shāfi'is in religion; the rest of the tribe are Hanbalis.

DHAID*
ديد

An isolated village in the heart of the great **'Omān** Promontory; it belongs to the principality of **Shārjah** and geographically and politically it is a centre of some importance in Trucial **'Omān**.

Position, surroundings and climate.—Dhaid is about 30 miles east of **Shārjah** Town and 33 miles south by west of the town of Rās-al-**Khaimah**. It stands near the western side of a level plain, which is about 15 miles wide from west to east and the same in length from north to south; this plain is bordered on the west and north by sand dunes, on the east by the hills which form the backbone of the **'Omān** Promontory,

---

* *Authority*:—Major P. Z. Cox, Political Resident in the Persian Gulf, from personal observation. The only map is *Route taken by Major P. Z. Cox*, etc., 1905.

and on the south by the shingly plateau of Qallah Mahāfidh. The main features of the Dhaid plain and some other localities adjoining it are described in the last paragraph of the present article. The plain of Dhaid is well wooded, containing many acacias, and after rain it produces in abundance a coarse tussocky kind of grass. In the summer months a dry hot wind blows constantly at Dhaid, detracting from the amenity of the place which otherwise would be considerable.

Village and inhabitants.—The village of Dhaid consists of about 140 houses, nearly all date-leaf huts; of these about 70 belong to the **Tanaij** tribe, 40 to the Bani **Qitab**, and 30 to **Na'īm** of the Khawātir section. The **Tanaij** and **Na'īm** communities have each a fortified mud tower for the defence of their separate quarters; and on the east side of the village is a four-towered fort belonging to the Shaikh of **Shārjah**. Dhaid is the headquarters of the nomad portion of the **Tanaij**, but the Bedouins who frequent the plain surrounding it are chiefly, perhaps, Bani **Qitab**.

Agricultural resources.—The date groves of Dhaid form an oasis about 1 mile in diameter. They are irrigated by a fine Falaj which comes from Wādi Haqālah to the south-east and passes through the precincts of the Shaikh of Shārjah's fort on its way to the oasis; the stream before it is tapped for irrigation is about three feet wide and two feet deep, clear and transparent, and has a strong flow. The waters of the Falaj are carefully divided up among the lands of the oasis, and the local representative of the Shaikh of **Shārjah** is responsible for their correct distribution. In addition to dates a little wheat is grown at Dhaid, and the inhabitants have the usual complement of domestic animals.

Administration.—The settlement is governed and kept in order by a Wāli who is directly under the orders of the Shaikh of **Shārjah**. This official is, at the present time, a venerable old negro retainer of the **Shārjah** family, who resides in his master's fort and flies the flag of Trucial **'Omān** upon its north-western tower. The annual revenue derived by the Shaikh of **Shārjah** from Dhaid is said to consist of 100 Jirābs of dates, paid as a royalty, and of $228 in cash recovered as a water rate from users of the Falaj. The position of the Shaikh's fort is such as to dominate the Falaj; but it is questionable whether the possessors of the fort could seriously interfere with the flow or affect the course of so strong a stream.

Shaikh of Sharjah's Fort at Dhaid, Trucial Oman.
[Maj. P. Z. Cox.]

Political and military position.—Although Dhaid is controlled by the Shaikh of **Shārjah** he has not an exclusive interest in the place. His uncle Sālim-bin-Sultān and the Shaikhs of **'Ajmān** and **Hamrīyah** all own date plantations at Dhaid, and the unpleasantness of the climate in the hot weather months is given as the only reason why they do not visit the place frequently. There is reason to think that, in event of British or Indian troops being required in Trucial **'Omān,** Dhaid would be the most suitable station for them in the interior, at least during the cold weather. The water supply is excellent and ample; camel and other grazing is abundant; and the place is probably already accessible for wheeled transport from Rās-al-**Khaimah** Town by way of the **Sīr** and **Jiri** plains, besides which there are camel routes through the hills connecting it with the ports of the **Shamailīyah** District on the other side of the **'Omān** promontory. The subject of communications with Dhaid is more fully discussed in the paragraph on routes in Trucial **'Omān.**

Topography of the neighbourhood.—The following are the most important places in the vicinity of Dhaid:—

Name.	Position.	Nature.	Remarks.
'Ali (Tūi) طوي علي	In the Dhaid plain, 6 miles south-south-west of Dhaid village.	A well.	It lies immediately under the sand dunes which border the plain on the west.
Biruddi البردي	About 12 miles east-south-east of Dhaid village.	A locality.	This is the point at which, it is said, the Falaj watering the village of Dhaid enters the Dhaid plain.
Faraikh فريخ	3 to 7 miles north-north-east of Dhaid village.	A sandy valley which descends from north to south and finally debouches on the plain of Dhaid near Muraqqibāt.	The valley contains a number of acacias and some Arta which afford grazing to the camels of the Bani Qitab. About midway between the head and the foot of the valley is a well of the same name on the route between Rās-al-Khaimah Town and Dhaid village.
Maqālah حقاله	Said to be situated in the hills 15 or 20 miles south-east of Dhaid	A village of 10 houses of Na'īm of the Āl Bū Shāmis division.	The inhabitants are said to possess camels, donkeys, cattle, sheep and goats and a consi-

Name.	Position.	Nature.	Remarks.
	village and at a considerable elevation.		derable number of date palms. Near by are a valley called Wādi Haqālah, in which the stream that irrigates Dhaid village has its source, and a hill called Jabal Haqālah that is said to overlook Wādi Sfuni.
Kathairah (Wādi) وادي كثيرة	In the Dhaid plain south of Dhaid village.	A valley or water scour.	This hollow runs north-north-westwards for 2 miles from Wushāh and then turns westwards in the direction of the coast. In this part of its course its left bank skirts the foot of some sandhills.
Manghōl (Wādi) وادي منغول	Crosses the Dhaid plain from east to west 3 miles north of Dhaid village.	A Bat-ha or water scour in the sand, running out of the Dhaid plain in the direction of the coast.	Muraqqibāt and Thiqbat-as-Sanaibil are situated on this hollow, the former to the east and the latter to the west of the point where it is crossed by the route between Rās-al-Khaimah Town and Dhaid village. To the west of that route the Wādi is sometimes called Wādi-as-Sanaibi وادي السنيبيل
Muraqqibāt مرقبات	On the right bank of Wādi Manghōl, ¼ a mile east of the place where the route between Rās-al-Khaimah Town and Dhaid village crosses it.	A group of wells.	These wells are commonly used by travellers between Umm-al-Qaiwain and places on the east coast of the 'Omān Promontory from Fujairah as far south as Shinās.
Sanaibil (Thiqbat-as-) ثقبة السنيبيل	On the left bank of Wādi Manghōl, 1 mile below Muraqqibāt.	A group of borings which are the head of the Falaj watering Falai in the Umm-al-Qaiwain district.	The chalky clay thrown up from the excavations forms a cluster of white mounds which are an excellent landmark.
Wushāh وشاح	3½ miles south by east of Dhaid village, on the right bank of Wādi Kathairah.	A well on the route from Dhaid village to the Baraimi Oasis.	Just above Wushāh, Wādi Kathairah receives a tributary on its right bank.

DHA'IN (Ā) آل ضاعن

A very small tribe of non-Bedouin Arabs in **Bahrain**, said to be descended from an individual named Dhā'in, who was a servant of the Āl Bin-'Ali. They have 10 houses in **Muharraq**, and one of the quarters of that town is named after them. They are pearl fishers by occupation and Māliki Sunnis by religion.

DHAKHĪRAH الذخيرة

A village on the east coast of **Qatar**, situated on a Khor or inlet of the same name about 30 miles north of **Dōhah**, and consisting of about 100 houses of the **Mahāndah** tribe. The people are all pearl divers, following no other occupation except fishing and owning no flocks or herds. Fifteen pearl boats and two other sea-going boats of the Mashuwah type and 5 fishing boats are owned at Dhakhīrah. Transport animals are 10 camels. Drinking water is from Lubwairdah, 2 miles to the north-west.

DHALŪF (ABU) ابو ضلوف

A village on the north-west coast of the **Qatar** Promontory, near its tip and 1 or 2 miles south-west of **Ruwais**. It is difficult of approach from seaward being fronted by a reef $2\frac{1}{2}$ miles broad which is nearly dry at low water. The inhabitants are about 70 families of the **Manāna'ah** tribe owning 20 pearl boats, 5 other sea-going vessels and 10 fishing boats. Their drinking water is from the well of Umm Dhā'an, about $1\frac{1}{2}$ miles inland. Camels here number 30.

DHANK TOWN ضنك

Frequently pronounced Dhanch; the second largest town in the **Dhāhirah** district of the **'Omān** Sultanate, pleasantly situated at the mouth of a precipitous opening in the Western **Hajar** range which forms the exit of Wādi **Dhank**. Jabal Hafit is visible from Dhank on a clear day. Dhank is divided into an 'Alāyah علايه or upper town of about 5, and a Sifālah سفاله or lower town of about 7 quarters, each quarter being separately walled. The houses are mostly of sun-dried brick. Fine date plantations containing about 3,500 palms and orchards of limes and pomegranates surround the town, and on the outskirts is some cultivation of wheat, lucerne and indigo. Water for irrigation is raised from wells by bullocks. Livestock comprises 14 horses, 80 camels, 250 donkeys, 350 cattle and 1,100 sheep and goats. The population of Dhank is about 3,500 souls, belonging to various sections of the **Na'īm** and some other tribes: in the 'Alāyah, which consists of 400 houses, the people are all **Na'īm**; in the Sifālah, containing 300 houses, they are **Na'īm** of the 'Ayāl 'Azīz, 'Ayāl Hiyah, Shawāmis and Wahaishah sections and Shakūr.

DHANK (WĀDI)
وادي ضنك

Or Wādi Dhanch; also called Wādi Fida فدا. One of the two chief valleys in the district of **Dhāhirah** in the Sultanate of **'Omān**; it begins in Western **Hajar** near Najd-al-Wuqbah, on the opposite side of which pass Wādi-al-'**Āhin**, going to **Bātinah**, has its rise. From its head to about Yanqul the direction of Wādi Dhank is apparently from north to south, but below Yanqul it runs almost due westward; its final exit from the hills of Western **Hajar** is by a precipitous gorge just above the town of **Dhank**. On the upper side of the gorge the valley is half a mile broad, with banks 100 feet high and a fine stream of water in the middle, flowing above ground; at this spot was fought the battle of Dhank in 1870 between Saiyid 'Azzān and Saiyid Turki, of which the ultimate result was the ruin of 'Azzān's cause and the accession of Turki to the Sultanate.

The chief places in Wādi Dhank from above downwards are:—

Name.	Position.	Houses and inhabitants.	Remarks.
Wuqbah رقبه	On the right bank, 3 hours below Najd-al-Wuqbah.	150 houses of Bani 'Ali.	There are 4 horses, 50 camels, 60 donkeys, 100 cattle, 400 sheep and goats and 15,000 date palms.
Yanqul ينقل	On the left bank, 5 hours below Wuqbah.	200 houses of Bani 'Ali.	Yanqul was one of the chief places of the Nabāhinah during their predominance in 'Omān about 1600 A. D. There are 20 horses, 200 camels, 50 donkeys, 150 cattle and 600 sheep and goats; palms number 2,000.

Name.	Position.	Houses and inhabitants.	Remarks.
Fida فدا	On the right bank, 2 miles below Yanqul.	200 houses of Bani Zīd.	The date plantations of Fida form a long but narrow fringe in the valley and contain 2,500 palms. There are 100 camels, 100 donkeys, 200 cattle and 300 sheep and goats.
Dūt دوت	On the right bank, 2 miles below Fida.	100 houses of Bidāh and Sā'idah.	There are date plantations containing 1,000 palms.
Dhank Town ضنك	......	......	See article Dhank Town.

A mile or two below **Dhank** Town, Wādi Dhank is joined on its right bank by Wādi Abu Kurbah ابو كربه, which has a sandy bed and banks thickly clad with tamarisk. It also receives from the east, at some point below **Dhank** Town, a Wādi called Wādi-al-Jailah جيله, in the upper course of which is situated a village Khadal خدل composed of 100 houses of Jarāwinah (Bani **Kalbān**). Wādi Dhank then continues on its way towards the **Ruba'-al-Khāli** in which it is lost.

The total population of Wādi Dhank and its affluents is about 7,300 souls.

DHAWĀ-HIR ظواهر

A considerable Arab tribe who have their headquarters in the Baraimi Oasis and inhabit its neighbourhood: practically the whole Baraimi Oasis except the villages of Su'arah and **Baraimi** belongs to them. They number perhaps 4,500 souls and are divided into 3 sections, the Darāmikah درامكه, who inhabit Hīli, Ma'ataradh and Qatārah; the Jawābir جوابر, who are confined to 'Ain; and the Bani Sa'ad سعد, who own Jīmi. In politics the Dhawāhir are Hināwīyah; in religion Muwālik. In summer all of them inhabit villages; in winter the entire community become Bedouins. They own large flocks of sheep and many camels; they are charcoal-burners and carry their charcoal for sale to the coast of Trucial **'Omān**, and elsewhere, on their own camels. The Dhawāhir have probably little cultivation elsewhere than in **Baraimi**, unless, as some assert, the Bani Sa'ad of Ghūnah and Mad-hah in

Shamailīyah belong to this tribe. Politically the Dhawāhir of **Baraimi** are subservient to the Shaikh of Abu **Dhabi**, to whom they even pay tribute; and it is not unlikely that, if they were to avail themselves of their numerical superiority and of his assistance, they might be able to possess themselves of the whole oasis.

DHRU-
MAH
ضرمة

A large village in the **'Āridh** district of **Najd**, memorable chiefly for the resistance which it offered to the Egyptian forces in 1818 and for the severity with which it was treated after being taken by them.

Dhrumah appears to be situated about 35 miles to the south-east of Barrah and about the same distance to the west-south-west of **Riyādh**. It stands in a plain of some extent which receives the drainage of three valleys from the western slopes of Jabal **Tuwaiq**; of these the northernmost begins in Jabal Kharshah, a portion of the **Tuwaiq** range adjoining Haisīyah; the middle one is Bōdhah بوضة and the southernmost is Saqtah سقطة. To the south-east and north-east of Dhrumah are the **Tuwaiq** hills, to the south-west is a sandy desert, and to the northwest is a plain across which lies the route to **Shaqrah** in **Washam**. The hollow in the Dhrumah plain down which passes the combined drainage of the valleys from Jabal **Tuwaiq** leaves the village of Dhrumah on its right bank, but the date groves of the village are watered from wells in its bed; from Dhrumah it trends east-south-eastwards, traverses Jabal **Tuwaiq**, and enters Wādi **Hanīfah** a short way below Hāir but near enough to that place to irrigate a portion of its date gardens. Between Dhrumah and Hāir, at several miles from Dhrumah, a village called Mizāhmīyah is passed upon the right bank, and several miles further on another village, named Rōdhah, also on the right bank*; the lands of both these places are partly watered from the hollow, which as it approaches Hāir receives the name of Sail Hāir سيل حائر. Before reaching Hāir it is joined—apparently from the left—by another hollow, called Maghrifīyah مغرفية, from Jabal **Tuwaiq**. The route from Dhrumāh to **Riyādh** lies by Mizāhmīyah and thence over the high portion of Jabal **Tuwaiq** known as Abaljid; the whole journey occupies about 12 hours, and the latter three-fourths of the way are hilly and difficult. The way direct from Dhrumah to Hāir lies over a

---
* Another authority transposes the positions of these villages, and yet another reduces the distances and makes them suburbs of Dhrumah.

more southern and less elevated part of Jabal **Tuwaiq** called Maghrifiyah, and the journey is apparently a longer one than that to **Riyādh**. These are the routes used by travellers moving lightly or in fear of robbers; but a strong caravan with laden camels would, it is said, go by Hāir, following the natural valley which leads from Dhrumah to that place.

The following table gives the usual particulars of the villages of Dhrumah, Mizāhmīyah and Rōdhah :—

Name.	Position.	Houses and inhabitants.	Remarks.
Dhrumah ضرمه	See above.	300 houses, viz., about 150 of Bani **Khadhīr** and on the average about 25 each of 'Anizah of the Ifqɪhah section, **Dawāsir** of the Mɪdbal section, **Fadhūl Mutair** of the Nafīsah (Braih) section, **Sabai'** of the Āl ' Abdul Azīz section, **Sahūl** and Bani **Tamīm**. The main town is called Bilād بلد, and there are outlying quarters or dependent villages known as Qasr-bin-Shahail شهيل and Wusaitah وسيطه .	There is a bazaar containing a number of shops. There is extensive cultivation of wheat and barley; different estimates of the date palms average 30,000. Millet, lucerne, melons and the ordinary fruits are also grown. The wells are 11 to 18 fathoms in depth. Livestock are numerous. The Amīr or headman of the village is at present Muhammad-bin-'Abdul 'Azīz of the Nawāsir section of the Bani Tamīm.
Mizāhmīyah مزاهميه	Do.	100 houses, viz., 40 of Bani **Tamīm**, 40 of inferior tribes, and the remainder 'Anizah and Dawāsir.	There are 6,000 date palms, a few fruit trees and the usual cereals and lucerne. The water level is the same as at Dhrumah, or not quite so deep.
Rōdhah روضه	Do.	45 houses, viz., 30 of 'Anizah and 15 of inferior tribes.	Resembles Mizāhmīyah, except that date palms are estimated at 4,000 and that water is at 10 fathoms.

This seems the most convenient place in which to refer to the torrent bed of Abaljilāt الابجلات, which, though not directly connected with Dhrumah, adjoins it on the southward, being situated (apparently) in the hills of Jabal **Tuwaiq** between Dhrumah and the **Harīq** district. It is said to rise in the same neighbourhood as the Nisāh tributary of Wādi

Hanīfah; but its direction must be different, for, after passing a village called Jau-as-Saibāni جو السيباني, it runs southwards to Khashm-adh-Dhīb in the Harīq district, where it ends. Only in times of exceptional flood does its water reach to Khashm-adh-Dhīb.

The village of Jau-as-Saibāni is a poor and scattered one; it ordinarily consists of 40 houses of slaves only. Bani **Tamīm**, however, from Dhrumah and Mizāhmīyah, come here to cultivate in the cold weather. There are no date trees and no lucerne, but wheat, barley, millet and melons are grown. Water is at 4 fathoms from the ground level.

DHUFĀR* ضفار **or** ظفار **DISTRICT.** The term Dhufār is properly used to describe the maritime plain on the south coast of Arabia which extends, enclosed between the **Samhān** hills and the sea, from Rās Risūt eastwards for 30 miles to Khor Rori. It is also used in a restricted sense to designate the villages of Hāfah and **Salālah**, which together contain two-thirds of the entire settled population of the same plain. In a wider sense, however, as the name of a district, Dhufār denotes the whole coastal tract, from and including the village of Kharīfōt on the west to Rās Nūs on the east, which is in the possession of the Sultān of **'Omān** and forms a separate district of the **'Omān** Sultanate. It is in the last of these three meanings that the word is employed in the present article; **Dhufār** Proper is dealt with separately under that title. The eastern and western limits of the Dhufār district as just defined approximately coincide with those of the **Qara** tribe.

Extent.—The district of Dhufār, as defined above, has a length west by south and east by north of 134 miles and a maximum breadth inland, in **Dhufār** Proper, of about 20 miles.

Physical geography.—The greater part of the district does not merit a detailed description; it consists of barren hills at no great distance from the sea, interrupted here and there by short insignificant valleys. The only valley of importance is Wādi Raikūt which reaches the coast at Hāsik and is said to have its head in the far interior. The hills, though in places irregular in direction and discontinuous, really form one range

---

* For Dhufār district, see map in Mrs. Bent's *Southern Arabia* or in the Geographical Journal for August 1895. The Chart for Dhufār is No. 10B. For authoritie on the district see article **'Omān Sultanate** (first footnote).

which is generally known by the name of Jabal **Samhān**. In two places only does the range recede perceptibly from the coast; one of these is between Rās Nūs and **Murbāt**, where a belt of low land 6 to 12 miles broad, rocky and desolate in the extreme, but containing some hares and gazelles besides a few date trees in a ravine towards Rās Nūs, is left between the hills and the sea; the other is the plain of **Dhufār** Proper, of which the extreme points upon the coast have been already mentioned.

Climate.—Situated as Dhufār is on the shore of the Arabian Sea, its seasons are regulated chiefly by the monsoons. The south-west monsoon, which brings rain, ordinarily arrives about the 11th of June and is sometimes preceded by 10 days by a severe gale from the south or south-east. In December and January the air of Dhufār is pleasant and salubrious.

Inhabitants.—The two great tribes of the district are the **Qaras**, who are found chiefly in the **Samhān** hills, and the Āl **Kathīr**, who inhabit the plain of **Dhufār** Proper and the hills also. The **Qaras** have a language of their own and the Āl **Kathīr** are believed to speak an Arabic dialect which differs considerably from that of the Persian Gulf. The villagers are indolent agriculturists and like most town Arabs are timorous and much addicted to tobacco. Other tribes known in Dhufār are the Ja'afar جعفر and the Bait-al-Qalam قلم of the former of whom there are 20, and of the latter a few households at **Murbāt**; Saiyids or Sādāt سادات and Mashāikh, both sacred classes, mostly settled at **Murbāt** and Tāqa; the Hasārīt حساريت or Hasrīt حسريت, a Bedouin tribe who visit **Murbāt**, but ordinarily inhabit a country said to lie three or four days' journey to the east of Dhufār; and the Harāsīs حراصيص, a tribe of which stray members are seen now and again in Dhufār, having come, it is believed, from a long distance. A few **Mahras** and **Hikmān** are found at **Murbāt** in Dhufār, and the district is adjoined on the west by **Mahra** territory. Formerly there were a few Indian traders in Dhufār, now there are none.

The blood-feud flourishes in Dhufār and is at times so prevalent that two inhabitants can hardly pass one another without a Rabi' ربيع or guarantor. This was particularly the case in 1845, when frightful anarchy prevailed and there was a general desire for British protection. The condition of affairs has been somewhat ameliorated since the effective occupation of Dhufār by the Sultān of **'Omān**, but population is said to be still decreasing. The former rulers of the country, whose ruined villages cover the plain of **Dhufār** Proper, are called by the present people the Minquwi مِنقُوِي.

Population.—As will be apparent from the table at the end of this article and from that in the article on **Dhufār** Proper, the population of the whole district must be about 11,000 souls, composed as follows:—

Settled inhabitants of **Dhufār** Proper	3,000
Settled inhabitants of the remainder of the district . . .	1,500
Qara Bedouins	4,250
Āl Kathīr Bedouins	2,000
Other Bedouins (Hasārīt, etc.)	250
Total .	11,000

Communications and transport.—Communication between Dhufār and the outside world is hampered by various obstacles. The coast possesses no large harbour and landing is generally difficult on account of surf, though the bays of **Murbāt** and Risūt afford good anchorage for small vessels in the north-east and south-west monsoons respectively. Practically no sea-going boats are owned in Dhufār, but there are about 40 Horis and 10 Shāshahs.

The plain of Dhufār could be crossed with field guns, but the track along the coast which connects the plain with the **Murbāt** anchorage would be difficult for artillery. The paths in the **Samhān** hills become altogether impassable in the rainy season. The Āl Kathīr and **Qara** tribes possess many camels: other transport animals are scarce.

A land route connects **Salālah** in Dhufār with **Adam** in 'Omān Proper, but it is an arduous one and the journey occupies about a month; water in some parts is met with only at intervals of two marches. This route leaves Dhufār by Wādi Jarzīz, traverses the district called Qatan behind Jabal **Samhān**, approaches the sea at Jāzir and then bears direct for **Adam**, passing on the way through a locality called **Dhahr** ضهر . There is no direct route between Dhufār and Central Arabia.

Trade, shipping and resources.—There are no manufactures. By far the most valuable export is frankincense from the **Samhān** hills, which is mostly carried to Bombay in native boats. Other exports are hides, sheepskins, gums, bees' wax, bitter aloes, and at times ghi; these also are for the most part hill products. Imports are chiefly rice, sugar, jowari, dates and dyed cloth from Bombay; but small quantities of goods are brought also from Aden and Makalla مكلا, particularly tobacco from Makalla; and in summer a few traders in piece-goods visit Dhufār from Shihr شحر, returning to their homes in the cold weather.

One sea-going boat was formerly owned in Dhufār; it was a Badan which made voyages between Murbāt and Makalla, but it has now disappeared. Boats from Makalla, **Sūr, Bahrain** and **Kuwait** frequently call at Dhufār to trade or to obtain provisions, and business with Bombay is carried on chiefly by means of boats belonging to **Sūr**. Dhufār merchants used occasionally to charter Indian Kūtiyahs from Sind, but this is no longer done and trade is said to be falling off.

Boats from the Persian Gulf generally visit or pass Dhufār in November and December; some return before the monsoon, but others better equipped linger till the Tadbīrah تدبيره or premonitory symptoms of the monsoon in June, or even till the first blast of the monsoon itself. These boats carry dates on their outward, and coffee on their return voyage. The smaller craft of the coast about **Masīrah** fish in fleets along the shore towards Dhufār in winter and return home with the current in March or April.

The inhabitants of Dhufār believe themselves independent of foreign trade, and think that they could subsist by their own cultivation and flocks and herds if intercourse with the outer world were to be interrupted; this is possibly true in regard to food, but a blockade would certainly reduce them to great straits for clothing.

The products of the Dhufār district are described in the articles on **Dhufār** Proper and Jabal **Samhān**. No minerals of commercial value are certainly known to exist, but an easily worked not very durable building stone is quarried near **Salālah**.

Administration.—This remote district of the '**Omān** Sultanate is ruled by a Wāli who is appointed from '**Omān** by the Sultān. The late Wāli, Sulaimān-bin-Suwailim, had been almost continuously absent from Dhufār for 9 years before his death in 1907, and his duties were carried on by a resident deputy-governor. The revenue derived from sea-customs amounts to $5,000 a year, or more, and there are taxes on animals and a tax on agriculture; the last, known as Zakāt, is fixed at $\frac{1}{20}$ of the gross produce and is estimated to bring in about $15,000 a year. The taxes are mostly received in kind, and the late Wāli was accustomed to send the goods thus collected to an agent whom he maintained at Bombay, where they were converted into cash. The revenue realised only suffices to cover the expenses of government and no surplus is ever remitted to **Masqat**. The military force is fluctuating and consists of 50 to 200 'Askaris or armed levies who are paid from the local revenues: at present the number is about 60 distributed between

Murbāt, Salālah, Hāfah and **Rīsūt**. These levies are now mostly local men, not 'Omānis; in their number we have not included the personal retinue of the deputy-governor in the Hisn.

Topography.—The topography of the plain of **Dhufār** Proper and the **Samhān** hills is given in the articles under those names: the following is an alphabetically arranged table of the principal features and places in the remainder of the Dhufār district:—

Name.	Position.	Nature.	Remarks.
Kharifōt خريفوت	On the coast 17 miles west of Rās Sājar.	A ravine and village of 30 houses divided from Rakhyūt to the east by the tract called Sailikōt. The people are **Qaras** of the Shamāsah and Bani 'Īsa sections.	There is a stream of running water and, at the mouth of the ravine, a date grove. The village is the westernmost in the Dhufār district. There are 100 sheep and goats; no boats.
Murbāt مرباط	......	......	See article **Murbāt**.
Nūs (Rās and Bandar) بندر راس أوس	On the coast 43 miles east-north-east of **Murbāt**.	A cape with a small anchorage on the east side of it formed by a concavity of the coast and sheltered from southerly and westerly winds.	2 miles north of the point which forms the north end of the bay is the tomb of Sālih-ibn-Hūd صالح ابن هود There are date trees and a good spring, sufficient to supply 2 or 3 vessels in a day. The population, consisting of 20 households of **Jannabah**, is poor and nearly naked; they inhabit low circular huts, built of stone, date branches and sea-weed, upon the cape. They have 60 sheep and goats, but no boats.
Qinqari قنقري	On the coast 22 miles east of **Murbāt**.	A small sandy bay, 2½ miles wide at the entrance and 1¼ miles deep; it is sheltered from the north and east but open to the south: the soundings are irregular from 8 to 26 fathoms.	A limestone hill called Jabal Qinqari with veins of chalk and gypsum overlooks the bay; it is 1,300 feet high.

DHUFĀR DISTRICT

Name.	Position.	Nature.	Remarks.
Rakhyūt رخيوت	On the coast 13 miles west of Rās Sajar.	A village of 60 or 70 mud houses inhabited by Qaras of the Bait 'Ak'āk, Bait Hardān, Bait 'Īsa and Bait Shamāsah sections; it stands at the mouth of a ravine of the same name and is separated from Safqōt to the east by a mountainous ridge scarped on the side towards the sea.	The village stands on the west side of a creek, on the opposite side of which is a tower built by the 'Omāni Wāli of Dhufār to keep off the attacks of hostile **Mahras**. Rakhyūt has increased considerably in the last 20 years in consequence of the expansion of the frankincense trade. Rakhyūt is also called Qamar قمر and occasionally Sa'dūni سعدوني from the name of a former chief.
Risūt * ريسوت	At the western extremity of **Dhufār Proper**.	A bay facing the east with a promontory of the same name on the south side of it. The bay is about 1 mile broad by half a mile deep. The beach is sandy and is divided from the plain of **Dhufār Proper** by some hundred yards of low sea cliff. The promontory is 200 feet high and 1 mile broad at its base; it is covered with traces of human occupation, including a cemetery, 3 acres in extent.	In the bay stands a mud-built bazaar of 15 or 20 shops, constructed by the Wāli of Dhufār and permanently occupied by Dhufār traders. In the trading season, between March and September, the number of shops increases to 40 or 50. A guard of 10 or 15 'Askaris is always posted here. A torrent bed reaches the bay through a small lagoon: $1\frac{1}{2}$ miles up this ravine is a fresh water spring. Boats from **Sūr** and **Masqat Town** call here, but none belong to the place. There are 300 cattle and 200 sheep and goats.
Rori (Khor) خور روري	At the eastern extremity of **Dhufār Proper**.	A remarkable lake or inlet of the sea running a mile or more inland; it is the estuary of Wādi Dirbāt from Jabal **Samhān**.	The inlet is divided from the sea by a sand bar over which the water flows at high tide. A peninsula, once fortified, adjoins the east side of the entrance. Remains of ancient buildings surround the lake.

* A plan of the Risūt anchorage will be found as an inset in Admiralty chart No. 10 B.

Name.	Position.	Nature.	Remarks.
Sadah سدح	On the coast east of **Murbāt**, apparently 20 miles or more from that place by land.	A small village on the sea at the mouth of a Wādi of the same name. There are 1 or 2 houses and about 20 caves, on both sides of the valley, inhabited by **Qaras** of the Ahl 'Umr section.	The Wāli of Dhufār formerly maintained a post of 15 'Askaris here, but it has been abolished: there are a few store-houses. The place depends on the frankincense trade. There are no boats except from other places. Cattle number 600 and goats and sheep 1,000.
Safqot سفقوت	On the coast 9 miles west of Rās **Sājar**.	A small village said to consist of 10 houses of **Jannabah**; it is at the mouth of a deep ravine which here comes down to the sea.	The people inhabit caves in the sides of the valley. They do not recognise the authority of the Wāli of Dhufār, but they give no trouble.
Sājar (Rās) راس ساجر (Also pronounced Sāgar and Sāyir.)	On the coast 32 miles west-south-west of Rīsūt.	The largest, but not the most striking cape on the southern coast of Arabia. The sea around it is very deep. The summit is 3,380 feet above the sea, and the bluff extremity 2,770 feet, but the cape does not project much from the main land. The eastern side is not so high as the western, owing to the strata dipping to the east, but it is perpendicularly scarped. The south-west side descends in 3 or 4 grand steps to the sea.	Rās Sādar is a part of the **Sambān** mountains; it consists of white and grey limestone. Its sides, where not perpendicular, are covered with trees, and the plains at the top with long grass. There are caverns inhabited by **Jannabah** on both sides, but chiefly on the eastern. The people are poor fishermen, about 20 in number, owning a few small, roughly made Horis. The Government of India in 1879 fixed this cape as the boundary between the political jurisdictions of its officers at **Masqat** and Aden: the convenience of the arrangement is now open to question as the Wāli of Dhufār has established his control at Rakhyūt 13 miles to the westward.

Name.	Position.	Nature.	Remarks.
Sailikōt سيلكوت	Between Rakhyūt and Kharīfōt.	A stretch of coast.	Here the highlands fall back somewhat from the sea and the ground descends to the coast in long shelves covered with grass and trees.
Salah صلح	In the hills eastwards of **Murbāt**, from which it is said to be distant two days' journey.	A valley.	This valley can only be reached on foot. It contains 12 huts of **Qaras** who own 150 cattle and 200 sheep and goats and import maize from **Murbāt**.

Salālah is the largest place in Dhufār: the second is **Murbāt** which is the principal port of the district.

DHUFĀR*
ضفار or ظفار
PROPER

Boundaries.—A low-lying maritime plain in the **Dhufār** District, to which it gives its name; it is bounded by the sea on the south and the **Samhân** hills on the north, and extends from Rīsūt on the west to Khor Rori on the east. Its length is thus about 30 miles and its average depth less than 5 miles.

Physical characteristics.—The plain consists of miliolitic or freestone deposits covered by a rich alluvium; its elevation above the sea is trifling, and it is famed among Arabs as the most fertile and favoured district on the southern coast of Arabia. Numerous watercourses from the hills traverse the plain to the sea, and about a dozen of these, where they reach the shore, form creeks of which the water is partially fresh; some are well-wooded and grassy inland, and some are densely grown with mangroves at the coast. Parts of the country are covered with a coarse grass which dries up in winter, and in places there is a jungle of acacia. Water is found everywhere at a few feet from the surface; the wells

---

* The map and chart for Dhufār Proper are the same as for **Dhufār** District *q. v.*

are from 5 to 20 feet deep. At its west end the plain ends in a *cul-de-sac* 100 feet above sea level, behind a coast range of which the Rīsūt promontory is a prolongation. At the east end it is connected with **Murbāt** by a narrow maritime plateau which, from Khor Rori to a point four miles short of **Murbāt**, is 100 feet above the sea except at breaches made by ravines. The coast from Tāqa for 5 miles to the westward consists of cliff about 100 feet high; and from that point as far as Dahārīz it is low and is skirted by a mangrove swamp half a mile deep. There is generally a heavy surf upon the beach; and the landing, which is effected in catamarans, is ordinarily difficult or at least unpleasant.

Population.—From the topographical table at the end of this article it may be deduced that the fixed population of **Dhufār** Proper numbers about 3,000 souls, and it will be seen that nearly all belong to the **Āl Kathīr** tribe. The people, both nomads and non-nomads, wear their hair long and collect it by a fillet round their heads; Saiyids, however, and the poorest classes have their heads shaved. The ordinary inhabitant of Dhufār has only one garment, a dark-blue sheet six cubits long by three broad, which forms a kilt by day and is his only bedding at night.

Agriculture and animals.—The principal crops are bajri, maize, millet, cotton, and a little wheat and sugar-cane. There are no dates. Cocoanuts grow, but there is no surplus for export. Fruits are water and musk-melons, papai and a few plantains and mulberries. Some tobacco is produced, but the quantity is insufficient even for local consumption. Vegetables include bindis, and red pepper is grown; brinjals are seen, but only in the Wāli's garden. Ploughs are not in use; the ground is tilled with spade or hoe. The people own camels, cattle, sheep and goats, but have no horses and few donkeys; the goats are of a peculiar and rather handsome variety known throughout 'Omān as Dhufār goats. Fish abound and acres of a small fish called 'Aid عيد, resembling the sardine, may be seen drying near villages. Gazelle, hyænas and foxes are met with where there is cover.

Administration.—Dhufār Proper is the only part of the Lhufār District which is effectively controlled by the Wāli. The late Wāli had his headquarters in the Hisn or fort upon the shore between **Salālah** and Hāfah, a country residence and fort at Rizāt, and a house and gardens at Hamrān.

DHUFĀR PROPER

Topography.—The following are the principal places in Dhufār Proper :—

Name.	Position.	Nature.	Remarks.
'Auqad عوقد	The westernmost village in Dhufār plain, 4 miles west of Salālah, four miles north-east of Rīsūt, and about one mile from the sea.	A village of about 75 occupied mud houses divided into two quarters with an interval of half a mile between. The quarter to the west is 'Auqad Bait Fādhil and has 60 houses; the other is 'Auqad Bait Marhūn which has now only 15 occupied houses. The quarters are named from the sections of the Āl Kathīr tribe who inhabit them.	The inhabitants cultivate maize and bajri and collect frankincense. The water-supply is from wells two or three fathoms deep. There are no boats. Cattle number about 600 and sheep and goats the same. Midway between Salālah and 'Auqad a stream beginning in a fresh water spring runs down with a zig-zag course to the sea; its banks are marshy and abound in water-fowl. Half a mile north of 'Auqad are the ruins of a fort.
Bilād * بلاد or Balad-al-Qadīmah بلد القديمه or Balaid بليد	On the coast ⅓ a mile east of Hāfah, from which it is divided by cotton fields and groves of cocoanut palm.	A ruined site covering an area two miles in length by 600 yards in breadth. The fortified portion of the ancient town, at its east end, stretched for 1,240 yards along the sea, had a depth inland of 500 yards and was encircled on the three landward sides by a great ditch of fresh water. The citadel at the north-west corner of this quarter still rises 30 feet above the plain. The ruins of the unfortified part of the town are extensive but insignificant.	The ruins contain many sculptured remains, some Muhammadan, some possibly pre-Islamitic: among the former, near the north-east corner of the ruins, is the marble tombstone, admirably preserved and bearing the date 710 A. H., of Malik Ibrāhīm-bin-Mudhaffar, who according to tradition was the first Arab ruler of Dhufār. Not far from Bilād is the shrine of 'Abdullah-ās-Sāmiri عبد الله السامري a saint from Malabar, whose intercession is sought in the time of drought. To the north and east of Bilād is an accacia jungle containing gazelle and foxes.

* A full description of the ruins of Bilād, with drawings, will be found in an article by Dr. Carter in the transactions of the Bombay Geographical Society for 1846.

Name.	Position.	Nature.	Remarks.
Daharīz دهاريز	On the coast, 4 miles east of Hāfah.	Village of 100 mud and stone houses of the Āl Fādhil and other sections of the Āl Kathīr. The place is in a ruinous condition. On the west side are cotton fields and a grove of cocoanut palms.	The people are fishermen and cultivators: there are 10 small fishing boats, 1,000 cattle and 300 sheep and goats. Daharīz was once the capital of Dhufār.
Hāfah حافه	About 2 miles east of Salālah on the coast, along which it extends quarter of a mile.	Village of 150 houses of stone and mud; some however are uninhabited. About 25 families are low caste fishermen; the rest are Āl Kathīr Arabs of the Shanāfirah section.	There are a few cocoanut gardens. There are no manufactures.
Hamrān حمران	About 12 miles east of Salālah and two miles from the sea.	House and gardens, with a spring and watercourse, which belonged to the late Wāli of Dhufār.	Fruit, tobacco and vegetables are grown here by Bayāsirah cultivators, immigrants from 'Omān.
Hisn الحصن	About 100 yards from the beach at a point half a mile west of Hāfah and 1½ south-east of Salālah.	The principal fort in Dhufār of the Sultan of 'Omān: it was built several years ago by the Wāli Sulaimān, covers about an acre of ground, and contains a substantial three-storeyed building. The entrance is on the east side.	Outside the fort is a small enclosed bazaar of 6 shops, near which are a few huts.
Rizāt رزات	About eight miles east of Salālah and one-and-a-half miles from the sea.	A fort built by the late Wāli of Dhufār and garrisoned by 10 levies. Near by are some 10 mud houses inhabited by cultivators of the late Wāli's gardens, who are Āl Kathīr.	The lands are irrigated by a water-course from a Wādi of the same name.
Rubāt ربط	Two miles north-east of Salālah and one-and-a-half miles from the sea.	A deserted site with standing columns, etc. The remains cover many acres, but are not apparently very ancient.	There was a small village here as lately as 1844, but it has since been abandoned on account of the depredations of the hill Qaras.

Name.	Position.	Nature.	Remarks.
Salālah سلالة	.....	......	See article Salālah.
Tāqa طاقة	The easternmost village in the Dhufār Proper two miles west of Khor Rori and 20 miles west of Murbāt.	A village of about 20 mud huts and one stone building, chiefly inhabited by Ma'ashani Qaras. There are three or four families of Sharīfs and a few of Mashāikh; these latter classes act as mediators and go-betweens to the Bedouins, among whom their persons are sacred, and they take charge of the flocks and herds of Bedouins while in the plains.	The mountains here come down close to the sea and make a pleasing background. There are many ancient remains, standing columns, stone sarcophagi, etc.

DIBAH
دبة

A coast village of the Rās-al-Khaimah District in Trucial 'Omān, situated 1 mile south of Bai'ah on the western shore of a sandy bay which is 6 miles in breadth and open from north-north-east to east; it is connected by a route, which runs *viâ* the Qaliddi pass, with Rās-al-Khaimah Town on the other side of the 'Omān Promontory. Dibah is the frontier village, in this part, of Shārjah; Bai'ah, the next to the north, divided from Dibah merely by a small Wādi coming down to the sea, belongs to the Ruūs-al-Jibāl district of the 'Omān Sultanate. Bai'ah is ordinarily included under the name "Dibah"; but it is really distinct from Hisn-ad-Dibah or Dibah proper and should not be confounded with it. Dibah is held as a fief by Rāshid-bin-Ahmad, a first cousin of the Shaikh of Shārjah; he resides in the place and is described as Wāli: the neighbouring village of Wamm is subject to his administration, and he receives the Zakāt on dates from the village of Muhtarqah in Wādi-al-Qaliddi. The population of Dibah may be about 1,000 souls: there are 100 houses of the peasant class called Bayādir, 50 of the Awānāt tribe, 15 of Naqbiyīn and 10 of Sharqiyīn. To the south of the place are extensive date plantations containing, it is estimated, about 10,000 palms. The water is good and the wells about 4 fathoms deep. Livestock are 20 camels, 50 donkeys and 700 sheep and goats.

DIBAI
دبي
PRINCI-
PALITY*

An independent Arab principality on the coast of Trucial 'Omān; its political position is explained in the article on that country. Dibai is situated between the Shaikhdoms of **Shārjah** on the north and Abu Dhabi on the south, meeting **Shārjah** on the coast at Abu **Hail** which lies partly on one side of the border and partly on the other, and Abu **Dhabi** at Khor Ghanādhah, a creek described in the article on the Abu Dhabi Principality, which runs inland for many miles and divides the principalities one from the other. Jabāl-al-'Ali جبل العالي, the only hill on this coast, is in Dibai territory: it is 220 feet high, flat-topped, and lies 19 miles south-west of **Dibai** Town and 4 miles inland, being separated from the sea by a strip of low desert. It is often called Jabail جبيل. †

Inland the extent of the influence of the Shaikh of Dibai is doubtful. The village of Hajarain, 50 miles south-east of **Dibai** Town in Wādi **Hatta**, at the present time recognises him as overlord; but the origin of the connection is exceptional, and the place must be regarded as an isolated dependency, for there are villages nearer to **Dibai** Town which do not acknowledge the Shaikh's authority.

Besides **Dibai** Town and the village of Hajarain, the latter being merely a distant protectorate, the only permanently inhabited place in the principality is Jumairah جميره, a coast village about 3 miles south-west of **Dibai** Town; it consists of 45 date branch huts and is inhabited by Bani **Yās**, **Manāsīr** and mixed tribes who are all fishermen and own among them 5 camels, 60 donkeys, 45 cattle and 200 sheep and goats. None of the Bedouin tribes are expressly attached to Dibai, and the only recognised subjects of the Shaikh are accordingly the inhabitants of **Dibai** Town, of Jumairah and of Hajarain. The trade, shipping, etc., of the principality are simply those of the capital.

The Shaikh maintains about 100 retainers armed with Martini rifles, and about 1,500 of his ordinary subjects are reported to be similarly armed. There are no customs at **Dibai** Town, but the revenues of the principality are said to amount to $51,400 a year, largely derived from the pearl fisheries.

DIBAI
دبي
TOWN

The capital and only town of the principality of the same name: it is situated on the coast of Trucial 'Omān, 7 miles south-west of the

---

* For authorities, maps, charts, etc., see first footnote to article Trucial 'Omān.
† A representation of this hill will be found in Chart No. 2373—2837-A.

DIBAI TOWN

town of **Shārjah** and 79 miles north-east of the town of **Abu Dhabi**. At sea 20 miles to the west-south-west of Dibai town is 'Alaiwi, the easternmost and nearest of the Persian Gulf pearl banks.

Dibai stands on both sides of a creek, with a shallow and difficult entrance, which extends for some miles beyond the town in a south-easterly direction; there is a small quay for vessels able to go inside. The town consists of 3 main quarters: of these the principal is Dairah دیره , which stands on a tongue of land about 20 feet high on the north-east side of the creek between it and the sea, and has a date grove a mile in extent behind it. Dairah contains about 1,600 houses,—inhabited by Arabs, Persians, **Balūchis** and others,—and the main bazaar of 350 shops. The other two quarters, Shandaghah شندغه and Dibai proper, lie on the south-west side of the creek, Shandaghah being the nearer to the sea. Shandaghah is the residence of the Shaikh of the Abu **Dhabi** Principality and contains some 250 houses all occupied by Arabs; Indians are not allowed to establish themselves here. Dibai proper contains about 200 houses and 50 shops, also the principal mosque and some ruins said to be those of a Portuguese fort; the Indians are all collected in this quarter. Ferry boats ply between Dairah and Dibai proper, and on Fridays the crossing is free to inhabitants of Dairah who go to worship in the Jāmi' mosque. There is good water at Dibai in wells from 5 to 30 feet deep. The town was once walled, but the wall is now in ruins; on the landward side, however, are a number of towers of defence.

The population of Dibai town, in all about 10,000 souls or rather more, consists of the following elements: Bani **Yās** of the Āl Bū Falāsah and Sabāis sections, 440 houses; Āl Bū **Mahair**, 400 houses; mixed tribes, chiefly Arabs and including **Mazārī'** and natives of **Bahrain** and **Kuwait**, 400 houses; Persians, from various districts of Persia, 250 houses; **Sūdān**, 250 houses; **Balūchis**, 200 houses; natives of the **Hasa** Oasis, 50 houses; **Marar**, 30 houses; and Shwaihiyīn 10 houses. Nearly all of these are Sunnis of the Māliki sect. There are also 67 settled Hindus and 23 **Khōjahs**, British subjects, inclusive of women and children, and in the pearl season about 20 other Hindus visit the place.

Date trees number about 4,000, but the yield is scanty: the only other cultivation is a little lucerne. Dibai town is reckoned to possess 1,650 camels, 45 horses, 380 donkeys, 430 cattle and 960 goats. About 335 pearl boats, 50 fishing boats and 20 seagoing vessels, the last being chiefly Sambūks and Badans, belong to the place, and 10 to 12 boats are built annually.

The trade of Dibai is considerable and is rapidly expanding, chiefly in consequence of the enlightened policy of the late Shaikh, **Maktūm-bin-**

Hashar, and the stringency of the Imperial Persian Customs on the opposite coast; Dibai is now in process of supplanting **Lingeh** as the chief entrepôt of the foreign trade of Trucial **'Omān**. Dibai is now a port of call for the steamers of the British India and of the Bombay and Persia Steam Navigation Companies, the vessels of the former calling regularly once a fortnight and those of the latter at intervals as opportunity offers. The only exports of local origin are pearls, mother-of-pearl shells and dried fish. The imports are dates from **Basrah, Mīnāb** and **Bātinah**; also rice, wheat, piece-goods, spices, metals, coir-rope and timber, chiefly from India. The town contains some 400 shops and 200 warehouses. A portion of the imports are destined for the interior, particularly for the **Baraimi** Oasis. Of the local merchants 23 are Hindus and 7 are **Khōjahs** under British protection.

DIBDIBAH
دبدبه

A large district in the **Kuwait** Principality, situated between **Shaqq** on the east, **Shiqqaq** on the north, the **Bātin** on the north-west and **Summān** on the south-west; on the south it ends near **Dhula'-al-Mi'aijil**. It extends little, if at all, further north than the latitude of **Kuwait** Town, and its northern end is about 25 miles west of **Jahrah**. Its total length is thus about 100 miles, and its breadth is perhaps 50.

Dibdibah consists of featureless plains, with undulations so slight as to be almost imperceptible and yet sufficient to conceal camels at comparatively short distances; it is almost destitute of landmarks. The district contains some pasture in the season; but it is a very poor country, there are no wells, and the nomads who frequent the northern part of it actually procure their drinking water from **Jahrah**. A certain number of gazelle are found in Dibdibah.

The chief points of interest are the following:—

Name.	Position.	Nature.	Remarks.
'Amārah (Umm-al-) ام انعماره	10 miles west of **Shaqq** on the same parallel of latitude as **Riqa'i** in the **Bātin**.	A depressed tract adjoined by very slightly elevated ground.	Water collects here after rain and there are said to be traces of old and deep wells.
Hamīr (Umm-al-) ام الحمير	6 miles east of **Riqa'i** in the **Bātin**.	A Khabrah or hollow in which water collects.	The land rises from this place to the bank of the **Bātin** at **Riqa'i** in 5 or 6 distinct terraces or ridges. These drain towards Umm-al-Hamīr.

Name.	Position.	Nature.	Remarks.
Hīrān (Abul) ابو لحيران	About 22 miles west of Shaqq, on the direct route from Kuwait Town to Hafar in the Bāṭin.	A large Khabrah fed by at least one line of drainage.	It is enclosed on the east by a natural ridge. The water holes contain water for a month after ordinary rain.
Musannāh مسناه	Extends from a point on Falaij-al-Janūbīyah, a few miles south of Hafar, to Umm-al-'Amārah, and thence subsides to the Shaqq valley.	An undulation which runs from west-south-west to east-north-east, rising as it goes, and forms the highest part of Dibdibah.	Musannāh is a ridge, but it is barely perceptible and easily escapes notice.
Qara'ah قرعه	15 miles south-east of Sala', on the western border of Shaqq.	A low plateau.	Nasi grass is produced here which the Bedouins collect and sell at Kuwait Town.
Sala' سلع	8 miles east-north-east of Abul Hīrān.	A ridge.	It is rather higher than the ridge to the east of Abul Hīrān.

DIH KUHNEH
ده كهنه

The principal village in the **Shabānkāreh** district of the **Persian Coast,** and the residence of the Khān who is its ruler. It is situated on a plain about 15 miles north-west of **Burāzjān,** ½ a mile from the foot of the southernmost part of the coast range, at this point called Tavīseh; the defences consist of one or two insignificant forts built of stones and mud. The inhabitants are about 1,500 persons of the Haijab and Khājavān tribes, speaking Persian. Dih Kuhneh is the trade centre of the **Shabānkāreh** district, but depends chiefly on the cultivation of wheat, barley and dates. Water is from wells. There are about 20 horses and 400 donkeys besides some camels, and a regular caravan track exists between this place and Shīf.

DILAIM
دليم

An Arab tribe located in Mesopotamia between **Baghdād** and Hīt and generally outside the limits of the present Gazetteer. They sometimes

encamp, however, near the **Baghdād-Karbala** road about **Mahmūdīyah**.*
They are closely connected with the **Zubaid** and would probably act with
them in case of war.

**DILAM
or
DAILAM**
دیلم

A small port situated on the coast of the **Līrāvi** District in Persia, but not forming part of it administratively; it lies about 85 miles north-north-west of **Būshehr** Town and a similar distance east-north-east of the bar of the **Shatt-al-'Arab**.† Dīlam stands upon a low coast which extends north and south and consists of a strip of rocky land raised 10 to 15 feet above the sea-level, having swamps behind it that run inland for several miles. Half a mile to the south of the place is a little cultivation with some trees; and to the eastward is a plain containing a few villages dependent on Dīlam. A square fort stands in the middle of Dīlam, and 1¼ miles to the north-eastwards is the fort of Tanūb, again mentioned below, which protects the water-supply.

Anchorage.—The anchorage for vessels, about 3¼ miles off the shore, is sheltered from the Shamāl and partially from the Qaus; the bottom is of soft mud and the depth of water 4 fathoms: native craft lie close to the beach in a creek in the mud-flats. Landing is difficult because of the mud, and cargoes are loaded and unloaded by means of donkeys.

Inhabitants.—The population amounts to about 1,500 souls and is entirely Shī'ah; all the people are Persian-speaking, but about one-third of them can talk Arabic also. Some are cultivators in the surrounding **Līrāvi** District, others sailors or fishermen, and the remainder merchants or shop-keepers. Their houses are erections of sun-dried brick without an upper storey. The population seems to be decreasing as there are now about 100 unoccupied and ruinous houses. A number of recent emigrants from **Dīlam** have settled at **Fāo** in Turkish **'Irāq**.

Resources.—The resources of the place are inconsiderable. Drinking water is scarce and indifferent; it is brought from Tanūb. About 20 horses, 40 mules, 200 donkeys, 160 cattle and 500 sheep are owned by the inhabitants. There are 10 Būms, 10 Māshuwahs and 20 small fishing boats.

---

* For information about the Dilaim, see Gazetteer of Baghdād (1899), pages 134-5 and 190.

† It would seem natural to identify Dīlam with the Mahrubān of the mediæval Arab geographers; but Mr. Le Strange, the best authority, identifies it with Sīnīz. See his *Lands of the Eastern Caliphate*. *Vide* also footnote to article **Līrāvi**.

DĪLAM

Trade.—Dīlam is the port of the wheat-growing district of **Behbehān**, and to this circumstance it owes such trade as it enjoys. Oversea traffic is principally with **Būshehr** but also, to limited extent, with **Kuwait**, **Bahrain** and **Masqat**. The chief exports are wheat, barley, straw, insoluble gum, linseed, ghi and dried figs; imports include rice, coffee, sugar, tea, pepper, turmeric, dried limes of **Masqat** origin, and kerosine oil. The bazaar contains 90 shops. Ordinary Persian coin, mostly Qrāns, is current. The standard of weight is a local Man of 14 lbs. $8\frac{1}{2}$ oz. English; there is also a Hāshim Man of 16 ordinary local Mans or $232\frac{1}{2}$ lbs. English.

Communications.—The route from Dīlam to Zaidān (21 miles) and thence to **Behbehān** Town (22 miles) has been recently described,* and a coast route connects Dīlam with **Rīg**, 54 miles distant on the one side, and with **Hindiyān** Village at 27 miles on the other. Both of these routes are suitable for pack carriage and neither presents any serious difficulties.† Postal communication with **Būshehr** is by courier, and there is a post in each direction every week. Dīlam is a station on the Persian Government's branch telegraph-line from **Burāzjān** to **Ahwāz**; it is intermediate between the **Rīg** and Behbehān Town stations.

Administration.—Dīlam is ruled by two local Khāns (at present 'Abdul Husain and 'Abdur Riza, brothers), who are under the authority of the Governor of the **Gulf Ports**; the Khāns, who defer considerably to Saiyids and Mullas, dispose of criminal matters, and civil causes are settled by the Qāzi and Mullas. ‡ The general revenue of Dīlam is inconsiderable, being farmed by the Khāns from the Governor of the Gulf Ports for 1,250 Tūmāns a year, but, since the establishment of a post of the Imperial Persian Customs, the sea customs have yielded a substantial return. The Khāns previously farmed the sea customs for 12,000 Qrāns per annum; since direct management was instituted they have been receiving compensation at the rate of 500 Qrāns annually, while the duties collected by the customs in 1905 amounted to 60,000 Qrāns. The people of Dīlam are fairly well armed with Martini rifles and revolvers: there is about one rifle to every house.

---

* *Vide* a report by Lieutenant C. H. Gabriel, I.A., in the records of the Intelligence Branch, Simla.

† See *Routes in Persia*, I, No. 21. A route from Būshehr to Dīlam has recently been described by Col. Bailward, R.F.A.

‡ Before the end of 1905 the Khāns were removed by the Governor of the **Gulf Ports** who proceeded to appoint an outside nominee: it is impossible to say whether this innovation will become permanent.

Dependencies.—Two small places in the neighbourhood dependent on Dilam are the following:—

Name.	Position.	Houses and inhabitants.	Remarks.
'Amiri عامري	6 miles north-east of Dilam on the route to Behbehān.	60 mud huts of Lurs and 1 or 2 of Arab Saiyids.	The village stands on slightly rising ground. Some grain is cultivated. There are a few horses and about 200 sheep; also 2 wells of brackish water.
Tanūb تنوب	1¼ miles north-east of Dilam.	Half a dozen huts of cultivators who are dependents of a Saiyid of Dilam.	There is a little cultivation and a small fort built by a Saiyid, as an act of merit, to protect the water-supply of Dilam which is at this place and was formerly liable to be seized by enemies.

DILAM دلم

The capital and administrative centre of the **Kharj** district of Southern **Najd,** and itself sometimes loosely called "Kharj"; it is situated about 50 miles south by east of **Riyādh** and perhaps 35 miles east-north-east of **Hautah** town.

Dilam is walled and is said to consist of three wards styled respectively Samhān سمحان Sūq سوق and Tuwālah طوالة. There is a fort within the walls occupied by Ibn Sa'ūd's representative, and some of the ordinary houses of the place have upper storeys; but the principal mosque is a mean construction in the poor Wahhābi style of architecture. There is one large school, the Madrasah Shaikh Makhdhūb مخذوب, besides a number of small ones. The population of Dilam is about 1,500 souls; there are 100 houses of ' **Āid,** 60 of Bani **Tamīm,** 20 of **Dawāsir,** 20 of **Sabai** ' and 100 of inferior tribes.

Reports agree in describing the date groves of Dilam as extensive and as containing between 10,000 and 15,000 palms. Wheat and maize are grown and even a little rice; there are also citrons, grapes, lemons, figs, pomegranates, melons and lucerne. Irrigation is from wells of good water, 6 to 8 fathoms in depth, and from the Farzān rivulet described in the article on **Kharj.** Livestock are estimated at 600 camels, 100 donkeys and 300 cattle; there are few horses or none. The bazaar contains about 30 shops, supplied with piece-goods and sundries from **Hasa** and with coffee from Yaman *via* **Hautah.**

Dilam is at present governed in the name of the Wahhābi Amīr by one Hasan, a Yamani of the **Qahtān** tribe, specially appointed by Ibn Sa'ūd. He is not a local man, but he has with him at Dilam about 20 households of his relations and personal dependents.

DIMA (WADI)
وادي دما

In the Eastern **Hajar** of the **'Omān** Sultanate: a valley which rises in a Saih or desert plain to the north of the Baldan-al-Masākirah division of **Sharqīyah** and, running northwards, joins Wādi **Tāyīn** on the right bank at the village of Sīdafi. The following are the villages of Wādi Dima in descending order from its head to Sīdafi :—Dairah ديره (70 houses), Samūt سموط (50 houses), Ghamsah غمصه (60 houses), Oaryah قريه (150 houses), Hail حيل (20 houses), Qutaifi قطيفي (40 houses), Barkyāt بزكيات (60 houses), Ahla اهلا (20 houses), Samhān صمحان (50 houses), Hisn حصن (180 houses), Hārrah حارّه (20 houses), Qabsah قبصه (10 houses), 'Auf عوف (80 houses) and Hājir حاجر (100 houses). All the villages are on the left bank except Dairah, Hārrah and 'Auf which are on the right bank and Hājir which is on both sides; the inhabitants, some 4,500 souls, all belong to the Bani Shahaim except those of Hājir who are Bani **Ruwāhah**. Hājir is within sight of Sīdafi. Livestock are estimated at 350 camels, 550 donkeys, 600 cattle and 2,500 sheep and goats, distributed approximately in proportion to the size of the villages. Date palms number about 50,000, of which the majority are at Hisn (10,000), Qaryah (9,000) and Barkyāt (8,000).

DIMNAH
دمنه

A small village in the **Qrā'ah** district of the **Kuwait** Principality, situated on a low bank of sand about 200 yards from the sea and 6 miles east-south-east of **Kuwait** Town. The village belongs to the '**Awāzim**, contains 25 houses, and is inhabited in the cold weather only. In the hot weather the people find employment at the pearl fisheries or in the date gardens on the Shatt-al-'**Arab**. The inhabitants have only 1 or 2 Horis; they fish principally by means of Hadhrahs or tidal weirs upon the beach. A few donkeys and some poultry belong to the village. There are a number of wells but only a few hold water, which is brackish and hardly more than sufficient for the requirements of the village. There is no recognised headman, and the Shaikh of **Kuwait** deals direct with the village through the first inhabitant whose presence he can secure.

The houses of Dimnah are typical of the country about **Kuwait** and may therefore be described. They consist of a single room each with a floor-space of 30 feet by 10 feet. The walls are of mud, 4 feet high, and support a gable roof, 7 feet high at the ridge, of light rafters and **Basrah** reeds covered with date-leaf matting. The door is low, and there is no window. A fireplace and a slightly raised stand for coffee pots, constructed of mud, occupy one end of the apartment.

DĪWĀNĪ-YAH
ديوانيّة
QADHA

A division of the Sanjāq of the same name in the Wilāyat of Baghdād, in Turkish 'Irāq.

Position and boundaries.—The Qadha of Dīwānīyah is situated upon the **Euphrates** between **Hillah** and **Samāwah**, chiefly, if not entirely, upon the left or eastern bank. It is bounded on the east by the Qadha of **Hai** in the Basrah Sanjāq of Muntafik; on the south by the Qadha of **Samāwah**; on the west by that of **Shāmīyah**; on the north-west by that of **Hillah**; and on the north by the Qadha of **Kūt-al-Amārah** in the Baghdād Sanjāq.

Topography and tribes.—The only places of size in the Qadha are the town of **Dīwānīyah**, described elsewhere under its own name, and the Daghārah and 'Afaj settlements of which mention is made in the article on the **Daghārah** canal; to these may be added the village of Fuwwār referred to in the article on the **Euphrates**.

The following (apart from the **Daghārah** tract, the article on which may be consulted) are the Muqāta'ahs or tracts of which the Qadha is composed and the tribes that inhabit them:—

Tracts.	Tribes.
'Abrah عبرة	Farāhinah.
Dajjah دجّه	Abu 'Alaiwi, Sindān and Ziyād.
Jalīhah جليحه	Jalīhah.
Kharkharah خرخره	Same as Dajjah.
Murādīyah مراديّه	Āl Bū Husain.
Nakhailah نخيله	Āl Bū Rīshah.

Further information about tribes will be found in the article on the **Daghārah** canal, the whole of the tract watered by which is situated in this Qadha.

DĪWĀNĪYAH TOWN

Population.—The total fixed population of the district is estimated at 50,000 souls, of whom all are Muhammadans and all (except about 500 Sunnis at **Dīwānīya**h Town) are Shī'ahs.

Resources.—Dates, wheat, barley and rice are cultivated, and the usual animals are owned. According to the latest Turkish official statistics the date palms in the Qadha number 100,000.

Administration.—Dīwānīyah being the Markaz Qadha in the Sanjāq of the same name has no Qāim-Maqām, but is personally governed by the Mutasarrif resident at **Dīwānīya**h Town, who is also in direct charge of the Markaz Nāhiyah or subdivision likewise called Dīwānīyah. There are 3 other Nāhiyahs in the district, *viz.*, 'Afaj (3rd class), Budair بدير (1st class) and Daghārah (1st class); the Mudīrs of the first and last of these are stationed at the villages bearing the same names which are described in the article on the **Daghārah** canal, and the Mudīr of the second has his headquarters at a place called Budair. The town of **Dīwānīyah** is the *chef-lieu* of the whole Qadha.

DĪWĀNĪYAH TOWN ديوانيه

The chief town of the Sanjāq of the same name in Turkish 'Irāq; it stands upon the **Euphrates** about 65 miles below **Hillah** Town and 75 miles above **Samāwah** Town by the course of that river, and it consists of two portions upon opposite banks united by a boat-bridge of nine pontoons. Dīwānīyah has now, in consequence of the drying up of the reach of the **Euphrates** on which it stands, nothing to recommend it as an administrative centre except its central position in the Sanjāq. Upstream as far as the boundary of the **Hillah** Qadha and downstream as far as **Rumaithah**, agriculture has ceased for want of water; and the villages, though many of them are still standing, are practically deserted. At the town itself the pontoons composing the boat-bridge may sometimes be seen reposing upon dry sand.

The main quarter of Dīwānīyah, about $\frac{4}{5}$ of the whole, half composed of brick-built houses and including the Sarāi or government offices and the barracks, is upon the left bank of the river bed; the right bank quarter consists altogether of houses of sun-dried brick. The town is open and undefended except by a ruinous wall on the left bank: the open desert surrounds it on every side.

The population does not exceed 4,000 and is decreasing. It consists almost entirely of Arabs, of whom all but 150 are Shī'ahs: there are also some 50 Turks, 45 Jews, 30 Persians, and half a dozen Christians. There are two public baths.

The trade of the place, which has dealings with **Najaf** and **Baghdād** as well as with **Basrah**, is insignificant and is confined to the export of ordinary agricultural and pastoral produce and to the import of a few common articles. Even this small degree of trade depends largely on the still flourishing settlements upon the **Daghārah** canal, some way to the north-east, and on properties of the **Dāirat-as-Sanīyah** at some distance off. The town itself has only a few date trees, and for supplies it depends upon outlying places connected with it. There are about 200 ordinary shops, besides eight cafés, four Khāns or caravansarais and four 'Alwahs or grain stores. For eight months in the year the **Euphrates** river is dry and the inhabitants get their drinking water from wells, which are fortunately sweet.

The Turkish Government had some difficulty in compelling the chief officials of the **Dīwānīyah** Sanjāq to remove from **Hillah**, where they had established themselves, to their proper headquarters here; indeed this measure was not successfully enforced until about 12 years ago. Among the civil officers is a Mamūr of the Public Debt Department. The military garrison of Dīwānīyah consists nominally of one battalion of regular infantry and three guns; but three of the four infantry companies are generally on duty in the district, collecting revenue, etc., and the normal garrison is only about 80 men. Perhaps 100 Radīfs can be called up at Dīwānīyah, which is the headquarters of the 3rd battalion of the 86th Radīf regiment. Dīwānīyah is connected with **Hillah** by a double line of telegraph and with **Samāwah** by a single line. The town is constituted as a municipality.

YĀLAH
ديالة

This river, coming down from the Persian frontier north-east of **Baghdād** City, lies outside the scope of the Gazetteer except at its mouth, which opens into the **Tigris** at a point 10 miles south-east of **Baghdād** in a direct line and over 20 miles distant from it by river. Just above the confluence the banks of the Diyālah are united by a boat-bridge of 16 pontoons divided into four sections, which are connected by planks; each boat is 32 feet long, 12 feet wide, 6 feet deep and flat bottomed. Except at the bridge, where the approaches though ramped are difficult for wheels, the banks (in this part of the Diyālah) are mostly precipitous and rise about 30 feet above the stream. For two miles from the bridge on the left bank the country is much cut up by water channels, and beyond this again the country is open desert—

cultivable but uncultivated—in all directions. At the end of the bridge on the right bank are about 30 huts and on the left bank 15: these compose a small village called Diyālah which is inhabited by mixed tribes, chiefly **Zubaid** of the Āl Bū Khattāb section. From the beginning of December to the middle of April the Diyālah is navigable by native craft as far as the town of Ba'qūbah, but during the rest of the year, partly in consequence of the water drawn off by important canals, it is a shallow stream of no consequence. The Diyālah apparently serves as a boundary between the **Baghdād** and **'Azīzīyah** Qadhas.

The Diz river rises in the mountains of South-Western Persia in the vicinity of Burūjird, enters **'Arabistān** at a point about 15 miles north of **Dizfūl** Town, and joins the **Kārūn** exactly at **Band-i-Qīr**.

DIZ RIVER or ĀB-I-DIZ
آب دز

Course and general characteristics.—After passing the town of **Dizfūl** on its left bank, it being here a swift and not very deep river but partially obstructed by rocks, the Diz runs for about 12 miles to the south-west; in this reach its bed is broad and shingly, the stream flowing in several channels, and a number of small canals take off on either bank, especially on the left bank where there is a tract of heavily irrigated country.

At about 11 miles below **Dizfūl** Town the Diz is joined on its right bank by the **Balārūd** and near the same place it changes its direction to south-south-east; 11 or 12 miles further on it passes the village of 'Abdush Shāh upon its left bank, and 3 or 4 miles beyond 'Abdush Shāh it receives the perennial **'Ajīrub** stream as a tributary upon that side.

At a place about 30 miles south-south-eastwards in a direct line from **Dizfūl** Town the Diz leaves the village of Dih Nau upon its left; and several miles further on it reaches Kūt Bandar کوت بندر, virtually the upper limit of navigation, at which point a rocky ridge not more than a hundred feet high, with a north-westerly and south-easterly direction, is pierced by the river in its course: this ridge is named Umm-al-'Ayāi ام العيني. A couple of miles before arriving at Kūt Bandar a place Lim (or Ilm) Kathīr, which is only about 16 miles south-west of **Shūshtar** Town, is passed on the left bank: a left-bank tributary known as the Shūreh شوره, which may perhaps be identified with the **Kāunak** stream, enters the river immediately above Lim Kathīr, and a small right-bank affluent called the Mukhaibāt مخيبات, of which the source is not known, falls into it just above Kūt Bandar.

From Kūt Bandar the Diz continues its south-south-easterly course to within 10 miles or less of the right bank of the **Kārūn** above **Wais**, when it swerves to the north-east and enters the **Kārūn** at the confluence of its **Shatait** and **Gargar** branches; before turning north-eastward it is joined on its right bank by the **Shāūr** river, the most important of its tributaries, in two channels which are described in the article under the name **Shāūr**. For some distance above Kūt Bandar, and below that place for the whole way to **Band-i-Qīr**, the course of the Diz is serpentine in an extraordinary degree; thus Kūt Bandar, which in a straight line is only about 25 miles from **Band-i-Qīr**, is distant from that place by river no less than 85 miles. To speak generally, the Diz is swifter, shallower and (above Kūt Bandar) more broken up by obstacles than the **Kārūn**.

The average fall of the Diz appears to the eye to be more rapid than that of the **Shatait** or **Gargar**. It cuts its way through an alluvial plain between steep banks which rise 10 to 20 feet above flood level and outside of which there is no marked valley or river basin. The banks are frequently several hundred yards apart at bends, and the re-entrant curves are occupied by low deposits of mud overgrown with scrub. From about 20 miles south of **Dizfūl** Town to within about the same distance of its junction with the **Kārūn** the course of the Diz lies in a belt of brushwood, not usually more than 2 or 3 miles wide and in places less, frequently broken by gaps through which glimpses are caught of limitless plains. Trees from 30 to 40 feet in height are scattered through this jungle, yet there is no wood fit for use except as firewood: the principal trees and shrubs are the Gharab or Euphrates poplar, the Sarīm, the tamarisk, the liquorice bush, and a sort of blackberry. Fuel for the steamers on the **Kārūn**, for the towns of **Shūshtar** and **Nāsiri**, and to a certain extent for **Dizfūl** Town is obtained from this tract.

The climate of the Diz country is undoubtedly much more humid than that of '**Arabistān** generally, and in spring there is abundant pasturage upon both sides of the river. Fuel and fodder are obtainable, and the Arabs of the neighbourhood own numbers of buffaloes, cattle, sheep and goats. On the left bank immediately above Kūt Bandar there is much unirrigated cultivation of wheat and barley.

Irrigation.—At all seasons of the year the Diz is of a darker colour than either the **Gargar** or **Shatait**; it assumes, when in flood, a deep red hue near **Dizfūl** Town and one verging on chocolate at **Band-i-Qīr**.

DIZ RIVER

The proportion of silt carried is about the same as in the **Kārūn**. In 'Arabistān the Diz is hardly utilised for irrigation except in the reach immediately below **Dizfūl** Town, where the level of the country on either side is not much higher than that of the stream. The following is a list of the principal canals which tap the Diz in the **Dizfūl** District, but their exact relative positions and the spelling of some of the names are uncertain :—

Right Bank.

Qanāt Sinjar.
Nahr Qal'eh Tūq.
„   Shūhān.
„   Shākhak.
„   Zāwiyeh Bakhtiyāri.
„   „   Shaikh.
„   „   Kalāntarhā.
„   Bunwār Nāzir.
„   „   Khwājeh Husain.
Jāteh.

Left Bank.

Qanāt Shāhābād.
„   Siyāh Mansūr (watering Siyāh Mansūr village).
„   Bunwār Shāmi.
„   Kumish Hājiyān.
„   „   Mūminān.
Qanāt-i-Gāvdūl (with head at **Dizfūl** Town).
„   Bāgh Gāzir.
„   Hammām Kinār Āb (not used for irrigation).
„   Hammām Pilleli (also not used for irrigation).
Nahr Bāgh Saiyid.
„   Khān.
„   Ilyāsi.
„   Dahli.
„   Kulangān (partially irrigating Qal'eh Shaikh).
„   Kūtiyān.
„   Jībar.
„   Sharafābād (watering a number of villages, among them 'Abbās, Asad Khān, Hājiābād, Jībar, Kuwīgh and Sharafābād).
Nahr-i-Kilmilak (with head at **Dizfūl** Town).

Navigation.—In a favourable state of the river there is no obstacle, except a strong current, to navigation between **Band-i-Qīr** and Kūt Bandar—a distance, as already remarked, of 85 miles by water. At Kūt Bandar the channel is interrupted by a reef of rock; the rock however is pierced by an opening, about 20 yards from the left bank, which in a good river carries from $4\frac{1}{2}$ to 6 feet of water, but is somewhat difficult owing to the strength of the current. A little higher up there is a second reef, but the soundings in the passage through it are better. Above Kūt Bandar, in consequence of a steeper inclination of the river bed, the current becomes more rapid; the depth also is less, and the gravelly and in places the stony nature of the bottom would make it dangerous to force a lightly built vessel should she show signs of grounding. Kūt Bandar may therefore be taken as the practical limit of navigation for steamers of the type of the "Shushan",[*] which last visited the place in March 1905.

Villages and inhabited tracts.—The villages on both banks of the Diz below **Dizfūl** Town are described in the article on the **Dizfūl** District; the last of these is Dih Nau, below which there is nothing adjacent to either bank that can be reckoned as a permanent village. There are, however, both above and below Dih Nau, a number of habitable tracts distinguished by names, and these are described in descending order in the table below :—

Name.	Position.	Nature.	Remarks.
Hiddeh	On the right bank, below Jirqeh Saiyid Muhammad.	A tract of land.	Also called Haddāmeh, **Kathīr** of the Āl Bū Nassi section dwell here.
Husainīyeh حسينية	On the right bank, about midway between the confluences of the **Balārūd** and 'Ajīrub with the Diz; it extends as far westwards as the **Shāūr** river.	Do.	Belongs to the **Kathīr** tribe, by whose Bait Karīm, Ma'alleh, Āl Bū Nāsir and Māhūr sections it is occupied. The name is derived from a building erected for the holding of Rozehkhāni.
Abul Bishr ابوالبشر	On the left bank, below the 'Ajīrub and above Dih Nau.	Do.	Occupied by the Bait Sa'ad.
Umm-al-Wāwi ام الواوي	On the left bank, in the neighbourhood of Dih Nau.	Do.	Do.
Lim Kathīr لم كثير	On the left bank, 5 miles below Umm-al-Wāwi and 2 by land above Kūt Bandar; **Shūshtar** town lies 16 miles north-eastwards.	A combined fort and caravansarai built of mud, known also as Khāneh-i-Shaikh Farhān خانه شيخ فرحان	This was until very recently the headquarters of Shaikh Farhān Asad, one of the heads of the **Kathīr** tribe, but he has now removed to the village of Dih Nau. Another form of the name of the place is Ilm Kathīr الم كثير.

[*] The "Shushan" is a stern-wheeler of 100 feet length over all, 23 feet beam and 2½ feet draft.

Name.	Position.	Nature.	Remarks.
Abur Ridha ابوالرضا	2 miles from the right bank, not far below Kūt Bandar.	An Imāmzadeh.	Locally the name is pronounced Rīdā. Bani Sa'ad of the Ka'ab-as-Sitātleh section dwell here.
Jājīs جاجیس	Said to be about 2 miles from the right bank of the Diz, at a point about 10 miles below Kūt Bandar.	A mound, said to have been crowned at one time by an impregnable fort.	The neighbourhood is occupied by Bait Sa'ad tribesmen and watered by the Ishāreh canal from the Shāūr.
Huwaisiyāt ...	On the right bank immediately above the 'Anāfijeh border.	A tract of land.	Irrigation is by the Hawasīyeh canal from the Shāūr. The inhabitants are Bait Sa'ad.
Abu Tayūr ابو طیور	On the right bank, 12 miles by water above the junction of the Diz with the Kārūn.	Do.	A settlement of the 'Anāfijeh.
Yaqauwīyeh يقوريه	On the left bank, about 4 miles from Band-i-Qīr.	Do.	The people are of the Hardān tribe; they are surrounded by the 'Anāfijeh.
Nais نیس	Between the preceding and the following place.	Do.	'Anāfijeh of the Nais section camp here.
Abul Jazīreh ابو الجزیره	On the right bank about 1 mile from Band-i-Qīr.	Do.	Occupied by 'Anāfijeh. The name is pronounced Ubūizīreh.

DIZFŪL
دزفول
DISTRICT

A district of Persia, composing with the adjacent district of **Shūshtar** and the neighbouring districts of **'Aqīli** and **Rāmuz** a northern division of the province of **'Arabistān**. The physical geography, climate, inhabitants, and government of the district being dealt with in the article on Northern **'Arabistān**, while its agriculture, communications and trade are described in that on the province of **'Arabistān** generally, it only remains to treat in the present place of its boundaries and topography.

Boundaries.—On three sides the Dizfūl District is enclosed by other Persian territory, *viz.*, on the north by the hill tract of Western Luristān and the **Bakhtiyāri** country, on the east by the district of **Shūshtar** in Northern **'Arabistān**, and on the south by the district of **Ahwāz** in Southern **'Arabistān**; on the west it is conterminous with the Basrah Wilāyat of the province of Turkish **'Irāq**. The northern limit of Dizfūl is a line running eastwards from a spot on or near the **Dawairīj** stream so as to include Pā-i-Pul, the tract of Mazra'eh Sālihābād and the villages of Sar Bīsheh and Āb Bīd; on the east the boundary is at first an imaginary line passing between the villages of **Kāunak** and Shalgahi in Dizfūl and those of Pahwindeh and Farajābād in the **Shūshtar** District, and thereafter it may be taken to be the **Diz** river as far southwards as a point between Lim Kuthār and Kūt Bandar; the line then turns to the west, leaving the **'Anāfijeh** in the **Ahwāz** District, and continues in the same direction, crossing the **Shāūr** and **Karkheh** rivers on the way, until it joins the undemarcated Perso-Turkish frontier. That frontier itself constitutes the boundary of the Dizfūl District upon the west.

Topography.—Below is a tabular statement of the principal places in the Dizfūl District, from which it will appear that the settled population probably amounts to about 61,500 souls, inclusive of the inhabitants (45,000) of **Dizfūl** Town.

Name.	Position.	Houses and inhabitants.	Remarks.
Āb Bīd آب بید	About 8 miles east and somewhat north of **Kāunak**, with a precipitous hill called Kūh War-i-Zard immediately to the north of it.	160 houses of Haftlang **Bakhtiyāris**. The people have 20 rifles and there are 2 forts, one held by the **Bakhtiyāri** Khāns and the other by the villagers.	Water is from a spring which is surrounded by willows; there is a garden with trees, and wheat and barley are grown. Some cattle, donkeys and sheep are kept. A Hammām exists. The village is the property of the **Bakhtiyāri** Khāns.
'Abbās (Qal'eh) قلعه عباس	About 9 miles south of **Dizfūl** Town on the east side of the **Diz** river.	30 houses of **Lurs**, mostly Sagwand but a few Faili. There is a small fort and the people have 3 rifles.	Water is from the **Diz** river by the Sharafābād canal; there are 20 mules and 3 flocks of sheep.

DIZFŪL DISTRICT

Name.	Position.	Houses and inhabitants.	REMARKS.
Abbāsābād عباس آباد	About 7 miles south of Dizfūl Town and less than 1 mile east of the Diz river.	25 houses. The people are mostly Lurs of the Sagwand and Dīnārwand sections, but there are a few Arabs: among them they have 8 rifles.	Irrigation is from the Diz river and there are some gardens.
'Abdush Shāh (Qal'eh or Kūt) قلعه — كوت عبد الشاه	About 16 miles south of Dizfūl Town, 1 mile from the left bank of the Diz river and 2 miles from the upper end of the jungle tract on the Diz.	80 houses. The people are Kathīr Arabs with some Kurds and a few Dizfūlis. There is a fort and 50 rifles are owned.	The people live by agriculture and wood cutting; they also own camels, buffaloes, cattle and sheep. In winter there is a ferry over the Diz at this place; the rafts are supported by skin floats. The village belongs to Shaikh Haidar of the Kathīr; but a water mill which is reputed to grind 400 Dizfūli Mans of flour in the 24 hours is the property of the Bakhtiyāri Khāns. There is a shrine here of Ishāq-bin-Ibrāhīm.
Ahmad (Jirqeh Saiyid) جرقه سيد احمد	About 10 miles west-south-west of Dizfūl Town in a tract called Ja'farābād, near the tomb of Saiyid Tāhir. It is situated in the tract known as Milk Bin-Mu'alla.	120 houses, of which 30 recently built are mud with timber roofs, the rest being huts. Except 4 families of Saiyids and a few Lurs the people are Kathīr. There are 25 rifles, all belonging to Saiyid Ahmad.	Wheat, barley, rice, millet and Māsh are grown, and water and marsh melons have lately been introduced. Irrigation is from the Karkheh and Shāūr rivers. Livestock are cattle, mules, sheep and a dozen buffaloes. The place is named after its present head, who is a younger son of Saiyid Tāhir.
Aiwān-i-Karkheh ايوان كرخه	...	...	See article Karkheh.
Ali (Qal'eh Hāji) قلعه هاجي علي (also called Khānābād) (خان آباد)	About 6 miles south-west of Dizfūl Town to the west of the Diz river.	20 houses of Sagwand Lurs. There are two small forts, one of which is out of repair, and 10 rifles which are the property of Khānjān Khān.	There is irrigation from the Diz river and wheat, barley, rice, Kunjid, Māsh and millet are grown. Some cattle and donkeys are kept. The village is owned in 4 shares of which one belongs to Khānjān Khān, the Sagwand

Name.	Position.	Houses and inhabitants.	Remarks.
Ali-ibn-al-Husain (Qarīyeh) قریه علي ابن الحسین	About 10 miles south-west of Dizfūl Town, to the west of the Diz river.	10 houses of Sagwand Lurs and Saiyids. There is a small mud fort with timber roof and the people have 2 rifles.	Lur chief, one to Muhammad 'Ali, and two to the heirs of the late Āgha Riza, Mustaufi. The village is irrigated from the Diz and there are a garden with trees and a water mill. Cattle and donkeys are kept. The owners are the heirs of the late Āgha Riza, Mustaufi. The shrine known as Buq'eh-i-'Ali-ibn-al-Husain is 1 mile from the village.
Ali Quli (Qal'eh) قلعة علي قلي	5 miles south of Dizfūl Town on the east side of the Diz river.	20 houses of Dizfūlis and Lurs. There are 4 rifles and a small fort.	Water is from the Diz river. There are some gardens.
Anjīreh انجیره	6 miles south-east of Dizfūl Town.	20 houses of Sagwand Lurs and Dizfūlis. There are 5 rifles and a small fort.	Irrigation from the Diz river.
Āqa Abu Talab (Qal'eh) قلعه آقا ابو طلب	Adjoins 'Abbāsābād on the south-east.	25 houses. The people are Sagwand Lurs with a few Saiyids and Arabs. They have 4 rifles.	...
Asad Khān (Qal'eh Nau) (I) قلعه نو اسد خان	Adjoins Dih Jībar.	40 houses. The inhabitants are Arabs, Kurds, Bakhtiyāris and a few Dizfūlis. There are 5 rifles and a small fort.	Water is from the Diz river by the Sharafābād canal. This village and the next take their name from the same founder.
Asad Khān (Qal'eh Nau) (II) قلعه نو اسد خان	About 8 miles south-east of Dizfūl Town.	20 houses of Sagwand Lurs and Dizfūlis. There are 4 rifles and a small fort.	Water is by Qanāt from the Diz river. There are some gardens. This village is named after the same individual as the last.
Bakhtiyāri (Zāwiyeh) زاویه بختیاري	About 8 miles south-west of Dizfūl Town, west of the Diz river.	40 houses of Dizfūli Lurs and Arabs. The people have 6 rifles and there is a fort.	Wheat, barley, beans, rice, indigo, Kunjid, Māsh and millet are grown; irrigation is from the Diz river by a canal. Livestock are donkeys, buffaloes and cattle.

DIZFŪL DISTRICT

Name.	Position.	Houses and inhabitants.	Remarks.
Bālingān Bālāi بالنگان بالای	12 miles south of Dizfūl Town on the east side of the Diz river.	25 houses of Kurds, Nais Arabs under the protection of the Kathīr and Dizfūlis. There are 6 rifles and a small fort.	Water is from the Diz river.
Bālingān Dūman or Pāīn بالنگان دومن — پائین	About 1 mile east of Qal'eh 'Abdush Shāh.	30 houses of Lurs. There is a small fort and 20 rifles are owned.	Do.
Bandobār or Bandobāl (Qarīyeh) قریه بندوبار — بندوبال	2 miles south of Dizfūl Town.	30 houses of Dizfūlis. There is a mud fort; the people have only 2 rifles.	Water is by a canal from the Diz river, and wheat, barley, beans, rice, indigo and Kunjid are grown, also melons and fruit. There are some donkeys, cattle and sheep.
Banūt (Qal'eh) قلعه بنوت	About 4 miles south of Qal'eh 'Abdush Shāh.	50 houses of Kathīr of Shaikh Farhān's section and of Dizfūlis. There are 14 rifles and a small fort.	Irrigation is from the Diz river and the crops grown include indigo and linseed.
Bīsheh Nau (Qal'eh) قلعه بیشه نو	About 4 miles south of Dizfūl Town on the east side of the Diz river.	50 houses of Dizfūlis and Sagwand Lurs. There is a small fort and 10 rifles are owned.	Water is from the Diz river. There are two gardens.
Biyāwtiyūn بیار تیون	Roughly 4 miles to the east of Qal'eh 'Abdush Shāh.	50 houses of Bakhtiyāris, Arabs, Sagwand Lurs and Kurds, among whom are a few Dizfūlis. The inhabitants have a small fort and 20 rifles.	Irrigation is from the 'Ajīrub.
Chūgheh Sabz (Qal'eh) قلعه چوغه سبز	Close to Chūgheh Surkh below.	45 houses of Bakhtiyāris, Dizfūlis and Sagwand Lurs. There is a small fort and 5 rifles are owned.	...

Name.	Position.	Houses and inhabitants.	Remarks.
Chūgheh Surkh (Qal'eh) قلعه چوغه سرخ or Chawāsir چواسر	About 10 miles south-south-east of Dizfūl Town.	30 houses of Dizfūlis, Bakhtiyāris and Lurs. There are 4 rifles and a fort.	A number of mules are owned here.
Dāyiji دايجي	About 6 miles south-west of Dizfūl Town to the west of the Diz river.	50 mud houses of Dizfūlis. There is a small fort.	Water is from the Diz river.
Dihbār (Qal'eh) قلعه ده بار	About 4 miles south of Dizfūl Town on the east side of the Diz river.	25 houses of Lurs and Dizfūlis. The people have a small fort and 7 rifles.	Do. There is a shrine of Suwār-i-Ghāib سوار غائب or the Invisible Rider.
Dizfūl Town دزفول	...	...	See article Dizfūl Town.
Dūbandar دوبندر	About 8 miles west-south-west of Dizfūl Town on the way to Aiwān-i-Karkheh.	100 mud houses of Lurs, Bakhtiyāris and Dizfūlis. There are 3 small forts.	The village is owned by Āqa 'Ali of Dizfūl Town; it has a water mill and an Imāmzādeh.
Fariāsh (Qal'eh) قلعه فراش	About 6 miles from Dizfūl Town on the east side of the Diz river.	40 houses of Arabs, Dizfūlis and Sagwand Lurs, chiefly the last. They have a small fort and 6 rifles.	Water is from the Diz river. A considerable number of buffaloes and transport animals are owned here.
Ganjeh (Qarīyeh) قريه گنجه	Adjoins Bunwār Nāzir.	40 houses of mud with timber roofs, forming a fort; the people are Dizfūlis. The only arms are a few muzzle-loaders.	There is a good supply of water from the Diz river by a canal which takes off from the right bank below the bridge at Dizfūl Town; and wheat, barley, beans, rice, indigo, millet, Māsh, Kunjid and marsh melons are grown. There are also a few date palms and the orchards contain sweet and bitter limes, oranges, citrons, pomegranates, quinces, apples, figs, grapes, apricots, plums and mulberries. There are some cattle, donkeys, sheep, and a few buffaloes. The place is owned by inhabitants of Dizfūl Town.

Name.	Position.	Houses and inhabitants.	Remarks.
Gumār گمار	About 8 miles south of Kāunak.	See next column.	The place consists of 4 hamlets, *viz.*, Qal'eh Riza رضا (Dizfūlis), Qal'eh Murād مراد (Dizfūlis), Saiyid Ramzān رمضان (Saiyids and a few Arabs), and Kā Arzan Nūr کا ارزن نور (Lurs and Shūshtaris). Irrigation is from the Kāunak stream.
Hājiābād حاجي آباد	About 9 miles south of Dizfūl Town on the east side of the Diz river.	20 houses. The people are Kurds, Nais Arabs connected with the Kathīr tribe and Dizfūlis. They have 3 rifles and there is a small fort.	Water is from the Diz river by the Sharafābād canal. There are some gardens.
Jībar (Dih) ده جیبر	About 10 miles south of Dizfūl Town to the east of the Diz river.	30 houses of Kurds and Sagwand Lurs, among whom are a few Dizfūlis. There is a fort and the inhabitants have 4 rifles.	Water is from the Diz by the Sharafābād canal. There are two water mills.
Kālehwand (Qal'eh) قلعه کاله وند	About 5 miles south of Dizfūl Town to the east of the Diz river.	40 houses of Kurds, Sagwand Lurs and Dizfūlis. There are 10 rifles and a small fort.	Water is from the Diz and there are 4 gardens.
Karīm Khān ('Amleh) عمله کریم خان	About 12 miles from Dizfūl Town between west and southwest, and 5 from Bunwār Nāzir. It is situated in the tract known as Milk Bin-Mu'-alla.	A settlement of 200 households, mostly Dīnārwand Lurs, the remainder being Sagwand Lurs, Kurds, and a few Arabs. They inhabit huts in summer and tents in winter and possess 60 rifles. The Dīnārwands immigrated from Pusht-i-Kūh with the grandfather of Karīm Khan. "'Amleh" is the word in Pusht-i-Kūh for personal following.	The village lands are well irrigated by canals from the Karkheh and Balārūd and produce wheat, barley, rice, millet, Kunjid, Māsh and musk melons. Livestock are mares, mules, donkeys, and many cattle and sheep, also buffaloes. Karīm Khan and his brother Pāpi Khan are alive; they are Faili Lurs. The former holds a commission for the maintenance of 40 mounted men but is never paid by the Persian Government.

Name.	Position.	Houses and inhabitants.	Remarks.
Kāunak كاونك	...	...	See article **Kāunak**.
Khairābād خیرآباد	...	...	See article **Karkheh**.
Khānābād خان آباد	...	...	The same as Qal'eh Hāji 'Ali *q.v.*
Khizar Baigi (Zāwiyeh) زاویه خضر بیگي	Adjoins Zāwiyeh Murādi.	8 houses of Sagwand **Lurs**. There is a mud fort with timber roof, but the people have no rifles.	Irrigation is by a canal from the **Diz** river; and wheat, barley, rice, indigo, Kunjid, Māsh and musk melons are grown. The people have at present no livestock, having been recently raided. The village, which is owned by respectable inhabitants of **Dizfūl** Town, is exempt from Government revenue.
Khusrauābād (Qal'eh) قلعه خسرو آباد	A little east of Sālarābād and less than 4 miles from Kūt 'Abdush Shāh.	50 houses of **Bakhtiyāris, Kurds** and Dizfūlis. There are 14 rifles and a small fort.	Irrigation is from the **Diz** river. There is one water mill.
Khwājeh Husain (Bunwār) بنوار خواجه حسین	About 8 miles west-south-west of **Dizfūl** Town.	60 houses of Dizfūlis. There is one small fort.	Water is from the **Diz** river.
Kilmilak كلملك	About 5 miles southwards from **Dizfūl** Town.	10 houses of Dizfūlis.	The houses have mud and timber roofs. There are a garden and a small mud fort. Animals are cattle, donkeys and a few sheep. The lands are watered by a canal of the same name from **Dizfūl** Town.

Name.	Position.	Houses and inhabitants.	Remarks.
Kūtiyān (Qal'eh) قلعه کوتیان	4 miles or more east of Qal'eh 'Abdush Shāh.	60 houses of Bakhtiyāris, Sagwand Lurs, Arabs and Dizfūlis. The dwellings are of mud with timber roofs. There is a small fort and the people have 20 rifles.	Water is from the Diz river by canal: the crops grown are wheat, barley, beans, rice, millet, Kunjid, cotton and Māsh. There are a few date and some other trees, also a water mill. Livestock are mules, donkeys, buffaloes, cattle and sheep. The village is owned by the Bakhtiyāri Khāns.
Kūwigh (Dih, Qal'eh or Qarīyeh) ده - قلعه - قریه کریغ	9 miles south of Dizfūl Town, east of the Diz river.	30 houses of Arabs and Kurds. There is a mud fort with a timber roof and the people have 3 rifles.	Wheat, barley, beans, rice, Kunjid, and indigo (the last for seed only) are grown by irrigation from the Sharafābād canal from the Diz river. Donkeys, buffaloes, cattle and sheep are owned. The village is the ancestral property of one Hāji Saiyid 'Abdul Ghafūr.
Miyān Chughān میان چغان	About 6 miles west-south-west of Dizfūl Town.	45 mud houses of Dizfūlis. There is a fort.	Two gardens exist.
Mu'alla (Milk Bin-) ملك بن معلی	Between the Diz and Karkheh rivers, containing the villages of Jirqeh Saiyid Ahmad and 'Amleh Karīm Khān.	A tract irrigated by two permanent canals from the Karkheh river.	The owners are said to be the Shahāb-us-Saltaneh, Bakhtiyāri (2 shares); Saiyid Ahmad, Arab (2 shares); the Sardār-i-Mukarram (1 share); and Karīm Khān (1 share).
Muhammad (Jirqeh Saiyid) جرقه سید محمد	About 12 miles south-west of Dizfūl Town, west of the Diz river: it is above the tract on the Diz called Hiddeh and near the ruined shrine of Buq'eh-i-Julbās بقعه جلباس	80 houses, mostly Arabs, with a few Saiyids and Lurs. The Shaikh has a large house, besides which there are 5 other mud houses: the rest of the dwellings are huts. The inhabitants own 20 rifles.	Mares, mules, cattle and a few sheep are kept. The village lands are irrigated by the Harmūshi canal from the Karkheh and the crops are wheat, barley, beans, millet and Māsh.

Name.	Position.	Houses and inhabitants.	Remarks.
Murādi (Zāwiyeh) زاويه مرادي	About 7 miles south-west of Dizfūl Town and west of the Diz river.	15 houses of Dizfūlis and Sagwand Lurs. There is a fort, but the people have no rifles.	Irrigation is by canal from the Diz river; the crops grown are wheat, barley, beans, rice, indigo, Kunjid, Māsh and musk melons. The people formerly had some cattle and donkeys, but most of these have been plundered by Arabs.
Najafābād (Qal'eh) قلعه نجف آباد	Adjoins Qal'eh Kūtiyān.	25 houses of Bakhtiyāris and Dizfūlis. There are 5 rifles and a small fort.	...
Nāzir (Bunwār) بنوار ناظر	About 6 miles west-south-west of Dizfūl Town.	180 houses of mud with timber roofs. The people are Dizfūlis, were formerly well-to-do and had many rifles; now they have only a few muzzle-loaders for protecting their crops and stand in fear of the Sagwand Lurs. The place was once plundered by the Dīrakwand Lurs.	The place consists of 7 Qal'ehs or walled hamlets, situated close together and appearing from a distance to form one village; these bear the following names:—Agha Mūsa, Hāji, Agha Muhammad, Baqqāl, Agha Bāqir, Hashtdar and Galleh. Water is from the Diz river and wheat, barley, beans and lentils are cultivated in winter, and rice, indigo, Kunjid, Māsh and musk melons in summer. There are gardens with trees in which formerly stood large buildings such as Hammāms. The place is owned by various inhabitants of Dizfūl Town.
Qāzi (Qal'eh) قلعه قاضي	Between Shalgahi and Najafābād.	20 houses of Sagwand Lurs and Dizfūlis. There are 4 rifles and a small fort.	Irrigation is from the 'Ajīrub.
Qumāt قماط	...	...	See article Qumāt.

Name.	Position.	Houses and inhabitants.	Remarks.
Saiyid (Qal'eh) قلعه سید	7 miles south-east of Dizfūl Town.	20 houses of Sagwand Lurs and Dizfūlis. The people have a small fort and 6 rifles.	Water is from the Diz river.
Sālārābād (Qal'eh) سالار آباد	About 2 miles east of Qal'eh 'Abdush Shāh and a little south of Shama'ūn.	45 houses of Sagwand Lurs, Bakhtiyāris and Arabs. There are 10 rifles and a small fort.	Do.
Sālihābād (Mazra'eh) مزرعه صالح آباد	About 11 miles north-west of Dizfūl Town.	No houses at the present time.	This is a fertile tract about 6 miles by 4 in extent, partially watered by Qanāts from the Balā-rūd. The soil is very good, but the supply of water is limited and most of the tract is unirrigated. The cultivators are inhabitants of Dizfūl Town: the crops include wheat, barley, water and musk melons and sometimes Kunjid. The place belongs to the descendants of one Hāji Saiyid Husain, Shūshtari, who obtained it in perpetual Tiyūl from Shāh Muhammad Shāh: of the actual owners some reside at Shūshtar and some at Dizfūl Town. The original founder was one Sālih Muhammad Khān and the ruins of a fort, Hammām, etc., built by him are still visible.

Name.	Position.	Houses and inhabitants.	Remarks.
Sar Bīsheh سربیشه	About 20 miles from Dizfūl Town on the direct route to Āb Bīd, also 4 miles north-north-east from Kāunak.	12 houses of **Bakhtiyāris** with a few Dizfūlis. There is a weak mud fort, but the people have no rifles.*	Wheat and barley are grown, but the place is poor and has been several times plundered by the Dīrakwand **Lurs**. The village is the property of the Samsām-us-Saltaneh, Īlkhāni of the **Bakhtiyāris**.
Shāhābād شاه آباد	12 miles south-east of Dizfūl Town on the route to Shūshtar Town.	40 houses of **Bakhtiyāris** and Dizfūlis. There is a small fort.	Water is by Qanāt from the **Diz** river. There is an Imāmzādeh here with a few Kunār trees. Near Shāhābād are the ruins of Jundi Shāpūr جندي شاپور, at one time the Sassanian capital of 'Arabistān. In the 10th century A. D. Jundi Shāpūr had begun to decline in consequence of the attacks of neighbouring tribes, but even in the 14th century it still retained part of its prosperity and population.†
Shaikh (Qal'eh) قلعه شیخ	4 miles south of Dizfūl Town on the east side of the **Diz**.	30 houses of Dizfūlis and a few **Lurs** who have been settled here from old time. There are two forts.	The village lands are irrigated by the Kulangān canal and produce indigo and pen reeds.
Shalgahi Buzurg شلگهي بزرگ	12 miles south-south-east of Dizfūl Town.	50 houses of **Kurds**, Dizfūlis and **Bakhtiyāris**. The inhabitants have a fort and 14 rifles.	...

* A more recent report (1907) gives Sar Bīsheh 100 houses, partly Arabs and partly **Bakhtiyāris**; also considerable resources of every kind. The place may have increased lately. Water is from a spring.

† *Vide* Le Strange.

Name.	Position.	Houses and inhabitants.	Remarks.
Shalgahi Kuchik شلگهي كوچك	Less than ½ a mile from the last.	20 houses of Bakhtiyāris. There is a fort and the people have 5 rifles.	...
Shama'ūn شمعون	About 2 miles east of Qal'eh 'Abdush Shāh.	50 houses of Lurs. There is a small fort and 14 rifles are owned.	The village lands are irrigated by the 'Ajīrub. There are 3 mounds, locally called Chūghehs چوغه probably indicating old remains: viz., Chūgheh Dih ده Chūgheh Ibrāhīm ابراهيم, and Nishān-i-'Aqāb نشان عقاب. There are also 3 other smaller mounds, one of which is called Tappeh 'Ali Sāla-ba-Sar, from a Qadamgāh adjoining it where the saint is supposed to have appeared carrying a basket on his head.
Shāmi (Bunwār) بنوار شامي	About 3 miles south-south-east of Dizfūl Town.	25 houses of Sagwand Lurs, Dizfūlis and Bakhtiyāris. The people have a fort of mud with a raftered roof and 6 rifles.	Water for irrigation is brought from the Diz river by a canal which takes out of it about 7 miles above Dizfūl Town.
Shamsābād شمس آباد	About 8 miles south-east of Dizfūl Town.	Consists ⅔ of Bakhtiyāris and ⅓ of other Lurs. There is a small fort and the people have 15 rifles.	There are here 4 gardens, a water mill and a shrine called Imāmzādeh Amīr (i.e. 'Ali).
Sharafābād شرف آباد	About 3 miles from Dizfūl Town and 2 miles east of the Diz river.	50 houses of Sagwand Lurs with a few Arabs and Dizfūlis. There are 12 rifles and a fort.	The village is surrounded by fruit gardens and trees, the lands are irrigated by the canal from the Diz called the Sharafābād, and there is a water mill. The inhabitants own a considerable number of mules and buffaloes.

2 I

Name.	Position.	Houses and inhabitants.	Remarks.
Shūhān شوهان	About 7 miles south-west of Dizfūl Town, west of the Diz river.	12 houses of Dizfūlis; they have a small fort but no rifles.	Irrigation is from the Diz and possibly also from the Karkheh. Wheat, barley, beans, rice, Kunjid and Māsh are grown, and there are some donkeys and cattle.
Shūsh شوش	...	...	See article Shūsh.
Siyāh Mansūr سیاه منصور	8 miles south-east of Dizfūl Town on the route to Shūshtar Town.	35 houses of Bakhtiyāris and Lūrs and a fort.	Irrigation is by a Qanāt, likewise called Siyāh Mansūr, which takes out of the Diz river above Dizfūl Town.
Ta'ameh (Jirqeh or Qarīyeh Saiyid) جرقه - قریّه سیّد طعمه	About 8 miles west-south-west of Dizfūl Town, above the bridge over the Harmūshi canal from the Karkheh.	70 houses of Kathīr of Saikh Haidar's section, Bani Lām of the Sharkhah section, Kurds and Sagwand Lars, they live all the year round in huts. They have 5 rifles.	Water is from the Karkheh river by the Harmūshi canal; the crops grown include wheat, barley, beans, millet and Māsh. Mares, mules, donkeys and cattle are owned, and Saiyid Ta'ameh, who is the eldest son of Saiyid Tāhir, has 100 sheep; formerly there were many more sheep, but they were plundered in 1904 by the Kathīr of Shaikh Farhān's section.
Tāhir (Jirqeh or Qarīyeh Saiyid) جرقه - قریّه سیّد طاهر	About 10 miles west-south-west of Dizfūl Town, in a tract called Husainābād and 1,000 paces nearer to Dizfūl town than a shrine known as Buq'eh-i-'Ali-bin-Mūsa-ar-Ridha.	60 houses of mixed Arabs among whom are Kurds and a few Lūrs. The people are cultivators and unwarlike; they own 6 rifles. Of the houses 10 or 12, recently built, are of mud; but the rest are still huts.	Water is from the Karkheh by the Harmūshi canal; wheat, barley, millet and Māsh are cultivated, and there are 100 buffaloes. The present headman is Ja'far, a son of Saiyid Tāhir.
Tūq or Tū (Qal'eh) قلعه توق - تو	2 miles south-west of Dizfūl Town on the right bank of the Diz.	60 mud houses of Dizfūlis and a small fort.	There are 2 gardens. Water is brought from the Diz river by canal.

DIZFŪL TOWN

DIZFŪL
دزفول
TOWN

The town of Dizfūl is situated on the left bank of the **Diz** river about 20 miles below the point where that river leaves the hills.

Site and buildings.—The site of Dizfūl is elevated and somewhat uneven, falling away on the river face in conglomerate cliffs about 100 feet high, the foot of which is washed by the river when in flood; on the left bank these cliffs do not extend beyond the town in either direction, but they are found again on the right bank a short distance up-stream. The length of Dizfūl upon the river is about 1½ miles, and its depth inland about three-fourths of a mile. The houses are closely packed, and most of them have an upper storey; many are of brick and well built. The streets are narrow and crooked, and the central portions, which are neither paved nor cobbled and are used as common sewers, become in wet weather canals of black and putrid filth; raised side walks for foot passengers, however, about 18 inches wide, run along their sides. On the side next the **Diz** the houses are built on the face of the precipitous bank, the foundations of the lowest being on a level with the water's edge; and several steep, narrow paths afford access from the town to the river. Dizfūl contains 38 mosques and no less than 24 shrines, some of which are Imāmzādehs and some Qadamgāhs. The shrines are said to be still used to some extent as places of Bast or sanctuary from the law: the most important are the Imāmzādeh of Bāba Yūsuf بابا يوسف, in the south-east corner of the town, and that of Sultān Husain سلطان حسين situated on the left bank of the river above the town in a suburb called Rūband روبند. A canal called Qanāt-i-Gāvdūl گاودل takes off from the left bank of the river between Rūband and the main town.

At the southern extremity of Dizfūl town the river is spanned by an ancient bridge, which, with the numerous water-mills above it, is the chief feature of the place. The bridge is about 430 yards in length and consists of 24 arches, all slightly pointed but not uniform in shape or span. The piers are built of large blocks of cut stone; the superstructure is of brick, and different parts of it evidently belong to different periods. The roadway is about 16 feet wide and roughly cobbled: the parapets in some places have disappeared. The bridge generally is in bad repair; and an arch built of brick by the townspeople, to replace one which collapsed two years ago, is of inferior workmanship. Convenience of communication with the country to the west, and consequently, to some extent, the prosperity of Dizfūl town, depend on the existence of this bridge. The mills, of which particulars are given below, are 39 in number, and stand upon rocks and artificial islands, mostly near the left bank; some of them are connected with others by gangways, and all are liable to be submerged in the spring floods. A permanent canal, known as Nahr-i-Kilmilak كلملك, leaves the river on the east side below the bridge.

The only edifice on the right bank of the river is the mansion of the Persian Governor of Northern **'Arabistān**, a modern construction, known as the Kūshk كوشك. It consists of an enclosure, about 500 feet in length by 300 in breadth, and contains several buildings; it is surrounded by an ordinary high brick wall, the only semblance of a fortification which exists at Dizfūl.

People.—The population of Dizfūl is about 45,000 souls and is increasing. It has absorbed many heterogeneous elements, and some of the groups of which it is composed still bear names or cherish traditions indicative of foreign origin: such are the Jamā'at Gīwehkashān كيوه كشان who claim to be of **Lur** extraction; the Afshārs افشار, who call themselves descendants of Nādir Shāh; and the Khawānīn خوانين, some of whom name Jenghiz Khān as their ancestor. Nevertheless, the people of Dizfūl have been brought by a process of assimilation and fusion to resemble one another so closely that they now form a community homogeneous in language, customs, and details of dress, and by themselves may even be considered to constitute a Persian type. No **Lurs** proper, **Kurds**, or Arabs reside within the town. The most prominent sections of the populace are the Saiyids, who number 6,000 souls and are divided into a multitude of subsections; the Tujjār تجّار or merchants, who are 500 households or less; the Mashāikh مشائخ, who are reckoned at 250 houses; and the Khawānīn, who are estimated at 100 houses. The lower orders belong to a base type; they are dirty, discontented, unhealthy, and peculiarly ill-favoured in appearance. The better classes, such as the Saiyids, are many of them respectable and well-mannered. The only religion is the Shī'ah faith in its standard form, and "there are no Bābis, 'Ali Ilāhis, or avowed infidels." Although the people generally are bigoted and fanatical in regard to their particular form of religion, no signs of hostility to foreigners are apparent at ordinary times. Politically the ordinary townsmen of Dizfūl are a negligeable quantity.

Occupations, industries and trade.—A considerable number of the inhabitants of Dizfūl exercise vocations connected with religion: shopkeepers number about 2,000: the remainder are employed in the local industries. The indigo of Dizfūl, though inferior to that imported from

Dizfūl Town.

[Maj. G. Arbuthnot.]

India, enjoys local favour, and the average annual output is estimated at 3,000 Dizfūli Mans: it is graded in three qualities and fetches from 30 to 60 Qrāns per Dizfūli Man.* Agricultural implements, stirrups, bits, horse and mule-shoes, knives, and tools are manufactured at Dizfūl from imported iron and steel; rifles are repaired; copper is converted into cooking-pots; and brass and German silver are made into samovars and pipe-bowls and are used for inlaying iron. Floor-cloths, 'Abas and hats of felt, various cotton textiles both plain and striped for clothing, cotton webbing, 'Abas of woollen thread, riding and pack-saddles or Palāns, earthenware and blue enamelled pottery, linseed oil, gunpowder and bullets, lacquered pen-cases and similar articles of papier-mâché, also native soap for washing clothes, are among the other manufactures of the town. Some of the inhabitants are occupied in the stamping of designs on cloth with wooden blocks, in dyeing, lime-pounding, rice-cleaning, cotton-ginning, in the making of cotton shoes and in the cleaning of hides for tanning. There are also builders, bricklayers, millers, basket-makers, bath-keepers, and butchers. The curious profession of the Sagpā سگ با deserves mention; he keeps a large number of dogs which he hires out for the protection of flocks or cultivation.

The 39 mills already mentioned grind flour and are actuated by wooden water-wheels. Only 12 of them can ply when the water is at its lowest in summer. The ordinary charge for grinding is 7 Siyāh Pūl and a handful of flour for every Dizfūli Man ground. The annual cash earnings of a mill vary from 20 to 50 Tūmāns, of which half goes to the owner and half to the Persian Government; the owners are people of the town, and some of them are exempt from the Government demand.

All foreign goods and most goods from a distance are imported from **Shūshtar** or **'Amārah** by the large merchants, and as a rule are deposited by them in their private houses; for—except Messrs. Lynch Brothers, and four of the principal local merchants—the business men of Dizfūl have no warehouses other than their ordinary residences. The smaller dealers and shopkeepers purchase from the larger merchants, and even they do not, as a rule, keep their more valuable goods at their shops. Small shops are found scattered in various streets, but there is also a large bazaar which consists of three or four lines of booths, each row of stalls standing back-to-back with the next; it is always crowded with purchasers from town and country. Caravans from **'Arabistān** for Khurramābād start from Dizfūl.

---

* At the present time the indigo works are closed and the owners have removed their plant on account of the excessive imposts placed by the Sardār-i-Mukarram, the new Governor of Northern **'Arabistān**, upon the industry (1906).

Supplies and transport.—There is an unlimited supply of river water, which is used for all domestic purposes * and is also taken off for irrigation by Qanāts or subterranean conduits on both banks above and at the town. A large supply of grain and meat is always available; and recently (1905) a Persian military force of over 2,000 men for some time drew its supplies from Dizfūl. Firewood is obtained from the banks of the **Diz** river below Kūt 'Abdush Shāh and from the **Karkheh** district; and, during floods, the supply is increased by a quantity of inferior drift-wood retrieved from the river. It is estimated that 300 camels and 1,000 mules accompanied by professional drivers could, in ordinarily favourable circumstances, be obtained at Dizfūl upon short notice.

Administration and political influences.—The Persian administrative staff at Dizfūl, besides the Nāib-ul-Hukūmat or Deputy Governor—who is at present (1905) the Telegraph Master—consists of only 2 Mīrzas or clerks and 4 Farrāshes or orderlies. The real power, both in the town and in the surrounding country, is held by the religious leaders of the community, the most important of whom are the Mujtahids. The civil authorities can only make themselves obeyed when they have bought or otherwise secured the countenance of the predominant religious faction of the day; and **Lur** or Arab chieftains of the neighbourhood, if they have reason to distrust the intentions of the Persian Governor towards them, will only obey his summons to appear when it is accompanied by a safe-conduct from the chief Mujtahid (Āgha Shaikh Muhammad Hasan, Hujjat-ul-Islām). † The supreme power is in the hands of the chief Mujtahid, who is generally liked and respected, and has up to the present shown himself agreeable and polite in his dealings with the representative of the British Government. The Mujtahids are the dispensers of public charity, and collect for the purpose the Zakāt or alms prescribed in the Qurān; most of them however, having little private property, are supposed to act upon a familiar proverb to the prejudice of the destitute and distressed. There are 27 schools at Dizfūl in which reading, writing, and religious subjects are taught; a few are kept by ordinary Mullas, but the rest are held in the houses of the Mujtahids, that of the chief Mujtahid being attended

---

* In mediæval times the water was raised from the river to the level of the town by a mechanical contrivance worked by a water wheel. See Le Strange.

† Since the above was written the position has been modified by the appointment of the Sərdār-i-Mukarram to the Governorship of **'Arabistān** under whom the Deputy Governorship has been abolished and respect for authority enforced; but it is uncertain how long the more vigorous régime which has been initiated will last (1906).

by 150 to 200 pupils. Notwithstanding their great local influence the Mujtahids of Dizfūl are of less importance politically than those of **Shūshtar.**

There is also at Dizfūl an official called the Imām Jum'eh امام جمعه, whose office is virtually hereditary and at present a sinecure; he is supposed to lead the Friday prayers in the principal mosque, but this function has fallen into desuetude. The appointment was originally ecclesiastical, but the recognition of the Persian Government has rendered it semi-secular. The present holder of the office (Saiyid Abus Salām) is possessed of considerable private property, receives a salary of 300 Tūmāns a year in quarterly instalments from the Imperial Customs treasury, is on good terms with the Mujtahids, and has some influence with the surrounding Arab tribes.

A Persian telegraph office and post office exist at Dizfūl; and there is a custom house presided over by a director, under whom are a dozen guards.

DŌHAH
الدوحة

Generally so styled at the present day, but Bedouins sometimes call it Dōhat-al-Qatar, and it seems to have been formerly better known as Bida' (*Anglice* " Bidder ") : it is the chief town of **Qatar** and is situated on the eastern side of that peninsula, about 63 miles south of its extremity at Rās Rakan and 45 miles north of Khor-al-'**Odaid.**

Harbour.—Dōhah stands on the south side of a deep bay, at the south-western corner of a natural harbour * which is about 3 miles in extent and is protected on the north-east and south-east sides by natural reefs. The entrance, less than a mile wide, is from the east between the points of the reefs; it is shallow and somewhat difficult, and vessels of more than 15 feet draught cannot pass. The soundings within the basin vary from 3 to 5 fathoms and are regular: the bottom is white mud or clay.

Town site and quarters.—The south-eastern point of the bay is quite low; but the land on the western side is stony desert 40 or 50 feet above the level of the sea. The town is built up the slope of some rising ground between these two extremes and consists of 9 Farīqs or quarters, which are given below in their order from the east to the west

---

* A plan of the harbour of Dōhah is given in Chart No. 2374—2837-B.

and north: the total frontage of the place upon the sea is nearly 2 miles.

Name of quarter.	Position.	Remarks.
Al Bin-'Ali آل بن علي	On Rās-an-Nisa'ah راس النسعه, a small promontory at the extreme east end of the town.	Inhabited chiefly by Āl Bin-'Ali, whence the name.
Sulutah السلطه	Do.	Named after the Sulutah, who are the principal occupants. There are also some Baqāqalah here.
Murqāb-ash-Sharqi مرقاب الشرقي	Adjoins and is continuous with Farīq-as-Sulutah.	The people are mostly Ma'ādhīd, Manāna'ah and Sulutah.
Dōhah الدوحه	Follows Murqāb-ash-Sharqi without an interval.	Founded later than Bida' by Āl Bū 'Ainain who afterwards removed to Wakrah. The present inhabitants are Hūwalah, Ma'ādhīd and Persians; there are also Āl Bin-'Ali, Arabs from Najd, Bahārinah and Dawāsir. In this quarter is the main bazaar of about 50 shops; also a hereditary mansion of the Āl Thāni, the most important Arab family in Qatar.
Duwaihah الدويحه	Separated from Dōhah by a slight interval in which is a cemetery.	Inhabited by Bahārinah, Hūwalah and other tribes. This quarter was formerly known as Dōhat-as-Saghīrah درحة الصغيرة.
Qal'at-al-'Askar قلعة العسكر	Stands inland of Duwaihah, of which quarter it was originally part, upon somewhat higher ground.	Here is the fort of Dōhah; by the Turks called Qasr Kunārah قصر كنارة, which accommodates the Turkish military garrison and some Turkish officials. It was built originally about 1850 by Al Musallam whom the Shaikh of Bahrain brought in to counterbalance the Sūdān of Bida'. The accommodation of the troops is wretched.
Murqāb-al-Gharbi مرقاب الغربي	Extends along the shore, forming a gap about 600 yards long in the town front.	At present deserted.

Dohah in Qatar.
(Herr H. Burchardt.)

Name of quarter.	Position.	Remarks.
Bida' البدع	Divided from Qal'at-al-'Askar by Murqāb-al-Gharbi.	The oldest of the quarters, said to have been founded by Sūdān refugees from Abu Dhabi; it is a compact settlement of some 150 houses and is still tenanted chiefly by Sūdān (80 houses), the remainder of the inhabitants being Āl Bū Kuwārah (20 houses), 'Amāmarah, Baqāqalah, Hūwalah, Bani Yās and negroes.
Rumailah رميلة	Separated from Bida' by an interval of 200 or 300 yards: one mile beyond Rumailah is Rās-ash-Shūwa' راس الشوع, a small cape which forms the north-western limit of the town as Rās-an-Nisa'ah does the eastern.	Contains about 100 houses, some of which are at present occupied by Khalīfah, eldest son of Jāsim, the Āl Thāni Shaikh, and his retainers. The inhabitants are Ma'ādhīd.

The general appearance of Dōhah is unattractive; the lanes are narrow and irregular, the houses dingy and small. There are no date palms or other trees, and the only garden is a small one near the fort, kept up by the Turkish garrison.

Population and tribes.—The inhabitants of Dōhah are estimated to amount, inclusive of the Turkish military garrison of 350 men, to about 12,000 souls. The population may be distributed as follows by tribes or classes:—

Name of tribe.	Number of souls.	Where located.
'Ali (Āl Bin-)	1,750	In the Āl Bin-'Ali and Dōhah quarters.
'Amāmarah	100	Scattered through the town.
Arabs from Najd	250	In the Dōhah quarter, on the inland side.
Bahārinah	300	Scattered through the town, especially in the Dōhah quarter.
Baqāqalah	50	Scattered through the town, especially in the Bida' and Sulutah quarters.
Dawāsir	150	In the Dōhah quarter.

Name of tribe.	Number of souls.	Where located.
Hūwalah, of whom ¼ are Al Bū Fakhru	1,000	Scattered through the town, especially in the Dōhah and Bida' quarters.
Kuwārah (Āl Bū)	100	In the Bida' quarter.
Ma'ādhīd	500	In the Dōhah, Murqāb-ash-Sharqi and Rumailah quarters.
Manāna'ah	50	Scattered through the town, especially in the Murqāb-ash-Sharqi quarter.
Negroes (free)	1,000	Scattered through the town.
Negroes (slaves, but living separately from their masters)	2,500	Do.
Persians	300	In the Dōhah quarter.
Sūdān	400	In the Bida' quarter.
Sulutah	3,250	In the Sulutah and Murqāb-ash-Sharqi quarters.
Yās (Bani) of the Āl Bū Falāsah section.	50	Scattered through the town, especially in the Bida' quarter.

Besides the above a few families of Sādah are found.

There were formerly a few British Indians at Dōhah of whom 2 or 3 were permanent settlers; but their occupations, in consequence of the Āl Thāni Shaikhs having entered personally on the business of pearl merchants, ceased to be profitable and all of them have now taken their departure.

The people of Dōhah are, as a general rule, unhealthy in appearance— a circumstance which is attributed to their assiduity in pearl diving, this being a form of employment which places a severe strain on the human constitution.

Occupations, shipping and trade.—The **Bahārinah** are blacksmiths, coppersmiths, and petty pearl dealers; the other tribes live by pearl diving, sea fishing and a small maritime carrying trade. About 350 pearl-boats, 60 sea-going boats running to **'Omān,** the Persian coast and **Basrah**, and 90 fishing boats are owned at Dōhah. Pearls are the only export; and the imports resemble those of the coast towns of Trucial **'Omān.** Foreign trade is chiefly with **Bahrain** and, in a lesser degree, with **Lingeh**. Dōhah is naturally the chief market town of the Bedouins of the **Qatar** peninsula.

Supplies, water and transport.—Little can be obtained locally in the shape of supplies. Firewood is brought from the interior and from **Clarence Strait.**

Dōhah itself possesses only one well of brackish water, named 'Ain Walad Sa'īd عين ولد سعيد, which is ½ a mile to the south of the Dōhah quarter; but there is a group of others called Mushairib مشيرب, with fairly good water, at 1 mile to the west of the Dōhah quarter. Three miles further inland is Bīr-al-Jadīdah بير الجديده, a large masonry well of indifferent water on which the town mainly depends for its supply. A mile beyond to the southwards are the wells of Na'aijah, from which the Shaikhs of the Āl Thāni, the other notables of Dōhah town and the officers of the Turkish garrison obtain their drinking water. The best of the Na'aijah wells is called 'Asailah عسيله. The Turkish troops obtain most of their water from Mushairib, where there is a military outpost of 8 men in a tower to watch the wells. The soldiers have now a vegetable garden at this place; and scurvy, which was formerly common among the garrison, has disappeared.

About 150 horses and 800 camels are kept at Dōhah.

Political position.—Dōhah may be regarded as in most respects the capital of **Qatar** and its place in the political system will be apparent from the general article on **Qatar**. The Turkish garrison which bespeaks, though it cannot enforce, the Turkish claim to sovereignty over all **Qatar** is stationed here; but Jāsim-bin-Thāni, the most influential Shaikh of the promontory, avoids residing in the place. The town is at present ruled by Jāsim's fourth son 'Abdullah, he being recognised as Shaikh of Dōhah both by his father and by the Turks. The appointment of a Raīs-al-Līmān or Turkish harbour master is said to be contemplated (1907).

DŌRAQ or DORAQ
درق

This name is sometimes used to designate the town of **Fallāhīyeh** and the country about it, inhabited by the **Ka'ab** tribe, or even the whole of the **Fallāhīyeh** District in Southern **'Arabistān**. It is possible that it was formerly used to describe the whole principality of the **Ka'ab**

Shaikh, including the districts of **Fallāhīyeh**, **Jarrāhi**, **Ma'shūr**, and even **Hindiyān**. Khor Dōraq, a branch of Khor **Mūsa**, is described in the article under that name.

Dāraq-al-Furs, possibly **Fallāhīyeh** Town, was in the 10th century A. D. a very flourishing place, through which most pilgrims from **Fārs** and Kīrmān passed on their way to Makkah. It then possessed remains of Sassanian buildings and, according to one authority, a fire temple.*

DŌRAQIS-TĀN
درقستان

In Southern 'Arabistān, the tract upon the sea between Khor Dōraq on the east and the **Bahmanshīr** upon the west. The name is not in common use.

DUKHĀN† JABAL-AD-
جبل الدخان

The highest hill on **Bahrain** Island and in the **Bahrain** archipelago. It is situated 13 miles south of **Manāmah** Town and is a square-looking mass of black rock, 440 feet high, situated in the middle of the great central depression of **Bahrain** Island. Its colour and appearance are however deceptive, for in common with the rest of the island it is not volcanic, but consists entirely of limestone. A good view is obtainable from its summit of all **Bahrain**, of the encircling sea, and even of the coast of the Arabian mainland; the hill itself is visible from the sea at a distance of 24 miles and it forms, in conjunction with the minarets of the Madrasah Abu Zaidān mosque, a leading mark for vessels entering **Manāmah** harbour. In certain circumstances it might be of value as a signalling station.

DURŪGĀH
درکاه
or
DURŪD-GAH
درد کاه

The principal place in the small Persian district of **Zīra**; it is situated about 10 miles north-west of **Burāzjān** and 1½ miles from the right bank of both the Rūd Shīrīn stream and **Rūd-hilleh** River near the point where the former merges in the latter. Durūgāh consists of about 150

---

* *Vide* Le Strange.
† A distant view of Jabal-ad-Dukhān from the sea will be found in Admiralty Plan No. 2377—20.

houses of a tribe claiming Arab descent who live by cultivation of wheat, barley, dates and cotton ; it is also the bazaar of the **Zīra** District, but there are no regular shops. The date-palms are said to number 25,000, and livestock comprises 20 horses, 200 donkeys, 120 cattle and 500 sheep and goats. The village is held in Tiyūl by a relative of the Sālār-i-Mu'azzam and is farmed by the Khān of **Shabānkāreh** to prevent its falling into the hands of any rival Khān. Revenue is collected at the rate of 20 to 100 Qrāns per Gāu of cultivation. The defences of the place consist of 4 towers.

DUVVĀN
دوان

A considerable village of over 200 stone and mortar houses on the coast of the **Lingeh** District in Persia, about 7 miles north-west of Bustāneh and 4 miles east of **Mughu** ; to the south-west of the village is a pearl bank, known as the Duvvān bank, close to the shore. The village is divided into two quarters; that on the west is called Kāfarghān کافرغان or Duvvān Qawāsim, is inhabited by **Qawāsim**, and pays revenue to the Deputy-Governor of **Lingeh** ; that on the east is called Duvvān Āl 'Ali after the tribe inhabiting it and is under the Shaikh of **Chārak**. The Āl 'Ali, who are only about half as numerous as the **Qawāsim**, have a large fort in which they reside for fear of their enemies, the Marāzīq of **Mughu**. Except a few Wahhābis all the people are Sunnis. The Āl 'Ali have 12 pearling vessels (Sambūks) which work on the Arabian side of the Gulf and sometimes at **Farūr** island ; they also possess about 26 smaller craft (Baqārahs, 'Āmilahs, Shū'ais and Varjis) which they use for fishing and pearling near Bustāneh and for fishing at **Farūr** island. The **Qawāsim** own 8 Sambūks which run as far as **Basrah** on the one side and the **Bātinah** coast of **'Omān** on the other ; also 2 'Āmilahs and 3 Shū'ais. The Āl 'Ali have about 70 rifles and are a warlike tribe : of the **Qawāsim** only about 15 possess rifles. The people are sailors, fishermen, pearl-divers, agriculturists and date-growers ; some of them are Nākhudas in command of boats belonging to ports on either side of the Gulf which ply upon the **Lingeh** and **Shībkūh** coasts. Animals are 100 camels, 100 donkeys and 700 sheep and goats ; the camels are kept in the hills near Bustāneh. There are wells of sweet water and, in addition to these, each of the quarters possesses 2 reservoirs.

**EUPHRA-
TES
or
FURAT***
الفرات

The length of this famous river between **Fallūjah**—the point where it enters our purview—and its junction with the **Tigris** at **Qūrnah** is, by the winding course which it follows, nearly 400 miles; its general direction between the extreme points mentioned is from north-west to south-east, but it runs in a curve of which the hollow is on the north-eastern or Mesopotamian side.

To describe fully and with correctness this, the lower course of the Euphrates, is at present impossible. The survey made in 1836 of the river below **Samāwah** and the survey dated 1860-65 of the portion between Khān **Maqdam** and **Samāwah** are now antiquated, and reliable detailed information about the changes that have taken place in recent years is not, when it relates to the more inaccessible reaches of the river, easy to procure. So far, however, as these difficulties permit we shall endeavour to describe the Euphrates,—first in its general and topographical aspects, and then with reference to navigation and irrigation.

General course and character.—The principal points that mark the line of the Euphrates in its lower course are the towns of **Musaiyib, Hillah, Dīwānīyah, Samāwah, Nāsirīyah** and **Sūq-ash-Shuyūkh**, by which it passes. This part of the river may be divided into three sections; an upper section from **Fallūjah** to **Musaiyib**, a central section from **Musaiyib** to **Samāwah** and a lower section from **Samāwah** to **Qūrnah**.

The following are the principal points, in descending order, and the character of the river in the first of these divisions:—

Name.	(1) On which side situated; (2) distance by stream, and (3) average direction from the last place.	Nature.	REMARKS.
Fallūjah فلوجه	Left bank.	See article **Fallūjah**	The river, which is spanned here by a bridge of 25 boats and divided into 2 channels by an island, flows with a breadth of 240 yards and a maximum depth (in November) of about 25 feet.

* *Authorities.*—This article is founded chiefly on information supplied by Colonel L. S. Newmarch and Sir W. Willcocks, on an article by Mr. H. W. Cadoux in the Geographical Journal for September 1906, and on personal inquiries. Some of the data regarding the course of the river below **Nāsirīyah** were supplied by Dr. Bennett and Mr. Van Ess of the American Presbyterian Mission at **Basrah**. The best maps of the Euphrates are that from Chesney's survey (1836) of the whole; that from the surveys of Selby, Collingwood and Bewsher (1860-65) of the portion between Khān **Maqdam** and **Samāwah**; and that which illustrates Mr. Cadoux's article. A useful sketch map of the part between **Hillah** and **Qūrnah** accompanied letter No. 8 of 29th April 1863 from the Political Agent at Baghdad to the Secretary to the Government of India in the Foreign Department.

Name.	(1) On which side situated; (2) distance by stream, and (3) average direction from the last place.	Nature.	Remarks.
Khān Maqdam خان مقدم	Left bank. 30 miles. South-east.	See article Khān Maqdam.	The Euphrates has a width at this place of about 190 yards.
Khidhar Aliyās خضر الياس or Khidhar الخضر	Left bank. 24 miles. South-east.	A mosque with date palms and a few mulberry trees. Above the mosque is a wood of tamarisk and poplar about 800 yards long by 200 yards wide. The neighbouring Arabs are **Mas'ūd**. The lands in the vicinity belong to the Dāirat-as-Sanīyah.	The banks here rise about 10 feet above the level of the river.
Imām Ibrāhīm-al-Khalīl امام ابراهيم الخليل	Left bank. 6 miles. South-south-east.	A tomb surrounded by a small graveyard. On the opposite side of the river, about 1,000 yards to westward, are some walled date gardens belonging to **Baghdād** owners.	The Khān at **Sikandarīyah** on the Bagdād-Karbala road is visible from this place.
Musaiyib مسيب	Both banks. 8 miles. South-south-east.	See article **Musaiyib**.	From Imām Ibrāhīm-al-Khalīl the land on both sides of the river is cultivated and there are many gardens, walled and unwalled, of dates, oranges, pomegranates and figs. At **Musaiyib** the river is 180 yards broad and is crossed by a bridge of 24 boats. In the low season the banks, which here consist of alluvial sand of varying fineness with no cohesion, are 8 to 14 feet above the level of the stream, the

Name.	(1) On which side situated, (2) distance by stream, and (3) average direction from the last place.	Nature.	Remarks.
			extreme depth is 14 feet and the current flows about 1,500 yards an hour. In the flood season the river rises 10 feet and the current increases to 4 miles an hour. There is a considerable island in the river about 1½ miles above **Musaiyib** and a similar one about 1 mile below: both are suitable places for bridging operations and date timber in plenty is available near the former.

In this section, 68 miles in length, the Euphrates flows through a dry but arable country; its bed is broad and open, and the current is ordinarily slight. In the table above reference has not been made to some small canals which take off on the left bank: they will be mentioned in the paragraph on irrigation below.

After passing through the town of **Musaiyib** the Euphrates runs for two miles and then throws off from its right bank the important **Husainīyah** canal: just below this point a former loop of the river, called the Shatt-al-'Atīq شط العتيق or Old River, takes its departure on the opposite side; this branch is now altogether dry. Three miles below the head of the **Husainīyah** canal the river reaches a crucial point in its career and its waters divide into two streams which separate at an acute angle that to the west or right is the great **Hindīyah** canal; the other—here known as the Shatt-al-Hillah—is the one which we shall follow, for it is the true Euphrates of the last thousand years, though its stream is now thin and sluggish. About a mile below the bifurcation of the **Hindīyah** canal and the Euphrates, the Shatt-al-'Atīq already mentioned rejoins the Euphrates from the left: most of the land enclosed between the Euphrates and the Shatt-al-'Atīq now belongs to the Dāirat-as-Sanīyah.

EUPHRATES

The following diagram will help to explain what takes place :—

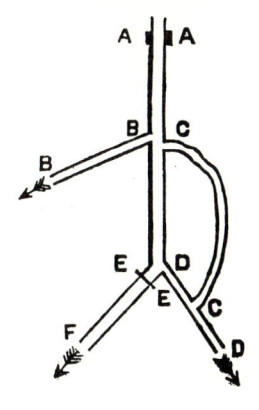

Scale ¼" = 1 mile.

A = Musaiyib.
BB = Husainīyah canal.
CC = Shatt-al-'Atīq.
DD = Shatt-al-Hillah.
EE. = Hindīyah barrage.
F = Shatt-al-Hindīyah.

A tabular account of the second section of the Euphrates follows here in continuation of the preceding table :—

Name.	(1) On which side situated; (2) distance by stream, and (3) average direction from the last place.	Nature.	Remarks.
Husainīyah Canal حسينية	Right bank. 2 miles. South-south-west. (This is the position of the head.)	See article Husainīyah canal.	From Musaiyib to the head of the Husainīyah the left bank of the river has some wooding, but the right bank is almost treeless. The breadth of the river immediately below the head of the Husainīyah is about 120 yards.
Hindīyah (Shatt-al-) شط الهندية	Right bank. 3 miles. South-south-west. (The position given is that of the head.)	See article Shatt-al-Hindīyah.	Here the Hindīyah canal withdraws nearly the whole water of the river; throughout the remainder of this section the Euphrates, as a large river, is non-existent. This point is more fully discussed at the end of the present table.
Hillah حلة	Both banks. 24 miles. South-south-west.	See article Hillah.	The ruins of Babylon begin about 8 miles, and end about 3 miles, above Hillah: the great bulk of the remains

2 K

Name.	(1) On which side situated ; (2) distance by stream, and (3) average direction from the last place.	Nature.	Remarks.
			are on the left bank of the river. On the right bank opposite to the site of Babylon is the village of 'Anānah عنانة. For 2½ months in summer the Euphrates at **Hillah** and in the reach above it is quite dry, and the boat bridge of 15 pontoons at **Hillah** settles down upon the sand. In winter, after rain, the stream at **Hillah** is 60 yards broad and less than four feet deep.
Daghārah دغارة Canal	Left bank. 35 miles. South-east. (This is the position of the head.)	See article **Daghārah.**	For about 20 miles below Hillah there are date groves and many villages : one of the latter called Imām Hamzah (I) is not to be confounded with the village of the same name below. The palms then cease and for 10 miles the country has a less cultivated and prosperous appearance. Towards the end of latter stretch are numerous fortified hamlets, 200 to 300 yards apart. Then follow 5 miles of still more desolate country, where many of the hamlets are now deserted and where the fighting towers are beginning to show symptoms of decay. The villages on the right bank belong to the **Wjsāmah** tribe and one of them, called Shukri شكري , marks the boundary between the two main sections

Name.	(1) On which side situated; (2) distance by stream, and (3) average direction from the last place.	Nature.	Remarks.
			of the Wisāmah. In summer some disconnected pools are all that remains of the river in the reach between **Hillah** and the head of the **Daghārah**, they are sometimes crowded with fish which either are caught with nets by the Arabs or die as the water evaporates.
Dīwānīyah ديوانيه	Both banks. 30 miles. South-south-east.	See article **Dīwānīyah**.	In the neighbourhood of **Dīwānīyah** the average breadth of the river bed is 90 to 95 yards, and the deepest part is almost invariably within 10 feet of the steep bank on the outside of a curve. On the lands enclosed by hollow curves of the river much tamarisk grows. The height of the banks here above the bed, which is altogether dry in summer, is 13 to 16 feet.
Imām Hamzah (II) امام همزه	Right bank. 20 miles. South by east.	A small village on the river bank taking its name from a shrine in the desert about 1 mile to westwards. It is not to be confounded with the village of the same name a little below Hillah Town.	The stretch from **Dīwānīyah** to Imām Hamzah (II) is dry in summer, and in that season it is almost deserted by the inhabitants who migrate westwards towards the **Hindīyah** canal to find water for their cattle. Near Imām Hamzah (II) deposition of wind-borne sand is proceeding rapidly in the bed of the river. The village of **Lāmlūm** لاملوم which has now ceased to exist, stood on the left bank of the

Name.	(1) On which side situated; (2) distance by stream, and (3) average direction from the last place.	Nature.	REMARKS.
Samāwah سماوه	Both banks. 30 to 40 miles. South-east.	See article Samāwah.	river 6 miles below Imām Hamzah (II). Below Imām Hamzah (II) the bed of the river narrows in places to 50 or even 40 yards, and the banks are sometimes more than 18 feet high. Here, as in the immediately preceding reaches, the river —except in winter— has virtually ceased to flow; but 5 or 6 miles above Samāwah its channel is joined by the 'Atshān عطشان coming from the Bahr-an-Najaf, which gives back to it, so far as not expended or absorbed, the water taken out by the Hindīyah canal above Hillah. The first half of the way from Imām Hamzah (II) to Samāwah is desert and the towers and houses which still stud the banks of the river, are now all unoccupied; but after Abu Juwārīr ابو جوارير, a mud village of about 80 houses situated on the right bank 14 miles by road from Imām Hamzah (II), the country improves and possesses both cultivation and inhabitants. Abu Juwārīr is the headquarters of a Nāhiyah in the Qadha of Samāwah; the inhabitants are Bani 'Āridh and Khazā'il. A short way above Abu Juwārīr is the small

Name.	(1) On which side situated; (2) distance by stream, and (3) average direction from the last place.	Nature.	REMARKS.
			village, also on the right bank, of Saiyid Abu Tabakh زبو طبخ and a little below Abu Juwārīr, on both banks, is the half-deserted town or settlement **Rumaithah** to which a separate article is devoted. At **Samāwah** there is a boat bridge.

In this, as in the first section, some canals have been omitted which are dealt with further on in the paragraph on irrigation.

Except in the first 5, and again in the last 5 miles of this section the bed of the Euphrates is for practical purposes dry during a great part of the year; indeed for $2\frac{1}{2}$ months in summer it is altogether empty, and even in winter it only carries one thirty-fifth part of the water of the river. The total length of the section, waterless at times with the exception of 10 miles, is about 150 miles. The place of the Euphrates in this part of the country is taken by the Shatt-al-**Hindīyah**, which opens into the river at both ends and draws off nearly all the water at the head of the reach to restore a portion of it again at the tail. The causes of the supersession of the river by the canal,—a process which does not appear to have been foreseen in 1836 and which may have begun but was not, apparently, far advanced in 1860-65,—are partly natural and partly artificial. The chief factor was probably a gradual rise in the level of the river bed about **Hillah** by a natural deposition of silt; and examination has shown that in the neighbourhood of **Hillah** the loss of depth amounts in places to as much as 12 feet. A second influence came into operation with the opening of the **Hindīyah** canal, by which the volume and velocity of the Euphrates stream were reduced and its scour was diminished. A barrage constructed by the Turkish Government about 1890 at the head of the **Hindīyah** canal partially remedied the evil for a time; but in July 1903 this work gave way and the injury was aggravated, for the whole Euphrates now began to pour down the **Hindīyah** channel. Since this event occurred the silting up of the old Euphrates bed below the take-off of the **Hindīyah** has been accelerated by dams or Sukūr سكور which the Arabs build in it, especially below **Hillah,** for the purpose of flooding their lands and by the wasteful manner in which they withdraw water from the river, particularly by means of the **Daghārah** canal, without returning the surplus. Sand also, carried by the wind from the adjoining desert, is now doing its part in choking up the ancient channel; and in places the accumulations due to this cause have attained a depth of 2½ feet.

It is interesting to observe that these changes constitute a return to the conditions of 1,000 years ago, when the main stream of the **Euphrates** flowed—as it has again begun to do—by **Kūfah,** and when the channel on which **Hillah** Town subsequently grew up was a canal known as the ‚Sūrān سوران. The move of the **Euphrates** into the Hillah channel appears to have taken place gradually between the 8th and the 12th centuries A.D.

The principal features of the river in its third and last section, about 165 miles in length, are given in the table below which is a continuation of the last preceding one :—

Name.	(1) On which side situated; (2) distance by stream, and (3) average direction from the last place.	Nature.	Remarks.
Durrāji دراجي	Left bank. 25 miles. East-south-east.	A small village on the left bank about 25 miles below **Samāwah** Town. It belongs to the Dāirat-as-Sanīyah and contains a telegraph office.	On the left bank about 18 miles below **Samāwah** Town and 7 miles above Durrāji is Khidhar خضر, a village of about 100 mud houses, named after a small shrine which it possesses; the inhabitants are cultivators, boatmen and traders and mostly belong to the Āl Bū Muhsin tribe. The Mudīr of the Durrāj Nāhiyah of the **Samāwah** Qadhā has his residence at Khidhar. On or near the right bank of the Euphrates a little way above Durrāji is 'Ain Said عين صيد, a locality in the desert inland of which salt is obtained. Below **Samāwah** the Eu

Name.	(1) On which side situated: (2) distance by stream; and (3) average direction from the last place.	Nature.	Remarks.
			phrates flows in a turbid stream, varying from 60 to 120 yards in width, between banks which in the low season are 7 to 14 feet high. Near the river on either side are cultivated fields with the desert and scrub jungle beyond.
Nāsirīyah ناصریه	Left bank. 50 miles. East-south-east.	See article Nāsirīyah Town.	The reach below Durāji is similar to the one above it; but the river widens as it advances, and at Nāsirīyah, 4 miles below which the westernmost branch of the Shatt-al-Gharāf joins it as a left bank tributary, it is about 300 yards broad. There is a boat bridge at Nāsirīyah of 25 pontoons. The celebrated ancient ruins of Muqaiyar مقیر are situated on a slight eminence, to the south of the river, about 6 miles southwest of Nāsirīyah.
Sūq-ash-Shuyūkh سوق الشیوخ	Both banks. 20 miles. East-south-east.	See article Sūq-ash-Shuyūkh.	The left bank between Nāsirīyah and Sūq-ash-Shuyūkh is a swamp, formed by the spreading out and commingling of the Shatt-al-Gharāf and the Euphrates. At Sūq-ash-Shuyūkh the river proper cannot be very broad as the bridge contains only a dozen boats. About 10 or 15 miles below Sūq-ash-Shuyūkh and perhaps 3 miles inland from the right

Name.	(1) On which side situated; (2) distance by stream, and (3) average direction from the last place.	Nature.	Remarks.
Madīnah مدينة	Right bank. 70 miles (and about 12 miles above Qūrnah). Village. East by north.	See article **Madīnah**.	bank of the river is the Turkish military station of Khamīsīyah خميسية. Three creeks which lead from the river to Khamīsīyah unite at that place and the canal formed by their junction is said to connect with the Shatt-al-'Arab just above Kūt-al-Farangī. In the reach from Sūq-ash-Shuyūkh to Madīnah the Euphrates runs through marshes notorious for their extent. Hammār, a village or small town which is the headquarters of a Nāhiyah of the same name in the Qadha of Sūq-ash-Shu-yūkh and has a telegraph station, is situated on the left bank of the Euphrates about half-way between Sūq-ash-Shuyūkh and Madīnah, at the junction of the easternmost channel of the Shatt-al-Gharāf with the great river. A large stretch of the marshes below this point is known as Birkat-al-Hammār بركة الحمار. Below Hammār again, on the same bank, is Jazāir جزائر or Kibāish كبائش, a considerable place inhabited by Bani Asad. The breadth of the Euphrates from Sūq-as-Shuyūkh

Name.	(1) On which side situated ; (2) distance by stream, and (3) average direction from the last place.	Nature.	Remarks.
			to **Madīnah** and thence to **Qūrnah** is described as on the average about 150 yards. In the swamps above **Madīnah** the depth is sometimes only 2½ feet. Near **Madīnah** there are great marshes on the south side of river partly known as Hor-aal-Jazāir هور الجزائر. which communicate with the Shatt-al-'**Arab** by backwaters and from which also, in floods, Euphrates water finds its way down to the hollow between **Basrah** and **Zubair** Towns.

Navigation.—The navigation of the Euphrates is nowhere free above the town of **Sūq-ash-Shuyūkh**, which was the highest point reached— and that not without difficulty—by the R.I.M.S. *Comet* in her last attempt to ascend the river in recent years. In the swamps above **Madīnah** the depth of water, as already mentioned, is sometimes only 2½ feet. Native Safīnahs can ordinarily reach the mouth of the 'Atshān at any season, but between July and November they cannot go much further. In March and April, however, the two months of highest river, communication is still open through **Hillah** to **Musaiyib**; but the channel, as we have seen above, is silting up, and unless energetic measures are taken it will soon be blocked altogether. Boats now generally reach **Musaiyib** *via* the 'Atshān, Bahr-an-Najaf and Shatt-al-**Hindīyah** thus passing **Shināfīyah, Kūfah, Kifl** and **Tawairij** on the way instead of Imām Hamzah (II), **Dīwanīyah** and **Hillah**. The result is thus a diversion rather than a closing of communication, and the loss other than agricultural which is caused by the change is more to a few old towns and some villages than to the country at large : it is obvious however that neither of the rival waterways is as satisfactory as it would be if the other did not exist, and the damage to vested interests by the transference of business from one line to the other is in some cases very great. It is believed that by efficient repairs to the **Hindīyah** barrage, before it is too late, a minimum depth of 4 feet could even now be secured in the whole lower course of the Euphrates.

The depth of the Euphrates is variable and appears to have decreased generally throughout its course, and not only in the section from **Musaiyib** to **Samāwah,** since the survey of 1836; but above the head of the Shatt-al-**Hindīyah** there are still soundings of 30 feet in places where the stream is confined.

Navigation depends largely on wind, and when both wind and current are adverse progress becomes almost impossible. In the absence of wind and with an average current a native boat can drop down stream at the rate of about 4 miles an hour: the current in the wide reaches above **Musaiyib** is only about 3 miles an hour even in time of flood, but there are places where it reaches a velocity of 8 or 9 miles. The influence of the sea tides is felt as far up as Durrāji.

Even if physical obstacles to navigation did not exist it is improbable that a steamer service on the Euphrates would be remunerative in the present circumstances of the country; for Turkish '**Irāq**, in its undeveloped condition, cannot support more than one large centre of trade and one line of communication, and these it possesses already in **Baghdād** City and the **Tigris** river. Moreover, the imports which would follow the Euphrates line are neither so heavy nor so bulky as to demand steam carriage; and the most considerable export is grain which must be picked up from point to point,—a task that steamers cannot profitably perform.

Irrigation.—The Euphrates from **Fallūjah** to **Diwānīyah** is a river well calculated to serve as a source of perennial irrigation upon a large scale, and the fact is one which during long ages received a full and practical recognition. The canals to which Mesopotamia owed its prosperity and importance in ancient times mostly tapped the Euphrates on its left bank between the two places mentioned and after traversing Mesopotamia at this, its narrowest part, flowed with open mouths into the **Tigris;** in this way, besides watering the fertile country through which they passed, they afforded a means of communication by boat between the two great rivers. The remains of these canals are still the dominant feature of the landscape, and huge piles of silt-clearance, resembling railway embankments, cross the otherwise featureless desert in every direction and intersect at many angles. Some of the old canals are yet in operation on a greatly reduced scale and irrigate perhaps a hundredth part of the area which was formerly served.

EUPHRATES

The maximum discharge of the Euphrates at **Musaiyib** is 2,500 to 3,000 cubic metres per second and the minimum discharge about 300. The mean velocity of the river at a typical place in the same neighbourhood was ·85 metres per second on the 5th January 1905, giving by calculation a maximum flood velocity of 1·33 and a minimum low-water velocity of ·66 metres per second. The average fall of the river is about 1 in 13,000, or much the same as that of the Nile, to which in the reaches between **Fallūjah** and **Mussaiyib** it is said to bear a striking resemblance. In the latitude of **Baghdād** the average level of the Euphrates is about 20 feet above the average level of the **Tigris**, so that the Tigris at its highest is exactly on a level, its maximum rise being 6½ metres, with the Euphrates at its lowest in the corresponding stage of its course. The Euphrates runs in a shallower and more open bed than the **Tigris**, and having a more constant stream it is the more suitable for irrigation. To the east of **Baghdād** the lowness of the left bank of the **Euphrates** is a serious but remediable defect; when it rises it lets loose destructive floods which sometimes sweep across Mesopotamia almost to the **Tigris**, and one of the first steps in the reclamation of Mesopotamia would be the prevention of such occurrences. Between **Fallūjah** and Khān **Maqdam** attempts have already been made to confine the river by means of earth embankments about 8 feet high and 20 feet wide which are revetted on the side towards the stream.

The river is at its highest in April and at its lowest in September: the following diagram will explain the character of its ordinary rise and fall:—

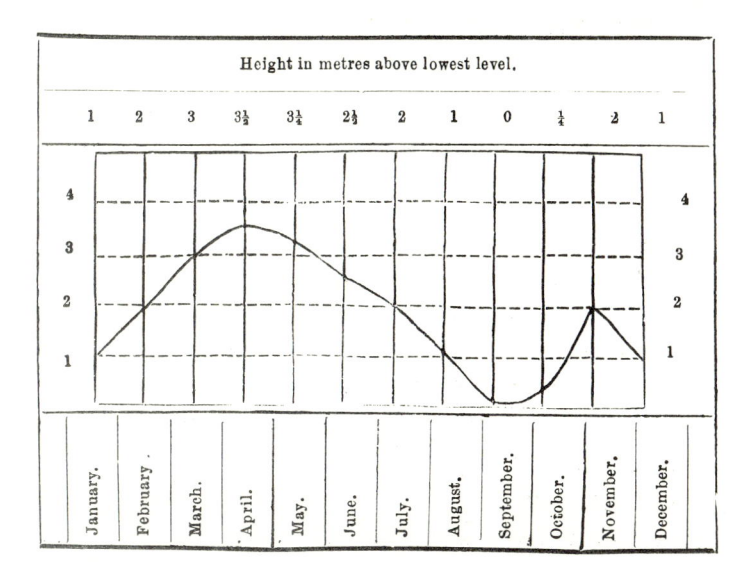

The rise in spring is due to the melting of the winter snows in Armenia, and the sudden rise in November followed by a temporary decrease in December and January is attributable to the autumn rains, of which the effect is suddenly checked by winter frosts. The maximum annual rise of the Euphrates, which does not last long enough to appear in our diagram, is about 5 metres.

If the restoration of irrigation in Mesopotamia were to be seriously undertaken the operations would probably be begun on the part of the Euphrates between **Fallūjah** and **Dīwānīyah**; some of the more important existing canals in this quarter consequently must be noticed here. The first of these is the Saqlāwīyah سقلاویه, which used to take out some 8 miles above **Fallūjah** and, passing to the north of the ruins of 'Aqār Nimrūd عقار نمرود, formed an extensive lake on the west side of **Kādhimain** Town and then entered the **Tigris** about 5 miles below **Baghdād**. In July 1838 the British surveying steamer *Euphrates* passed through this canal and met with no soundings of less than 6 feet; but since then the canal has been closed, on account of the floods which it assisted on their way towards **Baghdād**. The upper end is now blocked by wheat fields, while the lower is filled for a short distance by a back-flow from the **Tigris**, and forms a creek, known as the Khar خر, which is spanned by an iron bridge at a short distance from **Baghdād** on the route to **Musaiyib**. The following is a list of the existing canals from **Fallūjah** to **Hillah** with their discharges as registered on the 3rd January 1905 when the Euphrates at **Fallūjah** was 1½ metres above its lowest level and was itself discharging 700 cubic metres per second:—

Name and description of canal.	Discharge on 3rd January 1905 in cubic metres per second.
1. The Abu Ghuraib ابو غریب, takes out 4 miles below **Fallūjah** and runs to near **Baghdād**. Close to its head it is spanned by a strong brick bridge carrying a roadway, 10½ feet broad; the bed width of the canal here is about 30 feet, and it runs in a cutting 40 feet deep. It is separated from the Saqlāwiyah by a high pebbly desert yielding gypsum	6
2. The Radhwānīyah رضوانیه, of which the head is a mile or two below Khān **Maqdam**	Nil.

Name and description of canal.	Discharge on 3rd January 1905 in cubic metres per second.
3. The Mahmūdīyah محموديه, takes out below the Radhwānīyah, crosses the **Baghdād-Karbala** road at **Mahmūdīyah** and approaches the **Tigris at Madāin**. Near its head it is crossed by a brick bridge without a parapet: the roadway is 11 feet wide. The bed width of the canal at the same place is 12 feet	2
4. The Latīfīyah لطيفيه	Nil.
5. The Sikandarīyah سكندريه, further down, crosses the **Baghdād-Karbala** road at **Sikandarīyah** . . .	1
6. The Musaiyib مسيّب, leaves the river just above the town of **Musaiyib** and crosses the **Baghdād-Karbala** road	2
7. The Nasrīyah نصريه, takes off between **Musaiyib** and the head of the Shatt-al-**Hindīyah** and crosses the **Baghdād-Hillah** road	2
8. The Mahāwīl ماحول, quits the reduced river several miles below the point of separation of the **Hindīyah** and crosses the **Baghdād-Hillah** road	Nil.
9. The Khātūnīyah خاتونيه, leaves the Euphrates a short distance above the ruins of Babylon and crosses the **Baghdād-Hillah** road	2
10. The Nīl نيل, takes out still nearer to the ruins of Babylon than the Khātūnīyah and crosses the same road .	1
11. The Wardīyah ورديه crosses the **Baghdād-Hillah** road between the ruins of Babylon and **Hillah** . . .	Nil.

All the canals in the list above are on the left bank of the Euphrates and, with the exception of the Radhwānīyah, the Mahāwīl and the Khātūnīyah, they are the property of the Dāirat-as-Sanīyah. The Abu Ghuraib has a good regulating-head of masonry, consisting of two spans each $2\frac{1}{2}$ metres wide and probably identical with the bridge described above; but the regulators of the remainder are indifferent. As will be seen, the aggregate discharge of these canals with a rather low river is only 16 cubic metres a second; this might rise in time of flood to about 200 cubic metres per second, but the result would be flooding, owing to imperfect subsidiary arrangements, of the whole country; and cultivators in the present state of affairs prefer not to irrigate their lands at all when the river is high. The silt in these small canals is heavy, and there are symptoms that clearance is not keeping pace with deposit and that the canals are gradually deteriorating.

The large **Husainīyah** canal and Shatt-at-**Hindīyah** on the right bank, whose heads are 2 and 5 miles respectively below **Musaiyib**, form the subjects of special articles; and the small canals on both banks between **Hillah** and the head of the **Daghārah**, being described in the article on the **Hillah Qadha**, do not call for notice here, except the **Tājīyah** which takes out just above **Hillah** and the **Jarbū'īyah**, an important asset of the Dāirat-as-Sanīyah, about half way from **Hillah** to the head of the **Daghārah**, both of which are on the right bank. The **Daghārah** itself, on the left bank, is separately dealt with elsewhere. It only remains to mention the Abul Fadhal ابو الفضل, a canal thrown off by the Euphrates from its left bank some 2 miles above **Dīwānīyah** and swallowed up in the marshes to the south-eastwards which contain the village of Fawwār نوار distant about 30 miles from **Dīwānīyah**.

FADHŪL
فضول

A considerable Arab tribe of Southern **Najd**, not apparently found anywhere elsewhere. In **Sadair** they occur at 'Ashairah, 'Attār, **Majma'**, Tuwaim and **Zilfi**; in '**Āridh** at Bīr, Jarīnah, Mahrīqah and Malham in Mahmal, at Malqa and 'Audah in Wādi **Hanīfah**, and at **Dhrumah**; in **Harīq** at Harīq town; in **Hautah** at Hautah town and Hilwah; and in **Aflāj** at 'Amār, **Lailah**, **Raudhah** and Umm Shinādhir. Those of **Majma'** belong to sections called Fadhl فضل and Kathīr كثير and those of Hautah town to sections styled Āl Tālib آل طلب and Kathrān كثران, while the Fadhūl of 'Amār and **Raudhah** are said to be of a Shaikhly section known as Mughairah مغيرة. The Kathīr and Kathrā sections are probably identical. The origin of the Fadhūl is forgotten, but a vague tradition connects them with the Bani **Lām**.

FAID

FAHAIHĪL
فحيحيل
or
FAHĀHĪL
فحاحيل

A coast village in the 'Adān district of the Kuwait Principality, 21 miles south-south-east of Kuwait Town. It consists of about 50 houses and has 20 wells of good water about 18 feet deep. There are 200 well-grown date palms and some cultivation of wheat, barley and melons, irrigated from the wells. The inhabitants, who belong to various Arab tribes, own some flocks of sheep and goats. As mentioned in the article on 'Adān, Fahaihīl is a resort at certain seasons for townsmen of Kuwait.

FAHAL*
فحل

An island seven miles north-west of Masqat Town and two miles from the nearest point on the 'Omān coast. It is 280 feet high and precipitous, with overhanging cliffs all round except at the south-west corner where the only landing place is. Fahal is one-third of a mile in length from north to south, is light-coloured, and has deep water all round. It was known to the Portuguese as "the Isle of Victory" on account of a naval success which they gained near it over the Turks.

FAID
فيد

A large and scattered village in Jabal Shammar proper, about 45 miles south-east by east of Hāil on the route to Buraidah. It stands on high ground to the west of a Wādi called Abal Krūsh ابا الكرش; 2 miles to the south-west of the place is Jabal Qafail قفيل, a hill 200 feet high. The soil is sand, 15 to 30 feet deep, with a stratum of 6 feet of very hard black basalt beneath. The quarters of Faid and their date groves are spread over a space 2 to 3 miles in extent: the quarters are, besides that specifically called Faid which contains 40 houses,—'Ain عين, Ghazaizīyah غزيزيه, Hamrah حمره, Hadhaifān حذيفان, Marjūm مرجوم, Najīb نجيب, Qalaiyib قليّب, Shajarah (Abu) ابو شجره, and Sinaiyān سنيان. The population, who may number 1,000 souls, are partly Bani Tamīm and partly Shammar. Cereals, vegetables and melons are grown. Water is at 6 to 9 fathoms, and the best well is in Marjūm. In ancient times Faid was a large and famous

---

* A view of Fahal from the sea will be found in Chart No. 2373—2837-A.

place and a station on the pilgrim route from **Kūfah** to Makkah. There are some ruins on a black lava hill called Kharāsh خراش, 600 yards south of 'Ain.

FAILAKAH ISLAND
فيلكه

To British mariners formerly known as "Pheleechi," from the local pronunciation which is Failachah. An island, 7 miles in length with a maximum breadth of 3 miles, lying on the north side of the entrance to **Kuwait** Bay: its western end, the nearest to **Kuwait** Town, is about 10 miles east-north-east of Rās-al-Ardh, while its northern end is about 7 miles south-east of the mouth of Khor-as-**Sabīyah**.

Physical characteristics and surroundings.—The shape of Failakah is that of a badly-shaped wedge, having its point to the south-east and its base to the north-west. The island stands on an extensive flat of mud and sand with rocky patches, which is called Dhārub ضارب and stretches south-eastwards from the entrance of Khor-as-**Sabīyah**. Failakah is low, the highest point being a mound 30 feet high in the westernmost part; at high spring tides it is broken in upon by the sea, and, not being visible more than 6 or 8 miles, it is frequently not sighted in entering **Kuwait** Bay. Failakah has two outliers, 'Auhah عوهه, a small sandy islet about 3 miles from its south-eastern extremity at the place where the Dhārub flat comes to an end, and Mashjān مشجان, a low sandy islet on the flat about 2 miles from Failakah in the direction of Khor-as-**Sabīyah**.

Inhabitants.—Estimates of the population of Failakah vary; but there appear to be about 200 men or, say, 500 souls altogether. There is now only one village, Zor زر, on the north-west coast facing Mashjān; a Niqa'ah or boat-harbour, difficult of entrance, is situated on the shore three-quarters of a mile to the north-east of the village. Landing at Zor is easy. The place possesses some 70 or 80 ordinary boats, smaller on the average than the boats of **Kuwait** Town, and over 20 Wahrīyahs or fishing-boats built of Jarīds or date-branches. There are several deserted villages on the island. One of these, named Subaihiyah صبيحيه, sisituated on the western shore nearer to the southern than to the northern

FAILAKAH ISLAND

end of the island. It is marked by a group of 90 superannuated palms, perforated by insects. Close to Zor, beyond its boat-harbour, is the deserted site of Sa'īdi سعيدي; about a mile further is a similar place called Dasht دشت; finally, in this direction, we reach Qrainīyah قرينيه where Jābir, the eldest son of Shaikh Mubārak of **Kuwait**, has built himself a house: this is now, except Zor, the only inhabited place on the island. The people of Zor, mostly fishermen but a few of them pearl divers, are of mixed origin: the majority are said to have come from the island of **Khārag**, but others are from **Fāo**, the **Hindiyān** District and even **'Omān**. They are civil and well-disposed, but superstitious and fanciful, and their condition generally is wretched. Indeed the aspect of the island from every point of view is one of melancholy but gentle decay.

Water supply.—Water is found in most parts of the island at a depth of only 6 feet: it is said to be better than the water of **Kuwait** Town and to be less brackish near the sea than it is at some distance inland. In the hot weather it turns so salt in some places as to kill lucerne.

Fisheries and agriculture.—The resources of Failakah are fisheries and agriculture on a modest scale.

After deduction of Mākalah مكاله, or the food expenses of the crew, the catch of fish is divided into equal shares, of which one goes to the Shaikh of the island, one to the owner of the boat, one to the Captain, and one to each of the crew.

Wheat and barley are grown with some success on clayey patches. About 6,000 lbs. of wheat are said to be sown annually in the whole island, and the total yield of grain is about 30 tons. The produce after deduction of taxes, when taxes are paid, is divided equally between the cultivators on the one hand and the suppliers of seed, plough-animals and food for the animals on the other: the crop is sown in October and reaped in April. Melons are grown, also lucerne and some of the ordinary vegetables such as onions, carrots and radishes. There are a few rose trees and some dates; but the latter, which are chiefly towards the south end of the island, are not in a flourishing condition, and the agriculture of Failakah generally is inferior to that of **Jahrah**. The

Sidar or ber and the tamarisk are the principal trees other than dates, but hardy as they are they do not grow without attention.

Domestic and other animals.—Failakah boasts a dozen camels, a number of donkeys, a few flocks and herds, and some poultry. Flamingos, pelicans, gulls and flocks of a bird resembling the curlew haunt the shore, and the island is said to be visited in the hot weather by large flocks of sand-grouse. There are a number of gazelles, descended from a pair which a member of the Shaikh of **Kuwait's** family turned loose some years ago: only relations of the chief are permitted to shoot them.

Administration.—Failakah is governed (1904) on behalf of the Shaikh of **Kuwait**, to whom it belongs, by one of his relations. This individual, Sa'ūd **Qalātah**, who is a man of about 35 with some negro blood and partially paralysed in his lower limbs, succeeded his father in the governorship. About one-third of the arable land on Failakah is held Mu'āf or revenue-free: the remainder pays Zakāt to the Shaikh of **Kuwait** at the rate of one-tenth of gross produce, besides which the Shaikh takes for himself all the straw of the island, even on revenue-free holdings, except a small quantity that the inhabitants are allowed to retain for their own necessities. The Shaikh has declined to allow rich merchants of **Kuwait** or foreigners to settle in Failakah on the ground that they would probably oppress the original inhabitants.

Sacred places.—Failakah is remarkable chiefly for its tombs and shrines. First, there are the graves of the Auliya الأولياء or Saints, who play a large part in the traditions of the island; of these some 60 or 70 are scattered round the village of Zor. Then, about a mile to the south of Zor, there are the tombs of Sa'ad سعد, Sa'īd سعيد, and Sa'īdah سعيدة; that of Sa'ad is to the east of the others, and the whole group stand up conspicuously as Failakah is approached in a boat from **Kuwait**. It is principally to visit these tombs, said to commemorate two brothers and a sister who were murdered here, that pilgrims from Yaman and India, and more frequently from Afghanistān and Balūchistān, visit Failakah. There is another tomb, also possessing virtue and visited by pilgrims; it is said to be that of a certain Muhammad-al-Badawi, whose only claim to distinction is that his finger after death resisted the removal of his signet ring. Lastly, there is the Muqām-al-Khidhar, مقام الخضر, which overlooks the boat harbour of Zor, and is now a roofless tower threatened by the encroachments of the sea. Persians do not resort to it but it is frequented by Arab sailors who come to perform their vows, made in sickness or in danger at sea, by sacrificing a sheep or a goat, by burning incense and by feeding the poor. The tutelary spirit is probably the same Khidhar who has a shrine on **'Abbādān** island; in Failakah, however, his reputation is chiefly as a patron saint of mariners. The shrine of Khidhar is not so much visited by foreign pilgrims as those mentioned before it.

Traditions.—Qrainīyah is said to have been the seat of a tyrant who wore golden boots: his city was destroyed by God because he cut a child in half to prove the temper of his sword. There is a local tradition, supported by traces of good stone houses in the middle of the island, that the Portuguese once occupied the place. They are said to have been driven, first from Dasht and then from the centre of the island to which they retired, by a plague of rats sent upon them by the Auliya.

FAILĪYEH
فيليه

A village in the **Muhammareh** District of Southern **'Arabistān**; it is situated on the left bank of the Shatt-al-**'Arab**, 3 miles above **Muhammareh** Town, between the Shatt-al-**'Arab** and the right bank of the Abu Jidi' ابو جديع canal. It consists of about 300 brick, mud, and reed houses, with 12 or 15 general shops and two coffee shops: the inhabitants are **Muhaisin** and mixed Arabs, **Balūchis**, and negroes. Failīyeh is the headquarters of the Shaikh of **Muhammareh's** administration; here are the offices of his Government, and here is quartered his mercenary force of about 400 armed Arabs and **Balūchis**. A small quay of date logs occupies the angle between the river and the canal, and about a mile up the Abu Jidi' is a small dock in which the Shaikh's steamers are repaired. The Shaikh has at Failīyeh about 20 brass and iron muzzle-loading guns, and his saluting battery stands just below the entrance to the canal: below the battery is an orchard and young date grove. Failīyeh is connected with **Muhammareh** Town by a private telephone belonging to the Shaikh. The principal buildings are two palaces which are still occupied by part of the household of the Shaikh, but Khaz'al Khān now resides in an imposing new mansion called Qasr Khaz'alīyeh, خز عليه three-quarters of a mile further up the bank of the Shatt-**'al-Arab**; his Persian wife, the Jamīl-as-

Saltaneh, also has her abode there. Failīyeh was founded about 1860 by Hāji Jābir, the first great Shaikh of the **Muhaisin**.

FAKKĀN* (KHOR)
خور فكّان

A coast village in the centre of the **Shamailīyah** tract in Trucial 'Omān, about 23 miles north of Khor **Kalba** and 20 miles south-south-east of **Dibah**. Khor Fakkān stands on the southern shore of a sandy bay two miles wide, one mile deep and open to the north-east: the bay has a perfectly sheltered boat harbour at its east end and just outside its eastern point is an island 240 feet high known as Sīrat-al-Khor صيرة الخور. The water supply of the village is good and the date plantations contain about 5,000 trees; fish, vegetables, cattle and poultry are procurable. There are about 150 houses of **Naqbiyīn** and Arabi-cised Persians, and the population may amount to 800 souls. The people live by their dates, by cultivation of wheat and by pearl diving: they own four or five coasting vessels which run to **Masqat** Town and to places in the Persian Gulf. There are seven shops. The place is at present held in fief by Sa'id-bin-Ahmad, a first cousin once removed of the present Shaikh of **Shārjah**. One of the quarters or suburbs of Khor Fakkān is called Hiyawah.

FALAIJ (WĀDI)
وادي فليج

A valley in the Eastern **Hajar** district of the 'Omān Sultanate, through which runs the main line of communication between the coast at Sūr and the inland districts of **Ja'alān** and **Sharqīyah**; its direction is south-south-west and north-north-east, and it reaches the sea slightly to the west of **Sū**.

Wādi Fisão فساو, the principal tributary of Wādi Falaij, rises on the eastern side of a pass in Jabal **Khamīs** about 20 miles south-south-east of **Sūr**, and about 1 mile below the pass opens out into a stony plain called Ma'qal معقل, which is surrounded by hills and ravines and in which are some of the coal exposures referred to in the article on Jabal **Khamīs**. Bedouin encampments are sometimes found in this vicinity. About eight miles below Ma'qal, Wādi Fisão joins Wādi Falaij, of which the upper portion has not been described by any European traveller, from the right bank. In the foot-hills of Jabal **Khamīs**, to the east or north-east of this junction, is a Mashārifah village, of about 60 houses, called

* A plan of the Khor Fakkān Bay will be found in Chart No. 2373—2837-A.

Ghassah غسّه, which is distinguished by a tower and is said to possess 20 camels, 20 donkeys, 30 cattle, 600 sheep and goats and 800 palms; and in the bed of the Wādi itself, below the junction, is the oasis of Falaij with date palms, oleanders and other trees, good and ample water, abundant camel-grazing and evidences of former cultivation extending for about a mile : Bedouins belonging to the Mashārifah or to the Rawājih section of the Bani Bū Hasan frequently encamp here, but there are no permanent habitations. Four and-a-half miles below the oasis of Falaij, on the right bank of the Wādi, is the tower of Rafsah رفصه ; it is said to have been built by an Imām of 'Omān to resist the incursions of the Wahhābis, but it is now in the hands of the Mashārifah tribe who oblige all caravans using this route to pass through a square gate-house 100 yards from the tower and pay toll, in consideration of which they do not plunder them. The tower itself is a quaint erection 50 feet high by 30 feet in diameter and it completely commands the passage up the Wādi, which at this point is narrow. On the left bank of the Wādi, opposite the tower, are cave-dwellings containing some eight or ten families of Mashārifah, who possess 3 camels, 40 donkeys, 8 cattle and 200 goats. This is the frontier village of the tribe in the direction of Sūr. About two miles below Rafsah, Wādi Falaij is joined from the west by a ravine with conspicuous yellow sandstone cliffs, two or three miles up which lies the Mashārifah village of Mislaq مسلق. The people of Mislaq are wood cutters and carriers; they own 8 camels, 16 donkeys, 12 cattle and 200 sheep and goats. One mile further on Wādi Falaij debouches from the hills and, leaving Sūq Sūr on its right bank, tends north-eastwards to the coast.

The total fixed population of the valley and its affluents appears to be only about 500 souls.

The valley of Wādi Falaij varies greatly in breadth : at Rafsah it is only a few hundred yards broad, while further up it exceeds two miles; the actual bed of the Wādi is generally 200 to 300 yards across and is enclosed between banks 20 or 30 feet high. From the oasis of Falaij downwards the Wadi contains a limpid, running stream, which has frequently to be crossed in ascending or descending the valley and is in places two feet deep. The road generally runs in the bed of the stream, but at Rafsah it ascends to the level of the Mashārifah tower by a steep zigzag path.

FALLĀ-HĪYEH ولّاحيّه DISTRICT

The most central of the districts of Southern '**Arabistān**, having on the south-west and west the district of **Muhammareh**, on the north the district of **Ahwāz**, on the north-east the **Jarrāhi** District, on the south-east **Ma'shūr** and the territory connected with it, and on the south Khor **Mūsa** and the open sea.

Boundaries.—The border of the district apparently begins on the sea at the mouth of Khor Silaik and follows that creek, and subsequently the Khuwairīn branch of Khor Qanāqah with which Khor Silaik is virtually connected, to the ruins of **Qubbān**. From **Qubbān** onwards the boundary seems to be the Salmānīyeh canal until some marshes near the bank of the **Kārūn** river are reached; these it skirts, running more to northwards than before, and passes in succession by Maqtū' مقطوع and 'Ataishi عطيشي, at the latter of which there is a ruined tomb, to a locality named Khuwaiseh خويسه, where there is some rising ground. Beyond Khuwaiseh the line turns eastwards and arrives by way of Qusaibeh قصيبه, where again there is some elevated land, at the right bank of the **Jarrāhi** River immediately below the village of Qarqar. Crossing the river it continues at first in a south-easterly, and then in a southerly direction; passes by 'Aquleh, a spot 8 miles west of **Ma'shūr**; and finally reaches the bank of Khor **Mūsa** at or near the point where that inlet breaks up into the two Khors of Dōraq and Ma'shūr. From this point back to the mouth of Khor Silaik the boundary is at first Khor **Mūsa** and then the Persian Gulf.

Physical geography, climate and natural products.—The Fallāhīyeh district consists of the country traversed by the **Jarrāhi** River in the lower one-third of its course. From the point where it enters the district, immediately below Qarqar, down to Khazīneh, where its stream is finally broken up a little above **Fallāhīyeh** Town, the **Jarrāhi** is bordered on both banks by a belt of canal-irrigated cultivation. Outside this cultivated belt are, at the eastern end of the district, flat alluvial plains which stretch to the horizon and are waterless except after rain; and this dry and nearly desert portion of the district reaches, on the south side of the **Jarrāhi**, about as far west as Imāmzādeh 'Abdul Hasan, near which it is terminated by an extension southwards, known as **Shatūt**, of the irrigated tract connected with the river. On the north of the **Jarrāhi**, on the borders of the **Ahwāz** District, there are large swamps both to the west and to the east of Gharaibeh; of these the former is probably fed by the spill of the Mālih and the latter by the

A Canal in the Fallahiyeh District.
(Maj. P. Z. Cox.)

FALLĀHĪYEH DISTRICT

surplus waters of the **Gūpāl,** both streams of the **Ahwāz** District, as well as by the overflow of the **Jarrāhi** which they adjoin. The Fallāhīyeh-Mārid canal, a continuation of the **Jarrāhi** River, traverses Hors or swamps which extend to an uncertain distance on either side of it. The large tract between Khor Qanāqeh and Khor Dōraq is as yet unexplored; but the north-eastern bank of Khor Dōraq is known to be marshy throughout almost its entire length, and is practically unapproachable except at one point near Imāmzādeh 'Abdul Hasan.

In the damp parts of the district the heat of summer is almost intolerable, and mosquitoes abound to such an extent that even natives of the country take refuge inside nets immediately before sunset and eat their evening meal there. From June to September military operations would be practically impossible for climatic reasons.

In the drier parts of the district tamarisk, dwarf tamarisk and camel-thorn are seen, especially on the banks of hollows. Other naturally growing plants are Qāqilah, 'Ausaj, Rimth and a kind of Salsola from which Shinān or herb-potash is obtained by burning.

Inhabitants.—The population of the district is almost entirely of the **Ka'ab** tribe and therefore Shī'ah by religion; the people, though their houses are not solidly constructed, form fixed agricultural communities and should perhaps be regarded as settled. If this view be taken, the district has no considerable Bedouin population. The following is a rough estimate of the number of souls in the district:—

Fallāhīyeh Town	2,000
Buziyeh	8,000
Jarrāhi settlements (see next paragraph)	28,000
Janjīreh settlements	4,500
Shatūt settlements	2,500
Total souls	45,000

In the two towns first mentioned **Ka'ab** are a majority of the population, but intermixed with them are some Persians, some Arabs from **Kuwait**, and some **Sabians**; in the Jarrāhi settlements the people are all **Ka'ab** except 1,000 persons, or fewer, who are Saiyids or belong to various Arab tribes; the **Janjīreh** and **Shatūt** tracts are in the exclusive possession of the **Ka'ab.** Among the non-**Ka'ab** residents near the **Jarrāhi** are some Bani **Turuf,** settled by the Shaikh of **Muhammareh** on the Khaz'ali canal, and a few **'Anāfijeh** of the Simairāt section on the Shabaisheh canal, to whom may be added the Bait Iblāl بیت ابلال (about 150 souls) at Khuwainis and Khamis and the Ma'āwiyeh (some 70 persons) at Madīnat-al-Mūmin: both of the last named tribes are here dependent on the **Ka'ab**. Even in this, their principal district, the black turban which used to be distinctive of the **Ka'ab** has been generally discarded for the Arab kerchief and fillet: headmen, however, still wear the old-fashioned head dress. Houses are sometimes of mud and sometimes of matting and reeds: they have generally sloping thatched roofs. The mud brick is here of the same pattern as in the **Jarrāhi** District.

Canals, settlements and general topography.—Most of the villages of the district are settlements situated upon canals from the **Jarrāhi** River and known by the same names as the canals. The canal system consequently furnishes the key to the topography of the district, and in the table below an attempt is made to explain it; but two tracts or groups of distributaries which are of special importance have been reserved for separate description elsewhere under the names **Janjīreh** and **Shatūt**. The remaining canals are given below in the order in which they occur in descending the **Jarrāhi**:—

Name of canal.	Position on the Jarrāhi.	Particulars of the dependent population.	Particulars of cultivation, livestock, etc., and remarks.
Dilis دلس	Left bank, 1 mile below Qarqar in the Jarrāhi District.	Ka'ab of the Bait Hilāyil section, inhabiting reed and mat huts. Fighting strength is 20 men, all armed with rifles and mounted.	20 Faddāns of cultivation. There are 20 cattle and 1,000 sheep and goats.
Zabdi زبدي	Left bank, 1½ miles below Dilis.	Ka'ab of the Āl Bū Ghubaish subdivision chiefly occupying mat huts. There are 30 fighting men, all armed with rifles and mounted.	30 Faddāns of cultivation. Livestock are 30 cattle and 100 sheep and goats.
Zubaidīyeh زبیدیه	Right bank, partially opposite Dilis and partially opposite Zabdi.	Ka'ab of the Khanātireh division, living chiefly in mat huts. There are 20 fighting men, all mounted and armed with rifles.	20 Faddāns of cultivation. There are 100 cattle and 100 sheep and goats.
Qatrāni قطراني	Left bank, ¾ of a mile below Zabdi.	Ka'ab of the Bait Hilāyil and Moni sections, mostly occupying mat huts. They have 90 fighting men, all with rifles and mounted.	On the average 90 Faddāns of cultivation including gardens, but the canal can water up to 150. Animals are 100 cattle and 1,000 sheep and goats.

FALLĀHĪYEH DISTRICT

Name of canal.	Position on the Jarrāhi.	Particulars of the dependent population.	Particulars of cultivation, livestock, etc., and remarks.
Mansūreh منصوره	Right bank, perhaps $\frac{3}{4}$ of a mile below Qatrāni.	Ka'ab of the Hazbeh division; they have 2 or 3 mud houses and the rest are reed and mat huts. There are 20 fighting men armed with rifles and mounted.	30 Faddāns are cultivated and there are gardens. No animals are kept here; the owners have their livestock at Umm-as-Sakhar.
Mansūreh Saiyid Ja'far منصوره سيد جعفر	Right bank, about 1 mile below Mansūreh.	Arabs of various tribes. Fighting strength is 60 men, all mounted but only half of them with rifles. There are 2 mud houses; the other dwellings are reed and mat huts.	60 Faddāns of cultivation: there are some gardens. Animals are 50 cattle and 300 sheep and goats.
Mansūreh Kinaiyin منصوره كنين	Right bank, about 1 mile below Mansūreh Saiyid Ja'far.	Ka'ab of the 'Asākireh subdivision; occupying reed and mat huts. There are 30 fighting men all armed with rifles and mounted.	There are gardens and 30 Faddāns of cultivation. Livestock are 30 cattle and 100 sheep and goats.
Farhāni فرحاني	Left bank, perhaps $\frac{3}{4}$ of a mile below Mansūreh Kinaiyin.	Ka'ab of the Āl Bū Ghubaish subdivision, inhabiting reed and mat huts. Fighting strength is 20 men, all with rifles, of whom 15 are mounted.	20 Faddāns of cultivation. Livestock are 30 cattle and 100 sheep and goats.
Nahr-ash-Shaikh نهر الشيخ	Left bank, $\frac{3}{4}$ of a mile below Farhāni.	Arabs of different tribes, living in reed and mat huts. There are 40 fighting men of whom 30 are mounted and 30 are armed with rifles.	There are gardens and 40 Faddāns of cultivation. Animals are 30 cattle and 100 sheep and goats.
Chilbān چلبان	Left bank, perhaps $\frac{1}{2}$ a mile below Nahr-ash-Shaikh.	Ka'ab of the Āl Bū Ghubaish subdivision; their dwellings are reed huts. Fighting strength is 20 men, all mounted and armed with rifles.	20 Faddāns are cultivated and there are gardens and 50 cattle and 100 sheep and goats.
Khuwainis خوينس	Left bank, $\frac{3}{4}$ of a mile below Chilbān.	Bait Iblāl Arabs dependent on the Ka'ab. They live in reed and mat huts and have 30 fight-	There are gardens and 30 Faddāns of cultivation. Livestock are 40 cattle and 100 sheep and goats.

Name of canal.	Position on the Jarrāhi.	Particulars of the dependent population.	Particulars of cultivation, livestock, etc., and remarks.
Mansūreh Hasan-ibn-Mādhi منصورة حسن ابن ماضي	Right bank, exact position uncertain.	ing men of whom 20 are mounted and have rifles. Ka'ab of the Muqaddam division. They have 30 fighting men, all with rifles and mounted. Their houses are mat and reed huts.	There are gardens and 30 Faddāns of cultivation. Animals are 20 cattle and 100 sheep and goats.
Khamis خمس	Left bank, below Khuwainis and above Qarakhān.	Bait Ibl āl Arabs dependent on the Ka'ab.	This canal irrigates 22 Faddāns.
Qarakhān قرخان	Left bank, 3 miles below Khuwainis.	Ka'ab of the Āl Bū Banaidar section. They live in reed huts and have 40 fighting men, all armed with rifles and mounted.	There are gardens and 40 Faddāns of cultivation. Animals are 40 cattle and 300 sheep and goats.
Nahr Saiyid Hasan نهر سيد حسن	Right bank.	Fighting strength is 15 men who have all rifles but are not mounted.	There are 15 Faddāns of cultivation.
Khashāb خشاب	Right bank, perhaps ½ a mile below Nahr Saiyid Hasan.	Ka'ab of the Āl Bū 'Ubaid section; they inhabit reed huts and have 30 fighting men of whom 20 have rifles and are mounted.	There are 2 boats here, Ballams, also 30 Faddāns of ordinary cultivation and gardens. Livestock are 30 cattle and 100 sheep and goats.
Madīnat-Dishmān مدينة دشمان	Left bank, 1 mile below Khashāb.	Ka'ab of the Āl Bū Sūf section, occupying reed huts. Fighting strength is 20 men, all mounted and armed with rifles.	There are gardens and 20 Faddāns of cultivation. Animals are 30 cattle and 100 sheep and goats.
Braijeh بريجه	Right bank, practically opposite the two Madīnehs.	Ka'ab of the Kharaijeh section; their fighting strength is 50 men, of whom 40 have rifles and 40 are mounted.	50 Faddāns of irrigation.
Madīnat-al-Mumin مدينة المومن	Left bank, adjoining Madīnat Dishmān above.	Ma'āwiyeh dependent on the Ka'ab and living in reed huts. They have 20 fighting men of whom 15 are mounted and 15 have rifles.	There are gardens and 20 Faddāns of cultivation. Animals are 30 cattle and 200 sheep and goats.

Name of canal.	Position on the Jarrāhi.	Particulars of the dependent population.	Particulars of cultivation, livestock, etc., and remarks.
Āl Bū Ghuwāzi آل بو غوازي	Left bank, ½ a mile below Madīnat-al-Mumin.	Saiyids.	15 Faddāns of cultivation.
Nahr Shitawi نهر شتوي	Right bank, 1 mile below Āl Bū Ghuwāzi.	...	9 Faddāns of cultivation.
Gharaibeh غريبه	Right bank, at the point where the Jarrāhi changes its direction from west to south-west. The bulk of the habitations are between canals (2) and (3) below.	As below.	Gharaibeh is a river port and Ballams are always procurable. Merchandise coming by mule caravan from Northern 'Arabistān is shipped here in Ballams for Buziyeh.
Consists of :— (1) Nahr-al-Husaini نهر الحسيني	Right bank, just below Nahr Shitawi.	Ka'ab of the 'Awāmir section, with 50 fighting men of whom 20 are mounted and 20 have rifles. The houses are reed and mat huts.	There are 50 Faddāns of cultivation, 50 cattle and 100 sheep and goats.
(2) Nahr Mahmūd نهر محمود	Right bank, just below Nahr-al-Husaini.	Ka'ab of the Āl Bū Banaidar section, inhabiting reed and mat huts. They have 50 fighting men of whom 40 are mounted and 40 have rifles.	The cultivated area is 50 Faddāns. There are 80 cattle and 200 sheep and goats.
(3) Gharaibeh (proper) غريبه	Right bank, just below Nahr Mahmūd.	Arabs of various tribes. They have 50 fighting men, 20 with rifles and 30 mounted. The houses are reed and mat huts.	50 Faddāns are cultivated. Livestock are 50 cattle and 100 sheep and goats.
'Aquleh عقله	Right bank, ½ a mile below Gharaibeh.	Ka'ab of the Rubaihāt section. Fighting strength is 40 men, of whom 30 are mounted and all are armed.	Do.
Shākhat-as-Saiyid Fākhar شاخة السيّد فاخر (also called Qāhan قاهن and Shārūkhīyeh شاروخيه	Left bank, below 'Aquleh.	Saiyids.	This canal waters 20 Faddāns of cultivation and besides supplies the canals of the Shatūt tract with water.

Name of canal.	Position on the Jarrāhı.	Particulars of the dependent population.	Particulars of cultivation, livestock, etc., and remarks.
Bin-Nāsir بن ناصر	Right bank, below Shākhat-as-Saiyid Fākhar and within 1½ miles of Gharaibeh.	Ka'ab of the Khanāfireh division.	80 Faddāns are irrigated.
Baiyūdhi بيوضي	Right bank, below Bin-Nāsir and within 1½ miles of Gharaibeh.	Do.	Do.
Bin-'Arbīd بن عربيد	Right bank, below Baiyūdhi and within 1½ miles of Gharaibeh.	Do.	Irrigation of 60 Faddāns.
Fārsi فارسي	Right bank.	Do.	15 Faddāns are irrigated.
Maksar مكسر	Do.	Ka'ab of the Āl Bū Na'īm section.	Do.
Safarat 'Abdun Nabi صفرة عبدالنبي	Do.	Do.	Irrigated area is 52 Faddāns.
'Ameh عمه	Left bank.	Saiyids.	15 Faddāns of cultivation.
Subaikhīyeh صبيخيه	Do.	Do.	5 Faddāns are irrigated.
Safreh صفرة	Do.	Ka'ab of the Khanāfireh division.	This canal waters 30 Faddāns.
Āl Bū Sūf آل بو صوف	Right bank.	Ka'ab of the Al Bū Sūf section.	The irrigated area is Faddāns.
Mughaidhi مغيضي	Do.	Ka'ab of the Khanāfireh division.	Do.
Khaz'ali خزعلي	Do.	Bani Turuf, settled here by the present Shaikh of Muhammareh who also constructed this canal.	Rice is grown as well as wheat and barley, which last are the only crops on the canals above this one; the annual rice crop is estimated at 1,000 Hāshim Mans. The Khaz'ali canal is 10 yards wide at the

FALLĀHĪYEH DISTRICT

Name of canal.	sition on the **Jarrāhi**.	Particulars of the dependent population.	Particulars of cultivation, livestock, etc., and remarks.
			entrance and flows at first north or north-west; its surplus waters are said to reach the **Kārūn** river near 'Ali-ibn-al-Husain. This and the canals below it are said, unlike those above, to flow in summer as well as winter.
Ja'fari جعفري	Right bank.	Ka'ab of the 'Amāreh section.	Rice is grown, the annual output being estimated at 5,000 Hāshim Mans, and there are 3,000 date palms.
Muhammadi محمدي	Do.	Ka'ab of the Muqaddam division.	There are 2,000 date trees. The annual crops are estimated at 1,000 Hāshim Mans of wheat and 2,000 of rice.
Umm-as-Sakhar ام الصخر	Do.	Ka'ab of the Hazbeh division who are said to possess 550 rifles.	There is extensive rice cultivation yielding perhaps 14,000 Hāshim Mans of rice per annum. Date palms number 5,000. Livestock are 15,000 buffaloes and 1,500 cattle.
Nāsirīyeh ناصریه	Do.	Ka'ab of the Hazbeh division.	The cultivated area is 15 Faddāns yielding about 500 Hāshim Mans of wheat and barley in the year.
Jafāl جفال	Do.	Ka'ab of the Dawāriqeh (Āl Bū Nāsir) section.	There are 5,000 date palms and the yearly rice crop is estimated at 4,000 Hāshim Mans.
Subāhīyeh صباحیه	Do.	Ka'ab of the Muqaddam division.	The annual crops are 500 Hāshim Mans of rice and the same of wheat and barley.
Shitālīyeh شتالیه	Do.	Do.	3 Faddāns of cultivation yielding 500 Hāshim Mans of wheat and barley annually.

FALLAHIYEH DISTRICT

Name of canal.	Position on the Jarrāhi.	Particulars of the dependent population.	Particulars of cultivation, livestock, etc., and remarks.
Shākhat Ghānim شاخة غانم	Left bank.	Ka'ab of the Āl Bū Ghubaish subdivision.	This canal irrigates 25 Faddāns of wheat and barley cultivation.
Munāfīyeh مناڧیه	Right bank.	Ka'ab of the Al Bū Na'īm section.	7 Faddāns of cultivation producing about 700 Hāshim Mans of wheat and barley per annum.
Janjīreh	Left bank.	See article Janjīreh.	See article Janjīreh.
Khalfīyeh خلڧیه	Right bank.	Ka'ab of the Āl Bū Na'īm section.	There are 6 Faddāns of wheat and barley cultivation producing 300 Hāshim Mans of grain annually.
Kuwait Hāshim كويت هاشم	Do.	Ka'ab of the Khanāfireh division.	This canal waters 20 Faddāns of land yielding 2,000 Hāshim Mans of grain each year. There are also dates.
Bida' بدع	Do.	Do.	Here are 10 Faddāns of cultivation producing about 500 Hāshim Mans of wheat and barley a year.
Sūdānīyeh سودانیه	Do.	Do.	The irrigated area is 8 Faddāns and the estimated annual yield of wheat and barley is 400 Hāshim Mans.
Mubaqqi مبقي	Left bank.	Ka'ab of the Āl Bū Tāheh section.	There are 10 Faddāns of wheat and barley and 10 of rice cultivation; the annual output of each is about 500 Hāshim Mans. Linseed and dates are also grown.
'Alwān علوان (also called Haidari حيدري)	Do.	Ka'ab of the Al Bū Banaidar section.	20 Faddāns of irrigated cultivation.

FALLĀHĪYEH DISTRICT

Name of canal.	Position on the Jarrāhi.	Particulars of the dependent population.	Particulars of cultivation, livestock, etc., and remarks.
Mizar'anwi (spelling uncertain)	Right bank.	Saiyids.	20 Faddans of irrigated cultivation producing about 1,000 Hāshim Mans of wheat and barley in a harvest.
Shabaisheh شبيشه	Left bank.	Bāwīyeh of the Simairāt section.	There are 20 Faddāns of cultivation.
Badarīyeh بدريه	Right bank opposite Shabaisheh.	Ka'ab.	The annual yield of cereals is estimated at 500 Hāshim Mans of rice and the same of wheat and barley.
Shākhat Hamad شاخة حمد	Right bank.	Ka'ab of the low-class Musallim section.	The cultivation here produces about 700 Hāshim Mans of wheat and barley and 1,000 of rice in the year.
Jadīdeh جديده	Do.	Ka'ab.	There are 5,000 date palms and the annual output of cereals is estimated at 500 Hāshim Mans of wheat and barley and 1,250 of rice.
Shākhat Shāhbāz شاخة شاه باز	Do.	Do.	Date trees number 2,000 and the yearly production of cereals is placed at 500 Hāshim Mans of rice and the same of wheat and barley.
Shikālīyeh شكاليه	Do.	Do.	There are no date palms. About 700 Hāshim Mans of wheat and barley and the same of rice are produced annually.
Topchīyeh توپچيه	Right bank, at the point on the Jarrāhi River called Khazīneh.	Ka'ab of the 'Abraiheh, Āl Bū' Ashaireh, Dawāriqeh, Manī'āt, Muhammad-ibn-Hāji Ya'qūb, and Āl Bū 'Ubaid section.	About 500 Hāshim Mans of wheat and barley and 2,500 of rice are raised annually. There are 6,000 date palms, 300 buffaloes and 200 other cattle.

Name of canal.	Position on the Jarrāhi.	Particulars of the dependent population.	Particulars of cultivation, livestock, etc., and remarks.
Minduwān مندوان	Right bank, immediately below Tōpchīyeh.	Ka'ab of the Dawāriqeh and Rubaihāt sections.	About 1,500 Hāshim Mans of rice are produced annually and there are 5,000 date palms and 300 buffaloes.
Shāuli شاؤلي	Right bank, just below Minduwān.	Ka'ab of the Dawāriqeh, Rubaihāt and Yūsuf-bin-Aqaiyi b sections.	There are 6,000 date trees and the annual yield of cereals is computed at 500 Hāshim Mans of wheat and barley and 1,000 of dates.
Ghaiyādhi غياضي	Right bank immediately below Shāuli.	Ka'ab of the Āl Bū Jinām, Āl Bū Khadhīr, Āl Bū Kiraimi, Mutārīd, Sawālim, Shāwardīyeh, Āl Bū Sūf and Āl Bū Zambūr sections.	The lands irrigated produce about 1,000 Hāshim Mans of rice in each year.
Khalfi خلفي	Left bank, at the point on the Jarrāhi River called Khazīneh, and apparently a little below the Ghaiyādhi on the opposite side.	Ka'ab of the Dawāriqeh section.	The irrigated area is 15 Faddāns and rice, linseed and dates are grown. This canal passes a little to the east of Buziyeh, below which it falls into Khor Dōraq. The head which it has in common with the 5 following canals is about 15 yards broad.
Buziyeh بزيه	Its head is the same as that of the last, but its lower course is further to the westward.	Ka'ab of the Āl Bū Ghubaish and Nassār subdivisions, the latter of the Dawāriqeh section.	There are 10,000 date palms and the lands irrigated yield about 1,000 Hāshim Mans of wheat and barley and 2,000 of rice per harvest. This canal passes less than half a mile to the west of Buziyeh and further down falls into Khor Dōraq.
Aushār اوشار	Do.	Ka'ab of the 'Asākireh subdivision. Those on the branch called Khor are of the Āl Bū 'Abbādi section; others are the Fait 'Abdush Shaikh, Bait Afsai-	On the main body of this canal there are 10,000 date palms, and the annual yield of cereals is about 500 Hāshim Mans of wheat and barley and 1,500 of rice.

FALLĀHĪYEH DISTRICT

Name of canal.	Position on the Jarrshi.	Particulars of the dependent population.	Particulars of cultivation, livestock, etc., and remarks.
		yil, Āl Bū Araiyin, Bait 'Azīz, Āl Bū Hamad, Āl Bū Jinām, Āl Bū Kuwaisih, Āl Bū Mutādir, Āl Bū Musallam, Āl Bū Na'īm, Āl Bū Sharhān, Āl Bū Shilāqeh and Āl Bū Subaiyah.	Some distance below **Buziyeh**, on the west side of which it passes at half a mile distance, the Aushār forms two branches known as Khor خور and Nahr Mūsa نهرموسى; the former has 8,000 date palms, and the latter irrigates land producing 1,000 Hāshim Mans of rice a year.
'Anaiyiti عنيتي	Its head is the same as that of last, but its lower course is further to the westward.	Ka'ab of the Āl Bū Hāji 'Ali, Hassān, Makāsibeh and Sawailāt sections.	There are 3,000 date trees and about 2,000 Hāshim Mans of rice are produced in each harvest. This canal passes about 1½ miles west of **Buziyeh**.
Musaiyir مسير	Do.	Ka'ab of the Āl Bū 'Ali and Makāsibeh sections.	Date palms number 5,000 and the annual yield of rice is about 2,000 Hāshim Mans.
Sa'adi سعدي	Do.	Ka'ab of the Dawāriqeh and Mutārid sections.	About 1,500 Hāshim Mans of rice are produced annually and there are 6,000 date palms.
Maghaiti مغيطي	Right bank, below Khazīneh.	...	...
Qaidāri قيداري	Do.	...	...
Nāsiri ناصري	Do.	...	...
'Abūdi عبودي	Left bank, about 1 mile above **Fallāhīyeh Town**.	...	...
Kharūsi خروسي	Left bank.	Ka'ab of the Āl Bū Hamdi, Kawāmil and Shawārdīyeh sections.	...

Canals which it is desired to close are quickly and effectually dammed at their heads with a mixture of earth and brushwood.

2 M

The chief places or tracts in the district besides those given in the table above are the following :—

Name.	Position.	Character.	Remarks.
'Abdul Hasan (Imāmzādeh) امام زادۀ عبد الحسن	20 miles west by north of Ma'shūr and several miles inland from the north bank of Khor Dōraq: it is situated on the eastern margin of the Shatūt tract.	A neglected shrine supplying a land-mark.	The direct route between Buziyeh and Ma'shūr passes by this place. A practicable track, 10 miles in length, connects the Imamzādeh with a point on Khor Dōraq.
'Aquleh عقله	8 miles west and slightly north of Ma'shūr on the border of the Fallāhīyeh district with the Ma'shūr tract.	A spot, with one or two holes containing bitter water, in the midst of an absolutely featureless plain.	The direct route from Buziyeh to Ma'shūr passes through 'Aquleh.
Buziyeh بزیه	On both sides of Khor Dōraq at its head, 28 miles west by north of Ma'shūr.	...	See article Buziyeh.
Fallāhīyeh Town فلاحیه	On both banks of the Fallāhīyeh-Mārid canal, 3 miles west of Buziyeh.	...	See article Fallāhīyeh Town.
Janjīreh جنجیره	On the left bank of the Jarrāhi River, 8 miles north-east of Fallāhīyeh Town.	...	See article Janjīreh.
Qubbān قبان	At the head of the Qanāqeh branch of Khor Mūsa, 15 miles south-east of the Mārid creek on the Kārūn.	...	See article Qubbān.
Ramleh رمله	4 miles south-east of Imāmzādeh 'Abdul Hasan.	A place marked by sand hills.	A variant of the direct route between Buziyeh and Ma'shūr runs by Ramleh instead of by Imāmzādeh 'Abdul Hasan.
Shatūt شطوط	Between the Jarrāhi River, Imāmzādeh 'Abdul Hasan, Khor Dōraq and Buziyeh.	...	See article Shatūt.

Agriculture, livestock and trade.—Dates are the principal crop of the district, and from Umm-as-Sakhar southwards and westwards there are large plantations upon all the more important canals. Rice, wheat and barley as well as dates are cultivated on a considerable scale, not only on the canals but also beside sheets of standing water which occur here and there. The gardens in the villages contain garlic and beans.

Sheep and goats are plentiful, and numerous herds of cattle are to be seen, besides buffaloes in the marshy tracts : some of the last are brought into the district, at particular seasons only, by migratory Ma'adān. Horses and donkeys are also owned, but in smaller numbers.

The chief exports of the Fallāhīyeh district are dates, rice, wheat, barley, wool, ghi, hides, palm leaves, matting for roofs, date wood for fuel, melons, garlic and other vegetables : to these may be added the skins and feathers of the Baiyūdhi (probably an egret) and of other birds which are found in the marshes. The dates are chiefly disposed of to sailing vessels from the Gulf, but some go to **Rāmuz ; Kuwait** is the destination of most of the rice ; the greater part of the wheat and barley is purchased and fetched away by visitors from **Kuwait, Būshehr, Bahrain** and **Masqat ;** the remaining articles go to **Muhammareh.** Imports are piece-goods, through **Muhammareh,** and spices, coffee, tea, sugar and metals from **Kuwait.** Buziyeh is the only port situated in the district and the greater part of the foreign trade is carried on there : but some, as we have seen, passes through **Muhammareh** Town. Light 'Abas for summer wear are the sole manufacture of Fallāhīyeh district. The Fallāhīyeh or Dōraq Man is equal to about 248 lbs. avoirdupois English, and it is considered to be equivalent to 16 Shushtar Mans ; it is divided into 12 Waqīyahs of 20 lbs. each. Half a Fallāhīyeh Man is called a Qusārah and 10 Fallāhīyeh Mans make a Kārat-ad-Dōraq. There are two units of lineal measure, a Dhara' or Zar', which is equal to 9/10 of an English yard, and the ordinary Gaz-i-Shāh.

Land communications, transport and supplies.—The principal land routes in the district are dealt with in the general article on **'Arabistān.** The drier tracts can be traversed in any direction without impediment except such as may arise from scarcity of water, forage, and fuel. In the moister regions progress is more difficult ; but even there, in places, there are winding paths practicable for laden animals. Of this last kind are some tracks which lead westward from **Buziyeh** and **Fallāhīyeh** Town, between the marshes, to the left bank of the **Kārūn.**

No statistics of animal transport are available, and there is no more exact information concerning supplies than that contained in the paragraph above upon agriculture. Canals being numerous, water is not ordinarily a difficulty in the inhabited parts of the district.

It has been pointed out that the first step in a military occupation of Fallāhīyeh would probably be to seize a position near **Janjīreh** commanding the irrigation of the district; this would prevent the inhabitants from resorting to their traditional tactics of flooding the country to embarrass an enemy, and by manipulation of the water supply combined with a blockade they could probably be brought to submission.

Water communications and transport.—The oversea communications of the district depend on the port of **Buziyeh** and the Khor **Mūsa** inlet, and information regarding them will be found in the articles under those names.

The main artery of internal communication by water is the **Jarrāhi** River, which boats of considerable size can navigate to the uppermost limit of the Fallāhīyeh district, and even beyond it. The **Jarrāhi** is not connected by a navigable channel with Khor **Mūsa** or any of its branches; but it is prolonged to the **Kārūn**, which it enters at the Mārid creek, by the Fallāhīyeh-Mārid canal, locally called Shākheh شاخة. This canal passes through the middle of **Fallāhīyeh** Town, 4 miles below which it emerges from the date groves and enters the open grassy desert; its direction is at first somewhat south-westerly, but the southing disappears as the **Kārūn** is approached. For a number of miles after the date groves of **Fallāhīyeh** Town are left behind, the canal is only a ditch 6 to 8 feet wide with a depth of 1½ to 2 feet, and its small capacity in this part makes it impracticable for boats of over 5 tons; but it could probably be improved without much difficulty, and even in its present neglected condition it is the principal means of communication between the towns of **Fallāhīyeh** and **Muhammareh**. At 10 miles from the **Kārūn** the Shākheh begins to feel the influence of the sea tides, and its channel becomes wider and deeper. The whole length of the canal from Khazīneh, where the **Jarrāhi** River ends, to Mārid has been computed by a traveller at 37 miles; but this appears to be an overestimate, easily explicable by the slowness of the journey.* Mosquitoes are said to render the passage of the canal almost impossible at certain times of the year.

---

* Descriptions of this canal by Major E. B. Burton will be found in the Government of India's Proceedings in the Foreign Department for June and July 1904.

Very few boats are owned by the riverside villages on the **Jarrāhi**, yet there is said to be no lack of small craft when occasion demands; none of them however can carry more than 60 Fallāhīyeh Mans or about 7 tons English. About 300 Ballams are said to have their headquarters at **Fallāhīyeh** Town and to ply chiefly on the section of the river between that place and Gharaibeh which, being situated on a route to **Shūshtar**, is a sort of river port. Between Gharaibeh and **Fallāhīyeh** Town goods are carried entirely by water. The local boats work upon the upper reaches of the river as well, and also in the opposite direction from **Fallāhīyeh** Town to **Muhammareh**; and large numbers of small craft from **Muhammareh** visit **Fallāhīyeh** Town and even ascend the **Jarrāhi** for some distance, principally in the date season.

There is a uniform rate of freight for all places on the **Jarrāhi** irrespective of distance: it varies from 1 to 2 Qrāns per Fallāhīyeh Man. Goods are forwarded from **Shūshtar** to **Fallāhīyeh** Town by land and water at a through rate of 15 to 20 Tūmāns per 100 **Shūshtar** Mans.

Administration.—The district, which now forms part of the territories of the Shaikh of **Muhammareh**, its revenues being held by him in farm, is administered by two Shaikhs of the **Ka'ab** tribe who are answerable to him and are jointly responsible with him to the Persian Government. The Shaikh of **Muhammareh** is represented personally by an agent at **Fallāhīyeh** Town. Criminal cases in the district are tried by the ecclesiastical authorities, and their sentences are carried out under the orders of the senior of the two local chiefs.

The principal taxes are those on agriculture. The date crop pays 33 Qrāns per Kāreh; and of rice half the produce in kind is invariably demanded. Lands cultivated with wheat or barley are subject to a fixed cash assessment of 12 Qrāns per Faddān and a share of the crop is also taken: on the **Jarrāhi** below the Safreh canal this share is $\frac{1}{3}$, and above that canal $\frac{1}{4}$, of the total yield. There is also a shop tax at the rate of 3 Qrāns a month on every shop. The revenue derived from these sources is assigned to the Shaikh of **Muhammareh** in compensation for the loss of the **Muhammareh** customs which he formerly held. The annual value of the collections has been estimated at 4,500 Tūmāns, and one report places it at 6,000 Tūmāns.

The only institutions in Fallāhīyeh belonging to the central Persian Government are a customs house and post office at **Buziyeh** and a post office at **Fallāhīyeh**.

FALLĀ-HĪYEH
فلاحیه
TOWN

The chief town of the district of the same name in Southern 'Arabistān and the capital of the **Ka'ab** tribe.

It stands almost buried from view by date groves, on both banks of the **Fallāhīyeh**-Mārid canal about 3 miles below Khazīneh, the place where the **Jarrāhī** River ends and the canal begins: by the time it has reached the lower end of Fallāhīyeh town the canal has parted with most of its water, and a few miles further on the date groves cease. The part of the town on the left bank is surrounded on three sides by a dilapidated stone wall which encloses, as well as houses, a large area of marsh: in the circumstances it is not surprising that Fallāhīyeh should be reckoned the most unhealthy town of **'Arabistān**. Among the diseases prevalent are ulcers, caries bone, rheumatism and ophthalmia. About 250 mud houses and 130 shops compose the bulk of the town: there is only one important mosque. In one place, on the left bank of the canal, there are several brick houses of considerable size, the largest of which, now empty, formerly belonged to Ja'far, a Shaikh of the **Ka'ab**. The people are mostly **Ka'ab** of the Khanāfireh division, and a reference to the article under that name will show some of the sections to which they belong; in number they may be about 2,000 souls. Movement is chiefly by water, and the town possesses many Ballams: Mahailahs also come up from **Muhammareh** by the Fallāhīyeh canal, and there is a good waterway conducting from Fallāhīyeh to **Buziyeh** viâ Khazīneh and the Buziyeh canal. The town lands produce abundant dates and rice; but trade is slack, and the bazaar is generally closed at noon from lack of business. During the last 8 or 9 years the power of the Shaikh of **Muhammareh** has become absolute at Fallāhīyeh, which he now administers through a member of the ruling family of the **Ka'ab**. In the matter of customs Fallāhīyeh town is within the jurisdiction of the post at **Buziyeh**, but there is a separate post office.

FALLŪJAH
فلّوجه

A village in Turkish 'Irāq, on the left bank of the **Euphrates**, nearly 70 miles by water above the town of **Musaiyib**; it is surrounded by cultivation, but there are not many dates. The Abu Ghuraib canal still takes off from the **Euphrates** about 4 miles below Fallūjah, and the Saqlāwīyah used to take off about 8 miles above it: both are noticed in the article on the river. At Fallūjah the **Euphrates** is spanned by a boat bridge, 227 yards long, carrying a roadway 10 feet in width; the bridge is divided into 2 parts by an island and consists altogether of 25 boats, each of which is 30 feet long, 11 feet broad and 5 feet deep: this bridge is at present in poor repair and has practically no handrail. The inhabitants number about 600 souls: their houses are built of sun-dried bricks. An isolated house, the property of Kāzim Pāsha, brother-in-law of the present Sultan of Turkey and political détenu at **Baghdād,** stands on the right bank of the **Euphrates** opposite to Fallūjah, near the further end of the bridge. In Fallūjah village proper are a mosque, two or three Khāns, and a bazaar of about 30 shops. There is also a Sarāi or Government building, for Fallūjah is the headquarters of a Nāhiyah similarly named in the Qadha of Dilaim and is consequently the seat of a Mudīr. The place is on the **Baghdād**-Aleppo telegraph line, being the station intermediate between the offices at **Kādhimain** Town and Rumādīyah: the connection is double in either direction.

FANTĀS
فنطاس

A coast village in the **'Adān** district of the **Kuwait** Principality, 16 miles south-south-east of **Kuwait** Town. It contains about 100 houses; the inhabitants belong to the mixed Arab tribes which are found in **Kuwait** Town. There are about 30 wells; some are brackish, but others contain good water at a depth of 20 feet. The wells have openings 20 feet square, and three gangs of donkeys can work at one simultaneously. Cultivation consists of barley, lucerne, melons, radishes and onions, and is richer than at **Jahrah**, though the area cultivated is smaller. The village has 300 date palms and many Sidar or ber trees. As mentioned in the article on **'Adān**, it is to some extent a country resort for townsmen of **Kuwait**.

FĀO*
فاو

This name, which as used by Europeans refers only to the well-known telegraph station near the mouth of the Shatt-al-**'Arab**, denotes properly the whole of a cultivated tract or estate extending along the right bank

---

Authority.- Most of the information contained in this article is derived from an elaborate report by Mr. W. D. Cumming of the Indo-European Telegraph Department. **Fāo.**

of the river from the sea upwards to a distance of 8 miles; the telegraph station is situated above the middle of this tract at about 5 miles from the sea. By the Turks the name Fāo is also applied to a whole Qadha in the Basrah Wilāyat of which the administrative headquarters are at Fāo.

Boundaries of the Fāo tract.—The Fāo tract is enclosed on its north-eastern side by the waters of the Shatt-al-'**Arab** and is bordered upon the south-west by the open desert; its breadth between the two varies from ¼ of a mile to ¾ of a mile and is generally greater in its lower than in its upper reaches. At its upper end Fāo is divided from Ma'āmir, the next tract above it, by a creek known as Hadd or Mūsa, and its length thence to the sea is, as already stated, about 8 miles.

Character, topography and population of the Fāo tract.—The tract consists of a narrow strp of clayey soil adjoining the bank of the Shatt-al-'**Arab**. Everywhere it is cut across at right angles by irrigation creeks from the river; these creeks form a continuous series from one end of the tract to the other and are on the average less than ¼ of a mile apart; on each is situated a small hamlet bearing the same name as the creek.

The following is a list of the creeks and hamlets in order from the upper to the seaward end of the tract :—

Serial No.	Name of creek and hamlet.	Number of households forming the hamlet.	Inhabitants and remarks.
1	Hadd or Mūsa حد - موسى	1	Persians from the **Hindiyān** District.
2	Muhammad Muhibb 'Ali محمد محب علي	5	Do. do.
3	Shinnu شنو	3	Bahrakūn Arabs from the **Hindiyān** District.
4	Khanāzi خنازي	5	Do. do.
5	Harabu حربو	2	Persians from the **Hindiyān** District.

A Creek at Fāo.
(Mr. W. D. Cumming.)

Serial No.	Name of creek and hamlet.	Number of households forming the hamlet.	Inhabitants and remarks.
6	Sināfi صنافي	1	Ka'ab Arabs of the Nassār division from Qasbeh on 'Abbādān island.
7	Sirsakūh سرسكوه	3	Persians from Dīlam.
8	Munnakh منّخ	1	Arabs from Kuwait.
9	Saqar and Karaim صقر - كريم	1	Do. do.
10	Salā'īd صلاعيد	3	Bahrakūn Arabs from the Hindiyān District.
11	'Abdul Hasan عبد الحسن	2	Do. do.
12	Nāsir Julsah ناصر جلسه	2	Persians from Dīlam.
13	Dushman دشمن	3	Bahrakūn Arabs from the Hindiyān District.
14	Manqūs منقوس	1	Do. do.
15	Abdus Saiyid عبد السيّد	2	Do. do.
16	'Aid عيد	2	Arabs from Kuwait.
17	Khadhairi خذيري	3	Bahrakūn Arabs from the Hindiyān District.
18	Mahfari محفري	2	Arabs from Kuwait.
19	Shairān and Muhammad Sālih. شيران - محمّد صالح	4	Do. do.
20	'Ali Safar علي صفر	2	Bani Hājir Arabs from Kuwait.

Serial No.	Name of creek and hamlet.	Number of households forming the hamlet.	Inhabitants and remarks.
21	Muhammad Gudayān محمد گديان	4	Arabs from **Kuwait**.
22	Hāji Rashīd or Telegraph Creek حاجي رشيد	2	Persians from **Kangūn**.
23	Hāji 'Abdullah or Quarantine Creek حاجي عبد الله	3	Do. do. The Fāo station is between this creek and the last.
24	Ahmad Bārūn and Shumail احمد بارون - شميل	5	Persians from **Dīlam**.
25	'Abdun Nabi عبد النبي	7	Arabs from the **Dawāsir** District on the Shatt-al 'Arab.
26	Bin-Āyāi بن آياي	12	**Ka'ab** Arabs from Qasbeh on **'Abbādān** island. This creek has a southerly branch called Yūsuf Bahraini.
27	Tanaksīr تنکسير	6	Persians from the **Tangistān** District.
28	Hāji 'Abdullah حاجي عبد الله	2	Persians from **Kangūn**.
29	Khalīfah-bin-Ibrāhīm خليفه بن ابراهيم	3	Khashnām خشنام Arabs, who are possibly **Muhaisin** of the same branch as are found at Faddāghīyah.
30	Zarzūr زرزور	9	**Ka'ab** Arabs from Persia.
31	Kathaif and Dardshād کثيف - دردشاد	23	**Ka'ab** Arabs of the Nassār division from Qasbeh on **'Abbādān** island.
32	'Ali Shīr علي شير	6	Persians from **Dīlam**.
33	Tāhir and Nāsir Safar طاهر - ناصر صفر	15	On the former Persians from **Dīlam**; on the latter **Kuwait** Arabs.
34	Muhammad Sulaimān محمد سليمان	7	Persians from the **Hindiyān** District.

Serial No.	Name of creek and hamlet.	Number of households forming the hamlet.	Inhabitants and remarks.
35	'Abdur Rahīm and 'Abdul 'Azīz عبد الرحيم - عبد العزيز	4	Persians from **Kangūn**.
36	Mābin Sanaisar and Astāwi مابن سنيسر - استاوي	6	Ka'ab Arabs from Persia.
37	Hāji Sultān and Hāji Sulaimān حاجي سلطان - حاجي سليمان	18	Do. do.
38	Sālih-bin-Nāsir and Shanāni Nahār صالح بن ناصر - شناني نهار	25	Settlers from **Bahrain**.
39	Bin Gajairi and Nahr Athār بن گجيري - نهر اثار	23	Persians from the **Hindiyān** District.
40	Ibn Ahmad ابن احمد	9	Ka'ab Arabs from Persia.
41	Habash and Bū Agap حبش - بو اكپ	20	Do. do.
42	Muhammad 'Abd-ud-Dāim and Ahmad Zaich محمّد عبد الدائم - احمد زيج	7	Arabs from the **Dawāsir** District on the Shatt-al-'Arab.
43	Bū Sa'īd بو سعيد	7	Do. do.
44	Mulla 'Īsa and Husain 'Abd-ud-Dāim ملّا عيسى - حسين عبد الدائم	5	Do. The Fāo fort is between this creek and the last.
45	Mulla Husain and 'Ajam Maghlūb ملّا حسين - عجم مغلوب	14	Persians from **Dīlam**.
46	Bait Subiyān بيت صبيان	4	Ka'ab Arabs of the Nassār division from Qasbeh on **'Abbādān** island.

Serial No.	Name of creek and hamlet.	Number of households forming the hamlet.	Inhabitants and remarks.
47	Bin 'Alawi بن علوي	16	Arabs from the **Dawāsir** District on the Shatt-al-'Arab.
48	Husain Ahshamari حسين اهشموي	18	Persians from **Kangūn**.
49	'Abdul 'Azīz عبد العزيز	4	Do. do.

A civil station, containing the Fāo telegraph office, is situated between the adjacent creeks of Hāji 'Abdullah and Hāji Rashīd and a fort between the creeks Bū Saiyid and Mulla 'Īsa: there are thus 22 creeks in Fāo above the civil station, 21 between it and the fort, and 6 below the fort.

From the above table it will be apparent that the fixed population of Fāo, exclusive of the civil station and fort which are dealt with further on, amounts to about 1,700 souls, and that it consists of very heterogeneous elements.

Agriculture of the Fāo tract.—Agriculture is almost confined to the growing of dates; the groves generally begin between 200 and 800 yards from the water's edge, but the clear space between is also being planted with palms and in places the trees already come down to the bank. The present number of palms in the whole tract is estimated at 10,000. The date palms of Fāo have a luxuriant growth, but most of them yield the inferior qualities of fruit known as Sāir which are exported in baskets to Asiatic countries; some of the better sort however are now bought up by **Basrah** dealers for export in boxes to Europe and America.

A little wheat and barley is produced for local consumption; and a small quantity of vegetables is raised by the people, both in summer and winter, for their own use. The cultivators do not keep livestock on the same scale as the inhabitants of **'Abbādān** island on the other side of the Shatt-al-'Arab, but they own some cattle and a very few sheep: for these some lucerne is cultivated, but their pasture consists chiefly of the grass that grows everywhere on the banks of the Shatt-al-'Arab.

In recent years reclamation of land from the river and the sea has been undertaken by Shaikh Mubārak of **Kuwait** who is owner of all the land at Fāo. By means of Sadds or embankments a quantity of arable land has been added below the fort both on the bank of the river and on the side towards the sea, but not in the direction of Khor 'Abdullah; and at another place the Shaikh has endeavoured to check erosion of the river bank by causing large Ballams filled with earth to be sunk close in shore. Creek No. 49 is a new one and is called after the present land-agent of the Shaikh of Kuwait. Shaikh Mubārak is also preparing to cultivate a new strip of land on the side next the desert; it extends with a breadth of 600 yards from the civil station to the Hadd creek, a distance of 5 miles; at present this plot is saline and produces nothing.

Climate.—The year at Fāo may be divided into seasons as follows:—

Winter—December, January and February.
Spring—March, April and May.
Summer—June, July, August and September.
Autumn—October and November.

This distribution of months being taken as a basis, the highest and lowest temperatures recorded (in degrees Fahrenheit) since observations began to be taken have been:—

Season.	Highest Temperature.	Lowest Temperature.
Winter of 1904-05	84	51
Spring of 1905	106	70
Summer of 1905	116	93
Autumn of 1905	105	78
Winter of 1905-06	84	47
Spring of 1906	107	68
Summer of 1906 (to end of July)	120	73

The winters of 1904-05 and 1905-06 are believed to have been colder, and the summers of 1905 and 1906 less hot, than those of ordinary years.

January and February are the wettest months ; but rain may fall at any time between the middle of November and the middle of March, and in 1905 some rain was received in May. The total cold weather rainfall in 1904-05 was 3·65 inches, and in 1905-06 it was 1·63 inches. There are occasional showers at all seasons. During July and the first half of March north-west winds ordinarily prevail, with dry heat ; and from the middle of July to the end of September the atmosphere is damp as well as hot. In September and October there are frequently fogs at night and in the early morning.

The civil station of Fāo.—The station of Fāo covers the riverward end of the spit between the Hāji Rashīd creek (No. 22 above) and the creek of Hāji 'Abdullah (No. 23 above) immediately below, and its frontage upon the river is about 600 yards.

The telegraph offices—for the sake of which, chiefly, the station exists—are situated on the southern bank of the Hāji Rashīd creek, the quarters of the Turkish signalling staff being exactly in the corner between that creek and the bank of the Shatt-al-'**Arab**. These quarters are built of wood in two storeys, each storey containing four rooms ; the staff accommodated consists of a superintendent, a mechanician and **six** clerks. A little further from the river (and also from the Hāji Rashīd creek) is the instrument room, a single-storeyed wooden building divided in half by a partition ; the end nearest to the river is occupied by the Turkish, and the other end by the British staff. At a slightly greater distance from the river (but again considerably nearer to the creek) are the quarters of the British telegraph staff, which consists of one clerk in charge and three other clerks of the Indo-European Telegraph Department, one Assistant Surgeon of the Indian Medical Service, and seven menials, among the last being four boatmen. A garden, lawn tennis court and other appurtenances adjoin the British quarters on the two landward sides, and there are 7 tanks of 400 gallons capacity each for storing water. The average number of messages transferred monthly at Fāo from the Turkish line to the Indo-European Company's cable is about 800, and of those transferred in the opposite direction about 600.

On the south side of the British compound, about equidistant from the two creeks and from the river, is the Sarāi or Turkish Government building, which is a substantial single-storeyed brick structure of five rooms ; and beyond this again, on the northern bank of the Hāji 'Abdullah creek and at about the same distance from the Shatt-al-'**Arab** as the

British telegraph quarters, is a village of huts with a population of about 150 souls consisting partly of minor Turkish officials, police, etc.

The quarantine establishment and premises, the latter consisting of two mud rooms, are located in the corner between the Hāji 'Abdullah creek and the Shatt-al-'**Arab** which corresponds to the position occupied by the Turkish telegraph quarters at the other end of the station: the Customs House is between the Sarāi and the quarantine office and has an upper storey of one room. On the river front, nearer to the quarantine than to the telegraph station, are the quarters of the Turkish harbour master: they stand on a tongue of firm ground between two marshes presently to be mentioned.

A marsh lies behind the entire station, reaching practically from creek to creek; and upon the river also there are two marshes, of which the larger lies between the telegraph station, the Sarāi and the harbour master's quarters, and the smaller between the quarantine offices and the same quarters. At the back of the inland marsh, at about 700 yards from the river, date groves begin; they extend for some hundreds of yards to the desert beyond. On the southern bank of the Hāji Rashīd creek, on the verge of the desert and about 1,000 yards from the river are the ruins of an old mud fort, now used as a graveyard and planted with date palms. On the same bank of the same creek, but nearer the river and about the middle of the date plantations, is a mosque adjoined by one or two huts.

The Fāo fort.—The Fāo fort, of which the construction was commenced in 1886, stands about four miles below the station, between the creeks of Bū Sa'īd (No. 43 above) and Mulla 'Īsa (No. 44 above), of which the former runs along its north-western and the latter along its south-eastern side; it is about 500 yards distant from the Shatt-al-'**Arab** proper, but at high tide the water of the river washes up to its walls. The plan of the fort is roughly rectangular and its main face is apparently that on the Mulla 'Īsa creek, which looks to the south-east and towards the mouth of the river; this front, which is faced with light coloured stone and rises about 15 feet above the crest of the glacis, shows from the river as a white line against a dark background of date plantations. The fort is already completely shut in by date groves upon its south-west side, and new plantations reaching to the Shatt-al-'**Arab** have been laid out upon its north-western and south-eastern sides; it appears, in fact, that in a few years the fort, except for a clear alley leading down to the nearest part of the river, will be completely surrounded by a forest of dates. The fort is still without any artillery armament. The actual garrison consists of a Yūzbāshi, about 45 rank and file of regular infantry, and a Medical Officer; there is also a Bimbāshi who is called "Bimbāshi of the Fāo Fort," but he lives at **Basrah**.

Political position.—Fāo, as the key of the Shatt-al-'**Arab** and as the point where the cable of the Indo-European Telegraph Department meets the Turkish land line, is a place of international importance; it is at the same time the only Turkish station of any size below **Basrah**. The Shaikh of **Kuwait** has valuable interests at Fāo inasmuch as the whole of the tract, after remaining for some years in litigation in the Turkish courts between him and some of his nephews who are Turkish subjects, passed in 1904 to the Shaikh in virtue of an amicable agreement by which the family estates on the banks of the Shatt-al-'**Arab** were partitioned among the various claimants. The agent of the Shaikh of **Kuwait** at Fāo is one 'Abdul 'Azīz of **Kangūn** in Persia, a circumstance which may account for the nationality of a number of the cultivators employed.

Turkish administrative arrangements.—Fāo is the headquarters of a Turkish Qadha, and the Qāim-Maqām who governs it has his residence and office at the Sarāi in the civil station; this official is at present a civilian, but military officers have at times held the appointment. The duties of the Qāim-Maqām are political rather than executive. His staff consists of a Māl Mudīr or general secretary, a Sandūq Amīn or treasurer, and a clerk. The civil police under his orders are two non-commissioned officers and 15 men of the Dhābitīyahs.

The strength and location of the Turkish telegraph staff and military garrison at Fāo have already been described above. The place is the headquarters of the 2nd battalion of the 85th Radīf regiment.

The Turkish Customs establishment consists of a **Mudīr** or superintendent and one clerk, besides menials; and the quarantine establishment of 1 officer and 2 guards.

The present harbour master is a Lieutenant in the Turkish Navy; his duties are to register all local craft belonging to Turkish subjects and to levy port dues on exports and imports leaving or arriving by water.

The Fāo Qadha consists of the districts on the right bank of the Shatt-al-'**Arab** from Fāo up to Mutāwa' inclusive, with the dependent islands, and its population is thus about 15,000 souls.

Communications.—At high water landing is easy everywhere in the neighbourhood of Fāo; but, when the tide is low, banks of mud that extend from 50 to 100 yards into the river are uncovered between the station and the mouth of the Shatt-al-'**Arab**, and the shore here becomes inconvenient (though not impossible) of approach. At the station the breadth of the mud flats is only about 20 yards and it gradually decreases to 10 yards at the head of the Fāo tract. The difference between ordinary high and low tide is, at the station, about 10 feet. With a south-west wind blowing, the tide sometimes rises 20 feet and submerges the station along with the surrounding country.

The course of the paths in the Fāo tract is determined by the creeks, the arrangement of which and of the villages upon them is extremely regular and symmetrical. A path follows the bank of each creek from the edge of the Shatt-al-'**Arab** up to the beginning of the desert; and there is also a pathway leading from the river to the desert up the centre of every spit between two adjacent creeks. Longitudinal communication is supplied by 3 roads or paths, all of which are roughly parallel to the river: of these, the one nearest to the river runs between the date plantations and the stream and is interrupted by every creek which it encounters; the second, which is the most shady and frequented, connects the village on each creek with the villages upon the creeks adjoining it on either side and its course is consequently not very straight, but upon this route every creek is bridged by a single date log thrown across it; the third route lies along the edge of the desert behind the date plantations and is not interrupted by the creeks. Of these longitudinal routes the second and third are said to be prolonged the whole way to **Basrah Town**.

FARA' (WĀDI) وادي فرع

Also called Wādi Rustāq رستاق: an important valley in the Sultanate of **Omān** which has its head on the north side of the Najd al-Fara' in the Western **Hajar** hills, some fifteen miles to the north of Hamrat-al-'Abriyīn in '**Omān** Proper and a few miles east of Jabal Shām شام, the highest peak of Jabal **Akhdhar**: from the Najd Wādi Fara' runs in a general north-north-east direction, finally reaching the sea on the west side of **Masna'ah** on the **Bātinah** coast, at a point about 45 miles distant in a straight line from its origin. The valley contains an intermittent stream which appears above ground at **Rustāq**, Ghashab, Wushail and **Jammah**.

The villages of Wādi Fara' in descending order are as follows:—

Village.	Position.	On which bank.	Houses and inhabitants.	Remarks.
Fara' فرع	Half an hour below the Najd.	Right.	70 houses of Bani 'Auf.	The people grow wheat, barley and millet and are carriers. They have 6 camels, 30 donkeys, 70 cattle and 700 sheep and goats. There are 2,000 date palms.
Hail حيل	Two hours below Fara'.	Left.	100 houses of Mishāqisah.	The people are carriers, grow wheat, barley and millet, and possess 10 horses, 10 donkeys and 20 cattle. Date palms number about 1,000.
Nāzīyah نازيه	Adjoins Hail.	Do.	30 houses of Bani 'Auf.	Cultivation and occupations as at Hail. Livestock are 10 cattle and 50 sheep and goats. 1,000 date trees.
'Alāyat-al-Mazārī' المزاريع علاية	Opposite Nāzīyah.	Right.	300 houses of Mazārī'.	There is a fort called Burj-al-Mazārī', held by 30 men of the Mazārī' tribe, immediately above the village: it has a date plantation and spring of fresh water. There are 40 donkeys, 100 cattle and 200 sheep and goats. Date palms, 20,000.
Sawālih صوالم	Adjoins 'Alāyat-al-Mazārī'.	Do.	40 houses of Bani 'Adi.	Cultivators of grain as at Fara' and possess 12 donkeys, 20 cattle and 40 sheep and goats. 9,000 date trees.

FARA' (WĀDI)

Village.	Position.	On which bank.	Houses and inhabitants.	REMARKS.
Hājrat-ash-Shaikh حجرة الشيخ	Adjoins the last village.	Right.	50 houses of Bani Hina.	Cultivation as at Sawālih: date palms number about 10,000: live-stock are 20 donkeys, 20 cattle and 40 sheep and goats.
Hārat-al-Jabah حارة الجبه	Do.	Do.	100 houses of Bani Hina and Āl Bū Sa'īd.	Cultivation as at Sawālih: there are 30 donkeys, 30 cattle and 80 sheep and goats: dates are estimated at 5,000 trees.
Mahādhar محاضر	Quarter of an hour below the last village.	Do.	200 houses of Dalālil, an inferior community who trade in cattle.	Here are 20 donkeys, 40 cattle, 150 sheep and goats and 2,000 date palms.
Bait-al-Qarn بيت القرن	Do.	Do.	60 houses of 'Abriyīn and Sharāinah, also a few Āl Bū Sa'īd.	The people are traders and own 8,000 date trees, 10 donkeys, 10 cattle and 50 sheep and goats.
Hawājiri حواجري	Opposite Bait-al-Qarn.	Left.	30 houses of Manādharah and Dalālīl.	The inhabitants weave and cultivate grain, and own 7 donkeys, 4 cattle and 25 sheep and goats. Dates are 2,000 trees.
Qal'at Kasra قلعة كسرى or Rustāq رستاق	Adjoins the last village.	Do.	...	See article Rustāq.
Qasra قصرى	Nearly opposite Hawājiri.	Right.	150 houses of Bani 'Adi and Bani Lamak.	The people trade and cultivate grain and have 15 donkeys, 15 cattle and 100 sheep.
Rummāniyah رمانيه	Opposite Qal'at Kasra.	Do.	50 houses of Salaimiyīn.	Cultivators, possessing 8 donkeys, 7 cattle and 50 sheep and goats. Date trees, 4,000.

FARA' (WĀDI)

Village.	Position.	On which bank.	Houses and Inhabitants.	REMARKS.
Umm Himār ام حمار	Adjoins Rummānīyah.	Right.	60 houses of Bani **Shakail** and Bani **Lamak**.	The people are carriers and cultivators and own the same livestock as those of Rummānīyah. The date palms of this village are estimated at 20,000.
'Ain-ar-Ramāh عين الرماح	A short distance below Umm Himār.	Left.	300 houses of Ramāh, a tribe not found elsewhere in 'Omān.	The inhabitants are silversmiths and cultivators; they have 40 donkeys, 20 cattle, 200 sheep and goats, and date palms are said to number 30,000.
Murbah مربه	Half an hour below 'Ain-ar-Ramāh.	Do.	150 houses of Bani **'Adi**.	Grain is cultivated. There are 20 donkeys, 15 cattle and 100 sheep and goats, and date palms are placed at 25,000.
Saqairīyah سقيريه	Opposite Murbah.	Right.	30 houses of Bani **Hina**.	Cultivation; there are 5,000 palms, 5 donkeys, 4 cattle and 20 sheep and goats.
Hallah حله	Adjoins Murbah.	Left.	100 houses of **Manādharah**.	Cultivation of wheat, millet and lucerne. Livestock are 8 donkeys, 10 cattle and 100 sheep and goats. Date trees, 6,000.
Ghashab غشب	Half an hour below Hallah.	On both banks.	500 mud houses of Bani **'Adi** of the Bani Bakar section and of Bani **'Umr**.	Same cultivation as at Hallah. Animals are 25 donkeys, 25 cattle and 250 sheep and goats. There are said to be 40,000 date palms here.

FARA' (WÂDI)

Village.	Position.	On which bank.	Houses and inhabitants	Remarks.
Tîkhah طيخه	Adjoins Ghashab.	Left.	20 houses of the Wîlâd 'Abd-as-Salâm section of the Ya'âribah.	Same crops as at Hallah above; livestock are 20 donkeys, 20 cattle and 120 sheep and goats; and dates are estimated at 30,000 trees.
Wabil ربل	Opposite Tîkhah.	Right.	150 houses of Bani 'Adi.	Same cultivation as preceding villages. Animals are the same as at Tîkhah. Date trees, 8,000.
'Ain Wabil عين ربل	Adjoins Wabil.	Do.	No houses.	There are plantation of date palms, amounting to about 8,000 trees. The animals on this estate are 30 donkeys, 30 cattle and 200 sheep and goats.
Mizâhît مزاحيط	Adjoins 'Ain Wabil.	Do.	200 houses of Manâdharah, Mishâqisah and the Bani Salmân section of the Miyâyihah.	There is a post of 15 'Askaris here, representing the authority of the Sultân of 'Omân. Livestock are 30 donkeys and 500 sheep and goats. The number of date palms is stated at 12,000.
Falaj Shirâh فلج شراه	Half an hour below Mizâhît.	Do.	100 houses of Siyâbiyîn and 'Abâbid.	The lowest village within the hills of Hajar. Here are 10 donkeys, 70 sheeps and goats and 8,000 date palms.
Wushail وشيل	Opposite Falaj Shirâh.	Left.	700 houses of Mishâqisah and Mazârî'.	There are only a very few cattle here, but dates are placed at 60,000 trees.

Village.	Position.	On which bank.	Houses and inhabitants.	REMARKS.
Falaj-al-'Ālī فلج العالي or Falaj Banī 'Umr فلج بني عمر	One hour below Falaj Shirāh.	Right.	150 houses of Banī 'Umr.	No animals. Date palms are said to number 18,000.
Falaj-al-Wusta فلج الوسطا or Falaj-al-Hawā-shim فلج لهواشم	Quarter of an hour below Falaj-al-'Ālī.	Do.	150 houses of Hawāshim.	No animals and the number of palms is somewhat smaller than at Falaj-al-'Ālī.
Dāris دارس	Adjoins Falaj-al-Wusta.	Do.	40 houses of Yāl-Sa'ad and Hawāshim.	5 camels only, but about 12,000 date palms.
Shabaikah شعيكه	Three-quarters of an hour below Dāris.	On both banks.	50 houses of Banī Hina and Hawāshim.	No livestock: 2,000 date palms.
Hazam حزم	Half a mile below Shabaikah.	Left.	...	See article Hazam.
Misfāh مسفاه	Half an hour below Hazam.	...	100 houses of Siyābiyīn and Banī 'Auf.	...
Jammah جمه	Opposite Hazam.	Half an hour east of the right bank.	...	See article Jammah.
Buwairid بويرد	Do.	Quarter of an hour east of Jammah.	50 houses of Banī Harrās and of Balūchis, servants of the Āl Bū Sa'īd.	30 sheep and goats only. Date palms, 8,000.
Mansūr منصور	Do.	Half an hour east of Jammah.	40 houses of Banī Harrās.	The people form a garrison and are cultivators on behalf of Saiyid 'Alī-bin-Badar, of the Āl Bū Sa'īd whose private estate the village is. There is cultivation of dates, wheat and lucerne; the palms number

Village.	Position.	On which bank.	Houses and inhabitants.	REMARKS.
				about 8,000. Animals are 5 camels and 300 sheep and goats, also 1 horse.
Tarīf طريف	Three hours below **Hazam**.	Left.	...	See article **Bātinah**.
Tau-ash-Shawī طو الشوي	Opposite Tarīf.	Right.	...	Do.
Masna'ah مصنعه	One hour below Tarīf.	Do.	...	See article **Masna'ah**.

The settled population of the valley down to and including Mansūr is thus approximately 25,000 souls.

There is also a ruined village called Munāqi مناقي near Wushail, half of which belonged to the government of the 'Omān Sultanate and half to the inhabitants of Wushail; it has about 12 wells, one of which is very large and is still used for irrigation. Another village now deserted was Hājar هاجر, about a mile south of Jammah; it was held by the Bani Harrās and Siyābiyīn.

The trade of Wadi Fara' is with **Masna'ah**. The name **Rustāq** is of uncertain application; it is sometimes used to designate particularly the fortified village of Qal'at Kasra, which is the capital of the valley, but more generally it refers to the whole aggregate of villages from **Hazam** inclusive upwards. All **Rustāq**, in the latter sense, is in the possession of Saiyid Sa'īd bin-Ibrāhīm-bin-Qais-bin-'Azzān, who receives an allowance of $200 a month from the Sultān of Masqat and has given him his sister in marriage.

A place in Turkīsh 'Irāq on the right bank of the Shatt-al-'Arab 4 miles above **Basrah**; by Europeans it is called " Magil " but this name is not used by natives and its origin is uncertain.* Kūt-al-Farangi was, until about 35 years ago, the site of the British Consulate at **Basrah** and

FARANGI (KŪT-AL-) كوت الفرنگي

---

* In Colonel Chesney's Chart of 1849 the name appears as "McGill." Colonel Chesney also gives Ma'kil, i.e., معقل (stronghold), as an alternative, but locally this explanation is repudiated. The Ma'qil canal, however, which led to Old **Basrah**, must have separated from the Shatt-al-'Arab somewhere in this neighbourhood.

derives its name ("European Fort") from the fact: the Euphrates and Tigris Steam Navigation Company have docks and workshops at this place, where they have been established for many years. One of the river steamers of the E. and T. S. N. Co. was lately reconstructed here, but as a rule the Kūt-al-Farangi yard is only used for small repairs, and the heavy work of the Company is carried out at their **Baghdād** premises. There are two cemeteries, one belonging to the Company and the other to the Anglican community of **Basrah**; and a native village and some brick kilns also exist. Some of the Arab inhabitants have recently emigrated to Persia to avoid conscription by the Turks for military service. On the south side of the place is an insignificant creek which does not run very far inland: on the north side is a channel by which water from Khamīsīyah on the **Euphrates** is said to reach the Shatt-al-'**Arab**. The frontage of Kūt-al-Farangi on the Shatt-al-'**Arab** seems to have been reclaimed at no very distant time and it is now again threatened by the encroachments of the river.

FĀRS
فارس

By Arabs called Fāris فارس. A large and important division of Persia ranking as a Province or Ayālat ایالت and ruled by a Governor-General or Farmān-Farmā فرمان فرما. The following districts of the Persian Gulf are in the jurisdiction of the Governor-General of Fārs:—**Lirāvi**, **Shabānkāreh**, **Mazāra'i**, part of **Dashtistān**, **Tangistān**, **Dashti**, the greater part of **Shībkūh** and, though in name only, the maritime portion of **Bastak** about **Khamīr**. The physical geography, the administration, and the currency, weights and measures of these districts of Fārs are dealt with in the article on the **Persian Coast**.

The modern European name of the whole country (Persia) is derived from the name of this province (Fārs) through the Greek "Persis."

FĀRSI
فارسى

An islet in the middle of the Persian Gulf, about 67 miles north-east of **Musallamīyah** bay on the coast of the **Hasa** Sanjāq and an equal distance to the south-west of the Bāraki villages on the coast of the **Tangistān** district in Persia: Jazīrat '**Arabi** is about 15 miles south of it. The island is a quarter of a mile across, 10 feet above sea level and overgrown with coarse grass and brushwood; it is frequented by fishermen, chiefly from **Khārag**, who come to catch turtle, abundant here, for their oil and shell. There is no fresh water. The ownership of this island, like that of **'Arabi**, appears to be undetermined.

FARŪQ (WĀDI) وادي فروق

A valley apparently running north by west and south by east and divided from the **Hasa** Oasis, to the east of it, by an interval of about 30 miles. On the north Wādi Farūq meets **Summān** in the neighbourhood of Jabal Hamrat Jūdah; on the west it is bounded by **Summān** throughout its length of, possibly, 100 miles; on the south it ends at a hilly ridge called Jau-ad-Dukhān جو الدخان perhaps 30 or 40 miles short of **Jabrīn**. Its average breadth is perhaps 10 or 15 miles. Wādi Farūq is said to consist of a labyrinth of sandhills, but it produces firewood which is brought in by Bedouins for sale at **Hofūf**. The valley is occupied in autumn by the **'Ajmān**, and at times it is infested by raiding parties of the Āl **Morrah** and **Manāsīr**.

FARŪR [*] فرور

To British navigators at one time known as "Polior." An island in the Persian Gulf almost 20 miles south of the **Shībkūh** port of **Mughu**: in shape it is an ellipse with its greater diameter of $4\frac{1}{2}$ miles running from north to south and a lesser diameter of 3 miles. Except for a reef with a few detached rocks on the west side, the island has deep water all round it; and the coast consists of rocky cliffs 30 or 40 feet high. The tides here are strong and there is one dangerous shoal between Farūr and the mainland, apparently identical with the pearl bank known as Nīveh Jazīrat Farūr نيوه جزيرة فرور ; otherwise the island is easy of approach. Farūr is covered with dark volcanic hills which in one conical but table-topped peak attain a height of 465 feet. Most of the island is bare rock and talus, but the ravines contain numerous trees and one on the east side has wells and some date-palms. There is little bird-life but there are a few gazelle. On the east side of the island is a small village of about 40 souls of **Sūdān** and of miscellaneous Arabs from the Persian side. They own a couple of fishing boats (Shū'ais); most of their

---
[*] A distant view of part of Farūr Island is given in Chart No. 2373—2837-A, *Persian Gulf*.

provisions are imported from **Mughu**. The people of **Mughu** send their cattle to Farūr to graze and they obtain some firewood from the island. Farūr is under the Marzūqi Shaikh of **Mughu**. The Persian Government have not up to the present time shown any interest in this island.

FARŪR (NĀBIYU) نابيو فرور

In English formerly known by the extraordinary name of "Nobfleure." An uninhabited islet lying in the Persian Gulf about 10 miles south-south-west of the southern extremity of **Farūr** island. It has a reef one mile in extent on the north-west side and narrow reefs on the west and south sides, otherwise it is surrounded by deep water. Nābiyu Farūr is circular in shape with a diameter of half a mile, and towards its east side is a dark-coloured, saddle-shaped hill 120 feet in height; the greater part of its surface is sandy and covered with salsola bushes. A few larks and chats (genus Saxicola) and a colony of ospreys are the only living creatures. No attention has as yet been paid by the Persian Government to this island.

FASHT (FASHT KHOR) فشت خور فشت

A large coral reef of irregular shape, with an average diameter of about 3 miles, lying about 7 miles north-west of **Bahrain** Island. Near its eastern extremity is a remarkable Kaukab or spring of fresh water, which is 3 feet below the surface of the sea at low tide. As much as 700 gallons of excellent water have been obtained from it in a day. Pearl divers make use of the spring in the pearling season: during the rest of the year it is seldom visited by sailing boats.

FAWĀRS فوارس

Or Āl Fāris آل فارس ; singular Fārisi فارسي. A general term used in the Persian Gulf to describe Arabs of the Persian littoral from **Kangūn** to Bandar 'Abbās who do not belong to any well known Arab tribe; such, for instance, are the Abu Dastūr who are found on **Sirri** island.

The name is in use in the Sultanate of **'Omān** also, but there it is applied to Arabicised Persian immigrants and their descendants; in the dominions of the Sultān the Fawāris are Sunnis and number about 5,000 souls, being found at Sawaiharah, **Sohār** Town and Sallān in the **Sohār** sub-Wilāyat of **Bātinah** and at Sharu and Fanjah in Wādi **Samāil**.

FUJAIRAH
جيره

A village of the **Shamailīyah** tract in Trucial 'Omān, 15 miles south of Khor **Fakkān** and 27 miles north-north-east of **Shināṣ**; it is situated near the place where Wādi **Hām** reaches the coast and is about two miles from the sea. The landing place opposite Fujairah is called Gharaifah; but its port is **Ghāllah**, a little to the southward, from which it is distant four miles by land and whence goods are brought on camels. Fujairah possesses date plantations containing some 3,000 palms, amid which stands the village adjoined by a small but strong fort upon a hill. The village is completely surrounded by a strong wall, 9 feet high, to which have been added on the south and west sides an exterior ditch and breast-work. There is plenty of fresh water in wells 4 fathoms deep. The houses, in number about 150, are mostly of mud and stone, but a few are of gypsum cement. During the date harvest, when peace reigns, the inhabitants are accustomed to camp in mat huts among their plantations outside the village walls. The people of Fujairah, who are **Sharqiyīn**, mostly of the Hafaitāt section, live by the cultivation of dates and by pearl diving; some tobacco, wheat and jowari are raised also. There are no manufactures and no shops. Fujairah is the stronghold of the Sharqi leader Hamad-bin-'Abdullah, who since 1901 has been endeavouring to assert the independence of a part of the **Shamailīyah** tract against the Shaikh of **Shārjah**. The following places in **Shamailīyah** are reported to be now in the possession of Hamad and accordingly to look to Fujairah as their capital: Bithnah, Gharaifah, Marbah, Qaraiyah, Qidfa' and Saqamqam. This tract in revolt under Hamad enjoys the countenance of the Shaikh of Abu **Dhabi**.

FUWAIR-AT
الفويرط

A village on the east side of the **Qatar** promontory about 10 miles from its northern extremity. Immediately to the north of it is a hill called Jabal-al-Fuwairat, separating it from the site of the now deserted village of Ghārīyah which is also on the coast; according to another account, however, the Jabal is merely a vertical cliff 30 feet high, against the foot of which the sea breaks. The village is surrounded by towers, but it is not continuously walled and there are no gates. The houses upon the circumference of the village are substantially built of stone and mud. The population of Fuwairat consists of about 100 houses of the Āl Bū **Kuwārah** tribe and 50 of **Kibísah**: these communities are divided from one another by a well-marked street and form a southern and a northern quarter respectively. The people live chiefly by pearl diving, but they also own some 20 horses, 100 camels, 60 donkeys and 80 cattle. About 35 pearl boats, 9 other sea-going vessels, and 12 fishing boats belong to the place. There are no shops. Indifferent water is obtained from the Zarka زرقا well, 1 mile west of the village, and good water from the wells of Filīhah, فليحه and 'Ain Sanān عين سنان distant 2 and 4 miles respectively to the south-west. The 'Ain Sanān well is protected by a fort originally built by the **Ma'adhīd**, but now occupied and kept in repair by the Āl Bū **Kuwārah**.

GĀBANDI كابندي

A valley in the **Shībkūh** district of Persia: it runs parallel to the coast at an average distance throughout its course of about 10 miles inland, finally reaching the sea in **Nāband** bay: the length of the valley is about 45 miles, and its direction is from east-south-east to west-north-west. The principal points in the Gābandi valley are the village of Chāh Mubārak, at about 13 miles from its mouth, and Gābandi village about 16 miles above Chāh Mubārak.

The villages of Gābandi are divided into four political groups known as Harami هرمي, Māliki مالكي, Nasūri نصوري and Tamīmi تميمي. The Harami villages lie on the south side of the valley for a short distance both above and below Chāh Mubārak and on the north side of the valley from Chāh Mubārak to the sea; the Māliki villages are mostly on the south side of the valley below Chāh Mubārak, but one or two of them are interspersed with Harami villages on the south side of the valley near Chāh Mubārak; the Nasūri villages form a cluster below, but also for a short distance above, Gābandi village; and the Tamīmi villages occupy the north side of the valley immediately above Chāh Mubārak. The portion of the valley above the Nasūri group contains no villages. The following tables give the topography of the groups in greater detail:—

GĀBANDI

Harami Villages.

Name.	Position.	Houses, resources, etc.
'Askar (Bū) بو عسکر	6 miles west-north-west of Chāh Mubārak, on the north side of the valley.	80 houses; 4 camels, 4 donkeys, 90 cattle, 600 sheep and goats and 1,300 date palms; 10 wells of sweet water, $3\frac{1}{2}$ to 4 fathoms deep, of which 4 are specially devoted to watering tobacco crops.
Bazbaz بربز	2 miles west of Dih Nau, on the north side of the valley.	50 houses; 30 donkeys, 70 cattle, 1,500 sheep and goats and 3,000 date palms; 2 springs and 3 wells of 2 to 3 fathoms' depth.
Dih Nau ده نو	9 miles west-north-west of Chāh Mubārak and 5 miles from the mouth of the Gābandi valley, on the north side of the valley.	70 houses; 3 camels, 50 donkeys, 45 cattle, 800 sheep and goats and 3,000 date trees; numerous wells of sweet water 2 to 3 fathoms deep.
Ghuwairizeh غویرزه	Some distance to the east of Kashkunār.	50 houses; 6 camels, 40 donkeys, 40 cattle, 500 sheep and goats and 700 date trees; 8 wells of 6 fathoms' depth.
Kashkunār کشکنار	6 miles south-east of Chāh Mubārak, on the south side of the valley.	425 houses; 60 camels, 500 donkeys, 900 cattle, 5,000 sheep and goats and 16,000 date palms; 5 water reservoirs and numerous wells of 2 to 5 fathoms' depth. A track over the hills connects Kashkunār with the port of Tibin, 10 miles distant. By Arabs Kashkunār is called Qasr Kunār.
Khiyāru خیارو	4 miles west-north-west of Chāh Mubārak, on the north side of the valley.	120 houses; 10 camels, 60 donkeys, 100 cattle, 1,600 sheep and goats and 4,000 palms; 14 wells of sweet water $3\frac{1}{2}$ to 4 fathoms deep, of which 5 are specially used for watering tobacco.
Khund خند	A mile or two east of Tang Sharzeh, at the foot of the Sharzeh hill.	260 houses, of which 30 are inhabited by Jews; 15 camels, 130 donkeys, 280 cattle, 3,000 sheep and goats and 15,000 date palms; 2 springs and 30 wells of fresh water 2 to 3 fathoms deep, of which 10 are used chiefly for tobacco cultivation.
Sarvbāsh سروباش	One and a half miles west-north-west of Kashkunār, upon a sandhill, on the south side of the valley.	110 houses; 6 camels, 40 donkeys, 90 cattle, 500 sheep and goats and 3,500 date palms; 3 reservoirs and 25 wells varying from $2\frac{1}{2}$ to $3\frac{1}{2}$ fathoms in depth, the deeper being near the reservoirs.

Name.	Position.	Houses, resources etc.
Sharzeh (Tang) تنگ شرزه	1 or 2 miles east of Dih Nau, near a hill called Sharzeh.	10 houses; 15 donkeys, 35 cattle, 500 sheep and goats, and 2,500 date palms; 3 springs, on which depends the water supply.
Tumbu تمبو	2 miles south-west of Chāh Mubārak.	70 houses; 3 camels, 25 donkeys, 40 cattle, 800 sheep and goats and 1,600 date palms; 14 wells 2 to 2½ fathoms deep.
Tumbu Gharbi تمبو غربي	1 mile west north-west of Tumbu.	40 houses; 3 camels, 25 donkeys, 150 cattle, 2,500 sheep and 2,500 date palms; 12 wells of fresh water from 1½ to 2 fathoms deep.

Māliki Villages.

Name	Position	Houses, resources etc.
Akābir اكابر	2½ miles south by west of Chāh Mubārak, on the south side of the valley.	60 houses; 5 camels, 15 donkeys, 40 cattle, 300 sheep and goats and 2,500 palms; 18 wells 2 to 2½ fathoms deep. The name is also pronounced Achābir and sometimes takes the form of Akbari.
Banūd بنود	7 miles west by north of Chāh Mubārak, on the south side of the valley.	80 houses; 10 camels, 90 donkeys, 100 cattle, 1,500 sheep and 7,000 date palms; 18 wells of 3 to 4 fathoms depth. There is a reservoir called Birkeh Akhavain on the side towards Kunehkhaimeh. The name of the village also occurs as Banūt بنوط.
Basātīn بستاتين	Near the mouth of the Gābandi valley, a mile or two west of Hālat Nāband on the coast.	100 houses; 7 camels, 40 donkeys, 60 cattle, 800 sheep and goats and 6,000 dates; 8 wells, all situated in the date gardens, of 3 to 4 fathoms' depth.
Fawāris فوارس	3 miles south by east of Chāh Mubārak on the south side of the valley.	70 houses; 5 camels, 30 donkeys, 40 cattle, 300 sheep and goats and 2,300 date trees; 15 wells of fresh water 2½ to 3 fathoms deep. The place is also called Fārsi.
Khareh خره	3½ miles west by south of Chāh Mubārak, on the south side of the valley.	160 houses; 10 camels, 100 donkeys, 130 cattle, 800 sheep and goats and 10,000 date trees; 22 wells of 2 to 3 fathoms' depth.
Kunehkhaimeh كنه خيمه	6 miles west by north of Chāh Mubārak, on the south side of the valley.	70 houses; 5 camels, 25 donkeys, 40 cattle, 400 sheep and goats and 5,000 date trees; 12 wells 3 to 4 fathoms deep.

Name.	Position.	Houses, resources, etc.
Safiyeh سعیه	On the south side of the valley towards its mouth, 2½ miles inland westwards from the foot of Nāband bay.	70 houses; 15 camels, 30 donkeys, 65 cattle, 600 sheep and goats and 5,000 date palms; 1 reservoir and 6 wells of fresh water 4 to 5 fathoms deep.
Savāhil سواحل	1 mile east-south-east of Chāh Mubārak, on the north side of the valley.	50 houses; 3 camels, 25 donkeys, 45 cattle, 550 sheep and goats and 500 date palms; 4 wells 2½ to 3 fathoms deep.
Zūbār زوبار	1 mile east-south-east of Safiyeh, on the south side of the valley.	90 houses; 15 camels, 70 donkeys, 75 cattle, 800 sheep and goats and 5,000 date trees; 1 water reservoir and 8 wells 4 to 5 fathoms deep. There is also a fort, belonging to the administration, with a well 7 fathoms deep.

Nasūri Villages.

Name.	Position.	Population, resources, etc.
Ahshām احشام	1 mile south-east of Gābandi village.	150 houses; 40 camels, 150 donkeys, 100 cattle, 3,000 sheep and 2,000 date palms; 2 water reservoirs. The place is also known as Ada.
Amūni اموني	In two parts at 4 and 6 miles north-west of Gābandi village, on the north side of the valley.	50 houses; 12 camels, 20 donkeys, 80 cattle, 1,200 sheep and goats and 700 date trees; also called 'Alumanīyeh.
Bambari بمبري	½ a mile south-west of Gābandi village.	20 houses; 4 camels, 10 donkeys, 30 cattle, 200 sheep and goats and 1,500 date trees.
Bardūl بردل	1½ miles north-west of Gābandi village, on the north side of the valley, under a hill called Marzuvabānu.	50 houses; 20 donkeys, 60 cattle, 20 sheep and goats and 3,000 date palms; 1 water mill. There are vines, and the dates grow by running water.
Dailam (Nakhl) نخل ديلم	About a mile west of Gābandi village.	20 houses; 7 camels, 20 donkeys, 40 cattle and 500 date trees.
Dashti دشتي	1½ miles south-south-west of Gābandi village, on the south side of the valley.	200 houses; 70 camels; 200 donkeys, 320 cattle, 2,000 sheep and goats and 1,000 palms.
Dūkūn (Birkeh) برکه دوکون	7 miles north-west of Gābandi village, on the north side of the valley.	90 houses; 20 camels, 30 donkeys, 150 cattle, 2,000 sheep and goats and 2,000 date trees; also called Baraidkan.

Name.	Position.	Population, resources, etc.
Fūmistān فومستان	About 1½ miles north of Gābandi village, under the hill Marzuvabānu.	70 houses; 30 donkeys, 100 cattle, 300 sheep and goats and 5,000 palms, water chiefly from springs, but there is also a reservoir. Limes, vines and pomegranates grow, and there are 3 watermills.
Gābandi village گابندي	13 miles north-north-west of Shīvuh, on the north side of the valley.	300 houses; 15 horses, 2 mules, 30 camels, 200 donkeys, 400 cattle, 2,500 sheep and goats and 11,000 date palms; 8 water reservoirs and some wells, of which the best is called Chāh-i-Nau and is in the direction of Ahshām. The residence of the Nasūri Shaikh is here.
Garīt (Nakhl) نخل گریط	About 1 mile south of Gābandi village.	30 houses; 7 camels, 20 donkeys, 45 cattle, 200 sheep and goats, and 1,000 palms.
Khalaf (Yard) يرد خلف	About 1½ miles south-east of Gābandi village.	20 houses; 20 camels, 30 donkeys, 30 cattle, 1,500 sheep and goats and 800 date trees; drinking water is from Gābandi village and only animals are watered from the local wells.
Kunār Bahār كنار بهار	Near Yard Khalaf.	35 houses; 30 camels, 40 donkeys, 70 cattle, 2,000 sheep and goats and 1,000 palms; water as at Yard Khalaf.
Mīlaki ميليكي	3 miles north-west of Gābandi village, on the north side of the valley.	40 houses; 5 camels, 15 donkeys, 30 cattle, 1,500 sheep and goats, and 800 date palms.
Muqbil (Nakhl) نخل مقبل	¼ of a mile west of Gābandi village.	20 houses; 3 camels, 15 donkeys, 15 cattle, 70 sheep and goats, and 300 date palms.
Sitlu ستلو	3 miles west of Gābandi village, on the south side of the valley, at the foot of a hill called Qal'eh Surkh.	60 houses; 30 camels, 20 donkeys, 45 cattle, 1,500 sheep and goats and 800 date palms.
Surkhūhā سرخوها	Near Yard Khalaf.	30 houses; 12 camels, 40 donkeys, 35 cattle, 400 sheep and goats and 1,000 date palms. The people are ruddy complexioned, whence the name of the village: they talk good Persian and are believed to be from the north.

GĀBANDI

Tamīmi Villages.

Name.	Position.	Population, resources, etc.
Ain-as-Saudeh عين السودة	In a hill of the same name, to the east of Bundu.	20 houses; 500 sheep and goats and 1,000 date trees; 3 springs from the hill.
Bundu بندو	5 miles east-south-east of Chāh Mubārak, on the north side of the valley.	80 houses; 20 donkeys, 80 cattle, 1,000 sheep and goats and 500 date palms; 7 wells of 3 to $3\frac{1}{2}$ fathoms' depth.
Bustānu بستانو	$2\frac{1}{2}$ miles west-north-west of Chāh Mubārak, on the north side of the valley.	110 houses; 10 camels, 70 donkeys, 100 cattle, 2,000 sheep and goats and 4,500 date trees; 12 wells of sweet water $3\frac{1}{2}$ to 4 fathoms deep.
Chāh Mubārak چاه مبارك	16 miles north-west by west of Gābandi village, on the north side of the valley, and the same distance east by south of **Nāband**.	230 houses; 8 horses, 20 camels, 160 donkeys 250 cattle, 1,500 sheep and goats and 12,000 date palms; 4 water reservoirs, of which one called Gharāmeh is large, and 20 wells $3\frac{1}{2}$ to 5 fathoms deep, including one called Chāh-i-Bābūl which is said to be ancient and of great size. Chāh Mubārak was the residence of the late Tamīmi Shaikh, Saqar-bin-Mubārak, who built here a fort with a deep ditch round it.
Jalālāt جلالات	4 miles east-south-east of Chāh Mubārak, on the north side of the valley, under the hill called 'Ain-as-Saudeh.	50 houses; 15 donkeys, 40 cattle, 1,500 sheep and 600 date palms; 3 wells 4 to $4\frac{1}{2}$ fathoms deep.
Mardu مردر	In the hills to the east of Tāzu.	1 house, 300 date palms, and running water.
Murva'eh مروعه	A mile or two to the east of Chāh Mubārak.	40 houses; 25 donkeys, 45 cattle, 500 sheep and goats and 600 date palms; 5 wells of $2\frac{1}{2}$ to 4 fathoms depth.
Sahmu سهمو	1 mile east-south-east of Savāhil, on the north side of the valley.	90 houses; 6 camels, 50 donkeys, 100 cattle, 800 sheep and goats and 3,000 date palms; 7 wells of sweet water $2\frac{1}{2}$ to 3 fathoms deep.
Sahmu Sharqi سهمو شرقي	1 mile east-south-east of Sahmu.	70 houses; 5 camels, 40 donkeys, 70 cattle, 600 sheep and goats and 3,500 date palms; 5 wells of sweet water 3 to 4 fathoms deep.
Tal-i-Yardu تل يردر	Between Bustānu and Chāh Mubārak.	A fort built in 1905 by the late Shaikh Saqar, Tamīmi: it is supplied with water from Chāh Mubārak.
Tāzu تازر	In the hills a mile or two to the east of 'Ain-as-Saudeh.	1 house, 100 pomegranate and lime trees, 500 date palms, and running water.

From the number of houses it would appear that the normal population of the valley is about 19,500 souls, *viz.*—

Harami villages	. . . .	6,400
Māliki „	. . . .	3,700
Nasūri „	. . . .	5,900
Tamīmi „	. . . .	3,500

Recently, however, the valley has been to a considerable extent depopulated by emigration, due to political troubles, chiefly to **Bahrain, Kuwait** and **Fāo**; and in most of the villages a proportion of the houses are empty. In all the divisions the people are of mixed origin, speaking both Persian and Arabic, and nearly all are Sunnis of the Shāfi'i sect. The inhabitants of the Nasūri group of villages call themselves Nasūris, but in reality only the family of their chief and a very few others belong to that tribe. In most of the places there is a sprinkling of negroes.

Wheat, barley, maize, rice, flax and tobacco are grown in the Gābandi valley, chiefly by rainfall but in places by irrigation; date palms everywhere abound; and in some villages there are limes, pomegranates and vines. Most of the people are agriculturists, but some of them take part in the pearl fishery on the Arabian side of the Gulf. **Shīvuh** and Tibin are the ports of Gābandi. An estimate of local resources can be formed from the data given in the village tables above.

Until 1905 the whole valley was administered by the Nasūri Shaikh of Gābandi village, Hasan-bin-Mazkūr, under whom were also **Shīvuh** and certain other places on the **Shībkūh** coast and the villages of Darveh **Āsūh**; for the places then subject to his control the Shaikh paid 12,000 Tūmāns a year to the Governor of **Bastak**. In 1906 a new arrangement was made, the Harami, Māliki and Tamīmi villages being taken from Hasan-bin-Mazkūr, whose annual revenue was at the same time reduced to 7,000 Tūmāns, and conferred on the Tamīmi Shaikh, Saqar-bin-Mubārak, of Chāh Mubārak, who thereupon became responsible to the Governor of **Bastak** for 5,000 Tūmāns a year on account of the Māliki and Tamīmi groups and to the Imperial Persian Customs for 3,560 Tūmāns a year on account of the Harami villages in Gābandi and upon the coast of **Shībkūh**. Shaikh Saqar was however assassinated in March 1907, and it is not yet known how the local administrative arrangements will be affected by the event. Shaikh Hasan-bin-Mazkūr is a Sunni; but his wife, a daughter of Tāhir Khān of Galehdār, is a Shī'ah; consequently his sons are being brought up as Sunnis and his only daughter as a Shī'ah.

GANĀVEH گناوه

A group of 3 villages on the coast of the Persian district of **Hayāt Dāvud**, 15 miles north-north-west of the town of **Rīg**; the villages, in order from north to south, are distinguished as Shamāli شمالي, Miyāni مياني and Qausi قوسي. The place is defended by half a dozen towers and comprises altogether about 150 houses: the inhabitants are **Lurs**. A short way to the south of the villages is a creek deep enough to admit native boats of 25 tons burden; but the anchorage for larger vessels is at some distance off-shore, there being only 3 fathoms at 1½ miles, and the landing is bad at low water. Dates, wheat and barley are the chief products; there are about 40 horses, 30 mules and 200 donkeys, and the fowls are said to be remarkably fine. Ganāveh is governed at present by Murād Khān, son of Kā Murād, an uncle of the Khān of **Hayāt Dāwud**; and he resides here. A Customs official is now stationed at this place partly in order to prevent the smuggling of rifles into the country, but as yet the trade has suffered little from his interference. Near Ganāveh are some extensive ruins, probably marking the site of the Jannābah of the mediæval Arab and Persian geographers.[*]

GARGAR or ĀB-I-GARGAR آب گرگر

This channel, the uppermost part of which is artificial, issues from the **Kārūn** on its left bank just above **Shūshtar** Town and rejoins that river at **Band-i-Qīr**. Its direction is thus almost exactly from north to south, and its length in a straight line about 30 miles, but between its extreme points it bends eastwards in a regular curve of which the maximum divergence from the direct line is about 8 miles. The Gargar forms the eastern boundary of the **Miyānāb** island.

Features of course.—At its head are the remains of a massive barrage, apparently known at the present day as the Band-i-Mīrza بند ميرزا;[†] it is built of hewn stone with six narrow openings, through which water passes leaving the crest dry except when the river is high and pours over it. The openings, however, are unbridged and are too wide to cross. Below this barrage the stream flows for half a mile through a channel, 100 feet deep, artificially excavated in the sandstone rock: it then reaches a second dam, called Pul-i-Būlaiti پل بوليتي, which carries the routes from

---

[*] See Le Strange's *Lands of the Eastern Caliphate*. The Carmathian Abu Tāhir is said to have been born at Jannābah, which was also celebrated in the middle ages for the manufacture of linen stuffs.

[†] The names Band-i-Qaisar and Band-i-Shāhzādeh are not now recognised as applying to this barrage. See also footnote to article **Shatait**.

Shūshtar Town to all places east of it. At the Pul-i-Būlaiti the water is forced into tunnels in the precipitous rock on both sides of the river and by these is conducted to the flour-mills of Shūshtar and Būlaiti a little further down. Below the mills, at 200 yards or more from the dam, rock yields to earth; but the banks continue to be nearly 100 feet in height till the end of Shūshtar Town is reached. Half a mile below Pul-i-Būlaiti a natural ledge of rocks crosses the channel with an opening in it 20 yards wide but passable for native river boats. At a point 4 miles lower down the river bed is again nearly traversed by a natural barrier, carrying masonry remains, by which the course of the stream is considerably deflected to the east and made to form an acute angle; this place is called Māhībāzān ماهي بازان or Bāzāniyāt بازانيات, meaning a place where fish play, from the numbers of fish which come there to spawn and are caught. On the right bank at 7 or 8 miles below Shūshtar is the important landing place of Shalaili, above which there is not, for practical purposes, any navigation either native or European. From Māhībāzān to a short distance above Band-i-Qīr the Gargar meanders through a stretch of low ground: this bottom varies in width from a mile to several hundred yards and is enclosed upon either side by steep clay banks from 40 to 50 feet high, with which the river in its windings from time to time comes in contact. As Band-i-Qīr is approached the high banks close in upon the river and show remains of brick buildings, vestiges of the ancient city of 'Askar Mukram عسكر مكرم; parts of these are sunk as much as 10 and even 20 feet below the present surface of the ground. At Band-i-Qīr itself the banks do not ordinarily rise more than 18 feet above the river in its lowest season; and in the high season, during floods, they are frequently overflowed. The width of the Gargar stream varies from 50 to nearly 100 yards, and at Band-i-Qīr it is about 60. The banks are now entirely denuded of wooding.

Discharge, rise and fall, current and silt.—The flood discharge of the Gargar is estimated at about 7,000 cubic feet a second, but in March 1905 the discharge at Band-i-Qīr was only about 2,000 cusecs. Owing to the height of the banks the river does not lend itself naturally to purposes of irrigation, but in some places there are small inundation canals watering low-lying lands. The times of the river's rise and fall vary from year to year, and the difference between the summer and the winter level is also inconstant; but by the middle of June the water has ordinarily subsided to a low level and thereafter continues to decrease until the first rains of winter fall at the end of October or beginning of November. Ordinarily the current varies from 5 to 2 knots and is strongest in the upper reaches towards **Shūshtar** Town, but when the Haddām is in flood it is said to attain 8 knots below the confluence of that tributary. The silt of the Gargar at its maximum is about one-eightieth of the volume of water; most of it is of purely local origin and is very quickly dropped. The discoloration of the water in floods is a light buff.*

Navigation.—The navigation of the Gargar is difficult, chiefly on account of the sinuosity and the narrowness in places of the channel, of which the breadth varies from 20 to 40 yards; with a low river obstacles in the shape of stones, sand spits and tree stumps are superadded. Tree stumps and similar snags are especially common in the middle reaches of the Gargar; many of them are known and can be avoided, but new ones are frequently met with when the river falls. The average depth of the Gargar in the low season is from 6 to $4\frac{1}{2}$ feet, but at particular points soundings of 3, 2 and even $1\frac{1}{2}$ feet may be expected. The channels are subject to perpetual alteration in consequence chiefly of sandbars, which are thrown across the river by small tributaries during the last freshets of spring; these the reduced river of the summer season is unable to scour away. Among the larger of the tributaries are the Mālih مالح, 6 miles below Hilāleh; the Chāi-an-Naft چاي النفط, coming in 2 miles below Kraidi, from the neighbourhood of some naphtha springs below the Bakhtiyāri hills; and the Haddām هدّام, 1 mile below Saiyid Hasan: these are all upon the left bank and contain water only after rain. About $1\frac{3}{4}$ miles above **Band-i-Qīr** the river contains piles of old cut stones which make the passage dangerous in the low season and also afford a *point d'appui* for the formation of sand banks.

The "Shushan," which runs from **Ahwāz** to Shalaili in ordinary states of the river, is a stern-wheeler 100 feet in length over all, with a beam of 23 feet, and draws 3 feet when carrying 30 tons of cargo; † a longer vessel could not negotiate some of the turns, and an ordinary paddle-steamer would find many if not most of the channels too narrow. Since 1892 the "Shushan" has plied regularly on the Gargar at most seasons, but when the river is low she frequently runs aground or strikes the banks and sometimes sustains injury. The only fuel is wood, which all comes from the banks of the **Diz** and of which about 15 tons are consumed

---

* The waters of the Gargar, then known as the Mashrūqān مشروقان, were described as "white" by an Arab traveller so long ago as the 10th century A.D. See Le Strange.

† Her barge, $65\frac{1}{2}$ feet by $15\frac{1}{4}$ feet, carrying 50 tons of cargo, can only be used in a good river.

on the round trip from **Ahwāz** to Shalaili and back again : a fuel-depôt is maintained at **Band-i-Qīr**. The steaming hours between **Ahwāz** and Shalaili are from 20 to 26 in ascending, of which 7 are occupied by the reaches of the **Kārūn** below **Band-i-Qīr**; the return journey to **Ahwāz** takes from 9 to 20 hours according to the state of the river.

Villages.—The following are the villages situated on both banks of the Gargar in order from **Shūshtar** Town down to **Band-i-Qīr** :—

Name.	Miles below Shūshtar Town by water, and on which bank.	Houses and inhabitants.	Remarks.
Būlaiti بوليتي	Nil. Left.	200 houses, some of mud, some of stone and some of gypsum cement. The people are Gūnduzlus and have about 200 rifles.	Būlaiti is connected with **Shūshtar**, of which it forms a suburb, by a dam across the Gargar. The routes from **Shūshtar** Town to Qal'eh Tūl and **Rāmuz** Town pass through this village. Wheat, barley and beans are cultivated, and some of the inhabitants are carriers owning 100 mules. There are some flour mills. Būlaiti is owned by the Mu'īn-ut-Tujjār of Tehrān, the Rais-ut-Tujjār of **Muhammareh** and two others.
Muhammad Husain (Kūt Hāji) كوت حاجي محمد حسين or Saiyid Amīn (Qal'eh) قلعه سيد امين	5¼. Right.	6 mud houses of Shūshtaris: they have 3 rifles.	This place stands on the high bank, about 1 mile down stream from the place called Māhībāzān and overlooking the river. There is a garden below in the river bed. Three Persian soldiers are quartered here, nominally as a guard for the Shalaili landing place.
Shalaili Buzurg شليلي بزرگ or Shalailīyeh Kabīr شليليه كبير	7. Right.	20 houses of Shīr 'Ali Bakhtiyāris, Persians and Kurds, owning 3 or 4 rifles, also 2 or 3 houses of Arabs.	The village is about ½ mile from the river bank. Wheat, barley and beans are grown, also sesame and cotton near the edge of the river. Some buffaloes are kept by the Arab

Name.	Miles below Shūshtar Town by water, and on which bank.	Houses and inhabitants.	REMARKS.
			inhabitants. A little below this village and above the next is the landing place for Shūshtar Town where steam and sailing boats from the lower Kārūn discharge their cargoes. A Persian military guard is supposed to be stationed here for the protection of vessels and goods; it is represented at present by 3 men living at Kūt Hāji Muhammad Husain above. This and the smaller Shalaili below are owned by a member of the family of the late Muhammad 'Ali, Mujtahid, of Shūshtar Town.
Shalaili Khurd شليلي خرد or Shalaili Kūchik شليلي كوچك or Shalailīyeh Saghīr شليليه صغير	8¼. Right.	10 houses of the same tribes as in the last village. They have 3 or 4 rifles.	See last village.
Qurūmizi قرومزي or Qul Rūmizi قل رومزي	9¼. Right.	40 houses of Shīr 'Ali Bakhtiyāris. The inhabitants have 30 rifles.	Wheat, barley and beans are grown. The village is owned by Mīrza Tāhir Khān, Mustaufi, of Shūshtar.
Hasmāwa حسماوا or Hasmābād حسم آباد	11½. Right.	30 houses of Shīr 'Ali Bakhtiyāris and Miyānāb Arabs, owning 10 rifles.	Wheat, barley and beans are cultivated by the Bakhtiyāris; the Arabs only keep buffaloes. Formerly sailing boats discharged their cargoes here for

Name.	Miles below Shūshtar Town by water, and on which bank.	Houses and inhabitants.	REMARKS.
			Shūshtar which is 10 miles distant by road. Near the village is the conspicuous Qadamgāh of Nabi Shu'aib نبي سعيب. Same owner as Qurūmizi above.
Chahārgāweh چهارگاوه	13¼. Right.	15 houses of Shīr 'Ali Bakhtiyāris and Shūshtaris. They have 4 rifles.	This place is occupied only at seed time and harvest. Same owner as at Qurūmizi above.
Nāsir or Nasair (Bunneh) بنّه ناصر - نصیر	14¾. Right.	12 grass huts of Miyānāb Arabs, possessing 10 rifles.	Wheat, barley and beans are grown. The owner is the same as at Qurūmizi above.
Ijbāreh (Bunneh) بنّه اجباره	15¾. Right.	30 mud houses of Miyānāb Arabs owning 10 rifles.	There are about 10 mules. The village belongs to the family of Hāji Saiyid 'Abdus Samad, Mujtahid, of Shūshtar Town.
Abdullah Jarrāh (Bunneh or Kūt) بنّه - کوت عبد الله جراح	16½. Right.	15 huts, mostly mud, of Arabs, Shūshtaris and Shīr 'Ali Bakhtiyāris. There are 6 rifles.	Same owners as Bunneh Ijbāreh above.
Sūfān صوفان or Nasr Ullah (Bunneh Mulla) بنّه ملا نصر الله	18. Right.	30 mud huts of Shīr 'Ali Bakhtiyāris, who have 10 rifles.	The name Sūfān is derived from a tomb in the vicinity. Wheat, barley and beans are grown and there are about 10 mules. The owners are the same as at Bunneh Ijbāreh above.
'Abbās (Bunneh Mulla) بنّه ملا عباس	19¾. Right.	50 mud huts of Shīr 'Ali Bakhtiyāris and some Arabs. They own 20 rifles.	Wheat, barley and beans are cultivated and 10 mules are kept. There is a ferry here. Same owners as at Bunneh Ijbāreh above. This village is situated in a tract known as Daulatābād.

Name.	Miles below Shūshtar Town by water, and on which bank.	Houses and inhabitants.	REMARKS.
Hilāleh هلاله	19¾. Left.	60 grass huts and tents of **Salāmāt** Arabs and Shīr 'Ali **Bakhtiyāris**. There are 30 rifles.	The crops are wheat and barley. The owners are those of Bunneh Ijbāreh above, but for the last two years half the revenue has been paid to the Shaikh of **Muhammareh** who has leased it.
Sōzi سوزي	21. Right.	35 mud huts of Shīr 'Ali **Bakhtiyāris**, **'Anāfijeh** of the Mahdīyeh and Wahabīyeh sections, and a few **Salāmāt**: the headman is a Bakhtiyāri. Rifles number 10.	Wheat and barley are grown. The owners are the same as those of Bunneh Ijbāreh.
Daulatābād دولت آباد	22. Right.	The remains of a village or town and, perhaps, the tract surrounding it (See Bunneh Mulla 'Abbās above and 'Adhāfeh below).	The place was deserted about 20 years ago on account of failure of irrigation from the Mīnau canal.
'Adhāfeh عضافه	23. Right.	50 houses, 4 or 5 of mud, the rest grass huts and tents. The people are **'Anāfijeh** Arabs of the Dailam and Mahdīyeh sections and Bait Sa'ad of the Nais section: they own 20 rifles. The headman belongs to the Dailam.	Wheat and barley are grown and there are 20 mules. Ownership as at Bunneh Ijbāreh above. This village like Bunneh Mulla 'Abbās stands in the tract called Daulatābād.
Salāmāt سلامات or Saiyid Muhammad سید محمد	23. Left.	25 tents of **Salāmāt** Arabs. They have 10 rifles.	...
Abdun Nabi (Bunneh Mulla) بنّه ملّا عبد النبي	24½. Right.	20 grass huts of **Miyānāb** Arabs, partly connected with the **'Anāfijeh** and partly with the	The crops are wheat and barley. The owners are those of Bunneh Ijbāreh above.

Name.	Miles below Shūshtar Town by water, and on which bank.	Houses and inhabitants.	REMARKS.
		Kathīr of Farhān Asad's faction. Rifles number 10.	
Dīwān (Bunneh Saiyid) بنّه سیّد دیوان	27¾. Right.	20 mud huts of mixed Arabs and some Shūshtaris. They have 5 rifles.	Cucumbers, water melons and onions are grown by the Shūshtaris. Same owners as Bunneh Ijbāreh above.
Janām (Bunneh Shaikh) بنّه شیخ جنّام	28. Left.	35 grass and mud huts and tents. The inhabitants are Arabs chiefly of the Zahairīyeh section of the Al Khamīs tribe; they have 20 rifles.	Wheat and barley are cultivated. The owners and the relations of the Shaikh of Muhammareh with the place are the same as at Hilāleh.
Sultān (Bunneh Saiyid) بنّه سیّد سلطان	31. Right.	15 huts of Miyānāb Arabs with a few Shūshtaris; most are of grass, a few of mud. There are 6 rifles.	Wheat and barley are grown. Ownership is the same as at Bunneh Ijbāreh.
Kraidi کریدی	31½. Left.	25 grass huts of Hardān Arabs of the Bani Na'āmeh section with some Salāmāt. They have 10 rifles.	The crops are wheat and barley. Ownership and the position of the Shaikh of Muhammareh with regard to the place are the same as at Hilāleh above. The inhabitants are mostly temporary and do not generally remain more than a year or so on account of the hardness of the Saiyid landlords. There is one small ferry boat.
Udīhi ادیحی	32. Left.	A small village.	Same owners as Bunneh Ijbāreh. This place seems to be identical with Saiyid Dakhīl دخیل where there is a ferry with 1 small boat.
Simaideh سمیده	34¼. Right.	10 mud houses of Miyānāb Arabs. Rifles number 5. The chief man is 'Ali, son of one	There is a boat ferry here. Wheat and barley are grown. Same owners as Bunneh Ijbāreh above.

GARGAR

Name.	Miles below Shūshtar Town by water, and on which bank.	Houses and inhabitants.	REMARKS.
		Mashhūt, who was a refugee from **Wais** and had been an attendant at the Imāmzādeh there.	
Hasan (Saiyid) سید حسن	34¼. Left.	40 huts with mud walls and roofed with mats or tent cloth. The inhabitants are mostly Bait **Sa'ad** of the Mahāmīd section, connected with the party of Shaikh Farbān of the **Kathīr**. There are also some **Salāmāt** and a few Shūshtaris, **Bakhtiyaris** and **'Anāfieh**. There are 20 rifles.	There are here 15 mares, 10 mules, 60 cattle and 1,000 sheep and goats. Ownership as at Bunneh Ijbāreh above. There is a ferry here with one small boat.
Naghaishi نغیشي	36. Right.	10 grass huts and 10 tents of Maiyāh Arabs, a subdivision of the Dailam section of the 'Anāfijeh. They have 10 rifles.	The proprietors are the same as at Bunneh Ijbāreh above; this is the last village in this direction which they own. Opposite, upon the left bank, is the Chāi-al-Haddām which forms the boundary between the Shaikh of **Muhammareh's** jurisdiction and Northern 'Arabistān.
Rūbīyeh (Umm-ar-) أم الربیه	39. Left.	A fort built by the Shaikh of **Muhammareh** near his border for the protection of river traffic. At present the fort is not garrisoned, as it is not required, nor are there any civil inhabitants.	To attract settlers the revenue at this place was fixed at the low rate of two Qrāns per plough. At the time the 2-Qrān piece was about equal in value to the Indian rupee and was sometimes called "Rūbīyeh". Hence the name of this fort.
Band-i-Qīr بند قیر	44. Right.	...	See article **Band-i-Qīr**.

From a point called **Umm-al-Hamām** about a mile above **Band-i-Qīr** and up to Saiyid Hasan the ruins are visible of the city of Lashkar لشكر or 'Askar Mukram عسكر مكرم ; they occur upon both banks. 'Askar Mukram took its name from Mukram, an Arab commander sent by Hajjāj, the celebrated governor of **'Irāq** under the Omaiyids, to subdue a rebellion in **'Arabistān**. In the 10th century A. D. the main town stood on the western bank and was connected with the remainder by 2 bridges of boats. 'Askar Mukram still existed in the 14th century and was then generally called Lashkar.*

GAT'AH
كطعه

An island adjoining the right bank of the Shatt-al-**'Arab** off the tract called Gat'ah ; it begins immediately below **Bahrīyah**, is opposite to the upper portion of Hāji **Salbūq** island, and has a length of nearly 2 miles but very little breadth. The inhabitants number about 200 souls and belong to various tribes. They own about 7,000 date palms, 40 cattle, 50 sheep and goats and 1 or 2 horses. Grapes, apples, figs, melons and pomegranates are grown as well as dates. Gat'ah is Turkish territory.

GHAFA-LAH
غفله

Singular Ghafaili غفيلي. A nomadic Arab tribe inhabiting the plain country inland of Rās-al-**Khaimah** and Umm-al-**Qaiwain** but not extending into the hills ; the **Jiri** plain and its immediate neighbourhood are their favourite habitat. They are a small tribe and probably do not number more than 500 souls. In politics they are Ghāfiriyah and they are generally well disposed to the Shaikh of Abu **Dhabi**, whom they have frequently assisted in warfare, but at the present time their closest relations are with Umm-al-**Qaiwain** ; in religion they are Hanbali Sunnis. They own camels and live by selling firewood and charcoal in the coast towns. They are credited with the possession of 700 camels, 40 donkeys, 100 cattle, and 1,000 sheep and goats.

GHĀFIR (WĀDI BANI)
وادي بني غافر

A valley which has its head in the Western **Hajar** district of the **Omān** Sultanate, traverses **Bātinah**, and reaches the sea at Bat-ha Yāl Sa'ad : the pass in **Hajar** at which it rises is called Najd-al-Hayāl, being adjacent to the village of Hayāl in the Wādi-al-**Kabīr** of **Dhāhirah**.

---
* *Vide* Le Strange.

GHĀFIR (WĀDI BANI) 573

Its principal tributory is Wādi **Sahtan** which joins it on the right bank near the village of Tabāqah.

The villages of Wādi Bani Ghāfir in order from the Hayāl pass downwards are as follows: the distances between them are stated in hours:—

Village.	Position.	On which bank.	Houses and inhabitants.	REMARKS.
Sa'abah صعبه	At the head of the valley.	Left.	25 houses of Bani Shahūm of the Naiyāyirah section.	Nil.
Rimi رمي	2 hours below Sa'abah.	Right.	60 houses of Bani Shahūm.	Do.
Bilād-ash-Shahūm بلاد الشهوم	2 hours below Rimi.	Left.	100 houses of Bani Shahūm.	Do.
Murri مري	3 hours below Bilād-ash-Shahūm.	Do.	60 houses of **Maqābīl**.	There are two forts here.
Mahbab مهبب	2 hours below Murri.	Right.	60 houses of **Maqābīl**.	Situated on a route between **Dhank Town** and **Rustāq**.
Dhab'a ضبعا	1 hour below Mahbab.	Do.	25 houses of **Miyāyihah**.	There is a tower here.
Maihah ميحه	1½ hours below Dhab'a.	Do.	60 houses of Bani Shakail.	This village has a square fort.
Maqham مقحم	Half a mile below Maihah.	Do.	18 houses of Bani Shakail.	There is a tower here.
Midān ميدان	Adjoins Maqham.	Do.	30 houses of Bani Shakail.	Nil.
Sani سني	Adjoins Mīdān.	Do.	120 houses of Bani Shakail.	Do.
Kahaf كهف	Three-quarters of an hour below Sani.	Do.	30 houses of **Miyāyihah**.	Do.

GHÂFIR (WÀDI BANI)

Village.	Position.	On which bank.	Houses and inhabitants.	REMARKS.
Dhawaihir ضويهر	Quarter of an hour below Kahaf.	Left.	20 houses of Miyāyihah.	Nil.
Taiyib طيب	Quarter of an hour below Dhawaihir.	Do.	25 houses of Miyāyihah.	Do.
Rijlah رجه	Half an hour below Taiyib.	Do.	20 houses of Miyāyihah.	Do.
Qarti قرطي	Half an hour below Rijlah.	Do.	40 houses of Miyāyihah.	Do.
Ruwaibi رويبي	Half an hour below Qarti.	Do.	15 houses of Miyāyihah.	Do.
Difa' دفع	One hour below Qarti.	Right.	30 houses of Miyāyihah.	Do.
Marji مرجي	One hour below Difa'.	Do.	50 houses of Miyāyihah of the Bani Salmān section.	Do.
Khafdi خفدي	Two hours below Marji.	Left.	30 houses of Miyāyihah.	Do.
'Ain Sharāinah عين شرائنه	Quarter of an hour below Khafdi.	Right.	150 houses of Sharāinah.	Do.
Tabāqah طباقه	2 hours below 'Ain Sharāinah.	Left.	40 houses of 'Abriyīn and Miyāyihah.	Wādi Sahtan comes in here, on the right bank. This village has 4,000 date palms and there is some cultivation of wheat. There are a few camels and a large number of sheep and goats.
Dihās دهاس	2 hours below Tabāqah.	Right.	20 houses of Miyāyihah of the Salāmiyīn section.	There are dates here but no other cultivation. A fort stands on an eminence in the middle of the village.

GHĀFIR (WĀDI BANI) 575

This concludes the upper portion of the valley or Wādi Bani Ghāfir proper, of which the population is apparently about 5,000 souls. Everywhere in this section there is cultivation of wheat, barley, millet, beans and lucerne, and the date palms are estimated at about 25,000. Livestock is evenly distributed among the villages and amounts to some 1,000 camels, 5,000 donkeys, 2,000 cattle and 8,000 sheep and goats.

Near Dihās, which is about 12 miles in a direct line from the sea, the valley enters **Bātinah** and changes its name to Wādi-al-Hōqain حرقين, from the Bani **Hina** village of Hōqain which is mentioned below. At its mouth upon the sea it is called Bat-ha **Suwaiq** or Bat-ha Yāl Sa'ad. The villages in the Wādi-al-Hōqain section are :—

Name.	Position.	On which bank.	Houses and inhabitants.	Remarks.
Lamki لمكي	2 miles below Dihās.	Right.	30 houses of Bani Lamak.	Nil.
Ain عين	1 mile below Lamki.	Both.	20 houses of Sharāinah.	Do.
Amār عمار	3 miles below 'Ain.	Do.	houses of Miyāyihah.	Do.
Nizūk نيزرك	3 miles below 'Amār.	Do.	40 houses of Maqābil and Miyāyihah of the Khanābishah section.	Do.
Madīnah مدينه	3 miles below Nizūk.	Right.	50 houses of Maqābil and Miyāyihah of the Khanābishah section.	Do.
Misinnah مسنه	1 mile below Madīnah.	Do.	25 houses of Bayāsirah.	Do.
Zūla زلا	1 mile below Misinnah.	Left.	20 houses of the Bani Tiyūm section of the Bani Kalbān.	Do.
Salam سلم	1 mile below Zūla.	Do.	30 houses of Maqābil.	Do.

Name.	Position.	On which bank.	Houses and inhabitants.	REMARKS.
Zawājir زراجر	1 mile below Salam.	Right.	35 houses of Miyāyihah.	Nil.
Mali ملي	1 mile below Zawājir.	Do.	40 houses of Bayāsirah.	Do.
Hawail حويل	1 mile below Mali.	Do	45 houses of Bani Hina.	Do
Hōqain حوقين	4 or 5 miles below Hawail.	Both.	200 houses of Bani Hina.	The inhabitants are said to possess 20 camels, 80 donkeys, 100 cattle and 1,000 sheep and goats.

The crops are the same in Wādi-al-Hōqain as in the upper valley: the population works out at 2,800 souls.

The trade of Wādi Bani Ghāfir as a whole is partly with Wudām and partly with Suwaiq. A route from Miskin in Dhāhirah to Rustāq falls into Wādi Bani Ghāfir at Mahbab and leaves it again at Dihās.

GHĀLLAH غاله — Also known as Kalba, but never called Ghāllat Kalba, and not to be confounded with Khor Kalba. Ghāllah is a village of the Shamailīyah tract in Trucial 'Omān, situated on the coast about half way between Khor Kalba and Fujairah, 4 miles from either; it consists of about 300 houses, chiefly date branch huts, and a few mud godowns. The inhabitants are Naqbiyīn, Sharqiyīn, Kunūd (20 families), 'Abādilah (20 families), Balūchis and Persians—the last from the Bastak district and the vicinity of Lingeh: they live by fishing and the cultivation of dates, wheat, jowari and tobacco, their date palms numbering about 25,000. They own 10 sea-going boats which run to Masqat, Makrān and the Persian Coast ports, also 14 fishing boats. Exports are chiefly tobacco, grown on the hills behind, to Bahrain, and dried fish to the Bātinah ports and Masqat. Ghāllah is still under the domination of Shārjah; it has not been affected by the recent rebellion which has its headquarters at **Fujairah**. The small fort with an upper storey is held by a representative of the **Shārjah** governor of **Shamailīyah**. Ghāllah is the port of **Fujairah**.

GHANAM (JAZĪRAT-AL-)
جزيرة الغنم

An island off the western coast of the **Ruūs-al-Jibāl** district of the **'Omān** Sultanate near its northern extremity: it is separated from the mainland by Khor **Quwai**. Its length north and south is 2½ miles, its breadth ¾ of a mile; low in the north it rises to 600 feet in the southern part, and the shore at nearly all points is precipitous. Jazīrat-al-Ghanam is totally barren and devoid of water; but the people of **Kumzār**, to whom it belongs, send goats here for grazing after rain.

GHARĀF* (SHATT AL-)
شط الغراف

Also called the Shatt-al-Hai شط الحَي ; but this name, though it is still understood, seems to be passing out of general use. The Shatt-al-Gharāf is a great stream, almost a river, in Turkish 'Irāq : it leaves the right bank of the **Tigris** opposite **Kūt-al-Amārah** and, running on the average about south-east by east, joins the **Euphrates** at two places, *viz.*, at Hammār and at a point a little below **Nāsirīyah** Town. The relations to one another of the various channels of the Gharāf are explained below. The length of its course from **Kūt** to **Nāsiriyah** is about 120 miles; in parts where the bed is single its average width is as much as 75 yards; and the banks, which are of sandy alluvium, rise in places as much as 18 feet above the level of the bed. In summer the Shatt-al-Gharāf is dry, but in winter the main stream is said to have an average depth of about 6 feet and could probably be navigated by a river steamer of light draught : it is believed however that the waterway is silting up. The difference of level between the upper end of the Shatt-al-Gharāf on the **Tigris** and its lower end at **Nāsirayah** Town is inconsiderable, and it is said that floods in the **Euphrates** reverse for a time the current of the stream in its lower reaches.

A branch of the Shatt-al-Gharāf formerly separated from the present bed immediately below **Hai** Town and rejoined it 2 or 3 miles below

---

**Authorities.*—Mr. H. W. Cadoux in an article in the Geographical Journal for September 1906 and personal inquiries by the writer; also information obtained by Mr. Crow, Consul at Basrah, from Dr. Bennett of the American Mission there, who lately visited the Gharāf (1907).

Qal'at **Sikar**; this channel is now silted up and is called the Shatt-al-A'ma شط الاعمى or Blind River; while it still flowed the alternative branch was known as Abu Juhairah ابو جهير and the island enclosed between the two as Jazīrat Kinānah كنانه. At the same period the reach near **Shatrat-al-Muntafik** was styled the Shatt-as-Sabīl شط السبيل, but this name seems to have fallen into desuetude. The stream is said now to divide some way above **Shatrat-al-Muntafik** Town into two branches, of which the eastern takes ⅔ of the water and is called the Shatt-al-Bada'ah البداعه, while the western carries the remainder and is known as the Shatt-ash-Shatrah. The Shatt-al-Bada'ah runs through swamps to the **Euphrates** at Hammār; and the Shatt-ash-Shatrah, after passing the town from which it is named, bifurcates at a place Hamzah همزه into two channels. Of the two sub-divisions of the Shatt-ash-Shatrah the larger, known as the 'Ajūzah عجوز, goes eastwards and joins the Shatt-al-Bada'ah while the other—which is probably the original bed of the Gharāf—enters the **Euphrates** about 4 miles below **Nāsirīyah**. The lower part of the Shatt-al-Gharāf in both its present branches is environed by marshes over which the inhabitants move in canoes, except in the dry season; but communication between the towns of **Nāsirīyah** and **Shatrat-al-Muntafik** is ordinarily by land. The marshes on the Bada'ah branch vary in depth from 3 feet in summer to 6 or 7 feet in time of flood.

The following are the chief points of interest on or near the westernmost (or original) bed of the Shatt-al-Gharāf, in order from its head downwards:—

Name.	Position.	Nature.	Remarks.
Mhairijah مهيرجه	On the right bank, about 10 miles from the **Tigris**.	A small village, the head-quarters of a Nāhiyah of the same name in the Qadha of Hai. There are about 50 houses and 5 or 6 shops.	The surrounding Arabs are Bani Rabī'ah of the Maiyāh section.
Hai Town حي	On the left bank, about 20 miles below Mhairijah.	...	See article Hai Town.
Qal'at Sikar قلعة سكر	On the left bank, about 25 miles below Hai Town.	...	See article Qal'at **Sikar**. The Bada'ah branch of the stream probably separates from the Shatrah branch somewhere between this place and **Shatrat-al-Muntafik** below.

Name.	Position.	Nature.	Remarks.
Tallūh تلوُّ	About three miles from the left bank, some 25 miles below Qal'at Sikar.	A site with ancient ruins which extend for 4 miles from north-west to south-east along the left bank of a former bed of, or ancient canal from, the Shatt-al-Gharāf. These have been explored by French archæologists.	The country around Tallūh is a swamp during half the year and a desert during the other half. The town of Shatrat-al-Muntafik lies about 8 miles to the south-west of this place.
Shatrat-al-Muntafik شطرة المنتفك	Four or five miles from the right bank about 30 miles below Qal'at Sikar.	...	See article Shatrat-al-Muntafik. Somewhere below this place occurs the bifurcation of the Shatrah branch into the 'Ajūzah and Nāsiriyah channels.
Nāsiriyah Town ناصريه	On the western side of the westernmost channel of the Shatt-al-Gharā near its junction with the Euphrates, and about 30 miles below Shatrat-al-Muntafik.	...	See article Nāsiriyah Town.

Cereals are extensively cultivated on both sides of the Shatt-al-Gharāf, and a kind of water lift is here in use for irrigation which resembles the balanced lever seen on the banks of the Nile and the *dhenkli* of the Panjāb in India. The chief crops are wheat, barley, maize, millet, and sesame.

In the country of the Bani **Rabī'ah**, which adjoins the **Tigris**, the Shatt-al-Gharāf divides the territory of the Maiyāh section of that tribe on the west from that of the Sarāi section on the east side; the rest of its course lies through the country of the **Muntafik**.

Some authorities consider that the Shatt-al-Gharāf was originally an irrigation canal dug from the **Tigris** and that it has been enlarged to its present dimensions by the rush down it of the surplus waters of that river in time of flood. The main stream of the **Tigris** apparently began to flow down the bed of the Shatt-al-Gharāf about 600 A.D. and returned to its original (and present) bed about 1550 A.D.

The celebrated ancient town of Wsit-al-Hai واسط الحي was probably situated on the Shatt-al-Gharāf not far from the present town of **Hai**; it was founded by the celebrated governor Hajjāj about 703 A.D. and was called Wāsit or Central because it was regarded as approximately equidistant from **Kūfah**, **Basrah** and **Ahwāz**. At the end of the 14th century it was held with a garrison by Taimūr Lang (Tamerlane).

GHARĪF
غريف

A level tract, described as strewn with broken black shingle, between the sandy, flat country of the Trucial '**Omān** coast and the hills in the interior: it lies on the route from **Shārjah** Town to the **Baraimi** Oasis, rather nearer to the former than to the latter, and is now inhabited by the Bani **Qitab**. It originally belonged to the **Na'īm** of **Baraimi** who were expelled by the Bani **Ka'ab** about 1790. In 1840 the place was already in the occupation of the Bani **Qitab** and was then covered with thick thorn jungle and had several wells and a ruined fort; the last has now disappeared. The nearest well in Gharīf to **Shārjah** Town is one called Thaqaibah ثقيبة, and the furthest from it is that of 'Aiyōh.

GHUBBAT GHAZĪRAH
غبة غزيره

Also called Malcolm Inlet.* An arm of the sea forming a remarkable indentation in the eastern coast line of the **Ruūs-al-Jihāl** district of the '**Omān** Sultanate towards its northern extremity. It is 3 miles wide at the entrance and has a depth from east-south-east to west-north-west of 9 miles: its head is divided from Khor-ash-**Sham** in the Persian Gulf only by the narrow isthmus of **Maqlab**. On the north side two large coves 3 miles deep, and on the south side two shorter ones, project inland at right angles to the main inlet. Ghubbat Ghazīrah is surrounded on every side by precipitous hills; but here and there are small sandy bays formed by ravines which come down from the mountains, and the coast-line of

---

* Remarks on this inlet by Admiral Atkinson-Willes, R.N., will be found in the Government of India's Political Proceedings for June 1904.

GHUWĀR

the inlet is so irregular as to attain a length of over 40 miles. The soundings are from 30 to 36 fathoms in the main inlet and from 20 to 25 fathoms in the smaller coves. Ghubbat Ghazīrah would shelter a large fleet, but it is not suitable for a fixed coaling station as it would not be easy to defend. Vessels could safely coal in it from colliers, and it would serve as a good temporary anchorage. The villages of Film, Habalain, Mansal and Maqāqah, belonging to the **Dhahūriyīn**, are situated in Ghubbat Ghazīrah.

GHURAĪB (ABU) ابو غريب

A station of the Dāirat-as-Sanīyah in the Qadha of **Kādhimain** in Turkish **'Irāq**: it is situated on the route from **Baghdād** City to **Fallūjah** on the **Euphrates**, at about 28 miles from the former by road and 15 miles from the latter. There are two large walled Khāns and two smaller ones, which together would accommodate 200 horses and 400 men; these stand on a high, dry and gravelly site. The surrounding country is cultivated and cut up by small canals, and in parts it is even marshy: the main source of irrigation is the Abu Ghuraib canal which is described in the article on the **Euphrates**. Large quantities of grain are sometimes stored in this place. The Sanīyah estate is managed by two Turkish military officers, assisted by two clerks and having 7 mounted Dhābitīyahs under their orders; the income of the estate is about 8,000 Līrahs per annum as against an expenditure of 800 Līrahs.

GHUWĀR الغوار

A tract in the Sanjāq of **Hasa** lying on the west side of the **Hasa** Oasis and conterminous with that district between Jabal Qārat-ar-Rukbān and Jabal Bū Ghanīmah, both of which are situated on the common border. The eastern boundary of Ghuwār is, however, prolonged far to the southward and reaches to a hill called Qusūr Bin-'Ajlān قصور بن عجلان, which is probably about 50 miles north of **Jabrīn**; south of the **Hasa** Oasis, Ghuwār is adjoined on the east by the tract known as **Kharmah**. The north-western corner of the **Ghuwār** tract is marked by the hill of Ghār-ash-Shuyūkh, and thence the western boundary runs southwards to another hill named Qārat-al-'Othmānīyah and gradually converges towards the eastern boundary which it meets at Quṣūr Bin-'Ajlān. The length of the Ghuwār tract according to these specifications is about 90 miles; and its maximum breadth, which is opposite to the **Hasa** Oasis, is 20 to 25. The western border of Ghuwār is parallel to the edge of **Summān**, but is separated from it by the tracts of **Na'alah** and Wādi **Farūq**, which are also long and narrow and follow the same direction as **Summān**; of the two, **Na'alah** is the one which is immediately in contact with Ghuwār.

Nearly in the centre of that part of Ghuwār which has for its corners the hills of Qārat-ar-Rukbān, Bū Ghanīmah, Qārat-al-'Othmānīyah and Ghār-ash-Shuyūkh is a hill known as Jabal Ghuwār. Ghuwār is described as a sandy district abounding in stony hillocks.

Some authorities would carry Ghuwār as far north as the Gharaimīl hill, thus absorbing in Ghuwār the greater part of the tract which we have dealt with elsewhere under the name of Badd-al-**Asīs**.

GULF PORTS
گلف پورت

Called in Persian Banādir-i-Khalīj-i-Fārs بنادر خلیج فارس. This is an administrative division of the **Persian Coast** which ranks as a Mamlakat and is ruled by a Governor with the style of Hukmrān. It comprises at the present time the following districts or towns:—**Dīlam** Town; the **Hayāt Dāvud, Rūdhilleh, Angāli** and **Zīra** districts; part of the **Dashtistān** district; **Būshehr** Peninsula and Town; part of the **Shībkūh** district; **Lingeh** district and Town; the islands of **Qishm, Hanjām, Lārak** and **Hormūz**; a maritime portion of the **Bastak** district, although the whole of **Bastak** nominally belongs to **Fārs**; Bandar 'Abbās Town; and the **Shamīl, Mīnāb, Biyābān** and currency, **Jāshk** districts. The physical geography, the administration, and the weights and measures of the Gulf Ports division generally are described in the article on the **Persian Coast**.

GULSHAN
گلشن

A valley in the **Shībkūh** district of Persia, in the article on which its position and course are described: it seems to be known also as the Sadāq صداق valley.

GULSHAN

The following are some of the villages in the Gulshan valley :—

Name.	Position.	Inhabitants.	Remarks.
Armaki (Baikheh) بيخه ارمكي	Described as some miles to the west of Gulshan village, and possibly not in the Gulshan valley.	...	The headquarters of 'Abdullah-bin-Muhammad, 'Obaidli, Shaikh of Chīru.
Bahmani بهمني	9 miles north-north-west, in a direct line, of Chārak.	Āl 'Ali, half of whom are under the Shaikh of Chārak and half under the Bushri Shaikh.	...
Gulshan گلشن	Said to be about 1 mile south-west of Dih Nau Mir : if so, it is about 10 miles north-north-west of Chārak.	150 houses ; a few of them of genuine 'Obaidlis and the rest of mixed tribes who call themselves so ; the people are all Shāfi'i Sunnis.	Resources are 12 camels, 40 donkeys, 75 cattle, 1,000 sheep and goats and 1,200 date palms. There are 5 water reservoirs and 3 wells of 3 to 5 fathoms' depth.
Mir (Nakhl-i) نخل مير	10 miles north by west of Chārak.	...	The residence of Muhammad-bin-Rahmah, head of the Bushri section of the Āl 'Ali.
Murāgh مراغ	5 miles east by north of Nakhl-i-Mīr.	...	The inhabitants have some cultivation at Chāh-i-Varzang which is 4 miles to the east-south-eastward.

Other villages in the Gulshan valley are 'Askar (Bul) بو العسكر , 'Izz-ud-Dīn (Nakhl) نخل عزّ الدين ; Kandeh كنده ; Mīr (Dih Nau) ده نو مير , at 1½ miles south-west of Nakhl-i-Mīr; Murāgh (Dih Nau) ده نو مراغ , at 2 miles south-west of Murāgh ; Rustami رستمي and Sihkunār سه كنار . All the villages in the valley, except Gulshan itself which is under the Shaikh of Chīru, appear to be subject either to the Āl 'Ali Shaikh of Chārak or to the head man or the Bushri section of the Āl 'Ali : in the latter class seem to be the villages of Nakhl-i-Mīr, and Sihkunār. The Āl 'Ali villages are known collectively as Baikheh Sadāq.

The population of the Gulshan valley is roughly estimated at 4,000 souls.

GŪPĀL

گوپال

By Arabs pronounced Gōbāl. A brackish stream which traverses the great plain common to the **Rāmuz** and **Ahwāz** Districts of 'Arabistān, forming a sometimes serious obstacle on the route between **Nāsiri** and **Rāmuz** Town. The Gūpāl consists at first merely of the surplus water of a canal which takes off from the right bank of the Rāmuz river at a point about 5 miles east of **Rāmuz** Town and waters the plain to the north-east of the town between it and the hills. At about 4 miles north of **Rāmuz** Town the overflow water of the canal is augmented by a brackish tributary which has its rise in the Gypsum Hills bounding the **Rāmuz** District on this side; the increased stream continues to flow north-westwards, keeping within a mile of the hills and parallel to them, until the mounds of Kūt-ash-Shaikh are passed, lying $1\frac{1}{2}$ or 2 miles to southward. Three or four miles further on the Gūpāl changes direction to the south-west, and so passes about 6 miles to the north-west of the village of **Mīrbacheh**. Near this it probably receives on the left bank two tributaries, *viz.*, the fresh stream which has its course a mile eastward of **Mīrbacheh** and the salt Muwailheh stream which is described in the article on **Rāmuz** District. About 9 miles after passing **Mīrbacheh** a salt stream from the north, called the Kindak كندك and having its source in the Gypsum Hills which enclose the plain on the north-east, falls into the Gūpāl on its right bank.

Eventually, about 12 miles west of **Mīrbacheh**, the Gūpāl intersects the usual route between **Nāsiri** and **Rāmuz**: there is some choice of crossing places. A barrage, partly of masonry, was constructed hereabouts in 1905 by the Shaikh of **Muhammareh**, and a canal was cut from the same to irrigate the lands of Banneh which lie a few miles to the south. The barrage can be used as a bridge by men, but not at present by animals; it is intended, however, to improve it. At this point in its course the water of the Gūpāl is salt, even after recent rain.

The banks, which in most places are perpendicular and of clay, rise about 20 feet above the level of the bed, and the distance between them varies from 20 to 70 yards. In summer the Gūpāl is probably almost dry; in winter it sometimes rises 15 or 20 feet and overflows the banks, and at that season it may be found either fordable or unfordable. When unfordable, yet without being much swollen, the actual stream is 10 to 15 yards in breadth and runs with a considerable volume and a decided current. Quicksands occur.

About 300 yards below the barrage the stream bends to the west, and 8 miles further on it is drawn off in a southerly direction in numerous small canals, some of which, being 3 feet, deep are difficult to cross. The

Gūpāl now ceases to exist, and the surplus water which is not absorbed by the cultivation spreads out to form the Shākheh marsh; it is said when in great excess, to travel far southward and flood miles of country to the north-east of Gharaibeh on the **Jarrāhi**. In March 1906 from a point 4 miles north of Gharaibeh more than 90° of the horizon, chiefly between north and east, was seen to be flooded in this manner.

Extent.—The Gwādar district includes not only the town and port of that name, but the whole of the country in Makrān which is subject to the Sultān of **'Omān**. It consists of the shores of East and West Gwādar Bays and of a sandy strip of flat country in which rise the hills of Jabal-i-Mahdi مهدي, Koh-i-Drām درام, and various low eminences further to the westward. At the foot of the Koh-i-Drām lies Gwādar-i-Nigwār نگور, the only cultivated locality.† The rest is known as Gwādar-i-Raik ريك *i.e.*, Gwādar Sands. The whole district covers an area of some 307 square miles.

**GWĀDAR*
گوادر
DISTRICT**

Limits.—Great divergence of opinion exists regarding the boundaries on every side except the south. Those given by Captain Ross, who was for several years Assistant Political Agent at Gwādar, are: north, Koh-i-Drām; east, Barambāb برمباب or Barambābād Kaur آباد کور ; west, Cape Pīshukān پيشکان . These appear to be the limits generally recognised by the townspeople of Gwādar. Some Balūchi subjects of the 'Omān Sultanate regard the watershed of the Talār تلار range, called Sāiji صائجي, in Dasht دشت from the Talār Pass to Kandāsōl کندسول as the northern boundary; a line drawn south from the Talār Pass to near Sarchib سرچپ, eventually terminating at the mouth of the Kārwāt کاروات torrent, as the eastern limit; and a line running south through Koh Tungi کوه تنگي near Gabd گبد to Ispar Kōh اسپر کوه, a hillock east of Ganz گنز, as the frontier on the west. Subjects of the Khān of Kalāt کلات give the Drām hill as the northern, the Drabbailo دربيلو stream as the eastern, and the Ānkārau آنکارو stream as the western boundary; the tract from the mouth of the Pālairi پاليري to Pīshukān is regarded by them as an isolated locality also belonging to the Sultanate of 'Omān. The bulk of local opinion seems to incline to

---

* The greater part of the materials for this and following article has been supplied by the courtesy of Mr. R. Hughes-Buller, I.C.S., editor of the Imperial Gazetteer of Balūchistān. The map for Gwādar district is sheet No. 16 N. E. of the North-Western Frontier series of the Survey of India: the Chart is No. 2383—38. The latter contains a view of the coast hills.

† Nigwar is the cultivated skirt of a hill.

this view. At Pīshukān again the boundary is disputed, the people of that place claiming up to Ispar Kōh, while those of Ganz and Jīnwri جينزري consider their limit to be the western margin of Dagāro Tal دگارو تل about 2 miles west of Pīshukān.

The coast line, which extends some 40 miles in a direct line, is low and consists of sand-dunes. The most conspicuous headlands are Sur سر or Jabal Sur, the north-east point of Gwādar East Bay; Gwādar Head, a hammer-headed rocky promontory 7 miles in length east and west and about a mile wide; and Rās Pīshukān, a narrow rocky spit.

Physical features.—The Drām or Drāmb hills form part of the Makrān coast range. Owing to their inaccessibility they have long formed an asylum for the people of southern Makrān from Persian and other incursions. It was here also that the Kulānchis كلانچي took refuge from Mīr 'Abdullah Khān between 1715-16 and 1730-31. The highest peaks are Bārn بارن (3,152 feet), Drām (3,125) and Mukh مکه (3,200). The Drām range is much frequented by the nomads of Gwādari-i-Nigwar. Chish چش and Kahūr کهور trees are abundant and the water-supply is fairly plentiful. Jabal-i-Mahdi, so called from an original settlement of the Mahdizais مهدي زي, an offshoot of the Sangur سنگر tribe, on its skirts, is a mass of white clay hills of somewhat remarkable outline, and with perpendicular cliffs on the south side; a gap 2 miles in width divides it from the Sur headland. The Kōh-i-Bātil باطل forms part of the Gwādar Head: it is an irregular mass of cliffs of a dark brown colour and about 480 feet high overlooking **Gwādar** Town. Five miles east of **Gwādar** Town there is a small mud volcano * near the beach, and one of the features of the harbour itself is another, which after heavy weather becomes active and emits poisonous gases, sometimes destroying thousands of fish.

The area contains no rivers; the Karwāt, Barambāb or Barambābād, Sur, and Ānkārau are the most important of the hill torrents. All rise in the Drām hills with the exception of the Ānkārau, which rises further north in the southern slopes of the Sāiji ridge and falls into the sea through a large salt-water creek to the west of **Gwādar** Town.

Climate and water supply.—The climate is hot throughout the year, but the proximity of the coast and the consequent sea-breezes render the heat less oppressive than in the Kaich کیچ valley. The European Telegraph officials formerly stationed at **Gwādar** Town found the place

---

* See article Persian **Makrān**, physical characteristics, footnote.

so unhealthy that it had to be abandoned; the stench arising from the sea, apparently caused by mud-volcanoes, is at times intolerable. More recently some improvement has taken place, but malaria is always prevalent and strangers are generally attacked.

The water supply everywhere is brackish. In **Gwādar** Town water is obtained from shallow wells and in Gwādar-i-Nigwar from deep ones; in the latter place it is not only brackish but fetid. The rainfall is very scanty and sometimes none occurs for several consecutive years: most is received in winter.

Plants and animals.—There is nothing distinctive about the flora, which is scanty in the extreme. Tamarisk is found in the beds of the torrents and Chish, Chigird چگرد and Kahūr in the plains, except in Gwādar-i-Raik, where there are no trees. Gwādar-i-Nigwar possesses a few date-groves. The hills contain mountain sheep and Sind ibex, which are celebrated for their size. The sea swarms with fish, and fishing is carried on not only in the Gwādar Bays and at Pishukān but also at Sur and off the mouth of the Bārambāb.

Population.—The total population of the Gwādar district, including Gwādar-i-Nigwar and Pishukān, was about 1,030 families or 5,150 persons in 1903. With the exception of the **Gwādar** Town, the headquarters of the administration, and Pishukān there are no permanent villages. Of the few temporary hamlets in Gwādar-i-Nigwar, Khiya Qalāt کهیا قلات alone is important, as the headquarters of the Nigwar headman. The groups inhabiting Nigwar in 1903 were Kalmatis, کلمتی, 20 families; Mahdizais, 30 families; Zainūzais زینوزی (a section of the Kulanch کلانچ Bands بند) 10 families; Raikānis ریکانی or indigenous **Balūchis**, 50 families; and 10 families of servile origin.

Gwādar Town contains about 870 families or 4,350 persons, and Pishukān about 40 families or 200 persons. The majority of these are Maids مید, who number some 3,700 persons: others are Koras کورا or sailors, 80 families; Hindus, 40 families; **Khōjahs** or Lūtiyahs لوتیا, 50 families. The Arab Wāli's following and escort of sepoys number about 30. The Nigwar Balūch are Zikris ذکری; the **Khōjahs** are followers of the Āgha Khān; the Arabs are Ibādhīyah; and the Maids and Koras are Sunni Muhammadans. The occupation of most of the population is fishing; the **Balūchis** are engaged in flock-owning, cultivation and transport, and the **Khōjahs** and Hindus in trade.

Agriculture.—Cultivation is confined to Gwādar-i-Nigwar; its extent is insignificant and as a means of livelihood it is precarious. Large tracts of arable land are, however, available for cultivation. The whole of the land is dry-crop and dependent on floods caught by embankments. The cultivators generally combine flock-owning with agriculture.

The principal crops are jowari, cotton, and Māsh. A little wheat, barley, Parmash, Arzun and some melons and dates are also grown. In Nigwar there are about 200 camels, 100 cattle and 1,000 sheep and goats; there are almost no donkeys.

Manufactures.—Salt is manufactured in pans out of salt water drawn from wells on the shore. It was untaxed until 1903, when the Arab authorities proposed to take one-twentieth of the produce as revenue. The salt is used for local consumption and for fish-curing.

Communications.—The main route from Gwādar to Turbat تربت traverses the south-east of the area. An alternative route leads northward to the Ānkārau river and, crossing the Drām, joins the first route at the Talār Pass. Several tracks lead westward to Persian **Makrān**, the principal one following the telegraph line *via* Gabd and Drābol درابول to Bāhu باهو and another going to the same place *via* Suntsar سنتسر and the Dasht. Transport animals are chiefly camels, but there are a few mules and donkeys.

Administration.—The country is administered by an Arab deputy of the Sultān of **'Omān**, known as the Wāli, who lives in **Gwādar** Town and is supported by an Arab garrison of 20 footmen. A sub-governor, a Maid by origin, lives at Pīshukān. Civil cases are referred to a local Qādhi, whose decision must be confirmed by the Wāli. The interests of the British subjects, *i.e.*, the Hindus and the **Khōjahs**, are looked after by a resident Native Assistant to the Director of Persian Gulf Telegraphs, the Director deciding any civil or criminal cases which may occur among them. The Wāli is helped by the Nigwar headman in all cases relating to the people of that place, and by the Kauhdas كوهداس or headmen of the Maids and the Koras in cases relating to the latter. In return for his services the Nigwar headman is given the Dahyak دهيك or tithes and the grazing-tax of Nigwar. The Kauhdas of the Maids and the Koras get four dollars per annum as an allowance. The only revenue realized by the Arab authorities is derived from customs duties, levied on goods entering or leaving the port, at the rate of 5 per cent. *ad valorem*; from octroi on goods imported into **Gwadār** Town; and from a tithe on fresh fish.

The customs revenue of Gwādar has undergone various vicissitudes since it ceased to be farmed and was brought under direct management in 1903; it is understood that the gross collections are now about $37,000 a year, while the net income is about $28,000.

GWĀDAR* گوادر **TOWN**

Capital of **Gwādar** District and the principal place on the Makrān coast.

Gwādar is a town with an open roadstead, standing on a sandy isthmus to the northward of Gwādar Head about 310 miles east of Karāchi. On either side of the isthmus are bays, both of which are shallow. Large steamers cannot approach near the shore and landing has to be effected in country boats. The population numbered about 4,350 persons in 1903: the details of its composition are given in the article on **Gwādar** District. Most of the dwellings are mat-huts: but round a square fort with a high tower garrisoned by Arab 'Askaris of the Sultān of **'Omān** there are clustered a number of mud and stone houses, among which the **Khōjah** mosque is conspicuous. There are a few date and banyan trees, and fair water is obtainable by digging about 12 feet. The climate of Gwādar town is unhealthy; and an intermittent fever, attended by headache, want of appetite and violent retching, is prevalent, especially when the wind is in the south-west. †

The value of the trade, which is carried on chiefly by Hindus and **Khōjahs**, was estimated in 1903 at 5½ lakhs of rupees exports and 2 lakhs imports. Exports are ghi, wool, goats' hair, hides, cotton, salt fish, fins, dates, Pish-leaves and mats; imports are cotton piece-goods, silk, sugar, rice, jowari, iron, and kerosine. Some coarse cloth is woven and Pish mats are made. Trade with the interior is carried on by Balūch caravans. There are 5 Hindu and 10 Muhammadan Indian houses of business under British protection. Dues are levied both on imports and exports, generally at 5 per cent. *ad valorem*, and a tithe is taken of all fresh fish landed in the port. The number of large native craft (1905) belonging to the place is 23; there are also 50 smaller fishing boats, 6 lighters and 400 fishing Horis. The sea-going vessels of this port run to **Basrah, Masqat,** Karāchi, Bombay and the Malabar coast. The Gaz or cubit of Gwādar is very nearly equal to 2 feet.

---

* The map and chart are the same as for **Gwādar** District *q. v.* The chart contains a view of Gwādar Head.

† The climate of Gwādar is described in the Foreign Proceedings of the Government of India for February 1880.

Formerly Gwādar was the chief port of Makrān and the trade from Persian as well as British Makrān gravitated to it, but since the construction of the bridle-path from Pasni پسنی to Turbat and Panjgūr پنجگور, nearly the whole trade of Makrān has found its way to Pasni, which is fast increasing at the expense of Gwādar.

Gwādar is a fortnightly port of call of the British India Steam Navigation Company's steamers. There is a combined post and telegraph office, located in a building belonging to the Indo-European Telegraph Department at the north-east side of the town, near which is the British political bungalow.

The authority of the Sultan of **'Omān** is repressented by a Wāli and 20 'Askaris.

GWATAR* گوتر

Gwatar Bay is a great indentation in the **Makrān** coast line at the point where Persian territory ends and Kalāt territory begins : the bay is about equally divided between the Persian and British spheres of influence. At the entrance the width is 19 miles and within it is somewhat less : the depth inwards is about 11 miles and the whole area of the bay is entirely open to the south : the bottom is of mud, very flat and even. The soundings, which are 6 fathoms in the entrance, begin to diminish at half way towards the foot of the bay, and thereafter they shoal regularly to the low swampy coast which forms its northern shore ; the land on the east and west sides of the bay is rocky and hilly, and on the west side it rises to a tableland from 300 to 400 feet in height.

With the eastern half of the bay, which lies in Balūchistān, we are not concerned : the chief feature of the remainder is the Dashtyāri Chīl دشتیاري چیل, a river, which, coming down from Bāhu, the capital of the Bāhu district, and passing 4 miles to the east of Mīr Bāzār, the capital of the Dashtyāri district, enters the bay at its north-western corner.

On the west coast of the bay, 3 miles south of the estuary of this river, is the village of Gwatar ; it consists of about 200 mat huts. There are two mosques built of mud. The inhabitants, who belong to the Maid tribe, number about 1,000 souls and are nearly all fishermen. There are 10 Hindu traders, unaccompanied by their families, and

---

* A plan of the bay is given as an inset in Chart No. 2383—38, *Maskat to Karachi*.

HABL 591

28 Khōjhas, both men and women; these are all British subjects. Shipping comprises 4 seagoing boats, called Safri Bōjis سفري برجي, of about 75 tons burden each and carrying crews of 8 to 20 men; also 22 fishermen's boats called Gazdānis گزداني of 10 to 20 tons burden, and 4 smaller boats called Yakdārs يكدار.

The trade of Gwatar, which is one of the three principal ports of Persian **Makrān**, formerly nearly equalled that of **Chabbār**; but it is at present hampered by disturbances in the interior, and the value of the annual exports does not now exceed Rs. 50,000, nor that of the annual imports Rs. 30,000. The Persian Imperial Customs Department is represented here by a Mudīr assisted by three **Balūchi** guards.

Gwatar is in the district of the Bāhu chief.

HABĪB (BANI)* بني حبيب

In the 'Omān Sultanate two contiguous villages, known as 'Ain and 'Aqar, situated in Wādi Bani Habīb in Jabal **Akhdhar**, about 16 miles north-north-west of Tanūf. The elevation above the sea is about 6,200 feet. The place consists altogether of about 40 houses of the Āl Bū Shāmis section of the **Na'īm** tribe. The dwellings are small and stand about half-way down one slope of the Wādi. Both sides of the valley are laid out in terraces and planted with pomegranates, figs, peaches, apricots, walnuts, and sweet limes. A little wheat and barley is grown, and the hills are covered with vines. There are about 15 camels, 15 donkeys, 20 cattle and 200 sheep and goats.

HABL حبل

An irregularly shaped and extensive tract of desert country in the Sanjāq of **Hasa**: its position may be approximately defined by saying that its centre lies about 70 miles inland, in a west-south-westerly direction, from the coast town of **Qatīf**.

Boundaries.—Habl is described as somewhat resembling in outline a smoker's pipe, with the stem running from north-north-east to south-

---

* For a view of this place see page 60.

south-west and the bowl, which is at the south end, turned to the west; still observing the terms of this metaphor we may say that stem and bowl combined are 80 miles in length, while the stem is about 15 miles in diameter and the bowl has a depth (from west to east) of 50 and a diameter (from north to south) of 30 miles. On the north the Habl tract may be regarded as bounded by **Sanfān-al-Hanna**,—which however some authorities would include in it ;—and from Jabal Labtalah at the southern apex of **Sanfān-al-Hanna**, the boundary between Habl on the east and Wādi-al-**Miyāh** on the west runs direct to Jabal Qadām. At this last point the boundary of Habl turns west and runs along the southern end of Wādi-al-**Miyāh** to the Taff hills which it follows southwards to Naslatain-al-Farha, one of the spurs of that system; it then goes eastwards, defining the extent of Habl to the south and separating it, between Naslatain-al-Farha and Jabal Mathlūth, from the **Taff** plain tract, and, between Jabal Mathlūth and Jabal Dām, from the tract of Jau-as-**Sa'adān**. At Jabal Dām the line takes a northerly direction and becomes the eastern border of Habl, the adjoining tract on this side being **Biyādh** until the southern end of Jau **Shamīn** is reached; to exclude that district the line turns westwards for some miles and then resumes its northerly course which finally ends at the point of junction of the regions of Habl, **Sanfān-al-Hanna**, **Radāif** and Jau **Shamīn**, that is at the well of Hajrah. It should be noted that some Bedouins would include the south-western part of Habl, which lies beyond Jabal Qadām, in Wādi-at-**Miyāh**; but this view does not appear to command general acceptance.

Physical characteristics and divisions.—Habl is described as an expanse of dark-coloured sand in which mounds alternate with low valleys; the hollows are full of the tree called Markh and the shrub known as Ghadha, besides which they produce 'Arfaj and Rimth bushes and Nasi, Subat and Thamām grass. Wells however are few and far between, and they are much deeper than those of **Jauf**, a tract which Habl in other respects resembles. In the extreme west of the tract, immediately before the Taff hills are reached, is a bare stretch of heavy sand styled Jau-al-Ghānam جر الغانم ; and near the centre of the tract is a large salin depression commonly known as Khor خور, of which the position is more exactly fixed by the wells that it contains, viz., Umm-al-Qāh and Himārah. Two hills in the district are Ghumīs غميس , 10 miles north of Jabal Mathlūth, and Qabūrah قبورة which lies 17 miles westwards of the northern extremity of Jabal Dām.

HABL

Wells.—The principal wells in Habl are these :—

Name.	Position.	Remarks
Abwāb ابواب	Near the south-west corner of Habl, about 30 miles west of Jabal Dām, nearly equidistant from Jabal Mathlūth and Naslataia-al-Farha and a little to the north of a line joining them.	...
Alaimīyah عليميه	Near the north end of Habl, 5 miles west of Jabal Labtalah near its southern end.	...
Ariq عرق	In the middle of the broadest part of the district, 9 miles south by west of Jabal Qadām.	...
Haba-i حبئي	Near the trijunction point of the Habl, Jau Shamīn and Biyādh tracts.	...
Habaiyah حبيه	Near the east border of Habl and about 10 miles west of the Hūshūm area in Biyādh.	...
Hafairah حفيره	On the southern boundary of Habl, 8 miles east of Jabal Mathlūth.	...
Himārah حماره	8 miles south-east of Jabal Qadām.	This is one of the two wells situated in the depression called Khor. The water is barely drinkable.
Mughar المغر	13 miles north of Jabal Qadām close to the edge of Jau Shamīn.	...
Musallakh مسلخ	At the north end of Habl at the eastern foot of Jabal Labtalah.	...
Qāh (Khor Umm-al-) خور ام القاح	In a line between Habaiyah and Himārah and 8 miles from each of them.	A well in the Khor tract yielding water which is almost undrinkable.

2 Q

Name.	Position.	Remarks.
Radha ردها	Just within Habl at its north end, being situated 5 miles south of the Hajrah wells where the Habl, Sanfān-al-Hanna, Radāif and Jau Shamīn districts all meet.	The water of this well is said to be good.
Rubatah ('Aqalat) عقلة ربطة	On the eastern border of Habl in a line between Haba-i and Habaiyah and 6 miles from either.	...
Shafīyah شفيه	12 miles west by south of 'Ariq.	...
Tulah طوله	2 miles west of Jabal Dām.	This well is 12⅓ fathoms deep; its water is the best in Habl.

Inhabitants.—Habl north of the Habaiyah well belongs to the **Bani Khālid**; the southern half is in the country of the **'Ajmān**. When however, as at present, the two tribes are on good terms, they wander without let or hindrance each in the domains of the other.

HABŪS
حبوس

Singular Habsi حبسي. A tribe of Yamani race, in politics Hināwi and in religion Ibādhi; they inhabit the western part of the **Sharqīyah** district of the **'Omān** Sultanate known as Baldān-al-Habūs, possess the villages of Wāfi and Mutaili' in Wādi **'Andām**, and are found at **Manah** in **'Omān** Proper and in Wādi **Mi'aidin**.

Their principal divisions are:—

Section.	Fighting strength.	Habitat.	Remarks.
'Abdu ('Ayāl) عيال عبدر	100	**Manah**.	Nil.
'Asīrah عاسيرة	100	**Sharqīyah** villages, especially **Mudhaibi**.	Do.

HABŪS

Section.	Fighting strength.	Habitat.	Remarks.
Dhanain (Yāl) يال ضنين	200	Sharqīyah villages, especially Rôdhah in Wādi Samad.	Nil.
Ghanānimah غنانمه	200	Sharqīyah villages.	Do.
Ghasāsimah غساسمه	100	Do.	Do.
Haban (Aulād) اولاد حبن	100	Mudhaibi.	Do.
Jawābir جوابر	200	Do.	Do.
Mahrah ('Ayāl) عيال مهرة	160	Mudhaibi and Raddah.	Do.
Maqādamah مقادمه	30	Sharqīyah villages, especially Lizq.	Do.
Nājiyah ناجيه	100	Sharqīyah villages, especially Qufaifah.	Do.
Sa'īd (Bani Bū) بني بو سعيد	60	Qābil Bani Bū Sa'īd.	Do.
Sawālim سوالم	140	Qufaifah.	Do.
Shabīb (Yāl) يال شبيب	80	Sharqīyah villages, especially 'Ainain and Lizq.	Do.
Shamātarah شماطره	80	Various villages in Sharqīyah.	Do.
Thāni (Bani) بني ثاني	100	...	This section are Bedouins: they possess about 60 camels, 30 donkeys, 50 cattle and 2,000 sheep and goats.

2 Q 2

The chief villages and towns inhabited by the **Habūs** may be ascertained by reference to the articles on the **Sharqīyah** district and **Wādi Samad**. There is no reliable estimate of their number but it may be placed provisionally at 7,000 souls.

The Habūs are a wild, uncivilised tribe, less wealthy and important than their neighbours, the **Hirth** and **Hajrīyīn**: such influence as they possess depends on their numbers rather than on their character. They are principally engaged in date cultivation, but are also camel-owners. They have now many rifles of various cheap kinds (1905) and maintain an offensive and defensive alliance with the **Hirth**. The small Warūd tribe is tributary to the Habūs. The principal Shaikhs of the Habūs (1905) are Sālim-bin-Hamaid, Ghanānami, and Mas'ūd-bin-Rāshid, Jābiri. **Mudhaibi** is the political headquarters of the tribe, but Rōdhah in Wādi **Samad** is their largest settlement.

HADD (I)
الحد

A village in the Sultanate of **'Omān**, situated at the foot of Khor-al-Hajar, and about one mile inland in a south-westerly direction from Rās-al-Hadd, the low sandy point which marks the entrance of the Gulf of **'Omān** and is almost the easternmost point in Arabia. Hadd is 16 miles east by south of **Sūr** and may be reckoned as belonging to the coast of the Eastern **Hajar** District.

The village stands in a sandy plain and consists of over 200 habitations, some of which are of mud but most of date branches: it boasts a stone fort, three or four round towers, and some date trees. The water-supply is fairly good but not very abundant. The inhabitants of Hadd belong to the Muwālikh tribe; they live by fishing and possess 8 Badans and 15 small boats; about 30 sheep and goats constitute the whole of their livestock. The cod and other rock-fish here are of the largest size, sometimes almost gigantic.

The authority of the Sultān of **'Omān** at Hadd is marked by the presence of a detachment of 15 'Askaris, commanded by a Jama'dār under the orders of the Wāli of **Sūr**; and for purposes of revenue and taxation Hadd is treated as subordinate to **Sūr**.

HADD (II)
الحد

A town on the south-eastern point of **Muharraq** Island in **Bahrain**. It covers the narrow promontory for a distance of about ¾ of a mile, and at high tide is only connected with **Muharraq** Island by a neck of land

400 yards wide. There are a number of well-built masonry houses, perhaps 200, and a very much greater number of mud and stone houses and mat huts, perhaps 700 of each. The water supply is from wells in a date grove called Zimmah ½ a mile to the north. The people are Sunnis, chiefly **Sādah** (150 houses) and Āl Bin-'**Ali** and Āl Bū Falāsah (Bani **Yās**) (200 houses), after each of whom a quarter is named: there are also 20 houses of **Hūwalah,** 10 of Āl Bū **Kuwārah,** 10 of **Sūdān,** 10 of **Manāna'ah** and 1 or 2 of Āl **Musallam,** and a fourth division of the town is called Farīq-al-Musallam. The total population is estimated at 8,000 souls. Shops only number 5 or 6. Next to **Muharraq** Town this is the greatest pearl diving place in **Bahrain,** and to it belong 167 pearl boats; vessels of all sorts are 3 Batīls, 42 Baqārahs, 183 Shū'ais and Sambūks and 21 Māshuwahs and jollyboats. There are 2 horses, 110 donkeys and 35 cattle. No dates are grown, there being no space for plantations, but the grove at Zimmah belongs to Hadd. The islet and spring of Abu Shāhīn lie 1 mile south-east of Hadd.

HADĪYAH
حديّه

A small hamlet on the west coast of **Qatar** about 3 miles north of Zubārah. It consists of about four houses, merely, of the **Kibísah** tribe.

HAFAR
حفر

An important halting place and group of wells in the **Bātin** section of Wādi-ar-**Rummah,** near the point where it leaves **Dahánah** and reaches **Dibdibah.** Hafar lies about 160 miles west-south-west of **Kuwait** Town, from which it is reached in from 3 to 5 stages.

The wells of Hafar are about 40 in number, but at the present time only 11 are "alive," that is to say, yield water. They are scattered in the bed of the **Bātin,** which here forms a circular plain about 3 miles in diameter, at intervals of 100 yards to ¼ of a mile apart; each well is in the centre of a mound, about 10 feet high, which has been formed by the spoil removed from it. The wells are lined with rough stone masonry and are about 6 feet across at the top; their average depth is about 150 feet to water, but if left undisturbed for a time the level rises by about 30 feet. The water they contain is almost tepid, and in the chilly air of morning vapour can be seen rising from their mouths. South by east from the wells, between them and the right bank of the **Bātin,** is a long, low, sandy hill.

No firewood is available in the immediate vicinity and the only fuel at hand is camel dung.

The **Mutair, Dhafīr** and various tribes of **Kuwait** territory make some use of these wells, and they would be more frequented if they were of a less inconvenient depth. Hafar is one of the recognised stages on the route to **Qasīm** *via* the **Bātin** from **Kuwait** Town and **Basrah**, and the place marks approximately the frontier on this side between **Kuwait** and Jabal **Shammar**; at times, in the course of the recent wars, it has been held by the Shaikh and at times by the Amīr.

At Hafar two hollows join the **Bātin**, one apparently coming from due north and the other from due south; the former is called Falaij-ash-Shamālīyah فليج الشمالية and leads to a line of wells styled Atwāl-adh-Dhafīr اطوال الضفير running northwards, of which the first is Dalaimīyeh دليمية ; the other hollow, named Falaij-al-Janūbīyah فليج الجنوبية, conducts similarly to a line of wells having a southerly direction and known as Atwāl-al-Mutair of which the first is Sāfah صافه in **Summān**: the wells of each of these series are said to lie from 2 to 3 days' march apart.

HAFFĀR
حفار

The true Haffār is a tract on the right bank of the **Kārūn** river beginning about 7 miles above **Muhammareh** Town and ending about 1 mile above the point of divergence of the **Kārūn** and **Bahmanshīr**; it contains the riverside villages of Ramsān, Askaleh, Bū Mahsin, Bū Charīm, Muqāmiseh and Umm-at-Talūl. From this reach the name has been transferred, possibly by the native pilots of European vessels, to a lower one; and it is now commonly but erroneously applied by geographers to the last two or three miles of the course of the **Kārūn**, those namely between the point where the **Bahmanshīr** leaves it and the place where it enters the Shatt-al-'**Arab**. Such an application of the term is in no way sanctioned by local usage; and it has been particularly ascertained that residents of **Muhammareh** Town, though they sometimes call the **Kārūn** where it flows past their walls the "Bahmanshīr," thus giving rise to confusion on a different point, never speak of it as the "Haffār". The villages of the true Haffār are described in the article on **Muhammareh** District and those of the so-called Haffār in the articles on **Muhammareh** District and '**Abbādān** island.

HAI QADHA

A division of the Muntafik Sanjāq of the Basrah Wilāyat in Turkish 'Irāq.

Position and boundaries.—The Qadha of Hai is situated on both sides of the Shatt-al-**Gharāf**, the river which connects the **Tigris** transversely with the **Euphrates**, in the upper half of its course. The district is apparently enclosed between the Qadha of **Kūt-al-Amārah** on the north, that of '**Amārah** on the east, that of **Shatrat-al-Muntafik** on the south and that of **Dīwānīyah** on the west.

Topography and inhabitants.—Besides the town of **Hai** and the villages of Qal'at **Sikar** and Mhairijah, the two first of which are the subjects of separate articles while the last is noticed in the article on the Shatt-al-**Gharāf**, there are no places of importance in the Qadha. The only conspicuous natural feature is the Shatt-al-**Gharāf**. The dominant tribes are the **Muntafik** in the southern and the Bani **Rabī'ah** in the northern part of the district; and the tribe of Bani Hāshim are found in the neighbourhood of Qal'at **Sikar**.

Population.—The total fixed population is estimated at 44,000 souls, of whom at least 42,000 are Shī'ah Arabs, while about 1,500 are Sunnis, and there are perhaps 500 Jews. The last two classes are not found in any number outside the town of **Hai**.

Resources.—The district is dry and healthy, and the crops and livestock are such as can flourish without a superfluity of moisture. The staples of production and trade are wheat, barley, millet, maize, sesame, dates, ghi, wool, skins and hides.

Administration.—The Qadha of Hai is subdivided into 3 Nāhiyahs, namely the Markaz Nāhiyah of Hai, that of Qal'at Sikar, and that of Mhairijah; the seats of the Mudīrs of the last two are the villages similarly named.

HAI TOWN or KŪT-AL-HAI

A town situated on the left bank of the Shatt-al-**Gharāf** about 30 miles from its head opposite **Kūt-al-Amārah**: it is the chief place in the Qadha of the same name in Turkish '**Irāq**. About two-thirds of the town consists of brick houses and the rest of huts. The population is 4,000 souls, of whom three-fourths are Shī'ahs; but there is a considerable Jewish community, which maintains a Jewish school, besides about 100 households of Faili **Kurds**. The surrounding Arabs belong to the Sarāi section of the Bani **Rabī'ah** tribe. The neighbourhood of Hai produces wheat, barley, millet, maize, sesame and some dates; the export trade is chiefly in these and in pastoral produce such as ghi, wool, skins and hides. There is a bazaar of about 300 shops. Hai is the seat of a Qāim-Maqām, and possesses a branch of the Public Debt Office, a customs house, telegraph and post offices and several Khāns and public baths. A harbour master is common to this place and **Shatrat-al-Muntafik** Town. The telegraphic connection is with **Kūt-al-Amārah**. The town is constituted as a municipality. The garrison ordinarily consists of 1 squadron of cavalry and a battalion of infantry, for whom there are barracks and a military hospital: a captain and five lieutenants of the Radīf also are posted here, and about 100 reservists belong to this centre, which does not however appear in the general scheme of distribution of the Radīf. The climate of Hai is dry and healthy.

HĀIL
حائل

The capital of the Jabal **Shammar** province of Central Arabia; it is situated about 400 miles west-south-west of **Basrah**, 350 miles north-west by west of **Riyādh**, 450 miles north-north-east of Makkah and 500 miles south-east of Jerusalem; its elevation above the sea is 3,530 feet. *

Site and surroundings.—Hāil lies in the plain called Batn on the open valley of Wādi Da'aijān, and is overlooked by the cliffs of Jabal **Aja**, which rise 1,000 feet high about 3 miles to the westward. The town is enclosed on its north and east sides by Jabal Samra سمرا, a double hill of dark-coloured plutonic basalt; Umm Arkab ام اركب the eastern eminence, with its summit 3,990 feet above the sea, is the higher of the two, and between it and its neighbour passes Wādi Da'aijān on its way beyond Hāil to the open desert. A basaltic ridge, 300 feet high at the loftiest part, connects Jabal **Aja** with Jabal Samra, screening Hāil from view from the northward; this ridge is crossed by a pass with an elevation of about 60 feet. Hāil, though as a whole unwalled, is a town, not an oasis; but on the south and west date palms are so numerous as largely to conceal the houses.

Quarters and streets.—In shape the town is roughly a parallelogram with one of its longer sides upon Wādi Da'aijān, which passes it upon the

---

* As deduced by Lieut. F. Fraser Hunter from Huber's observations (see footnote to article Jabal **Shammar**).

north.* The quarters of the town, roughly in order from west to east, are Samāh سماح, Barzān برزان, Sabhān سبهان, 'Abid عبد, Lubdah لبدة, Maghīthah مغيثه, 'Atīq عتيق, Jabārah جبارة, Jarād جراد, Qaraishi قريشي, Rakhīs رخيص, Faraikh فريخ, Dhuba'ān ضبعان, Ziqidi زقدي, and Wasaitah وسيطه; and there are to the east two detached quarters or villages named Kharaimi خريمي and Suwaiflah سويفله. Barzān, Lubdah and Maghīthah are the largest of the wards. Barzān contains the Qasr or fortified palace of the Amir of Jabal **Shammar**; Lubdah contains the principal bazaar. Wasaitah is a small quarter, with a large date plantation; it is situated opposite to the rest of the town, on the further side of Wadi Da'aijān and under the northern portion of Jabal Samra. For some time about 1878 Wasaitah remained uninhabited, having been depopulated by an epidemic of cholera, probably that of 1871: it is adjoined by the common cemetery of Hāil. At Kharaimi is a large date plantation, watered by springs, which is the property of the Amīr. Suwaiflah is about 2 miles northeast from the main body of the town, and beyond Jabal Samra; it also was devastated by the epidemic which temporarily ruined Wasaitah and is still deserted. The main place of the town is the Mis-hab مسحب, 250 yards long by 25 broad, on one side of which is the Amīr's Qasr, while opposite is a row of rooms, called Makhāzin مخازن, where the guests of the Amir are lodged. At the south end of the Makhāzin is an enclosure set apart for female stall-keepers who deal in ornaments, perfumes, female attire, dates and vegetables; and immediately beyond this enclosure is the head of the main bazaar, locally called Mabī' مبيع, which is a continuation of the Mis-hab 200 yards in length and contains about 140 shops. These shops are the property of the Amīr and are rented from him. The chief mosque of Hāil stands at the south end of the Mis-hab.

Buildings.—The houses of Hāil have often an upper storey and are built of small sun-dried bricks and date or Ithl timber; the coffee rooms and the guests' quarters pertaining to them are usually in an adjoining quadrangle with a separate entrance. Rooms, which are ordinarily few but large and commodious, are lighted only by the door-ways and by unglazed openings in the walls just below the ceilings. The general view of the town is not imposing. The only large building is the Amīr's Qasr, built of clay and overlaid with white gypsum plaster; part of it rises to a height of 40 feet. Only the quarters containing the palace

* A plan of Hāil will be found in Palgrave (I. 139), a plan of part of the town adjoining the Qasr in Doughty (I. 587), and a plan of the environs in Doughty (I. 615). There is also an unfinished sketch plan at the end of Huber's *Journal de Voyage*.

and the main bazaar are enclosed, and the walls surrounding them are of no great height. The gates of the walled quarters are kept closed at night.

Population.—The size of Hāil is small in proportion to its political importance; it seems clear that the population does not exceed 3,000 souls. It is composed of agriculturists, tradesmen, men-at-arms and household slaves; the last are not numerous. The people are mainly **Shammar**, but among them are some natives of **Qasīm** besides Gallas and a few Persians. The typical Hāil townsman is of slender build. All classes and both sexes wear next their skins the Haqu, a plaited leather belt, and in this they resemble the Arabs of the desert. Food is universally served on the floor and, contrary to the practice of **Jauf-al-'Āmir** and other northern places, it is exposed for sale in open markets. The morals of Hāil are reputed lax. There are four ordinary schools.

Trade and industries.—The commerce of the town is small and its manufactures are few. The butchers' trade is considered degrading and the cook-shops in the bazaar are mostly kept by Persians. The shopkeepers are generally natives of **Najaf, Qasīm** or Madīnah. Cloth, calico, spices, metals and European goods are imported from **Basrah, Najaf** and Madīnah; corn from **Sūq-ash-Shuyūkh.** Artisans are not many; they belong to the smiths' caste and their implements are few and clumsy; nevertheless copperware, spear-heads, and horse-shoes are manufactured, wooden bowls are turned, and camel-saddles are built. There are a few house builders and gypsum plasterers. Women embroiderers in silk and metal-thread do a small business. The largest trading capital in Hāil probably does not exceed £300.

Supplies.—Ordinary supplies are obtainable. There are the ordinary livestock, also horses and riding camels, but home-grown dates are not very abundant and stocks are imported from **Qasīm**. Wood and grass are mostly collected by Qasīmi labourers, and the town has many wells of 10 to 15 fathoms' depth; but, with the exception of one sweet well of 15 fathoms belonging to the Samāh quarter, they are either bitter or saline.

General.—The present town of Hāil is probably of late foundation. A more ancient town is said to have existed to the east of modern Hāil and to have included Suwaiflah. Hāil has risen to importance chiefly as the permanent residence of the Amīrs of Jabal **Shammar**. When the fortunes of Ibn Rashīd were in the ascendant there was much going and coming of strangers and the Amīr entertained about 180 guests a day at an annual expense of about £1,500. Hāil in time past also derived much profit from the transit of Persian pilgrim caravans on their way to and from Makkah, but in recent years the route has been to a great extent in abeyance owing to the incessant wars and prevailing insecurity.

HĀIL (ABU)
ابو حيل

A sandy locality with date plantations, on the coast of Trucial 'Omān, on the boundary between the principalities of **Shārjah** and **Dibai**. It lies a short distance south-west of **Khān**, from which it is divided by the Khān creek, and is 2½ miles from **Shārjah** Town and 5 miles from the town of **Dibai**. In the date season it is occupied by people from both **Khān** and **Dibai**: at other times it is uninhabited.

HAIL-AL-GHĀF
هيل الغاف

A flourishing village of about 60 houses in the Sultanate of 'Omān on the western side of Wādi **Tāyīn** at a place, about 7 miles from the coast, where it widens before leaving the hills. There is an unfailing supply of water brought by a Falaj from the hills. The inhabitants are Āl Bū **Sa'īd**, Bani **Battāsh** and other tribes. There is extensive cultivation of dates and other crops, and olives and mangoes flourish. Livestock are 20 donkeys, 25 cattle and 300 sheep and goats. Hāil-al-Ghāf was founded early in the 19th century by Saiyid Khalfān, an Āl Bū Sa'īdi, who was a conspicuous Anglophile in his day. The land was purchased from the Bani **Battāsh**, who as late as 1884 still exercised a sort of protectorate over the place.

HAIYADH
حيض

A place in Wādi-al-**Hilti** in the Western **Hajar** district of the 'Omān Sultanate; it is situated upon the right bank about 3 miles above the exit of the valley from the hills. The village consists of only 30 houses of the Jahāwar and Shabūl tribes; but it contains a fort which is in the possession of the Sultān of **'Omān** and is the only point held by him in this part of Western **Hajar**: the garrison of the fort consists of 10 'Askaris. A few dates and a little grain are grown, and the livestock of the village comprises 6 camels, 10 donkeys, 5 cattle and 300 goats and sheep.

604 HAJAR

HAJAR
هَجَر

Also called, in plural form, Hujūr هُجُور. A remarkable hilly tract or range of the mountains in the Sultanate of **'Omān**, extending from **Shinās** on the north-west to **Sūr** on the south-east; it is nowhere far distant from the coast, and east of **Masqat** Town it closely adjoins the sea. Hajar in the aggregate forms one of the most extensive districts in the **'Omān** Sultanate; for, while its breadth varies from 20 to 50 miles, its length exceeds that of any other two districts together. According to native ideas the Hajar is all one; but for convenience we may divide it at Wādi **Samāil** (including that valley and its affluents in the eastern portion) and deal with it in two articles under the names of Eastern and Western **Hajar.**

HAJAR
هَجَر
and
KHATT HAJAR
خَطّ هَجَر

These are ancient names which have not entirely died out but have become somewhat indefinite in their application. The accepted view is that Hajar originally referred to the oasis of **Hasa** and that Khatt Hajar designated the coastal tract from Rās **Tanūrah** to Dōhat **Salwa** and therefore included the **Qatīf** Oasis, Barr-adh-**Dhahrān**, Barr-al-'**Oqair** and Barr-al-**Qārah**. It is said that the whole of this littoral was once thickly populated; but now, except the **Qatīf** Oasis, Khatt-al-Hajar is a desert. The name is sometimes given as Khatt Hajar-al-Bahrain; and this corroborates a hypothesis, founded partly on other facts, that the name **Bahrain** was once applied to a part of the mainland as well as to the archipelago which now bears it.

HAJAR (EASTERN)*
هَجَر

The article on the **Hajar** division of the **'Omān** Sultanate contains a general definition of the whole tract so named; we now proceed to describe in detail the eastern portion which we have arbitrarily separated from the rest.

Limits and extent.—The Eastern Hajar of **'Omān** extends about 120 miles from Wādi **Samāil** and its tributaries on the north-west to the Jabal **Khamīs** range on the south-east, both of which it includes. Its watershed, continuous with the watershed of Western **Hajar** to which it is linked by the Najd-al-Mughbārīyah, is 50 miles distant from the coast at the head of Wādi **Samāil** and thence runs at first almost due east to a point 40 miles south-south-west of **Masqat** Town: beyond this place its direction is from north-west to south-east and the distance between

---
* For authorities, maps and charts see first footnote to article **'Omān** Sultanate.

it and the coast diminishes, being ultimately reduced at its termination near **Sūr** to about 20 miles.

The disposition of the valleys and ridges of Eastern Hajar with reference to the main axis of the range is very imperfectly understood but it is probably less regular than in Western **Hajar**: Wādi **Tāyīn**, for instance, in its upper course runs parallel to the general direction of the range instead of at right angles to it, an eccentricity which has no counterpart in Western **Hajar**. Between **Daghmar** and **Sūr** the hills of Eastern Hajar fall directly into the sea, and beyond the aspect which they present seawards nothing is known of them in this part: where they are crossed by the route from **Sūr** to **Ja'alān** they have been partially surveyed.

Little is known, similarly, of the inland flank of Eastern Hajar except that it forms the boundary upon the north of the interior districts of **Ja'alān** and **Sharqīyah**. The uncertainty as to the position of the inland border of Eastern Hajar makes it impossible to estimate the whole breadth of the district with accuracy, but it probably varies from 30 to 40 miles.

The hills of Eastern Hajar are fairly constant in elevation from the north-west end, where they reach 5,250 feet at the head of Wādi **Tāyīn** and 6,300 feet inland of **Quryāt**, to the south-east as far as Jabal **Khadhar**: beyond this point they fall away to 2,845 feet in the Jabal **Khamīs** range behind **Sūr**.

Configuration and features.—The principal feature of the north-western and only explored part of Eastern Hajar is Wādi **Tāyīn**, which, running at first between two important ridges of the **Hajar** system, Jabal Baidha and Jabal Sauda, turns suddenly at right angles to burst through a remarkable cañon and debouch on the coast at **Daghmar**. Immediately to the north-west of Wādi **Tāyīn**, near the sea, is Wādi Bani **Battāsh**. In proceeding south-eastwards Wādi **Tāyīn** is followed, still on the seaward side of the hills, by a group of three valleys included under the common name of Wādi Bani **Jābir** (I): they are Wādi **Shāb**, Wādi **Tīwi** and Wādi **Hilam**, which reach the sea at Ghail-ash-Shāb, **Tīwi** and **Kalhāt** respectively. The only remaining valley of importance on this side of the range is Wādi **Falaij**, which has its mouth near **Sūr**, and is enclosed between the parallel ranges of **Khadhar** and **Khamīs**, the two easternmost members of the **Hajar** system and disposed at right angles to the main range.

As already remarked, the inward slopes of Eastern Hajar are practically unknown, but they are probably less abrupt than the outward face; on this inner side three Wādis, called **Mahram**, **'Andām** and **Samad**, run down, the last by **Samad** town, to the western end of the **Sharqīyah** district, Wadi **'Andām** (of which the other two are tributaries), eventually joining Wādi **Halfain**; while Wādi Bani **Khālid** descends south-eastwards to the **Ja'alān** plain.

The Eastern Hajar consists, so far as is known, of limestone; with reference to this point the geological Appendix may be consulted.

Topography.—The following is a list of the places on the coast of Eastern Hajar in their order from north-west to south-east:—

Name.	Position.	Houses and inhabitants.	Remarks.
Quryāt قريات	31 miles south-east of **Masqat** Town.	...	See article **Quryāt**.
Daghmar دغمر	Extends from 4 to 8 miles south-east of **Quryāt**.	...	See article **Daghmar**.
Dhibāb ضباب	16 miles south-east of **Quryāt**.	50 to 60 huts of Bani Jābir of the Ghazāl section.	The inhabitants are fishermen and also cultivate dates, melons and cotton. They have 25 small fishing boats, 500 date palms and 100 sheep and goats.
Bimah بمه	24 miles south-east of **Quryāt**.	100 houses, mostly stone and mud, of the Bani Ghadānah section of the Bani Jābir.	The people are fishermen and own date plantations in the hills; they have 30 fishing boats and 1,000 date palms, but very little ordinary cultivation. There are wells here of brackish water.
Fins فنس	Exactly midway between **Quryāt** and **Sūr**, 31 miles from either.	50 or 60 stone houses of the Bani Ghadānah section of the Bani Jābir.	Here are 30 donkeys, 30 cattle, 200 sheep and goats, some cultivation of grain and a little of dates.
Ghail-ash-Shāb غيل الشاب	25 miles north-west of **Sūr**.	...	See article Wādi **Shāb**.
Tīwi طيوي	23 miles north-west of **Sūr**.	...	See article **Tīwi**.

HAJAR (EASTERN) 607

Name.	Position.	Houses and inhabitants.	Remarks.
Haiwa حيوى	20 miles north-west of Sūr.	An anchorage merely, without houses or inhabitants.	Fine limestone is or used to be shipped from this place to India.
Kalhāt كلهات	12 miles north-west of Sūr.	...	See article Kalhāt.
Sūr سور	94 miles south-east of Masqat Town.	...	See article Sūr.
Hadd (I) الحد	16 miles east by south of Sūr.	...	See article Hadd (I). The place is really beyond the limits of Eastern Hajar, but it cannot be reckoned to any other district.

Names and descriptions of the principal inland places of Eastern Hajar will be found in the articles on Wādis **'Aqq, Dima, Falaij, Hilam, Bani Jābir (I), Khabbah,** Bani **Khālid, Mansah, Saijāni, Samāil, Shāb, Tāyīn** and **Tīwi,** and in those on Jabal **Khadhar** and Jabal **Khamīs;** a few not included in these are given in alphabetical order in the following table :—

Name.	Position.	Character.	Remarks.
Fita فت	On Wādi Manqāl منقال, which is between Kalhāt and Sūr, considerably nearer to the former, and several miles inland from the sea.	Fita is a sort of plain traversed by the Wādi mentioned; it contains a village about 2 miles from the right bank of the Wādi.	The village consists of 30 houses of the Farārijah section of the Bani Bū Hasan. There are 40 camels, 100 donkeys, 100 cattle, 1,000 sheep and goats and 200 date palms.
Jarda جردا	In the hills near the head of the Wādi-al-'Aqq tributary of Wādi Samāil.	60 houses of Nidābiyīn and others.	There are 20 camels, 30 donkeys, 35 cattle, 200 sheep and goats and 150 date palms.
Kabda كبد	In Wādi Manqāl a few miles inland from Kalhāt.	130 mud houses of the Sha'ībiyīn section of the Bani Jābir.	There are 350 date palms, 100 camels, 150 donkeys, 80 cattle and 600 sheep and goats.

To these should possibly be added Dūh and Saima, which are described in the article on 'Omān Proper.

Population.—The principal tribes of Eastern Hajar are the Bani **Ruwāhah,** Bani **Jābir, Nidābiyīn, Rahbiyīn** and **Siyābiyin** in Wādi **Samāil** and its tributaries; the Bani **Battāsh** and Bani **Jābir** in the central portion; the Mashārifah near the eastern end; and the **Rahbiyīn,** Bani **Battāsh** and Bani 'Arābah in Wādi **Tāyīn;** Sa'ādiyīn and **Hishm** also are found in Wādi Bani **Khālid** on the side next **Ja'alān.**

The following is an estimate of the settled population of the Eastern Hajar district:—

Wādi-al-'Aqq	1,500
Wādi Bani Battāsh	3,000
Wādi Dima	4,500
Wādi Falaij	500
Wādi Hilam (excluding Kalhāt)	2,100
Wādi Bani Jābir (I)	9,000
Wādi Khabbah	1,900
Jabal Khadhar	1,700
Wādi Bani Khālid	6,400
Wādi Mansah and its tributary Wādi Rak	3,900
Wādi Saijāni	850
Wādi Samāil and its tributary Wādi Dhaba'ūn	30,000
Wādi Shāb (excluding Ghail-ash-Shāb)	250
Wādi Tāyīn (excluding Daghmar)	8,600
Wādi Tīwi (excluding Tīwi)	2,200
Places on the coast (see 1st table in paragraph on Topography above)	20,900
Miscellaneous places (see 2nd table in paragraph on Topography above)	1,100
Total	98,400 souls

The Bedouins of the district are Bani Bū **Hasan, Hishm** and Aulād Kāsib: their number is uncertain.

Products and animals.—Our knowledge of Eastern Hajar as a whole is too incomplete to admit of a general account being given of its vegetable and animal products or agriculture. The facts that are known will be found in the articles on the particular valleys and places which have already been indicated.

Administration.—Except at **Quryāt** and **Sūr** upon the coast, the Sultān of 'Omān has at present no representatives and very little influence in Eastern Hajar: the whole interior of the district is virtually independent.

HAJAR* (KHOR-AL-) خور الحجر

An inlet on the coast of the 'Omān Sultanate, 2½ miles west of Rās-al-Hadd and about the same distance east of the entrance of Khor-al-Jarāmah. The entrance to Khor-al-Hajar is ¼ of a mile wide and lies between low cliffs; the inlet runs inland for ¾ of a mile in a south-south-easterly direction and then opens eastwards into a large shallow basin which extends for more than a mile to the east, almost reaching Hadd Town. The entrance is open to the north and its depth rapidly diminishes from 3½ to 1½ fathoms, while the inner basin is altogether dry at low-water spring-tides. It follows that Khor-al-Hajar is of little value even for the smallest vessels and is not used except by fishing-boats.

Disputes similar to those affecting Khar-al-Jarāmah occurred in regard to this inlet between 1877 and 1880.

HAJAR† (WESTERN) حجر

This is a division, arbitrarily formed to facilitate description, of the Hajar region of the 'Omān Sultanate.

Boundaries and extent.—The Western Hajar district reaches from Wādi-al-Qor on the north-west to Wādi Samāil on the south-east, and has thus a length of 160 miles approximately. Its watershed is roughly parallel to the Bātinah coast and runs at an average distance of 40 miles inland; the distance however is greater than this towards the extremities and less towards the centre where the sea-coast curves inwards slightly towards the mountains. The boundary of Western Hajar on the seaward side is the line along which its hills subside into the Bātinah plain at a distance, on the average, of some 15 miles from the sea. The boundary with Dhāhirah on the inland side is somewhat indefinite, the decline being more gradual than on the seaward face: the valleys on this side up to their heads are generally reckoned in the district of Dhāhirah; but the Hajar hills undoubtedly extend south-westward to the immediate neighbourhood of 'Ibri and Dhank Town. Including therefore, for the moment, in Hajar the slopes which are ordinarily considered a part of Dhāhirah, we may say that the Western Hajar has an average breadth of 40 to 50 miles.

Configuration and general characteristics.—The physical geography of Western Hajar appears to be simple and regular. Its axis runs

---

* Admiralty plan No. 2371—228 contains a delineation of this inlet on a large scale; also a view of the adjoining coast.

† For authorities, map and charts, see first footnote to article 'Omān Sultanate.

2 R

north-west and south-east and the valleys to which its slopes give birth run off at right angles on both sides, those on the north-east to **Bātinah** and those on the south-west to **Dhāhirah** and **'Omān** Proper. The highest portion of Western Hajar is a considerable block at the south-east end which is called Jabal **Akhdhar**; Jabal **Akhdhar** reaches an elevation of nearly 10,000 feet, but the remainder of the range to the north-west is considerably less and at the head of Wādi-al-**Jizi**, perhaps the lowest point, it is only 1,860 feet.

The chief valleys which run down from Western Hajar across **Bātinah** to the sea are, in order from east to west, as follow: Wādi **Tau**; Wādi **Lājāl**; Wādi **Ma'āwal**; Wādi Bani **Kharūs** (near the coast called Wādi-al-Qāsim) with its eastern affluent Wādi **Mistāl**; Wādi Bani **'Auf**; Wādi **Fara'** or **Rustāq**; Wādi Bani **Ghāfir** (in **Bātinah** styled Wādi-al-Hōqain) with its right bank tributary Wādi **Sahtan**; Wādi **Mabrah**; Wādi-al-**Hawāsinah** with its tributary from the west, Wādi Bani **'Umr**; Wādi **Shāfān**; Wādi **Sarrāmi**; Wādi **'Āhin**; Wādi-al-**Hilti**; Wādi-al-**Jizi**; Wādi Bani ' **Umr**-al-Gharbi; Wādi **Hatta**; and Wādi-al-**Qor**. There is also a Wādi called Faidh فيض in the neighbourhood of **Shinās** Town.

Proceeding next from west to east along the inland slopes of Western Hajar, we find that the range sends down Wādis **Dhank** and **Kabīr** to **Dhāhirah** and Wādis **Tanūf** and **Mi'aidin** to **'Omān** Proper.

The Western Hajar is a limestone range and its geological character is noticed in the Appendix on geology. The Jabal **Akhdhar** portion is fully described under its own name: the remainder is generally very peaked and sharp ridged, with some herbaceous but very little ligneous vegetation. Trees and plants include Samar, acacia arabica, rhamnus, screw-pine, oleander, calotropis, euphorbia, castor-oil plant, wild lavender, a kind of rush called Rasal رسل, used for mat-making, and a plant named Marannahah مرنّحه, bearing a fruit like a small bitter lime, of which the seeds, administered in food or drink, cause stupefaction. Birds are few in Western Hajar; ravine deer and foxes are among the commoner animals.

Villages and population.—The articles on the Wādis of Western Hajar, a list of which is given in the preceding paragraph, contain full information regarding the tribes who inhabit Western Hajar, their villages and their mode of life. To complete the topography of

Western Hajar we subjoin a table of places not situated in any of the better known valleys:—

Name.	Position.	House and inhabitants.	Remarks.
Buwah برة	Between Tau and Bidbid, below a pass of the same name on the side of it next Tau.	50 houses, mostly of mud and stone, of the Bani **Jābir**.	The inhabitants have 30 camels, 30 donkeys, 30 cattle and 2,000 sheep and goats.
Tuwaiyah طوية	3 miles west of **Nakhl** on the way to 'Awābi.	80 houses of mixed tribes, chiefly **Ya'āribah**.	The drainage of Tuwaiyah goes eastwards to Wadi **Ma'āwal**. Livestock are 20 camels, 40 donkeys, 50 cattle and 700 sheep and goats.

The following is an estimate of the settled population of Western Hajar:—

Wādi 'Āhin	3,000
Jabal Akhdhar (including upper villages of Wādi Mi'aidin)	3,500
Wādi Bani 'Auf	1,000
Wādi Fara'	25,000
Wādi Bani Ghāfir	5,000
Wādi Hatta (below but not including Hajarain)	500
Wādi-al-Hawāsinah (down to and including Ghaizain)	2,300
Wādi-al-Hilti	1,800
Wādi-al-Jizi	4,000
Wādi Bani Kharūs	6,400
Wādi-al-Qor (Aswad only)	400
Wādi Lājāl	400
Wādi Ma'āwal	12,000
Wādi Mabrah	1,700
Wādi Mistāl	1,500
Wādi Sahtan	700
Wādi Sarrāmi	5,500
Wādi Shāfān	4,500
Wādi Tau	1,500
Wādi Bani 'Umr	3,600
Wādi Bani 'Umr-al-Gharbi	800
Miscellaneous places (see preceding table)	650
TOTAL	85,750 souls.

There are some Bedouins also in Western Hajar belonging to the Bidūwāt, **Hawāsinah** and Bani **Kharūs** tribes.

Administration.—The authority of the Sultān of **'Omān** over Western Hajar is slight. The only places there held in his name are **Nakhl**, where he is represented by a Wāli, and **'Awābi**, **Hībi** and **Haiyadh**, at each of which, as also at Mizāhit in Wādi **Fara'** and Burj-ash-Shikairi in Wādi-al-**Jizi**, there is a fort in his possession.

HĀJIR (BANI) بني هاجر or HUWĀJIR هواجر

A nomadic Arab tribe of Eastern Arabia. By Bedouins the name is generally pronounced Bani Hāyir and Huwāyir; the singular is Hājiri (Hāyiri) حاجري .

Distribution.—The Bani Hājir are mostly found in one part or another of the **Hasa** Sanjāq, but they have not exclusive possession of any particular territory, excepting only a considerable portion of **Qatar** which is occupied by their Makhadhdhabah division; they are accustomed to obtain Rafīqs from the **'Ajmān**, under whose auspices they wander dispersed in the country of that tribe. The Bani Hājir sometimes camp as far south as Khor-al-**'Odaid**, and in the opposite direction they pay occasional visits to the dominions of the Shaikh of **Kuwait**; some also appear annually at 'Anik in the **Qatīf** Oasis. Settled Bani Hājir, now altogether unconnected with the tribe, are said to be found at Wusailah in the **Aflāj** District and at Haraimlah and Thādiq in the **'Āridh** District of Southern **Najd**. Arabs claiming to be Bani Hājir are found on the **Persian Coast**, *e.g.*, in the **Rūd-hilleh** District.

Religion, character and mode of life.—The Bani Hājir are Hanbali Sunnis.

In character they are lawless, troublesome, mischievous and uncivilised; but in their favour it is stated that they are enterprising and of a humourous disposition, and they are said to show some respect for engagements and promises. Their women enjoy considerable liberty. Though they have no vessels of their own the Bani Hājir are addicted to piracy, which they carry on by means of boats temporarily seized from the coast villages of other tribes. Their principal occupations however are pastoral, and they live chiefly by their flocks and herds and by the breeding of horses and camels; but they also own a number of small date groves in Barr-al-**'Oqair** and Barr-adh-**Dhahrān**, and the palms at

HĀJIR (BANI)   613

Ja'aimah in **Biyādh** to the north of the **Qatīf** Oasis are their property. Their tents are generally black, or black lined with white.

Divisions and numbers.—The following table shows the structure of the tribe together with some details of fighting strength and other particulars :—

Section.	Subsection.	Fighting strength.	Subsectional Shaikhs and remarks.
Makhadhdhabah مخضبه	Dibisah دبسه	15	...
Do.	Fahaid (Al) آل فهيد	20	...
Do.	Hamrah (Āl) آل حمرة	25	...
Do.	Hasaiyin (Āl) آل حصين	15	...
Do.	Jarārhah جرارحه	20	...
Do.	Khaiyārīn خيارين	45	Mushāsh-bin-Mubārak.
Do.	Madhāfirah مضافره	50	...
Do.	Mānaʿ (Āl) آل مانع	25	...
Do.	Mazāhimah مزاحمه	25	...
Do.	Qumzah (Al) آل قمزة	15	...
Do.	Saʿaiyīd (Al) آل سعيد	15	...
Do.	Shabāʿīn (Āl) آل شباعين	100	Shāfiʿ-bin-Sālim-bin-Shāfiʿ ; the chief Shaikhship of the whole Makhadhdhabah section belongs to him.
Do.	Shahwān (Āl) آل شهوان	50	Saif-bin-Shahwān.
Do.	Sharaʿān (Al) آل شرعان	30	...

Section.	Subsection.	Fighting strength.	Subsectional Shaikhs and remarks.
Makhadhdhabah مخضبه	Sharāhīn شراهين	35	...
Do.	Sultān (Āl) آل سلطان	25	...
Do.	Tawwa (Al) آل طوا	20	...
Do.	Zabar (Al Bū) آل بو زبر	40	...
Do.	Zakhānīn زخانين	30	...
Do.	Various	50	...
Muhammad (Āl) آل محمد	'Amīrah عميرة	30	The 'Amīrah are divided into Āl Jida-i آل جدئي and Āl Dhumain آل ضمين, whose fighting strengths are given in this order in the preceding column. The Shaikhs of the same are Dhīb-bin-Raddah, and Muhanna-bin-Bālūd, respectively.
		120	
Do.	Filahah (Āl) آل فلحه	60	Battāl-bin-Hashar.
Do.	Kidādāt كدادات	70	'Abdullah-bin-Jidaiyid.
Do.	Kilabah (Āl) آل كلبه	50	...
Do.	Misārīr مسارير	150	Suwaiyid-bin-Mutrab.
Do.	Qarūf (Al) آل قروف	50	Mubārak-bin-Dughmah.
Do.	Sha'āmil شعامل	200	Muhammad-bin-Mādhi-bin-Ta'azah; he is also chief Shaikh of the whole Al Muhammad section.
Do.	Simāhīn سماهين	30	'Awaidhah-as-Simhāni.
Do.	Tāya' (Al) آل طايع	20	Fahad-bin-Tāya'.
Do.	Various	70	...

The total fighting strength of the Bani Hājir is thus about 1,500 men, of whom 650 belong to the Makhadhdhabah and 850 are of the Al Muhammad section; and the number of the whole tribe probably amounts to some 5,000 souls.

Political condition.—The two great divisions of the Bani Hājir, namely, the Mukhadhdhabah and the Āl Muhammad, are ordinarily at enmity with one another, and this is the case at the present time; there is consequently no paramount Shaikh of the whole tribe. It is understood that the leading men of the Bani Hājir, receiving as they do allowances from the Turkish Mutasarrif of **Hasa** and presents from the Shaikh of **Kuwait** and the Āl Thāni Shaikhs of **Qatar**, are inclined to regard themselves as independent of all authority; but the payment by them of Zakāt to the Wahhābi Amīr is regarded as a not impossible contingency of the future. About 1865 the value of their annual contribution to the **Riyādh** treasury was estimated at $3,000.

HAJR

Singular Hajari حجري. A tribe of the **'Omān** Sultanate, Yamani by descent, Ibādhi in religion and Hināwi in politics. They inhabit the whole **Badīyah** division of the **Sharqīyah** district, are found also at **Mudhaibi**, and deal with the port of **Sūr**. They have not a good name for honesty and are rapacious and turbulent; nevertheless they are one of the wealthiest and most enterprising communities in this part of the country. They are engaged in cultivation and trade and own a number of boats: some of them visit Bombay and Zanzibar. The Hajriyīn, though possessing fixed villages, have retained to a considerable extent the tendencies and characteristics of Bedouins.

The Hajriyīn are now estimated at 7,500 souls and the subdivisions of the tribe are as follows:—

Section.	Fighting strength.*	Villages in **Badiyah**.	Remarks.
Baharimah بهارمه	200	Wāsil, Haili and Hātūh.	Nil.
Bahārinah بحارنه Habābasah حبابسه	80	Wāsil, Dabīk and Qā'.	Do.

* These are apparently somewhat under-estimated.

Section.	Fighting strength.*	Villages in **Badiyah**.	Remarks.
Haid (Wilād Bū) ولاد بو حيد	300	Rāk and Mintirib.	Nil.
Mahādinah مهادنه and Mahāddah مهادّه	400	Yāhis, Shāraq and Shāhik.	These two sections resemble Bedouins more than the others.
Mahāsinah مهاسنه	400	Ghabbi and Mintirib.	Nil.

* These are apparently somewhat under-estimated.

Wāsil is the tribal capital; but the Hajriyīn have at present no Tamīmah.

It was the Hajriyīn who in 1813 suddenly attacked Mutlaq, the Wahhābi leader, slew him and expelled his force from the country: Sa'ad, the son of Mutlaq, in revenge completely broke their power, and they have never entirely recovered their former position.

HALAIFAH (ABU)
ابو حليفه

A coast village in the **'Adān** district of the **Kuwait** Principality, lying about 18 miles south-south-east of **Kuwait** Town; it consists of about 50 houses and is inhabited by Arabs of miscellaneous origin. There are about 1,000 flourishing date palms and 30 wells containing good water at about 20 feet; but of the latter only 7 yield water for irrigation. Barley, melons and a few vegetables are grown and some Sidar or ber trees are seen. This village, as mentioned in the article on **'Adān**, is to some extent a country resort for townsmen of **Kuwait**.

HALFAIN (WĀDI)
وادي حلفين

A valley in **'Omān**, probably the longest in that part of Arabia. Its head is divided from the head of Wādi **Samāil** by the Najd of Mughbārīyah only, and it finally reaches the sea at **Mahōt**: its general direction is thus south by east and its length about 185 miles in a straight line. Five miles below the Najd, of which the elevation is 2,400 feet above sea-level, Wādi Halfain passes Mutī (2,300 feet); 7 miles further on it reaches the town of **Izki** (2,150 feet), which it divides into two

Muti at the head of Wādi Halfain.
[Maj. P. Z. Cox.]

parts; about 10 miles below **Izki** it passes a group of small villages belonging to the **'Awāmir** tribe and called collectively Falāj-al-'Awāmir فلاج العوامر, some of which are described in the article on **'Omān** Proper; below this point it is untenanted except by Bedouns. At **Izki** the right bank of the Wādi is 200 feet high; but below that town the bed opens out and becomes flat, sandy, and hardly distinguishable from the surrounding desert. It is stated however that after heavy rain its flood water sometimes reaches the sea at **Mahōt**.

Wādi **Mi'aidin** from Jabal **Akhdhar** joins Wādi Hafain at no great distance below **Izki**: while further down, below Dūh دہ, near **Adam**, Wādi Halfain receives Wādi Kalbu on the right bank from **'Omān** Proper and, somewhere not far from **Sanāu**, Wādi **'An'ām** from the Eastern **Hajar** upon the left.

Wādi Halfain, it is said, everywhere contains sweet water near the surface and has pasturage at all seasons. It is the chief highway between the inhabited portion of **'Omān** and the South-east Coast; and at one time it was customary to land cargoes of slaves at **Mahōt** and march them by this route to their destination to avoid the risk of capture by British cruisers.

HĀLŪL
حالول

An island in the Persian Gulf, about 61 miles east-north-east of **Dōhah** in **Qatar**. It is about a mile in diameter and consists partly of hills, of which one peak rises to 180 feet; but a considerable portion of its surface is fairly level. There is no fresh water, nor is there grazing even after rain; but some of the fishing grounds in the vicinity are excellent, and the island itself is a favourite breeding place for terns and yields large quantities of their eggs in the season. Pearl boats call here, and fishing vessels take refuge under the lee of Hālūl in Shamāls; the usual anchorage in such cases is on the south-east side, where a quiet berth can be found in 6 fathoms at half a mile from shore, and where there is a natural landing place and boat harbour formed by a gap in the cliffs of the coast. The island is surrounded by a fringe of pearl banks, and about 16 miles north by east of it is a detached pearl bank known as Najwat Bin-Hilāl or Riqqat Hālūl. An intermittent spring of bitumen exists under the sea in the neighbourhood of Hālūl; but its exact position is uncertain. The political position of Hālūl appears to be indeterminate; the pearl-divers and fishermen both of **Qatar** and of Trucial **'Omān** are in the habit of resorting to it; and, so far as can be learnt, no exclusive or

618   HĀLŪL

preferential rights are claimed by any of the classes who use it, or by any territorial chief.

HĀM (WĀDI)
وادي حام

A valley in Trucial 'Omān which apparently pierces the hills of the 'Omān Promontory obliquely from north-west to south-east: it has its head in the neighbourhood of the village of Adhan in the Jiri plain, and after traversing the whole mass of mountains it reaches the sea on the east coast near **Fujairah**. Its total length, windings being followed, seems to be about 35 miles. The lower part of the valley is in **Shamailīyah** and the upper in Rās-al-**Khaimah**, both districts of the **Shārjah** Principality.

The following are, in alphabetical order, the principal villages in Wādi Hām or connected with it:—

Name.	Position.	Houses and inhabitants.	Remarks.
Adhan اذن	Outside Wādi Hām at its head, 14 miles north-east by north of Dhaid village. In the Rās-al-Khaimah District.	...	Although reckoned the uppermost settlement of Wādi Hām this village is situated in the Jiri plain, in the article on which it is described.
'Asimah عصمة	In Wādi Hām, about 6 miles below Adhan. In the Rās-al-Khaimah District.	50 houses of Mazārī and Shahāirah.	There are 20 camels, 40 donkeys, 40 cattle, 400 sheep and goats and 4,500 date palms.
Bilaidah بليدة	In Wādi Hām, about 3 miles above Bithnah. In the Shamailīyah District.	4 houses of Sharqiyīn.	This is the uppermost village of Shamailīyah in Wādi Hām.
Bithnah بثنة	In Wādi Hām, about 6 miles from the coast. In the Shamailīyah District.	50 houses of Sharqiyīn.	The place is walled and fortified and commands the route up Wādi Hām: at present it is held by the Shaikh of **Fujairah** against his overlord, the Shaikh of **Shārjah**. The estimated resources of Bithnah are 15 camels, 30 donkeys, 20 cattle, 600 sheep and goats and about 4,000 date trees.

HĀM (WĀDI).

Name.	Position.	Houses and inhabitants.	Remarks.
Diftah دفتة	In or near Wādi Hām between Bithnah and Masāfi, but nearer to the former.	10 houses of **Naqbiyīn**.	Here there are about 20 donkeys, 30 cattle, 150 sheep and goats and 1,000 palms.
Fara' فرع	In Wādi Hām, about half way between Adhan and 'Asimah. In the Rās-al-**Khaimah** District.	20 houses of **Mazārī'**.	Resources are 10 camels, 40 donkeys, 20 cattle, 250 sheep and goats and 1,500 date trees.
Khalaibīyah خليبيه	In a small valley called Wādi Khabb, close to 'Asimah in Wādi Hām. In the Rās-al-**Khaimah** District.	30 houses of **'Abādilah** and **Sharqiyīn**.	There are said to be 30 cattle, 200 sheep and goats and 2,000 date palms.
Manāmah منامه	In a small valley connected with Wādi Hām.	7 or 8 houses of **Sharqiyīn** of the Hafaitāt section.	Sufad is in the same valley, and both places perhaps belong to **Shamailīyah** generally rather than to Wādi Hām.
Masāfi مسافي	In Wādi Hām, about 15 miles above Bilaidah and 12 below Adhan. In the Rās-al-**Khaimah** District.	50 houses, half of **Sharqiyīn** of the Hafaitāt section and half of Mahārizah.	Livestock are placed at 20 camels, 50 donkeys, 30 cattle and 350 sheep. Date trees are estimated at 5,000.
Sfuni صفني	Near Sīji in a small Wādi of the same name (Sfuni) which joins Wādi Hām. In the Rās-al-**Khaimah** District.	40 houses of Dhabābihah and 30 of **Mazārī'**.	Palms number about 3,000, and livestock are said to amount to 30 camels, 200 donkeys, 60 cattle and 1,000 sheep and goats. Sfuni is overlooked by Jabal Haqālah. Wādi Sfuni has a branch called Wādi Naidain نيدين.
Shōkah شوكه	Near Sīji, outside Wādi Hām proper and to the west of it. In the Rās-al-**Khaimah** District.	10 families of Qawāid, practically Bedouins.	There are a few camels and donkeys, also about 150 sheep and goats and 1,000 date palms.

Name.	Position.	Houses and inhabitants.	Remarks.
Sīji سيجي	Apparently in a plain, about 7 miles west of Wādi Hām at Masāfi. In the Rās-al-Khaimah District.	20 houses of Zahūm.	Resources are estimated at 10 camels, 2? donkeys, 30 cattle, 30? sheep and goats and 2,000 date trees.
Taiyibah طيبة	In Wādi Hām, 1 or 2 miles below Asimah. In the Rās-al-Khaimah District.	50 houses of Sharqiyīn and Mahārizah.	Palms are said to number 3,000 and livestock to be about 10 camels, 60 donkeys 70 cattle and 65? sheep and goats.

The route from **Fujairah** to **Dhaid** follows Wādi Hām for about ⅔ of the way to its head.

HAMĀD
حماد

A great desert plain in Northern Arabia to the north-east of Wādi **Sirhān** and to the north of **Jauf-al-'Āmir**; northwards it reaches as far as the **Baghdād-Damascus** line, and a small branch of it intervenes between **Jauf** and the **Nafūd**. The elevation of the last mentioned part above the sea is about 2,220 feet; it is absolutely level and bare of vegetation, a flat black expanse of gravelly soil covered with small round pebbles. The Hamād, where it abuts on Wādi **Sirhān** near Kāf, in an immense stony plateau, with white calcareous protuberances of remarkable shape; about 45 miles south-east of Kāf a chain of hills called **Jabal Misma** runs into it north-eastwards from the edge of Wādi **Sirhān**.

HAMAID
حميد

A considerable nomad Arab tribe of Southern **'Arabistān**; their range is from the **Gargar** (in its lower course) and from the **Kārūn** (about Naddāfīyeh) eastwards as far as Raghaiweh, and their tribal focus is on or near the Haddām affluent of the **Gargar**. They are politically allied to the **Bāwīyeh**. The Hamaid own a few camels besides considerable numbers of cattle and large flocks of sheep and goats, but they subsist chiefly by the cultivation of wheat and barley. Their fighting men

HAMAID

number about 1,700 of whom some 550 are mounted and nearly 500 are armed with rifles. Some of the **Hamaid** go to the Shatt-al-'**Arab** in summer to work in the date plantations there.

The following are the principal tribal divisions with such information regarding each as it has been possible to procure :—

Name.	Location.	Fighting strength.	Remarks.
Attāb عتاب	Hasanīyeh, 11 miles east of Saiyid Hasan on the **Gargar**.	100, of whom 30 are mounted and 30 have rifles.	The 'Attāb have 100 cattle and 500 sheep and goats.
'Awāmir عوامر	Zuwair, 4 miles east of Naddāfīyeh on the **Kārūn**.	200, of whom 50 have rifles and 100 are mounted.	Livestock are 40 camels, 200 cattle and 6,000 sheep and goats. The principal Shaikh of the tribe belongs to this section.
Hawālāt حوالات	4 miles north of the Haddām and the same distance east of the **Gargar**.	150, of whom 50 have rifles and 50 are mounted.	Animals are 200 cattle and 4,000 sheep and goats.
Kharāmizeh خرامزة	Nihairīyeh near Raghaiweh.	500. Of these 200 are armed with rifles and 150 are mounted.	This section have 40 camels, 400 cattle and 10,000 sheep and goats.
Maiyāh مياح	Both sides of the Haddām near its junction with the **Gargar**.	Do.	Possess about 500 cattle and 6,000 sheep and goats.
Nisailāt نسيلات	Naddāfīyeh on the **Kārūn** and Zuwair near it.	40, of whom 10 are mounted and 15 have rifles.	They have 40 cattle and 200 sheep and goats.
Sa'id ساعد	Both sides of the Haddām.	200, of whom 30 have rifles and 50 are mounted.	Their livestock amount to 100 cattle and 3,000 sheep and goats.

The total number of the tribe may be estimated at 6,000 souls. Of the above sections the Kharāmizeh alone pay revenue to the **Bakhtiyāri** Chief, the Samsām-as-Saltaneh; the others render tribute, to the amount of about 600 Tūmāns a year, through Mulla Thāni of Naddāfīyeh to the Shaikh of **Muhammareh**. All sections inhabit tents exclusively. The 'Abādat section of the '**Anāfijeh** have now been living with the **Hamaid** for some years.

HAMAIDĀT
حميدات

Singular Hamaidi حميدي. A branch of the Āl Subaih section of the Bani **Khālid** tribe; they are found chiefly at **Lūsail** in **Qatar**, where they have 50 houses; there are some also at the village of **Dha'āin**. The Hamaidāt are Māliki Sunnis and live by pearl diving and fishing. In winter they camp in the interior of the peninsula of **Qatar** with their sheep and goats.

HAMDĀN
حمدان

A town in Turkish 'Irāq on the south side of the Shatt-al-'**Arab**, about $\frac{2}{7}$ of the way from **Basrah** to **Muhammareh** Town; it is situated $2\frac{1}{4}$ miles up a creek of the same name, of which the entrance is $6\frac{1}{4}$ miles by river below the British Consulate at **Basrah** and opposite to Yamīn on '**Ajairāwīyah** island.

The town stands on both sides of the creek, the portion on the north-western bank being however $\frac{1}{2}$ a mile distant from it. The population of Hamdān is about 11,000 souls, of whom the majority are **Muhaisin** of the Bait Kana'ān section. There are 30 to 40 houses well built of bricks and mud, but the rest of the dwellings are huts. Grazing is good and cattle numerous. Date palms are estimated at 150,000 trees, and livestock at 2,500 cattle, 1,000 sheep and goats, 40 horses and 200 donkeys.

Within the Hamdān creek, and so not visible from the Shatt-al-'**Arab**, are a tomb visited by Shī'ahs and a shrine respected by Sunnis; the former appears to be a cenotaph, as it is admitted that the Imām Hamzah whom it commemorates neither lived nor died at Hamdān.

HAMIDAH
حمده

A tribe settled in the Rās-ar-Rummān suburb of **Manāmah** town in **Bahrain**—also known for this reason as Farīq-al-Hamidah—where they have 120 houses. They are an offshoot of the **Manāna'ah** but have been converted to Shī'ism, and they are classed at the present day as **Bahārinah**. Their occupations are sea-fishing and pearl-diving.

HAMRA (JAZĪRAT-AL-)
جزيرة الحمرا

Also called Jazīrat-az-Za'āb حزيرة الزعاب. An island and village in the principality of **Shārjah** in Trucial '**Omān**, 12 miles west-south-west of Rās-al-**Khaimah** Town. It is included in the district of Rās-al-**Khaimah**. The island,—about 2 miles long, parallel to the coast and very narrow,—is low and sandy, and its south-west end at low-water is nearly connected with the mainland ; the creek between the island and the coast is shallow and can be forded in all states of the tide. On the mainland opposite are some red sand hills. The village, which is in the middle of the island, consists of about 500 houses of the **Zaʼāb** tribe and is divided into a small quarter called Umm ʼAwaimir ام عويمر on the north and a large one called Manākh مناخ to the south. The inhabitants possess about 100 camels, 100 donkeys, 150 cattle and 500 sheep, but have no dates except at **Khatt** in the **Jiri** plain. They own about 25 pearl boats and some 10 small boats in which they bring firewood for sale to the towns of **Shārjah** and **Dibai**. They depend for their livelihood chiefly on pearl-diving.

**HAMRĪ-
YAH**

حمريه

A village on the coast of Trucial **ʼOmān**, 8 miles south-west of Umm-al-**Qaiwain** town and 6 miles north-east of the town of **ʼAjmān**. It stands on the north side of a small creek, consists of about 300 houses, and is defended by a fort on the shore and by several towers. There are 6 shops. The inhabitants, including the Shaikh, are **Naʼīm** of the Darāwishah section, with a few **Tanaij** : they own about 17 pearl boats besides some 3 horses, 40 camels, 50 donkeys, 60 cattle and 150 sheep. There are now 1,000 date palms. The Naʼīmi Shaikh of Hamrīyah, at present ʼAbdur Rahmān-bin-Saif, is not recognised as an independent chief; he has no separate treaty with the British Government, he is entitled to no salute, he used to accompany the Shaikh of **Shārjah** at interviews with British officers, and he must still be regarded as a dependent of **Shārjah**. Now, however, he denies his subordination to the Shaikh of **Shārjah** and looks for protection to the Shaikh of Umm-al-**Qaiwain**. There are no customs at Hamrīyah, but the Shaikh derives about $4,520 a year from taxation of pearl boats. He also owns a date plantation at **Dhaid**.

**HANĪFAH
(WĀDI)**

وادي حليفه

Next to Jabal **Tuwaiq**, in which it has its origin, this valley is the most important physical feature of Southern **Najd**, or at least of the ʼ**Āridh** district.

General course.—Wādi Hanīfah emerges from the main range of Jabal **Tuwaiq** at a point marked by a conspicuous bluff to the west of Sidūs; it appears to be formed by the union of four valleys of Jabal **Tuwaiq** which are, in order from north to south, Khumar خمر, the eastern Haisīyah حيسيّة, Ghurūr غرور and Bōdhah بوضة; of these Haisīyah, which is thickly grown with acacia and other trees, is the best known as containing the road between 'Ayainah and Barrah, a section of one of the principal routes across Arabia. From the head of Haisīyah down to **Riyādh**, a distance of about 50 miles, the general direction of the Hanīfah valley is east. At Malqa about 15 miles above **Riyādh** it apparently forks,[*] enclosing a small island; and near 'Ilb, some 4 miles further on, the same thing occurs again. Between 'Ayainah and **Riyādh**, Wādi Hanīfah receives three tributaries, all on its right bank; these are Wahairish رحيرش, which comes in immediately above Taraf, Ubaitah ابيطع, midway between Jabailah and Malqa, and 'Ammārīyah or Mazaira'ah مزيرعة, which contains the village of 'Ammārīyah and joins immediately below Malqa. At **Riyādh**, or just beyond it, Wādi Hanīfah turns to the south-south-east; and, after passing Hāir at less than 20 miles from **Riyādh**, it is joined by a valley from **Dhrumah** and acquires the alternative name of Wādi Hāir: beyond this point it receives, apparently on the borders of **Kharj**, a tributary named Nisāh نساح, which begins in the same part of the **Tuwaiq** hills as the Abaljilāt valley going to **Harīq**. Wādi Hanīfah is finally lost in the desolate **Sahábah** tract at a distance of perhaps 30 miles from Hāir; its drainage is said to reach the **Dahánah** beyond, where it disappears. Some natives of the country hold that the fresh-water springs of **Hasa** are fed subterraneously by the drainage of Wādi Hanīfah,—a theory which is at least plausible.

General characteristics.—Above 'Ayainah low hills separate the Wādi on its right bank from the higher summits of Jabal **Tuwaiq**, while on the left bank there is a raised plateau. At 'Ayainah the bed of the valley is gravelly, and thence to **Dara'īyah** sandy. From 'Ayainah down as far as Malqa the general character of the Wādi is fairly uniform; it has an average width of a few hundred yards and on either side of it there are flat-topped cliffs, alternating with low slopes, while the immediately adjacent hill crests never rise more than 200 feet above the level of its bed. From **Dara'īyah** to **Riyādh** the Wādi appears to be of a

---

[*] The point is obscure both in Palgrave and Pelly. Fresh inquiry tends to show that the loop formed is unimportant, and that the island enclosed is short and liable to submersion in heavy floods.

different character and to become, in places at least, a scarp-sided and contracted ravine rather than an open valley.

Floods in Wādi Hanīfah are said to rise 7 to 8 feet and to occur on the average four or five times in the year. After exceptionally good winter rains flowing water in the river bed may be expected to last, in the neighbourhood of **Riyādh**, throughout the succeeding spring and even summer. The lower part of the valley is celebrated for its luxuriant date groves; in the upper and less frequented portion gazelle and partridges are met with.

Wādi Hanīfah has always been the seat of political power in Southern **Najd** and the successive capitals of 'Ayainah, **Dara'īyah** and **Riyādh** have all been situated upon it.

Towns and villages.—The following table contains particulars of the principal inhabited places on Wādi Hanīfah and its 'Ammārīyah tributary:—

Name.	Position.	Houses and Inhabitants.	Remarks.
'Ayainah عيينة	On the left bank of Wādi Hanīfah, about 18 miles south-east of Sidūs.	No permanent inhabitants, but in favourable seasons, when there is water, cultivators immigrate from Sidūs and Malham, and to a lesser extent from Dara'īyah.	There are no date palms, but tamarisks abound. Wheat, barley and millet are grown. The water supply is from springs and from numerous wells 12 fathoms deep; one of the springs, called 'Ayainat Bin-Mu'ammar بن معمر is supposed to be dependent on a reservoir on the Ghāllah torrent in the direction of Sidūs. By some 'Ayainah is said to have been the birth-place* of the founder of the Wahhābi sect and at one time the capital of the country. Detached heaps of ruins and extensive retaining walls built to confine the flood of Wādi Hanīfah seem to prove that it once was, in fact, a considerable place.

* It seems more probable, however, that Muhammad-bin-'Abdul Wahhāb was born in Hautah.

Name.	Position.	Houses and inhabitants.	Remarks.
Taraf طرف	About a mile below 'Ayainah.	Resembles 'Ayainah, but the occasional cultivators in this case are all from Malham.	Like 'Ayainah in respect of agriculture and water supply.
Jabailah جبيله	On the left bank of Wādi Hanīfah about 3 miles below Taraf.	The permanent inhabitants are only 4 houses of inferior tribes; in winter, however, there is an influx of about 50 households of cultivators, chiefly from Malham but a few from Salbūkh.	There was formerly a large village here. Crops are wheat, barley, lucerne, marsh melons and water melons, but dates are very few. The village lands are on both sides of the Wādi. Numerous wells 12 fathoms deep yield fresh water, but the level of the Wādi bed is too low to admit of irrigation from them.
Malqa ملقى	On the left bank of Wādi Hanīfah 9 miles below Jabailah.	About 30 houses, *viz.*, 15 of Fadhūl, 4 of Qahtān, and 10 of inferior tribes.	The name is due to the separation of Wādi Hanīfah at this point into two branches which re-unite further down. Wheat, barley, millet, lucerne and melons are cultivated; there are date palms in abundance but no other fruit trees. The date plantations are the property of the ruler of Riyādh. Supplies are very limited. Water is from wells 8 to 14 fathoms deep. Some of Ibn Sa'ūd's horses are kept here.
Kabash (Abul) ابو الكباش	On the right bank of the 'Ammāriyah tributary of Wādi Hanīfah at a distance of several miles up it.	No permanent inhabitants, but visited in the agricultural season by about 10 cultivating families from other places, *viz.*, Fadhūl from Dara'īyah and Malham and inferior tribes from 'Ilb.	There are no dates, but the usual cereals and melons are grown. The wells are 6 to 12 fathoms deep.

Names.	Position.	Houses and inhabitants.	Remarks.
'Ammārīyah عمارية	At the head of the 'Ammārīyah tributary a few miles above Abul Kabāsh.	60 houses, viz., 20 of Dawāsir, 10 of Sabai', 10 of Bani Tamīm and 20 of inferior tribes.	There are 5,000 date palms and some other fruit trees, but no vines. Water is in wells at 8 to 18 fathoms.
'Ilb علب	On the right bank of Wādi Hanīfah 4 miles below Malqa.	50 houses, viz., 20 of Sabai' and 30 of inferior tribes.	The date palms are estimated at 6,000 and there are also citrons and figs. Lucerne, melons and the usual cereals are grown. Part of the cultivation is on the further side of the Wādi. The depth of the wells varies between 4 and 12 fathoms.
'Audah عودة	On the right bank of Wādi Hanīfah 1 mile below 'Ilb.	30 houses, viz., 10 of Fadhūl, 10 of Sabai' and 10 of inferior tribes.	Part of the cultivation is on the further side of Wādi Hanīfah. The usual cereals are grown and there are also citrons, figs, melons and water melons. The number of the date trees is estimated at 4,000.
Dara'īyah درعة	On the left bank of Wādi Hanīfah 1 mile below 'Audah.	...	See article Dara'īyah.
'Arjah عرجة	On the right bank of Wādi Hanīfah 3 miles below Dara'īyah.	100 houses, viz., 30 of Sabai', 30 of Bani Tamīm and 40 of inferior tribes.	There are the usual fruit trees and cereals and the datepalms are estimated at 15,000. The wells vary in depth between 4 and 12 fathoms.
Shuyūkh (Bātin-ash-) باطن الشيوخ	Chiefly on the left bank of Wādi Hanīfah 4 miles below 'Arjah, but part of the village is on the opposite side.	100 houses, viz., 30 of the family of Ibn Sa'ūd and 70 of inferior tribes.	The date groves belong to the family of Ibn Sa'ūd; there are also other fruit trees and cultivation of lucerne cereals. The dwellings are mostly garden houses.
Riyādh رياض	About 2 miles from the left bank of Wādi Hanīfah at a point 2 miles below Bātin-ash-Shuyūkh.	...	See article Riyādh.

Names.	Position.	Houses and inhabitants.	Remarks.
Manfūhah منفوحة	On the left bank of Wādi Hanīfah 2 or 3 miles below Riyādh from which it is separated by an enormous burial ground.	450 houses, viz., 100 of 'Anizah, 50 of Dawāsir, 100 of Qahtān, 50 of Bani Tamīm and 150 of inferior tribes.	Manfūhah had in 1819 some good upper-storeyed houses of mud and stone with flat roofs. Dates, wheat and barley are the present staples, the palms (which are irrigated from wells) being estimated at over 30,000; in 1819 cotton, maize, musk melons, water melons, peaches and figs were grown, and brinjals, spinach and clover were obtainable, but the fruits were not of good quality. The wells vary in depth from 4 to 12 fathoms according to their distance from the Wādi. The Wahhābi ruler keeps some 30 horses at this place. To the village belong some 30 camels, 50 donkeys and 150 cattle.
Masāni' مصانع	On the left bank of Wādi Hanīfah 3 miles below Manfūhah.	100 houses, viz., 30 of Sabai', 30 of Bani Tamīm and 40 of inferior tribes.	The village lands lie on both sides of the Wādi. Water is near the surface. There are the ordinary fruit trees and cereals and perhaps 10,000 date palms. The groves of Masāni' are continuous with those of Manfūhah.
Hāir حائر	On the right bank Wādi of Hanīfah 12 miles below Masāni' and one day by caravan north-westwards from the Sahábah tract.	200 houses, viz., 100 of Sabai' and 100 of inferior tribes. In the hot weather the population is largely increased by an influx of Bedouin Sabai' who own date palms here.	The date plantations are on both sides of the Wādi and are estimated to contain 10,000 palms. There are a few fruit trees, and cereals, lucerne and vegetables are grown, but the cultivation is poor. The water level is only 2 or 3 fathoms below the surface of the ground.

HANJĀM   HANJĀM*
هنجام

To British navigators of a former generation known as "Angaum" and even as "Angar." A remarkable island situated off the south coast of **Qishm** Island, in close proximity to Khārgu point, from which it is divided by a strait a mile wide and 6 to 12 fathoms deep in the fair-way. Hanjām has been not inaptly called the "Perim of the Persian Gulf"; and it would form a good base of naval observation, the Gulf being here so narrow that the Arabian coast is ordinarily visible; it would not however be a suitable site for a defended naval establishment.

Configuration.—Hanjām island is of a nondescript but compact shape; it measures 5½ miles in length from north-north-east to south-south-west and about 3 miles in breadth. The island consists of an agglomeration of rugged hills decreasing in elevation from north to south: the highest summit is Table Hill, one mile from the north end, which reaches 350 feet. The dismal aspect of Hanjām from the sea, whence it appears as a mass of barren, broken and almost black rocks, streaked here and there with white and red, does not belie its real character.

Geology.—Geologically the island is as rich in interest and variety as botanically it is poverty-stricken. The prevailing rock is a miliolitic limestone; but patches of maroon coloured stone and soil are numerous and are generally indicative of the presence of rock salt. In the northern part of the island are several salt caves, notably one † towards the centre of the island which is entered by a long, low, narrow passage in the face of a hill; it contains a grotto of rare beauty adorned with stalactites and tracery of the purest white salt. The mouths of some of the caves are adjoined by piles of stones and metallic substances of various colours which have excited the admiration of more than one visitor; among them appear

---

* For naval considerations relating to Hanjām, Commanders T. W. Kemp and H. B. T. Somerville's report of 20th June 1903 may be consulted: see the Political Proceedings of the Government of India for June 1904. Some remarks by Sir L. Dane and Admiral Atkinson-Willes are given in the same. A tracing of the Hanjām anchorage with additional soundings taken in June 1903 is contained in the Government of India's Foreign Proceedings for June 1904, and remarks on Hanjām by Admiral Willes will also be found there. A plan of the anchorage is given as an inset in Chart No. 2573-2837 A., *Persian Gulf*, where also a distant view of the island from the sea will be found. A general report on Hanjām by Lieutenant V. Hunt is contained in the Foreign Proceedings of the Government of India for May 1901: see also reports by Mr. Lobo, Sir L. Dane and Lieutenant Shakespear in the Foreign Proceedings for December 1904, June 1904 and March 1905. There is a plan of the telegraph station in the Proceedings for September 1905.

† Described by Floyer; see his *Unexplored Baluchistan*, pages 124-6.

to be sulphur, red ochre and blocks of specular iron ore ; the last, on account of their weight, are used by the fishermen of the island as sinkers for their nets. A valley near the western coast, about 300 yards north-west of the foot of Table Hill, presents another geological curiosity in the form of clay pillars which stand erect and bear a singularly close resemblance to the trunks of fossilised date trees. In 1904 two of these pillars, on being broken open, were found to hold a core or second pillar of flint of the same length as the first ; and one of the clay pillars contained in addition a fossilised bivalve shell. The outer clay case was extremely hard, but peeled off in layers under the blows of a hammer.*

Climate.—The climate of Hanjām in summer is barely tolerable ; the heat is terrific and is aggravated during the months of June, July and August by the moisture with which the atmosphere is laden, by the assaults of sand-flies and other insects, and, in the neighbourhood of the coast, by the stench of decomposing sea-weed. The rainy season begins in October and ends in March. In the winter of 1903-1904 the fall was considerable and filled the reservoirs, but for 4 or 5 years previously there had been very little rain.

Flora and fauna.—The only self-sown trees are the ber and acacia; and, grass, even in spring, is only sufficient to tinge one or two of the main valleys with a slight shade of green.

In the hills are some wild goats, in reality domestic goats which have escaped from the villages and their descendants, and the island is now overrun by hares which were introduced here and on **Tunb** island about 1882 by Mr. Ffinch, then Director of the Persian Gulf Telegraphs. There are no wild carnivora. Birds are not uncommon, especially towards the open ground at the south-west of the island ; among them are the kite, hawk, stone-plover, lark, dove and blue-rock pigeon, the latter inhabiting the caves and sometimes the deep wells of the island. The edible oyster is plentiful along the shores, and pearl-oysters also abound. Sand-flies and other insects exist in myriads and are troublesome at certain seasons.

Telegraph station.†—Only three points on Hanjām are at present inhabited. Of these the first is the British telegraph station, which was re-established at the north end of the island in April 1904 after having

---

* Mr. R. W. Lobo of the I. E. T. D., on whose excellent account of Hanjām the greater part of this article is founded, has seen similar freaks of nature at Ormārah on the coast of Makrān.

† A plan of the station and discussion of its boundaries will be found in the Government of India's Political Proceedings for September 1905.

been in abeyance for 13 years. The buildings are situated on a cliff ¼ of a mile inland from the north coast of the island, and are only a few yards to the northward of the plinth which marks the site of the original station. The staff consists of an Assistant Superintendent and two clerks. On the south side of the station is a valley of considerable extent and about 550 yards across; it runs across the island from west to east and contains two or three wells, the best of which is affected to the use of the telegraph establishment. The water is about 18 feet from the surface and varies from sweet to brackish : advantage has been taken of it to lay out a small garden and plant some trees.* The northern side of the valley consists of high cliffs, the lower strata of which are composed of Shūr or saline matter. A village called Masheh, مشه, consisting of a few huts, stands 300 yards east of the telegraph station and is occupied by native employés of the Indo-European Telegraph Department who were brought here from **Jāshk** but were originally natives of **Bāsīdu**.

Hanjām village.—The most populous place on the island is the village of Hanjām, situated on a stretch of flat open country by the coast on the south-east side of the island. The plain adjoining it is all under cultivation. Hanjām is a typical Arab village, comparatively clean and well-built, and consists of about 200 houses. It possesses 8 or 9 gardens well stocked with fruit trees and irrigated from wells 20 to 25 feet deep which are worked by bullocks; there are about 1,400 date-palms, and the other principal crops are wheat, barley, onions and pumpkins. The Arabs of Hanjām belong to the Bani **Yās** tribe of the Arabian coast, whence they are said to have immigrated about 3 generations ago; their intercourse is still chiefly with that coast and particularly with the town of **Dibai**. They are manly, independent, intelligent, industrious and extremely hospitable. They own 36 pearl boats which constitute their principal means of livelihood; the bulk of the male population is absent on the Arabian pearl-banks every year from June to October, not returning to the island until they have disposed of their takings to Indian merchants in Trucial **'Omān** or at the pearl mart of **Lingeh**. The women during the same season seek employment at **Mīnāb** and other places as date-pickers and return to the settlement about the same time as their male relatives. In summer, consequently, Hanjām village is practically deserted except by aged caretakers. In winter the men of Hanjām, who are said to be very dexterous in the use of the harpoon, mostly devote themselves to

---

* The valley and wells have been minutely described by Mr. Lobo : *vide* the Government of India's Foreign Proceedings for December 1904.

shark-fishing, but some remain on shore to tend the cold weather crops. For shore-fishing the people of Hanjām use a torpedo-shaped fish trap of wickerwork with one inch meshes and a cone-shaped entrance projecting inwards from one end; this is sunk at a moderate depth in a passage between two rocks and is taken out at the end of the day with such fish as having wandered in have been unable to find their way out again. To Hanjām village and that of Ghail, mentioned below, belong 7 camels, 40 donkeys, 50 cattle and 400 goats, all of which are allowed to roam at large over the island. About a mile south of Hanjām village, in the first series of hills from the coast, are some masonry remains which the Arabs attribute to the Portuguese.

Ghail. village.—The third settlement is Ghail غيل, an offshoot of Hanjām village situated on the west coast about 3 miles southwest of the telegraph station and 3 miles north-west of Hanjām village. It contains about 30 houses and depends like Hanjām chiefly on pearl-diving. Here there is a well of excellent water within a few feet of the sea beach. Four or five walled gardens have sprung up about 100 yards east of the village; in these there are fruit trees, onions and a few pumpkins and beans. In the gardens are some eight shallow wells, and between them and the village an artificial lake for storing rain water has been created by damming up a hollow which passes the village. The supply of water at Ghail is almost inexhaustible, and native vessels anchoring between Hanjām and Qishm Island procure their supply from this place by boat when the tanks at the north end of the island are empty.

Besides the telegraph station and the villages of Hanjām and Ghail there are now no other settlements on the island; but traces of former hamlets exist in more than one place, and in the valley south of the old telegraph station are the remains of walled plots of cultivation.

Anchorage, etc.—Some idea of the resources and trade of Hanjām has been given in describing the island and villages. The salt-caves and pits, it may be observed, have not been worked in recent years. It remains to add that there is a valuable anchorage, called Masheh bay, between Hanjām and Qishm; it is visited by most native vessels proceeding up the Gulf in order to take water on board, or, in some cases, to obtain shelter from the Shamāl which here blows from the west-south-west. This place was formerly a rendezvous of pirates and is still occasionally used by slavers. The anchorage is a double one, lying on both sides of a sandy spit at the northernmost point of the island, on which a beacon and high-water mark have recently been erected by the cable ship of the

Indo-European Telegraph Department. The amount of the anchorage sheltered from the prevailing winds is very limited, and the bottom is hard and a ship is liable to drag her anchor, especially in consequence of the tides which run strongly during ebb and are said to attain about 3 knots at springs. Vessels drawing about 10 feet can be beached on the spit. The western part of the anchorage is the better, but it is partially exposed to the Shamāl, to avoid which vessels must change their position to the other side of the cape. The depth in the anchorage is about 9 fathoms. Masheh bay is the place where vessels load salt from the Namakdān mines on **Qishm** Island for the Calcutta and other markets; there being no safe anchorage off Namakdān the salt is brought here in lighters, a distance of over 20 miles, and transhipped.

Political position.—The principal authority on the island is the Shaikh of the village of Hanjām, who has hitherto endeavoured, with some success, to avoid relations with the Persian authorities. No revenue or tribute is paid by the islanders, and a Persian Customs post and two Persian flag-staffs at the north end of the island are as yet the only evidences of Persian sovereignty.

Ruins.—No account of Hanjām would be complete which failed to mention the ruins on the north coast. The principal are two mosques 275 yards apart, of which the eastern seems to have been a Persian construction and the western stands on a cliff overhanging the sea. On the northern side of the former, along the beach, extend traces of a settlement which appears to have consisted of 200 or 300 houses: among the remains here some copper coins, dating from 113 to 164 years back, have been discovered. Immediately to the south of these ruins is a hollow 250 yards square containing graves and headstones, and in the vicinity of the mosque are 9 reservoirs hewn out of the solid limestone rock and lined with an imperishable hydraulic cement locally called Sarūch. The largest of these reservoirs is 60 feet long, 12 feet wide and 12 feet deep and has a cylindrically vaulted roof of common Gach and stones. The western mosque appears to have been built with the ordinary maroon-coloured cement of the island; it is also adjoined by reservoirs, 3 or 4 in number, and by a graveyard which, with the remains of houses on the hill behind, indicate that it may have been the nucleus of a distinct settlement. About a mile from the village of Ghail are three blocks of granite, the largest weighing several tons, of which the presence is not in any way accounted for except by a superstitious tale.

HARB
حرب

Singular Harbi حربي. A great Arab tribe, mostly nomadic, found in the Hijāz province and on the western confines of **Najd**.

Distribution.—Part reside between Makkah and Madīnah within the basin of the Red Sea, others to the south of Khaibar about the head of **Wādi-ar-Rummah** and that of Wādi-al-Hamdh حمض which goes down to Madīnah; the remainder, with whom we are chiefly concerned, inhabit the country upon the upper course of Wādi-ar-**Rummah** and the tract called Hazam-ar-Rāji حزم الراجي to the south of it, sometimes pushing as far east as Dilaimīyah, Ab-ad-Dūd and Subaih in **Qasīm** and as 'Aqlah, Balāzīyah, Fuwārah and 'Odhaim in Jabal **Shammar**. Harb Bedouins are occasionally seen in 'Āridh. Settled Harb are found at Barrūd in Wādi-as-Sirr, at **Zilfi** in **Sadair**, and at Rghabah in 'Āridh; and some of the inhabitants of permanent villages in **Qasīm** claim to be of Harb descent, especially at Basr, Bukairiyah, 'Ain Ibn-Fahaid, Hamar, Hilālīyah, Jau'i, Qaryah, Quwai'ah, Muraid Saiyid, Nabhānīyah, Shaihīyah, Shiqqah, Subaih and Ummahāt-az-Ziyābah. The Bedouins who adjoin the Harb in **Najd** are the **Hataim** upon the north, the **Mutair** upon the east and the **'Ataibah** upon the south-east and south.

Divisions and number.—The Harb tribe consists of two main divisions, the **Masrūh** مسروح and the Bani Sālim بني سالم.

The subdivisions of the Masrūh are three, the Bani 'Ali بني علي, the Bani 'Amr بني عمر and the Bani-as-Safar بني السفر; these again are composed of the sections given below.*

Bani 'Ali subdivision of the Masrūh.

'Abidah	عبده	Karāshīf	كراشيف
Dahaim	دهيم	Kitimah	كتمه
Dawā'irah	دواعره	and	
Kalakhah	كلخه	Turafah	طرفه

The Bani 'Ali appear to lie the furthest to the north and east of the whole tribe. Some of them are "pithless day-sleepers and coffee-drinkers;" some are ultra-religious; others on the contrary are unable to say their prayers, and not all keep Ramdhān. Some of the Bani 'Ali pitch their tents in a circle and keep their animals in the middle, an unusual form of camp among the Bedouins of Central Arabia. The

---

* Doughty received an almost entirely different statement (II. 513). Possibly the sections he mentions are those in Hijāz.

ruling family of the whole Masrūh division belong to a subsection of the Karāshīf called Furōm فروم .

Bani 'Amr subdivision of the Masrūh.

Atūr	عطور	Sha'āfīn	شعافين
Bidārīn	بدارين	Shiddah	شدّه
Ghiyādīn	غيادين	and	
Sh 'ab	شعب	Sillāh	سلّاح

Bani-as-Safar subdivision of the Masrūh.

| 'Auf | عوف | Makhallaf | مخلّف |
| Faridah | فرده | Wahōb | وهوب |

The 'Auf are reputed robbers, especially of pilgrims, but in reality only part of the section engage in nefarious practices.

The subdivisions of the Bani Sālim are two only, the Maimūn ميمون and the Mizainah مزينه . The Bani Sālim appear to be as a rule honest, kindly, hospitable and, for Bedouins, well clad. Their sections are *:—

Maimūn subdivision of the Bani Sālim.

Ahāmidah	احامده	Salaim (Aulād)	اولاد سليم
Gharbān	غربان	Wasadah	وسده
Hanishah	حنشه	and	
Jimlah	جمله	Zighaibāt	زغيبات

Mizainah subdivision of the Bani Sālim.

'Araimāt	عريمات	Hawāmil	هوامل
Bishārīyah	بشاريّه	Hawāzim	حوازم
Dhawāhirah	ضواهره	Husnān	حصنان
Hanāniyah	حنانيه	Nahāitah	نهائته

Of these the 'Araimāt have no camels, but only sheep; and the Hawāzim, † who are perhaps not true Harb, are taunted by their enemies

---

* Doughty's account differs considerably from this (II. 512).
† See the footnote to the article on the **Awāzim**.

with being **Saluba** or **Hataim**, and are sometimes described as Ibādhi in religion like the tribes of the **'Omān** Sultanate.

The settled Harb of **Zilfi** are said to belong to a section called Bani Hammād بني حمّاد .

The numbers of the Harb are difficult to estimate, but those in **Najd** may be placed at about 3,500 souls.

Livelihood and character.—The Harb are camel and sheep-owners; their camels are nearly all swarthy or black, and some of their sheep are black also. A number of the tribe are professional robbers and highwaymen, and others act as escorts to pilgrim caravans passing through their country. In complexion the Harb are extremely dark, but they have the features of true Arabs. In religion they are Hanbali Sunnis; in character and disposition they seem to vary considerably from section to section; many of the poorer Harb live among the **Hataim**, but they abstain from intermarriage with them. The Harb are not as yet a well-armed tribe; their weapons are still for the most part muzzle-loading guns, flint-locks and spears; such rifles as they possess have been imported through Yanbō' on the Red Sea.

Political position.—As the greater part of their territory and nearly all their immovable property are in Hijāz, where they have a number of fixed villages, the political relations of the Harb with the Turks are necessarily close. The Bani Sālim division and the Bani 'Amr sub-division are subsidised by the Turkish Government in consideration of their keeping open the various pilgrim routes through the Harb Dīrah; but the subsidy is really paid by the pilgrims in the form of tolls collected at Makkah by the Turkish authorities on behalf of the Harb. The Damascus Hajj is severely taxed for this purpose, that from **Hāil** less so, the **Qasīm** Hajj escapes still more cheaply, and that from **Riyādh** is altogether exempt. The Harb who live in **Najd** beyond effective Turkish jurisdiction were in the beginning tributaries of the Wahhābi; but in 1864 they allied themselves to the **'Ataibah**, then hostile to Ibn Sa'ūd. In 1878 they were subject to taxation by Ibn Rashīd and used to be periodically collected by his order at Samīrah for military and revenue purposes. They have lately returned to their original allegiance and render annual tribute to the Wahhābi Amīr at the rate of one sheep or goat in every 50 and one dollar in cash on every 5 camels: the total value of their present annual contribution has not been ascertained.

HARDĀN
حردان

A considerable Arab tribe located chiefly upon the boundary, to the west of the **Kārūn**, between Northern and Southern 'Arabistān; a few are found to the east of the **Gargar**. Shārtāgh a few miles to the east of Kūt Nahr Hāshim appears to be their principal centre. The Hardān cultivate wheat and barley: they also own 300 camels, cattle in considerable numbers, and large flocks of sheep and goats. The fighting men of the tribe are reckoned at nearly 700, of whom over 200 are mounted on horses and 100 or 200 have rifles, and the total number of souls may be estimated at 2,500. The Hardān pay revenue to the Shaikh of **Muhammareh**.

The following are the divisions of the tribe with some particulars concerning them:—

Name.	Location.	Fighting strength.	Remarks.
'Abūdeh عبوده	Shārtāgh, 7 miles east of Kūt Nahr Hāshim.	150, of whom 40 are mounted.	Livestock are 50 camels, 100 cattle and 3,000 sheep and goats. The revenue of the section is paid through Shaikh 'Anāyeh at Umm-at-Tamair, who is in charge of the right bank of the Kārūn in the Ahwāz District.
Hāji (Āl Bū) آل بو حاجي	Among the 'Anāfijeh, usually at Yaqauwiyeh on the Diz River.	150, of whom 30 are mounted.	This section own 200 cattle and 2,000 sheep and goats and pay their revenue through the 'Anāfijeh.
Hardān حردان	Shārtāgh.	200, of whom 50 are mounted.	The chief Shaikh of the whole tribe is of this section. They own 200 camels, 200 cattle and 5,000 sheep and goats and pay their revenue in the same manner as the 'Abūdeh section.

Name.	Location.	Fighting strength.	Remarks.
Na'āmeh (Bani) بني نعامه	Kharrān, near the Qadamgāh called Shiraif.	80, of whom 30 are mounted.	The lands occupied by this section are the property of 'Abdus Samad, Mujtahid, of Shūshtar and they pay revenue to him. Their water is from wells and they own 10 camels, 200 cattle and 5,000 sheep and goats. Others of this section, as they now live apart from the tribe, are not reckoned to it; they are mentioned in the article on the Hawīzeh District.
Shijairāt شجيرات	Chiefly about Sīdīyeh, a place on the right bank of the Kārūn below Li'aimi; but the section is a scattered one.	100, of whom 30 are mounted.	The Shijairāt have 200 cattle and 3,000 sheep and goats. Robbery and theft were formerly rife in the vicinity of their headquarters, but have decreased since the Marawuneh tribe moved into the same neighbourhood.
Tamīm (Bani) بني تميم	Shārtāgh.	100, of whom 40 are mounted.	The revenue of the Bani Tamīm is paid in the same manner as that of the 'Abūdeh section. They have 40 camels, 100 cattle and 2,000 sheep and goats.

All the sections of this tribe are dwellers in tents: the only exceptions are a very few families who are settled at Kraidi on the **Gargar**.

HARĪQ حريق Generally pronounced Harīj or Harīg; a valley in Southern **Najd** forming a district of the Wahhābi dominions.

Boundaries and physical features.—On the north Harīq is divided from the district of **'Āridh** by Jabal 'Alaiyah; and on the south it appears to be bounded by a range, called Hilaiyah حليه, which is interposed between it and part of the **Hautah** district. The fall of the Harīq valley appears to be from west to east, and its drainage is reported to join that of **Hautah** upon its way to **Kharj**.

Jabal 'Alaiyah, already mentioned, is an important physical feature connected with this district and with **Hautah**; it is uncertain whether it pertains to the **Tuwaiq** system or is an isolated range. It is described as enclosing a basin of which the drainage escapes by a fissure called Sha'īb 'Alaiyah in the eastern side of the mountain; in the north-western part of the basin is a locality named Māwān ماوان where there are wells 4 fathoms deep and date groves at which Bedouins assemble in the season to gather the fruit. Jabal 'Alaiyah is reported high and difficult and is said to contain a number of strongholds, which are called Qarānīyah قرانيه or Qurūnīyah قرونيه and are occupied by robber bands composed of the off-scourings of many of the tribes of Arabia. A part of Jabal 'Alaiyah apparently projects southwards into the Harīq valley, for it is crossed immediately after leaving Harīq town on the way from that place to **Dilam** in **Kharj**.*

Communications. — Routes radiate from Harīq town to **Dilam in Kharj**, to Hāir on Wādi **Hanīfah**, and to the village of Jau-as-Saibāni which is described in the article on **Dhrumah**.

The route to **Dilam** goes east with a slight southerly inclination; the journey occupies a caravan 10 or 11 hours and the distance may be about 30 miles. The first 3 hours are spent in ascending and then descending a portion of Jabal 'Alaiyah; thereafter the route runs through a plain where neither villages nor torrent beds are encountered. It is also possible to go from Harīq to **Dilam** by descending the Harīq valley to its junction with the valley of **Hautah** and thence following the **Hautah** valley to **Dilam**: on this route also no villages are passed.

The route from Harīq to Hāir is identical with the first route to **Dilam** until the crossing of part of Jabal 'Alaiyah has been effected and the south-eastern corner of the mountain is reached; it then diverges northwards, 'Alaiyah for some time remaining on the left hand. A waterless stage which is reckoned half way to Hāir is reached in 10 caravan hours; it is named Ausat اوسط from a hill that adjoins it on the west. Unless however the road is very winding, it does not appear that the journey can amount to so much as 60 miles.

---

* Harīq has not, so far as is known, been visited by any European traveller. It is ard, however, to understand how Palgrave reached **Kharfah** in **Aflāj** without pparently passing through either Harīq or Hautah

The route from Harīq to Jau-as-Saibāni runs for 8 hours through hilly ground, Jabal 'Alaiyah being on the right hand side of the traveller, to the hill of Faraishah فريشه ; thence the way continues westwards for 5 hours over a level plain to Jau-as-Saibāni. The times being those taken by a caravan, the total distance is probably between 30 and 40 miles. At 3 hours short of Jau-as-Saibāni on the south side of the route is Khashm-adh-Dhīb خشم الذيب which is regarded as the north-westernmost corner of the hills of Harīq and is the furthest point reached by the torrent of Abaljilāt from 'Āridh.

Topography, population and resources.—The following is a table of the principal places in the Harīq district with some particulars concerning them :—

Name.	Position.	Houses and inhabitants.	Remarks.
Harīq town حريق	About 30 miles west by north of Dilam in Kharj.	Population is about 3,000 souls, but a number of the people live scattered in the date gardens. There are 100 houses of Ruwalah 'Anizah of the Hazāzinah section; 40 of Sahūl; 20 of Sabai' of the Khathlān section; 15 of Dawāsir; 10 of Fadhūl and 175 of Bani Khadhīr. The Sabai' are settled in the date groves to the south-east. One of the Qasrs in the middle of the settlement is called Mishrāq مشراق.	The date groves are very extensive and contain a large number of trees. The usual fruits of Southern Najd, including peaches, are found; also the usual cereals. Water is at 16 to 20 fathoms and the well-lifts are worked by camels. Livestock are estimated at 50 horses, 50 donkeys, 500 camels and 300 cattle. There is a bazaar of about 40 shops, supplied from Hasa with piece-goods and 'Abas, from Hasa and Qatar with arms and ammunition, and from Yaman with coffee. The place contains a number of upper-storeyed houses; timber for building is obtained locally and not imported.
Mufaijir مفيجر	About 8 miles east of Na'ām.	45 houses, *viz.*, 15 of Hazāzinah of the Ruwalah section of the 'Anizah, 10 of Sahūl and 20 of inferior tribes.	The water supply and crops are the same as at Harīq town, but the date plantations are neglected and the place is going to decay.

Name.	Position.	House and inhabitants.	Remarks.
Na'ām نعام	About 8 miles east of Harīq town between the two routes from Harīq town to Dilam in Kharj.	About 80 houses of **Ashrāf** and their dependents. The owners are well-to-do.	The founder, a certain Muhammad bin Husain, is dead and the village is in the possession of his three sons with their families and servants. There are considerable date plantations. Agricultural conditions are similar to those prevailing at Harīq town.
Sha'ībāt شعيبات	In the direction of Wādi Braik, in a valley from **Hautah** which goes to **Kharj**.	A deserted village.	There are some wells at this place.
Wuthailān وثيلان	On a hollow which runs down from Jabal 'Alaiyah to the valley of **Hautah**.	Do.	There are the remains of a Qasr and some untended date groves, but no permanent habitations which are at present occupied. A little wheat is grown by cultivators from Hautah. Water is from a perennial spring.
Zalāl (Qā'-az-) قاع الزلال	Close to the town of Harīq on the side towards Na'ām.	Nil.	This is a Khabrah where grass grows and there is a well. Cultivators from Harīq town cultivate wheat here in the cold weather.

It will be observed that among the genuine Arab villagers of the Harīq district **'Anizah** of the Ruwalah section predominate, but the inferior tribes who are grouped together under the designation of Bani **Khadhīr** are probably more numerous than they. The whole settled population of the Harīq district probably does not exceed 4,000 souls. It is believed that Harīq was once more thickly peopled than it is now; local opinion attributes the decline to the Egyptian invasions. The valley is noted for the excellence of its fruits. The revenue which Harīq at present yields to the Wahhābi Amīr is estimated at $5,000 a year.

HARQŪS
حرقوص

A mere sandbank in the Persian Gulf, situated about 30 miles west and slightly south of **Fārsi** island; it is about 200 yards in length and is hardly above the level of high water. There are a few birds. The ownership of Harqūs is undetermined, never having come into question.

HARRĀS (BANI)
بني حراص

Singular is Harrāsi حراصي. A Ghāfiri tribe in the Western **Hajar** district of the Sultanate of 'Omān, Ibādhis in religion: they are found at Hillat Bani Harrās (100 houses) in Wādi **Samāil**; at **Nakhl** (65 houses) and Hibra (40 houses) in Wādi **Ma'āwal**; at 'Awābi, in Wadi Bani **Kharūs**; at Buwairid (25 houses), Mansūr (40 houses) and **Jammah** (500 houses), in Wādi **Fara'**; and at Fīq in Wādi **Mistāl**. They also occur at Taimsa (40 houses), in 'Omān Proper. The Bani Harrās number about 4,000 souls. The ruling family is called Aulād Thinaiyān اولاد ثنيان; the present chief is Khalfān-bin-Thinaiyān, and the tribal capital is **Jammah**.

HASA
الحسا
or
AHSA
الاحسا
OASIS*

This and the **Qatīf** Oasis are the only fertile and well watered tracts in the Sanjāq of **Hasa**; and of the two the Hasa Oasis, now under consideration, is by far the more valuable and important.

Boundaries, extent and position.—The Hasa Oasis has its north-western corner at Jabal Qārat-ar-Rukbān and its south-western corner at Jabal Bū Ghanīmah, while its southern boundary runs from Jabal Bū Ghanīmah to Jabal Arba' and thence for several miles further to the east; on the remaining sides the borders of the district are not precisely defined by conspicuous features. With these limits its extent is about 35 miles from north to south, and its breadth may be taken at 20 miles. The Hasa Oasis is enclosed by the desert tracts of **Ghuwār** on the west, **Kharmah** on the south, and **Biyādh** on the east and north; at Jabal Qārat-ar-Rukbān it touches Badd-al-**Asīs**, and at its opposite or south-eastern extremity it meets **Jāfūrah**. The town of **Hofūf**, of which the position is well ascertained, is situated in the district near its south-western corner; and the eastern border of the oasis approaches within about 30 miles of the Persian Gulf coast at the port of **'Oqair**.

Physical features and climate.—It should be clearly understood that although the whole is spoken of as Hasa, only a portion of the district just defined is cultivated or permanently inhabited. The greater part of

---

* The principal authorities, maps, etc., relating to this tract are included among those mentioned in the first footnote to the title of the article on the **Hasa** Sanjāq.

Near the village of Qārah in the Hasa Oasis.
(Herr H. Burchardt.)

it is in fact merely desert except, perhaps, between Qaran and 'Ayūn, where it is marshy. The chief block of cultivation is in the south, to the east of the towns of **Mubarraz** and **Hofūf**; it does not extend much further north than the first of these, and southwards it hardly reaches beyond the second and does not cross to the south of the **Hofūf**-Jishshah road until near Bāb-al-Jafar; its extreme length from west to east does not exceed 12 miles. Besides this block there are 2 or 3 detached areas of cultivation, but in comparison with it they are insignificant; and, when in the following paragraphs mention is made of limits of cultivation, the phrase is to be taken as referring to the limits of the main block. Of the cultivated areas the nearest to the main block is one which adjoins the west side of Sha'abah; it is separated from the cultivated country to the south of it by a narrow belt of stony, waste land, across which water for irrigation is brought in deeply-dug channels. This patch is about 2 miles north of **Mubarraz**; and 2 miles further, in the same direction, a somewhat larger one occurs which contains the villages of Matairafi, Jalaijilah, Qaran and Qarain and possesses springs of its own. The lands of 'Ayūn village compose the largest and most isolated of the minor cultivated areas, for they cover a space of perhaps 4 square miles and the nearest part of them is about 15 miles north of **Mubarraz**; in connection with these may be mentioned a small patch of cultivation at Qattār. which is 6 miles further to the northward but belongs to the same owners as 'Ayūn.

The hills of Qārat-ar-Rukbān, Bū Ghanīmah and Arba', inasmuch as they lie on the borders of the oasis and are common to it and other districts, are described in the general article on the **Hasa** Sanjāq. Eminences actually included within the district are few and unimportant. The nearest to **Hofūf** is a mound called Abul Kubāri ابو الكباري about 1½ miles north-east of the town; and the largest is Jabal Qārah, قارة which lies 6 miles east-north-east of **Hofūf**, covers a considerable area, and has at its base upon different sides the villages of Qārah, Dālwah Taimiyah and Tuwaithīr: Jabal Qārah consists, partly at least, of sand stone rocks weathered into fantastic shapes, and it contains roomy caves which are used as dwellings in the hot weather. The only hill of importance besides Jabal Qārah is Jabal Buraijah بريجه also called Jabal Sha'abah; it is a high ridge running eastwards for perhaps a mile from the village of Sha'abah which is situated at the foot of it. Mention may also be made of some hillocks a mile to the south-east of Jishshah which are known as Talūl-ad-Duwwār.

The aqueous features of the oasis, such as springs, streams and lakes are noticed in the paragraph below on irrigation.

The elevation of Hasa above the sea has not been observed; but it is certainly not great. The general slope of the oasis, to judge from the flow of the springs, is downwards from west to east; but in the northern portion, to the south of 'Ayūn, there appears to be a descent northwards as well as eastwards. The soil is light and inclines to sandiness; but, though barren saline patches occur arbitrarily here and there, it is generally fertile. A multitude of springs exist, all of which are more or less warm and some of which are extremely hot; they probably represent, along with those of **Qatīf** and **Bahrain**, the drainage of **Najd** eastwards which disappears on reaching the **Dahánah** desert. Running waters fed by the springs abound, especially on the east side of **Hofūf**; in places the roads run upon embankments through deep, saturated country; and in some localities there are marshes and large stagnant ponds, the most notable being Birkat-al-Asfar.

Natural grass is plentiful in spring; reeds and rushes grow in the swamps; and among wild trees the tamarisk and the Sidar or ber are the most common.

The climate of the Hasa Oasis is not favourable to physical activity or to health, but it is colder, drier and less relaxing than that of **Qatīf** or **Bahrain**.

Population.—The people of the Hasa Oasis are partly nomads and partly settled townsmen and villagers. The Bedouins are dealt with elsewhere in the article on the **Hasa** Sanjāq, and here we have only to do with the fixed inhabitants, who are called in Arabic Hasāwīyah حَسَاوِيَّة. Among the Hasāwīyah little stress is laid on tribal divisions, and the principal distinction observed is that of religion, between Shī'ahs and Sunnis. The total sedentary population of the oasis, the towns of **Hofūf** and **Mubarraz** being included, may be placed at 67,000 souls, of whom 25,000 (three-fourths Sunnis) inhabit the town of **Hofūf** and 8,500 (four-fifths Sunnis) that of **Mubarraz**. Of the 33,500 persons living in the 35 other towns and villages of the oasis, it appears that almost exactly ⅔ are Shī'ahs and ⅓ Sunnis; but the Sunnis generally preponderate in the larger of these country places. Both sects have schools at **Hofūf**, and the Sunnis have small schools in some of the larger villages as well, but the Shī'ahs have none outside of the capital.

It may be mentioned, notwithstanding the unimportance in Hasa of differences other than those of religion, that most of the Shī'ahs probably belong to the race known as **Bahārinah**, being so regarded by the people of **Qatīf** and **Bahrain** though not, perhaps, so styled by themselves; and that among the Sunnis there are included a few of the class called **Hūwalah**. The **Bahārinah**, notwithstanding the name and their undoubted racial identity with the original inhabitants of **Bahrain**, as proved by the existence among them of some of the same family divisions, appear to be indigenous to Hasa and not to be immigrants even of old standing. There are a few Jews in the oasis who have come from Turkish 'Irāq since the Turkish occupation of Hasa; and it is said that a **Sabian** community once existed, but if so it has now disappeared. Negro slaves are fairly numerous and for statistical purposes have not been distinguished from their owners, whose form of religion—whether Shi'ah or Sunni—they usually follow.

It is reported that in the villages of the oasis nearly every male adult possesses a rifle.

Inhabited places.—The following is an alphabetically arranged list of the principal towns, villages and nomad camping grounds in Hasa :—

Name.	Position.	Nature and inhabitants.	Remarks.
'Amrān-al-Janūbīyah عمران الجنوبيه	2 iles north-east by north of Jishshah.	A village of 200 houses of Shī'ahs.	Also called Hautah حوطه. This village is on the eastern edge of the cultivated portion of the oasis, or just outside it.
'Amrān-ash-Shamālīyah عمران الشماليه	Immediately north of 'Amrān-al-Janūbīyah.	A village of 350 houses of Shī'ahs.	The village lands are irrigated by water from the Haqal spring.
'Aqār العقار	2 miles west-northwest of Jishshah, on the north side of the Jishshah-Hofūf road.	A village of 40 houses of Sunnis.	The water supply for irrigation of the village is from the Khadūd spring.
Ayūn العيون	20 miles north of Hofūf.	A town of 500 houses of Sunnis.	The northernmost settlement in the Hasa Oasis and a place of some importance; it is surrounded by a deep moat and is the headquarters of a Nāhiyah, but there is no bazaar. Ayūn receives much of the surplus water of the oasis from the south-

Name.	Position.	Nature and inhabitants.	Remarks.
			ward; and the moat, which is generally dry, can easily be filled in times of danger. The cultivation at Qattār, mentioned below, belongs to 'Ayūn.
Battāliyah بضّليه	3 miles east-north-east of **Mubarraz**.	A village of 325 houses of Shī'ahs.	Irrigation is from the Hārah and Jauharīyah springs, of which the former rises close to the village.
Dalaiqīyah (Qasr ad-) قصر الدليقيه	5 miles south by west of Jishshah and ½ a mile north of Jabal Arba'.	A small fort-like enclosure containing 10 houses of non-Bedouin Arabs. There is no garrison, either police or military.	The building has 4 bastioned corners and a gate on the north side. There are 2 or 3 springs and perhaps 3,000 date trees; but the place lies outside the southern limit of cultivation.
Dālwah الدالوه	At the south end of Jabal Qārah, 3½ miles west-north-west of Jishshah.	A village of 225 houses of Shī'ahs.	For irrigation this place depends on the surplus water of various other villages.
Fudhūl فضول	Adjoins the Jishshah-**Hofūf** road on the south side at a point 3 miles from Jishshah and 6 from **Hofūf**.	A village of 250 houses, mostly of Sunnis.	There is flowing water, but little cultivation except of dates.
Gharābi غرابي	4½ miles east-south-east of 'Ayūn.	A well and camping ground visited by Bedouins.	The place is surrounded by desert.
Ghuwaij الغويج and Ghuwājīyah الغراجيه	About 16 miles north of Jishshah and 11 miles south-east by east of 'Ayūn.	Two wells close together on the border of **Biyādh**.	Do.
Halailah حبيله	6 miles north-east of **Hofūf**, just within the northern limit of cultivation.	A village of 300 houses of Shī'ahs.	Water for irrigation is from the Haqal spring. The Dāirat-as-Sanīyah has rice lands here.

Name.	Position.	Nature and inhabitants.	Remarks.
Hamādah ('Aqalat or 'Ain) عقلة - عين حمادة	About a mile south of Naslat Bū Ghanīmah and a short distance to the west of Sarāt-al-Kasht.	A Bedouin camping ground with wells.	...
Hautah حوطه	...	...	See 'Amrān-al-Janūbīyah above.
Hazam حزم	On the west of, and immediately adjoining, the Sāhūd fort near **Mubarraz** town.	A Bedouin camping ground.	Numbers of the poorer Bedouins of the **'Ajmān, Dawāsir,** Bani **Hājir** and **Āl Morrah** are to be found here in the hot weather. In summer as many as 1,500 tents may be counted at this place, but in winter not one remains.
Hofūf الهفوف	Near the southwest corner of the oasis and about 40 miles south-west by west of **'Oqair** Port on the coast.	..	See article **Hofūf**.
Jabail جبيل	5 miles east-north-east of **Hofūf** and a short distance from the western foot of Jabal Qārah.	A village of 200 houses of Shī'ahs.	Irrigation is by a channel from the Khadūd spring. The Dāirat-as-Sanīyah has rice lands here.
Jafar (Bāb-al-) باب الجفر	Immediately south of the Jishshah-**Hofūf** road at a point 1 mile west of Jishshah.	A large walled village of 350 houses; about half the people are Shī'ahs and half Sunnis.	This place is the headquarters of a Nāhiyah and there is land here under the management of the Dāirat-as-Sanīyah. The lands of the village are watered by a channel from the Haqal spring, but those of the Dāirat-as-Sanīyah lands by one from the Barābar spring. There is a post here of 50 mounted and 10 unmounted Dhābitīyahs.
Jalaijilah جليجله	5 miles due north of **Hofūf**.	150 houses of Shī'ahs.	This village stands in the centre of a detached area of cultivation which it shares with the other villages of Matairafi,

Name.	Position.	Nature and inhabitants.	Remarks.
			Qarain, Qaran and Shaqīq. There are rice lands here under the Dāirat-as-Sanīyah.
Jishshah جشة	9 miles due west of Hofūf on the route from Hofūf to 'Oqair Port, and situated on the eastern limit of cultivation or just outside it.	A town of 400 houses. The people are Sunnis with a small proportion of Shī'ahs. Some of the Sunnis are settled Pani Khālid of the Āl Jabūr section.	The inhabitants mostly either cultivate dates or own camels on which they carry goods for hire between 'Oqair Port and Hofūf. Good water, grass, fuel and other supplies are obtainable, but there are no shops. Jishshah is the first stage on the way from Hofūf to 'Oqair when the journey is performed in 4 stages.
Juwāthah (Masjid) مسجد جواة	2 miles north-north-east of Halailah beyond the northern limit of cultivation.	An ancient village site.	Here are a spring and the ruins of a mosque which is locally believed to have been one of the first 3 ever built by Muhammadans.
Kanzān كنزان	10 miles north-east of Hofūf and 5 miles north of Jabal Qārah.	A well and Bedouin camping ground.	...
Kalābiyah كلابية	1 mile north-west of Halailah.	A village of 250 houses. About two-thirds of the people are Sunnis and the remainder Shī'ahs: some of the Sunnis are Bani Khālid of the Āl Miqdām section.	This place is situated on the northern border of cultivation.
Luwaimi (Qasr-al-) قصر اللويمي	1 mile east of Hofūf at the south side of the road to Jishshah.	A fort occupied by Turkish troops and police, namely, it would seem, a quarter of a battalion of regular infantry and 25 mounted Dhābitīyahs.	The land connected with the fort is watered by the Luwaimi spring.
Manaizlah منيزلة	On the north side of the Jishshah-Hofūf road at a point 3 miles west of Jishshah.	A village of 225 houses, mostly of Shī'ahs.	Jabal Qārah rises about 1 mile to the north of this village. The Dāirat-as-Sanīyah has rice lands here.

HASA OASIS

Name.	Position.	Nature and inhabitants.	Remarks.
Maqdam المقدم	Midway between Kalabiyah and Halailah.	A village of 100 houses, mostly of Shī'ahs.	Situated on the northern verge of cultivation.
Markaz المركز	½ a mile north-west of Jishshah.	A village of 325 houses. About half of the people are Sunnis and the other half Shī'ahs.	The plantations of this place are watered by channels from the Khadūd and Haqal springs. There is a post here of 25 mounted and 10 unmounted Dhābitīyahs.
Matairafi مطيرفي	¾ of a mile south-south-west of Jalaijilah, in the same detached area of cultivation.	A village of 125 houses of Shī'ahs.	The Huwairah spring rises a few hundred yards west of this place, which is also supplied with water for irrigation by the Umm-al-Līf spring. There are lands here belonging to the Dāirat-as-Sanīyah.
Mazāwi المزاوي	2 miles north-west by west of Jishshah.	A village of 50 houses of Shī'ahs.	Cultivation depends on the Haqal spring. At this village too are Sanīyah rice lands.
Mubarraz مبرز	2 miles north of Hofūf.	...	See article **Mubarraz**.
Na'ām (Bani) بني نعام	On the north side of the Hofūf-Jishshah road at 2½ miles from Hofūf.	A village of 200 houses of Shī'ahs.	The Nasairīyah spring rises close to the east side of this village and irrigates its fields.
Nahu (Bani) بني نهر	1 mile east of Hofūf and a short distance to the north of the Hofūf-Jishshah road.	A hamlet of 20 houses of Shī'ahs.	This place has declined greatly, but it is still irrigated and some date plantations remain. The Haqal, Umm-al-Līf, Qasaibah, Luwaimi and Barābar springs are situated in a cluster between it and Hofūf; and the Mansūr spring rises immediately to the south-east of it.
Qārah القاره	6 miles north-east by east of Hofūf.	A village of 300 houses of Shī'ahs.	Jabal Qārah rises immediately behind this village, on its south-east side.

Name.	Position.	Nature and inhabitants.	Remarks.
Qarain القرين	½ a mile south-east of Qaran.	A village of 130 houses of Shī'ahs.	This place is situated in the same detached area of cultivation as Jalaijilah.
Qaran القرن	1 mile north-east of Jalaijilah.	A village of 120 houses of Shī'ahs.	Jabal Qārah rises immediately behind this village, on its south-east side.
Qasr-ash-Sharqi قصر الشرقي	At the south side of the Hofūf-Jishshah road, 4 miles due east of Hofūf.	A fort occupied by a Turkish garrison which consists apparently of a quarter of a battalion of regular infantry and 25 mounted Dhābitīyahs.	This post is also known as Qasr Ghasaibah غصيبه and as Qasr-al-Wajāj وجاج
Ramailah الرميله	1 mile north-north-east of Jishshah, just within the eastern limit of cultivation.	A village of 100 houses. The people are mostly Shī'ahs.	…
Ruqaiqah الرقيقه	1 mile south of Hofūf and perhaps somewhat to westward.	A large camping ground always occupied by Bedouins of the poorer class; of these about 500 families are permanently resident and 1,000 more are added to their number in the hot weather. Dawāsir, 'Ajmān, Āl Morrah, Bani Hājir, Sahūl, Mutair, Sabai', 'Ataibah and Qahtān are all found here.	The name is pronounced Rujaijah and even Rugaijah. Water is from pits. The permanent residents grow barley in winter in the surrounding desert.
Sābāt الصاباط	1 mile west-north-west of Jishshah.	A village of 100 houses; the people are mostly Shī'ahs.	…
Sha'abah الشعبه	4 miles north-north-east of Mubarraz at the western end of Jabal Buraijah.	A village of 150 houses of Shī'ahs.	The cultivated lands of this village, which stretch from it south-westwards for a couple of miles or more, are separate both from those of the main block and

The village of Qarah in the Hasa Oasis.
(Herr H. Burchardt.)

Name.	Position.	Nature and inhabitants.	Remarks.
			also from those of the area surrouding Jalaijilah. Irrigation water is brought across the intervening waste from the springs of Hārah and Jaubarīyah.
Shahārīn الشهارين	1 mile south-west of Jabail.	A hamlet of 20 houses of Shī'ahs.	This place has a good water supply, but the population is nevertheless small.
Shaqīq شقيق	¾ of a mile south-east of Matairafi.	A village of 100 houses. Half the people are Shī'ahs and the other half Sunnis.	The Dāirat-as-Saniyah has lands here on which rice is grown. Shaqiq is in the same group with Jalaijilah, etc.
Siyāirah سيائرة	1½ miles north of Jishshah.	A village of 150 houses, mostly of Shī'ahs.	...
Taimīyah التميه	3 miles north-west of Jishshah, at the south-eastern corner of Jabal Qārah.	A village of 225 houses of Shī'ahs.	Irrigation is by channels from the Khadūd and Haqal springs.
Taraf الطرف	1 mile south-west of Jishshah.	A village of 450 houses. The bulk of the people are Sunnis; a small proportion are Shī'ahs.	Irrigation is dependent on the Barābar spring.
Thanain (Abu) ابو ثنين	4 miles south-east of Hofūf.	A Bedouin camping ground with wells.	Surrounded by desert.
Thaqbah ثقبه	2 miles west of Hofūf and perhaps slightly to southward.	Do.	Do.
Thūr (Abu) ابو ثور	2 miles north by west of Jishshah.	A village of 40 houses of Shī'ahs.	...
Traibīl طربيل	Closely adjoining Jabail and to the south-east of it.	A village of 50 houses of Shī'ahs.	The supply of water for irrigation is brought from the Khadūd spring.
Tuwaithīr تويثير	4 miles north-west of Jishshah, at the foot of Jabal Qārah on its east side towards the north end.	A village of 250 houses of Shī'ahs.	...

The houses of the Hasa oasis are built chiefly of sun-dried bricks and mud and the villages have walls and gates; but in most places there is also a proportion of huts outside the village wall. The villages are generally hidden away in date groves and gardens. Except in the town of **Hofūf**, where there are wells, water for drinking is generally taken from the springs which irrigate the date groves.

Irrigation.—The most remarkable features of the oasis are unquestionably its water supply and the utilisation of the same for agriculture. Reference has already been made to the warm springs which break out here and there all over the surface of the country, sometimes singly and sometimes in groups; and a table is now subjoined showing the names, positions and characteristics of the more important, and of certain lakes and channels which are connected with them:—

Name.	Position.	Remarks.
Asfar (Birkat-al-) بركة الاصفر	12 miles east-north-east of Hofūf.	A large lake or swamp formed by the excess waters of the springs to the east of Hofūf and fed in particular by the northern branch of Salaisil.
Bahair بحير and Bahairīyah بحيريه	Close together a few hundred yards west of Hofūf, near the north-western corner of the Khazām fort. Bahairīyah is to the north of Bahair.	Springs irrigating a cultivated area which extends from them in a north-westerly direction. The surplus waters find their way into Salaisil.
Barābar برابر	A few hundred yards east of Hofūf and the same south-west of Bani Nahu village.	A large spring. Its waters eventually reach the south-eastern villages of Bāb-al-Jafar and Taraf.
Faraihah فريحه	About ½ a mile east of Hofūf.	A spring which contributes to form Salaisil.
Haqal الحقل	A few hundred yards east of Hofūf, west and somewhat north of Bani Nahu.	A large spring watering among other villages those of Bāb-al-Jafar, Markaz, Mazāwi, 'Amrān-ash-Shamālīyah, Taimīyah and Halailah.
Hārah الحاره	Immediately to the north of Mubarraz.	A spring affording irrigation to Mubarraz, Battālīyah and Sha'abah.
Huwairah هويرة or Huwairāt هويرات	A few hundred yards to the west of Matairafi.	A large spring of hot water. It helps to form Salaisil; and, in the opposite direction, its waters reach to 'Ayūn.

Name.	Position.	Remarks.
Iblāl ابلال	Less than one mile to the south-east of **Hofūf**	A spring of which the surplus waters are tributary to Salaisil.
Jabarīyah جبريه	Between the villages of Bani Nahu and Bani Na'ām, rather nearer to the latter.	A large spring which is one of feeders of Salaisil.
Jamāl (Umm-al-) ام الجمال	A few hundred yards east of **Hofūf**, between the Haqal and Khadūd springs.	...
Jauharīyah جوهريه	Close to the south-west side of Battālīyah village.	A spring of which the water reaches to Sha'abah.
Jazīrah جزيره	In a garden of the same name about 1 mile south-west of **Hofūf**.	A double spring of which the surplus waters fall in to Salaisil.
Kasht (Sarāt-al-) صرات الكشت	About 1 mile north west of **Hofūf** and the same south-west of **Mubarraz**.	A large shallow lake near the western side of the oasis; it receives the water of several springs. In the hot weather the lake dries up, and in the process of doing so its waters become undrinkably salt.
Khadūd الخدرد	A few hundred yards east of **Hofūf** and the same west of Bani Nahu village.	A large spring of which the waters benefit the villages of Jabail, Traibīl, 'Aqār, Taimīyah and Markaz.
Kharaisān (Umm) ام خريسان	Just outside **Hofūf** on the north-east side.	A large spring which is among the feeders of Salaisil.
Līf (Umm-al-) ام الليف	Immediately to the north-east of the Khadūd spring.	Do.
Luwaimi اللويمي	Immediately to the east of the Barābar spring.	A large spring, from which the lands about Qasr-al-Luwaimi are irrigated.
Mahza' (Birkat Umm-al-) بركة ام المهزع	Several miles east of the town of 'Ayūn.	A lake which receives the superabundant waters of the northern part of the Hasa oasis. From the side of 'Ayūn it is fed by a channel called Maqta'-al-Mahza', which flows about 10 feet broad and varies in depth with the season of the year, but is said to be sometimes impassable.
Mansūr منصور	A short distance to the south-east of Bani Nahu village and rather more than 1 mile east of **Hofūf**.	A spring from which is irrigated a part of the lands of **Hofūf** town.

Name.	Position.	Remarks.
Marjān مرجان	Just outside **Mubarraz** town, at its south-west corner.	Also called 'Ain-as-Saiyid عين السيّد. A spring from which the people of **Mubarraz** obtain drinking water.
Mishaitīyah مشيطيّه	About 1 mile south-east of **Hofūf**.	A spring.
Nādharah ناضره	Close to the south-west corner of **Mubarraz** town.	There was formerly a village here called 'Ain Nādharah, but it has disappeared. The plantations still exist and are tended by people of **Mubarraz** and **Hofūf**.
Najm ('Ain-an-) عين النجم	About 1⅓ miles west of **Mubarraz**, near the tip of Naslat Bū Ghanīmah.	A hot sulphur spring; the water is clean, beneficial in cutaneous diseases, and can also be used for irrigation. A dome which covered the spring was destroyed in 1862 by the Wahhābis.
Naqairāt (Khīsat or Saba') خيسة – سبعه نقيرات	4½ miles east of Jishshah.	A small well-like spring. It is not applied to irrigation.
Nasairīyah نصيريّه	On the east side of Bani Na'ām village, immediately adjoining it.	A spring watering the lands of Bani Na'ām village.
Qasaibah قصيبه	Immediately north of the Luwaimi spring.	...
Qattār قطّار	About 6 miles north of the town of 'Ayūn.	A spring of which the waters do not reach very far. The land adjoining it belongs to the people of 'Ayūn, who grow wheat and rice in it; when the Bedouins are on the war path, however, it is allowed to lie fallow.
Saba' (Umm) أمّ سبع	½ a mile south of the village of Matairafi, and the same distance west of that of Shaqīq.	A large and very hot spring. From its basin, 50 feet in diameter, 7 streams radiate in different directions: it owes its name to this circumstance. Some old masonry work and thick vegetation surround the pool. The water of Umm Saba' is distributed among the villages of Matairafi, Shaqīq and Qarain and reaches to 'Ayūn.

Name.	Position.	Remarks.
Saiyid ('Ain-as-) عين السيد	...	See Marjān above.
Salaisil الساىسل	It begins a mile east of Hofūf on the north side of the Bani Nahu village.	A river-like torrent formed by the commingling of the surplus waters of many springs. At first it flows east in a single channel, has a strong current, and is 30 to 40 feet wide and very deep; as it passes Bani Na'ām village, however, on the north side, it divides into two branches known as Nahr Salaisil and Nahr Dughāni نهر دغاني. Of these the latter, which is the more southerly, waters all the south-eastern villages of the Hasa Oasis; it appears to be about 10 feet broad and 2 or 3 feet in depth. Nahr Salaisil on the other hand passes close to the south of Jabal Qārah, and branches of it even run round that hill to Halailah and other villages; so much of its water as is not expended in irrigation finds its way into the Birkat-al-Asfar.
Sarah الصرة	5 miles east-south-east of Jishshah.	A spring which may be taken as marking the south-easternmost limit of the Hasa oasis. A few date trees adjoin it and a village is said to have existed formerly.
Ta'ādhīd تعاضيد	1 mile east of Hofūf.	A spring.
Za'ablah زعابله	3 miles east of Hofūf.	Do.

The irrigation channels leading from the springs to the fields continually cross one another by means of aqueducts, and the result is a very complex network of waterways. Each spring is the separate property of one or more villages. The water seems to be ample for the cultvated land, and much of it even runs to waste. Each plot of land has had from time immemorial a regular water supply from a particular spring attached to it, which is reckoned by hours of flow; the distribution of water consequently follows that of land and not hereditary tribal shares or any other scheme of division. Water rights cannot be sold apart from land, for the two are indissolubly connected and are necessarily transferred together. The water is not subject to taxation, being regarded as " Māl Allah ", or a natural benefaction free to all who are landholders. Small striped or speckled fish exist in the streams.

Agriculture and livestock.—The cultivated parts of Hasa are a mass of date plantations interspersed with rice fields: every village possesses some date groves. The dates are the most valuable product of the oasis and are considered by the Arabs of the Persian Gulf to be the best in the world, superior to those of **Basrah** and **'Omān**; about ⅓ are of the most esteemed variety styled Khalās, and ½ are of the kind called Razaizi. The average annual date crop of the Hasa oasis has been estimated at 51,000 tons. Besides dates some rice is cultivated; also lucerne and a "sour grass"—possibly a sorrel—called Rashaidi رشيدي. Wheat and barley are raised, part of the barley being grown in winter, without irrigation, in the desert portions of the oasis where there are semi-permanent Bedouin encampments; but the cereals produced are not sufficient even for local consumption. Sugar and indigo are not seen. The fruits of the oasis include the citron, peach, apricot, fig, pomegranate, grape, sweet lime and sour lime: and there are also common vegetables such as radishes, onions and garlic, but both fruits and vegetables are of poor quality.

The chief domestic animals are cattle, sheep, donkeys, horses and camels: despite the swampy character of the country and its political connection with Turkish **'Irāq** there are no buffaloes. Cattle are abundant, and there is said to be on the average a cow to every house; but sheep, which belong chiefly to the Bedouins, are not so plentiful as in **Najd**. The donkeys, which are in possession of the villagers, are estimated to number about 3,000 of the famous white **Hasa** breed and about 10,000 of ordinary breeds. Horses owned by villagers are about 100.

Communications, transport and supplies.—The main routes which traverse the Hasa Oasis are described in the article upon the **Hasa Sanjāq**. Here it may be added that travellers proceeding northwards from **Hofūf** do so by way of 'Ain Hamādah and the Barr or desert to the westward, avoiding the cultivated country.

Reliable estimates of the transport and supplies available in the oasis are not available, but a rough indication of the nature and extent of its resources is contained in the foregoing paragraphs.

Manufactures, trade, civil administration and military arrangements.—These subjects are dealt with in the article on the Hasa Sanjāq except the trade in dates, the nature of which is explained by the following table :—

Quantity in tons.	Disposal.	Remarks.
3,000	Exported to Jiddah *via* 'Oqair Port and Basrah.	The passage from 'Oqair to Basrah is by sailing boat. On this route there is a saving in transhipment dues.
1,000	Exported to Jiddah *via* Bahrain.	...
5,000	Exported to Bahrain.	For local consumption in Bahrain.
2,000	Exported to Qatar.	For local consumption in Qatar.
40,000	Locally consumed in the Hasa oasis, sold to Bedouins, or exported overland to Najd, Kuwait, etc.	...

None of the dates exported from the Hasa Oasis are boiled dates.

HASA SANJĀQ

A detached province of the Turkish Empire, situated on the coast of Eastern Arabia between the Kuwait Principality on the north and the promontory of Qatar and the Jāfūrah desert on the south ; on the east it is bounded by the sea, and on the west by the tract known as Summān. The official designation of this province among the Turks—at least until the Ottoman occupation of a part of the true Najd in 1905—was "Sanjāq of Najd."

* The region dealt with in this article being in some respects a territorial unit it was necessary to give it a specific name for the purpose of separate description. Without such an article no general view of this part of Eastern Arabia in its physical aspect could have been set before the reader, nor could the Turkish administration of the scattered localities in which representatives of the Porte are actually stationed have been presented in any intelligible light. Moreover, it would have been impossible to deal satisfactorily with the main routes which traverse this piece of country ; and more than 20 articles in the Gazetteer, dealing with the tracts of which it is composed, would have remained uncorrelated to one another.

The term "Hasa Sanjāq" is not unobjectionable, but it seems to be the least unsuitable that can be suggested : the only possible alternative is "Eastern Arabia"—a phrase at once too comprehensive and too vague. Each component of the name "Hasa Sanjāq" is liable to criticism, the first component because the Turks call their

Boundaries and natural divisions. —On the north the boundary of the Sanjāq begins at Jabal Munīfah upon the coast and runs inland westwards to the Na'airīyah hill; then, changing its direction to south-west, it passes by the 'Udūmāt hill to the north end of the Abu Dhahair ridge. The western boundary is marked by Jabal-al-Taff throughout the length of that range, and beyond by a line joining the south end of Jabal-al-Taff to Jau-ad-Dukhān. From Jau-ad-Dukhān the boundary runs first north-east by Qusūr Bin-'Ajlān to the south-eastern corner of the **Hasa** Oasis; then eastwards; and finally south-eastwards to the foot of **Salwa** bay.

province the 'Sanjāq of Najd," while the Arabs do not admit the applicability of the term "Hasa" to anything but the small oasis so styled, and the second component because it seems to suggest that the Turks have effectively occupied the entire region in question. The former of these objections to "Hasa") does not carry much weight; for, the existence of a Turkish Sanjāq in Eastern Arabia being admitted and the Turkish name "Sanjāq of Najd" being rejected for obvious reasons, it is clearly best that the Sanjāq should be called after its headquarters and most valuable constituent district—the oasis, namely, of **Hasa**. The second objection (to 'Sanjāq") has perhaps more force; but it must be remembered that, while on the one hand the Turkish occupation is not at present effective except in the oases of **Hasa** and **Qatīf**, at **'Oqair** Port and on the islands of **Tārūt, Musallamīyah** and **Jinnah**, on the other hand there are strong reasons for regarding the whole of the region under discussion as subject to Turkish influence and even authority. The Turks themselves claim the sovereignty of the whole, and the validity of their title to the country north of **'Oqair** Port has been allowed by the British Government; while to the south of that place, though called in question, it has not been explicitly denied. The Turks also subsidise the '**Ajmān, Bani Hājir, Bani Khālid** and **Āl Morrah** tribes, who together occupy the whole of the country except the two oases and **Tārut** Island, and maintain by their means a system of postal communications outside the oases. Within the limits of what we have called the "Hasa Sanjāq," for the last 30 years, the political relations of those tribes have been exclusively with the Turkish Government.

The political status of the region (other than the oases, **'Oqair** Port and the islands) somewhat resembles that of parts of the tribal territory between the administrative border of British India and the frontier of Afghanistan, where the political suzerainty of Great Britain is proved, not by administrative occupation, but by the payment of subsidies and by the occasional employment of military force. In other words, tracts such as **Biyādh** and **Ghuwār** seem to belong to the jurisdiction of the Mutasarrif at **Hofūf** in much the same manner as the Afridi and Mahsud countries belong to the jurisdiction of the Chief Commissioner at Peshawar.

Such information relating to the Hasa Sanjāq as was available in 1904 was thrown by the writer into the form of notes and appeared as 16 foolscap pages of print in November of that year: these notes were taken by him on tour to the Persian Gulf and formed the basis of fresh investigations which he initiated there during a halt in Bahrain. After the writer's return to India in 1905 detailed information regarding the **Qatīf** Oasis was obtained by Mr. J. C. Gaskin, Political Assistant in the Persian Gulf; and an exhaustive study of everything connected with the Hasa province and its geography was commenced by Captain F. B. Prideaux, Political Agent in Bahrain, assisted by Mr. In'ām-al-Haqq, Agency Interpreter, an Aligarh graduate. In November 1905 a provisional draft of articles on the Sanjāq and places, etc., in it

The administrative divisions of the Sanjāq will be mentioned further on, but the present is a suitable place in which to enumerate the various natural tracts, having distinctive names, of which the region is composed: each of these has a character more or less peculiar to itself, and each forms the subject of a separate article in this Gazetteer, which may be consulted for details concerning it. The order of these tracts upon the coast from north to south is:—Zor-al-**Audhān, Huzūm, Biyādh, Qatīf** Oasis, Barr-adh-**Dhahrān**, Barr-al-**'Oqair** and Barr-al-**Qārah**. The tracts upon the landward frontier in succession are:—on the north Sabākhat-al-**Mutāya, Radāif** and Wādi-al-**Miyāh**; on the west, Wādi-al-**Miyāh, Habl, Taff**, Wādi **Farūq, Na'alah, Ghuwār, Kharmah**, the **Hasa** Oasis (at its south-east corner), **Biyādh** and Barr-al-**Qārah**. The tracts in the interior which do not at any point reach to the circumference are **Sanfān-al-Hanna** and Jau **Shamīn** south of **Radāif**, and Jau-as-**Sa'adān, Badd-al-Asīs** and **Jauf** to the north-east and north of the **Hasa** Oasis. The Sanjāq, it will be seen, consists of no less than 22

---

was finished by the writer and sent to the Gulf, where it was carefully revised by Captain Prideaux; Major P. Z. Cox also, Resident in the Persian Gulf, dealt with some of the points that had been raised. Meanwhile a set of maps and plans had been compiled by Captain Prideaux, with great labour, from native information; and at the beginning of 1907, chiefly in consequence of the work of Captain Prideaux during the previous two years, a fresh set of drafts was completed at Simla extending to over 130 octavo pages of print as against 50 similar pages at the end of 1905. This draft of 1907 was subjected, during the remainder of the year, to further revision by Captain Prideaux.

Apart from the present Gazetteer the chief general authorities on the Hasa Sanjāq are the following: Niebuhr's *Description de l'Arabie*, 1774; Sadlier's *Diary of a Journey across Arabia* (in 1819), 1866; *Bombay Records, XXIV*, 1856; Palgrave's *Central and Eastern Arabia*, 1865; Pelly's *Report on a Journey to the Wahabee Capital*, 1866; Captain J. A. Douglas's *Journey from India to the Mediterranean*, 1897; the Rev. S. M. Zwemer's *Arabia*, 1900; and Herr H. Burchardt's article *Ost-Arabien von Basra bis Maskat*, 1906. The *Persian Gulf Pilot*, 1898, deals fully with the coast, islands and other maritime features of the region; a report by Dr. Cassim Izzedine, contained in the Political Proceedings of the Government of India for June 1898, treats of the country primarily from the sanitary standpoint; and for discussions of ancient geography, the identification of places, etc., Spreng *Alte Geographie Arabiens*, 1875, and Colonel Miles' *Note on Pliny's Geography of the East Coast of Arabia*, 1878, may be consulted.

The map issued with this Gazetteer is the best of the region under consideration. It is founded on the following valuable compilations by Captain Prideaux from native information: *Map of Eastern Arabia north of Qatar*, 1905; *Plan of the Hasa Oasis*, 1905; *Plan of the Katif Oasis*, 1905; *Index Map of the Tracts in Eastern Arabia north of Qatar*, 1906: these are filed in the Library of the Foreign Department, Simla, under the following numbers 1369, 1370, 1371 and 1372. The only Charts relating to the coast of the Hasa Sanjāq are No. 2374—2837-B., *Persian Gulf*, and Preliminary Chart No. O. 1, *Bahrein to Ojar*, Poona, 1902.

separate natural divisions; of these all are desert with the exception of the two oases and, to a certain extent, of Wādi-al-**Miyāh**. Besides these tracts on the mainland, the islands of **Musāllamīyah, Jinnah, Janāh,** Abu **'Ali Jaraid** and **Tārūt**,—all separately described,—must be taken to be included in the Hasa Sanjāq.

Physical features.—As a whole, the region is one of sandy or earthy deserts, containing numerous shallow wells of drinkable water and a fair quantity of grazing and therefore habitable by Bedouins. Here and there the surface is broken by isolated hills: such of these as belong entirely to one tract are described in the article on the tract, while the remainder, situated on boundaries and common to more than one tract, are dealt with in the general table below:—

Name.	Position.	Character.	Remarks.
'Ajlān (Qusūr Bin·) قصور بن عجلان	About 70 miles south of Jabal Bū Ghanīmah.	A hill.	It marks the southern extremity of **Ghu-wār**, dividing it from **Jāfūrah**.
Arba' (Jabal)* جبل اربع	5 miles south of Jishshah village in the Hasa Oasis.	An isolated hill with four points.	It stands on the border between the Hasa Oasis and Kharmah. Qasr Dalaiqīyab in the oasis is immediately north of it.
Barāim (Jabal) جبل برائم	15 miles west of Jabal Gharaimīl.	A solitary hill of no great size.	On the border between Badd-al-**Asīs** on the east and Jau-as-Sa'adān on the west.
Dām (Jabal-ad-) جبل الدام	40 miles inland, west by north, from the foot of Dōhat **Ruhum**; 50 miles south-west of **Qatīf** Town, and nearly 60 miles north by east of **Hofūf**.	An isolated hill, one of the principal landmarks in the centre of the Sanjāq; it is probably several miles in length from north to south.	At its north end are two small peaks called Jabailain-al-Faraj جبيلين الفرج. Jabal-ad-Dām marks the junction of no less than 5 distinct tracts,—**Habl, Biyādh, Jauf,** Badd-al **Asīs** and Jau-as-**Sa'adān**.

* A view of Jabal Arba' accompanies Herr H. Burchardt's article *Ost-Arabien*, 1906,

Desert between the Hasa Oasis & Qatar.
(HERR H. BURCHARDT.)

Name.	Position.	Character.	Remarks.
Dhahair (Jabal Abu) جبل ابو ظهير	60 or 70 miles inland, due westwards, from the coast between **Musallamīyah** and Abu 'Ali island.	A range of hills, perhaps 20 miles long from north to south. It forms a northerly prolongation of Jabal-ai-Taff, from which it is divided only by a slight gap. The two most conspicuous peaks are one at the north called Jabal Umm-az-Zor ام الزور and one at the south called Halaiyāt حليات.	It skirts Wādi-al-**Miyāh** on the west from opposite **Ntā'** southwards as far as the 'Awainah wells. Beyond it, but separated from it by an interval of some miles, is **Summān**.
Dukhān (Jau-ad-) جو الدخان	About 90 miles south by west of Jabal Bū Ghanīmah.	A hill.	It marks the southern extremity of the **Na'alah** and **Wādi Farūq** tracts.
Ghanīmah (Jabal Bū) جبل بو غنيمة	About 6 miles west of the towns of **Hofūf** and **Mubarraz**.	A ridge of white craggy hills, probably some miles in length from north to south: a spur known as Naslat Bū Ghanīmah نصلة بو غنيمة comes down to the Najm spring on the west side of **Mubarraz**.	At the southern end is the meeting place of the **Hasa** Oasis and the **Ghuwār** and **Kharmah** tracts.
Gharaimīl (Jabal) جبل غريميل	40 miles north of **Hofūf** and 20 miles south-south-east of Jabal-ad-Dām.	An isolated hill, apparently of considerable size or at least extent.	The tracts of **Jauf**, **Biyādh** and **Badd-al-Asīs** meet round this hill.
Hass (Jabal-al-) جبل الحصّ	About 15 miles south-east by east of **Ntā'**.	An isolated hill.	It marks the trijunctional point of the **Radāif** and **Sanfān-al-Hanna** tracts and **Wādi-al-Miyāh**.
Jūdah (Jabal) جبل جودة	About 12 miles south-south-west of the Umm Rubai'ah wells in **Taff**.	An outlier of Jabal-al-Taff, but probably disconnected from that range.	Between **Taff** and **Summān**. (See next entry.)

Name.	Position.	Character.	Remarks.
Jūdah (Jabal Hamrat) جبل حمرة جودة	About 12 miles south-south-west of Jabal Jūdah, between **Taff** and **Summān**.	An outlier of Jabal-at-Taff, but probably disconnected from that range.	Between **Taff** and **Summān**. (See last entry.) The Jūdah wells in **Taff** are between this hill and Jabal Jūdah.
Labtalah (Jabal) جبل لبطاه	Some 5 miles south-east of Thāj in Wādi-al-**Miyāh**.	An isolated hill.	This hill, which is of some extent from north to south, is on the boundary between **Habl** and Wādi-al-**Miyāh**.
Mathlūth (Jabal) جبل مثلوث	25 miles west by south of Jabal-ad-Dām.	An isolated three-pointed hill not covering much space.	This hill is the meeting place of the **Habl**, Jau-as-Sa'-adān and **Taff** tracts.
Murair (Jabal) جبل مرير	10 miles inland, due westwards, from the foot of Dōhat-ad-Dafi.	A small isolated hill.	Stands on the border between **Biyādh** and **Huzūm**.
Na'airīyah (Jabal) جبل نعيرية	About 18 miles north-north-east of **Ntā'**.	A detached hill or group of hills.	Wādi-al-**Miyāh** and the **Radāif** tract meet at this spot, which is also upon the southern border of the **Kuwait** Principality.
'Othmānīyah (Qārat-al-) عثمانية	About 25 miles west by south of Jabal Bū Ghanīmah.	An isolated hill.	It is on the border between **Ghuwār** and **Na'alah**.
Qadām (Jabal) جبل قدام	About 35 miles north-west of Jabal-ad-Dām.	Do.	It stands at the head of a reentrant in the border of **Habl**, the other district which reaches it being Wādi-al-**Miyāh**.
Rukbān (Qārat-ar-) قارة الركبان	About 20 miles north-north-west of **Hofūf**.	A hill of insignificant height and circumference, but one which sometimes plays an important part in intertribal fights among the Bedouins.	It marks the north-western corner of the **Hasa** Oasis and is its meeting place with the **Biyādh**, Badd-al-**Asīs** and **Ghuwār** tracts.

Name.	Position.	Character.	Remarks.
Shuyūkh (Ghārash-) غار الشيوخ	About 25 miles north-west of Jabal Bū Ghanīmah.	A hill. It perhaps extends southwards for some distance, for some authorities assign to it a position a good deal more southerly than that given in the last column.	This hill seems to be the meeting place of the Badd-al-**Asīs**, **Ghuwār**, **Na'alah** and **Jau-as-Sa'adān** tracts.
Taff (Jabal-at-) جبل الطف	Roughly parallel to the coast at a distance of about 100 miles inland: its northern end is approximately in the latitude of Qasr Al **Subaih** and its southern in that of **Zakhnūnīyah** island.	A range of hills, the most extensive in this part of Eastern Arabia, running for about 100 miles from north by west to south by east. From its eastern side the range sends off two principal spurs, namely, Daqlam دقلم near the wells of Qubaibah in Wādi-al-**Miyāh** and Nasatain-al-Farha نصلتين العرحا on the border between **Habl** and **Taff**. At the western foot of it, in nearly the same latitude as Naslatain-al-Farha, is a circular depression called Subsub, and yet a little further west is a detached hill known as Jabal Wushaihah.	Jabal-at-Taff divides **Taff**, **Habl** and the southern half of **Wādi-al-Miyāh** on the east from **Summān** on the west. Jabal Jūdah and Jabal Hamrat Jūdah, though apparently detached, seem to belong to the southern part of the Taff system.
'Udūmāt عدرمات	About midway between Jabal Na'airīyah and the northern end of Jabal-al-Taff.	An isolated hill.	It stands on the northern border of Wādi-al-**Miyāh** between that district and the **Warai'ah** tract in the Kuwait Principality.

Other hills which, standing within a district, belong to it and are described in the article under its name are the following:—Jubail-al-Bahri, Dhalaifain, Mubārakīyah and Qarain in **Biyādh**, the two former on the coast and the two latter in the interior; Ghumīs and Qabūrah in **Habl**, in the interior; Dhahrān in Barr-adh-**Dhahrān**, near the coast; Qārah and Buraijah in the **Hasa** Oasis; Ghuwār in **Ghuwār** and

Kharmah in **Kharmah,** both in the interior : and finally Jabal-al-Qārah in Barr-al-**Qārah,** near the coast. Springs, streams and lakes occur only in the **Hasa** and **Qatīf** Oases, in the articles on which they will be found. The depth of the water level has been indicated, so far as possible, in the articles on the numerous desert tracts. The climate is warm and in the oases moist also ; more rain, it is said, falls than in **Bahrain,** and some food grains are even raised near the **Hasa** Oasis without recourse to artificial irrigation.

Inhabitants.—The following is an estimate of the population of the whole Sanjāq, distinguishing between villagers (or townsmen) and Bedouins, according to such information as is available :—

Settled population.

Area.	Souls.
Hasa Oasis, including the towns of **Hofūf** (25,000) and **Mubarraz** (8,500)	67,000
Jinnah island	500
Miyāh (Wādi-al-)	1,000
Musallamīyah island	2,000
Qatīf Oasis, including **Qatīf** Town (10,000)	26,000
Subaih (Qasr Āl)	1,000
Tārūt island	3,500
Total settled population	101,000

Nomadic population.

Tribe.	Souls.
'Ajmān	35,000
Hājir (Bani)	5,000
Khālid (Bani), after deducting settled Bani **Khālid** on the islands of **Musallamīyah, Jinnah** and **Tārūt** and at Qasr Al **Subaih,** etc.	10,000
Morrah (Āl)	7,000
Total nomadic population	57,000

The whole of the **'Ajmān** and Āl **Morrah** tribes have been included among the Bedouins of Hasa, for the great bulk of the former have their headquarters in the Sanjāq, and the Āl **Morrah,** though the **Jāfūrah** desert and **Jabrīn** are among their peculiar possessions, have hardly any relations with the external world except through Hasa. Conversely the **'Awāzim** and **Rashāidah,** although they wander to some extent in Hasa, have been excluded from the table because their permanent headquarters and proper locations are in **Kuwait** territory and certain Bedouin tribes of **Najd**—such as the **Dawāsir, Sahūl**

Mutair, Sabai', 'Ataibah and Qahtān, who are represented by camps in Hasa in the hot weather,—have been similarly treated.

The Bahārinah—who form nearly the entire population of the Qatīf Oasis, compose perhaps ⅜ or more of the population of the Oasis of Hasa and occupy Tārūt island, but are not found elsewhere—are the chief racial ingredient in the settled population : their number may amount to 58,000 souls. The next most considerable element is the settled portion of the Bani Khālid, about 4,500 persons, chiefly on the islands of Musallamīyah, Jinnah and Tārūt, at Qasr Āl Subaih, and at Kalābīyah and Jishshah in the Hasa Oasis and Umm-as-Sāhak in the oasis of Qatīf. In Wādi-al-Miyāh there are about 1,000 miscellaneous Arabs, drawn from the 'Ajmān, 'Awāzim, Bani Khālid, Mutair, Rashāidah and Shammar tribes ; and these, with a few Bani Yās and Sādah on Tārūt Island and still fewer Hūwalah at Qatīf Town and in the Hasa Oasis, complete the tale of the settled inhabitants. Negro slaves, who are fairly numerous, have been included, for statistical purposes, in the tribes and communities by whom they are owned. There was formerly a flourishing though fluctuating community of Hindu traders, British subjects, unaccompanied by their families, at Qatīf Town ; but it has now disappeared for reasons which are explained in the article on that place.

The distribution of the Bedouin tribes of the Sanjāq is explained in detail in the articles under their names ; to speak generally, the Bani Khālid are located in the north, and the Āl Morrah to the south, with the Bani Hājir between them towards the coast and the ' Ajmān between them in the interior.

The inhabitants of the Sanjāq are heavily armed , and it is reported that, in the villages of the Hasa and Qatīf Oases, nearly every male adult possesses a rifle. When the arms trade was permitted in Bahrain rifles were easily obtained thence; now they are mostly smuggled in through Qatar.

Agriculture and livestock.—Agriculture is practically confined to the Oases of Hasa and Qatīf, in the articles on which irrigation and crops are described. Here it may be repeated that dates, which are excellent and plentiful, are the chief staple; but rice, wheat, barley and a considerable variety of fruits and vegetables are also grown. Cattle and donkeys are owned in considerable numbers by the villagers of both oases; but camels, horses and sheep are chiefly in the possession of the Bedouins.

Transport.—A proportion of the donkeys in the Oases of Hasa and Qatīf are excellent and belong to the white indigenous breed now found also in Bahrain; their good quality is attributed to the dates and lucerne on which they are fed. The price of donkeys per head ranges from 10 to 150 Riyāls and the total number in the two oases is estimated at 3,200 of superior, and 10,650 of inferior breeds; but it is not probable that the owners could spare more than a small proportion of either class from field labour and other necessary employments. Of the number of horses and camels either existent or available among the Bedouins no estimate is possible; in the two oases, exclusive of animals belonging to the Turkish Government, there are said to be about 150 horses (chiefly mares). The horses vary from the pure-bred Arab, difficult to obtain and fetching a very high price, to the common Kadīsh or baggage horse. A large number of hardy and serviceable animals, showing some breeding, may be had at prices ranging from 20 to 40 Līrahs; and the Turkish Dhābitīyahs, who are mounted on horses of this stamp, can perform journeys of 100 miles in 3 days with ease. Good riding camels, inferior only to those of 'Omān, are numerous, as are also ordinary baggage camels; but a well-bred riding camel costs on the average 20 Līrahs, and frequently much more.

Natural products.—The products of the Sanjāq are chiefly agricultural, from the oases, and pastoral from the surrounding deserts: their nature will become apparent in considering the question of exports.

Pearl fisheries.—On the coast pearl fishing is carried on to some extent; it employs 167 boats and affords occupation to about 3,500 men. The average crew of a pearl boat in Hasa is about 21 men.

Manufactures.—The only industry of importance in Hasa is a manufacture of 'Abas which has its seat at **Hofūf**; the material used is generally all wool, but mixtures of silk and wool and of silk and cotton are also employed; the finished article is sometimes embroidered with gold or silver thread. There are also some expert workers in copper and brass who make coffee-pots of an elegant shape; but a number of these, having emigrated, are now plying their craft in different parts of the Persian Gulf, and the monopoly formerly enjoyed by Hasa in this line has ceased to exist.

Trade.[*]—Trade has its principal seat at **Hofūf**, which is the chief market of the **Hasa** Oasis and surrounding country as well as an entrepôt of the foreign trade of **Najd**; but there is a secondary centre, of more restricted importance, at **Qatīf** Town. The whole Sanjāq has only two ports, **'Oqair** and **Qatīf** Town: of these the former serves

---

[*] Some particulars about the trade of Qatīf are contained in the Government of India's Foreign Proceedings for January 1901 and January 1904.

Hofūf together with the regions directly or indirectly dependent on that place, while the port of Qatīf exists solely for the benefit of the Qatīf Oasis and its smaller outside clientèle. The present volume of foreign trade (in both directions) at Qatīf Town is estimated at about 35 lakhs of rupees annually. Some account of the export and import trade of the Hasa province will be found in the articles on Qatīf Town and 'Oqair Port: this trade is principally and almost exclusively with Bahrain, where is Manāmah, the actual steam port of the Sanjāq.

The only exports of importance are dates and other products of the date palm; reeds and reed-matting; donkeys, ghi, hides and 'Abas. The destinations and quantities of the dates exported are detailed in the articles on the Hasa and Qatīf Oases. Date branches for firewood are despatched to Bahrain and Persia; reeds for mat-making from Qatīf to Bahrain; finished reed-mats to Masqat, Qatar and Basrah; donkeys, ghi and hides to Bahrain; and hides to Persia.

Imports are piece-goods, rice, wheat, barley, coffee, sugar, spices, metals and hardware: except a part of the cereals, which is received from Turkish 'Irāq and from Persia, these are obtained almost entirely through Bahrain and are largely of Indian provenance.

The slave trade is said to be carried on freely in Hasa at the present day, even in the town of Hofūf. A good many of the negroes sold in Hasa are taken to Qatar to be employed in pearl diving.

Weights.—In the tables of weights which follow, the English equivalents, given in avoirdupois weight, have been calculated from different data and are not entirely consistent.

The weights used in the Hasa Oasis for general and retail purposes are called Asqāt اسقاط and are these:—

1 Ruba' ربع	=	...	= ·68 lb. (but it is sometimes taken as equal in weight to 12 Riyāls or 28¾ Indian rupees, that is, to 28¾ Indian Tolas or ·73 lb.)
1 Thamīn ثمين or 1 Huqqah حقة	=	4 Ruba'	= 2·75 lbs. (or rather more).
1 Qiyāsah قياسة	=	{ 8 Thamīn or 8 Huqqah }	= 23 lbs. (or rather less).
Hasa Mann من الحسا	=	24 Qiyāsah	= 552 lbs. (or rather less).

Other weights, with special uses, in the **Hasa** Oasis are the (local) Mithqāl Shīrāzi مثقال شيرازي, equal to ⅖ of an Indian Tola or 72 grains, for transactions in gold and silver; the Mūsmīyah موسميه, of 10 Qiyāsah or 230 lbs., for wholesale dealings in locally grown cereals; and the Waznah وزنه, which is ⅐ of a Qiyāsah and so equivalent to about 3 2/7 lbs., for wholesale operations in dates, these being always estimated by the Waznah, not by the Qiyāsah or Mann.

The Qiyāsah is considered to be the true unit of weight in **Hasa**.

In the **Qatīf** Oasis the ordinary weights used in retail trade are :—

1 Qiyās قياس	=	...	= 1·07 lbs. (but it is sometimes taken as being equal in weight to 18 Riyāls or 102 Mithqāl Shīrāzi, both rather less than this).
1 Alf الف	= 2 Qiyās	=	2·14 lbs.
1 Qatīf Mann من القطيف	= 16 Alf	=	34·37 lbs.
1 Qallah قله	= 2 Qatīf Mann	=	68·75 lbs.

Wholesale business in dates is conducted in Qallahs. Besides the above the **Qatīf** Oasis possesses two other tables of weight for special purposes.

The first, for the weighment of precious metals, runs :—

1 Mithqāl Mishkhas مثقال مشخص or 1 Hamar حمر	=	...	= 54 grs. (viz., 3/10 of an Indian Tola).
1 (local) Mithqāl Shīrāzi مثقال شيرازي	=	...	= 72 grs. (viz., ⅖ of an Indian Tola).
1 Khamsīn خمسين	=	10 Mithqāl Shīrāzi	= 1·65 oz.
1 Mīyah ميه or 1 Amyah اميه	=	2 Khamsīn	= 3·29 oz.

The second, which is for retail dealings in meat, fish, etc., is as follows :—

1 Waqīyah وقيه	=	...	= ·68 lb.
1 Huqqah حقه	=	4 Waqīyah	= 2·75 lbs.
Qatīf Mann من القطيف	=	12½ Huqqah	= 34·37 lbs.

In **Qatīf** the Mann is regarded as the real unit of weight.

The Qiyāsah of the **Hasa** Oasis and the Qiyās of **Qatīf** are, it will be observed, entirely different weights; but the Ruba' for general purposes of **Hasa** and the Waqīyah for the sale of certain articles in **Qatīf** are identical, and each of them is equal to $\frac{1}{6}$ of a **Bahrain** Ruba'. The Qallah is altogether peculiar to **Qatīf**, and there is no Qiyās or Alf in **Hasa**.

Wholesale weighments in the Hasa Sanjāq are made by means of a machine which is in fact a rudimentary steelyard; the moveable weight in this instrument consists of a perforated stone slung by a string from the lever; and the lever, in the **Hasa** Oasis, is graduated in Waznahs, Qiyāsahs and Manns.

Measures.—In both oases the unit of linear measure is the Dhirā' ذراع which in **Hasa** is of the same length as in **Bahrain**, *viz.*, $18\frac{3}{4}$ inches, and in **Qatīf** is $19\frac{3}{4}$ inches.

Currency.—The currency of the Sanjāq is very mixed. The official standard is the Turkish Līrah of 100 gold piastres worth 18*s.* English; but the term Qursh or gold piastre is still unknown in the bazaar and the popular standard is the Riyāl or Maria Theresa dollar, here worth on the average about 1*s.* $10\frac{1}{4}d.$ English. **Qatīf** Town accepts Indian rupees readily, at least 3 lakhs of rupees having been sent there for the purchase of dates in 1905, and Indian currency notes are favourably received in the towns of **Qatīf** and **Hofūf**. The following is a table of the principal coins, real and imaginary, in the Sanjāq :—

Name.	Turkish official valuation.	Average bazaar rate.	REMARKS.
Mardhūf مرضوف	$\frac{1}{16}$ of a gold piastre.	$\frac{1}{4}$ of a Muhammadīyah (see below).	An imaginary unit of account peculiar to Qatīf Town.
Muhammadīyah محمدية	$\frac{1}{4}$ of a gold piastre.	$\frac{1}{30}$ of a Riyāl (see below).	Do.
Riyāl ريال	$\frac{1}{10}$ of a Līrah.	The bazaar unit of currency.	Nil.
Rupee	$5\frac{1}{2}$ gold piastres.	$\frac{5}{7}$ of a Riyāl.	Do.

Name.	Turkish official valuation.	Average bazaar rate.	REMARKS.
Tawīlah طويلة or "Long-Bit"	$\frac{11}{142}$ of a gold piastre.	$\frac{1}{100}$ of a Riyāl, but varying between $\frac{1}{70}$ and $\frac{1}{130}$.	An ancient coin current only in the **Hasa** Oasis and said to be of Carmathian mintage, It is of copper and about an inch and a half in length; the shape is difficult to describe. The Tawīlah appears to have been formed by doubling a strip of metal in the middle, after which the two limbs were compressed and welded together for $\frac{2}{3}$ of the distance from the place of flexure, the points remaining slightly separated after the manner of a split-pin. The free ends are rounded, the compressed part is flattened, on both sides; an illegible inscription apparently impressed before the strip was bent, is found on the exterior faces of the flattened portion.

The Turkish Government allows taxes to be paid in Riyāls or rupees as well as in their own coin, but Mardhūfs and Muhammadīyahs are not admitted in official accounts, and the Tawīlah is not recognised as legal tender. It will be observed that the Indian rupee stands relatively higher in popular than in official estimation.

Communications.—A few remarks upon the principal lines of communication in the Hasa Sanjāq follow:—

I. *Route from Hofūf to Kuwait Town.**—The way to the **Kuwait** border, which is generally reached at or near the Na'airīyah hill, lies across a number of desert tracts in the Hasa Sanjāq, all more or less equally provided in respect of water and grazing, and all equally deficient in supplies; it follows that there are no hard-and-fast lines of march and no established halting places. Different caravans follow different strings

* *Authority.*—Captain F. B. Prideaux, Political Agent in Bahrain, from native information.

of wells according to season and the state of Bedouin politics, but as a rule they pass by **Ntā'** in Wādi-al-**Miyāh**, the only village of any size which can be taken in the course of the journey, and one which divides it into two nearly equal halves. The distance from **Hofūf** to **Kuwait** Town in a straight line is a little under 300 miles; but the track of a caravan making the journey is probably not less than 360 miles, in consequence of the slight but frequent changes of direction that are made for the sake of camping at wells. The character of the tracts traversed and the nature of the wells may be learned from the articles under their names: the tracts are, after leaving the **Hasa** Oasis,—either **Biyādh** or **Badd-al-Asīs**; either **Jauf** or **Jau-as-Sa'adān**; **Habl**; and Wādi-al-**Miyāh**: **Sanfān-al-Hanna** is sometimes, perhaps, crossed between the two last-named. On the **Kuwait** side of the border similar conditions prevail and the coastal tracts of **Sūdah**, **Hazaim**, **Salū**, **'Adān** and **Qrā'ah** are ordinarily traversed in succession. The route is only suitable for desert caravans; but to these it does not present, in ordinary seasons, any serious difficulties. For the direction of the start from **Hofūf** the article on the **Hasa** Oasis may be consulted.

II.—*Route from Hofūf to Qatīf Town.**—This route, though the stages are not invariable, is better defined than the last; it runs to the north-north-east and its actual length is about 105 miles, as against a direct distance of 85 miles between the two termini. The following are the principal points on the journey:—

Name.	Nature.	Tract.	Miles from the last point.
Hofūf	Town.	Hasa Oasis.	...
Kalābīyah	Village.	Do.	6
Kanzān	Wells.	Do.	4
Ghuwaij	Do.	Do.	8
Hamām (Abul)	Do.	Jauf.	23
Hayāt (Abul)	Do.	Biyādh.	16
Zughail	Do.	Do.	6
Ji'ō-ai	Do.	Do.	16
Lājām	Village.	Qatīf Oasis.	20
Qatīf Town	Town.	Do.	6

There is a sufficiency of water and fuel by the way, but the water is generally indifferent, and the country is infested by Bedouin

* *Authorities.*—Captain F. B. Prideaux, Political Agent in Bahrain, from native information; and Captain J. A. Douglas in his *Journey from India to the Mediterranean*. See also Lieutenant Jopp in *Bombay Selections XXIV*, 1856, pages 114-115. Herr H. Burchardt's article *Ost-Arabien*, 1906, also contains a general description of this route and is accompanied by a view taken on the way.

marauders. The distance can be covered in 3 days, but caravans ordinarily take longer.

III.—*Route from Qaṭīf Town to Kuwait Town.**—The average direction of this route, which like No. I is by no means strictly defined, is a little west of north-north-west. Starting point and destination are about 230 miles apart; but the deflection caused by the inward trend of the intermediate coast, added to a slight zigzagging from well to well, probably raises the actual distance to about 300 miles. Travellers making this journey appear to pass, as a rule, by the Abu Ma'an wells and Mubārakīyah hill in **Biyādh**, and thereafter by the Mistannah wells which are at the meeting place of the **Radāif** and **Huzūm** tracts.

IV.—*Route from Hofūf to 'Oqair Port.*†—The direction of this route is between north-east and east-north-east, and its length in actual travelling is apparently about 50 miles. The usual line taken is by Jishshah village in the **Hasa** Oasis (9 miles); the wells of Shātar (12 miles) and Baraimān (14 miles), both in **Biyādh**, at each of which as also at Jishshah a halt may be made if it is desired to break the journey into 4 short stages; and, finally, 'Oqair (14 miles). Between **Hofūf** and Jishshah the road runs at first over a stony plain with a well-marked track across it; and for the last 3 or 4 miles through a cultivated country; between Jishshah and Shātar there are first 2 miles of open stony plain, then 6 miles between sand hills, then 4 miles across the nitrous Sabákhat Shātar which is fairly clear of sand: the remainder of the way is very heavy going over loose sand, and the track is liable to be obliterated by wind. The places mentioned are described under **Biyādh**.

An alternative line after Jishshah village is by Khuwainij (23 miles), Muwaih (5 miles), Bisaitīn (2 miles) and **'Oqair** (11 miles); the 3 places named before **'Oqair** all possess water and are described in the article on the **Biyādh** tract, in which they are situated. The journey by this alternative line is ordinarily broken by a halt at Khuwainij.

V. *Route from Hofūf to Dōhah in Qatar.*‡—The general direction of this route is east-south-east, but as in Nos. I and III the course pursued

---

* *Authority.*—Captain F. B. Prideaux, Political Agent in Bahrain, from native information.

† *Authorities*—Captain F. B. Prideaux, Political Agent in Bahrain, from native information; and Captain J. A. Douglas in his *Journey from India to the Mediterranean.* See also Lieutenant Jopp in *Bombay Selections XXIV*, 1856, pages 111-112.

‡ Captain F. B. Prideaux, Political Agent in Bahrain, from native information. Herr H. Burchardt (*vide* his *Ost-Arabien*, 1906) travelled this way, but gives no detailed account of the route; a view giving a general idea of the country however accompanies his article.

by caravans is apparently variable. Some appear to travel circuitously, in order to avoid the **Jāfūrah** desert, by Hamrūr to Ba'aij—both of which are in Barr-al-**Qārah** and are described in the article under that name—; but the ordinary route is by Mana'āyah and Bahath in **Jāfūrah** and there is a yet more direct route to Ba'aij by Ghaiyāthīn in **Jāfūrah**. The distances from **Hofūf** are about 35 miles to Mana'āyah, 45 to Bahath and 65 to Ba'aij, or 35 to Ghaiyāthīn and 55 to Ba'aij: about 10 miles beyond Ba'aij the foot of Dōhat-as-**Salwa** is turned and the district of **Qatar** entered. The water on these routes is of bad quality and there are no supplies.

VI.—*Routes from Hofūf to Riyādh.**—Travellers from the **Hasa** Oasis to Southern **Najd** do not ordinarily, it would seem, shape a direct course from **Hofūf**, but start either in a north-westerly direction for the wells of Jūdah in **Taff** or in an almost southerly one for the wells of 'Awaisah in **Kharmah**; these at first exceedingly divergent routes are said to unite at Sa'ad سعد in the neighbourhood of Abu Jifān. This route is further described in the article on **Najd**.†

The wells upon these and all routes in Hasa are described in the articles upon the districts composing the Sanjāq. In cases where the water is described as "good" it is understood to be not inferior to that of the springs on **Bahrain** Island. The wells of the Sanjāq have generally a dry masonry lining of largish stones; where a village formerly existed, however, the blocks are sometimes set in mortar.

---

* Captain F. B. Prideaux, Political Agent in Bahrain, from native information.

† It is interesting to identify, where possible, the actual routes which have been followed and described by travellers. Captain F. B. Prideaux, who has given much attention to the subject in this part of Arabia, believes that the following were the points reached by Sadlier in 1819 on the dates given below :—

June.
28th—Saihāt (**Qatīf** Oasis).
29th—Badrāni (**Biyādh**, IV).
30th—'Aziz-al-Mā (**Hushūm**).

July.
1st—Mulaibah (**Biyādh** III).
2nd—Abwāb (**Habl**).

July—continued.
3rd—Rubai'ah (Umm) (**Taff**).
8th—Hafairah (**Habl**).
9th—'Ain Dār and Dumaiyagh (**Jauf**).
10th—'Ayūn (**Hasa** Oasis).
11th—**Hofūf**.
24th—Rubai'āh (Umm) (**Taff**).

Palgrave's route in 1862 cannot be identified unless on the supposition that he has transferred the name Oweysit ('Awaisah) to some earlier stage in his journey than the one to which it belonged.

Pelly's route in 1865 appears to have lain approximately by Abu Jifān and Jūdah; the wells which he passed on the 10th of March may have been the former, and on the 13th or 14th (according to his map) he must have been in the vicinity of Jūqan.

General system of administration.—The Hasa Sanjāq, by the Turks hitherto called the "Sanjāq of Najd", is an administrative division of the Basrah Wilāyat in Turkish 'Irāq; the local governor has his seat at Hofūf in the Hasa Oasis and, as combining in his own person the chief civil and military authority upon the spot, is styled Muta*ṣ*arrif Liwa Najd متصرف لواء نجد or "Deputy-Governor and Brigadier of Najd."

The Turks divide the Sanjāq into 4 Qadhas, namely, **Hofūf** (or the **Hasa** Oasis and its dependencies), **Qatīf** (or the **Qatīf** Oasis and its dependencies), **Qatar** and **Najd**; but the validity of the Ottoman claim to **Qatar** is not admitted by the British Government, and **Najd**, even supposing the recent Turkish occupation of **Qasīm** to be renewed or continued, has no actual administrative connection with Hasa. The Qadha of **Hofūf** is divided into 4 Nāhiyahs named after their respective headquarters **Hofūf**, **Mubarraz**, Bāb-al-Jafar and **'Oqair**; the **Qatīf** Qadha has no subdivisions, but in it are included the islands of **Tārūt**, **Musallamīyah** and **Jinnah**. The duties of Qāim-Maqam in the **Hofūf** Qadha, and even of Mudīr in the **Hofūf** Nāhiyah of the same, are discharged by the Mutaṣarrif of Hasa in person; but in the **Qatīf** Qadha there is a separate Qāim-Maqām, who has his headquarters in **Qatīf** Town and is a purely civil official without authority over the troops stationed in his jurisdiction. Civil duties in the **'Oqair** Nāhiyah are performed by the officer commanding the Dhābitīyahs at **'Oqair** Port.

The administration of Hasa is organised on the usual Turkish pattern, and some of the ordinary civil departments are represented in the Sanjāq; but the system of government is less elaborate than in Turkish 'Irāq and partakes somewhat of the nature of a military occupation. In the oases of **Hasa** and **Qatīf** the power of the Turks is firmly established and the agricultural population are held in awe by military force. In most of the villages of these two districts there are hereditary Shaikhs; but, except at Saihāt in the **Qatīf** Oasis, they have been deprived by the Turks of the executive powers which they wielded under the Wahhābis and in earlier times. The official head of each village is now a Mukhtār مختار, elected by 4 respectable persons called Ikhtiyār-īyah اختياريه who have themselves been nominated by the Turks. The Bedouins of the Sanjāq while within the oases are submissive to the Porte; but in the surrounding deserts, even at comparatively short distances from military posts, they are virtually independent and sometimes attack Turkish convoys; nor are the Turkish desert mails safe unless carried by tribal Sā'īn or escorted by tribal Rufaqa. Chiefly in the interests of their postal service the Turks subsidise the **'Ajmān**, Bani

HASA SANJĀQ

Ḥājir, Bani Khālid and Āl Morrah tribes: the total annual amount of the tribal subsidies is stated to be 437½ Līrahs or about £400 English.

Military and police forces.—The military garrison of the Sanjāq, with Qatar, consists of 4 battalions of regular infantry, 2 squadrons of cavalry and 1 battery of light guns drawn by mules: the last is classed by the Turks as a mountain battery. Besides these there are 2 old guns at Dōhah in Qatar. The troops are relieved at intervals from Basrah, British mail vessels, chartered steamers and frequently native sailing boats being employed for the purpose; and no military unit is supposed to remain in Hasa for more than two years, service there being very unpopular and regarded as a sort of exile. There is an auxiliary corps of about 50 Bedouin guides, who are mounted on camels and armed with Snider rifles.

The police force, in Hasa an important adjunct to the military garrison, consists of 6 Bulūks or companies of Dhābitīyahs or gendarmes furnished by Basrah; of these 4 Bulūks are mounted. The chief duties of this armed constabulary are to occupy small posts for the protection of roads and villages and to supply escorts for travellers and caravans. The mounted men receive pay of Rs. 30 a month, and the unmounted of Rs. 15; both branches wear uniform and carry Snider rifles. The Dhābitīyahs, as in Turkish 'Irāq, are mostly Kurds and non-local Arabs; but Bahārinah and other indigenous classes are now being enlisted.

The units, whether military or police, in Hasa are ordinarily much below their proper strength. The following is believed to be a fairly accurate statement of the distribution of the troops and gendarmerie at the present time:—

Station.	Post.	Military garrison.	Police garrison.
Hofūf.	Kūt-al-Hofūf.	1 battalion of infantry. 2 squadrons cavalry. 1 battery.	Nil.
Do.	Qasr-al-Khazām.	¼ battalion of infantry.	25, mounted.
Do.	Qasr-al-'Abīd.	Nil.	100, unmounted.
Mubarraz	In the town.	Do.	25, mounted, and 10, unmounted.
Do.	Qasr Sāhūd.	¼ battalion of infantry.	25, mounted.

2 x 2

Station.	Post.	Military garrison.	Police garrison.
Hasa Oasis	Qasr-al-Luwaimi.	¼ battalion of infantry.	25, mounted.
Do.	Qasr-ash-Sharqi.	Do.	Do.
Do.	Bāb-al-Jafar village.	Nil.	50, mounted, and 10, unmounted.
Do.	Markaz village.	Do.	25, mounted, and 10, unmounted.
'Oqair Port	...	Do.	50, mounted, and 20, unmounted.
Qatīf Town	Kūt-al-Qatīf.	A detachment of 50 infantry from the battalion at 'Anik.	36, unmounted.
'Anik	...	A battalion of infantry, less a detachment of 50 at Qatīf Town.	150, mounted, less a detachment of 5 at Saihāt.
Saihāt	...	Nil.	A mounted detachment of 5, principally employed in assisting the customs.
Tārūt Island	...	Do.	10, unmounted.
Jinnah Island	...	Do.	3, unmounted.
Musallamīyah Island	...	Do.	Do.

The battalion which is stationed at Dōhah in Qatar belongs to the Hasa command.

The land communications with Turkish 'Irāq, the internal political situation, and the military resources of the Turks in Hasa being such as we have depicted them, it seems probable that the Turkish administration of the Sanjāq would be reduced to serious straits by a naval blockade of the coast.

Revenue and finance.—Details of the fiscal system are not available, but it is clear that the public revenue of Hasa is derived mostly from agriculture, of which date cultivation is the principal branch. Taxation is not, apparently, uniform throughout the Sanjāq. In the Hasa Oasis the Turkish Government takes a share of all agricultural produce. In the Qatīf Oasis, on the other hand, there is a cash tax on dates, its incidence following the results of a quinquennial survey at which the plantations are arranged in 3 grades; each palm

* The Government of India's Foreign Proceedings for May 1904 contain information about the finances of Hasa.

tree is assessed at 2 gold piastres, 1¼ gold piastres or ¾ of a gold piastre per annum according as it belongs to a plantation of the 1st, 2nd or 3rd grade. The total yearly revenue derived from agriculture in the Hasa Sanjāq has been roughly estimated as follows, Riyāls being converted into rupees at the rate of $10 = R14 : —

Item.	Rs.
Share of dates in the Hasa Oasis, about 20,000 Mann at $9½ per Mann.*	2,66,000
Share of rice in the Hasa Oasis, about 1,680 Mūsmīyahs at $8 per Mūsmīyah	13,440
Share of wheat in the Hasa Oasis, about 560 Mūsmīyahs at $12 per Mūsmīyah	6,720
Proceeds of tax on palms in the Qatīf Oasis	80,000

To the total thus obtained of Rs. 3,66,160 or £24,411 English must be added whatever the taxes on livestock and on Bedouin tents yield; it is known that such taxes exist, but their rates and the amounts which they produce have not been ascertained.

The customs of the Sanjāq are not directly managed by the Ottoman customs service, as is the case with those of Turkish 'Irāq; they are annually put up to auction by the Mutasarrif who reports the result to the head of customs at Baghdād and receives instructions accordingly. In 1905 the Hasa customs were knocked down to two leading Shi'ahs of Qatīf for a year on an undertaking to pay 13,500 Līrahs or about £12,544 English. The customs farmers are represented by officials called Mudīrs at Hofūf, 'Oqair Port and Qatīf Town; and the Hofūf Mudīr, who deals with Bedouin produce, has a subordinate styled a Wakīl at Mubarraz.

There is a tax on pearl boats of half a Līrah per annum per boat, irrespective of size; it is reported to yield about £75 sterling a year.

In 1903 it was stated in Bahrain by a retiring Mutasarrif of Hasa that the annual revenue of the Sanjāq amounted in all to 60,000 Līrahs (£54,000 English); that of this sum 54,000 Līrahs (£48,600 English) was required to cover military expenditure; and that the balance of 6,000 Līrahs (£5,400 English) was insufficient to meet the expenses of the civil administration. It is asserted, on different authority, that the small amounts disbursed by the Hasa administration in subsidies to Bedouins actually exceed those which are recovered by taxation from the same

* It should be noted the Turks profess to take the value of one-tenth of the crop; but they really obtain more by overestimating the pecuniary value of the Government share. Thus in 1907, when the export of dates from the Hasa Oasis ceased on account of the insecurity of the roads, etc., the price of dates fell locally to $3 per Mann, but the tax for the year was nevertheless calculated at $7 per Mann.

tribes; but, if this is the case, either the total revenue must be considerably less than £54,000 or some important item of revenue must have been omitted above.

Miscellaneous civil departments.—Some of the ordinary civil institutions of a Turkish Sanjāq exist in Hasa, but they are not prominent. The courts of judicature are understood to be constituted as they are elsewhere in the Turkish dominions, and the department of Public Debt is represented by a Mudīr at **Qatīf** Town. The ports of **Qatīf** Town and '**Oqair** are each in charge of a Raīs-al-Līmān or Turkish harbourmaster, and it is reported that a similar official is about to be stationed at **Dōhah** in **Qatar**. The department of Public Instruction maintains schools at various places in the Hasa Sanjāq but nothing more is known of its operations. No post or telegraph offices exist. Private correspondence is despatched by private arrangement; but official mails are carried by Sā'is ساعي or mounted couriers, who are drawn from the subsidised tribes and are in waiting every day at the office of the Mutasarrif. The journey between **Hofūf** and **Qatīf** Town is made once a week, and that between **Hofūf** and **Dōhah** in **Qatar** once a month, by Sā'is; the first of these journeys occupies 3 days, and the second either 3 or 4 days, in each direction. Official correspondence between **Hofūf** and **Basrah** was sent from 1871 until 1900, or later, entirely *viâ* **Bahrain**; it was then for a time despatched, partially at least, by land through an agency of which the headquarters were at **Kuwait** Town; finally by 1907, if not earlier, the land route had been again entirely abandoned in favour of the route by sea.

The Dāirat-as-Sanīyah.—The Dāirat-as-Sanīyah or Civil List Department, which plays so important a part in the economy of Turkish 'Irāq, made its appearance in Hasa about 20 years ago. In the **Hasa** Oasis it owns plantations, partly in the village of Bāb-al-Jafar, which yield 2,000 to 2,500 Manns of dates per annum, and the yearly crop of its palms in the **Qatīf** Oasis is estimated at about 16,000 Qallahs; the average total annual value of the dates obtained by it in both oases has been calculated at £3,000. In the villages of Jabail, Jalaijilah, Halailah, Manaizlah, Matairafi, Mazāwi and Shaqīq in the **Hasa** Oasis are rice lands under the Department which are said to produce 1,000 Musmīyahs of rice per annum. The Dāirat-as-Sanīyah also owns about 25 houses in **Qatīf** Town which formerly belonged to the Āl Bin Ghānim Shaikhs of the **Bahārinah**. The Mudīr Amlāk-as-Sanīyah مدير املاك السنية or manager of the Sanīyah properties is in the **Hasa** Oasis invariably, and perhaps *ex officio*, the Tābūr Aghāsi or Major of Gendarmerie at **Hofūf**: in the **Qatīf** Oasis the office has been held from the first, and still is held, by a certain Hāji Mansūr Pāsha Bin-Juma' of **Qatīf** Town.

HASAN (BALAD BANI BU)
بلد بني
بو حسن

A straggling town or settlement in the **Ja'alān** district of the **'Omān** Sultanate, the capital of the Bani Bū **Hasan** tribe; it is situated about 35 miles south-west by south of **Sūr** and extends perhaps five miles in a north and south direction with a breadth of about one mile. On the north side the settlement is defended by a wall and boasts two forts, one of mud, the other of gypsum stucco; there are also towers, defending the springs on which the irrigation of the place depends, about one mile to the westward; and to the south-east stands a stone and gypsum fort surrounded by about 30 houses which is called Hisn-al-Mashāikh حصن المشائخ. The hostile settlement of Balad Bani Bū **'Ali** lies about seven miles to the south-south-east, the distance being measured from the centre of the one oasis to the centre of the other.

The houses of Balad Bani Bū Hasan are said to number 1,000, and, some allowance being made for exaggeration, the population may amount to 4,000 souls; the ordinary building material is mud, but some gypsum stucco is also seen. The dwellings, throughout the greater part of the settlement, are interspersed with date plantations; the groves are densest towards the west and south. Streams of clear and sweet water, sent forth by a dozen or more springs, irrigate the date groves; and drinking water is drawn from wells 4 to 5 fathoms deep. Lucerne and a little maize and cotton are cultivated as well as dates; the date plantations are reported to contain 10,000 trees. Only about 15 horses are owned by the inhabitants: other livestock are 250 camels, 400 donkeys and 2,000 sheep and goats. There is a respectable bazaar of about 40 shops in which cloth and food-stuffs are sold. There are no manufactures; but a little cloth is woven for local consumption, and boiled dried dates called Bisr بسر are exported to Bombay through **Sūr** and **Masqat** Town. **Sūr** is the usual port of Balad Bani Bū Hasan, and the route thither lies down Wādi **Falaij**, passing a short distance to the east of Kāmil and **Wāfi**.

One of the south-western quarters of the town, called Jawābi-al-Khuwaisah جوابي الخوصيه, was the scene in July 1881 of a severe struggle between the Bani Bū **Hasan** and the Bani Bū **'Ali** in which the former are said to have lost 75 and the latter 60 in killed.

HASAN (BANI BŪ)
بني بو حسن

Singular is Hasani حسني. A tribe of the 'Omān Sultanate, Yamani by descent and Hināwi in politics. They number about 4,000 souls in the Ja'alān district at Balad Bani Bū Hasan, which is their principal settlement, and perhaps 500 in Bātinah at Barkah and Hadhīb (I). They are also found at Jināh near Sūr (40 houses) and at Fita (30 houses) in Eastern Hajar. Their total number is thus about 5,000, or, with some subordinate tribes mentioned below, about 7,000 souls.

In Ja'alān the Bani Bū Hasan are date-growers and cultivators and are well provided with camels. They are for the most part stationary; but in language and general characteristics they resemble the Bedouin tribes of their neighbourhood.

The Bani Bū Hasan are now fairly well armed with rifles of various cheap kinds, yet of late they have shown themselves on the whole less restless than the other Hināwi tribes of Ja'alān and Sharqīyah.

The sections of the Bani Bū Hasan proper are the following :—

Section.	Fighting strength.	Habitat.	Remarks.
Ḍarū' درع	30	Balad Bani Bū Hasan.	Nil.
Farārijah فرارجه	40	Fita and in Ja'alān.	Do.
Huwājir حواجر	60	Jināh.	Do
Jābir (Bani) بني جابر	70	Do.	Do.
Matāni (Hāl Bū) حال بو متاني	200	Jināh and Balad Bani Bū Hasan.	Do.
Masārīr مسارير	200	Balad Bani Bū Hasan.	Do.
Rawājih رواجح	100	They encamp at Falaij in Wādi Falaij.	Bedouins.
Shikālah شكاله	100	...	Nil.
Suwābi' سوابع	100	Balad Bani Bū Hasan.	Do.

HATAIM

Besides these there are four petty client tribes who are reckoned almost as sections of the Bani Bū Hasan, namely :—

Name.	Location.	Households.	Remarks.
Jabal (Ahl) اهل جبل	Near 'Aqībah in Ja'alān.	60	This section are robbers but are said to possess 90 camels, 10 donkeys, 50 cattle and 1,000 sheep and goats.
Mashāikh-al-Balad مشائخ البلد	Do.	40	This also is a predatory section.
Mashāikh-al-Jabal مشائخ الجبل	In Jabal Mashāikh in Ja'alān.	250	These are Bedouins and robbers; they own a considerable number of animals.
Sarhān (Bani) بني سرحان	Do.	40	...
'Umr (Hāl) حال عمر	In Ja'alān and Badīyah.	100	This section cultivate, and own about 2,000 date palms.

The Bani Bū Hasan are Ibādhis, with the exception of the Ahl Jabal section who are Azraqah Wahhābis. There is perpetual desultory warfare between the Bani Bū Hasan and their neighbours, the Bani Bū 'Ali. The present Tamīmah of the Bani Bū Hasan is 'Āmir-bin-'Ali-bin-Rāshid.

HASSĀN (KHOR) خور حسان or **KHUWAIR** خوير

A village on the west coast of the **Qatar** promontory about 10 miles from its northern extremity. It is frequently spoken of simply as "Khuwair" in contradistinction to "Khor," *i.e.* Khor **Shaqīq** on the opposite side of the promontory. Khuwair possesses a tribal fort in a good state of repair and is inhabited by about 80 families of the **Kibīsah** tribe, who live solely by pearl diving and fishing; they have 20 pearl boats, 5 fishing boats and 20 camels, but no other resources of any sort. Drinking water is fetched from Thaghab, about 3 miles to the southeast. A small islet off Khuwair Hassān is known as Jazīrat-al-Khuwair.

HATAIM هتيم

The singular is Hataimi هتيمي and there is a distributive plural Hatmān هتيمان. A nomad tribe of Central Arabia; their origin is uncertain and they are not regarded as true Arabs.

Location.—The Hataim (exclusive of the Hawāzim section whose distribution is discussed below) inhabit the country from Khaibar eastwards as far as the Abanāt hills upon Wādi-ar-**Rummah** and are hemmed in between the **Harb** on the south and the **'Anizah** on the north. Some settled Hataim are said to be found in the villages of Hāyat and Thurghud in Harrat Khaibar, of Ghazālah and Mustajiddah in Jabal **Shammar,** and of 'Ayūn-as-Suwaina' and Faidhah in Wādi-as-**Sirr.**

Divisions and number.—Among the sections* of the Hataim are the—

'Awāmirah	عوامره	Mahaimizāt	مهيمزات
Barrāqah	برّاقه	Madhāribah	مضاربه
Dalāmīk	دلاميك	Nuwāmisah	نوامسه
Hawāzim	حوازم	Qa'ābīd	قعابيد
Jalādān	جلادان	and	
Khiyārāt	خيارات	Simrah	سمره

The Shaikhs of the tribe are said to belong to the Barrāqah section. The Hawāzim section (by some authorities treated as **Harb** and not Hataim) are either frequently confounded, or are really identical, with the **'Awāzim,**† tribe of **Kuwait;** these Hawāzim or **'Awāzim** are found at **Jauf-al-'Āmir,** Sakākah, **Taimah** and Baidha Nathīl in Jabal **Shammar** and also, perhaps, at the village of Ghāt in the **Sadair** district of Southern **Najd.** It is curious that the **Rashāidah,** who resemble the **'Awāzim** and like them live near **Kuwait,** are also said to be connected with the **Hataim.**

The Hataim in the west of Central Arabia may be roughly estimated at 3,000 souls.

Life and character.—The Hataim live in the ordinary Bedouin manner, but they are distinguished from Arab Bedouins by their long blue shirts. They are less cheerful, frank, dignified and honourable than the Arabs, and also less civil to guests. The Hataim are good fighting material and often excellent shots; in person they are more robust than the Arabs and their women are better looking. As hunters they are second only to the **Sulaba** and sometimes they even succeed in killing ostriches. Their dromedaries have always been among the best, rivalling those of the **Shararāt,** but they have never been well provided

---

* Other sections are mentioned by Doughty and Huber, but have not been identified in the course of our inquiries from the Persian Gulf side.

† Regarding this difficulty see article **'Awāzim** (footnote). The Hawāzim of the Hataim are apparently also known as Hawāzin هوازن.

with horses; in 1863 they had only a score of mares and in 1878 were still almost without any. Some sections of the Hataim make cheeses of sheep and goats' milk which they sell at Khaibar. The women's apartment in their tents is on the right side in entering.

Political position.—Notwithstanding their comparatively thriving condition the Hataim are despised by the Arabs, who class them with the **Sulaba** below all Arab tribes and taunt them with being eaters of carrion. The Arabs never intermarry with the Hataim, although some **'Anizah** and **Harb** families dwell among them; and, on the other hand, poor Hataim women sometimes condescend to mate with negroes. The Hataim generally render Khuwwah خُرَّة or Akhāwah اخاوة , that is blackmail, to all from whom they have anything to fear, and this is doubtless the secret of their relative prosperity. In 1878 some of those about Khaibar paid taxes both to the Amīr of Jabal **Shammar** and to the Turks, and they still give Khuwwah simultaneously to the **Harb, Shammar** and **'Anizah** tribes.

A plain, the only one of any extent in the interior of the **Masqat** District of the **'Omān** Sultanate, it includes part of the upper basins of Wādis **'Adai, Maih** and **Mijlās** and a small portion of the course of Wādi Sarain. It begins on the north at Mutahaddamāt in Wādi **'Adai** and runs southwards to include Bīrain; it then curves round eastwards embracing the last 8 miles of Wādi Jannah—here called also Wādi Hatāt—before its junction with Wādi **Maih;** finally it takes in the whole of Wādi **Maih** above Tawīlah, the whole of Wādi Sarain below Qābil 'Ali-bin-Zamān, and the upper part of Wādi **Mijlās** with its tributary Wādi Haithadh. The north-western part of the plain is the broader and more open, its width hereabouts approaching or attaining 8 miles: south-eastwards of Wādi Jannah it is narrower and more broken up. The length of Saih Hatāt along the curve in which it lies is about 30 miles. Where it adjoins Eastern **Hajar** it has a few stunted trees and shrubs, greatly diminished by the ravages of **Masqat** wood-cutters; and in some places on the same side it is studded with natural pillars of rock, 20 to 25 feet high. The inhabitants of the villages of Saih Hatāt, which can be ascertained from the articles on the Wādis traversing it, are mostly Bani **Wahaib**: there are also Bani Khazam.

HATĀT (SAIH)
سيح حطاط

HATTA (WĀDI)
وادي حتّى

The north-westernmost valley—unless we reckon the lower part of Wādi-al-**Qor**—in the Western **Hajar** district of the **'Omān** Sultanate: it begins below a sandy tract in the heart of the **'Omān** Promontory from which it is separated by a **Najd**, and, breaking into two channels near the coast, reaches the sea at **Shinās** and **W**idaiyāj. The upper portion, from Hajarain to the head of the valley, can hardly be regarded as belonging to the **'Omān** Sultanate.

The places which Wādi Hatta passes in its descending course are the following :—

Name.	Position.	On which bank.	Houses and inhabitants.	Remarks.
Hadaf حدف	Near the head of the Wādi.	Right.	20 houses of Bani Ka'ab.	Nil.
Masfūt مصفوط	1 hour below Hadaf.	Do.	50 houses of Bidūwāt.	The people of this village, who are at enmity with those of Hajarain adjoining it, depend on the support of the **Na'īm** of the **Baraimi** Oasis.
Hajarain هجرين	¼ of an hour below Masfūt.	Do.	100 houses of Bidūwāt.	The Shaikh of this village is a vassal of the Shaikh of **Dibai**, to whom he looks for protection against the people of Masfūt and their allies the **Na'īm**.
Falaij Bin-Qafaiyir فليج بن ققير	1 hour below Hajarain	Do.	8 houses of Bidūwāt.	Nil.
Tamait طميط	½ an hour below Falaij Bin-Qafaiyir.	Do.	10 houses of Washāhāt.	Do.
Mushabbah مشبح	½ an hour below Tamait.	Do.	Do.	Do.

Name.	Position.	On which bank	Houses and inhabitants.	REMARKS.
'Ajīb عجيب	1 hour below Mush-abbah.	Left.	70 houses of Washābāt.	This village commands a fine view of the Bātinah. The hills end a short distance below it and 4 hours from it is **Shinās Town**.

Of the entire population of about 1,400 souls, only some 500 appear to be subject to the Sultān of **'Omān**; the rest belong rather to Independent **'Omān**.

These villages are poor in animals: altogether they are said to contain only 50 camels, 100 donkeys, 50 cattle and 200 sheep and goats.

Wādi Hatta carries the drainage of Wādi Qahfi and its tributary Wādi-al-Hayūl, which comes from the neighbourhood of **Mahádhah**.

A district in the interior of Southern **Najd** forming part of the Wahhābi dominions.

HAUTAH
حوطة

Boundaries and physical features.—Hautah is adjoined on the north by the district of **Harīq**, being separated from it by Jabal Hilaiyah; on the east it meets the district of **Kharj**; and on the south it is divided from the district of **Aflāj** by the range of Jabal Birk. The western limit of the Hautah district has not been ascertained, but it is perhaps the **Tuwaiq** range. The main feature of Hautah is a valley running apparently east-north-east from Hautah town to **Dilam** in **Kharj** and about 35 miles distant; by this valley, which immediately below Hautah town seems to be called Braik بريك, the drainage of Hautah is conveyed to the **Kharj** district. The Hautah valley has two main feeders: that of Hilwah حلوة joining it, apparently from the south, several miles below Hautah town, and that of **Harīq** which comes in from the north-west at a point still further in the direction of **Kharj**. The mountain ranges which bound the district on north and south are said to constitute a serious obstacle to egress upon those sides; but a pass called Salāmīyah, mentioned in the article on **Aflāj**, connects the valley of Hilwah with the Farshah division of **Aflāj**.*

---

*Hautah does not appear to have been visited as yet by any European traveller. But see the footnote to the article on **Harīq**.

Topography, population and resources.—The following table contains an account of the principal places in Hautah :—

Name.	Position.	Houses and inhabitants.	Remarks.
Hautah town حوطة	About 35 miles west-south-west of **Dilam** in **Kharj** and perhaps 20 miles south by west of Harīq town in **Harīq**.	The population is about 4,000 souls. The principal tribes are: **Dawāsir** of the Ghaiyithāt section, 30 houses; **Fadhūl**, of the Āl Tālib section, 20 houses, and of the Kathrān section, 20; **Sahūl**, 30 houses; **Sabai'** of the Khathlān section, 20 houses; **'Anizah** of the Dāūd section, 10 houses; **Qahtān**, 20 houses; **Bani Khadhīr** or inferior tribes generally, 600 houses. The chief divisions of the town are said to be Farīq Āl Husain فريق آل حسين Salaiyib سليّب Qil'ah قلعة, Dhāhirah ظاهرة and Sadr صدر.	The majority of the inhabitants live not in the town proper, which is called Hillah حلة, but in detached quarters among the date groves. The greater part of the plantations seem to belong to a part of the settlement called Braik بريك which apparently gives its name to, or is called after, the valley below the town; the bulk of the palms are said to be situated in the Hautah valley below its junction with the tributary from Hilwah and above its meeting with that which comes from **Harīq**. Besides dates the ordinary crops and fruits of Southern **Najd** are grown. The wells are deep and camels are used to work the water lifts, which are beyond the power of bullocks and donkeys. The town is largely commercial and has a bazaar of about 80 shops. The inhabitants own about 500 camels, 50 horses, 50 donkeys and 100 cattle : a number of the camels are employed in trading caravans.
Hilwah حلوة	Apparently a very few miles to the south of Hautah town.	There are about 300 houses, *viz.*, 170 of Bani **Tamīm**; 30 of **Dawāsir** of the Ghaiyithāt section; 20 of **Fadhūl**; 20 of **Sabai'** of the Khathlān section; 10 of **'Anizah** of the Dāūd section; and 60 of Bani **Khadhīr**.	There are the usual dates, fruits, cereals and lucerne; the wells are not quite so deep as those of Hautah Town, say 18 fathoms. Camels number about 300, donkeys 50 and cattle 100. The date plantations are very dense.

Name.	Position.	Houses and inhabitants.	Remarks.
Quwai' قريع	To the north-east of Hilwah and connected with that village, but actually nearer to Hautah town.	30 houses, *viz.*, 20 of Bani **Tamīm** and 10 of Bani **Khadhīr**.	Resembles Hilwah in its general characteristics, but livestock are proportionately fewer.
Wusaitah وسيطه	Between Hilwah and Quwai'.	A Qasr of Bani **Khadhīr**.	A considerable date grove belongs to this place.

It will be seen from the above table that the settled population of the district is tribally very composite, and that it probably amounts to rather less than 6,000 souls, of whom the majority inhabit the town of Hautah and its suburbs. The agriculture and livestock are those of Southern **Najd** generally, but the date trees are exceptionally large and fine, some of them (it is said) yielding an incredible quantity of dates in a single season. The other fruits of the district are also above the average.

Trade.—There is a considerable trade with **Hasa** and **Qatar** on the one side and with Yaman and Hijāz on the other; piece-goods are chiefly obtained from **Hasa**—with which district nearly all the local merchants have business relations,—arms and ammunition are imported through **Qatar,** and coffee is brought from Yaman. A certain number of Hautah merchants are accustomed to visit India for trade. Among the principal firms in Hautah are the Ghanaim, who are Bani **Tamīm**, and the 'Atiqah and Wahaibis, who belong to the Bani **Khadhīr**. There are also some merchants of repute among the Dāūd.

Administration.—The Amīr of Hautah town and principal man in the district is at present one Muhammad Abu Shaibah of the Bani **Tamīm.** He stands high in the favour of Ibn Saūd and has authority under the Wahhābi rulers over all Hautah, even the Amīr of Hilwah (now 'Abdul 'Azīz-bin-Kharaiyis) having been made subordinate to him. This is regarded as an exceptional and temporary arrangement, due to the personal influence of Abu Shaibah with Ibn Saūd. The people of Hautah are well armed with rifles, but swords are still carried.

HAWĀSI-NAH حواسنه

Singular Hausini حوسني. A Hināwi tribe of the 'Oman Sultanate, partly Ibādhi and partly Sunni in religion; they occupy the whole of Wādi-al-**Hawāsinah** and nearly all of Wādis **Sārrāmi** and **Shāfān** in

Western **Hajar**; also most of the town of **Khābūrah** in **Bāṭinah**; and they are found also at Qasbiyat-al-Hawāsinah in the sub-Wilāyat of **Saham**. Their tribal capital is Ghaizain in Wādi-al-**Hawāsinah**. They number about 17,500 souls, exclusive of some Bedouins who belong to the tribe.

Below is a table of the Hawāsinah which explains the classification and distribution of about 10,500 members of the tribe; the remainder (7,000) are mostly at **Khābūrah**, where the Hawāmid and Sawālim sections in particular are represented.

Section.	Number of houses.	Habitat.
Hawāmid حوامد	310	Mijzi in Wādi-al-Hawāsinah; Hībi and Khadd in Wādi Sarrāmi; and Khishai in Wādi Shāfān.
Najāja'ah نجاجعه	60	Suwari, Shakhbōt and Sadān in Wādi-al-Hawāsinah.
Rashaid (Aulād) اولاد رشيد	160	Ghaizain in Wādi-al-Hawāsinah and Qasbiyat-al-Hawāsinah in the sub-Wilāyat of Saham.
Sa'īd (Bani) بني سعيد	1,440	Khadhra, Sakhīyat, Qal'ah, Khabt Saiharah, Falaj Harmal, Dhuwaihirah, Fajaij and Hail Rāsha in Wādi Sarrāmi, and Nakhshah, Ghashain, Safa, 'Iqli and Bī'aik in Wādi Shāfān.
Sawālim سوالم	70	Ghaizain in Wādi-al-Hawāsinah.
Sinān (Bani) بني سنان	100	Harmali and Bada'ah Aulād Juma'ah in Wādi-al-Hawāsinah.

The Hawāsinah are generally at feud with the Bani **'Umr** who adjoin them on the west. Their present chiefs are Almirr and Nāsir, brothers, sons of Muhammad.

HAWĀ-SINAH (WĀDI-AL)
وادي الحواسنه

A valley in the Western **Hajar** district of the **'Omān** Sultanate, which, beginning at the north side of a pass some miles north of **Miskin** in Dhāhirah, reaches the sea at **Khābūrah** in **Bāṭinah** a little to the east of the bazaar of that town.

Wādi-al-Hawāsinah contains the following places, which we give in their order from above downwards: the inhabitants are all Hawāsinah:—

Place.	Position.	On which bank.	Number of houses.	Remarks.
Mijzi مجزي	6 hours below the head of the Wādi.	Left.	40 (of the Hawāmid section).	Livestock are 20 camels, 40 donkeys, 100 cattle, and 500 sheep and goats. Palms, 3,000.
Suwari سوري	1 hour below Mijzi.	Do.	15 (of the Najāja'ah section).	There are 4 camels, 20 donkeys, 15 cattle, and 40 sheep and goats. Palms, 2,000.
Harmali حرملي	3 hours below Suwari.	Do.	70 (of the Bani Sinān section).	Animals are 30 camels, 40 donkeys, 70 cattle, and 800 sheep and goats. Palms, 4,000.
Shakhbōt شخبوت	1 hour below Harmali.	Right.	25	There are 5 camels, 10 donkeys, 10 cattle, and 100 sheep and goats. Palms, 700.
Falaj-al-Hawāsinah فلج الحواسنه	½ an hour below Shakhbōt.	Do.	40	20 camels, 25 donkeys, 20 cattle, and 300 sheep and goats are owned here. Palms, 3,000.
Bada'ah Aulād Juma'ah بدعه اولاد جمعه	½ an hour below Falaj-al-Hawāsinah, but not in the main valley.	...	30 (of the Bani Sinān section).	Animals are 3 camels, 5 donkeys, 10 cattle, and 100 sheep and goats. Palms, 5,000.
Badai'ah بديعه	½ an hour below Badaah Aulād Juma'ah.	Right.	20	There are 5 camels, 20 donkeys, 15 cattle, and 200 sheep and goats. Palms, 1,000.
Sadān صدان	3 hours below Badai'ah.	Do.	20	Animals are 3 camels, 10 donkeys, 10 cattle and 200 sheep and goats. Palms, 1,000.

HAWĀSINAH (WĀDI-AL-)

Place.	Position.	On which bank.	Number of houses.	REMARKS.
Ghaizain غيزين	3 hours below Sadān.	Left.	200 (of the Aulād Rashaid and Sawālim sections.	The principal place of the Hawāsinah tribe. Livestock 30 camels, 25 donkeys, 40 cattle, and 1,000 sheep and goats. Palms, 8,000.
Qasaf قسف	6 hours below Ghaizain and 1 hour above Khābūrah.	Right.	...	See article Bātinah.

Of these places Ghaizain is the last within the **Hajar** hills : Qasaf is in **Bātinah**. The population of the valley above the point where it enters **Bātinah** seems to be about 2,300 souls.

Wādi-al-Hawāsinah has two principal tributaries, both from the west. The upper of these is Wādi-adh-Dhula' وادي الضلع, which comes in below Harmali and above Shakhbōt and contains only one village, namely Bada'ah Aulād Juma'ah, given in the table above. The other, Wādi Bani 'Umr, enters Wādi-al-Hawāsinah between Ghaizain and Qasaf, outside the hills ; it is elsewhere described under its own name, but we may here note that its uppermost village is another Mijzi مجزي which can be reached from the Mijzi in Wādi-al-Hawāsinah in about 5 hours by a pass across the hills.

Wādi-al-Hawāsinah is deep and narrow, and the hills which form its sides are of dark-coloured rock. The villages are built upon the hill-sides, and their date trees grow on artificial terraces to which spring-water is conducted in channels : there are no wells. The houses are of stone and mud ; the crops besides dates are wheat, barley, bajri, maize, millet, lucerne, beans, sweet potatoes, and various grasses which are cultivated as fodder for animals ; the people keep camels, cattle, sheep, goats and donkeys. Fruits are limes, mangoes, grapes, olives, plums, pomegranates, figs, quinces and almonds. The trade of Wādi-al-Hawāsinah is with **Khābūrah** and **Suwaiq**.

HAWĪZEH حويزه **DISTRICT.**   The westernmost of the districts of Southern 'Arabistān.

Position and extent.—Hawīzeh district surrounds **Hawīzeh** Town, which is about 65 miles north of **Muhammareh** Town and equidistant from the **Kārūn** river at **Nāsiri** and the **Tigris** at **'Azair**. It is enclosed by Turkish **'Irāq** on the west and on the remaining sides by districts of **'Arabistan,** *viz.,* **Dizfūl** on the north, **Ahwāz** on the east, and **Muhammareh** on the south. On its north-east side it is bordered and separated from the **Dizfūl** District by two parallel hill ranges, called Manyūr منیور and Mishdākh مشداخ, which run from north-west to south-east, at distances respectively of 15 and 20 miles from **Hawīzeh** Town, and end on reaching the right bank of the **Karkheh**: these ranges are included under the common name of Khadhar * خضر. The limits of the district are otherwise indefinite, but some of the places comprised in it are specified in the paragraph on topography below.

Physical characteristics.—The general features and condition of the district at the present day are not well understood, as tribal disturbances and chronic lawlessness have made it for the time being inaccessible to civilised travellers; and it does not seem to have been visited by Europeans since the Anglo-Russian survey of the Turko-Persian border half a century ago. The river **Karkheh**, turning the corner of the Manyūr and Mishdākh ranges, enters the district near Kūt Nahr Hāshim at the eastern end; a part of it emerges again at the western end under the name of Swaib or Shwaiyib and eventually flows into the Shatt-al-**'Arab**. The bulk of the Hawīzeh district, between the disappearance of the **Karkheh** and the formation of the Swaib, is believed to consist of marshes and water channels in which the river loses itself, interspersed with pasture grounds and surrounded by barren deserts.

Population.—The inhabitants of the Hawīzeh district, those of **Hawīzeh** Town alone excepted, nearly all belong to nomadic tribes; and all but a few **Sabians** and two or three **Najd** Arabs, who are shopkeepers in the town, are Shī'ahs by religion. In summer and autumn the tribes encamp in the marshes, and in winter and spring they roam the deserts with their flocks and herds: some of them cross at times into Turkish territory. The 5,000 persons who live in **Hawīzeh** Town may be taken as representing almost the whole fixed population of the district; the nomadic remainder appear to reach the large total of about 60,250 souls. The tribes of Hawīzeh are represented by their neighbours as being uncivilised, dangerous, and bitterly hostile to Sunni Muhammadans.

---

* But see article Southern **'Arabistān**. The name Manyūr seems to be applied at times to the continuation of the Kūh-i-Ahwāz from the **Kārūn** towards the **Karkheh** river.

The following is a conspectus of the main tribes, both nomadic and settled, of the Hawīzeh District :—

Tribe.	Location.	Fighting strength.	Remarks.
Bāji (Āl) آل باجي	...	...	Believed to be a section of the Bani Lām tribe. They are found also in the Dizfūl District at Khairābād on the Karkheh.
Halāf حلاف	Scattered, in the Bani Sāleh and Bani Turuf country.	Included in the Bani Sāleh and Bani Turuf.	Formerly an independent tribe but now distributed among, and forming sections of, the Bani Sāleh and Bani Turuf, and possibly of the Bani Tamīm. The Halāf are Shī'ahs.
Hiyādir حيادر	Scattered, chiefly in the Bani Turuf country.	600	The Hiyādir live chiefly among the Bani Turuf and are not apparently connected with the Hiyādir section of the Bani Sāleh or with the Haiyādir tribe of Southern 'Arabistān. The Hiyādir are Shī'ahs.
'Ikrish عكرش	About Suwaimīyah and in the country a few miles to the east of Kūt Nahr Hashim.	150 of the Bait Ghālib and 150 of the Bait Hasan division; also the bulk of 1,100 of the Daghāghleh division, the rest of these last being in the Ahwāz District.	For further information see article 'Ikrish.
Juruf (Ahl-al-) اهل الجرف	Scattered, but partly in Hawīzeh Town.	Perhaps 400 altogether, of whom 150 in Hawīzeh Town.	This tribe is Shi'ah.
Kūt (Ahl-al-) اهل الكوت	Hawīzeh Town.	350, other small tribes of the town being included with them.	Do.
Mālik (Bani) بني مالك	...	...	This is a section of the Bani Tamīm, and it is possible that other sections of the same tribe also enter the district.

Tribe.	Location.	Fighting strength.	REMARKS.
Mazra'eh مزرعه	In the Bani Turuf country.	Included in the Bani Turuf.	Formerly an independent and powerful tribe who are said to have owned ⅓ of the lands of the Hāwīzeh District. They have now become subject to the Bani Turuf and are reckoned as one of their sections. They are Shī'ahs.
Na'āmeh (Bani) بني نعامه	Among the Shurafa.	250, of whom 60 are mounted.	They originally belonged to the Hardān, but they have been excluded from the article on that tribe as they are now separate from it. The Bani Na'āmeh are Shī'ahs.
Nais نيس	Scattered, but partly in the town of Hawīzeh.	400, of whom only about 60 are in the town.	These Nais are believed to be of the same origin as the sections similarly named of the 'Anāfijeh, Bait Sa'ad and Bani Turuf tribes. They are Shī'ahs. There are Nais also at Bālingān Balāi and Hājiābād in the Dizfūl District
Qāti' (Āl) آل قاطع	Below (that is downstream from) the Shurafa.	100, of whom 30 are mounted.	The Āl Qāti' are Shī'ahs.
Sabians سبا	Hawīzeh Town.	...	See article Sabians.
Sākīyeh ساكيه	Do.	300	This tribe is Shī'ah.
Sāleh (Bani)	A considerable tract south of Hawīzeh Town.	4,350, of whom 1,000 are mounted.	See article Bani Sāleh.
Shurafa شرفا	Apparently not far from Kūt Nahr Hāshim between that place and Hāwīzeh Town.	500, including 100 mounted, if their dependents be reckoned.	They are reckoned Saiyids and are said to have come from Makkah a very long time ago. They are engaged in agriculture

Name.	Position.	Nature.	Remarks.
			and by religion are Shī'ahs. The Shawā-kir of the **Ahwāz** district are attached to them politically. Compare article **Ashrāf**.
Suwā'id سواعد	In the Bani **Turuf** country.	400	These in '**Arābistān** live among the Bani Turuf, but they are said to be merely a branch of a larger tribe in Turkish 'Irāq, towards 'Amārah. In religion they are Shī'ahs.
Suwāri سواري	Scattered throughout the district.	900	Of the fighting men 500 are said to belong to a section called Bait ' Awāyeh بيت عوايه of whom the bulk are in Turkish territory near 'Amārah, and the rest to a section called Bait Nusir بيت نصر. They are all Shī'ahs.
Turuf (Bani) بني طرف	The district generally.	5,600, of whom only about 50 are mounted.	See article Bani **Turuf**.

Topography.—The following are a few points in the district of which the names are known:—

Name.	Position.	Nature.	Remarks.
Dahabīyeh دهبيه	Apparently some miles to the west of **Hawīzeh** Town.	A canal dependent on the **Karkheh**.	It is said to be a considerable centre of population.
Hāshim (Kūt Nahr) كوت نهر هاشم	On the **Karkheh**, about 25 miles west-north-west of **Nāsiri** and 15 miles east by north of **Hawīzeh** Town.	The site of a great dam on which the proper irrigation of the **Hawīzeh** district depended: it gave way in 1837 and has not been restored.	Some 700 families of 'Ikrish of the Daghāghleh section are generally in camp a few miles to the east of this place.

Name.	Position.	Nature.	Remarks.
Hawīzeh Town حويزه	In the centre of the district and about 40 miles west by north of Nāsiri.	...	See article Hawīzeh Town.
Khafājīyeh خفاجيه	On the left bank of the present main stream, in the district, of the Karkheh river; it is situated several miles to the west of Kūt Nahr Hāshim.	The seat of the principal family of the Bani Turuf tribe.	There are said to be 90 mud-built shops at this place.
Muhammad (Shaikh) شيخ محمد	Apparently to the south-east of Hawīzeh Town.	A locality.	It marks the eastern boundary of the territories proper of the Bani Sāleh tribe.
Suwaimīyeh سويميه	About 7 miles north of Hawīzeh Town.	Do.	About 100 families of 'Ikrish of the Bait Ghālib section are settled hereabouts.

Trade and communications.—The chief exports of the district are rice, fish, and the plumage of a bird called Baiyūdhi, probably an egret, but commercially described as an "osprey." In the season great quantities of large 'Anz fish are caught and sell locally at 2 Qrāns per Hawīzeh Man; the Hawīzeh Man is equal to 7 Man of Shūshtar.

The trade of Hawīzeh is mainly with 'Amārah on the Tigris by way of the marshes and the Jahálah canal. There are also routes, to some extent in use, which connect the district with the towns of Muhammareh and Dizfūl: these are noticed in the article on 'Arabistān.

History and administration.—The district was once well cultivated and prosperous, but by the bursting of the dam at Kūt Nahr Hāshim on the Karkheh in 1837 it was rendered almost impassable, and its agriculture was destroyed. After this event the power of the local Wāli or Maula مولى, who was an independent chief, belonged to a Saiyid family of Hawīzeh Town, and had formerly exercised authority over an extensive region, shrank within narrow limits. Since 1902, in which year the Shaikh of Muhammareh assumed responsibility for the revenue of the district, the Persian Government being unable to recover the same by their own arrangements, Hawzeh has been included, theoretically, in the administrative division of Southern **'Arabistān;** and in 1904 the Shaikh of **Muhammareh,** by a successful expedition against the principal tribe, the Bani **Turuf,** succeeded in reducing the tract to actual submission. Thereafter the district was managed for a time through the chief Shaikh of the Bani **Sāleh;** but more recently the Shaikh of **Muhammareh** has appointed Maula 'Ābid 'Ali-bin-Maula Mutab to be his Deputy-Governor with headquarters at **Hawīzeh Town.** The annual assessment is nominally 30,000 Tūmāns on the Bani **Turuf** and 16,000 on the more settled inhabitants of the district about **Hawīzeh** Town; but it is stated that from the former only about 20,000 Tūmāns, and from the latter about 10,000 are collected.

HAWĪZEH
حويزه
TOWN

Situated about 40 miles west by north of **Nāsiri** in the centre of the **Hawīzeh** District of which it is the capital. Formerly a large town, it was ruined by the bursting in 1837 of the dam at Kūt Nahr Hāshim on the **Karkheh** river, which upset the whole irrigation system of the district, caused the main stream of the **Karkheh** to take a more northerly course, and reduced the town, which stood on the left bank of the original river bed, to comparative insignificance. The greater part of the population are said to have been dispersed by this event and to have joined the wandering Arabs of the district; but the town still boasts of 1,000 inhabited houses, representing a population of about 5,000 souls; there are also many deserted dwellings. The Kūt كوت quarter, the only part of Hawīzeh which now resembles a town, lies furthest to the south; the others are Sākīyeh not so far to the south, Nais on the south-west, and Ahl-i-Juruf on the north; these last three are named from the tribes inhabiting them, of whom some details are given in the article on the **Hawīzeh** District. A large part of the population which is reckoned to the town is said to be massed on a canal called Dahabīyeh on the west side of the settlement. The whole population is Shī'ah except 3 shopkeepers who are Arabs of **Najd** and 20 families of **Sabians;** of the latter 12 are silversmiths and 2 ironsmiths but none are agriculturists. The water of Hawīzeh town is now bad as well as scanty, but it remains the seat of the official who governs the district in the name of the Shaikh of **Muhammareh.**

Hawīzeh in the 14th century A.D. was one of the most flourishing places in **'Arabistān** and the centre of a district which produced corn, cotton and sugar cane. The **Sabian** community already existed at that time.

HAYĀT DĀVUD
حیات داود

The northernmost part, if we except the town of **Dīlam**, of the **Gulf Ports** governorship in Persia; it has **Rīg** for its capital and is situated on the coast of the Persian Gulf between the district of **Līrāvi** on the north and the district of **Rūdhilleh** on the south.

Limits.—The Hayāt Dāvud district is bounded on the west by the sea. The eastern boundary in the northern part is a range of hills, about 15 miles inland, which rises in places to the height of about 1,000 feet; in the southern part it is a salt stream called **Rūd Shūr** رود شور which comes down from a hill called Bīkarz-wa-Mīshān بیکرز و میشان or Tavīseh تویسه and divides it from the **Shabānkāreh** District. The northernmost village of the district is Bahmiyāri, and on the south Hayāt Dāvud extends almost to the **Rūdhilleh** River; its maximum length is consequently 40 miles, but its extent upon the coast is less as in the north it is overlapped upon the sea by the portion of the **Līrāvi** district which contains Jabal Bang. The island of **Khārag** belongs to Hayāt Dāwad.

Physical geography.—The whole district appears to be a plain; it has good soil in certain localities and is intersected by watercourses, some of considerable size, which cross it from the hills to the sea. There is an outcrop of light grey sandstone close to **Rīg**. The chief features of the coast are a creek, called Khor-al-Qusair قصیر or Khūr Jasair جسیر, frequented by large boats and yielding a few mother-of-pearl shells, midway between **Rīg** and the **Rūdhilleh** River, and Khūr Khalīl خلیل, a tidal inlet 1 mile south of **Ganāveh**, which is used by the boat-owners of that place.

Population.—A list of the villages of Hayāt Dāvud is subjoined under the heading of topography. The people, as will be seen, are mostly **Lurs** whose ancestors immigrated from the **Behbehān** province, partially submerging an ancient Persian population whom local tradition represents as having continued to be Gabrs گبر or fire worshippers till about 5 centuries ago. In some places there is an infusion of Arab blood, and the village of Gumārūn is a settlement of **Saiyids**.

The total number of the inhabitants appears to be about 12,000 souls. The Persian language with Lurish modifications is practically universal, so also is the Shī'ah form of the Muhammadan religion. Inland the people are cultivators, and upon the coast cultivators, seafarers and fishermen. Outside of **Rīg**, huts are the only kind of dwelling. The generality of the inhabitants are peaceable and partially civilised, but they are well-armed with Martinis and possess, it is said, on the average about one rifle to every house. From January to April the population is swelled by Darashūli and Kāshkūli Īliyāt, or nomadic hill tribes, who camp in the vicinity of **Rīg** and make their purchases for the year in that town.

Agriculture and livestock.—Wheat and barley are the agricultural staples, but dates also are cultivated. The banyan, fig and castor oil plant flourish. There appear to be few cattle, but sheep are numerous and are estimated to amount to 10,000 in the whole district. Water is all from wells.

Trade.—The subject of trade is disposed of in the article on **Rīg**, through which all the external trade of the district passes. The internal trade is of no account.

Transport and communications.—The district, it is believed, can furnish about 350 horses, 150 mules, 250 camels and 2,000 donkeys. There appear to be no serious obstacles to the movement of transport. It is possible to march along the coast,* and an inland route from **Burāzjān** to Zaidān traverses the district *viâ* the villages of Chāhrūsahi, Gāh Safīd, 'Abbāsi, Muhammad Sādiq and Bahmiyāri ;† there is also a route from **Rīg** to **Dih Kuhneh** in the **Shabānkāreh District**.

Administration.—The district is governed by a hereditary Khān (at present Haidar Khān, son of Khān 'Ali Khān) of **Lur** descent, who has his residence at **Rīg** and is subject to the Governor of the **Gulf Ports**. At present 8,000 Tūmāns a year is paid by him for the farm of the district. Criminal justice is dispensed by this Khān and by one of his brothers (Muhammad Khān) who acts as his deputy at Chāhrūsahi. Documents are attested and civil disputes are settled in every village

---

* *Vide* Colvill in Volume XVII of the Transactions of the Bombay Geographical Society, pages 137-39.

† See *Routes in Persia*, I, Nos. 19A. and 21A.

by the local Qāzi or Mulla, except matrimonial cases which it is usual to refer to the decision of the Qāzi or Mulla of some neighbouring village. The general administration is conducted through the headmen of villages. There are no regular police, but the retainers of the Khān look to the safety of the roads. Land revenue is collected at the rate of 60 to 70 Qrāns per Gāu of cultivation; there are no other taxes. The only direct representatives of the Persian Government are a postmaster and a telegraph master at Rīg and Persian Customs officials at Rīg and Ganāveh.

Topography.—The following are the principal places in the Hayāt Dāvud district with some details :—

Name.	Position.	Houses and inhabitants.	Remarks.
'Abbāsi عباسي	8 miles north-east of Rīg.	100 houses of Lurs and ancient Persian tribes. Some of the dwellings, still inhabited, are said to date from pre-Islamic times.	The village stands in a plain and is defended by 3 towers. Dates, wheat and barley are grown, and there are 30 horses, 20 mules, 100 donkeys, 70 cattle and 800 sheep and goats.
Allahyāri الله ياري	10 miles east by south of Rīg.	15 houses.	There are 7 horses, 15 donkeys, 12 cattle and 150 sheep and goats.
'Arash عرش	On the coast, 2 miles north of Rīg.	12 huts of Sunnis, settlers from Rīg.	A little wheat and barley are grown.
Bahmiyāri بهمياري	15 miles north by west of Ganāveh.	75 houses, mostly of Lurs from Behbehān. Here as at 'Abbāsi some of the buildings are said to be ancient.	There are 4 small towers. Dates, wheat and barley are grown and there are 30 donkeys and 800 sheep. The people are quiet and civil.
Bang بنك	About 2 miles from Jabal Bang in the Līrāvi district.	10 houses of Lurs from Behbehān.	There are a few dates and some other cultivation, also a few horses and donkeys and 100 sheep.
Bīdu بدر	6 miles east by south of Rīg near the Rūd Shūr.	20 houses of Sunni Arabs, said to be Bani Tamīm and to have come from Fallāhīyeh.	Only grain is cultivated. There are a few horses and some 30 donkeys and 30 camels.

Name.	Position.	Houses and inhabitants.	Remarks.
Chahārburj چهار برج	12 miles east by north of Ganāveh.	30 houses of Lurs from Behbehān.	There is grain cultivation and some 40 donkeys and 500 sheep are kept besides a few horses.
Chahārmal چهارمل	10 miles east of Rīg.	30 houses of Behbehānis.	Wheat and barley are grown and there are some 40 donkeys and 400 sheep, also a few horses.
Chāhrūsahi چاهروسهي	15 miles north-east of Rīg and 2 miles from the right bank of the Rūd Shūr.	100 houses of Lurs from Behbehān.	The village is on rising ground and is protected by a small fort and 4 towers. Dates, grain and tobacco are grown and there are 30 horses, 100 donkeys and 500 sheep. There is a small shrine. A deputy of the Khān has his residence here.
Darehdūn دره دون	12 miles from Rīg.	30 houses of Lurs.	Wheat and barley are grown: there are 10 horses and 30 donkeys.
Fahrābari فهرابري	15 miles north by east of Ganāveh.	70 houses of Lurs and old Persian tribes.	Stands on the plain. Wheat and barley are grown. There are here some houses said to date from pre-Muhammadan times. Animals are 10 horses, 15 mules, 100 donkeys, 50 cattle and 600 sheep and goats.
Ganāveh گناره	On the coast 15 miles north-west of Rīg.	...	See article Ganāveh.
Gāh Safīd گاه سفید	9 miles south-east of Rīg.	A group of three villages containing together about 250 houses of Lurs and the descendants of ancient Persian tribes.	The villages stand on high ground and are defended by towers. There is cultivation of wheat and barley, and the inhabitants possess some 30 horses, 150 donkeys and 2,000 sheep and goats These villages are said to be very old.

HAYĀT DĀVUD

Name.	Position.	Houses and inhabitants.	Remarks.
Gumārūn كمارون	12 miles east-north-east of Ganāveh.	80 houses of Shī'ah Saiyids, well-known throughout the Persian Gulf as Gumārūnis. Some others of them are found at Chāh Zangi in the Shabānkāreh District.	Wheat, barley and dates are grown here and about 20 horses, 100 donkeys and 700 sheep and goats belong to the village. The headman is a learned Saiyid and farms the village from the Khān of **Hayāt Dāvud**. The people are said to be charitable but somewhat fanatically disposed.
Haidari (Qal'eh) قلعه حيدري	On the coast 20 miles north-west of Rīg.	A small hamlet.	There are a few date trees.
Imāmzādeh امامزاده	Adjoins the middle village of Ganāveh.	12 huts of mixed Lurs and Arabs.	Wheat and barley are grown. Some arches are standing of a mosque said locally to have been the first built in this part of Persia.
Jazīreh جزيره	On the south side of a creek which runs inland for ¼ of a mile from the sea.	15 houses of Arabs who claim to be of Bani Hājir and Bani Tamīm descent; they are Sunnis and speak Arabic as well as Persian.	The people cultivate and fish and possess about 30 donkeys and 300 sheep and goats, besides a dozen fishing boats. Their surplus produce they sell at **Būshehr**. The creek is 2 fathoms deep at entrance.
Kamāli كمالي	10 miles north-east of Rīg.	20 houses of Lurs.	There are about 30 donkeys and 400 sheep and goats, and a little grain is grown.
Kūhak كوهك	5 miles south-east of Rīg, with the salt stream called Rūdkhāneh Shūr passing its east and south sides on the way to the sea.	15 huts of Lurs from Behbehān.	The inhabitants have about 100 camels and 30 donkeys besides cultivating on a small scale. They send some wool to the **Būshehr** market. Also called Abu Gharīb ابو غريب.

Name.	Position.	Houses and inhabitants.	Remarks.
Kūlar کولر	On the plain about 6 miles north of Rīg.	30 houses of Lurs from Behbehān who are said to be religiously inclined and charitable.	The people deal in wool and gum and cultivate a little: they have 40 donkeys and 300 sheep and goats.
Mahmad Sādi مهمد صادي	On the plain about 12 miles northeast of Rīg.	100 houses of Lurs. They are said to be charitable and rather fanatical in religion.	There is considerable cultivation of wheat and barley and some of dates. Horses number 30 and donkeys about 150. Also called Muhammad Sādiq محمّد صادق.
Mahmīd (Māl-i-) مال مهمید	On a hill, 7 miles from Rīg.	30 houses of Lurs from the Behbehān province.	There is cultivation of cereals, and 80 donkeys, 400 sheep and goats and a few horses belong to the village.
Pūzehgāh پوزه گاه	On the coast 6 miles south-south-east of Ganāveh.	50 huts of Lurs from the Behbehān province.	Some wheat and barley are grown and livestock are 20 horses, 80 donkeys and 600 sheep and goats.
Rīg ریگ	31 miles north-north-west of Būshehr Town.	......	See article Rīg.
Rūsūr روسور	10 miles from Rīg.	30 houses of Lurs.	The people grow wheat and barley, send some wool to Būshehr, and own 20 horses, 40 donkeys, 30 cattle and 600 sheep and goats.
Shūl شول	14 miles inland from Rīg, on the south side of a salt stream that comes down from the Bībī Hakīmeh hills.	Perhaps 400 houses of Lurs from the Behbehān province.	Wheat and barley are cultivated and about 500 Hāshim Mans of gum, collected in the hills, are exported annually. Ancient foundations are traceable here. Animals are 20 horses, 15 mules, 300 donkeys 100 cattle and 1,500 sheep and goats.
Tāj Maliki تاج ملکی	3 miles south of Shūl.	30 houses of Behbehāni Lurs.	Cereals are grown and about 30 donkeys and 400 sheep owned.
Yazdpūshān یزد پوشان	10 miles north-east of Ganāveh.	25 huts of mixed Lurs.	There are some donkeys and ordinary cultivation.

HAZAIM

A district of the **Kuwait** Shaikhdom, enclosed by the sea on the east, by the **Salū'** district on the north, and by the **Shaqq** district on the west; the briny rivulet of **Maqta'** marks its southern limit and divides it from the plain of **Labībah**. The middle of the district is about 60 miles south by east of **Kuwait** Town; its total extent is doubtful.

Hazaim consists of a large plain without trees but not destitute of camel grazing; the soil is firm and dark-coloured and free from stony patches. At the south end, near the **Maqta'** stream, is a Sabákhah or saline wet-weather marsh.

Hazaim contains the following places which we have tabulated in their alphabetical order :—

HAZAIM
حزيم

Name.	Position.	Character.	Remarks.
'Aqrabi عقربي	Within sight of the sea near the northern border of Hazaim.	Wells.	The depth is 1½ to 2 fathoms and the quality of the water varies with the amount of rain.
'Asailān عسيلان	About 4 miles to the west and somewhat north of Rāfa'iyah.	Do.	Contain good water at 1½ fathoms.
'Atāridh عطارض	To the west and somewhat north of 'Asailān.	Do.	Contain good water at 2 fathoms.
Dhalī'-al-Ashāri ضليع العشاري	A little to the south of Rāfa'iyah.	Do.	Contain good water at 1½ fathoms.
Marāghah مراغه	About the middle of the western border of Hazaim, probably 20 to 25 miles west by north of the mouth of the **Maqta'** stream and 10 to 15 miles south-east of Wafrah.	Do.	The water stands at 1½ fathoms and is not good.
Qu'amah قعمه	Close to the sea-shore, a couple of miles to the south of 'Aqrabi.	Do.	The water, at 2 fathoms, is of indifferent quality.
Rāfa'īyah رافعيه	About 10 miles west-south-west of the mouth of the **Maqta'** stream.	Do.	Fairly good water at 2 fathoms.

Name.	Position.	Character.	Remarks.
Rahaiyah رحيه	5 miles west of Wafrah.	A small hill.	...
Rughwah رغوه	Some miles north or north-east of Rāfa'īyah.	Wells.	Water bitter, at 1 fathom.
Rughwān رغون	Adjoining Rughwah.	Do.	Do.
Sa'ūd صعود	West and slightly north of Taiyibat-al-Ism.	Do.	Good water at $2\frac{1}{2}$ fathoms.
Shadhaf شضف	9 miles south-south-east of Wafrah and 7 miles west of Marāghah.	Do.	Depth 2 fathoms; water brackish.
Taiyibat-al-Ism طيبة الاسم	A short distance inland from Qa'amah.	Do.	Indifferent water at 2 fathoms.
Wafrah وفره	Apparently between 50 and 60 miles due south of Kuwait Town.	Numerous wells.	The wells are 2 fathoms deep and yield water of passable quality.

Those who make Umm **Janaib** a small separate district to the west of Hazaim assign to it the hill of Rahaiyah and the wells of Shadhaf and Wafrah described above.

IAZAM حزم

A valuable fort and small village in the Sultanate of 'Omān, situated on the west side of Wādi **Fara'** at less than 1 mile from the bed of the Wādi and some 15 miles to the south-west of the town of **Masna'ah** in **Bātīnah**, which is the port of Hazam. Hazam is the lowest point in the tract known as **Rustāq**, and there is a difference of opinion regarding the district in which it is situated, some assigning it to **Hajar**, which is probably correct, and others to **Bātinah** : this much is clear that it stands in a plain, at some distance from the hills of **Hajar** properly so called.

The village is walled and consists of about 80 houses of the **Miyāyihah** and **Ya'āribah** tribes, in the centre of which is the celebrated fort. There are no wells here, and the water supply depends on subterranean conduits from Wādi **Fara'** which enter the village. The date plantations are extensive, containing (it is estimated) 70,000 palms; and wheat, barley, sesame, beans, sugarcane and lucerne are grown. Horses are said to number 4, donkeys 150, camels 100 and sheep and goats 900.

The fort is one which can be held by a small garrison and its possession gives command of routes, especially that to **Suwaiq**, which are important to the neighbouring tribes of **Bātinah** and particularly to the **Yāl Sa'ad**. Hazam originally belonged to the **Ya'āribah**, from whom it was captured by 'Azzān-bin-Qais in 1870 after a long siege. It is now in the possession of Saiyid Sa'īd-bin-Ibrāhīm of **Rustāq**, a relation and virtually independent vassal of the present Sultan of **'Omān**.

HIBI
حيبي

Or Hibi حيبي : a village in the Western **Hajar** district of the **'Omān** Sultanate, one day's journey inland from **Saham** Town, at the head of Wādi **Sarrāmi**. The place consists of 80 houses of Bani 'Īsa, **Hawāsinah** of the Hawāmid section and Bani **'Umr**; and the local resources include about 20 camels, 10 donkeys, 40 cattle, 300 sheep and goats and 3,000 date palms. There is a fort garrisoned by 40 men under an 'Aqīd on the part of the Sultan of **'Omān**.

HIKMĀN
حكمان

Singular is Hikmāni حكماني . A tribe found on the South-Eastern Coast of **'Omān**, where the Barr-al-Hikmān بر الحكمان or mainland between **Masīrah** island and Ghubbat Hashīsh is named after them, especially at **Mahōt**: they also occur along the coast for 40 miles to the south-west of Ghubbat Hashīsh. Sixty years ago they were an independent tribe, Ghāfiri in politics and Sunni in religion, regarded as cognate with the **Jannabah**; but since that time they have partially lost their separate existence, those of Barr-al-Hikmān having attached themselves to the Bani Bū **'Ali**, while others have become Hināwis under the protection of Shaikh Zāid-bin-Khalīfah of Abu **Dhabi**, to whom they pay annual visits and from whom they receive presents. **Mahōt** is their principal settlement. Their number may be 800 souls. Some Hikmān are found also at **Murbāt** in Dhufār and at **Barkah** and Wādi Manūmah in **Bātinah**. One authority gives the name of this tribe as 'Ukmān عكمان.

3 z

HILAM (WĀDI) Or Halam; the easternmost of the three valleys which compose Wādi Bani Jābir (I) in the Eastern Hajar district of the 'Omān Sultanate. Wādi Hilam reaches the coast at Kalhāt, and the following are the principal places which it contains, in order from above downwards:—

Name.	Position.	Houses and inhabitants.	Remarks.
Hilam حلم	Near the head of the valley.	250 houses of Bani Jābir of the Salūt section.	The head-quarters of the Salūt or ruling section of the Bani Jābir.
Hūl حول	1½ hours below Hilam.	30 houses of Bani Jābir.	Nil.
Qasa'ah قصعه	¼ of an hour below Hūl.	Ditto	Do.
Qa'ab قعب	½ an hour below Qasa'ah.	20 houses of Bani Jābir.	Do.
Sufun سفن	¾ of an hour below Qa'ab.	30 houses of Bani Jābir.	Do.
Shūfi شوفي	½ an hour below Sufun.	40 houses of Bani Jābir.	Do
Mahat محط	½ an hour below Shūfi.	20 houses of Bani Jābir.	Do.
Qōdhah قوضه	4 hours below Mahat.	Ditto	Do.
Kalhāt كلهات	On the sea, 2 hours below Qōdhah.	...	See article Kalhāt.

The Bani Jābir here mostly belong to the Aulād Nāsir section of the tribe, but some are Aulād Rāshid; and the total population of the valley (exclusive of Kalhāt) is about 2,000 souls.

The general character of Wādi Hilam is described in the article on Wādi Bani Jābir (I).

HILLAH QADHA حله A division of the Dīwānīyah Sanjāq of the Baghdād Wilāyat in Turkish 'Irāq.

Position and boundaries.—The Qadha of Hillah is situated on both banks of the Euphrates below Musaiyib and above Dīwānīyah. It is bounded on the north and north-east by the Qadhas of Kādhimain and Jazīrah, both in the Baghdād Sanjāq; on the south-east by the

Dīwānīyah Qadha; on the south by the Shāmīyah Qadha; and on the west by all three Qadhas of the Karbala Sanjāq.

Topography and tribes.—With the exception of **Hillah** Town, described elsewhere under its own name, this Qadha contains no very large places; but the villages of Husain and Imām Hamzah (I), mentioned below, contain each about 2,000 inhabitants. The district is divided into 4 rural Nāhiyahs, each containing a number of villages and inhabited by various tribes.

The villages and tribes of the Bārmānah بارمانه Nāhiyah, which is of the 2nd class, in alphabetical order are:—

Villages.	Tribes.
1. 'Atābij عتابج 2. Bārmānah بارمانه (headquarters of the Mudīr) 3. Dūlāb دولاب 4. Fanharah فنهره 5. Garaita'ah گريطعه 6. Husain حصين 7. Jam'iyāt جمعيات 8. Kuwaikhāt كويخات 9. Nukhailah نخيله 10. Rawāshid رواشد 11. Sādah سادە	Āl Bū **Sultān** of the following sections:— 'Abdullah (Āl Bū), 'Anah (Āl Bū), 'Awaisāt, Daghairāt, Darwīsh (Āl Bū), Gharān (Āl Bū), Hamdah (Āl Bū), Harīsh (Āl Bū), Husain 'Ali (Āl Bū), Janāhiyīn, Khalīl (Āl Bū), Maraizah (Āl Bū), Sālih (Āl Bū), Samandar (Āl Bū), Saqar (Āl Bū), Shakair (Āl Bū), Shāwi (Āl Bū), Talabah (Āl Bū), Thābit (Āl Bū), Zuwain (Āl Bū). Also **Zubaid** of the Jahaish section (Āl Bū Dadah and Āl Bū Sanaid subsections).

The Khawās خواص Nāhiyah, also of the 2nd class, is inhabited by about 5,000 persons of the Yasār and 4,000 of other tribes: its villages are 'Anānah عانائه (on the right bank of the **Euphrates** opposite to the ruins of Babylon), Sinjār سنجار and Tahmāsīyah طهماسيه, (about 3 miles west of **Hillah** Town). 'Anānah is the residence of the Mudīr.

The villages of the Mahāwil محاويل Nāhiyah, likewise of the 2nd class, are as below; the tribes are not specified:—

Villages.	Villages.
1. Ahmad (Battah) بته احمد	6. Mustafa (Al Bū) آل بو مصطفى
2. Barnūn برنون	7. Sādāt-al-Hisn سادات الحصن
3. Jamjamah جمجمه	8. Saiyid (Battah) بته سيد
4. Khātūnīyah خاتونيه	9. Sūrah سوره
5. Kuwairish كويرش	10. Wahbi (Battah) بته وهبي

Besides these there are the following villages on the Mahāwil canal: Sabbāghiyah صباغيه, Khān-al-Mahāwil, Imām امام, and Manfīyah منفيه. Sabbāghīyah is the residence of the Mudīr.

The Mamdūhīyah ممدوحيه Nāhiyah, which is of the 1st class, contains the villages and is inhabited by the tribal sections which follow:—

Villages.	Tribal sections.
1. 'Alāk علاك	Hamad (Al Bū),
2. 'Alāwanah علاونه	'Īsa (Āl Bū),
3. Imām Hamzah (I) (See article **Euphrates**) امام حمزه	Jaraiyāt,
	Jarbū',
4. Khaikān-al-Kbīr (headquarters of the Mudīr) خيكان الكبير	Jāsim (Āl Bū),
	Kasairāt,
5. Khaikān-as Saghīr خيكان الصغير	Masā'id (Al Bū),
	Mansūr (Āl Bū),
6. Khashkhashīyah خشخشيه	Samandar (Al Bū),

Villages.	Tribal sections.
7. Mazīdīyah مزيديه 8. Sa'air (Abu) ابو سعير 9. Shurfat-as-Saghīrah شرفة الصغيرة	Sharīfāt and Zabairīyah, all of whom are sections of the Al Bū Sultān tribe.

The remaining Nāhiyah, that of Nahr Shāh نهر شاه, is of the 2nd class and contains these villages:—

Villages.	Villages.
1. 'Abaid (Jadīdat-al-Hājj-) جديدة الحاج عبيد 2. 'Afaināt عفينات 3. Busairah بصيرة 4. Dablah (headquarters of the Mudīr) دبله 5. Ghalais غليس 6. Hiddah حدة	7. Huwaish-as-Saiyid حويش السيد 8. Janājah جناجه 9. Ma'aimarah معيمرة 10. Rashīdīyah رشيديه and 11. Sa'īdīyah سعيديه

The tribes inhabiting this Nāhiyah are the Jamai'āt, Jawāzarīyah, **Khazā'il**, Bani Mansūr, Shaghab, Shukar, 'Umr Lang, and 'Uwaidiyan, all of whom perhaps, with the exception of the **Khazā'il**, are subsections of the two Jabūr sections of the **Zubaid**. Janābiyīn, Wisāmah and **Zubaid** of the Khafājah and Yasār sections are also found.

Population.—The fixed population of the Hillah Qadha is estimated at 75,000 souls. Of these it is believed that about 48,500 are Shī'ah Muhammadans, 26,000 Sunni Muhammadans, and 500 Jews.

Resources.—The chief products of the district are dates, wheat and barley. A recent official enumeration of the date palms appears to have given the following results:—

Nāhiyah of Barmānab	. . . . .	146,329 trees.
„ „ Khawās	. . . . .	12,538 „
„ „ Mahāwīl	. . . . .	4,207 „
„ „ Mamdūhīyah	. . . . .	57,026 „
„ „ Nahr Shāh	. . . . .	48,488 „

This makes a total of 268,588 palms, or, with those of **Hillah** Town, of about 333,000 for the whole Qadha. Livestock are horses, donkeys, camels, cattle, buffaloes, sheep and a few mules and goats. Liquorice grows wild.

The principal canals in the various Nāhiyahs are given below in their alphabetical order :—

Bārmāṇah.	Khawās.	Mahāwil.	Mamdūhīyah.	Nahr Shāh.
1. Bārmānah بارمانه	1. Khawās خواص	Those apparently of Mahāwil, Khātūnīyah, Nīl and Wardīyah mentioned in the article on the river Euphrates.	1. Abu Chumāq ابو چماق	1. Abu Zawāyah ابو زوايه
2. Fanharah فنهره	2. Mahnāwiyah مهناويه		2. 'Awādil عوادل	2. 'Aliyah عليه
3. Ghunaiyah غنيه	3. Sāṭūrīyah ساطوريه		3. Badhal بذل	3. Batrah بترة
4. Hasan (Al Bū) آل بو حسن	4. Tahmāsīyah طهماسيه		4. Bāshiyah باشيه	4. Daurah دورة
5. Mishaimish مشيمش	5. Tājīyah تاجيه		5. Hor-as-Saiyid Hijāb هور السيد حجاب	5. Ghurbīdah غريبده
			6. Kadas كدس	6. Hamzāwiyah همزاويه
			7. 'Othmānīyah عثمانيه	7. Haqānīyah حقانيه
			8. Rūbiyānah روبيانه	8. Hor-al Hindīyah هور الهنديه
			9. Shūmli شوملي	9. Hor-an Nāil هور النائل
			10. Shuwaimli شويملي	10. Hor-as Salmān هور السمان
			11. Zu'ailāwi زعيلاوي	11. Hor-al Wastāni هور الوسطاني
				12. 'Ilāj علاج

Bārmānah.	Khawās.	Mahāwil.	Mamdūhīyah.	Nahr Shāh.
				13. Jāzarīyah جازريه
				14. Jarbū'ī-yah جربوعيه
				15. Jōb جوب
				16. Manāsīm Sālih مناصيم صالح
				17. Multahī-yah ملتهيه
				18. Nahr Saif نهر سيف
				19. Rustamī-yah رستميه
				20. Shabābī-yah شهابيه
				21. Zarūfīyah زروفيه
				Besides these there are eight others of which the names have not been ascertained, making 29 in all. Thirteen of them take directly out of the **Euphrates** and 16 out of the Nahr Shāh, which gives its name to the Nāhi-yah.

Administration.—Hillah is a Qadha of the 1st class; it consists of a headquarters Nāhiyah of Hillah and of the 4 rural Nāhiyahs (already mentioned) of Bārmānah, Khawās, Mahāwīl, Mamdūhīyah and Nahr Shāh, each of which is governed by a Mudīr. The relative positions of the Nāhiyahs are not altogether certain, but Khawās is evidently upon the west side of the **Euphrates** immediately above **Hillah** Town, while Mahāwīl apparently extends up the eastern bank from **Hillah** Town to the northern limit of the Qadha. The Nāhiyahs of Bārmānah and Mamdūhīyah seem to succeed one another in this order on the left bank of the **Euphrates** below **Hillah** Town, Nahr Shāh being partly opposite to both of them on the other side of the river.

The Dāirat-as-Sanīyah owns various estates in the Qadha: among them are the Muqāta'ahs or tracts of Abu 'Arāis ابو عرائس, Abu Gharq ابو غرق, 'Ilāj علاج, Umm-al-Hawa ام الهوى, Mālih مالح and Yūsufīyah يوسفيه. They are said to be cultivated by Arabs of the Ma'adān tribe, and are all situated in the lower part of the Khawās Nāhiyah and watered from the Shatt-al-**Hindīyah**.

HILLAH حله TOWN

One of the most important towns of Turkish '**Irāq** at the present day: it stands upon both banks of the **Euphrates** about 30 miles below **Musaiyib** and perhaps 65 miles by the course of the river above **Diwānīyah** Town. A road, unmade but fit for driving, and a service of public conveyances connect it with **Baghdād** City about 60 miles distant.

The principal part of the town, called Shāmīyah شاميه (because it is the nearer to the Syrian desert), stands on the right bank of the river, of which the bed is here about 100 yards wide, and is connected with the eastern portion, called Jazīrah جزيره (because situated in Mesopotamia), by a bridge of 15 boats. In summer the river bed is now entirely dry, and the people of Hillah obtain their drinking water by digging holes in it to an average depth of 3 feet. Both parts of the town are largely constructed of ancient bricks dug up on the adjacent site of Babylon: the only features of architectural interest belong to the western quarter, namely a tall minaret in the centre and a mosque called the Masjid-ash-Shams مسجد الشمس outside the north-western gate on the road to **Karbala**. The town of Hillah stands towards the upper end of a magnificent stretch of date trees that fringes the banks of the **Euphrates** for some 30 miles: it is estimated that the town itself possesses 65,000 palms and that the district has not less than 333,000.

The population is 30,000, and more than three-fourths of the whole are Shī'ah Arabs; the remainder are mostly Sunni Arabs, but there are perhaps 750 Persians, 30 Oriental Christians, and 20 Panjābi and Kashmīri Indians, besides a dozen Afghāns. Among the Persians are included a few **Balūchis**, who are Persian subjects.

Surrounded by gardens and fruit-trees, Hillah is the centre of a district which produces wheat and barley in abundance; and a surplus of these, as well as of dates, is ordinarily available for exportation. The agricultural prosperity of Hillah is however on the decline in consequence of the failure of the **Euphrates** and may conceivably become, at no very distant date, a thing entirely of the past. At present, it is calculated, the following supplies could be collected at Hillah in a week if the conditions were favourable: 400 tons of wheat, 600 tons of barley, 100 tons of rice, 1,000 oxen and cows, 600 buffaloes, 300 horses, 1,000 donkeys, 50 mules, 700 camels and 5,000 sheep. The covered bazaars are extensive and well-stocked, containing it is said as many as 2,000 shops; they furnish all ordinary articles and some of European manufacture. The number of 'Alwahs or grain stores is stated at 120, of coffee shops at 20 and of Khāns or caravansarais at 18. There is also a warehouse for the storage of petroleum. Hillah imports piece-goods and some other merchandise from **Baghdād** City, but the rest of its trade is with **Kūfah** on the Shatt-al-**Hindīyah**, a means of communication being provided by marshes which in some seasons extend from the **Hindīyah** to within about 4 miles of Hillah. The chief exports are barley, wheat, dates and ghi; the principal imports are piece-goods, sugar and coffee; the only manufactures of importance are a fine felt, used for rugs and for horse-furniture, and a particular kind of Arab saddle.

Hillah is the *chef-lieu* of the Qadha of the same name in the Sanjāq of **Dīwānīyah** and is a municipal town; besides the Qāīm-Maqām of the Qadha there are here Mamūrs of the Public Debt department and Tobacco Régie and a harbour master for the river. The military garrison consists of a regiment of cavalry, 3 guns and a battalion of infantry, and Hillah is probably, after **Baghdād** and **Basrah**, the most important military station in Turkish 'Irāq. The place is a centre for about 1,200 reservists, being the headquarters of the 1st battalion of the 84th regiment of Radīf; and a large stock of ammunition besides several hundred spare rifles for the reservists and, it is said, a reserve battery of field-guns are kept there. The barracks, well built of Babylonian bricks, are in the western town and form the back of a large open square which fronts the river at the boat bridge. The Sarāi or offices of the civil administration consist of a large block of buildings in good repair a little to the north of the barracks. There are a telegraph and a post office. Schools number 3 and mosques nearly 30. The Persian Government are represented here by an honorary Nāib-Kārpardāz or Consular Agent.

Hillah stands amidst historic sites. The ruins of Babylon begin only 3 miles to the north, while the Tall Nimrūd تل نمرود or prominent mound which marks the place of the ancient Borsippa is 8 miles to the south-west; and Hāshimīyah هاشميه, the first capital of the 'Abbāsid Khalīfahs, is believed to have stood about 10 miles to the northward, a few miles to the east of the **Euphrates**. The eastern quarter of the town existed already, as Jāmi'ān جامعان in the 10th century A.D.; and Hillah proper, on the west bank, was founded in 1102 A.D. The name means "The Settlement."

HILTI (WĀDI-AL-)
وادي الحلتي

A valley in the Western **Hajar** district of the **Omān** Sultanate; it descends to **Bātinah** and reaches the sea by various branches near Sawaiharah and 'Awaināt. It rises on the north side of a pass between **Bātinah** and **Dhāhirah** called Najd-al-Hilti and passes in succession the following villages:—

Name.	Position.	Houses and inhabitants.	Remarks.
Halāhil حلاحل	6 hours below the Najd, on the right bank.	90 houses of Bani Ghaith.	Here are 15 camels, 15 donkeys, 40 cattle and 700 sheep and goats.
Muta'ārishah متعارشه	2 hours below Halāhil, on the right bank.	60 houses of **Maqābīl** of the Bani Khail section.	Livestock are 8 camels, 10 donkeys, 12 cattle and 500 sheep and goats.
Hail حيل	1 hour below Muta'ārishah on the right bank.	40 houses of **Maqābīl**.	Animals are 3 camels, 7 donkeys, 5 cattle and 300 sheep and goats. Some date plantations and arable land here, worth $300 a year, belong to the present Sultān of **'Omān** (Saiyid Faisal) in his private capacity.

HILU (WĀDI-AL-)

Name.	Position.	Houses and inhabitants.	Remarks.
Lithaibāt لثيبات	1 hour below Hail, on the left bank.	50 houses of Maqābīl and Jahāwar.	The people possess 8 camels, 10 donkeys, 10 cattle and 500 sheep and goats.
Aqair عقير	1 hour below Lithaibāt on the left bank.	40 houses of Maqābīl and Jahāwar.	There are 8 camels, 10 donkeys, 6 cattle and 400 sheep and goats.
Haiyadh حيض	Slightly below 'Aqair, on the right bank.	...	See article Haiyadh.
Khabt خبط	2 hours below Haiyadh, on the right bank.	30 houses of Jahāwar and Bani 'Īsa.	Livestock are 3 camels, 6 donkeys, 4 cattle and 100 sheep and goats.
'Ablah عبله	2 hours below Khabt, on the left bank.	20 houses of Jahāwar.	Animals are 5 camels, 8 donkeys, 7 cattle and 30 sheep and goats.
Abailah عبيله	1 hour below 'Ablah on the right bank.	10 houses of Jahāwar and Bani 'Īsa.	There are 2 camels, 5 donkeys, 5 cattle and 200 sheep and goats.
Riqqah رقه	1 hour below 'Abailah on the left bank.	A non-permanent encampment of shepherds.	The hills end here, and from this point across Bātinah to the sea is reckoned 12 hours.

The head of this Wādi does not appear to adjoin any inhabited place in Dhāhirah: the nearest villages to it are those of the Hawāsinah. Dates are cultivated throughout the valley, but not in profusion; a small amount of grain also is grown, but the people are mostly shepherds.

The total population of Wādi-al-Hilti is about 1,800 souls.

HILU (WĀDI-AL-) وادي الحلو

A small valley about 12 miles in length in the Masqat District of the 'Omān Sultanate; it runs from south to north and enters Wādi Maih from the east just below Yiti and only one mile from the coast. Wādi-al-Hilu contains two villages Hiwar, حور, 2 miles above Yiti, and Hilu, 2 miles above Hiwar: both are on the right bank. Hiwar consists of 10 houses of Bani **Battāsh** of the Ma'āshirah section; near it is Falaj-al-Hilam حلم, a village of 8 houses of Ma'āshirah, owned by a Hindu of **Masqat** Town, with date cultivation.

HINA (BANI) بني هنا

Singular is Hināi هنذئي. A tribe of Yamani descent in the Sultanate of 'Omān, Ibādhis by religion and belonging to the Hināwi political faction.

The Bani Hina are found principally in **Hajar** and in **'Omān Proper**. In **Hajar** they occur at Qurain (100 houses), Habbās (80 houses), Haili (200 houses), Qadīmah (40 houses), Jammah (50 houses), Naghzah (50 houses), Hārithīyah (20 houses) and Khōdh (120 houses) in Wādi **Samāil**; at Hajrat-ash-Shaikh (50 houses), Hārat-al-Jabah (80 houses), Saqairīyah (30 houses) and Shabaikah (40 houses) in Wādi **Fara'**; at Hawail (45 houses) and Hōqain (200 houses) in Wādi Bani **Ghāfir**; and at Khān (40 houses) in Wādi-al-**Jizi**. Their chief centre is **Nizwa** in 'Omān Proper where they have 300 houses; at Bilād Sait they have 40 and at Ghāfāt 50 houses; and Jabal-al-Kor is regarded as being in their country. Bani Hina are found also at **Liwa** Town (160 houses) in **Bātinah**, and at Hail (100 houses) and Dham (80 houses) in **Dhāhirah**.

The Bani Hina number in all about 9,000 souls. A few of them at **Nizwa** belong to a section called Hawāqinah حواقنة; and the Jabūr, whom we have treated as distinct, are perhaps a branch of the tribe The Bani Hina are brave and warlike and are at feud at the present time (1905) with the **Jannabah, Darū'** and Bani **Kalbān**. The Hināwi faction, formed in **'Omān** at the beginning of the 18th century, derived its name from the Bani Hina, whose chief Shaikh at that time, Khalf-al-Qusair, was the first Tamīmah or generalissimo of the whole faction. The Shaikh of the Bani Hina from 1881 to 1894 was Hilāl-bin-Zahair, a descendant of Khalf and, like his ancestor, noted throughout 'Omān for his resolution and daring: the headship is now held by his sons, who reside at **Nizwa**.

HINDARĀBI *
هندرابي

In English formerly known as "Inderabia." An island near the coast of the **Shībkūh** district in Persia: its eastern extremity is about 4½ miles west-north-west of **Chīru**. Hindarābi is over 4 miles in length from east to west and nearly 3 miles in breadth: it is of a brown colour and rises gradually from the sides to a flat centre about 100 feet above sea-level. There is no natural vegetation except a certain amount of grass in spring. The island is fringed by a reef which impedes landing at low water and is surrounded by pearl banks except at one place upon the east side. About the middle of the north shore of the island is situated the village of Hindarābi in which are about 100 houses of 'Obaidli Arabs, Sunnis; it possesses wells of which the water is brackish in summer, a few banyan trees, and some cultivation of wheat and barley; the flocks and herds amount to about 50 cattle and 100 goats. There are about 400 date palms, chiefly on the west side of the village. The people are mostly fishermen and pearl-divers, owning 20 small craft. (4 Baqārahs and 16 Shū'ais), which they use for fishing in winter and for pearling near the island in summer. Hindarābi island is subject to the 'Obaidli Shaikh of **Chīru**, whose local representative is styled Nāib. About ¼ of the fighting men are armed with modern rifles.

HINDĪYAH QADHA
هنديه

A division of the Karbala Sanjāq of the Baghdād Wilāyat in Turkish 'Irāq.

Position and boundaries.—The Qadha of Hindīyah is situated on both banks of the Shatt-al-**Hindīyah** beginning a little way below **Musaiyib** and ending some distance above **Kūfah**; it is bounded on the north by the Qadha of **Karbala**, on the east by that of **Hillah**, on the south by those of **Shāmīyah** and **Najaf**, and on the west by the **Shāmīyah** Desert.

Topography and population.— Hindīyah contains no places of any size except the town of **Tawairīj**, the administrative centre of the district, and the large village of **Kifl**, both of which are described in separate articles under their own names. The main and central feature of the district is the Shatt-al-**Hindīyah**, which traverses it from end to end and is possessed of numerous distributaries.

---

*To the mediæval Arab and Persian geographers Hindarābi seems to have been known under the name of Abrūm. See Le Strange's *Lands of the Eastern Caliphate.*

The following is a table of the principal Muqata'ahs or agricultural tracts of which the Qadha is composed and of the tribes by whom they are inhabited and tilled :—

Tracts.	Tribes.	Tracts.	Tribes.
1. Fatlah فتله	Āl Bū Fatlah.	7. Masai'īdat-a sh-Sharqīyah مسيعيدة الشرقيه	Jalīhah and Barāji'.
2. Harqa حرقا	Tufail.	8. Mshora b-al-Gharbi مشورب الغربي	Da'ūm, Karākishah and Mas'ūd.
3. Janājīyah جناجيه	Janājah.	9. Mshora b-ash-Sharqi مشورب الشرقي	'Āmirīyah, Bani Sadd and Bani Taraf.
4. Ka'abūri كعبوري	Bani Hasan.	10. Nafāsh (Abu) ابو نفاش	Bani Hasan.
5. Manfahān منفهان	Qarait.	11. Rōbah (Abu) ابو ربه	Qarait.
6. Masai'īdat-a l-Gharbīyah مسيعيدة الغربيه	Jalīhah.	12. Zubailīyah زبيليه	'Amirīyah.

The Bani Sālah tribe are also found in this district.

Population.—The total fixed population of the district is estimated at 95,000 souls, of whom about 89,000 are Shī'ah Muhammadans, 5,500 are Sunni Muhammadans and 500 are Jews.

Resources.—Date palms are estimated at 400,000 trees. Rice was formerly the chief crop of the Qadha; but the upper part of the district in the neighbourhood of **Tawairīj** town, formerly marshy, is now drying up, and the place of rice in that part is being taken by other cereals. There is nothing remarkable about the livestock.

Administration.—The district, which is a Qadha of the 1st class, consists of two regular Nāhiyahs, that of the Markaz or headquarters administered from **Tawairīj** by the Qāim-Maqām of the Qadha, and that of Kifl governed by a Mudīr, who has his seat at **Kifl**. The Nāhiyah of Kifl is of the 3rd class. There are also a number of small subdivisions called Qol Mu'ashirliyis, including Harqa حرقة which extends for some distance along the left bank of the Shatt-al-**Hindīyah** above the Nāhiyah of Kifl, and Mshorab مشورب on both banks of the Shatt-al-**Hindīyah** from the Dawaihīyah canal upwards: the latter is divided into 2 tracts, Mshorab-al-Gharbi on the west, and Mshorab-ash-Sharqi on the east side of the stream. The *chef-lieu* of the Qadha appears to have been originally at an unhealthy spot in the marshes, whence it was removed some years ago to the healthier site of **Tawairīj** on the banks of the Shatt-al-**Hindīyah**.

HINDĪYAH* (SHATT-AL-)

شط الهندية

A great waterway in Turkish 'Irāq, formerly a canal but now become a river: it leaves the right bank of the **Euphrates** at a point about 5 miles below **Musaiyib**, and draws off at the present time nearly the whole stream of that river.

The Hindīyah barrage.—The angle contained between the **Euphrates** and the Hindīyah immediately below the point of bifurcation is acute. At a short distance within the entrance of the Hindīyah, the banks being here about 200 yards apart, it is spanned by a large Saddah سدة or barrage built of massive limestone blocks: in the centre of this work there is now a gap about 20 yards in extent. As there is a concave flexure in its lower or downstream aspect the length of the barrage must exceed 200 yards: its form is somewhat as below:—

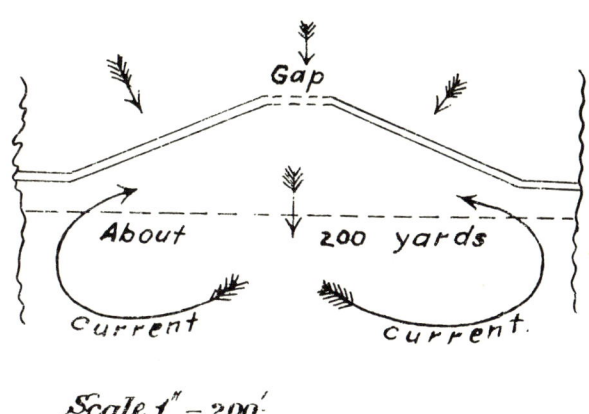

Authorities.—An article by Mr. H. W. Cadoux in the Geographical Journal for September 1906, Mr. G. Le Strange's *Lands of the Eastern Caliphate*, and personal investigations by the author.

The water rushes in a rapid—almost in a waterfall—through the gap and trickles over the wings, and a deep whirlpool is thus formed on the lower side, in which the dancing Quffahs of fishermen may often be seen. A village called Saddah stands on both sides of the Hindīyah at the barrage: on the right or western bank are some 50 houses with shops and cafés; on the left bank are about 25 houses, including the quarters of a superintending engineer and his establishment.

Topography of the Hindīyah proper.—The principal features of the Hindīyah in the next 68 miles of its course can be most conveniently explained by means of a table, as follows:—

Name.	Position.	Nature.	Remarks.
Mshorab مشرب Canal	Takes off from the right bank about 7 miles below the barrage.	A canal, sometimes dry, of which the bed is 15 or 20 yards broad and 10 feet deep.	Much water runs to waste through this canal and helps to flood the country to the south-east of Karbala Town. The substitution of rice for barley on the lands irrigated by it and the progressive enlargement of the mouth, which is unscientifically constructed, are accountable for a gradual increase in the damage done by this canal. The protective works which have been necessitated are referred to in the article on Karbala Town.
Sulaimānīyah سليمانيه Village	About 5 miles west of a point on the Hindīyah 8 miles below the barrage.	A village of about 40 mud huts, standing on a mound. The people own some buffaloes, sheep and donkeys, and some work as boatmen when the country in the neighbourhood is flooded. The donkeys are hired out to pilgrims to Karbala.	The route between Karbala Town and Tawairij passes the south side of this village at 6 miles from the former and 7 from the latter place. The Hor-al-Husainīyah extends away to the south-west of the village, and there are other swamps adjoining.

Name.	Position.	Nature.	Remarks.
Dawaibīyah دريبيه Canal	Takes off from the right bank about 2 miles below the Mshorab canal.	A canal about 25 yards wide with banks 7 or 8 feet high: in winter the water in it runs 3 or 4 feet deep. This canal goes to the south-west. The Dawaihīyah has a branch known as the Abul Khasāwi ابو الخصاوي which communicates with the swamps adjoining Sulaimānīyah village.	Similar to the Mshorab canal above. Near this canal is a village, called Bani Sālah سالح with cultivation of wheat and barley: the people, probably of the tribe so named, are about 200 souls. A little south of the canal is Umm Jamāl ام جمال a village of 400 inhabitants who grow cereals, dates and melons. Also near the Dawaihīyah, but to the north of the Karbala-Tawairīj road are the villages of Saiyid Jōdah جودة and Bani 'Aufi عوفي; the former has 400, the latter 100 inhabitants. Here are poplar trees and cultivation of wheat, barley, Māsh and millet: Bani 'Auhi has also a date grove. On both sides of the Dawaihīyah are the Maulah tribe (400 souls), who own date groves and work as boatmen.
Abd 'Auniyāt عبد عونيات Canal	Takes off from the right bank about 3 miles below the Dawaihīyah canal.	A canal similar to the last, on which it apparently converges, for upon the Karbala-Tawairīj road the two are less than 2 miles apart.	Similar to the Mshorab canal. Midway between the Dawaihīyah and the 'Abd 'Auniyāt, near the road, is a village called Al Bū Sahwah آل بو صحوة of about 450 inhabitants: the people are gardeners, cultivators and boatmen. A mile and a half from Al Bū Sahwah on the way to Tawairīj is Ibn 'Amti ابن عمتي a small hamlet of market gardeners; and about 2 miles south-west of

Name.	Position.	Nature.	REMARKS.
Tawairīj طويريج	Chiefly on the right bank, 1 mile below the 'Abd 'Auniyāt canal.	See article Tawairīj.	Tawairīj on a branch of the 'Abd 'Auniyāt is Rajībah رجيبه, a place partly cultivated by the Jalībah, where there are some gardens. As Tawairīj is approached wooding and cultivation increase upon the banks of the Hindīyah. At the town itself the stream is about 150 yards wide and is spanned by a boat bridge of 21 pontoons: here the water flows strong and deep between firm banks.
Shatt-al-Mulla شطّ الملّا Canal	Takes off from the right bank 3 or 4 miles below Tawairīj.	A canal which, within a few miles of its head, is 40 yards wide and 8 feet deep. Not far from its head it throws off from its right bank a considerable distributary called Zibdīyah زبديه or Zibdīyāt which is about 12 yards wide and 3 feet deep. A little below the point of separation of the Zibdīyah there is a village of the Qarait tribe upon the Shatt-al-Mulla. On the left bank of the Hindīyah, opposite the Shatt-al-Mulla, and between Tawairīj and Hillah, is a tract of land known as Mahannāwīyah مهناويه and watered by a canal of the same name: it produces wheat, barley, millet, Māsh and beans.	This canal is said to curve round westwards and then southwards, passing close to Khān Hamad and Khān Musalla on the route from Karbala Town to Najaf Town and eventually rejoining the Hindīyah near (probably just above) Kūfah. In going from Najaf Town to Kifl this canal is crossed at about 7 miles from Najaf: at the crossing place it has easily sloping banks, runs about 50 yards wide and 2 feet deep, and is about ¼ of a mile west of the Hindīyah.

Name.	Position.	Nature.	Remarks.
Tall Nimrūd تَلّ نمرود or Birs Nimrūd برس نمرود	On the left bank, 11 or 10 miles below the take-off of the Shatt-al-Mulla canal.	A remarkable mound, on which are Babylonian ruins. This is the ancient Borsippa.	A little way above Tall Nimrūd the left bank of the Hindīyah is broken by an inlet called Guss كَصّ. Water leaving the Hindīyah by this opening forms a large lake or swamp between the Hindīyah and the road connecting Tawairīj with Hillah Town. A part of this watery region is apparently called 'Aufi عوفي.
Kifl كفل	On the left bank, 12 miles below Tall Nimrūd.	See article Kifl.	The stream is 200 yards wide here, and there is much cultivation especially upon the right bank. About 3 miles below Kifl, near the right bank, is the village of 'Amrān عمران consisting of a few Arab huts and 1 walled and fortified enclosure. The Abu Shūrah canal, which waters the Hor-ad-Dukhn tract and is noticed in the article on the Qadha of Najaf, takes off from the left bank in the same vicinity. About 4 miles below 'Amrān again is a place where the Hindīyah narrows down to about 80 yards: here the banks rise 10 feet above the water.
Kūfah كوفه	On the right bank, about 14 miles below Kifl.	See article Kūfah.	At Kūfah, where there is a boat bridge of 16 pontoons, the Hindīyah is about 150 yards wide and flows in winter with a maximum depth of about 6 feet; but a quarter of a mile above the bridge the breadth of the stream is nearly twice as great.

3 A 2

Name.	Position.	Nature.	Remarks.
Abu Sikhair ابر سخير	On the right bank, about 12 miles below Kūfah.	The headquarters of a rich tract of country, known as Mushkhāb مشخاب, which belongs to the Dāirat-as-Sanīyah. This place is situated in the Shāmīyah Qadha.	The Dāirat-as-Sanīyah have an important station in a fort at this place. The head of the Hamīdīyah canal, running to **Najaf** town, is immediately above Abu Sikhair: this useful public work also belongs to the Department of the Civil List.
Ja'ārah جعاره	On the right bank, about 1 mile below Abu Sikhair.	A prosperous village, the property of the Dāirat-as-Sanīyah; it has about 1,500 inhabitants, some of whom are **Balūchis** under the protection of Persia. Like Abu Sikhair this village lies in the Qadha of Shāmīyah.	Ja'ārah has 3 mosques and about 100 shops.

About 15 miles below **Kūfah** the Hindīyah enters the Bahr-an-Najaf, which is described below and in the article on **Najaf** Town.

Banks and country adjoining the Hindīyah proper.—The country on both sides of the Hindīyah from its head down to **Tawairīj** appears to be generally firm and dry; but, as has been indicated above, there is considerable flooding due to unskilful management of canals between the lower part of this reach and the town of **Karbala**. The rest of this region is becoming gradually less and less moist, and rice is being supplanted here as the staple crop by other cereals which require less water.

Between **Tawairīj** and **Kifl** the country to the west of the Hindīyah is flat and somewhat sandy, but it is well cultivated and is liable to inundation in floods: the camel-thorn grows throughout it in profusion. The corresponding stretch on the east side of the Hindīyah consists of impassable and almost continuous swamps.

Below **Kifl** as far as the Bahr-an-Najaf the lands between the right bank of the Hindīyah and the **Shāmīyah** Desert appear to be stable and firm, and as far as **Kūfah** they are well cultivated; but their present character below **Kūfah** and that of the whole country on the left bank below **Kifl** are not well ascertained.

The right bank of the Hindīyah appears to be fairly well consolidated throughout and it is possible for caravans to travel parallel to it at no great distance from the stream; but between **Tawairīj** and **Kifl** the route runs as a rule at some three or four miles inland, chiefly (it is understood) because the canals which have to be crossed are unbridged near their heads: between **Kifl** and **Kūfah** the road appears to follow the actual right bank. The state of communications upon the left bank has not been recently investigated; but it seems clear that for the greater part of the way between **Tawairīj** and **Kifl**, at least, there is no possibility of travelling by land in the neighbourhood of the bank.

The Bahr-an-Najaf.—In order to reconduct the waters of the Hindīyah into the **Euphrates**, we may now follow their course across the so-called Sea of Najaf, which they enter about 15 miles below **Kūfah**, to **Shināfīyah**—a distance of about 21 miles. The Bahr, even when it contains most water, is shallow; and it is reported to be steadily silting up: as a lake it now exists from January to May only, and during the other 7 months of the year the greater part of it disappears leaving merely a stream or channel. The water, owing to the gypsiferous character of the region in which the lake is situated, is almost undrinkable. When the lake is at its highest its navigation is somewhat dangerous, especially at night; and a sort of primitive lighthouse to aid belated voyagers is (or was formerly) maintained at its southern end by the inhabitants of **Shināfīyah**.

The Bahr-an-Najaf did not exist in the middle ages; or at least it had not, apparently, any existence separate from the Great Swamp in which the **Euphrates**, in those days, disappeared at a short distance beyond **Kūfah**.

The Atshān.—The channel by which the bulk of the water issuing from the Bahr-an-Najaf is carried to the **Euphrates** is known as the 'Atshān عطشان; its course is extremely winding and measures about 60 miles. At about 2 miles below its exit from the Sea of Najaf stands the village of **Shināfīyah**, on both banks, and here there is a boat bridge of 12 pontoons. Ten miles below the present **Shināfīyah** is the deserted site of a former village of the same name. The junction with the **Euphrates** now takes place about 5 miles before the town of **Samāwah** is reached and not, as at the time when the survey of 1860-65 was made, about 10 miles after passing it. The 'Atshān has a northerly branch of some importance known as the **Abur Rafūsh** ابو الرفوش which reaches the **Euphrates** by an independent channel, but its course has not been clearly described.

Irrigation and cultivation.—Exact information is wanting as to the amount and value of the irrigation dependent on the Hindīyah, but it appears to be both extensive and successful. The date palms on the **Tawairīj** to **Kifl** section of the Hindīyah are estimated at 400,000 and those on the **Kūfah** reach at 170,000. Rice used to be grown extensively on the Hindīyah about **Tawairīj** and even above it; but the effect of the barrage, though now broken, has been to reduce irrigation in the upper reaches and to drive the rice-growers further down stream. The principal canals derived from the right bank have been described in the paragraph on topography above: those on the left bank are not well known. To the list of right bank canals should be added, perhaps, the **Si'adah** سعده. This canal skirts the **Shāmīyah** Desert, running more or less parallel to the section of the Hindīyah between **Tawairīj** and **Kūfah**; its source and ending have not been exactly ascertained; in its lower course, however, it is probably fed by inlets from the right bank of the Hindīyah. In the neighbourhood of **Najaf** Town it is sometimes empty and appears to be broken: it passes 4 miles to the east of **Najaf**, and where crossed by the **Najaf-Kūfah** road it is 40 yards wide from bank to bank, and about 50 feet deep. To speak generally, the country on both sides of the Hindīyah is well cultivated; but it is liable to be flooded when the stream rises above its normal level.

Navigation.—The breadth of the Hindīyah, as we have seen, varies from 80 to nearly 300 yards; its bed contains many shoals and shallows; the current in midwinter runs on the average about $1\frac{1}{2}$ miles an hour. It is navigable throughout by Safīnahs of medium size, of which about 20 are generally obtainable at **Tawairīj**, and it could probably be negotiated by river steamers of 2 or 3 feet draft. River traffic between the towns of **Nāsirīyah** and **Musaiyib** now generally follows the Hindīyah line, the course of which we have just traced; but in the dry season large vessels, that is vessels of a carrying capacity of 400 "sacks" and upwards cannot ascend above **Shināfīyah** or sometimes even **Samāwah**; and bulk must in any case be broken at the Hindīyah barrage, cargoes being there transferred across *terra firma* to boats on the upper **Euphrates**. Between Tall Nimrūd and **Shināfīyah** journeys are generally made by boat; for roads are few and unsatisfactory, and where they exist they are unstaged and somewhat unsafe.

Hydrographical changes.—The alternation of the **Euphrates** between two courses dividing at a point a few miles south of the present **Musaiyib** is an interesting historical and hydrographical problem. It seems clear that before the 9th century of the Christian era the main stream of the **Euphrates** flowed past **Kūfah** and must therefore have followed, more or less, the course of the present Hindīyah. The bed of the modern **Euphrates** by **Hillah** Town, however, existed even then as the Sūrān canal نهر السوران; and in the 9th century the **Hillah** channel became, or had become, more capacious than that which went by **Kūfah**. By the 12th century of the Christian era the **Hillah** channel had come to be regarded as the main **Euphrates** river, and so matters remained until the end of the 19th century. At the time of the British survey, made in 1860-65, the **Hillah** channel still carried the bulk of the river; but the **Euphrates** was now apparently showing a tendency to return to its old, original bed, for a barrage (marked as 'Umr Pasha's Sadd) already existed at or close to the site of the present Hindīyah barrage, near the head of what was still the Hindīyah *canal*. At some time between 1865 and 1890 the **Euphrates** succeeded, notwithstanding the Sadd, in entering the Hindīyah, which being nearly straight in its uppermost reaches had a rapid flow and was quickly scoured out to a greater and greater depth; in this way, assisted by the silting up of the **Hillah** channel, it soon attracted to itself the bulk of the river, and the country along its course was submerged and temporarily ruined. The construction of the present barrage was next undertaken by the Turkish Government with the assistance of M. Shouderfer, a French engineer: * a brick monument now standing on the high spit of land which divides the two channels at the point of their separation records the date of this work as 1303 A.H. (1890-91 A.D.). The barrage, while it remained entire, raised the level of the upper river by about 2 metres and caused about ⅓ of the water of the **Euphrates** to pass slowly down the **Hillah** channel. In July 1903 the central portion of the barrage gave way; the work became practically inoperative; and the **Euphrates**, after the interval of a millennium, resumed its ancient course. In 1905 the question of

---

*See Cuinet, III, 157 (footnote).

restoring the barrage was considered by a commission appointed by the Porte; but the final result of their deliberations is not yet known.

HINDIYĀN هنديان DISTRICT

This district, of which the name is sometimes spelt هنديجان and is locally pronounced Hindiyūn, is the easternmost of Southern '**Arabistān**.

Extent and boundaries.—The Hindiyān district is enclosed on the south by the Persian Gulf; on the west by a Khait خيط or strip of slightly elevated land which runs more or less parallel to the **Hindiyān River** about midway between it and **Ma'shūr**; on the north by a line traversing part of a plain called Shāh Nabi شاه بني and running eastwards to some hills, along which it continues to a point near Gargari, a distance in all of about 15 miles; on the east by a line which cuts obliquely across the maritime range from Gargari to a point on the coast between **Shāh Abul Shāh** and **Dīlam**. The district has thus a length upon the coast of about 50 miles and a depth inland of about 30 miles.

Physical characteristics and climate.—Neglecting the hills which run from the north-east corner to the neighbourhood of the sea at **Shāh Abul Shāh** and encroach but little on the surface of the district, we may say that the Hindiyān district consists wholly of plains. The soil is saline in places, but generally it is good and firm; and the prairies, grass-covered after rain, seem to offer every advantage for the breeding of cattle and horses. The chief feature of the district is the **Hindiyān River**, which is separately described under its own name. The sea is shallow upon the Hindiyān coast and as a rule a depth of so much as 3 fathoms is not found within 4 miles of land.

The climate is not unhealthy. Hot and dry winds from the north-west prevail in summer; but as early as September, in some years, the temperature has ceased to be unpleasant.

Population.—An idea of the numbers and composition of the population of the district may be obtained from the article on the **Hindiyān River**, which contains a table of the villages on its banks with some particulars of the inhabitants. The only village on the coast is **Shāh Abul Shāh**, which is elsewhere described under its own name. The fixed inhabitants of the district number some 14,000 souls, and to these must be added a small quota on account of nomad tribes, chiefly **Sharīfāt**,

HINDIYĀN DISTRICT

who wander in the district. The following is a succinct account of the principal tribes, but few of whom are common to the other districts of 'Arabistān :—

Tribe.	Villages.	Number of souls.	Remarks.
Ābād آباد	Cham Tang and Kurehpā.	1,100	Immigrated from the Kūhgalu Lur district 60 years ago in consequence of a famine.
'Aushār عوشار	Sarkhareh.	400	They are said to have left Shīrāz, their former home, on the death of Karīm Khān, Zand. They are described as being now Bābis.
Bahrakūn بهركون	'Abbād Ilāhi, Badrāni, Pūz Sufaid and Tuwaisheh, also some scattered huts below the last.	750	An Arab tribe said not to be found outside the Hindiyān district except at Fāo, whither a few have emigrated.
Bakhtiyāri بختياري	Gargari Bālāi.	150	They are of the Shīr 'Ali section.
Dailami ديلمي	Gargari Pāīni.	125	They trace their descent to the Dailami dynasty and claim to have been settled in Gargari for 500 years.
Ghālibi غالبي	Ditto.	125	They immigrated six years ago from Behbehān in consequence of bad treatment there.
Gurgi گرگي	Sāhabābād.	200	...
Haidari حيدري	Jīri.	500	By religion they are Sunnis. They are said to have come from the Rūd-hilleh District 60 years ago, but the cause is not known. By some they are identified with the Haiyādir, of the Jārrahi District.
Ja'fari جعفري	Jābirābād, Kaparkah and Nāsirābād.	850	They came from the Kūhgalu Lur country 60 years ago in consequence of a famine.
Ka'ab كعب	Both Gharābis, Cham Sha'abāni, Hindiyān Village and Dih Mulla.	1,550	See article Ka'ab. In this district they are of a section called Sha'abāni and are locally known as Shābūnis.

HINDIYĀN DISTRICT

Tribe.	Villages.	Number of souls.	Remarks.
Laki لکي	Asyāb, Gargari Pāini and Suwaireh.	1,025	They are said to have immigrated from Khurramābād 100 years ago. They were originally known as "Nādir Shah's Laki", which perhaps may indicate that they were among the followers whom that sovereign's death dispersed. By some accounts they are of Afghān origin.
Lur لر	Dārlakeh, Faili, Gargari Bālāi, Māliki, Cham Murād and Cham Sha'abāni.	1,250	Nearly all of the Āgha Jari section of the Kūhgalu group of Eastern Lurs.
Nidhārāt نظارات	Buzi and Kūt.	1,000	An Arab tribe who are said to have immigrated from Najd 300 years ago.
Qanawāti قنواتي	Chihl Mani, Darīhak, Gaz 'Ali, Hindiyān Village, Husainābād, Cham Kalgeh, Cham Khalaf 'Īsa, Cham Kharnūb, Dih Mulla, Cham Rahmāni and Zulmābād.	4,500	Now the principal tribe of the district and found also at Ma'shūr, where they number about 750 persons. They are said to have immigrated 50 years ago from Behbehān to escape oppression. According to tradition their original home was in the neighbourhood of Kūfah.
Sharīfāt شريفات	Shīrābād and Hindiyān Village.	350	See article Sharīfāt. Besides these about 500 nomad Sharīfāt come in at Qal'eh Mashraqi in the harvest season.

The Qanawātis, as will be seen, enjoy a great numerical predominance. The **Fāo** tract in Turkish territory on the Shatt-al-'**Arab** has been to a large extent settled by Arab and Persian families from the Hindiyān district.

Agriculture.—Cultivation is confined to the vicinity of the river. From **Dih Mulla** downwards it is all Daimi, that is dependent on rainfall: above that place it is Pāryāb or irrigated. There appears to be no impediment to the construction of canals on the lower course of the river except the poverty and indolence of the cultivating classes. The nature of the canals is noticed in the article on the **Hindiyān** River.

On the Lanjīr canal rice is grown; elsewhere the chief cereals are wheat and barley, the quantity of wheat standing to that of barley in the proportion of 4 to 1. Other common crops are beans, sesame, linseed, musk-melons and water-melons. Owing to the uncertainty of the rainfall in recent years, cultivators in the Hindiyān district have adopted the practice of storing the grain of one season in large mud receptacles outside their houses until the prospects of the next crop are assured. Each village possesses a due complement of donkeys, cattle, sheep and goats besides a few mares, and in the wet tract at the head of the district there are some herds of buffaloes. Grain is sold by weight. The unit of land-measurement is the Gāo.

Trade.—The only exports of value are grain and wool, which leave the district in considerable quantities. Horse breeding is on the decline, notwithstanding the facilities for it which exist, and the stamp of animal produced is not saleable in the Bombay market. The imports consist of the ordinary necessities and simple luxuries which the district does not produce. There are no local manufactures. The **Hindiyān** Village Man is equal to about 240, and the **Dih Mulla** Man to about 247½ lbs. avoirdupois English.

Communications.—The plains of the district present no obstacles to movement of man or beast except such as arise from their being slippery after rain and waterless at other times. The principal routes are dealt with in the general article on **'Arabistān**.

The supplies and transport available can be gauged by means of the village list in the article on the **Hindiyān** River and of the remarks on agriculture above.

Administration.—The Hindiyān district is subject to the Shaikh of **Muhammareh**, who has officials representing him at **Hindiyān** Village and **Dih Mulla**. The tenure on which he holds it has not been precisely ascertained. The revenue is fluctuating and is assessed at so many Tūmāns per Gāo of actual cultivation. In 1905 the revenue of the **Dih Mulla** neighbourhood was farmed for 5,000 Tūmāns and the revenue of the rest of the district for 18,000 Tūmāns; this was an enhancement on former years and has not been realised without hardship and oppression. The Imperial Persian Customs have posts at **Hindiyān** Village and at Tuwaisheh near the coast.

Antiquities.—In the 10th century the Hindiyān district contained the remains of fire temples and some water wheels of ancient construction; and at one time the Ismailians had strongholds in the adjoining hills.* A local tradition current at the present day, that the Portuguese once held the district, receives some support from the facts that the name of "Purgāl" پرگال is still recognised, and that there are traces of buildings and several old iron guns of the usual Portuguese type at **Dih Mulla**. Dih Mulla may perhaps have been a Portuguese factory, the river being then navigable above **Hindiyān** Village as it was, to some extent, as late as 1836.

HINDIYĀN هندیان RIVER

Headwaters.—Nearly always pronounced "Hindiyūn," and sometimes spelt Hīndījān هندیجان. This river is formed by the junction in the plain of Zaidān زیدان (generally pronounced Zaitūn), at a point 22 miles north by west from **Dīlam** on the coast, of two streams, the Khairābād خیرآباد or Āb Shīrīn آب شیرین and the Shūlistān شولستان or Āb Shūr آب شور both from the eastward: to the mediæval Arab geographers the entire Hīndiyān river appears to have been known as the Shīrīn.* The more northern of the two confluents, the Khairābād, is sweet; it is said to take its name from a ruined settlement upon its right bank a few miles above its junction and to rise in a high range of mountains in the country of the Kūhgalu **Lurs**. In its course the Khairābād gathers to itself the water of several other streams, of which the chief are the Zuhreh زهره and the Kumbal کمبل. The Shūlistān, which has bitter water, is stated to have its origin in a mass of hills to the west of the Kāzarūn-Shīrāz road; these were formerly, it is stated, inhabited by a tribe called Shūl but have now been occupied for some centuries by the Mamasani **Lurs**. The Shūlistān like the Khairābād river, has several tributaries, and one of these, the Shashpīr شش پیر, which comes down from the north of Shīrāz, is exceedingly bitter, strongly impregnating the Shūlistān and even affecting the Hindiyān but not in such a degree as to make its water undrinkable. Even at the driest season of the year the Khairābād and Shūlistān are both considerable streams with a breadth, at their junction, of 25 yards and a shingly bottom.

---

* See Le Strange's *Lands of the Eastern Caliphate.*

The Imāmzādeh of Haidar Karār at the place of formation of the Hindiyān River.

(Maj. P. Z. Cox.)

Upper course in the Zaidān district.—The upper course of the river formed by their union is generally known by the name of Zaidān not of Hindiyān, and may be taken as extending from Haidar Karār حيدر كرار, a small Imāmzādeh situated on the tongue of land between the Khairābād and the Shūlistān, to the border of the **Hindiyān** District, where it issues from the hills; in other words the length of this section is about 30 miles and its direction is from east-south-east to west-north-west. Here the Zaidān flows with a breadth of about 70 yards and a strong current of $3\frac{1}{2}$ miles an hour through the Zaidān plain, a valley 5 miles wide, governed from **Behbehān** and enclosed between a northern and a southern range of hills: the former called Kūh Zaidān has an elevation of about 1,500 feet and the latter, which is the subsidiary maritime range forming the inland boundary of the **Lirāvi** district and for that reason sometimes called Kūh Lirāvi, of about 1,000. The caravan route from **Dīlam** to **Behbehān** crosses the river near Cham **Zaidān**, where there are two or three fords: the bottom there is shingly and good, but the strength of the current necessitates care in crossing with laden animals.

Riverside villages in the Zaidān district.—The villages and other notable places in the Zaidān plain are, in descending order, the following:—

Name.	Position.	Houses and inhabitants.	REMARKS.
'Askari عسكري	On the right bank of the river, $\frac{1}{2}$ a mile north-west of the junction of the Khairābād and Shūlistān streams.	40 houses of Kurwais كروي, a tribe from the Kūhgalu **Lur** country.	The people are cultivators and own 2,000 sheep.
Abāzar اباذر	On the right bank of the river, 1 mile west by north of 'Askari.	80 houses of Kurwais.	40 donkeys, 30 cattle and 200 sheep and goats, but no horses are owned here.
Imāmzādeh Zaidān امامزاده زيدان	1 mile west by north of Abāzar and nearly 1 mile from the right bank of the river.	10 houses of Saiyids and Darvīshes.	There are 30 donkeys, 25 cattle, 100 sheep and goats. Some wheat and barley are grown.
Shāh Ibrāhīm شاه ابراهيم	$1\frac{1}{2}$ miles south of Imāmzādeh Zaidān, on the opposite side of the river.	A shrine with 2 rooms attached, occupied by Darvīshes.	...

Name.	Position.	Houses and inhabitants.	Remarks.
Sardasht سر دشت	Near the right bank of the river, 3 miles below the junction of the Khairābād and Shūlistān streams.	160 houses of a tribe called Qal'eh Gulābi قلعه گلابي	Rice is grown as well as winter crops of wheat and barley. There are 3,500 sheep and 20 horses.
Cham Zaidān چم زيدان	Near the right bank of the river, 2 miles below Sardasht.	...	See article Cham Zaidān.
Dih Bīsheh ده بيشه	½ a mile north-west of Cham Zaidān.	70 houses, mostly of the Agha Jari Lurs.	Wheat, barley, rice and beans are cultivated and 100 donkeys, 100 cattle and 500 sheep are owned here.
Lanjīr لنجير	On the left bank of the river about 14 miles below Cham Zaidān.	60 houses.	A canal takes off from the right bank opposite this place. Crops are wheat, barley, linseed and beans. There are 10 horses, 70 donkeys and 50 cattle.
Cham Charāteh چم چراته	On the right bank of the Lanjīr canal, 2 miles below Lanjīr.	14 houses of Shīr 'Ali Bakhtiyāris.	Wheat, barley, rice, linseed, tobacco and beans are grown. Livestock are 20 horses, 100 buffaloes, 300 donkeys and 250 cattle besides sheep and goats.
Ghōléh غوله	On the left bank of the river, about 14 miles below Lanjīr, at its exit from the hills.	60 houses of Shīr 'Ali Bakhtiyāris from Behbehān.	Crops as at Cham Charāteh. Animals are 10 horses, 100 donkeys and 70 cattle besides sheep and goats.

Opposite Lanjīr the river throws off from its right bank an artificial canal, which, circling round to the west-north-west and then to the west-south-west passes the villages of Cham Charāteh, Upper Gargari, Lower Gargari and Āsyāb and reaches Suwaireh; near the last it is absorbed by

The Hindiyān River near Zaidān.
(Mr. P. Z. Cox.)

numerous small distributaries when on the point of rejoining the parent stream.

Lower course in the Hindiyān District.—The lower course of the river in the **Hindiyān** District begins between the **Behbehān** village of Ghōleh and the **Hindiyān** village of Shīrābād, where the stream, turning the north end of some hills, emerges on the open plains of the **Hindiyān** District. From Shīrābād it runs first for 5 miles west-north-westwards to Suwaireh; it then turns, and its average direction from Suwaireh to **Hindiyān** Village, a distance of 22 miles in a straight line, is due southwards. At **Hindiyān** Village its course becomes winding; and, after all but reaching the sea at a place 10 miles south-south-west of **Hindiyān** Village, it meanders due westwards for another 9 miles, keeping within two or three miles of the coast the whole way, and eventually attains the Persian Gulf at a point 16 miles south-west of **Hindiyān** Village as the crow flies but double that distance from it by water. At its embouchure the Hindiyān cuts its way through mud-flats and its mouth is difficult to discover from seawards owing to the lowness of the coast.

Characteristics in the Hindiyān District.—Above Suwaireh the Hindiyān is broken up into more than one channel; but from Suwaireh downwards it flows in a single bed, having high banks and a nearly constant width of about 60 yards until past **Hindiyān** Village, where the breadth varies from 70 to 100 yards. The bottom from the beginning of the **Hindiyān** District till 6 miles below Suwaireh is shingly, and thence to the sea it is of hard mud. The water of the Hindiyān, as already observed, is drinkable, but impregnated with a salt or alkali brought down by the Shūlistān which gives it a bitter taste yet does not prevent the lathering of soap. In winter the river flows with a strong current throughout its course. From Gargari to a point 6 miles below Suwaireh there is irrigation by means of Jūbs جرب or water-cuts taking off from various natural branches of the river. The country on both sides of the river consists of featureless plains which the stream, except near the north end of the district, has not been utilised to irrigate. Here and there are patches of musk and water-melons in the actual bed, but the banks bear nothing except an occasional tamarisk until a fine grove of tall date trees belonging to Tuwaisheh is reached near the river mouth. The banks for the last 2 or 3 miles before reaching the sea are covered with bulrushes.

Riverside villages in the Hindiyān District.—The following is a table of the villages on or near the Hindiyān river from Gargari downwards :—

Name.	Position.	Population.	Remarks.
Shīrābād شيراباد	On the left bank of the Hindiyān one mile below Ghōleh.	200 houses of Sharīfāt.	200 sheep and goats are owned here and there is winter cultivation of grain. There are no cattle or donkeys.
Qal'eh Mashraqi قلعه مشرقي	On the right bank 1 mile north of Shīrābād.	Fluctuating: at harvest time there are 500 to 600 Sharīfāt nomads present.	The Sharīfāt who frequent this place own 70 horses, 1,000 camels and 10,000 sheep and goats: they cultivate grain here in winter. There is a prominently situated post for the defence of the crops.
Gargari Bālāi گرگري بالاي	6 miles east-north-east of Shīrābād, on the Lanjīr canal.	60 houses of Shīr 'Ali Bakhtiyāris and Āgha Jari Lurs.	Rice and linseed are grown and there are 100 sheep.
Gargari Pāīni گرگري پائيني	5 miles north-east of Shīrābād, on the Lanjīr canal.	80 houses of Lakis, Ghālibis and Dailamis.	There is irrigated cultivation, and 100 sheep and goats and 300 buffaloes are kept.
Asyāb آسياب	5 miles north of Shīrābād, on the Lanjīr canal.	120 houses of Lakis.	Grain is cultivated and there are 200 sheep and goats.
Suwaireh سويره	5 miles west-north-west of Shīrābād, on the right bank of the Hindiyān river and at the tail of the Lanjīr canal.	60 houses of Lakis.	There is riverside cultivation, and the people keep 100 cattle and 100 donkeys.
Buzi بزي	3 miles south-south-west of Suwaireh and 1 mile from the left bank of the Hindiyān river.	100 houses of Nidhārāt Arabs.	Grain is cultivated and there are 10 horses, 250 donkeys, 250 cattle and 100 sheep and goats.
Kūt کوت	¾ of a mile west of Buzi, near the left bank of the river.	100 houses of Nidhārāt Arabs and some Behbehānis.	The inhabitants grow corn, rice, beans and linseed and own 150 cattle and 200 donkeys.
Dih Mulla ده ملا	3 miles south-west of Kūt.	...	See article Dih Mulla.

Name.	Position.	Population.	Remarks.
Cham Khalaf 'Īsa چم خلف عیسی	2 miles south of Dih Mulla on the right bank of the river.	160 houses of Qanawātis and other Pehbehānis.	The people cultivate grain and have 20 horses, 30 mules, 200 donkeys, 150 cattle and 2,000 sheep and goats.
Darīhak دریهك	On the left bank opposite Cham Khalaf 'Īsa.	Ditto.	There is grain cultivation and 20 horses, 200 donkeys, 150 cattle and 300 sheep and goats are kept.
Cham Kharnūb چم خرنوب	On the right bank 1 mile south of Darīhak.	4 houses of Qanawātis.	Grain is cultivated and there are a few cattle and donkeys.
Faili فیلي	On the left bank 1 mile south of Cham Kharnūb.	30 houses of Faili Lurs.	Cereals are grown and 50 donkeys, 50 cattle and 30 sheep and goats are kept.
Jīri جیري	On the right bank 1 mile south-east of Faili.	100 houses of Haidari Arabs.	Grain is grown and there are 30 horses, 300 cattle, 300 donkeys and 1,000 sheep and goats. To the west at a short distance is an Imāmzādeh called Shāh Ibrāhīm.
Sarkhareh سرخره	On the left bank ½ a mile east of Jīri.	80 houses of 'Aushārs.	Grain is raised and the people keep 300 donkeys, 300 cattle and a few horses.
Nāsirābād ناصرآباد	On the right bank 1½ miles south-south-east of Sarkhareh.	100 houses of Ja'faris.	The inhabitants cultivate grain and own 150 cattle and 250 donkeys.
Cham Tang چم تنگ	On the right bank 1 mile south of Nāsirābād.	100 houses of Ābāds.	Resources are cultivation of grain, 200 cattle, 250 donkeys, 500 sheep and goats, and a few horses.
Cham Kalgeh چم کلگه	On the right bank 2 miles south of Cham Tang.	120 houses of Qanawātis.	Grain is cultivated. Livestock are 150 cattle, 200 donkeys and 1,000 sheep.
Kurehpā کرهپا	On the left bank ½ a mile south-east of Cham Kalgeh.	120 houses of Ābāds.	There are 150 cattle, 200 donkeys and 1,000 sheep and goats. Grain is cultivated.
Jābirābād جابر آباد	On the left bank ½ a mile south-east of Kurehpā.	60 houses of Ja'faris.	There are 30 cattle and 70 donkeys and grain is grown.

HINDIYĀN RIVER

Name.	Position.	Population.	Remarks.
Sāhabābād صاحب آباد	On the right bank 1 mile south-west of Jābirābād.	40 houses of Gurgis	Cattle and donkeys number 60 and 150 respectively and there is cultivation of grain.
Chihl Mani چهل مني	On the left bank 1½ miles south-west of Sāhabābād.	100 houses of Qanawātis.	There are 150 cattle, 250 donkeys and 500 sheep and goats. Grain is grown.
Husainābād حسين آباد	On the right bank a little below Chihl Mani.	80 houses of Qanawātis.	Grain is cultivated and 150 cattle, 175 donkeys and 500 sheep are kept.
Zulmābād ظلم آباد	On the right bank 1 mile south of Husainābād.	Qanawātis.	There is the ordinary cultivation of grain. No animals.
Cham Murād چم مراد	On the left bank 1½ miles south-west of Zulmābād.	60 houses of Āgha Jari Lurs.	There are 275 donkeys and 160 cattle. Grain is grown.
Cham Rahmāni چم رحماني	Not far from the left bank a little south of Cham Murād.	40 houses of Qanawātis.	There are 40 cattle and 75 donkeys. Grain is produced.
Hindiyān Village	On both banks 1 mile south-west of Cham Rahmāni.	...	See article Hindiyān Village.
Māliki مالكي	On the left bank 1 mile south-east of Hindiyān Village.	20 houses of Āgha Jari Lurs.	The inhabitants possess 150 cattle, 250 donkeys and 2,000 sheep and goats. They also cultivate grain.
Dārlakeh دارلكه	On the left bank ¾ of a mile south-west of Māliki.	Ditto.	There are 100 cattle, 100 donkeys and 300 sheep, and grain is grown.
Gharābi Kūchik غرابي كوچك	On the left bank 1½ miles west of Dārlakeh.	60 houses of Ka'ab Arabs.	Livestock are 200 cattle, 100 donkeys and 160 sheep. Corn is grown.
Gharābi Buzurg غرابي بزرگ	On the right bank almost opposite Gharābi Kūchik.	Ditto.	The people own 100 donkeys and 100 cows.
Cham Sha'abāni چم شعباني	On the right bank ¾ of a mile south-west of Gharābi Buzurg.	60 houses of Āgha Jari Lurs and 20 of Ka'ab Arabs of the Sha'abāni section.	Grain is cultivated and 200 cattle, 100 donkeys and 100 sheep and goats are kept.

Name.	Position.	Population.	Remarks.
Gaz 'Āli گز عالي	On the right bank ½ a mile west of Cham Sha'abāni.	100 houses of Qanawātis.	There are 10 horses, 100 cattle and 200 donkeys. Corn is grown.
'Abbād Ilāhi عباد الاهي	On the right bank 2 miles south-west of Gaz 'Ali.	30 houses of Bahrakūn Arabs.	The people grow grain and have 10 horses, 40 cattle, 40 donkeys and 1,000 sheep and goats. A track runs from here to Ma'shūr.
Badrāni بدراني	On the right bank 2 miles south of 'Abbād 'Ilāhi.	40 houses of Bahrakūn Arabs.	There are a few horses and donkeys, 40 cattle and 300 sheep and goats, besides grain cultivation.
Pūz Sufaid پوز سفيد	On the left bank almost opposite Badrāni.	Ditto.	The inhabitants cultivate grain and possess a few horses, 30 donkeys, 40 cattle and 800 sheep and goats.
Faraiz فريز	On the right bank 2 miles below Pūz Sufaid.	A very small hamlet.	There is cultivation and the people own 300 sheep and goats and a few other animals.
Kaparkāh کپرکاه	On the left bank 1⅓ miles south of Faraiz.	12 houses of Ja'faris.	There are here about 20 donkeys, 20 cattle and 100 sheep and goats.
Shāh Mīr Na'amān شاه میر نعمان	In the river 4 miles west-south-west of Kaparkāh.	...	An uninhabited island. A shrine of the same name stands on the right bank.
Tuwaisheh تويشه	On the left bank 1½ miles south-south-west of Shāh Mīr Na'amān and 5 miles east-south-east of the true mouth of the river (as distinguished from the bar).	20 houses of Bahrakūn Arabs.	There is a fine palm grove and some cultivation: a few horses, donkeys and cattle are owned. A post of the Imperial Persian Customs watches the river at this place.

There are also some huts occupied by Bahrakūn Arabs below Tuwaisheh near the mouth of the river.

Navigation.—The entrance to the river Hindiyān is closed by a bar which is situated about 30 miles east by north of the entrance of Khor Mūsa, 3 miles south-south-west of Rās Bahrakūn بهرکون and 6 miles nearly due south of the point where the firm banks of the river cease and mud flats begin. The bar has about 3 feet of water on it at low water springs and a heavy sea breaks on it when wind and tide are contrary. The bar and channel through the mud flats are at present marked by several small pile beacons which are not visible for more than 1½ miles. Within the bar a channel depth of not less than 6 feet at low water springs may be relied on the whole way to **Hindiyān** Village.

HINDIYĀN
هنديان
VILLAGE*   Locally pronounced Hindiyūn; the principal place in the **Hindiyān** District, situated on both banks of the **Hindiyān** River at a point 16 miles north-west of its mouth; the position has recently been determined as 30° 14′ 24″ north and 49° 43′ 5″ east. The population is about 1,000 souls and consists of Qanawātis, **Sharīfāt**, Hayād حياد and **Ka'ab** Arabs of the Sha'abāni section, the last predominating. The people are cultivators of grain, boatmen and traders, and they possess some 20 horses, 300 cattle, 500 donkeys and 1,000 sheep and goats. Ophthalmia is prevalent among them. Vessels from **Kuwait, Būshehr, Bahrain** and **Lingeh** come up the river to Hindiyān, and there is a considerable exportation of wheat, barley, wool and live sheep, also a smaller one of oak bark, sesame and ghi. The bazaar contains 30 shops. Forty years ago only the portion of the village on the right bank was subject to the **Ka'ab** Shaikh; but now the whole, like the rest of the district, is under the Shaikh of **Muhammareh**. An agent on the part of the Shaikh has his residence at Hindiyān village and collects taxes on shops and on all transactions in grain and wool. The Persian Imperial Customs have a post here which is reported to produce 18,000 Tūmāns a year. There is no telegraph, but postal communication is maintained with **Behbehān** and **Būshehr** by the Persian Post Office.

HIRTH,
HARTH
or
HURTH
حرث   Singular Hārithi حارثي. An important tribe of the **Sharqīyah** District in the **'Omān** Sultanate, said to be of Nizāri descent, but now belonging to the Hināwi faction; in religion they are Ibādhis. The central division

*A small town of Hindijān, famous for its market of sea fish, already existed in the 10th century A.D., but was situated apparently on the Tāb, i.e., on the **Jarrāhi**, not on the **Hindiyān** River. See Le Strange's *Lands of the Eastern Caliphate*.

of **Sharqīyah** called Baldān-al-Hirth, with its villages and towns, belongs entirely to the Hirth: their principal places are **Ibra** and Mudhairib, the former being the tribal capital. Hirth are found also at **Mudhaibi, Nizwa, Samad** and **Sīb.** The bulk of the Hirth are thus located between the **Hajriyīn** on the east and the **Habūs** on the west; and the total number of the tribe, exclusive of dependents mentioned below, appears to be about 9,000 souls.

The Hirth, though they have to some extent retained the characteristics of Bedouins, are chiefly occupied in date-growing and ordinary cultivation; but a number of them are wealthy traders owning vessels, and some who emigrated to Zanzibar have become men of substance and position in East Africa. The Hirth do not deal with **Sūr**: their ports are **Matrah** and **Masqat.** They are a warlike tribe and are now armed with various kinds of rifles.

The following are the principal sections of the Hirth proper :—

Section.	Fighting strength.	Habitat.	Remarks.
'Āsirāh عاسره	150	Subākh and Manzafah quarters of **Ibra.**	Nil.
Barāwanah برأونه	250	**Ibra.**	Were involved in the rebellion of 1877.
Ghayūth غيوث	150	Do. and Falaij in Baldān-al-Hirth.	Nil.
Hadām (Aulād) اولاد حدام	200	Sāh in Baldān-al-Hirth.	Do.
Hadri (Aulād) اولاد حدري	150	Qanātir in Baldān-al-Hirth.	Do.
Harfah (Aulād) اولاد حرفه	150	**Ibra** and Mudhairib.	Do.
Khanājirah خناجره	300	Do. and Nakhl in Western Hajar.	Do.
Ma'āmir معامر	280	**Ibra,** Mudhairib and Falaj Mas'ūd.	Do.
Maghārah مغاره	100	**Ibra** and 'Izz.	This section are Bedouins.

Section.	Fighting strength.	Habitat.	Remarks.
Maqādihah مقادحه	150	Sira in Baldān-al-Hirth.	Nil.
Marāhibah مراهبه	100	Ibra and Mudhairib.	Do.
Mashāhibah مشاهبه	150	Falaij in Baldān-al-Hirth.	Do.
Matāwabah متاوبه	150	Ditto	Do.
Rashāshidah رشاشده	200	Darīz and other places.	Do.
Saqūr سقور	100	'Izz.	Do.
Samrah سمرة	300	Qābil and Darīz.	The principal Shaikh of the tribe belongs to this section.
Sinān (Hāl) حال سذار	300	Ibra.	Nil.

Besides these there are five client tribes, all Ibādhis, and largely Bedouins, which are in partial subordination to the Hirth and may be regarded as Hārithi sections, namely :—

Tribe.	Fighting strength.	Habitat.	Remarks.
Dawakah دوكة	100	Barkah, Shakhākhīt, Rumais and Bū Mahār in Bātinah.	Singular is Dōki دوكي.
Muwālik موالك	500	Wādi Bani Khālid.	Singular is Māliki مالكي.
Nuwāfil نوفل	80	Mostly in Bātinah at Bū 'Abāli, Sha'ibah and Majiz-an-Nawāfil.	Singular is Naufili نوفلي.
Rashaid (Al Bū) آل بو رشيد o Rawāshid رواشد	170	At 'Abbāsah and Khadhra in Bātinah.	Singular is Rashaidi شيدي. Were implicated in the attack on Masqat Town in 1895.
Shabūl شبول	280	Haiyadh, Sohār Town and Wādi Bōshar.	Singular is Shabli شبلي.

The chief Shaikh of this tribe was, until his death in 1896, the notorious Sālih-bin-'Ali-bin-Nāsir, Simri, who had his home at Qābil: he was succeeded by his son 'Īsa, who has also given much trouble to the present Sultān of **'Omān**. 'Īsa, in consequence of a long continued drought, now resides at 'Izz instead of Qābil (1905).

HISHM هشم or **HĀSHIM (BANI)** بني هاشم

Singular Hāshimi هاشمي. A tribe of the **Ja'alān** and the Eastern **Hajar** districts in the **'Omān** Sultanate; they are Nizāri by descent, Ghāfiri by political faction, in religion partly Ibādhi and partly Sunni. Their principal place is Kāmil (200 houses) in **Ja'alān,** but they also occupy the **Ja'alān** villages of Dīdu (50 houses), Humaidha (15 houses) and Buwairid (55 houses) and the village of Tahwa (60 houses) near Jabal **Khadhar**. In the lower course of Wādi Bani **Khālid**, where their numerical strength lies, they have Zilaft (50 houses), 'Adhfain (200 houses), Halfah (95 houses), Badh'ah (150 houses), Sīq (180 houses) and Sibt (160 houses); and a few are found at Khabbah in Wādi **Khabbah**. In Bilād-as-Sūr at **Sūr** they have perhaps 80 houses. There are also about 1,500 Bedouins belonging to the tribe who own some 500 camels, 250 donkeys, 700 cattle and 8,000 sheep and goats.

The Hishm are supposed to number 8,000 persons and their subdivisions are the following:—

Section.	Fighting strength.*	Habitat.	REMARKS.
Hirzah حرزه	150	Kāmil.	Sunnis.
Hishāshimah هشاشمه	200	Do.	Do.
Kuwāshim كواشم	200	Humaidha.	Do.
Marāhibah مراهبه	300	Dīdu and Sīq.	Do.
Nāsir (Aulād) اولاد ناصر	200	Buwairid.	Do.
Rāshid (Bani) بني راشد	300	Badh'ah and Sīq.	Ibādhis.

* The numbers in this column appear to be exaggerated.

Section.	Fighting strength.	Habitat.	REMARKS.
Saif (Bani) بني سيف	300	Halfah.	Ibādhis.
Sarāhimah سراهمة	200	'Adhfain and Sibt.	Do.
Thuwāni ثواي	50	Zilaft.	Do.
Tuwā'i طواعي	200	Sibt.	Do.
'Umr (Bani) بني عمر	400	Kāmil and Sīq.	Do.
Zahaimiyīn زهيميين	200	Wādi Khabbah.	Do.
Zaiyūd زود	150	Dīdu and Kāmil.	Sunnis.

The Hishm command the road from **Sūr** to **Ja'alān** above Rafsah and can close it at pleasure. The whole of Wādi Bani **Khālid** is under their control, for the other tribes inhabiting it, though collectively of some account, are always disunited; these tribes are said to pay dues to the Hishm.

The Hishm always supported Saiyid Turki when Sultān of **'Omān** (1871-1888) and were even present on his side at the capture of **Matrah** from 'Azzān in 1871. They took part with his son and successor, Saiyid Faisal, in the crisis at **Masqat** in 1895, where they were under the leadership of 'Abdullah-bin-Sālim of the Bani Bū **'Ali**. The present chiefs of the Hishm are Sa'īd-bin-Rāshid and Sultān-bin-Rāshid of the Bani 'Umr section; the former resides at Sīq, the latter at Kāmil.

HOFUF هفوف

This town, the capital both natural and administrative of the Sanjāq of **Hasa**, is situated in the south-eastern corner of the **Hasa** Oasis at a distance of about 40 miles inland in a south-west by west direction from the port of **'Oqair**.

Site and surroundings.—The site of the town is rocky but low; it appears to be only a little higher than the waterlogged country which

General View of Hofūf.
(Herr H. Burchardt.)

COPYRIGHT.

adjoins it. The space covered by buildings is described as oblong, with a length from north to south of 1 to 1½ miles and a breadth of ½ a mile. The land to the south of the town is waste and quickly merges in the desert: on the other three sides cultivation and date groves, which are densest on the northern and eastern sides, approach close to the walls. The springs of Haqal, Umm-al-Jamāl, Khadūd, Umm-al-Līf, Qasaibah, Luwaimi and Barābar, described in the article on the Hasa Oasis, all rise within a mile of the eastern side of Hofūf, and those of Umm Kharaisān and of Bahair and Bahairīyah adjoin respectively its northern and western faces. A few hundred yards to the south-east of the town are a large well and a group of gardens called Suwaidarah سويدرة. Graveyards closely surround the town upon most sides, especially on the east, south-east and north-west.

Quarters and buildings.—Hofūf is divided into 3 large wards, of which the names are Kūt كوت or Kūt-al-Hofūf, Rifā'ah رفاعة and Na'āthil نعاثل.

Kūt, which forms the north-western corner of the town, is really a large fortified enclosure with sides about 600 yards long and completely surrounded by a ditch; it is inhabited by the Turkish troops, the Turkish official community, and others. It contains a fine Sunni mosque having a dome and called for that reason Qubbah قبّة, also another good building which is used as a military hospital, and a couple of forts which are mentioned further on among the defences of the town. On the east side of the Kūt, at the north end of the town, is a market place with a Qaisarīyah or arcade of shops. On the south of the Kūt, between it and the next quarter, is a date plantation. The Rifā'ah quarter forms the entire eastern side of the town; it is healthier and somewhat higher than the others, and in it are the residences of a number of the better families. Na'āthil includes the southern and western parts of the town and is, in extent, a good half of the place; it is inhabited promiscuously by all classes. As already mentioned, it is separated from Kūt by a date grove; and within its limits are enclosed occasional gardens and a few trees, the latter chiefly figs and citrons. The principal mosque of Hofūf, which belongs to the Shi'ah sect and is probably the largest mosque in Eastern Arabia, is in Na'āthil. Kūt is said to contain about 1,200, Rifā'ah about 2,100 and Na'āthil about 1,700 houses.

The houses of Hofūf are flat-roofed and are mostly built of stone and mud, and plastered with gypsum mortar; some of those in the Rifā'ah quarter are tolerably good and even handsome, with arches entering into their architecture. Nearly every house possesses a private well about 4 fathoms deep. The streets, except 2 main avenues, are narrow and filthy. The whole town has 8 gates, of which 2, called Bāb-ash-Shamāl باب الشمال and Bāb-ash-Sharq باب الشرق, belong to the Kūt.

Defences.—Hofūf is enclosed by a thin wall of sun-dried bricks and clay; it is only about 12 feet high and has now no ditch, as it once had, upon its outer side. At the north-western corner of the town the place of this wall is taken by the northern and western walls of the Kūt, which are continuous with it but twice as high. The principal military work is the Kūt, which forms one of the quarters of the town and has been partially described in that character: the Kūt comprises the chief citadel, known as Kūt-al-Hisār كوت الحصار and 2 minor structures styled Qasr-al-Qubbah and Qasr-al-'Abīd قصر العبيد. Qasr-al-Qubbah has the alternative name of Qasr Ibrāhīm ابراهيم, and Qasr-al-'Abīd serves the purpose of a jail as well as of a fort. These smaller fortifications are surrounded by moats, now dried and choked up with rubbish. The only detached work is Qasr-al-Khazām قصر الخزام, a fort situated a few hundred yards from the west side of the town and having the Turkish cemetery immediately to the south of it. The military garrison of the Kūt is reported to consist of two squadrons of cavalry, one battery of mule guns and one battalion of infantry; and that of Qasr-al-Khazām appears to be a quarter of a battalion of infantry. There are besides one hundred unmounted Dhābitīyahs on duty at Qasr-al-'Abīd and 25 mounted men of the same corps in Qasr-al-Khazām. A military band performs in the afternoons: this is the only recreation of the garrison.

Inhabitants.—The total population of Hofūf is estimated at about 25,000 souls. The people are a mongrel race and are not divided into any well ascertained tribes, nor are there many foreign immigrants among them. Genuine Persians are not found, but there are a fair number of Arabs from **Najd**; most of the latter are shopkeepers and camel-owners, but some of them are proprietors of date plantations. There are said to be in the Rifā'ah quarter some 50 families descended from the Ja'far section of the **Shammar** tribe.

About three-fourths of the people are Sunnis; the rest, with the exception of a few Wahhābis, are Shī'ahs. There are 2 large Sunni schools called Madrasat Shaikh Abu Bakr and Madrasat Shaikh 'Abdul Latīf, at both of which boys from **Bahrain**, **Masqat** and other distant places are received and educated. The principal Shī'ah schools

The Na'āthil Quarter, Hofūf.
(Herr H. Burchardt.)

are those of Shaikhs Muhammad-bin-'Abtān, 'Amrān-bin-Hasan, Mūsa-abu-Khamsīn and Muhammad-bin-Shaikh Husain.

Trade and manufactures.—Under normal conditions there is a considerable trade with **Riyādh** in **Najd** whence ghi is received at Hofūf and to which cloth, sugar and rice are sent in return. Before the recent wars in **Najd** the number of caravans coming into Hofūf from **Riyādh** was on the average about one a week. Bedouins from all the surrounding country supply their wants at Hofūf, and a general market is held every Thursday in an open space outside the town upon the north side which is called the Sūq-al-Khamīs شرق ;الخميس * but local trade is mostly carried on in private houses. Hofūf is celebrated for the manufacture of elegant 'Abas, richly embroidered with golden or coloured thread, and of brass coffee pots of curious shape which are exported as far as **Basrah** and **Masqat**.

Administration.—Hofūf is the civil and military capital of the whole **Hasa** Sanjāq; it is also the headquarters of the Hasa Qadha and of the Hofūf Nāhiyah. For purposes of internal administration it is constituted as a municipality.

HORMŪZ ISLAND †

هرموز

The north point of this island, the site of the celebrated Ormuz of former times, is situated 11 miles east-south-east of Bandar **'Abbās** and 4 miles south of the nearest part of the Persian mainland; the mouth of Khūr **Mīnāb** is distant from it 19 miles due eastward.

Hormūz island is nearly circular in shape with a diameter of $4\frac{1}{2}$ to 5 miles. The coast is free from pronounced indentations and the only promontory is the northern point, already mentioned, which is low and flat and projects nearly a mile from the general body of the island, its width across its base being also about a mile. The passage between Hormūz and the mainland navigable for vessels of moderate draft is only a mile wide, and its depth, which at the narrowest part of the

---

* A view of the Sūq-al-Khamīs accompanies Herr H. Burchardt's article *Ost-Arabien*, 1906.

† A plan of **Hormūz** anchorage occurs as an inset in Admiralty Chart No. 2373—2837 A., *Persian Gulf*, where also a distant view of the island from the sea will be found. A general report on Hormūz by Lieutenant V. Hunt is contained in the Foreign Proceedings of the Government of India for May 1901.

strait is 10 fathoms, diminishes to 4 and even $3\frac{1}{2}$ at the end towards Bandar **'Abbās**. The island, except at its northern and southern extremities, is surrounded by a belt of shoal water of considerable width. Except for the flat promontory on the north side and a strip of fairly level ground, half a mile to a mile in width, which follows the eastern shore, Hormūz is covered with jagged hills of brilliant and variegated hues. The dominant colour is a reddish-purple largely streaked with white, while the principal geological ingredients are rock-salt, red ochre and a greenish, very adhesive clay. The hills are on the average over 300 feet in height and one peak in the centre reaches 690 feet. All the ravines, and indeed whole valleys, in the interior of the island are incrusted with salt and present the appearance of being lightly powdered with snow. Upon the banks of the ravines are pure white saline incrustations varying in thickness from 3 to 12 inches and some of the ravines, in breadth from 6 to 15 feet, are spanned by natural bridges of salt strong enough to support a man.

Hormūz is almost perfectly barren; its aspect of all but metallic sterility is relieved only by a few stunted Kunār trees and some patches of barley on the plain near **Hormūz** Village. A few gazelle are the only natural fauna.

There is no permanently inhabited place on the island except **Hormūz** Village which, with its population, is described in a separate article; in that place also will be found some remarks on trade and resources. Here it may be added that of copper, specular iron ore, red oxide of iron and salt existing on the island only the last two are worked. The supplies and transport which the island affords only suffice for the needs of the inhabitants, and the quantity of sweet water available, chiefly rain water collected in reservoirs, is strictly limited. Vegetables and fodder are practically unavailable.

The revenue of Hormūz is at present farmed by the Mu'īn-ut-Tujjār of Tehrān from the Persian Government for 14,000 Tūmāns a year, and the island is consequently regarded as under his jurisdiction; but the political control is vested in the Governor of the **Gulf Ports**. The representative of the Mu'īn-ut-Tujjār is a resident agent by whom the taxes are collected; these are general revenue, a royalty on the red oxide workings (which are called Ganj or Galak), and a sort of poll tax on the miners. The agent has a salary of 50 Tūmāns a month, besides perquisites arising from the salvage of wrecks, etc., and he is responsible for the entire administration of the island. The present agent is a Persian, Mīrza Khalīl, whose father was at one time employed in the

British Residency at **Būshehr** as a munshi. The Deputy-Governor of Bandar **'Abbās** sometimes seeks to interfere in Hormūz affairs in the name of his master, the Governor of the **Gulf Ports**, the usual pretext being complaints of oppression or the wreck of a native boat. The Persian Government are represented by an Inspector of the Imperial Customs Department.

The simple topography of Hormūz Island is summed up in the table below :—

Name of place.	Position.	Houses and inhabitants.	Remarks
Bībī Gul (Qasr) قصر بيبي گل	On the south-west coast of the island.	Nil.	A site with a well of slightly brackish water and the ruins of former habitations.
Hormūz هرموز Village	On the northern point of the island.	...	See article **Hormūz** Village.
Salāh-ud-Dīn صلاح الدين	On the east coast of the island, 3 miles from Hormūz Village.	Nil.	A place where there are salt-pans and where salt is manufactured by a rough process.
Sar Pūzeh سر پوزه	At the southern extremity of the island.	No permanent habitations.	This is the present site of the red oxide workings of the island which employ about 200 hands. Water is brought from Trumbak. The road from Hormūz Village follows the east coast and the distance from it to Sar Pūzeh is about 9 miles.
Trumbak (Chāh) چاه ترمبك	On the south-east coast, 6 miles from Hormūz Village.	Nil.	There is a well here 40 feet deep with water which is fairly good but slightly brackish. There are also ruins of what appears to have been a small town.

The name Hormūz belonged originally to a town on the mainland, situated probably upon Khūr **Mīnāb**, *q. v.*; but, though the town was abandoned about 1315 A.D. only, the ruler transferring his seat to the island, the latter also appears to have borne the name of Urmuz or Urmus as early as the 9th century A.D. At the time of the transfer of government, however, the island appears to have been generally known as Jirūn or Zarūn. Probably about the 14th century A.D. the island of Hormūz supplanted Qais as the principal trade emporium of the Persian Gulf, just as Qais had supplanted Sīrāf.*

HORMŪZ
هرموز
VILLAGE

The only inhabited place on the island of **Hormūz** and the sole remaining vestige of the once celebrated city of Ormuz. The village is situated on the neck of the northern promontory, between the Portuguese fort at its extremity and the ruins of the ancient city upon its landward side. The place consists of about 200 houses, and the population may rise, while the salt and oxide mines are being actively worked, to 1,200 souls; but it falls in summer to less than half that number in consequence of emigration to the mainland, especially to **Mīnāb**, due to the heat and the prospects of employment in the date harvest. Persians predominate, many of them being natives of Bashākard and Rūdbār; but there are also **Balūchis** and Arabs who have long since forgotten to what tribes their ancestors belonged. The proportions of the mixture are roughly indicated by the fact that about ⅔rd of the population is Shi'ah as against ⅓rd Sunni. The inhabitants of Hormūz village are mostly sailors, fishermen and miners; they are reported to own 8 large Māshuwahs, 6 Baqārahs and 1 Ghunchah, with an aggregate burthen of 620 tons and employing 172 hands. The ordinary anchorage at Hormūz is half a mile to the east of the Portuguese fort, where the bottom is of mud and the depth of water from 4 to 5 fathoms. A little barley is grown on the plain near the village; there are hardly any date palms. A few reservoirs exist for the storage of rain water and there are some wells yielding brackish water. A Qadamgāh of merely local importance stands 1 mile south of the village. The village is the seat of the Persian agent who governs the island in the name of the Mu'īn-ut-Tujjār. The Portuguese fort is now in a dilapidated condition owing to the removal of stones from the walls for building purposes, but it still contains 2 magnificent reservoirs, empty but in good repair, one of which has lately been made serviceable under the orders of the Mu'īn-ut-Tujjār. For the better handling of the red oxide a truck line has recently been constructed under his directions, which runs for about 300 yards along the south face of the fort.

* See Le Strange's *Lands of the Eastern Caliphate.*

Hormuz — View from the old Fort.
(Raja Deen Dayal & Sons.)

HUSAINĪYAH (NAHR-AL-) نهر الحسينية

A large canal in Turkish 'Irāq; it takes off from the right bank of the **Euphrates** at **Musaiyib** and runs to **Karbala** Town where it divides into two branches. The construction of the Husainīyah is said to have been undertaken by order of the Ottoman Sultān Sulaimān I during his residence at **Baghdād** in 1544 A.D.; but it is known that the date groves of **Karbala** were already irrigated from the **Euphrates** in the 14th century of the Christian era.

Course and branches.—The original head of the Husainīyah was above **Musaiyib**, and a brick bridge still spans the former bed of the canal close to the west side of the town; the present head is 2 miles below **Musaiyib**. The course of the canal is at first towards the south-west; but at 7 miles it changes to west-south-west, a direction which it preserves thereafter until **Karbala** Town is reached at 18 miles from its head. For the first few miles there is little cultivation on either bank; but it rapidly increases as Khān-al-'Ataishi is approached. Khān-al-'Ataishi عطيشي, by Persians called Khān Ātishi خان آتشي, is a dilapidated caravansarai standing on a mound 100 yards from the right bank of the Husainīyah at 10 miles below its head; it is a square enclosure with sides about 80 yards long and a circular bastion at each of the 4 corners. A mile or two beyond Khān-al-'Ataishi begin the dense date plantations of **Karbala** Town; in the midst of these is reached, at 15 miles, a brick bridge known as the Pul-i-Sufaid پل سفيد which crosses the canal. Three miles beyond this bridge the Husainīyah passes the north side of **Karbala** Town and divides, at the north-western corner of the same, into 2 branches. One of these runs off in the direction of the tomb of Hurr, about $3\frac{1}{2}$ miles north-west of the town; it is called the Rashdīyah رشديه and is much larger than the other. After running for some distance to the north-west it turns to the south-west and approaches **Razāzah** upon its east side; in this reach it has the land called Qurtah, inhabited by the Yasār tribe, upon its right bank: it then turns southwards and ends in a marsh called Hor Abu Dibis هور ابو دبس at a little distance from **Razāzah**. The other branch, known as the Hanaidīyah هنيديه circles round **Karbala** Town upon its western side and then turning southwards runs to the Hor-al-Husainīyah, or Hor-as-Sulaimānīyah as it is also called from a village which is described in the article on the Shatt-al-**Hindīyah**. The waste water from the Husainīyah, in the neighbourhood of **Karbala** Town, generally goes to form this Hor-al-Husainīyah, which is fed also by the Shatt-al-**Hindīyah**. The Hor is a large lake or open swamp on which water fowl may be seen floating, and it causes the **Karbala-Tawairīj** road to be deflected to the north at a point about 3 miles from **Karbala** Town.

Dimensions.—The width of the Husainīyah at its mouth upon the **Euphrates** is only about 30 feet, but at about ¼ of a mile from the intake it has increased to 45 feet, and at this place the water runs about 4 feet deep in winter and the channel is filled by it from bank to bank. The Husainīyah branch which goes towards the tomb of Hurr is 24 feet wide and has banks 20 feet high at its entrance, and the stream in it runs about 12 feet wide and 3 feet deep in winter. The Hanaidīyah branch is about 20 feet wide near **Karbala** Town, and the top of the banks is about 25 feet above the level of the bed; but the flow of water in it in winter is only about 4 feet broad by 1 foot deep. From June to November the whole Husainīyah canal is practically dry.

Navigation and communications.—The Husainīyah canal is navigable for vessels of as much as 400 " sacks " burden down to the Pul-i-Sufaid; but, the current being slack, the voyage from the **Euphrates** to this place may take as much as 10 hours in the absence of a favourable wind.

The Husainīyah is spanned in 3 places by bridges fit for the passage of field guns. The uppermost bridge is the Pul-i-Sufaid, or White Bridge, 3 miles from **Karbala**, which is a high-arched construction in brick with a roadway about 20 feet wide; it is now in bad repair. The next is the Qantarat Bāb Baghdād قنطرة باب بغداد or Baghdād Gate Bridge, 2 miles nearer to **Karbala**; it is similar in design and materials to the first, but is at present in good repair and is used by vehicles plying between **Karbala** and **Musaiyib**; it leads from the right bank of the canal into the town of **Karbala**. The third is a curious double bridge at the place where the Rashdīyah and Hanaidīyah branches of the canal separate. This last bridge, of which the head on the southern bank of the canal is about 100 yards from the town wall,—an enclosed garden intervening,—is built so as to cover the whole trijunction of the canal and its 2 branches, and it has thus 3 entrances or exits; it is in fairly good repair and able to carry carts as well as foot passengers.

The Husainīyah, where it lies across the traveller's route, is an inconvenient obstacle; for the banks are high, perhaps 15 feet on an average, and descend very steeply to the stream. Near villages, however, they are often ramped, and at such places a Quffah also can generally be obtained to ferry passengers and baggage across; but transport animals must be unloaded and swum. In some parts deep, narrow, unbridged distributaries make the left bank difficult for mounted men to follow.

Cultivation and population.—The cultivation upon the upper part of the canal is chiefly of cereals. The date plantations which begin as **Karbala** is approached present a remarkable contrast to the well-ordered groves of **Basrah** Town, for the trees are of all ages and irregularly spaced as if self-sown; nevertheless they are valuable and productive.

Villages of the **Mas'ūd** tribe, built of thorns and matting, are sprinkled along the banks the whole way from the **Euphrates** to **Karbala**; while here and there is to be seen the more solidly built enclosure of a Shaikh, having towers at the corners for defence. At one place between Khān-al-'Ataishi and the Pul-i-Sufaid the hamlets are so thickly set as almost to form a continuous settlement.

HUSHŪM
هشم

One of the two areas containing the best wells in the **Biyādh** tract of the **Hasa** Sanjāq: the other is **Dabaisi**. The centre of Hushūm is situated about 30 miles west by south of **Qatīf** Town, and from this centre it extends approximately 5 miles in each direction.

The following wells are in Hushūm:—

Name.	Vernacular equivalent.	Position, etc.
'Adaiwi	العديوي	About 29 miles west of Qatīf Town.
Adhbūlah (Bū)	بو اضبوله	4 miles west-south-west of 'Adaiwi.
'Ashairi	العشيري	4 miles west of 'Adaiwi.
'Azīz-al-Mā	عزيز الماء	3 miles east of 'Adaiwi. Brackish.
Hashm-al-Haddah	هشم الهدّة	5 miles south-south-west of 'Adaiwi.
Jida' (Abu)	ابو جدع	6 miles south of 'Adaiwi.
Murtajjah	المرتجّة	6 miles south-west by south of 'Adaiwi.
Rūwa	روا	7 miles south-east of 'Adaiwi.
Taraifah (Bū)	بو طريفه	3 miles south of 'Adaiwi.

**HUWAI-
LAH**

الحويله

In English at one time known as "Owhale". A deserted town on the east coast of **Qatar** about midway between **Dhakhīrah** and the extremity of the peninsula. There are numerous wells in the vicinity, 2 miles inland from the sea, but the water is of indifferent quality. Before **Zubārah** and **Dōhah** rose to importance, Huwailah was the chief town of **Qatar**. It is believed that the inhabitants were originally Āl **Musallam,** who were expelled by the Shaikhs of **Bahrain,** and that thereafter they were Āl Bin 'Ali up to about 1850.

**HŪWA-
LAH**

هولة

or

HŪLAH

هولة

Singular Hōli هولي. A class of Sunni Arabs found in **Bahrain, Hasa, Qatar** and Trucial **'Omān**, and on the island of **Sirri**; they are a community who, after being domiciled for years or even generations on the Persian coast of the Gulf, have returned whether as individuals or groups to the Arabian side; the name of "Hūwalah" is not one acquired by them during their sojourn in Persia, but has been conferred on them by the Arabs among whom they settled on their return to Arabia.

Divisions.—Many of the Hūwalah are unable to say from which of the Arab tribes they are descended. Some claim to be Bani **Tamīm** and others to be Marāzīq. As Hūwalah they have no tribal institutions or organisation, but it is observed that they intermarry freely among themselves. They are not divided into sections properly so called, but some of them form groups named after a common ancestor, more or less remote, or after the place from which they have come; such are the Āl Bū Fakhru آل بو فخرو group, to which a fourth of the Hūwalah settled at **Dōhah** in **Qatar** belong, and the group of the Kashkunārīyah كشكناريه, who are said to have immigrated from a place Kashkunār, situated in **Gābandi** in Persia, inland of the **Shībkūh** coast. It is uncertain whether the **Mahāndah** and **Sulutah**, who have preserved their tribal character though according to some accounts they lived for a time in Persia, should be classed as Hūwalah or not. The Bani **Mālik** of **Qatar,** other than the **Sulutah,** are always ranked among the Hūwalah.

Religion and character.—The Hūwalah are, as already indicated, all Sunnis; but some belong to the Māliki and some to the Shāfi'i school for the sect. They have altogether lost their fighting instincts and are entirely given up to commerce, the handicrafts and other money-making pursuits, some on a large and some on a humble scale.

Numbers and distribution.—In **Bahrain** Hūwalah are found at Hālat-bin Anas, 10 houses; **Budaiya'**, 50 houses; **Hadd**, 20 houses; **Manāmah**, 1,000 houses; and **Muharraq** Town, 2,000 houses. In **Qatar** there are 200 houses of Hūwalah at **Dōhāh** and an equal number at **Wakrah**; and in Turkish territory a few, chiefly artisans, are found at the towns of **Hofūf** and **Qatīf**. Those of Trucial **'Omān** are 300 households and are all settled at **Shārjah** Town; while those of **Sirri**, numbering 30 families, are said to be immigrants from Trucial **'Omān**. The total number of Hūwalah in the part of Arabia where they are called by this name may be roughly estimated at 18,000 souls.

HUZŪM

الحزم

A small coastal district of the **Hasa** Sanjāq in Eastern Arabia: it extends, upon the sea, from the foot of **Musallamīyah** bay on the north to the foot of Dōhat-ad-Dafi on the south, a distance of about 25 miles; inland its dimensions from north to south are less. Its western boundary is at the wells of Mistannah, a little over 20 miles from the coast, where it is met by the districts of **Radāif** and Jau **Shamīn**. On the north it is bounded by the Sabakhat-al-**Mutāya**, and on the south by **Biyādh**, the hill of Murair being situated on the boundary between it and the latter.

Huzūm is a sandy district, but without hillocks, and its colour is described as brown and darker than that of **Biyādh**. The Markh tree is common, and the prevailing shrubs are 'Abal 'Ādhar and Artah, while the principal grass is Thamām. The Bedouins frequenting Huzūm are of the Bani **Khālid** and **'Ajmān** tribes.

The wells of Huzūm are on the average about six feet deep, and the following are among the more important:—

Name.	Vernacular equivalent.	Position.
'Ayāshīyah	العياشية	Near the southern border of the district, 6 miles south of Tūi.
Fuhūmīyah	الفهومية	8 miles south-west of Tūi.
Hāshāt (Umm-al-)	ام الحاشات	4 miles north-north-west of Tūi.
Jida' (Darb-al-)	درب الجدع	6 miles east of Tūi.

Name.	Vernacular equivalent.	Position.
Khasīyah	الخسية	6 miles west-north-west of Tūi.
Khufairīyah	الخفيريه	8 miles south-west by west of Tūi.
Khursānīyah	الخرصانيه	7 miles east-south-east of Tūi and 7 miles north-west of the Murair hill.
Mistannah	المستنة	At the meeting place of the Sabákhat-al-Mutāya, Radāif, Jau Shamīn and Huzūm tracts; about 16 miles south-west of the foot of Musallamīyah bay, and over 30 miles west-north-west by west of Dōhat-ad-Dafi.
Mutāya	المطايا	Near the border of the Sabákhat-al-Mutāya, 3 miles south-west of the foot of Musallamīyah bay.
Nuqūrīyah	النقوريه	In the base of the promontory which ends in Rās-al-Abkharah and forms the southern point of Musallamīyah bay, at a distance of 1 or 2 miles inland from the sea on every side.
Tūi	الطوي	In a central position between Mistannah and the coast, about 12 miles from either, and 8 miles south of the foot of Musallamīyah bay.
Zabaidīyah	الزبيديه	6 miles south-west of Tūi.

IBRA
ابرا
or
BIRA
برا

The largest town in the **Sharqīyah** district of the 'Omān Sultanate; it lies partly in that portion of the district which is called Baldān-al-Hirth and partly in that which is known as Baldān-al-Masākirah and it is situated almost exactly half way between the two ends of **Sharqīyah** about 35 miles east-south-east of **Samad**. The drainage of Ibra goes south-eastwards by Wādi Ibra to **Ja'alān** and thence to the sea, and the hills of Eastern **Hajar** are distant from the town, on the north and east, about 25 miles. The town stands in a well cultivated area bearing dates, fruits and cereals and measuring several miles in length and breadth: this oasis is studded with villages of the **Masākirah** and **Hirth**.

Ibra is divided into two main quarters, *viz.*, the 'Alāyah عليه or upper town on the north and east, inhabited by **Masākirah**, and the Sifālah

سفاله or lower town on the south, occupied by **Hirth**: the separate bazaars of these two quarters are about half an hour's walk apart. The 'Alāyah is unwalled; it comprises over 300 houses, mostly of mud and gypsum-stucco, with a few huts and a bazaar of some 30 shops. The number of houses in the Sifālah is over 500, and many of them are excellent, resembling those of **Masqat** Town. The entire 'Alāyah consists of various small wards which are dispersed in all directions; but a part of the Sifālah, called Manzafah منزفة, is walled and boasts a bazaar of 60 shops, besides a large fort on which some guns are mounted. The other wards of the Sifālah, namely, Subākh صباخ, Ahl Sināu اهل سناو and Ma'taradh معترض stand at a few minutes' distance apart from one another. The whole population of Ibra may be estimated at 4,000 to 5,000 persons of whom the majority are **Hirth**.

Silk and cotton, imported from India through **Masqat** Town, are woven into cloth at Ibra: this is a profitable industry and almost the only one exercised. Livestock are 10 horses, 300 camels, 800 donkeys, 600 cattle and 2,000 sheep and goats. Date palms are estimated at the large figure of 100,000.

'IBRI
عبري

A considerable town, the largest in the **Dhāhirah** district of the **'Omān** Sultanate: it is situated 37 miles south-south-east of **Dhank** Town and 50 miles west by north of **Bahlah** in **'Omān** Proper. The elevation of 'Ibri is 1,180 feet above sea-level: it stands in Wādi **Sanaisal** and is adjoined by Salaif in Wādi-al-'**Ain** which practically forms a suburb. 'Ibri is enclosed, except on the south, by hills rising from 300 to 400 feet above the plain at a short distance from the town. The bazaar and dwellings of the poorer classes form a compact block surrounding the fort; but the houses of the wealthier inhabitants are dispersed and lost to view in a sea of date groves, the most extensive, probably, in **'Omān** except those of Wādi **Samāil** and containing perhaps 50,000 palms. Fruit, cereals and grass are largely cultivated, both amidst the date plantations and in the open space beyond them. Livestock are estimated at 30 horses, 400 camels, 300 donkeys, 500 cattle and 2,000 sheep and goats. 'Ibri contains one of the largest Jāmi' mosques in **'Omān**. The population of the town is estimated at 5,000 persons, of whom at least 3,500 belong to the Ya'āqib tribe and some of the remainder to the Bani **Kalbān**. The bazaar is large and good, containing all the commodities for which there is a demand among Arabs.

Dates, mangoes, limes, apricots, peaches, and figs are exported; but the principal local industry is indigo-dyeing. Blacksmiths, carpenters and other artisans are to be found here; also goldsmiths. In 1885 'Ibri enjoyed the reputation of being a thieves' market for all **'Omān**; at that time all plunder from **Bātinah** or **'Omān** Proper was brought here for disposal by auction, but this has now ceased to be the case.

'ĪDĀN
عيدان

An Arab tribe of Turkish **'Irāq** having their headquarters upon the Shatt-al-**'Arab** immediately below **Basrah**; the right bank villages from **Basrah** down to Labāni are mostly in their occupation, and they hold almost exclusive possession of the upper half of **'Ajairāwīyah** island together with the left bank villages on the mainland which are abreast of the same. The **'Īdān** are found also at Kataibān and some other villages on the left bank of the river above **Basrah** and some are settled at Dorah towards the mouth of the river, not far above **Fāo**. With the **'Atub** and the Qatārnah they are the principal constituent of the mixed population of the right bank of the Shatt-al-**'Arab** generally; and indeed it may be said that they are found almost everywhere on both banks of the river above and below **Basrah** Town. A large number of the tribe have recently emigrated from Turkish to Persian territory in order to escape conscription for military service by the Turkish Government; these have mostly been enrolled by the Shaikh of **Muhammareh** as members of the **Muhaisin** tribe and have been settled by him as cultivators at Qasbeh on **'Abbādān** island and elsewhere. In religion the 'Īdān are Shī'ah; and by profession, like most of the tribes upon the Shatt-al-**Arab**, they are almost as much robbers as agriculturists. Their principal Shaikh resides either on Jazīrat-al-'Ain opposite to Kūt-al-**Farangi** above **Basrah**, or at Kibāsi-as-Saghīr on the mainland adjoining that island.

'IKRISH
عكرش
or
ARŪS
عروس

Sometimes pronounced 'Ichrish. A considerable tribe of perhaps 5,000 souls inhabiting the **Hawīzeh** District. The Bait Ghālib and Bait Husain sections, to which belong the ruling clans, are collected at Suwaimīyeh; the rest are scattered. The 'Ikrish live in tents; they own large numbers of cattle and sheep and some donkeys and they cultivate wheat and barley. Their divisions are :—

Division.	Subdivision.	Habitat.	Fighting strength.	Remarks.
Daghāghleh دغاغلة	Barkeh (Āl Bū) آل بو بركه	A few miles east of Kūt Nahr Hāshim, and at Saiyid 'Abbās on the Kārūn river and in the Zūwīyeh tract adjoining it.	300	...
Do.	Dawairīj (Āl Bū) آل بو دويريج	Do.	250	...
Do.	Sa'īdāt سعيدات	Do.	150	...
Do.	Subheh صبحه	Do.	100	...
Do.	Tōqān (Bait) بيت طوقان	Do.	300	...
Ghālib (Bait) بيت غالب	...	Suwaimīyeh, 7 miles north of Hawīzeh Town.	150	To this division belongs one of the ruling families.
Husain (Bait) بيت حسين	...	Do.	150	Do.

The 'Ikrish at Saīyid 'Abbās are an inconsiderable number, and practically the whole tribe is nomadic.

'IRĀQ (TURKISH)‡
العراق

The ancient name 'Iraq *—of which the etymology, or at least the meaning in the present case, is doubtful †—is used by the Ottoman Government to denote the country of the lower Euphrates

* The boundaries and geography of ancient 'Irāq are very fully discussed by Mr. Le Strange in chapters II to V of his book, *Lands of the Eastern Caliphate*.

† The ordinary meaning of 'Irāq is "cliff" or "shore".

‡ This article on 'Irāq and the other articles on places, etc., in 'Irāq have been compiled largely from original information now obtained for the first time.
  The work of collecting and arranging data was begun by the writer on a tour, in the course of which, in December 1904 and January 1905, he visited Zubair Town, Basrah, Baghdād, Musaiyib, Karbala and Hillah ; 'Irāq was entered by land from the Kuwait side and left by the usual route *viâ* the Shatt-al-'Arab. Among the European informants to whom the writer is personally indebted are Sir W. Willcocks, whom he found at Baghdād and by whom he was supplied with valuable information relating to the rivers Euphrates and Tigris and to the irrigation

and **Tigris**—the richest and most valuable in the whole basin of the Persian Gulf—which is comprised in the Turkish Wilāyats or provinces of Baghdād and Basrah. In British official terminology Turkish 'Irāq, with the addition of the more northern Wilāyat of Mūsal موصل, is conventionally known as "Turkish Arabia"; but the expression is an unfortunate one, for it obviously suggests the Red Sea provinces of

of the country generally; Captains Braine and Cowley of the E. T. S. N. Company's Service, whose familiarity with the topography and navigation of the Tigris were of great service; and Messrs. Hamilton and Millen at Basrah, who were able respectively to elucidate questions of trade at Basrah and the working of the Hamīdīyah or navigation branch of the Dāirat-as-Sanīyah.

The collection of information was carried on during 1905 by Colonel (then Major) L. S. Newmarch, Political Resident at Baghdād; and on him and on his subordinates, especially Mr. Muhammad Hasan Muhsin, Vice-Consul at Karbala, most of the labour at this time devolved. In particular, a quantity of authentic information in regard to routes was furnished by Major Newmarch from personal knowledge; and by his efforts, assisted by those of Mr. Yacoub Thaddeus, an ex-dragoman of the Residency, and of Mr. Thomas Khalīl, a broker well acquainted with the country, by whom a useful sketch map explanatory of tribal distribution was prepared, as well as of Mr. Muhammad Hasan, much new light was cast upon the difficult subject of Arab tribes. Some of the inquiries relating to the Wilāyat of Basrah were made at the beginning of 1905 by Mr. J. H. Monahan, then Acting British Consul at Basrah.

Preliminary drafts of the topographical articles relating to 'Irāq, founded on the investigation just described, were ready in print in August 1905 and were immediately sent to the local officers for revision; this process, attended by extraordinary difficulties arising from the nature of the country, occupied many months and entailed very heavy work on Colonel Newmarch and on Mr. F. E. Crow, who had now resumed his duties as British Consul at Basrah and gave close attention to the matter. Colonel Newmarch's principal assistant was as before Mr. Vice-Consul Muhammad Hasan, but questions of trade were referred to Mr. Parry of the E. T. S. N. Company. At Basrah the investigations were largely entrusted to Naoum Abbo Effendi, the dragoman of the Consulate, and some help was rendered by Dr. Bennett of the American Presbyterian Mission. The draft articles were also revised by the staff of the British Embassy at Constantinople, especially by Colonel F. R. Maunsell who dealt with the military paragraph. In 1906 minute and valuable reports on the Shatt-al-'Arab and on Fāo were received from Lieutenant Commander Bowden of the R.I.M.S. "Lawrence" and Mr. W. D. Cumming of the Indo-European Telegraph Department, respectively.

The revision of 1905-06 was so thorough, and the fresh inquiries produced so much additional information, that it became necessary to redraft nearly all the articles; and when they were reprinted in April 1907, it was found that they had increased in bulk from less than 150 to over 300 octavo pages. A large number of doubtful or obscure points discovered in the new drafts were referred to the local officers, among whom Major J. Ramsay had now taken the place of Colonel Newmarch and carried on the work with energy. The articles, as they now stand, include the results of this final examination. It has also been possible to incorporate some of the data obtained by Lieutenants A. Hamilton and Gardner of the R.I.M.S "Comet" in a new survey of the Tigris river which was completed only in 1907.

Yaman and Hijāz rather than Mesopotamia which is no part, either physically or politically, of the Arabian peninsula. In the vernacular, Turkish 'Irāq is known as 'Irāq-al-'Arabi in contradistinction to 'Irāq-al-

It remains to mention a few of the principal books, etc., which may be consulted in regard to 'Irāq. The more valuable of the older authorities are : Ainsworth's *Researches*, 1838 ; Chesney's *Expedition for the Survey of the Rivers Euphrates and Tigris*, 1850 ; Layard's *Nineveh and Babylon*, 1853 ; Loftus' *Travels and Researches*, 1857 ; *Bombay Selections, XVIII,* 1857 *;* Chesney's *Narrative of the Euphrates Expedition,* 1868 ; and Layard's *Early Adventures,* 1887. Recent authorities on the topography, population, agriculture, etc., of the country are not numerous : the best are the *Gazetteer of Baghdād,* 1889 ; Cuinet's *La Turquie d'Asie* (Vol. III), 1894 ; and the Turkish *Sālnāmahs* or official almanacs, published periodically, of which that of 1903 for the Baghdād Wilāyat and that of 1898 for the Basrah Wilāyat—the latest available—have been utilised in the compilation of the present Gazetteer. A *Reconnaissance Report*, 1904, by Captain H. Smyth, contains much general information and deals particularly with communications, transport and the probable line of the projected Baghdād Railway : it will be found in the Political Proceedings of the Government of India for February 1905. In all matters of Turkish administration the highest authority is Mr. G. Young's *Corps de Droit Ottoman,* 1905 : this invaluable work was unfortunately brought too late to the knowledge of the writer to be consulted in writing the Gazetteer. The best source of information in regard to military organisation is Colonel F. R. Maunsell's *Handbook of the Turkish Army,* 1904 ; and the annual Consular Reports for Baghdād and Basrah deal fully with the subject of trade. Mr. G. Le Strange's books *Baghdād during the Abbasid Caliphate,* 1900, and *Lands of the Eastern Caliphate,* 1905, have superseded all other and less comprehensive works on the geography of 'Irāq in mediæval times. Some information about the country in general and about particular places will be found in the Foreign Proceedings of the Government of India for February 1905. See also the Report of the German Railway Commission in the Proceedings for May 1901.

The most serviceable maps of 'Irāq (or of parts of that province) on any considerable scale are those which accompany Chesney's *Expedition for the Survey of the Rivers Euphrates and Tigris,* 1850 ; Sheets VII and VIII of the *Map of the Turco-Persian Frontier* made by a joint British and Russian mission, 1849-55 ; *Survey of Ancient Babylon, etc.,* by Selby, Collingwood and Bewsher in 6 sheets, 1885 ; a *Sketch Map of the Tract of Country between Baghdād and Najaf,* Intelligence Branch, March 1886 ; Sheets No. 72 of the *Map of South-Western Asia,* Survey of India, 1895, also Sheets No. 56 (1893) and No. 73 (1895) ; Sheets I and IV of the *Map of Persia,* in 6 sheets, Survey of India, 1897 ; Admiralty Chart No. 2374-2837 B., *Persian Gulf,* published 1862 and corrected to 1903 ; Admiralty Chart No. 2380-1235, *Mouth of the Euphrates, etc.*, published in 1898 and corrected to 1903 ; Admiralty Chart No. 2381-3293, *Approaches to Kuweit Harbour and Shatt-al-Arab* issued in 1902 and corrected to 1904 ; finally a *Sketch Survey of the Khor Zubeir,* Survey of India, 1906, and Captain Bowden's *Village Map of the Shatt-al-'Arab below Basrah,* 1906, the last (in two parts) being numbered 1387 in the Foreign Department Library, Simla. The best general map of all 'Irāq is *S. E. Turkey in Asia, Persian Gulf Sheet,* War Office, 1907.

'Ajami, which is a province of Persia; but originally the term 'Iraq was applied to Turkish 'Iraq only.

In the present article we shall deal with almost the whole of the region known as Turkish 'Iraq, certain only of the northern districts of the Baghdād Wilāyat being lightly touched on, to which Indian interests do not directly extend. The so-called Sanjāq of "Najd", that is to say, the **Hasa** Sanjāq described elsewhere under its own name, and the nominal Sanjāq of **Qasīm**—which also forms the subject of a separate article—are not, of course, in any sense parts of 'Iraq; but they are mentioned below incidentally on account of their administrative dependence on the Wilāyat of Basrah.

'Iraq is a purely geographical expression, and, so far as possible, we shall use it as such only; but occasionally, for political and administrative purposes, we shall be obliged to use the term as a synonym for the Baghdād and Basrah Wilāyats taken together without "Najd" (*i.e.* **Hasa**) or **Qasīm**.

Boundaries.—'Iraq is bounded on the west by the **Shāmīyah** Desert, on the south by the frontier of the **Kuwait** Principality and by the waters of the Persian Gulf. On the east its limit is the Persian border; and on the north our detailed inquiries will not extend beyond the town of **Kādhimain** on the **Tigris**.*

The Porte probably regard the **Shāmīyah** Desert as embraced in the Wilāyats of Baghdād and Basrah; but their authority over the nomad tribes inhabiting it is so slight that to treat any of the country to the west of the settled **Euphrates** valley as attached, even administratively, to 'Iraq would be a mistake: the most outlying Turkish stations, civil or military, upon this side are **Shifāthah**, **Najaf** Town, Rahabah and **Zubair** Town.

The exact position of the southern frontier is discussed in the article on the **Kuwait** Principality, and in this direction the most advanced Turkish outposts recognised by the British Government are those at **Safwān** and Umm **Qasr**; His Majesty's Government do not admit the title of the Porte to **Būbiyān** island, where a small detachment of Turkish troops is at present stationed.

The eastern frontier, that with Persia, was fixed by the Erzeroum Treaty of 1847 in general terms; but, though the country through

---

*As will be seen from Mr. Le Strange's book, already quoted, the ancient 'Iraq ended northwards at Tikrīt on the **Tigris**, and on the **Euphrates** at a point which may have been either due south or west by south of Takrīt.

which it runs was surveyed for the purpose of delimitation by an Anglo-Russian Commission in 1849-1855, no actual line has as yet been laid down. From this remark, however, the portion of the frontier between the Persian Gulf and **Kārūn** river must be excepted, for here the Shatt-al-'**Arab** divides the possessions of the Sultan and the Shah; this part alone of the Turco-Persian border is fixed with precision. North of this, the line of division observed in practice is understood to follow the Shatt-al-'**Arab** as far as the upper entrance of the Khaiyain creek, 6 miles by river above the mouth of the **Kārūn,** leaving the islands of Umm-al-**Khasāsīf** and **Shamshamīyah** upon the Turkish side, and thence to run in a north-westerly direction to the foot hills of Western Luristān and Kurdistān which, from the point where it reaches them, it skirts as far as Mandali مندلي. The line of contact between hill and plain is fairly well marked as it approaches Mandali; but in the neighbourhood of the Bani **Lām** country it is indefinite, and some of the pastures in the **Dawairij** neighbourhood are understood to be in dispute between the Turkish and Persian Governments. The districts of Jāngulah جانگله or Jangūlah جنگوله and Dih Bāla ده بالا or Taih Bāla تيه بالا, though not exactly in the plains, should perhaps belong to Turkey.*

Physical geography and character.—'Irāq is a plain of alluvial clay, unrelieved by a single range, hill or natural eminence of the slightest importance. On the east, however, the plain is dominated by the hills of the Persian district of Pusht-i-Kūh which, snow-clad in midwinter approach within about 30 miles of the **Tigris** at '**Ali-al-Gharbi** and are in full view, running nearly parallel to the river, all the way between the towns of '**Amārah** and **Kūt-al-Amārah.**

The chief features of 'Irāq are, of course, the great rivers **Euphrates** and **Tigris,** upon which the prosperity and even the habitability of the entire country depend. Minor but still important features are the **Diyālah,** a left bank tributary of the **Tigris** a short way below **Baghdād**; the **Shatt-al-Hindīyah,** formerly a canal but now a substitute for the dried-up reach of the **Euphrates** between **Musaiyib** and **Samāwah**; the channel, known as the Shatt-al-**Gharāf,** which connects the **Tigris** at **Kūt-al-Amārah** with the **Euphrates** at **Nāsirīyah** and Hammār; the enormous marshes upon the lower course of both **Euphrates** and **Tigris** from **Qūrnah** up to the towns of '**Amārah** and **Nāsirīyah** respectively; the swamps in which the **Daghārah** canal has its ending, and those which

---

* See a valuable Memorandum by Sir H. C. Rawlinson on the Turco-Persian frontier, printed as a Government of India Consultation in the Political Department, October 1844: see also Lord Curzon's "Persia," pages 558 to 570.

are said to have submerged a large part of the country between the Shatt-al-**Gharāf**, **Tigris** and **Euphrates**; the **Jahálah** which draws off a large proportion of the **Tigris** water at **'Amārah** Town, restoring part of it to the Shatt-al-**'Arab** *viâ* the Suwaib, together with the swamps to which this canal gives rise: finally a long, but narrow, saline marsh reaching apparently most of the way from Mandali to **Kūt-al-Amārah** upon the **Tigris**, of which the large swamp near Jassān جسّان town, known as Hor Jassān, is perhaps a part.

The soil of 'Irāq is in general a rich clay of fine quality, remarkably free, even in its natural state, from sterilising salts; this statement holds particularly of a large tract to the east of **Baghdād** City and of the country between the **Tigris** and **Euphrates** in the same latitude. Near the **Euphrates**, however, a saline efflorescence is in places observable; and below **Kūt-al-Amārah** Town, on the **Tigris**, and **Diwānīyah** Town, on the **Euphrates**, the proportion of sand in the soil to clay and humus is said to be excessive, except in the marshes. The valley of the **Euphrates** is much more extensively cultivated than that of the **Tigris**; but a little to the west of the former river, or rather of its **Hindīyah** branch, begins the irreclaimable **Shāmīyah** Desert. Wherever in 'Irāq the soil is irrigated there is rich cultivation and the date and other trees flourish; but the productive area is confined, in existing circumstances, to narrow belts which adjoin rivers, canals or marshes. In a few localities also, especially in depressions, occasional crops are grown by rainfall; but the aspect of 'Irāq remains, on the whole, that of a barren wilderness or Chōl چول of sun-baked clay, sprinkled with camel-thorn and wild caper and carpeted—but only after rain and chiefly on the side towards the Persian frontier—with a little thin herbage.

Flora.—Natural wooding hardly exists except upon the banks of rivers and canals, where the Gharab غرب or Euphrates poplar, a tree that does not attain any great size, grows interspersed with low tamarisk or Tarfah طرفه jungle: the Gharab is perhaps the Babylonian willow of Scripture. There is also a kind of osier or willow, known as Safsāf صفصاف, which gives a good shade. Some of the more important groves upon the **Euphrates** and **Tigris** are officially protected and are mentioned further on in this article in connection with the work of the Forest Department; they are sometimes very dense, but they are never extensive. The white and black mulberry, the ber, and various kinds of acacia (Barhām برهام) are among the self-propagating trees of the country, and there is also a mimosa which goes by the name of Shōk-ash-Shāmi شوك الشامي.

A small thorny plant, called simply Shōk شوك, is common everywhere and affords fuel and camel grazing. In the desert between **Basrah** and **Kuwait** are found, in addition to other common forage plants, a shrub called Haram هرم and a grass called Sahbah صهبه, both of which are eaten by camels: the leaves of the Haram are small and globular and contain fluid.

Two vegetable products, natural but possessing a commercial value, are colocynth or Handhal حنظل and Sūs سوس or liquorice. The colocynth occurs everywhere and is obtained in large quantities from the waste country between **Baghdād** and **Hillah**; but it is inferior to the Syrian colocynth, and the dried pulp only is exported instead of the whole fruit. The trade in liquorice is dealt with in one of the paragraphs on trade below. The liquorice plant grows chiefly in river bends, on the concave side of the curves, and is said never to be found at more than two miles distance from the water's edge; it requires a good deal of moisture and benefits by occasional floods. Its maximum height is about 10 feet, but on the average it does not exceed 4 or 5. Liquorice wood is a staple article of fuel at **Baghdād**.

Fauna.—Wild animals are rare in 'Irāq except gazelles, pigs (which abound in the marshes) and jackals; hyænas, foxes and hares also are said to exist.

Duck, black partridge and snipe are among the feathered game; and the bustard is found in the desert, while heron and other aquatic birds are numerous in the marshes.

The rivers produce fish, but not many kinds that are good to eat. The best known are the Bizz بز, which is often 6 to 7 feet long and over 100 lbs. in weight; the Shabūt شبوط, a fish weighing from 2 to 6 lbs.; the Bunni بني, a smaller but better tasting fish than the Shabūt; the Qattān قطان, a long, round fish measuring about 4 feet; the Jurri جري, a kind of scaleless catfish about 2½ feet long, eaten by Sunni Muhammadans but rejected by Shī'ah Muhammadans and Christians: and the Abu Zumair ابو زمير, a mustachioed fish which only the desert Arabs will eat. There are also a fish about 6 inches long, called Biyāh بياح, and a kind of flat fish known as Mazlag مزلگ. Sharks over 6 feet in length visit **Baghdād** in the hot season and make bathing in the **Tigris** dangerous; they have been found as far up stream as Sāmarrah.

In the marshy districts mosquitoes abound and sometimes make life a burden.

Minerals.—The minerals of 'Irāq are bitumen, mineral oil, and salt ; of these the first two occur outside the limits to which this article is confined, the bitumen at Hīt هيت and 'Anah عنه on the upper **Euphrates**, and the oil at Hīt and in the neighbourhood of the Persian frontier at Mandali, etc. The principal salt fields are those described in the articles on the **'Azīzīyah, Karbala, Najaf, Nāsirīyah, Samāwah Shatrat-al-'Amārah** Qadhas ; there is one also, but of less importance, on the outskirts of **Baghdād** City near the Bāb-at-Tilism.

It may be added that Juss or gypsum mortar is found in many parts of 'Irāq, especially at **Mahmūdīyah**, Sāmarrah and Tikrīt ; that a whitish-yellow clay, suitable for pottery, is obtained from the banks of the **Tigris** ; and that the desert about **Baghdād** and Ba'qūbah yields a clay good for making bricks.

Climate and health.—The climate of 'Irāq is on the whole not unhealthy, but it may be described as extreme, for the temperature in the shade ranges at **Baghdād** City from a minimum of 18·6°F. in winter to a maximum of 123° in summer. December, January and February are cold, crisp, and even bracing months, during which some rain falls ; March and April are warm and unsettled, with occasional thunder and dust-storms ; May and June are hot but fine, often with a refreshing north-west wind or Shamāl at night ; in July, August and September the heat is excessive and almost insupportable, driving the inhabitants of the towns to live in subterranean rooms or Sardābs سرداب by day, and upon the roofs of their houses from sunset to sunrise ; during October the heat begins to abate, and in November the weather becomes cool again. More precise details of temperature and rainfall will be found in the article on **Baghdād** City, the only place in 'Irāq for which exact statistics exist.

In 'Irāq the prevailing winds are those from the north-west and north; but calm weather is the rule. High temperatures accompany the east wind or Sharqi when it blows in the months of June, July and August ; and the south wind is invariably oppressive and is generally accompanied by dust.

The foregoing remarks relate primarily to **Baghdād** City and are not applicable without modification to the whole of the 'Irāq. In December 1905 the temperature in the **Euphrates** region between **Musaiyib** and **Kūfah** sometimes fell to 18°F. and biting winds blew from the north, but without injury to the health of caravans. The meteorological tables of the Government of India show that the conditions of **Baghdād** as to temperature are very similar to those of Jacobabad in Sind, and that the hot weather is more prolonged and intense than that of the Indian Panjāb. At **Basrah** Town and generally in the region of the Shatt-al-'**Arab**, the daily range of temperature is less, the summer nights are hotter, and the climate is more enervating than at **Baghdād.** Further meteorological details will be found in the articles on **Basrah** Town and **Fāo**.

Malarial fever in autumn is the principal disease of the country; and epidemics of cholera, and formerly of plague, have been of not unfrequent occurrence. Other diseases are small-pox and diphtheria, with typhoid, tuberculosis and syphilis in the towns. The celebrated Baghdād boil described in the article on **Baghdād**, is hardly known in 'Irāq outside of that city, but a similar affection exists in Eastern Anatolia and at Aleppo, Diyārbakr and other places in Asiatic Turkey.

Population.—It is difficult to form even an approximate estimate of the population of 'Irāq,—an intricate and extensive country, parts of which are hardly ever visited by civilised travellers. In attempting to give some idea of the number of the inhabitants a distinction may first be drawn between what we may call the fixed and the nomadic elements; and among the former of these will be included not only the residents of towns and large villages but also a very great number of tribesmen who dwell in huts or even tents, yet devote themselves to agriculture and stock-raising and are generally found in the same localities, though not exactly at the same places.

The following are three separate estimates of the fixed population in the Baghdād and Basrah Wilāyats:—

	I.	II.	III.
Baghdād Wilāyat	267,000	1,365,000	890,000
Basrah Wilāyat	935,000	1,500,000	590,000
Total souls .	1,202,000	2,865,000	1,480,000

The first of these estimates (total 1,202,000) was deduced by the (German) Baghdād Railway Commission of 1900 from the Turkish official registers; the second (total 2,865,000) was specially supplied, it would appear, to the same body by the Wālis of Baghdād and Basrah*; the

---

* See Proceedings of the Government of India in the Foreign Department for May 1901.

third (total 1,480,000) has been compiled, district by district, from information collected for the present Gazetteer, and a tabular analysis showing how it was reached will be found in the paragraph on civil administration below. The first two of these estimates no doubt include the populations of the **Hasa** Sanjāq and the **Kuwait** Principality in the figures for the Basrah Wilāyat, and to that extent they are excessive as estimates for 'Irāq proper, which indeed they are not meant to be ; but the first, on the other hand, is probably an underestimate for part of the country which it was intended to cover, for the Turkish official almanacs freely recognise the existence in some places of an "unregistered" population. Upon the whole the third estimate, referring as it does to 'Irāq only and based on all the available information of every kind, is probably not very far from the truth.

The exact number of Bedouins in 'Irāq is impossible to calculate, and the great majority of those seen in the country belong in reality to Central or Eastern Arabia and have been included already in our estimates of the population of Jabal **Shammar** and **Kuwait**. The true nomads whose homes are in 'Irāq are far from numerous ;* and they mostly belong to tribes of which the bulk is fixed or only semi-nomadic.

On full consideration of all the facts the population of 'Irāq may be placed at 1,500,000 souls or slightly more, of whom only a very small proportion are wandering Bedouins.

"*Urban*" *population and* "*urban*" *life.*—In approaching the subject of races and tribes among the people of 'Irāq, we may discard the distinction adopted above for purposes of numerical calculation and adopt another more suitable to our new topic—one, namely, between "urban" and "rural" population. By "urban" population are meant here not only the residents of towns, properly so called, but also those of permanent villages ; the "rural" population is taken to consist of the semi-nomads already mentioned, whose dwellings are huts or even tents, and of Bedouins pure and simple. The "urban" population, in what follows below, is thus very far from being identical with the "fixed"

---

* The (German) Baghdād Railway Commission, already quoted, estimated the "nomads and semi-nomads" in the Baghdād Wilāyat at 750,000 and those in the Wilāyat of Basrah at over 1,000,000. In the case of Basrah these figures probably include many tribes outside of 'Irāq : and in both Wilāyats the semi-nomads, it will be observed, have been bracketed (by the Commission) with the nomads and not (as in our estimate) with the fixed population. In any case the estimates of the Commission for fixed and nomadic population together are much in excess of the probable numbers. It is a well-known fact that the strengths of Bedouin tribes are as a rule grossly exaggerated except by the most cautious observers.

population above; and similarly there is no correspondence between the "nomadic" and "rural" populations.

The inhabitants of the towns and permanent villages, who thus form by themselves a natural division of the people, may be subdivided according to race into Arabs, Persians, Jews, Turks, **Kurds**, Chaldæans, Armenians and **Sabians**, besides Asiatic and European foreigners.

Arabs form the bulk of all the urban communities in 'Irāq with the two important exceptions of **Baghdād** City and the towns of **Karbala** and **Kādhimain**: in the first of these they are outnumbered by Jews, and in the other two by Persians. The distinctions of the urban Arabs among themselves are mainly religious and will be noticed further on; but a large proportion of them are descended from the rural tribes, dealt with in a later paragraph, and to some extent preserve their characteristics. The Arab of 'Irāq is not fanatical, but he is grasping in money matters and frequently overreaches himself by the extravagance of his own demands; he labours also under a rooted disinclination for hard work.

At **Karbala** Town, and at **Kādhimain** Town as well, Persians predominate in numbers over all other races. There is a considerable Persian colony in **Baghdād** City and one-eighth of the population of **Basrah** Town and a considerable proportion of that of **Tawairīj** are believed to be Persian; Persians engaged in retail trade are found even in such minor places as **Rumaithah**, **'Alī-al-Gharbi** and Qal'at **Sālih**. Many of the Persians are Turkish subjects; but they are generally unpopular with the Turks, and some of them maintain on their part a covert religious and political opposition to the Ottoman Government, especially at **Karbala** and **Najaf**.

The Jews are from every point of view an extremely important element in the population, and in the city of **Baghdād** they are believed to outnumber the Turks and even the Arabs. In 'Irāq, which contains the tombs of Ezra and Ezekiel and reaches to within a short distance of the tomb of Daniel, the Jews are surrounded by monuments of the Captivity, and this may account for the exceptional bigotry and devotion to the minutiæ of their law which they here display. They are almost entirely engaged in trade and money-lending, and many of them are altogether absorbed in these pursuits; but some of them are men of high and honourable character, in every way worthy of the distinguished and responsible positions to which they not infrequently attain. Many of them begin life as hawkers of stockings and such wares; all marry young and receive some capital at marriage from their fathers-in-law; when the latter are too poor to pay, the dowry or Muhr مهر is subscribed by their neighbours. The trade of Baghdād is passing every year more under Jewish control; and many Jews now visit England, and some of them even reside there as business agents for partners or relations. The native Christian merchants of **Baghdād** have mostly disappeared during the last 15 years in consequence of Jewish competition, and already Muhammadan merchants are taking Jews into partnership as a measure of self-defence; the Muhammadans, however, are still able to hold their own to some extent in the up-country trade carried on from **Baghdād**. The leading native firms at **Basrah** are Jewish also. Jews are found at various other places throughout the country such as **'Amārah** Town, where they have a synagogue and two rabbis; **Kūt-al-Amārah,** where they have a synagogue; **Nāsiriyah, Sūq-ash-Shuyūkh, Hai, 'Alī-al-Gharbi** and **Qal'at Sālih.** They venerate the tomb of Ezekiel at **Kifl** and many of them are buried there.

The Turks are not found in any numbers outside **Baghdād** City, where they compose about one-fifth of the population, and many of these are Turks only in name. The modern Turk is generally a hybrid and must often have in his veins much Christian blood, derived from the conquered and converted subjects of the old Byzantine Empire; and in 'Irāq his lineage is probably less pure than in some other Ottoman provinces. Turks in 'Irāq are mostly found in the government services and in official positions; those in the higher grades are often from Europe, and many of these know little or no Arabic. In 'Irāq the Turk does not figure as an agriculturist or trader as he does in Anatolia and other parts of the Empire. From excess of caution the Turk often appears reserved and even sullen, and he does not shine as a civil administrator; but he is believed to be still a brave and energetic soldier.

Among the finest classes of men in the towns and villages are the **Kurds,** most of whom seem to belong to the Failīyah فيليه branch of the tribe. The distribution and character of the **Kurds** is described in a separate article. As an agriculturist in 'Irāq the **Kurd** is said to be inferior to the Arab.

The Armenians, of whom there are some at **Baghdād,** have lost much of their importance in trade in consequence of Jewish competition, and with it, to some extent, their position as a community, but some of them are still well-to-do merchants or clerks. Chaldæan Christians are not very much in evidence except as domestic servants and upon the river steamers, where they enjoy a complete monopoly as deck-hands and firemen; those who serve on the steamers are all Talkaifis, or natives of

Talkaif تلکیف, a village near Mūsal, and strongly resemble one another in their features, which are of an unmistakeable cast. These Chaldæans are now improving their position by means of education, and some of the younger generation are clerks in banks, etc. The profession of the law is almost monopolised at **Baghdād** by the Christian races.

It remains to mention the curious sect or community of the **Sabians**, or Subba صبّاء, regarding whose religion much controversy has taken place and who are more fully described in a separate article: they are found also in the Persian province of **'Arabistān**. The **Sabians** are an artistic and mechanical people, hardly distinguishable in appearance from their Arab neighbours. The commonest profession among them is that of gold and silversmith, and the silver and antimony ware of he **Sabians** of **'Amārah** Town is celebrated; but others are employed as gunsmiths, carpenters and boat-builders; a few are bakers. Their chief settlements in 'Irāq are at **Nāsirīyah**, at **'Amārah** Town and at **Sūq-ash-Shuyūkh** where their Qāri or religious head has his abode; but they are also found at Qal'at **Sālih**, **'Alī-al-Gharbi** and Shaikh **Sa'ad**.

Asiatic foreigners, exclusive of Persians, are generally natives of India, Afghānistān, or the Indo-Afghan frontier who have been attracted to the country by the sacred places of Shī'ism or by the Sunni shrine of 'Abdul Qādir Gīlānī at Baghdād, and the descendants of such. The Indians are not generally held in much esteem, but the Afghāns and Pathāns, by their superior physique and force of character, command some respect. In **Baghdād** there is a considerable body of Afghāns and Pathāns, mostly employed as watchmen and door-keepers, who have been known, on such an occasion as the murder of one of their number, to occasion anxiety to the authorities by a disposition to make common cause.

Europeans in **'Irāq** are almost confined to the towns of **Baghdād** and **Basrah** and are chiefly English.

In the towns and villages of 'Irāq the houses are nearly always built on the same plan and consist of a square or oblong courtyard surrounded by rooms: in the larger towns the houses are often two-storeyed, and in that case the upper flat has generally a verandah which looks into the central yard. Handsome projecting windows called Shanāshīl شناشیل, an Arabic corruption of the Persian Shāhnishīn شاهنشین, and sitting-rooms built across the street at a considerable height above the ground so as to form a bridge between apartments on the opposite sides are features of the domestic architecture of **Baghdād** City and are reproduced in some of the other towns. Houses are generally built by the owners who buy

3 D 2

the materials and pay daily wages to the workmen; the architect who directs operations is frequently illiterate and works by rule of thumb without the aid of plans.

The members of each of the different races and religions which inhabit the towns generally congregate together in a particular quarter, and as a rule they are recognisable at sight by their dress and general appearance. In **Baghdād** the 'Aba عباء and Zabūn زبون, the outer and inner garment of the ordinary Muhammadan native, have begun to give way, partly perhaps in consequence of the wearing of European uniform by the troops, to European dress; the case of foot-gear is similar.

Work ceases at sunset throughout the year and few persons leave their houses after dark. Men are never seen abroad in the company of women, not even of their wives or nearest relations. Rice enters largely into the diet of the town classes, among whom the well-to-do mostly have a Pilāo or Shorbah at least once a day. Coffee is the universal beverage.

"*Rural*" *population and* "*rural*" *life.*—The people, outside the towns and permanent villages, are all Arabs, except in some of the eastern districts where there are **Kurds**; and the great bulk of them—as already explained—are at least semi-settled, and a few only, temporary visitors being excepted, are entirely nomadic.

The tribal system of 'Irāq, as we must at once warn the reader, is not so exact, so rigid, or so well ascertained as that, for example, of the Pathān tribes on the North-Western Frontier of India, or that even of the Bedouins of Central Arabia. Thus it happens that enumerations of tribal subdivisions received at different times or from different sources seldom tally, and that the Turkish Government do not understand, and that the tribesmen themselves are often unable to explain, the relationship subsisting between different sections. As concrete examples of the uncertainties encountered we may mention that diverse accounts represent the Dafāfi'ah and the Āl Bū Darrāj as wholly independent tribes and as sections of the **Shammar Tòqah** and Banī **Lām** respectively; that the Sarāi Arabs figure in some statements as a subdivision of the Banī **Lām** and in others as a section of the Banī **Rabī'ah**; and that the Khasraj are sometimes named in connection either with the Banī **Lām** or with the **Zubaid**, and at other times are spoken of as a tribe by themselves. The fluidity of tribal conditions is illustrated by the fact that the Banī **Mālik**, Ahl-al-Jazāir and Banī Mansūr, who a few years back were apparently considered to be sections of the **Muntafik**, are now generally regarded as possessing each a separate existence. Part of the

'IRAQ (TURKISH)

confusion arises from a tendency to class a small tribe which depends upon the assistance of a larger tribe in war as a section of the larger; and the political alliances which thus partly determine classification are unstable and fluctuating. Doubts of the kind we have indicated could be finally settled only by elaborate local enquiries among the tribes. In the present Gazetteer we have been guided by the best opinions available; but accuracy, in the circumstances, cannot be guaranteed.*

The following is a table of the principal "rural" tribes of 'Iraq:—

Tribe.	Location.	Remarks.
'Abdullah (Āl) آل عبد الله	In the **Najaf** Qadha.	A settled tribe of Shī'ah agriculturists, by some regarded as a section of the Jalīhah below.
'Afaj عفج	In the 'Afaj collection of villages on the **Daghā-rah** canal, and in that neighbourhood. The country inhabited by this tribal group is marshy. There are no horses and Mashḥūf canoes are the chief means of locomotion.	'Afaj is not really the name of a tribe, but it is used loosely to designate the whole body of tribes who inhabit 'Afaj. The principal among them are the 'Ajārij عجارج, Bahāhithah بهاحثه, Hamzah همزة, Makhādihah مخادحه, Āl Bū Nāshi آل بو ناشي, Āl Bū Rāshid آل بو رشد, and Shaibah شيبه. These people are described as courageous, independent and trustworthy, but always engaged in feuds.
'Ājīb or 'Ajāīb عجائيب عاجيب	In the Qadhas of **Najaf** and **Samāwah**.	The 'Ajīb are generally stated to be a subsection of the Jabūr-al-Wāwi section of the **Zubaid**: in religion they are Shī'ahs. In the **Najaf** Qadha they figure as nomads: in **Samāwah** they are settled.
'Akaidāt عكيدات	In the Qadha of **Kādhi-main**.	A settled tribe, Sunni by religion.
'Akārāt عكارات	In the Qadha of **Najaf**.	The 'Akārāt number about 200 men; they are Shī'ahs and agriculturists. They are said to be a subsection of the Jabūr-al-Wāwi section of the **Zubaid** and to be included in a subdivision of the tribe called the Āl 'Īsa آل عيسى.

* The separate articles on the tribes of 'Irāq, viz., the **'Atub, 'Īdān, Khazā'il, Bani Lām, Bani Mālik, Mas'ūd, Muhaisin, Āl Bū Muhammad, Muntafik, Bani Rabī'ah, Shammar Tōqah, Al Bū Sultān** and **Zubaid** must be read subject to these remarks.

Tribe.	Location.	Remarks.
Alaiwi (Abu) ابو عُلَيوِي	In the Qadha of Diwaniyah.	......
'Amirīyah عامريه	In the Qadha of Hindīyah, partly in Mshorab-ash-Sharqi on the left bank of the Shatt-al-Hindīyah between Musaiyib and Tawairīj.	The 'Āmirīyah are Shī'ahs, live in reed huts, cultivate, and keep cattle. They were originally connected with the Zubaid, but are now an independent tribe and are at present in alliance with the Bani Hasan below.
'Anizah عنزه	Some of the Bedouins of this tribe visit the parts of the Karbala and Najaf Qadhas which are nearest to the Shāmīyah desert.	See article 'Anizah.
Aqra' اقرع	The Daghārah group of villages on the Daghārah canal.	A general term covering a number of tribes of which the principal are these:—Hamad حمد, Hilālāt حلالات, Mujāwir مجاوير, Nail (Al Bū) آل بو نيل, Sa'īd (Al) آل سعيد, Shibānah (Āl) آل شبانه, 'Umr (Āl) آل عمر, and Zaiyād زياد. To these should perhaps be added the Farāhinah, Āl Bū Husain, Āl Bū Rīshah and Sindān below. In their general characteristics the Aqra' resemble the tribes of the 'Afaj group above, whose neighbours they are. They are all Shī'ahs and have an evil reputation as robbers.
Asad (Bani) بني اسد	Apparently in the Hindīyah Qadha between the Mshorab canal from the Shatt-al-Hindīyah and the Abu Khasāwi branch of the Dawaihīyah canal.	These Bani Asad are only about 300 souls and have no horses; they are Shī'ahs and allied with the Bani Taraf. They are apparently identical with the Bani Sadd (see below). There is another tribe of the same name in the Qadha of Sūq-ash-Shuyūkh, especially in the neighbourhood of Hammār and Jazāir upon the Euphrates.
'Atīj عتيج	In the Qadha of Najaf.	The 'Atīj number about 70 persons and are Shī'ahs by religion and engaged in agriculture. They are probably a subsection of the Jabūr-al-Wāwi section of the Zubaid and not an independent tribe.

'IRĀQ (TURKISH)

Tribe.	Location.	Remarks.
'Atub عطب	On the Shatt-al-'Arab, chiefly between Basrah and Muhammareh.	See article 'Atub.
'Awābid عوابد	In and about the Muqāta'ah of Rghailah in the Qadha of Shāmīyah.	The 'Awābid, who are Shī'ahs inhabiting tents and huts and engaged in agriculture and stock breeding, are estimated at 5,000 souls. They possess about 500 horses. The 'Awābid are probably not an independent tribe but a section of the Bani Hasan below.
'Ayāsh عیاش	In the Qadhas of Najaf and Shāmīyah.	In the Najaf Qadha the members of this tribe are nomadic, visiting the district with their cattle in the winter only; in the Shāmīyah Qadha, where their fixed settlements are, they are said to number 9,000 souls. All the 'Ayāsh are Shī'ahs and the majority are engaged in cattle breeding, but the poorer among them cultivate. The tribe is independent but closely connected with the Bani Hasan below.
Balūchis بلوش	Chiefly in the towns of Karbala, Hillah and Kūfah and at Shifāthah and Ja'ārah.	The ancestors of these Balūsh or Balūchis, who are Persian subjects and now number about 3,000 souls in 'Irāq, are said to have come from Baluchistān about 100 years ago at the invitation of Sāhib-ar-Riyādh, a celebrated scholar of Karbala, to assist in defending that town against the Wahhābis.
Barāji' براجع	In the Qadha of Hindīyah.	The Barāji' are Shī'ahs and can muster 400 men; they are friendly with the Āl Bū Fatlah and at feud with the Bani Hasan. All are agriculturists. They are probably a section of the Jalīhah below.
Barbari برري	At Najaf Town.	The Barbaris are not numerous in 'Irāq; they are believed to have entered the country as political refugees from Afghānistān. Barbaris are not now, perhaps, found in Afghānistān; but they were the original inhabitants of the Hazārajāt and were practically annihilated by Jangiz Khān (or one of his successors) who swamped them with military colonists (Hazāras). The Band-i-Amīr Lakes in Afghanistān are still some times called the Band-i-Barbar.

Tribe.	Location.	Remarks.
Budair (Al) آل بدير	In the Rghailah Muqāta'h of the Shāmīyah Qadha and in the Qadha of Dīwānīyah upon the Daghārah canal.	The Āl Budair are Shī'ahs, inhabiting tents and huts, and engaged in agriculture and stock raising. They are said to number about 3,000 souls and to have 300 horses. Those in Shāmīyah number about 300 men and are only cultivators: they are moreover so closely connected with the Bani Hasan as to be almost indistinguishable from them.
Daghārah دغاره	The Daghārah villages on the Daghārah canal.	This, like 'Afaj above, is not a genuine tribal name; but it is used as a synonym for the Aqra' mentioned above because they inhabit the Daghārah villages.
Darrāj (Āl Bū) آل بو درّاج	The right bank of the Tigris from Kumait down to a point opposite 'Amārah Town.	By some authorities these Āl Bū Darrāj are treated not as an independent tribe but as belonging to the Khasraj division of the Bani Lām.
Da'ūm دعوم	On the Mshorab canal from the Shatt-al-Hindīyah in the Qadha of that name.	In general characteristics this tribe resembles the Jalībah. Politically they are dependent on the Āl Kinānah, but they are sometimes said to be a subsection of the Jabūr-al-Wāwi section of the Zubaid. They are Shī'ahs by religion and agriculturists and cattle breeders by occupation. Their fighting men are said to number 400.
Dhafīr ضفير ظفير	Some of the Bedouins of this tribe visit the right bank of the Euphrates in the neighbourhood of Nāsirīyah.	See article Dhafīr.
Dhawālim ظوالم	In the Qadha of Samāwah.	A settled Shī'ah tribe, engaged in agriculture and cattle breeding: said to muster 2,200 men. They consist of several sections among whom are the Āl Bū Husain آل بو حسين and the Āl Juma'ah آل جمعه.
Dhuwaihir ظويهير	In the Qadha of Najaf.	A settled Shī'ah tribe: they are cultivators and cattle breeders and number about 100 men.
Dilaim دليم	In the Qadha of Kādhimain.	See article Dilaim.

'IRĀQ (TURKISH)

Tribe.	Location.	Remarks.
Fadāghah فداغه	In the Qadha of Kādhimain.	Some of the Fadāghah are Shi'ahs and some are Sunnis; they are said to number 1,500 persons.
Farāhinah فراحنه	In the Qadha of Dīwānīyah.	A settled Shi'ah tribe on the Daghārah canal, engaged in cattle breeding and agriculture. They are perhaps one of the Aqra' tribes mentioned above.
Fatlah (Āl Bū) آل بو فتله	In the Hindīyah Qadha, especially between Tawairīj and Hillah and near Tall Nimrūd, and in the Shāmīyah Qadha about Ja'ārah.	This tribe is generally at feud with the Bani Hasan and on good terms with the Jalīhah, Qarait and Tufail below. They are supposed to number some 10,000 souls; but their horses are only about 200. They are divided into about 25 sections, all agricultural and inhabiting either reed huts or mud houses.
Ghazālāt غزالات	In the Najaf Qadha and about Ja'ārah in the Shāmīyah Qadha.	The Ghazālāt are a Shi'ah tribe at enmity with the Dilaim and closely associated with the Khazā'il. In all they are said to muster about 2,000 men. The majority are Bedouins and the rest agriculturists and cattle-breeders.
Hakīm (Bani) بني حكيم	In the Qadha of Samāwah.	Vulgarly known as the Bani Hachaim حچيم, a large settled Shi'ah tribe engaged in stock raising and agriculture. They comprise many sections of which the following are the chief:—'Abas عبس, 'Ata Ullah عطا الله, 'Atāwah عطاوه, Burkāt بركات, Falāhāt فلاحات, Fartūs فرطوس, Ghalīdh غليظ, Āl Bū Hāchmah, Hamīd حميد, Hashīsh حشيش, 'Iqāb عقاب, Jazburah جزبره, Muminīn مومنين, Mushā'alah مشاعله, Sufrān صفران, and Taubah توبه.
Hamaidāt حميدات	In the Shāmīyah Qadha, especially in the Muqāta'ah of Rghailah.	The Hamaidāt are about 5,000 in number. They cultivate rice and other cereals, own 500 horses and breed cattle and sheep. They live in tents and huts and are Shi'ahs. According to some the Hamaidāt are a section of the Bani Hasan below.

Tribe.	Location.	Remarks.
Hasan (Bani) بني حسن	In the Najaf Qadha, particularly in the sub-district of Hor-ad-Dukhn, in the Qadha of Shāmīyah, and in parts of the Qadha of Hindīyah.	The Maulah, Mawāsh, Qaraishāt and Bani Taraf tribes below and the Hamaidāt above are closely associated with the Bani Hasan and by some are even reckoned sections. Divisions of the Bani Hasan in Hor-ad-Dukhn are :— 'Abbās عبّاس, Al Bū 'Adhaib آل بو عذيب, Al Bū 'Āridhi آل بو عارضي, Al Bū Hadāri آل بو حداري, Hawātim حواتم, and Majātīm مجاتيم. Other divisions of the tribe elsewhere are :— Bani 'Amr بني عمر, Al Dahīm آل دهيم, Al Bū Hadādi آل بو حدادي, Al Jamīl آل جميل, Al Jarrah آل جرة, Bani Salāmah and Sārāwān ساراوان, of whom the Bani Salāmah at least are Bedouins. The 'Awābid, already described above are probably a section of the Bani Hasan; and similarly the 'Ayāsh and Al Budair, though independent tribes, are very closely connected with the Bani Hasan. The Bani Hasan are usually on bad terms with their neighbours the Barāji'; and the Al Bū Fatlah above and the Karākishah below are their friends. The Bani Hasan are roughly estimated at 10,000 souls, but they have only about 200 horses. About $\frac{1}{5}$ of the tribe sometimes move with their cattle in search of pasture.
Hasan (Shaikh) شيخ حسن	At Buwārīn on the left bank of the Shatt-al-'Arab and on the islands of Umm-al-Khasāsīf and Shamshamīyah in that river.	The Shaikh Hasan are probably not a separate tribe. Some describe them as a section of the Ka'ab and others would merge them in the Muhaisin. They are Shī'ahs.

'IRĀQ (TURKISH)

Tribe.	Location.	Remarks.
Hāshim (Bani) بني هاشم	In the Hai Qadha in the neighbourhood of Qal'at Sikar.	A small tribe allied to the Muntafik. One account, which is not confirmed, says that they are identified with the section of the Quraish of which the prophet Muhammad came and are honoured as Saiyids. It has also been stated that they are found in many places throughout Turkish 'Irāq, but in this perhaps there is some confusion with the Bani Hakīm or Hachaim above.
Hassān (Al Bū) آل بو حسّان	In the Qadha of Samāwah.	The Āl Bū Hassān are a large settled Shī'ah tribe comprising, among others, these sections:— 'Abas عبس , Āl Bū 'Ainain عنين , Jalābitah جلابط , Khamis خمس and Suhūr سحور .
Husain (Āl Bū or Bani) آل بو حسين	In the Qadha of Dīwānīyah.	These may perhaps be regarded as belonging to the Aqra' group above. They live in tents and keep sheep. They have no horses, but they have many canoes and are fairly well armed. They are a settled tribe. Some say that the Bani Sadd on the Shatt-al-Hindīyah are Bani Husain.
Ibrāhīm (Āl) آل ابراهيم	In the Shāmīyah Qadha, especially about Ja'ārah.	The Āl Ibrāhīm are Shī'ahs and are supposed to number about 4,000 souls. They live in tents and huts and cultivate rice and pulse and breed cattle. They have about 300 horses. They may be a section of the Āl Shibil below.
'Īdān? عيدان	On both banks of the Shatt-al-'Arab, especially on the right bank immediately below Basrah Town, and upon 'Ajairāwīyah Island.	See article 'Īdān.
Jabūr جبور	Their distribution is explained in the article on the Zubaid tribe.	It seems preferable to class the Jabūr as a double section of the Zubaid, the article on which tribe may be consulted. But some authorities regard them as a distinct tribe, divided into two sections which are now unconnected with one another: viz., the Jabūr-al-Wāwi of the Euphrates valley, who are all Shī'ahs, and the Jabūr of the Tigris side, who are Sunnis.
Jadi جدي	In the Nasrīyah tract in the Qadha of Karbala.	A tribe of about 200 fighting men, Shī'ahs. They cultivate and breed cattle and have about 100 horses.

Tribe.	Location.	Remarks.
Jahaish جهيش	In the Nasrīyah tract in the Qadha of Karbala.	A Shī'ah tribe of about 1,500 souls, cultivators and cattle breeders. They have only about 50 horses. The Jahaish were formerly a section of the Zubaid, but they are now generally regarded as an independent tribe. They are on terms of enmity with the Āl Bū Sultān.
Jaiyāsh (Al Bū) آل بو جياش	In the Qadha of Samāwah.	A large settled Shī'ah tribe of cultivators and cattle breeders. The Āl Bū Jaiyāsh include the following sections:—'Antar عنطر, Hamāmrah حمامره, Huwaish حويش, Āl Bū Jarād جراد, Jarīb جريب, Najairis نجيرس, Rubāyi' ربايع, and Shanābirah شنابره.
Jalīhah جليحه	In the Qadhas of Dīwānīyah and Hindīyah: in the latter their settlements are chiefly between Tawairīj and Rajībah, on a branch of the 'Abd 'Auniyāt canal from the Shatt-al-Hindīyah.	The Jalīhah are allies of the Āl Bū Fatlah mentioned above. They are roughly estimated at 3,000 persons, but have only about 100 horses. They live chiefly in huts, but at Rajībah they have some houses. The Jalīhah are Shī'ahs. According to some authorities the Āl 'Abdullah above are a section of this tribe, also the Barāji'.
Janābiyīn جنابيين	On the left bank of the Euphrates below the Dilaim tribe and above the town of Musaiyib: this is the tract called Jarūf.	The Janābiyīn are mostly Sunnis, but some of them are Shī'ahs. They are reputed brave and generous; they live as agriculturists, as watchmen, and sometimes as thieves. They have no fixed houses. The Janābiyīn are said to be about 10,000 souls. A large number of this tribe are said to have settled in Baghdād City. The rural Janābiyīn are friends and allies of the Mas'ūd.
Janājah جناجه	In the Qadha of Hindīyah.	A Shī'ah tribe of about 1,500 souls. Many of them find employment in the date groves about Hillah.
Jarāwinah جراونه	In the tract called Nasrīyah in the Qadha of Karbala.	A Shī'ah tribe of about 5,000 souls. They live in tents and huts, cultivate and breed stock, and are said to have 500 horses.
Jashshām جشام	Uncertain.	Sunnis.

Tribe.	Location.	Remarks.
Jazāir (Ahl-al-) اهل الجزائر	In the Qadhas of Qūrnah and Sūq-ash-Shuyūkh, especially in the subdistrict of Hammār.	This tribe was formerly less scattered; but about 5 years ago, their chief Hasan Khaiyūn, who was then Mudīr of Hammār, having engaged in intrigues and caused the death of some Ottoman officials, they were attacked and dispersed by the Turks. They were formerly (but are not now) under the protection of, and closely associated with, the Muntafik. In religion they are Shī'ahs.
Ka'ab كعب	In the Fāo tract on the right bank of the Shatt-al-'Arab at its mouth.	See article Ka'ab. The not very numerous representatives of the tribe at Fāo are merely immigrants from Persian 'Arabistān.
Karākishah كراكشه	On the west bank of the Shatt-al-Hindīyah from the barrage to Sulaimānīyah village.	A small, quiet, and agricultural Shī'ah tribe, dependent on the Āl Kinānah below but, possibly a section of the Āl Bū Sultān; they are about 1,500 souls in all and are said to resemble the Jalīhah. The Karākishah are friends of the Bani Hasan.
Khadhīrāt خضيرات	Among the Mas'ūd.	A small Shī'ah tribe dependent on the Mas'ūd among whom they live. They are cultivators and number about 150 men.
Kawām كوام	In the Qadhas of Kūt-al-Amārah and Kādhimain especially on the left bank of the Tigris between Kūt-al-Amārah and a point opposite Shaikh Sa'ad.	The Kawām are all Sunnis. They are probably a section of the Bani Rabī'ah q. v.
Khawādhir خواظر	In the Qadhas of Karbala and Dilaim. The Khawādhir own a number of buffaloes which they pasture in the cold season round Shifāthah, removing in summer into the Dilaim Qadha.	......
Khazā'il خزاعل	In the marshes between Kūfah and Samāwah Town, chiefly in the Samāwah Qadha; also, to some extent, in the Shāmīyah Desert where it adjoins the Euphrates in the same neighbourhood.	See article Khazā'il.

Tribe.	Location.	Remarks.
Kinānah (Āl) آل كنانة	On the west side of the Shatt-al-**Hindīyah**, between Sulaimānīyah village and the Abu Khasāwi branch of the Dawaihīyah canal.	The name is pronounced Āl Chinānah. The Da'ūm, Karakishah and Āl Bū Samān are dependent on this tribe, who themselves have no horses and number only about 100 men. They are a very quiet people, Shī'ahs, non-nomadic, and engaged in agriculture. By some they are represented as a section of the Bani Taraf below.
Kurd (I) كرد	At various towns and villages on the **Tigris** and Shatt-al-**Gharāf**.	See article **Kurd** Tribe.
Kurd (II) كرد	In the Hor-ad-Dukhn subdivision of the **Najaf** Qadha.	An Arab tribe, notwithstanding their name; about 3,000 in number and owning 500 horses. In religion they are Shī'ahs; by occupation they are cultivators and cattle breeders, living in mud houses and huts. Their men number about 1,200.
Lām (Bani) بني لام	On the left bank of the **Tigris** from a point opposite Shaikh **Sa'ad** down to '**Amārah** Town: they reach northwards to the hills of the Persian frontier and eastwards to the **Karkheh** River.	See article Bani **Lām**.
Ma'adān معدان	......	See Al Bū **Muhammad** below.
Mahaiyi (Āl Bū) آل بو محيّي	In the neighbourhood of **Musaiyib** Town.	A settled, cultivating tribe, by religion Shī'ah.
Mālik (Bani) بني مالك	On both banks of the **Tigris** from **Qūrnah** village up to '**Azair**, and at various places on the right bank of the Shatt-al-'**Arab** below Basrah Town.	See article Bani **Mālik**.
Mansūr (Bani) بني منصور	In the Qadhas of **Qūrnah** and **Sūq-ash-Shuyūkh**, intermingled with the Ahl-al-Jazāir above.	The Bani Mansūr are Shī'ahs. They were once closely connected with the **Muntafik**.
Maqāsīs مقاصيص	On the right bank of the **Tigris** for some distance upwards from Shaikh **Sa'ad** and on the left bank between **Kūt-al-Amārah** and a point opposite Shaikh Sa'ad.	This tribe are generally regarded as a section of the Bani **Rabī'ah**, in the article on whom they are mentioned; but some of them are perhaps more closely connected with the Bani **Lām**. The distinction perhaps depends on the bank of the **Tigris** which they inhabit.

IRAQ (TURKISH) 783

Tribe.	Location.	Remarks.
Mashāhidah مشاهدة	In the Qadha of Kādhimain.	These are perhaps a tribe by themselves; but inhabitants or natives of Mashhad 'Ali or Najaf are commonly called Mashāhidah.
Mashid (Spelling uncertain)	At Ruwais on the right bank of the Shatt-al-'Arab and upon the island of Tawailah.	The Mashid are possibly not a tribe but a subdivision of some tribe.
Masri (Āl Bū) آل بو مصري	In the Qadha of Karbala, upon the Husainīyah canal.	A settled tribe engaged in agriculture. In religion they are Shī'ahs.
Mas'ūd مسعود	In the Karbala Qadha along the Husainīyah canal from the Euphrates to the Pul-i-Sufaid; and in the Qadha of Hindīyah on the west side of the Shatt-al-Hindīyah in the tract watered by Mshorab canal; also, possibly, on the left bank of the Euphrates a little above Musaiyib.	See article Mas'ūd.
Maulah مولة	In the Hindīyah Qadha, on both sides of the Dawaihīyah canal from the Shatt-al-Hindīyah.	The Maulah number about 150 men and are Shī'ahs: they are boat-makers, fishermen and muleteers. Some make them a section of the Bani Hasan.
Mawāsh مواش	In the Hor-ad-Dukhn subdivision of the Najaf Qadha, and probably in the Shāmīyah Qadha also.	A cultivating, gardening and cattle breeding tribe, inhabiting tents and huts. They are politically dependent on the Bani Hasan and are Shī'ahs by religion. They are estimated at 3,000 persons and their horses at 300.
Muhammad (Āl Bū) آل بو محمد	On the banks of the Tigris from 'Amārah Town down to 'Azair, and in the marshes inland of both banks for some distance below 'Azair. They are said to occur in the direction of Sūq-ash-Shuyūkh, and a few are found on either bank of the Shatt-al-'Arab to a short distance below Qūrnah. They are most numerous in the Qadhas of Shatrat-al-'Amārah and Zubair.	See article Āl Bū Muhammad. The term Ma'adan appears to be practically a synonym for Āl Bū Muhammad.

Tribe.	Location.	Remarks.
Muhaisin محيسن	On the Shatt-al-'Arab, chiefly on the left bank between the towns of Basrah and Muhammareh, but also to some extent on the left bank above Basrah and on the right bank below it.	See article Muhaisin.
Muhsin (Āl Bū) آل بو محسن	About Khidhar in the Qadha of Samāwah.	The Āl Bū Muhsin are a considerable and distinct tribe, engaged in cultivation and cattle breeding. They are Shī'ahs.
Muntafik منتفك	Upon both banks of the Euphrates from Durrāji down to Qūrnah Village; upon both banks of the Shatt-al-Gharāf from Hai down to Nāsirīyah Town; also to some extent, perhaps, on the right bank of the Tigris between 'Azair and Qūrnah.	See article Muntafik.
Nahairāt (Ahl) اهل نهيرات	About the village of Qūrnah.	A small tribe of Shī'ahs, or, possibly, a section of the Bani Sa'īd or Sa'ad below.
Nāsirīyah ناصريه	In the tract likewise called Nāsirīyah or Nasrīyah in the Karbala Qadha.	The Nāsirīyah are Shī'ahs and their number is estimated at 3,000 souls. They have perhaps 100 horses. They cultivate the Sanīyah lands and some of them are fishermen and some weavers.
Qaidhah قيضه	With the Yasār tribe below, and in the Nasrīyah tract in the Qadha of Karbala.	The Qaidhah number about 600 souls and are politically dependent on the Yasār. They are Shī'ahs and only cultivate.
Qaraishāt قريشات	In the Kūfah subdivision of the Najaf Qadha.	A Shī'ah tribe, able to muster about 200 fighting men: they make their living by trade in wood, grass and garden produce. They have been domiciled for 3 generations among the Bani Hasan, of which tribe they are now virtually a part.
Qarait قريط	In the Qadha of Hindīyah, on the west side of the Shatt-al-Hindīyah above Tawairij, and also on the Shatt-al-Mulla below that place.	The Qarait are said to be of Shammar origin, but they are now a separate tribe. In religion they are Shī'ahs and by occupation cultivators and stock farmers. Their fighting men are said to number 1,500 and they are well armed with Martini rifles. The Qarait are allied politically with the Al Bū Fatlah above.

Tribe.	Location.	Remarks.
Qatārnah قطارنه	In the Qūrnah Qadha, and particularly at the villages of Kataibān, Jazīrat-as-Saghīr and Kibāsi-as-Saghīr on the left bank of the Shatt-al-'Arab above Basrah Town: they, the 'Atub and the 'Idān, are the principal ingredients of the mixed population on the right bank of that river generally.	The Qatārnah are Shī'ahs.
Rabī'ah (Bani) بني ربيعه	On the right bank of the Tigris from Bghailah to Shaikh Sa'ad, and on the left bank from a point opposite Bghailah to Kūt-al-Amārah; also in the Kādhimain Qadha.	See article Bani Rabī'ah.
Rīshah (Āl Bū) آل بو ريشه	On the Daghārah in the Qadha of Diwānīyah.	A settled cultivating Shī'ah tribe perhaps belonging to the Aqra' group.
Sa'ad (Bani) بني سعد	......	See Bani Sa'īd below.
Sadd (Bani) بني سد	On the left bank of the Shatt-al-Hindīyah above Tawairīj and below Musaiyib.	Some accounts make them a division of the Bani Husain, but it seems that they are identical with the Bani Asad above.
Sa'īd (Bani) بني سعيد	In the Qadha of Sūq-ash-Shuyūkh.	Probably a division of the Muntafik, *q. v.* They are found on the Euphrates between Hammār and Madīnah, and some of them are Sunnis and some Shī'ahs. They appear to be known also as Bani Sa'ad سعد.
Salāmah (Bani) بني سلامه	In the Qadhas of Najaf and Shāmīyah.	A settled Shī'ah tribe of cultivators and cattle-breeders. In the Shāmīyah Qadha they are said to number 10,000 souls. Those found in Najaf are merely winter visitors from Shāmīyah.
Sālah (Bani) بني ساله	In the neighbourhood of Tall Nimrūd on the Shatt-al-Hindīyah and of the Dawaihīy ah canal from the same.	The Bani Sālah are about 400 men: their horses are only 100. Some say they are a section of the Bani Taraf below.
Saman (Āl Bū) آل بو سمن	In the Qadha of Hindīyah.	They are about 1,500 souls altogether and they generally resemble the Jalīhah. Politically they are dependent on the Āl Kinānah. They are Shī'ahs, non-nomadic, and engaged in agriculture. Some make them a section of the Tufail below.

3 E

Tribe.	Location.	Remarks.
Sha'ār شعار	In the Qadha of Kādhimain about Abu Ghuraib.	The Sha'ār are Sunnis: they have no Shaikh of their own and obey the Shaikh of the Zōba'.
Shalāl شلال	Parts of the Ghamās Nāhiyah of the Shāmīyah Qadha.	.....
Shammar (Northern) شمر	Not actually resident in 'Irāq, but some of their Bedouins frequent the Najaf Qadha.	See article Northern Shammar.
Shammar Tōqah شمر طرقه	On the left bank of the Tigris from Baghdād City to a point opposite Bghailah.	See article Shammar Tōqah.
Shibil (Al) آل شبل	In the Qadhas of Shāmīyah, Karbala and Najaf.	The Āl Shibil are divided into many sections: one of these, the Āl Khuzaim آل خزيم or Khazaiyim occupy nearly all the Ghamās subdivision of the Shāmīyah Qadha; other two, the Ahl-ad-Dawāb اهل الدواب and the Āl Lajām آل لجام are found at Ja'ārah in the same district. The Al Ibrāhīm above should perhaps be regarded as a section of the Āl Shibil. Other subdivisions are the Āl Bū Dahaidi' دحيدع, Dahaiyim دهيم, Khālid Lahaibāt لهيبات, Musāgh مصاغ and Zaiyād زياد. The Āl Shibil in the Qadha of Karbala winter around Shifāthah and move in summer into the neighbourhood of Karbala Town. The Āl Shibil of the Karbala and Najaf Qadhas and some of the others, in all about ¼ of the tribe, are nomadic; those visiting the Karbala Qadha are about 500 persons. The tribe are supposed to number about 7,000 souls and to possess about 1,000 horses. They live in tents and huts, cultivate rice and other grains, and breed cattle: some are robbers. In religion Āl Shibil are Shī'ahs, and in politics they are friendly with the Khazā'il and hostile to the 'Anizah and Shammar.

Tribe.	Location.	Remarks.
Shīti شيتي	In the Qadha of Kādhimain about Abu Ghuraib.	The Shīti have no Shaikh of their own and are subject to the Shaikh of the Zōba'.
Shūshtari شوشتري	Chiefly in the Qadha of Kūfah.	Under this name are known about 600 immigrants from Shūshtar and other parts of Southern Persia.
Sindān سندان	In the Qadha of Dīwānīyah upon the Daghārah.	They are Shī'ahs and belong to the Aqra' group (see above). They cultivate and keep cattle.
Sultān (Āl Bū) آل بو سلطان	In the Hillah and Najaf Qadhas generally.	See article Āl Bū Sultān.
Tamīm (Bani) بني تميم	In the neighbourhood of Karbala Town.	These Bani Tamīm, who are not to be confounded with the Bani Tamīm subsection of Karaish section of the Bani Rabī'ah, number about 1,000 souls and are believed to be of the same descent as those of Najd. By religion the Bani Tamīm are Shī'ahs and by occupation agriculturists and cattle-breeders. They live partly in houses and partly in huts called Kūkh.
Taraf (Bani) بني طرف	On the left bank of the Shatt-al-Hindīyah above Tawairij and below Musaiyib.	This tribe, who are settled and engaged chiefly in agriculture and cattle-breeding, are dependent on the Bani Hasan; and by some the Āl Kinānah and Bani Sālah above are treated as among their sections. They are Shī'ahs, quiet and inoffensive, and number about 2,000 souls. The Bani Asad above are their allies.
Tarājamah تراجمه	With the Yasār tribe below, especially in a tract called Bada'at Aswad on the Husainīyah.	The Tarājamah are about 800 persons; Sunnis in religion, and said to be of Shammar origin. They are politically dependent on the Yasār. They cultivate and keep some cattle.
Tufail طفيل	On both banks of the Shatt-al-Hindīyah about Tall Ni·rūd and Kifl, especially in the tract called Harqa on the left bank.	The Tufail are stated to be about 3,000 souls in all: they are said to resemble the Jalīhah. According to some the Āl Bū Sıman above are a section of the Tufail. They are Shī'ahs and depend chiefly on agriculture. In politics they side with the Āl Bū Fatlah.

Tribe.	Location.	Remarks.
Uwaisāt عويسات	In the Qadha of Karbala in the neighbourhood of Musaiyib, and in the Rghailah tract of the Shāmīyah Qadha.	The 'Uwaisāt are Shī'ahs and settled cultivators, numbering about 100 men. Some class them as a section of the Āl Bū Sultān.
Wisāmah وسامه	On the right bank of the Euphrates between Hillah and Dīwānīyah, in the Nahr Shāh Nāhiyah of the Hillah Qadha and partly perhaps in the Qadha of Dīwānīyah.	A Shī'ah tribe who are said to possess about 500 fighting men. They are divided into two main sections, the Wisāmat Hanatah حنطه and the Wisāmat Dughnān دغنان of whom the former live above, and the latter below the village of Shukri شكري. The Wisāmah bear an unenviable reputation as robbers.
Yasār يسار	On the right bank of the Husainīyah canal at Quitah and westwards of Karbala Town in the direction of Razāzah, but chiefly at Mahannāwīyah between Tawairīj and Hillah, in the neighbourhood of Hillah, and on the Harqa reach (left bank of the Shatt-al-Hindīyah).	This is a scattered tribe: they are generally at feud with the Mas'ūd and usually have the better of them. The Yasār are estimated at 8,000 souls. They are exempt from conscription for the Turkish military service.
Zagārīt زگاريت	In the Karbala Sanjāq.	Sunnis. Divided into several sections.
Zaiyād (Āl) آل زياد	In the Qadhas of Dīwānīyah, Samāwah and Shāmīyah.	The Āl Zaiyād are supposed to number about 11,000 persons of whom 9,000 are in the Qadha of Shāmīyah: in religion they are Shī'ahs. They cultivate rice, keep cattle, own about 1,500 horses, and live in tents and huts. Among their sections are the Adaim اديم, Asaidah اصيده, Bahlah بحله, Darāwishah دراوشه and Hassān حسان.
Zaraij (Bani) بني زريج	In the Qadha of Samāwah.	A large, separate Shī'ah tribe of many sections, all settled and engaged in cultivation and cattle-breeding.
Zōba زربع	In the Qadha of Kādhimain.	This tribe sometimes have an encampment on the left bank of the Euphrates at Khān Maqdam. The Sha'ār and Shīti above are subject to the Shaikh of the Zōba'. The number of the Zōba' and their subordinate tribes is large. Some of the Zōba' are Sunnis.

Tribe.	Location.	Remarks.
Zubaid زبيد	Baghdād City, Bghailah, the Daghārah district and Musaiyib are approximately the 4 points within which the Zubaid range, between the Tigris and Euphrates rivers. One subsection is represented in the Najaf Qadha and two are found in the Qadha of Samāwah.	See article Zubaid.
Zubār زبار	In the Qadha of Kādhimain upon the Radhwānīyah canal from the Euphrates.	They are Sunnis.
Zumailāt زميلات	With the Mas'ūd.	A small tribe dependent on the Mas'ūd, of whom some would classify them as a section. They are Shī'ahs, and though settled are much addicted to robbery. Their men are only about 50 in number.

The following general remarks upon the customs of the rural Arab population relate in the first instance to the tribes of the **Euphrates** and Shatt-al-**Hindīyah** country in the neighbourhood of **Karbala** Town, but in some degree they are true of all.

Two stringent articles of the tribal code are those relating to protection and assistance: under the first a person on whose protection another expressly throws himself must receive him into his house and refuse to surrender him even at the cost of his own life; under the second a guest who, after declining proffered food and coffee, is addressed with the phrase "Eat, thy demand shall be satisfied" is entitled to the utmost assistance of his entertainer in the design which he may thereupon unfold. An important feature of the tribal system is the payment of Dīyah دية or blood-money for murders, a matter which the Turkish Government has so far been content to leave in the hands of the Shaikhs. The ordinary price of a man's life ranges from 100 to 1,000 Bashliks say £4 to £40 (English); but among the **Muntafik** it is £37, among the Bani **Mālik** £60, and among the **Khazā'il** is said to rise to as much as 1,000 Majīdīs or about £170. The value of a woman is generally the same as that of a man, but sometimes it is half; the Dīyah of a Saiyid is double that of an ordinary person. If the victim and the murderer belong to different tribes the relations of the victim receive ½ the blood-money, the Shaikhs of his tribe take ⅛, and the remaining ⅜ is divided among his fellow tribesmen at large. Money compensation may be declined, and the heir of a murdered man may demand instead two unmarried girls of his own selection from the murderer's tribe; on their being made over to him the claim to pecuniary compensation is transferred from him to the girls' next-of-kin. For a woman received in marriage a sum of 100 to 1,000 Bashliks, called Mihr مهر, is paid to her father or next-of-kin; the bride is carried in procession to the house of the bridegroom with jumping, singing, dancing and firing of guns,—a display known as Hōsah هوسه; on the next day one of the relatives of the bridegroom spreads a cloth on the ground and exclaims "Shōbāsh", whereupon the guests come forward with their wedding presents. Strange to say the same performance of Hōsah attends the conveyance of a corpse to burial; the Fātihah is then read and mourning continues for from three to five days: the mourners are treated as guests, but they bring with them money or other presents. A pilgrim returned from Makkah holds a reception for three days; his visitors also are his guests, and they too offer gifts.

The clothing of the ordinary countryman consists of a cotton shirt or tunic known as Thōb ثوب, a woollen cloak called 'Aba عباء or Bishit بشت, a Kafiyah كفيه or kerchief, and an 'Aqāl عقال or headband. Milk (Halīb حليب), curds (Libn لبن), bread ('Aish عيش) and dates are the chief articles of diet; the bread is generally of barley kneaded with milk, wheat bread being reserved for exceptional occasions and given to guests. The people inhabit for the most part black tents of hair-cloth, styled Buyūt-ash-Sha'ar بيوت الشعر (houses of hair), or huts of grass, thorns, reeds or date-matting, called Kūkh كوخ. The agriculture of most tribes is shifting and desultory; their cultivation includes wheat, barley, maize, sesame, Māsh, pulse, linseed, vegetables, rice and dates, varying according to the character of the soil and the means of irrigation. Their domestic animals are the camel, buffalo, horse, cow, sheep and goat, the kind of live-stock kept by a particular tribe depending on the nature of its lands; the pastoral portions of most tribes generally wander in the desert in spring, accompanied by their flocks and herds. At times, in certain localities, a considerable number of Arabs earn a livelihood by digging liquorice root for exportation to America: some of these belong to the Fallāhīn or cultivating tribes, and certain of the semi-settled and Bedouin tribes also allow their women to earn money by thi occupation. The more nomadic tribes are incorrigibly lazy and averse to every sort of manual labour.

Most of the tribes, except perhaps on the lower **Euphrates** and along the margin of the **Shāmīyah** Desert are now under the effective control of the Turkish Government; but they are managed chiefly through their Shaikhs who still, with the countenance and support of the Ottoman officials, exercise considerable executive authority. A number of the semi-nomadic cultivating tribes now abstain from settling down only in order to escape liability to conscription for military service and administrative interference with their life. On the side towards the **Shāmīyah** Desert the fear of Bedouin raids has an appreciable effect in preventing the extension of agriculture.

Arms.—The armament of several of the tribes to which special articles have been devoted is noticed in those articles.

To speak generally, the tribes nearest to the Persian Gulf are the most heavily armed with modern rifles; this is probably due to the facilities which at present exist for secret importation into lower 'Iraq, either from **Kuwait** by way of the desert or from **Masqat** and **Muhammareh** by sea and river. A possible new source of supply has lately come into existence in the shape of rifle-factories worked by **Kurds** at Kirind in Persian Kurdistān: the parallel with the Indo-Afghan frontier which this suggests is completed by the occasional loss by Turkish troops of rifles which pass into the hands of the tribesmen, especially of the Bani **Lām**. The tribes in the **Basrah** Wilāyat have probably as many rifles as they can afford to purchase; but the Bani **Rabī'ah** about **Kūt-al-Amārah** have fewer, and the **Zubaid** and **Shammar Tōqah**, who lie above them, are still comparatively unprovided with arms of precision. The favourite pattern of breech-loader in 'Iraq is the Martini, but there is also a sprinkling of Mausers. Where breech-loaders are deficient, the favourite substitute is a double-barrelled muzzle-loading gun, and this is the weapon most in evidence at the present day between **Baghdād** and **Karbala** and in the neighbourhood of **Karbala** and **Hillah**. A Turkish law strictly regulates the carrying of firearms in 'Iraq, but it is not properly enforced; it is, in fact, little more at present than an engine of official extortion.

Swords are still worn by some tribes; and the Bedouin lance, 12 feet in length with a broad and formidable blade, is still common in the desert and may be seen even upon the banks of the rivers. Curved daggers about a foot in length, double-edged and very sharp at the point, are frequently carried, particularly by Persians. The weapon of the herd-boy and of the very poor is a kind of knobkerry, consisting of a stick about 2 feet long on one end of which is fixed a hard and heavy lump of bitumen.

The ordinary tribes measure their strength in rifles and men, distinguishing the latter as mounted or unmounted; their more aquatic brethren keep account chiefly of rifles and of boats or canoes.

Religion.—The country population is almost universally Shī'ah except in the outlying north-western districts of the Sanjāq of Baghdād, and Shī'ism may accordingly be styled the religion of 'Irāq. The principal exceptions to the rule in our list of tribes are the **'Anizah, Dhafīr** and **Shammar** who can hardly be said to belong to the tract; the Sa'īdūn or ruling section of the **Muntafik**; two sections (in part only) of the **Zubaid**, and a majority of the Janābiyīn: these and a few other petty clans are Sunnis.

The case of town populations is somewhat different, but not sufficiently so to reverse the broad statement that 'Irāq is a Shī'ah country. In the Baghdād Wilāyat only about $\frac{1}{3}$ of the total population appears to be Sunni, and the Sunnis are confined almost entirely to the Sanjāq of Baghdād, a large number of them belonging to **Baghdād** City itself. In the Basrah Wilāyat the proportion of Sunnis is only about $\frac{1}{13}$, and only a very few are found outside the towns of **Basrah** and **Zubair**.

The chief features and institutions of Islām in 'Irāq are described in the special Appendix of this Gazetteer which deals with religions.

The Muhammadans of 'Irāq generally are ignorant and uninformed in their own religion, but not fanatical: neither statement however applies to the inhabitants of the religious centres of **Karbala, Najaf,** and **Kādhimain**. Superstitions are universal, especially regarding the evil eye, charms against which are worn even by adults and are placed upon children and young or pet animals, besides being affixed to houses, sailing-boats and even Quffahs or coracles.

The principal religions of 'Irāq, other than the Muhammadan, are the Jewish and the Christian. Jews are numerous, but Christianity numbers only a few thousand adherents distributed among the following sects, whom we mention in their probable order of numerical importance,—Gregorian Armenian Church, Chaldæan Catholic Church, Syrian Catholic Church, Roman Catholic Church, Catholic Armenian Church, various Protestant Churches, Greek Church.

Language.—The prevailing language of 'Irāq is Arabic of a not very pure type. The official classes however speak and write Turkish, and the superior officers sent from European Turkey often do not understand Arabic. Persian is largely spoken in the towns, especially at **Karbala**, **Najaf**, and **Kādhimain**, where it is generally understood. Kurdish is spoken by the **Kurds**, Hebrew by the Jews, and a language of their own—perhaps Syriac—by the **Sabians**. The most diffused European language at **Baghdād** is French, and after it English; the use of English, however, is, on the increase at **Baghdād**, and at **Basrah** English has already distanced all European competitors.

Agriculture.—Cultivation, as already remarked, is restricted to a comparatively small fraction of the total area of 'Irāq: with a proper system of canal irrigation it might be immensely extended. The backward condition of agriculture is attributable chiefly to want of irrigation in some parts and to want of drainage in others, but also in a certain degree to scarcity of labour, and on the verge of the desert to the insecurity produced by Bedouin raids. It has been estimated that at present not more than one-tenth of the Baghdād Wilāyat is cultivated, and even that not continuously nor the whole of it in the same year; and some authorities would even place the proportion of productive lands throughout 'Irāq as low as 3 per cent. of the whole.

There are two harvests in 'Irāq, the spring or Shitwi شتوي and the autumn or Saifi صيفي.

The principal spring crops are wheat, barley, beans, and Hurtumān هرطمان. Wheat and barley are sown on plains that have a moderate supply of water, either before or after Jawairīd جويرد, the name given by the Arab cultivator to "the first cold days of winter, when the trees lose their last leaves;" the earlier sowings, called Hirfi هرفي, are made in September and October, the later, called Athli اثلي, between November and the end of January. The wheat and barley harvest begins in April; the grain after being dried in stacks in the sun is threshed by being trodden with buffaloes or cows, except near the towns where a threshing-machine (Jarjar جرجر) of native (Mūsal) manufacture is sometimes used. In an average year the return for seed sown is about 8 or 10-fold; and the 'Alwas علوى or grain-stores which are a feature of many country-towns, along with the statistics of the export trade attest a frequent surplus of cereals in some districts. The best wheat and barley lands probably are (or till recently were) those about **Hillah** on both sides of the **Euphrates**, the surplus produce of which is sent down the

Euphrates in native boats to **Basrah** for local consumption or shipment. The neighbourhood of **'Amārah** Town also is becoming known for its wheat and barley. Beans are planted at the end of September and are harvested in the beginning of April, but green beans appear in the market about the middle of February. Beans are of various kinds, including the broad, French, and haricot varieties; and large quantities of them, when dried, are exported to Indian ports and to Jiddah on the Red Sea. Hurtumān, described as a sort of oats, is sown in January and reaped about the end of May.

The autumn crops are rice, called Timn تمن or Shilib شلب, maize or Idhrah, sesame, a millet known as Dukhn دخن, Māsh ماش, (a lentil), Lūbiyah (a kidney pea) لوبيه, and, of course, dates: some cotton also is grown, but chiefly outside the limits with which we have to deal. Rice is the chief item of the autumn harvest and in the **Baghdād** market is of 4 principal kinds: the best are Nakkāzah نكازه and 'Ambarbū عمبربو, the second of these being a peculiarly scented variety esteemed by Indians and Persians; the third is Shimbah شمبه, which is the commonest kind; and the fourth is Huwaizāwi حويزاوي, a cheap, reddish rice consumed by the poorer classes. Rice straw, called Būh بوه, is utilised as fodder for cattle. The principal rice grounds are on the Shatt-al-**Hindīyah** between **Tawairīj** and **Kūfah**, especially about Hor-ad-Dukhn; on the **Daghārah** canal; in the Qadhas of **Shāmīyah** and **Samāwah**; and in the part of the country adjoining **'Amārah** Town. Idhrah is sown in March and reaped in August or September. Sesame is grown on plains which are inundated by the rivers in their rise and dry up again in the course of the summer, and it is seen also along the banks of creeks from the Shatt-al-**'Arab** in the **Basrah** Qadha; most of it is pressed for oil, which is used in cooking and for lighting purposes, but some is roasted and eaten with bread, and some is used in the manufacture of sweetmeats or Halāwah حلاوه. Dukhn, sown at the end of March and reaped in August or September, is cultivated on a large scale upon the **Tigris** and even more upon the **Euphrates**: some is used locally as food for cattle and poultry or is mixed with wheat to make bread: the remainder is exported by way of **Basrah**. Māsh is of two kinds, green and black, both of which are sown in the end of June; the green ripens at the middle or end of September, the black in the beginning of November. Māsh is cultivated on damp, sandy plains and does not require watering; the natives mix it with rice to make soup, and a large quantity is exported to India. Lūbiyah is sown in June and harvested in October; it grows on river banks and on plains inundated by the rise of the rivers; it begins to be sold green as a vegetable in June or July; when dry it is assorted into red and white, the red kind being the cheaper. Lūbiyah is locally consumed, but some is exported to India. The lentil proper or 'Adas عدس of 'Irāq is inferior.

Dates are of many sorts, and the immense plantations which fringe the banks of the Shatt-al-'**Arab** below and above **Basrah** Town are probably the finest in the world. There is also a noble stretch of date groves some 30 miles in length upon both sides of the (old) bed of the **Euphrates** above and below **Hillah** Town, but these are declining in consequence of the diversion of the **Euphrates** into the Shatt-al-**Hindīyah**. Another large date growing tract is at **Shifāthah** to the west of **Karbala**. Good date plantations exist also around **Baghdād** City, **Karbala** Town and **Kūfah** and at other places. The subject of date culture and the date trade is more fully dealt with elsewhere in a special Appendix of the Gazetteer. Common fruits are water-melons, marsh-melons, pomegranates, oranges (in the Baghdād Wilāyat), sweet and sour limes, apricots, quinces and grapes; almonds, figs, olives, citrons, apples, nectarines and peaches grow—the citrons at **Hillah** and the peaches at **Bghailah** among other places—but the last three are of poor quality; there are also mulberries at **Karbala** and upon the course of the **Diyālah**.

Among the vegetables of 'Irāq are onions, radishes, beetroot, garlic, cucumbers, cabbage, cauliflower, turnips, carrots, tomatoes, artichokes, ladies' fingers, brinjols, lettuce, cress, pumpkins of 3 kinds and potatoes; but garlic, though used in great quantities, is imported to a larger extent than it is grown, mostly from Persia, while potatoes are of recent introduction and have not yet come into general use except among the well-to-do.

Tobacco, known as Dukhān دخان or Tutun تتن, which is a state monopoly, is grown in certain localities only, principally about **Karbala** and **Najaf**, but also to the north-east of **Baghdād** City in the **Diyālah** valley.

In the Baghdād Wilāyat cultivated lands are classified according to the means of irrigation: thus we have, though rarely, lands watered only by rainfall and called Daim ديم; lands watered by lifts with "pulleys" and therefore called Bakrah بكرة or, if the means of irrigation is a bucket, Saqi سقي; finally we have lands irrigated from canals and known as Saih سيح. Marshes and drying pools, when cultivated, are styled Kibis كبس (pronounced Chibis); and land moistened by little runnels, such as are used in rice fields, is known as Chaltīq چلتيق.

Canals are numerous, but they are seldom in good working order. A number of them are specified by name in the articles on the rivers **Euphrates, Tigris**, and Shatt-al-**Hindīyah**; the most important, to which separate articles are devoted, are the **Daghārah, Husainīyah**, and **Jahālah**. Water-lifts are generally used for date gardens, and some arable land also along the banks of the two great rivers is irrigated by their means. Lifts are of two kinds, the Karad كرد (pronounced Charad) and the Na'ūr ناعور. In the Karad the water is hoisted in a camel-skin bucket, termed Dalu دلو, by means of a rope which passes over a pulley; while in the Na'ūr it is raised by a series of buckets slung from a revolving wheel: the Na'ūr is of comparatively recent introduction and is cheaper in working than the Karad but not so effectual: both kinds of apparatus are actuated by animal power, and both have their counterparts in India. In the neighbourhood of **Baghdād** City centrifugal pumps worked by oil engines have been introduced and promise to become popular. The easiest and most natural irrigation of all is in the Shatt-al-'**Arab** region where the sea-tides raise the fresh water of the river, twice in the 24 hours, almost to the level of the cultivated land.

The proportions in which the produce that remains after Government has taken its share is divided between the Mallāk مالك or proprietor and the Fallāh فلاح or actual cultivator vary with the class of land and are sometimes not the same in the spring as in the autumn harvest. The grain for seed is sometimes supplied by the owner, and in other cases provided by the cultivator.

Livestock.—Domestic animals are cattle everywhere; buffaloes in the marshy tracts, which are of an excellent class but are said to suffer from the cold in winter and from the attacks of insects in summer; fat-tailed sheep yielding mutton almost equal to that of Europe; donkeys of average, and mules of good quality; camels, a proportion of which are very light in colour; and horses, which have a high reputation but are not equal to those of **Najd** or Syria. Some good horses, however, are reared in the **Hillah** and **Dīwānīyah** Qadhas: the best cattle are those of the tract about '**Amārah** Town. The Bani **Lām** tribe are celebrated for their horses, camels and sheep, and the Āl Bū **Muhammad** for their buffaloes. Tame birds are pigeons, fowls, turkeys, ducks and geese; the turkeys and fowls are exceptionally fine.

Trade generally.—During the last 20 years a substantial, and on the whole steady, increase has been observable in the volume of trade in 'Irāq;

and it still, apparently, continues. It is attributed to the spread of what has been styled "comparative civilisation" in the country itself; and to a larger demand in Persia for the "comparative luxuries" which that country obtaines through 'Irāq.

Bombay is felt, throughout 'Irāq, to be the nearest great centre of commerce and civilisation; and since the recent institution of a rapid steamer service to India it is a common though not strictly accurate remark among natives, that Bombay and **Baghdād** are equally distant from **Basrah**. Two facts in regard to the trade of 'Irāq should be clearly realised at the outset: first that it consists to a large extent merely of a transit trade between the Persian Gulf and Western Persia, secondly that it has only one real centre, namely, **Baghdād**. The position of unique importance occupied by **Baghdād** as a point of divergence and convergence in transit, in foreign, and even to some extent in internal trade is indeed remarkable; no less so is its mercantile predominance over **Basrah**, which, but for a local trade in dates and grain, would be little more than the seaport of **Baghdād**. The hides of **'Amārah** often ascend the **Tigris** to be pressed at **Baghdād** for shipment to Europe, and the retail traders of **Basrah** itself obtain quantities of European goods, especially piece-goods, from the wholesale merchants of **Baghdād**. On the **Tigris** from **'Amārah** town upwards, and in the **Euphrates** valley above **Kūfah** and its neighbourhood, most commercial dealings are with **Baghdād**. Even the remainder of 'Irāq, though nearer to **Basrah**, is partially served from **Baghdād** through **Basrah** and other places. The commercial influence of **Baghdād** balances at Mūsal with that of Aleppo; and the whole of Kurdistān and the parts of Western Persia about Kirmānshāh and Hamadān are dependent on **Baghdād** for their supply of foreign goods. As **Basrah** is the limit of ocean-borne traffic, so **Baghdād** marks the point where carriage by river, against the stream, ceases to be profitable; and, except for rafts which descend the **Tigris** from Mūsal to **Baghdād**, all commerce to the east, north, and west of the capital is carried on by mule or camel caravan.

From a political point of view imports by sea and, in a lesser degree, exports by sea are the most important features of the trade of 'Irāq; but, in order to understand the basis on which ocean-borne imports and exports rest, we must first examine the questions of internal trade, local manufactures and imports by land.

Internal trade.—The functions of **Baghdād** are, in relation to internal trade, comparatively restricted; but it is the principal centre for the distribution of cotton piece-goods in the whole country. Moreover, it sends to Mūsal sugar, coffee, spices, twists, window-glass and metals,—but not piece-goods, which the people of Mūsal procure mostly through Syria,—and receives in return the best of the 'Awwāsi عوّاسي or 'Awaisi عويسي * wool and the whole of the mohair and gall-nuts which constitute important items of the general export trade, besides oak and walnut wood, partly for exportation, and beams and rafters of poplar for local use. Ba'qūbah is dependent on **Baghdād** for manufactured articles, and sends much fruit and firewood to **Baghdād** by way of the **Diyālah** river.

The chief centres of internal trade in the west are **Karbala**, which imports piece-goods, sugar, kerosine, Indian spices, tea, Persian medicines and Persian fruit, and exports dates, consecrated objects, skins, wool and inferior tobacco; **Musaiyib**, which takes piece-goods and sends away wheat and barley; **Tawairīj**, which buys piece-goods and sells wheat, barley and dates; **Hillah**, which imports piece-goods, sugar and coffee on a large scale and exports wheat, barley, ghi, dates, sheep-skins and goat-skins on a still larger; finally **Najaf**, which receives large quantities of piece-goods, sugar, tea and Indian spices and disposes of lambskins and 'Abas. All of these receive their piece-goods from **Baghdād**, and the general trade of **Musaiyib** and **Karbala** seems to be mostly with **Baghdād**; but **Hillah** and probably **Najaf** receive most of their goods (other than piece-goods) by way of the **Euphrates** *viâ* **Kūfah**, and **Hillah** exports its dates direct to **Basrah**. It is from these western districts that the capital draws a large part of its supplies of wheat and rice.

On the **Tigris** below **Baghdād**, the towns of **Kūt-al-Amārah** and **'Ali-al-Gharbi** are the principal seats of the trade with Southern Kurdistān; hereabouts many **Kurds** are settled, and **Kurds** from the Persian frontier come in to satisfy their wants, bringing with them ghi, skins, wool, galls, gum, aniseed, pistachios, walnuts and other nuts, in all of which there is a considerable trade. **Kūt-al-Amārah** deals chiefly with the Kurdish towns of Badrah بدرة and Jassān جسّان, which lie within the Turkish frontier but at a distance from the **Tigris**; at **'Ali-al-Gharbi** wheat and barley from the surrounding plains are accumulated. **'Amārah** Town is to some extent a centre of the Kurdish trade, but it is also a market

---

* 'Awwāsi wool is obtained from a crossbreed between the Arab or plain-reared sheep and the Kurdish or hill-reared sheep. Arab wool is fine and curly, Kurdish is coarse and straight; while 'Awwāsi, which is considered to form a class by itself, is intermediate between the two.

for the produce of the surrounding Bani **Lām** and **Āl Bū Muhammad** tribes; consequently we find it to be a considerable emporium of ghi, hides, wool, rice and, to some extent, of barley and wheat. **Qal'at Sālih**, further down the **Tigris**, is a centre of the rice trade; and dates, wheat, barley, rice, straw, date-mats and reed-mats can all be procured at **Qūrnah**, though the trade of that place is not so large as might from its position have been expected.

Camels for export are mostly collected at **Samāwah**, **Dīwānīyah** and **Najaf**; sheep, cattle and buffaloes in the neighbourhood of **'Amārah**.

The Shī'ah pilgrimages to **Karbala**, **Najaf**, **Kādhimain** and Sāmarrah are an important factor in the internal trade of 'Irāq; they are the cause, for example, of an immense demand for forage at **Kādhimain**, where most of the pilgrims leave their riding-animals for several days during their absence at **Karbala** and **Najaf**, and of the existence at the same town of a good supply of carpets brought by the pilgrims from Persia. The trade in sacred objects and souvenirs, such as Turbahs (praying-tablets made of the earth of the holy places) and winding sheets stamped with verses from the Qurān, which is of some value at **Karbala** and **Najaf**, likewise depends upon the custom of pilgrims.

There are no wholesale carriers or forwarding agents in the country, and transport must be specially engaged whenever merchandise is to be moved. Additional light will be cast upon internal trade by the remarks on local manufactures which follow.

Manufactures.—**Baghdād** City is the chief seat of industries, but these are not mechanical; in fact, apart from a private ice-factory, the Army Clothing Factory and Army Flour Mills of the Turkish Government, and two out of several wool-presses, the town cannot boast of any machinery driven by steam. At or near **Basrah** Town there are two British wool-presses and one American liquorice-press, also a soda-water factory owned by an Indian and a flour mill and an ice-machine belonging to a Jew. At **'Amārah** Town there is one British wool-press; and at **Kūt-al-Amārah** are one British-owned and one native-owned wool-press.

An important element in some of the most characteristic manufactures of **Baghdād** is a kind of silken thread, called Sha'ri شعري; the true Sha'ri is said to be a vegetable product, but Assam or "Moga" silk, imported from Calcutta, is also used and is described as Sha'ri. At **Baghdād** silk thread is woven into a stuff called Aghabāni اغباني, from which light summer clothing, especially 'Abas, is manufactured

Silk is also used to embroider turbans, girdles, tablecloths, curtains and counterpanes in a special style; the art is almost entirely confined to Jewesses and a few female Christians. Long pieces embroidered with silk are called Kashīdah كشيده and are used as headdresses, square pieces are known as Charqand چرقند: many of the embroidered turbans are exported to Northern Africa. Striped cotton piece-goods are manufactured at **Baghdād**, in imitation of those of Damascus, and are made into Zabūns زبون or Antāris انتاري, that is into the long body-garments worn by men, and into long waistcoats or jackets called Duglahs دگله: other materials locally woven and applied to the same use are Ālajah آلجه, a cotton fabric, and Qutni قطني, a mixture of silk and wool. Women's veils, called Yāshmaq ياشمق, women's shawls or sheets, called Chārshāfs چارشاف, and Izārs ازار are made at **Baghdād**; also ladies' ornamental belts and kerchiefs of various kinds in silk, cotton and wool; the handkerchiefs for ladies are embroidered with silk, and the kerchiefs for Arabs, called Kafīyahs كفيه and generally fringed or tasselled, are dearer but more durable than those of Manchester make. Coarse cotton cloth for the wear of the poorer classes is made at **Baghdād,** also canvas for tents; but tents of Indian or Persian material are preferred by the well-to-do, who use them for camping out in spring and autumn. There is some silk-weaving at **Kādhimain**, and the silk-embroidered handkerchiefs of that town have a sale in Algeria and Tunis. Harāmāt حرامات or woollen rugs and Zull زل or coarse carpets are manufactured at **Kūt-al-Amārah**, and rough Kurdish carpets, both cheap and durable, at **'Amārah** Town: these close the list of textiles.

'Abas or Arab cloaks are manufactured at **Baghdād** City, at the towns of **Kādhimain, Karbala, Najaf, 'Amārah, Sūq-ash-Shuyūkh** and at the village of **Qūrnah**: those of **Baghdād** are sometimes of silk, but generally of wool, with gold or silk embroidery; those of **Najaf** are frequently of silk embroidered with gold; those of **'Amārah** are in great demand at **Baghdād** and in the neighbourhood; those of **Qūrnah**, called Khāchīyah خاچيه or Batīyah بتيه are famous for their lightness and can, it is said, be passed through a finger-ring.

Jewellers are found in all the principal towns, and the **Sabian** gold and silver-smiths of **Sūq-ash-Shuyūkh, Shatrat-al-Muntafik** and **'Amārah** Towns are among the best; the jewellers of **'Amārah** have an art, possibly peculiar to themselves, of inlaying silver with antimony. Combs and small objects of ivory, wood and tortoise-shell are made at **Kādhimain**, chiefly by Persians; and filigree work in the precious metals and elaborate engraving on mother-of-pearl are executed at **Karbala**.

More solid industries are those of tanning and working leather, which have their principal seat in **Baghdād** City and its suburbs. The tanneries are chiefly at **Mu'adhdham**, where a large number of hands are employed in 40 establishments and 5,000 sheepskins and goat-skins are turned out every week. At **Kādhimain** are similar tanneries on a smaller scale. The leather, though only rough-tanned, finds a ready sale in Europe. From local leather are made, at **Baghdād** and in **Mu'adhdham**, the Yamanīs يمني or red and yellow shoes worn by Arabs and old-fashioned Baghdādīs of other classes; also the slippers called Pāpūsh پاپوش or Babuj بابج and a kind of boot known as Masht مشت, the latter being a kind of yellow top-boot which is worn by old Muhammadan females.

The **Baghdād** coppersmiths are experts in their craft and make boilers, kettles, coffee-pots and large copper dishes.

House-building is understood in many places, and the Juss جصّ or gypsum-mortar commonly used is prepared in quantities at **Mahmūdīyah** between **Baghdād** and **Musaiyib** and at **Zubair** near **Basrah**. Encaustic or Kāshi كاشي tiles are made by Persians, mostly at **Karbala**, but also at **Kādhimain** and **Baghdād**. At **Kādhimain** are numerous good Persian painters and decorators. The clay earthenware of **Baghdād**, very light-coloured and porous, is exported to **Basrah** and other nearer places; the commonest articles are water-coolers and filters called Hubbs حبّ, often of large size, and Jarrahs جرّه or goblets.

Boats and canoes are built at **Qal'at Sālih, Shatrat-al-Muntafik, Sūq-ash-Shuyūkh** and other places.

Much of the 'Araq عرق or native spirit consumed in the Baghdād and Basrah districts is distilled at **Qarārah** on the **Tigris** three miles from **Baghdād**; the basis of the spirit is derived from Zahdi dates; aniseed, orange-peel, mastic and cardamoms are other ingredients: there is also some distillation at **Hillah**, but the produce is said to be inferior.

Import trade by land.—The import trade by land is chiefly on the Persian side, whence gums, opium and carpets are brought in some quantity, also fruit including apples and pears. Wheat also is obtained from Persia for local consumption in years of scarcity, but not generally, except at **Basrah**, for exportation abroad. The most valuable of the imported gums is gum tragacanth, which is handled in flake, not in powder, and is used for the best varnishes; there is no gum Arabic, but a considerable trade is done in another gum which exudes from the bitter-almond tree and was believed, until a few years ago, to be insoluble. Samagh صمغ is the generic name in Arabic of all tree-gums. A number of the articles, already enumerated in a previous paragraph, which reach **Baghdād** from Mūsal are actually of Persian origin. Some imports which are received partly by land and partly by sea are mentioned in the paragraph below on imports by sea.

External trade generally.—With the agricultural resources, local manufactures and overland imports of the country before us, we are now in a position to approach the subject of sea-borne imports and of all kinds of exports; and, in view of the smallness of the cultivated area and of the trivial character of the manufactured articles, we shall not be surprised to find that the foreign trade of 'Irāq is of moderate dimensions and that the land-borne traffic upon the Persian side is one of its most important items—in other words, that the trade of the country is largely a transit trade. Imports and exports at the port of **Basrah** are the measure of the foreign trade, goods for the interior being all included in the shipping returns of that place; consular statistics, however, in 'Irāq have to be compiled without access to reliable returns, and it is sometimes impossible to reconcile the figures for **Basrah** with those for **Baghdād** which they are supposed to include.

Import trade by sea.—The total annual value of goods imported by sea may be taken at £1,300,000 sterling, of which nearly a half represents cotton-goods from Great Britain alone. The trade in cottons is chiefly in the hands of the Jews, some of whom have agents, generally near relations, in London or Manchester: at **Baghdād** cottons probably amount to as much as three-fourths of the total imports in value. The trade in white and grey shirtings is practically a Jewish monopoly, but about one-fourth of the prints are imported by British firms. Next in order of value after cotton goods is sugar, both loaf and crushed: some is from Belgium, Austria and Egypt, but the great bulk of it is from France which also supplies (but in small quantities) leather for the manufacture of European boots and shoes, silk goods, satins, gold brocade, broadcloth, brandy and Bordeaux wine. The Oriental Christian merchants of **Baghdād** mostly trade with France, as the Jews do with England; but there is not in this any basis of political sentiment. Wood and timber, coffee, gunnies, metals, yarn and twist, spices, kerosene and tobacco are the principal remaining imports. The imported wood is mostly for date-boxes and comes from Austria; but bastard teak, locally called Jāwi

جاري, is imported by an Indian firm at **Basrah** from Calicut and Singapore: nearly all building-timber, planks and charcoal are from Indian ports, the charcoal being from Karāchi, but part of the building timber is from Russia, Sweden and Norway. Coffee is principally Brazilian; but India supplies the gunnies, the cotton yarn and twist and the spices. Indigo also is brought in considerable, and tea in increasing, quantities from British India: about ¾ of the tea is now from India. Iron, the metal most imported, is of British origin. Kerosene is from Russia, but only part of it is received through a Russian medium: the Indian firm already mentioned imports some kerosene direct from Batoum. America, whose trade with 'Irāq is every year greater, sends cheap blankets, bed-sheets and watches, and nearly all the stockings now sold in the **Baghdād** bazaar are of American manufacture, but the quantity of these last is small. Germany and Austria supply cheap fancy articles, fezes, crockery, low-priced clothes sometimes second-hand, penknives, articles of German silver, sewing-machines and all sorts of haberdashery: the best candles are from Holland, and the best window glass is from Belgium.

There are, in addition to the sea-imports just enumerated and to the land-imports from Persia already specified, some imports, partly by sea and partly by land, from other provinces of the Ottoman empire; goods from Constantinople, however, are now received chiefly by sea, and those from Aleppo largely so *viâ* Alexandretta. Such imports are blankets, flannels, fezes, bath-towels, ladies' shoes, slippers, knives and fancy articles from Constantinople, and native soap, rope, pistachios, silk and gold-thread from Aleppo and Damascus; Aleppo to a greater extent than **Baghdād** supplies the cotton piece-goods of Mūsal. Silk for embroidery is from Syria and Northern Persia, except the "Moga" silk from the East which is so largely used in **Baghdād** embroideries.

It is estimated by experts that no less than three-fourths of the foreign goods imported into **Baghdād** are re-exported to Persia.

Export trade by sea.—Dates are the most valuable export by sea, and in 1905 those despatched by sea from **Basrah** were estimated to be worth £345,184; most are grown in the **Basrah** neighbourhood and sent to England and America, but some Zahdi زهدي and Kursi كرسي dates from the plantations about **Baghdād** are consigned, packed in skins, to Egypt, the Levant and the Black Sea ports. Wheat and barley taken together generally hold the second place, barley, much of which is from the Shatt-al-**Gharāf** and 'Amārah districts, greatly predominating over wheat in spite of the fact that wheat is the only grain which leaves **Baghdād** for abroad. Wool and mohair, Persian opium, seeds (including Idhrah, Dukhn, Mash, sesame, linseed and hemp), Kurdistān gall-nuts, skins and hides, succeed grain and follow one other in order of importance; next are horses, and Persian carpets, the last mostly through **Baghdād**; then gum, then liquorice-root. Other exports are intestines, to be utilised as sausage-skins, and dogs' dung which goes to Austria for use in the tanning of fine leather. There is a small trade with Bombay in Persian raisins, and **Baghdād** oranges and pomegranates have been exported experimentally to the same place. Ghi from **'Amārah** and other places reaches Bombay, the Red Sea and even the ports of the Levant. Maize, colocynth and almond-kernels, the last for the manufacture of prussic acid, are also exported to a limited extent.

The destination of the wool is London, Marseilles, America, Germany or Austria; of the gall-nuts London, Bombay or Persia; of the gums London, Marseilles and sometimes New York and Austria; of the wheat the Red Sea coast and London; of the opium Hongkong, except a little which goes to Singapore and Europe; of the skins and hides Constantinople, France and the United Kingdom. Some walnut wood is sent to Marseilles, and 85 per cent. of the liquorice-root is taken by America, where the liquorice-paste with which American tobacco is sweetened is manufactured from it. The liquorice business in 'Iraq is now managed by an agency of the American Tobacco Trust. The root is collected in the winter months when it contains most juice and, after being weighed and cured at the receiving stations, is forwarded to **Basrah** where it is baled by hydraulic power. The value at **Basrah** at the time of export is about £6 a ton and the average quantity of the root exported is at present about 4,000 tons per annum. The trade in horses to India is important though not very large; the number shipped from **Basrah** in 1905 was 2,262. Persian carpets and hides and dates find a market at Constantinople; and Persian carpets, "Moga" silk articles, ladies' Izārs, dates and spices in Syria: the spices are largely Indian. Most of the Persian carpets, however, go to America and London, and high prices are realised in those markets for old ones; new carpets are not appreciated as they frequently owe their colours to aniline dyes. The total value of the exports by sea is about £1,300,000 annually, or the same as the value of the sea-borne imports.

Export trade by land.—The wares for places on the Mediterranean are sent partly by sea and partly by caravan, but one of the principal exports,—that of camels, buffaloes, cattle and sheep,—takes place entirely overland: the camels are collected at **Samāwah** and **Najaf**, and the other animals are assembled mostly in the neighbourhood of **'Amārah** Town whence they are marched in huge droves up the **Tigris** to Mūsal and from there across country to Aleppo and Alexandria, the agents of the purchasers accompanying them to settle the difficulties of the road. The ultimate destination of the camels and part of the cattle is Egypt : the remainder of the cattle and the sheep are disposed of in Syria.

The trade of 'Irāq with **Najd** is not what it once was, owing to the competition of the **Kuwait** and **Hasa** routes, by which Central Arabia now receives a large proportion of the manufactured goods that it consumes; but of late years the disturbances in **Najd** and Jabal **Shammar** and the insecurity of the more southern roads have brought about a certain revival by which **Samāwah** and other towns on the lower **Euphrates** have benefited; and occasional visits of the Hadrah, حضرة also called Risālah رسالة, a commercial and purchasing mission from Jabal **Shammar** to **Najaf**, have not ceased. At some places on the western frontier, such as **Shifāthah**, there is a periodical Bedouin fair or market known as Musābalah مبابلة . Formerly there was a much frequented route from **Basrah** to **Najd** on which the first stage was **Zubair** Town. The exports to **Najd** are few and simple, consisting chiefly of cotton-prints for clothing, cotton and silk handkerchiefs for head-coverings, sugar, coffee, enamelled iron ware and in some years grain, the last from **Karbala** and **Najaf**.

The outward trade to Persia is, as already pointed out, simply a later phase—and an important one—of the inward trade to **Baghdād**.

Shipping and river traffic.—In 1905 the number of ocean steamers that entered the port of **Basrah** was 169 with a net tonnage of 189,440, and of these 163 were British. In the same year sailing-vessels numbered 618 and had a net tonnage of 37,731 ; 120 of these were under the British flag, and the remainder were nearly all Persian, Turkish or Arabian. The greater share of the **Tigris** traffic, so far as carried by steamer, falls to the Dāirat-as-Sanīyah, which has 6 boats, and the remainder to the (British) Euphrates and Tigris Steam Navigation Company, who are not allowed by the Turkish Government to employ more than 2 steamers.* Cotton and sugar upwards, and wool, carpets, skins, mohair, gum, opium and gall-nuts downwards are chiefly conveyed by steamer; but other commodities, such as grain and liquorice, which are either more bulky or have to be picked up at many points, travel by native boat.

---

* They have now permission to use three (1908).

Trade customs, credit, and commercial system.—A short statement of mercantile customs and of the manner in which trade generally is conducted will not be out of place here: information regarding import, transit and export duties will be found under the head of taxation below.

At **Baghdād,** the trade of which is typical of the trade of the country, all weighments, except of consignments between principal and agent or *vice versâ,* are made by public weighmen. These individuals, called Qabānchis قبانچي, visit the premises where their services are required and receive fees from the merchants who employ them; their testimony is supposed to prevent subsequent disputes. Another universal institution is Dallālah or agency; and without the presence of a Dallāl دلّال, at least on one of the sides, no bargain is ever struck. The principals may be in accord before they meet, but the agreement is only concluded by a Dallāl's declaration of the fact, which he generally accompanies by an emphatic gesture; the commission of the Dallāl runs from ½ to 1 per cent. Even European merchants at **Baghdād** find it advisable to defer to these two local customs: at **Basrah,** however, there are no Qabānchis.

Cash transactions are uncommon in the course of internal trade, a reduction being expected if cash is paid, and the usual method of settlement is by Kambiyālah * كمبيالة, a species of bill or promissory note issued between parties residing in the same place, maturing in from three months to two years and perfectly negotiable when backed by a good name; or, when the parties belong to different places, by an ordinary inland bill or by sending specie insured through the Turkish Post Office, for there is no system of money orders in 'Irāq; but the last mentioned method is not much in vogue. In foreign trade, orders for goods are sent direct to Europe by the larger firms only, and small merchants generally avail themselves of the credit of the larger to obtain European goods. This is arranged by each of the smaller merchants paying a percentage against his order to the patron; the patron then obtains and pays for the whole consignment, and on its arrival distributes the goods to the clients who ordered them, — at **Baghdād** sometimes on credit, but at **Basrah** only on receiving cash payment or a Kambiyālah. Some merchants who are without credit in Europe obtain goods thence direct by causing the bill of lading to be sent to a bank or well-known firm from whose custody they release it by paying the value of

---

* The word Kambiyālah is used in Egyptian Arabic also. It is derived no doubt from the Italian *cambiale,* a bill of exchange.

the goods according to the invoice. Payment for goods exported to Europe is obtained by the larger merchants through their own agencies there, but they generally draw against the bills of lading to the extent of three-fourths, the balance of the transaction being settled afterwards. Among the smaller merchants a custom prevails of consigning goods to commission agents in Europe and drawing against the bill of lading as soon as the goods are shipped; but this is a risky method and users of it have frequently been ruined by the failure of their consignments, owing to a fall in values, to realise prices equal to the amounts drawn against them. Small merchants also sometimes obtain three-fourths of the value of their bills of lading from the shippers, to whom they make them over, and a complete settlement takes place later between the parties.

A European firm at **Baghdād** is generally engaged in both import and export trade and conducts its business through native correspondents, each of whom serves it in all the lines in which it may happen to deal. A European house in general business at **Baghdād** has probably correspondents at **Hillah**, Mūsal, Kirkūk, Sulaimāniyah, Kirmānshāh and Hamadān through whom, in case of the local rates being favourable, it will order its requirements; otherwise the arrival of the commodities at **Baghdād** in the ordinary course of trade will be awaited. European houses seldom, it is said, have cause to complain of dishonesty in their native agents. At **Basrah** none of the British firms are interested in the import trade to any large extent.

Weights.—No account of the commerce of 'Irāq would be complete without a reference to the system of weights and measures, and to the currency, all of which are extremely complicated and confusing. The standards of weight vary from place to place, and we shall therefore deal chiefly with those of **Baghdād**, the commercial capital.

At **Baghdād** two systems of weighment exist side by side which may be called the local and the non-local. The first is applied, with certain exceptions, to local produce and is founded upon the **Baghdād** or large Huqqah بغداد حقّه or حقّه كبير — in English generally called "Oke"—of 8lb. 12oz. 8dr. English: the other has for its basis the Constantinople Huqqah حقّه استنبولي of 2lb. 12oz. 12dr. English and is used for all imported, and even for certain other articles. The

Baghdād local weights remain the same whatever the substance weighed and are as follows :—

						lbs.	oz.	dr. English.
			1	Ruba' ربع	=	0	8	12½
4	Ruba'	=	1	Waqīyah رقيّه	=	2	3	2
4	Waqīyah	=	1	Huqqah حقّه	=	8	12	8
1½	Huqqahs	=	1	Chārak چارك	=	13	2	12
4	Chāraks	=	1	Mann من	=	52	11	0
4	Manns	=	1	Waznah وزنه	=	210	12	0
20	Waznahs	=	1	Taghār طغار	= 4,215	0	0

The non-local weights are variable: gall-nuts are weighed by the Qantār قنطار of 223⅕ Constantinople Huqqahs or 624 lb. 4 oz. 3⅕ dr. English; wool by the Mann of 12½ Constantinople Huqqahs or 33 lb. 15 oz. 6 dr. English; wood and charcoal by a Waznah of 50 Constantinople Huqqahs or 139 lb. 3 oz. 8 dr. English; wheat and barley by a different Waznah of 78 Constantinople Huqqahs or 218 lb. 2 oz. 8 dr. English. In the case of wool the Constantinople Huqqahs is also called an Astānah اسـتانه; in the case of gall-nuts it is sub-divided into 4 Waqīyahs of 11 oz. 3 dr. English each; in the case of wood, 20 Waznahs or 1,000 Constantinople Huqqahs make a Taghār of 3,784 lb. 6 oz. 0 dr. English. The French kilogramme, equal to 2·20485 lb. English, is in use to a limited extent as an official measure under the name of Huqqah 'Ashshārī حقّه عشاري or decimal Huqqah, and 100 kilogrammes are treated in the case of grain as equivalent to 1 Waznah. Apothecaries employ the French kilogramme with its sub-divisions and multiples. Thus there are at least two kinds of Waqīyah, three of Huqqah, two of Mann, three of Waznah and two of Taghār in simultaneous use at **Baghdād**.

The foregoing weights correspond to our Avoirdupois; those that follow, used at **Baghdād**, correspond to our Troy :—

1	Qīrāt * قيراط	or Habbah حبّه	= 3·09375 grains English.
16	Qīrāt	= 1 Dirham درهم	= 49½ ,, ,,
1½	Dirham †	= 1 Mithqāl Baghdād	= 74¼ ,, ,,
		مثقال بغداد	
100	Mithqāl Baghdād	= 1 Chaki چكي	= 150 oz. 225 ,, ,,

These are used for weighing precious metals and stones: there is also a Mithqāl 'Ajami مثقال عجمي of 22½ Qīrāts or 69½ grains used only for weighing pearls.

---

* From this word is derived the name of our *carat* of 4 grains.

† Probably from the Greek *drachma*, whence also our drachm and dram.

At **Basrah** the unit of local weight is a Huqqah of 2 lb. 12 oz. English and the local Waqīyah is 2½ Huqqahs. A Mann of ghee at **Basrah** is 50 local Huqqahs and a Mann of grain 60; and the **Basrah** Taghār, containing 1,200 Huqqahs is treated as roughly equivalent to 1½ tons English.

Measures.—At **Baghdād** there are three measures of length, each founded upon a different Dhara' or "yard." The Dhara' Baghdād بغداد ذرع or Baghdād yard is the most generally used and is equal to 29¾ English inches; it is subdivided into 4 Chāraks چارك of $7\frac{7}{16}$ inches apiece, and each of these again into 4 'Aqads عقد of $1\frac{55}{64}$ inches apiece. The Dhara' Halab ذرع حلب or Aleppo yard is employed in measuring silks and woollens and is equal to $26\frac{7}{8}$ inches; it is subdivided in a similar manner to the Baghdād yard, giving a Chārak consequently of $6\frac{3}{4}$ and an 'Aqad of $1\frac{11}{16}$ inches. In measuring carpets and in other transactions with Persians the standard is the Dhara' Shāh ذرع شاه of about 41 inches; its Chārak, also called a Ruba', equals 10¼, and its 'Aqad $2\frac{5}{8}$ inches. British goods are estimated in British yards, and other European goods in French metres. Thus we have three different Chāraks of length, as well as the Chārak of weight, and a Ruba' of length besides the Ruba' of weight.

There are no standard measures for liquids, and these are sold by the pot or the bottle, the pots being of all sizes and the bottles generally reputed pints or quarts.

Distances, except in official measurements which are made by kilometres, are estimated in hours and days; the unit is the space covered by a walking horse in sixty minutes and so fluctuates from about 3 to 4¼ miles.

The commonest unit of land measurement is the Faddān فدان, which varies in size from one place to another and at **Baghdād** is variously defined as "the area that two men can cultivate" or "a surface that can be completely sown with 500 Huqqahs of wheat and 700 Huqqahs of barley," in all 1,200 (Constantinople) Huqqahs. The Baghdād Faddān is also described as containing 200 Dōnums دنم, each of 919 square metres, and as being equal to 18 Jarībs جريب, each of 10,000 square metres or rather more: this would give the Faddān an area of about 44½ acres. The Dōnum, it should be mentioned, is subdivided into 1,600 Dhirā' Ma'māri ذراع معماري. There is also a Juft جفت, the area that a yoke of bullocks can plough, which is from 70 to 100 Dōnums. At **Basrah** the Faddān is unknown and the unit of land measurement is a Jarīb جريب, which is about equal to 1½ English acres and is supposed to contain 100 date palms.

Currency.—The question of the currency in 'Irāq is difficult and complicated. The only fixed standard of value is the Līrah or Turkish pound, ordinarily worth about 18*s.* of British money, and to it all other coins and denominations must be regarded as subsidiary; they are numerous and some of them are fictitious, while the values of others are fluctuating. The subject is discussed below with reference to **Baghdād** rather than to **Basrah.**

The Līrah is habitually resolved into no less than six different varieties of piastre or Qursh قرش, all of which are fictitious. The first of these is the "gold" piastre, which is simply $\frac{1}{100}$ of a Līrah and is the official piastre of the Turkish Government; all taxes and all payments to State departments must be rendered in gold piastres; for example a one piastre postage stamp can only be purchased for a coin which, whatever its denomination may be, is currently worth $\frac{1}{100}$ of a Līrah. The next three kinds of piastre are all termed Majīdīyah مجيديّه, but properly the name belongs to the first of them alone, of which 102·6 go to a Līrah; the Imperial Ottoman Bank keeps its accounts in these as well as in gold piastres. The remaining sorts of Majīdīyah piastre are one of which 103·5, and another of which 108, are equal to a Līrah; the former of these is used by merchants in keeping their own books and for wholesale transactions generally, while the latter is employed partly for ease of calculation and partly on account of its close correspondence in value to the actual silver coin called a Qursh Sāgh قرش صاغ . The two remaining kinds of piastre, both called Rāij رائج, are employed in retail accounts; of the one there are 414 and of the other 432 to the Līrah, from which it will be seen that they are merely quarters of the Majīdīyah piastres standing at 103·5 and 108 to the Līrah.

We now come to the actual medium of circulation. There are five Turkish gold coins of 5, 2½, 1, ½ and ¼ Līrahs respectively; but the first two are rarely seen, and the last is not very common. The chief Turkish silver coin is the Majīdī مجيدي which is worth 18·5185 gold piastres, 19, 19·166 and 20 respectively of the various kinds of Majīdīyah piastre, and 76·666 and 80 respectively of the two sorts of Rāij piastre. In cash transactions, in the absence of a special understanding, 5·4 Majīdis are accepted as the equivalent of one Līrah. The table of smaller coins and their approximate English values is as follows: the Pārah

پاره, with which it opens, is an imaginary coin, but the others (in the second column) have a material existence:—

		£	s.	d.
5 Pārahs	= 1 Fulsain فلسين . . . =	0	0	0¼
2 Fulsain	= 1 Qursh Rāij قرش رائج or Mitlīq * متليق . . =	0	0	0½
2 Mitlīqs	= 1 Qamarī قمري . . . =	0	0	1
4 Mitlīqs	= 1 Qursh Sāgh قرش صاغ . . =	0	0	2
5 Mitlīqs	= 1 Ruba' Bashlik ربع بشلك or Abu Khamsah ابو خمسه =	0	0	2½
8 Mitlīqs	= 1 Qurshain Sāgh قرشين صاغ or Abu Thamāniyah ابو ثمانيه =	0	0	4
10 Mitlīqs	= 1 Nusf Bashlik نصف بشلك or Abu 'Ashrah ابو عشره . =	0	0	5
2 Nusf Bashliks	= 1 Bashlik بشلك or Ruba' Majīdi ربع مجيدي . =	0	0	10¼
2 Bashliks	= 1 Nusf Majīdi نصف مجيدي . =	0	1	8¼
2 Nusf Majīdis	= 1 Majīdi مجيدي . . . =	0	3	5¼

Of these small coins the Fulsain and Mitlīq are believed to consist of nickel, the Qamari, Abu Khamsah and Abu 'Ashrah of some alloy; and the remainder of silver. The half and quarter Bashlik and the Fulsain are uncommon, and the others, except the Mitlīq, are by no means plentiful.

The deficiency is made up with foreign coin, chiefly Persian, which circulates freely in spite of a prohibition against the use of foreign silver. Only a little Persian gold is seen; but various Persian coins make up the bulk of the silver currency, namely, the double Qrān of 8½d., the Qrān قران of 4¼d., the half Qrān of 2d., the quarter Qrān of 1d. and a Sittah Fulūs ستة فلوس worth ¾d. A Persian copper coin (erroneously called a Shahi شاهي) is also in use; it is worth $\frac{1}{16}$ of a penny. One Persian Tūmān, as will be seen, is at the present time about equal to one Turkish Majīdi, and there are over 50 Qrāns to the Līrah; merchants' accounts, however, where kept in Qrāns, are kept in a fictitious Qrān of which 34·4 go to the Līrah. Indian silver is current, but is occasionally seized by the authorities under the law already mentioned; Persian silver, being absolutely indispensable to the continuance of business, is never interfered with. Some English, French and Russian gold is in circulation. It remains to notice one more coin and that fictitious,—the Shāmi شامي which is the unit of computation in the date trade. There was once

---

* Doubtless from *métallique*.

an actual coin of this name with a nominal value of 10 gold piastres, but that value having been reduced by order of the Turkish Government after the last Russo-Turkish war to 5 gold piastres, which was less than the price of the metal it contained, it was everywhere melted down and has now altogether disappeared except from the quotations of the date market.

Banking and exchange.—The only bank represented in the country is the Imperial Ottoman Bank, which has branches at **Baghdād** and **Basrah**. The Imperial Bank of Persia formerly had an establishment at **Baghdād**, but withdrew it in August 1893 in consequence of an agreement with the Imperial Ottoman Bank.

The rate of exchange with Europe is variable, falling as low as 105½ per cent. in the date season and rising to as much as 110 and even more in winter. The **Baghdād** money market is controlled by rich Sarrāfs صراف who keep themselves informed by telegraph of exchange rates at Bombay, Constantinople, Paris and London and so carry on a large business. The drafts most in request at **Baghdād** are those payable by the Kirmānshāh, Tehrān and Tabrīz branches of the Imperial Bank of Persia at three and four months' sight.

Time.—The day, in 'Irāq is divided into 12 hours of which the 12th ends at sunset; thus when the sun sets at 6 P.M. seven o'clock by local time corresponds to 1 P.M., European style, and when it sets at 6-30 P.M. to 1-30 P.M., European style.

Land communications.—The subject of land communications is of less importance in 'Irāq than in most other countries. From the Persian Gulf to **Baghdād** and **Musaiyib**, admirable means of longitudinal communication are supplied by the great rivers, while the need for cross-routes is partially met by the Shatt-al-**Gharāf**, which links together except in the low season the best navigable portions of the **Tigris and Euphrates**; by the meeting of the two rivers themselves at **Qūrnah**; and by various canals such as the **Jahálah** and **Husainīyah**, not to mention innumerable marshes and lagoons connected with the rivers, on which boats can ply. In 'Irāq, to speak generally, land routes of any length neither exist nor are required; in the populous districts they would generally be obstructed as well as out-rivalled by water-ways, natural and artificial; while at a distance from the rivers the population is sparse and shifting, and there is consequently no need for fixed lines of communication. A few very important exceptions must be signalised in the north: namely the routes from **Baghdād** to the Persian frontier, the routes from Baghdād to the north and north-west, the routes from **Baghdād** to **Hillah** and **Karbala**, and the route from **Karbala** to **Najaf**. In the south, land routes as a rule lie only between adjacent places and are of no consequence; but the route from **Basrah** to the Turkish frontier at **Safwān** forms an exception to the rule, and there is a road between **Basrah** and **Fāo** behind the date plantations of the Shatt-al-'**Arab** which is frequented to a considerable extent.

I. *Routes from Baghdād to the Persian Frontier.*—We are not directly concerned here with the routes from **Baghdād** towards the Persian frontier; but we may note that the principal are (1) one to Khānaqīn خانقين, 95 miles, *viá* Ba'qūbah بعقربه, Shahrabān شهربان and Qizil Rubāt قزل رباط; and (2) another to Mandali مندلي, 79 miles, *viá* Khān Bani Sa'ad خان بني سعد, Buhrīz بهريز, and Baladruz بلدرز.

II. *Routes from Baghdād to Armenia and Syria.*—These also do not come within the scope of the present Gazetteer. The chief route from **Baghdād** to the north is by Dujail دجيل, Harbah حربه and Sāmarrah سامره to Tikrīt تكريت, 104 miles; while the main route to the north-west passes by Abu **Ghuraib, Fallūjah,** Rumādīyah رماديه, and Hīt هيت and reaches 'Anah عنه at 216 miles; the Tikrīt route follows the **Tigris**, the 'Anah route the **Euphrates** line. Forty days is about the time taken by a laden caravan to reach the Mediterranean from **Baghdād**.

III. *Route from Baghdād to Karbala.**—The following is an account of the route from **Baghdād** City to **Karbala** Town, divided according to the salient points by the way: the total distance is approximately 61 miles.

Name of place.	Distance by road and direction from last point.	Nature of place.	Remarks on road.
Baghdād City بغداد	...	See article **Baghdād** City.	...
Kharr Bridge خر	3 miles. South by west.	The ends of the bridge are two stone piers, 16 feet broad and 54 feet long, project-	About 500 yards outside **Baghdād** a brick bridge, with a ramp leading up to

---

* *Authorities.*—A report by Major Newmarch, Political Resident (*vide* his letter No. 258 of 13th April 1905, to the Secretary to the Government of India in the Foreign Department), and personal observation.

Name of place.	Distance by road and direction from last point.	Nature of place.	Remarks on road.
		ing from either bank; the central portion consists of a single iron girder 171 feet long, carrying a metalled roadway 9 feet wide with an iron footway 2 feet wide upon either side of it. In April, when the water in the Kharr stream (see article **Tigris**) is 10 feet deep, the height of the roadway above the water is 12 feet. At the south end of the bridge, on the east side of the road, is a two-storeyed brick house, behind which are about 20 mud huts.	it is crossed. Water sometimes collects on either side of this bridge in pools $1\frac{1}{2}$ feet deep, and might be an obstacle to guns but not to cavalry or infantry. From a short distance beyond this bridge to the Kharr Bridge (2 miles) the road runs along the top of an embankment which is revetted with brushwood and pierced at intervals by brick culverts, giving passage to floods that cross the line of the road here in wet weather. The top of the embankment is about 15 feet above the surrounding country and where it leads on to the Kharr Bridge it attains its maximum breadth of 45 feet.
Mahmūdī-yah محمودیه	18 miles. South.	See article **Mahmūdīyah**.	After crossing the Kharr Bridge the road trends to the left, separating from the bridge-embankment which continues westwards for about 2 miles and ends in the desert. A mile or so further on the road strikes a bend of the **Tigris**, but again immediately leaves it. At 6 miles K h ā n-al-Kharābah خان الخرابه, a ruined caravansarai, is passed on the east of the road. About 4 miles further on there is marshy ground (sometimes dry) on both sides of the road, where snipe and duck are found in the season; be-

'IRĀQ (TURKISH) 815

Name of place.	Distance by road and direction from last point.	Nature of place.	Remarks on road.
			yond this as far as **Mahmūdīyah** the country traversed is dry desert. At 13 miles there is another deserted caravansarai, Khān Āzād خان آزاد on the west side of the road. As **Mahmūdīyah** is entered the canal of the same name from the **Euphrates** is crossed: the canal is here 27 feet broad and 4 feet deep, and the bridge over it, at present in good repair, is 18 feet wide and has a small arch of 6 feet span in the middle. A little higher up, the canal is only 10 feet broad.
Musaiyib مسيب	20 miles. South-south-west.	See article **Musaiyib**.	At 5 miles **Khān-al-Bīr** خان البير a deserted caravansari which has been superseded by **Mahmūdīyah**, is passed, standing on the west side of the road; and at 12 miles the route runs through **Sikandarīyah** village, described elsewhere under its own name. Just beyond the village the Sikandarīyah, a deep canal from the **Euphrates**, is crossed by a brick bridge, at present in a fair state of repair. Between **Sikandarīyah** and **Musaiyib** there is sometimes an extensive slough, known from the tract of country in which it is situated as **Abu Lūqah** ابو لوقه. The road strikes the

Name of place.	Distance by road and direction from last point.	Nature of place.	Remarks on road.
Karbala Town كربلا	{ 20 miles. West-south-west.	See article Karbala Town.	left bank of the **Euphrates** immediately above **Musaiyib** town; about 50 yards before reaching the bank it crosses a deep canal by a high brick bridge of which the roadway is 10 feet wide. The approach to the town is along a broad embankment, carefully revetted, which contains the river at this point. In the middle of **Musaiyib** town the **Euphrates** is crossed by a boat bridge of 24 pontoons, at present a somewhat rickety and ill-maintained structure. The road for vehicles from **Musaiyib** to **Karbala** skirts the northern edge of the cultivation dependent on the **Husainīyah** canal at a distance of 2 or 3 miles from the canal; passes the tomb of 'Aun عون at 12 or 13 miles; and finally enters **Karbala** by the **Bāb Bāghdād** bridge over the **Husainīyah**, described in the article on that canal. [An alternative route, for horsemen and foot passengers, follows more closely the north bank of the **Husainīyah**. At about 7 miles from **Musaiyib** it crosses a medium-sized distributary from the **Husainīyah**, empty and ruined; and imme-

Name of place.	Distance by road and direction from last point.	Nature of place.	Remarks on road.
			diately beyond this it runs over the Wall رُل distributary by a brick bridge, 18 feet wide, with no handrail or parapet: the banks of the Wall are 45 feet apart, 25 feet high and precipitous; and the stream at the bottom flows 6 feet wide and 3 feet deep. A short distance beyond the Wall, the road crosses the Hamūdīyah حمودية distributary, which has banks 28 feet apart and 16 feet high, the flow of water in the same being similar to that in the Wall: the bridge over the Hamūdīyah is of brick and carries a roadway 8 feet wide. At about 11 miles from Musaiyib there is another distributary, known as the Abu Sulaimān ابو سليمان which is smaller than the preceding ones and is spanned by a very narrow bridge of wood and earth. Less than a mile further on, at 12 miles from Musaiyib, the road reaches Khān-al-'Ataishi, which is described in the article on the Husainīyah canal. For the next 5 miles the way lies along the right bank of the Husainīyah and a number of small canals are passed, the bridges over which are bad

Name of place.	Distance by road and direction from last point.	Nature of place.	Remarks on road.
			and unfit for wheels; the road then crosses to the left bank of the **Husainīyah** by the Pul-i-Sufaid. For the last several miles the way lies through dense date plantations; and in the last 3 miles, that is from the Pul-i-Sufaid to **Karbala** Town, there are continuous walled enclosures adjoining it on either side.]

The route described above is not a made road; but in ordinary weather it is perfectly suitable for vehicles and is daily used by such: it is the main line of communication between Persia and the holy places of the Shi'ahs. Travellers by carriage ordinarily make the whole journey in one day, while others divide it into three stages by halts at **Mahmūdīyah** and **Musaiyib**. Between **Baghdād** and **Musaiyib** the road lies over level clay plains which are generally barren, only for lack of irrigation, but in the neighbourhood of **Mahmūdīyah, Sikandarīyah** and **Musaiyib** are actually to some extent cultivated. The only shrub seen by the wayside between **Mahmūdīyah** and **Musaiyib** is the small thorny plant, called simply Shōk, which is used for facing embankments. In the cold weather large caravans of camels and small ones of donkeys are met with upon this road, carrying wheat and rice to **Baghdād**; and mules conveying Persian corpses in the opposite direction for burial at **Karbala** or **Najaf** are a common sight. Cold northerly winds, accompanied if the weather is dry by clouds of dust, sometimes make travelling by the desert portion of this road extremely uncomfortable in winter. The Arabs of the country along this line were still, in 1905, armed chiefly with muzzle-loading guns, many of them double-barrelled. The **Baghdād-Hillah** line of telegraph, which is a double one, follows the alignment of the road pretty closely, as far as **Musaiyib**, now on one side and now on the other.

IV.—*Route from Baghdād to Hillah.**—This route is the same as the last up to a point seven or eight miles beyond **Mahmūdīyah**: there it

---

* *Authorities.*—As for Route No. III.

'IRĀQ (TURKISH)

diverges to the left and begins to run almost due south. **Mahmūdīyah** being taken as the point of departure the following are the principal places passed on the way to **Hillah** :—

Name of place.	Distance by road and direction from last point.	Nature of place.	Remarks on the road.
Khān-al-Haswah خان الحصوه	14 miles. South.	Khān-al-Haswah is a one storeyed Khān of the usual shape : it has a courtyard surrounded by 38 arched recesses which are intended as lodging places for travellers. Behind the recesses are rows of vaulted stables, dark but convenient. A parapet wall about four feet high runs all round the roof. The courtyard would accommodate 100 men, and the stables 150 animals. Attached to the Khān is a village of about 60 domed brick dwellings : the inhabitants are nearly all Sunnis. Two coffee shops exist, and there is a small Dhābitīyah post. A few animals are owned in the village ; supplies, except firewood, are practically nil. The soil in the neighbourhood is gritty, consisting of pebbles mixed with a sandy clay. The cultivation, of which there is a good deal in the direction of **Sikandarīyah**, all belongs to the Dāirat-as-Sanīyah.	The road separates from the **Karbala** road about three miles south of Khān-al-Bīr and gradually diverges from it till at Khān-al-Haswah it is two miles south-east of **Sikandarīyah** village on the other road. The country beyond Khān-al-Bīr is featureless ; but Khān-al-Haswah itself stands somewhat high, on the top of a slight eminence.
Khān-al-Mahāwīl خان المحاويل	14 miles. South.	A Khān with walls 18 feet high outside, very similar to that at Khān-al-Haswah, but in worse repair. Attached to the Khān is a village of about 600 inhabitants : it is surrounded by mud walls which are 10 feet high and are topped with thorns. The place is the headquarters of the Mahāwīl Nāhiyah of the **Hillah** Qadha and consequently the seat of a Mudīr. There is one	From Khān-al-Haswah to Khān-al-Mahāwīl the country is desert but cultivable ; and to some extent it is actually cultivated on the eastern side of the road. Between five and nine miles from Khān-al-Haswah three canals from the **Euphrates** cross the road ; the second and third are traversed by brick bridges, and the third is apparently the

Name of place.	Distance by road and direction from last point.	Nature of place.	Remarks on road.
		coffee-shop and a small Dhābitīyah station. A few animals and plenty of fuel are available ; but grain, notwithstanding a considerable cultivated area, is generally scarce, being exported for sale. On the south side of the village flows the Mahāwīl canal from the Euphrates with a stream, in April, about 20 feet wide by 12 feet deep : some 50 date palms belonging to the village stand on the bank of the canal.	Nasrīyah canal from the Euphrates. At eight miles from Khān-al Haswah is Khān-an-Nasrīyah خان النصرية a deserted hostelry upon the east side of the road. About half a mile short of Mahāwīl a small water channel is crossed.
Hillah Town الحلة	13 miles. South.	See article Hillah Town.	After crossing the Mahāwīl canal by a high brick bridge in bad repair, which carries a roadway 10 feet wide and rises 12 feet above the level of the water, the road traverses a plain strewn with débris which possibly mark the site of the city of Hashimīyah, the capital (before Baghdād) of the 'Abbāsid Khalīfahs. At about four miles from Mahāwīl the Khātunīyah canal from the Euphrates is crossed by a brick bridge ; and at seven miles is the Nīl canal which has a similar bridge. For the next three miles the way lies amid the remains of the city of Babylon, now represented only by a mud-walled village called Kuwairish كويرش with about 300 inhabitants, most of whom are employed on the German excavations now in progress. Between Babylon and Hillah the principal canal crossed is the Wardīyah from the Euphrates.

The distance of **Hillah** from **Baghdād** by road is thus roughly 62 miles; and, like the **Karbala** route, this route is regularly used by wheeled carriages; but beyond the point where it separates from the **Karbala** road the track is not so distinctly marked. Its character as far as Babylon resembles that of the **Karbala** route up to **Musaiyib**; for the country crossed is, apart from a few feeble canals and some sporadic cultivation, merely a dry desert of clay. Emerging from the ruins of Babylon, however, it enters cultivated country and runs for the remainder of the distance along the eastern edge of the celebrated **Hillah** date plantations. Inconvenience from wind and dust is sometimes experienced on this road as upon the **Baghdād-Karbala** road. A double line of telegraph accompanies the road the whole way from **Baghdād** to **Hillah**.

V.—*Route from Karbala to Hillah*.*—This route consists of two parts: the first section, from **Karbala** Town to **Tawairīj**, is about 13 miles in length and has an almost south-easterly direction; the second, from **Tawairīj** to **Hillah** Town, is about 14 miles, and its direction is the same.

For about one mile the date groves of **Karbala** flank the road on either side, and, at four miles from the town, the lake known as the Hor-al-Husainīyah approaches the right of the road; the water which escapes from this lake at its north-western corner is used for irrigation, but it sometimes spreads over the road and spoils it in places. At five or six miles from **Karbala** the road grazes the village of Sulaimānīyah, described in the article on the Shatt-al-**Hindīyah**, upon its southern side; and beyond this village is a bad slough which in time of flood can only be passed in boats. At 2½ miles short of **Tawairīj** the Dawaihīyah, and at one mile short of **Tawairīj** the 'Abd 'Auniyāt—both canals from the Shatt-al-**Hindīyah**, in the article on which they are described—are passed by fording. The last two miles of the road are very sandy. The single line of telegraph which connects **Karbala** with **Tawairīj** follows the route described and is carried upon iron posts; but at the Dawaihīyah and 'Abd 'Auniyāt crossings it is slung upon high wooden masts.

At **Tawairīj** the route crosses from the right to the left bank of the Shatt-al-Hindīyah by a bridge of 21 boats at the town. The country traversed between **Tawairīj** and **Hillah** is flat, rather sandy, and partly cultivated. The track itself is intersected by various canals from the Euphrates, which are wider and deeper as **Hillah** is approached. Those

* *Authorities*.—As for route No. III.

nearest to the town have frail and narrow bridges, neither strong enough nor wide enough for guns, and without parapet or handrail. The largest of these canals, the Tājīyah تاجية still in use, is crossed two miles before entering **Hillah** Town; the enormous accumulations of silt-clearance which line its course make it appear from the distance like a high railway embankment. During the last three-quarters of the journey from **Tawairīj** to **Hillah** the Birs Nimrūd mound and ruins are visible, first to the right front and then on the right.

In ordinary weather and in the absence of floods this route is an easy one for all but vehicular traffic; in favourable circumstances and with preparation of the canal crossings near **Tawairīj** and improvement of the bridges near **Hillah**, it might perhaps be made passable for wheeled carriages.

VI.—*Route from Karbala to Najaf.**—This route runs for the greater part of the way along the edge of the **Shāmīyah** Desert, skirting lands irrigated from the **Husainīyah** canal and from the Shatt-al-**Hindīyah**. The following are the chief points by which it passes:—

Name of place.	Distance by road and direction from last point.	Nature of place.	Remarks on road.
Karbala Town كربلا	...	See article **Karbala** Town.	...
Khān Nukhailah خان نخيله	10 miles. South-east by south.	There is a large caravan-sarai 100 yards square, with walls 19 feet high on the outside; it would accommodate 400 horses and 300 men. There are the usual open cubicles for sleeping in round the courtyard, and the usual back galleries of stables. Water is from a well ¼ of a mile distant. There are two other small Khāns at this place, each of which would hold 50 horses and 20 men. No supplies are obtainable except a little chopped straw.	The road from **Karbala** to Nukhailah runs through flat featureless desert: to the west of it is a veritable ocean of golden sand.

---

* *Authority.*—A report by Colonel L. S. Newmarch, Political Resident (*vide* his letter No. 1031, dated 29th December 1905, to the Secretary to the Government of India in the Foreign Department).

'IRĀQ (TURKISH)

Name of place.	Distance by road and direction from last point.	Nature of place.	Remarks on road.
Khān Hamad خان حمد	14 miles. South-east by south.	Khān Hamad consists of a large walled enclosure, 250 yards long by 100 yards wide, with 5 caravansarais inside it opening one into the other. In these are the usual arched cubicles with stables behind them. The outer walls of the enclosure are 18 feet high, and, as there are parapets above the roofs of the stables, the whole could be easily defended against rifle fire. There is accommodation for 500 horses and 1,000 men. Besides the large enclosure there are 2 or 3 small Khāns and about 50 ordinary mud houses. Water is from wells and is said to be always sufficient; but food and fodder are scanty. To the south of the place is sandy desert, and to the north and east of it are about 400 date trees.	About midway between Nukhailah and Khān Hamad a stream 50 yards wide and 4 feet deep, said to be a branch of the Shatt-al-**Hindī-yah**, is twice struck on the left of the road; this appears to be a part of the Si'adah, mentioned again under the next route. Near Khān Hamad the country is flat and featureless; in the direction of the **Hindīyah** it is cultivated to a considerable extent with low-growing crops.
Khān Musalla خان مصلا or Khān Mirza خان ميرزا	12 miles. South-south-east.	Here is a large walled enclosure, containing two carvansarais which lead one into the other. Outside are 2 small Khāns and a few coffee shops; and about 200 yards to eastwards are some 30 Arab huts. The place would hold 800 horses and 600 men, but there are practically no supplies. Water is obtained from wells and from a canal which comes frm the Shatt-al-**Hindīyah**.	The road is sandy for some distance after leaving Khān Hamad; it runs between the pure desert on the right and low-lying lands, connected with the **Hindīyah**, on the left; these last are liable to inundation, but have good grazing during the cold season. About 3 miles short of Khān Musalla the going becomes better.
Najaf Town نجف	11 miles. South-south-west.	See article **Najaf**.	From Khān Musalla to Najaf the road lies over fine sand and the going is heavy.

This is the route used by stage carriages making the journey between **Karbala** and **Najaf**.

VII.—*Route from Najaf to Tawairij.**—The following is not apparently an established route; but it may be used as a line of communication in the cold weather. The places passed are:—

Name of place.	Distance by road and direction from last point.	Nature of place.	Remarks on the road.
Najaf Town نجف	...	See article **Najaf Town**.	...
Kifl كفل	18 miles. North by east.	See article **Kifl**.	At 7 miles the Si'ādah سعده canal, empty and broken, is crossed without difficulty; and the country, hitherto desert, changes to fertile cultivated land and pasture. One mile further on the Shatt-al-Mulla, a canal from the Shatt-al-Hindīyah is crossed; at this point it has easily sloping banks and the water in it runs 50 yards wide and 2 feet deep. From the Shatt-al-Mulla the road runs eastwards for a quarter of a mile to the right bank of the Shatt-al-**H i n d i y** ah, following which in an upward direction for 4 or 5 miles the village of 'Amrān is passed, lying about half a mile to the westward. The way continues up the right bank of the **Hindīyah** until a point opposite to **Kifl** on the left bank is reached; at this spot the **Hindīyah** is 200 yards wide. The minaret of **Kifl** comes in sight shortly after the departure from **Najaf**; and Khān Musalla, on the **Karbala-Najaf** road, is descried to the left soon after striking the **Hindīyah**.

* *Authority.*—The same as for Route No. VI above.

Name of place.	Distance by road and direction from last point.	Nature of place.	Remarks on the road.
Tawairīj طويريج	13 miles. North-north-west.	...	For about 5 miles above **Kifl** the road still follows the right bank of the **Hindīyah**; but beyond that place unbridged canals from the river make a diversion to the left necessary. At 11 miles from **Kifl** the road has diverged from the **Hindīyah** 3 miles to westward: and Birs Nimrūd and Khān Hamad are then, apparently, both visible, the former on the right and the latter on the left hand. Nine miles beyond this point the Shatt-al-Mulla, here a large canal 40 yards wide and 8 feet deep is crossed at a village of the Qarait tribe; and 1 mile further on a branch, the Zibdīyah, here 12 yards wide and 3 feet deep, is crossed also; a boat is sometimes used to take baggage over the Zibdīyah. The road then bends round to the east of north, and so continues until **Tawairīj** is reached.

VIII.—*Route from Basrah to Safwān.**—The route from **Basrah** to **Safwān** runs through **Zubair** Town which, at 9 miles, is the first stage on the way to either **Kuwait** or **Najd**. For 6 miles from the outskirts of **Basrah** Town the road traverses a depression, sometimes flooded to a depth of 2 or 3 feet by the overflow, not of the Shatt-al-'Arab, but of the **Euphrates** near **Madīnah**. At 6 miles, higher ground is reached at the ruins of Old **Basrah** which continue for 3 miles up to the walls of **Zubair** Town.

Zubair is about south-west by west from the present **Basrah**, and **Safwān** is almost due south from **Zubair**.

Scattered cultivation of lucerne, etc., surrounded by tamarisks, adjoins the left side of the road for the first 3 miles after leaving

* *Authority.*—Personal observation in 1904.

Zubair, and 1 mile further on a slight descent begins which continues for 6 miles. At 4 miles Rāfidhīyah رافضيه, a country residence of the Naqīb of **Basrah**, is passed 2 miles to the left; it is a quadrangular enclosure with bastions at the north and south angles and boasts of some trees on its north side. At 11 miles the road enters a damp sandy depression or Sabákhah, which continues for 3 miles and ends 3 miles short of **Safwān**, which is 17 miles from **Zubair**. The whole of the country traversed between **Basrah** and **Safwān** is open, and it is generally barren; to the south of **Zubair** there is some gravel. Wheeled vehicles, if strong, could probably be taken by this route.

IX.—*Route from Basrah to Fāo.*—There is a route from **Basrah** to **Fāo** which runs along the eastern edge of the desert immediately behind the date plantations of the right bank of the Shatt-al-'**Arab**. It has not been possible to obtain a full account of this road; but so far as can be ascertained it presents no difficulties and is not anywhere interrupted by serious obstacles: the towns of Abul **Khasīb** and **Hamdān** can be reached by its means. Another continuous road or path, called Wasti رسطي or Intermediate, is said to run from village to village the whole way from **Basrah** to **Fāo**; this one is nearer to the Shatt-al-'**Arab** than the first mentioned, and it is shaded throughout by date groves; but its course is crooked, and it is poorly provided with bridges, many of the numerous creeks and deep irrigation trenches encountered being spanned only by a single date log or crossed by means of ferry boats. There is also a third route, known as Hadar حدر or Lower, which runs between Wasti and the river bank and appears to be the most difficult and discontinuous of the three.

Transport and supply.—The general question of transport and supply in 'Irāq is a large one, and it is impossible here to enter on details such as are given in special works on the subject.* Trade is carried on between **Baghdād** and **Karbala** chiefly by camels and donkeys, between **Baghdād** and Khānaqīn entirely by mules; and mules predominate

---

* See in particular pages 17 to 25 and 96 to 97 of the Gazetteer of Baghdād, 1889. Since the statistics there given were compiled the price of horses has risen, and that of mules has fallen, about 20 per cent. Neither the pack-horse nor the mule of the country can carry more than 300 lbs. satisfactorily. The price of donkeys is now from £7 to £10, and they cannot ordinarily carry more than 200 lbs. The local farriers mentioned as available should be discounted, for they are so ignorant as to be more dangerous than useful. A quantity of new information on the subject of transport and supplies has recently become available in Captain H. Smyth's *Reconnaissance Report*, 1904, which contains some useful estimates; and a few fresh facts will be found in this Gazetteer in the articles on **Hillah Town**, **Tawairīj** and **Nāsirīyah Town**.

in the caravans going from **Baghdād** to Badrah and Mandali. A fair supply of camels, horses and mules is forthcoming in most of the drier parts of the country. At **Baghdād** passable riding-horses and excellent mules can be hired for a tour at the rate of one rupee per diem each; if however the journey is of an unusual kind, or less than 10 animals are engaged, the rate may be as much as one and a half rupees. A **Baghdād** mule-caravan can, on flat ground, cover from 3 to 3½ miles in the hour and as much as 40 miles in the day. It is advisable to take a written agreement when transport is engaged, even for a private journey.

Tibn تبن or chopped wheat and barley straw is the usual fodder and can be had at all seasons; green food, called Hashīsh حشيش, is at many places obtainable only in the early spring. In cultivated districts there is generally a certain surplus of these two articles and of grain; but the supply is liable to fail in seasons when irrigation or rainfall is deficient.

None of the roads of 'Irāq are made roads, but those described above as Nos. III, IV and VI, to the south and south-west of **Baghdād**, are fit in ordinary weather for vehicular traffic. Most of the coming and going between **Baghdād** and **Hillah**, **Baghdād** and **Karbala**, and **Karbala** and **Najaf** is by stage-coach. In 1905 there were 26 coaches plying between **Baghdād** and **Musaiyib**, 12 between **Musaiyib** and **Karbala**, 9 between **Karbala** and **Najaf**, and 6 between **Baghdād** and **Hillah**: those on the **Musaiyib** and **Karbala** line go and return the same day, while the rest go one day and return the next. The coaches resemble covered waggonettes, have four wheels, and are drawn by four horses or mules: they run together in convoys and are generally spoken of as belonging to a Qumbanīyah or company, but in reality they are owned in twos and threes by private individuals. The usual fare between **Baghdād** and **Karbala** is one Majīdī. A similar service exists between **Baghdād** and Sāmarrah.

In all 'Irāq there is only one horse tramway, connecting the western suburb of **Baghdād** with **Kādhimain**; it is 3 miles in length and was constructed about 1870 by Midhat Pāsha, at that time Wāli of **Baghdād**.

At present there is no railway in 'Irāq, but the Anatolian Railway is being extended in the direction of the **Euphrates** and **Tigris** valley.

Accommodation for travellers.—At halting-places on the main routes, as well as in most towns and large villages, Khāns خان or hostelries for travellers are generally found: on the main route to **Karbala** there are several at each stage. They consist of quadrangular enclosures surrounded on the inside by small rooms and stables; in the better sort there are a few superior rooms forming a second storey; but the sanitary condition of all alike is indescribably bad. Some Khāns are public, and at these the accommodation is free; but the majority are privately owned, and the Khānchi lives by the payments he receives for supplies and by the tips which satisfied travellers usually give him.

Boat bridges.—Where bridges over the larger rivers exist in 'Irāq they are invariably bridges of boats. The pontoons are lightly constructed of wood and smeared with bitumen; they are secured to one another by lashings, and the whole bridge is held in position by cables made fast to the bank and by moorings in the stream; a section of several boats is generally made so as to open and fall away, when required, for the passage of steamers and large native craft. The bridge at **Baghdād** is passable for all vehicles; but on others the gangways connecting the boats are sometimes so narrow and badly adjusted as to be difficult for animals, and considerable preparation would be required to fit some of them for wheeled traffic. Boat-bridges exist at Sāmarrah, **Kādhimain**, Baghdād, Qarārah, Kūt-al-Amārah and 'Amārah on the **Tigris**; at Fallūjah, Musaiyib, Hillah, Nāsirīyah and Sūq-ash-Shuyūkh on the **Euphrates**; at **Tawairīj** and **Kūfah** on the Shatt-al-**Hindīyah**; and on the **Diyālah** just above its confluence with the **Tigris**.

Water communications.—The navigation of the **Tigris, Euphrates, Hindīyah, Gharāf** and **Diyālah** rivers and of the **Husainīyah** and **Jahálah** canals is dealt with in the articles under those names. As already observed, the principal communications of the country are by water.

The **Tigris** is navigable to Mūsal, but up-stream traffic practically ceases at **Baghdād** in consequence of rapids and the increased force of the current above that point, especially at Qanātir; down-stream traffic, however, from Mūsal to **Baghdād** is carried on by raft, almost to the exclusion of other means of transport; and some of the rafts descend as far as 'Amārah Town.

Regular boat carriage on the **Euphrates** does not now extend above **Hillah** Town and with difficulty reaches that point: between July and October some of the reaches between **Samāwah** and **Hillah** cannot be negotiated by boats of size, which must unload at **Samāwah** or **Shināfīyah**. By entering the **Hindīyah** through the Bahr-an-Najaf boats from the lower **Euphrates** can reach the river again at the **Hindīyah** barrage or Saddah; as however the barrage has no lock, they must here transfer their cargoes to other boats which come to meet them from above. The Shatt-al-**Gharāf** is not passable in the low season. About **Kifl** and **Kūfah**, where the roads are uns'aged and unsafe, and in the marshy districts generally, the people for the most part move about in boats or canoes.

The question of steamers is treated of elsewhere; but we may here remark that native sailing-boats have the advantage of steamers in the carriage of articles, such as grain and liquorice, which are bulky and have to be collected from point to point, also in down-stream work generally, and in most cases where the desideratum is cheapness rather than speed. That the native carrier is willing to dispense with bagging of grain is another point in his favour. The present steamer freight from **Baghdād** to **'Amārah** Town, for instance, is 14s. 8d. a ton, while boat freight is only 9s. 4d.

Passengers by steamer from Bombay sometimes accomplish the journey to **Baghdād** in 14 days, and goods from Bombay arrive in from 14 days to 6 weeks, or more, with only one transhipment from ocean to river-steamer at **Basrah**; goods from England are delivered at the **Baghdād** custom-house in periods varying from 40 days to four months and over.

*Native river boats.**—The chief kinds of native boat in use on the rivers and marshes of 'Irāq are the Mahailah مهيله, Ballam بلّم, Dānak دانك, Mashhūf مشحوف or canoe, Quffah قفّه or coracle, and Kalak كلك or raft. †

The Mahailah مهيله, in some up-country places called a Tarādah طرادة or Safinah ‡ سفينه, is found everywhere from **Fāo** to **Baghdād**. It is the largest boat seen on the Mesopotamian rivers and varies in length from 30 to 80 feet with a beam slightly less than ⅓ of the total length; it is built with great sheer, giving the midship portion a freeboard of only about one foot when fully loaded, while the gunwale at bow and stern is from 10 to 12 feet above the water. The Mahailah is an open boat and is strengthened with three or four stout cross-beams; but the larger sizes have a poop, and all have a steering platform aft, as well as a forecastle deck for working the ground tackle and for poling. The stern is pointed and the lines of the vessel are extremely fine. The Mahailah is steered with an ordinary tiller and rudder and has only one mast carrying a lateen sail; there is also a staysail which is hoisted when the wind is too heavy for the larger sail. The Mahailah floats so

---

* *Authority.*—Chiefly a special report by Commander A. Rowand, R.I.M.
† See illustrations in Vol. III of this Gazetteer.
‡ Plurals Tarārīd طراريد and Sufun سفن

lightly that a mere rag of canvas will enable it, when unloaded, to advance at a fair speed even against a strong current. When wind or river are adverse the Mahailah is poled along in the shallow water close to the bank, or a long coir rope is led from the masthead to the shore by which the crew tow, one man remaining on board to steer. The crew varies from 3 to 8 men according to the size of the vessel, and from 10 to 100 tons of cargo can be carried. A large Mahailah will contain 60 passengers. The cost of construction of a Mahailah is from £100 to £250 English.

The Ballam بلّم is the boat *par excellence* of the Shatt-al-'**Arab** and its ordinary range is from **Qūrnah** to **Fāo**, but it is found on the **Euphrates** as far up as **Nāsirīyah** Town. The typical Ballam is a small boat about 20 feet long by 3 feet across at the greatest beam; in shape it is long and narrow and pointed at both extremities.* It has a platform for poling at either end and is strengthened by cross-beams. The Ballam draws very little water and is generally poled along the bank, but it can also be rowed or sailed: a rudder is shipped when sailing. Three or four men constitute the crew of a Ballam, and it costs from £10 to £15 English to build one. The small passenger Ballams of **Basrah** are gaily painted and have a scroll ornament at each end.

A larger cargo-carrying vessel of the Ballam type is called an 'Arāgīyah عراكيه : it may be as much as 60 feet in length and carry a load of 50 tons. The home of the 'Arāgīyah is on the **Euphrates** and **Hindīyah** from **Samāwah** to **Hillah**; and it is said to take its name from the river ports of this neighbourhood which are called collectively 'Arāg, a word which has possibly some connection with the name 'Irāq: on the **Tigris**, however, the term 'Arāgīyah is used somewhat loosely to describe any boat from the **Euphrates**.

The Dānak دانك has much the same distribution as the Mahailah, but it is not nearly so common, unless perhaps on the **Euphrates** in the neighbourhood of **Hillah** and **Dīwānīyah**. It is an open boat, 30 to 40 feet in length, and pointed at bow and stern, with a platform at each end and cross-beams in the waist. The stem and stern-post rise 3 to 3½ feet above the gunwale in order that they may stand clear when the vessel is loaded up with datestalks or such produce. There is one mast carrying a lateen sail, the steering-gear consists of a rudder and tiller,

---

* This is the Ballam 'Ashārī عشاري; it is used for passenger traffic and as a lighter; it is sometimes as much as 50 feet long; a large one will carry 20 passengers. There is also a pattern called Ballam Nassāri, 40 or 50 feet long, in which cargo is carried between Basrah and Kuwait. Both types are built at Kuwait, but Ballams are not owned at that port.

and the hull, which is of wood, is coated with bitumen. Poling is resorted to in shallow water. The crew consists of about 5 or more men, and both cargo and passengers are carried, but the capacity of the Dānak does not commonly exceed 12 tons. A Dānak costs £15 to £20 English to build.

The mast in all the vessels described above is called Shaiyāl شيّال; the sails are Shirā' شراع; and the poles for propelling are Marādi مرادي.

The Mashhūf مشحوف is a light plank or reed-canoe, covered with bitumen, which is used in the marshy tracts upon the **Tigris and Euphrates** above their confluence at **Qūrnah**. Mashhūfs are built in considerable numbers at Qal'at **Sālih** and **Sūq-ash-Shuyūkh**, and the positions of these two places sufficiently indicate the country to which the Mashhūf belongs. The length of the Mashhūf is from 15 to 18 feet,* and it can be very rapidly propelled by one man, who sits as far aft and as low as possible, and strikes the water with a paddle upon either side alternately. The Mashhūf, if managed with care, will carry altogether 4 or 5 men, and occasionally a second oarsman sits in the bow. There is a species of large Mashhūf called a Qaiyarīyah قيريه, also bitumen-covered but built of thin planking; it has a mast, sail, rudder and tiller, but is reckoned an inferior boat. The name is derived from Qīr, meaning bitumen.

Baghdād is the headquarters of the Quffah قفة, and 500 are said to belong to that place; but it is seen as far south as **Basrah** and as far west as the **Husainīyah** canal. It is a circular coracle, shaped like an Indian water-jar, or in more precise terms a hollow oblate spheroid with the central portion of the top removed. Quffahs are ordinarily 4 to 5 feet in diameter, but some are as small as 3 feet 8 inches and others as large as 10 feet; the former may be as little as 2 feet 6 inches in depth and the latter as much as 3 feet 6 inches. In construction the Quffah is nothing else than a strong wickerwork basket thickly coated with bitumen and costing £5 or less. The ordinary Quffah is propelled by two men with paddles and will carry 4 or 5 passengers, but a very large one can convey 20 persons, or one camel and several passengers. The Quffah does not advance well against the current; but it is very safe, being little liable to accident in case of a collision. By fishermen descending the stream a bundle of hurdles, marking the end of the net, is sometimes sent in advance of the Quffah, while the vessel itself is retarded by a heavy stone attached to a rope and dragging along the bottom of the river. The larger Mahailahs sometimes have a Quffah as dinghy.

There is also a class of small boat on the **Euphrates** about **Musaiyib** which is called Sājah ساجه.

---

* A Mashhūf seen at Basrah, however, measured 32 feet in length, 3½ feet in beam, and 1 foot and 7 inches depth.

The last and most primitive kind of river craft in 'Irāq are the Kalaks كلك or rafts which come down from Mūsal to Baghdād and sometimes to 'Amārah Town. They consist of a square or oblong platform, either of timber or built up with layers of crossed branches to a thickness of 1½ or 2 feet and then covered with rough planks: the usual size is 14 by 15 feet to 16 by 18 feet, but some are even 30 feet long. The buoyancy of the materials is increased by 30 to 50 inflated skins which are attached to the submerged portion of the platform; the Kalak can only move with the current and is kept in mid-stream by means of two roughly fashioned sweeps. These rafts bring with them pottery, wood, fruit, empty oil-tins, etc., which they sell on the way to villagers and Bedouins; on arrival at their destination they are broken up, the wood being sold as scantlings to house-builders and the skins conveyed up the river again to the original point of departure. The load of a Kalak varies from 5 to 30 tons.

It is impossible, owing to defective registration, to obtain a clear idea of the number of boats which exist on the rivers. * At **Basrah** Town, in 1903-04, there were 635 mastless and 475 masted vessels upon the Government' books; but the Naqīb of **Basrah** alone then owned 200 boats, other notables among them perhaps 50, and a large number of private individuals 3 or 4 each, none of which were registered. Mash-hūfs, too, are never registered. The chief seats of boat-building are **Basrah** Town and Sangar on the Shatt-al-'**Arab** below **Basrah**. The times taken by native boats to ascend and descend the large rivers are extremely uncertain, varying with wind and current: thus the upward journey from **Basrah** to **Baghdād** varies between 15 and 45 days, and the downward journey from **Baghdād** to **Basrah** between 10 and 30 days, but river and wind both being favourable **Basrah** may even be reached from **Baghdād** in 5 days.

Post office.—The Turks have not been remiss in establishing post offices; but the efficiency of the postal service leaves something to be desired, and, at least off the main routes, private messengers are still in request and considerable use is made of the good offices of travellers and passing muleteers. There is no system of money orders, but specie can be sent insured through the post.

---

* Estimates of the river transport which might be obtainable at **Baghdād** and **Basrah** are given by Captain H. Smyth in his *Reconnaissance Report*, 1904.

Telegraphs.—The origin of the telegraphic system in 'Irāq is explained in the Appendix to this Gazetteer which deals with the subject of telegraphs.

Baghdād City is the centre of the whole network. From **Baghdād** radiate a line which meets the Indo-European Telegraph Department's cable at **Fāo** and affords communication between India and Europe, another running to the Persian frontier at Khānaqīn and meeting there with a line from Tehrān worked by the Persian Government, and a third which reaches Constantinople *viâ* Mūsal and Diyārbakr. A fourth line, from **Baghdād** to Europe by way of Aleppo, has now been completed after being for some years under consideration.

Baghdād is connected with **Fāo** by a line through **Qūrnah** Village and **Basrah** Town: at **Qūrnah** this line, a double one, crosses to the right bank of the Shatt-al-'**Arab** which it follows thence all the way to **Fāo**. There is a small branch office, distinct from the general office at **Basrah** Town, which is situated in the Maqām quarter of the same and receives messages in Arabic and Turkish only.

Between **Baghdād** and **Qūrnah**, on the way to **Fāo**, there are alternative lines, one following the **Tigris**, the other the **Euphrates** valley. The stations on the **Tigris** line between **Baghdād** and **Qūrnah** are '**Azīzīyah** Village, **Kūt-al-Amārah** Town, '**Ali-al-Gharbi**, '**Amārah** Town, Qal'at **Sālih** and '**Azair**: those on the **Euphrates** line are **Musaiyib**, **Hillah** Town, **Dīwānīyah** Town, **Samāwah** Town, Durrāji, **Nāsirīyah** Town, **Sūq-ash-Shuyūkh** and Hammār. A branch to the town of **Hai** leaves the **Tigris** line at **Kūt-al-Amārah**; and a wire from **Hillah**, on the **Euphrates** line, runs to **Tawairīj, Karbala** and **Najaf**. The **Tigris** line is apparently double throughout, and the **Euphrates** line as far as **Hillah**. It is the intention of the Turkish Government to prolong the **Kūt-al-Amārah** to **Hai** line by way of Qal'at **Sikar** and **Shatrat-al-Muntafik** to **Nāsirīyah** Town, thus providing a cross-connection; and it is also stated that **Kifl** and **Kūfah** will shortly be linked up with **Karbala** and **Najaf**, * probably by means of the wire which connects those two places. The **Tigris** telegraph, it should be mentioned, is on the left bank of the river from **Baghdād** to Qal'at **Sālih**, and there crosses to the right bank which it follows to **Qūrnah**.

On the line from **Baghdād** to Khānaqīn, which is single, the intermediate stations are Ba'qūbah, Shahrabān and Qizil Rubāt; and from Shahrabān a branch, also single, is thrown off to Mandali and Badrah.

---

* This has now been done (1907).

3 H

The stations in 'Irāq upon the Aleppo line, which is double, are **Fallūjah** and Rumādīyah.

The Turkish telegraphs in 'Irāq are indifferently maintained. In 1905 the line between **Karbala** and **Najaf** was interrupted, and for several months no attempt was made to restore communication.

Civil administrative divisions.—Before entering on the subject of administration it is necessary to understand the system on which, in the Turkish Empire, the country is distributed and organised for purposes of government, and how in particular that system has been applied by the Porte in 'Irāq.

The largest territorial unit is the Wilāyat ولاية or province; each Wilāyat consists of divisions, known as Sanjāqs سنجاق or Liwas لواء; each Sanjāq again is subdivided into Qadhas قضاء or districts; and each Qadha includes as a rule one or more Nāhiyahs ناحية or small outlying administrative charges. Within the Nāhiyah are generally found, in 'Irāq, a number—sometimes very large—of Muqāta'ahs مقاطعة or estates;* but these have little or no administrative significance. The Muqāta'ah in fact is simply a tract of land which happens to be included under one common name; it may contain a village or villages or it may be uninhabited, it may be cultivated or desert, and it may belong to one or to many owners. Wilāyats are of the first or of the second class, Sanjāqs are classified in 3 grades according to their importance, and Qadhas and Nāhiyahs are similarly treated; but in every Sanjāq there is a Markaz مركز or headquarters Qadha which has the same name as the larger division and has no grade, either high or low, in its own class. Baghdād is a Wilāyat of the first, and Basrah apparently of the second class.

In the tables which follow below of the administrative divisions of 'Irāq opportunity has been taken to insert some details elucidative of facts given in the paragraph on population above.

The Baghdād Wilāyat consists of 3 Sanjāqs, *viz.*, those of Baghdād and Dīwānīyah, which are both of the first class, and that of **Karbala**

---

* The word Muqāta'ah does not originally mean an estate; it is properly a term of Turkish revenue or finance and denotes the farming out of a portion of the public revenue for a period at a fixed rate. Such contracts being common in connection with the land revenue the word has now acquired, in 'Irāq, a territorial signification also.

which belongs to the second class. The following are the details of their composition:—

Name of Qadha.	*Chef-lieu* of Qadha and its population in souls.	Population of Qadha in souls and class to which it belongs.	Nāhiyahs composing the Qadha and class to which each belongs.
	(1.) Sanjāq of Baghdād.		
'Anah عنه	'Anah Town. 5,000.	20,000. 3rd class.	Hadaithah (3rd). حديثه Jubbah-Ālūs (3rd). جبّه آلوس Qāim (2nd). قائم
'Azīzīyah عزيزيه	'Azīzīyah Village. 200.	20,000. 2nd class.	Salmān Pāk (1st). سلمان پاك
Badrah بدره	Badrah Town. 2,500.	15,000. 3rd class.	Gharaibah (2nd). غريبه Jassān (2nd). جسّان
Baghdād بغداد	Baghdād City. 140,000.	150,000. (Markaz).	Mu'adhdham (2nd). معظّم
Dilaim دليم	Rumādīyah. 1,000.	50,000. 1st class.	Fallūjah (2nd). فلّوجه Hīt (2nd). هيت Kubaisah (3rd). كبيسه Rahālīyah (3rd). رحاليه
Jazīrah جزيره	Suwairah. 750.	15,000. 2nd class.	Nil.
Kādhimain كاظمين	Kādhimain Town. 8,000.	25,000. 3rd class.	Do.

Name of Qadha.	Chef-lieu of Qadha and its population in souls.	Population of Qadha in souls and class to which it belongs.	Nahiyahs composing the Qadha and class to which each belongs.
Khānaqīn خانقين	Khānaqīn Village. 1,600.	30,000. 1st class.	Bankdarah (1st). بندره Qizil Rubāt (1st). قزل رباط
Khurāsān خراسان	Ba'qūbah. 4,000.	40,000. 1st class.	Khālis (1st). خالص Shahrabān (1st). شهربان
Kūt-al-Amā-rah كوت الامارة	Kūt-al-Amār-ah Town. 4,000.	20,000. 2nd class.	Nil.
Mandali مندلي	Mandali Village. 1,500.	15,000. 2nd class.	Do.
Sāmarrah سامرة	Sāmarrah Town. 5,000.	15,000. 3rd class.	Tikrīt (1st). تكريت

(2) *Sanjāq of Dīwānīyah.*

Name of Qadha.	Chef-lieu of Qadha and its population in souls.	Population of Qadha in souls and class to which it belongs.	Nahiyahs composing the Qadha and class to which each belongs.
Dīwānīyah ديوانيه	Dīwānīyah Town. 4000.	50,000. (Markaz).	Budair (1st). بدير Dagharah (1st). دغارة
Hillah حلة	Hillah Town. 30,000.	75,000. 1st class.	Bārmānak (2nd). بارمانه Khawās (2nd). خواص Mahāwīl (2nd). محاويل Mamdūhīyah (1st). ممدوحيه Nahr Shāh (2nd). نهر شاه
Samāwah سماو	Samāwah Town. 10,000.	60,000. 2nd class.	Durrāji (3rd). دراجي Juwārīr (Abu) ابو جوارير or Rumaithah (2nd). رميثه

'IRÂQ (TURKISH)

Name of Qadha.	Chef-lieu of Qadha and its population in souls.	Population of Qadha in souls and class to which it belongs.	Nūhiyahs composing the Qadha and class to which each belongs.
Shāmīyah شامية	Formerly Umm-al-Ba'rūr, now Hamīdīyah. 4,000.	65,000. 1st class.	Ghamās (2nd). غماس Hor Allah (2nd). هور الله Salāhīyah (2nd). صلاحية Shināfīyah (2nd). شنافية

(3) *Sanjāq of Karbala.*

Hindīyah هندية	Tawairij. 4,000.	95,000. 1st class.	Kifl (3rd). كفل There are also several small subdivisions called Qol Mu'ash-shirliyis, *viz.*, Mshorab, Ka'abūri, Musai'idah, Āl Fat-lah, Abu Rūbah, Harqa and Abu Nifāsh.
Karbala كربلا	Karbala Town. 50,000.	80,000. Markaz.	Musaiyib (1st). مسيب Shi fāthah (1st). شفاثة
Najaf نجف	Najaf Town. 30,000.	50,000. 1st class.	Hor-ad-Dukhn (2nd.) هور الدخن Kūfah (1st). كوفة Rahabah (3rd). رحبه
Razāzah رزازة	Nil. Nil.	750. 3rd class.	Nil.

The Basrah Wilāyat consists, the Sanjāq of "Najd" or **Hasa** and the nominal Sanjāq of **Qasīm** being excluded, of 3 Sanjāqs, *viz.*,

'Amārah, Basrah and Muntafik: the composition of these by Qadhas is as follows:—

Name of Qadha.	Chef-lieu of Qadha and its population in souls.	Population of Qadha in souls.	Nāhiyahs composing the Qadha.

(1) Sanjāq of 'Amārah.

Amārah عمارة	'Amārah Town. 10,000.	41,000. (Markaz.)	'Ali-al-Gharbi علي الغربي 'Ali-ash-Sharqi علي الشرقي Majar-al-Kabīr مجر الكبير Majar-as-Saghīr مجر الصغير
Dawairīj دريريج	Tafrah. 100.	50,000.	Markaz only: no subdivisions.
Shatrat-al-'Amārah شطرة العمارة	Qal'at Sālih. 2,000.	45,000.	Ditto ditto.
Zubair زبير	Masa'īdah. 650.	14,000.	Ditto ditto.

(2) Sanjāq of Basrah.

| Basrah بصرة | Basrah Town. 58,000. | 150,000. (Markaz.) | Arab (Shatt-al-) شط العرب
Basrah (Markaz). بصرة
Hārthah. هارثه
Khasīb (Abul). ابو الخصيب
Zubair زبير |
| Fāo فاو | Fāo Station. 200. | 13,000. | Markaz only: no subdivisions. |

'IRĀQ (TURKISH)

Name of Qadha.	Chef-lieu of Qadha and its population in souls.	Population of Qadha in souls.	Nāhiyahs composing the Qadha.
Qūrnah قورنه	Qūrnah Village. 2,000.	30,000.	Dair and Sharish. دير و شرش Madīnah. مدينه Mansūr (Bani). بني منصور Nashwah. نشوه Qūrnah (Markaz). قورنه

N.B.—The Turks regard the principality of **Kuwait** as a Qadha of the Basrah Sanjāq.

(3) *Sanjāq of Muntafik.*

Hai حي	Kūt-al-Hai. 4,000.	44,000.	Hai (Markaz). حي Mhairijah. مهيرجه Sikar (Qal'at). قلعة سكر
Nāsirīyah ناصريه	Nāsirīyah Town. 10,000.	53,000. (Markaz)	Azairij ازيرج Butaibah. بطيحه Nāsirīyah (Markaz). ناصريه
Shatrat-al-Muntafik شطرة المنتفك	Shatrat-al-Muntafik Town. 4,000.	65,000.	Bada'ah. بدعه Dajjah. دجه Shatrat-al-Muntafik. (Markaz). شطرة المنتفك

Name of Qadha.	Chef-lieu of Qadha and its population in souls.	Population of Qadha in souls.	Nāhiyahs composing the Qadha.
Sūq-ash-Shuy-ūkh سوق الشيوخ	Sūq-ash-Shuy-ūkh Town. 12,000.	85,000.	Garmah. كرمه Hammār. حمّار Sūq-ash-Shuyūkh (Markaz). سوق الشيوخ

It has not been possible to ascertain the classes to which the divisions and subdivisions of the Basrah Wilāyat belong.

We may mention here that the Sanjāq of **Hasa** or "Najd" is divided by the Turks into the 3 Qadhas of Hofūf (Markaz), Qatar and Qatīf, and they treat the Hofūf Qadha as consisting of 5 Nāhiyahs, viz., Ayūn عيون, Hofūf (Markaz), Jafar جفر, Mubarraz مبرّز and 'Oqair عقير; but the Qatar and Qatīf Qadhas are not subdivided, even nominally, into Nāhiyahs.

The so-called Sanjāq of **Qasīm** consists, in the imagination of the Turkish Government, of 2 Qadhas, viz. Buraidah بريدة and Riyādh رياض. Buraidah again is composed of a Markaz Nāhiyah of Buraidah and a Nāhiyah of 'Anaizah عنيزه; and Riyādh is supposed to include a Markaz Nāhiyah of Riyādh and two other Nāhiyahs, Sadair, سدير and Washam, وشم.

The whole of 'Irāq was formerly included, along with Mūsal, in one enormous province known as the Pashāliq پشالق of Baghdād. In 1878, with a view to reducing this unwieldy charge, Mūsal and its dependencies were detached and formed into a separate Wilāyat; and in June 1884 the territory remaining under the government of Baghdād was further broken up into the two Wilāyats of Baghdād and Basrah which have been described above. The Baghdād and Basrah Wilāyats, it may be noted, had been separated before this in 1875, but in 1880 they had been reunited.

Civil officials.—Each Wilāyat is ruled by a Wāli والي or Lieutenant-Governor; each Sanjāq by a Mutasarrif متصرّف or Commissioner; each Qadha by a Qāim-Maqān قائم مقام or Deputy-Commissioner; and each Nāhiyah by a Mudīr مدير or Subdivisional Officer. These charges of

'IRĀQ (TURKISH)

varying importance are sometimes described by the rank of the officers who administer them, a Sanjāq being spoken of as a Mutasarrifliq متصرفلق, a Qadha as a Qāim-Maqāmliq قائم مقاملق, and a Nāhiyah as a Mudīrlik مديرلك or Mudīrīyah مديريه.

The salaries of the superior officials are determined by the grade of the territorial unit of which each holds charge, and the following are the present rates of pay attached to these :—

Charge held.	Monthly pay in gold piastres.	Annual pay in English money.
1st class Wilāyat	30,000	£3,240
2nd class do.	18,000 to 26,000	£1,944 to £2,088
1st class Sanjāq	7,500	£810
2nd class do.	5,000	£540
1st class Qadha	2,500	£270
2nd class do.	1,750	£189
3rd class do.	1,250	£135
1st class Nāhiyah	750	£81
2nd class do.	500	£54
3rd class do.	450	£48-12-0

In each Wilāyat there are a Maktūbji مكتوبجي, or principal secretary to the Wāli, and a Daftardār دفتردار or Accountant General; and at the headquarters of each Qadha are found a Māl Mudīri مال مديري or General Secretary and a Sandūq Amīn صندوق امين or Treasurer besides other petty employés and clerks, etc.

Civil and municipal administration.—The Wāli of each Wilāyat is the head of all the non-special branches of the administration represented in his province: such are the gendarmerie, the civil police, the revenue collecting establishment and the department of general accounts called Muhāsibah محاسبه. The courts of justice, the departments of Land Records, Posts and Telegraphs, Religious Endowments, Customs, Public Debt, Tobacco Régie and Public Instruction, and the Sanitary Service are exempt from the control of the Wāli, and the local chiefs of these offices receive orders direct from the principal bureaux of their departments at Constantinople; but duplicates of such orders are sometimes sent to the Wāli also for information, and it is his duty to investigate the complaints which may be preferred against the proceedings of any department in his Wilāyat, whether under his control or not. The Wāli is also the political representative of the Turkish Government in his own province, and all dealings with foreign consular officers or foreign subjects there, and with the uncivilised tribes of the country, are in his hands. The Wāli has no authority over the regular troops in the Wilāyat, but he may call upon the military commander to take such steps as may be necessary for the attainment of administrative or political objects. Occasionally, as in the Wilāyat of Basrah at the present time, the same individual is invested with the highest civil and military powers; and such an arrangement is not unknown even in the lower grades, the chief civil authority in the Sanjāq of **Nāsirīyah**, for instance, being now the military officer in command of the troops there (1905).

Every civil official, from Wāli down to Mudīr, is assisted by an Administrative Council or Majlis-al-Idārah مجلس الادارة of which he is *ex-officio* president; but the functions of these bodies are advisory only. The composition of the Council of the Wāli of Baghdād may be mentioned as typical: it consists of 14 ordinary members. Of these 6 hold their seats by virtue of office, *viz.*, the Mufti, Qādhi and Naqīb of Baghdād, the Daftardār and Maktūbji of the Wilāyat, and the Mushīr of the 6th Army Corps: the non-official members, of whom one must be a Christian and one a Jew, are selected by Government from short lists of names submitted by the Christian, Jewish and Muhammadan communities. The Administrative Council in a Nāhiyah is called Nāhiyah Idārah Majlisi ناحيه اداره مجلسي and meets four times a year. Every village or Qaryah قريه within the Nāhiyah is governed by a Mukhtār مختار or headman with the assistance of an Ikhtiyār Majlis اختيار مجلسي or Council of Elders, who have the right to send up not more than four of their number to represent them in the Nāhiyah Idārah Majlisi.

The headquarter towns or villages of Sanjāqs and Qadhas are organised as municipalities; and the affairs of each one of them are supposed to be managed by a Majlis Baladīyah مجلس بلديه or Municipal Council. These Municipal Council, however, have no more real power than the Administrative Councils of the territorial divisions.

The Turkish administration of 'Irāq would thus seem to be carefully organised and to be based to a large extent upon representative institutions. The case, however, is one in which but little correspondence exists between the outward appearance and the real fact. Mudīrs and even Qāim-Maqāms are sometimes merely illiterate tribal Arabs whom it is desired to placate : such is the Qāim-Maqām of **Razāzah** and such was, till recently, the Mudīr of Hammār.

Gendarmerie or Dhābitīyahs.—The maintenance of law and order throughout the country districts depends, in time of peace, on a force of police known as Gendarmerie جندارمه or Dhābitīyahs ضابطيه ; the former is a new, the latter is an old name for these police, but it has been clearly ascertained that both terms refer to the same body of men. The organisation of the Gendarmerie is military, and the force is under the control of a section of the Turkish War Office styled Jandārmah Dāirahsi جندارمه دائره سي ; but it is distributed among the Wilāyats of the empire for service as a civil police under the orders of the civil authorities, and the Gendarmerie of each Wilāyat are a charge upon the civil revenues of the same.

The Gendarmerie consists partly or Astarsuwārs, استرسوار or mounted men (literally "mule riders") and partly of Piyādahs پياده or unmounted; and some of the latter, styled Shabānah شبانه wear no uniform. The Gendarmerie are organised in Tāburs طابور or battalions and Bulūks بلوك or companies, mounted and unmounted, the number of Bulūks in a Tābūr varying from 4 to 10, and of men in a Bulūk from 20 to 100. Most of the Tāburs consist partly of mounted and partly of unmounted Bulūks. The force is commanded partly by officers seconded from the regular Turkish Army and partly by individuals holding special commissions for the purpose.* The following are the different ranks of the officers with the rates of pay atttached to each :—

Name of rank.	Corresponding English military rank.	Monthly salary in gold piastres.	Annual salary in English money.
Ālāi Baigi آلاي بكي	Colonel.	1,900	£205
Tābūr Āghāsi طابور أغاسي	Major.	950	£103
Yūzbāshi يوز باشي	Captain.	470	£51
Suwāri Mulāzimi سواري ملازمي	Lieutenant (mounted).	280	£30
Piyādah Mulāzimi پياده ملازمي	Lieutenant (unmounted).	237	£25

* In the Baghdād Wilayat there are no officers taken from the regular army.

A Captain is also known as Bulūk Āghāsi بلوک آغاشی and a Lieutenant as Bulūk Āghāsi Mu'āwini معاوني. An Ālāi Baigi, commanding the whole force of gendarmerie in the province, is generally stationed at the capital of the Wilāyat with the Wāli; while there is usually a Tābūr Āghāsi at the *chef-lieu* of the Sanjāq with the Mutasarrif, and a Bulūk Āghāsi at the headquarters of the Qadha with the Qāim-Maqām.

Of the rank and file of the Gendarmerie a majority belong to the Radīf or military reserve; and the men as a whole, though not smart in appearance, are useful and hardy. In 'Irāq many of the Dhābitīyahs are **Kurds**. In ordinary stations the pay of the mounted private is 180 gold piastres a month or nearly £20 English a year, of an unmounted private 80 gold piastres or about £9 English a year. The mounted men generally ride mules and both branches are armed with Martini rifles. The mounted men, in consideration of their higher pay, provide their own mounts and saddlery.

In 'Irāq the Gendarmerie are employed on all sorts of miscellaneous duties besides civil police work: they assist in the realisation of revenue from the tribes, and they furnish escorts and even garrisons for posts. The commandant of a Gendarmerie battalion seldom has many of his men under his direct command; as a rule they are scattered up and down the country in small detachments of 3 to 50 men; and thus it happens, for example, that at **Karbala** Town, which is the headquarters of a battalion, the number of Dhābitīyahs present is rarely over 100 and often falls below that number.

The following is a statement of the distribution (by headquarters only) and of the strength of the Gendarmerie in 'Irāq:

Gendarmerie of the Baghdād Wilāyat.

Tābūr.	Headquarters.	Number of Officers.	Mounted strength.	Unmounted strength.
1st	Baghdād City.	34	6 Bulūks (=270 men)	4 Bulūks (=300 men).
2nd	Ba'qūbah.	32	7 Bulūks (=280 men).	3 Bulūks (=174 men).
3rd	Baghdād City.	20	6 Bulūks (=336 men).	Nil.
4th	Karbala Town.	14	2 Bulūks (=95 men).	2 Bulūks (=138 men).

'IRĀQ (TURKISH)

Tābūr.	Headquarters.	Number of officers.	Mounted strength.	Unmounted strength.
5th	Dīwānīyah Town.	23	4 Bulūks (=180 men).	3 Bulūks (=207 men).
6th	Khānaqīn.	14	1 Bulūk (=54 men).	3 Bulūks (=183 men).
7th	Baghdād City.	17	5 Bulūks (=280 men).	Nil.

Gendarmerie of the Basrah Wilāyat.

Tābūr.	Headquarters.	Mounted strength.	Unmounted strength.	Shabānah.
1st	Basrah Town.	2 Bulūks.	4 Bulūks.	1 Bulūk.
2nd	'Amārah Town.	2 do.	2 do.	1 do.
3rd	Nāsirīyah Town.	3 do.	Nil.	1 do.

The following is an abstract of the entire strength by provinces:—

Wilāyat.	Officers.	Mounted.	Umounted.	Shabānah.
Baghdād	154	31 Bulūks (=1,495 men)	15 Bulūks (=1,002 men)	Nil
Basrah	Not known.	7 Bulūks (Say 350 men)	6 Bulūks (Say 400 men)	3 Bulūks (=175 men)
Totals		38 Bulūks (about 1,850 men)	21 Bulūks (about 1,400 men)	3 Bulūks (=175 men)

These figures do not include the Gendarmerie of the **Hasa** Sanjāq, consisting of 4 Bulūks of mounted and 2 of unmounted Dhābitīyahs, who are the 4th Tābūr of the Basrah Wilāyat.

The annual cost of the Gendarmerie in the Wilāyat of Baghdād is about £60,000 sterling, and of those in the Wilāyat of Basrah rather less than £40,000.

Civil police, Qānūns and passport system.—In the larger centres of population and in places of administrative importance in 'Irāq there exists, alongside of the Gendarmerie, a purely civil police force differently constituted; where the latter are found the employment of Gendarmerie is excluded, but the authority of the civil police does not extend to surrounding villages or to the open country. The civil police force consists of Police Commissioners of 3 grades and of constables; their pay is as follows:—

Turkish title.	Corresponding English rank.	Monthly pay in gold piastres.	Annual pay in English money.
Sar-Commissaire سر قومیسر	Police Superintendent of the 1st grade.	1,000	£108
Ikinji Commissaire اکنجی قومیسر	Police Superintendent of the 2nd grade.	500	£54
Ūchunji Commissaire اوچنجی قومیسر	Police Superintendent of the 3rd grade.	300	£33
Pōlīs پولیس	Constable.	200	£22

There is a Sar-Commissaire of Police at **Baghdād** City and another at **Basrah** Town, each being the head of the civil police in his Wilāyat. In **Baghdād** City there are, in addition to the Sar-Commissaire, 2 Commissaires of the 2nd grade, 6 of the 3rd grade, and 29 constables. The distribution of the remainder of the civil police in that Wilāyat appears to be somewhat as follows: at **Karbala** Town a Commissaire of the 2nd grade; at each of the towns of 'Anah, **Kādhimain, Kūt-al-Amārah, Najaf** and Sāmarrah, 1 Commissaire of the 3rd grade and 1 constable; at Ba'qūbah and Khānaqīn, 1 Commissaire of the 3rd grade each; at Badrah 1 constable, at Mandali 1 constable and at **Tawairīj** 3 constables. The officers of the civil police are entitled to make use of Dhābitīyahs when they require men. The annual cost of the civil police is less than £2,000 sterling in the Wilāyat of Baghdād, and less than £500 in that of Basrah.

A small force of Qānūns or military police, drawn from the local troops, has recently been created to assist the civil police in garrison towns. They are specially charged with the supervision of soldiers in streets and bazars, and are distinguished by a crescent-shaped brass badge bearing the word Qānūn قانون whence their name, and by a yellow worsted aiguillette. In **Baghdād** City the Qānuns number 16.

Before leaving the subject of civil police we may note that a system of travelling passports or Tadhākir-al-Marūr تذاکر المرور

obtains in 'Irāq but is very imperfectly enforced. Every person, whether an Ottoman subject or not, desiring to cross the boundary of the Wilāyat in which he resides is supposed to provide himself with such a Tadhkirah : the necessary document is issued in the large towns by a department known as Nufūs نفوس, and in smaller places by the petty civil officials. Few travellers take the trouble to comply with the law and the right of examining passports is consequently a lucrative one.

Justice.—The principal remaining departments for the working of which the Wāli of the Wilāyat is responsible will be noticed incidentally, further on, in connection with the subject of finance. Consequently we now pass on to consider those institutions and branches of the administration which are directly controlled from Constantinople ; and of these the courts of justice are perhaps the most important.

Courts are of four kinds,—ecclesiastical, criminal, civil, and commercial,—and we proceed to deal with them in this order, taking the ecclesiastical first because they are the oldest and are indigenous to the country.

Ecclesiastical courts.—In 'Irāq, as elsewhere, only questions of Shara' شرع or Quranic law are entertained by the ecclesiastical courts, and the judges are Qādhis قاضي recognised and paid by Government, of whom there is one at the headquarters of each Wilāyat, Sanjāq and Qadha. The scale of pay of Qādhis is personal : the present Qādhi of **Baghdād** draws 60 Līrahs a month. From the decision of the Qādhi of a Wilāyat an appeal lies to the Shaikh-al-Islām شيخ الاسلام at Constantinople only ; but local appeals in 'Irāq, from the lower Qādhis to the higher, are permitted.

Another set of functionaries of the Quranic law, but jurisconsults rather than judges, are the Muftis مفتي, who resolve legal difficulties and give Fatwas فتوى or decisions authorising or prohibiting acts of disputed legality, especially such as are connected with marriage. An officially recognised Mufti is found at the *chef-lieu* of each Wilāyat and Sanjāq, and the Qādhi of every Qadha also exercises the functions of Nāib or Deputy Mufti in the same. The Mufti of **Baghdād** ordinarily receives 12 to 18 Līrahs a month as pay.

Criminal and civil courts.—The tribunals exercising criminal and civil jurisdiction in 'Irāq are the Bidāyat Mahkamahsi بدايت محكمه سي or Court of First Instance, one of which exists at the headquarters of every Wilāyat, Sanjāq and Qadha in 'Irāq; the Istināf استئناف or High Court at **Baghdād**, with original and appellate jurisdiction; and the **Tamyīz** تميیز or Supreme Court of Appeal at Constantinople, with appellate jurisdiction only. Each of these three tribunals has a criminal side or Jaza Qismi جزاء قسمي and a civil side or Huqūq Qismi حقوق قسمي; and in each the judges of these separate sides are two distinct sets of persons.

The Bidāyat as a criminal court consists of a President and either two or four members, half of the members being ordinarily Muhammadans and half non-Muhammadans; the members are appointed for two years each, after objections to their names have been invited and considered.

The President of the civil division of the Istināf is the **Qādhi** of the Wilāyat.

The Tamyīz deals with questions of both law and fact, and its decisions cannot be reversed except by Iradé ارادە or edict of the Sultān.

The language of all the courts in 'Irāq is Turkish, and the courts themselves are spoken of by their Turkish names.

Criminal proceedings.—Crimes are divided in Ottoman jurisprudence into three categories, *viz.*, Qabāhah قباحه, Junhah جنحه and Janāyah جنایه, corresponding respectively to petty, ordinary, and serious offences.

In the discharge of their criminal functions the courts are assisted by a Mud'i 'Umūmi مدعي عمومي or Public Prosecutor and his subordinates, by a Mustantiq مستنطق or Examining Magistrate, and by a body called the Haiah Ittihāmīyah هیئه اتهامیه or Court of Testing Charges. A Public Prosecutor and an Assistant Public Prosecutor are stationed in each Wilāyat, and it is their duty to collect and arrange the evidence for government prosecutions and to conduct such cases in court; an officer, known as a Mu'āwin معاون, of lower status but having the same functions, is attached to every Court of First Instance. The Examining Magistrate, who is appointed by Imperial decree and represents a department styled the Istintāq Ōtahsi استنطاق اوطه سي, is empowered to make preliminary arrests and to hold magisterial inquiries with a view to determining whether accused persons should be released or should be committed for trial by competent courts; this he does at the request of the Public Prosecutor, to whom he is subordinate, and he cannot himself convict or pass sentence in any case. The Court of Testing Charges consists of three judges taken from the criminal side of the Court of First Instance of a Markaz Sanjāq; it meets on fixed day without being specially convoked, and its duties, as will be seen further on, are analogous to those of an English grand jury.

Cases of Qabāhah are generally sent by the Public Prosecutor direct, that is without reference to the Examining Magistrate, to the Court of First Instance of the Sanjāq or Wilāyat, and may be tried and disposed of by the President and two members of that tribunal. From decisions of the Court of First Instance in such cases there is no appeal, except on a point of law to the Court of Tamyīz at Constantinople.

Cases of Junhah are first referred by the Public Prosecutor to the Examining Magistrate for investigation ; when the latter has submitted his report the prisoners are sent for trial to the Court of First Instance, which, as in Qabāhah cases, consists of a President and two members only. In cases of the Junhah class, including such as arise in the Basrah Wilāyat, an appeal lies from the finding of the Court of First Instance to the High Court at **Baghdād**, and thereafter to the Supreme Court of Appeal at Constantinople.

Cases of Janāyah are referred by the Public Prosecutor to the Examining Magistrate, and are reported on by the latter, in the same manner as cases belonging to the Junhah category ; but here the similarity in procedure ends, for a person accused of Janāyah is not placed on his trial until the Court of Testing Charges have examined the papers in the case and have held that a *primâ facie* case against him exists. The trial of cases of Janāyah which arise in the Baghdād Wilāyat is conducted by the Istināf at **Baghdād** in the exercise of its original criminal jurisdiction ; but in the Basrah Wilāyat, where no High Court at present exists, such cases are heard by a Janāyah Mahkamahsi جنايه محكمه سي specially constituted for the purpose and composed of the President and four members of the Court of First Instance. In Janāyah cases there is a direct appeal to the Tamyīz Court at Constantinople.

British subjects are not exempt from the jurisdiction of the Turkish criminal courts; but, by Article 42 of the Capitulations with Turkey, no criminal case against a British subject may proceed except in the presence of the British Ambassador or of a British Consul. No sentence passed on a British subject is valid until concurred in by the British diplomatic or consular representative ; and, should the latter disapprove of the order which the court proposes to pass, the matter must be settled between the British Ambassador at Constantinople and the Turkish Ministry of Justice.

Civil proceedings.—The Bidāyats or Courts of First Instance may entertain and decide all civil causes whatever their value or nature ; and the judgment of the Bidāyat in civil cases is subject to appeal only if the value of the claim exceeds 50 Līrahs. Civil appeals from the Bidāyat lie to a superior Bidāyat, to the Istināf or to the Tamyīz according to circumstances. Basrah civil cases reach the Baghdād courts by way of appeal only.

Commercial courts and proceedings.—Besides the ordinary civil courts there are in 'Irāq two Commercial Courts, one at the headquarters of the Baghdād, and the other at the headquarters of the Basrah Wilāyat. This form of tribunal, known as the Tijārat Mahkamahsi تجارت محكمه سي tries most mercantile suits, as well as cases relating to bills of exchange and promissory notes which are not strictly of a commercial character; but its jurisdiction is not altogether exclusive, for commercial cases in which the value of the subject matter does not exceed 10 Līrahs may, but only if all the parties are Ottoman subjects, be disposed of by the ordinary civil courts.

The Commercial Court consists of a President appointed from Constantinople and of two nominated members, these 3 being all Muhammadans, with the addition of 2 non-Muhammadan elected members, generally a Christian and a Jew, who are appointed for one year each by their respective communities. The procedure of the Commercial Court is based upon the Code Napoléon, but it also follows to some extent the principles of Islamic jurisprudence. The President and the Members have each one vote, and the decision of the court is by a majority of votes. It is within the competence of this court to declare Ottoman subjects bankrupt. When all the parties to a suit are Turkish subjects there is a first appeal from the Commercial Court to the Istināf at **Baghdād** and a second to the Tamyīz at Constantinople.

Certain differences in procedure are involved if a foreign subject is a party to a case in the Commercial Court. In such circumstances one or two assessors are added to the ordinary members of the court, these being of the same nationality—if it can be arranged—as the foreigner interested; the proceedings are watched by a representative of the foreigner's consulate, and an appeal lies not to the superior civil courts but to the Tijāratin Birinji Majlisi تجارتن برنجي مجلسي or Commercial Court at Constantinople, of which the decision is final. A judgment creditor who is a Turkish subject can only, it should be observed, obtain a declaration of the bankruptcy of a foreign debtor and the appointment of a receiver and trustee, by application to the foreigner's consulate through the local Turkish authorities. It may be added that in matters of succession and bankruptcy the Porte allows its subjects to submit to the jurisdiction of the consular court of the deceased or the bankrupt.

Imperial Departments.—The Imperial Departments, which have branches in 'Irāq but of which the working is not subject to the control of the local Wālis, may be divided into 2 classes, *viz.*, those of which the whole *raison d'être* is to produce revenue and those which are intended to serve the public convenience. To the former of these classes belong the Customs, Public Debt, Tobacco Monopoly, and Land Record Departments; the second includes Posts and Telegraphs and the Departments of Public Health, Religious Endowments and Public Instruction.

Department of Customs.—The Imperial Customs department, known as Gumruk كمرك, is charged with the collection of the duties payable at the frontier, both sea and land, of 'Irāq. The highest local Customs official is a Nādhir ناظر or Director-General, who is stationed at **Baghdād**, deals direct with Constantinople and has under his orders two executive officers called Mudīrs مدير, one of whom is quartered at **Baghdād** and the other at **Basrah**. Customs officials of a lower rank, called Mamūrs مامور, are found in the direction of the Persian frontier at Khanaqīn, Qizil Rubāt, Mandali and Badrah; on the Shatt-al-**'Arab** at Nashwah and **Qūrnah**; on the **Euphrates** at **Sūq-ash-Shuyūkh**; and on the **Tigris** at **Qal'at Sālih, 'Amārah, Kūt-al-Amārah, Suwairah** and **Kādhimain**.

The general rate in 'Irāq of Āmadīyah آمديه (also called Idkhālīyah ادخاليه) or import duty is 8 per cent.,* and that of the Raftīyah رفتيه (also called Ikhrājīyah اخراجيه) or export duty is 1 per cent. *ad valorem*; but there is no customs duty on salt as it is already a Government monopoly. On imported goods re-exported within six months a refund of 7 per cent. is allowed; in other words, goods in transit are placed on the same footing as original exports. Extra customs duties have recently been imposed by means of 2 kinds of stamps, required to be affixed to documents presented at the Customs House, which entail in some cases an addition of nearly 50 per cent. to the customs duty proper: one of these duties has no special object, but the proceeds of the other are professedly devoted to the construction of the railway from Syria to the Hijāz. The Customs receipts in the Baghdād and Basrah Wilāyats amounted in a recent year to £149,514 sterling, and the expenses of the department to £14,614.

---

* From the 12th of July 1907 it was raised to 11 per cent.

Department of Public Debt.—The Duyūn-al-'Umūmīyah ديون العمومية or Department of Public Debt, which is subject to international control and exists in the Ottoman dominions chiefly for the benefit of European bondholders, is represented in 'Irāq by a Nādhir at **Baghdād**, under whom are 5 Mudīrs, posted respectively at Ba'qūbah, **Basrah, Hillah, Kūt-al-Amārah** and Sāmarrah, besides Mamūrs of inferior rank or agents at **'Amārah,** 'Anah, **Umm-al-Ba'rūr** (or rather Hamīdīyah), **Dīwānīyah, Hai,** Hit, **Kādhimain,** Khānaqīn, Abul **Khasīb,** Mandali, **Musaiyib, Najaf, Nāsirīyah,** Qizil Rubāt, **Qūrnah, Samāwah, Shatrat-al-Muntafik, Sūq-ash-Shuyūkh** and **Tawairīj,** not to mention **'Oqair** Port and the town of **Qatīf** which are in the **Hasa** Sanjāq. The Nādhir has also at his disposal a Mufattish مفتش or travelling inspector.

The principal sources of revenue which have been made over to this department for management are fisheries, liquor, salt, silk, and stamps, and it may be regarded as an Excise Department. The distilleries at **Qarārah** and elsewhere are under its control, and the proceeds of the salt tax and of licenses for the vend of liquor go into its treasury.

The annual receipts of the Public Debt Department in the Wilāyats of Baghdād and Basrah amounted recently to £39,849 sterling, and its expenditure to £16,645.

The Tobacco Monopoly.—The Tobacco Monopoly, generally known as "the Régie Cointéressée des Tabacs de l'Empire Ottoman," is a joint stock company holding a monopoly for the manufacture and sale of tobacco in the Turkish Empire: it is represented at **Baghdād** by a Nādhir. There is also an office at **Basrah,** and Mudīrs, Mamūrs or other subordinate officials of the Company are stationed at **'Amārah,** Badrah, Ba'qūbah, **Hillah, Karbala,** Khānaqīn, **Kūt-al-Amārah,** Mandali, **Najaf,** Sāmarrah, **Samāwah** and **Tawairīj** and are under the orders of the Nādhir; their principal duties are to supervise the cultivation of tobacco and to collect the taxes payable thereon at the various dépôts of the Department. There is also, as a rule, a travelling inspector of the Régie with headquarters at **Baghdād.**

The tax on tobacco cultivation recovered by the Régie is at the rate of 7·8 gold piastres per kilogramme on the best homegrown tobaccos such as Shāūr شاور and Qūzi قوزي and of 3·9 gold piastres on inferior sorts like Khurdah خردة. Persian tobacco, which is largely imported for smoking in nargilés, pays an import duty of 2 gold piastres per kilogramme as customs to the Turkish Government and 1 piastre as "droit de monopole" to the Régie. The Tobacco Monopoly is virtually a branch of the Public Debt Department and it is not to be confounded with the Société du Tombac, an Ottoman company which holds an exclusive concession for the importation of Persian tobacco into Turkey. In 'Irāq the Qadhas most important to the Régie are those of **Hillah, Hindīyah, Karbala** and **Najaf**, but its rights are more restricted in this province than in other parts of Turkey.

Department of Land Records.—In order to understand the work of the Daftar Khāqāni دفتر خاقاني or, as we may call it, the Land Records Department, it is necessary first to explain the classification of land according to ownership which prevails in 'Irāq as in other parts of the Turkish Empire. There are 5 principal kinds of landed property.

The first kind is Mulk ملك or freehold property, over which the owner has full power in life and in death. It may be transmitted by inheritance or by legacy, and only in event of failure of heirs does it escheat to the Bait-al-Māl or Treasury. Mulk is of 4 sorts, but on this minuter classification it is unnecessary to enter. Mulk, in 'Irāq, consists chiefly of land in the neighbourhood of villages which has been purchased by the villagers from Government.

The second sort of land is Mīri ميري or that which belongs to the state; it comprises arable lands, pastures, and forests, and the ownership thereof is vested in the Bait-al-Māl.

Lands of the third kind are Waqf وقف : those, namely, of which the profits are assigned for religious purposes. Waqf lands that are under the management of the Department of Religious Endowments, to which we shall refer in another paragraph, are *ipso facto* free of taxation; while those in the hands of private individuals are taxed to the same extent as similar lands which are not Waqf. The large landed properties owned by or vested in the Naqīb of **Baghdād**, however, have been specially exempted from taxation by an Imperial edict and may therefore be regarded as Waqf in the public sense.

Matrūkah متروكه lands, or such as are not individual property and are left unoccupied for the public benefit, compose the fourth class.

The fifth category consists of Mawāt موات , or Dead Lands, which have remained uninhabited and uncultivated from time immemorial.

The lands owned by the Sultan of Turkey as an individual and managed on his behalf by the Dāirat-al-Saniyah or Civil List Department, of which we shall have something to say further on, may now almost be taken as constituting a sixth variety of land. These lands are known as Arādhi Sanīyah اراضي سنيّه ; they are private domains, and they must not be confounded with Arādhi Mīrīyah, or lands of the second kind, which are public or state domains.

The Daftar Khāqāni and its functions in regard to these various kinds of land and land tenure now fall to be considered. The Daftar, which in 'Irāq seems to be represented only by a Mamūr at **Baghdād**, is divided into two sections, the Tāpu طاپو and the Amlāk املاك. The duty of the Tāpu is (1) to register all facts connected with the ownership of land in general and (2) to manage the Arādhi Mīrīyah or public domains on behalf of the state. The bulk of the Arādhi Mīrīyah is in the possession of cultivators who have rights of occupancy, and these rights are obtained by payment of a price or sum in consideration of which a Sanad سند or title deed is conferred on the tenant by the Tāpu. At the death of a tenant under the Tāpu, or Mustahiqq Tāpu مستحقّ طاپو as he is called, his rights of occupancy pass to his heirs; but, on the other hand, a tenant of Mīrī land who leaves it uncultivated during three years forfeits thereby his occupancy rights. The disposal of government lands to occupancy tenants and, where that is impossible, the farming of them to Arab tribes upon produce rents are, together with the registration of all transactions in and arrangements relating to land, the work of the Tāpu.

The Amlāk section resembles the Tāpu in that it registers transfers, but these are only of house property.

Both Tāpū and Amlāk levy a registration fee, which in the case of the Amlāk is usually at the rate of about ½ per cent. *ad valorem*; and the receipts of both sections are remitted to Constantinople after deducting the local working expenses. The net revenue of the Department appears to have been £4,816 in the Baghdād Wilāyat in 1903, and £1,060 in the Basrah Wilāyat in 1901.

The Tāpu was established in 'Irāq in 1889 only, and the Amlāk even more recently.

Department of Posts and Telegraphs.—The postal and telegraphic services of 'Irāq have already been described under the heading of communications, and it only remains here to mention the organisation of the department which is responsible for the working of both. The chief official of the department in 'Irāq is a Director or Bāsh Mudīr باش مدیر

at **Baghdād**, under whom are two executive Mudīrs—one for Posts, the other for Telegraphs—and an Inspector most of whose time is given to the work of the Telegraph section. The receipts of the Department in 'Irāq in a recent year were apparently £18,097 sterling, and the working expenses £15,097.

Department of Public Health.—The sanitary department, which is chiefly occupied with quarantine, is controlled by a doctor of medicine at **Baghdād**, known as the Mufattish or Inspector, who receives his orders direct from the international Board of Health at Constantinople. Information in regard to the working of this department in 'Irāq will be found in the Appendix to this Gazetteer which deals with epidemics and sanitary organisation in the Persian Gulf. One of the principal subordinates of the Inspector is a doctor with three assistants at Khānaqīn, whose duty it is to inspect corpses entering the country from Persia for interment at the holy places of the Shī'ahs; and there are establishments for the maintenance of sea quarantine at **Fāo** and **Basrah** Town, the station at **Basrah** being located on 'Ajairāwīyah Island. After these the sanitary posts at **Najaf** and **Karbala**, where most of the Shī'ah burials take place, are the most important. Mamūrs of the department are stationed also at **'Amārah** on the **Tigris**; at Hāji Qarah حاجي قرة (in the Khānaqīn Qadha), Mandali and Badrah near the Persian frontier; and at Sāmarrah, **Kādhimain**, and **Musaiyib**, places visited by the Persian pilgrims or through which Shī'ah pilgrims and corpses pass. There is also a sanitary post at **Qatīf** Town in **Hasa**.

Not long ago the receipts of the Department of Public Health in the Baghdād and Basrah Wilāyats for one year amounted to £6,830 sterling and the expenditure to £3,819. The accounts of the department are kept by a Muhāsibji محاسبجي or Accountant at Baghdād.

Department of Religious Endowments.—The chief local official of the Religious Endowments or Auqāf اوقاف Department in 'Irāq is merely a Muhāsibji or Accountant at **Baghdād**; but much important work is performed by the department in superintending the finances of the great Shī'ah shrines. The Auqāf is able to hold its own with the local executive government in 'Irāq and has successfully obstructed, up to the present time, a scheme for the extension of the congested town of **Najaf**. The income of the Auqāf Department in 'Irāq in a financial year not long past was £7,981 sterling, and its expenditure in the same year £3,042.

Department of Public Instruction.—The Educational Department or Ma'ārif معارف maintains a primary school or Maktab Rushdī مكتب رشدي in which Turkish and Arabic are taught at the *chef-lieu* of every Sanjāq and Qaḍha. In addition to these there are a Maktab I'dādī Mulki مكتب اعدادي ملكي or secondary civil school for boys and an Ināth Maktab Rashdīsi اناث مكتب رشدي سي or primary school for girls at **Baghdād** and at **Basrah**; all of these are government institutions managed by the Department and in them no fees are charged. The secondary boys' school at **Baghdād** was founded in 1890 and the number of pupils is about 250, most of whom eventually enter the public service or proceed to study law or medicine at Constantinople. The primary girls' school at **Baghdād** was opened in 1898. Besides the above there are a Maktab Rashdīsi 'Askari مكتب رشدي سي عسكري or primary military school and a Maktab I'dādi Askari مكتب اعدادي عسكري or secondary military school at **Baghdād**; and **Baghdād** and **Basrah** each possesses a Maktab San'īyah مكتب صنعيه or industrial school. The military schools are free. The Dāirat-as-Sanīyah maintains primary schools on some of the rural estates which are under its management.

Besides the schools of the Education Department there are many schools, both Muhammadan and non-Muhammadan, in 'Irāq, especially at the larger centres of population. Thus at **Karbala** the Sunnis have one, and the Shī'ahs a number, of religious high schools or Madrasahs مدرسه; and, as the unmarried students mostly live in the school building, these may be described as boarding schools. At **Baghdād** the Jewish, Chaldæan, Syrian, and Armenian communities, consisting of Ottoman subjects, each maintain a good school of their own.

Schools in 'Irāq kept by non-Turkish subjects are noticed under the head of British and other foreign interests below.

Finance and taxation.—Below are two tables of annual revenue and expenditure in the Wilāyats of 'Irāq; in the first table the provinces are treated separately, in the second they are combined. The figures for the Sanjāq of **Hasa** or "Najd" are, it should be remembered, included in both tables. In the first table the Baghdād figures are taken from the official budget of the Wilāyat for 1903 while those for Basrah, also from official sources, are about 2 years older. The date of the statistics contained in the second table is uncertain but recent.

'IRÂQ (TURKISH)

Table I.

Annual Revenue in Pounds Sterling.			Annual Expenditure in Pounds Sterling.		
Item.	Baghdād.	Basrah.	Item.	Baghdād.	Basrah.
Tent and hut tax.	6,851	3,989	Salaries of officials under the Ministry of the Interior.	17,934	24,599
Military service commutation tax.	5,216	436	Shara' courts.	4,150	
Sheep tax.	30,962	14,688	Justice.	8,386	
Buffalo tax.	929	1,682	Revenue establishments.	12,336	
Camel tax.	4,180	1,049	Monthly allowances to individuals.	4,612	
Fixed tithes (i.e. farmed out).	59,647	99,675	Military.	108,085	98,875
Revenue tithes (i.e. collected direct).	Nil.	44,882	Marine.	Nil	8,037
Security deposits.*	65,182	Nil	Gendarmerie.	59,883	38,363
Leases.	196	Nil	Civil police.	1,823	474
Income tax.	30,250	Nil	Sanitary.	248	60
Forest receipts.	498	Nil	Pensions, etc.	11,818	14,545
Royalties on minerals.	179	Nil	Miscellaneous.	Nil	916
Tāpu and Amlāk receipts.	4,816	1,060			
Court-fees.	2,021	1,152			
Miscellaneous.	981	17,216			
Totals	£211,908	£185,829	Totals	£229,275	£185,869

In the budget of Basrah Wilāyat for 1905-1906, however, revenue was estimated at £168,402 and expenditure at £185,842.

* This item consists of sums paid into the treasury by persons to whom Government lands are leased.

Table II.

Department.	Annual revenue in pounds sterling.	Annual expenditure in pounds sterling.
Customs	149,514	14,614
Public Debt	39,849	16,645
Posts and Telegraphs	18,097	15,097
Sanitary	6,830	3,819
Religious endowments	7,981	3,042
Totals	£222,271	£53,217

Of the items contained in the tables above those connected with the Imperial Civil Departments have been already noticed in the foregoing paragraphs on the departments, while those relating to the military and marine services will be dealt with in their appropriate places further on ; but a few words may be added here in explanation of some of the other entries.

The tent and hut tax, generally known as Baitīyah بيتية or Buyūtīyah بيوتية, is a tax collected, where collection is feasible, by the Turkish Government from its agricultural Arab subjects, both fixed and semi-fixed. It is levied at the rate of 50 gold piastres per annum on every house or hut, but it is a tax on households rather than on dwellings ; for a house inhabited by two married couples is reckoned as two dwellings and one containing only unmarried members of a family which already pays Baitīyah is exempt. Widows and helpless persons are excused from this tax. Along with the Baitīyah proper of 50 gold piastres per house is recovered an annual cess of $5\frac{1}{2}$ gold piastres ; this is described as a contribution towards educational and military expenditure.

The various taxes on domestic animals are all included under the common term of Kōda كودا ; they fall (or ought to fall) largely on the nomad tribes, and consequently nothing like realisation in full can be effected. The Shaikhs of the Bedouin tribes ordinarily wring from the tribesmen under them as much as they can on their own behoof; but in matters of Turkish taxation, on the contrary, they screen and protect them to the best of their ability. Kōda is paid at two different rates, *viz.*, at half a Majidi per annum for each camel, horse, mule, cow, buffalo, pig or monkey (*sic*) and at 12 Rāij piastres per annum for each sheep, goat or donkey.

The agricultural taxes—generally described, whatever their incidence may be, as 'Ushr عشر or tithes—are the most valuable source of revenue and also the most difficult to understand. Mulk lands are assessed at $\frac{1}{10}$ to $\frac{1}{5}$ of gross produce, the former rate being applicable to all holdings which are irrigated by means of water-lifts and to Daim lands in the autumn harvest, and the latter to Daim lands in the spring harvest; some Chaltīq lands, however, of the Mulk class, pay as much as $\frac{1}{3}$rd of gross produce. The revenue, or rather rent, charged by the Government for the use of Mīri lands is a matter of arrangement between the Tāpu and the tenant, but it ranges ordinarily from $\frac{1}{10}$th of gross produce on lands unfavourably situated to $\frac{1}{5}$th on lands which are easily irrigated or highly cultivated; in exceptional circumstances, however, it may amount to $\frac{1}{3}$rd or even to $\frac{1}{2}$. The lessees of Mīri lands are frequently tribal Shaikhs who either give security for the rent or pay part of it in advance; and the leases granted them are commonly for one year only, but may be for two or even for three. In table No. I above, "fixed tithes" are understood to represent agricultural revenue farmed out, "revenue tithes" the same collected direct, and "security deposits" the advances or guarantees furnished by lessees of Mīri lands. There is an annual tax of 7 Rāij piastres on every date palm, and one of 2 to 4 Rāij piastres on every orange tree; honey also is taxed at the rate of $\frac{1}{10}$th of its market value. Agricultural revenue of all kinds is collected at the time of harvest.

Landed property may be held in Turkey by foreign governments, foreign religious bodies, etc., as Mulk or Waqf; and when this is the case a yearly tax, described at Muqāta'ah مقاطعة, is paid as compensation to the Ottoman Government for the tithes, right of escheat, etc., thus lost to it.

The official forests from which, as Table No. I above shows, a small revenue is derived are for the most part plantations by the banks of the large rivers: they consist chiefly of Euphrates poplar and of tamarisk, and the timber is usually very small. Such forests exist at or near **Suwairah**, **'Azīzīyah** and **'Amārah** Town upon the **Tigris**, and also at several other places which are indicated in the article on that river.

The royalty on minerals extracted in 'Irāq varies between 5 and 15 per cent. *ad valorem.*

Miscellaneous taxes, somewhat exceptional in their character and of which the proceeds are not shown in the tables above, are Turābīyah ترابية and Shahrīyah شهرية. Turābīyah consists of burial dues realised by the Turkish Government on account of Shī'ah interments at **Najaf, Karbala** and **Kādhimain**: it varies from 31½ to 5,000 gold piastres per corpse according to the sacredness of the place of burial. The Shahrīyah is a punitive tax, from which British subjects are exempt, collected at **Karbala** only; it was imposed by the Porte about 40 years ago in consequence of resistance offered by the inhabitants to conscription for military service, and it is payable by traders at a rate varying from ⅕th to ½ Majīdi monthly.

No harbour dues are charged by the Turkish authorities at **Basrah** Town, who in this case appear to have overlooked their opportunity.

Municipal taxation does not enter into the provincial budgets given above, but a few remarks on the subject will not be out of place here. An octroi or Ihtisāb احتساب, the liability to which of British subjects is not admitted, is levied at the rate of 7 per cent. on local products entering an inland town where there is no customs house; but articles imported from abroad, which have already paid customs duty, are exempt from this charge. Examples of other municipal or partially municipal taxes follow: they are taken from **Baghdād** City, where all of them are in force. An 8 per cent. duty is levied on Sha'ri thread worked up into Āghabāni cloth: the thread, at the time of being imported, had already paid customs duty at the rate of 8 * per cent. A tax called Tamgha طمغا, of which the amount varies with the article, is taken on all cloth and woollen goods manufactured or embroidered locally; the farm of this tax in **Baghdād** City produces about £900 sterling a year. There is also the Pāsbānīyah پاسبانیه, a tax collected monthly and graduated according to incomes, of which the object is to provide for municipal scavenging and lighting and for watch and ward. Other taxes to which the citizen of **Baghdād** is liable are the Asnāfīyah اصنافیه, a trade tax of ¼th to ½ a Majīdi on each trader annually, and a tax ranging from 2¼ to 45 Rāij piastres per head on the slaughter of animals for food. The majority of the preceding are purely municipal taxes, but the proceeds of the Asnāfīyah and slaughter tax go partly into the funds of the municipality and partly into the general revenues of the province. Taxes on fish, firewood, Quffahs and boats also are paid in **Baghdād** City; but these are provincial, except the tax on fish, which is taken by the Department of Public Debt, and none of them are municipal.

When any tax is paid a receipt is given; and to the receipt must now be affixed, in 'Irāq, not only an ordinary receipt stamp of ¼th gold piastre but also a Hijāz Railway stamp of 1 gold piastre.

---

* Now 11 per cent. (1907)

Dāirat-as-Sanīyah.—Before leaving the subject of the civil and general administration it will be advisable to notice, in some detail, an official agency which in 'Irāq possesses great economic and political importance: this in the Dāirat-Qomīsyōn-as-Sanīyah دائرة قميسيون السنيه, generally known as the Dāirat-as-Sanīyah. The Dāirat-as-Sanīyah is a section of the Khazīnah-i-Khāssah-i-Shāhānah خزينة خاصّة شاهانه or Ottoman Civil List Department, by which the large private properties of the Sultān of Turkey are administered. It is presided over, in 'Irāq, by a Central Committee at **Baghdād**, which corresponds direct with the Minister of the Civil List at Constantinople; and in the part of the Turkish Empire with which we are concerned it consists of two principal branches, one dealing with lands and irrigation and the other with navigation. We shall now examine separately the assets and methods of each of these branches, and at the same time we shall mention some facts relating to the local staff, income and policy of the department.

The private domains of the Sultān, administered on his behalf by the Dāirat-as-Sanīyah, are known as Arādhi Sanīyah اراضي سنيّه; and it is stated that they now amount, in the Baghdād Wilāyat, to about 30 per cent. of the whole cultivable area as against 30 per cent. owned by the state, 20 per cent. belonging to private individuals, and 20 per cent. which is unclassed. In the Basrah Wilāyat also considerable areas, including some of the finest wheat, rice, and date-growing tracts, are under the management of the department. The Sanīyah lands in 'Irāq may be conveniently divided into 4 groups depending for irrigation on the **Tigris**, the Shatt-al-**Gharāf**, the **Euphrates** and the Shatt-al-**'Arab** respectively; but, in addition to these lands on the main rivers, there are Sanīyah properties on the Mahrūt مهروط canal in the valley of the **Diyālah**, and even on the 'Aliyāwah علياوه canal close to the Persian frontier at Khānaqīn. The Dāirat-as-Sanīyah has also charge of agricultural and other properties in **Hasa** which are referred to in the article on that Sanjāq.

On the **Tigris** the Dāirat-as-Sanīyah has acquired the Dujail canal, which takes out on the right bank of the river above **Baghdād**, and holds possession of the estates, irrigated from the same, of Dujail, Balad بلد and Sumaikah سميكه in the Sāmarrah Qadha and of Tārmīyah in the Qadha of **Kādhimain**. Below **Baghdād**, between 'Azīzīyah Village and **Kūt-al-Amārah** Town, the valuable estate of Shādi in the Qadha of 'Azīzīyah is controlled by the Dāirat-as-Sanīyah, and Sanīyah lands extend along the right bank of the river from Tawīl to Umm-al-'Ajāj and along the left bank from Summar or Samr to Imām Mahdi; these last are said to reach, on either side of the river, from 20 to 30 miles inland; and in the right bank block is situated the rising village of **Bghailah** which is altogether under the department. The right bank of the **Tigris** from the point where the Shatt-al-**Gharāf** leaves it to Shaikh **Sa'ad,** together with the country behind it to a depth of perhaps 40 miles, is under the Dāirat-as-Sanīyah. The **Tigris** properties down to Shaikh **Sa'ad** are all situated in the Wilāyat of Baghdād. From **Kumait** to the Bitairah canal Sanīyah lands occupy the right bank and extend inland some 30 miles; and further down the lands about Daffās, opposite to **'Amārah** Town, also those of **Majar-al-Kabīr** and Majar-as-Saghīr, and others on the right bank in the neighbourhood of Qal'at **Sālih** are included in the Sultān's private domains. On the left bank the Sanīyah properties are believed to extend almost continuously from **'Amārah** Town to a point opposite **'Azair,** while inland in the same neighbourhood they reach almost to the **Hawīzeh** marshes, including in particular the tracts of Akhdhar, Bahāthah, Jahálah, Misharrah and Shatt which are in the **'Amārah** Qadha and a large portion of the Qadha of **Zubair.** All the estates mentioned above from **Kumait** downwards are in the Wilāyat of Basrah.

The Dāirat-as-Sanīyah also holds a quantity of land in the Muntafik Sanjāq, probably irrigated by the Shatt-al-**Gharāf.**

The Sanīyah estates watered by the **Euphrates** are numerous, and most of them are named from the canals on which they depend; the cultivators as a rule, inhabit temporary and not permanent villages. Above and below **Musaiyib** are properties of which the centres are Abu **Ghuraib, Mahmūdīyah** and **Sikandarīyah,** the first probably including the lands managed by the Department at Khidhar Aliyās, and others irrigated by the Latīfīyah, Musaiyib and Nasrīyah canals from the **Euphrates.** In the neighbourhood of **Hillah** Town are Sanīyah lands watered by the Nīl and Wardīyah canals, and in the Khawās Nāhiyah of the **Hillah** Qadha are domains known as Abu Gharq, Umm-al-Hawa, 'Ilāj, Yūsufīyah, and Abu 'Arāis. The Hamīdīyah canal which brings drinking water to **Najaf** Town is a Sanīyah property; so also is a large tract of country known as Mushkhāb which has its headquarters at Abu Sikhair and includes the prosperous village of Ja'ārah; Abu Sikhair and Ja'ārah are both in the **Shāmīyah** Qadha.

On the Shatt-al-**'Arab** 1,500 acres of valuable land, chiefly at Da'aiji village, at Sanīyah (I) and at Sanīyah (II) in the **Dawāsir** District are said to be in the possession of the department.

The methods of the Dāirat-as-Sanīyah in agriculture are energetic. Its custom is to acquire the most easily worked canals and to push each one that comes into its possession as far as it will go, never irrigating the same land a second time until the canal has attained its maximum length. A survey is carried on concurrently with the expansion of irrigation, but the undeveloped portions of each estate are left for the time being unsurveyed; it follows that, although the limits are marked out on the ground with boundary pillars, the total areas in its charge are generally as yet unknown even to the department. The lands to be irrigated during the year are leased out to cultivators on a rent of two-fifths, or, if the seed is supplied by the Dāirat-as-Sanīyah, of seven-tenths of the produce; and money advances are sometimes given to the cultivators and recovered in the harvest. The landed property under management of the Dāirat-as-Sanīyah has mostly been obtained on extremely favourable terms, for, when—as often happens—Arādhi Mīrīyah or state domains are disposed of by auction, no one ventures to bid against the representatives of His Majesty the Sultān.

The branch of the Dāirat-as-Sanīyah which is concerned with land and irrigation engages in miscellaneous enterprises also. It has constructed a number of handsome dwelling-houses at **'Amārah** Town, which bring in good rents; and it has recently undertaken the collection of tolls at the Kharr Bridge near **Baghdād**, a right which was formerly leased to a contractor for about 2,100 Līrahs or £1,900 sterling a year.

The navigation branch of the Dāirat-as-Sanīyah, known as the Hamīdīyah حميديه Navigation Office, came into existence with the purchase by the department, in March 1904, of the whole stock and assets upon the Shatt-al-'**Arab** and **Tigris** rivers of a former " 'Omān-Ottoman " branch of the Turkish Ministry of Marine. The principal items then transferred to the Dāirat-as-Sanīyah and the valuations at which they changed hands were as below :—

	£ Turkish.	£ English.
River steamers (3) and barges (3)	5,050	4,545
River steamer (1)	1,500	1,350
Workshop at **Basrah** with engineering plant complete	1,500	1,350
Dry dock in the Khandaq creek at **Basrah** with some machinery	1,000	900
Office, brick-built storage godown, and open space of about 4,000 square yards for cargo on the Shatt-al-'Arab at Basrah	150	135
Office at '**Amārah** Town	100	90
Do. at **Kūt-al-Amārah** Town	100	90
Do. at **Baghdād** City	100	90

Influences similar to those which enable the Dāirat-as-Sanīyah to buy land cheaply were evidently at work on this occasion, for the office at **Kūt-al-Amārah** had been built only 2 years before at a cost of £T. 1,500, while the market value of the Baghdād office has been estimated at £T. 1,500 to 2,000. In 1905 the Hamīdīyah office added two new Glasgow-built steamers to its fleet and was arranging to obtain 2 new barges: the vessels in its possession at the end of that year were :—

(1) River steamer "Baghdādi" بغدادي, age 44 years, speed 6 knots, carrying capacity = 100 passengers.

(2) River steamer "Furāt" فرات, age 38 years, tonnage 125, horse power 200, speed 5 knots an hour, carrying capacity = 400 passengers, 4 horses and 70 tons of cargo.

(3) River steamer "Rusāfah" رصافة, similar in all respects to the "Furāt."

(4) River steamer "Mūsal" موصل, age over 30 years, speed 7 knots an hour, carrying capacity = 600 passengers, 8 horses and 100 tons of cargo.

(5) River steamer "Hamīdīyah" حميدية, new, tonnage 430, horse power 700, good cabins and electric light. The contract speed of this steamer was 12 knots and the carrying capacity should have been 900 passengers, 10 horses and 230 tons of cargo; but capacity is deficient and the maximum speed is 9 knots an hour only.

(6) River steamer "Burhāniyah" برهانية, similar in all respects to the "Hamīdīyah", except that she has attained a speed of $10\frac{1}{4}$ knots an hour.

Besides the above there were 2 barges, each about 40 years old.

The Hamīdīyah office competes closely with the (British) Euphrates and Tigris Steam Navigation Company for the **Tigris** carrying trade, and it is stated that its agents sometimes appeal to the loyalty or religious feelings of native merchants and passengers in order to obtain their patronage. Turkish troops on mobilisation or relief and Turkish government stores are carried by the Hamīdīyah steamers at commercial rates; and in the Hamīdīyah workshop at **Basrah**, where castings of as much as 5 cwt. can be executed, engineering and mechanical work of all sorts is undertaken for private employers.

The highest local authority in Sanīyah matters in 'Irāq is a Central Committee at **Baghdād**; but the principal place of business is now at **'Amārah** Town, whither it was transferred from **Basrah** about 1899. Both at **'Amārah** and at **Basrah** there is a Committee subordinate to the Central Committee at **Baghdād**: that at **'Amārah** consists of a President, a Mudīr and 3 members. The general staff of the department in 'Irāq is considered to be small in proportion to the amount of business transacted, but the members are well paid. The Central Committee at **Baghdād** includes a Raīs رئيس or President with a salary of £T. 55 a month, a Mudīr مدير or Director on £T. 40 a month and a Kashf-Mudīr كشف مدير or Chief Surveyor, besides several merchants who receive small monthly honoraria for their services. A feature of the Dāirat-as-Sanīyah administration is the number of military officers on the active list whose services are utilised, a special allowance being given them by the department in addition to their military pay; thus the Kashf-Mudīr at **Baghdād** is a military Colonel receiving £T. $17\frac{1}{2}$ monthly from the department, and not long ago the Mushīr of the 6th Army Corps himself held a well paid appointment under the Dāirat-as-Sanīyah. The object of this arrangement is possibly to secure a supply of military labour for the work of the Dāirat-as-Sanīyah; for some use is made of such labour, yet nothing is paid to the rank and file employed.

No complete account is available of the executive staff of the Dāirat-as-Sanīyah in 'Irāq, but it comprises at least the following:—

Group.	Estates.	Staff.	Remarks.
Tigris properties.	Dujail, Balad, Sumaikah and Tārmīyah.	Wakīl or Agent at Dujail, and a Mamūr or Manager each at the other places.	......
Do.	On both sides of the **Tigris** above and below **Bghailah**.	A Mamūr, with headquarters at **Bghailah**.	......
Do.	Akhdhar in the **'Amārah** Qadha.	A Mamūr and a clerk.	......
Do.	Bahāthah and Jahálah in the **'Amārah** Qadha.	A Mamūr and 2 clerks.	......
Do.	Misharrah in the **'Amārah** Qadha.	A Mamūr and 1 clerk.	......
Do.	Shatt in the **'Amārah** Qadha.	Do.	......
Do.	Tafrah, etc., in the **Zubair** Qadha.	A manager at Masa'īdah on the **Jahálah**.	......
Do.	About Qal'at Sālih.	An official at Qal'at Sālih.	......

Group.	Estates.	Staff.	Remarks.
Shatt-al-Gharāf properties.	...	A Mamūr at Dujailah دجيله in the Hai Qadha, perhaps the locality so called on the right bank of the Tigris.	......
Do.	...	A Mamūr at Shatrat-al-Muntafik.	......
Do.	...	A Mamūr at Hammār.	......
Euphrates properties.	Abu Ghuraib.	A Mamūr and assistant with headquarters at Abu Ghuraib, also 2 clerks and 7 mounted Dhābitīyahs.	The manager is at present a military Adjutant-Major, receiving an allowance of £T. 10 a month from the department: his assistant is a military Captain.
Do.	Mahmūdīyah.	A Mamūr with headquarters at Mahmūdīyah, under whom are some Dhābitīyahs and a few soldiers.	......
Do.	Latīfīyah.	A Mamūr.	......
Do.	Sikandarīyah.	A Mamūr with headquarters at Sikandarīyah.	......
Do.	Nasrīyah and others in the Karbala Qadha.	A Wakīl.	......
Do.	Nīl, Wardīyah, Abu 'Arāis, Abu Gharq, Umm-al-Hawa, 'Ilāj, Mālih and Yūsufīyah in the Hillah Qadha.	A Mamūr.	......
Do.	Jarbū'īyah in the Hillah Qadha.	A Wakīl.	The manager is at present a junior military officer who receives a monthly allowance of £T. 9 from the Dāirat-as-Sanīyah.

Group.	Estates.	Staff.	Remarks.
Euphrates properties.	Je'ārah (including Mushkhāb).	A manager with headquarters in a fort belonging to the department at Abu Sikhair; he has a staff of 2 clerks, a touring inspector, etc., and about 100 soldiers, mounted and unmounted, under him.	The manager is a military Major. There is also a Wakīl.
Do.	Durrāji.	......	......
Shatt-al-'Arab properties.	...	A Mamūr at Basrah with a staff of 2 or more clerks.	......

In addition to these local agents the Dāirat-as-Sanīyah has in 'Irāq a field-engineer and an assistant field-engineer. The former is a military Lieutenant-Colonel, but receives a salary of £180 sterling a year. His assistant is a military Adjutant-Major. The Sanīyah officials in **Hasa** are mentioned in the article on that Sanjāq.

The estate managers of the Dāirat-as-Sanīyah have no criminal or civil jurisdiction. The petty employés who work under them, called Shabānah شبانة, are generally Arabs and do not wear uniform.

The Director, at **Basrah**, of the Hamīdīyah Navigation Office has lately been endeavouring to free himself of the control of the Central Committee at **Baghdād** and to obtain the right of dealing direct with the Ministry of the Civil List at Constantinople: the pay of this Director is hardly inferior to that of the (British) Euphrates and Tigris Steam Navigation Company's manager at the same place. The Hamīdīyah steamers are undermanned, but the hands employed on them receive pay only about 10 per cent. lower than is given on the British boats. The two new Hamīdīyah steamers both carry British engineers, and one of them is commanded by a British Captain; the Basrah workshop also was in charge, in 1905, of a British marine engineer, and the number of hands was at that time sufficient; service in the workshop is pensionable.*

The annual income of the Dāirat-as-Sanīyah in the Baghdād and Basrah Wilāyats was said to amount in 1905, according to the books

---

* The employés are now all Turkish subjects (1907).

of the department itself, to £94,500 sterling; and its expenses, chiefly salaries and repairs of canals, to £27,900 sterling; but the operations of the department are perpetually extending and its turnover is increasing very rapidly. Some of the estates are particularly profitable, for instance that of Abu Ghuraib, of which the income is said to be about £T. 8,000 and the expenses only £T. 800 per annum. The annual *gross* returns of lands on the **Tigris** below **'Amārah** Town were said to be £36,000 sterling in 1905, the *net* annual profits of the Shatt-al-'**Arab** properties being in the same year about £9,000 sterling. It is stated on good authority that the annual revenue of the Dāirat-as-Sanīyah from agricultural estates is already about double of what has been spent in acquiring them.

The policy of the Dāirat-as-Sanīyah in 'Irāq is one of enlightened self-interest; its relations with its tenants are generally good, and it appears to aim at increasing its business by giving satisfaction to those who make use of its steamer service. On some of its estates it has opened free primary schools, and one-third of the revenue which it realises from the tolls on the Kharr Bridge is assigned to a hospital for the poor at **Baghdād**. The Dāirat-as-Sanīyah is performing a useful function in opening up the country, and on the **Tigris** the villages of **Bghailah** and **Kumait** have been brought into existence, and the town of '**Amārah** has been greatly increased, by the development of the surrounding tracts under Sanīyah auspices. The superior management of the department is not entirely Muhammadan; it is believed to include some able Armenians, and the Inspector of highest rank visiting 'Irāq is a Jew. There is sometimes friction between the local representatives of the department and the ordinary civil officials, and victory does not always remain with the latter. In economic and commercial questions pertaining to 'Irāq the actual achievements and the future ambitions of the Dāirat-as-Sanīyah are important factors which foreign governments and concessionaires must take into account.

Military resources.[*]—The army of the Turkish Empire being a symmetrically organised whole, no account of the military resources of the Porte in 'Irāq can be given without first describing the general system of which they form a part.

A regular form of army service and a military organisation were instituted in Turkey in 1843. Improvements were introduced after the

---

[*] *Authorities.*—Colonel F. R. Maunsell's *Handbook of the Turkish Army* and reports by Colonel L. S. Newmarch, Political Resident at Baghdād, and Mr. F. E. Crow, Consul at Basrah.

Russian wars of 1854 and 1878; and in 1886 the actual system, which is territorial and follows European continental models, was established on the recommendation of Colonel Von der Goltz, an officer of the German General Staff whose services had been specially lent to the Ottoman War Office.

The Turkish army throughout the Empire is recruited by conscription, but only from the Muslim elements of the population; and the field of supply is further narrowed by local and other partial exemptions which affect even Musulmāns. Turkish subjects professing other faiths than Islām are excluded, *ipso facto*, from the Turkish military service and pay instead a service commutation tax or Badal 'Askarīyah بدل عسكرية of 40 gold piastres, or about 7 shillings English, per annum. In the classes subject to conscription liability to service commences from the 1st of March following the 19th birthday and continues for 20 years; the soldier passes successively through the Nidhām نظام or regular active army, in which he spends 3 years with the colours; through the Ihtiyāt احتياط or reserve of the Nidhām, the period of service in which is 6 years; through the Radīf رديف or reserve army, in which he remains for 9 years; and finally through the Mustahfidh مستحفظ or territorial (defensive) force, in which he performs the last 2 years of his service. This, in theory, is the system; but in practice the soldier is often kept for 6 years or longer with the colours and then passes directly into the Radīf without serving in the Ihtiyāt; it follows that the Ihtiyāt cannot be depended on to reinforce the regular army, and the same may be said of the Mustafidh, which has no battalion organisation and could only be used for filling up deficiencies in the Radīf. Apart from mobilisation for war, the Radīf are liable to be embodied by Imperial Iradé for the maintenance of order, for the suppression of riots or insurrection, and for the augmentation of any garrison that may stand in need of it; they are also supposed to be called up for a month's ordinary training once in every two years. Recruits, in 'Irāq, are taken only from among the townspeople, villagers, and settled or semi-settled tribes; the nomadic tribes neither serve nor pay any tax in lieu of service, and this exemption has had a marked effect in preventing the settlement on the land of certain Bedouins who would otherwise ere now have taken to agriculture. Another pernicious exemption in 'Irāq is one in favour of students of theology; it unduly swells the ranks of a useless class, and in the Sanjāq of Karbala, where it is easy to become a student without going far from home, the Turks obtain very few recruits. In 'Irāq the inhabitants of the town of **Zubair** enjoy a special exemption from conscription.

Turkey, European and Asiatic, is divided altogether into 7 Ordus اردو or military districts, to each of which a Qol Ordu قول اردو or army corps is assigned. The district and army corps with which we are concerned are those numbered VI; the district is co-extensive with the civil Wilāyats of Baghdād, Basrah and Mūsal, and **Baghdād** City is the military as it is the civil headquarters of the whole region. The 6th Army Corps is commanded by a Mushīr مشير or Field Marshal who is directly under the Minister of War at Constantinople and occasionally holds, in addition to his military appointment, the civil governorship of the Baghdād Wilāyat. The troops in the Ordu are Nidhām and Radīf, and the local, organisation of these we may now examine separately.

The Nidhām of the 6th Ordu consists of two divisions of infantry, each commanded by a Farīq فريق or Lieutenant-General; of a cavalry division, also commanded by a Farīq; and of a regiment of artillery, commanded by a Colonel or Mīr Ālāi ميرآلاي. It also comprises 2 companies of engineers (1 of pioneers and 1 of telegraph), 4 artificer companies (1 of tailors, 1 of shoemakers, 1 of clothworkers and 1 of tanners), and 1 battalion of train (viz., supply and transport).

The Nidhām infantry of the 6th Ordu is organised as follows by divisions and brigades:—

Number of division and divisional headquarters.	Number of brigade and brigade headquarters.
11th, Baghdād	21st, Baghdād.
	22nd, Hillah.
12th, Kirkūk	23rd, Kirkūk.
	24th, Mūsal.

Each Nidhām infantry brigade consists of two regiments, each regiment of four battalions; and to each infantry division is attached a single Nishānji or rifle battalion bearing the same number as the division. The arm of the Nidhām is, in 'Irāq, the Martini rifle.* The table below

---

* A large proportion have now received Mausers: the rest have still Martinis (1907).

gives the distribution and supposed strength of the Nidhām infantry of the 11th Division as they were in April 1905 :—

11th Division.

Brigade.	Regiment.	Battalion.	Where serving.	Rifles.
21st	41st	1st	In Najd	470
Do.	Do.	2nd	Do.	450
Do.	Do.	3rd	Khamīsīyah near Sūq-ash-Shuyūkh.	570
Do.	Do.	4th	In Najd	520
Do.	42nd	1st	Baghdād City	570
Do.	Do.	2nd	In Najd	480
Do.	Do.	3rd	Basrah Town	545
Do.	Do.	4th	Nāsirīyah Town	475
22nd	43rd	1st	Dōhah in Qatar	480
Do.	Do.	2nd	Qatīf Oasis in the Hasa Sanjāq.	480
Do.	Do.	3rd	Hasa Oasis in the Hasa Sanjāq.	436
Do.	Do.	4th	Do. do.	450
Do.	44th	1st	In Najd	480
Do.	Do.	2nd	Do.	460
Do.	Do.	3rd	Nāsirīyah Town	460
Do.	Do.	4th	In Najd	490

To these must be added the 11th rifle battalion, which was in the **Hasa** Oasis in the **Hasa** Sanjāq and had a strength of 580.*

The strength of the 12th Division, localised in the Mūsal Wilāyat, is approximately the same as that of the 11th, and the scheme of distribution is similar.

The war strength of a Turkish infantry battalion is fixed at 1,065 officers and men, but from the foregoing it would seem that the battalions

---

* But see the article on the Hasa Oasis. Only 2 (not 3) infantry battalions were traceable in the posts of that oasis in 1906.

sent to **Najd** proceeded on a peace footing, perhaps because the additional men were not available in the Ihtiyāt.

The Nidhām cavalry of the 6th Ordu forms the 6th Cavalry Division of the Turkish army and is organised as follows by brigades and regiments :—

Number of brigade and brigade headquarters.	Number of regiment and regimental headquarters.
16th, Baghdād	{ 31st, Baghdād. { 32nd, Hillah.
17th, Hillah	{ 33rd, Mūsal. { 34th, Kirkūk.
18th, Kirkūk	{ 35th, Baghdād. { 36th, Khānaqīn.

The distribution and strength of the cavalry of the whole Ordu are stated to have been as below in April 1905 :—

Regiment.	Where serving.	Sabres.
31st	Baghdād	450
32nd	Hillah	430
33rd	Mūsal	480
34th	Khānaqīn	450
35th	Baghdād and in Najd, *i.e.,* probably, Hasa	240 and 200
36th	Kirkūk	470

The peace strength of a cavalry regiment in the Turkish army is properly 597, and it would consequently seem that those of the 6th Ordu are at present under strength. The weapons of the cavalry are Martini rifles and swords.

The artillery regiment belonging to the Nidhām of the 6th Ordu consists of 5 battalions and is composed as follows, the battery being of 6 guns :—

1st battalion	. . . . .	. 3 horse batteries.
2nd do.	. . . . .	. 4 field do.
3rd do.	. . . . .	. 4 do. do.
4th do.	. . . . .	. 4 do. do.
5th do.	. . . . . .	. 5 mountain do.

The 2nd, 3rd, 4th and perhaps the 1st battalion of artillery are stationed at **Baghdād**, with the exception of 1 field battery detached to **Basrah**; and, of the 5 mountain batteries, 2 seem to be at **Baghdād** and 1 in **Hasa** or **Qatar**. The remainder have not been clearly traced and are probably distributed over the military stations of the Ordu. Some antiquated field guns and old pattern mountain guns are found with artillery detachments in charge of them, at various places, such as the towns of **'Amārah, Dīwānīyah, Karbala, Nāsirīyah, Samāwah, Shatrat-al-Muntafik** and **Tawairīj**. In April 1905 it was understood that 4 " large " and 4 " small " guns had proceeded to **Najd** with 100 artillery men (rank and file); and it was reported that the total number of artillery men belonging to the Ordu was 2,035, while guns of all kinds numbered 137. The modern guns of the 6th Army Corps are Krupps with a calibre of 7·5 cm. in the horse and mountain batteries and of 8·7 cm. in the field batteries.

The strength of the combatant part of the 6th Army Corps (rank and file only) is thus approximately :—

Infantry	. . . .	. 15,578
Cavalry	. . . .	. 2,720
Artillery	. . . .	. 2,035
	Total	. 20,333

and of these about half of the infantry and cavalry and a larger proportion of the artillery are localised in the Wilāyats of Baghdād and Basrah.

The account of the distribution of the Nidhām given above would have been more valuable had it related to a period of complete peace and not to a time when half a division were serving in Central Arabia, and 'Irāq, from which most of the units had been taken, was largely denuded of troops. There are usually infantry battalions or considerable detachments at 'Amārah, Ba'qūbah, Hai, Hillah, Karbala, Samāwah, Shatrat-al-Muntafik and Tawairīj; but these, in 1905, had probably been replaced by Radīf. No account need be taken of a number of small detachments which are furnished by the larger stations and are scattered about the country at places such as Kūfah, Kumait, Umm Qasr, Qūrnah, Safwān and Zubair Town.

The towns of Baghdād, Basrah and Hillah are the principal military centres; and at each of these there is an important magazine and a military hospital. Medical arrangements are almost entirely on the regimental system; and transport, except the single train battalion which is only sufficient for peace requirements, is simply hired or impressed when required. At Baghdād there is an 'Abakhānah عباخانه or Army Clothing Factory which supplies clothing for the whole of the 6th Ordu: connected with it are a military tannery and shoemakers' shops which cure local buffalo hides and turn out army boots and leather equipment. Army Flour Mills, in which the grain for the troops is ground, exist at Baghdād.

We now come to the Radīf which is, or should be, an important part of the Turkish military organisation, for it consists of mature men between 29 and 38 years of age who have served for 9 years in the standing army and its active reserve. In the 6th Army Corps the Radīf is composed entirely of infantry, but it is fed by the cavalry as well as by the infantry of the Nidhām.

The table below explains the organisation of the Radīf of the 6th Army Corps whose connection is with 'Irāq; the remainder, consisting of an equal number of units localised in the Mūsal Wilāyat, is constituted on exactly similar lines.

Number of division and divisional headquarters.	Number of brigade and brigade headquarters.	Number of regiment and regimental headquarters.	Number of battalion and battalion centre.
21st, Baghdād	41st, Baghdād	81st, Baghdād	1st, Baghdād.
Do.	Do.	Do.	2nd, do.
Do.	Do.	Do.	3rd, do.
Do.	Do.	Do.	4th, Mu'adhdham.

'IRĀQ (TURKISH)

Number of division and divisional headquarters.	Number of brigade and brigade headquarters.	Number of regiment and regimental headquarters.	Number of battalion and battalion centres.
21st, Baghdād	41st, Baghdād	82nd, Ba'qūbah	1st, Ba'qūbah.
Do.	Do.	Do.	2nd, Daltawa.
Do.	Do.	Do.	3rd, Mandali.
Do.	Do.	Do.	4th, Khānaqīn.
Do.	42nd, Kādhimain	83rd, Kādhimain	1st, Kādhimain.
Do.	Do.	Do.	2nd, Kiuruk.
Do.	Do.	Do.	3rd, Sāmarrah.
Do.	Do.	Do.	4th, Rumādīyah.
Do.	Do.	84th, Hillah	1st, Hillah.
Do.	Do.	Do.	2nd, Tawairīj.
Do.	Do.	Do.	3rd, Karbala.
Do.	Do.	Do.	4th, Najaf.
22nd, Basrah	43rd, Basrah	85th, Basrah	1st, Basrah.
Do.	Do.	Do.	2nd, Fāo.
Do.	Do.	Do.	3rd, 'Amārah.
Do.	Do.	Do.	4th, (non-existent).
Do.	Do.	86th, Nāsirīyah	1st, Nāsirīyah.
Do.	Do.	Do.	2nd, Kūt-al-'Amārah.
Do.	Do.	Do.	3rd, Dīwānīyah.
Do.	Do.	Do.	4th, (non-existent).

A 44th Brigade also, forming half of the 22nd Radīf division, exists on paper; the battalions composing it have not yet been formed. No similar deficiency is found in the Radīf of the Mūsal division. The Radīf are armed with Martini rifles: their clothing and equipment are usually very deficient. It is believed that the Radīf battalions of the 6th Army Corps have not, when mobilised, more than about 500 men each; and the total strength of the Radīf in this Ordu therefore probably does not exceed 27,000 men (54 battalions), considerably less than half of whom are in 'Irāq.

At each centre to which a battalion is allotted a cadre or permanent staff of about 35 officers, non-commissioned officers and men of the Radīf is maintained, or supposed to be maintained, and an arms, ammunition and clothing dépôt has been formed. The permanent officers of the Radīf are apparently responsible for the training and for the appearance, when called out, of the reservists living in their neighbourhoods, and they are also utilised to superintend conscription for the army generally. Each regiment of the Nidhām obtains its recruits from the centres assigned to the Radīf brigade of the corresponding number; thus the 41st Nidhām regiment is supplied with recruits from **Baghdād, Mu'adhdham,** Ba'qūbah, Daltawa, Mandali and Khānaqīn which are in the territorial district of the 41st Radīf Brigade. The district under each Radīf centre is divided into company subdistricts for purposes of conscription and superintendence of reserves.

More than half the men of the 6th Army Corps, both Nidhām and Radīf, are Arabs, the remainder being mostly **Kurds;** and the composition of the commissioned ranks is believed to be similar. The officers of the Nidhām are, as a rule, incompetent; those of the Radīf are worse. As a class the officers are ill-educated; and they are at all times surrounded by an atmosphere of dishonesty and corruption.

The resources of the 6th Ordu were taxed to the uttermost in 1904 and 1905 by the Turkish operations in **Najd.** The original Central Arabian field force marched from **Samāwah** on the **Euphrates** at the beginning of May 1904 between 1,500 and 2,000 strong: by the end of September 1904, in consequence of severe losses in action, it had practically ceased to exist. The formation of a second expeditionary force was then commenced and was completed about the end of January 1905, when 3,000 to 3,500 men were encamped at **Najaf** under the personal command of the Mushir of the Army Corps. In all about 5,000 Nidhām troops, nearly all of whom were infantry, were withdrawn from the Ordu; and, as all but a few were taken from the 11th Division, the number of Nidhām infantry remaining in the Baghdād and Basrah Wilāyats was reduced to about 3,000 rifles. The place of the absent Nidhām battalions was taken by the Radīfs, who were called out, partly in the Mūsal division, to the number of about 2,000 men; but these bore little resemblance to soldiers, and no efforts apparently were made to improve their efficiency by training during the period of their embodiment. The concentration at **Najaf** in the winter of 1904-05 disclosed corruption and a serious want of discipline in the Nidhām. It was stated at **Baghdād** at the time that some of the battalions lost as much as 20 per cent. of their strength by desertion before reaching **Najaf** and that the Mushīr himself was conniving at the desertion of private soldiers in consideration of small bribes.

Officers * of the Turkish Army receive, besides their pay, rations in kind (Ma'īshah معيشه) or a ration compensation allowance (Ta'īnāt تعينات) in lieu thereof. Their pay is frequently much in arrears, and they are often paid in orders (Sanad سند) on the local treasuries which are cashed by bankers or shops at a heavy discount only. The pay of the ordinary soldier is treated as if it were a luxury rather than a necessity; in fact the men frequently see no pay until the end of their service, and then receive it in Sanads which can only be used for payment of taxes. The Turkish soldier, as a rule, is well fed.

Military expenditure in the Baghdād Wilāyat amounted in a recent year (apparently 1903) to £108,085 sterling, and in the Basrah Wilāyat (apparently in 1901) to £98,875 sterling. In the same Wilāyats, in the same years, the proceeds of the military service commutation tax were £5,216 and £436 sterling respectively.

There are no fortifications in 'Irāq, except a small fort at **Fāo** which was built 20 years ago and is still unarmed; and, if there were any permanent works, the 6th Army Corps is entirely destitute of fortress artillery by which they could be defended.

Naval resources and river conservancy.—The Turkish naval establishment in 'Irāq consists of a Commodore at **Basrah**, having two vessels under his command, and a shore establishment which fluctuates between 100 and 250 of all ranks. The principal duties of the establishment are to police the river and to look after stores and materials. The larger vessel is the " Kilīd-al-Bahr " كليد البحر, a screw corvette with a complement of about 80 officers and men; she carries Krupp guns of the

---

* The following are the rates of annual pay (in sterling) of the commissioned ranks:—

Mushīr مشير (Field Marshal)	£1,584
Farīq فريق (Lieutenant-General)	£634
Liwā لواء (Major-General)	£420
Mīr Ālāi مير آلاي (Colonel)	£210
Qāim-Maqām قائم مقام (Lieutenant-Colonel)	£132
Bimbāshi بكباشي (Major)	£105
Qol Āghāsi قول آغاسي (Adjutant-Major)	£63
Yūzbāshi يوزباشي (Captain)	£42
Mulāzim Awwal ملازم اول (Lieutenant)	£32
Mulāzim Thāni ملازم ثاني (Second Lieutenant)	£26

1874 pattern, but is totally unseaworthy * and hardly ever leaves her moorings. The other is the paddle-steamer "Ālūs" آلوس, carrying about 20 officers and men and a small gun mounted forward; she is used for patrolling the river. The post of Commodore was still in 1905 occupied by a Crimean veteran. The only officers of any education under the Commodore are two in the "Kilid" and one in the "Ālūs" who are from Constantinople: the men on board are recruited from coast districts of the Turkish Empire. The naval expenditure of the Basrah Wilāyat, apparently in 1901, was £8,037 sterling.

We may mention here, although their duties are of a civil nature, the harbour-masters who are stationed at a number of places on the rivers of 'Irāq. The principal functions of the Raīs-al-Līmān رئيس الليمان are to collect tonnage dues on native craft, to control bridges, to supervise river embankments and generally to attend to river conservancy. Officials of this service are found at **Qūrnah, Basrah,** Abul **Khasīb** and **Fāo** on the Shatt-al-**'Arab**; at **Baghdād, Kūt-al-Amārah** and **'Amārah** on the **Tigris**; at **Musaiyib, Hillah, Samāwah, Nāsirīyah, Sūq--ash-Shuyūkh** and **Madīnah** on the **Euphrates**; and at **Tawairīj, Kūfah** and **Shināfīyah** on the Shatt-al-**Hindīyah**. One harbour-master is in charge of **Hai** and **Shatrat-al-Muntafik**, both on the Shatt-al-**Gharāf**; and it is proposed to appoint one to **Dīwānīyah** on the **Euphrates**.

British and other foreign interests and political representation.— British interests predominate in 'Irāq over those of every other European country: they may be divided into two classes, *viz.*, those which concern principally His Majesty's Government, and those with which the Government of India have more particularly to do.

British interests of the former class are mainly commercial, comprising an export—chiefly direct—of local and Persian products to the United Kingdom; an import—also chiefly direct—of goods manufactured in Great Britain; ocean shipping; and the general business of local British firms having no connection with India, the number of which at the present time is 7. Among British commercial interests must be mentioned also those of the Euphrates and Tigris Steam Navigation Company, which holds a concession for its operations from the Turkish Government and has no relations with India or the Indian Government except such as arise from a contract for the carriage of the mails of

---

* When she was examined in 1904 by a British marine engineer in the service of the Dāirat-as-Sanīyah it was found that a hand-hammer could be driven through her plates above the waterline with the greatest ease.

the British Indian Post Office and for other contingent services between **Basrah** and **Baghdād**. The history of this company's concession will be found elsewhere : here it is sufficient to mention that they have hitherto been, and still are, restricted by the Porte to the use of two steamers,* but that a lighter at present (1906) accompanies each with the consent of the Turkish Government: by this means each boat is enabled to convey 400 tons of cargo in the high, and 280 in the low season of the river, the greater part in the former case being carried upon the lighter. Besides their offices at **Basrah** and **Baghdād** the company own repairing yards at **Baghdād** and **Kūt-al-Farangi**, a coal dépôt and a wool-press at **'Amārah**, and a coal dépôt at **Kūt-al-'Amārah**. The number of European British subjects in 'Irāq at the present time is 49, *viz.*, 22 in the Baghdād, and 27 in the Basrah Wilāyat.

British Indian interests in 'Irāq are also largely commercial; but except shipping they are chiefly indirect, for the number of Indian traders actually settled in the country is small. There are 4 Indian firms in 'Irāq, of which 3 do a good business at **Baghdād** while the fourth, engaged in general trade, is established at **Basrah**.

Probably the most important Indian interests are those, of a different character, which arise from the pilgrimage of British Indian subjects and protected persons to the Shī'ah shrines and from the occasional settlement of such persons in the country. The pilgrims arrive in hundreds, indeed in thousands, from India and adjoining countries every cold season; two special caravansarais for their use exist at **Basrah**; and during the time of the influx, that is from October to March, the good offices of the British political representatives are in constant request on their behalf. Asiatics entitled to British protection and resident in 'Irāq are mostly Shī'ah Muhammadans who have first been attracted by the shrines of **Najaf** and **Karbala** and in the end have made their stay permanent for religious reasons or because they liked the country, or the descendants of such; in a few cases the settlers are men of means, but as a rule they are poor and they often maintain themselves by petty trade, chiefly as druggists and dealers in spices. These British Indian subjects, as they may be loosely termed for the sake of shortness, are mostly found at **Karbala**; on that side of 'Irāq, if the towns of **Najaf, Hillah, Tawairīj** and **Musaiyib** (at each of which there are a few) be included, their number is about 1,500 souls, men, women and children, of

---

* Since the spring of 1907 a third steamer with barge has been permitted, but she does not carry mails and must fly the Turkish flag while under steam.

whom it is estimated that about 900 are Indians other than Panjābis, 250 are Panjābis from the Lahore, Sialkot and other districts, 200 are Kashmīris, * 100 are Afghāns and 50 are Tibetans. At **Baghdād** and **Kādhimain** there are about 1,200 Muhammadan British subjects who are nearly all Indians; and at **Basrah** there are a few of the same class and one or two Hindus. Of these Asiatics, approaching 3,000 in number and entitled to British protection in 'Irāq, only a small proportion are actually registered in the British Consular books; but the remainder, on production of proof and payment of a fine for neglect to register their names, can obtain recognition at any time. Except in the case of Indians, British Consular protection is not ordinarily continued to the children or descendants, born in the country, of the protégés mentioned above. Nowhere do the Indians form, as might have been expected, a compact community having their social and commercial intercourse chiefly with one another; on the contrary they generally marry Persian and Arab wives and rapidly assimilate themselves to their surroundings, maintaining their status as British subjects only for the sake of the privileges, particularly exemption from military service, which it confers.

Great Britain is represented in 'Irāq by a Political Resident and Consul-General at **Baghdād**, who is a member of the Indian Political Department; by a Consul of the Levant Service at **Basrah**; and by a native Vice-Consul at **Karbala**. A Residency Surgeon of the Indian Medical Service is attached to the **Baghdād** Residency; also, since 1906, an Assistant to the Resident for Trade and Commerce. The Residency building is one of the finest modern edifices in **Baghdād**. The Government of India maintain extra-territorial post offices at **Baghdād** and **Basrah**, the mails between the two being carried, as already mentioned, by a British line of river steamers.

Russia is the only European power besides Great Britain which possesses a Consulate-General in 'Irāq: it is located at **Baghdād**. A Russian Vice-Consulate,† also, exists at **Baghdād**; and there is a Russian Consulate at **Basrah**. Russian subjects number about 50 at **Kādhimain** and 30 at **Karbala**, but they are all Persian speaking and of Persian race. The actual material interests of Russia in 'Irāq are small, and Russian trade is represented only by agencies of the Russian Steam Navigation and Trading Company at **Basrah** and **Baghdād**.

---

* The inhabitants of the Kashmir Valley proper are Sunnis, but in some of the borderlands, and at places in the Gilgit Agency, Shī'ahs are found.

† Now abolished (1907).

'IRĀQ (TURKISH)

Belgium, France, Germany, Spain and Sweden are each represented at **Baghdād** by a Consul; so also are the United States of America, who have besides a Consular Agent at **Basrah**. Each of these countries has a moderate commercial interest in 'Irāq. Greek interests are at present protected by the British Consul-General at **Baghdād** and the British Consul at **Basrah**; those of Italy are in the hands of the British Consul at **Basrah**; those of Austria are watched by the French Consul at **Baghdād**. The French representative, in virtue of the claim of France to protect Roman Catholics everywhere in the Turkish Empire,* is charged with the interests of a Carmelite foundation and school at **Baghdād** as well as of the Latin Church and the affiliated Syrian and Catholic-Armenian churches there; the Latin church and school at **Basrah** also are under French protection. An American Presbyterian mission, dispensary and school exist at **Basrah**. The interests of Germany in 'Irāq, apart from a moderate share in the trade and a leading part in the investigation of the antiquities of the country, are prospective only: their extent and nature will be determined by the basis on which the projected extension of the (German) Anatolian Railway to **Baghdād** and the Persian Gulf may be carried out.

Persia is the Asiatic power which has the greatest stake in 'Irāq; her interests there depend chiefly on the multitudes of Persians who make pilgrimages to the holy places of the Shī'ahs and on the large numbers of Persians who have settled at these, but also on the many retail traders of Persian race and nationality who carry on their business in the towns and villages. The Persian Consular representatives in the country are numerous and, with the exception of those at **Baghdād** and **Basrah** who are described as Consuls-General, are graded either as Kārpardāz کارپرداز or Nāib-Kārpardāz نائب کارپرداز ; both these terms are loosely applied and the first may signify either a Consul or a Vice-Consul, the second a Vice-Consul or a Consular Agent. The following is a table of the Persian Consular representatives, except the two Consuls-General, in 'Irāq :—

Paid Kārpardāz at—	Unpaid Kārpardāz at—	Paid Nāib-Kārpardāz at—	Unpaid Nāib-Kārpardāz at—
Karbala.	Khanaqīn.	Najaf. Sāmarrah.	Badrah. Hiliah. Kādhimain. Kūt-al-Amārah. Mandali.

* In practice the French claim, in so far as it relates to institutions and to Roman Catholics who are not British subjects, is conceded in 'Irāq by the British Government; but no French right of protection is acknowledged in the case of Roman Catholics who are British subjects.

There are also Persian representatives whose precise rank has not been ascertained at the towns of **'Amārah** and **Nāsirīyah**.

IZKI ازكي or ZIKI زكي

An important town of **'Omān** Proper in the Sultanate of **'Omān**; it is situated on both sides of Wādi **Halfain** about 12 miles below its head and at an elevation of 2,150 feet above the sea. The quarter situated on the right bank is walled and contains a compact and massive fort with walls 5 feet thick, standing upon a cliff 200 feet high above the Wādi bed: this quarter is called Yaman يمن, has about 350 houses and is inhabited by the Bani **Ruwāhah**, Darāmikah and Manādharah tribes. The quarter on the left bank stands on low ground and is occupied by Bani **Riyām**: it is called Nizār نزار and has about 450 houses. These opposite quarters are constantly at feud, the one being Hināwi and the other Ghāfiri in politics. The entire population of Izki proper may be about 4,000 souls: the people are cultivators and carriers. The bed of Wādi **Halfain** at Izki is broad and contains extensive palm-groves and other cultivation, especially on the left bank which is low and fertile: the general aspect of the town is highly picturesque. Crops are wheat, barley, millet, lucerne, beans, sesame and sugarcane, the date palms are estimated at 10,000. Irrigation is from springs which are among the most copious in **'Omān**. Outside Izki are several small hamlets and watch-towers of the Yāl 'Umair and other tribes, among them Zikait زكيت, a small quadrangular walled village containing 15 houses of the Bani **Riyām**, which is situated further down Wādi **Halfain** and about 1 mile south-east of Izki. The possession of the Izki fort, commanding as it does the main or Wādi **Samāil** route between the coast and the interior, is of vital importance to the Sultān of **'Omān**. At the present time the fort is held in his name by a garrison of 20 'Askaris and his authority is represented by a resident Wāli. The Zakāt collected by the Wāli amounts annually to about $1,600, but the whole of this sum goes in local administrative expenses.

JA'ALĀN * جعلان

A district in the **'Omān** Sultanate lying to the south-east of **Sharqīyah**, of which some authorities consider it to be a division. Its greatest length is about 50 miles from the coast at **Lashkharah** north-

---

* For authorities, maps and charts, see footnote to article **'Omān** Sultanate.

JA'ALĀN

eastwards to the confines of **Badīyah** in **Sharqīyah**: its limits on the north-east and south-west are undetermined, so also is its extent upon the sea where, however, it certainly includes the strip from Rās-ar-Ruwais to Lashkharah; but its breadth appears to be somewhat less than its length. On the north it is shut in and overlapped by the easternmost hills of **Hajar**: on the south it is enclosed by sandy desert.

Physical characteristics.—There is a hill called Jabal Qahwān قهوان belonging to this district which is situated 20 miles inland from the coast a little north of Lashkharah: its height is 2,600 feet and it is probably a southern spur of the Jabal **Khamīs** range of **Hajar**. Hills called Jabal Mashāikh مشائخ are said to occur near the west end of the district. Around Humaidha, Kāmil and **Wāfi**, streams afford abundant irrigation and the country is well cultivated. Between these villages and Balad Bani Bū **Hasan** is an extensive plain, covered with acacia and consisting alternately of very loose drift-sand and of whitish, indurated clay. From Balad Bani Bū **'Ali** to Lashkharah the ground is at first level and firm with a few acacias, then broken and sandy. For 25 or 30 miles south-south-west of Balad Bani Bū **'Ali** there is an open waste without trees or water, then a narrow ridge of low calcareous hills, then mounds thickly interspersed with gum Arabic trees: these sandy mounds continue for several hours' journey. To the west of the last-mentioned tract are arid plains without trees or bushes, displaying alternately a pebbly surface and saline incrustations.

Topography.—The chief permanently inhabited places which Ja'alān contains are given in the following table: with the exception of Rās-ar-Ruwais, Suwaih, Jumailah and Lashkharah, which are on the coast, they are situated close together on a plain in the heart of the district. About Jabal Qahwān are some small and unimportant settlements of the Mashāikh-al-Jabal and Bani Sarhān who are connected with the Bani Bū **Hasan** tribe. The small places on the coast are described in the article on the South-Eastern Coast of **'Omān**.

Place.	Position.	Houses and inhabitants.	REMARKS.
'Ali (Balad Bani Bū) بلد بني بو علي	40 miles south-south-west of Sūr.	...	See article Balad Bani Bū **'Ali**.
'Aqībah عقيبه	In Jabal Mashāikh.	Ahl Jabal and Mashāikh-al-Balad, dependent on the Bani Bū Hasan.	...

Place.	Position.	Houses and inhabitants.	Remarks.
Buwairid بویرد	2 miles north of Kāmil.	50 to 60 houses, mostly mud, of the **Hishm** tribe.	The people are chiefly carriers but own also 500 date palms and a few sheep and goats.
Dīdu دیدر	Half a mile west of Kāmil.	100 houses of **Hishm** and **Balūchis**.	Palms number 4,000. Livestock are 40 camels, 30 donkeys, 50 cattle and 500 sheep and goats.
Hasan (Balad Bani Bū) بلد بني بو حسن	7 miles north-north-west of Balad Bani Bū 'Ali.	...	See article Balad Bani Bū **Hasan**.
Humaidha حمیضا	4 miles north of Kāmil.	15 mud and date-branch huts of the **Hishm** tribe.	The hills are distant from this about 7 miles on the north and 6 miles to the east. There is a fort here and about 300 date palms; the inhabitants own a few sheep and goats.
Jumailah جميله	On the south-eastern coast of 'Omān, 88 miles south by west of Suwaih.	25 houses of Bani Bū'Ali.	See article South-Eastern coast of 'Omān.
Kāmil كامل	3 miles north of Wāfi.	200 houses of the **Hishm** tribe, cultivators and camel carriers plying for hire.	The village has a bastioned wall on the north and west sides and date-groves on the south and east. There are 15 shops. Streams afford good irrigation and dates and lucerne are cultivated with success. There are 1,000 date palms, 40 camels, 40 donkeys, 50 cattle and 200 sheep and goats.

Place.	Position.	Houses and inhabitants.	Remarks.
Lashkharah لشخره	On the South-Eastern Coast of 'Omān, 48 miles from Rās-al-Hadd and 20 miles from Balad Bani Bū 'Ali inland.	200 houses, a few of stone but mostly huts, inhabited by the Ja'āfarah section of the Bani Bū 'Ali.	The place depends chiefly on the sea-fisheries: about 50 fishing-boats and one large Sambūk are owned here. Lashkharah is also a port for all the Ghāfiri tribes subject to the Tamīmah of the Bani Bū 'Ali.
Mashāikh (Falaij-al-) فليج المشائخ	About 8 miles to the south and a little to the west of Wāfi.	70 to 80 houses, ⅔ of which are of clay, inhabited by semi-Bedouins of the Hāl 'Umr section of the Bani Bū Hasan.	There are date plantations irrigated by springs. The palms number about 1,000, and there are 50 camels but few other animals.
Ruwais (Rās-ar-) راس الرديس	On the South-Eastern Coast of 'Omān, 24 miles south by west of Rās-al-Hadd.	20 houses of Bani Bū 'Ali.	See article South-Eastern coast of 'Omān.
Suwaih سويح	On the South-Eastern Coast of 'Omān, 8 miles south-west of Rās-ar-Ruwais.	A few Bani Bū 'Ali.	See article South-Eastern Coast of 'Omān.
Wāfi وافي	6 miles north of Balad Bani Bū Hasan.	...	See article Wāfi.

Population.—The fixed population of the district thus amounts to about 12,000 souls and belongs chiefly to the Bani Bū 'Ali, Bani Bū Hasan, Hishm and Bani Rāsib tribes. There are also Bedouins, chiefly 'Awāmir, Bani Bū Hasan, Hishm, Āl Bū 'Isa, **Jannabah** and Āl Wahībah; in the aggregate these are numerous but their numbers cannot be ascertained.

Singular **Jābiri** جابري. An important and in every way superior tribe of the 'Omān Sultanate, also the strongest numerically; they are found chiefly in **Hajar** and their principal seat is the group of 3 valleys known as Wādi Bani **Jābir** (I) which they occupy to the exclusion of other tribes. Their villages in Wadi **Hilam** are Hilam (250 houses), Hūl (30 houses), Qasa'ah (30 houses), Qa'ab (20 houses), Sufun (30 houses), Shūfi (40 houses), Mahat (20 houses), Qōdhah (20 houses) and

JĀBIR (BANI) بني جابر

Kalhāt (130 houses); in Wādi **Shāb** they have Hillat-ash-Shāb (50 houses), Jahl (30 houses) and Jailah; in Wādi **Tīwi** their settlements are **Tīwi** (320 houses), Fahdah (20 houses), Hillāt-al-Hisn (75 houses), Hārat Bidih (50 houses), Hārat Bani 'Īsa (20 houses), 'Aqr (10 houses), Saima (150 houses), Mībām (100 houses) and 'Amq (7 houses). They possess a number of villages in Wādi **Samāil**, namely, Hijrat-ad-Dābah (80 houses), Murriyah (50 houses), Khallūt (10 houses), Bistān (15 houses), Jabailiyāt (60 houses), Hājir (40 houses), Misā'ad (50 houses), Hijrat-as-Sufa (100 houses), Mahbūb (20 houses), Hisn Bin Hammās (10 houses), Ghubrah (25 houses), Dan (20 houses), Fāru (40 houses), Hillat-al-Majālibah (30 houses), Sarūr (250 houses), Bidbid (20 houses) and 'Amqāt (15 houses), to which may be added Hamīm (40 houses) and Thumaid (15 houses) in the Wādi Dhaba'ūn tributary of Wādi **Samāil**. They have also exclusive possession of Wādi Bani **Jābir** (II), their settlements in that valley being Saijah (120 houses), Hīl (500 houses), Hōb (300 houses), Bīr (30 houses), Jailah (400 houses), Firjāt (150 houses), Misfāh (100 houses) and Qaiqa (200 houses). On the coast of Eastern **Hajar** they occupy Dhibāb (55 houses), Bimah (100 houses), Fiṇs (55 houses) and Kabda (130 houses) inland of **Kalhāt**; and in the **Masqat** District they are found at Ghallah and Lansab in Wādi **Bōshar** and have 30 houses at **Matrah**. To the west of Wādi **Samāil** they are found in the adjacent **Hajar** at Buwah (50 houses), Halbān (30 houses), **Nakhl** (10 houses) and at Tau in Wādi **Tau** (300 houses); to the east of it they inhabit Majāzah in Wādi **'Andām**. Some are found also in Wādi Bani **Khālid** and Wādi **Khabbah**. Colonies of Bani Jābir exist in the sub-Wilāyat of **Sohār** at 'Amq (40 houses) and Falaj-al-Qabāil (300 houses) and in the sub-Wilāyat of **Shinās** at Widaiyāj (40 houses) and Bū Baqarah (100 houses); also at **Sīb** (30 houses).

In politics the Bani Jābir are Ghāfiri, in religion Ibādhi. They are smarter in dress, more intelligent, and better educated than most of the tribes of **'Omān**.

The following are their subdivisions:—

Section.	Fighting strength.	Habitat.	Remarks.
Burhān (Aulād) اولاد برهان	400	Saijah, etc. in Wādi Bani Jābir (II).	Nil.
Dafāfi دفافي	50	Hājir in Wādi Samāil.	Do.

Section.	Fighting strength.	Habitat.	REMARKS.
Fahd (Bani) بني فهد	200	Firjāt in Wādi Bani Jābir (II).	Nil.
Falīt (Bani) بني فليت	240	Qaiqa in Wādi Bani Jābir (II).	Do.
Ghadānah (Bani) بني غدانه	240	Bimah and Fins on the coast of Eastern Hajar.	Do.
Ghazāl غزال	150	Daghmar and Dhibāb on the coast of Eastern Hajar.	Do.
Hadhdrami (Bani) بني حضرمي	400	Saima (see article 'Omān Proper) and Wādi Samāil.	There is perhaps some confusion between this section and the distinct tribe of the Bani Hadhram.
Hamaid (Aulād) اولاد حميد	180	Muqazzih in 'Omān Proper.	Nil.
Harb (Bani) بني حرب	240	Majāzah in Wādi 'Andām.	Do.
Ibrāhīm (Bani) بني ابراهيم	240	Wādi Samāil.	Do.
Khamīs (Aulād) اولاد خميس	160	Do.	Do.
Lurhān (Aulād) اولاد لرهان	300	Do.	Do.
Ma'āmarah معامره	400	'Amq and Falaj-al-Qabāil in the Sohār sub-Wilāyat.	Do.
Mazrū' (Bani) بني مزروع	240	Hīl in Wādi Bani Jābir (II).	Some regard the Mazārī' of Wādi Fara' as belonging to this section of the Bani Jābir.
Muqīm (Bani) بني مقيم	600	Ghail-ash-Shāb, Jahl and Jailah in Wādi Shāb and Tīwi Saima, Mībām and 'Amq in Wādi Tīwi.	Nil.

Section.	Fighting strength.	Habitat.	Remarks.
Nāsir (Aulād) اولاد ناصر	320	Wādi **Hilam**.	Nil.
Qurwāsh (Bani) بني قرراش	160	Wādi **Samāil**.	Do.
Rāshid (Aulād) اولاد راشد	480	Wādis **Hilam**, **Tīwi**, and **Tau**.	Do.
Rāshid-Bin-'Amir (Aulād) اولاد راشد بن عامر	240	Wādi **Samāil**.	Do.
Sa'ad (Bani) بني سعد	240	Do.	Do.
Saba' (Āl) آل سبع	70	Samā'īyah and **Khabbah** in Wādi **Khabbah**.	Do.
Sahaim (Aulād) اولاد سهيم	140	Bīr and Misfāh in Wādi Bani **Jābir** (II).	Do.
Sa'īd (Aulād) اولاد سعيد	160	Hōb in Wādi Bani **Jābir** (II).	Do.
Salīm (Aulād) اولاد سليم	240	Jailah in Wādi Bani **Jābir** (II).	Do.
Salūt سلوط	640	**Hilam** in Wādi **Hilam** and most of the villages of Wādi **Tīwi**; also Ghallah in Wādi **Bōshar**.	The Tamīmah of the tribe, Salat-bin-Muhammad, belongs to this section and has his residence at Hilam.
Sha'ībiyīn or Shu'aibiyīn شعيبيين	350	Kabda and **Kalhāt**, also Halfah in Wādi Bani **Khālid**.	Those of **Kalhāt** have recently (1907) gone over to the Hināwis and do not at present consider themselves Bani Jābir: they have allied themselves with the Bani Bū Hasan.
Shajbiyīn شجبيين	200	Wādi **Samāil**.	Nil.
Wādi (Aulād) اولاد وادي	80	Bidbid and elsewhere in Wādi **Samāil**.	Do.

JĀBIR (WĀDI BANI) (II)

The total number of the tribe is estimated at 25,000 souls.

The Bani Jābir boast their descent from the tribe of Dhubyān, famous in Arab poetry, and are at bitter enmity with the Bani **Ruwāhah** who are derived from the rival tribe of Abs. Hilam and Tau are equally regarded as capitals of the tribe; but the Bani Jābir, though dispersed, keep up communication with one another and act as a body. Saiyid Turki, during his troublous reign, from 1871 to 1888, frequently employed the Bani Jābir to close the passes leading to **Masqat** against his enemies in **Sharqīyah**.

JĀBIR (WĀDI BANI) (I)
وادي بني جابر

A main seat of the Bani Jābir tribe; it is a tract consisting of the three Wādis of **Hilam, Tīwi** and **Shāb**, each of which is described elsewhere under its own name.

JĀBIR (WĀDI BANI) (II)
وادي بني جابر

In the **Hajar** district of the 'Omān Sultanate, the only important tributary from the west of Wādi **Samāil**, which it joins at Miltiqa: its head is below 'Aqabat-al-Qatt, on the east side. The course of Wādi Bani Jābir is approximately parallel to that of Wādi **Samāil** above Miltiqa: Saijah, near its beginning, is divided from Darwāzah in Wādi **Samāil** only by about 4 miles of open country and is visible from it.

The villages in Wādi Bani Jābir in order from its head downwards are given below; almost the entire population are Bani **Jābir**:—

Village.	Position.	On which bank.	Number of houses.	REMARKS.
Saijah سيجة	At the head of the Wādi.	Left.	120 houses of Bani Jābir of the Aulād Burhān section.	This place, though reckoned to Wādi Bani Jābir, drains to Wādi Samāil a few miles above Hisn Samāil. Resources are 30 camels, 50 donkeys, 50 cattle, 300 sheep and goats and 15,000 palms.
Hīl هيل	2½ miles north of Saijah.	Do.	500 houses of Bani Jābir, some of them of the Bani Mazrū' section.	Qurain in Wādi Samāil can be seen from here. The intervening distance is 4 miles. Livestock are 40 camels, 80 donkeys, 70 cattle and 600 sheep and goats. Date trees are estimated at 20,000.

Village.	Position.	On which bank.	Number of houses.	Remarks.
Hôb هوب	1 mile north-west of Hîl.	Left.	300 houses of Bani Jābir, some of them of the Aulād Sa'īd section.	The inhabitants possess 30 camels, 50 donkeys, 40 cattle and 400 sheep and goats; also about 10,000 date palms.
Bīr بير	3½ miles north-north-east of Hîl and 2 miles up left bank tributary of Wādi Bani Jābir called Wādi Maih.	Do.	30 houses of Bani Jābir of the Aulād Sahaim section.	Animals are 20 camels, 20 donkeys, 30 cattle and 100 sheep and goats; and there are about 8,000 date trees.
Jailah جيله	5 miles below Hîl.	Do.	400 houses of Bani Jābir, partly of the Aulād Sālim section.	The principal village of the Bani Jābir in this part of the country. A pass leads across the intervening hills to Hillat-al-Hājir in Wādi Samāil. The resources of the village are estimated at 60 camels, 70 donkeys, 50 cattle, 800 sheep and goats and 20,000 palms.
Firjāt فرجات	¼ of an hour below Jailah.	Right.	150 houses of Bani Jābir.	The people have 50 camels, 70 donkeys, 30 cattle and 200 sheep and goats, also 300 date trees.
Misfāh مسفاه	½ an hour below Firjāt.	Do.	100 houses of Bani Jābir of the Aulād Sahaim section.	Here are about 20 camels, 30 donkeys, 10 cattle, 100 sheep and goats, and 200 palms.
Qaiqa قيقا	2 miles below Jailah and 4 miles above the junction of the Wādi with Wādi Samā'l.	Do.	200 houses of Bani Jābir.	This place is said to have been the scene of a great battle in the 18th century between the 'Omānis and the Persians. Resources of the village are 60 camels, 70 donkeys, 40 cattle, 300 sheep and goats, and 2,000 date trees.

The upper part of this valley, above Jailah, is properly called Wādi Sakhnān. وادي سخنان .

JABRĪN
جبرين

Sometimes pronounced Yabrīn. A remarkable oasis, said to lie five caravan days to the east of **Aflāj** and eight to the south-west of **Dōhah** in **Qatar**: one of the nearest well known points to it upon the coast is Khor-al-'**Odaid**. Jabrīn is 150 to 160 miles south-south-west of **Hofūf** and about 180 miles south-west by west from the foot of Khor-al-'**Odaid**. On the western side of Jabrīn the country consists of barren clay plains traversed by the route from **Aflāj**; on the other three the oasis is surrounded by sandy desert. The districts or tracts surrounding Jabrīn are **Dahánah** on the north and west, Ahqāf on the south and **Jāfūrah** on the east. Jabrīn is about 10 miles in length from north to south and 7 or 8 in breadth from east to west. It is a plain, lower in level than the surrounding country and watered by springs and streams; the drainage goes to the eastern desert in which it is swallowed up. There is good grass, and over the whole surface of the plain wild date palms are scattered in patches. Jabrīn is frequented by the Āl **Morrah** Bedouins who collect the dates in the season; it is said that it was once permanently inhabited and that coins and other relics of civilisation are still found there: its abandonment is attributed to a change of climate by which it became malarious. The nearest village in **Aflāj** is **Saih**, and there is an intermediate halting-place at Mishāsh, two days from **Saih** and three from Jabrīn, where **Dawāsir** Bedouins encamp in the midst of clay plains. The wells on routes leading to it from **Hofūf** and the Persian Gulf are specified in the article on **Jāfūrah**. No European has as yet visited Jabrīn.

JADGĀL TRIBE
جدگال

In '**Omān** the name is Arabicised and becomes Zidjāl زدجال, which is treated as a plural with the singular Zidjāli زدجالي. The Jadgāls are a tribe of Persian **Makrān**, now reckoned **Balūchis** but said to have come originally from Sind; they are numerous in '**Omān** also, where they have been introduced at various times as mercenary soldiers in the employment of the Sultāns. In Persian **Makrān** the Jadgāls have their headquarters in the Dashtyāri and Bāhu districts, where the ruling chiefs are of their number; in '**Omān** they occupy an entire suburban quarter of **Masqat** Town, and are found also at **Matrah**, and generally throughout the country wherever a **Balūchi** colony exists. In religion the Jadgāls are Sunnis.

JĀFŪRAH*
الجافورة

A great desert in Eastern Arabia; it extends the whole way from the **Hasa** Oasis to the confines of Trucial ' **Omān**, and its eastern edge is nowhere very far inland from the coast of the Persian Gulf. By some Arabs Jāfūrah is regarded as a projection in the direction of **Qatar** of the **Ruba'-al-Khāli** or Great Desert of Southern Arabia; and those who view the matter in this light say that Jāfūrah ends, and that the **Ruba'-al-Khāli** proper begins, in the region known as Ahqāf احقاف or the Sand Dunes.

Limits.—Whether or not it be a part of the **Ruba'-al-Khāli**, Jāfūrah is in itself a remarkable and very extensive desert. In shape it is roughly triangular, with its apex on the north almost touching a line drawn between **Hofūf** and **'Oqair** Port, and its other corners (to the south-west and south-east) adjoining the oasis of **Jabrīn** and the southern extremity of Sabákhat **Matti** respectively. Along its western side Jāfūrah is met in succession from north to south by the tracts of **Biyādh, Kharmah, Ghuwār, Na'alah, Summān** and **Dahánah**; on the east it is separated from the sea, in the same order, by Barr-al-**Qārah, Qatar, 'Aqal** and **Mijan**; on the south it is bounded by the **Ruba'-al-Khāli**. It may be added here that Jāfūrah encloses **Jabrīn** upon the north and east, and that, in the opinion of some, Barr-al-**Qārah** is a portion of Jāfūrah and not a separate tract.

Physical characteristics and inhabitants.—Jāfūrah differs from the waterless **Ruba'-al-Khāli** only in possessing a few wells of very bitter water and a little scanty grazing; its surface consists of red and burning sand.

The **'Ajmān** venture into the northern extremity of Jāfūrah; but the only tribe who frequent it to any considerable extent are the hardy Āl **Morrah**, and even they avoid entering it unless in winter or in search of a refuge from more powerful enemies. The Āl **Morrah** are said to wear when in Jāfūrah a specially thick foot-gear made of camels'-hair; and, if popular rumour may be trusted, those of the tribe who spend most time there are of an unusually swarthy complexion, while their camels are nearly jet black. While sojourning in Jāfūrah the Āl **Morrah** as a rule drink nothing but the milk of their camels and even cook their rice in the same; if compelled to swallow water from the

---

* Nearly the whole of the information contained in this article was supplied by Captain F. B. Prideaux, Political Agent in **Bahrain**, in whose *Map of Jāfūrah, etc.*, the region in question is included.

JĀFŪRAH

wells they first mix it with dried dates to make it more palatable. The Wahhābis have frequently waged war upon the Āl **Morrah**; but Faisal alone, if local tradition is to be believed, succeeded in penetrating with his troops as far as Banaiyān, and his force was so reduced by the hardships of the desert march that he was compelled, on his arrival there, to grant the tribe exceedingly easy terms.

Topography.—The following are some of the best known wells in Jāfūrah: the water of all is bitter:—

Name.	Vernacular equivalent.	Position.	REMARKS.
'Adhbab (Mishāsh-al-)	مشاش العذبه	About 40 miles south-south-west of the foot of Khor-adh-Dhuwaihin in 'Aqal.	...
'Akrish (Abul)	ابو العكرش	About 35 miles west by south of the foot of Khor-adh-Dhuwaihin in 'Aqal: (But one authority would place it within 20 miles of Sakak in Qatar.)	...
'Ariq	العرق	About 50 miles north-east by east of Jabrīn.	...
Arzīlah (Bū)	بو ارزيله	About 20 miles west of Sakak in Qatar.	...
Azīz (Bīr)	بير عزيز	About 50 miles east of Jabrīn.	...
Bahath	البحث	About 12 miles inland, westwards, from Dōhat Hamāh on the coast of Barr-al-Qārah.	Or Bajāsh-al-Bahath. A stage on the ordinary route from **Hofūf** to **Dōhah** in Qatar.
Banaiyān	بنيان	About 70 miles south-south-west of Dōhat-as-Sila' on the coast of Mijan. (But one authority would make it about this distance west of Sila'.)	Also called Khairān Āl Morrah خيران آل مره The depth of the wells is here 1¼ fathoms.
Baqar (Abul)	ابو البقر	About 30 miles east-south-east of Banaiyān.	...

Name.	Vernacular equivalent.	Position.	Remarks.
Baqash	بقش	Between 15 and 20 miles north-north-east of 'Ariq.	The best grazing in Jāfūrah is in this neighbourhood.
Da'ailij	دعيلج	About 4 miles east of Bahath.	...
Fādhil (Bīr)	بير فاضل	About 35 miles east by south of Bīr 'Azīz.	...
Ghaiyathīn	غيثين	About 7 miles south-west of Bahath.	A stage on the most direct route from Hofūf to Dōhah in Qatar.
Hardh	الحرظ	Half way from Hofūf to Jabrīn in a straight line between the two and about 80 miles from either.	...
Hidbah	الهدبه	Between 25 and 30 miles north-east of Jabrīn.	...
Jadairāt	الجديرات	10 or 15 miles west of Abul 'Akrish.	...
Jira (Umm-al-)	ام الجرا	40 miles west of Banaiyān.	...
Khashbīyah	خشبيّه	3 miles east-south-east of Muraiqib, on the eastern border of the Sabákhat Shātar in Biyādh.	...
Khuwaitmah	خويتمه	20 miles south-south-west of Mishāsh-al-'Adhbah.	...
Mabāk	المباك	About 45 miles inland, westwards, from the foot of Khor-al-'Odaid.	There is a small oasis here with wells, a few date palms, and the ruins of a village.
Mana'āyah	منعايه	8 miles east-north-east of Muraiqib.	A stage on the ordinary route from Hofūf to Dōhah in Qatar.
Muraiqib	مريقب	On the eastern edge of Sabákhat Shātar and 4 miles south of the Shātar wells in Biyādh.	...
Nābit (Bīr Āl)	بير آل نابت	6 miles north-east by north of Bahath.	...

Name.	Vernacular equivalent.	Position.	Remarks.
Nathīl (Hamar)	حمر نثيل	4 miles west by south of Bahath.	...
Nuwādis (Abu)	ابو نوادس	6 miles south-south-east of Muraiqib.	...
Qalāib	قلائب	25 to 30 miles west of Abul 'Akrish.	...
Rākān ('Aqalat)	عقلة راكان	About 35 miles south-west of the foot of Khor-adh-Dhuwaihin in 'Aqal.	...
Sufuk	السفك	Near the southern border of the Sabakhat Matti, about 35 miles east of Banaiyān.	...
Wusī'ah	وسيعه	About 30 miles west-south-west of Mish-āsh-al-'Adhbah.	...

    Besides the above there are two wells, Umm-as-Suwaijah ام السويجه and Dhībi ذيبي, which are unplaced but are probably inland of **'Aqal**, and perhaps in the neighbourhood of Qalāib or 'Aqalat Rākān.

    It should be observed that the wells of Hardh, Baqash, 'Ariq and Hidbah are stages on the second part of the route from **Hofūf** to **Jabrīn**, either 'Awaisah and Shajah or Khuwainah and Zarnūqah in **Kharmah** being points on the first half of it. Similarly the wells of Banaiyān, Umm-al-Jira, Bīr Fādhil and Bīr 'Azīz form a chain connecting the **Jabrīn** oasis with the desert highway between **'Omān** and **Hasa** in the vicinity of Sabákhat **Matti**.

JAHÁLAH
جهله

    The name is generally pronounced Chahálah and should perhaps be spelt جهله. This large canal, by Europeans called "the Hadd," waters part of the **'Amārah** and **Zubair** Qadhas in Turkish **'Irāq**: it takes out of the **Tigris** on its left bank at the northern end of **'Amārah** Town, and, circling round the east side of the place, is spanned at the back of it by a short pontoon bridge. The Jahálah was made less than a century ago; but, forming a straight continuation of the **Tigris** at a point where there is a bend in its natural course, it has been enlarged by the action of the river and is now about 80 yards wide at its mouth and abstracts, along with the Bitairah canal on the opposite bank a few miles further up, nearly half of the whole water of the river. The Jahálah runs inland to the **Hawīzeh** marshes in which it eventually loses itself; but it is understood to pursue a well-defined course, more or less parallel to the **Tigris**, as far south as Qal'at **Sālih**. For some two-thirds of this distance, to a village called Masa'īdah in the **Zubair** Qadha, it has a depth of about five feet at low water and the channel though narrow is clear; to this point it might be navigated by a small river steamer, but the passage beyond, if there is one, is obstructed by reeds. Much of the land in the neighbourhood of the Jahálah is owned by Dāirat-as-Sanīyah.

JAHRAH

جهرة

Sometimes pronounced Jahārah. A considerable village in the **Kuwait** Principality, situated near the foot of **Kuwait** Bay, about 2 miles inland, 40 feet above sea level, and distant 20 miles by road from **Kuwait** Town: it is the chief and almost the only seat of agriculture in **Kuwait** territory.

Situation.—Jahrah stands in an open plain of sand sprinkled with camel grazing, 3½ miles to the south-east of the gap in the **Zor** hills through which caravans from **Kuwait** to **Basrah** pass: the desert rises gradually from the village towards the west and south-west. One mile to the north of the village is a plain called Maraitabah مريطبة, on which Bedouins camp in the hot weather: it is riddled with wells containing water at a depth of 12 feet. The few trees about Jahrah, except the dates belonging to the village, are either tamarisks or bers. The air of the place is dry and the climate healthy.

Defences.—Jahrah is commanded at artillery ranges by the **Zor** hills, and, owing to the shoal water at the foot of **Kuwait** Bay, the place could not be effectively supported by naval fire. The only defensive work is a fortified residence of the Shaikh of **Kuwait** on the south-east side of the village outside the limits of cultivation. In form it is approximately a square, having the angles to the cardinal points and sides of about 200 feet in length; the height of the walls is 15 feet, and there is a tower 20 feet high at each corner enfilading the wall; the only entrance, commanded from within by an old muzzle-loading gun, is in the north-west face. The enclosure contains stabling for about 100 horses. The fort is in bad repair, and its chief uses appear to be as the residence of a **Mutair** wife of the Shaikh and as a place for keeping his brood mares and young stock. A new date plantation and garden, the property of the Shaikh, stand in front of the entrance at a few yards distance; they are about 12 acres in extent and are enclosed by walls. There is no well in the fort.

Population.—The permanent inhabitants of Jahrah are mostly cultivators of Najdi extraction, who till the lands possessed here by the Shaikh and various merchants of **Kuwait** and by relations of the Naqīb of **Basrah**. The houses, 86 in number, are built of clay and accommodate about 100 families or 500 souls. In the hot weather the population is increased by about 700 households, mostly of the **Mutair** tribe, who pitch their tents near the village; and even in winter there are generally one or two Bedouin encampments within sight.

Agriculture.—As the importance of Jahrah is chiefly agricultural, and as most of the cultivation in the Shaikh's dominions is concentrated here, we proceed to give a full account of the place in this aspect.

There is no fixed scale for the division of produce between landowner and tenant.

The staple crops are wheat, barley and lucerne, the amount of barley being about double that of wheat; the total yield of wheat in a good year is about 120 maunds only. The wheat, called Hintah or Hubb, is sown at the beginning of September and is reaped along with the barley or Sha'ir at the beginning of March. A part of the cereal crops is cut green for fodder as in India, and is called Qasīl; the barley is twice cut for this purpose before it is allowed to mature; but the young wheat is seldom so treated except in unusually good years. The lucerne, called Qatt, is of excellent quality and is cultivated on the same ground for four years, after which the plot is left Hāilah or fallow for one year.

Other crops are the musk melon or Batīkh and the water melon or Raqi which are sown once a year, ripen about the beginning of November, and continue in season for three weeks; the quantity grown is too small to admit of export to **Kuwait** Town. The pumpkin or Qara' comes in at the beginning of December, lasts for three months, and is exported to **Kuwait** Town. Beans or Bājilla (*i.e.*, Baqilla) ripen in February, but the crop is small and only sufficient for village requirements. The onion or Basal is ready at the end of December and continues till spring ; the radish, called Arwaid, begins early in the year and outlasts the onion. The leek or Baqal is sown afresh every year ; it is cropped like lucerne and yields 16 crops in the season. Clover or Halbah and cress or Rashād are small and short-lived crops ; these herbs are only used for seasoning. The brinjal or Bahdiyān, bindi or Bāmiyah, and the tomato—which has no Arabic name—come early in the year and do not last long, but are exported to **Kuwait** Town.

There are about 2,000 date-trees at Jahrah producing about 500 maunds of dates per annum ; practically the whole of the fruit is eaten as Ratab, that is, in the yellow or semi-ripe state. Date plantations, now number eleven, of which the best belongs to Saiyid Khalaf, a relation of the Naqīb of **Basrah** : three new date groves are being laid out this year (1904).

At present only about 30 tons of grain are exported yearly to **Kuwait** Town, but the agriculture of Jahrah might be greatly extended if more capital were sunk in it.

Irrigation.—The crops enumerated above are mostly irrigated and are grown in enclosures formed by clay walls about 9 feet high ; most of these gardens are on the south side of the village. Some of the wheat and barley is grown by rainfall alone, but the area of such cultivation is small compared with the rest. The water for irrigation is brackish ; it is raised in skins by donkeys which pull by walking down an inclined plane that slopes away from the well. There are 19 large wells with an average depth of about 20 feet. A waterlift is called an Arjīyah, and the channels which carry the water from the well head to the crops are Sāqīyah. Sometimes the water raised is collected in a reservoir or Birkah to give it a good flow : natural or artificial hollows where water collects are known as Khabrahs. A Sharb is a small embanked terrace on which irrigation water is allowed to spread before being let go to a lower level.

Agricultural terms.—Late-sown crops are described as Musaiyaf. The chief varieties of soil are Harrah, or good arable land ; Daim, which is land either situated on the edge of a Khabrah or watered only by rain ; Hazam, or stony ground ; and Sabākhah, which is swampy, saline and non-productive. The commonest instruments of agriculture are a rudimentary plough, called Ifdān ; an iron spade, called Fakhīn, used in making, repairing, opening and closing water channels; and a wooden rake or hoe, called Masāh, for levelling the ground. The Makhyūl is a bogey made of an 'Aba hung on a staff to prevent sheep and goats from straying, or to scare birds from growing crops. An economical substitute for a wall to protect crops against animals is a Khadad or ditch, 2 feet deep and 2 feet broad, with sand walls on either side about 1 foot high.

Livestock, water supply, etc.—The supply of fowls, eggs and milk at Jahrah is limited, and wood is very scarce, but there are plenty of sheep and goats and a few cattle. Lucerne and some vegetables are procurable. The local transport available consists of some 30 or 40 donkeys, but camels can be hired from the Bedouins. Drinking water of fair quality is yielded by certain wells about half a mile south-west of the village.

Administration and political importance.—The Shaikh of **Kuwait** is represented at Jahrah by one Amīr 'Abdul Karīm, a native of the village but of Najdi parentage, who exercises considerable undefined powers in the place. This man is also the Shaikh's agent for the cultivation of his garden, already mentioned, and takes half the profits of the same while the Shaikh bears all the expenses. No revenue is collected on behalf of the Shaikh. In former times the disorderly conduct of the Bedouins frequently caused annoyance at Jahrah; but under the strong rule of Mubārak this drawback has been removed.

The Shaikh of **Kuwait** regards Jahrah as one of the most important spots in his territory, not only on account of its agricultural resources, but also because of the prestige which its possessor enjoys among the Bedouins frequenting its vicinity and of the hold which it gives him over them.

Topography of the neighbourhood. Several places and landmarks which bear names and do not belong to any of the recognised divisions of the **Kuwait** Shaikhdom may conveniently be described here on account of their proximity to Jahrah.

They are, in alphabetical order, as follow :—

Name.	Position.	Nature.	Remarks.
Atrāf اطراف	8 miles west-south-west of Jahrah.	Some broken mounds.	These form the western extremity of the Zor hills.
Atwainij (Umm) ام اتوينج	Between Atrāf, Farīdah, and a curving ridge which runs south-east and then east from Farīdah.	A plain.	There are one or two Khabrahs here and the remains of some habitations.

Name.	Position.	Nature.	REMARKS.
Ba'al (Khabrat-al-) خبرة البعل	5 miles south-west of Jahrah.	A natural basin which intercepts a certain amount of the drainage descending from the desert towards Jahrah.	In favourable seasons scanty crops of wheat or barley are raised here.
Farīdah فريدة	9 miles west-south-west of Jahrah.	A small hill.	Detached and solitary.
Rahaiyah رحيه	6 miles south-west of Jahrah.	Do.	Do.
Ruūs (Umm) ام رووس	12 miles south-south-west of Jahrah.	A three pointed hill.	It forms a good landmark.
Sāddah (Khadd-as-) خد السادة	Cuts the Jahrah-Riqa'i route at 16 miles from Jahrah.	A ridge running due north and south.	The slope of the country is upwards all the way from Jahrah to Sāddah. At a point on the ridge 4 miles north of the Jahrah-Riqa'i route is a triple summit known as Inhaidain نهيدين which forms a good landmark. Small camps of **Mutair** may be found in winter under the shelter of Sāddah.

JAMMAH
جمه

A town of the Western **Hajar** or possibly of the **Bātinah** district in the **'Omān** Sultanate, situated 1 or 2 miles to the east of Wādi **Fara'** some distance outside the hills and opposite to **Hazam**; it consists of about 590 houses of the Bani **Harrās** tribe and is surrounded by a wall. The date plantations are large and are said to contain 80,000 trees. Livestock are 100 camels, 300 donkeys, 500 cattle and 2,000 sheep and goats. The fort, which is on a hill, belongs to the Sultān of **'Omān**; but he keeps no Wāli or garrison here as the place is loyal to him. The nearest garrison is at Mizāhīt above Jammah in Wādi **Fara'**.

JANĀ'AT
جناعات

Singular Janā'i جناعي. A tribe who claim connection with the **Sahūl** of **Najd**; in religion they are Sunni Muhammadans of the Māliki school. The Janā'āt were formerly somewhat numerous in **Bahrain**, but the majority have migrated to **Kuwait** Town where they now number about 150 souls. In **Bahrain** only 2 or 3 families, who are shopkeepers, now remain at **Manāmah**. An idea prevails in some quarters that the Janā'āt were once **Sabians**; this the Janā'āt would explain away by suggesting that a fresh complexion and robust physique common to themselves and the **Sabians** of the north have led to confusion between the two.

JANĀH

جناه

A small sandy islet about 10 feet high, ½ a mile long and very narrow. It is situated 10 miles east by north of Abu 'Ali island off the coast of the **Hasa** Sanjāq, to which it may be taken as belonging.

JANAIB (UMM)

ام جنيب

A general term including several of the districts of the **Kuwait** Shaikhdom, namely, **Kabd**, **Qrā'ah**, **'Adān**, **Salū'**, **Hazaim**, and possibly the northern part of **Sūdah**. It is thus bounded on the east by the sea, on the north by **Kuwait** Bay, and on the south by **Dhula'-al-Mi'aijil**. This is one view of the meaning of the name.

According to another authority Umm Janaib is a small separate district, somewhat higher than **Hazaim** and to the west of it, and of **Labībah**, containing the hill of Rahaiyah and the wells of Shadhaf and Wafrah which we have included in **Hazaim**.

JANJĪREH

جنجيره

A point on the left bank of the **Jarrāhi** River, about 8 miles northeast of **Fallāhīyeh** Town, from which a number of small canals radiate into the country to the southwards. The following is a table of the canals belonging to the Janjīreh system; they are given approximately in order from east to west:—

Name of canal.	Dependent population.	Number of date palms.	Annual yield of cereals in Maus of Fallāhīyeh.
Sikanām	Ka'ab of the Makāsibeh section.	...	400 of rice.
...			
Muraiyeh	Ka'ab of the Āl Bū Ghubaish subdivision.	...	500 do.
...			

Name of canal.	Dependent population.	Number of date palms.	Annual yield of cereals in Mans of Fallāhī-yeh.
Manqūshi مذقوشي	Ka'ab of the Āl Bū Bālid section, owning 100 cattle.	300	600 of rice and some wheat and barley.
Mūsa-ibn-Afsaiyil موسى ابن افصيل	Ka'ab of the Āl Bū Dahaleh section.	Nil.	300 of rice.
Musallim-ibn-Sālim Fauqāni مسلم ابن سالم فوقاني	Do.	...	400 do.
Al Bū Dalli آل بو دلّي	Do.	200	Do.
Nahr-al-Ōrān ...	Ka'ab of the Al Bū Hamādi section.	...	150 of rice.
Bait Haraib بيت حريب	Ka'ab of the Āl Bū Ghubaish subdivision.	300	200 do.
Mahrūqi محروقي	Ka'ab of the Āl Bū Ghubaish subdivision, of the 'Amāreh, Bait Iba' in, Bait Rawaishid-ibn-Kabain and Bait Shafi sections.	6,000	500 do.
Asaifir ...	Ka'ab of the Muaisir and Salaiyih sections.	...	300 of rice and 100 of wheat and barley.
'Abdun Nabi عبدالنبي	Ka'ab of the Āl Bū 'Abbādi section.	500	200 of rice.
Musallim-ibn-Sālim Hadrāni مسلم ابن سالم حدراني	Ka'ab of the Āl Bū Dahaleh section.	Do.	Do.
Khāni خاني	Both the owners and cultivators are Ka'ab, the former of the Bait Hilāyil and the latter of the Kināneh section. There are also Ka'ab of the Is-hāq and Bait Suwayir sections.	...	600 of rice and 200 of wheat and barley.
Makāsibeh مكاسبه	Narakīyeh, an Arab tribe, dependent on the Makāsibeh section of the Ka'ab.	..	100 of rice and 100 of wheat and barley.
Bait Qatān بيت قطان	Ka'ab of the Dawāriqeh section but dependent on the Bait Hilāyil.	..	200 of rice and 100 of wheat and barley.
Afraiāt ...	Ka'ab of the Bait Shuwaish section.	...	100 of rice.
A'rār اعرار	Ka'ab of the Āl Bū Subaiyah section.	500	300 do.

Name of canal.	Dependent population.	Number of date palms.	Annual yield of cereals in Mans of Fallāhīyeh.
Jadīdi جديدي	Ka'ab of the Āl Bū Ghubaish subdivision, belonging to the Bait Khawaitār and Bait Shuwaish sections.	6,000	500 of rice and 500 of wheat and barley.
Asairafi ...	Ka'ab of the Āl Bū Sa'īd section.	...	150 of rice and 150 of wheat and barley.
Sha'ab ...	...	...	Do.
Habāch حباج	Ka'ab of the Āl Bū Jabbār section.	...	600 of rice and 200 of wheat and barley.

The spot known as Janjīreh has some date groves but is situated in fairly open country; it is connected by winding paths with **Buziyeh** and **Fallāhīyeh** Town. It has been pointed out that, as the heads of a number of canals are commanded at Janjīreh, the place is one which it would probably be advantageous to occupy in case of military operations in the neighbourhood.

JANNABAH جنبه

Singular Jannaibi جنيبي. A large tribe of the **'Omān** Sultanate, Yamani by extraction, but now belonging to the Ghāfiri political faction and Sunnis in religion. They are partly settled and partly nomad. Their metropolis is **Sūr**; but they also possess **Masīrah** island and, interspersed with **Hikmān** and **Āl Wahībah**, occupy in a desultory fashion the South-East Coast of **'Omān** from Rās Jibsh, where they have a village, to the commencement of the **Dhufār** District; some of them visit **Murbāt** in **Dhufār**, and the cave dwellings on Rās Sājar and the small hamlet of Safqōt at the west end of **Dhufār** are said to be occupied by members of this tribe. A few reside among the **Hikmān** of **Mahōt**. Detached colonies of Jannabah are found at **Bahlah**, Khadhra-bin-Daffā' and 'Izz in **'Omān** Proper and at Wādi Manūmah in **Bātinah**.

It is necessary to distinguish the settled portion of the tribe, chiefly at **Sūr**, from the migratory pastoral and fishing sections further to the south. The former, known in common with some of the Bani Bū **'Ali** as "Sūris," own and navigate a large number of sea going vessels which run to Bombay, Zanzibar and the Red Sea: they are also merchants, having large commercial dépôts at **Sūr**, and the **Hajriyīn** of the interior carry on all their foreign trade through them. The pastoral portion of the tribe are dark-skinned, thin and undersized but not ill-looking; they wear their hair long and confine it round the head with a leathern thong. They are disliked by their neighbours and appear to have little or no religion. In the cool season they come down to the coast with their herds of camels and goats, which are said to be very large, retreating again to caves in the hills on the approach of the south-west monsoon. It has been noticed that those who fish are of a lighter complexion than their purely pastoral brethren and that their cranial and facial type is more or less peculiar to themselves.

As a tribe the Jannabah bear an evil reputation. Those of **Sūr** indulged in slave-dealing and even piracy as long as these courses were open to them, and the Jannabah of the south-eastern coast are wreckers and robbers to a man.

The Jannabah are divided into the following sections:—

Section.	Fighting strength.*	Remarks.
'Arāmah عرامه	400	At Sūr.
Fawāris فوارس	600	At Sūr, in Ja'alān, and on **Masīrah** island.
Ghaiyālīn غيالين	450	At Sūr and on **Masīrah** island.
Maja'alah مجعله	300	Nil.
Makhānah مخانه	500	At Sūr and on **Masīrah** island.

* Evidently under-estimated.

These sections are generally found intermingled at the places occupied by the tribe. Some of each section are Bedouins. The total number of the Jannabah may be about 12,000 souls, of whom over 9,000 are settled; but the strength of the nomad portion who inhabit the southern desert is necessarily difficult to estimate. The Jannabah have a perpetual feud with the Āl **Waḥībah**, the enmity between these two tribes being the most deadly and constant in 'Omān. The Tamīmah of the Jannabah is Mahmad-bin-Mubārak, of the Makhānah section, who resides at **Sūr**.

JARAID
جريد

A small sandy islet, about 12 feet high and ¼ of a mile in extent, lying 10 miles off the coast of the **Hasa** Sanjāq about midway between **Qatīf** and **Musallamīyah** bay: it is 14 or 15 miles south-east by east of the seaward end of Abu 'Ali island. It may be regarded as belonging to the Sanjāq which it adjoins.

JARĀMAH*
(KHOR-AL-)
خور الجرامه

An inlet of the sea which breaks the coast-line of the 'Omān Sultanate at a point 12¼ miles east of the **Sūr** creek and 4 miles west of Rās-al-Hadd. The entrance, which runs from north to south, is a mile long and winds between cliffs 60 feet high; its breadth is about 150 yards, but the channel at one point contracts to 60 yards and at the inner end it is divided into two by an island. Inland the Khor expands into a large, shallow basin with a length of 2½ miles from north-west to south-east, surrounded for the most part by cliffs 100 to 200 feet high but having, at its south end, a low and shelving beach with a few scattered trees. The interior of the inlet forms a perfectly sheltered harbour which is easily accessible to steam-vessels drawing less than 15 feet of water. Fish abound, and there are wells on the southern beach yielding brackish but drinkable water sufficient for a caravan of 200 camels and an equal number of men. The owners of the place are the Muwālikh tribe of **Hadd**, and the only actual occupants at the present time are a few fishermen who have some miserable huts near the wells already mentioned; but the ruins of a considerable village, said to have been called Labīd لبيد, are traceable close to the same spot.

Disputes regarding the free use of Khor-al-Jarāmah by mariners occurred between 1877 and 1880, and the British authorities, as related in the historical portion of this Gazetteer, were obliged to intervene.

---

* A plan of Khor-al-Jarāmah will be found in Admiralty Chart No. 2369—10-C.; and a route from this place to the coal-fields of the Jabal **Khamīs** range, described by Capt. Dowding, is among the records of the Intelligence Branch, Simla

JARRĀHI DISTRICT
جراحي

This district of Southern 'Arabistān has on the north-east of it the Rāmuz district, on the north-west the Ahwāz district, on the west the Fallāhīyeh district, on the south Ma'shūr and its connected territory, and on the east the Hindiyān district; it is itself situated upon both sides of the Jarrāhi River in the upper two-thirds of its course.

Boundaries.—The north-easternmost corner of the district is at the tomb of Shāh Nabi شاه نبي, at the foot of some hills to the east of the Jarrāhi, whence the boundary runs westwards through the southern extremity of Cham Manī' in the Rāmuz District to a mound named Rumais رميس. From Rumais it goes south to Qarqar village on the right bank of the Jarrāhi, immediately below which it crosses that river to the left bank and continues southwards for 5 miles: it then runs south-eastwards to 'Auleh about 8 miles west of Ma'shūr where it turns to the north-east: finally it passes through a large mound named Radhwān رضوان, 8 miles east of Khalfābād and so returns, following a range of low hills, to the point from which it started.

Physical features.—With the exception of a few miles of broken ground and ravines in the extreme north-east, the district consists of open and generally level plains of alluvial soil. Parts of these are tilled by rainfall, and there is some permanent cultivation along the banks of the Jarrāhi. The only trees are a few dates near villages and a little scrub along the river.

People.—The fixed population of the district is collected entirely upon the banks of the Jarrāhi River; it does not appear now to exceed 4,000 souls, and the number is said to have declined during the last 5 years in consequence of a series of bad harvests. Of the whole nearly 2,500 persons, or more than half, are Ka'ab, while other tribes deserving of separate mention are the Haiyādir حيادر at Butlīyeh, Cham, Rahāneh, Gumbuzōn and Thilith; the Maqātīf مقاطيف who are perhaps a branch of the Bani Tamīm (II), at Auleh Takhait and Abu 'Alāiq; and some Bandarīyeh, or immigrants from Ma'shūr, at Hadāmeh. The Haiyādir, who number 300 souls or more, are identified by some with the Haidaris of the Hindiyān District: they are said to be well armed with rifles and to own 50 cattle and 3,000 sheep and goats. The Maqātīf are about 400 persons; the Bandarīyeh about 300. The balance of the district population is made up of miscellaneous Arabs and Persians. Khalfābād is the principal village: among its inhabitants are a family or clan, known as Amāreh امارۀ, on whom the Haiyādir are dependent.

From Hadāmeh upwards the houses of the settled population are all of mud, and for some distance below it low mud walls and gables are seen; but still further down the dwellings are booths or wigwams of matting and reeds. These differences in domestic architecture are due less to differences in civilisation than to the nature of the materials available. Where mud is used it is mixed with broken straw and is made up into flattish oval blocks which do not possess a single straight line; this is the form of brick used by Arabs on the **Kārūn** and in the **Fallāhīyeh** District as well as on **Jarrāhi**; but in **Fallāhīyeh** Town there are one or two buildings of the ordinary square-shaped thin burnt bricks of Persia. Matting is made of a stiff reed called Qassāb, crushed flat; but in the construction of houses a large kind of bulrush called Bardi or Labbūn is employed, of which the blade is flat on one side and convex on the other but contains little substance. Roof supports are made by binding up Labbūn into faggots about 1 foot in diameter.

The nomad population consists chiefly of **Bāwīyeh** of the 'Amūr and Bani Khālid sections from the **Ahwāz** District. Some **Sharīfāt** of the Rajaibāt and Bani Rashīd sections are found almost permanently in the neighbourhood of **Khalfābād**, and it is a question whether they should be reckoned as among the sedentary or the Bedouin inhabitants of the district.

Villages and settlements.—The permanent villages of the district are described at length in the articles upon the **Jarrāhi** River, and a short table now follows of some of the inland settlements where cultivation is carried on:—

Name.	Position.	Remarks.
'Aquleh عقله	North of the Jarrāhi River and west of Haskeh village.	About 40 Faddāns of land are regularly cultivated here by some 20 families of Maqātif who return after the harvest to Haskeh. This community are said to own 20 rifles and about 5,000 sheep and goats.
Asghāyar (Hāji) حاجي اصغاير	On the south side of the Jarrāhi River, west of Hamād.	Inhabited by the **Ka'ab** tribe.
Dauweh درة	6 miles from the Jarrāhi River, east of the village of Abu Dubaiyān.	Various sections of the **Ka'ab** tribe are represented here.

Name.	Position.	Remarks.
Hamād حماد	On the south side of the Jarrāhi River, east of Hāji Asghāyar and west of Khalāfiyāt.	There are 20 Faddāns of cultivation here. Inhabited by the Ka'ab tribe.
Idāideh اداىدى	On the south side of the Jarrāhi River, west of Hor Trawaishid and east of Abu Saīleh.	This place belongs to Maqtū' on the river and is frequented by Ka'ab of the 'Asākireh subdivision.
Khalāfiyāt خلافيات	On the south side of the Jarrāhi River, west of Abu Saīleh and east of Hamād.	The cultivation here amounts to about 35 Faddāns. Inhabited by the Ka'ab tribe.
Saīleh (Abu) ابو سىيله	On the south side of the Jarrāhi River, west of Idāideh and east of Khalāfiyāt.	40 Faddāns of cultivation here. Inhabited by the Ka'ab tribe.
Trawaishid (Hor) هور ترويشد	On the south side of the Jarrāhi River, about 4 miles south of Maqtū' Fauqāni.	Similar to Idāideh above.

Agriculture and trade.—Canal irrigation is confined, in the Jarrāhi district, to a space of about three square miles in the neighbourhood of Cham-as-**Sābi**, and the crops, except on the banks of the river, depend entirely on rainfall. Wheat, barley, and a little sesame are the staples of cultivation; onions and inferior tobacco are grown in the gardens of villages. The irrigation of gardens is by means of skin lifts worked by cattle. The exported produce of the district finds its way chiefly to the towns of **Ma'shūr** and **Buziyeh** from which are procured in return piece-goods, spices, tea, and sugar. Dates are brought from the **Fallāhīyeh** and rice from the **Rāmuz** District.

Communications.—The **Jarrāhi** River is navigable by boats up to **Khalfābād**, and the country on both sides of it is free from obstacles to movement. The articles on the **Jarrāhi** River and **Fallāhīyeh** District and the paragraph on routes in **'Arabistān** may be consulted.

Administration.—The Jarrāhi district was once a part of the old Dōraq principality which belonged to the Shaikh of the **Ka'ab**. In 1865 the Persian Government separated it from the **Fallāhīyeh** District and constituted it, together with **Ma'shūr** and the district of **Hindiyān**, into a separate governorship. Now it is a district by itself and is under the Shaikh of **Muhammareh**, who is locally represented by a visiting agent from **Ma'shūr**; but it is understood that the Shaikh holds it in farm only from the Nizām-us-Saltaneh and the Mushīr-ud-Dauleh, whose joint property it is said to be. Revenue is assessed at one-fourth of gross produce on canal-irrigated lands at Cham-as-**Sābi** only; at one-fifth on river-bank lands; and elsewhere, that is at inland settlements, at a fixed cash rate of 44 Qrāns per Faddān annually. The district is said to be worth 14,000 to 15,000 Tūmāns a year.

JARRĀHI RIVER
جراحي

Frequently pronounced Yarrāhi. This river is formed within the bounds of **Rāmuz** District by the junction, near Qal'eh-i-Shaikh, of the Rāmuz * river from the north-east with the **Mārūn** river from the south-east. The Jarrāhi, possibly with its tributary the **Mārūn**,—and not, as has sometimes been supposed, the **Hindiyān**—appears to be the Tāb طاب river of the mediæval Arab and Persian geographers.†

Course.—Passing a place known as Cham Manī' منبع, 3 or 4 miles below the point of its formation, the Jarrāhi breaks through the belt of low hills which form the boundary on this side of the **Rāmuz** District and emerges near the village of Cham-as-**Sābi** into the **Jarrāhi** District. The range of hills, it may be remarked, comes from the north-west and dies away in undulating ground at some distance short of the right bank of the river; its course is resumed on the left bank somewhat higher up-stream, and the gap in the middle—through which the river passes—is occupied by a tract of broken, hilly ground about 10 miles in extent. From Cham-as-**Sābi** the river runs *viá* **Khalfābād** to the village of Maqtū', which is about 11 miles north-north-west of **Ma'shūr**; the length of this reach is nearly 30 miles, it is free from serious bends, and its general direction is from north-east to south-west. At Maqtū' the river changes direction and runs for about 10 miles west-north-west to Qarqar, where it leaves the district of **Jarrāhi** and enters that of **Fallāhīyeh**. In the **Fallāhīyeh** District its course is somewhat winding,

---

* "Rāmuz river" appears to be the name least open to objection, as well as that most generally understood, for the river which passes a few miles east of **Rāmuz** Town flowing southwards. It is sometimes spoken of, but only in the hills, as the Āb-i-'Ala آب اعلا or Āb-i-Zard آب زرد ; in strictness, however, these appear to be the names of streams which go to form the river and not of the river itself. The Rāmuz river has also been described as the "Jibur", but this name does not appear to be locally recognised. Of the manner of formation of the Rāmuz river we have as yet no authentic information, and the statements which have been obtained from native sources are conflicting. The water which it brings down is fresh and good.

† See Le Strange's *Lands of the Eastern Caliphate*.

but its average direction to a point distant 14 miles in a straight line from Qarqar is due west; at the point in question it turns to the south-west and runs for 5 miles further to a place called **Khazīneh** خزينة or the Reservoir, about 2 miles north of **Buziyeh** Town, where it is mostly dissipated in canals. The remaining stream now ceases to be the Jarrāhi river and becomes the Fallāhīyeh-Mārid canal, which is described in the article on the **Fallāhīyeh** District and on which **Fallāhīyeh** Town is situated at 3 miles below its head.

Volume and banks.—Above Cham-as-**Sābi** the river is broad and rapid with a breadth of about 80 yards; and the banks, which are of no great height, are covered with tamarisks. For some few miles below Cham-as-**Sābi** the same characteristics are preserved and the stream is divided by tamarisk-covered islands into several arms. Below **Khālfabād** the Jarrāhi runs with a slow current, is 60 to 70 yards broad, and resembles a sinuous canal cut deep through the alluvial soil; receiving no affluents, its stream from this point onwards continually diminishes in volume while its breadth decreases to about 40 yards. Above **Khalfā-bād**, though bare, level plains adjoin it on both sides, some fuel and grass are obtainable; but below **Khalfābād** both fuel and forage are scarce until a more productive region is entered again near Tuwaiqīyeh. Date groves begin on the right bank at the place where the river changes its direction from west-north-west to south-west, but at first they are scattered.

Crossings and navigation.—The Jarrāhi is fordable in summer at numerous places, and some fords near **Khalfābād** are practicable for laden animals during the greater part of the year, except after recent rain. There is a ford, sometimes difficult in winter but probably easy in the low season, one mile below Cham-as-**Sābi**; and another, passable only in summer and autumn, exists at Rahāneh, 8 miles above Maksar, where the breadth of the river is 50 yards; its greatest depth here in winter is 13 feet, and the height of the almost perpendicular banks is 15 feet.

A Ballam which can be used as a ferry boat is kept at Maksar, and there is a second at Hadāmeh. Boats 40 feet in length, with a beam of 6 to 8 feet and drawing 2 to 3 feet of water, can ordinarily ascend the river as far as **Khalfābād** at all seasons of the year.

Irrigation.—One mile above Cham-as-**Sābi** there are the remains of an old canal which took out on the right bank of the river; and in the neighbourhood of **Khalfābād** are traces, running inland from the present left bank, of a large canal, or possibly of a former bed or natural branch of the river. At Hadāmeh, also, a dam is said to have existed, by means of which irrigation was brought to the lands of **Ma'shūr** to the southward. The Jarrāhi, throughout its length, has now only one channel; and there are no canals in operation above the point where the river enters the **Fallāhīyeh** District. The **Jarrāhi** District appears to be commanded by the river at Cham-as-**Sābi**; but below that point, until the **Fallāhīyeh** District is reached, the level of the river as compared with that of its banks, is generally too low to admit conveniently of irrigation.

Riverside villages in the Jarrāhi District.—The villages on the Jarrāhi which are in the **Rāmuz** and **Fallāhīyeh** Districts are described in the articles under those names. The intermediate ones, which are in the **Jarrāhi** District are tabulated below:—

Name.	Miles below last village and on which bank situated.	Houses and inhabitants.	REMARKS.
Sābi (Cham-as-) چم الصابي	...	...	See article Cham-as-Sābi.
Khalfābād خلف آباد	7 Left.	...	See article Khalfābād.
Khar Faraih خر فريح	5 Right.	30 tents and huts of Ka'ab Arabs and Saiyids.	...
Wakhāmeh وخامه	Nil. Left.	20 mud houses of mixed Persians.	...
Hamūd (Saiyid) سيد حمود	2 Right.	10 mud houses of mixed Arabs.	...
Tiltīyeh تلتية	Nil. Left.	5 mud houses of mixed Arabs.	...
Dubaiyān (Abu) ابو دبيان	1 Left.	6 mud houses of poor Persians.	...
Butlīyeh بطلية	4 Left.	10 mud houses of Haiyā dir.	...
Cham چم	Nil. Right.	10 Do.	...

Name.	Miles below last village and on which bank situated.	Houses and inhabitants.	REMARKS.
Rahāneh رحانه	2 Left.	35 mud houses of Haiyādir.	There is a ford here, described in the article above.
Gumbuzōn گنبزون	1 Right.	15 Do.	...
Hirrīyeh حریه	2 Right.	20 mud houses of mixed Arabs.	...
Bunwār بنوار	Nil. Left.	15 mud houses of Ka'ab of the Āl Bū Ghubaish sub-division.	...
Bunwār Rizaiq بنوار رزیق	3 Left.	40 mud huts of the same. They have 50 rifles and 50 of their fighting men are mounted.	There are gardens and 100 Faddāns of ordinary cultivation. Thirty cattle and 500 sheep and goats are owned. The second part of the name is pronounced Rizaij.
Maksar مکسر	Nil. Right.	15 mud huts of the same. There are 30 fighting men, all mounted and armed with rifles.	There are gardens and 40 Faddāns of ordinary cultivation. There are 30 cattle and 500 sheep and goats. There is one boat, a Ballam.
Maksar 'Atīqeh مکسر عتیقة	2 Right.	20 mud huts of the same. There are 40 fighting men, of whom all have rifles and 30 are mounted.	Livestock are 50 cattle and 1,000 sheep and goats and 50 Faddāns of land are cultivated.
Hadāmeh هدامه	Nil. Left.	50 mud huts of Bandarīyeh, i.e., of natives of Ma'shūr or their descendants, divided into 3 sections called Shaikh 'Abdullah, Mulla Faraij and Hāji Sultān. They have 100 fighting men, of whom 60 are mounted and 70 have rifles.	The village is in 2 parts. Resources are 3 gardens, 80 Faddāns of cultivation, 50 cattle, 500 sheep and goats, and 1 boat, a Ballam. It is stated that a dam once existed at this place, by means of which the lands of Ma'shūr were irrigated.
Suwaireh صویره	2 Left.	20 mat huts of Ka'ab of the Al Bū Subaiyah section. They have 40 fighting men, all with rifles and mounted.	Cultivation extends to 40 Faddāns and there are gardens. Animals are 20 cattle and 200 sheep and goats. Half a mile inland is an Imāmzādeh of Wais.
Kurdūnīyeh کردونیه	... Right.	25 reed and mat huts of Ka'ab of the Al Bū Ghubaish sub-division, Hāji Ghadīr section. They have 50 fighting men, all mounted and armed with rifles.	70 Faddāns are cultivated and there are gardens. Livestock are 20 cattle and 1,500 sheep and goats.

Name.	Miles below last village and on which bank situated.	Houses and inhabitants.	REMARKS.
Maqtū' Fauqāni مقطوع فوقاني	4 (below Suwaireh). Left.	50 mat huts of Ka'ab of the 'Asākireh sub-division, Hāji 'Abūd section. Fighting men number 100 and are all mounted and armed with rifles.	There are gardens and 100 Faddāns of ordinary cultivation. A few cattle and 1,000 sheep and goats are owned.
Haskeh حسكه	Nil. Right.	30 mud and mat huts of Ka'ab of the Al Bū Ghubaish sub-division, Khazaiyil section. They have 60 fighting men, all with rifles and mounted.	80 Faddāns of land are cultivated and there are gardens. Livestock are 30 cattle and 500 sheep and goats.
Maqtū' Hadrāni مقطوع حدراني	1. Left.	45 mat huts of Ka'ab of the 'Asākireh subdivision. There are 90 fighting men, all of whom have rifles and 60 of whom are mounted.	Cultivation at the village amounts to 90 Faddāns and the people are said to have another 200 Faddāns of arable land at a distance to the southward. Their livestock amount to 30 cattle and 5,000 sheep and goats and are distributed for pasturage among all the Diis Ka'ab.
Takhait ...	... Right.	30 mat huts of Maqātif Arabs, dependent on the Amāreh, a leading family at Khalfābād. Their fighting men number 60, 40 of whom have rifles and 40 are mounted.	There are 20 Faddāns of cultivation at the village and livestock are estimated at 40 cattle and 3,000 sheep and goats. The people are said to have another 40 Faddāns of land irrigated from wells at some distance to the northward.
Khan-zeh خمزة	... Right.	20 mat huts of Ka'ab of the Khanāfireh division, Bait Dhuwaiyib section. Fighting men are 40, all armed with rifles and mounted.	60 Faddāns of land are cultivated. Animals are 30 cattle and 100 sheep and goats.
Sidaireh صديرة	Nil. Left.	1 Kūt of mud with an enclosure and 4 or 5 mat huts: the inhabitants are Ka'ab of the 'Asākireh subdivision. There are 20 fighting men all armed with rifles and mounted.	There are no livestock. Cultivation amounts to 30 Faddāns.
Thilith ثلث	... Right.	10 mat and mud huts of Haiyādir. They have 20 fighting men, all with rifles and mounted.	There are 100 sheep and goats, but no cattle. 30 Faddāns of land are cultivated.

Name.	Miles below last village and on which bank situated.	Houses and inhabitants.	REMARKS.
Saraimeh صريمة	5½ (below Maqtū' Hadrāni). Left.	50 mat huts of Ka'ab of the 'Asākireh subdivision. They have 100 fighting men, all with rifles and mounted.	Cultivation amounts to 100 Faddāns: 30 cattle and 200 sheep and goats are owned. There are gardens here.
Dōb-al-Mīr دوب المير	¼. Right.	15 houses of Ka'ab of the Āl Bū Ghubaish subdivision. 3 or 4 of the dwellings are of mud, the rest are reed and mat huts. Fighting strength is 30, ⅔ mounted and with rifles.	There are 20 cattle and 200 sheep and goats. Cultivation amounts to 30 Faddāns.
'Alāiq (Abu) ابو علائق	... Right.	20 mat huts of Maqātīf. Fighting men are 40, of whom 30 have rifles and 30 are mounted.	There are 40 Faddāns of cultivation. Cattle number 30 and sheep and goats 500.
Tuwaiqīyeh طويقية	2. Left.	30 mat huts of Ka'ab of the Khanāfireh subdivision, with 60 fighting men of whom 40 have rifles and 40 are mounted.	Cultivation is estimated at 50 Faddāns and livestock at 30 cattle and 200 sheep and goats. There are gardens at this place. The name is pronounced Tuwaijīyeh.
Qarqar قرقر	Nil. Right.	75 houses of Ka'ab of the Khanāfireh subdivision; a few are of mud, the rest are reed and mat huts. The fighting strength is 150, and 130 of the men are mounted and 100 have rifles.	Pronounced Gargar. Cultivation extends to 150 Faddāns and there are 50 cattle and 1,000 sheep and goats. There are gardens here.

The drinking of Jarrāhi water is locally believed to be conducive to health. The explanation given is that it contains sulphur.

JĀSHK (I) جاشك نو or NEW JĀSHK*

A port of Persian Makrān and a station of the Indo-European Telegraph Department; it is situated on a promontory about 140 miles south-east of Bandar 'Abbās, 145 miles north-north-east of Masqat Town, and 290 miles west by north of Gwādar.

* This is the correct pronunciation, but by Persians the word is sometimes sounded as if it had two syllables, Jā-shak.

Site.—The Jāshk peninsula divides Jāshk East Bay on the one side from Jāshk West Bay on the other, and it is itself nearly cut off from the mainland by a winding creek which runs inland from the western bay at a point 3½ miles northwards from the tip of the promontory. The land on which New Jāshk stands is low; the upper stratum consists of a loose sand mixed with clay and the lower stratum of hard calcareous matter, chiefly a shelly conglomerate.

Climate.—The climate of the place is extreme; the thermometer, which may fall to 44·3° Fahrenheit in winter, sometimes rises to 110° in summer; and the heat is rendered more trying by the moistness of the atmosphere, the mean humidity of which often exceeds 70 per cent. of saturation. The prevailing winds are easterly, but in winter it frequently blows from the north-west. Sandstorms are of frequent occurrence and during their continuance the air is heavily charged with a fine red dust. Malarial fever is prevalent in the cold weather. The normal rainfall is about 4½ inches per annum.

Surroundings.—The extremity of the Jāshk peninsula is called Jāshk-i-Sar جاشك سر ; it carries a small tomb, about 15 feet above sea-level, which is styled Shaik Sa'īd, **Hindi**, and which is an occasional object of pilgrimage. The recognised boundary of the British telegraph station, marked by a wire fence, crosses the peninsula in a zigzag line about ¾ of a mile from its extremity.[*] In the centre of the space enclosed by this land boundary and the sea stand the telegraph buildings with the British military barracks about 300 yards to the south-east of them.

In Persian territory, on the eastern side of the peninsula at 1¼ miles from Jāshk-i-Sar, is a strip of coast distinguished by the name of Damīlān دميلان , and beyond it is another known as Kurāzi كرازي .

On the western side of the peninsula, partly within and partly without the boundary of the telegraph station, is the West Bay in which is the ordinary landing place for New Jāshk; and on this bay, just outside the station boundary, is a tumble-down mud fort, the property of the Persian Government, which, not being required for military purposes, is used as a place for drying and storing whitebait. On the same shore, half a mile beyond the fort, begins a date grove called **Maksa**

---

[*] The actual boundary is thus seemingly not in accordance with the Agreement of 1887 (*vide* Aitchison's Treaties, Vol. X, pages 93-94 and footnote), but closer examination of the question with plans shows that the apparent discrepancy is due to the distance of the telegraph station from the point having been underestimated; that distance instead of being 300 is nearly 700 yards.

جاسك, a mile in extent, where there is a large mansion with Bādgīrs, owned by a private merchant but sometimes used as a place of quarantine.

Inhabitants.—New Jāshk is divided into two parts, namely, the European station, with a native settlement depending on it, and a Persian village which surrounds the Persian fort.

In the European station, the position of which has already been described, reside all the members of the telegraph establishment with their families and servants.

The Persian village consists of 45 mud houses and 150 date-leaf huts; it is inhabited by **Balūchis**, Saiyids, Mulāis, Raī-is, Maids who are fishermen, and negroes who are either labourers or domestic slaves: in addition to these there are some natives of the **Mīnāb** District and other Persians, also a large number of half-breeds of various kinds. Except the Persians, who are Shī'ahs, the people are Sunnis; and of the latter sect two divisions are represented, the **Balūchis** being Hanafis and the Saiyids Shāfi'is. The Persian, Balūchi, Arabic and Hindustani languages are all spoken and some of the people understand a little English. The inhabitants of the Persian village are mostly traders, agriculturists, graziers and fishermen. Agriculture is now at a low ebb in consequence of a succession of bad seasons; and a formerly considerable trade, especially by the Saiyids, in goods imported from Karāchi and Bombay, has declined since the establishment of an Imperial Persian Customs post in 1902.

Shipping, anchorages and trade.—New Jāshk is a fortnightly place of call for the steamers of the British India Company and is the chief port of Persian **Makrān** after **Chahbār**. Four Baqārahs of about 12 tons burden and trading only to the Arabian coast belong to this place.

There are anchorages suitable for steam vessels on both sides of the Jāshk promontory in which shelter can be found from all but southerly winds: the customary berth is in the West Bay about 2 miles from the landing place. Native boats use the creek already mentioned as leading out of the West Bay; the course is winding, its length 4 or 5 miles, and it has some depth of water inside, but the bar is almost dry at low tide.

The estimated value of the trade of the port in the year 1906 was— imports, about £3,264, exports, about £841 sterling. A Goanese firm under British protection act as agents for the British India Steam Navigation Company. There is also 1 British Indian (Muhammadan) general merchant.

Water and supplies.—The resources of New Jāshk are inconsiderable. Water, which is brackish, is from wells, the least bad of which is situated nearly 1 mile north-east of the telegraph station buildings and about 300 yards from the west coast of the peninsula; the water from this well is raised by bullock power into an elevated iron tank from which it is carried by iron pipes to a cistern at the back of the telegraph office; this water is not used for drinking except by natives. Drinking water for the telegraph staff is obtained from two rain storage covered masonry reservoirs, sunk in the ground, one of these has a capacity of 81,000 and the other of 58,000 gallons, and another similar tank of about 84,000 gallons capacity is now being constructed for the benefit of the Indian Military guard.

Food stuffs and even vegetables for the European community have, during the recent bad agricultural years, been mostly imported from India and Bandar 'Abbās. Livestock are about 200 cattle and 200 goats and sheep; there being no fodder there are no transport animals, and some of the residents who own camels keep them at Old **Jāshk**.

British telegraph station.—The telegraph station is an important one. The staff consists of 10 or 12 European clerks under a Superintendent or Assistant Superintendent, and there is an Assistant Surgeon in medical charge of the establishment. The inspecting officer of the land line from **Gwādar** to New Jāshk also has his headquarters here. The Jāshk office is connected with Karāchi by a cable; with **Chahbār**, **Gwādar**, Pasni, Ormārah and Karāchi by a two-wire land line; with **Masqat** by a cable; and with **Būshehr** by two cables, one of which runs direct and the other *via* **Hanjām**. The cables enter the sea at a point 550 yards south-east of the telegraph office; and of the 3 which at first turn westwards the nearest to shore is that to **Hanjām**, the next the direct cable to **Būshehr**, and the outermost that to **Masqat**. Messages are now transmitted direct between Karāchi and Tehrān, the current being reinforced at Jāshk and again at Būshehr: from 500 to 1,000 messages pass in the 24 hours, in one direction by day and in the other by night, this being arranged in alternation with another line. The telegraph office and quarters form three blocks of substantial and commodious flat-roofed buildings. For the protection of the place a detachment of 50 sepoys of the Indian Army under a native officer are posted at New Jāshk; they are accommodated in well-built barracks which are capable of containing double the number.

Political relations and administration.—The head of the telegraph station is the political representative of the British Government at New Jāshk, and as such exercises jurisdiction over British subjects and deals with the Persian officials and local authorities under the orders of his superior, the Director at Karāchi.

The Persian Imperial Customs establishment consists of a Mudīr and 4 armed guards locally recruited; the revenue collected by them during the year 1906 amounted to 8,728 Qrāns, 3,414 Qrāns and 1,779 Qrāns on account of imports, exports, and stamp duty respectively. Apart from these Customs employés the Persian Government have no agents at Jāshk. The quarantine arrangements are in charge of the British medical officer of the telegraph station, on behalf of the Persian Government. Authority over Persian subjects in the settlement is exercised by the Mīrs of Old Jāshk whose position is described in the article on Jāshk District.

JĀSHK (II)
جاشك
or
OLD JĀSHK

In English generally "Jask" and at a former period "Jasques". The administrative capital of the Jāshk District and residence of the chiefs; it is situated 7 miles north of New Jāshk and one mile inland from the shore of Jāshk West Bay. The village is completely surrounded by date groves which contain about 2,000 trees. The chief points of interest are the ruins of a reputed Portuguese fort, with an old gun lying buried in the ground, and a Ziyārat called Shāh Mardān شاه مردان which is much frequented by Balūchis. There are about 10 mud houses and 150 mat huts and the population may be estimated at 800 souls, of whom rather more than half are Balūchis; the remainder are Shaikhs, Jats and slaves. Dates, wheat and Arzun are cultivated, and to a lesser extent cotton and barley. The village possesses 200 camels, 50 donkeys, 60 cattle and 300 sheep and goats. Water is from 2 wells, 8 feet deep, and is muddy but sweet. The inhabitants are chiefly agriculturists, except some weavers called Jūlahag جولاهگ; but they deal also in carpets called Zilu زيلو and Khirsak خرسك, in date mats called Tak تك, and in firewood and ghi which they export to Qishm Island and to the Arabian coast, especially to Bātinah, their trade relations being chiefly with these places and with the Persian districts of Bashākard and Mīnāb. The trade with Masqat Town is now insignificant. Some silk embroidery is done by the women and fishing nets are made. The administration is noticed in the article on **Jāshk** District. There is good partridge shooting, and some hares are obtainable, near Old Jāshk.

JĀSHK جاشک DISTRICT

The Jāshk district, except in the administrative sense, is a division of Persian **Makrān**, and most of the general remarks contained in the article on the coast of that region apply to it without modification.

Limits.—The Jāshk district extends from Kūh Mubārak (or rather from a stream called Maināhi ميناهي , 1 mile north of Kūh Mubārak) on the west nearly to the Sadaich river on the east; inland it meets the Bashākard district at about 50 miles from the coast. Our attention will, however, be confined to the plain which here, as elsewhere in Persian **Makrān**, skirts the sea and extends to the outer hills that rise at some miles inland.

Physical characteristics.—The remarks under this head in the article on the Persian **Makrān** coast hold good of the Jāshk district and need only to be supplemented by a slight description of some of the principal natural features. These are given below, in tabular form, in their order from west to east:—

Name.	Position.	Nature.	Remarks.
Kūh Mubārak* كوه مبارك	3½ miles north of Rās-al-Kūh, the corner at which the coast turns northwards from the Gulf of 'Omān to the entrance of the Persian Gulf.	A very remarkable precipitous rocky hill of light colour, shaped like a cylinder placed upon one of its ends.	It is 333 feet high and stands perfectly isolated in a swampy plain at one mile from the coast. It is perforated and the perforation can be seen through from the south-east.
Chālapi چالپي	7 miles east of Kūh Mubārak.	A small stream.	...
Tawarkand Stream تور كند	Rises at 30 miles from the coast and, passing the western shoulder of the Parkau mountain, reaches the sea 9 miles west of Old Jāshk.	A stream, dry except after rain.	Rabg village is situated on this stream within the hills. At a few miles from the sea its bed width is 100 yards.

* A distant view of Kūh Mubārak from the sea is given in Chart No. 2375-753 (*Entrance of the Persian Gulf.*)

Name.	Position.	Nature.	Remarks.
Parkau Hills or پرکو Jabal Baḥmadi جبل بهمدي	The highest and central summit is 13 miles north of the mouth of the Tawarkand stream at the coast.	A barren group of hills of which the highest point is 3,048 feet. The range runs for a few miles both west and south-south-east from this peak. The strata appear to be inclined upwards from west to east.	On the seaward slopes of the range is a remarkable rock-pillar of natural origin. These hills are divided from the rest of the coast range by the Tawarkand stream on the west and the Bahmadi stream on the east.
Bahmadi Stream بهدي	Rising not so far north as the Tawarkand stream it comes down by the east shoulder of the Parkau hills and reaches the sea about the same place as the Tawarkand.	A stream, dry except after rain.	Between the southeastern extremity of the Parkau hills and the Gaigan hill the stream runs in a deep and narrow defile called Tang Bahmadi.
Gaigan Hill گیگن	About 8 miles north-east of Old Jāshk.	An isolated barren hill of remarkable aspect, 1,630 feet high.	The hill is quoin-shaped with a sheer fall to westward: the precipices are of a yellow colour. As seen from New Jāshk it somewhat resembles the Rock of Gibraltar.
Kwaik Stream کویک	Comes down in a west-south-westerly direction from a few miles inland and reaches the sea a mile or two west of Old Jāshk.	A stream, dry except after rain.	Towards the coast the bed of this torrent is 200 yards wide and the banks 40 feet high. There is good but scanty water in wells.
Jāshk Stream جاشك	Comes down from the back of the Gazdān hill and flows into the head of a small creek near Old Jāshk.	A stream.	There is no water except after rain.
Gazdān Hill گزدان	13 miles north-east of New Jāshk and 4 miles from the coast.	A summit of the coast range rising to 1,725 feet.	There is a small village on this hill where a few Shikāris live. Some pools and natural reservoirs contain good water.
Shehrnau Stream شهرنو	Rises in the hills behind Tār village and reaches the sea 15 miles east of New Jāshk.	A stream with low banks about 100 yards apart.	The Shehrnau is dry except after heavy rain. Its mouth is a tidal creek with shifting sandhills on the west side.

Name.	Position.	Nature.	Remarks.
Jagīn River جگين	Rises in the Bashākard district more than 70 miles inland and reaches the coast 29 miles east of New Jāshk.	A river which near the coast is low in summer and autumn, but after heavy rain becomes impassable and overflows its banks. Ordinarily it is a rapid stream 50 yards wide and 3 feet deep with well-defined banks 20 feet high which are in places half a mile apart. The water is good.	The river is sometimes impassable for 5 or 6 and even for 10 to 15 days. In the plain there is a thick belt of tamarisk and acacia jungle on both banks. Near its mouth are two mangrove swamps called Janakāni جنكاني and Nazai نزي separated by a marshy plain 7 miles wide through which the river wanders. The local chiefs are said to derive some revenue from the creek formed by the mouth of the river; they impose dues on the boats which call to cut mangroves.
Sīramch Stream سيرمچ	Between the Jagīn and Gābrīg rivers nearer the former.	Resembles the Shehrnau above.	This stream has a number of small tributaries; it is dry except after heavy rain
Gābrīg River گابريگ	Rises in the Bashākard district, nearly 80 miles from the coast and reaches the sea about 45 miles east of New Jāshk.	A river somewhat resembling the Jagīn, but with low banks which at 10 miles from the coast are $\frac{1}{4}$ of a mile apart.	After entering the maritime plain this river has a sandy bottom abounding in quicksands, and the banks are lined with tamarisks and acacias.
Sadaich سديچ	Rises 70 miles from the coast in the Bashākard district and reaches the sea about 60 miles east of New Jāshk.	A river which overflows its east bank in the maritime plain during high rises but is dry except after rain. The water is sweet. At 4 miles from the sea the Sadaich receives a tributary called the Haimin هيمن on its right bank and at 6 miles from the sea another called the Gilik گلك on its left; the latter has a tributary called the Raiku	The mouth of this river is a tidal creek with a shallow bar; the coast on the east side of it is swampy, and on the west bare white sandhills called Sūrāp, سوراپ, in which water can be obtained by digging, extend along the beach for 6 miles.

Name.	Position.	Nature.	Remarks.
		ریکو which enters it on its left bank at 5 miles from its junction with the Sadaich. These smaller streams contain water after rain only and their banks are low and ill-defined.	

Before leaving the subject of physical conformation we may note that the coast of the Jāshk district is in general low and marshy. From Rās-al-Kūh to the mouth of the Jāshk creek the shore consists of a narrow strip of sand, in places bearing tufts of grass, which has mangrove swamps behind it and in places is penetrated by inlets; of these Khor Hāmid حامد, some miles east of Rās-al-Kūh, is the most considerable and is to some extent frequented by boats. At New Jāshk there is a short interval of well-defined coast; and east of this again mangrove swamps, with creeks which are visited only for fishing and cutting firewood, resume their place till the Sūrāp sandhills are reached near the mouth of the Sadaich river.

Population.—The inhabitants of the Jāshk district are comprised in the population which is described in the general article on the coast of Persian **Makrān**. The Hōts may in this district be regarded as the dominant tribe, inasmuch as the chiefs are of their number. The total population (including hill villages not given in the table below) is roughly estimated at 22,000 souls; the fighting strength of the first line, that is, of men armed with modern rifles, at 500; and that of the second line at 3,000. The population of the coastal strip with which we are concerned is about 9,000 souls.

Agriculture, livestock and fisheries.—For general information under these heads the article on Persian **Makrān** may be consulted. Additional details will be found in the topographical table at the end of the present article.

Trade, communications, supplies and transport.—The reader is referred to the remarks under these heads in the articles on Persian **Makrān** and New **Jāshk**, and to the topographical table at the end of the present article.

JĀSHK DISTRICT

Of the camels about ⅔ are females which are seldom used for transport.

Administration.—The Jāshk district, though situated in Persian **Makrān**, is under the jurisdiction of the Governor of the **Gulf Ports**, by whom the local rulers are appointed. There are at present two joint chiefs or Mīrs of Jāshk, Mustafa Khān and Mīr Hōti, who reside at Old **Jāshk** and are relations; the former is the principal chief. These chiefs belong to the Hōt tribe. Nothing is, or ever has been, paid by them to the Persian Government on account of the farm of the district; the nominal ground of their exemption from payment is that they are responsible for the Persian fort at New **Jāshk**, but this is not the real reason. The chiefs collect several taxes for their own benefit, notably a land tax which produces about 1,500 Tūmāns per annum, a poll tax of 10 Qrāns yearly on all men of substance and traders, a poll tax of 2 Riyāls a year on male adults in the villages of Lūrān, Bahāl and Kūh Mubārak, and a tithe or Dahyaki دهیکی on grain produce and dates. In the fishing season they also take 10 Riyāls on account of every fishing boat; and they receive annually 15 camels under the Balūchi title of Gurjawi گرجوی. Some of the slaves of the chiefs constitute a sort of police force.

The political institution of greatest importance in the district is the British telegraph station described in the article on New **Jāshk**, and the chiefs of Jāshk receive an annual telegraph subsidy of Rs. 840 through the representatives of the Indo-European Telegraph Department. The Persian Government is as yet unrepresented save by a Mudīr of the Imperial Persian Customs and his subordinates, 4 armed guards, who are posted at New **Jāshk**.

Topographical.—The following is an alphabetical table of the principal places in the part of the Jāshk district adjoining the sea:—

Name.	Position.	Houses and inhabitants.	REMARKS.
Ādūri آدری	2 miles west of the Jagīn river and 13 miles from the coast.	10 huts of Qalandarzais.	Resources are 20 camels, 10 cattle, 50 goats and sheep, 150 date palms, and a little ordinary cultivation. The Jagīn river used to pass this place, but changed its course about 20 years ago.

Name.	Position.	Houses and inhabitants.	Remarks.
Bahāl بهال	On the coast, 6 miles east-north-east of New Jāshk.	70 huts of Maids and negroes.	The people are fishermen and net-makers; they have also some date groves and a little cultivation. The principal export is whitebait, for the storage of which there are two mud godowns. Water is from wells and is good. There are 3 small fishing boats; and 10 camels, 10 cattle and 50 goats and sheep are owned.
Bagāni بگاني	Near the right bank of the Gābrīg river 10 miles from the coast.	5 huts of Balūchis, chiefly weavers.	This village was destroyed by a chief named Mīr Barkat, a relation of the Mīrs of Jāshk, a few years ago. Resources are 400 date palms, 20 camels, 15 cattle and 50 goats and sheep.
Bahmadi بهمدي	At the foot of Kūh Bahmadi and 10 miles north-west of Old Jāshk.	100 huts of Hōts and Raīs.	The huts are scattered about in various places. Crops are dates (500 palms) wheat, maize and Arzun; animals are 10 camels, 20 cattle, 200 sheep and goats and 20 donkeys. Ghi is made. The people are fond of sport. Water is good, from wells.
Balūchi بلوچي	13 miles west-north-west of Old Jāshk near the left bank of the Tawarkand stream.	30 huts of the Raīs tribe.	Wheat, maize, Arzun and a little cotton are grown and date palms number 1,000. There are 20 camels, 10 donkeys, 50 cattle and 100 sheep and goats, and ghi is manufactured. There is a considerable trade with the Arabian coast, chiefly through Sohār, and with Qishm Island. Water is good, from wells.

Name.	Position.	Houses and inhabitants.	Remarks.
Chāhru چامرو	On the coast 12 miles east-north-east of New Jāshk.	10 huts of Maids, occupied only during the season of the whitebait fishery, viz., from October to April.	The people are fishermen.
Chaikalau چیکلر	2 miles west of the Gābrīg river and 4 miles from the coast.	6 huts of Maids.	The people are fishermen; they also own 50 date trees, 20 camels, 20 cattle and 30 goats and sheep.
Dārōbast داروبست	On the right bank of the Gābrīg river at 7 miles from the sea.	15 huts of Hōts.	There is a little cultivation of barley and jowari; dates number 150 trees; live stock are 10 camels, 20 cattle and 50 goats and sheep; and wells of good water exist.
Dārzīn دارزین	4 miles east-south-east of Yakdar.	5 huts of Jangizais.	The people own 50 camels, 20 cattle and 50 goats and sheep.
Gabrīg کابریگ	On the right bank of the Gabrīg river at about 10 miles from the coast.	200 huts with a fluctuating population of Jangizais, Hōts, the Rais tribe and negroes.	The place is much scattered. Wheat, barley, maize and cotton are grown, and other products are wool, goat and camel hair, ghi and goat skins. Date palms number 1,000. The people own 200 camels, 30 donkeys, 50 cattle and 200 sheep and goats. There is some trade in slaves. Water is from wells in the river bed and is good. The local headman is Nūr Muhammad.
Gaigan کیگن	5½ miles north-north-west of Old Jāshk at the southern foot of a mountain similarly named.	20 huts of low-class Balūchis.	The mountain is 2,300 feet high. The people own 20 camels, 20 cattle and 500 goats and sheep and are proficient as Shikāris of the mountain goat and gazelle. There is a Ziyārat of Mīr 'Umr at the village. Water is from wells and is very good.

Name.	Position.	Houses and inhabitants.	REMARKS.
Gangān گنگان	19 miles west by north of Old Jāshk and 3½ miles inland from the coast.	Fluctuates from 120 to 200 huts of the Rais tribe, reaching its maximum size in the season of agriculture.	The village is a scattered one. Dates are in plenty (1,000 trees), and there is much cultivation of wheat, maize and Arzun. The people own 300 camels, 200 cattle and 200 goats and sheep, and some of them are weavers and others wood-cutters. Sheep's wool, goats' and camels' hair and ghi are exported, and there is some trade, chiefly in ghi, with Qishm Island and the coast of Arabia. Water is from wells and is good. Two routes from the Biyābān district and Mīnāb Town converge here.
Garuk گرک	...	...	Part of the village of Gangān, q.v., is so called.
Grīshkin گریشکن	On the bank of the Gābrīg river at its mouth.	10 huts of fishermen.	There is a considerable trade with Masqat Town and Qishm Island after the monsoon. Ghi, wool, sheep and goats are exported, and dates, rice, jowari and cloth imported. The chief is Nūr Muhammad of Gābrīg. Water is good, from wells.
Gūrandu گورندر	On the left bank of the Gābrīg river at 15 miles from the coast.	20 huts of Hōts and Balūchis of a low class, chiefly weavers.	Resources are 400 date palms, 50 camels, 20 cattle and 50 goats and sheep.
Haimin هیمن	On the right bank of the Haimin stream at 8 miles from the sea.	12 huts of Hōts and Balūchis.	Date palms number 200, and livestock are 50 camels, 20 cattle and 50 goats and sheep.
Hasā حصار	6 miles north-east of Yakdar.	50 huts of Singalaus.	There is a little cultivation of cotton and the people possess 500 date trees, 100 camels, 50 cattle and 300 goats and sheep.

JĀSHK DISTRICT

Name.	Position.	Houses and inhabitants.	Remarks.
Hushdān هشدان	On the coast, 10 miles east-north-east of New Jāshk.	Half-a-dozen huts of Maids, fishermen, and of cultivators.	The inhabitants own 100 date palms, a few cattle and 20 sheep and goats; grow wheat, maize and cotton; and deal in whitebait. Water is good.
Hūn هون	3 miles north-east of Gūrandu.	10 huts of Hōts and Balūchis in the dry season, increasing to 100 in the rains.	There is a little cultivation of barley and jowari and 100 date palms, 50 camels, 20 cattle and 50 goats and sheep are owned.
Jagīn جگين	On both banks of the Jagīn river at 4 miles from the sea.	100 huts of Jangizais, Maids, Balūchis and negroes.	Wheat, maize, Māsh, Arzun and cotton are grown and there are 1,000 scattered date trees. Livestock are 150 camels, 50 cattle and 200 goats and sheep. Some ghi and raw cotton are exported. Water is good, from the river and from wells.
Jāshk جاشك نو or New Jāshk.	About 140 miles south-east of Bandar 'Abbās, 145 miles north-north-east of Masqat Town and 290 miles west by north of Gwādar.	...	See article New Jāshk.
Jāshk (II) جاشك or Old Jāshk	7½ miles north of New Jāshk and a mile or more from the sea.	...	See article Old Jāshk.
Kāhōti كاهوتي	6 miles north-east of New Jāshk near the head of the Jāshk creek.	10 huts of Balūchis.	The people own 30 camels, 10 cattle, 5 donkeys and 50 sheep and goats, and deal in firewood. Water is good, from wells, and there are about 400 date trees.
Kalābatān كلابتان	2 miles west of Kāhōti, midway between that place and Old Jāshk.	20 huts of Hōts.	The inhabitants possess 20 camels, 10 cattle and 50 sheep and goats and traffic in wood fuel. Date trees number 200.
Kordap كوردپ	4 miles north-west of the mouth of the Jagīn river.	5 huts of Maids.	The people are fishermen.

Name.	Position.	Houses and inhabitants.	Remarks.
Lapink لاپنک	2 miles north-west of Old Jāshk.	20 huts of Balūchis.	The people are chiefly pastoral and nomadic, frequently changing their location for the sake of better grazing. They have 10 camels, 20 cattle, and 500 sheep and goats. They also grow some corn and cotton and own 200 date palms. There is good water from wells.
Lāsh لاش	3 miles east of Shehrnau.	20 huts of Maids and Balūchis.	The people are fishermen and cultivate a little; they also own 30 camels, 20 cattle, 50 sheep and goats and 200 date palms.
Lōnd لوند	On the right bank of the Jagīn river, 9 miles from the coast.	5 huts of Balūchis.	There are some date palms, at present about 50, but the trees are frequently carried away by floods in the river. Livestock are 30 camels, 20 cattle and 40 goats and sheep.
Lūrān لوران	2 miles north-east of New Jāshk.	60 huts of Maids and negroes.	The village is divided into two portions about half a mile apart: that nearer to New Jāshk consists of the mud bungalow of Khān Sāhib Hasan Khān, a pensioned Indian artificer of the Indo European Telegraph Department, with a dozen huts occupied by his dependants. The people are date-growers, fishermen and agriculturists, and formerly they were slave-traders also. Nets are made and some business is done in whitebait. Water is good, from wells in K. S. Hasan Khān's garden. There are 400 date trees, 6 donkeys, 10 cattle and 50 goats and sheep.

Name.	Position.	Houses and inhabitants.	Remarks.
Lūti لوتي	Near Lāsh, but a little further from the sea.	10 huts of Maids and low-class Balūchis.	Fishermen and cultivators on a small scale. Resources are 400 date palms, 50 camels, 20 cattle and 100 goats and sheep.
Malagimach ملگي مچ	10 miles west by north of Old Jāshk and 3 miles from the coast.	10 huts of Hōts.	There are about 600 date trees, 200 camels, 10 cattle and 100 goats and sheep. Wells yield good water.
Maliki Chīdag ملكي چيدك	Between the Sadaich river and the Haimin stream.	An uninhabited spot.	This place is regarded as being on the boundary between Jāshk and Gaih districts.
Mubārak (Kūh) كوه مبارك	7 miles west of Gangān at the foot of the hill after which it is called.	100 huts of Shaikhs, Raīs, Balūchis and negroes.	The dwellings are scattered about amidst low hills. The inhabitants cultivate wheat, maize and Arzun, and own 1,000 date palms, 50 camels, 50 cattle, and 800 sheep and goats. They export some ghi, wool and goat hair to Qishm Island and the Arabian coast. Water is good, from wells. A creek, which can be entered by boats of considerable size, runs 2 miles inland from the sea in the direction of the village; it is said to have 2 feet of water at low tide.
Mugmālam مگمالم	...	...	Part of the village of Kūh Mubārak, q. v.
Mugrōbāh مگروباه	Between Kāhōti and Kalābatān.	None, except in the date season when the owners encamp there.	A plantation of 50 date palms belonging to Old Jāshk. The European Telegraph establishment at New Jāshk used to hunt hares and foxes here, but now they are scarce.

Name.	Position.	Houses and inhabitants.	Remarks.
Nigor نگور	At the foot of the Bahmadi hill between the villages of Bahmadi and Balūchi.	100 huts of Raīs and Balūchis.	The village is closely connected with Bahmadi and has much cultivation. Water is good, from wells, and there are 1,000 date palms. Livestock are 10 camels, 50 cattle and 200 goats and sheep.
Rabg رېگ	5 miles north of Balūchi village on the Tawarkand stream.	50 huts of Balūchis.	The people cultivate wheat, maize, Arzun and occasionally cotton, besides owning 10 camels, 50 cattle and 200 sheep and goats. They are also woodcutters. Water is good, from wells, and there are 500 date trees.
Sadaich سديچ	On both banks of the Sadaich river at 7 miles from the sea.	80 huts of Balūchis.	Wheat is grown and there are 200 scattered date palms. Livestock are 50 camels, 20 cattle and 150 goats and sheep. Water is from pools in the river and from wells.
Shehrnau شهر نو	South-east of Hushdān.	20 houses of fishermen, Maids.	Wheat, maize, Māsh and cotton are grown, also barley and Arzun. The livestock amount to 30 camels, 30 cattle and 200 goats and sheep. There are 200 date trees.
Sīramch سيرمچ	Between the Jagīn and Gābrīg rivers at 12 miles from the coast.	10 huts of Jangizais.	Camels vary from 50 to 500 according to the season, and there are in the season 50 cattle and 100 goats and sheep.
Tār تار	3 miles north-west of Yakdar.	8 huts of Balūchis, increasing to 50 in the rains.	There are a few goats and sheep and a little cultivation of barley and jowarï. Date trees amount to 50.

Name.	Position.	Houses and inhabitants.	Remarks.
Yakbūni يكبوني	3 miles east-north-east of New Jāshk.	20 huts of negroes, Balūchis and Maids.	The inhabitants cultivate dates (100 trees) and sometimes wheat; are fishermen and deal in whitebait. They have 10 camels, 10 cattle, and 30 sheep and goats. They buy and sell cloth and formerly they trafficked in slaves.
Yakdar يكدر	23 miles east by north of New Jāshk, on the telegraph line and nearly 10 miles from the coast.	200 huts of negroes, Balūchis, Jangizais and Maids.	Wheat, maize, Māsh, Arzun and cotton are grown, and 50 camels, 40 cattle and 200 sheep and goats are owned. There are some traders in cloth, ghi, cotton, fish and dates.
Zawāru زوارو	Between the Jagīn and Gābrīg rivers at 6 miles from the sea.	6 huts of Jangizais and negro slaves.	There are 100 date palms, 50 camels, 20 cattle and 50 goats and sheep.
Zīrkūh زيركوه	14 miles west-north-west of Old Jāshk.	10 huts of Balūchis and Raīs.	Date palms number 500 and there are 10 camels, 10 cattle and 100 goats and sheep. Water, from wells, is good.

JAU*
جو

Locally pronounced Yō: a small district of Independent 'Omān situated between the 'Omān Sultanate and Trucial 'Omān and including, at its north-western and most important part, the oasis of **Baraimi**. The boundaries of Jau are indefinite, but the tract embraces Jabal Hafīt with the villages near the southern end of that range: the country visible from the top of the **Baraimi** fort is mostly situated in Jau. Jau is a plain. On the south-east, the side on which it adjoins **Dhāhirah**, it is stony with a little scrub jungle.

---

* The maps for Jau are *Compass Sketch of Part of the Route taken by Major P. Z. Cox, etc.*, 1902, and *Route taken by Major P. Z. Cox, etc.*, 1905.

The following are the principal places and features of Jau:—

Place or feature.	Position.	Nature.	Remarks.
Baraimi Oasis بريمي	...	...	See article **Baraimi** Oasis.
Hafit (Jabal) جبل حفيت	Begins 4 miles south of **Baraimi** Village and runs thence about 24 miles in a southerly direction.	A range of hills.	The direction of the range is north and south and its maximum elevation above the Jau plain is about 1,500 feet. The plain close to its western flank is strewn with talus.
Hafit حفيت	About 25 miles south-south-east of **Baraimi** Village, near the south-eastern foot of Jabal Hafit.	A village of 150 houses of Na'īm of the 'Aryān, Khawātir and Kilābinah sections.	It is divided into 3 contiguous hamlets which are, in order from north to south, Bū Gharah, Hafīt Proper and Gharbī. Water is good and abundant; wheat and bananas are grown, and there are 9,000 date palms. There are 200 camels and 1,000 sheep and goats.
Hawaithah حويثة	22 miles east by south of **Baraimi** Village.	A halting place in the Hawaithah plain above the head of Wādi-al-Jizi.	......
Khurūs خروض	16 miles east by south of **Baraimi** Village on the route from that place to **Sohār** Town, between Khatmat-ash-Shiklah and Hawaithah.	A well or water hole.	This place is between two ridges, at the head of a hollow which runs down from it south-westwards to the Jau plain.
Muzdailah مزديلة	Crossed about 7 miles east of **Baraimi** Village on the route from that place to **Sohār** Town.	A plain.	It extends several miles northwards from the place where it is crossed, with a breadth of about 2 miles, between two parallel ridges.

Place or feature.	Position.	Nature.	Remarks.
Qābil قابل	About 2 miles south of Hafīt village and close to the southern extremity of Jabal Hafīt on its east side.	A village of 180 houses of Na'īm of the Āl Bū Shāmis division.	The water is good; wheat and bananas are grown; there are 10,000 date palms.
Qatār قطار	8 or 9 miles east by north of Baraimi Village.	A bluff.	This is point in the ridge which overlooks the Muzdailah plain from the east.
Shiklah (Khatmat-ash-) خطمة الشكلة	A mile north of Khatmat-as-Suwwād.	The southern extremity of a ridge which runs from south to north.	The Baraimi-Sohār route passes between this place and Khatmat-as-Suwwād. A short distance to the east of Khatmat-ash-Shiklah is a low red hill of compact nummulitic limestone.
Suwwād (Khatmat-as) خطمة السواد	12 miles east-south-east of Baraimi Village.	The northern end of a ridge which goes off to southwards.	See Khatmat-ash-Shiklah above.

JAU
جوف

A tract in the Ḥasa Sanjāq, beginning about 8 miles north of the Oasis of that name; it is divided from the latter by a small strip of the Biyādh tract which intervenes. On the west side of Jauf a line connecting Jabal Gharaimīl with Jabal Dām divides it from the tract of Badd-al-Asīs; and, at its north-western corner, only the interposition of Jabal Dām prevents its meeting the Habl tract. On the remaining sides it is enclosed by Biyādh. The length of Jauf from north-west to south-east is rather over 30 miles; and its average breadth, taken at right angles to its length, is about half as much.

Jauf is a sandy depression and its surface is composed of mounds and hollows, all of sand. The general colour of the tract is darker than that of Biyādh. The hollows contain trees of Markh and bushes of Ghadha, and in the grazing are included the shrubs called 'Arfaj, and Rimth and the grasses known as Nasi, Subat, and Thamām. In most respects Jauf resembles Habl, which it adjoins, but it is better provided with water.

Wells are numerous in Jauf and the average depth is about 12 feet. The following are among the better known:—

Name.	Vernacular equivalent.	Position.
Asaifirāt	اصيفيرات	In the centre of the northern part of Jauf, 8 miles east of Jabal Dām and 8 miles north of Jabal Gharaimīl.
Dār ('Ain)	عين دار	Near the northern end of Jabal Gharaimīl, 7 miles south of Asaifirāt.
Dhalūf (Abudh)	ابو الضلوف	Between Shahamah and Shāra'.
Dumaiyagh	دميغ	Near the north-eastern corner of Jabal Gharaimīl, 5 miles east of 'Ain Dār.
Faqāt	فقات	10 miles south-west by west of Taba'āt in Biyādh and 3 miles or so east of Jabal Gharaimīl.
Fūdah	فوده	4 miles north-north-west of Faqāt, near the eastern foot of Jabal Gharaimīl.
Hamām (Abul)	ابو الحمام	In the extreme south-eastern corner of Jauf, close to the Habail tract in Biyādh.
Madassah	مدسة	3 miles north-east of Asaifirāt.
Murair	مرير	2 miles north-east by north of Faqāt.
Muwattarah	موترة	1 mile west of Faqāt. It is adjoined by a hillock of the same name.
Nasab	نصب	6 miles north-west by north of Asaifirāt.
Ruwāqi	رواقي	5 miles east-south-east of Asaifirāt.
Salaisil	سليسل	6 miles south-east of Asaifirāt.
Sawūd	سوود	3 miles west of Asaifirāt.
Shahalah	شهله	3 miles south-east of Asaifirāt.
Shahamah	شحمة	4 miles north-east of Asaifirāt and 5 miles west of Sarrah in Biyādh.
Shāra'	شارع	5 miles east by north of Asaifirāt.
Shuraiya'	شريع	6 miles south-west of Asaifirāt.
Shuraiyāt	شريات	5 miles south by east of Asaifirāt.
Thalaimah	ثليمة	4 miles south-west of Asaifirāt.

Of these wells Asaifirāt, 'Ain Dār, Ruwāqi and Shāra' are said to be the best, while Nasab and Sawūd are among the worst.

Jauf belongs to the **'Ajmān** tribe of Bedouins and the Bani **Hāji** also visit it under their auspices.

JAUF-AL-'ĀMIR or 'AMAR
جوف العامر
جوف العمر

The largest town in the dominions of the Amīr of Jabal **Shammar** in Central Arabia; it lies, entirely surrounded by deserts, about 365 miles south-west of **Baghdād**, 225 miles north-west of **Hāil** and 310 miles south-east of Damascus.

Site.—Jauf-al-'Amir is about 1,850 feet above sea-level. It is situated on a dead flat plain forming the bottom of an extraordinary depression of oval form which has a maximum diameter, from north-west to south-east, of about 3 miles. The walls of the depression are sandstone hills supporting a desert plain some 500 feet higher than Jauf. These hills are called on the north side Jāl-al-Jauf جال الجرف, and on the south side Tabaiq طبيق; behind Tabaiq, between it and the **Nafūd** which begins two hours from Jauf, is a clayey and pebbly tract called Safīhah صفيحة where Bedouins cut brushwood and dry grass for sale at Jauf. The Syrian road leaves Jauf by a defile in the Jāl on the north-west side of the valley. At the opposite end is the descent into the Jauf basin from the **Hāil** side which occupies about half an hour. The symmetrical form of the Jauf depression is broken, on the west only, by a limestone spur which projects from the encircling heights and subsides by degrees into the centre of the plain. The soil of the valley is a sterile, crusty sand with clayey hollows here and there in which water collects, leaving salt behind when it dries; rain however is rare.*

Town.—The town forms a curve with the concavity to the south-west; for two-fifths of its length it runs from west-north-west to east-south-east and the remainder lies north-west and south-east. Its length is over 2 miles and its breadth less than half a mile, the latter being greatest near the point where the change occurs in the direction of its axis. The orchards and palm groves form a continuous line parallel to the town on its west side and mostly stand clear of it towards the western side of the valley. Jauf-al-'Āmir is divided into a number of quarters, each of which is separately walled, and contains houses irregularly placed and interspersed with small orchards and with deep pits from which earth has been dug for building

---

* A sketch of the Jauf oasis and basin is given in Lady Anne Blunt's *Pilgrimage* (I. 120).

material. The houses are of sun-dried brick and many of them possess a detached coffee-room. The quarters, in order from north-west to south-east are apparently Husaini' حسيني, Gharbi غربي, Dharai ذري, Qa'aiyid قعيّد, Dīrat Mārid ديرة مارد, Dīrat Hattāb ديرة حطّاب, Salmān سلمان, Habāb هباب, Sa'aidān سعيدران, Rahaibiyīn رهيبيين, 'Alāq علاق, Zuqmah زقمه, Khadhmah خذمه and Dalhamīyah دلهميّه. Dīrat Mārid is the most ancient quarter and to it belongs Mārid castle, an erection originally all of hewn stone but coarse in construction, which stands upon a precipice of the limestone spur already mentioned, is connected with the quarter by a wall, and looks north over the town. Dīrat Hattāb is the broadest part of the town and at Salmān occurs the more southward bend previously described. Habāb possesses a strong tower and was in former days at feud with the quarter of Dīrat Mārid. Dalhamīyah was destroyed in 1838 and has not been rebuilt. To these quarters may be added the village of Ghuti غطي, a small walled hamlet of a dozen houses with a tower at each corner, which lies a few hundred yards to the east-south-east of Khadhmah. About half a mile south of Khadhmah, on rising ground, stands a large fort built by Ibn Rashīd about 40 years ago; it has walls 40 feet high and there is a tower considerably higher at each of the angles; it is furnished with loopholes and machicoulis. About 100 yards to the north-west of this fort is a copious spring which waters some date gardens.

Inhabitants.—The population of Jauf-al-'Āmir is estimated at about 6,500 souls. The inhabitants are **Sahrārāt**, Hawāzim (who are possibly **Harb**) and **'Anizah** of the Ruwalah section; also, it is said, some Bani **Tamīm**, besides negroes and Mutawalladīn. About a quarter of the fighting men of the town are armed with breech-loading rifles. The Jaufis are not naturally travellers, and those among them who are better off seldom leave the oasis unless to visit **Hāil** or to make the pilgrimage to Makkah; some of the poorer sort however go every year to the Syrian Haurān to labour for hire among the Druses.

Cultivation and supplies.—The resources of Jauf-al-'Amir are chiefly agricultural. The place is famous for its dates, which are unusually large and good, and particularly for a luscious and juicy sort called Hilwah; in all some 15 varieties are grown. Wheat, barley, maize, millet and lucerne are cultivated in the date plantations, but the cereals are not raised in quantities equal to the local consumption. Fruits include figs, apricots, peaches, oranges and grapes; a few vegetables also are grown. All the crops are irrigated from wells worked by bullocks: travellers disagree as to the distance of the water from the surface, but it appears to be ordinarily 3 or 4 fathoms. The best wells for drinking purposes belong to the Khadhmah quarter. Besides wells there are some springs and tanks, but the latter, owing to the infrequency of rain, are not of much service. The water of Jauf is generally insipid and sometimes evil-tasting. The only cattle kept are those employed on the wells. There are practically no horses or camels, and transport, when required, is obtained from the surrounding Bedouins.

Trade.—Jauf-al-'Āmir is a market town for the Arab tribes of the country round, who bring in wool, hides, ghi, milk and occasionally ostrich feathers, and provide themselves here, generally by way of barter, with dates and other provisions, gunpowder, calico of various sorts, 'Abas, leather, and camel furniture. The Bedouins, as already remarked, are the carriers of Jauf, and the balance of food grain which the town requires is imported through them from abroad. A strange product of the desert which the Bedouins bring to Jauf for sale in large quantities is a wild grain called Samh; it resembles canary seed, has the colour of wheat, and can be made into bread. Travelling Syrians and occasionally Persians from **Najaf** visit Jauf and do business there. The artificers of Jauf have a great reputation throughout north-western Arabia for their work in metal and marble; from the latter coffee-mortars and pestles are made. Light 'Abas, spears, copper-ware, leather, camel-furniture and sandals are the other manufactures of the place.

Administration.—The Amīr of **Hāil** is (or was till recently) represented at Jauf-al-'Āmir by a governor and a military garrison of about 50 men. Some of the date plantations are owned by the Amīr as his private property.

Dependencies.—The following places, one of which is important, may most conveniently, as they lie in the vicinity of Jauf-al-'Āmir and do not belong to any region which has a recognised name, be described here:—

Name.	Position.	Houses and inhabitants.	Remarks.
Jāwah جاوه	4 miles east of Jauf-al-'Āmir on a plateau.	20 houses of mud and stone.	There is some cultivation of dates and grain. A well 3 fathoms deep yields drinkable water.

Name.	Position.	Houses and inhabitants.	Remarks.
Qārah قارة	15 miles east by north of Jauf-al-'Āmir.	80 houses.	The place has good palms: at the north end is a rocky mound with a ruin. Ruwalah Bedouins ('Anizah) camp about here.
Sakākah سكاكة	15 miles east-north-east of Jauf-al-'Āmir and 6 north of Qārah.	600 houses of sun-dried brick. Many of the inhabitants are negroes or half-castes.	The town lies in a broad hollow, somewhat broken up by sand-hills and protruding rocks and surrounded by sandstone cliffs. The surface soil is nearly pure sand. The town is scattered amidst the date-plantations which are more extensive than those of Jauf-al-'Āmir; but there are 4 more or less compact groups of dwellings called 'Umran عمران, Hirkan هركان, Faiyād فياد and Suhaiyān سهيان. The water is good, but some of the wells are deep, rendering irrigation laborious.
Tuwair طوير	Between Qārah and Sakākah.	A small village.	The inhabitants are mostly artisans who work in wood and iron.

A well-beaten track leads from Jauf-al-'Āmir by Jāwah to Sakākah, and the march from Sakākah to Qārah and thence to Jauf presents no difficulties. The valley in which stand Qārah and Sakākah contains many inscribed rocks.

JAZĪRAH
جزيره

A division of the Baghdād Sanjāq of the Baghdād Wilāyat in Turkish 'Irāq; it was created in 1884, at the time of the separation of the Baghdād and Basrah Wilāyats, out of territory which had previously formed part of the Qadha of Kūt-al-Amārah. There is no "island" in the Tigris in this part of its course, and the name Jazīrah appears to have been given to the Qadha merely because it is situated in "Mesopotamia".

JAZĪRAH

Position and boundaries.—The **Qadha** of Jazīrah lies entirely on the right bank of the **Tigris** at a short distance below **Baghdād** City; it is bounded on the north-east by the **Tigris**, which divides it on that side from the Qadha of **'Azīzīyah**. On the south-east Jazīrah meets the Qadha of **Kūt-al-Amārah**; on the south-west that of **Hillah** in the Sanjāq of Dīwānīyah; and on the north-west that of **Kādhimain**.

Topography and tribes.—The only places worthy of mention in the Qadha are **Suwairah**, the administrative headquarters, and **Bghailah**; both of these are described in articles under their own names. It should be noted that the ordinary civil officials have little or no power in **Bghailah** and the Sanīyah properties attached to it, which may therefore be regarded as virtually excluded from the Qadha.

The following, given in their alphabetical order, are the chief Muqata-'ahs or tracts with the tribes by whom they are inhabited and tilled:—

Tract.	Tribe.	Tract.	Tribe.
1. 'Abdullah (Nahr) نهر عبدالله	Shuyūkh.	10. Qusaibah (Nahr) نهر قصيبه	Dawaikāt Āl Bū Wais (Zubaid).
2. Barnabj (Nahr) نهر برنبج	Āl Bū Sālih.	11. Rahmānīyah رحمانيه	Bani 'Ajīl (Zubaid).
3. Bghailah (See article **Bghailah**)	Kalābiyīn, Karaish and Āl Bū Sultān, the first and last being sections of the Zubaid.	12. Rajaibah (Nahr) نهر رجيبه	Dāwar Shīshah.
4. Dīwānīyah ديوانيه	Bani 'Ajīl (Zubaid.)	13. Sainam (Nahr Umm) نهر ام سينم	Dilaim.
5. Ghubaish (Nahr) نهر غبيش	Kalābiyīn (Zubaid).	14. Shahaimah (Nahr). نهر شحيمه	Al Bū Na'aim (Zubaid).
6. Hamad (Bad'-at). بدعة حمد	Dawaikāt Al Bū Jamal (Zubaid).	15. Sharhān (Nahr) نهر شرهان	Al Bū Khidhr (Zubaid).
7. Jōz (Nahr) نهر جوز	Dawaikāt Āl Bū Jamal (Zubaid).	16. Shiyānah (Nahr) نهر شيانه and	Āl Bū 'Āmir.
8. Juwaimisah (See article **Suwairah**)	Bani 'Ajīl (Zubaid).		
9. Khusaimah خصيمه	Qaraghōl (Shammar Tōqah).	17. Tuwail (Nahr) نهر طويل	Dāwar (Zubaid).

Population.—The whole fixed population of the Qadha is estimated roughly at 15,000 Muhammadan souls, of whom the majority are Shī'ahs. There are also a few Jews.

Resources.—The assets of the Qadha are altogether agricultural and pastoral. Wheat and barley are grown, and horses, donkeys, camels, cattle, buffaloes and sheep and goats are bred. Gram, ghi and wool are exported. The liquorice bush grows wild.

Administration.—Jazīrah is a Qadha of the 2nd class and has **Suwairah** for *chef-lieu*. Besides the Nāhiyah of Jazīrah, of which the headquarters are located at **Suwairah,** there is only one other Nāhiyah in the Qadha, that of A'aiwij اعيرج (2nd class), and it is said to have no existence except on paper. Much of the cultivable land in Jazīrah belongs to the Dāirat-as-Sanīyah.

JINNAH جنّة

Also called Jazīrat-al-'Amair جزيرة العمائر but this second name is ambiguous being borne by both Jinnah and **Musallamīyah** islands. Jinnah is an island a mile off the coast of the Sanjāq of **Hasa** near **Musallamīyah** bay; it lies about 9 miles north-west of Abu'**Ali** island and 3 miles south of Rās Bidya'. Jinnah is level on the top, of a light colour, and has cliffs 35 feet high on the north-east side; the western part of the island is low. The length, east and west, is about 1½ miles; and on its north-east side it is adjoined by a pearl bank known as Waih-al-Jazīrah. On the north side is a mud house, occupied since 1902 by Turkish Dhābitīyahs, at first 8 and now 3 in number, over which the Turkish flag is flown; also a village of about 100 families of the Bani **Khālid** tribe, belonging to the Āl **Shāhīn**, the Āl Hasan and perhaps to other 'Amāir sections, who with the inhabitants of **Musallāmīyāh** island own about a dozen pearl boats. Access to the village for native boats is afforded by a channel coming from the direction of Rās Bidya' and there is a small basin with 3 fathoms of water close to the north-east of the island; but the entrance of this basin, open to the eastwards, is nearly dry at low water. Jinnah island is under the Qāim-Maqām of **Qatīf**; and the local Shaikh, who belongs to the Āl Shāhīn section of the Bani **Khālid**, has the title of Mudīr and is paid an allowance of 30 Riyāls a month by the Turks.

JIRI

JIRI*
جري

A small but somewhat singular plain in the Rās-al-**Khaimah** District of the **Shārjah** Principality in Trucial **'Omān**.

Position and extent.—Jiri is shut in between a sandy desert on the west and the high hills of the **'Omān** Promontory on the east, and it forms a connecting link between the plains of **Sīr** and **Dhaid** which enclose it on the north and south respectively; with these boundaries it is about 15 miles in length, from north to south, and 7 to 8 miles in breadth. At both ends it is contracted by an inclination of the western desert and the eastern hills towards each other, but in either case a passage into the next tract remains open.

Physical characteristics.—The soil of Jiri is of a dark colour, forming a sharp contrast with the light red of the sandhills which border it upon the west; of this characteristic the detritus brought down from the hills on the east appears to be the explanation. The surface is generally sandy though firm; but in places it is more clayey, retains water after rain, and cracks when it dries. Jiri is thickly sprinkled with acacias and other wild vegetation, and in the neighbourhood of the Hadaithah wells Samr and Ghāf trees are particularly abundant; hereabouts, too, the soil is more loamy than in some other parts and produces, after rain, a good deal of rank grass and weeds. Among the plants which grow towards the western edge of the plain are Rimth, Halam, Thamām and Qasad, all of which are useful as grazing, also dwarf tamarisk. The slope of the Jiri plain is towards the coast of the Persian Gulf, but the whole of the drainage is intercepted and utilised by the inhabitants.

Inhabitants.—The only fixed villages are those of Khatt, Habhab and Adhan described in the table below, and the settled population, consisting of 'Awānāt, **Mazārī'**, **Naqbiyīn**, **Sharqiyīn** and some **Za'āb**, hardly amounts to 1,000 souls. The predominant Bedouins of the district are **Ghafalah** and **Na'īm**, the latter of the Khawātir section.

Communications and water supply.—Routes which cross Jiri are dealt with in the paragraph on communications in the general article on Trucial **'Omān**.

The wells, some of which are mentioned in the paragraph on topography below, are generally about 60 feet deep and are worked with a

---

* *Authority.*—Major P. Z. Cox, Political Resident in the Persian Gulf, from personal observation and enquiry. A portion of Jiri is shown in the map *Route of Lieutenant-Colonel Herbert Disbrowe, etc.*, 1865, and the whole in the map *Route taken by Major P. Z. Cox, etc.*, 1905.

bucket and rope arrangement, which limits their daily yield to about 1,200 gallons each; but this amount they are capable of supplying, at least in the cold weather, and the water as a rule is of good quality.

Administration.—Jiri is included in the dominions of the Shaikh of **Shārjah** and its government is in the hands of his Deputy Governor at Rās-al-**Khaimah** Town.

Topography.—The following are the villages and other principal points of interest in Jiri :—

Name.	Position.	Nature.	Remarks.
Adhan اذن	At the head of Wādi Hām, of which it is often reckoned the highest up settlement; it is 10 miles south of Khatt and 14 miles north-east by north of Dhaid village.	A village of 40 houses of the Mazārī' tribe, chiefly of mud and date branches.	Resources are estimated at 15 camels, 50 donkeys, 30 cattle, 400 sheep and goats, and 2,000 date palms. Behind the village rises a hill known as Qumr قمر.
Habhab هبهب	One mile south-east of Khatt village, and about 1 mile north-east of the Qaliddi route between Rās-al Khaimah Town and Dibah.	A village of 35 houses of Sharqiyīn.	Habhab stands at the eastern foot of the hills of the 'Omān promontory. It has a Falaj of its own, distinct from the source which waters Khatt. Animals are stated to be 30 donkeys, a few camels, 20 cattle and 250 sheep and goats, and date palms in number about 3,500.
Hadaithah حديثه	At the western edge of the Jiri plain, under the sand hills which bound it.	Two wells each about 10 fathoms deep and lined near their mouths with stone from the hills of the 'Omān Promontory.	The wells are in the open plain, but they are surrounded by Ashkar shrubs and some fine Ghāf trees. They are used by nomads of the Ghafalah tribe and of the Khawātir section of the Na'īm.
Hamrānīyah حمرانيه	Seven miles west by south of Khatt village, near the western edge of the Jiri plain.	A couple of wells situated in a small green oasis.	Good shade is afforded by 4 or 5 substantial acacias near by. The tribes frequenting these wells are the same as at Hadaithah.

Name.	Position.	Nature.	Remarks.
Khatt خَتّ or	At the eastern side of the Jiri plain close under the foot of the hills, about 12 miles south-south-east of Rās-al-Khaimah Town and 14 miles south-east by east of Jazīrat-al-Hamra.	A village of 100 houses of 'Awānāt, **Naqbiyīn** and **Sharqiyīn**. Some **Za'āb** from Jazīrat-al-Hamra sojourn here in the hot weather months for the date harvest.	The date plantations form a large oasis and are said to contain about 20,000 trees, of which $\frac{3}{5}$ are owned by the **Za'āb** of Jazīrat-al-Hamra. Livestock are estimated at 20 camels, 30 donkeys, 25 cattle and 300 sheep and goats. Water for all purposes including irrigation is supplied by a hot spring, overlooking which is a tower built by the Shaikh of **Shārjah**; the water of the spring is sweet and wholesome when cooled, and to bathe in the spring is believed to be a cure for certain diseases. The main range of hills receives behind Khatt the name of Jabal Khatt.
Sā'adi ساعدي	At the western edge of the Jiri plain, 5 miles south of Hadaithah.	A pair of wells.	In regard to situation and ownership they resemble the wells of Hadaithah and Hamrānīyah.
Saram صرم	In a Wādi of the same name, said to be between Adhan and Khatt, about 6 miles north of the former.	A watering place.	It is used by passing caravans.
Ya'ilān (Bū) بو يعلان	Two miles north-north-west of Hamrānīyah, under the sandhills which bound the Jiri plain on the west.	2 wells.	They are of the same character as the Hadaithah and Hamrānīyah wells and are used by caravans and frequented by **Ghafalah** and by **Na'īm** of the Khawātir section.

JISSAH (BANDAR)*

بندر جصه

An anchorage on the coast of the **'Omān** Sultanate five miles south-east of **Masqat** Town: it is formed by a precipitous light-coloured island, 600 yards long and 140 feet high, which lies east and west across the entrance of a bay one mile in length and the same in depth. The entrance round the east end of the island is 280 yards broad with a depth of 7 fathoms: the passage at the west end is nearly blocked by a flat rock which has only 1½ fathoms on each side of it. The outline of the bay is indented, and there is an islet towards the western side behind which, on the mainland, is a village of 60 houses of **Qawāsim** with a date grove: this village stands on a sandy beach at the mouth of a valley and consists of a few stone houses and many mat huts. Hills rise all round the harbour and at the back of the village to a height of some hundred feet. The harbour is sheltered except from the north-east and would afford anchorage in 6 to 7 fathoms for all classes of vessels except the largest: if proper moorings were laid down a fair number of ships could be accommodated at the same time. The bottom appears to be of sand throughout; there are a few detached rocks which could easily be removed. The site is naturally adapted for fortification. Fresh water is somewhat scarce.

JIZI (WĀDI-AL-)†

وادي الجزي

A valley in the Western **Hajar** district of the Sultanate of **'Omān** which, rising in a locality 30 miles east by south of the **Baraimi** Oasis, reaches the sea immediately to the north of Sallān in **Bātinah**: its length is thus between 35 and 40 miles in a straight line, and its general direction is from west-south-west to east-north-east.

Wādi-al-Jizi is apparently formed by the confluence of two other valleys, *viz.*, Wādi 'Abailah عبيلة from the north-west and Wādi Kitnah كتنة from the south-west; between these two, just before their junction, is a level expanse several square miles in area known as the 'Abailah plain. Wādi 'Abailah has its head in a larger plain named Hawaithah حوثية, and a well-marked ridge of hills runs parallel to it at a short distance from its left bank. The valley contains the villages

---

* A plan of Bandar Jissah will be found in Admiralty Chart No. 2369--10·C.; and the best account of the place, with sketches, is contained in the Proceedings of the Government of India in the Foreign Department for February 1899.

† The only good map of Wādi-al-Jizi is *Route taken by Major P. Z. Cox, etc.*,

of Subaithah سبيثه and Kabaidah كبيده on its left bank, at 4 and 7 miles respectively above its junction with Wādi Kitnah; and 5 miles north-west of Kabaidah is another village, Zāhar زاهر, on the western border of the Hawaithah plain. These are villages of the Bani **Ka'ab** tribe, mostly of the Nawaijiyīn section. In Wadi Kitnah there is a village Kitnah consisting of 30 houses of Bani Kalaib of the Shawāmis section.

The following places are passed in descending Wādi-al-Jizi :—

Place.	Position.	On which bank.	Houses and inhabitants.	Remarks.
Rābi الرابي	1½ miles below the junction of Wādis 'Abailah and Kitnah.	Right.	50 houses of Bani Kalaib of the Hadādinah section and of Bani Ghaith.	Here are the remains of a tower, perched on a pinnacle-rock 200 feet high. There are 300 date palms and grain is grown.
Hail Bin-Suwaidān حيل بن سويدان	Very slightly below Rābi.	Left.	80 houses of Bani Kalaib of the Rashaidāt and Hadādinah sections and of Bani Ghaith.	The people are often at feud with those of Khawairij and annoy them by cutting off their water-supply. There are 500 date palms.
Khawairij خويرج	A short distance below Hail Bin-Suwaidān.	Right.	40 houses of Bani Kalaib of the Shawāmis section.	There is considerable cultivation on terraces, irrigated from the Wādi: various kinds of grain are grown: there are 400 date palms.
Wāsit واسط	1 mile up a side valley which enters Wādi-al-Jizi from the south-west 1 mile below Rābi.	Do.	100 houses of Bani Kalaib of the Shawāmis section.	Nil.
Khān خان	7 miles below Khawairij.	Do.	80 houses of Bani **Hina** and **Maqābīl**.	Here are the graves of many 'Omānis slain in resisting an advance of the Wahhābis upon **Sohār** Town early in the 19th century. Just below Khān is a tower called Burj-ash-Shikairi برج الشكيري on a peak 200 feet high on the right

Place.	Position.	On which bank.	Houses and inhabitants.	REMARKS.
				bank of the Wādi; it is joined by a stone wall to a tower lower down and is said to have been constructed as a defence against the Wahhābis. It is occupied by a garrison of 10 men on behalf of the Sultān of 'Omān.
Sahailah سهيله	9 miles below Khān.	Left.	100 houses of Kunūd.	Nil.
Milaiyinah ملينه	6 miles below Sahailah.	Right.	15 houses of Kunūd.	Just below Milaiyinah is an ancient arched aqueduct of masonry which conveys water to Gharrāy.
Gharrāq غراق	2 miles below Milaiyinah.	Do.	20 houses of Bani Ghaith.	Nil.
Sihlāt سهلات	2 miles below Gharrāq.	Do.	30 of do.	Picturesquely situated on the top of a hill.
Falaj-as-Sūq فلج السوق	4 miles below Sihlāt and 10 miles from the coast.	Do.	A ruined Falaj and deserted village.	This place really lies some distance to the north of Wādi-al-Jizi.

At each village there are a few hundred date palms and everywhere wheat, barley, millet and lucerne are grown. Animals are not very numerous; there are a few camels and some donkeys, besides goats and sheep.

The above are the principal villages in the main valley, and the chief tributary valleys with their villages are: Wādi Hail 'Adha حيل عضا, from the north between Wāsit and Khān, with a village Hail 'Adha composed of 40 houses of Maqābīl and Shabūl; Wādi Hansi حنسي, from the south-west about midway between Khān and Sahailah, having a village Hansi with 40 houses of Shabūl and Maqābīl, and another Furfar فرفار with 15 houses of Shabūl, on its left bank at 3 and 7 miles respectively from its mouth; Wādi Thiqbah ثقبه, from the north, coming in exactly opposite Wādi Hansi and containing the villages of Hail-ash-Shiya حيل الشيا, 10 houses of Kunūd, Hail-ar-Rafsah حيل الرفصه,

60 houses of **Kunūd**, and Thiqbah, 20 houses of **Kunūd**; the village of Thiqbah is on the left bank of the Wādi of the same name at a little more than a mile from Wādi-al-Jizi.

The settled population of the entire valley with its tributaries seems to be about 4,000 souls.

Wādi-al-Jizi runs in the hills until a short distance below Milaiyinah, when it leaves them and enters the **Bātinah** plain. On its way across **Bātinah** to the coast Wādi-al-Jizi is said to pass on both sides of the Hūrah Barghah hill.

From Hail down to Sihlāt the valley contains flowing water; above Khawairij the stream is copious though never more than a few inches deep; below Khawairij it disappears and reappears at intervals. The fields are irrigated both by wells and by conduits from the stream.

The route from **Sohār** Town to the **Baraimi** Oasis lies up Wādi-al-Jizi and over the 'Abailah plain; it is reported to be easy and not to present any obstacle which need delay field-artillery more than an hour. Travellers leave **Sohār** by Sallān, whence they pass by 'Auhi and Falaj-al-Qabāil to Falaj-as-Sūq; 2 or 3 miles beyond Falaj-as-Sūq they strike Wādi-al-Jizi, which they follow for 4 miles and then again leave, diverging to the right for 9 miles; rejoining the Wādi at Sahailah they follow it with little deviation to its head; the further way lies across the 'Abailah and Hawaithah plains, and then by Kharūs and between Khatmat Shiklah and Khatmat Suwwād, which are described in the article on the **Jau** district.

JUNAIDĀT
جنيدات

Singular Junaidi جنيدي. A tribe, said to be of 'Omāni extraction, but not traceable in **'Omān**, of whom a few families are settled at Dārin on **Tārūt** island. They live by fishing and pearl diving and are Hanbali Sunnis by religion.

KA'AB
كعب

Pronounced Cha'ab; the singular is Ka'abi كعبي (Cha'abi). The Ka'ab are the largest and most important tribe of Southern **'Arabistān**;

they are Arabs, but at the present day they are to some extent Persianised.

Distribution.—The Ka'ab form almost the entire population of the **Fallāhīyeh** District, which is their headquarters, and they also occupy the greater part of **'Abbādān** island, especially towards its lower end; the articles under these names with those entitled **Janjīreh** and **Shatūt** include the great bulk of the villages of the Ka'ab. A few occur in the Haffār tract on the right bank of the **Kārūn** in the **Muhammareh** District, and some on the left bank of the **Bahmanshīr**. Ka'ab are found in considerable numbers in the **Jarrāhi** District, where they occupy the riverbank villages of Khar Faraih, Bunwār, Bunwār Rizaiq, Maksar, Maksar 'Atīqeh, Suwaireh, Kurdūnīyeh, Maqtū' Fauqāni, Haskeh, Maqtū' Hadrāni, Khamzeh, Sidaireh, Saraimeh, Dōb-al-Mīr, Tuwaiqīyeh and Qarqar, and have settlements in the interior at Dauweh, 'Aquleh, Hor Trawaishid, Idāideh, Abu Saīleh, Khalāfiyāt, Hamād and Hāji Asghāyar, and they spread northward into the **Ahwāz** District at Banneh and Shākheh: the tribe is represented also at Cham Sha'abāni, Gharabi Kūchik and **Hindiyān** Village in the **Hindiyān** District. Detached colonies of Ka'ab emigrants occur further down the coast of Persia in the **Lirāwi, Rūd-hilleh** and **Angāli** districts; but these are tribally isolated and unimportant. In Turkish **'Irāq** some immigrant Ka'ab are settled at **Fāo**.

Subdivisions and numbers.—The structure of the Ka'ab tribe has been carefully investigated, but the results elicited are conflicting even as regards main divisions and subdivisions. The ordinary tribesman has no ideas whatever on the subject of the composition of his tribe, and the theories which are entertained by intelligent individuals here and there do not command general acceptance. One fact stands out clearly, that the tribe consists partly of original and partly of adscititious families and groups, the divisional name Drīs being closely associated with the former, and that of Khanāfireh with the latter of these two classes. The more minute classification of the Ka'ab depends not on blood relationship but on political accidents, for the name of a headman's family or section is generally extended to include all who find (or place) themselves under his authority; it follows that there are many semi-obsolete names, as well as aliases both exact and partial.

The following is the classification of the tribe which appears most satisfactorily to express the facts in so far as they are known:—

Division.	Subdivision.	Section.	Fighting strength.	Habitat and remarks.
Drīs دريس	'Asākireh. عساكرة	'Abbādi (Āl Bū) آل بو عبّادي	80	On both banks of Khor Dōraq below **Buziyeh**, on the Khor branch of the Aushār canal, and on the 'Abdun Nabi canal of the **Janjīreh** group. They occur also at Āl Bū 'Abbādi on the eastern bank of the **Bahmanshīr**.
Do.	Do.	'Abdush Shaikh (Bait) بيت عبد الشيخ	40	On the Aushār canal in the **Fallāhīyeh** District.
Do.	Do.	'Abūd (Hāji) حاجي عبود	100	At Maqtū' Faūqāni on the **Jarrāhi** River.
Do.	Do.	Afādileh	30	Manyūhi on 'Abbādān island.
Do.	Do.	Afsaiyil (Bait) بيت افصيل	50	On the Aushār canal in the **Fallāhīyeh** District. Musa-ibn-Afsaiyil, the chief Shaikh of the 'Asākireh subdivision belongs to this section.
Do.	Do.	'Ali (Āl Bū) آل بو علي	200	On the Musaiyir canal in the **Fallāhīyeh** District.
Do.	Do.	'Āmir (Āl Bū) آل بو عامر	100	On the **Janjīreh** canals. They are allied to the Āl Bū Mubādir.
Do.	Do.	'Araiyin (Āl Bū) آل بو عرين	70	On the Aushār canal in the **Fallāhīyeh** District and on the left bank of the Shatt-al-'Arab.
Do.	Do.	'Atqīyeh عتقيّة	300	On the Jafāl canal in the **Fallāhīyeh** District and on the Bahmanshīr.
Do.	Do.	'Azīz (Bait) بيت عزيز	80	On the Aushār canal in the **Fallāhīyeh** District. They are allied to the Āl Bū Mubādir.

Division.	Subdivision	Section.	Fighting strength.	Habitat and remarks.
Dris دريس	'Asākireh. عساكره	Banaidar (Āl Bū) آل بو بنيدر	...	On the Qarakhān, Nahr Mahmūd and 'Alwān canals in the Fallāhīyeh District.
Do.	Do.	Dahaleh (Āl Bū) آل بو دهله	100	On both banks of Khor Dōraq below Buziyeh and on 4 of the canals of the Janjīreh group.
Do.	Do.	Dalli (Āl Bū) آل بو دلّي	100	On the Janjīreh canals.
Do.	Do.	Dawāriqeh دوارقه	120	On the Sa'adi canal in the Fallāhīyeh District and on the eastern bank of the Bahmanshīr.
Do.	Do.	Hamādi (Āl Bū) آل بو جمادي	60	On Khor Dōraq, eastern bank, and on the Oran canal in the Janjīreh group.
Do.	Do.	Hamaidi (Āl Bū) آل بو حميدي	100	On the western bank of the Bahmanshīr, etc.
Do.	Do.	Hamūd (Āl Bū) ال بو حمود	100	On the Aushār canal in the Fallāhīyeh District.
Do.	Do.	Hassān حسان	50	On the 'Anaiyiti canal in the Fallāhīyeh District and on the east bank of the Shatt-al-'Arab.
Do.	Do.	Jinām (Āl Bū) آل بو جنام	150	On the Aushār canal in the Fallāhīyeh District and on the left bank of the Shatt-al-'Arab.
Do.	Do.	Kawaisib (Āl Bū) آل بو كويسب	80	Do.
Do.	Do.	Mahmūd (Āl Bū) آل بو محمود	40	On the west bank of the Bahmanshīr, etc.
Do.	Do.	Muaisir	...	On the Asaifir canal of the Janjīreh group.
Do.	Do.	Mubādir (Āl Bū) آل بو مبادر	100	On the Aushār canal in the Fallāhīyeh District. To this section are allied the Al Bū 'Āmir, Bait 'Azīz, Āl Bū Dalli, Al Bū Hamūd, Āl Bū Na'īm and Āl Bū Shilāqeh sections.

KA'AB

Division.	Subdivision.	Section.	Fighting strength.	Habitat and remarks.
Drīs دريس	'Asakireh. عساكره	Musallim (Āl Bū) آل بو مسلّم	300	On the Shākhat Hamad and Aushār canals in the **Fallāhīyeh** District, on the western bank of the **Bahmanshīr**, and on the eastern bank of the Shatt-al-'**Arab**.
Do.	Do.	Mutārīd مطاريد	70	On the Ghaiyādhi and Sa'adi canals in the **Fallāhīyeh** District.
Do.	Do.	Na'īm (Āl Bū) (I) آل بو نعيم	100	On the Aushār canal in the **Fallāhīyeh** District. They are allied to the Āl Bū Mubādir.
Do.	Do.	Na'īm (Āl Bū) (II) آل بو نعيم	140	On the right bank of the **Jarrāhi** River opposite to **Janjīreh**.
Do.	Do.	Nasairi (Āl Bū) آل بو نصيري	140	On the canals of the **Janjīreh** group.
Do.	Do.	Nawaisir نويصر	50	Uncertain. They are the private followers of Mūsa, the chief Shaikh of the 'Asākireh subdivision.
Do.	Do.	Salaiyih صليّح	200	On the Asaifir canal of the **Janjīreh** group and on the western bank of the **Bahmanshīr**.
Do.	Do.	Sharhān (Āl Bū) آل بو شرهان	300	On the Aushār canal in the **Fallāhīyeh** District near to **Buziyeh**, and on the left bank of the Shatt-al-'**Arab**.
Do.	Do.	Shilāqeh (Āl Bū) آل بو شلاقه	120	On the Aushār canal in the **Fallāhīyeh** District. They are allied to the Āl Bū Mubādir section.
Do.	Do.	Shiyākhīn شياخين	300	$\frac{1}{5}$ of them are at a place Lubtaināt and $\frac{4}{5}$ in the locality called Maidān between **Fallāhīyeh** Town and the Sa'adi canal. They are buffalo-herds and wanderers, but own some property in the **Fallāhīyeh** District.

Division.	Subdivision.	Section.	Fighting strength.	Habitat and remarks.
Drīs درىس	'Asākireh. عساكره	Subaiyah (Āl Bū) آل بو صبيّح	150	On the Aushār canal in the **Fallāhīyeh** District on the A'rār canal in the **Janjīreh** group and at Suwaireh on the **Jarrāhi** River.
Do.	Do.	Suwailim (Al Bū)	200	At Qasbeh on 'Abbādān island.
Do.	Do.	Tāheh (Āl Bū) آل بو طاهه	40	On the Mubaqqi canal in the **Fallāhīyeh** District.
Do.	Do.	Taraiki (Al Bū) آل بو تريكي	70	Mālteh, south of **Buziyeh**, on the eastern side of Khor Dōraq.
Do.	Do.	Thawāmir ثوامر	400	'Abbādān island chiefly at Manyūhi, but also at Qabāneh on the east side of the island and at Baraim and Nāsirīyeh on the west side. They are found also at Lower Silaik on the east bank of the **Bahmanshīr**.
Do.	Do.	'Ubaid (Al Bū) آل بو عبيد	120	On the Khashāb and Tōpchīyeh canals in the **Fallāhīyeh** District.
Do.	Al Bū Ghubaish. آل بو غبيش	Abid (Bait Hāji) ...	12	On the Buziyeh canal in the **Fallāhīyeh** District.
Do.	Do.	Abraiheh	200	On the Tōpchīyeh canal in the **Fallāhīyeh** District.
Do.	Do.	Afādileh	20	On the **Janjīreh** canals.
Do.	Do.	'Ali (Al Bū Hāji) آل بو حاجي علي	200	On the 'Anaiyiti canal in the **Fallāhīyeh** District.
Do.	Do.	'Amāreh عمارة	40	On the Mahrūqi canal in the **Janjīreh** group and on the Ja'fari canal in the **Fallāhīyeh** District.
Do.	Do.	Aqqār (Bait) ...	20	Dauweh in the **Jarrāhi** District.
Do.	Do.	Badar (Āl Bū) آل بو بدر	60	On the Khātar distributary in the **Shatūt** tract.

Division.	Subdivision.	Section.	Fighting strength.	Habitat and remarks.
Drīs دريس	'Asākireh. عساكرة	Bairi (Āl Bū) آل بو بيري	200	On the Janjīreh canals.
Do.	Do.	Bālid (Āl Bū) آل بو بالد	50	On the Manqūshi canal in the Janjīreh group.
Do.	Do.	Bandarīyeh بندريه	30	On the Buziyeh canal in the Fallāhīyeh District.
Do.	Do.	Dailam ديلم	50	On the Wuli distributary in the Shatūt tract. Supposed to be of the same origin as the Dailam section of the 'Anāfijeh.
Do.	Do.	Dishmānziārīyeh ...	100	On the Buziyeh canal in the Fallāhīyeh District.
Do.	Do.	Ghadīr (Hāji) حاجي غدير	50	At Kurdūnīyeh on the Jarrāhi River.
Do.	Do.	Haiyāch ...	30	Do. They are weavers.
Do.	Do.	Hamūd (Āl Bū). آل بو حمود	20	On the Jābar distributary in the Shatūt tract.
Do.	Do.	Hilāyil (Bait) ...	100	On the Buziyeh, Dilis and Qatrāni canals in the Fallāhīyeh District and on the Khāni and Bait Qatān canals of the Janjīreh group.
Do.	Do.	Hiliyū ...	40	Lithainīyeh in the Jarrāhi District.
Do.	Do.	Hizaiyim (Bait) ...	15	On the Buziyeh canal in the Fallāhīyeh District.
Do.	Do.	Iba'in (Bait) ...	50	On the Mahrūqi canal in the Janjīreh group.
Do.	Do	Is-hāq أسحاق	20	On the Khāni canal in the Janjīreh group.
Do.	Do	Ithāmneh (Bait) ...	40	On the Khātar distributary in the Shatūt tract.

Division.	Subdivision.	Section.	Fighting strength.	Habitat and remarks.
Dīs دريس	'Asākireh. عساكره	Ja'ameh	40	On the Janjīreh canals.
Do.	Do.	Jabbar (Āl Bū)	40	On the Habāch canal in the Janjīreh group.
Do.	Do.	Jawaisif (Dōb)	30	Near Tuwaiqīyeh on the Jarrāhi River.
Do.	Do.	Ka'ab-al-Karūm	30	On the Buziyeh canal in the Fallāhīyeh District.
Do.	Do.	Khātar (Āl Bū)	20	On one of the 'Azzāz distributaries in the Shatūt tract.
Do.	Do.	Khawaitar (Bait)	100	On the Jadīdi canal of the Janjīreh group.
Do.	Do.	Khazaiyil.	60	At Haskeh on the Jarrāhi River.
Do.	Do.	Kināneh كنانه	20	On the Buziyeh canal in the Fallāhīyeh District and the Khāni canal in the Janjīreh group. Of Bani Lām origin.
Do.	Do.	Mahmūd (Bait Hāji)	30	On the Janjīreh canals.
Do.	Do.	Marzeh	40	In the Jarrāhi District east of Abu Dubaiyān.
Do.	Do.	Moni	...	On the Qatrāni canal in the Fallāhīyeh District.
Do.	Do.	Muhaidi (Bait)	30	On the Buziyeh canal in the Fallāhīyeh District.
Do.	Do.	Mukhaiyat (Āl Bū)	20	On one of the 'Azzāz distributaries in the Shatūt tract.
Do.	Do.	Musallim-al-Yūrāni	30	Dauweh in the Jarrāhi District.
Do.	Do.	Nawāsir نواصر	20	On the Khuwainis canal in the Fallāhīyeh District.
Do.	Do.	Ōd (Bait Abul)	20	Apparently at Khar Faraih on the Jarrāhi River.

KA'AB 955

Division.	Subdivision.	Section.	Fighting strength.	Habitat and remarks.
Drīs دريس	'Asākireh. عساكرة	Qarāghūl قراغول	20	On the Khātar distributary in the **Shatūt** tract.
Do.	Do.	Quwām (Āl) آل قوام	40	Do.
Do.	Do.	Rāhan (Bait) ...	70	Do.
Do.	Do.	Rawaisbid-ibn-Kabain (Bait) بيت رويشد بن كبين	20	On the Mahrūqi canal in the **Janjīreh** group.
Do.	Do.	Rijaibāt or Riyabāt, رجيبات	40	On the **Janjīreh** canals and in **Behbehān**.
Do.	Do.	Sadeh ...	30	On the Buziyeh canal in the **Fallāhīyeh** District.
Do.	Do.	Sa'īd (Āl Bū) ...	30	On the Jābar distributary in the **Shatūt** tract and on the Asairafi canal in the **Janjīreh** group.
Do.	Do.	Salaiyah ...	100	Dauweh in the **Jarrāhī** District.
Do.	Do.	Sāleh (Bani) ...	40	On the **Janjīreh** canals.
Do.	Do.	Sālih (Āl Bū) ال بو صالح	50	On the Jābar distributary in the **Shatūt** tract.
Do.	Do.	Sālih (Bait Hāji) بيت حاجي صالح	100	On the Buziyeh canal in the **Fallāhīyeh** District.
Do.	Do.	Sawālih صوالح	40	On the right bank of the **Jarrāhī** in the **Jarrāhī** District below Maksar.
Do.	Do.	Shabaiyib (Bait) بيت شبيب	20	On the Jābar distributary in the **Shatūt** tract.
Do.	Do.	Shafi (Bait) ...	20	On the Mahrūqi canal of the **Janjīreh** group.
Do.	Do.	Shamāl (Āl Bū) ال بو شمال	30	On the Jābar distributary in the **Shatūt** tract.

Division.	Subdivision.	Section.	Fighting strength.	Habitat and remarks.
Drīs دريس	'Asākireh. عساكرة	Shuwaish (Bait) بيت شويش	30	On the Arfaiat and Jadīdi canals of the **Janjīreh** group.
Do.	Do.	Suwaiyir (Bait) ...	200	On the Khāni canal of the **Janjīreh** group.
Do.	Do.	Tibīyeh (I) ...	50	On the Buziyeh canal in the **Fallāhīyeh** District.
Do.	Do.	Tibīyeh (II) ...	20	Locality uncertain.
Do.	Do.	Umaiyid Rafaii ...	40	Do.
Do.	Do.	Umtaiyir-an-Nas-sāri (Bait) ...	20	Dauweh in the **Jarrāhi** District.
Do.	Do.	Yūsuf-bin-Aqai-yib ...	20	On the Shāuli canal in the **Fallāhīyeh** District.
Do.	Do.	Yūsuf-bin-Rajaib يوسف بن رجيب	50	On the **Janjīreh** canals.
Do.	Do.	Ziba'ad (Bait) زبعد	70	On the Jābar distributary in the **Shatūt** tract.
Do.	Do.	Zuwaihid (Bait) زويهد	15	On the Buziyeh canal in the **Fallāhīyeh** District.
Do.	Nassār نصّار	Dawāriqeh دوارقه	200	On the **Buziyeh** canal in the **Fallāhīyeh** District.
Do.	Do.	Ja'ūdeh جعودة composed as below :—		
		(1) Dhafāli'eh ضفالعه	200	Qasbeh on **'Abbādān** island.
		(2) Masā'id (Āl Bū) آل بو مساعد	150	Do.
		(3) Said (Āl Bū) آل بو صيد	100	Do.

KA'AB

Division.	Subdivision.	Section.	Fighting strength.	Habitat and remarks.
Drīs دريس	Nassār أنصار	Maghālīyeh مغاليّه consisting of :—		
		(1) 'Abūd (Āl Bū) آل بو عبود	200	About Ma'āmareh on 'Abbādān island.
		(2) Ghānim (Āl Bū) آل بو غانم	100	Near Qasbeh on 'Abbādān island.
		(3) Khalīfeh Āl Bū) آل بو خليفه	100	Near Ma'āmareh on 'Abbādān island.
		(4) Mishailish (Āl Bū) آل بو مشيلش	150	About Ma'āmareh and Qasbeh on 'Abbādān island.
Khanāfireh خنافره	...	Amāreh اماره	120	On the Ja'fari canal in the Fallāhīyeh District.
Do.	...	'Ashaireh (Āl Bū) آل بو عشيره	200	Buziyeh and on the Tōpchīyeh canal in the Fallāhīyeh District.
Do.	...	Darādisheh درادشه	50	Fallāhīyeh Town.
Do.	...	Dawāriqeh دوارقه	600	On the Tōpchīyeh canal in the Fallāhīyeh District.
Do.	...	Dhuwaiyib (Bait) ...	40	At Khamzeh on the Jarrāhi River.
Do.	...	Hamdi (Āl Bū) آل بو حمدي	120	On the Kharūsi canal in the Fallāhīyeh District.
Do.	...	Jinām (Āl Bū) آل بو جنام	200	...
Do.	...	Kawāmil كوامل	400	On the Kharūsi canal in the Fallāhīyeh District.
Do.	...	Khadbīr (Āl Bū) آل بو خضير	180	On the Kharūsi canal in the Fallāhīyeh District and on the Ghaiyādhi canal also.
Do.	...	Khanfar (Āl Bū) آل بو خنفر	200	On the Qaidāri canal in the Fallāhīyeh District.

Division.	Subdivision.	Section.	Fighting strength.	Habitat and remarks.
Khanāfireh خنافره	...	Kharaijeh	...	On the Braijeh canal in the Fallāhīyeh District.
Do.	...	Kiraimi (Āl Bū) آل بو كريمي	200	On the Ghaiyādhi canal in the Fallāhīyeh District.
Do.	...	Makāsibeh مكاسبه	150	On the 'Anaiyiti and Musaiyir canal in the Fallāhīyeh District and on the Sikanām canal in the Janjīreh group.
Do.	...	Manai'āt منيعات	150	On the Tōpchiyeh canal in the Fallāhīyeh District and on the western side of 'Abbādān island.
Do.	...	Muhammad-ibn-Hāji Ya'qūb (Bait) بيت محمد ابن حاجي يعقوب	600	On the Tōpchīyeh canal in the Fallāhīyeh District.
Do.	...	Rubaihāt ربيحات	200	On the 'Aquleh, Minduwān, Shāuli canals in Fallāhīyeh District.
Do.	...	Sālim or 'Abūd (Bait) بيت سالم-عبود	40	Fallāhīyeh Town. These are the relations of the chief Shaikh of the Khanāfireh division, at present 'Abūd-bin-Sālim-bin-'Abūd.
Do.	...	Sawailat صويلات	150	On the 'Anaiyiti canal in the Fallāhīyeh District above the Makāsibeh section.
Do.	...	Shāwardiyeh شاورديه	400	On the Ghaiyādhi and Kharūsi canals in the Fallāhīyeh District.
Do.	...	Sūf (Āl Bū) آل بو صوف	200	On the Madīnat Dishmān, Āl Bū Sūf and Ghaiyādhi canals in the Fallāhīyeh District.

Division.	Subdivision.	Section.	Fighting strength.	Habitat and remarks.
Khanāfireh خَناشِرة	...	Suwālim سوالم	200	On the Ghaiyādhi and Kharūsi canals in the **Fallāhīyeh** District.
Do.	...	Zambūr (Āl Bū) آل بو زمبور	180	On the Ghaiyādhi cana in the **Fallāhīyeh** District.
Muqaddam (Pronounced Mujaddam) مقدم	...	Is-hāq اسحاق	400, of whom all have rifles and 40 are mounted.	Banneh in the **Ahwāz** District.
Do.	...	Maiyāh مياح	100, of whom all have rifles and 300 are mounted.	Do.
Do	...	Muqaddam مقدم	800, of whom 700 have rifles and 100 are mounted.	¾ of these are at Banneh and have all rifles and include all the mounted men: the remainder with 100 rifles and no mounted men, are settled on the Fallāhīyeh-Mārid canal below **Fallāhīyeh** Town.
Hazbeh خزبه	...	Ghuwainim (Āl Bū) آل بو غوينم	150, none mounted but all with rifles.	On the Umm-as-Sakhar canal in the **Fallāhīyeh** District. They have 100 cattle and 3,000 sheep and goats.
Do.	...	Hazbeh حزبه	400, of whom all have rifles and 40 are mounted.	These live on the Umm-as-Sakhar canal in the **Fallāhīyeh** District and own 200 cattle and 3,500 sheep and goats.
Do.	...	La'ateh (Āl Bū) ...	200, all with rifles but none mounted.	Locality uncertain. Their livestock are 60 cattle and 6,000 sheep and goats.

The Dawāriqeh, of whom the name occurs more than once in the table above, are stated to be an aboriginal race distributed among the various branches of the Ka'ab as herdsmen and almost as serfs. It should be added that of the above only the Drīs and Nassār divisions are universally regarded as true Ka'ab; the Khanāfireh and Muqaddam are frequently described not as Ka'ab but as Tawāif, that is "(dependent) tribes." There are said to be other adscititious Ka'ab also who are not included among either the Khanāfireh or the Muqaddam.

This is the system of classification of the Ka'ab which seems to be the most worthy of adoption out of two or three that have been propounded; but in order to exemplify the discrepancies of opinion which exist another is now added in brief. It is as follows :—

I. Drīs درّيس
(fighting strength 6,000 men)
  1. Drīs درّيس
  2. Nāsir (Āl Bū) ناصر
  3. Nassār نصّار

II. Muqaddam مقدّم
(fighting strength 1,100 men)
  1. Is-hāq اسحاق
  2. Maiyāh ميّاح
  3. Muqaddam مقدّم

III. Khanāfireh خنافرة
(fighting strength 3,000 men).
  1. Hamdi (Āl Bū) حمدي
  2. Kawāmil كوامل
  3. Shāwardīyeh شاورديه

IV. Hazbeh حزبه
(fighting strength 3,000 men)
  1. Ghuwainim (Āl Bū) غوينم
  2. Hazbeh حزبه
  3. La'ateh (Āl Bū)

The total strength of the Ka'ab tribe is, and must be, largely a matter of conjecture; but, if the first table of sections given above be accepted as correct, the number of fighting men arrived at is 15,722 as below :—

Drīs	'Asākireh	4,750
	Ghubaish (Āl Bū)	3,042
	Nassār . , ...	1,200
Khanāfireh	. . . .	4,680
Muqaddam	. . . . . .	2,050
	Total	15,722

According to the principle on which fighting strength is usually calculated the figures given would represent a total of about 55,000 souls,—a number which is not patently either in excess or in defect. These statistics do not include the Ka'ab colonies outside Southern **'Arabistān** nor those of the **Hindiyān** District: the members of the latter in number about 1,500, mostly belong to a section called Sha'abāni شعباني, not shown in any classification table of the tribe that has been obtained.

Arms.—It may be added here that a large number of long-barrelled muzzle-loaders are still seen among the Ka'ab, and that almost every fighting man of the Drīs and Khanāfireh divisions is armed either with one of these or with a superior weapon. The numbers of rifles possessed by the Muqaddam and Hazbeh are indicated above in the table of sections.

Religion and life.—The Ka'ab, like all the other tribes of Southern 'Arabistān are Muhammadans of the Shī'ah persuasion. They cannot except in a few places be described as altogether settled, nor on the other hand are any considerable proportion of them truly Bedouin. The bulk of the tribe are now in that stage of development, intermediate between nomadism and fixity, which is typified by the huts—less removeable than tents and more easily abandoned than houses—in which they dwell. In out-of-the-way tracts like **Shatūt** the Ka'ab are still very primitive in their ideas and habits; and in some places a tradition as to the iniquity of buying and selling things for money lingers amongst them. Like the Pathans of the Indo-Afghan frontier they have a strong objection to being seen in a state of nudity, and this prejudice is even said to give rise to embarrassment among themselves when rivers have to be crossed by swimming. Where the Ka'ab possess arable lands they cultivate wheat, barley and rice; where pasture exists they own buffaloes, cattle, sheep, goats and even donkeys; in the marshes they move about in light canoes, catching fish and snaring or shooting wild fowl; at **Fallāhīyeh** Town they are otherwise noted as the manufacturers of very fine and light woollen 'Abas for summer wear.

Origin, history and political position.—The Ka'ab claim to be 'Awāmir عوامر or Bani 'Āmir بني عامر, descended from a certain Ka'ab-bin-Rabī'-bin-'Āmir who was himself, they say, the 24th in descent from Ishmael. It is stated that the original home of the Ka'ab was in **Najd** and that some of the tribe are still to be found there at a place called Bishaurānīyah; all efforts to identify this locality have, however, up to the present, been unsuccessful. According to tribal tradition the majority of the descendants of Ka'ab eventually established themselves in Northern Africa; but Nassār and Drīs, the legendary progenitors of the Ka'ab of Southern **'Arabistān** made their way from **Najd** to **Dōraq** and occupied it after expelling some other Arab tribes and some Afshār or 'Aushār Turks whom they found in possession. The date of these supposed events is altogether uncertain. Early in the seventeenth century, apparently, the capital of the Ka'ab tribe was at **Qubbān**; and there it remained until 1747, when a move was made to **Fallāhīyeh** Town or Dōraq-al-Fallāhīyeh as it was then styled. Another old settlement of the Ka'ab, since abandoned, was Sāblah سابلة or Sablah سبلة; it stood on the right bank of the **Kārūn** river, opposite to the island of Dāir and the Mārid creek. The history of the Ka'ab tribe in the eighteenth and nineteenth centuries is a part of that of

'Arabistān, which is related at length elsewhere. Here it is enough to add that shortly after 1775 the jurisdiction of the Ka'ab chiefs seems to have extended from the neighbourhood of **Basrah** to the confines of **Behbehān**; but their influence declined as that of the **Muhaisin** rose, and the chiefs of the Ka'ab, stripped of political power, have sunk in recent years into undistinguished vassals of the Shaikh of **Muhammareh**.

The divisional Shaikhs have no political power: the most important among them are Shaikh Rizaij of the Āl Bū Ghubaish (Bait Hilāyil), who is in charge of **Buzīyeh** and lives there; Shaikh 'Abūd, the head of the Khanāfireh; Shaikh Mūsa of the 'Asākireh, and Shaikh Sultān of the Muqaddam, who is at present in jail.

KA'AB (BANI) بني كعب

Singular Ka'abi كعبي. A tribe in the interior of the 'Omān Promontory, having their headquarters at **Mahádhah**, in the neighbourhood of which they are nearly all found. In politics they are Ghāfirīyah; in religion Sunnis. Their principal sections are:—

Section.	Habitat.	Approximate number of souls.	REMARKS.
Drisah درسه	Wādi Shīya.	150	Nomadic.
Makātīm مكاتيم	Mahádhah and Kahal villages.	600	Settled.
Misā'id مساعيد	Wādi Bū Jila'ah.	350	Do.
Miyādilah ميادله	Wadi-al-Hayūl and Shibakah in Wādi Qahfi.	500	Do.
Miyāisah ميائسه	Jawaif and Sharam in Wādi Khadhra.	150	Do.
Mizāhamiyīn مزاحميين	Mahádhah village.	50	Do.
Nawaijiyīn نويجيين	Khatwah in Wādi Bū Sa'ad, also Khabbain, also Zāhar and Subaithah in the Wādi 'Abailah affluent of Wadi-al-Jizi.	1,400	Do.

Section.	Habitat.	Approximate number of souls.	Remarks.
Salālāt صلاحات	Mahádhah village.	300	Settled.
Sawālim سوالم	Nawai-i.	300	Do.
Shwaihiyīn شويهيين	Wādi Shwaihah and Shibakah in Wādi Qahfi.	1,000	Mostly nomads. A sub-section of this section, known as Hibnāt حبناة, are found at the village of Shibakah.
Yidhwah (Ahl) اهل يذوه	The villages of Mahádhah and Kahal and Sharam in Wādi Khadhra.	600	Settled.
Zahairāt زهيرات	Mahádhah village and Nawai-i.	300	Do.

Bani Ka'ab are found about the head of Wādi-al-Qor; also in the 'Omān Sultanate at Hadaf in Wādi Hatta and at Hasaifīn Sūr al-'Abri and Taraif in the Liwa sub-Wilāyat of Sohār. They probably number about 6,000 souls in Trucial 'Omān and 1,250 in the 'Omān Sultanate. The chief Shaikh of the tribe, at the present time Sālim-bin-Diyain, belongs to the Mizāhamiyīn section and resides at Mahádhah village.

KA'ABĀN كعبان

Singular Ka'abi كعبي. A small tribe of Bahrain and Qatar who regard Ka'ab-al-Habār كعب الحبار, a companion of the prophet Muhammad, as their ancestor and claim tribal connection with the Ka'ab of Persian Arabistān and the Bani Ka'ab of Trucial 'Omān. About 60 nomad families of Ka'abān belong to Qatar; 30 other nomad families wander in the neighbourhood of Jabal-ad-Dukhān in Bahrain; and 30 families, employed in the pearl fisheries, are settled at Jasairah on Bahrain Island. In religion the Ka'abān are Māliki Sunnis. They are said to have accompanied the 'Utūb from Qatar to Bahrain, but their earlier movements are untraceable.

KABB (KHOR-AL-)
خور الكب

This is the name of the large salt water inlet on the east side of **Bahrain** Island which travellers between **Manāmah** and the two **Rifā's** must either cross or go round. It is a fine sheet of water with wooded banks and is sometimes dotted with waterfowl. At low tide the foot of the creek, called Khor-al-Maqta' Tūbli خور المقطع توبلي, is a stretch of mud covered with stumpy mangroves, which a donkey-rider can cross at a ford 1 mile from its end without wetting his feet.

KABD
كبد

A locality about 25 miles south-west of **Kuwait** Town, between the district of **Qrā'ah** on the east and that of **Shaqq** on the west. Kabd is a row of hills or belt of high ground extending east and west over a distance of 6 miles. Immediately to the south of Kabd is a parallel ridge called Kabaidah كبيدة or Little Kabd, having to the east of it some wells called Jāhliyah جاهلية, and to the south of it a well-known Bedouin landmark called Rijm-al-Jahtān رجم الجحطان. South of Rijm-al-Jahtān, again, is Fawāris فوارس, a small plain diversified by hillocks. A group of five small hills at the western end of Kabaidah is called Mināqīsh مناقيش; they are of a whitish hue and stand between the route from **Jahrah** to **Riqa'i** and that from **Kuwait** Town to **Hafar**.

KABĪR (WĀDI-AL-)
وادي الكبير

A valley in the **Dhāhirah** district of the **'Omān** Sultanate which runs south-westwards and debouches on Wādi **Sanaisal**, a little above **'Ibri** in Dhāhirah. The places situated in Wādi-al-Kabīr from its head downwards are the following:—

Place.	Position.	On which bank.	Houses and inhabitants.	REMARKS.
Miskin مسكن	Near the head of the Wādi.	Left.	...	See article Miskin.
Najaid نجيد	3 hours below Miskin.	Do.	40 houses of Bani Kalbān.	There is a fort held by the Bani Kalbān. Animals are 10 camels, 30 donkeys, 60 cattle and 300 sheep and goats: there are 800 date palms.

Place.	Position.	On which bank.	Houses and inhabitants.	Remarks.
Haiyāl هيال	7 hours below Najaid.	Right.	50 houses of Bani 'Umr.	There is a fort of the Bani 'Umr. Resources the same as at Najaid.
'Āridh عارض	3 hours below Hayāl.	Do.	...	See article 'Āridh.
Darīz دريز	4 hours below 'Āridh in a side valley called Qarn-al-Kabsh قرن الكبش.	Left.	200 houses of Miyāyihah, and 30 of Bani Rashid mostly mud but a few huts.	In 1885 there was a tumble-down fort here with 2 guns. Livestock are 10 camels, 30 donkeys, 60 cattle and 300 sheep and goats, and there are 500 date palms.

Wādi Bilād Shahūm, in which stands **Maqnīyāt,** is a tributary of this valley.

KĀDHAMAH* كاظمة

The innermost cove (Dōhat Kādhamah) of **Kuwait** Bay, to the west of Rās 'Ashairij: also a point (Rās Kādhamah) which projects into the same cove from its north side.

The cove shoals gradually from its entrance, where it is 4 miles broad and 6 fathoms deep in mid-channel, to its head, which is 9 miles west by south of Rās 'Ashairij and within about 2 miles of the village of **Jahrah.** There is an anchorage, well sheltered from the Shamāl, which would accommodate a large number of ships of 24 feet draught; but there is no deep water close to the shore, and cargo would have to be worked in lighters or a large pier built.

Rās Kādhamah is a low swampy point running out some 3 furlongs southwards into the cove at about 3 miles from its head: it is hardly above sea level, but it is partially protected by a natural bank of sand which follows the highwater line.

* A sketch survey of Dōhat Kādhamah will be found in the Government of India's Foreign Proceedings for July 1902. The suitability of the place as a terminus for the proposed Baghdād Railway is discussed by Captain E. W. S. Mahon, R.E., in a report dated 24th July 1905. See also Government of India's Foreign Proceedings for February 1905.

KĀDHI-MAIN
كاظمين
QADHA

A division, by the Turks called Kāzimīyah كاظميه, of the Baghdād Sanjāq of the Baghdād Wilāyat in Turkish 'Irāq.

Position and boundaries.—The Qadha of Kādhimain embraces the greater part of that narrow section of Mesopotamia which is enclosed between the rivers **Tigris** and **Euphrates** where they approach one another in the neighbourhood of **Baghdād** City. On the north-east side the **Tigris** divides Kādhimain from the Qadha of **Baghdād**; on the north Kādhimain appears to be in contact with the Qadhas of Sāmarrah and Dilaim; the adjacent districts on the west, south-west, south and south-east are Dilaim, **Karbala, Hillah** and **Jazīrah** respectively

Topography and tribes.—The only places of importance in this Qadha are Abu **Ghuraib, Kādhimain** Town and **Mahmūdīyah**, all of which are described under their proper names.

The parallel columns below contain a list of the Muqāta'ahs or tracts in this Qadha and of the tribes and sections by whom they are cultivated, but it has not been found possible to arrange the tribes by territorial groups:—

Tracts.	Tribes or sections.
1. Ghuraib (Abu) (See article Abu Ghuraib).	1. 'Akaidāt.
2. Hasaiwah حصيوه	2. 'Azzah.
3. Hor هور	3. Dilaim.
4. Mahmūdīyah (See article **Mahmūdīyah**).	4. Fadāghah.
5. Mazrafah مزرفه	5. Kawām.
	6. Ma'āmirah.
6. Radhwānīyah (See article **Euphrates**).	7. Mashāhidah.
7. Saraiwīl (Abu) ابو سريويل	8. Rabī'ah (Bani) of the Karaish section, and Bani Tamīm subsection.
	9. Sha'ār.
8. Tāji تاجي	10. Shamāmtah Jabūr.
	11. Shīti.
9. Tārmīyah طارميه	12. Zōba'.
	13. Zubār.

Population.—The fixed population of the Kādhimain Qadha is estimated at 25,000 souls, all Muhammadans, of whom 17,000 may be Sunnis and 8,000—chiefly in the town of **Kādhimain**—are probably Shī'ahs.

Resources.—Apart from the town of **Kādhimain** the district is rural, and its assets consist in cultivation and livestock of the same kinds as are found in the other Qadhas of the Baghdād Sanjāq, such as **Jazīrah** The principal canals which traverse the Qadha are described in the articles on the **Euphrates** river: they are those apparently from the Saqlāwīyah to the Latīfīyah inclusive.

Administration.—The Qadha is of the 3rd class and is not, apparently, subdivided into Nāhiyahs: the town of **Kādhimain** is the *chef-lieu.* The Dāirat-as-Sanīyah have established a firm hold on the district and are represented by Mudīrs at Abu **Ghuraib** and **Mahmūdīyah.**

KĀDHIMAIN TOWN

Called Kazimīyah كاظميّة by the Turks, and known also as Imām Mūsa امام موسى. This town in Turkish 'Irāq, situated on the right bank of the **Tigris** about 3 miles north-west of **Baghdād** City, is important both as a Shī'ah place of pilgrimage and as the headquarters of a Qadha of the same name in the Sanjāq and Wilāyat of Baghdād. It is connected with **Baghdād** by a horse-tramway (which was constructed by Midhat Pasha, Wāli of Baghdād about 1870, and runs most of the way along the top of an embankment) and with **Mu'adhdham** on the opposite bank of the **Tigris** by a bridge of 21 boats.

The permanent population of the town is about 8,000 souls, all Muhammadans, of whom about 7,000 are Shī'ahs: about 1,000 are Persian subjects; 200 are British subjects, being Indians or of Indian descent; and 50 are Russian subjects of Persian race.

The town is a hot-bed of vice; venereal and ophthalmic maladies are common, and the passage through the place of nearly all the Shī'ah corpses sent from Persia to be buried at the holy places of **Najaf** and **Karbala** in no wise adds to its salubrity. In the cold weather the population is largely increased by Shī'ah pilgrims on their outward and return journeys.

The chief feature of the place is the tomb of the 7th and 9th Shī'ah Imāms, namely Mūsa-bin-Ja'far and his grandson Muhammad-bin-'Ali, from whom the town derives its name of Kādhimain or "the Two Self Restrained Ones," although in strictness the epithet of Kādhim belongs to the 7th Imām alone. Christians are not admitted within the precincts of the shrine, which is surrounded by a lofty wall; but a good general view of the buildings can be obtained from the roof of a Khān which faces the main entrance. The structure has the form of double cube, each of the two portions of which is surmounted by a cupola; and four tall galleried minarets spring from near the corners of the building. After his visit to the shrine in 1874 Nasr-ud-Dīn, Shāh of Persia, imitating the munificence of Nādir Shāh at **Karbala,** caused the twin domes to be plated and the minarets to be richly ornamented with gold, and the general effect produced by the large surfaces of the precious metal is brilliant in the extreme. The coloured encaustic tile work of the entrance gate and minarets, also the stalactite corbelling below and the carved wood-work above the galleries of the minarets, are equally remarkable. The shrine is richly endowed and the endowments are under the management of the Auqāf Department of the Turkish Government by whom the salaries of the custodians and attendants are paid. There are graveyards here for devout Shī'ahs, of which the principal is the Maqābir-i-Quraish مقابر قريش; but they do not possess equal sanctity with those of **Najaf** and **Karbala**.

Combs and small artistic objects of ivory, wood and tortoise-shell are manufactured for export, chiefly by Persians; Kāshī كاشي or encaustic tiles and bricks are also made by Persians; and there are some skilful Persian painters who decorate walls and roofs. The weaving of silk kerchiefs and handkerchiefs is a considerable industry and some of the handkerchiefs are sent abroad as far as to Tunis and Algeria; there are also tanneries. There is a trade in Persian carpets which the pilgrims, combining business with the performance of a religious duty, bring with them from their country; and the fact that the pilgrims mostly leave their riding animals to wait for them at Kādhimain while they proceed by stage-coach to **Karbala,** creates a large demand for forage. The pilgrims, many of whom are visitors from cold climates, are considerable purchasers of tea, sugar and woollen cloths. Kādhimain contains 30 Khāns or hostelries and over 300 shops.

The principal civil officials are the Qāim-Maqām of the Qadha and representatives of the Departments of Customs and Public Debt. The ordinary police force of Kādhimain consists of about 50 Dhābitīyahs:

but at the Muharram, and on other occasions of religious excitement, large reinforcements are drafted into the town from **Baghdād** City, with which there is telegraphic communication. There is also a post office. The town is constituted as a municipality. Kādhimain is the headquarters of the 1st battalion of the 83rd regiment of the Radīf and also of the 42nd brigade of the same.

An honorary Nāib-Kārpardāz or Consular Agent is charged with the interests of Persian subjects.

KAHÁFAH
كفعه

Generally pronounced Chaháfah. A well-known village in the Jabal **Shammar** principality, about midway between **Hāil** and **Buraidah** and some 75 or 80 miles from either; it is the ordinary third halting place on the **Hāil-Buraidah** route. The village is unwalled and contains about 50 houses of the Mas'ūd section of the Aslam division of the **Shammar**. Some of the wells, which are 8 to 9 fathoms deep, have good water, and the place is reputed healthy; there are only about 10 days' rain in the year, at the beginning of winter. Dates, cereals and vegetables are cultivated; the best kind of date is a large, yellow variety called Fankhah; palms of all sorts are said to number about 3,000. There are the usual animals. The Turks, after their defeat in **Qasīm** in the summer of 1904, fell back upon Kaháfah.

KAIR
كير

A river of Persian **Makrān** which comes down from Gaih and reaches the sea by two mouths, of which the eastern is on Puzim Bay, 28 miles west by north of **Chahbār,** and the other 18 miles farther to westward on the east side of Tank point. The village of Tank is situated on the right bank of the western branch at about 3 miles from the coast, and some 50 huts, frequently empty, forming a settlement known as Kair are scattered upon both banks of the eastern branch at about 7 miles from the sea; barley, wheat, cotton and jowari are grown in small quantities round this settlement, which is occupied chiefly by Buzdārs but partly also by Hōts. Much water comes down the Kair river when in flood; it sometimes rises over its banks and remains impassable for five or six consecutive days. The usual ford is at the telegraph crossing, but there is a better one $1\frac{3}{4}$ miles below it.

KĀKI
كاكى

A small town in the **Dashti** district of the **Persian Coast**, 26 miles south-south-east of **Khurmūj** town and 20 miles from the sea; it is situated about 5 miles from the left bank of the **Mūnd** river. The population is very mixed, including some of the Nasūri tribe, who are Sunnis. Kāki, 40 years ago, was larger than **Khurmūj** town but not so well built; the Khān of the place had at that time commenced the erection of an elaborate fort and residence. Now there are about 300 houses, but no shops; some trade in sugar, tea and piece-goods is carried on in private houses. There are 8,000 date palms: livestock are 20 horses, 15 mules, 120 donkeys, 100 camels, 70 cattle and 3,000 sheep and goats. Native vessels of 40 tons can ascend the **Mūnd** river almost to Kāki. A cousin of the Khān of **Dashti** has his seat at Kāki and acts as the Khān's deputy.

KALBA (KHOR)
خور كلبا

Khor Kalba is not to be confounded with Kalba, otherwise called **Ghāllah**. It is the southernmost village of the **Shamailīyah** district in the **Shārjah** Principality of Trucial **'Omān** and is situated on the coast of the Gulf of **'Omān** 20 miles north-north-west of **Shinās** in the **Bātinah** district of the **'Omān** Sultanate and 24 miles south of Khor **Fakkān**. Khor Kalba stands on a creek which boats can enter at high water and it is defended by a fort: it consists of 150 houses of the **Za'āb** tribe, who own 5 or 6 sea-going boats employed in the coasting trade.

KALBĀN (BANI)
بني كلبان

Singular Kalbāni كلبانى. A tribe of the **'Omān** Sultanate inhabiting both slopes of Western **Hajar**; they are found on the **Dhāhirah** side at **Maqnīyāt** (740 houses), which is their principal place, at Sammah (60 houses), at Khadal (100 houses) in an affluent of Wādi **Dhank**, and at **Miskin** (200 houses), Najaid (40 houses) and **'Āridh** (300 houses) in Wādi-al-**Kabir**. They occur also at **'Ibri** in **Dhāhirah**. On the **Bātinah** side their villages are Zūla (20 houses) in Wādi Bani **Ghāfir**; Daiqarah (25 houses), Hiyāl (70 houses), Minzifah (25 houses) and Raqaiyid (25 houses) in Wādi **Mabrah**; and Rattah (90 houses) in Wādi **Sarrāmi**. There are also 30 houses of Bani Kalbān at **Bahlah** in **'Omān** Proper. In politics the Bani Kalbān are Ghāfiri, in religion Ibādhi. None of them are Bedouins.

The following are their subdivisions :—

Section.	Number of households.	Habitat.	Remarks.
'Amairah (Aulād) اولاد عميرة	300	Maqnīyāt and Miskin.	Nil.
Ghabābīn غبابين	200	Maqnīyāt.	Do.
Jarāwinah جراونه	720	Maqnīyāt, 'Āridh and Khadal.	Do.
Sinān (Wilād) ولاد سنان	200	Maqnīyāt.	Do.
Subaih (Wilād) ولاد صبيح	150	Maqnīyāt and Miskin.	Do.
Tīyūm (Bani) بني نيوم	20	Zūla in Wādi Bani Ghāfir.	Do.

There is also a section or subsection called Quyūdh قيوض who are found at Raqaiyid. Their total number is about 8,000 souls. In the troubles of 1883 the Bani Kalbān sided with the Sultān of 'Omān. They are sometimes at feud with the Miyāyihah.

A village on the coast of the 'Omān Sultanate 12 miles north-west of Sūr. It has no dates or cultivation of any sort, is unwalled and consists of 120 to 130 houses, all of mud, and a dozen shops. The Hajar hills rise behind the village at less than a mile's distance and Wādi Hilam reaches the sea at its east side. There are a few wells. The inhabitants are Bani Jābir of the Sha'ibiyīn section: they are fishermen and sailors and own about 12 Badans running to Masqat Town and Sūr and about 40 Hawāri. They have recently become Hināwis and have allied themselves with the Bani Bū Hasan against their own tribe (1907). Kalhāt is the port of Wādi Bani Jābir (I), of Kabda, and of Wādi Manqāl in which is Fita.

KALHĀT
كلهات
also
QALHĀT
قلهات

KANGŪN
کنگون

In English formerly spelt "Congoon." With the exception of its small dependency Banak, Kangūn is the northernmost of the **Shībkūh** ports on the **Persian Coast** and the only one of them lying north of the region in which the main maritime range falls directly into the sea; these high hills first approach the coast about 5 miles west of Kangūn. Kangūn is situated at the eastern end of a large bay, open to the south but fairly well sheltered from the Shamāl, at the opposite end of which, 9 miles to the westward, stands the rival port of **Daiyir**. Kangūn is about 20 miles north-west of the next considerable **Shībkūh** port, that of **Tāhiri** and is exactly opposite to **Bahrain** from which it is distant about 140 miles.

The place, at the present time partially abandoned, normally consists of some 300 houses of Arabs of mixed tribes; about two-thirds of the population are Sunnis and the remainder Shī'ahs. Some of the recent emigrants are now settled at **Fāo** in Turkish 'Irāq. The inhabitants of **Kangūn** are fishermen, pearl divers and sailors owning 8 Sambūks which run to **Qatar, Bahrain, Qatīf, Basrah** and various Persian ports, also 10 Baqārahs of the kind called 'Āmilah which are used for fishing; they also cultivate dates and grain. Palms number about 2,000, and livestock are estimated at 5 horses, 200 camels, 100 donkeys, 200 cattle and 2,000 sheep and goats. Good water is contained in 3 wells of 4 to 5 fathoms depth; and there is a hot spring which is resorted to for its curative properties. Kangūn possesses a fair anchorage (but inferior to that of **Daiyir**) in a Shamāl. The number of shops is about 20. Imports are sugar, tea, piece-goods and rice; exports are wheat, barley, sheep, cattle, firewood, charcoal and onions. Kangūn is the port of Jam جم and Rīz ريز in the interior, 10 to 20 miles distant northwards. A square fort stands in the middle of the town. Kangūn was till lately farmed by the Khān of **Dashti**, whose sub-lessee was one of his own relations. A post of the Persian Imperial Customs was established here in 1904.

KARBALA
کربلا
QADHA

The headquarters division of the Sanjāq of Karbala in the Baghdād Wilāyat in Turkish 'Irāq.

Position and boundaries.—The Qadha of Karbala extends, at a short distance west of the **Euphrates**, from the parallel of **Musaiyib** (or a little above it) down almost to that of **Najaf** Town: at **Musaiyib** however it actually touches the river and even reaches a few miles to the east of it. On the north the Qadha is in contact with that of Dilaim; on the north-east with that of **Kādhimain**; on the east with that of **Hindīyah** and possibly with that of **Shāmīyah**; on the south with that of **Najaf**; and on the west with the **Shāmīyah** Desert.

Topography and inhabitants.— By far the largest and most important place in the Qadha is the town of **Karbala**, described elsewhere under its own name; but the town of **Musaiyib**, the settlement of **Shifāthah**, and the village **Sikandarīyah** are also deserving of mention and form subjects of separate articles. **Razāzah** in practice belongs to the Karbala Qadha and is mentioned below in the list of Muqata'ahs, but nominally it is a separate Qadha. The chief feature of the Karbala district,— apart from the **Euphrates** river with which its connection is slight,— is the **Husainīyah** Canal, running from **Musaiyib** to **Karbala** Town and beyond.

The following is a list of the principal Muqata'ahs or agricultural tracts in the Qadha:—

Tracts.	Tracts.	Tracts.
1. 'Aishah (Bad'at) بدعة عيشه	8. Bikairah بكيره	15. Jardān (Abu) ابو جردان
2. 'Amaishīyah عميشيه	9. Faraibah فريحه	16. Jawaib جويب
3. 'Asāfīyah عسافيه	10. Haidarīyah حيدريه	17. Ji'aitinah جعيتينه
4. Aswad (Bad'at) بدعة اسود	11. Hamūdīyah حموديه	18. Kamālīyah كماليه
5. 'Awairat-al-Kabīrah عويرة الكبيره	12. Harūdi حرودي	19. Karbala كربلا
6. 'Awairat-as-Saghīrah عويرة الصغيره	13. Ibrāhīmīyah ابراهيميه	20. Khair-ud-Din خير الدين
7. Bahādari بهادري	14. Janganah جنگنه	21. Lāyah لايه

Tracts.	Tracts.	Tracts.
22. Qādhi قاضي	27. Sālihīyah صالحيّة	32. Tahīn (Abu) ابو طحين
23. Qa'qa'aiyah قعقعيّه	28. Sharīf (Bad'at) بدعة شريف	33. Tuwairij طويريج
24. Qartah قرطه	29. Shītah شيطه	34. Wand وند
25. Razāzah رزازة	30. Sulaimān (Abu) ابو سليمان	and
26. Sālih (Karaid Muhammad) كريد محمّد صالح	31. Sumānah (Bū) بو صمانه	35. Zanit (Abu) ابو زنت

There is also a tract called Jarūf جروف, inhabited by the Janābiyīn tribe, on the east bank of the **Euphrates** above **Musaiyib** Town. Another tract known as Nasrīyah نصريّه or Nâsirīyah ناصريّه, occupied by the Jadi, Jahaish, Jarāwinah and Qaidhah tribes, is situated further south on the same side between **Musaiyib** and the **Hindīyah** barrage; it is the country surrounding the Khān-an-Nasrīyah on the **Baghdād-Hillah** route.

The characteristic tribes of the part of country adjoining the **Husainī-yah** canal are the Āl Bū Masri, **Mas'ūd and** Yasār: those of the **Musaiyib** neighbourhood are the Janābiyīn, Āl Bū Mahaiyi and 'Uwaisāt. The desert round **Shifāthah** is occupied by nomads of the Khawādhir and Āl Bū Shibil tribes.

Population.—**Karbala** Town (50,000), **Musaiyib** (4,500), and **Shifāthah** (8,000) being included, the fixed population of the Karbala Qadha is believed to amount to 80,000 souls. The great majority of these are Shi'ah Muhammadans; but Sunni Muhammadans number about 10,000 and there are about 300 Jews.

Resources.—The rural population, including the inhabitants of **Shifāthah**, are altogether engaged in agricultural and pastoral occupations. Dates, wheat, barley, cotton, opium and tobacco are cultivated by them; and their livestock include horses, cattle, buffaloes and sheep.

The date palms of the Qadha are estimated at 750,000 trees, of which some 50,000 belong to the rich settlement of **Shifāthah**. There is in this Qadha a remarkable salt-field which is said to yield about 500 tons English of salt every year. It begins on the west side of **Razāzah** and passing to the north-east of **Shifāthah** is said to reach for many miles to the north-westwards: it is described as a great hollow with broken, rocky banks resembling the bed of a dried-up sea. The hollow is said to contain water which in summer partly evaporates leaving masses of crystalline salt along the margin. In consequence of its position and extent the Turkish Government are unable to make efficient arrangements for the prevention of smuggling.

Administration.—Containing as it does the town of **Karbala**, the headquarters of the whole Sanjāq, the Qadha has no separate Qāim-Maqām and is subject to the personal rule of the Mutasarrif, as is also its headquarters subdivision which consists chiefly of the town and is known as the Karbala Nāhiyah. The other two Nāhiyahs of the Qadha are Musaiyib and Shifāthah, each governed by a Mudīr who is stationed at the place from which his charge derives its name: both of these are of the 1st class. The Dāirat-as-Sanīyah, as mentioned in the article on **Musaiyib**, is strongly established in the part of the Qadha to the east of the **Euphrates**; it appears to be in possession of the whole Nasrīyah tract referred to above in the present article.

KARBALA كربلا **TOWN**

One of the chief towns of Turkish 'Irāq, renowned as the scene of the martyrdom, or rather massacre, of Husain and his companions,—an event to which it owes its alternative name of Mashhad Husain مشهد حسين and in virtue of which it has become one of the principal places of Shi'ah pilgrimage; it is situated about 55 miles south-south-west of **Baghdād** City and about 25 miles west-north-west of **Hillah** Town. Karbala is known also by the name of Ghādharīyah غاضرية and by the old-fashioned appellation of Nainawā نينوا.

Site and buildings.—The town stands on the left bank of the **Husainīyah** canal, which circles round its northern and western sides. On the north, east and south it is surrounded by cultivated lands, date plantations and gardens of fruit trees; and its general shape and disposition cannot be observed from any point of view accessible to Europeans. On the west the **Shāmīyah** or Syrian Desert approaches almost to the walls. About 2 miles to the south-east of Karbala begins the Hor-al-Husainīyah, a marsh formed by the **Husainīyah** canal and the Shatt-al-**Hindīyah**; an embankment running north and south for a distance of 6,000 metres is supposed to prevent the ingress of the waters of the **Hindīyah**, but this work is at present in a ruinous and inefficient state.

Karbala consists of an old town on the north, still walled on the east, north and west, but open on the south—the side on which the new town adjoins it: the old town is crowded and irregularly built, the new is well laid out, with a broad main street running north and south, and is by comparison clean. A mile or more to the south of the new town the large mansion of a Panjābi Indian family is conspicuous, standing in its own grounds and known as Afzal Khān's Fort.

The walls of the old town are of brick, between 20 and 30 feet high, with towers projecting at intervals as bastions; there are two tiers of loopholes, and on the inside is a banquette supported by arches which affords standing room for the defenders of the upper tier. The perimeter of the walls is about 2 miles; they are pierced by 5 gates, and about 25 towers still remain; but the whole work is now in bad repair, and the arches on the inner side serve chiefly as dormitories for vagabonds and as latrines.

The bridges connected with the town are described in the article on the **Husainīyah** canal.

The site of the town is level, but the ground is somewhat higher towards the north-western corner.

Inhabitants.—No close estimate of the population is possible; but it appears to amount to about 50,000 souls, not reckoning pilgrims and other visitors. At least three-fourths of the fixed population are Persians, and almost the whole of the remainder are Arabs. There are only about 100 Turks and 50 Jews, but Indians or persons of Indian extraction number about 1,200 souls, and there are a number of **Balūchis**. With the exception of a few hundred Sunnis, of the Jews already mentioned, and of about a dozen Christians, the people of Karbala are all Shī'ah Muhammadans. The Persians who compose the bulk of the population are almost altogether Persian subjects, so also are the **Balūchis**; but the rest are of Turkish nationality, except the Indians, who are nearly all British subjects, and about 30 Persian-speaking subjects of the Russian Empire. In all there are about 9,000 dwelling-houses; but they are not sufficient and the extension of the town, although constant, does not keep pace with the growth of the population. Drinking water is from the **Husainīyah** canal, or, in the months when it is dry, from some 20 or 25 wells, mostly sunk in its bed.

Trade, manufactures, and resources.—Karbala is a place of considerable trade, the most valuable imports being piece-goods, sugar, petroleum, spices, coffee, tea, Persian carpets, and candles, almost entirely for local consumption; while the leading exports are dates, consecrated articles — such as rosaries, praying-tablets, and inscribed shrouds — skins and hides, wool and tobacco. The bazaars are extensive and well-stocked, and attached to the main bazaar in the old town is a Qaisarīyah قيصرية or arcade, in which are about 20 good shops dealing in European and other wares.

Filigree work and engraving upon mother-of-pearl are the only two arts; but all the ordinary trades are carried on with success, and even mechanical professions, such as watchmaking and photography, are exercised with a fair degree of skill.

The agricultural and garden produce of the environs is large, and the output of dates is on such a scale as to leave a large balance for exportation. Karbala is not, however, a good centre for the collection of ordinary supplies or transport: there are no mules, and camels can only be procured in autumn when Bedouins of the **'Anizah** and **Shammar** tribes are in the vicinity.

Administration.—Karbala is the chief town and the headquarters of the administration, both civil and military, of the Karbala Sanjāq in the Wilāyat of Baghdād: internally it is administered as a municipality. The Mutasarrif of the Sanjāq has his residence here, and there is a Mudīr of the Sanitary department, also a Mamūr of the Tobacco Régie. A whole Tābūr of Dhābitīyahs is supposed to be located at Karbala, but it is rare that more than 100 of the force are present. There is a post office, and telegraphic connection is maintained with **Baghdād** and **Basrah** *viâ* **Hillah**: a branch line of telegraph also connects Karbala with **Najaf**.

One battalion of regular infantry is, as a rule, stationed at Karbala; but it is partly scattered in detachments over the country, and the garrison of the town does not often exceed 240 men; these, in a manner characteristic of Turkish administration, are quartered in a hired caravansarai in the new town. There are also two muzzle-loading field guns but no cavalry. A reserve of 600 rifles is said to be maintained, probably for arming the Radīfs inscribed at this and subordinate centres n the event of their being called out; the place is the headquarters of the 3rd battalion of the 84th Radīf regiment.

The interests of British subjects, both residents and pilgrims, are watched over by a native Vice-Consul, and the Persian Government also maintain at Karbala a paid Kārpardāz or consular official of somewhat similar rank.

Religious importance.—We may now mention the holy places which are the sole cause of the existence of a large Persian city on the verge of the **Shāmīyah** Desert at a distance of nearly 150 miles from the nearest part of the Persian frontier. The historical events with which they are connected are related elsewhere: but for those events Karbala, which does not appear to have been a seat of pre-Islamic civilisation, might never have existed, even as a petty town. The chief shrines within the town are the tombs of Husain and 'Abbās and the Khaimahgāh; in the country outside the walls are the tombs of 'Aun and Hurr.

The shrine of Husain, called Bārgāh Hazrat Husain بارگاه حضرت حسين, stands in the old town towards its western end. The interior is not accessible to Christians, but it is known to consist, in the first place, of a large enclosure called the Sahn صحن or Outer Court; this enclosure has 7 entrances, the main one surmounted by a clock-tower, and the enceinte-wall is lined upon the inner side by no less than 53 arched recesses forming rooms, some of which are of considerable size. In the midst of the Sahn stands the Haram حرم or Sanctuary proper: it is a roofed building surmounted by a lofty dome of gilded tiles and its façade, from either end of which shoots up a gilded minaret of great height, faces the main entrance of the Sahn. A tile-work minaret, larger than those of the Haram but not so magnificent, rises in the corner of the Sahn which is at the back of the Haram and behind its proper left; and near this corner is a small external Sahn adjoining the main Sahn to which it serves as an entrance. In the centre of the building, underneath the dome, lies the Imām Husain with his son 'Ali Akbar on one side of him. The tombs of both have an outer cover of steel lattice-work overlaid with silver and an inner one of carved wood; both are of hexagonal shape. Behind a silver grating in one of the corners are the tombs of the 72 Shuhada شهدا, or so-called martyrs, who died with Husain.

The tomb of 'Abbās, half-brother of Husain, to the east of that of Husain and so nearer to the middle of the town, is similar but slightly smaller and has a dome of glazed brick only; the minarets however are gilded.

Each of these principal shrines has a treasury supposed to contain untold wealth: but, as the treasury of Husain was looted by the Wahhābis in 1801 and is still admittedly the richer of the two, it does not seem that in either case the popular idea can be well founded. Such treasures as remain are, along with the other endowments, in charge of the Auqāf Department of the Turkish Government. Both buildings owe their gold plating to the piety of Nādir Shāh. At night a festoon of lanterns is slung from minaret to minaret in both shrines; but the most impressive sight of all is immediately after sunset when the golden outlines of the great edifices, catching the afterglow, burn in the gathering dusk with a fiery incandescence.

The Khaimahgāh or site of Husain's tent before the battle lies still further west than his tomb and is divided from it by rising ground, from the brow of which the women of his party are said to have witnessed the tragedy: the building of the Khaimahgāh is small and unpretentious.

The tomb of 'Aun عون, a sister's son of Husain, is 7 miles northeast of Karbala on the road to **Musaiyib,** while that of Hurr حر, who deserted to the side of Husain immediately before the battle, lies 3½ miles to the north-west.

As might be expected, Karbala is a great centre, though in this respect subordinate to **Najaf,** of Shī'ah culture and learning. The Mujtahids or Shī'ah doctors are here a numerous and influential body; and there are 29 Shī'ah schools, of which 8 are Madrasahs or high schools, against a single Sunni school. In addition to the shrines there are 3 important mosques and over 150 others. Karbala possesses the second greatest of the holy cemeteries in which Shī'ahs are interred; it is inferior in sanctity to that of **Najaf** only, and is known by the name of Wādi-i-Aiman وادي ايمن or Vale of Security.

The early history of the Shī'ah shrines of Karbala is obscure, but a shrine of Husain existed in 850 A.D., for the Khalīfah Mutawakkil ordered it to be flooded with water and forbade pilgrimages to it. By 979 A.D. a magnificent shrine had been built, which was burnt down in 1016 A.D.; but by 1086 A.D. it had been restored.

The Karkheh river rises in the hills of the Western **Lur** country and enters the plains of **'Arabistān** about 15 miles further to the west than

KARKHEH

كرخه

the **Diz** river. It forms the western limit of effective Persian jurisdiction as exercised from **Dizfūl** or **Shūstar**: beyond it, within the hills, is the autonomous district of Pusht-i-Kūh; and in the plains, upon that side, are the locations of the Bani **Turuf** and other virtually independent tribes. In the middle ages the Karkheh was known as the Dujail of Basinna بصنّا, from an important town which was then situated near it a short day's journey to the south of **Shūsh**.

Course.—Near its exit from the hills the Karkheh was formerly spanned by a bridge, of which the remains still exist and are known as **Pā-i-Pul** پای پل. About 4 miles south of Pā-i-Pul the river passes the Sassanian ruins of Aiwān-i-Karkheh or Kasra ایوان کرخه کسری, which lie half a mile from its right bank; and about 14 miles further on, the direction of the stream being now somewhat easterly as well as southerly, **Shūsh**, the site of the ancient Susa, is left 2 miles from the left bank. Aiwān-i-Karkheh was still in the 10th century A.D. a small but populous town with a weekly market.

The Karkheh after this pursues a general south-south-easterly course to a place, about 50 miles from **Shūsh** and perhaps 20 miles north-west of **Nāsiri** on the **Kārūn** river, at which it swings suddenly to the south-west and from which it runs in that direction for about 20 miles; after turning this corner it passes between the hills which form the north-eastern border of the **Hawīzeh** District and the low range which is their prolongation and which crosses the **Kārūn** river at **Ahwāz** Village. This bend of the Karkheh to the south-westwards appears to be a recent feature: there is reason to think that the river formerly fell into the **Kārūn** a few miles below **Ahwāz**, and it is believed that at the present day this condition of affairs could be restored without difficulty by artificial means.

At the end of the reach which goes south-westwards the Karkheh arrives at Kūt Nahr Hāshim in the **Hawīzeh** District,—the site, not long since, of a massive dam by which the whole irrigation of the **Hawīzeh** District was regulated. When this dam was in existence the further course of the river lay first southwards and then through **Hawīzeh** Town; but since the dam gave way, in 1837, the main stream of the river has taken a north-westerly course from Nahr Hāshim, and its waters, dissipated in streams and marshes, have submerged and ruined the country. At the western end of the **Hawīzeh** District the river gradually reassembles its water, and finally, under the name of Suwaib or Shwaiyib شویب, augmented by the overflow of some of the **Tigris** marshes, it enters the Shatt-al-'Arab about 4 miles below **Qūrnah.**

Character of stream.—At its entrance into 'Arabistān the Karkheh is a broad and rapid stream of whitish water. Near Aiwān-i-Karkheh it is split into several branches by low islands. Further down it continues to be broad, and islands and banks in midstream remain frequent; nor does its level fall much below that of the surrounding country until near the point at which it turns in the direction of **Hawīzeh.** It is crossed by shifting and dangerous fords at Pā-i-Pul and Aiwān-i-Karkheh and near **Shūsh.** At Aiwān-i-Karkheh, 60 years ago, it was observed that the Karkheh appeared to be navigable for vessels of light draught; and in the autumn of 1841, when the stream was at its lowest, a small steamer ascended the Suwaib section for a distance of 10 miles. The waters of the upper Karkheh are celebrated for their purity; but lower down the stream is contaminated by the stagnant swamps through which it passes. The volume of the Karkheh exceeds that of the **Jarrāhi** River.

Character of the banks.—The banks of the Karkheh are wooded with tamarisk jungle and small trees, and in places they are lined with dense brakes of cane-reeds and willow. A remarkable belt of scrub, known as Jangal-i-Gharabi جنگل غربي, extends for a distance of about 50 miles between the Karkheh and **Shāūr** rivers and has an average breadth of 4 or 5 miles; it begins above a place called Buq'eh-i-Ghaib Ibn-'Ali بقعه غيب ابن علي and reaches to a locality called Gharaibeh غريبه, which is in the country of the 'Anāfijeh. The lion and fallow deer, formerly found here, are now practically extinct; but wild boars, hyænas, and small game abound, and considerable herds of gazelles frequent the plains on both banks of the river.

Irrigation and villages.—The level of the Karkheh being, in the upper part of its course, but little below that of the surrounding country, its waters there are applied to irrigation on a considerable scale. Several of the more western villages of the **Dizfūl** District are watered by canals from the Karkheh, notably Jirqeh Saiyid Ahmad, 'Amleh Karīm Khān, Jirqeh Saiyid Muhammad, Jirqeh Saiyid Ta'ameh, Jirqeh Saiyid Tāhir, and possibly Shūhān; two or three of these are served by a channel called the Harmūshi هرموشي which takes off from the left bank of the Karkheh near Pā-i-Pul. Near **Shūsh** are the remains of great canals, down which were probably floated the stone columns for the Sassanian palace of Susa, brought from the mountains of the Western **Lur** country. Above the point where it turns towards **Hawīzeh** the Karkheh throws off a number of canals still actually in operation. In the **Hawīzeh** District again it is said practically to dissolve into a network of canals. The whole way from Pā-i-Pul to its junction with the **Tigris** the river flows through alluvial plains which are for the most part capable of irrigation; and the entire Karkheh region, though **now** almost a desert, is studded with the remains of human habitations and of irrigation works.

The only village of importance now existing on or near the Karkheh above the point where it enters the **Hawīzeh** District appears to be Khairābād خیرآباد, which is on the left bank below **Shūsh**, perhaps not so far from that place as has hitherto been supposed, for one report makes the intervening distance only 8 miles.* This place consists of about 80 houses and some tents; 20 families are of the Āl Bū Rawāyeh tribe, and the remainder are Bani **Lām** of the Āl Bāji section, 'Ikrish of the Daghāghleh section and Arabs of various other tribes. The inhabitants possess about 100 rifles, and of the fighting men 60 are mounted. Livestock are 200 camels, 100 cattle and 6,000 sheep and goats. A noted outlaw, Saiyid Na'ameh, who was released from imprisonment by the Shaikh of **Muhammareh** about 1905, has been established by him here under surveillance of Shaikh Farhān Asad of the **Kathīr**.

KĀRŪN
کارون

The largest river of Persia and the only one navigable by steamers. It has its rise in the mountains of the **Bakhtiyāri** country about 100 miles due west of Isfahān and enters the plains of **'Arabistān** some 15 or 20 miles north of **Shūshtar** Town. The name Kārūn appears to have been unknown to the Arab and Persian geographers of the middle ages, who called the river the Dujail, adding the epithet "of **Ahwāz**" or "of **Shūshtar**" to distinguish it from the Dujail canal near **Baghdād**.

Upper course.—Not far below its exit from the hills, which takes place by a defile 3 miles in length known as Tang-i-Qal' eh-i-Dukhtarān تنگ قلعه دختران, the Kārūn passes the village of Gotwand on its right bank: here there is, upon that side, a fertile alluvial plain sloping down slightly

---

* It is difficult to locate Khairābād. Another report puts it on the left bank of the **Shāūr**, *q.v.*, in the Bait Sa'ad country.

from the west, and opposite to it the fertile plain of 'Aqīli round which the river flows in a remarkable curve. At 4 miles below Gotwand the Kārūn leaves the village of Jallakān on its right bank, the plain of 'Aqīli being still upon its left, and 8 miles further down it breaks through a range of pinkish sandstone hills, which rise on the right bank to a height of only 200 or 300 feet, but on the left bank attain an elevation of about 1,000 : the portion of the range nearest to the river upon its eastern bank is Kūh-i-Fidalak. The villages mentioned are described in the article on the **Dizfūl** District and the plain of 'Aqīli under its own name.

Two and a half miles beyond the Kūh-i-Fidalak barrier and at about half a mile from the town of **Shūshtar** the river, which has since emerging from the hills preserved a generally north and south direction, swings to the westwards. About 600 yards above the town it divides into two streams, the **Gargar** to the east and the Kārūn proper to the west. On the north side of the town the Kārūn proper forms a broad sheet of water, and then, turning to the south and passing an ancient dam and a bridge known as the Pul-i-Dizfūl, it changes its name to **Shatait**. The **Gargar** and **Shatait** form the subjects of separate articles, and the island enclosed by these branches and called **Miyānāb** is dealt with under its own name.

At a point 30 miles south in a direct line from the town of **Shūshtar** the **Gargar** rejoins the **Shatait**,—the village of **Band-i-Qīr** standing between them in the angle above their confluence,—and the Kārūn river once more resumes its course under its own name. At the point of junction of the **Gargar** and **Shatait** the **Diz** river, coming from the west, adds its waters to the Kārūn; and from this place to **Wais**, 12 miles further down upon the left bank, the course of the river is straight and almost due southwards. From **Wais** to **Ahwāz** Village on the left bank, the direction of the river is on the average south-west; but it winds considerably, and the distance, which is only about 14 miles as the crow flies, is fully doubled in travelling by water.

Rapids of Ahwāz.—Immediately above **Ahwāz** village the Kārūn divides into two streams, enclosing the small island of Umm-an-Nakhl; it reunites to pass through a gap in the ridge of sandstone hills which here traverse the country at right angles to its course; and in its descent over the sill of rock here forming its bed it gives rise to the famous rapids of Ahwāz,*

---

* A plan of the Ahwāz rapids by H. S. Wells, R.E., was lithographed by the Public Works Department of the Government of India in 1883.

by Arabs called Sidd سد and by Persians Band بند, which are situated opposite the village so named. The rapids, which are not quite 1½ miles in length, terminate at the lower end of another small island, called Umm-as-Sabā'; just below them stands the village of **Nāsiri** on the left bank.

Lower course.—From **Nāsiri** to the tomb of 'Ali-ibn-al-Husain, a place on the left bank about 40 miles south-south-west of **Nāsiri** in a straight line, the Kārūn describes an extraordinary series of bends and convolutions; but at 'Ali-ibn-al-Husain it resumes a more straightforward and ordinary course, eventually reaching the Shatt-al-'Arab at a point situated 25 to 30 miles in a direct line to the south-west of 'Ali-ibn-al-Husain. About 15 miles below 'Ali-ibn-al-Husain it throws off the Salmānīyah سلمانیه or Salmānah سلمانه canal, now almost dry, from its left bank; and 3 miles further down, opposite the island of Dāir, there is an outlet from the left bank of the Kārūn, called Mārid-al-A'ma مارد الاعمی or the Blind Mārid, which runs inland as a creek for about a mile and forms the mouth of the Fallāhīyeh-Mārid canal which is supplied with water by the **Jarrāhi** River: on the south-west bank of this creek at three-quarters of a mile from the entrance are some heaps marking the site of the old village of Mārid. A dry hollow, containing bushes at the end towards the Kārūn, connects the Blind Mārid with the Qanāqeh branch of Khor **Mūsa**; at one time, no doubt, the Kārūn discharged a part of its waters by this route to the sea. On the right bank, opposite to the Mārid creek, is the site of the old **Ka'ab** settlement of Sāblah. About 7 miles below the Mārid creek and 2 or 3 miles short of the Shatt-al-'Arab, the so-called **Bahmanshīr** quits the Kārūn on the left bank and follows an independent course to the Persian Gulf. The short remaining reach of the Kārūn below the head of the **Bahmanshīr** is called by Europeans the "**Haffār**" and by some natives the **Bahmanshīr**: the town of **Muhammareh** stands about the middle of its right bank.*

Animal life.—Duck, teal, snipe, pelicans, and gulls are seen upon the river; the banks hold francolin, hares, lynxes, and wild boars. In warm weather sharks travel up-stream to **Nāsiri** and even to **Shūshtar** Town.

Navigability and character of banks.—From **Band-i-Qīr** to **Ahwāz** village the width of the Kārūn is about 300 yards and there are ordinarily

---

* Tradition has it that this reach was artificially dug as an irrigation canal. Some authorities believe that the Shatt-al-'**Arab** once flowed into the Kārūn by this channel, instead of *vice versâ* as at present, and that the mingled waters of both rivers were discharged by the channel which we have called the **Bahmanshīr**.

no serious obstacles to navigation; but sandbanks and heaps of stone occur, and the depth of water is sometimes insufficient. The banks here vary in height from 10 to 30 feet and have gravelly plains behind them: towards **Ahwāz** they are of marl: the brushwood which once clothed them has mostly disappeared.

The rapids of **Ahwāz**, though passable by towing, are a serious obstacle even to native boats, especially with a very high or a very low river,[*] and bulk is commonly broken at this point, goods for up-country being conveyed by a light railway, of which the trucks are at present drawn by horses, from **Nāsiri** on the lower river to a place a quarter of a mile above **Ahwāz** village upon the upper. The length of the rapids is about 2,000 yards; they are reckoned to be five in number and the real obstacle to navigation is the second rapid from the top. At this place a reef runs out from the left bank, leaving between its point and the right bank a channel, only 100 yards wide, through which the water rushes with a fall of 1 in 50: this channel is moreover broken up by rocky islets into two or three passages, of which the one adjoining the right bank is the easiest of ascent, but has a width of only 50 yards. Both reef and islets carry masonry remains, those of a great irrigation barrage which here raised the surface of the river to the level of the surrounding country.[†] Above the rapids the river is 400 yards broad, between them in places as much as 700, and below them only 200 to 300; from head to tail the total loss of level is 1 foot with a high river and 7 or 8 feet with a low one.

From **Ahwāz** to Muhammareh, a distance of over 100 miles by river, the Kārūn averages a quarter of a mile in width and flows through an open uncultivated country. The banks are generally low upon this part of its course, and in winter they are occupied by Arab encampments around which some slight and shifting cultivation takes place; but in summer, with the exception of the permanent villages mentioned below, they are totally deserted. The worst reach for steamers is the 20 miles immediately below **Nāsiri**; vessels of only $3\frac{1}{2}$ feet draft sometimes have difficulty in navigating it during the low season and are even obliged to unload part of their cargo.

Date groves commence on the right bank of the Kārūn at Qisbeh, 7 miles above **Muhammareh** Town; and in the final section between the

---

[*] The steamer "Assyria" ascended the rapids successfully in 1842, and the steamer "Shushan" in 1890.

[†] This barrage was called the Shādhurwān, and it existed in the 10th century A.D. (*vide* Le Strange).

Bahmanshīr and the Shatt-al-'Arab both banks carry fine plantations. Above Qisbeh as far as Band-i-Qīr the banks are bare and desolate and devoid of wooding.

There are ferries on the river at various places noted in the table below: no bridges however exist except the Pul-i-Būlaiti and the Pul-i-Dizfūl—the latter broken—both at Shūshtar.

Volume, current, and variations of stream.—The minimum discharge of the Kārūn has been calculated at 10,000 cubic feet a second, and the flood discharge at 120,000 to 140,000.

The average surface slope of the river below the Ahwāz rapids is about 5 inches in the mile; and the current varies from 4 or 5 knots in the season of floods to 2 knots between August and November.

The Kārūn, along with its affluents, is liable to more violent and irregular changes of level than the great rivers of Turkish 'Irāq. In most places the difference between low and high river is ordinarily from 12 to 14 feet; but there is a difference of 24 feet between the lowest recorded reading in October 1901 and the highest in February 1903. The river is generally at its minimum from the middle of October to the end of November; and the highest floods usually occur in March and April,* but sometimes earlier. The influence of the sea tides is perceptible as far up the river as Ismā'īlīyeh, and lower down they cause a rise and fall of 4 to 5 feet; but no salt water ever enters the Kārūn.

Irrigation.—The Kārūn is not at present utilised for irrigation except on a petty scale, and that principally by means of water lifts upon the banks which are worked by animals. When the river is full it carries a brown silt and in its lower course runs flush with the banks; its water is at all times more or less discoloured. The silt does not, it is believed, ever exceed $\frac{1}{800}$ of volume and its fertilising value appears to be low.

Districts and villages.—Above Band-i-Qīr the course of the Kārūn in 'Arabistān lies in the Shūshtar District; the river then enters the Ahwāz District, which it traverses. The next and last district upon the Kārūn is that of Muhammareh which begins on the right bank immediately above Sab'eh, and on the left bank just above the ruined tombs at ' Ali-ibn-al-Husain.

The riverside villages from Shūshtar Town to Band-i-Qīr are dealt with in the articles on the Gargar and Shatait; those from Band-i-Qīr

---

* These data depend on records kept by the river steamers.

KĀRŪN

to Sab'eh are given in the table which follows below in the present article: the remainder will be found in the articles on the **Muhammareh** District and **'Abbādān** island. The tribes inhabiting the banks of the Kārūn can be ascertained from the paragraphs on the populations of Northern and Southern **'Arabistān**.

Name.	Miles by river below **Band-i-Qīr** and on which bank situated.	Houses and inhabitants.	Resources and general remarks.
Naddāfīyeh Kabīr (Kūt-an-) كوت النداڧيه كبير	3 Left.	50 houses, mostly grass huts, of Hamaid of the Nasailāt section. There are 150 fighting men, of whom 100 have rifles and 60 are mounted. Mulla Thāni, through whom the revenue of a number of tribes is paid, resides here.	Wheat and barley are cultivated. There is a ferry with one small boat.
Khalaf (Kūt Saiyid) كوت سيّد خلف	4½ Left.	5 grass huts of mixed Arabs; they have no rifles.	Ordinary cultivation.
'Abbās (Kūt Saiyid) كوت سيّد عباس	5½ Right.	Deserted since two years. Formerly there was a considerable village of 'Anāfijeh.	Trade was with **Wais**.
Naddāfīyeh Saghīr (Kūt-an-) كوت النداڧيه صغير	6½ Left.	15 grass huts of mixed Arabs: there are 30 fighting men, of whom 10 are mounted and 10 carry rifles belonging to the Shaikh of Muhammareh.	The inhabitants are under an agreement with the Shaikh of Muhammareh to protect native vessels between **Wais** and Saiyid Hasan on the Gargar.
Hilleh-wa-Dilleh حله و دله	7⅔ Right.	Now deserted.	There is one small ferry boat here.
Wais ويس	11½ Left.	...	See article **Wais**.
Li'aimi لعيمي	11½ Right.	Until lately deserted, but reoccupied about November 1905, by the Āl Bū Rawāyeh with a number of tents.	This place was formerly the chief centre of the 'Ānāfijeh.
Muwailheh مويلحه	11¾ Left.	Two small adjacent hamlets containing together about 50 grass huts of Hawāshim. There are 100 rifles.	Practically a suburb of **Wais**. Wheat and barley are grown, and there are 50 mules which ply to **Nāsiri**, **Rāmuz** and **Shūshtar**.

Name.	Miles by river below Band-i-Qīr and on which bank situated.	Houses and inhabitants.	Resources and general remarks.
Ismā'īl (Kūt Saiyid) كوت سيّد اسماعيل	21½ Right.	At present deserted.	This place is also known as Kūt Zāir Farbān and is situated in a tract called Luqbair لقبير .
Suwaini'ai صوينعي or Karādeh (Kūt) كوت كرادة	23¾ Left.	Do.	...
'Anāyeh (Kūt Saiyid) كوت سيّد عنايه	26¼ Left	100 grass huts of mixed Arabs, subjects of the Bāwīyeh. Of the fighting men 80 are mounted and 150 have rifles.	Wheat and barley are grown. There is a ferry here with 1 small boat.
Ibrāhīm (Kūt Saiyid) كوت سيّد ابراهيم	31¼ Right.	At present deserted.	Opposite the island of Khuwaiseh.
Qrāneh قرانه	32¾ Left.	100 houses of Zarqān of the Āl Bū Lahaiyeh and Sumāq sections; 40 are of mud, the rest are mat huts or tents. There are 50 mounted men and 100 rifles.	Wheat and barley are cultivated. One small ferry boat is kept here.
'Abbās (Saiyid) سيّد عبّاس	34½ Left.	14 grass huts of 'Ikrish of the Daghāghleh section, Persians, etc. They have 7 rifles and 10 mounted men.	Wheat and barley are grown. This place is situated in a tract known as Zūwīyeh زويه. There is 1 small ferry boat here.
Ahwāz Village اهواز	42 Left.	...	See article Ahwāz Village.
Nāsiri ناصري	43¼ Left.	...	See article Nāsiri.
Amīnīyeh امينيه	43¼ Right.	65 mud houses mostly of Hawāshim, among whom are 4 families of Sabians. There are 15 mounted men and 30 rifles.	The Sabians are silversmiths; the other inhabitants cultivate wheat and barley and own 20 mules, 15 donkeys and some cattle and sheep. The place is below the Ahwāz rapids and nearly opposite to Nāsiri, with which is its trade.

Name.	Miles by river below **Band-i-Qīr** and on which bank situated.	Houses and inhabitants.	Resources and general remarks.
Shikāreh شكاره	46¾ Left.	30 houses of mixed Arabs and Persians; some are of brick or mud, the rest are mat huts. Mounted men number 15 and rifles 20.	The village depends on agriculture. One small ferry boat is kept. The D'Arcy Oil Syndicate made their cart-road to **Rāmuz** for the despatch of plant from this place.
Harsheh حرشه	48¼ Left.	20 mud houses of mixed Arabs and Āl Bū **Kurd**. There are 10 mounted men and 10 rifles.	The village depends on agriculture.
Suwaiyid (Kūt) كوت سويد	48¾ Left.	At present deserted.	...
'Abdullah (Kūt) كوت عبد الله	49 Left.	60 mud houses of Āl Bū **Kurd** and **Bāwīyeh**. There are 40 rifles and 30 mounted men.	Adjoins Kūt Suwaiyid, from which it is separated only by a small ridge. Detached on the south side at about ¼ of a mile is a part of the village, called Bait Haidar, which is owned by Mīrza Hamzah, the principal Arab agent of the Shaikh of **Muhammareh**. There is a ferry at Kūt 'Abdullah with one small boat.
Sālih (Kūt Saiyid) كوت سيد صالح	49½ Left.	60 mud houses of **Bāwīyeh** and Āl Bū **Kurd**. They have 20 rifles and 15 mounted men.	This is an agricultural community. There is a small one-boat ferry.
Dibbis (Abu) ابو دبس	51 Left.	15 mud houses of poor Arabs and Āl Bū **Kurd**. No rifles or mounted men.	The people are cultivators. This village lies further north than the last, though it is further down the river.
Karaishān كريشان	52¾ Right.	20 mud houses of Āl Bū **Kurd**. Eight of the fighting men are mounted and 10 have rifles.	Wheat and barley are cultivated and 15 mules, a number of donkeys and some sheep and goats are owned. One small ferry boat is kept.

Name.	Miles by river below Band-i-Qīr and on which bank situated.	Houses and inhabitants.	Resources and general remarks.
'Amaireh (Kūt-al-) كوت العميرة	57¾ Left.	100 mud houses. Chiefly of Bāwīyeh of the Lijbārāt and Al Zahrāo sections, and 50 tents of Āl Bū Kurd. There are 150 mounted men and 150 rifles.	Part of the village is called Kūt Shaikh 'Ali from the late principal Shaikh of the Bāwīyeh who had his seat here. There is cultivation and about 200 camels are owned. On account of a great loop made by the river this place is about 2 miles due west of Kūt Saiyid Sālih. There is one small ferry boat.
Muzaffari (Bandar) بندر مظفري or Muzaffarīyeh مظفریه	85⅓ Left.	20 brick houses, 180 mud houses and 20 shops, also a large caravansarai and a Qahwehkhāneh built by Miz'al, the late Shaikh of Muhammareh. The people are Āl Bū Kurd with a few Dizfūlis. They have 10 mounted men and 100 rifles and are reputed warlike.	This place was formerly known as Ithleh اثله; it stands on a narrow tongue of land between two bends of the river. After Muhammareh and Nāsiri, Muzaffarīyeh is now the most important place on the Kārūn below Band-i-Qīr. The Shaikh of Muhammareh has a brick house here and maintains an agent, one of the Āl Bū Kurd; he frequently camps here himself in winter when he has business at Nāsiri or with the Bāwīyeh. There is some trade at Bandar Muzaffari with the surrounding tribes and merchants occasionally land with goods in retail quantities. One small ferry boat is kept here.
Tamair (Umm-at-) أم التمير	61 Right.	60 mud houses occupied and 30 or 40 deserted. The inhabitants are Bāwīyeh and have 10 mounted men and 20 rifles.	The caravan route from Muhammareh to Hawizeh leaves the Kārūn at this place, which, after Muhammareh, Nāsiri, and Muzaffari, is the most important on the Kārūn below Band-i-Qīr; and Shaikh 'Anāyeh, who is in direct charge of the right bank

KĀRŪN 991

Name.	Miles by river below Band-i-Qīr and on which bank situated.	Houses and inhabitants.	Resources and general remarks.
			of the **Kārūn** as representing the Shaikh of **Muhammareh**, resides here. Wheat and barley are grown; and a few mules, a number of donkeys and cattle and some sheep and goats are owned. There is one small ferry boat.
Maqtū' مقطوع	63 Right.	At present deserted, but **Muhaisin** and Bani **Tamīm** (II) of the 'Ayāisheh section still encamp here occasionally and cultivate wheat and barley.	This place was once (it is said) the seat of the Maulas of **Hawīzeh**. It is stated that a canal formerly ran from this place to **Hawīzeh** and had a branch which went off in a southerly direction.
Khifi خفي	65 Right.	10 mat huts of **Muhaisin** of the Manai'āt section. They have 5 rifles.	Inhabited only in the seasons of seed-time and harvest.
Ghazzāwīyeh غزاويه	66 Left.	30 mud houses of **Bāwīyeh** of the Nawāsir and Lijbarāt sections: they have 10 mounted men and 20 rifles.	The people are cultivators. There is a ferry here with one small boat.
Milaihān مليحان	68¼ Right.	20 houses of mud and reeds occupied by **Muhaisin** of the Manai'āt section. 10 men are mounted and there are 20 rifles.	This is a colony located by the Shaikh of **Muhammareh** for the protection of the river traffic. They cultivate wheat and barley. There is one small ferry boat.
Morān موران	73 Left.	30 mat huts of **Muhaisin** who have 30 mounted men and 15 rifles. **Bāwīyeh** of the Nawāsir section are also found here.	By the **Muhaisin** only occupied in the seasons of agriculture.
Bayūdh بيوض	78¼ Right.	A couple of huts, one of reeds and one of mud, occupied by Saiyid Nāsir, a member of a Saiyid family of **Ahwāz**. No arms.	Wheat and barley are grown.

Name.	Miles by river below **Band-i-Qīr** and on which bank situated.	Houses and inhabitants.	Resources and general remarks.
Braikeh بریکه or Braicheh بریچه	78¼ Left.	150 mud houses of Ma'āwīyeh. They have 60 rifles and 30 mounted men.	Wheat and barley are grown and livestock include 30 horses, 15 mules and some donkeys, cattle and sheep. The Ma'āwīyeh formerly paid their revenue to the Shaikh of **Muhammareh** through the **Bāwīyeh**, but their headman is now permitted to retain it as a personal allowance. One small ferry boat is kept.
Fārsiyāt فارسیات	83¼ Left.	4 mud houses and about 25 huts of **Muhaisin**, among whom are a few Saiyids. Rifles number 10 and mounted men 20.	This place is only occupied at the times of ploughing and reaping. There is then a small ferry boat here.
Ismā'īli * (اسماعیلي)	91¼ Left.	40 mat huts of **Muhaisin** of the Mutūr section: they have 20 rifles and 25 mounted men.	Sometimes pronounced Simā'īni. Except a garden (with two masonry water lifts) which is cultivated all the year round, Ismā'īli is deserted at the seasons of agricultural inactivity. A small ferry boat is sometimes to be found.
Chimaiyān چمیان	93¼ Left.	17 mat huts of **Muhaisin** and 3 of Saiyids, with 10 rifles and 15 mounted men.	...
Qajārīyeh قاجاریه	94¼ Right.	60 reed huts of **Muhaisin** of the Zuwaidāt section. There are 60 rifles and 50 mounted men. At seed-time and harvest the place is temporarily increased by about 35 houses of Bani Tamīm (II).	This place was formerly known as Saiyid Kādhim سید کاظم. Wheat and barley are grown. About 50 horsemen, *viz.*, the mounted men of the village, are stationed here by the Shaikh of **Muhammareh** for the protection of the river, and there is a small mud fort. A post and telegraph office constructed here by the Persian Government was never used as such and has now been converted into a rest house. There is a ferry with one small boat.

* A view of Ismā'īli will be found in Chesney's *Narrative*.

Islands.—The following is a list of the principal islands in the Kārūn:—

Name.	Vernacular equivalent.	Position, etc.
Wais	ريس	A little below the Muwailheh hamlets.
Luqbair	لقبير	Opposite the tract called Luqbair.
Khuwaiseh	خويسه	Opposite Qrāneh.
Agha (Jazīrat-al-)	أغا	Opposite the tract known as Zūwīyeh.
Umm-an-Nakhl	ام النخل	Immediately above the **Ahwāz** rapids.
Umm-as-Sabā'	أمّ السباع	Between the second lowest and the lowest of the **Ahwāz** rapids.
Abu Dibbis	ابو دبّس	2 miles below the village of Abu Dibbis.
Karaishān	كوياشن	2 miles below the village of Karaishān.
'Amaireh (Jazīrat-al-)	عميرة	Opposite Kūt-al-'Amaireh village.
Ithleh	اثله	Opposite Muzaffari.
'Adhrāt	عضرات	A long island 4 miles below Kūt-al-'Abīd.
Salmāneh	سلمانه	Half a mile below the point where the Salmānīyeh canal leaves the Kārūn: the island is about 300 yards long.
Dāir (Jazīrat-al-)	دائر	A very small island opposite to the Mārid creek on the left, and to Sāblah on the right bank of the river. A masonry dam here, of which the remains are still visible, is said to have been destroyed by Karīm Khān, Zand.

Political control.—The right of armed vessels or boats under foreign flags to enter even the lowest reach of the Kārūn is disputed by the Persian Government; and on each occasion that a British gunboat has anchored higher up than the British Consulate at **Muhammareh** a protest has been lodged by the local representative of the Persian Foreign Office. These protests have never been followed by any result.

3 s

KĀRWĀN
كاروان

A small district near the coast in Persian **Makrān**; it lies upon both sides of the **Rāpch** river, beginning on the south at about 10 miles from the coast and extending thence northwards for a distance of 10 or 15 miles; its breadth also, from near Balak on the east to the Kāshi stream on the west, is about 10 miles. Kārwān is, for Persian **Makrān**, a well cultivated and well wooded tract; it abounds with small game, such as black partridge and, in the season, duck. The inhabitants of Kārwān are known as Kārwānis; their tribal divisions are given in the article on Persian **Makrān**. The principal villages are :—

Name.	Position.	Number of huts.
Ganjak كنجك	11 miles north-west of the telegraph crossing on the **Rāpch** river.	35
Gāo گار	10 miles north of do.	12
Haivān هیان	2 miles west of Gāo.	20
Kārkindār كاركندار	12 miles north-west of the telegraph crossing on the **Rāpch** river.	40
Tambālān تمالان	8 miles north of do.	25

The chief village is Kārkindār, and besides the places mentioned above there are several small hamlets of which the names and particulars have not been ascertained. The village of Sāul, described in the article on Persian **Makrān,** should perhaps be reckoned to Kārwān. Five headmen of the Kārwān district receive annual subsidies aggregating Rs. 700 from the Indo-European Telegraph Department for the protection of the land line within their district. The district forms part of the chiefdom of Gaih.

KATHĪR
كثير

Generally pronounced Chathīr; an important Arab tribe of Northern 'Arabistān. The Kathīr occupy both banks of the **Diz** river, the Bait Sa'ad being in places interspersed with them, from the limits of the

'Anāfijeh up to a point 8 or 10 miles above Qal'eh 'Abdush Shāh; also the country in general between the **Diz** and the **Karkheh** rivers belongs to them. The majority are tent-dwelling nomads; but in the **Dizfūl** District they are found in the villages of Qal'eh 'Abdush Shāh, Jirqeh Saiyid Ahmad, Qal'eh Banūt and Dih Nau. Some Kathīr also are settled at 'Arab Hasan on the **Shatait**. The Kathīr, unlike other Arab tribes of **'Arabistān** such as the **Bāwīyeh**, not only take Persian wives themselves, but are accustomed to give their daughters in marriage to Persians.

The following is a statement of the divisions of the tribe:—

Section.	Subsection.	Location.	Fighting strength.	Remarks.
Ka'ab-ad-Dibais كعب الدبيس	...	Right bank of the Shāūr to the west of Shūsh near Qaryeh Saiyid Tāhir.	800, all with rifles, of whom 50 are mounted.	This section are said to own 3,000 buffaloes, 4,000 cattle and 10,000 sheep and goats.
Karīm (Bait) بيت كريم	Karīm or Mauleh (Bait) بيت كريم مولە	Husainīyeh, a tract on the right bank of the Diz 7 miles above the 'Ajīrub and extending from the Diz to the Shāūr.	500, all with rifles, of whom 300 are mounted.	This section takes one of its names from Mauleh who is a brother of Shaikh Haidar: the other name is generally pronounced Charīm or Jarīm. Their livestock are estimated at 500 camels, 400 mules, a few buffaloes, 1,000 cattle and 20,000 sheep and goats.
Do.	Ma'alleh معلە	Do.	50, all with rifles, of whom 30 are mounted.	The ruling family of the Kathīr in old times were of this section. They are stated to possess 30 camels, 140 mules, 100 cattle and 1,500 sheep and goats.
Do.	Mahmūd محمود	Right bank of the Diz, 7 miles above Kūt 'Abdush Shāh.	100, all mounted and armed with rifles.	Called after a Shaikh whose father was paternal uncle of Shaikh Haidar.

Section.	Subsection.	Location.	Fighting strength.	REMARKS
Karīm (Bait) بيت كريم	Nāsir (Al Bū) آل بو ناصر	Husainīyeh, as above.	100, all with rifles, of whom 30 are mounted.	The real Āl Bū Nāsir were almost exterminated 20 years ago by Ghāfil, grandfather of Shaikh Haidar; the section is now composed largely of outsiders who have become incorporated with it. The Āl Bū Nāsir own 40 camels, 100 mules, 200 cattle and 2,000 sheep and goats.
"Khaltaq" خالطق (i.e. miscellaneous dependents)	Bakhaitāt بخيتات	Left bank of the Diz between the Shūreh and the 'Ajīrub.	100, all with rifles but none mounted.	Their animals are 150 buffaloes, 200 cattle and 2,000 sheep and goats. The Bakhaitāt are attached to the Dailam subsection below.
Do.	Dailam ديلم	Do.	300, all with rifles but none mounted.	Their livestock are estimated at 600 buffaloes, 2,000 cattle and 2,000 sheep and goats. They are supposed to be of the same stock as the similarly named section of the 'Anāfijeh.
Do.	Dhabbeh ...	Left bank of the Diz above and close to Kūt 'Abdush Shāh.	150, all with rifles but none mounted.	They are said to own 200 buffaloes, 400 cattle and 3,000 sheep and goats. They are attached to the Dailam sub-section above.
Do.	Māhūr ماهور	Husainīyeh, as above.	100, all with rifles, of whom 60 are mounted.	These are really a division of the Sarkhah (Bani Lām), but at present they hold land under Shaikh Haidar of the Kathīr, pay revenue through him, and are attached to the Bait Karīm. At times they have lived under the protection of Haidar's rival, Farhān Asad. They own 100 camels, 100 cattle and 4,000 sheep and goats.

Section.	Subsection.	Location.	Fighting strength.	REMARKS.
"Khaltaq" خلطق (*i.e.* miscellaneous dependents)	Sa'ābireh سعابره	With the Dailam subsection above.	100, all with rifles but none mounted.	The Sa'ābireh are attached to the Dailam section above. They are s'ated to possess 100 buffaloes, 200 cattle and 3,000 sheep and goats.

Besides the above, or perhaps included in them, are said to be a section called Āl Bū Naṣṣi who live at Hiddeh or Haddāmeh on the **Diz** and have 300 rifles.

The whole tribe may be estimated at 7,000 souls, of whom perhaps not more than 1,000 have a fixed residence.

The senior member of the Ma'alleh section formerly commanded the obedience of the whole tribe; but at the present time two rival Shaikhs divide the Kathīr between them. Shaikh Farhān Asad is followed by the Bait Karīm subsection and part of the Dailam subsection and has his headquarters at Dih Nau; the village of Qal'eh Banūt also belongs to his party; and, outside of the Kathīr, the **Miyānāb** Arabs of 'Abdun Nabi on the **Gargar,** the Āl Bū Hamdān and Mahāmīd sections of the Bait **Sa'ad,** the Bait **Sa'ad** of Saiyid Hasan on the **Gargar,** and indeed the Bait **Sa'ad** generally, are his adherents. The remainder and great majority of the Kathīr upon the upper **Diz,** obey Shaikh Haidar, to whom the village of Qal'eh 'Abdush Shāh belongs. Both chiefs are recognised by the Persian Government, and the control of the country and tribesmen and the collection of revenue is left entirely in their hands; the total annual revenue demanded from the two is said to be 4,725 Tūmāns, for the greater part of which Shaikh Haidar is responsible. Shaikh Farhān Asad cultivates the friendship of the Shaikh of **Muhammareh** and his sister is married to Karīm Khān, Faili **Lur** of 'Amleh Karīm Khān; while Shaikh Haidar, whose daughter is married to a chief of the Sagwand **Lurs** and who has himself a Sagwand wife, is inclined to rely for support in difficulties on the Sagwands and indirectly on the Wāli of Pusht-i-Kūh. The relations of Shaikh Farhān Asad are with the Persian officials at **Shūshtar** and those of Shaikh Haidar with the authorities at **Dizfūl**; consequently the tribe may be regarded as divided between the two districts of Northern **'Arabistān.** It is a remarkable fact that of the Shaikhs—who are distantly related to one another—neither really belongs to the Kathīr tribe, but both are of Bait **Sa'ad** extraction.

KATHIR (ĀL) آل كثير

Singular Kathīri كثيري. The principal tribe in **Dhufār** Proper where all the villages except Tāqa belong to them; they are represented in the **Samhān** hills also by several sections, who act as a partial counterpoise there to the uncivilised **Qaras**. A few emigrants of the tribe are settled at Dōhah in the **Masqat** District near **Masqat** Town. The following table explains the subdivisions and distribution of the Āl Kathīr:—

Section.	Number of families.	Habitat.	Remarks.
'Ali-bin-Badr (Bait) بيت علي بن بدر	150	In the lower **Samhān** hills immediately behind **Salālah**.	Nil.
'Amr-bin-Muhammad (Bait) بيت عمر بن محمد	40	Salālah, etc.	Do.
Fādhil (Al) آل فاضل	120	At 'Auqad-al-Fādhil and Dahārīz.	Do.
Ghawwās (Bū) بو غواص	150	At Salālah, and in the Samhān hills.	Do.
Marāhīn مراهين or Marhūn (Bait-al) بيت المرهون	50	All at Salālah, except a few at 'Auqad-al-Marhūn.	Do.
Muhammad-bin-Hamad (Al) آل محمد بن حمد	150	In the Samhān hills.	Do.
Shanāfirah شنافرة	225	At Hāfah, etc.	This section are loyal to the Sultān of 'Omān. Their present Shaikhs are Bakhīt and 'Ali-bin-'Umr. The Shanāfirah are said to have been originally 'Awāmir but they are now reckoned to the Āl Kathīr.

Other sections, entirely Bedouin, are the Bait Bakhīt-bin-Sālim بخيت بن سالم, the Baīt-al-Hamar حمر the Baīt Jadād جداد and the Baīt Masan

مسن : of these the Bait Masan gave much trouble to the Sultān's Government between 1895 and 1897. Altogether the settled Āl Kathīr probably number about 2,500, and the nomadic about 2,000 souls.

The settled Āl Kathīr are agriculturists; their resources are described in the article on **Dhufār** Proper. The nomad sections in the hills own camels and cattle and collect frankincense like the **Qaras**, whom in their arms, clothing and habits they very closely resemble, except that they arrange their hair in a top-knot instead of binding it with a fillet; their language is possibly a dialect of Arabic, but it is reported to be quite different from that spoken by the Bedouins of **'Omān** and it has not as yet been properly investigated. Some of the Āl Kathīr Bedouins are almost jet black.

The Āl Kathīr are a Hināwi tribe and claim to have immigrated from Hadhramaut some 3 centuries ago, conquering **Dhufār** Proper and establishing a capital at Dahārīz: they are Ibādhis. There is constant friction between them and their **Qara** neighbours.

KĀUNAK
كارنك

A considerable village in the **Dizfūl** District of Northern **'Arabistān**, situated about 16 miles south-east of **Dizfūl** and 22 miles north-west of **Shūshtar** on the route connecting those towns; it is the ordinary halting place for travellers between the two places. Kāunak stands on the left bank of a stream of the same name, which is a left-bank affluent of the **Diz** river. The bed of the Kāunak stream at the village is usually a dry or nearly dry stretch of shingle about a mile across; after moderate rain, however, there is a good flow of water in several distinct channels, and heavy rain renders it impassable for short periods.

The village consists of about 100 mud houses; it is not surrounded by a wall, as are most of the villages of the **Dizfūl** District. A caravansarai stands about 200 yards north of the place; it is a mud-walled enclosure, but some of the interior buildings are of brick and there are a few small lodgings for better-class travellers in an upper storey. This building, along with the right to maintain 4 shops in Kāunak village, is held on lease by a private individual who pays 50 Tūmāns a year to the owner of the caravansarai and 20 to the Kadkhuda of the village. The only defences of Kāunak are a couple of upper-storeyed buildings in the village, which show a few loopholes, and a small mud tower with a timber roof. There are two water mills.

The inhabitants of Kāunak are **Bakhtiyāris** and a few Dizfūlis: there is one shopkeeper from **Shūshtar** Town. The fighting strength fluctuates; at the best there are but 10 or 12 rifles, and in September 1904, when an attack by Dīrakwand **Lurs** was expected, the place was almost deserted.

Rice, Kunjid, Māsh, wheat, barley, beans and cotton are cultivated on the village lands, which are irrigated from the Kāunak stream. A canal takes out of the stream a few hundred yards above the village, and beyond Kāunak it reaches a group of hamlets called Gumār which also it serves: there is a fair supply of water at all seasons of the year, but it is rather brackish. No transport is procurable at Kāunak except about 50 donkeys; cattle number about 150, and sheep and goats about 600.

There are four local shrines: the Imāmzādeh of Bībī Qulkhān قلخان, close to the caravansarai; a Qadamgāh of Hazrat 'Abbās and another of Imām Riza, both on the south side of the village and close to it; and a Qadamgāh, called Amīr Wazīr, half a mile from the village in the direction of **Shūshtar** Town. These shrines are visited by the surrounding Arabs as well as by Dizfūlis and Shūshtaris.

The revenue of Kāunak is paid into the **Dizfūl** treasury. With that of Gumār it amounts to 1,000 Tūmāns per annum for crops except rice, being assessed, it is said, at the rate of 2 Tūmāns a plough; half produce in kind is paid on account of rice cultivation.* A flour mill belonging to the village, which charges customers 1 Qrān and 1 Dizfūli Man of flour on every 12 Dizfūli Mans ground, is assessed to revenue at 500 Tūmāns a year. Kāunak belongs to the **Bakhtiyāri** Khāns and to Āgha 'Ali, Mustaufī, of **Dizfūl**.

KHABBAH (WĀDI)
وادي خبّة

A valley in the Eastern **Hajar** district of the **'Omān** Sultanate, a tributary of Wādi **Tāyīn** which it joins from the right bank at Ghubrat-at-Tām. Wādi Khabbah comes down from the watershed between the Wādi **Tāyīn** basin and **Sharqīyah**; its direction near its junction with Wādi **Tāyīn** is from south-south-east to north-north-west and in this

---

* The annual cash assessment of Kāunak, separately, is now reported to be 318 Tūmāns (1907).

part of its course it has no visible stream, but yields water in shallow wells and Falajs. The principal places in Wādi Khabbah are:—

Name.	Position.	On which bank.	Houses and inhabitants.	REMARKS.
Samā'īyah سماعية	At the head of the Wādi on the watershed.	Left.	200 houses of Hanādhilah, Bani Jābir of the Āl Saba' section, etc.	Nil.
Khabbah خبه	3 miles below Samā'īyah.	Do.	100 mud houses of **Hishm**, **Siyābiyīn**, Bani Bū 'Ali and Suwāwifah, also Bani Jābir of the Āl Saba' section and Hanādhilah: of the whole half are **Siyābiyīn**.	Do.
Waljah ولجه	7 miles below Khabbah and 3 above Ghubratat-Tām.	Do.	80 houses of Hanādhilah.	Do.

The fixed population of the valley is thus about 1,900 souls.

A good route from Wādi **Tāyin** into **Sharqīyah** lies up Wādi Khabbah: it is described as running westwards and south-westwards over a pass called Najd-al-'Awainah عوينه to Bataiyin بطيّن near Munjarid المنجرد.

KHABRAH خبره

A town of the **Qasīm** province in **Najd**, normally subject to **Buraidah** and distant about 35 miles south-westwards from that place. The site of Khabrah, which is near the left bank of Wādi-ar-**Rummah**, has no natural amenity, and the place consists of long, dreary streets of half-ruinous clay cottages. The town is surrounded by a mud wall and has a public square about an acre in extent, in the middle of which rises the watch-tower, commanding a view of the surrounding country. The population of Khabrah is about 3,000 souls and, though tradition represents it as originally a settlement of the Qahtān, the present inhabitants are described as of 'Anizah extraction: they are dull, ungracious and inhospitable. The majority live by agriculture, but many are camel-men. Dates, fruit and the ordinary cereals and vegetables of Qasīm are grown on the town lands by irrigation from wells 8 fathoms deep; the water of the town is sweet. The arable lands are in the bed of Wādi-ar-Rummah below those of Rass. A weekly market is held on Fridays. There are said to be 300 camels, a few donkeys and about 60 cattle, but no horses at this place.

KHĀBŪRAH
خابورة

A town on the Bātinah coast in the Sultanate of 'Omān, almost midway between its two extremities being situated 19 miles south-east of Saham Town and 22 miles north-west of Suwaiq. Wādi-al-Hawāsinah reaches the coast here, passing by the eastern side of the Khābūrah bazaar. The town consists entirely of huts; but it is now larger than Sohār Town and the inhabitants may number 8,000 souls, of whom 6,000 are Hawāsinah belonging, in part at least, to the Hawāmid and Sawālim sections. There are also a few Qatait. About 25 families of Khōjahs are settled here. Khābūrah is the port of Wādi-al-Hawāsinah and its tributaries and partially of Wādi 'Āhin; and 5 sea-going boats are owned which run to Masqat with dates and to the ports of Trucial 'Omān. There are also 30 Shāshahs and 15 small boats. Wheat is cultivated by irrigation from wells and there are 8,000 date trees: sheep and cattle are few and the only transport animals belong to visitors. The Sultān of 'Omān has a Wāli at Khābūrah supported by a detachment of 10 'Askaris. The revenue is only about $2,000 a year, collected as Zakat, and of this the whole is expended on the local administration.

KHADHAR (JABAL)
جبل خضر

A range forming part of the Eastern Hajar hills in the 'Omān Sultanate but running, apparently, at right angles to them; it constitutes the western side of Wādi Falaij. Jabal Khadhar is barren, rugged and precipitous, consisting of masses of limestone piled one upon another; its average height above the sea may be 5,000 to 6,000 feet. The highest summit of the range is situated about 9 miles west of Rafsah. Several villages and other frequented spots lie along the eastern foot of Jabal Khadhar; the principal in order from north to south are :—

Name.	Position.	Houses and inhabitants.	Remarks.
Lamīm لميم	In a Wādi of the same name.	Camping ground and date-grove of the Mashārifah, but no permanent dwellings.	There are 100 untended date palms.
Taima تيما	In a valley called Wādi-al-Manjūl وادي المنجول about 8 miles west of Sūr.	200 houses of Mashārifah.	Date palms are about 500.
Wādaila واديلا	A very short distance south of Taima.	80 houses of mixed tribes.	There are 800 date palms.
Tahwa طهوى	3 hours south-west of Taima.	60 houses of Hishm.	Palms are about 300.

Each of the above villages possesses a few donkeys, sheep and goats; and the total population of the tract seems to be about 1,700 souls.

KHADHIR (BANI)
بني خضير

A comprehensive term used in Southern **Najd** to describe the body of inferior tribes by whom chiefly, in a number of the districts, cultivation is carried on on behalf of the Arab masters of the soil. The Bani Khadhīr seldom own land themselves; but the Qāsim at **Saih** in **Aflāj**, who are Bani Khadhīr, constitute an exception to this rule.

Distribution.—Bani Khadhīr are found in the south-western part of **Najd** at Quwai'īyah; in **Aflāj** at 'Amār, **Badī'**, Haddār, Harādhah, **Kharfah, Lailah,** Rajaijīyah, **Raudhah, Saih,** Shutbah, Stārah, Wāsit and Wusailah; and in **'Aridh** at Haraimlah, Jarīnah, Malham, Rghabah, Salbūkh, Sidūs and Thādiq in the Mahmal division of the district, as well as at Jabailah, Malqa, 'Ammārīyah, 'Ilb, 'Audah, **Dara'īyah**, 'Arjah, Bātin-ash-Shuyūkh, **Riyādh**, Manfūhah, Masāni' and Hāir on Wādi **Hanīfah**, and at Dhrumah proper, Mizāhmīyah and Rōdhah in **Dhrumah**. In **Harīq** they occur at Harīq town and Mufaijir; in **Hautah** at Hautah town, Hilwah, Quwai' and Wusaitah; in **Kharj** at 'Adhār, **Dilam**, Na'ajān and Sulaimīyah; and in **Sadair** at 'Ashairah, 'Attār, 'Audah, Dākhilah, Ghāt, Harmah, Hasūn, Hautah, Jalājil, Janūbīyah, Khatāmah, Khīs, **Majma'**, Raudhah, Ruwaidhah, Tamair, Tuwaim and **Zilfi**.

Divisions.—The following are a few of the sections, or rather tribes which go to form the general body of the Bani Khadhīr, together with the names of some of the places at which they are found:—

'Atīj (Bani)	بني عتيج	at Zilfi.	Mizai'al	مزيعل	at Thādiq.
Had-hūd	هدهد	at Malham.	Muhārib	محارب	at Malham.
Hamadāt	حمدات	at Malham.	Natāqah	نتاقه	at Zilfi
Jamai'ah	جميعه	at Thādiq.	Qāsim	قاسم	at Saih.
Jidā'ah	جداعه	at Thādiq.	and		
Marshūd	مرشود	at Malham.	Rabaiya'	ربيع	at Thādiq.

KHAIMAH (RĀS-AL-) راس الخيمه DISTRICT*

The northernmost district in the principality of **Shārjah** in Trucial 'Omān: it forms part of the 'Omān Promontory, and in shape it is roughly triangular with its base to the west.

Boundaries and divisions.—The Rās-al-Khaimah district is divided from the **Ruūs-al-Jibāl** district of the 'Omān Sultanate on the northeast by a line which runs obliquely from Rās-ash-Sha'am on the west coast of the promontory to a point between the villages of **Dibah** proper and **Bai'ah** on the east coast. On the west, from Rās-ash-Sha'am on the north to the southern end of Jazīrat-al-**Hamra** on the south, it is bounded by the sea, and thence by a line, of which the course is indefinite, drawn across the desert to the southern extremity of the **Jiri** plain. The southeastern limit is an imaginary line connecting the south end of **Jiri** with the east coast at a point immediately south of **Dibah**.

The principal divisions of the Rās-al-Khaimah district are the plain of **Sīr**, the plain of **Jiri**, Jazīrat-al-**Hamra**, the island of **Tunb**, and the

---

* For authorities, maps, charts, etc., see first footnote to article Trucial 'Omān.

remainder of the tract of which the boundaries have been described above: the last mentioned division has no general name.

Physical characteristics.—**Sīr, Jiri,** Jazīrat-al-**Hamra** and **Tunb** are described elsewhere under their own names. The rest of the district consists, on the west, of low, sandy desert adjoining the sea; and, on the east, of a section of the mountains that form the spine of the 'Omān Promontory. The hilly tract is divided into two nearly equal sections, a northern and a southern, by the Wādi-al-**Qaliddi** route between Rās-al-**Khaimah** Town and **Dibah**.

Topography.—For the topography of the **Sīr** and **Jiri** tracts, Wādi-al-**Qaliddi** and **Hamra** island the articles under those names may be consulted: the following is a table of the principal places in the remaining portion of the district:—

Name.	Position.	Nature.	Remarks.
Dibah دبه	On the east coast of the 'Omān Promontory, between the districts of **Ruūs-al-Jibāl** and **Shamailīyah**.	...	See article **Dibah**.
Ghalīlah غليله	On the west coast of the 'Omān Promontory, about 1 mile south of **Sha'am**.	A village of 50 mud and stone houses of Shihūh of the Bani Shatair division and 'Ayāl Sā'ad section.	The inhabitants have 5 fishing boats and about 4,000 date trees.
Hamra (Jazīrat-al) جزيرة الحمرا	12 miles west-south-west of Rās-al-Khaimah Town.	...	See article **Jazīrat-al-Hamra**.
Khaimah (Rās-al) راس الخيمه Town	On the west coast of the 'Omān Promontory, about 48 miles north-east of Shārjah Town.	...	See article **Rās-al-Khaimah** Town.
Khuwair (Khor) خور خوير	On the west coast of the 'Omān Promontory, between Ghalīlah and **Rams**.	30 houses of Shihūh of the Bani Shatair section.	Date palms are estimated at 2,000 trees, and livestock at 10 camels, 10 donkeys and 300 sheep and goats. There is a creek here which can be used by boats at high water.

Name.	Position.	Nature.	Remarks.
Muzāhmi مزاحمي	On the west coast of the 'Omān Promontory, towards Umm-al-Qaiwain.	An inlet with a sandy beach.	It is uninhabited but is a resort for fishermen using small boats.
Rams رمس	On the west coast of the 'Omān Promontory, 8 miles north-east of Rās-al-Khaimah Town.	...	See article Rams.
Sha'am الشعم	On the west coast of the 'Omān Promontory, 17 miles north-north east of Rās-al-Khaimah Town.	...	See article Sha'am.
Shariyah شريه	In the hills north-west of Dibah, in a valley called Hajīl حجيل which is said to drain towards Rās-al-Khaimah Town.	10 houses of Sharqiyīn.	The place is under Rās-al-Khaimah Town: its resources are estimated at 10 donkeys, 20 cattle, 600 sheep and goats and 2,000 date palms.
Wamm رم	In the hills somewhat to the north of the Dibah Rās-al-Khaimah route at a point a few miles to the west of Dibah.	30 houses of Sharqiyīn.	Wamm is under Dibah. Donkeys number about 50, cattle 50, sheep and goats 400 and date palms 1,500.

Population.—The settled inhabitants of the district number about 16,000 souls as below :—

Sīr	2,50
Jiri	1,000
Jazīrat-al-Hamra	2,500
Remainder of the district (including Tunb island)	10,000

Among the fixed population the Za'āb with about 2,500 persons are numerically the most important tribe; after them come the Ahl Rās-al Khaimah, Shihūh and Tanaij with about 2,000 souls each. The Mahārah (1,250) and the Bani Shamaili (1,000) are also considerable tribes; and cultivators of mixed tribes, included under the general and merely descriptive term of Bayādir, are numerous. The remainder of the settled popula-

Crowd at Rās-al-Khaimah.
(Maj. P. Z. Cox.)

tion are 'Awānāt, Āl 'Ali, Āl Bū Mahair, Mazārī, 'Naqbiyīn, Sharqiyīn, and a very few Balūchis.

The nomads of the district, chiefly in Jiri, are either Na'īm of the Khawātir section or Ghafalah.

Agriculture and trade.—The agricultural resources of the district may be learned from the village and topographical tables in the articles upon the divisions of which it is composed.

The trade of the district is concentrated at Rās-al-Khaimah Town, to the article on which reference may be made.

Communications.—The subject of routes is dealt with in the general article on Trucial 'Omān.

Administration.—The Rās-al-Khaimah district is at present governed by Khālid-bin-Saqar, the eldest and only surviving son of the Shaikh of Shārjah, as his father's deputy; it brings in no surplus revenue, but the receipts, which are said to amount to Rs. 6,300 from the pearling interest alone, cover the expenses of the administration. The only military force is a body of armed retainers maintained by the Deputy-Governor at Rās-al-Khaimah Town, which is his headquarters. The town of Dibah and village of Wamm, it should be noted, are at present exempt from the Deputy-Governor's jurisdiction and are held in fief by Rāshid-bin-Mājid, a first cousin of the Shaikh of Shārjah; the feudatory personally resides at the place and is styled Wāli of Dibah.

KHAIMAH (RĀS-AL-) راس الخيمه TOWN

This town, the capital of the district similarly named in the principality of Shārjah, is situated on the coast of Trucial 'Omān about 48 miles north-east of Shārjah Town and 24 miles west-north-west of Dibah on the opposite side of the 'Omān Promontory.

Site and harbour.—The town stands upon a narrow spit of land, 2½ miles in length, which runs parallel to the coast and is connected with the mainland at its south-western end. The country in the vicinity of the town is low, flat and sandy. A dense grove of dates, mostly belonging to the tract called Sīr, begins opposite the town and extends a considerable distance inland, continuing northwards as far as Rams; while a line of reddish sandhills, commencing a little to the south-west of the town, reaches to Jazīrat-al-**Hamra** and beyond. The creek enclosed between the spit and the mainland contains an uninhabited island called Qurmah قرمه; and on the eastern side of the creek there formerly stood a village named Mahārah محاره, of which the deserted site, or its vicinity, is generally occupied by some colony of temporary visitors to Rās-al-Khaimah. At present such a settlement, known as Ma'airīdh معيريض and inhabited by Persians from **Rams**, etc., exists on this shore of the creek. Apart from the entrance at Rās-al-Khaimah town, the creek is connected with the sea by a backwater, 4 miles long, which has its opening on the coast 1½ miles south of **Rams**. The creek forms an excellent and well sheltered anchorage for native boats; but, though 9 feet deep inside, it has only 2 feet of water at the entrance at low tide: the approach, however, could probably be somewhat improved by dredging. The anchorage for large vessels is at sea, 2½ to 3 miles north-west of the town.

Defences.—A dilapidated wall crosses the isthmus to the south-west of the town, and there is a fort in the town itself. Neither is of any modern value.

Inhabitants.—There are altogether about 1,000 houses in Rās-al-Khaimah, of which half are built of stone and gypsum mortar, while the remainder are huts of date leaves. The largest section of the inhabitant are a mongrel race, known as Ahl Rās-al-Khaimah اهل راس الخيمه, formed by the fusion of various Arab tribes; these may number 400 houses. The other main elements of the population are Mahārah محاره (250 houses), Āl 'Ali (150 houses) and Āl Bū **Mahair** (120 houses). There are also a few **Na'īm** of the Darāwishah section of the Āl Bū Shāmis division. In the town are found also 10 families of **Balūchis** from the Bashākard district of Persia who live by working in the date gardens of **Sīr**. There are here no resident Hindu traders; but 33 **Kōhjahs**, British subjects, are settled in the place.

Resources.—Drinking water is scanty and indifferent. The date plantations belonging to the town are estimated to contain about 15,600 trees, and the inhabitants possess in addition livestock to the number of 20 horses, 130 camels, 175 donkeys, 150 cattle and 800 goats. About 33 pearl boats and 15 other sea-going vessels, of which 7 are Baghlahs and the rest Sambūks, belong to this port; 10 of the pearl boats belong to Ma'airīdh and are of small size. There are also about 120 fishing boats.

Rās=al=Khaimah, looking towards Ruūs=al=Jibāl.
(Mrj. P. Z. Cox.)

KHALFĀBĀD

Trade and manufactures.—The trade resembles that of other places on the coast of Trucial 'Omān. Of the local merchants 7 are **Khōjahs**. The only manufacture is of daggers, which find a sale in the other towns of the coast.

Administration.—Rās-al-Khaimah town is the seat of the Deputy Governor of the district of the same name. He is at present a son of the Shaikh of **Shārjah** and has under his orders a force of 70 'Askars or armed retainers to man the towers and otherwise defend the place if required. There are said to be several hundreds of rifles in the town also, the owners of which would participate in repelling an attack from outside.

KHALAI-FĀT
خليفات

Singular Khalaifi خليفي. An Arab tribe of **Qatar and Bahrain** who claim to be an offshoot of the Bani 'Abīdah of Yaman. Those of **Qatar** have 170 houses at **Wakrah** and those of **Bahrain** 40 houses at Hālat-al-Khalaifāt, but the latter village is not continuously occupied. In religion the Khalaifāt are Māliki Sunnis, and they live by pearl diving and pearl dealing and partly also by pastoral pursuits. In the cold weather most of them camp in the interior of **Qatar** with their cattle: in the hot weather they work on the pearl banks, leaving their flocks and herds in charge of Bedouins.

KHALFĀ BĀD
خلف آباد

The principal village of the **Jarrāhi** District and the seat, alternately with **Ma'shūr**, of the agent of the Shaikh of **Muhammareh** by whom the district is managed. Khalfābād stands on the left bank of the **Jarrāhi** River towards the upper end of the Jarrāhi District and 7 miles below Cham-as-**Sābi**. There are some fords near it which are practicable for laden animals during the greater part of the year, except after rain. The village consists of only about 40 mud houses, the inhabitants being mixed Arabs and Persians engaged in agriculture. To one of the tribes or families here, called the **Amāreh** اماره, belonged until recently the local governors of **Ma'shūr**.

3 T

KHĀLID (BANI) بني خالد or KHUWĀLID خوالد

The singular of the name is Khâlidi خالدي. An Arab tribe of Eastern Arabia who had formerly a very wide range but are now little found outside the Sanjāq of Hasa; they are still predominantly Bedouin, but appear to be in the process of settling down.

Distribution.—The domains proper of the nomadic Bani Khālid are the northern portion of Habl down to the Habaiyah wells and the northern half of Biyādh; when however, as at the present time, they are on good terms with the Ajmān, they make use of the southern parts also of these two tracts. They also roam in Kuwait territory, sometimes travelling as far north as Kuwait Town to obtain supplies, but the Maqta' stream is their ordinary limit in this direction. Summān, too, is visited by them. Permanent communities of Bani Khālid have for long existed on the islands of Musallamīyah, Jinnah and Tarūt; and during the last few years two fixed villages of Bani Khālid have sprung up on the mainland, namely, Umm-as-Sāhak in the Qatīf Oasis and Qasr Āl Subaih in Biyādh. The Bani Khālid are also represented at Jishshah and Kalābiyah in the Hasa Oasis and in the fixed villages of Wādi-al-Miyāh; and a few are permanently settled in Bahrain and some at Kuwait Town, while others pay regular annual visits to 'Anik in the Qatīf Oasis, and may be regarded as partially settled there.

In Najd part of the inhabitants of Malham in 'Āridh, of Zilfi in Sadair, of 'Anaizah, Qusaibah and possibly of Khabb and Qisai'ah in Qasīm, and of Quwai'īyah in the south-western desert are believed to be of Bani Khālid extraction; those at 'Anaizah bear a stronger resemblance to Bedouins than their fellow-citizens who are Bani Tamīm.

Religion, character and mode of life.—The Bani Khālid, unlike most of their neighbours, are Māliki and not Hanbali Sunnis: the difference is probably accounted for by their hereditary antagonism to the Wahhābis, from whom the Hanbalis are sometimes almost indistinguishable.

The Bani Khālid are described as more dignified and formal in their intercourse with strangers than the other Bedouin tribes of Eastern Arabia; and among themselves the share of the women in the social life of the tribe is said to be more restricted. Their tents are larger than the ordinary Bedouin tent. The Bani Khālid are considered to be handsomer and of fairer complexion than the average Bedouin, and in general appearance they resemble the settled Arab rather than the nomad. As a rule they are well dressed and ordinarily wear 'Abas: they are said to have a characteristic way of bringing down their kerchiefs so as partially to conceal their faces. They have some slight peculiarities of dialect.

In the 3 hot weather months the Bedouins of the Bani Khālid descend to the coast and tend the date plantations which they own at various places in its vicinity; during the rest of the year they roam in the interior. The principal occupations of the tribe as a whole are horse and cattle breeding and the cultivation of dates; but those who are settled on the coast engage also in pearl diving and in the sea-fisheries.

Divisions and numbers.—The following is a table of the divisions and subdivisions of the Bani Khālid together with such detailed information as it has been possible to procure regarding them :—

Section.	Subsection.	Fighting strength.	Remarks.
Amāir عمائر	Dawāwdah دواردة	100	A few Dawāwdah are settled at Yasrah in Bahrain and some others may be regarded as partially settled at 'Anik in the Qatīf Oasis; otherwise the subsection is entirely nomadic. The Dawāwdah are of low origin and only the family of their Shaikh, at present Muhammad bin-'Isa, are considered to rank equally with the Bani Khālid of other subsections and sections.
Do.	Hasan (Āl) آل حسن	600	A few Al Hasan are settled on the islands of Musallamīyah and Jinnah, but all the rest are Bedouins. Their chief Shaikh is Fuwairis-bin-Muhammad (others say Sudi-bin-Husain).
Do.	Khālid (Al) آل خالد	400	This subsection are settled on Musallamīyah island where their Shaikh, at present Shabīb-bin-'Aqal, is the principal personage and holds the appointment of Mudīr under the Turks; he is said to be the leading Shaikh of the Bani Khālid tribe.

Section.	Subsection.	Fighting strength.	Remarks.
'Amāir عمائر	Razīn (Al) آل رزين	150	Also settled on **Musallamīyah** island: their present Shaikh is Adwān-bin-Nāsir.
Do.	Shāhīn (Āl) آل شاهين	100	The Āl Shāhīn are settled on **Jinnah** island and have at present Miqdal-bin-Sulaimān for their Shaikh: he is Mudīr of the island under the Ottoman authorities.
Do.	Various.	530	Partly nomad, partly semi-settled at 'Anik in the **Qatīf** Oasis, and partly sedentary on the islands of **Musallamīyah** and **Jinnah**.
Humaid (Āl) آل حميد	...	20	The Āl Humaid were once the predominant section of the Bani Khālid; they had their headquarters at Thāj in Wādi-al-**Miyāh**, and the oasis of **Hasa** is said to have been subject to them. The Āl **Musallam** are stated to have been originally one of their sections, and it is believed that a considerable number of Al Humaid have become incorporated with the **Muntafik** of Turkish **Irāq**. The few who remain in the Hasa Sanjāq are all nomads, and Bārak-bin-Talmas-as-Sardh is their present Shaikh.
Jabūr (Āl) آل جبور	...	150	Now partially settled at Jishshah in the Hasa Oasis. The subsectional Shaikh is 'Abdul Muhsin-bin-Bidāh.
Muhāshīr. مهاشير	...	150	The majority of this subsection are nomads, but some are partially settled at 'Anik in the **Qatīf** Oasis, while others have become permanently residents of **Musallamīyah** and perhaps of **Jinnah** island and a few of their **Kuwait** Town: their Shaikh is Ali-bin-'Ali Āl Kulaib (others say Sannā-bin-Thanaiyān).

Section.	Subsection.	Fighting strength.	Remarks.
Miqdām (Āl) آل مقدام	...	300	The majority of this section are nomads; the Shaikh is Marzūq-bin-'Āmir, Āl Faiyādh. This section are represented at Kalābīyah in the Hasa Oasis.
Nahad (Bani) بني نهد	...	300	Mostly nomads; the Shaikh is Raja-bin-Musbih.
Subaih (Al) آل صبيح	'Ainain (Āl Bū) آل بو عينين	...	This subsection, found only in Qatar and Bahrain, must now be regarded as a separate tribe, and they are described in a separate article.
Do.	Dhahairāt ضحيرات	130	Settled at Qasr Āl Subaih. Their Shaikh is at present Zaitūn-bin-Shadaiyid.
Do.	Had-hūd هدهود	100	Also settled at Qasr Al Subaih, their present Shaikh being 'Abdullah, Al 'Azzām.
Do.	Haiyah (Al) آل حية	50	An entirely nomadic subsection, under Shaikh Jarbō'ah-bin-Marshad.
Do.	Hamaidāt حميدات	...	This subsection, located in Qatar and Bahrain, is now to all intents and purposes a distinct tribe and is described separately under its own name.
Do.	Katab (Al) آل كتب	180	It is stated that the Bani Qitab or Katab of 'Omān are of the same origin as this subsection. The present Shaikh of the Al Katab in the Hasa Sanjāq is Khālid bin-Fahad, Al Thawāb.
Do.	Makhāsim مخاصم	80	This subsection are altogether nomadic; but their Shaikh, at present Muhammad-bin-'Ajrān, is Shaikh also of the whole Āl Subaih section.

Section.	Subsection.	Fighting strength.	Remarks.
Subaih (Āl) آل صبيح	Zaban (Āl) آل زبن	160	Bedouins: their Shaikh at this time is Sultān-bin-Mansūr.
Do.	Various	500	Partly nomads and partly settled at Qasr Āl Subaih.

The settled Bani Khālid of Malham are stated to belong to a section called Qammāz قمّاز, those of Zilfi to sections styled Dūshān دوشان and Hamrān حمران and those of Quwai'īyah to one known as 'Arāfah عرافة. There is also a small nomadic section, the Kathīr كثير, who are found to the north of Kuwait among the Dhafīr tribe.

The fighting strength of the Bani Khālid, exclusive of divisions which have separated from them and become independent tribes, is thus about 4,000 men; and the total number of souls in the tribe, subject to a similar deduction, may be roughly estimated at 14,000.

History and present political position.—Less than 150 years ago the Bani Khālid were the paramount tribe of Eastern Arabia, and the extent of their territory at that time is marked by the fact that caravans between **Baghdād** and Aleppo used to suffer from their depredations. Their power was first broken by the Wahhābis in or before 1795, and in 1830 they were obliged to surrender the sovereignty of the **Hasa** Oasis to the Wahhābi Amīr. In 1874 the Turks attempted to govern the **Hasa** Sanjāq through one of the Bani Khālid chiefs, but the experiment was a failure.

The Bani Khālid are on bad terms with the **Mutair** and the Āl **Morrah,** and the recent establishment of the village of Qasr Āl **Subaih** was intended to facilitate the prosecution of hostilities against those tribes. With the Turks the Bani Khālid are in somewhat close relations, and the non-nomadic portion of the tribe for the most part pay them a regular Zakāt; but the allowances disbursed by the Porte to the tribe as a whole exceed the revenue which is recovered from the sedentary sections. The Shaikh of the Āl Khālid section is styled Mudīr of the island of **Musallamīyah** and receives a monthly allowance of $30, which he shares (unofficially) with the Shaikh of the Āl Razīn; and the other headmen on the island are given annual presents of about $50 each. The Shaikh of the Āl Shāhīn is similarly called Mudīr of **Jinnah** island, and he also receives an allowance from the Turks of $30 per mensem. The settled Bani Khālid of Qasr Āl **Subaih,** however, appear to consider themselves independent of the Turks; and so apparently do the nomadic branches of the tribe unless when they are in the neighbourhood of Turkish posts.

KHĀLID (BANI)

A valley in the Eastern **Hajar** district of the **'Omān** Sultanate which, beginning at the watershed between the coast and the interior at a point inland from **Tīwi** runs from north-west to south-east down into **Ja'alān**. The villages of Wādi Bani Khālid in succession from above downwards are:—

KHĀLID
(WĀDI
BANI)
وادي بني خالد

Village.	Position.	On which bank.	Houses and inhabitants.	Remarks.
Muqal مقل	Near the head of the Wādi.	Left.	150 houses of Sa'ādiyīn.	The people are carriers and shepherds owning 300 camels, 400 donkeys, 200 cattle and 2,000 sheep and goats.
Dawwah درة	Adjoins Muqal.	Do.	200 houses of Masālihah, Muwālikh and Nidhairiyīn with some Bani Jābir.	This village consists of 7 quarters and there is a fort belonging to the Muwālik. Animals are 40 camels, 70 donkeys, 100 cattle and 200 sheep and goats.
Zilaft زلفت	1 hour below Dawwah.	Do.	50 houses of Hishm of the Thuwāni section.	There are 30 camels, 50 donkeys, 50 cattle and 200 sheep and goats.
'Adhfain عذفين	1 hour below Zilaft.	Do.	200 houses of Hishm.	Here is a fort and a perennial spring called 'Ain Sārūj عين صاروج. Livestock are 70 camels, 100 donkeys, 100 cattle and 500 sheep and goats.
Halfah حلفح	½ an hour below 'Adhfain.	Do.	190 houses of Sha'ibiyīn (Bani Jābir) and Hishm.	Animals are 60 donkeys, 40 cattle and 300 sheep and goats.
Badh'ah بصعه	½ an hour below Halfah.	Do.	150 houses of Hishm.	There are 30 camels, 200 donkeys, 40 cattle and 500 sheep and goats.
Sīq سيق	1 hour below Badh'ah.	Do.	180 houses of Hishm.	Sa'īd-bin-Rashid, Shaikh of the Hishm, has a tower here. Livestock are 20 camels, 30 donkeys, 100 cattle and 1,000 sheep and goats. Date palms number about 4,000.
Sibt سبت	½ an hour below Sīq.	Do.	160 houses of Hishm.	The same Shaikh has a tower here. Animals are 70 camels, 100 donkeys, 20 cattle and 300 sheep and goats.

KHALID (WĀDĪ BANI)

The settled population of the valley is thus about 6,400 souls.

On passing Sibt, which is said to be about 10 miles north of Kāmil in **Ja'alān,** the Wādī emerges from the hills and enters the plain of **Ja'alān.** Wādi Bani Khālid contains running water; the principal crops are wheat, barley, lucerne and dates. The palms are said to number 100,000 distributed among the villages.

KHAMĪR
خمير

A large village situated on the coast of the **Bastak** district of Persia, about 12 miles west-north-west of **Lāft** on **Qishm** Island; mountains called Kūh-i-Khamīr كوه خمير run east and west immediately on the north of it. Khamīr is approached within half a mile by a creek, leading out of the Masakeh branch of **Clarence Strait,** which is navigable for native boats of 20 to 30 tons' burden. Sweet water is contained in 17 large reservoirs and brackish water in a dozen wells. Hills called Kūh-i-Dumdumdeh دمدمه, one mile to the north-west of Khamīr, yield lime; and 3 miles to the north-westward, in a spur of the higher mountains which is called Kūh-i-Ma'adan معدن, are deposits of sulphur (in conjunction with gypsum) and a hot sulphurous spring. The spring is called Āb Bād آب باد and rises in a tank of masonry.

On the east side of the place are date plantations, and in this direction at 3 miles from the village, is a wall in excellent repair which was built by Saiyid Sultān of **Masqat** during an 'Omāni occupation. This rampart is known as Sidār سدار. The only other defence is a fort with a high square tower, also in perfect preservation and built in the same circumstances. There are 2 or 3 shrines of merely local importance, also a fine mosque in which free instruction is given to the young.

Khamīr contains about 350 houses, and the total population may be 1,800 souls. The people, except a very few, are Sunnis and belong to various Arab tribes: they are chiefly engaged in navigation, fishing, date-growing, wood-cutting and lime-burning, and they own about 50 camels, 20 donkeys and 200 cattle, sheep and goats. Their diet is of fish, dates and coarse barley bread, the commonest and most esteemed fish being a large sort of mullet.

The shipping of **Khamīr** consists of 4 Ghunchahs and 22 Baqārahs, some of which run as far as **Basrah** and even to Indian ports. Exports are fish, lime in large quantities, mill-stones and a little sulphur, but the trade in sulphur has ceased to be remunerative under the expensive method of extraction employed*; firewood is also sent to the towns of Trucial **'Omān** and to **Bahrain**.

Khamīr belongs properly to the **Bastak** district, but it is under the political supervision of the Governor of the **Gulf Ports**, and the local administration is carried on by a Kalāntar appointed by the Mu'īn-ut-Tujjār of Tehrān who is revenue lessee of Khamīr and its dependencies: the present Kalāntar is one of the hereditary Shaikhs of the town. The Imperial Persian Customs have now a post here.

KHAMĪS (AL)
آل خميس

An Arab tribe found in the **Rāmuz** district, but said to be connected with the Ma'adān tribe on the **Tigris**. The principal divisions of the tribe are the following :—

Section.	Subsection.	Location.	Fighting strength.	REMARKS.
Ạbbād (Āl Bū) آل بو عباد	...	Near the Zarnīni, about 4 miles south-west of Rāmuz Town.	100, of whom 40 have rifles and 30 are mounted.	Their livestock amount to 50 camels, 100 cattle and 3,000 sheep and goats.
Ahmadīyah or Hmadīyeh احمديه	...	Mamūhīyeh village in the Rāmuz District.	100, of whom 30 are mounted and 30 have rifles.	This section own 40 camels, 150 cattle and 3,000 sheep and goats.
Kamīs (Al) آل خميس	Mansūr منصور	Near the Zarnīni, in the Rāmuz District.	50, of whom 30 are mounted and 30 have rifles.	The animals of the Mansūr are 40 camels, 100 cattle and 1,000 sheep and goats.
Do.	Rizaij-as-Sufur رزيق الصفر	'Ain-ul-Bārideh, close to the east bank of the Zarnīni, about 4 miles from Rāmuz Town.	50, of whom 20 are mounted and 20 have rifles.	They have 30 camels, 100 cattle and 1,500 sheep and goats.
Do.	Rizaij-as-Sultān رزيق السلطان	Tughali, in the Rāmuz District.	60, of whom 30 are mounted and 30 have rifles.	Their animals are 60 camels, 150 cattle and 2,000 sheep and goats.
Rashaid (Bani) بني رشيد	...	At Sultānabād upon the right bank of the Mārun River.	100, of whom 30 have rifles and 20 are mounted.	They possess 40 camels, 200 cattle and 3,000 sheep and goats.

* The method is described by Pelly at page 243 of the Bombay Geographical Society's Journal, Volume XVII, 1865.

1018 KHAMĪS (AL)

Section.	Subsection.	Location.	Fighting strength.	Remarks.
Zabairīyeh زهيريه	...	Mamūhīyeh above; also at Bunnat Shaikh Janām upon the Gargar.	100, of whom 40 have rifles and 30 are mounted.	This section have 50 camels, 200 cattle and 4,000 sheep and goats.
Zubaid زبيد	...	Apparently at Sar-i-Chishmeh in the Rāmuz District, and at Sidar Gūpāl not far from Mamūhīyeh in the same.	150, of whom 80 have rifles and 50 are mounted.	The lands of this section are irrigated from the Gūpāl stream. They own 150 camels, 400 cattle and 10,000 sheep and goats.

Most of these sections inhabit reed huts; and the tribe, of which the number may be estimated at 2,500 souls, should now perhaps be regarded as settled rather than as nomadic. About 1840 the Āl Khamīs emigrated to the country between Hawīzeh and the Kārūn, but they have since returned to their former seat, where they are at present subject and pay revenue to the Bakhtiyāri chiefs.

KHAMĪS (JABAL)* جبل خميس

This is the name of the range which forms the termination eastwards of the Eastern Hajar hills in the Sultanate of 'Omān; it begins immediately south of Sūr and runs due south into Ja'alān, a distance of over 20 miles; its direction is thus at right angles to the main axis of Eastern Hajar.† Jabal Khamīs is parallel to Jabal Khadhar, the portion of Hajar which next adjoins it on the west; and Wādi Falaij, the main route from Sūr to Ja'alān and Sharqīyah, descends to the coast between the two. The height of Jabal Khamīs, which at 9 miles from the coast has an elevation of 2,845 feet, increases apparently from north to south and attains 4,195 feet at a point about 25 miles from Sūr; 4 or 5 miles however to the north of this point it falls to a col with an elevation of only 2,340 feet above the sea. This pass, called Najd-al-'Ayūn عيون, is crossed by a route practicable for camels, which on the one side leads down via 'Ain-al-Mashārifah عين المشارفه (16 miles) to Khor-al-Jarāmah (30 miles) and on the other falls to Wādi Fisāo and passes by Wādi Falaij to Sūr; 'Ain-al-Mashārifah has shallow wells of indifferent water

---
* A distant view of Jabal Khamīs is given in Chart No. 2383—38.
† See *Sketch Map of the Country round Sūr*, 1903.

KHĀRAG 1019

sufficient for 200 camels and an equal number of men, and the route on which it lies crosses a number of dry water-courses that run down from Jabal Khamīs to the South-Eastern Coast of 'Omān. In Wādi Muswa مسوى and Wādi Fisāo, the valleys which begin respectively from the east and west sides of the pass and in their tributaries, are outcrops of coal which were scientifically examined in 1901.* The mass of the Jabal Khamīs range is composed of limestone, sandstone and shale.

KHĀN
خان

A village on the coast of Trucial 'Omān, in the **Shārjah** Principality. It stands about 2 miles south-west of **Shārjah** Town on the north side of a small inlet called Khor-al-Khān with two branches, one of which runs north-east and joins, or almost joins, at high tide the **Shārjah** backwater, while the other turns south behind Abu Hail. In passing between **Shārjah** and Khān the **Shārjah** creek must be crossed or a détour made so as to pass between it and the Khān creek. The land inshore of the village is for some distance low and swampy. Khān consists of about 200 houses, the majority of stone set in gypsum mortar or mud, the rest huts of date branches. The inhabitants, who belong to the Āl Bū **Mahair, Mazārī'** and **Manāsīr** tribes, are pearl divers and fishermen, owning about 74 pearl boats, but no other sea-going vessels. Their fishing boats number 40, and they also possess some 115 camels, 85 donkeys, 35 cattle and 170 goats.

KHĀRAG†
خارگ

By Arabs called Khārij خارج and in English formerly known as "Karrack." An island of some importance in the Persian Gulf; its south-eastern point is 34 miles west-north-west of **Būshehr** Town, and 2½ miles north of it begins the smaller island of **Khārgu**. Khārag is over 4 miles in length from north to south and its average breadth is about 2 miles. The greater part of the island consists of barren, table-topped hills, which are highest in the middle of the island and at the south end where they exceed 250 feet; northwards they decrease in elevation and terminate

---

* See the reports by Dr. A. von Krafft and Mr. R. D. Oldham, of the Indian Geological Survey, in the Proceedings of the Government of India in the Foreign Department for August 1901 and August 1902.

† A plan of Khārag Island is given as an inset to Admiralty Chart No. 2374—2837 B, *Persian Gulf.*

in cliffs only 20 to 30 feet high. The hills generally consist of a bed of soft sandstone or limestone overlain by a thin stratum of nearly horizontal calcareous breccia; this upper stratum, where the supporting material has been eroded by weather, has collapsed in slabs and masses which convey a singular impression of ruin and desolation. The only low ground is a plain about one square mile in extent which forms a protuberance on the east side of the island and carries at its extremity the only village on the island and the remains of a Dutch fort. The island is surrounded by a reef about $\frac{1}{2}$ a mile broad; the best anchorages and landings are off the village, but they are exposed, and the holding-ground is rocky and indifferent. Pearl banks occur between Khārag and **Khārgu** and also on the west side of Khārag to a considerable distance from shore. There are a few wild gazelle in the hills of the island. The climate resembles that of **Bahrain** but is rather cooler in summer.

The village consists of 120 houses and the inhabitants are partly recent settlers from **Bahrain, Mīnāb**, etc., and partly tribesmen who give conflicting accounts of their origin; some of the latter speak a language which is said to resemble that of the Kumāzirah section of the **Shihūh**. About $\frac{1}{8}$ of the people are Shī'ahs and the remainder are Sunnis. In character the Khāragis are quiet and unwarlike, but they possess a few Martini rifles. They are mostly pearl-divers and pilots, but a little agriculture is carried on; there are 1,500 date trees and some wheat and barley are grown. Irrigation is partly from springs, of which there are four large and three small, and some old Qanāts exist; there are also wells of good water close to the beach, and on these the supply of water for drinking principally depends. The inhabitants possess 50 donkeys, 50 cattle and 150 sheep and goats. Provisions however are mostly imported from **Būshehr**.

The earnings of the Khārag pilots are considerable; they are employed by steamers proceeding to **Basrah** and Rs. 140 is paid as pilotage for the voyage and return voyage. The people of Khārag also visit the Arabian coast for pearl-diving, and since 1901 pearling operations have been prosecuted with success on the reef of the island itself. The number of divers on the Khārag reef continued increasing until 1903, in which year. Khārag pearls to the value of Rs. 12,500 were sold to **Bahrain** merchants: in 1904 however the value of the take declined to half of what it was in the previous year. The Khārag pearls are said to excel those from the banks about **Bahrain** in colour and lustre. The only sea-going vessel belonging to Khārag is one Kūtiyah, but there are about 90 fishing boats of the Baqārah, Shū'ai and jolly-boat patterns, and about 40 boats are used for pearling.

The island is subject to the Khān of the **Hayāt Dāvud** who is represented on the spot by a deputy, at present his own cousin Mīrza Husain Khān. Taxation appears to be heavy. It is reported that a poll-tax of 2 Tūmāns a year is levied by the Khān on every male adult, besides which he takes the greater part of the pilotage fees and ¼th of the pearls obtained locally by divers. The Persian Imperial Customs have recently posted an official of the department on Khārag. No import duties are at present collected, but exports are taxed in the same manner as elsewhere.

In the interior of the island are some caves * which are possibly prehistoric places of sepulture. They were originally divided into recesses by thin partitions of living rock which were grooved for the reception of 4 tiers of shelves, but they are now used as cattle-pens and the old workmanship is much defaced.

A Muhammadan shrine of Mīr Muhammad, also in the middle of the island, appears to have been in existence for more than 600 years and is still a place of pilgrimage. Khārag in the 13th century A.D. was a place of call for ships between **Basrah** and **Qais** and was then already celebrated for its pearl fishery.†

KHARFAH
خرفه

A considerable village in the **Aflāj** district of Southern **Najd** with one or two small hamlets and a number of detached Qasrs dependent on it; it is situated about the middle of the district, 3 miles north of **Raudhah** and 5 or 6 miles south-south-west of **Lailah**. Kharfah with its Qasrs comprises about 100 houses of **Dawāsir** of the Ghaiyithāt section and 50 of Bani **Khadhīr**; of the whole about two-thirds are contained in the main village which is known as Hillah or Qil'ah. The lands of Kharfah are said to be about 1½ square miles in extent and to form a compact block; the date palms are estimated at 5,000 only and there are no other fruit trees. Wheat and barley and a little millet and maize are grown, also melons and lucerne; the wells are 7 to 8 fathoms deep. The settled inhabitants have no horses, but there is no scarcity of livestock of the other sorts common in **Najd**. The present

---

* Described by Captain Stiffe in the Geographical Journal, Vol. XII of 1898, page 179.
† See Le Strange's *Lands of the Eastern Caliphate*.

Amīr or headman of Kharfah is Shakhbūt-bin-Sultān. The nomenclature of Kharfah and its dependencies is given in the following table:—

Name.	Position.	Houses and inhabitants.	Remarks.
Hillah حلّة	See above.	See above.	The main quarter of Kharfah.
Hufūf هفوف	A few hundred yards beyond Samīnah in the direction of Raudhah.	50 houses of Bani Khadhīr.	The people are poor; they have but few animals and no fruit trees except 200 date palms. The water level is the same as at Kharfah proper. Lucerne and the ordinary cereals are grown.
Qil'ah قلعة	...	...	Another name for Hillah above.
Samīnah سمينة	On the southern margin of the Kharfah lands.	10 houses of negroes and half caste slaves.	The inhabitants cultivate for the owners who live elsewhere. There are cereals but no dates.

KHĀRGU*
خارگو

By Arabs called Khawairij خويرج and in English formerly known as "Korgu." A very low, white, sandy island situated with its southern point $2\frac{1}{2}$ miles north of the island of **Khārag**: it is $3\frac{1}{2}$ miles in length from north to south and only $\frac{1}{2}$ a mile wide. Khārgu is barren and uninhabited.

KHARJ
خرج

A district of the Wāhhabi dominions or Southern **Najd**; it is adjoined by **'Āridh** on the north and by **Harīq** and **Hautah** on the west; on the other sides it is enclosed by deserts. It is understood to extend about 40 miles from north to south and the same from east to west.

---
* A plan of Khargu will be found in Chart No. 2374—2837-B, *Persian Gulf*, where it is given as an inset.

KHARJ

Physical characteristics. Kharj is a sandy plain without any remarkable physical features. The **Sahábah** tract on the north-east is closely connected with Kharj, but should probably be regarded as distinct. On the east side Kharj passes into a sandy and at times stony country called Marāghah مراغة ; on the south it shades off into a bare sandy desert known as Dahi دهي ; on the west it is divided from **Hautah** by Saut سوت, a stretch of low flat country containing tamarisk and acacia trees. The drainage of the **Hautah** and **Harīq** districts is brought to **Dilam** in Kharj by a hollow (Wādi Braik) which has its beginning at **Hautah** town, or even further away, to the west-south-west; and the Sha'īb 'Alaiyah reaches from the eastern face of Jabal 'Alaiyah to the village of Yamāmah in Kharj: on the other hand Wādi **Hanīfah**, though it approaches the district from the north, is dissipated in **Sahábah** and does not enter Kharj. There is one flowing stream in the district, that of Farzān, which rises on the west side of the Kharj villages and after making its way across some miles of sandy country is utilised for the irrigation of crops. The air of Kharj is described as healthy and refreshing.*

Topography, population and resources.—The following table contains some particulars of the principal places in Kharj:—

Name.	Position.	Nature.	Remarks.
'Adhār عذار	On the west or south-west side of Dilam, the date groves of the two places being almost continuous.	A village of about 40 houses, *viz.*, 20 of Bani Tamīm, 10 of 'Aid and 10 of inferior tribes.	There is considerable cultivation of dates and wheat; livestock are estimated at 60 camels, 20 donkeys and 40 cattle. The wells are 6 fathoms deep.
Balaisah بليسة	A short distance to the south-west of 'Adhār.	Formerly a village, now deserted.	There is not even cultivation now at this place.
Dhabai'ah (Umm) ام ضبيعة	Some miles south of Sulaimīyah.	A Khabrah.	...
Dilam دلم	About 50 miles south by east of Riyādh, 30 miles east by south of Harīq town, and 35 miles east-north-east of Hautah town.	...	See article **Dilam**.

* So far as is known Kharj has not as yet been visited by any European traveller.

Name.	Position.	Nature.	Remarks.
Faraijah فريجه	Not far from Dilam, direction south-west.	An abandoned Qasr.	There are wells by means of which some cultivation is carried on in favourable years by agriculturists from Dilam.
Farjān ('Ain) عين فرجان	To the west of Zamaijah.	A spring which formerly sent out a stream, but now nearly dry.	This spring belonged originally to the Farjān subdivision of the Dawāsir, but it was seized by the Wahhābi Amīr after the withdrawal of the Egyptians from Najd.
Farzān ('Ain) عين فرزان	Rises about 8 miles west of Dilam.	A flowing stream, said to be the property of the Wahhābi Amīr.	This rivulet loses much of its volume on its way through sandy ground to Dilam. Its water is used for all crops by the cultivators of Dilam, and the people of Sulaimīyah and Yamāmah are able to irrigate their corn fields from it, but it does not reach their date groves. The inhabitants of Na'ajān derive no benefit from it.
Muhammadi محمدي	About 3 miles north of the date groves of Dilam.	A stretch of cultivated ground.	There was a Qasr here, but it is now ruined and deserted.
Na'ajān نعجان	About 5 miles north of Dilam.	A village of 25 houses nearly all of inferior tribes but one or two of Bani Tamīm.	The usual crops of the district are grown and there are the ordinary livestock.
Saih سيح	A mile or two or perhaps more to the west of Yamāmah.	A place with a few houses occupied by servants of Ibn Sa'ūd. About 50 horses of the Wahhābi Amīr are kept here on account of the lucerne which is good.	There are no dates, but some ordinary cultivation is carried on. Water is said to be derived from the Farzān stream. According to one account the place is now dried up and forsaken.

Name.	Position.	Nature.	Remarks.
Sulaimīyah سليمية or Salamiyah سلمية	About 8 miles east by north of Dilam.	A village of about 100 houses, viz., 30 of 'Āid, 20 of Bani Tamīm, 10 of Dawāsir, 10 of Sahūl, and 40 of inferior tribes.	There is the usual cultivation, fairly extensive here, of both dates and cereals. Livestock are estimated at 200 camels, 50 donkeys, and 300 cattle, besides sheep and goats, but no horses. This village benefits to some extent by the Farzān stream and its own wells are only 6 fathoms deep. The chief Shaikh is of the 'Āid tribe.
Yamāmah يمامة	1 or 2 miles north (or, according to another account, south) of Sulaimīyah.	A village of about 130 houses, viz., 30 of 'Āid, 20 of Sabai', 15 of Dawāsir, 15 of Sahūl, and 50 of inferior tribes.	There are large date plantations, and the usual fruits, cereals, melons and lucerne are grown. Livestock are said to amount to 300 camels, 80 donkeys, and 200 cattle, exclusive of sheep and goats, but there are no horses. The village is partially irrigated from the Farzān stream and for the rest depends on its own wells, 6 fathoms in depth. As at Sulaimīyah, the headman of the village belongs to the 'Āid tribe.
Zamaijah زميجة	Some miles to the south-west of Dilam.	A small settlement of about 10 houses.	The inhabitants are slaves belonging to Dawāsir residents of the Aflāj district.

Apparently the settled population of the Kharj district, among whom the 'Āid are the most characteristic tribe, amount to some 3,000 persons only, and half of them inhabit Dilam town; they are said to be of a milder disposition than the people of 'Āridh. Their houses are of sun-dried brick and mud with a coating of cement, which gives them a white appearance. The Bedouins of the district, who outnumber the townsmen and villagers and have been placed at 8,000 souls, are said

3 v

to be chiefly 'Ajmān of the 'Arjah and Āl Shāmir sections, Sabai', 'Ataibah, and Dawāsir of the Ju'aid section; they are well armed with breech-loading rifles.

In point of fertility Kharj ranks high among the districts of Southern Najd. The water level is only 6 to 8 fathoms below the surface, and dates and cereals are produced in large quantities; among fruits other than dates are grapes, lemons, pomegranates, and figs; lucerne and melons are also included among the products of Kharj. Domestic animals are camels, donkeys, horned cattle, and sheep and goats; but horses, unless belonging to Ibn Sa'ūd or the Bedouins, are hardly seen in the district. Such trade as exists is concentrated in Dilam town.

Communications.—The ordinary route from Kharj to Hasa leaves the district at Yamāmah and, skirting the Sahábah tract which is on the right hand, falls into the Riyādh-Hofūf route at Tarābi or Abu Jifān. The distance from Yamāmah to Abu Jifān is stated at 3 days by caravan.

Administration.—As explained in the article on Dilam, the Wahhābi Amīr at present governs Kharj through an official without local connections who is stationed at Dilam and occupies a fort within the walls. Taxes are collected from the nomadic as well as from the sedentary population of the district.

KHARMAH
خرمه

A tract in the Sanjāq of Hasa immediately to the south of the Oasis of the same name; it is bounded on the north by the Oasis, on the west by Ghuwār, and on the other two sides by Jāfūrah. The length of Kharmah from north to south is about 40 miles, and it tapers from about 30 miles in breadth at its northern end to about 15 at its southern extremity; the loss of breadth appears to be chiefly upon the east side. Jabal Arba' is situated on the border between this tract and the Hasa Oasis.

The principal feature of Kharmah is a hill named Jabal Kharmah, which is situated in the middle of the tract at about 30 miles from its northern end. The soil of Kharmah is a light red sand and the general level is higher than that of the Hasa Oasis. Water is found in a few places only; but depressions contain Hamdh, Rimth and Thamám

KHARŪS (WĀDI BANI) 1027

upon which 'Ajmān and Āl Morrah Bedouins pasture their flocks and herds.

The following are the chief wells of Kharmah:—

Name.	Vernacular equivalent.	Position and remarks.
'Awaisah	عويسة	On the west side of Jabal Kharmah, about 4 miles from it. This is a halting place on the southern route from the Hasa Oasis Najd.
Khuwainah	الخوينة	14 miles north-east of Jabal Kharmah.
Mutawi	المطري	9 miles south of Jabal Arba'.
Shajah	الشجة	8 miles south-south-west of Jabal Kharmah.
Zarnūqah	زرنوقة	8 miles south-east of Jabal Kharmah. Here the Turks, in September 1902, made successful reprisals on the refractory Āl Morrah tribe.

The neighbourhood of Zarnūqah is said to be almost permanently inhabited by 'Ajmān and Āl Morrah.

KHARŪS (BANI) بني خروص

Singular Kharūsi خروصي. A Ghāfiri tribe of the northern slopes of the Western Hajar district of the 'Omān Sultanate; in religion they are Ibādhis. They are found in Wādi Bani Kharūs at Misfāh (45 houses), 'Aliya (80 houses), Taqab (12 houses), Istāl (80 houses), Sanaiba' (80 houses), Shau (10 houses), Hijār (90 houses), Tau-ash-Shaikh (20 houses), 'Awābi (70 houses), and Falaj Bani Khazair خزير (20 houses), the last being named from one of their sections; at Nakhl in Wādi Ma'āwal they have 40 houses. Hijār is the tribal capital. There is also a Bedouin section called Yāl Khamaiyis يال خميس who number about 1,500 souls and possess 150 camels, 300 donkeys, 150 cattle and 2,000 sheep and goats. Altogether the Bani Kharūs may be estimated at 4,500 souls.

KHARŪS (WĀDI BANI) وادي بني ص

A valley of the Western Hajar district in the Sultanate of 'Omān, alternatively called Wādi Hajar حجر; it begins at 'Aqabat-al-Hajar on the north face of Jabal Akhdhar and reaches the Bātinah coast a mile or two east of Bū 'Abāli. In its lower course in

3 v 2

Bātinah it is called Wādi-al-Qāsim وادي القاسم from the fact, it is said, that in the time of Saiyid Sa'īd II (1807-56) it was the frontier between the Sultān of 'Omān and the territory of the then independent Yāl Sa'ad tribe.

The villages of Wādi Bani Kharūs in succession from its head downwards are:—

Village.	Position.	On which bank.	Houses and inhabitants.	REMARKS.
Misfāh مسفاة	Near the head of the Wādi.	Right.	100 houses of Bani Riyām of the Sharai-qiyīn section and 45 houses of Bani Kharūs.	Wheat and lentils are grown: there are 4 camels, 15 donkeys, 30 cattle, and 40 sheep and goats.
'Aliya عليا	2 hours below Misfāh.	Left.	80 houses of Bani Kharūs and 70 of Bani Bahri.	The only livestock are 20 donkeys and 40 camels. Millet, mangoes and limes are grown.
Taqab نقب	One mile below 'Aliya.	Right.	12 houses of Bani Kharūs.	The people have 30 donkeys, 20 cattle, 300 sheep and goats, and 1,500 palms.
Istāl استال	1 hour below 'Aliya.	Do.	80 houses of Bani Kharūs.	One of the principal routes across Jabal Akhdhar starts from this village. Wheat, millet, sugar-cane and sweet potatoes are grown: there are 40 camels, 100 donkeys, 20 cattle, and 1,000 sheep.
Sanaiba' صنيبع	One hour below Istāl.	Left.	80 houses of Bani Kharūs.	Resources are 20 camels, 100 donkeys, 50 cattle, 500 sheep and goats, and 2,000 palms.
Shau شو	Immediately below Sanaiba'.	Right.	10 houses of Bani Kharūs.	Livestock are 40 donkeys, 30 cattle, 200 sheep and goats, and 1,000 palms.
Hijār هجار	Immediately below Shau.	Do.	90 houses of Bani Kharūs.	Here are 70 donkeys, 40 cattle, 300 sheep and goats, and 2,000 date trees.

Village.	Position.	On which bank.	Houses and inhabitants.	REMARKS.
Tau-ash-Shaikh طو الشيخ	2 hours below Istāl.	Right.	20 houses of Bani Kharūs and 30 of Dhahūl.	Crops are wheat, millet, lucerne and garlic; animals are 15 camels, 30 donkeys, 20 cattle and 70 sheep and goats.
'Awābi عوابي	Immediately below Tau-ash-Shaikh.	Left.	...	See article 'Awābi.
Falaj Bani Khazair فلج بني خزير	1 hour below 'Awābi.	Do.	20 houses of Bani Kharūs of the Bani Khazair section.	Wheat, garlic, mangoes and limes are cultivated and there are 1,000 sheep and goats.
Mahālil مهاليل	1 hour below Falaj Bani Khazair.	Do.	20 houses of Siyābiyīn.	Millet is grown: there are 10 camels, 100 donkeys, 15 cattle and 40 sheep and goats.
Sabaikha صبيخا	1 hour below Mahālil.	Do.	20 houses of Bani Ruwāhāh and Bani Harrās.	Only millet is grown; animals are 20 cattle and 50 sheep and goats.
Salaiyah صليه	2 hours below Sabaikha.	Right.	10 houses of Siyābiyīn.	The only crop is millet; there are 10 camels, a few cattle and 20 sheep and goats.
Abyadh أبيض	1 hour below Salaiyah.	Left.	200 stone houses of Bani Subh and Bani Harrās.	A little below this place the Wādi emerges from the hills. Wheat and millet are grown; there are 70 camels, 20 donkeys, 20 cattle and 150 sheep and goats.
Hifri حفري	5 hours below Abyadh and at no great distance from the sea.	Right.	40 houses of Jabūr.	Crops are wheat and millet; livestock are 10 camels, 10 donkeys, 30 cattle and 80 sheep and goats.

The only important affluent of Wādi Bani Kharūs is Wādi **Mistāl**, which joins it from the east at Mahālil. Wādi Bani Kharūs is an important valley, containing as it does the best route from the north to Jabal **Akhdhar**: the key of this route is 'Awābi. The trade of Wādi Bani Kharūs is partly with **Barkah** and partly with **Masna'ah**.

KHASAB*

سَخَب

In English formerly known as "Kassaab." A small town on the coast of the **Oman** Sultanate, the capital of the Banī Hadīyah section of the **Shihūh** tribe, situated on the south side of a great bay which forms the approach to Khor-ash-**Sham** on the western coast of the **Ruūs-al-Jibāl** district. It stands upon a sandy beach nearly a mile long and is surrounded by date groves, which extend some distance up a wide valley, called Sal'alah سلعلة, behind the town; these plantations belong partly to **Shihūh** of other places in the **Ruūs-al-Jibāl** district. At the back of the groves there is some cultivation of wheat and vegetables. Landing at Khasab is difficult at low water even from small boats. The only defences are a fort in the centre of the date plantations and two or three small towers near the sea. Good fresh water is obtained from wells 30 to 60 feet deep, and, being abundant, it is applied to irrigation: wood, cattle and vegetables are obtainable. The town consists of about 300 houses of **Shihūh**, besides which there is a bazaar of 10 shops. The fixed inhabitants nearly all belong to the Banī Hadīyah section of the **Shihūh**, but a few are of the Banī Shatair section: of the former about 300 persons are of the Bayādīr or field labourer class. There is also a floating population, especially in the date season, when people flock in from the country round and from **Hanjām, Shārjah** and **Dibai** and camp in mat huts which they erect on the broad level in front of the town.

The inhabitants own six sea-going boats which run to **Dibai, Lingeh** and the **Bātinah** coast; they have no pearl-boats of their own, but some of them go to the pearl-banks in boats belonging to **Dibai**. They depend chiefly on their own cultivation of dates and wheat and upon fishing.

The Sultān of '**Oman** maintains a Wālī here, who has 15 'Askaris under his orders and is understood to collect $600 a year as Zakāt. The present Sultān (Saiyid Faisal) has assigned to this official a date plantation and land at **Khasab** worth $1,000 a year from his own private estate, and out of this and the Zakāt the Wālī pays his own salary and defrays all other expenses; he makes no remittances to **Masqat** and receives none thence. His functions mostly relate to visitors and strangers; with the affairs of the permanent Shihhi inhabitants he seems to occupy himself little, but he acts as an arbitrator when requested to do so.

---

* A view of Khasab will be found at page 112 of Goldsmid's *Telegraph and Travel*